AIA GUIDE TO NEW YORK CITY

New York Chapter,
American Institute of Architects

AIA GUIDE TO NEW YORK CITY

Third Edition

Elliot Willensky
Norval White

Harcourt Brace Jovanovich, Publishers
San Diego   New York   London

The New York Foundation for Architecture

Individuals interested in joining with members of the architectural profession and others to pursue a vision of a better New York City, improved neighborhoods, and a higher quality of environmental design are invited by the New York Chapter of the American Institute of Architects to enroll in the New York Foundation for Architecture.

Members of the NYFA receive a subscription to *Oculus,* the Chapter's lively and informative monthly publication, which features a calendar of events and activities of architectural and urban design interest, as well as free or reduced admission to the many lectures, exhibitions, architecture tours, and field trips regularly sponsored by the Chapter and the Foundation. Those who join also receive invitations to other New York Chapter/AIA events previously available only to the professional community: the Architectural Heritage Ball, the opening reception of the Design Awards Program exhibit, and the Annual Chapter Meeting/Installation of New Officers. In addition, Foundation members are entitled to discounts on books and gift items from the Institute's AIA Bookstore in Washington and its mail order catalog.

For information on how to join the NYFA, contact

New York Foundation for Architecture
The Urban Center
457 Madison Avenue
New York, N.Y. 10022

Copyright © 1988 by Elliot Willensky and Norval White

Library of Congress Cataloging-in-Publication Data
AIA guide to New York City.
Includes index.
"At head of title: New York Chapter,
American Institute of Architects.
1. Architecture—New York (N.Y.)—Guide-books.
2. New York (N.Y.)—Buildings, structures, etc.—
Guide-books. 3. New York (N.Y.)—Description—
1981–   —Guide-books. I. Willensky, Elliot.
II. White, Norval, 1926– III. American Institute
of Architects. New York Chapter.
NA735.N5A78 1988 917.47'1'0443 87-17807
ISBN 0-15-104040-0
ISBN 0-15-603600-6 (pbk.)

Printed in the United States of America

First edition

A B C D E

A B C D E (pbk.)

Dedication

To our colleagues at Lathrop Douglass & Associates, 1955–1960,
the architectural office where the authors first met and
where the idea for this book first emerged:
Lathrop Douglass and John Bennett,
Harry Agne, Reade Barnes, Gene Baryla, Al Cardenas,
Warren Wolfgang Calwil, Phil Cipolla, Helen Fante,
Vernon Gibberd, Costas and George Machlouzarides, Sandy Malter,
Paul Mammolo, Bob McKelvey, John O'Hagan, Barbara Quick, Fred Rinke,
Charlie Russo, Wandy Wandelmaier,
and our indefatigable receptionist, remembered fondly (and only) as
Irene.

CONTENTS

2

THE BRONX

3

BROOKLYN

QUEENS

5

STATEN ISLAND

NECROLOGY

THE CITY

LIST OF MAPS

USING THE GUIDE

The *Guide* is designed to serve a whole spectrum of readers, from the casual wanderer to the serious historian; from the provincial New Yorker who rarely, if ever, ventures west of the Hudson River, to the visitor who wants to see more than the well-touted monuments, musicals, and museums. From these pages you will be able to select and follow a wide variety of specific walking tours (and motor tours for the outer reaches of the city), or you may use the book to design your own.

Some of you may explore familiar neighborhoods before venturing into unfamiliar places. Braver souls will immediately "go abroad" as tourists in other parts of the city, savoring new and exotic precincts. Some may wish to start at the Battery, working their way geographically or following the chronological development of the city.

For the less athletic, you may leave the *Guide* on your coffee table to leaf through the pages at your leisure, and enjoy excursions of the city in the mind, without ever stepping outside your door. And you will also be able to use the guide to show visitors from Paris, Tokyo, San Francisco, or even Hackensack how to view and relish not only New York's major monuments, landmarks, and historic districts but also the richness of its buildings and precincts in every borough.

Organization. The *Guide,* like the city, is divided into five boroughs. Manhattan, at whose southern tip the city began, is first. The outlying boroughs (The Bronx, Brooklyn, Queens, and Staten Island) follow in that order. A section entitled "The City" deals with the whole.

Each section is organized to illustrate the complexity and richness of a particular borough and, within that borough, its various sectors (Lower Manhattan, Northern Brooklyn, Northeastern Queens, etc.). The sectors, in turn, are divided into neighborhood areas, called precincts (Financial District, Greenpoint, Fresh Meadows, etc.).

Boroughs, sectors, and precincts are prefaced by a short historical introduction, a capsule description of the topography, and a history of physical development.

Entries. Each entry in the *Guide* is numbered—the numbers appear within brackets—and is identified by name in boldface type. (Sometimes there is also a former or original name or names.) This information is followed by the address and/or block location, the date of completion (or projected completion), and finally by the designer's name. When no other title follows a designer's name, it should be assumed that title is architect. Identification lines at the bottom of left-hand pages indicate the borough and sector being discussed; the identifying letter for the sector (**N** for Northern, **SE** for Southeastern, etc.) keys it to the maps. Right-hand pages show the precinct(s) being dealt with and the map page on which the entries appear. When several entries are geographically close but are cited individually in the text, the same number is used for each member of the group, and a letter suffix distinguishes each entry (**[3a.], [3b., etc.]**). On the maps these groups are usually indicated only by the number. Bracketed notes, such as [see . . .], refer to entries of related interest.

In some cases, buildings were demolished or changed more rapidly than the conversion of manuscript to printed book. In the interest of the city's dynamics—even if in a negative sense—the entries have been overprinted with DEMOLISHED, CONSUMED, ENDANGERED, etc.

Photographs of specific entries are captioned with the number that identifies them in the text. Though photographs almost always appear on the same (or opposite) page as the building that they illustrate, they are not necessarily contiguous with the text. When photographs were not taken recently or show conditions that are not current, the year they were taken is also noted.

Maps. Each borough is preceded by a specially designed map that delineates its sectors; the sectors are indicated by the identifying letters found at the bottom of left-hand pages. In areas with heavy concentrations of entries, detailed maps of sectors and/or precincts also show streets, subway stations, major institutions, and tour routes. The numbers correspond to the bracketed numbers of the text entries. Special symbols used on maps are shown below.

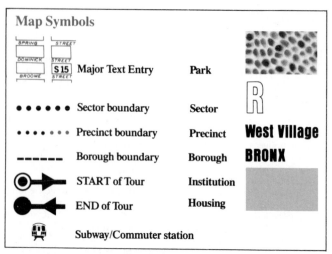

Map Symbols

S 15	Major Text Entry	Park
•••••• Sector boundary	Sector	ℝ
••••••• Precinct boundary	Precinct	**West Village**
------ Borough boundary	Borough	**BRONX**
⊙➤ START of Tour	Institution	
●◄ END of Tour	Housing	
🚇 Subway/Commuter station		

Tours. Walking and motor tours detailed in the text are indicated on the maps by solid black lines, their beginning by a bull's-eye and their end by a solid circle. All entries are arranged so that, by proceeding in their numerical sequence, the reader will naturally trace an easy-to-follow walking or motoring route. (In parts of Queens one-way streets are noted where this can be helpful.) Entries located away from the routes of walking tours are indicated at the end of some sections under the heading "Miscellany." For outlying parts of the city, we recommend a good street map. These are available at bookstores, stationery stores, and at map stores (Hagstrom's, 57 West 43rd St., or Rand McNally, 150 East 52nd St.).

Restaurants, Bistros, and Emporia. These are not numbered, except where they have been included particularly (but not exclusively) for their architectural distinction. Cultural facilities open to the public are especially noted.

Security. New York is a vast, busy, and complicated city, with much to see. But at certain times and in certain places, sightseers—gawkers, if you will —can inadvertently send out signals of distraction or vulnerability that are cues to those with less than lofty motives. Beware. Remember that there is safety in numbers. Don't walk in desolate areas. Don't tour at night. Do take a friend along—it's more fun that way.

Officially Designated Landmarks. Individual structures and natural objects, scenic landmarks, and historic districts, officially designated by the N.Y.C. Landmarks Preservation Commission (and confirmed by the Board of Estimate) are identified by a solid star ★. Designated interior landmarks are noted separately, also with a solid star ★. Entries lying within the boundaries of designated historic districts are noted with an open star ☆. Since landmark designations are subject to change, we recommend that you contact the Landmarks Preservation Commission at 225 Broadway, New York, N.Y. 10007, for up-to-date information.

Style Symbols. Marginal symbols printed in color signify that an entry is a notable example of a particular architectural style or stylistic group:

Colonial. Literally the architecture of New York as a colony, whether of The Netherlands or Great Britain. It doesn't necessarily imply either white clapboard or shutters and is best exemplified in Manhattan by St. Paul's Chapel (the only "Colonial" building remaining from before 1776) and by some of the Dutch Colonial farmhouses of southeastern Brooklyn.

Georgian/Federal/neo-Georgian/neo-Federal. The Federal style was the first—and therefore the "modern" (in its day)—architecture of our new republic, a modification of the contemporaneous Georgian architecture of London. Dignified and restrained, it emphasized geometric form and harmonious proportion and was executed in both wood and masonry. The neo-Federal and neo-Georgian are early 20th-century revivals of 18th- and 19th-century originals.

Greek Revival. The product of both political and aesthetic interests. The Greek Revolution made Greece independent of the Turks (the Ottoman Empire) in the 1820s. The newly won independence recalled, to fascinated American intellectuals, the patrician democracy of ancient Greece and its elegant architecture, created more than 400 years before the birth of Christ. In America, classical columns and orders were used mostly for decoration, often at entrance doorways in otherwise simply designed row houses. Whole buildings, however, sometimes were also recalled: Sailors' Snug Harbor in Staten Island and Federal Hall National Memorial on Wall Street are reincarnations of great Greek temples.

Gothic Revival/neo-Gothic/neo-Tudor. In its purest form Gothic Revival refers to the literary and aesthetic movement of the 1830s and 1840s, coincidental with that in England. Interest in the presumed "goodness" of long-gone medieval times suggested that the emulation of its Gothic architecture would instill a similar goodness among the present wicked. The posture gained enough adherents to inspire a re-revival around 1900 and later, particularly for colleges, urban high schools, and major churches, in styles labeled neo-Gothic and neo-Tudor.

Villa Style. This romantic residential style, based on the Italian villa, utilized a tall, usually asymmetrically placed tower and ensembles of gently pitched roofs redolent of classical pediments. Litchfield Villa in Brooklyn's Prospect Park is the city's finest example, despite the loss of its obligatory stucco surfacing, which had been inscribed so as to resemble stonework.

Romanesque Revival/neo-Romanesque. The late nineteenth-century Romanesque Revival is a vigorous style more common in Chicago than in New York and is based on the bold arch-and-vault construction of the early medieval Romanesque. Architect H. H. Richardson was its greatest American exponent, but Brooklyn's Frank Freeman was not far behind. A more decorative exploitation of the Romanesque's ornamental embellishments during the early 20th century characterizes the later neo-Romanesque style.

Renaissance Revival/Anglo-Italianate/Beaux Arts. Drawn from the architecture of 15th- through 17th-century Italy, France, and England. On this side of the Atlantic, Italian palazzi, French châteaux, and English clubs became the stylistic image for banking institutions, super town houses, clubs and government buildings, and even mercantile establishments (cf. The Federal Reserve Bank of New York, the YIVO Institute's headquarters on Fifth Avenue and 86th Street, and many of SoHo's cast-iron loft buildings). Proselytized through the École des Beaux-Arts in Paris, the Beaux Arts style, from about 1890 to 1920, inflated classical allusions to truly supergrandiose proportions, as in Grand Central Terminal, the Custom House at Bowling Green, and The New York Public Library, in search of a myth of palatial urbanism.

Roman Revival/Baroque Revival. Roman Revival was more pompous and posturing than Greek Revival. It brought back some of the histrionics of classical Rome, particularly through use of domes, columns, pedi-

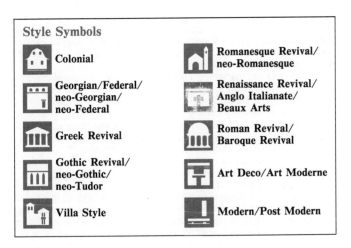

Style Symbols

	Colonial		Romanesque Revival/ neo-Romanesque
	Georgian/Federal/ neo-Georgian/ neo-Federal		Renaissance Revival/ Anglo Italianate/ Beaux Arts
	Greek Revival		Roman Revival/ Baroque Revival
	Gothic Revival/ neo-Gothic/ neo-Tudor		Art Deco/Art Moderne
	Villa Style		Modern/Post Modern

ments, and sculpture of a grandiose nature. Baroque Revival echoed similar elaborations found in the quirkier and even more ornate Baroque era that followed the Renaissance.

Art Deco/Art Moderne. The largely French-inspired styles of the era between World Wars I and II, when cubistic structures were embellished by the use of florid ornament inspired by the Paris Exposition of 1925 (Art Deco) and later by sleek streamlined ornament that also influenced the Paris Exposition of 1937 (Art Moderne). Many polychromed works of Ely Jacques Kahn exemplify Art Deco; the corner-windowed "modernistic" apartment houses of the Grand Concourse in the Bronx and the Majestic Apartments at Central Park West and 72nd Street are Art Moderne.

Modern/Post Modern. The breakdown of Modern (or Modernist) into component styles is a new phenomenon, based on the concept that Modern as we know it today has its own internal history: beginning with the works of Louis Sullivan (the Condict Building on Bleecker Street) and Frank Lloyd Wright (best known here for his much later Guggenheim Museum); followed by Art Deco and Art Moderne (see above) and the Bauhaus and/or International Style as imported by Walter Gropius, Marcel Breuer, and Ludwig Mies van der Rohe (cf. the Seagram Building); in addition to individual excursions into a nonhistorical personal architecture (Gordon Bunshaft's Lever House, and Charles Evans Hughes III's Manufacturers Hanover Trust, both from Skidmore, Owings & Merrill). The Post Modern style, with its allusions to classical forms and derivative appliqués, is the current Modern direction (cf. Stern & Hagman's Leonard N. Stern Park Avenue town house, and Kohn Pedersen Fox Associates' Heron Tower office building).

ACKNOWLEDGMENTS

Since 1966, when research on the first version of the *Guide* began, innumerable individuals have contributed information, ideas, comments, corrections, and considerable moral support. Previous editions and reprintings have recognized their contributions in the acknowledgments.

This Third Edition is a linear descendant of the original, self-published version feverishly prepared over a nine-month period for the 1967 convention of the American Institute of Architects in New York City. Because its approach profoundly influenced subsequent updatings of the *Guide,* it seems appropriate to credit once again those who helped the authors to set the book's tone, standards, and appearance: writers John Morris Dixon, Ann Douglass, Mina Hamilton, Roger Feinstein, Henry Hope Reed, Jr., and Sophia Duckworth and Richard Dattner; book designer Herb Lubalin and codesigner Fran Elfenbein; map and Manhattan cutaway designer Jerome Kuhl; and a devoted staff headed by Hope Asrelsky.

For this new edition other acknowledgments are in order. Special credit must again go to Margaret Latimer, who was responsible for preparing and writing the Necrology, as she did in the Second Edition, when that section was first introduced.

In revising and expanding a book of this length and complexity the role of copy editor has assumed special significance. This enormous responsibility Joel Honig has discharged with distinction, not only in minding the necessary Ps and Qs but in bringing inordinate expertise in the subject matter of New York's architecture and history, through rigorous discipline in correcting the manuscript and improving its quality, and accompanied always by welcome good humor.

Our work has been eased and improved by generous contributions from many individuals. Many thanks to:

Thomas J. Reese, S.J., who contributed many long, precise, and helpful communications documenting corrections and changes for many sections of the book which he had found through field checking.

Architectural historian Shirley Zavin, for her special efforts in supplying a massive amount of Staten Island information and for making available the research of others, particularly that of the late Dennis Steadman Francis.

Landmarks commissioner Anthony Max Tung, for conducting personalized and informative walking tours of Staten Island.

Many individuals at the Landmarks Preservation Commission: its research and survey staffs, particularly Marjorie Pearson, Anthony Robins, Louella Adams, Jim Dillon, Gale Harris, Don Plotts, Jay Shockley, counsel Dorothy Miner, archaeologist Sherene Baugher, and also Joe Bresnan, Jeremy Woodoff, as well as Marion Cleaver. Helpful at critical moments were landmarks commissioners David Garcia, Sarah Bradford Landau, Joe Mitchell, and Adolf Placzek.

Donald Presa, author of the National Register of Historic Places designation report for the Ridgewood community in Brooklyn and Queens, and Merrill Hesch, of the N.Y.S. Office of Parks, Recreation & Historic Preservation, who called the report to our attention.

As we have done in previous editions, we wish to recognize that legion of supporters who contributed anything from a correction of punctuation to a suggestion for a new entry. We, whose names begin with *W* and are usually listed last, therefore list these individuals in *reverse* alphabetical order:

John Zukowsky, Joseph Zito, G. Young, Miss Jean Wynn, William Wright, Ira Wolfman, Jay Weiser, Stephen Weinstein, Maron Waxman, V. Frederick Vender, Ernest Ulmer, Marcel Turbiaux, Charles Tresnowske, Barbara M. Topf, Woodlief Thomas, Jr., Stephen F. Temmer, Adam Taylor, John Tauranac, Peter Switzer, Richard Sullivan, Lawrence Stelter, Robert B. Snyder, Susan Smpadian, Jerry Slaff, Robert Sink, John Victor Singler, Donald E. Simon, Stanley Shor, Gaynor Wynne Shay, Rebecca Shanor, Vincent F. Seyfried, Susan Sekey, Joseph Schuchman, Ms. P. Sanecki, Larry Samuels, Peter R. Samson, M. Sallstrand, James Rossant, Jane M. Ross, Richard Rosenthal, Halina Rosenthal, Brenda A. Rosen, Ellen Fletcher Rosebrock, Anne Richter, F. Rex, Thomas E. Range, Gary Ostkoff, Fred Ost, Georgia O'Dea/Helen Mills, Peter Obletz, Daniel Nydick, Francis J. Murray, Louis Morhaim, Margaret and Truman Moore, Ava Moncrief, Joseph Merz, James D. Merritt, Joseph N. Merola, David Ment, Nancy McKeon, Priscilla McGuire, John Margolis, Jerry Maltz, Duncan Maginnis, Joseph Pell Lombardi, Nicholas Lobenthal, Martin H. Levinson, Walter E. Levi, Lenore Latimer, Andrew Lachman, James Kraft, Rev. Arthur Kortheuer, Joseph E. Konkle, Gwen and Maury Kley, Adriana R. Kleiman, Steven V. Kaufman, Bernard Kabak, David Edmund Jones, Christopher Jones, William H. Johnson, Jeanne Jantosca, Jack Intrator, Judith S. Hull, Christina Huemer, Alice C. Hudson, Holly Huckins, Sidney Horenstein, Dozier Hasty, Alex J. Hartill, Jay and Rosalie Harris, Hannelore Hahn, Cecilia Haas, David Gurin, Christopher Gray, Christabel Gough, Dorothy Twining Globus, Vernon and Diana Gibberd, Michael George, Ann George, Deborah Shaw Gardner, Charles P. G. Fuller II, Paul Fritz, Peter Freiberg, Gloria Okun Freedgood, John Frazier, Elizabeth Foster, Christopher Forbes, Richard C. Fitzpatrick, Jr., Anne E. Finelli, Gary Eriksen, Martin Dubno, Erin Drake, Ethelyn Underwood (Mrs. George E.) Dowling, Andrew Dolkart, John Diele, Norman Dick, Laurence G. Dengler, Harry Denker, Fred Del Pozzo, L. J. Davis, Philip I. Danzig, Dina Dahbany-Miraglia, Naomi Curtis, Arthur Cohen, Carol Clark, Albert Cattan, Mrs. Robert C. Carey, Michael J. Byczek, Natalie Bunting, Esther Brumberg, R. Michael Brown, Hal Bromm, Paul H. Bonner, Jr., Mary T. Bronham, Kevin Bone, Louis Blumengarten, Avis Berman, Daniel Beekman, Ann Bedell, L. A. Becker, Ernestine Bassman, Peter J. Bartucca, Patti Auerbach, Michael Armstrong, R. Boulton Anderson, Oliver Allen, William Alex, Emma Albert. And, at the last minute, Marjorie Johnson and Gregory Nolan.

The authors could not ask for more concerned support from our new publisher and its staff: our devoted and erudite senior editor John Radziewicz, our meticulous book designer Michael Farmer, our accomplished layout artist Janet Taggart, our patient cover designer Vaughn Andrews, and our ever reliable and congenial Vicki Austin. Typographic composition was in the hands of ComCom computer division of Haddon Craftsmen, whose staff set the complicated and demanding text with unflagging accuracy. And the anonymity of book production is here uncovered by recognizing Warren Wallerstein and Michele Weekes.

The book's original maps were totally reconstructed and updated by Shey Wolvek-Pfister of Michael Hertz Associates, under the guidance of Michael Hertz and aided by the graphic skills of Peter Joseph, who redid the cutaway view of Manhattan. The long index, whose format was established in the Second Edition by Vera Schneider, was diligently recompiled by Louise Ketz. The unending need for reams of Xeroxing under always restrictive time constraints was handled with dispatch by Sidney Solomon and his crew at Brooklyn's Remsen Books and by Longacre Copy Centers' Elliot (Chappy) Chapnick, his 40th Street store manager Jeff Gage, and their well-trained crew. Much of the photographic processing was performed by the downtown branch of Modernage Photographic Services, guided by Norman Krupit and his staff, always concerned with careful attention to quality. Photographer Jeff Perkell dispelled a highly vexing problem with graciousness and consummate skill.

Our architect colleague, George S. Lewis, former executive director of the New York Chapter/AIA and now a commissioner of the Landmarks Preservation Commission, volunteered to undertake the weighty task of reading the manuscript on behalf of the Chapter.

Of special regard to both authors is Howard Morhaim, friend, source of endless encouragement, a contributor in so many ways, and the perfect agent.

Of special assistance to Norval White on Brooklyn, Midtown, Upper West Side, Heights and Harlems, Upper Manhattan, and Outer Islands was Suzy Kunz, who is owed a debt for field checking, map editing, and for considerable photography and photo processing.

For special recognition Elliot Willensky cites:

Mitchell J. Paluszek, a dedicated lover of the city and an energetic and long-legged walker of its byways, to whom special thanks is extended for volunteering to verify and update in the field large portions of the Second Edition's text.

Phil Ressner, whose advice, support, and unflagging loyalty helped in so many different ways, as only a true friend can.

Peggy Latimer, already acknowledged for her considerable contribution to the text, whose confidence, sustenance, and love made the bad times few and brief.

And the long-lost—and, with Mitch Paluszek's help, finally regained—Cousin Arthur, a cherished and powerful influence.

Elliot Willensky/Norval White

AIA
GUIDE
TO
NEW
YORK
CITY

MANHATTAN

1

MANHATTAN

Borough of Manhattan/New York County

To most people, Manhattan *is* New York, the place to **"go to business,"** the downtown of all downtowns. This is where the **action** is, where money is **earned** and, in large part, **spent.**

To non-New Yorkers, Manhattan is known in excerpts from the whole: **Fifth Avenue, Broadway, Greenwich Village, Wall Street,** the caricatures of the chic, of bright lights, of the offbeat, of big business—excerpts symbolic of the public power and influence of Manhattan as the capital of **banking, corporate headquartering,** the **theater, advertising, publishing, fashion, tourism,** and, to a lesser degree, the **United Nations.** This passing parade of visitors mostly misses Manhattan's myriad local neighborhoods with handsome buildings and areas of visual delight. That there are distinguished architecture and urban design in **Harlem,** on the vast **Upper West Side,** or in the loft districts of **Lower Manhattan** will startle and, we hope, pleasantly surprise those visitors who have savored only the well-publicized monuments, musicals, and museums.

L

LOWER MANHATTAN

FINANCIAL DISTRICT • WATER STREET CORRIDOR
SOUTH STREET SEAPORT • BROADWAY-NASSAU
BATTERY PARK CITY • TRIBECA/LOWER WEST SIDE
CIVIC CENTER • CHINATOWN/LITTLE ITALY
LOWER EAST SIDE • SOHO

Manhattan's toe:

Manhattan's toe, that 1½-square-mile triangle pulsating south of Canal Street and contained by the confluence of the **Hudson** and **East Rivers,** is where Manhattan—all of New York for that matter—began. Here lay **Nieuw Amsterdam,** founded in 1625, the first permanent settlement of Europeans in this area, the first fortification, the first business district, the first community.

Where once all of the settlement's activities—even farming—took place in the toe, population growth and urbanization divined that **specialization would take command.** For Manhattan's tip the specialties would become shipping and warehousing, and the necessary backup of accounting, banking, and speculating that inevitably followed. And, of course, government.

Few people have actually lived in Manhattan's toe since before the turn of the century, making its **canyons** particularly **desolate** in nonbusiness hours. More recently, public policy has decreed that this shall change; and despite the explosive proliferation of office towers, evidence of residential infusion is appearing throughout the area in which it all began.

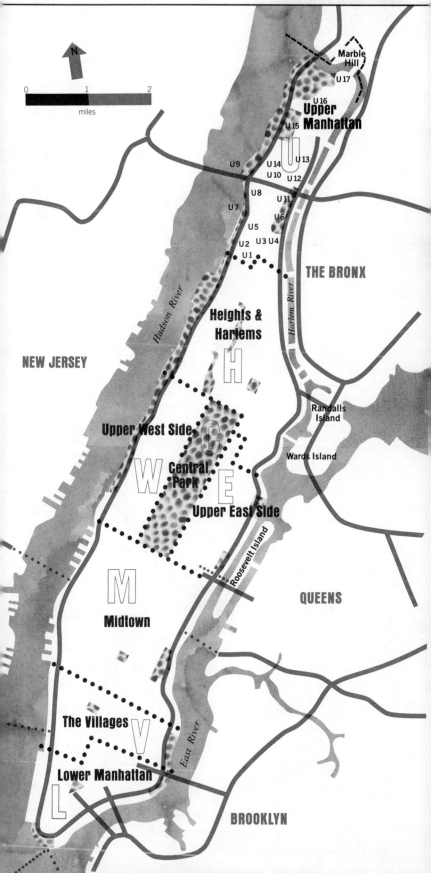

N

0　　　1　　　2
miles

Marble
Hill
U 17

U 16
Upper
Manhattan
U 15

U 9　U 14　U 13
U 10　U 12
U 8　U 11
U 7
U 5　U 6
U 2　U 3 U 4
U 1
THE BRONX

Hudson River

Harlem River

NEW JERSEY

Heights &
Harlems
H

Upper West Side
C
Central
Park
W
E
Upper East Side

Randalls
Island

Wards Island

Roosevelt Island

M
Midtown

QUEENS

East River

The Villages
V

Lower Manhattan
L

BROOKLYN

LOWER MANHATTAN

East Village

Place

3RD

2ND

1ST

STREET

STREET

E22

E27

E28

E30

E31

RIVINGTON STREET

E23

E29

E20

RIVINGTON

E21

E24

STREET

E14

E25

E26

NEW

STREET

WILLIAMSBURG

Lower East Side

E13

BROOME

E16

E17

E18

E19

STANTON

STREET

E11

E15

BROOME

Seward Park

E8

E9

E12

E6

BROADWAY

E1

E3

E5

E7

E10

E2

E4

L10

tOWN

L9

L8

L7

L6

L12

L4

L5

L3

ROBERT F. WAGNER

S8

S7

BROOKLYN BRIDGE

S6

South Street

S2

Seaport

S5

East River

BROOKLYN

N

East River

Park

Roosevelt

East River

MANHATTAN BRIDGE

0   1000   2000

feet

Exploring the toe:

Routes for visiting the area's architecture have been turned into a series of walking tours that radiate outward from the Battery to create armatures for exploration. The walks take convenient pathways; Lower Manhattan's development over time has taken more complex routes.

Note: For the Staten Island Ferry and the Ferry Terminal, see Water Street Corridor.

FINANCIAL DISTRICT

The Financial District's twisted streets, varying both in direction and width, occupy that part of Manhattan's tip originally laid out by early colonists, vividly recalling the irregular medieval street patterns of northern European settlements. It is this part of the toe, the **original** part, that became the foundation for the slender skyscrapers built between the turn of the century and the Great Depression of the 1930s. It is also the part abundantly served by the three subway systems whose stations dot the area.

Surrounding the district's early core on the waterside are a later series of concentric landfills. They support the successive waves of warehouses, countinghouses, and wharves that would serve the water-oriented enterprises that gave New York its early profits, power, and fame. In time these activities faded even as the core prospered, giving birth to the Financial District's canyons. Yet the twentieth century did not saturate the perimeter of the toe until after World War II, when large-scale skyscraper development bulldozed what had become outlying, seedy, low-scale areas, still abundant with architectural significance but marginal economically. The special visual character of these late 18th- and 19th-century **commercial precincts** is evident today only in the South Street Seaport Historic District.

Walking Tour A—Lower Manhattan's Medieval Street Plan: From **Battery Park** to the vicinity of Cass Gilbert's **90 West Street** Building, near the World Trade Center. **Start** at **Castle Clinton National Monument.** (The IRT Seventh Avenue local to South Ferry Station and BMT Broadway Line local to Whitehall Street Station will deposit you at Battery Park. The IRT Lexington Avenue Line express to Bowling Green Station leave you a short walk away.)

Battery Park and its perimeter:

[F 1.] Battery Park. [F 1a.] Verrazano Memorial. 1909, Ettore Ximenes, sculptor. **[F 1b.] John Wolfe Ambrose Statue** [Ambrose Channel]. 1936. Andrew O'Connor, sculptor.

The **Battery** signals the bottom of Manhattan to most New Yorkers, where tourists are borne by ferry to the **Statue of Liberty,** and "provincial" **Staten Islanders** start their homeward trek to that distant island which turns out to be, surprisingly, part of New York City. **Battery** was the namesake of a row of guns along the old shorefront line, now approximated by State Street between Bowling Green and Whitehall. During the **War of 1812,** the status of the gunnery was elevated: **Castle Clinton,** erected on a pile of rock some 300 feet offshore, was known as **West Battery,** while **Castle Williams,** on **Governors Island,** became **East Battery.** The intervening years have seen landfill entirely envelop **Castle Clinton** (and its various transmogrifications), forming **Battery Park,** a flat and somewhat confused stretch of **Robert Moses landscaping** that provides greenery and summer delight to New Yorkers from nearby offices. A fresh, if sometimes pungent, breeze from the Upper Bay is an antidote for the doldrums or any bad mood aggravated by heat.

The buff, bland **Coast Guard Building** at the east edge of the park's bayfront vies with the slated for demolition, eye-ease green, Staten Island Ferry Terminal [see W 1a.] as the city's most unfortunate structure in a prominent location. The Coast Guard site in earlier years was successively occupied by **two** richly conceived **U.S. Government Barge Offices** designed by the **Supervising Architect of the Treasury Department:** James G. Hill (1880) and James Knox Taylor (1914).

[F 1c.] Castle Clinton National Monument/earlier **New York Aquarium** (1896–1941)/earlier **Emigrant Landing Depot** (1855–1890)/earlier **Castle Garden** (1824–1855)/originally **West Battery** (1811–1815, renamed Castle Clinton, 1815). John McComb, Jr. ★ **Open to the public.**

Until recently, one of the most vitally involved structures in the city's life and history. Built as West Battery for the War of 1812 to complement Castle Williams across the waters on Governors Island (it never fired a shot in anger), it was originally an island fortification some 300 feet offshore, connected to Manhattan by a combination causeway-bridge. Twelve years after the war it was ceded to the city. As a civic monument it served for the reception of distinguished visitors at the very edge of the nation (General Lafayette, Louis Kossuth, President Jackson, Prince Albert). Remodeled as a concert hall and renamed Castle Garden, it enjoyed a moment of supreme glory in 1850 as the much ballyhooed, P. T. Barnum-promoted American debut of the Swedish soprano Jenny Lind. Only five years later it was transformed into the Emigrant Landing Depot, run by N.Y. State, where some 7.7 million new Americans were processed, some into the Union army, others into the Lower East Side. Scandal led to its closure, and the processing of immigrants was transferred to federal control, at the Barge Office in 1890 and at Ellis Island in 1892. Not to be forgotten, however, its innards were juggled and its decor changed by McKim, Mead & White, and it reentered the fray as the Aquarium, the much beloved grotto of New Yorkers until 1941.

[F 1c.] 1854 interior view of Castle Garden shown in use as a concert hall

It was then apparently doomed by Robert Moses' call for its demolition to build approaches for his ill-fated harbor bridge to Brooklyn—today's Brooklyn-Battery Tunnel. A loud civic clamor and the reported intervention of Eleanor Roosevelt miraculously saved it, though it languished inside a construction fence for decades. In 1946 the ruin was belatedly dubbed a National Historic Monument.

With its sea life displays removed to makeshift quarters at the Bronx Zoo, and then permanently installed in new facilities at Coney Island [see S Brooklyn C 3.], the fort awaited a new purpose. Urged on by the 1976 Bicentennial, the National Park Service schmaltzified this once lusty place into a tame tourist attraction, a neat lawn surrounded by a shingle roof within its rock-faced brownstone shell. In 1986 it lost out to commerce, reduced to service as a ticket office for the boats to National Park Service attractions in the harbor.

The Statue of Liberty and **Ellis Island** [see The Other Islands] are must-visit attractions only a short, privately operated boat ride away, sitting in the Upper Bay near the New Jersey shore but in plain view of visitors to Battery Park.

Miss Liberty: Perhaps three times the height of the Colossus of Rhodes, which was one of the "Seven Wonders of the World." **Liberty,** until the 1986 centennial, was considered corny but corn was a necessary ingredient here. Like an old shoe to **New Yorkers,** she is always there and continues to wear well, particularly since the restoration on the occasion of her birthday. Take the special boat out to her, ascend the spiral stairway through her innards to the crown, and you will look back on one of the romantic glories of the world: the **New York** skyline. She, still doing her own thing, is meanwhile saluting the rising sun of **France.**

[F 1d.] East Coast Memorial, Battery Park. 1960. Gehron & Seltzer, architects. Sculpture, 1963, Albino Manca.

Eight solid sawn-granite monoliths (steles) with the roles of those merchant mariners who died at sea off this coast in World War II.

[F 1d.] East Coast Mem'l, Battery Pk.   **[F 2.]** Memorial clocktower on Pier A

[F 1e.] Control House, Bowling Green Subway Station, IRT Lexington Avenue Line, Battery Park, State St., SW cor. Battery Place. 1905. Heins & La Farge. ★ **[F 1f.] IRT Bowling Green Subway Station, IRT Lexington Avenue Line,** under Bowling Green. 1908. Heins & La Farge. Redesigned, 1974, Transit Authority Architectural Staff.

A Flemish Revival **masonry** station entry, companion piece to the same firm's **cast-iron kiosks,** which once dotted Manhattan's street corners along the route of the city's first subway system, the **Interborough Rapid Transit** Company **(IRT).** Only one cast-iron version exists, and it is a replica [see V Manhattan/Astor Place A 12c.]. The subway station itself is a total redesign in lipstick red wall tile (1975, N.Y.C. Transit Authority Architectural Staff).

From the park savor the wall of buildings that defines its space.

Ringing Battery Park, clockwise, from west to east:

[F 2.] Originally **Pier A, N.Y.C. Department of Docks & Ferries,** off Battery Park, Battery Place SW cor. West St. 1886. George Sears Greene, Jr., engineer. Additions, 1900, 1904, 1919. ★

Both the pier, built atop granite arches sunk to river bottom, and the pier building, its once ornate, **Beaux Arts-ornamented** tinplate siding replaced (1964) with corrugated aluminum, are the oldest survivors of this kind of construction in Manhattan. The clock in the tower at the pier's tip was installed in 1919 as the nation's **first World War I memorial.** Plans are afoot to convert the pier to a visitors' center.

[F 3a.] Whitehall Building (offices), 17 Battery Place, NE cor. West St. 1902. Henry J. Hardenbergh. Rear addition, 1910, Clinton & Russell. **[F 3b.] Brooklyn-Battery Tunnel Ventilation Building,** Battery Place

bet. Washington and Greenwich Sts. 1950. Aymar Embury II. **[F 3c.]
Commodities Exchange Headquarters,** 10 Battery Place, bet. Greenwich and Washington Sts., behind the ventilation building and over the entrance ramp to the Brooklyn-Battery Tunnel. 1990. Roche Dinkeloo & Assocs. **[F 3d.] 1 Broadway (offices)/**formerly **United States Lines Building/**originally **Washington Building,** NW cor. Battery Place at Bowling Green. 1884. Edward H. Kendall. Refaced, 1922, Walter B. Chambers.

These structures on the north side of Battery Place define the southern edge of the Financial District against Battery Park. **No. 17** offers some of the best views of the harbor from any of the Battery's older buildings. The windowless structure is one of three constipated Classico/Modern necessities for Robert Moses' automobile and truck tunnel to Brooklyn. The Commodities Exchange centralizes a group of smaller Financial District Stock markets. **No. 1 Broadway,** having come to see a second life in 1922, was again redone in the 1980s: the upper-floor double-height arched windows that once illuminated a great booking hall for steamship tickets today reveal the insertion of an intermediate floor.

[F 3e.] Richly patterned brickwork enhances the Downtown Athletic Club arcade

[F 3e.] Downtown Athletic Club, 21 West St., SE cor. Morris St. 1926. Starrett & Van Vleck. Addition.

A chromatic range of salt-glazed tile, from burnt oranges to brown. This is the material of which **silos** are frequently made: a natural glaze, resistant to urban "fallout," without the crassness of the popular white-glazed brick of the 1950s and 1960s. The arcade with recessed ground floor is composed of corbeled arches, reminiscent of Moorish architecture. Corners are cantilevered—making corner windows a natural. An **Art Deco** delight.

Along Battery Park's eastern boundary, State Street:

Note: For the U.S. Custom House, the northernmost structure on State Street, see [F 7.].

[F 4a.] 1 Battery Park Plaza (offices), 24 State St., bet. Bridge and Pearl Sts. E side. 1971. Emery Roth & Sons. **[F 4b.] 1 State Street Plaza (offices)/**a.k.a. **Schroeder Building,** State, Pearl, Whitehall, and Water Sts. 1969. Emery Roth & Sons. **[F 4c.] 17 State Street (offices),** on former site of Seamens' Church Institute, SE cor. Pearl St. 1989. Emery Roth & Sons.

The first two are straightforward sleek curtain-walled office towers that add to their visual anonymity by adopting—thanks to the miscellaneous powers of the local Borough President—equally anonymous nonaddresses. The last structure (carrying a real address) replaced the Seaman's Church Institute hostel for mariners after only 16 years [see Necrology.]. In a house on the same site, in 1819, Herman Melville was born.

[F 4d.] Rectory of the Shrine of St. Elizabeth Bayley Seton (Roman Catholic)/originally **James Watson residence,** 7 State St., bet. Pearl and Whitehall Sts. NE side. 1793–1806. Attributed to John McComb, Jr. ★ Restoration and additions, 1965, Shanley & Sturges.

A single survivor of the first great era of mansions, this facade is original. Federal both in the archaeological and political senses, it was built in the fifth year of George Washington's presidency of the federal republic in a style that is separately considered Federal. Slender, elegant, freestanding Ionic columns and delicate late Georgian detailing.

Mother Seton, born on Staten Island, baptized Episcopalian, and converted to Roman Catholicism, was canonized as America's first saint in 1975.

Peter Stuyvesant's mansion, at 1 State Street, NW cor. Whitehall Street (ca. 1657), was renamed **Whitehall** by the first English governor and occupied a tiny peninsula projecting from the east end of the Battery at this point. **Robert Fulton** resided in a different building on the same site a century later.

Leave the Battery Park area and enter the space of Bowling Green, the widening of Lower Broadway in front of the Custom House.

Bowling Green:

[F 5.] Street Plan of New Amsterdam and Colonial New York, the full width of all street beds lying within an irregular curved triangle bounded by (and including the street beds of) Wall St. on the N; Broadway, Bowling Green, and Whitehall Street on the W; and Pearl Street on the E. ★

With the demapping of a part of Stone Street for the construction of **No. 85 Broad Street** [see F 8c.], the Landmarks Preservation Commission in 1983 designated as a **landmark** the old **boundary lines of the streets** that still mark the paths of the city's venerable Dutch and English colonial thoroughfares, many of which date from the 1600s. The officially designated **irregular street pattern,** in vivid contrast to later gridiron layouts, reflects an approach found in **medieval European city building** quite familiar to those who settled Manhattan in the 17th and early 18th centuries.

[F 5a.] Bowling Green, foot of Broadway. Altered, various years. Restored, redesigned, reconstructed, 1978, M. Paul Friedberg & Assocs., landscape architects. ★

Adjacent to the Dutch cattle market, this oval open space became a "parade" and was leased in 1733 for the annual fee of one peppercorn as a quasi-public bowling ground (or green), for the "Beauty & Ornament of the Said Street as well as for the Recreation & delight of the Inhabitants." The fence remaining today was erected in 1771–1772, although its decorative crowns were snapped off by exuberant patriots after the reading of the Declaration of Independence on July 9, 1776. The same patriots pulled down the gilded lead statue of **George III,** much of which was then reportedly melted down into bullets used against the redcoats.

The 1978 reconstruction removed an atrocious "1950s Modern" glassed-in, flat-topped subway entrance and relocated the 1896 **de Peyster** statue [see F 9c.] thereby restoring the simplicity of this patch of green amid the district's sunless canyons.

Clockwise, enclosing Bowling Green, from the west:

Note: For No. 1 Broadway, see [F 3d.].

[F 5b.] Bowling Green Offices, 11 Broadway, at Bowling Green. W side. 1898. W. & G. Audsley. Altered, 1920, Ludlow & Peabody.

"Eclectic" was invented for stylistic collections such as this. The battered **"Egyptian"** pylons framing the entrance are bizarre imports. Above the 3rd floor, however, the spirit changes: strong glazed-brick piers with articulated spandrels have much the bold verticality of the Chicago School. Built by financier **Spencer Trask,** founder of **Yadoo,** the writers' colony in Saratoga Springs, N.Y.

[F 5c.] Originally **Cunard Building (offices),** 25 Broadway, SW cor. Morris St. 1921. Benjamin Wistar Morris, architect; Carrère & Hastings, consulting architects. Great Hall: ceiling paintings, Ezra Winter; conversion to post office, 1977, Handren Assocs.

This "Renaissance" facade, and its neighbors, handsomely surround Bowling Green with a high order of group architecture. What matters most at **No. 25,** however, is its great **booking hall,** with its elaborately decorated groined and domical vaults, thankfully left undamaged by the U.S. Postal Service installation. It was in this **grand setting** that passage on such liners as the *Queen Mary* and the two *Queen Elizabeths* was purchased. (The Classical container is home to a freestanding post office **spaceframe** that could have been considered appropriate there only in the 1970s. Luckily it permanently damages nothing of the walls or vaults.)

[F 4d.] Rectory, Bayley Seton Shrine   **[F 7.]** The United States Custom House

[F 5d.] 29 Broadway (offices), NW cor. Morris St. to Trinity Place. 1931. Sloan & Robertson.

The tower's slim 31-story Broadway face widens to a broad Trinity Place backside, but what a **wonderfully ornamented Art Deco** experience it all is—except for the 6-story Broadway annex (where once was Schrafft's), which is just a timid refacing. *Survey the tower's lobby.*

[F 6a.] 26 Broadway (offices)/originally **Standard Oil Building,** NE cor. Beaver St. 1922. Carrère & Hastings and Shreve, Lamb & Blake.

This curving facade reinforces the street's group architecture, working particularly well with its friend, **No. 25,** across the green. Begun as **The** Standard Oil Building, built by the Standard Oil Trust Organization—**The** trust—the earliest structure on the site (1885) was only 9 stories tall. Enveloped and enlarged over the years, it served until John D. Rockefeller's trust was broken up, in 1911. Then, one of the trust's five offspring, Standard Oil Company of New York, **Socony** (later called Socony-Vacuum, Socony-Mobil, and now Mobil), lived here until it removed to its new building on East 42nd Street in 1956 [see M Manhattan/United Nations–Turtle Bay U 6.].

The 480-foot-high **pyramidal tower** is squared to the **city's uptown gridiron,** rather than to the loose geometry of lower Manhattan's street pattern. The designers were concerned with the tower as an element in the city's **skyline,** not as a **local form.**

[F 7.] Originally **U.S. Custom House,** 1 Bowling Green, bet. State and Whitehall Sts. to Bridge St. 1907. Cass Gilbert. Sculptures, E to W: Asia, America, Europe, Africa, Daniel Chester French; Adolph A. Weinman, associate. Cartouche at 7th-story attic, Karl Bitter. Rotunda ceiling paintings, 1937, Reginald Marsh. ★ Partial interior ★.

Until the establishment of a federal income tax, in 1913, the primary means of **financing the costs** of national government was through the **imposition of customs duties.** New York being the busiest point of entry for foreign goods, *this* Custom House became the nation's largest collector of such funds. It's no accident that this structure is so grand, one of the city's *grandest* Beaux Arts buildings, now reloved by modernists searching for fresh meaning in architecture. The **monumental sculptures** by French (better known for his seated Lincoln at the memorial in Washington) are very much **part of the architecture** of the facade, their whiteness—and that of those at the attic by other sculptors—a rich counterpoint to the structure's gray granite, both in form and color.

No less grand is the interior, whose giant oval rotunda, embellished by **Reginald Marsh's WPA-commissioned murals,** is both the crowning architectural space and the challenge for the structure's reuse. It has remained vacant except for temporary activities since the **Customs** Service vacated the **Custom** House in favor of the World Trade Center in 1973.

Now cross Broadway and turn southward.

The commanding site south of Bowling Green has been successively occupied by: **1)** Niuew Amsterdam's fortification, Fort Amsterdam (renamed Fort James, Fort Willem Hendrick, Fort James [again], Fort William, Fort William Henry, Fort Anne, and finally Fort George); **2)** Government House, built in 1790 to be George Washington's executive mansion (except that the nation's capital removed to Philadelphia); then used as the Governor's Mansion (until the state capital moved to Albany in 1797), briefly leased as John Avery's tavern; and then used as temporary Custom House until lost to a fire in 1815; **3)** a row of fine town houses, minor mansions, later occupied by the world's leading shipping companies (and so dubbed Steamship Row); and **4)** its current occupant, the U.S. Custom House building.

The **witty kiosk** sited on the Belgian block-paved forecourt echoes the building's forms and, thanks to the **N.Y. Landmarks Conservancy,** offers a fine introductory exhibit (*1983, Keith Godard/ Works, designer*).

The Produce Exchange of 1884 by architect George B. Post, which occupied the site of 2 Broadway (1959, Emery Roth & Sons. Entry mural, Lee Krasner), was one of the city's greatest architectural losses in the post-World War II years. That enormous red terra-cotta-and-brick Romanesque Revival construction is echoed today only in miniature by Post's extant Brooklyn Historical Society [see WC Brooklyn H 38.] The ruddy Exchange contrasted vividly with its newer, paler, limestone and granite neighbors until its demolition in 1957.

Walk south down the Custom House's left (western) flank, Whitehall Street, and turn left (west) on Pearl Street.

Pearl Street:

[F 8a.] Broad Financial Center (offices), 33 Whitehall St., NE cor. Pearl St. to Bridge St. 1986. Fox & Fowle.

BFC's developers wanted to **link its name to Broad Street,** a block away from the main entrance. The intervening, low, surrealist limestone Clearing House Association [see below] wanted to sell its air rights. A deal was struck whereby the pale-blue, mirrored office tower buys the air rights, overlaps its low neighbor, and obtains a tenuous tie to the desired street. Check out the BFC's **breathlessly wild and crazy lobby**—what a clock!

[F 8b.] New York Clearing House Association, 100 Broad St., bet. Pearl and Bridge Sts. W side. 1962. Rogers & Butler.

A funky little building whose occupant provides a vital financial service. It makes certain that banks observe a coherent system of clearing each other's checks.

[F 8c.] 85 Broad Street/Goldman Sachs (offices), bet. Pearl and S. William Sts. to Coenties Alley. 1983. Skidmore, Owings & Merrill.

The structure's enormous—and ungainly—bulk (close to a million square feet) results from the purchase and **transfer of air rights** from its Fraunces Tavern Block neighbors across the street; its tan cast-stone wall surfaces from an interpretation of the Zoning Law's mandate that they harmonize with the Historic District's protected facades.

While arcaded **No. 85** excises part of **ancient Stone Street's curving route** [see F 5.], it pays homage to that thoroughfare's path via a **curved elevator lobby** and the introduction of **vestigial curbs** where Stone Street once intersected Broad. *With eyes already directed to the ground, turn the Pearl Street corner and view* evidence of the 17th century in two glassed-in displays below the sidewalk surface, discovered in an archaeological survey required of the developer by the Landmarks Preservation Commission.

Broad Street was in Dutch times *de Heere Gracht* [The Gentleman's Canal], a drainage and shipping canal that reached today's Exchange Place, where a ferry to Long Island docked. The canal was filled in 100 years before the Revolution, but its path remains in the street's extraordinary width—at least for this part of town. Manhattan's oldest streets cross Broad: **Bridge** Street was at the first bridge immediately adjacent to the waterfront at Pearl Street; **Pearl** should be "Mother of Pearl," in fact, for the glistening shells that once lined its shore—and its pavement; **Stone** Street was the first to be cobbled. The geometry of the public space has not greatly changed, except that Broad's meeting with the shoreline is some 600 feet further into the harbor than at the time of the canal's fill, making **Water, Front,** and **South** Streets on landfill of a later date.

Corner of Broad and Beaver Sts. Outdoor dining had already gained fashion in 1906

The Stadt Huys, seat of Dutch colonial government, stood on the north side of Pearl St. (No. 71) between Broad Street and Coenties Alley. During preliminary explorations for foundations for an office building on this site, archaeologists found a number of colonial artifacts. Here the old shoreline was so close that tides at times lapped against the Stadt Huys steps.

Proceed north along Pearl Street, as it curves parallel to today's East River shoreline; remember that Pearl Street once marked the edge of Nieuw Amsterdam and was earlier called the wal (embankment) by the Dutch and The Strand by the English.

[F 8d.] Fraunces Tavern Block Historic District, bounded by Pearl, Broad, and Water Sts., and Coenties Slip. ★ Block created on landfill, ca. 1689. Structures (including Fraunces Tavern), 1719–1883 with 20th-century additions, restorations, alterations, Stephen B. Jacobs & Assocs., Samuel S. Arlen & Frederick B. Fox, Jr., and others.

Faced with the rapid diminution of Lower Manhattan's stock of Federal style and other early buildings, a circumstance prominently decried in Ada Louise Huxtable's 1964 book *Classic New York,* this block was singled out for historic designation. It is regrettable that no *two* sides of any blockfront were included, denying future visitors a sense of the true scale and environment of contained space of that era. *But do visit the nearby South Street Seaport Historic District.*

[F 8d.] Fraunces Tavern Block Historic District against New York Plaza towers

 [F 8e.] Fraunces Tavern (restaurant and museum), 54 Pearl St., SE cor. Broad St. 1907. William Mersereau. ★ ☆ **Museum open to the public.**

The tavern of Samuel Fraunces occupied this plot and achieved great historic note in the Revolution: for ten days in 1783 it served as Washington's last residence as general. On December 4 he bade farewell to his officers there and withdrew to his estate at Mount Vernon. He returned six years later and five blocks away to Broad Street's head, to take office as president of the United States at old City Hall, by then renamed Federal Hall [see F 12b.].

The present building is a highly conjectural construction—**not** a restoration—based on "typical" buildings of "the period," parts of remaining walls, and a lot of guesswork. With enthusiasm more harmless when attached to genealogy than to wishful archaeology, today's tavern has been billed as the Real McCoy. Such charades enabled **George Washington Slept Here** architecture to strangle reality in much of suburban America.

At Hanover Square, turn left (westerly).

[F 9a.] 7 Hanover Square (offices), bet. Water and Pearl Sts. N side. 1982. Norman Jaffe, design architect. Emery Roth & Sons, architects.

Twenty-six stories of latter-day neo-Georgian hype (red brick and limestonelike lintels over every one of the 1,000+ windows), squatting atop an overscaled reinterpretation of Frank Lloyd Wright's Midway Gardens. All of this is supposed to harmonize with the architecture of tiny, 3-story brownstone India House (whose air rights were transferred), quietly minding its own business across narrow Pearl Street.

 [F 9b.] India House/originally **Hanover Bank, New York Cotton Exchange,** and **W. R. Grace & Company,** 1 Hanover Sq., bet. Pearl and Stone Sts. 1851–1854. Richard F. Carman, carpenter.

A Florentine palazzo, typical of many brownstone commercial buildings that once dotted this area, now replaced by newer and denser construction. Brownstone is so associated with the New York row house that we almost do a double take on seeing it clothing a **Wall Street** building. Now a club, it harbors a maritime museum. Handsome stripped-Corinthian columns. **Carman,** the carpenter (as he sometimes listed himself in the city directory), was later responsible for **Carmans-**

ville, a village that stretched along Broadway between today's West 142nd to West 158th Streets.

Harry's [at Hanover Square] (bar/restaurant), 1 Hanover Sq., SW cor. Stone St.

Within part of the west flank of **India House,** this public restaurant shares some of the volume of that private club. Schnitzel, hasenpfeffer, dumplings, and other goodies are devised to adjust the jowls to bankers' proportions. Good and noisy.

[F 9c.] Hanover Square, NW cor. Pearl St. and Hanover Sq. 1976.

Until the 1970s ancient Stone Street, with both curblines intact, ran through this space. Now it is a pleasantly paved area that is a happy home to the seated bronze figure (*1896, George E. Bissel*); of **Abraham de Peyster,** a wealthy Dutch goldsmith; it had previously added to the clutter of Bowling Green.

Hanover Square was the original printing house square. At 81 Pearl, William Bradford established the first printing press in the Colonies in 1693. The Great Fire of 1835 substantially destroyed all buildings in an area of which this square was the center: the area between Coenties Slip, Broad, Wall, and South Streets, excepting the row facing Broad, and those facing Wall between William and Broad.

Five Corners: intersection of William, South William, Beaver Sts.

[F 9d.] Banca Commerciale Italiana (offices)/originally **Seligman Brothers Building/**later **Lehman Brothers Building,** 1 William St., SE cor. Hanover Sq. 1907. Francis H. Kimball & Julian C. Levi. Altered and expanded for Banca Commerciale Italiana, 1984, Gino Valle, architect; Jeremy P. Lang, associate architect; Fred L. Liebmann, consulting architect.

A Renaissance Revival structure in stone, rusticated from sidewalk to cornice. Although regrettably divorced from its original windows, it is now happily married to a brilliant addition that poetically harmonizes with many of its venerable architectural nuances.

[F 9b.] India House: ornate fire escape   **[F 9e.]** Delmonico's Restaurant, 1977

[F 9e.] Delmonico's (restaurant), 56 Beaver St., SW cor. South William St. 1891. James Brown Lord.

Occupying, like the **Flatiron Building** uptown, a valuable but awkward triangular space left between two converging streets. A distinguished restaurant for almost a century, this palatial headquarters was designed by Lord at the height of Delmonico's prestige and popularity. Orange terra-cotta and brick; the portal behind Delmonico's porch was *reputedly* brought from Pompeii by the Delmonico brothers themselves.

[F 9f.] Originally **Corn Exchange Bank Building (offices)/**later **Corn Exchange Bank Trust Company/**later **Chemical Corn Exchange Bank,** 15 William St., NW cor. Beaver St. 1894. R. H. Robertson. Addition to N, 1902, R. H. Robertson.

Built in two stages: the 11-story corner, followed by the 20-story midblock "tower." Note the magnificent winged stone cayatid supporting the all-important corner of this building at this five-fingered intersection.

Bear right (north) on William Street.

[F 10a.] **Canadian Imperial Bank of Commerce (offices)/**formerly **First National City Trust Company/**originally the **City Bank Farmers' Trust Company,** 22 William St., bet. Beaver St. and Exchange Place. 1931. Cross & Cross.

A slender fifty-seven-story tower of limestone, from the awkward period of architectural history between buildings-as-columns and steel-cage construction: neo-Renaissance *vs.* Art Moderne.

Look up to see the Gulliver-sized coins—not quoins—that ring the building's limestone base.

Wall Street

An area filled with history—and a host of historical plaques, markers (note those of the Municipal Art Society on the lampposts along Wall Street), cornerstones, and notices of building erection, mostly in A.D. MDCCCCLXXXXVIII terms.

[F 9f.] Originally Corn Exchange Bank   **[F 10a.]** Orig. City Bank Farmers' Trust

Wall Street: The Dutch wall of 1653 (a palisade of wood palings) was built as protection against attack from English colonies to the north. The English took it down, but the name remains.

Turn right (east) on Wall Street's south side to Pearl Street, make a U-turn, and return (west) on Wall Street's north side.

[F 10b.] **Citibank branch/**formerly **First National City Bank/**lower portion formerly the **U.S. Custom House** (1863–1899)/originally **Merchants' Exchange,** 55 Wall St., bet. William and Hanover Sts. 1836–1842. Isaiah Rogers. Converted to Custom House, 1863, William A. Potter. Remodeled and doubled in height, 1907. McKim, Mead & White. ★

Smoked granite. After the destruction of the **first Merchants' Exchange** in the Great Fire of 1835, Rogers erected a 3-story **Ionic** "temple" with a central domed trading hall on the same site. Later used as the **Custom House,** it was remodeled in 1907 (after the Fed's removal to Bowling Green) as the head office of the **National City Bank:** another tier of columns, this time **Corinthian,** was superimposed to double the cubic content.

During banking hours a visit to the main floor's banking hall is in order (*altered, 1981, The Walker Group, designers*).

[F 11a.] Originally **Seamen's Bank for Savings Headquarters (offices)**/now **Williamsburgh Savings Bank,** 74 Wall St., NW cor Pearl St. 1926. Benjamin Wistar Morris.

Craggy ashlar with a tall round-arched opening into the banking room. A friendly, romantic addition to the cold Wall Street canyon. Compare it with the same architect's later bank office building on the west end of this block [see F 11c.].

U-turn west on Wall Street.

[F 10b.] Once Merchants' Exchange   **[F 11a.]** Orig. Seamen's Bk. for Savgs.

[F 11b.] Morgan Bank Headquarters   **[F 12a.]** Pyramid-topped 40 Wall St.

[F 11b.] Morgan Bank Headquarters (offices), 60 Wall St., bet. Nassau and William Sts. N side to Pine St. 1988. Kevin Roche John Dinkeloo & Assocs.

Planted on 1¼ acres is this massive 1.7 million-square-foot, 52-story tower, which not only reinterprets in contemporary terms the Classical column elements of base, shaft, and capital but almost literally replicates the column itself. The bold streetfront arcade is meant to echo the forms of **No. 55,** across narrow Wall Street [F 10b.]. The transfer of Citibank's air rights made possible the total bulk on this side.

[F 11c.] Bank of New York Building (offices), 48 Wall St., NE cor. William St. 1928. Benjamin Wistar Morris.

Not especially noteworthy Renaissance Revival, but the banking room, particularly as seen through the large arched windows on both Wall and William Streets, is a special and serene space. The bank's sense of taste and feeling for history are evident in the display of cornerstones from earlier headquarters and a bronze plaque describing Lower Manhattan of yore.

Compare the coolness of this architecture with the same architect's other, more romantic bank office building at the block's east end [see F 11a.].

[F 12a.] 40 Wall Street (offices)/originally **Bank of the Manhattan Company,** bet. William and Nassau Sts. 1929. H. Craig Severance and Yasuo Matsui. Ground floor remodeled, 1963, Carson, Lundin & Shaw.

A skyline bank building, now best observed from an upper floor of the composite bank to which it has moved its quarters: the **Chase Manhattan** on Chase Manhattan Plaza to the north [see N 2.]. The pyramidal crown was the strong and simple symbol of the original bank. Chartered first as a water company (the Manhattan Company) and the city's first quasi-public utility, it became redundant in 1842 when the municipally owned **Croton aqueduct** began to bring water to Manhattan. Always permitted by a clause in its charter to engage in banking, it continued, after 1842, solely as the **Bank** of the Manhattan Company, the latter, parent organization becoming incidental to its offshoot. (In the years following World War II this tower fell victim to a collision by a small airplane.)

[F 12b.] The Pine Street elevation of Federal Hall National Memorial in 1966

[F 12b.] Federal Hall National Memorial/formerly **U.S. Sub-Treasury Building** (1862–1925)/originally **U.S. Custom House** (1842–1862), 28 Wall St., NE cor. Nassau St. 1834–1842. Town & Davis, with John Frazee and Samuel Thompson. ★

No, George Washington did not take his oath of office in front of *this* building but, rather, its predecessor, the former city hall, called Federal Hall. It had been remodeled by **Pierre L'Enfant** from the old shell, to which local government had been removed in **1701** from the Dutch **Stadt Huys** on Pearl Street. The current name, **Federal Hall National Memorial,** commemorates the earlier structure.

This **Doric-**columned temple and Staten Island's **Sailors' Snug Harbor** are the institutional stars of New York's **Greek Revival.** The **Wall Street** facade is a simplified **Parthenon,** without the sculptured frieze or pediment. Carved from marble quarried in Westchester County, it is raised on a high base to handle the change in grade from **Pine** to **Wall.** Inside the rectangular volume is a very non-Greek rotunda, the principal, and startling, space—rather like finding a cubical space in a helical conch shell.

The old **Assay Office** (*1823, Martin Thompson*) stood to the east until the building was demolished to make room for bigger things; its facade was rescued and is currently to to be seen at the **Metropolitan Museum's American Wing** [see E Manhattan/Met Museum M 12.].

J(ohn) Q(uincy) A(dams) Ward's statue of Washington (*1883*) stands on the approximate spot where the man himself took the oath, in 1789.

For a Broad Street excursion, detour to the left (south) or skip to the continuation of the tour at [F 15.].

Broad Street: South of Wall Street

[F 13a.] Morgan Guaranty Trust Company/formerly **J. P. Morgan & Company,** 23 Wall St., SE cor. Broad St. 1913. Trowbridge & Livingston. ★

Interesting more for its history than its architecture: **J. Pierpont Morgan** epitomized Wall Street to capitalists, communists, radicals, and conservatives alike. And, of course, when Wall Street was to be bombed, this was considered its **sensitive center of control:** on September 16, 1920, an **anarchist** ignited a wagonload of explosives next to the Wall Street flank. **33** persons were killed, **400** injured. The scars remain visible in the stonework.

[F 13b.] New York Stock Exchange, 8 Broad St., bet. Wall St. and Exchange Place. W side. 1903. George B. Post. Addition, 1923, Trowbridge & Livingston. Pediment sculpture, J. Q. A. Ward and Paul Bartlett. **Open to the public:** Use 20 Broad Street entry.

One of the few great architectural spaces accessible to the public in this city.

The original **Roman** temple facade by **Post** is a far cry from his **Queen Anne style Brooklyn Historical Society** 22 years before. [See WC Brooklyn/Brooklyn Heights H 38.]. The **Columbian Exposition** of **1893** had swept such earth-colored picturesque architecture under the rug. The rage for **neo-Classical** architecture and cities was compelling even to those who had been the Goths of architecture. The original mythological figures of the pediment became so deteriorated that their stone was replaced with sheet metal, secretively, so that the public would not know that any facet of the Stock Exchange was vulnerable.

[F 13b.] Stock Exchange pediment   **[F 16a., b.]** Irving Trust & Trinity Ch.

[F 14a.] 40 Broad Street (offices), bet. Exchange Place and Beaver St. W side. 1982. Gruzen & Partners.

A gold-toned entrance carved from a pale stone surround, rhythmically punctuated by detailless windows. (Bring back mullions!) The rear, fronting on New Street (a spectacular canyon), offers a very dramatic sloping facade.

[F 14b.] Bank of America International (offices)/originally **Lee-Higginson Bank** 37-41 Broad St., bet. Exchange Place and Beaver St. E side. 1929. Cross & Cross. Frieze, Leo Friedlander, sculptor.

This chaste convex bow that follows Broad Street's curve is a comforting gesture. Contrary to what usually transpires during a building boom, this *9-story* structure replaced the *26-story* Trust Company of America Building (*1907, Francis H. Kimball.*)

[F 14c.] American Bank Note Company Headquarters, 70 Broad St., bet. Marketfield and Beaver Sts. W side. 1908. Kirby, Petit & Green.

Look up to see the true shape of Classical columns: these resemble colossal Michelob beer bottles. Endangered.

Back up Broad Street's hill—its wide part was the site of the Curb Exchange, meeting indoors on Trinity Place since 1921 as the American Stock Exchange. The Curb's brokers literally met on the curb, out of doors, between 1865 and 1921.

Take a left (west) back on Wall Street.

[F 15.] Bankers Trust Company Building (offices), 16 Wall St., NW cor. Nassau St. 1912. Trowbridge & Livingston.

This is the tall one in the skyline, with the stepped pyramid top. When built, it was called the world's tallest structure (540 feet) on so small a plot (94 × 97 feet). A true New York City landmark but not officially designated. (The pyramid is invisible from the sidewalk.)

Broadway, at the head of Wall Street.

[F 16a.] Irving Trust Company (offices), 1 Wall St., SE cor. Broadway. 1932. Voorhees, Gmelin & Walker. Addition to S, 1965, Smith, Smith, Haines, Lundberg & Waehler.

Ralph Walker's experiments in the plastic molding of skyscraper form, both in massing and in detail, culminate here in this shimmering limestone tower, a fitting companion of quality to Trinity Church across Broadway. Don't miss the lobby, which resonates to the same Art Deco melodies. Now, as for the annex, that's another matter.

[F 16b.] Trinity Church (Episcopal), Broadway at the head of Wall St. W side. 1846. Richard Upjohn. ★ **William Backhouse Astor Memorial Altar and Reredos,** 1876, Frederick Clarke Withers. **Chapel of All Saints,** 1913, Thomas Nash. **Bishop Manning Memorial Wing,** 1965, Adams & Woodbridge. **Churchyard.** 1681–

Nestled in the canyons of **Broadway** and **Trinity Place,** Trinity's form is totally comprehensible to the pedestrian: on the axis of **Wall Street** the canyon walls read as surfaces, while Trinity sits importantly, an anthracite jewel, bedded in a green baize cemetery. The cemetery offers a green retreat for summer-tired office workers at noontime. Bronze doors designed by Richard Morris Hunt were executed by Charles Niehaus, Karl Bitter, and J. Massey Rhind (left entrance, main entrance, and right entrance, respectively).

Cemetery monuments of particular note include the pyramid of **Alexander Hamilton, Robert Fulton's** bronze bas-relief, and that of **William Bradford.**

The attached chapel must not be confused with **Trinity's** colonial chapels, which were separate and remotely located church buildings serving this immense **Episcopal** parish. Typical of the latter is **St. Paul's Chapel** at **Fulton** and **Broadway.** The parish is an enormous landowner (Fulton to Christopher Streets, Broadway west to the river was its original grant from Queen Anne in 1705). Thus, the proselytizing of the faith through missionary activities could be financed comfortably (**St. Augustine's** and **St. Christopher's Chapels** on the Lower East Side are further examples).

The original **Trinity** Church was founded in **1696,** erected in **1698,** enlarged and "beautified" in **1737,** and burned to the ground in **1776.** A second building, constructed in **1788–1790,** was demolished in **1839.**

[F 16c.] Trinity and U.S. Realty Buildings (offices), 111 and 115 Broadway, at Thames St. W. side. 1905, 1907. Both by Francis H. Kimball.

Rich buildings from top to bottom; their narrow ends at **Broadway** are broken **Gothic** forms with strongly scaled details. They have a great deal of personality vis-à-vis the passing pedestrian. Unlike the blank austerity of **1 Wall,** the temple entrance of **100 Broadway,** or the modern openness of **Chase Manhattan's** vast transparent lobby for bureaucrats en masse, these are buildings for individual people. One could feel possessive about them. **Bully!**

[F 16d.] Bank of Tokyo/originally **American Surety Company,** 100 Broadway, SE cor. Pine St. 1895. Bruce Price. Alterations, 1921, Herman Lee Meader. 1975, Kajima International, designers. Welton Becket Assocs., architects.

Kajima, through designer **Nobutaka Ashihara,** has recycled Price's "rusticated pillar" into modern and economic elegance. The Italians excelled at this in the 1950s (as at the **Castello Sforzesco** in Milan, converted to a museum); the Japanese now equal the Italians' best in New York.

The ladies above, by sculptor **J. Massey Rhind,** are a stern Athenian octet.

[F 12b., 16b.] G. Washington & Trinity   **[F 17c.]** 1 Exchange Plaza & neighbor

[F 16d.] The 1975 recycling of American Surety Building into Bank of Tokyo

[F 16e.] Wall Street Subway Station, IRT Lexington Avenue Line, under Broadway at Wall St. 1905. Heins & La Farge. ★ Redesigned, 1979, N.Y.C. Transit Authority Architectural Staff.

A restrained Heins & La Farge design upgraded by the TA in full height, ultramarine blue glazed brick. (*If you're feeling blue, don't venture here.*) The restored, golden oak and bronze change booth on the downtown side is a wonder to behold.

[F 17a.] Empire Building (offices), 71 Broadway, SW cor. Rector St. to Trinity Place. 1894. Renwick, Aspinwall & Tucker.

An ornate wall, a backdrop to **Trinity Churchyard** to the north.

Financier Russell Sage was almost assassinated in 1891 in the Empire Building that occupied this spot before replacement by this Empire Building. He quickly threw his male secretary at the bomber, muffling the intended damage to himself but almost killing his secretary. Sage withstood his assistant's law suit and died very rich. His widow later established the Russell Sage philanthopies, among them Forest Hills Gardens [see C Queens C 53.].

[F 17b.] Originally **American Railway Express Company Building (offices)/**now **American Bureau of Shipping Building,** 65 Broadway, bet. Exchange Alley and Rector St. W side to Trinity Place. 1917. Renwick, Aspinwall & Tucker. Altered, 1979, Carl J. Petrilli.

An H-plan results in a pair of slender 23-story wings, embracing (and arching over) light courts **fore and aft.** Note the **asymmetric** eagle on the lower arch and the **symmetric** one on the arch atop the building.

[F 17c.] 1 Exchange Plaza (offices), Broadway SW cor. Exchange Alley to Trinity Place. 1981. Fox & Fowle. **[F 17d.] 45 Broadway Atrium (offices),** bet. Exchange Alley and Morris St. W side to Trinity Place. 1983. Fox & Fowle.

A pair of sleek, exquisitely detailed, brick and glass towers by the same developer (HRO International) and architects. They would never have been separate structures were it not for the exorbitant price asked by the tiny fast-food holdout between. Note the brickwork mural on the wall facing the Atrium's windows—to appease those whose view is north.

Take a right (west) down the narrow, repaved brick Exchange Alley to Trinity Place, and turn right (north).

[F 18a.] Originally **American Express Company (warehouse),** 46 Trinity Place, bet. Exchange Alley and Rector St. W side. ca. 1880.

Note the terra-cotta seal (now weatherbeaten and painted) with the company emblem in relief.

[F 18b.] Trinity Place Bridge, Trinity Parish, linking Trinity Churchyard and 74 Trinity Place. Trinity Place bet. Rector and Thames Sts. 1987. Lee Harris Pomeroy Assocs.

As Trinity's congregation grew older and traffic on Trinity Place greater, the church felt **a need to separate** its aging parishioners commuting to their activity rooms across the street at **No. 74** from the danger of cars, trucks, and bicycles. This 80-foot-long bridge is the answer.

[F 19.] N.Y.U. Graduate School of Business Administration: [F 19a.] Charles E. Merrill Hall, 90 Trinity Place, SW cor. Thames St. 1975. Skidmore, Owings & Merrill. **[F 19b.] Nichols Hall,** 100 Trinity Place, bet. Thames and Cedar Sts. W side. 1959. Skidmore, Owings & Merrill.

A pair, connected by an enclosed bridge high over Thames Street. Stylish in 1959, the northerly **Nichols** has, in retrospect, become a dull, white-speckled brick ancestor to the off-black **Merrill** monolith to the south, a classic background Modern monument.

Turn into Thames Street between the two N.Y.U. buildings, and walk west; zigzag left on Greenwich and right (west) again on Albany street to the last stops on the tour.

[F 20a.] 90 West Street Building (offices), bet. Albany and Cedar Sts. E side. 1907. Cass Gilbert.

Limestone and cast terra-cotta. Increasingly interesting and complex the higher you raise your eyes: designed for **a view from the harbor** or the eyries of an adjacent skyscraper, rather than the ordinary West Street pedestrian. A similar, but less successful, use of terra-cotta than **Gilbert's** spectacular **Woolworth Building.**

In 1985 the upper-floor colonnades and mansard roof were brightly lighted, surprising many people who had never given this building any notice.

[F 20b.] Le Meridien Liberty (hotel), West St. bet. Carlisle and Albany Sts. E side. 1989. Ashihara Assocs.

Thirty or so stories of rooms looking out across the harbor tower above a base of banquet spaces and meeting rooms.

[F 19a.] Charles E. Merrill Hall, N.Y.U.   **[F 20a.]** Cass Gilbert's 90 West Street

The Hudson-Fulton Celebration 1609–1909, as part of the fall festivities, illuminated many of the city's prominent buildings and bridges—not with floodlights but with necklaces of bare electric bulbs, then a relatively new technique.

END of Tour A. The nearest subways are in the World Trade Center (IRT Seventh Avenue Line local, Cortlandt Street Station, BMT Broadway Line local, Cortlandt Street Station, or the IND Eighth Avenue Line, Chambers Street/World Trade Center Station).

WATER STREET CORRIDOR

Lower Manhattan's street of the million-square-foot towers.

Under Mayor Robert F. Wagner, City Planning Commission chairman William F. R. Ballard commissioned the **Lower Manhattan Plan of 1966,** prepared by Wallace McHarg Associates and Whittlesey, Conklin & Rossant. It promised a **lively** and **handsome pedestrian world** south of Canal Street, foot-eased by small and unnoxious electric buses and enlarged through landfill to the pierhead line. New residential communities surrounding riverside plazas—"windows on the water-front"—would be provided. With some **adjustments, detours, and compromises** we have the World Trade Center, Battery Park City, and a new Lower Manhattan skyline of million-square-foot, **flat-topped boxes** that line the Water Street Corridor.

From the harbor and the Brooklyn Heights Promenade it is these towers, the ones along Water Street and others, that have come to encircle the Financial District's heart. They have **muffled from view** the **constellation** of tall, slender, 1920s and 1930s Art Deco office buildings and the **flamboyant pinnacles** of their earlier, shorter, neo-Classical cousins, the structures that made up the inspired—if unplanned— Lower Manhattan skyline that was once the world-renowned symbol of New York City.

Walking Tour B: A **Water Street walk** northward from the **Staten Island Ferry Terminal** to **South Street Seaport,** at Fulton and Water Streets. START in Peter Minuit Plaza in front of the ferry terminal. (IRT Seventh Avenue local to South Ferry Station or BMT Broadway Line local to Whitehall Street Station. Alternates: A short walk from the start is the IRT Lexington Avenue Line express Bowling Green Station or the IRT Seventh Avenue express Wall Street Station. When leaving the alternates, ask which way to the ferry terminal.)

Before embarking up Water Street, spend a moment in front of the ferry terminal:

Staten Island Ferry, foot of Whitehall Street at Battery Park, not only ranks as a tourist mecca of great delight but also explains the overall arrangement of the water-bound city quickly, clearly, and with pleasure. For a modest 25¢ (round trip) you will experience one of the world's greatest (and shortest) water voyages, through the richly endowed harbor, past buoys, the West Bank Light House, Governors and Liberty Islands, and the U.S. Army Military Ocean Terminal (the old Bayonne naval base), to the community of St. George at Staten Island's northeastern shore. (If you decide to stay, turn to the Staten Island section of this guide. Otherwise, just travel the ferry route in reverse.) This is the low-income substitute for a glamorous arrival in New York by transatlantic liner, receiving first *Liberty*'s salute and then the dramatic silhouette of Lower Manhattan's skyline. On a lucky day you will surge through the wake of freighters, container ships, tankers, tugs, sludge boats, pleasure craft, and the few extant liners used for cruises, even an occasional warship.

[W 1a.] Staten Island Ferry Terminal, City of New York, South St. foot of Whitehall St. 1954. Roberts & Schaefer, consulting engineers.

Until removed for the proposed **South Ferry Plaza** tower complex [see below], the terminal will continue to rank as the world's **most banal portal to joy** (a public rest room en route to Mecca). Kafka would have had the shivers, although regular users seem inured to its **bile-colored** shortcomings. A blight on the celebration of arrival and departure at a great city, soon, one hopes, to be remedied.

[W 1b.] Proposed **South Ferry Plaza (mixed-use tower)** South St. foot of Whitehall St. Expected completion, 1992. Fox & Fowle and Frank Williams, associate architects.

A 50-story stake of metal and glass, driven into the very heart of that **vampire,** the Staten Island Ferry Terminal. Chosen in 1986 from submissions by 8 developer-architect teams responding to a City **R.F.P.** (Request for Proposals), written to derive **maximum income** from municipally owned property. The winning design harks back to those many unbuilt neo-Classical dreams of the 1920s. Portent of the future?

Upstream from the ferry terminal is another, older ferry terminal:

[W 2.] Originally **Municipal Ferry Piers, N.Y.C. Department of Docks & Ferries/**now **Battery Maritime Building, N.Y.C. Department of Ports, International Trade & Commerce,** 11 South St., foot of Whitehall St. S side. 1909. Walker & Gillette. ★

The false front on these aging ferry slips shows a raised porch with 40-foot columns to **Whitehall.** Green paint over sheet metal and steel structural members simulates verdigris copper. The **Governors Island ferry** today leaves from here. The only historical style which this inherits is the very idea of a colonnade; the columns, however, are original and relate to the material, sheet metal. Note the **Guastavino** tile soffits under the porch roof.

Ferry service to most points in Brooklyn ended on March 15, 1938.

[W 1b.] Prop. South Ferry Plaza proj.   **[W 2.]** Ornate Battery Maritime Bldg.

Find Water Street in the leaky open space that bears the Peter Minuit name, and proceed northeasterly. It's the wide street one full block inland from the river—just to the left of the very tall black tower—marked:

Water Street: curving version of midtown's Avenue of the Americas.

[W 3a.] 1 New York Plaza (offices), Whitehall St. bet. South and Water Sts. NE side to Broad St. 1969. William Lescaze & Assocs., design architects. Kahn & Jacobs, architects.

A behemoth. Thousands of interior decorators' picture frames form an unhappy facade on this **all too prominent,** dark, brooding office tower.

[W 3b.] 3 New York Plaza (offices)/originally **U.S. Army Building,** 39 Whitehall St., bet. Water and Pearl Sts. to Moore St. 1886. S. D. Hatch. Reconstructed and reclad, 1986, Wechsler, Grasso & Menziuso.

Concealed inches behind that slick green-and-white graph paper curtain wall is the masonry ghost of the building where hundreds of thousands of army inductees took their physicals for World War II and Korea. Occupying an entire (small) city block, it rests on the original foundations of the **1861 Produce Exchange,** by **Leopold Eidlitz.**

[W 4a.] 4 New York Plaza (offices), Water St. bet. Broad St. and Coenties Slip. S side. 1968. Carson, Lundin & Shaw. **[W 4b.] 2 New York Plaza (offices)/**briefly **American Express Plaza,** Broad St. NE cor. South St. 1970. Kahn & Jacobs.

Twenty-two-story **No. 4,** Manufacturers Hanover Trust's handsomely carved monolith of rich **earth-toned salt-and-pepper speckled brick,** is the earliest of the New York Plaza giants. Its careful choice of materials and details was meant to harmonize in quality, if not in scale, with the tiny Federal and Greek Revival survivors that were **still its neighbors** in the 1960s. Those survivors (except the Fraunces Tavern Block [see F 8d.]) and the color scheme rapidly gave way to non-ideas like the 40-story **No. 2.**

Coenties Slip: As the landfill crept seaward, this "slip," a tiny artificial bay for wharfing ships, was created with a diagonal breakwater paralleling the present west boundary. Eventually the breakwater was absorbed, as land projected even beyond its former tip.

[W 5a.] New York Vietnam Veterans Memorial, Vietnam Veterans Plaza/earlier **Jeanette Plaza/**originally **Jeanette Park,** on the bed of Coenties Slip bet. Water and South Sts. Jeanette Plaza, 1972, M. Paul Friedberg & Assocs. Memorial added, 1985. William Britt Fellows, Peter Wormser, architects. Joseph Ferrandino, writer.

A 70-foot-long, 14-foot-high rectangular prism surfaced in 12-inch-square glass blocks, lined with a granite shelf for visitors' offerings, and penetrated by two unadorned portals. The glass blocks, made **luminescent by night,** are **etched with excerpts** from speeches, news dispatches, and letters written home by those who were fighting in Nam. Chosen in a **national competition,** the winner is simple, thoughtful, carefully detailed, and neatly executed. But in sharp contrast to the emotionally powerful Vietnam Memorial in Washington, also a national competition winner, New York's fails to touch the heart.

At the river side of the plaza, looking across South Street and the FDR Drive viaduct is:

[W 5b.] Downtown Manhattan Heliport, Port Authority of N.Y. & N.J., East River opp. Vietnam Veterans Plaza. 1987. Port Authority of N.Y. & N.J. Architectural Design Team.

A modest but joyous Post Modern terminal building for those who hop around in whirlybirds. The Port Authority's staff can turn out some wonderful architecture.

[W 3a.] The brooding 1 N.Y. Plaza   **[W 6.]** Concrete-clad 55 Water Street

[W 6.] 55 Water Street (offices), bet. Coenties and Old Slips. SE side to South St. 1972. Emery Roth & Sons, architects. Terrace over South St., M. Paul Friedberg & Assocs, landscape architects.

Contains 3.68 million square feet; when opened, it was the world's largest private office building. But awkward. The deal for its bulk, arrived at through zoning modifications, also financed the redesigned Jeanette Plaza [see above]. *Take an escalator up between its south and north wings to visit its own elevated plaza.*

At Old Slip, turn right (southeasterly).

[W 7a.] Originally **1st Precinct, N.Y.C. Police Department/**now **Palatina (offices),** 100 Old Slip, bet. Front and South Sts. N side. 1911. Hunt & Hunt. ★

A rusticated Renaissance Revival palazzo, miniature in size, majestic in scale. It's considered the city's first modern police station.

[W 7b.] 1 Financial Square (offices), Front St. bet. Old Slip and Gouverneur Lane to South St. 1987. Edward Durell Stone Assocs.

One million square feet. Trading on the **transfer of development rights** from two low-rise neighbors, a demolished fire station (whose functions are now enveloped within the skyscraper) and 100 Old Slip [see above], this 36-story high rise is built on the former site of the **U.S. Assay Building** [see Necrology]. Financial Square's stone-clad base is supposed to harmonize with the stonework of the old station house.

Back to Water Street.

[W 7c.] 77 Water Street Building (offices), bet. Old Slip and Gouverneur Lane. E side to Front St. 1970. Emery Roth & Sons, architects. Street level and roof elements, Corchia-de Harak Assocs., designers.

A simple, sleek, workmanlike building that simultaneously delivers class and economic success. Thanks to developer Mel Kaufman, the street-level pools and bridges and an old-fashioned "candy store" under the arcade add a bit of **eccentric pedestrianism** to the neighborhood; a **mock** World War I **military airfield** atop the flat roof **(not open to the public)** amuses onlookers in neighboring skyscrapers.

[W 7a.] Orig. First Precinct, N.Y.P.D.   **[W 7c.]** Elegantly detailed 77 Water St.

[W 7d.] Barclay Bank Building, 75 Wall St., bet. Water and Pearl Sts. S side. 1987. Welton Becket Assocs.

A deep, generous entrance arch through a flamed granite base offers a promise, but the flat detailing above doesn't deliver.

A peek at the foot of Wall Street:

[W 8.] 120 Wall Street (offices), NW cor. South St. to Pine St. 1930. Office of Ely Jacques Kahn.

A powerful, symmetric, wedding cake silhouette. Very early for a large commercial building to brave a relatively inaccessible East River site. A Wall Street address and the nearby Second and Third Avenue elevated on Pearl Street, still operating in the 1930s, helped.

[W 9a.] Seaport South (apartments), 130 Water St., SW cor. Pine St. ca. 1955. Henry George Greene.

A corner infill structure whose curious zigzags and balconies begin to look better with time.

R.M.S. Queen Elizabeth Monument: Bronze letters from the majestic British ocean liner that sank in Hong Kong waters on January 9, 1972, are preserved in the plaza south of Wall Street Plaza, as is a bronzed telegram from Kurt Waldheim when secretary-general of the United Nations. The adjoining sculpture is *Disk and Slab* (1973, Yuyu Yang).

[W 9b.] Wall Street Plaza (offices)/originally **88 Pine Street Building,** Water St. bet. Pine St. and Maiden Lane. 1973. I. M. Pei & Assocs.

A white, **crisp elegance** of aluminum and glass (no mullions: one of the earliest examples here of butted glass that fills whole structural bays). Water Street's classiest building.

Red Grooms's "Ruckus Manhattan," a raucous collection of large scale, three-dimensional caricatures of the New York scene, was created by the artist and his good-humored team behind 88 Pine Street's giant ground-floor show windows in 1977–1978, to the acclaim of passersby.

A detour of a short block to the right (east) along Maiden Lane will reveal:

[W 9c.] Continental Center (offices), 180 Maiden Lane to Pine St., Front to South Sts. 1983. Swanke Hayden Connell & Partners.

One million square feet. A deceptively suave but actually neo-Tacky green monster with a greenhouse base, a project of the Rockefeller Center Development Corporation. (The resemblance to Rockefeller Center ends with the developer's name.)

[W 10a.] Skyward Café, 165 Water St., bet. Maiden Lane and Fletcher St. E side. 1983. Costas Terzis & Assocs.

The humble Greek diner elevated to a pretentious gentrified level—and skyward prices too.

[W 10b.] National Westminster Bank USA (offices), 175 Water St., bet. Fletcher St. and John St. S side to Front St. 1983. Fox & Fowle.

Half a million square feet. Mirrored glass cylinders (there are *two*) in embrace of the brick and glass horizontal-strip-window-jaws of the rest. Neither fox nor fowl.

(During excavation for this building the **remains of a mid 1700s ship** were found buried in the landfill. It had been scuttled to act as a cofferdam for late 18th-century earthmoving operations. The prow was successfully salvaged and removed to Mariners' Museum in Newport News, Va.)

[W 9b.] I.M. Pei's Wall Street Plaza

[W 10b.] National Westminster Bank

[W 10c.] 1 Seaport Plaza (offices), 199 Water St., to Front St. bet. John and Fulton Sts. 1983. Swanke Hayden Connell & Partners.

One million square feet. Developer Jack Resnick & Sons' **"first contextual office building."** Its main facades were designed to differ from one another, ostensibly to address the glitzier obligations of a **Water Street** frontage on the inland side, while granting low-scale **Schermerhorn Row** its due on Front Street. The height of 1 Seaport Plaza: 34 stories; the height of Schermerhorn Row: 4 stories plus. "Contextual?" Sure . . .

[W 10d.] 127 John Street Building (offices), NW cor. Water St. to Fulton and Pearl Sts. 1969. Emery Roth & Sons. Lobby, plaza, street level, and mechanical floor elements, Corchia-de Harak Assocs., designers.

No-nonsense building with a **happy nonsense-**filled lobby and sidewalk. Outside, pipe and canvas structures play with light and shelter pedestrians. Inside, a neon tunnel and other extravaganzas titillate the visitor. An adjacent electric display clock is a building in its own right. Developer Mel Kaufman is the person to thank.

The **Edison Electric Illuminating Company's** first large-scale, permanent commercial power and incandescent lighting system began operations on Monday, September 4, 1882, from a generating station located at 255-257 Pearl Street, between John and Fulton Streets. The area serviced included nearly a square mile, enclosed by Wall, Nassau, Spruce, and Ferry Streets, Peck Slip, and the East River. The generator ran until 1890, when it was partially destroyed by fire.

[W 11a.] 1 Seaport Tower (offices), 40 Fulton St., SW cor. Pearl St. 1989. Fox & Fowle.

A small office tower that wiped out a 1-story McDonald's serving alternative fast food to that available at the Seaport. Hooray!

[W 11b.] St. Margaret's House (senior citizens' housing), 49 Fulton St., NW cor. Pearl St. 1982. Gruzen & Partners.

A straightforwardly designed apartment tower plus a glassed-in lean-to of public space, sponsored by Trinity Church Parish and dedicated on Trinity Sunday 1982, according to the exquisitely lettered and carved slate panel outside the entrance.

[W 11c.] Pearl Street Playground, Fulton, Pearl, and Water Sts. 1982. Weintraub & di Domenico, N.Y.C. Department of Housing, Preservation & Development.

A sliver playground, in the latest Post Modern fashion, complete with a section in glass block and two—count 'em, **two**—polychromed colossal column capitals. A witty surprise.

END of Tour B. For refreshments, you couldn't be in a better place, at the gateway to South Street Seaport. And if you're in the mood for more touring see the South Street section, below. Otherwise, the closest subways are along Fulton Street in a complex, interconnected Fulton Street/Broadway-Nassau Station: the IRT Seventh Avenue express, the BMT Nassau Street local, the IRT Lexington Avenue express, and the the IND Eighth Avenue express.

SOUTH STREET SEAPORT

At the north end of boulevard-wide Water Street—at Fulton Street it reverts to its 50-foot width—lies the **South Street Seaport area.** The enclave of low-rise, small-scale structures—some dating to the 18th century, others new—owes its survival to a number of events: **1)** the establishment of the South Street Seaport Museum, spearheaded by **Peter Stanford, in** 1967; **2)** the subsequent banking of the area's **air-rights development** potential, later to be purchased by property owners to the south, where whopping office towers now stand; **3)** the State of New York's purchase of the **Schermerhorn Row block** in 1974; **4)** a series of official **landmark designations;** and **5)** the establishment, in cooperation with the City's Public Development Corporation, of a **"festival marketplace"** by the Rouse Company.

Transfer of development rights over buildings that occupy less bulk than zoning allows became a **favored technique** in the superheated 1980s. At South Street, the area encompassed by the transfer spanned a number of *blocks*—it normally includes merely a number of *lots.*

The South Street air-rights banking strategy, supported by influential board members of the museum, worked hand in hand with real estate interests attempting to **contain northward growth** of the Financial District. By limiting supply in an era of great demand, they sought—and in the end achieved—higher land values in Manhattan's toe. After a tentative period marked by designations of **sporadic individual structures** in the South Street area, the Landmarks Preservation Commission **acted decisively** in 1977 and designated **an (almost) all-embracing historic district.** *Entry to the Seaport area is best achieved by walking toward the East River on Fulton Street.* (The nearest subway stop is the rabbit warren of interconnected Fulton Street/Broadway-Nassau Stations of the IRT Seventh Avenue and Lexington Avenue express, the IND Eighth Avenue express, and the BMT Nassau Street local.)

Orientation: The thoroughfare called South Street is literally at the south flank of Manhattan Island, where the adjacent (and parallel) East River runs very roughly an east-west course (more pronounced above the Brooklyn Bridge). Logically, streets in this area that are perpendicular to perimeter South Street have (very roughly) east and west sides. For our purposes, and to tie this grid to the remainder, South Street will be considered running north and south, according to popular, but mildly inaccurate, convention.

Shop, shop, shop! Buy, buy, buy! Eat, eat, eat! As commendable as the preservation of the South Street Seaport area generally is, developer/landlord Rouse Company's **incessant invitations to spend** are quite intrusive: tourist baubles, T-shirts, fast food, as well as tonier items and pricey meals. Built with enormous municipal, state, and federal **subsidies,** like its clones in Boston and Baltimore, this festival marketplace caters primarily to middle-class families, to yuppies, and to the Financial District singles set, imparting to the development a neatsy-poo quality at odds with the **true grit** that the **waterfront** and the **fish market** once had. (While fish is still wholesaled here in the early morning hours, it is trucked in and trucked out.)

[S 1.] South Street Seaport Historic District, An irregular L-shaped area generally along parts of both sides of South St.: the East River waters from below Pier 15 including Piers 15, 16, and 17; W to Front St. bet. the S frontage of John St./Burling Slip and Fulton St.; W to Pearl St. bet. Fulton St. and Peck Slip; W to Water St. bet. Peck Slip and Dover St. ★

Ada Louise Huxtable's *Classic New York* warned in 1964 of the rapid demise of the physical vestiges of the city's 18th- and 19th-century waterfront heritage, much of which was still visible on South Street, the wide thoroughfare along the sheltered, narrow (relative to the Hudson) East River. This area, radiating out from the intersection of Fulton and South Streets, became the city's last holdout against mass demolition; its survivors evoke that period of commercial development which was generated by the city's role as a great domestic and international port.

Manhattan ever widening: The mucky shore became hard-edged and then was pushed outward, the new profile delicately balancing the needs of ships with those of shippers. Wild hills were tamed, and the earth from early cellar holes—and, much later, from deeper skyscraper excavations—was carted to the island's edge. Early on, Pearl Street (after the mother-of-pearl shells with which it was paved) marked the East River shore. As water lots were filled, the names of newly created streets reflected their succession to the perimeter: first Water Street, then Front, and finally—at least for now—South Street.

[S 1a.] Titanic Memorial Lighthouse, in Titanic Memorial Park, Fulton St. bet. Pearl and Water Sts. N side. Installed, 1976, Charles Evans Hughes III. ☆

Originally installed in 1913, by public subscription, atop the Seamen's Church Institute Building overlooking the East River at South Street and what was then Jeanette Park [see Water Street Corridor W 5a.] Visible from the river, it signaled noon to ships in the harbor with the falling of a black ball, at a signal received from Washington. It was taken down upon its host's demolition in 1968 and stored on a pier by the Seaport Museum until reerected here.

 [S 1b.] Seaport Park (apartments)/in part originally **Volunteer Hospital/**later **Beekman Street Hospital,** 117 Beekman St., bet. Water and Pearl Sts. S side. 1918. Adolph Mertin. ☆ Conversion and extension, 1983. Rafael Viñoly.

Long after ending its service as a hospital, the older part became part of a notorious nursing home scam and scandal. Converted, the combination of old and new is among the handsomest buildings in these parts.

South Street Seaport Museum Block:

Water to Front Streets, between Fulton and Beekman Streets.

[S 1c.] 207-211 Water Street (warehouses). E side. 1836. ☆
[S 1d.] Originally **A. A. Thompson & Company (metals warehouse),** 213-215 Water St. E side. 1868. Stephen D. Hatch. ☆ Restored, Beyer Blinder Belle, 1983.

Adaptively reused storehouses: **No. 207** is the **Museum Visitors' Center;** next door **No. 209** is the **Museum Books and Charts Store;** next, **No. 213-215** is the **Seaport Gallery,** an exhibition space; and **No. 211** is **Bowne & Co. Stationers,** the Museum's 19th-century print shop, where old techniques and equipment are still employed, to visitors' delight.

[S 1e.] Trans-Lux Seaport Theater, 133 Beekman St., bet. Water and Front Sts. S side. 1914. ☆ Restored, 1983, Beyer Blinder Belle. Altered into theater, 1984, Herbert Newman Assocs. Rumney Schiffer, graphic design.

Site of an introductory sight-and-sound event, *The Seaport Experience.*

Cannon's Walk:

A passageway between 19 Fulton Street, W of Front to 206 Front Street, N of Fulton.

[S 1f.] The "Bogardus" Building, 15-19 Fulton St., NW cor. Front St. 1983. Beyer Blinder Belle. ☆

It was this site that was chosen for the reerection of ironmonger James Bogardus' **demountable cast-iron facade** (removed from the warehouse that stood at Washington and Murray Streets) that was later **purloined** from the safekeeping of the Landmarks Preservation Commission (and melted down by the perpetrators). With the facade elements gone, the architects attempted to suggest its color, texture, rhythms, and proportions using similar—but not identical—ferrous materials. This successful effort—the wire-glass wraparound canopy is a particularly welcome addition—is made even more impressive because this building needed to enclose an existing 3-story IND subway-ventilation structure, which remained in operation during construction.

[S 2.] Fulton Market Building, 11 Fulton St., bet. Front and South Sts. N side to Beekman St. 1983. Benjamin Thompson & Assocs. ☆ **Open to the public.**

Echoing the vivacious **spirit** of the original **1883 Fulton Market Building,** which stood on this block until razed in 1948, is this brilliant essay, inside and out, of **marketplace architecture.** Its exterior, wrapped with a massive suspended iron canopy redolent of its predecessors, is intricate without being fussy; its majestic interior is filled with activity day and night. A tribute to the **Rouse Company,** who commissioned it as their initial addition to the Seaport area, to their architects, and to the Landmarks Preservation Commission, who recognized its genuine appropriateness. Among the places to eat: **Roeblings, The Coho, The Ocean Reef Grille.**

Streetscape: A particularly satisfying aspect of the Seaport Historic District is the use of substantial materials underfoot: Belgian block street pavement modulated by slabs of granite that evoke the horse-drawn era, with bluestone sidewalks and recreations of varying lamp-post designs of 19th-century Manhattan. All this is a result of Benjamin Thompson & Assocs. working closely with operating and regulatory City agencies.

[S 3.] The Schermerhorn Row block, 2-18 Fulton St., 189-195 Front St., 159-171 John Sts., 91-92 South St. 1811–1850. Variously altered and expanded. ★ ☆ **[S 3a.] "Schermerhorn Row" (east**

part), 2-12 Fulton St., SW cor. South St., and 92-93 South St., bet. Fulton and John Sts. W side. 1811. Altered and expanded. ★ ☆
[S 3b.] "Schermerhorn Row" (west part), 14-18 Fulton St., SE cor. Front St. 1812. 191 Front St., bet. Fulton and John Sts. E side. 1812. Variously altered and expanded. ★ ☆ Both parts restored, 1983, Jan Hird Pokorny. Storefront consultants, Cabrera-Barricklo.

Peter Schermerhorn filled the land on these, his "water lots," to a point **600 feet** out from the original shoreline and built his row in two stages a year apart. Served by these buildings, among many others, **South Street** was lined with ships, parked bowsprits in, oversailing the wheeled, hoofed, and pedestrian traffic below. (The bulkhead was at approximately the line of the west, or inner, row of columns supporting the highway viaduct.)

These were originally **Georgian-Federal** ware- and counting-houses, with high-pitched, loft-enclosing roofs, **built as an investment** by the Schermerhorn family. No storefronts at first: arched business entries of brownstone, quoined, and double-hung windows for light and air; only later did show windows appear at street level. Soon **Greek Revival** and **cast-iron** shopfronts brought a merchandising cast to serve the great crowds brought here, beginning in 1814, by the stream-powered **Fulton Ferry** from Brooklyn. To eat and drink: **Sweets** (upstairs), **North Star Pub** (South Street corner), **Sloppy Louie's** (South Street).

[S 1f.] The 1983 "Bogardus" Building   **[S 3.]** Restored Schermerhorn Row

[S 2.] The 1983 Fulton Market Building replaced the demolished 1883 original

[S 3c.] 191 and **193 Front St. (lofts),** bet. Fulton and John Sts. E side. Before 1793[?]. Altered and expanded upward, 19th century. ★ ☆ Restored, 1983, Jan Hird Pokorny.

The oldest on the block but not visibly so, since their fronts were drastically altered in the mid and late 19th century.

John Street between Front and South Streets widens to twice its normal dimension as a result of its earlier configuration as Burling Slip, an inlet for ships off the East River. In 1835 the slip was filled in.

[S 3d.] Originally **Mackle, Oakley & Jennison (grocers)**, 181 Front St., NE cor. John St. (a.k.a. 159-163 John St.). [S 3e.] Originally **Josiah Macy & Son (shipping and commission house)**, 189 Front St., bet. John and Fulton Sts. E side. (a.k.a. 159-165 John St.) Both behind Schermerhorn Row. S side. 1836. No. 181 expanded upward, 1917. ★ ☆ Restored, 1983, Jan Hird Pokorny.

A pair of Greek Revival commercial structures built when Burling Slip was filled in, their facades offering the pattern on which easterly neighbor **No. 165** was refaced.

[S 3f.] **Children's Center, South Street Seaport Museum**, 165 John St., bet. Front and South Sts., behind Schermerhorn Row. E side. 1811. Rebuilt, late 1830s–1840s. ★ ☆ Restored, 1983, Jan Hird Pokorny.

Following its reconstruction, it assumed a Greek Revival facade like its western neighbor. But, unlike its neighbor, it was never increased in height, so the original fascia, cornice, and roof line are all there.

[S 3g.] **The A. A. Low Building, South Street Seaport Museum**/originally **A. A. Low & Brothers (countinghouse)**/later **Baltimore Copper Paint Company**, 167-171 John St. (behind Schermerhorn Row), bet. Front and South Sts. E side. 1850. Altered. ★ ☆ Restored, 1983, Jan Hird Pokorny.

The youngest of Schermerhorn Row block's treasures, built by traders whose China clippers parked across South Street. Merchant **Abiel Abbot Low** (father of sometime mayor and Columbia University president **Seth Low**) lived only a ferryboat ride away at No. 3 Pierrepont Place [see WC Brooklyn H 24.]. There is brownstone under all that stucco and paint.

Note: The vacant lot in the Schermerhorn Row block, at the NW corner of South and John Streets, lost its group of 4-story brick, hip-roofed buildings from the block's heyday as recently as 1956 (in favor of a gas station, since demolished). There are plans to fill it in with an appropriate neighbor.

[S 3g.] Orig. A. A. Low & Bros., in old Baltimore Copper Paint Company livery

[S 3h.] Originally **Hickson W. Field Building**/formerly **Baker, Carver & Morrell (ship chandlery)**, 170-176 John St., bet. Front and South Sts. W side. 1840. ★ ☆ Expanded upward, 1981.

The last survivor of a commercial building type first imported from Boston by Town & Davis in 1829. The **austere granite blocks** and piers offer a dour face to the street.

To the south, along South Street:

[S 4a.] Originally **Maximilian Morgenthau tobacco warehouse,** 84-85 South St., bet. Fletcher and John Sts. W side. 1902. G. Curtis Gillespie. ☆

Despite the brutal surgery on its base this is one of South Street's—and the city's—unique treasures: terra-cotta Art Nouveau **tobacco leaf motifs** applied to a late Romanesque Revival storehouse.

Across South Street and onto the piers:

[S 4b.] South Street Seaport Museum ships, anchored along Piers 15, 16, 17, East River. Piers ☆ **Open to the public.**

The great glories of the Museum are the ships moored at the wharves and those, like the tall ships, which periodically tie up for brief visits. Floating architecture is honored here by the **Wavertree** and **Peking** (*1885 and 1911. Steel bathtub square-riggers—bathtubs to keep the water out rather than in*); the old humanoid **Ambrose Lightship** (*1907. Its successor is an electronic rig on stilts*); the **Lettie G. Howard** (*a venerable oysterman from Gloucester*); the **Maj. Gen. William H. Hart** (*1925. One of the city's smaller ferryboats*); and others. In addition there are excursions on the **Andrew Fletcher** and the 1885 schooner, **Pioneer.**

[S 5.] The forms of Pier 17's pavilion capture the spirit of a bustling harbor

[S 5.] Pier Pavilion, Pier 17, East River, opp. Fulton Street. 1984. Benjamin Thompson & Assocs., design architects. The Eggers Group, consulting architects. ☆

The Rouse Company's other great Seaport contribution, a pier large enough to moor a dirigible *in.* Conceived in a grand manner to bring back some of the vernacular waterfront architecture that was once ubiquitous along South (and other perimeter) Street. Gigantic, playful, adroitly detailed, and twinkling with lights well into the night. **An instant urban landmark.** The 3-story high interior space of the transept is quite remarkable.

North of the festival marketplace:

[S 6a.] 142-144 Beekman Street (lofts), NE cor. Front St. 1885. George B. Post. ☆

Built for a Schermerhorn descendant, **Ellen S. Auchmuty.** Particularly note the whimsical terra-cotta maritime ornament: decorative fish motifs, cockleshells, and starfish.

[S 6b.] 146-148 Beekman Street (lofts), bet. Front and South Sts. N side. 1885. George B. Post. ☆ **[S 6c.] 150-152 Beekman Street (lofts),** bet. Front and South Sts. N side. 1883. D. & J. Jardine. ☆

Colorful giant signs hawking wholesale seafood—FRESH, SALT AND SMOKED FISH/OYSTERS AND CLAMS—boldly painted across the brick street facades, are what count here. An advertising stratagem growing increasingly rare. Hold that line!

[S 6d.] 251 Water Street (tenement), SE cor. Peck Slip. 1888. Carl F. Eisenbach. ☆

Even a tenement design was infused by South Street fervor: the tympanum over the ornately framed apartment entrance is a joyous explosion of terra-cotta sunflowers. At the 4th-story windows, terra-cotta keytones carry faces surveying the streetlife below.

[S 6e.] 21-23 Peck Slip (lofts), NE cor. Water St. 1873. Richard Morris Hunt. ☆

Six wonderful stories of polychromed brick with carefully modulated windows and, on the Front Street facade, 45 neatly spaced star anchors tying in the timber floors to the masonry street wall. This structure was built for the trustees of Roosevelt Hospital, at the same time as Hunt's **Roosevelt Building** was [see SoHo H 4b.].

[S 7a.] Consolidated Edison electrical substation, 237-257 Front St., bet. Peck Slip and Dover St. E side to South St. 1975. Edward Larrabee Barnes, design architect. Con Edison, production architect. Mural, Richard Haas, artist. ☆

A reasonable attempt by the city's big electrical utility to be a harmonious neighbor to the Seaport, in the days before the historic district was enacted. (The Seaport's Restoration and Development Committee approved the design.) A mural on Peck Slip was a happy idea, but depicting the Brooklyn Bridge—with the real thing looming in the background—was a frivolous and silly conceit.

[S 7b.] Center for Building Conservation/originally **Jasper Ward residence,** 45 Peck Slip, NW cor. South St. 1807. ☆   Restored, 1983, Robert E. Meadows.

Built on a water lot on landfill and impaired by time and unequal settlement. Thoughtful restoration, **keeping the unevenness of decades,** adds to the apparent integrity of this doughty survivor.

[S 7c.] Formerly **Meyer's Hotel,** 116-119 South St., SW cor. Peck Slip. 1873. John B. Snook.

Its original use is unknown, but it became Meyer's Hotel in 1881. The building and its streetfront corner bar make perfect backgrounds for Hollywood nostalgia.

[S 8a.] Originally **Captain Joseph Rose residence** and **shop,** 273 Water St., bet. Peck Slip and Dover St. E side. As early as 1773/no later than 1781. ☆

A ruin. Fires in 1904 and 1976 have compromised this structure, the South Street District's oldest and Manhattan's third oldest (after the Morris-Jumel Mansion and St. Paul's Chapel). Rose was in the business of shipping Honduras mahogany to the New York market.

[S 8b.] Bridge Café, (restaurant), 279 Water St., SE cor. Dover St. Building, ca. 1801. ☆

The district's only extant wood frame building, built for grocer Peter Loring, remained a commercial structure until converted into a 3-family house in 1888. It then lost its peaked roof and was sheathed in novelty siding and other ornament of the era. Today, a good place for a drink and a repast.

BROADWAY-NASSAU

Lying between Wall Street and the southern tip of City Hall Park, from Church Street to South Street Seaport, is one of Lower Manhattan's least recognized—and therefore **most intriguing**—areas. Since it bestrides Fulton Street, under which lies the IND Eighth Avenue Line's Broadway-Nassau Station, this area **has been dubbed** after that **station's name.** It includes Chase Manhattan Plaza, the Nassau Street pedestrian mall, the Federal Reserve Bank of New York, and the old AT&T

Building. But, more important it includes many **minor but delicious** background buildings from the days of the earliest skyscrapers. Entries begin at Pearl and Pine Streets, one block north of Wall. (The closest subway stop to the first entry is the Wall Street Station of the IRT Seventh Avenue Line express.)

[N 1a.] American International Building (offices)/earlier **60 Wall Tower/**originally **Cities Service Building,** 70 Pine St., NW cor. Pearl St. to Cedar St. 1932. Clinton & Russell and Holton & George.

One of the Financial District's **most slender** towers, it sports Art Deco details everywhere—including its "Gothic" crown, unseen from the canyons in which the tower sits and therefore best appreciated as part of the skyline or from a neighboring eyrie. (To help passersby comprehend what they cannot fully see from the street, the architects provided 3-dimensional **stone replicas** of the building at the Pine and Cedar Street entrances.)

Double-decker elevators, serving two floors of the tower at a time, such as are found at Citicorp Tower [see M Manhattan/Park Avenue P 16.], **were first used here.** They proved unpopular and were later changed.

[N 1b.] Down Town Association (club), 60 Pine St., bet. Pearl and William Sts. N side. 1887. Charles C. Haight.

Anonymous and understated, this appropriately somber club serves many distinguished financial executives and lawyers, principally at lunchtime.

[N 2.] Chase Manhattan's executive suite offers fine view of 40 Wall's pyramid

[N 2.] Chase Manhattan Bank Tower (offices) and **Plaza,** 1 Chase Manhattan Plaza, bet. Pine and Liberty Sts., from William to Nassau Sts. 1960. Skidmore, Owings & Merrill.

David Rockefeller and his fellow board members, through their act of faith in building this Gargantua, here cried "Excelsior," and the flagging spirit of the **Financial District** took courage. Architecturally less successful than the later and more sophisticated **Marine Midland** [N 8.] by the same firm, it provides, however, the first gratuitous plaza hereabouts. Many have appeared since: the **Home Insurance Company, Marine Midland, Liberty Plaza, the World Trade Center,** and so forth.

A sheer **800 feet** of aluminum and glass rise from the paved plaza surface, which is accessible from both **Nassau** and **Pine Streets.** The topography unfortunately forces down the **Liberty** and **William Street** sides, detaching them from participation in the plaza's space.

A sunken circular courtyard is paved with undulating forms of granite blocks, crowned with sculpture, and caressed in summer by a fountain and pools: all by sculptor **Isamu Noguchi.** Goldfish were resident at first, but the urban fallout and sentimentalists' "coins in the fountain" destroyed even those resilient carp.

The plaza sculpture *Group of Four Trees* (1972. Jean Dubuffet), on the axis of **Cedar Street,** looks like papier-mâché but isn't: it gives out a temporary, expendable feeling.

[N 3a.] Louise Nevelson Plaza/Legion Memorial Square, Maiden Lane, Liberty St., William St. 1978. **Shadows and Flags,** 1978, Louise Nevelson, sculptor.

Inventory: 7 brown Nevelson sculptures, 8 black stone benches, 1 small drinking fountain, 12 trees, 3 lollipop lamps. An eerie assemblage but popular at lunch.

[N 3b.] 90 Maiden Lane (lofts), bet. William and Pearl Sts. S side, at Louise Nevelson Plaza. 1815. Cast-iron front, 1872, Charles Wright. Mansard added.

An unlikely spot for a carefully preserved cast-iron remnant, owned over time by Cornelius Van Schaick Roosevelt and his son, James Alfred Roosevelt. At only 4 stories in the Financial District's canyons, can it survive?

[N 4a.] 100 William Street (offices), bet. Platt and John Sts. E side. 1973. Davis, Brody & Assocs.

Green schist (split from natural geological strata) slate. A diagonal gallery slashes the form with a 4-story, stepped, street volume: a humanist place, rich, natural, and elegant, creating a vista terminating at:

[N 4b.] Plaza in front of **Home Insurance Group (offices),** 59 Maiden Lane, NW cor. William St. Redesigned, 1987, Kohn Pederson Fox Assocs. Building, 1966, Office of Alfred Easton Poor.

It's the plaza that counts here, redesigned as a miniforest in an urban setting. It again shows that public space contained by buildings can benefit from being small; increasing the size would diminish rather than enhance its quality. The back of the **Federal Reserve** forms a foil and wall for this space.

[N 2.] Dubuffet at Chase Manhattan   **[N 5.]** Federal Reserve Bank of N.Y.

[N 5.] Federal Reserve Bank of New York, 33 Liberty St., NE cor. Nassau St. to Maiden Lane. 1924. Extension E to William St., 1935. All by York & Sawyer. Decorative ironwork, Samuel Yellin. ★ **Open to the public by advance reservation.**

A **Florentine** palazzo conserves within its dungeons more money than **Fort Knox.** This is a great neo-Renaissance building of rusticated Indiana limestone, Ohio sandstone, and elegant ironwork. A bank for banks, this is the great stabilizer and equalizer of their separately erratic activities. In the five levels below the street, the gold of many nations is stored—and moved, in the balance of trade, from nation to nation—without ever leaving the building.

The stony south wall, on **Liberty Street,** is a magnificent foil to the crystalline glass and aluminum of Chase Manhattan Bank Tower. We hope that the **Federal Reserve** will live forever. (Florence, not having the luxury of 15th-century elevators, couldn't imagine such large-scale grandeur.)

Nassau Street Pedestrian Mall: From **Maiden Lane** to **Beekman Street, Nassau** serves as a most active local shopping strip: medium- to modest-priced chain stores, discount houses, and small, specialized shops. Panty hose, radio equipment, dresses, shoes, all of the personal and portable items that a lunch hour shopper would be most inclined to inspect and purchase. The ground-floor activity and clutter of show windows and signs keep the eye at street level. The form and detail of buildings above, no matter how tall, are rarely noticed, amost never observed. Closed to vehicles to fulfill its pedestrianism. Too bad it has no curbs any more or even some emblematic recognition of their earlier existence.

[N 6a.] 33 Maiden Lane (office tower), NE cor. Nassau St. to John St. 1986. Philip Johnson/John Burgee.

Occupies a site **intended** in the 1970s **for an annex** to the Federal Reserve Bank across Maiden Lane, a powerful Kevin Roche design. As it turns out, the substitute is a building suspended between a group of giant buff-brick **crenellated mailing tubes** (which permitted the developer to offer 7 "corner" offices per floor). The preposterously large-scale stone arch and greenhoused open-air lobby only add to the building's aesthetic problems.

[N 6a.] The 33 Maiden Lane offices   **[N 7b.]** N.Y.S. Chamber of Commerce

[N 6b.] 63 Nassau Street (lofts), bet. Maiden Lane and John St.   W side. ca. 1860. Cast iron by James Bogardus?

A tattered facade distinguished by 3-story, fluted cast-iron columns sitting on bases bearing relief portrait busts of Benjamin Franklin and George Washington. Indefatigable **Margot Gayle,** founder of **Friends of Cast Iron Architecture,** rediscovered this out-of-the-way structure.

[N 6c.] John Street United Methodist Church, 44 John St., bet. Nassau and William Sts. 1841. William Hurry. ★

The first church in **America** of the **Irish Wesleyans** was here in **1766,** later replaced by this building. The congregation is, therefore, the oldest **Methodist Society** in **America.**

[N 7a.] Liberty Tower (originally offices), 55 Liberty St., NE cor. Nassau St. 1909. Henry Ives Cobb. Restored and converted to residential, 1981, Joseph Pell Lombardi.

Glorious terra-cotta (similar to **Cass Gilbert's** gothicized **90 West Street**) over limestone as high as a person can reach.

[N 7b.] Originally **Chamber of Commerce of the State of New York,** 65 Liberty St., bet. Nassau St. and Broadway at NW cor. Liberty Place 1901. James B. Baker. ★

Rich, ornate **Beaux Arts;** a minor palace of imposing scale and rich detail. Rusticated, **Ionic** columns, mansard roof, oval porthole windows.

[N 8.] **Marine Midland Bank Building (offices),** 140 Broadway, bet. Liberty and Cedar Sts. E side to Nassau St. 1967. Skidmore, Owings & Merrill.

A taut skin stretched over bare bones. The sleek and visually flush facade is in melodramatic contrast to the ornamented masonry environment surrounding it. The matteness of black spandrels breaks up the reflections of the neighbors into **more random, mysterious parts.** The travertine plaza at Broadway was a perfect size to have a major impact on the feel of this neighborhood until the plaza across Broadway deprived it of its enclosing street walls. (The same architects' Chase Manhattan Plaza next door on Pine suffers from an amorphous shape, and a separation by elevation from the street life around it.)

The sculpture on the plaza's lap at Broadway is a **teetering** 28 feet tall **vermilion** *Cube* (1973. Isamu Noguchi) gored by a cylindrical punch.

[N 9.] **Equitable Building (offices),** 120 Broadway, bet. Pine and Cedar Sts. E side to Nassau St. 1915. Ernest R. Graham (of Graham, Anderson, Probst & White, successors to D. H. Burnham & Co.).

More famous for what it caused than what it is. An immense volume, it exploited the site as no building had before: **1.2 million** square feet of floor area on a plot of just under an acre, or a floor area of almost **30 times** the site's area. The hue and cry after Equitable's completion led to the adoption of the **nation's first comprehensive zoning resolution,** in 1916.

[N 10.] The One Liberty Plaza tower   **[N 10a.]** Bollards at 1 Liberty Plaza

[N 10.] **1 Liberty Plaza (offices)**/briefly **Merrill Lynch Plaza,** Broadway, Liberty, Church, Cortlandt, and Church Sts. 1974. Skidmore, Owings & Merrill. **[N 10a.]** **Liberty Plaza Park,** Broadway, Cedar, Church, and Liberty Sts. 1974; SE corner holdout, 1980. Skidmore Owings & Merrill.

A gloomy, articulate, cadaverous extravaganza of steel: handsome and somber as the renaissance of Florence. It replaced the great **Singer Tower** (1908–1970) by **Ernest Flagg,** an eclectic palace-tower and the tallest building ever demolished.

Bollards and chains surround the low, depressed basement that seems designed, consciously, to crush the passer and enterer (compare the great **Fosse Ardeatine** monument in **Rome**). A hovering hulk.

Across Liberty Street to the south is a large, bleak, red granite, treed plaza dedicated to the public, part of the zoning calculations, which allowed the developers (U.S. Steel) to add bulk to their behemoth. The plaza links, in a chain, Marine Midland and Chase Manhattan Plazas to the east, and the World Trade Center to the west.

 [N 11a.] Germania Building (lofts), 175 Broadway, bet. Maiden Lane and Dey St. 1865.

A miraculous tiny holdover from the city's Reconstruction days. For how much longer?

[N 11a.] The 1865 Germania Building　　[N 13d.] Orig. The Bennett Building

[N 11b.] East River Savings Bank, 26 Cortlandt St., NE cor. Church St. to Dey St. 1934. Walker & Gillette. Expanded upward.

Cool neo-Classical Art Deco with marvelous stainless steel winged eagles over both entrances, in the spirit of the Chrysler Building but nowhere near as daring.

[N 12a.] Originally **American Telephone & Telegraph Company Building (offices)**/now **195 Broadway Building,** bet. Dey and Fulton Sts. W side. Built in three sections: 1915–1922. All by Welles Bosworth. Addition to W, 1989, Eli Attia.

The square-topped layer cake of New York: a deep-set facade of 8 Ionic colonnades (embracing 3 stories within each set) is stacked on a Doric order. **Handsome parts** are assembled into a **bizarre whole:** more Classical columns than any facade in the world, and the columns within the lobby continue the record setting. (All was surmounted at the Fulton Street towertop by Evelyn Beatrice Longman's *Genius of the Telegraph* until the colossal gilded sculpture was moved to the *new* AT&T Building [see M Manhattan/Plaza Suite Z 9.].)

[N 12b.] Corbin Building (offices), 13 John St., NE cor. Broadway. ca. 1889. Francis H. Kimball.

A craggy and wonderful occupant of a not very important Broadway corner.

Note: For St. Paul's Chapel and northward, see Civic Center/Chinatown.

East on Fulton Street:

[N 12c.] Fulton Street Subway Station, IRT Lexington Avenue Line, under Broadway at Fulton St. 1905. Heins & La Farge. ★ Restoration, 1987, Lee Harris Pomeroy & Assocs.

A straightforward restoration with exceptionally fine new lighting.

[N 13a.] Originally **Whyte's Restaurant,** 145 Fulton St., bet. Broadway and Nassau St. N side. 1908. Clinton & Russell.

Though its facade is a bit worse for wear, the flavor of its nostalgic rendering of a baronial English inn is still largely there, concealed under layers of thoughtless kitsch.

[N 13b.] Originally **Fulton Building (offices),** 87 Nassau St., SW cor. Fulton St. 1893. De Lemos & Cordes. **[N 13c.]** Originally **Keuffel & Esser Building (offices),** 127 Fulton St., bet. Nassau and William Sts. N side. 1893. De Lemos & Cordes.

Richly ornamented masonry facades from the architects who later brought you **Siegel-Cooper** and **Macy's** department stores.

[N 13d.] Originally **Bennett Building (lofts),** 99 Nassau St., bet. Fulton and Ann Sts. W side. 1873. Arthur D. Gilman. Upper 4 floors added, ca. 1889.

A glassy building with a deeply 3-dimensional and very decorative cast-iron structural grid. For years its tacky Nassau Street stores diverted eyes from the splendor above. Now, a set of trendy mid-1980s store signs and a new **tutti-frutti pastel** paint job (including trompe l'oeil lot line extensions) remedy the situation markedly. The building's name, incidentally, is that of James Gordon Bennett (*New York Herald*) father and son, each of whom owned it.

[N 14a.] Temple Court (offices), 119–129 Nassau St., SW cor. Beekman St. to Theatre Alley. S part, 1882, Silliman & Farnsworth. N part, 1892, Benjamin Silliman, Jr.

Two mighty, pointed steeples cap this purply red-painted brick office building whose name (lifted from its London counterpart) suggests that it originally catered to the city's legal profession, way before Foley Square. A long-overlooked candidate for recognition as a landmark.

[N 14a.] The spires of Temple Court   **[N 14b.]** Potter Building terra-cotta

[N 14b.] Potter Building (offices) 38 Park Row, NE cor. Beekman St. 1883. N. G. Starkweather.

An elaborately ornate confection in cast and pressed terra-cotta, an early use in New York of a material that was to become the rage, producing repetitive elaboration economically. The invisibly used structural steel of this building is the first in New York to be fireproofed by terra-cotta.

[N 14c.] Originally **Morse Building (lofts)/now 12 Beekman Street (apartments),** NE cor. Nassau St. 1879. Silliman & Farnsworth. Converted, 1980, Hurley & Farinella.

A hearty red-brick loft structure, understated but very substantial.

[N 15a.] New York Infirmary Beekman Downtown Hospital/originally **Beekman Downtown Hospital,** 170 William St., bet. Beekman and Spruce Sts. E side to Gold St. 1971. Skidmore, Owings & Merrill.

A pleasant block full of Modern architecture, made a bit forbidding on the Gold Street side by its high base, unintentionally giving a humane place an inhumane posture.

 [N 15b.] Staff Residence, New York Infirmary Beekman Downtown Hospital, 69 Gold St., bet. Beekman and Ann Sts. 1972. The Gruzen Partnership.

An exciting work of reinforced concrete and brick masonry units responding to a simple set of programmatic requirements on a tiny site. It proves that imagination, the careful choice of materials, and skillful detailing can result in a handsome structure even when modest in size. Too bad it's so out of the way.

[N 16a.] Aetna Insurance Company Building (offices), 151 William St., NW cor. Fulton St. 1940. Cross & Cross and Eggers & Higgins.

A curious limestone cube with a rounded corner: son of the earlier **90 Church Street Federal Building,** also (in part) by Cross & Cross [see Civic Center C 2.]. Cloaked in stripped-down neo-Classical, it seems to have left Art Deco behind but hasn't found an adequate substitute.

[N 16b.] Originally **Royal Insurance Company Building (offices)**/later **Royal Globe Insurance Company Building,** 150 William St., bet. Fulton and Ann Sts. E side to Gold St. 1927. Starrett & Van Vleck.

A stately occupant of a full-block site. The gentle setbacks on all 4 facades terminate in a **pedimented Classical temple** at the roof.

[N 16c.] John J. DeLury, Sr. Plaza, at NE intersection of Gold and Fulton Sts. 1985. Bronson Binger, architect; Christopher Kusske, Elizabeth Hand, landscape architects; N.Y.C. Department of Parks & Recreation Capital Projects Division.

A **model public monument** rarely to be found so successfully executed in these times: austere in concept, substantial in materials, dignified in design and detailing. DeLury (1904–1980) was founder of the city's **Uniformed Sanitationmen's Association** and president for 40 years.

 [N 17.] Originally **Excelsior Power Company (powerhouse)**/now **apartments),** 33-48 Gold St., bet. Fulton and John Sts. W side. 1888. William Milne Grinnell. Converted, 1979, Wechsler, Grasso & Menziuso.

Coal-fired **electrical generators** once occupied this lusty Romanesque Revival brick monolith. Now, yuppies do, behind scraggy window sash and other bargain basement retrofits.

BATTERY PARK CITY

Once upon a time, not too long ago, Lower Manhattan's Hudson River shoreline was crammed—like teeth in a comb—with piers, wharves, and ferry slips. But with the **end of labor-intensive** break-bulk cargo in favor of **efficient containerization** and an increasing need to dispose of enormous volumes of **earthen fill from excavations** like that of the World Trade Center—and who knows from how many others?—a symbiotic opportunity arose to create a **92-acre add-on** to Manhattan Island: Battery Park City.

The idea had been kicking around from the late 1960s under Governor Nelson Rockefeller (riparian rights make the river's landfill state-owned), when the state's **Battery Park City Authority** commissioned Harrison & Abramovitz to design a development isolated from Manhattan's existing urban fabric. (It would be prophetic of their later Albany Mall—now named for Rockefeller—designed to be isolated from the urban fabric of the state capital.) After many enthusiastic announcements—but no demonstrated capacity to sell the necessary revenue bonds, BPCA finally began its **first aboveground project,** Gateway Plaza [see B 7.] (Meanwhile, the empty white sands had proved a boon to sunbathers and to **"Art on the Beach,"** the series of temporary but memorable sculpture installations and performance-art events conducted by **Creative Time.**)

The real beginning came in 1979, when a master plan was presented by Cooper, Eckstut Associates that proposed developing the area as an *extension* of Lower Manhattan, rather than as an isolated futuristic "project." The lines of existing east-west streets were to be **integrated** into the project, and new north-south avenues would be **oriented** to Manhattan's **street grid** north of Houston Street. A public **waterfront esplanade** and other **public park space** was envisioned. Not only were specific land uses proposed—a mix of commercial, residential, recreational, and arterial—but the visual character of the various developments was also defined in a set of **design guidelines.** The southern residential areas—guidelines by Stanton Eckstut—were to resemble such desirable Manhattan neighborhoods as Gramercy Park, Tudor City, and Riverside Drive. It is no accident, thankfully, therefore that the South Residential Quadrant looks like **"instant past."**

The commercial area, the **World Financial Center**—developed according to guidelines by Alexander Cooper—is a totally private effort by Canadian developers **Olympia & York.** It lies immediately west of the World Trade Center complex, embracing the earlier Gateway Plaza towers and largely concealing them from Lower Manhattan streets. To the south and to the north are a string of high-density residential communities with structures allocated to different developer-architect teams. Each team was beholden to the design guidelines' tenets but still exercised its own design and economic initiatives, later reviewed and approved by the Authority.

As the financial center and the southerly residential complexes emerged, the fundamental wisdom of the master plan made itself evident.

[B 1a.] The Esplanade, entire W edge of site. 1983–1990. Stanton Eckstut of Cooper, Eckstut Assocs., architects. Hanna/Olin, Ltd., landscape consultants.

Seventy-five feet wide, 1.2 miles long, and admittedly derivative— but **it works.** The design vocabulary draws from the best of the city's existing park design, particularly the **Carl Schurz Park** promenade atop FDR Drive, the city's traditional "B-pole" park lampposts, and Victorian-replica cast-iron and wood benches used in (of all places) the Art Moderne 1939–1940 New York World's Fair.

Entries begin beyond Pier A in the northwestern corner of Battery Park and proceed uptown through Battery Park City:

Battery Place residential neighborhood:

The southernmost residential area.

[B 1b.] South Park, N of Pier A. 1989. Jennifer Bartlett, artist. Alexander Cooper, architect. Bruce Kelly, landscape architect.

A series of interlinked gardens.

[B 1c.] Museum of the Jewish Heritage and **apartment tower,** Battery Place, W of 1st Place. 1990. James Stewart Polshek & Partners. **Museum open to the public.**

The museum presents a linear exhibition of the timeline of Jewish history plus a memorial to the victims of the Holocaust.

[B 2.] South Cove Park, surrounding South Cove bet. 1st and 3rd Place. 1988. Mary Miss, artist. Stanton Eckstut, The Ehrenkranz Group & Eckstut, architects. Susan Child, Child Assocs., landscape architects. Howard Brandston Lighting Design, Inc., lighting.

An effort to bring the changing character of the seasons, the tides, and the Hudson River itself into an artful interplay with the southern terminus of the Esplanade, the end of 1st Place, and the Museum of the Jewish Heritage complex.

[B 3a.] Apartments, Battery Place bet. 3rd Place and W. Thames St. E side. 1990. Paul Segal Assocs. and Costas Kondylis of Philip Birnbaum & Assocs. **[B 3b.] Apartments,** Battery Place SW. cor. W. Thames St. to South End Ave. 1990. James Stewart Polshek & Partners. **[B 3c.] Apartments,** South End Ave. SW cor. W. Thames St. 1990. Gruzen Sampton Steinglass.

Developments, all within the original design guidelines, that added to the initial housing inventory of the south residential complex as the BPC Authority, developers, and architects reached agreements.

[B 4.] "Living Room," E of the Esplanade at foot of W. Thames St. 1988. Richard Artschwager, sculptor.

Conran's furniture sized for Paul Bunyan, fashioned in granite, cast iron, and redwood and occupying a triangular "waiting area."

Rector Place residential neighborhood:

The first residential quarter built under the master plan and Eckstut's residential design guidelines. To comment at length on any individual group is to forget what was intended by the design guidelines and what, in the end, really counts: the totality of the complex.

[B 5a.] Liberty Court (apartments), 200 Rector Place, SW cor. West St. 1987. Ulrich Franzen. **[B 5b.] The Soundings (apartments),** 280 Rector Place, SE cor. South End Ave. 1987. Bond Ryder James. **[B 5c.] Battery Pointe (apartments),** 300 Rector Place, SW cor. South End Ave. 1987. Bond, Ryder James. **[B 5d.] Liberty Terrace (apartments),** 380 Rector Place, SE cor. The Esplanade. 1987. Ulrich Franzen/The Vilkas Group.

A fine, harmonizing—but not competing—group.

[B 5e.] Rector Park, Within the Rector Place loop, W and E of South End Ave. 1986. Innocenti-Webel with Vollmer Assocs., landscape architects. Gateway, 1987, R. M. Fischer, sculptor.

As befits the surrounding architecture, centrally placed Rector Park is veddy, veddy propuh, using the finest of materials very carefully detailed. Meant to be looked at, not played in.

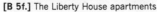

[B 5f.] The Liberty House apartments   **[B 5g.]** The River Rose apartments

[B 5f.] Liberty House (apartments), 377 Rector Place, NE cor. The Esplanade. 1986. James Stewart Polshek & Partners.

The detailing here is quite carefully thought out and pleasing to the eye.

[B 5g.] River Rose (apartments), 333 Rector Place, NW cor. South End Ave. 1986. Charles Moore and Rothzeid, Kaiserman, Thomson & Bee.

The most mannered and joyful of the Rector Park group.

[B 5h.] Parc Place (apartments), 225 Rector Place, NE cor. South End Ave. 1986. Gruzen Samton Steinglass.

The most understated and most appropriately detailed of the Rector Park group.

[B 6a.] Hudson View East (apartments), 250 South End Ave., SE cor. Albany St. 1987. Mitchell-Giurgola.

Bland of hue and spare of detail, save the subtle highlights of blue glazed brick and the handsomely wrought window grilles at street level.

[B 6b.] Hudson View West (apartments), 300 Albany St., SW cor. South End Ave. 1987. Conklin & Rossant.

Straightforward brickwork atop a 2-story limestone and granite plinth.

[B 6c.] 320-340 Albany Street (town house apartments), bet. The Esplanade and South End Ave. S side. 1986. Davis, Brody & Assocs.

Six 5-story apartment buildings meant to echo the forms and organization of the city's brownstones. The tiers of connected rear balconies lined with black ships' railings reveal a more masterful command of the problem. *Visible from the inner parking area.*

[B 6c.] 320–340 Albany Street apts   **[B 6d.]** The Hudson Tower apartments

[B 5h.] Parc Place apartments, in the Rector Place Residential Neighborhood

[B 6d.] Hudson Tower (apartments), 350 Albany St., SE cor. The Esplanade. 1986. Davis, Brody & Assocs.

A combination of bay windows and cantilevered corner windows proclaim that harbor views are important here. A happy building.

[B 6e.] "Upper Room," Albany Street Park, E of the Esplanade at foot of Albany St. Ned Smyth, sculptor.

No need to voyage up the Nile. Smyth's evocative, eclectic, open-to-the-sky forms summarize both Egypt's dynasties and Rome's empire.

Gateway Plaza

[B 7.] Gateway Plaza (apartments), 345, 355, 365, 375, 385, 395 South End Ave. 1982, 1983. Jack Brown and Irving E. Gershon, associate architects. Interior plaza, Abel, Bainnson & Assocs., landscape architects.

Sam Lefrak in Manhattan: 1,712 units divided among three 34-story lackluster towers and other containers; the scullery maids of Battery Park City residences. The central green space (except for the enclosed pool), however, is quite pleasant.

[B 8.] Pumphouse Park, E of Esplanade, N of Gateway Plaza. 1986. Synterra, Ltd., landscape architects.

Two 66-inch-diameter river water intake and outfall tubes for the World Trade Center were relocated to make possible the Liberty Street vehicular entry between the twin Gatehouses. These tubes, together with the required pumping apparatus, are in the area under this park.

World Financial Center:

The 7-million-square-foot commercial center, encompassed in a group of towers sheathed in reflective glass and thermal granite. The towers vary in height from 33 to 51 stories, and each has a different geometric termination—mastaba, dome, pyramid, stepped pyramid. The overall design concept was developed by design architect Cesar Pelli with Adamson & Associates as coordinating architects. As bulky as the towers are, they begin, in Pelli's irregular placement (dictated by landfill configurations), to soften the impact of the neighboring World Trade Center's raw, 110-story prisms. After years of lonely exposure, the Trade Center's out-of-scale twin towers have finally been shoehorned into a context with Lower Manhattan.

[B 9a.] North Bridge (200-foot clear span, 40 feet wide) connecting U.S. Custom House to the Wintergarden. **South Bridge** (220-foot clear span, 25 feet wide) connecting Liberty St. to South Gatehouse. Both 1985. Cesar Pelli, design architect. Haines Lundberg Waehler, architects. Lev Zetlin & Assocs. and Thornton Thomasetti, structural engineers.

Pedestrian access from "Little Old New York" across the great gulf formed by West Street. From the inside the bridges are long narrow ballrooms; from the outside they resemble levitating Brobdingnagian interstate buses minus their tires. (The bridges are formed of Vierendeel trusses of great span to accommodate the uncertainties of a multibillion-dollar Westway that was destined never to come.)

These bridges are the least successful part of the project.

[B 9b.] 1 World Financial Center/Dow Jones & Company Building and **Oppenheimer & Company Tower,** West St. opp. Cedar St. W side. 1985. Cesar Pelli, design architect. Adamson Assocs., architects.

Mastaba-topped, 40 stories high.

[B 9c.] North and **South Gatehouses,** West St. W side framing Liberty St. Cesar Pelli, design architect. Adamson Assocs., architects.

The marbled interiors of these bulky octagonal pavilions are spacious, lavishly clad, fussily detailed, and embarrassingly devoid of purpose.

[B 10a.] 2 World Financial Center/Merrill Lynch World Headquarters, South Tower, West St. bet. Liberty and Vesey Sts. W side. 1987. Cesar Pelli, design architect. Haines Lundberg Waehler, architects.

Dome-topped, the tallest tower at 51 floors.

[B 10b.] The Wintergarden, opp. North Bridge. 1988. Cesar Pelli, design architect. Adamson Assocs., architects. Lev Zetlin & Assocs. and Thornton Thomasetti, structural engineers. M. Paul Friedberg & Partners, landscape architects.

It's hard to fathom why London's 19th-century Crystal Palace was framed in so gossamer a structure, while this is encased in so heavy a steel pipe frame. Nevertheless, it's a welcome, sunny, barrel-vaulted, palm-filled interior public space measuring 130 × 230 feet, roughly the size of Grand Central's concourse. (The 90-foot-tall palms are *Washingtonia robusta,* specially chosen for heartiness from among the world's 2,780 species.)

[B 10c.] World Financial Center Plaza, W of 2 World Financial Center and the Wintergarden. 1988. Siah Armajani and Scott Burton, artists. Cesar Pelli, architect. M. Paul Friedberg & Partners, landscape architects.

Poised around the indented North Cove, the Plaza comprises the Terrace, the Court, Summer Park, and West Park.

Ferry service: Hoboken-Manhattan ferry service terminated in 1967, but the Port Authority plans to reinstate it from the North Cove area of BPC to the (fortunately) extant ferry terminal next to Hoboken's old Delaware Lackawanna & Western/Erie-Lackawanna/NJ Transit and Hudson Tubes/PATH terminals. Architects: Kohn Pederson Fox Assocs. 1990.

[B 11.] 3 World Financial Center: American Express Headquarters, West St. SW cor. Vesey St. 1985. Cesar Pelli, design architect. Adamson Assocs., architects.

Pyramid-topped.

[B 12.] 4 World Financial Center: Merrill Lynch World Headquarters, North Tower, Vesey St. SE cor. North End Ave. 1986. Cesar Pelli, design architect. Haines Lundberg Waehler, architects.

Step pyramid-topped.

[B 9–12.] World Financial Center softens the prismatic World Trade Center towers

[B 13.] 5 World Financial Center, Vesey St. bet. West St. and North End Ave. N side to Murray St. 1992. Cesar Pelli, design architect.

Speculative—unclear whether it will be undertaken.

North residential neighborhood.

The last of the master plan's residential areas to be developed. Lying on either side of North End Avenue, it consciously attempts to recall some urbane qualities of **Boston's Commonwealth Avenue.**

[B 14a.] North End Avenue mall. 1989. Weintraub & di Domenico.

The antecedents of this central green space are Boston's Back Bay, *not* our Park Avenue or upper Broadway.

[B 14b.] (Proposed new) **Stuyvesant High School.** West St. NW cor. Chambers St. 1992. Alexander Cooper & Partners and Gruzen Samton Steinglass.

A replacement for one of the city's special—admission by competitive test only—high schools, long on East 15th Street. Why here?

[B 15.] North Park. 1992.

Seven acres proposed as an echo of Olmsted & Vaux's Riverside Park, which adjoins the Hudson opposite the Upper West Side. Also considered as a park element back in 1981 was a latter-day Lewisohn Stadium to replace the original, demolished for City College's North Academic Complex; the idea was scrapped.

TRIBECA/LOWER WEST SIDE

Lower West Side:

A bit of history: After the Civil War, **shipping shifted** from the East River to the North (Hudson) River. Bowsprited South Street on Manhattan's southeast flank [see South Street Seaport] was abandoned for the longer, many-berthed piers of steam-powered shipping on this, the west flank. Later, Washington Market, a **venue for produce,** expanded from the market building and spread throughout the local streets, reusing the area's Federal and Greek Revival houses and warehouses as **storage** for fruits and vegetables.

Much later, truckers to the market and the still active piers brought **street congestion** that forced the building of the **West Side** (Miller) **Elevated Highway** atop West Street to accommodate through automobile traffic. The elevated highway was demolished in the early 1980s when **"deferred maintenance"** finally caused a partial collapse; its planned replacement, **Westway,** a multibillion-dollar underground superhighway (some called it boondoggle) yielded to the needs of the Hudson's **striped bass population** in a notable court ruling. After the produce market moved to new City-built facilities at **Hunts Point,** in the Bronx [see S Bronx S 23a., b.], the Lower West Side (a term less and less used) became TriBeCa.

See below for separate sections on the **World Trade Center,** the **Greenwich Street Corridor,** and the heart of **TriBeCa above Chambers Street;** see the preceding section for **Battery Park City.**

The World Trade Center

[T 1.] 1 and **2 World Trade Center (north** and **south towers), 4, 5** and **6 World Trade Center (plaza structures),** Church to West Sts., Liberty to Vesey Sts. WTC 1, 1973. WTC 2, 1972. WTC 4, 1977. WTC 5, 1972. WTC 6, 1974. Minoru Yamasaki & Assocs., design architects. Emery Roth & Sons, architects. Plaza sculptures: *Globe,* Fritz Koenig. *Ideogram,* James Rosati. Unnamed granite, Masayuki Nagare.

Two **shimmering** 1,350-foot-tall, 110-story stainless steel towers (which tourists simply call **"The Twin Towers"**) are flanked by somber, brown, low buildings and a plaza larger than **Piazza San Marco** in Venice. When completed, these stolid, banal monoliths came to **overshadow Lower Manhattan**'s cluster of **filigreed towers,** which had previously been the romantic evocation that symbolized the very concept of **"skyline."** The coming of the World Financial Center's shaped-top towers in Battery Park City [q.v.] softened the impact of the Trade Center's pair—at least for viewers in New Jersey.

Ten million square feet of office space are here offered: 7 times the area of the Empire State Building, 4 times that of the Pan Am. The public agency that built them **(Port Authority of New York & New Jersey)** ran amok with both money and aesthetics.

A visit to the top, however, is a must: to the indoor-outdoor **Observation Deck** and its exhibition area (*Warren Platner & Assocs., architects; Milton Glaser, graphic designer*) in WTC 2 and/or to **Windows on the World,** the pricey but memorable restaurant atop WTC 1 ("if only you could eat the view!"). The public accommodations at both are superb.

Below, in the enclosed WTC concourse, which drains the plaza of any meaningful activity (rush hour or noon is the time to see the crowds streaming through the concourse's corridors), are these eateries:

[T 1a.] The Big Kitchen (fast food), Market Bar & Dining Room (restaurant), Eat & Drink (bar/cafeteria), PATH Square concourse, World Trade Center. 1974–1976. Harper & George, designers. James Lamantia, architect. Big Kitchen graphics, Milton Glaser.

Refreshingly designed, these inventive, happy places to dine are intended for the thousands of WTC office workers. Closed off-hours and Sundays. Milton Glazer's black-and-white checkerboard-colored, larger-than-life block letters spelling BIG KITCHEN that made an adult playground out of the concourse around the phalanx of PATH escalators disappeared in 1987. A remediable loss.

[T 1b.] Vista International Hotel/3 World Trade Center, SW cor. WTC Plaza. 1981. Skidmore, Owings & Merrill.

With its elegant, horizontal-striped aluminum-and-glass curtain wall and its somewhat diagonal orientation, this handsome hotel looks out of place next to—but better than—its enormous WTC neighbors.

WTC 1–6 connect to **WTC 7** via a pair of 2nd-story pedestrian viaducts (one cocooned against wind and rain by **a Star Wars transparent cylindrical container**) that throw much of the sidewalks along this part of Vesey Street into shadow. This is particularly regrettable since WTC 7's overshadowed, arcaded neighbor to the west is the old Barclay-Vesey Building [see T 3.].

[T 1., 1b.] WTC 1 & 2, Vista Hotel   **[T 4.]** The 101 Barclay Street tower

[T 2.] 7 World Trade Center (office tower), Vesey to Barclay Sts., Greenwich St. to West Broadway. 1987. Emery Roth & Sons.

Contrasting with the 25-foot-tall, bright red Alexander Calder stabile, *Three Red Wings,* are the sheer 47-story-high walls of polished and flame-roughened red granite veneer that corset this 1980s addition to the original WTC project. Built atop complicated trusswork that spans the Center's original one-story utility and service ell, **No. 7** achieved fame not for its structural gymnastics or unrelenting form but for the unexpected cancellation, just a year before completion, of a **2 million sq. ft., $3 billion** rental deal by expected tenant Drexel, Burnham, Lambert, Inc., as a result of tax law changes and an insider-trading scandal.

Greenwich Street Corridor

Charles Harvey's experimental cable elevated railway began operation astride Greenwich Street's eastern curb in 1870 and soon evolved into the Ninth Avenue Elevated Line. In the interim Greenwich Street remained a narrow, dark, noisy thoroughfare lined with 3-, 4-, and 5-story commercial and residential structures along its 2½-mile length, from the Battery to Gansevoort Street. Though the street's share of light improved when the el structure was taken down just before World War II, it retained its threadbare character at the southern end until the assemblage of the World Trade Center site, when the surplus stores of Radio Row were demolished to clear the required super superblock for the WTC super supertowers. Greenwich was wiped out entirely between Liberty and Barclay Streets; and as new projects were okayed by the authorities (after a 100-foot-high lid was zoned between Reade and Murray Streets), the narrow roadway north of WTC was widened to near-boulevard width.

 [T 3.] New York Telephone Company (office building) a.k.a. **The Barclay-Vesey Building,** 140 West St., bet. Barclay and Vesey Sts. to (now demapped) Washington St. McKenzie, Voorhees & Gmelin. 1926.

Distinguished, and widely heralded, for the Guastavino-vaulted **pedestrian arcades** at its base, trade-offs for widening narrow Vesey Street. This **Mayan-inspired Art Deco** design by **Ralph Walker** proved a successful experiment in massing what was, in those years, a large urban form within the relatively new zoning "envelope" that emerged from the **old Equitable Building's greed** [see N 9.]. Critic Lewis Mumford couldn't contain himself. A half century later, Roosevelt Island's Main Street used continuous arcades as the very armature of pedestrian procession. Why not elsewhere in New York to protect against inclement weather and to enrich the architectural form of the street? Why, indeed, **not** next door, at 7 World Trade Center?

[T 4.] 101 Barclay Street (offices), NW cor. Greenwich St. to Murray St. 1983. Skidmore, Owings & Merrill.

Eight dinky gingki, on an otherwise empty, scored concrete piazzetta, announce entry to this Jordan almond-green graph-papered monolith. Actually two linked towers sandwiching what was once part of Washington Street, the building defines the path of the missing thoroughfare by creating a glaring white full-height atrium over the street's 60-foot width. At the far end the space is pierced by the half cylinder of 23-story-high elevator banks. (The experience is not unlike entering Cape Canaveral's Vertical Assembly Building and gazing up at a Saturn rocket ready for launch. The only thing missing is a cloud forming under the roof.)

Because the building is occupied by security-conscious Irving Trust and Dean Witter, everything depends on one's plastic access card—guard it with your life. Inserting it in the turnstiles to the left of "Saturn" gains you entry; inserting it again releases you from the building's clutches. Regimentation Takes Command.

[T 5.] 75 Park Place (offices), bet. Greenwich St. and West Broadway. N side to Murray St. 1987. Emery Roth & Sons.

A block-square silvery structure, somewhat squat in these parts at only 14 stories, but made debonair by thin blue stripes that alternate with the strip windows.

 [T 6.] The College of Insurance, 101 Murray St., bet. Greenwich and West Sts. N side. 1983. Haines Lundberg Waehler.

A clever, complicated, crystalline confection of pink precast panels. The designers of this complex of interlocking forms were evidently at the top of their class in descriptive geometry.

 [T 7a.] Greenwich Court I and II (apartments), Greenwich St. bet. Murray and Chambers St. E side. 1987. Gruzen Samton Steinglass.

WHERE BUSINESS MEETS TRIBECA its promotional signs once read. In theory, the design initiatives followed in this adjacent pair of block-front residential buildings should have heralded success as urban infill: a simple vocabulary of **large red brick** set in a red field, generous, rounded corners that ease the turning of odd-angled streets, green-framed sliding sash that adds depth to the facade. But, in the end, the structures seem labored: curved greenhouse cornices suggest a receding hairline; hemispherical pipe grids at the roof corners read as trivial pursuits.

The city's oldest extant cast-iron building, an officially designated landmark warehouse built by ironmonger James Bogardus in 1849, stood in the way of progress in the Washington Market area, at the northwest corner of Washington and Murray Streets (today a nonexistent intersection). In 1970 its cast-iron facade, and those of its neighbors, were disassembled; the parts, early examples of building prefabrication, were stored in a nearby vacant lot to be later reerected at Borough of Manhattan Community College's new campus [see T 9b.]. In the dead of a 1974 night two-thirds of the cast-iron pieces were spirited away (Landmarks chair Beverly Moss Spatt shouted "Someone has stolen my building!") and sold to a junk yard by the scrapnappers. Three years later much of the remainder vanished, this time from a City storehouse ("Someone has stolen my building again!").

[T 7b.] Public School 234, Manhattan, Greenwich St., bet. Warren and Chambers Sts. W side. 1988. Richard Dattner.

A fanciful mix of eclectic architectural elements **drawn from the daydreams of kids** who study here: watchtowers, sentry boxes, walled courtyards, arches from Historic Williamsburg, and Buck Rogers classroom wings.

Holdout: Ever since the inception of the Washington Market Urban Renewal Area project back in the 1950s, one lone structure has resisted the city, the developers, the lawyers, the courts, and the wrecking ball: 179 West Street, just north of Warren. Dingy, ill-kempt, bedraggled, sporting a twisted fire escape and leaky downspouts, a victim of continuing uncertainty, it alone in this multiblocked area of the new reminds us of the old.

[T 8a.] Dalton on Greenwich (apartments), 303 Greenwich St., NE cor. Chambers St. 1987. Beyer Blinder Belle.

A muted design vocabulary and a subtle palette of grays echoes—but doesn't mimic—the same architects' "Bogardus" building at South Street Seaport [see S 1f.]. But what works for 4 stories at the Seaport doesn't work for 11 here, and the flatness here works against the design.

[T 8b.] 311 Reade Street (apartments), SE cor. Greenwich St. 1989. Rothzeid, Kaiserman, Thomson & Bee.

Hard on the heels of its 3 successful downtown neighbors came this red brick development.

[T 9a.] Washington Market Park, N.Y.C. Department of Housing, Preservation & Development, Greenwich St. bet. Chambers and Duane Sts. W side. 1983. Weintraub & di Domenico.

Memorializing in its name the former market area, **a modern miracle,** a spirited amalgam of the natural and the artificial, in the spirit of **Olmsted & Vaux.** Voluptuous landforms, a witty enclosing fence, a gazebo—even a few relocated granite Art Deco ornaments from the erstwhile West Side Highway entry ramps—combine to make this one of the city's best small parks, perhaps *the* best.

[T 9b.] Borough of Manhattan Community College (CUNY), 199 Chambers St., NE cor. West St., along West St. to N. Moore St. Construction halted 1976; completed 1980. CRS (Caudill Rowlett Scott Partnership).

A **megastructure** interminably stretching north from Chambers Street over what were once more than five blocks (Reade, Duane, Jay, Harrison, Franklin, North Moore). A **curiosity** from that brief era when architects told us that megastructures would **cure all urban ills.**

[T 10a.] Independence Plaza North (housing complex), Greenwich St. bet. Duane and North Moore Sts. 1975. Oppenheimer, Brady &

Vogelstein (Barry Goldsmith, project designer), and John Pruyn, associated architects.

Overpowering 40-story middle-income **blockbusters** of brick and striated concrete block. The design was intended to minimize them by **plasticity,** through cantilevers and steady increases in bulk at the top, and **toothiness,** by silhouetting balconies against the sky.

But even with all that, they're still soooo BIG: Gullivers in a still-commercial Lilliput.

And in their shadow are:

[T 11a.] Harrison Street Houses, Harrison St. SW cor. Greenwich St. Partly relocated and restored, 1975, Oppenheimer, Brady & Vogelstein. ★ **[T 11b.]** Originally **Jonas Wood residence,** originally at 314 Washington St. 1804. ★ **[T 11c.]** Originally **315 Washington Street (town house).** 1819. John MComb, Jr. ★ **[T 11d.]** Originally **John McComb, Jr. residence,** originally at 317 Washington St. 1796. John McComb, Jr. ★ **[T 11e.]** Originally **Wilson Hunt residence,** originally at 327 Washington St. 1828. ★ **[T 11f.]** Originally **Joseph Randolph residence,** originally at 329 Washington St. 1828. ★ **[T 11g.]** Originally **William B. Nichols residence,** originally at 331 Washington St. 1828. ★ **[T 11h.]** Originally **Sarah R. Lambert residence,** 29 Harrison St. 1827. ★ **[T 11i.]** Originally **Jacob Ruckle residence,** 31 Harrison St. (original site). 1827. ★ **[T 11j.]** Originally **Ebenezer Miller residence,** 33 Harrison St. (original site). 1827. ★

[T 11a.] The Harrison Street houses in 1977, waiting to find their new owners

These were originally elegant Federal houses, recycled (and rejected) as produce market buildings, 2 on Harrison Street and a group from a now extinct part of Washington Street. Their reincarnation included **moving the Washington Street** group 2 blocks to this enclave. They have been lovingly restored—perhaps too lovingly: the patina from the passage of time has been totally erased (cf. **Williamsburg, Va.**). Note that McComb, City Hall's coarchitect, lived in one!

[T 12.] Shearson Lehman Plaza: [T 12a.] Faulkner Information Services Center, 390 Greenwich St., SW cor. Hubert St. to West St. 1986. Skidmore, Owings & Merrill. **[T 12b.] Office tower,** 388 Greenwich St., NW cor. N. Moore St. 1989. Kohn Pedersen Fox Assocs. building architects, architects for lobby, floors 1-4. Skidmore Owings & Merrill, architects for interiors above floor 4. **[T 12c.] Shearson Garden,** Greenwich St. NW cor. N. Moore St. 1986. Reduced in size, 1989. Both, Weintraub & di Domenico.

Modern Jeff and Post Modern Mutt. The newer 39-story, 1.5 million-square-foot tower occupies much of the original Shearson Garden, a larger parklet that **briefly greened** the construction site to be, and is remembered fondly by nearby TriBeCans. The substitute hemidemisemi parklet is much smaller.

TriBeCa

The acronym for the **Triangle Below Canal** was developed in the mid 1970s when an imaginative realtor, sensing a displacement of manufacturing and warehousing and an influx of artists from places like SoHo, decided to give the area an ear-catching identity (better than Lower West Side) to promote momentum. It did. Try-**beck**-a lies south of Canal Street, west of West Broadway, east of West Street (Little Westway), and north of the World Trade Center, but its heart is above Chambers Street and excludes the blockbuster new construction along the Greenwich Street Corridor.

[T 10a.] Independence Plaza North

[T 12a.] The Shearson Lehman Plaza

Hows Bayou (restaurant), 355 Greenwich St., NE cor. Franklin St.

Southern, Cajun, and south of the border in a very informal settin'—not even credit cards.

The Beach House (restaurant), 399 Greenwich St., NE cor. Beach St.

Mexican food in friendly surroundings.

[T 13.] Originally **Fleming Smith warehouse,** 451-453 Washington St., SE cor. Watts St. 1892. Stephen D. Hatch. ★

Fanciful Flemish. As much a surprise in TriBeCa as it would be anywhere in the city: a golden-hued, gabled, and dormered fantasy with weathered copper details at its picturesquely silhouetted roof. The ground floor has housed the **Capsouto Frères bistro** since 1980.

[T 14.] 135 Hudson St. (warehouse), NW cor. Beach St. 1886. Kimball & Inhen.

A laid-back masonry warehouse, converted and now occupied by laid-back artists who appreciate true grit in architecture. As just a sample of what to look for, note the cast-iron impost blocks at the top of the street-floor columns. *And be on the lookout for more.*

[T 15a.] Holland Tunnel exit rotary, Port Authority of New York & New Jersey/originally **St. John's Park/**later site of **New York Central & Hudson River Railroad Freight Depot,** Hudson to Varick Sts., Ericsson Place to Laight St.

A space occupied since 1927 by the exit roadways of the Holland Tunnel, this was once a square in a class with **Washington Square** and **Gramercy Park:** the houses surrounding it were grand **Federal** and **Greek Revival** places. Its owners, the **Trinity Church Corporation,** experiencing real estate decline, sold the great space to **Commodore**

Vanderbilt for a railroad terminal (1869). Later the railroads moved uptown (passengers), and to the north and west (freight), and the railroad's abandonment made it a found-place for the car to penetrate **New York's** edge by tunnel.

Until 1918 a handsome Georgian-Federal church, **St. John's Chapel** (1807. John McComb, Jr.) stood at the east side of the square (Varick Street) and gave the place its name. St. John's Lane, east of, and parallel to, Varick Street memorializes the chapel. An *Evening Post* of **1847** lyrically describes **St. John's Park** as a "spot of eden loveliness . . . it seems as if retiring from the din and tumult of the noisy town to enjoy its own secret solitude." At this, amid the noise and tumult of belching autos, we heave a historical (and sometimes hysterical) sigh.

[T 13.] Orig. Fleming Smith warehse.   **[T 17a.]** Federal survivor: 2 White St.

[T 14.] 135 Hudson St. warehouse   **[T 14.]** 135 Hudson St. terra-cotta

[T 15b.] Originally **4th Precinct, N.Y.C. Police Department**/now **1st Precinct,** 16 Ericsson Place (originally Beach St.), SW cor. Varick St. 1912. Hoppin & Koen.

A limestone Renaissance Revival palazzetto whose public interior in no way reflects the **opulence of the exterior**—except for the stable on the Varick Street side. The paddocks and other equine accouterments have a quality that exceeds that provided for the officers.

Smoke Stacks Lightnin' (restaurant), 380 Canal St., SE cor. West Broadway (in 285 W. Broadway building).

An atmospheric 1980s pub in a fine, terra-cotta-encrusted building.

[T 16.] New York Telephone Company Building/formerly a.k.a. **AT&T Long Lines Department,** 32 Sixth Ave., bet. Walker and Lispenard Sts. to Church St./originally 24 Walker St. 1918. Addition, 1932. Both by McKenzie, Voorhees & Gmelin.

High Art Deco on an irregular site by one of its New York masters, architect Ralph Walker, responsible for N.Y. Tel's sprinkling of office towers during this period and for nearby **Western Union** [see T 20c.], as well. The lobbies, too, are worth a visit.

[T 17a.] White Street, W. Broadway to Church St.

No. 2. 1809. ★ A genuine Federal store, now propped by a steel pipe-column; a real building with a real use. **Nos. 8-10.** Elaborated Tuscan columns. Watch for the neo-Renaissance trick of foreshortening each floor to increase the apparent height.

[T 17b.] Originally **High Pressure Service Headquarters, N.Y.C. Fire Department/**later **Department of Water Supply, Gas & Electricity,** 226 W. Broadway, bet. Franklin and White Sts. W side. ca. 1905.

This small gem is a sculpted, cream-glazed terra-cotta **galaxy of Fire Department icons** that remind of society's need for water under pressure: hydrants, pipe couplings, valves, and the City's seal.

[T 17c.] 218-224 West Broadway (lofts), NW cor. Franklin St. to Varick St. 1890.

The battered rusticated base distinguishes this bold, red brick behemoth, cousin to [T 20e. and T 20f.] below, and other members of their family in the great late 19th-century masonry tradition.

[T 17d.] El Internacional (restaurant)/formerly **Teddy's Restaurant,** 219 W. Broadway, opp. Franklin St. E side. Redesigned, 1985, Antonio Miralda, designer.

The earlier, pinkie-ring Teddy's (reputedly for the gravel-voiced set) reopened as El Internacional while the Statue of Liberty was briefly **closed for repair,** perhaps explaining artist Miralda's 1¼-ton **replica crown** on its roof. The seeming apparition is particularly startling if you're walking up Franklin Street, as it pokes out from above the restaurant's painted, Dalmatian-patterned stone veneer wall, also the artist's idea. **Whew!**

[T 18a.] Originally **Pierce Building (lofts)/**later **Powell Building,** 105 Hudson St., NW cor. Franklin St. 1892. Carrère & Hastings. Extension to N and upward, 1905, Henri Fouchaux.

Actually a 7-story, 50-foot-wide corner building **expanded** 25 feet in width and 4 stories in height. Can you find the joints in this Renaissance Revival brick and terra-cotta facade?

[T 18b.] 108 Hudson St. (lofts), NE cor. Franklin St. ca. 1895. Converted to residential, ca. 1980.

Get a load of those rusticated **marshmallow columns** at the entrance portico of this late Victorian Baroque heap.

[T 18c.] Originally **New York Mercantile Exchange,** 6 Harrison St., NW cor. Hudson St. 1884. Thomas R. Jackson. Converted to offices, 1987, R. M. Kliment & Frances Halsband.

Romantic and picturesque in pressed brick and contrasting granite, with a **prominent, incomparable tower.** A hearty pile and a must-see work.

[T 19a.] 39-41 Worth Street (lofts), bet. W. Broadway and Church St. N side. 1860. Samuel A. Warner.

The first floor has been castrated by a banal "modernization."

[T 19b.] 47 Worth Street (lofts), bet. W. Broadway and Church St. N side. ca. 1860.

A victim of "Colonializing" by an **innocent admirer** of history who, unfortunately, misunderstands architecture.

The varied facades that line the W side of Hudson Street between Harrison and Jay Streets are a joy to behold. They are anchored at the S end by:

[T 20a.] Originally **House of Relief, New York Hospital**/later **U.S. Marine Hospital No. 70,** 67 Hudson St., NW cor. Jay St. to Staple St. 1893. Cady, Berg & See. Converted to residential, 1985. **[T 20b.]** Originally **Ambulance Annex,** 9 Jay St., NW cor. Staple St. ca. 1905.

The **House of Relief** was the Lower Manhattan emergency room of **New York Hospital** (then on West 15th Street near Fifth Avenue). The small structure to the west (which carries the hospital's **NYH** monogram) was later the ambulance quarters and is still attached across narrow Staple Street by an enclosed overhead bridge.

Walk the 2-block-long, charming backwater that is Staple Street, named for the butter, eggs, cheese, and other staples shipped to the area.

[T 18c.] One of the city's many exchanges recycled as commercial space

[T 18b.] 108 Hudson Street entrance   **[T 20a.]** Orig. The House of Relief

[T 20c.] Western Union Building, 60 Hudson St., bet. Thomas and Worth Sts., E side to W. Broadway. 1930. Voorhees, Gmelin & Walker.

Nineteen shades of brick from brown to salmon form a subtly shaded palette. Note the handsome signs at the ground floor. From the same people who brought you **AT&T Long Lines** [see T 16.].

[T 20d.] 62 Thomas Street (lofts), bet. W. Broadway and Hudson St. S side. 1867.

A **rare** neo-Gothic cast-iron building suitably painted dark brown. Note the polygonal columns.

Duane Park area:

Once the butter, eggs, and cheese market; such dealers are still to be found.

[T 20e.] 165 Duane Street (lofts), NW cor. Hudson St. overlooking Duane Park. Stephen D. Hatch. 1881. **[T 20f.] 55 Hudson Street (lofts),** SW cor. Jay St. 1890. McKim, Mead & White.

A grand pair of 8- to 10-story bold, red brick monoliths, cousins to [T 17c.] above, and to the old Federal Archives Building in the West Village [V Manhattan/West Village C 13.].

[T 20c.] Art Deco Western Union

[T 20e.] S. D. Hatch's 165 Duane

[T 21a., b.] 171, 173 Duane Street, part of the city's old butter and egg market

[T 21.] Duane Park, bet. Hudson, Duane, and Staple Sts. 1795. Reconstructed, 1940.

Annetje Jans' farm was near here (despite the WPA carvings on the flagpole base) after 1636. Family farmers included Roeloff Jans, whose widow married a **Bogardus.** The farm was later sold to Governor Lovelace; then the Duke of York confiscated it and gave it to Trinity Church. The city purchased it as a public park in **1797** for **$5!**

North (odd) side:

[T 21a.] 171 Duane Street, NW cor. Staple St. ca. 1865.

Cast iron of an offbeat design.

[T 21b.] 173 Duane Street, bet. Greenwich and Staple Sts. N side. ca. 1885.

A brick monolith. Note the naturalistic incised terra-cotta archivolts banding the great arches.

South (even) side:

[T 21c.] 172 Duane Street, bet. Greenwich and Hudson Sts. S side, ca. 1870.

Elliptical over semicircular cast-iron arches. Elegant. **Brunelleschi** was simply but handsomely remembered here. Note the curved triangles in the spandrels (the space between the arches).

[T 21d.] 168 Duane Street (warehouse), W of Hudson St. opp. Duane Park. S side. 1886. Stephen D. Hatch. Converted to residential, 1986, John T. Fifield Assocs.

Before commissioning his more flamboyant Washington Street warehouse [see T 13.], developer Fleming Smith had Hatch do this one, perhaps as a trial run in the neo-Flemish style. After years as an egg-packing and cheese-making plant, it was converted into condos by John D. Rockefeller's great-granddaughter, Meile Rockefeller.

Good Enough to Eat (restaurant), 162 Duane St., SE cor. Hudson St.

American favorites served in the company of artifacts salvaged from Grammy's 1930s Midwest kitchen.

[T 22a.] 155 West Broadway (lofts), NE cor. Thomas St. 1865. Jardine, Hill & Murdock.

Two-faced and wonderful: noble Anglo-Italianate high style on wide West Broadway, brick-plain on industrial, narrow, side street Thomas.

[T 22b.] The Odeon Restaurant/originally **The Tower Cafeteria,** 145 W. Broadway, SE cor. Thomas St. Cafeteria, ca. 1935. Altered into restaurant, 1980, Lynn Wagenknecht, Brian McNally, Keith McNally, owner-designers. **[T 22c.] 145-147 West Broadway (lofts).** 1869. John J. O'Neil.

The only way to preserve even a vestige of New York's once ubiquitous streamlined, chrome, wood-paneled, and terrazzo self-service cafeterias is to gentrify them into popular, pricey, places like this. (An addition is the Bakelite mosaic of the Manhattan skyline recycled from the demolished Woolworth's flagship store at Fifth Avenue and 39th Street.) Among the missing items are the cafeterias' traditional blank checks (later to be punched to indicate cost of purchases). They emerged from a semiautomatic check dispenser at the door: BONG!
The building which the Odeon occupies is an interesting work of cast iron that replicates a quoined stone wall.

CIVIC CENTER

The flavor of city life rests largely in the **sharp juxtaposition** of different activities—government, commerce, industry, housing, entertainment—with differing ethnic and economic groups. These precincts are a caricature of that thought.
Spreading out from **City Hall, the neighborhood's center of gravity,** are government offices (**federal, state,** and **city**), middle-income and public housing, commercial warehousing, the fringes of the financial district, Chinatown, and that ancient viaduct that made New York's consolidation with the City of Brooklyn possible: **the Brooklyn Bridge.**
These streets are some of New York's most venerable, but only a smattering of the structures that originally lined them remain. Slowly the **blocks have been consolidated,** and larger and larger single projects of all kinds are **built or planned**—housing projects, government structures, and a college campus.

Civic Center Walking Tour: From **St. Paul's Chapel** to **Chambers Street and West Broadway,** encompassing City Hall, the old newspaper publishing district, the Municipal Building and Foley Square, and the *other* cast-iron district (as contrasted with SoHo). **START** at **Broadway and Fulton Street** (IRT Lexington Avenue express to Fulton Street Station or any train to Fulton Street or Broadway-Nassau Stations).

[C 1a.] St. Paul's Chapel (Episcopal) and **Churchyard,** Broadway, bet. Fulton and Vesey Sts. W side to Church St. 1764–1766. Thomas McBean. Tower and steeple, 1796, James Crommelin Lawrence. ★

Manhattan's only extant pre-Revolutionary **building.** Although the city's present territory contains a dozen older **structures,** they were isolated farmhouses or country seats that bear no more relation to the city than do still-rural 18th-century houses in outlands surrounding the enlarged city. Unlike Fraunces Tavern, St. Paul's is as close to the original as any building requiring maintenance over 200 years could be. Stone from the site (Manhattan schist) forms walls that are quoined, columned, parapeted, pedimented, porched, and towered in Manhattan's favorite **18th-** and **19th-**century masonry, **brownstone.**

A gilt weathervane forms a finial to the finial of a tower crowning a **"Choragic Monument of Lysicrates"** (Hellenistic Greek monument for Renaissance and neo-Renaissance copycats).

The graveyard is a green oasis, dappled with sunlight, an umbrella of trees over somber gravestones. Ivy. Squirrels. Lovely.

It is rumored that **Pierre L'Enfant,** the soldier-architect who designed the **Federal Hall,** America's first capitol [see F 12b.], designed the golden sunburst (gloire) over the high altar.

Governor Clinton's and **President Washington's** pews are within.

[C 1a.] The spire of St. Paul's Chapel   [C 1b.] Orig. N.Y. Evening Post Bldg.

[C 1b.] Originally **New York Evening Post Building (offices)**/later **Garrison Building,** 20 Vesey St., bet. Church St. and Broadway. 1906. Robert D. Kohn. Gutzon Borglum, sculptor.

The interest here is at the top. Kohn and Borglum collaborated to create sculptured limestone and copper **Art Nouveau.**

[C 2.] Federal Office Building, 90 Church St., bet. Vesey and Barclay Sts. W side to W. Broadway. 1935. Cross & Cross and Pennington, Lewis & Mills, Inc. Lewis A. Simon, Supervising Architect of the Treasury.

A cubical limestone monolith that has trouble deciding between a heritage of stripped-down neo-Classical and a new breath of Art Deco.

[C 3.] St. Peter's Church (Roman Catholic), 22 Barclay St., SE cor. Church St. 1838. John R. Haggerty and Thomas Thomas. ★

A granite **Ionic** temple. The wood-framed pediment and roof structure are sheathed in sheet metal molded to the appropriate profiles.

[C 3a.] 10 Barclay Street (mixed use), bet. Church St. and Broadway. S side to Vesey St. 1989. Perkins Geddis Eastman and The Vilkas Group, joint venture.

Topped by a globe, like the Paramount Building [see M Manhattan/Times Square T 9.], is this 44-story combination of commercial (in the stone sheathed base) and residential (in the multihued brick tower).

Columbia College (originally King's College) occupied the blocks between West Broadway, Barclay, Church, and Murray Streets. The river's edge was then 250 feet away, approximately at Greenwich Street, offering a view and sea breezes to the then-rural student and faculty bodies. In 1857 the college moved north, occupying the former buildings of the deaf and dumb asylum between 49th and 50th Streets, Madison and Park Avenues.

 [C 4.] Woolworth Building (offices), 233 Broadway, bet. Park Place and Barclay St. W side. 1913. Cass Gilbert. ★ Partial interior, ★

Much maligned for its **eclectic Gothic** detail and onetime **charcoal Gothic** crown, this sheer shaft is one of New York's most imposingly sited skyscrapers. Rising almost **800** feet, it soars; only the **Seagram** and **CBS Buildings** have the combination of articulate architecture and massing to achieve similar drama. The lobby is clothed in Skyros veined marble. Horace Walpole, who built a **Gothic "castle"** at "Strawberry Hill" and wrote *Castle of Otranto,* could have set his action here.

The **lobby sculpture** is amusing: Woolworth counting nickels, Gilbert holding a model of the building, Gunwald Aus, the structural engineer, measuring a girder, and others.

(The mid 1980s lighting of the tower fails to do justice to this, the world's tallest building from 1913 to 1931.)

[C 4.] The Woolworth Building (1913)   **[C 3.]** Dignified St. Peter's RC Church

[C 5.] Orig. Home Life Insurance Bldg.   **[C 6a.]** Orig. The Park Row Building

 [C 5.] Originally **Home Life Insurance Building (offices),** 256 Broadway, bet. Murray and Warren Sts. W side. 1894. Napoleon Le Brun & Sons.

A lordly midblock building, with a steep pyramidal top, that was among the world's tallest when it opened.

Park Row:

The east boundary of City Hall Park, from south to north.

[C 6a.] Originally **Park Row Building (offices)/**a.k.a. **Park Row Syndicate Building, Ivins Syndicate Building,** 15 Park Row, bet. Ann and Beekman Sts. E side. 1899. R. H. Robertson.

Twin towers for the romantic businessman—guarded by **4 carytids** on the 4th floor. From 1899 to 1908 it was the **world's tallest building,** at 386 feet.

Note: For the red terra-cotta Potter Building, at 38 Park Row, see [N 14b.].

[C 6b.] Pace University/originally **The New York Times Building,** 41 Park Row, bet. Beekman and Spruce Sts. 1889. George B. Post. Expanded upward, 1905, Robert Maynicke.

Rusticated granite but dull as ditchwater. **Post's** nadir.

[C 6c.] Benjamin Franklin statue, Printing House Sq. at the intersection of Park Row, Nassau, and Spruce Sts. 1872. Ernst Plassman, sculptor.

Here, where the *Times, Tribune, Herald, World,* and *Sun* were once published, is a square that commemorates old Newspaper Row and the many job printers who located hereabouts. A beneficent bronze Franklin holds a copy of his *Pennsylvania Gazette.*

[C 6d.] Originally **American Tract Society Building (offices),** 150 Nassau St., SE cor. Spruce St. 1896. R. H. Robertson.

The fascination here is at the roof, where giant "Romanesque" arches provide a geometry of architecture separate from the rusticated granite below.

[C 7a.] City Hall Park/formerly **The Common,** bet. Broadway and Park Row/Centre St., from Vesey/Ann St. to Chambers St. ca. 1730.

In the early 18th century the city itself extended barely to Fulton Street, when the eastern boundary of **The Common** was determined by the Boston (or Eastern) Post Road. On its northward trek it spawned other thoroughfares that linked the island's scattered villages and settlements.

Buildings, seemingly for random purposes at random locations, occupied pieces of this turf from time to time. One of special note was **Vanderlyn's Rotunda** (near the southwest corner of Chambers and Centre Streets), a mini-Pantheon for the display of panoramic views, such as that of Versailles, which, in a prephotography, preelectronic world simulated the experience of being there very nicely. The biggest guest building was the **Post Office** by **Alfred Mullett,** much maligned at the time; in retrospect it was a rich building inspired by Napoleon III's Paris. Mullett's more famous, and preserved, building is the **Executive Office Building** in **Washington.**

Assorted sculpture is also present: **Nathan Hale** (1893. Frederick MacMonnies, sculptor; Stanford White, architect of the base) is looking into the **BMT** for his tardy date; **Horace Greeley** (1890. J. Q. A. Ward) is grandly seated before the **Surrogate's Court.**

[C 7b.] City Hall, City Hall Park, bet. Broadway and Park Row. 1803–1811, 1812. Joseph François Mangin and John McComb, Jr. Altered, 1860, Leopold Eidlitz; 1898, John Duncan; 1903, William Martin Aiken; 1907, 1915, 1917, Grosvenor Atterbury; 1956, Shreve, Lamb & Harmon. ★ Interior, ★.

A minipalace, crossing **French Renaissance** detail with **Federal** form, perhaps inevitable where the competition-winning scheme was the product of a **Frenchman** and a **Scot. Mangin** (who had worked in Paris with **Gabriel** on the **Place de la Concorde**) was the principal preliminary designer and theorist; **McComb** supervised construction and determined much of the detailing.

The central domed space leads past the offices of mayor and city councilmen, up twin spiral, self-supporting marble stairs to the Corinthian-columned rotunda serving as entry to both the **City Council Chamber** and the **Board of Estimate** chambers. The **Governor's Room,** originally for his use when in New York City, is now a portrait gallery replete with portraits by Sully, Inman, Jarvis, Trumbull, and others.

[C 7b.] City Hall's graceful rotunda   **[C 7b.]** Mangin & McComb's City Hall

Interiors have been restored and refurbished, and the exterior peeled off and reproduced in new Alabama limestone (piece by piece). (The soft original **Massachusetts** marble had badly eroded by joint attacks of pollution and pigeons—the rear of the building had been built in brownstone to save money!).

A **bronze tablet** in front of City Hall commemorates the commencement of construction of the first viable subway system in America: the IRT (Interborough Rapid Transit) in 1900. At the foot of the entrance stairs to the IRT, at the southeast corner of Chambers and Centre Streets, is a second ornate plaque (Gutzon Borglum, sculptor) honoring the subway's constructors, led by Chairman August Belmont, Jr. (his father, né Schönberg, on his Americanization in a time of German unpopularity, changed his name to literal French: Schönberg = beautiful mountain = Belmont).

[C 7c.] City Hall Station, IRT Lexington Avenue Line local, below City Hall Park. 1904. Heins & La Farge. ★ **Not open to the public.**

Under City Hall Park, and sealed like King Tut's tomb, is the world's most beautiful (former) subway station at the south edge of the loop that turns the **Lexington Avenue IRT** locals around from **"Brooklyn Bridge"** pointed south to **"Brooklyn Bridge"** pointed north. **Heins & La Farge** were the architects (1904). You can sneak a peek by staying in the *last* car on a southbound local at Brooklyn Bridge Station and looping with it, instead of getting off at the "end of the line."

[C 7d.] Old New York County Courthouse ("Tweed" Courthouse)/now **municipal offices,** 52 Chambers St., bet. Broadway and Centre St. S side. 1858–1878, John Kellum, Leopold Eidlitz.

A building both maligned and praised at the same time: maligned mostly because of the great scandal in its construction (the **Tweed Ring** apparently made off with **$10** of the **$14** million construction "cost"); praised because of a new understanding of, and interest in, **Victorian** architecture.

Another view could consider this a late **Victorian** version of an **English Renaissance** country house.

[C 8a.] Brooklyn Bridge/originally **New York & Brooklyn Bridge,** Park Row, Manhattan, to Adams St., Brooklyn, 1867–1883. John A. and Washington Roebling. ★ Commercial infill of 29 arches below Manhattan approach, 1989, Perkins Geddis Eastman.

A walk across the raised central boardwalk to **Brooklyn Heights** is one of the great dramatic walks of New York. As a side tour from **City Hall,** it is a unique experience, viewing **Brooklyn, Manhattan,** their skylines, and the harbor through a filigree of cables.

The steel and cables have been repainted their original sprightly colors—beige and light brown—instead of the somber battleship gray that gloomed for a misguided generation.

A walk across at sunset, passing down the **Brooklyn Heights Esplanade** to a meal at one of Brooklyn Heights' restaurants is unbeatable. (But watch out for reckless bicyclists!)

"**Brooklyn Bridge,** which is old, . . . is as strong and rugged as a gladiator, while George Washington Bridge, built yesterday, smiles like a young athlete. In this case the two large Gothic towers of stone are very handsome because they are *American* and not "Beaux-Arts." They are full of native sap . . ."

—**Charles Edouard Jeanneret (Le Corbusier)**
When the Cathedrals Were White, 1947

1883 Brooklyn Bridge sparked the joining of N.Y.C. & Brooklyn (1893 cartoon)

[C 8b.] Brooklyn Bridge approaches, under the bridge, bet. Park Row and Water St./St. James Place, from Avenue of the Finest to Bache Plaza/Frankfort St. 1983. N.Y.C. Department of Transportation Urban Design Team; Ekkehart Schwarz, in charge.

A thorough, thoughtful design for the paving, landscaping, and lighting of an often passed-over site, on the occasion of the bridge's centennial.

[C 9.] Pace University, New Building, Nassau, Frankfort, Gold, and Spruce Sts. 1970. Eggers & Higgins. Expanded upward, 1984, The Eggers Partnership.

Limestone and bronze-anodized aluminum trying to look Modern. Benign.

[C 10a.] Bache Plaza (offices), 100 Gold St., SE cor. Frankfort St. 1969. Gruzen & Partners.

A delicate concrete cage reminiscent of **Alvar Aalto.** A pleasant and glassy understatement.

[C 10b.] Southbridge Towers (housing complex), Gold, Frankfort, Water, and Fulton Sts. 1969. Gruzen & Partners.

The charm of this scheme is in the contained urban spaces surrounded by **6-story** buildings—new at the time in publicly assisted housing. This is a **Mitchell-Lama** middle-income housing project.

[C 11a.] New York Telephone Company (switching center), 375 Pearl St., SW cor. St. James Place to Avenue of the Finest. 1976. Rose, Beaton & Rose.

Through its height and proximity to the Brooklyn Bridge's Manhattan tower, this humorless, windowless, high-rise monster diminished much of the majesty of that great span.

 [C 11b.] Murry Bergtraum High School, 411 Pearl St., S cor. Madison St. to Avenue of the Finest. 1976. Gruzen & Partners.

A sleek, purple-brown triangular "fort," complete with corner turrets, financed, through the Educational Construction Fund, by the overwhelming telephone building next door. (The **air rights** of the school provide **zoning credit** for the telephone building; the latter, in return, pays off the bonds that built the school.)

[C 11b.] Murry Bergtraum High School   [C 12a.] N.Y.C. Police Headquarters

 [C 12a.] N.Y.C. Police Headquarters, bet. Park Row, Pearl St., and Avenue of the Finest. 1973. Gruzen & Partners, architects, M. Paul Friedberg, landscape architect.

One of New York's most urbane civic buildings since the **City Hall** of **1812,** largely because of its elegant—but ill-maintained—plaza, stepped pedestrian passageways, and terraces that form an interlock for people in this otherwise car-infested area. An orange/brown-brick cube of office space hovers over special police facilities below.

Five in One, a sculpture by **Bernard (Tony) Rosenthal** in self-weathering (consciously rusty) steel, looms over the **Municipal Building** end.

[C 12b.] Metropolitan Correctional Center, bet. Park Row, Duane and Pearl Sts. 1975. Gruzen & Partners.

An annex to **Cass Gilbert's** U.S. Courthouse provides offices and a detention center. It forms a happy foil to the same firm's **Police Headquarters** and plaza adjacent.

 [C 13.] Municipal Building, Centre St., opp. Chambers St. E side. 1914. McKim, Mead & White (William M. Kendall and Burt Fenner). ★

This is urban architecture, boldly straddling a city street. In those days the ways of traffic were entwined with architecture (see **Warren & Wetmore's Grand Central Terminal** of **1913**). The "Choragic Monument" atop this composition is, in turn, surmounted by *Civic Fame* by **Adolph A. Weinman.**

 [C 14a.] Surrogate's Court/Hall of Records, 31 Chambers St., bet. Centre and Elk Sts. N side. 1899–1911. John R. Thomas and Horgan & Slattery. ★

Civic monuments were designed to impress the citizen in those days—not merely humor him, as is most often the case today. Therefore

his records were kept in a place of splendor. Go in. The central hall, in a small way, is worthy of **Charles Garnier's** earlier **Paris Opéra.**

[C 14b.] Originally **Emigrant Industrial Savings Bank Building**/now **City of New York office building,** 51 Chambers St., bet. Broadway and Elk St. N side to Reade St. 1912. Raymond F. Almirall. ★

The 3rd facility of the Emigrant Bank to occupy this site. Organized in 1851 to serve the city's **Irish Catholic** immigrant population, the Emigrant was once America's **wealthiest savings bank.** The building, a mix of Beaux Arts and Art Nouveau, is now used by the City's bureaucracy. Note the ranks of copper oriels in the light courts and the spirited—if somewhat flat—sculptures that top each wing: the source of Almirall's ornament was Vienna, not Dublin.

[C 14a.] *Horace Greeley* sits in front of the Surrogate's Court/Hall of Records

[C 14c.] N.Y.C. Department of City Planning, 22 (formerly 14, 16, 18, 20, 22) Reade St., bet. Lafayette St. and Broadway. N side. No. 14, 1878. Nos. 16, 18, 20, 22, ca. 1858. Restored, 1987, N.Y.C. Department of General Services Architectural Division.

After a quarter century next door, in the undistinguished Court Square Building—more familiarly known simply as 2 Lafayette Street (*1927, Buchman & Kahn*)—the Planning Department and its commissioners took up residence in this once-again distinguished row of 6-story, 19th-century business buildings. Though they're not designated landmarks, preservation certainly did prevail.

Foley Square

Big Tom's Square: The chaotic irregular subdivided excuse for a public space, around which are gathered many of the Civic Center's noble structures, is—in the old New York tradition—named for Thomas F. ("Big Tom") Foley (1852–1925). He was an alderman, sheriff, saloon-keeper, Tammany Hall district leader, and political mentor of Governor Alfred E. Smith. The square, site of Big Tom's last saloon, was named for him by his successors on the Board of Aldermen in 1926, before construction had even begun.

Clockwise around the square from the west:

[C 15.] Jacob K. Javits Federal Office Building and **Court of International Trade (Customs Court),** 26 Federal Plaza, Foley Sq. bet. Duane and Worth Sts. W side. 1967. Alfred Easton Poor, Kahn & Jacobs, Eggers & Higgins, associate architects. Western addition on Broadway, 1976, same cast. **"Tilted Arc,"** 1981, Richard Serra, sculptor.

The building: an **ungainly checkerboard** of granite and glass built on Foley Square, later extended westward to Broadway with a continued heavy hand.

The sculpture: a **prerusted** 75-ton sculpture resting on the building's Foley Square plaza in competition with its fountain. **"Tilted Arc"** became the subject of contention when added as part of a federal .5%-set-aside-for-art program.

Opponents: "A symbol of artistic noblesse oblige."

Serra: "This newly created concave volume has a silent amplitude which amplifies your awareness of yourself and the sculptural field of the space."

[C 16.] Originally **N.Y.C. Department of Health Building (offices)**/now **Health, Hospitals, and Sanitation Departments Building,** 125 Worth St., bet. Lafayette and Center Sts. N side to Leonard St. 1935. Charles B. Meyers.

The interest here, aside from the spandrel ornament and bas-reliefs on the boxy neo-Classical *cum* Art Deco cube, is in the finely crafted pairs of **anthropomorphic** bronze Art Deco torchères that flank the main entrances. Mmmmm, luscious!

[C 12b.] Metro. Correctional Center   **[C 16.]** Torchère, N.Y.C. Health Dept.

[C 17a.] New York County Courthouse a.k.a. **Manhattan Supreme Court,** 60 Centre St., bet. Pearl St., Hamill Place, and Worth St. in Foley Sq. E side. 1926. Guy Lowell. ★

This **Hexagon** anticipated the **Pentagon** by 30 years. Lowell's scheme won a 1912 competition (but wasn't built until much later), in the spirit of both City Hall and the Municipal Building. The imposing Corinthian portico is **handsome Roman archaeology** but doesn't measure up to the vigorous planning of the building. A grand form to view from above.

[C 17b.] U.S. Courthouse, 40 Centre St., SE cor. Pearl St., in Foley Sq. E side. 1936. Cass Gilbert and Cass Gilbert, Jr. ★

Capped by another Gilbert gold pyramid like the **New York Life Insurance Company Building** [see M Manhattan/Four Squares W 22.]. Dour granite.

The northern Civic Center:

[C 18a.] N.Y.C. Criminal Courts Building and **Men's House of Detention,** 100 Centre St., bet. Leonard and White Sts. E side to Baxter St. 1939. Harvey Wiley Corbett and Charles B. Meyers. House of Detention redesigned, 1986, The Gruzen Partnership.

The **"Tombs,"** after its "Egyptian" Revival long-gone twice-over ancestor across the street. This is a ziggurated construction overlaid with stylish detail of the 1930s: Art Moderne, as at the Paris Exposition of 1937.

[C 18b.] Civil Courthouse, City of New York, 111 Centre St., SW cor. White St. 1960. William Lescaze and Matthew Del Gaudio.

A **sleek but dull cube** fills the site facing an open plaza, under which the City conceals the area's air conditioning equipment. Bas-reliefs by William Zorach.

[C 18c.] Family Court, City of New York, 60 Lafayette St., bet. Leonard and Franklin Sts. 1975. Haines, Lundberg & Waehler.

Black, **very black.** And polished. And pretentious. A busy, somber, relentlessly competitive group of cubistic granite forms. What message does this building's architecture send to families with problems?

[C 17a.] New York County Courthouse   **[C 17b.]** The United States Courthouse

[C 21b.] Orig. Woods Mercantile Bldg.   **[C 19a.]** Orig. Engine Co. 31, N.Y.F.D.

[C 19a.] Originally **Engine Company No. 31, N.Y.C. Fire Department,** 87 Lafayette St., NE cor. White St. 1895. Napoleon LeBrun & Sons. ★

This *was* a house for fire engines, disguised as a **Loire Valley château.** It's now a surplus landmark awaiting a friendly use.

[C 19b.] White Street Correctional Facility, N.Y.C. Department of Corrections, bet. Centre and Baxter Sts. N side to Walker St. 1989. Urbahn Assocs., Inc. and Litchfield-Grosfeld Assocs., joint venture.

High-rise maximum-security detention for 500 inmates, rising from a base of little shops, a community clock, and a bridge of sighs connecting to the "Tombs" [see C 18a.].

Cast-Iron District 1 (South of Canal Street)

Cast iron gave an inexpensive means of reproducing elaborate detail, previously possible only as carving in stone. More Corinthian, Ionic,

Doric, Composite, Egyptian and Lord-knows-what-else columns were cast for New York facades of the 1850s and 1860s than Greece and Rome turned out in a millenium. The two great centers were between Broadway and West Broadway, Canal to Duane (here and in TriBeCa described) and, to the north, Crosby Street to West Broadway, Canal to Houston Streets, now rechristened **SoHo** (South of Houston). [SoHo is a separate precinct, below.]

These handsome loft spaces are used by assorted commercialdom, principally for warehousing, sometimes for light manufacturing, and for studios by the neighborhood's many real or would-be artists.

[C 20.] 254-260 Canal Street (lofts), SW cor. Lafayette St. 1857. Cast-iron facades attributed to James Bogardus. ★ Converted to offices, 1987, Jack L. Gordon.

One of the city's earliest surviving cast-iron facade buildings. If in fact the castings *are* Bogardus', this would be the largest and most important of his extant works. It's also very beautiful!

[C 21.] Church Street, bet. Walker and White Sts. E side.

A blockfront lesson in the virtues of a unified stylistic vocabulary. Note how differently the window openings are treated, building by building, and how the whole is greater than the sum of its parts.

[C 21a.] Ristorante Arqua, 281 Church St., SE cor. White St. 1987. Studio Morsa, designers.

Restrained introduction of a new restaurant into a fine old building. *Perfetto!*

[C 21b.] White Street, Church St. to Broadway.

No. 46. 1865. Formerly **Woods Mercantile Building.** ★ A set of buildings organized by its pediment. **No. 52.** Note the appropriate sign. **Nos. 54-56.** Italianate brownstone over cast-iron ground floor. **Nos. 55-57.** ca. 1865. John Kellum & Son. Mutilated ground floor. **Nos. 60-66.** 1869. Ground floors mutilated at **Nos. 64-66.**

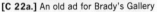

[C 22a.] An old ad for Brady's Gallery   [C 21c.] Civic Center Syn. in 1967

[C 21c.] Congregation Shaare Zedek (Civic Center Synagogue), 49 White St., bet. Church St. and Broadway. S side. 1967. William N. Breger Assocs.

A **ribbon** of marble tiles undulates to reveal a garden behind: unhappily (due to modern security needs) barred from the passerby by wrought-iron fencing. The sanctuary is on the second floor.

[C 22a.] Originally **James L. White Building (lofts),** 361 Broadway, SW cor. Franklin St. 1882. W. Wheeler Smith. ★

A corner building with two intersecting late cast-iron facades. Its most interesting attribute, however, may be the **faintly visible sign** painted atop its south, lotline wall:

359

BRADY'S

GALLERY

The reference is to the studio that photographer Mathew Brady maintained next door, beneath the sign. **Abraham Lincoln** came there to be photographed the morning after his famed **Cooper Union speech,** which many believe won him the presidency.

[C 22b.] Franklin Street, bet. Church St. and Broadway. 1860s.

More white, brown, and simulated (cast-iron) stone. Savor the Corinthian capitals, the glassy windows, the rich and variegated variations on a theme. A somewhat tired but elegant block that would blossom with paint and washed windows. It is said that Renwick and Co. did **No. 71. Nos. 112-114** are a rich stone and cast-iron set.

[C 22c.] Leonard Street, bet. Church St. and Broadway. 1860s.

Limestone (white), brownstone and cast iron. The game is to look closely to separate them: the iron tends to be more slender than the brittle stone. **No. 85** ★ was James Bogardus' own warehouse; **Nos. 87-89** are similar but simpler, and of stone, matching Bogardus' cast iron (all 1862). **Nos. 80-82.** 1862. James H. Giles. **No. 73.** 1863. James F. Duckworth. **No. 71.** 1860. Samuel A. Warner.

[C 22c.] Leonard Street's double-height columns: which are iron, which are stone?

[C 23.] Originally **New York Life Insurance Company Building,** 346 Broadway, bet. Catharine Lane and Leonard St. E side to Lafayette St. (orig. Elm St.) a.k.a. 108 Leonard St. E end, 1896, Stephen D. Hatch with McKim, Mead & White. W end, 1898, McKim, Mead & White. ★ Various interior spaces, ★

N.Y. Life occupied the Broadway end of this long narrow block since 1870. Hatch was engaged to design an eastern addition but died (1894) before construction was completed. MM&W joined in the completion of the addition and went on to demolish the original Broadway structure and design its successor, with its distinguished Classical clock tower overlooking Broadway.

N.Y. Life vacated the building in 1928 for its uptown tower [see M Manhattan/Four Squares W 22.]; **No. 346** has been owned since 1967 by the City. *Do look at the semicircular elevator bank and visit:*

Clock Tower Gallery, 108 Leonard St., bet. Broadway and Lafayette St. S side. **Open to the public.**

A not-for-profit gallery of avant-garde art located in the grand, cubical, top-floor room of the N.Y. Life tower, operated by the Institute for Art & Urban Resources, which also operates **P.S. 1** in L.I.C. [see W Queens W 25.].

[C 24a.] 65-85 Worth Street (lofts), bet. Church St. and Broadway. N side. ca. 1865.

This **handsome remnant** row of neo-Renaissance whitestone buildings once *faced* a fabulous cast-iron row (replaced by [C 24b.] below).

[C 24b.] American Telephone & Telegraph Company Long Lines Building, Church St. bet. Thomas and Worth Sts. E side. 1974. John Carl Warnecke & Assocs.

A giant electronic complex in the guise of a building. Pink, textured (flame-treated) Swedish granite sheathes a stylish leviathan that looms over the city with **architectural eyebrows.** The **only bow** to the neighboring humanity is a **bleak plaza** to the east. **Ma Bell,** why didn't you leave the air for people and place your electrons underground?

[C 23.] Orig. N.Y. Life Insurance Co.   **[C 24a.]** Worth Street "whitestones"

[C 24c.] N.Y. S. Insurance Fund (offices), 199 Church St., bet. Thomas and Duane Sts. E side to Trimble Place. 1955. Lorimer Rich Assocs.

A white glazed-brick tombstone atop a polished red granite base. The funky flaring stainless steel entrance canopy just screams "fifties."

[C 24d.] 8 Thomas Street, bet. Broadway and Church St. S side. 1875. J. Morgan Slade. ★

An **elaborate confection** composed of Romanesque, Venetian Gothic, brick, sandstone, granite and cast-iron parts, worthy of **John Ruskin,** whose polemics inspired such thoughts like the Jefferson Market Courthouse [see V Manhattan/Greenwich Village B 5.].

The Thomas Street Inn occupies the ground floor: a sensitive adaptation for lunch and early dinner. Beer and wine.

[C 24e.] 319 Broadway (lofts), NW cor. Thomas St. ca. 1865.

A **sentinel** marking the entrance of **Thomas Street,** seriously marred (as usual) by **grossly unsympathetic** commercial alterations at the street. Very elaborate, this is a cast-iron gem of the first order. New York Life Insurance Company began in rented rooms in this structure before graduating to [C 23.] above.

[C 25a.] Langdon Building (lofts), 305 Broadway, NW cor. Duane St. 1890s.

Handsome clustered Romanesque Revival colonnettes form piers that as ornament are equal to the natural incised bas-reliefs of **Louis Sullivan.**

[C 25b.] 291 Broadway (lofts), NW cor. Reade St. 1910. Clinton & Russell.

Some pleasant Renaissance trappings near street and cornice.

[C 25c.] 287 Broadway (lofts), SW cor. Reade St. 1872. J. B. Snook.

A glassy mansarded, wrought-iron-crested, Ionic- and Corinthian-columned, cast-iron delight. **Lovely.**

[C 26a.] Broadway Chambers Building (offices), 277 Broadway, NW cor. Chambers St. 1901. Cass Gilbert.

Carefully stacked Renaissance Revival. A Nedick's hot dog stand once scarred the corner, now carefully restored by the Manufacturers Hanover Trust Co. (note the carefully matched and replaced granite).

[C 26b.] 280 Broadway (lofts)/formerly **Sun Building**/originally **A. T. Stewart Dry Goods Store,** NE cor. Chambers St. 1846. Trench & Snook. Ottavio Gori, stonemason. Additions.

Here **Stewart** founded the first **great department store** of America, later to occupy grand premises at Broadway between 9th and 10th Streets (known to recent generations as Wanamaker's, who bought out all of Stewart's enterprises). **Henry James** and **Anthony Trollope** both lavished words of wonder on these premises. Later the *Sun* was published here. Now, in part a discount house, with City offices above.

Ellen's (luncheonette-bakeshop), 270 Broadway, S of Chambers St., across from City Hall Park.

The place to have a business breakfast if "business" means federal, state, or city government. Ellen is Ellen Hart Sturm, a "Miss Subways" beauty contest winner from the era (1959) when such concerns occupied subway car ads and were the subject of rush hour reading.

[C 27a.] John Kellum's spectacular cast-iron Anglo-Italianate Cary Bldg. (1857)

[C 27a.] Originally **Cary Building (lofts),** 105-107 Chambers St., NW cor. Church St. to Reade St. 1857. King & Kellum. Cast-iron facade by D. D. Badger's Architectural Ironworks. ★ Storefronts altered, 1985, Grandesign Architects.

This Anglo-Italianate palazzo, despite its losses (and pleasant retail gains) at street level, reflects the **talents of John Kellum,** who went on to design some of the city's finest cast-iron structures, such as the now demolished, full-block A. T. Stewart Store. Construction of The Cary heralded the establishment of a commercial center north and west of City Hall in the mid 19th century. **Once a midblock structure,** it has boasted an inadvertent east facade ever since **Church Street was widened** for the IND subway in the late 1920s.

Tenbrooks Restaurant, 62 Reade St., bet. Church St. and Broadway. 1980.

A neat and comfy new old-favorite in these political parts.

[C 27b.] Formerly **N.Y.C. Fire Department Museum Engine Company No. 7, Ladder Company No. 1,** 100 Duane St., bet. Church St. and Broadway. 1905. Trowbridge & Livingston.

An **English** version of an **Italian** palazzo with double-hung windows for fire engines.

Colonnaded block: Look carefully at the storefronts surrounding the block bounded by West Broadway and Reade, Duane, and Church Streets, and you'll discover along the ground floor a series of fluted Corinthian cast-iron columns carrying the masonry facades of the upper floors. Some are asphyxiated with modern materials or just hidden behind unwashed show windows, but **they are there.** What a wonderful contribution to the urbanity of this rediscovered district were they all to be revealed! The only exception, incidentally, is the northeast corner of West Broadway and Reade Street. But not to fret:

[C 28.] 109-113 West Broadway (lofts), NE cor. Reade St.

Surviving after countless years above the Greek restaurant is a faint but readable palimpsest on the oft painted stone wall advertising a long-gone paint store:

[C 28.] 109–113 West Broadway's wall is a palimpsest of an earlier billboard

END of Civic Center Tour. The nearest subways are along Chambers Street: IRT Seventh Avenue Line at West Broadway, and IND Eighth Avenue Line at Church Street.

CHINATOWN/LITTLE ITALY

Chinatown

In most large American cities Chinese have formed **enclaves** that are **sought by tourists** and **relished by city dwellers** with an appetite for China's diverting cuisines. Since the 1840s New York's Chinatown has traditionally been centered in the eight blocks encircled by Canal, Worth, and Mulberry Streets and the Bowery/Chatham Square. In the early 1970s Chinese began to push out the enclave's historic boundaries, although Mott Street below Canal remains Main Street, along whose flanks and side streets are located the most popular places to dine and shop. **Chinese expansion** is evident in every direction, dissipating the Italianness of Little Italy and replacing with Chinese ideographs the Yiddish signs that were once ubiquitous along East Broadway to the Forward Building and beyond. Except for Confucius Plaza and the Manhattan Bridge, the area east of Chatham Square and the Bowery is covered in the **Lower East Side.**

Park Row: Toward Chatham Square

[L 1.] Chatham Towers (apartments), 170 Park Row, bet. Park Row and Worth St. N side. 1965. Kelly & Gruzen.

Sculpted concrete, this joins the ranks of distinguished housing architecture: the **Dakota, Butterfield House, 131 East 66th Street,** Brooklyn's **Williamsburg Houses,** and **East Midtown Plaza** are its peers from all eras. All are participants in the city's life and streets, rather than towered islands, as in most public housing. And like all strong architectural statements, **Chatham Towers** rouses great admiration and great criticism.

A funeral cortege proceeding S along Mott Street, in the century's first decade

[L 1.] Chatham Towers apartments

[L 2.] Chatham Green apartments

[L 2.] Chatham Green (apartments), 185 Park Row, bet. Pearl St. and St. James Place. S side to Madison St. 1961. Kelly & Gruzen.

A great undulating wall: open-access galleries are served by vertical circulation towers. **Barney Gruzen** designed it after seeing **Alfonso Reidy's** undulating slabs at **Pedregulho** in Rio de Janeiro.

East of St. James Place (formerly New Bowery)

[L 3.] Governor Alfred E. Smith Houses, N.Y.C. Housing Authority, bet. South, Madison, and Catherine Sts. and St. James and Robert F. Wagner, Sr., Places. 1952. Eggers & Higgins.

Al Smith lived a stone's throw away—this is his turf. These are typical of New York's public housing of the 1940s and 1950s: **dull warehouses** for people—expensive for the taxpayer, cheap for the poor, and well maintained. For the school and recreation center on the northeast boundary of the site:

[L 3a.] Public School 126, Manhattan, The Jacob Riis School, and **Alfred E. Smith Recreation Center** (within Governor Smith Houses site), 80 Catherine St., bet. Cherry and Monroe Sts. W side. 1966. Percival Goodman.

A neatly articulated school and community recreation center, both of high design quality. Note the bold outdoor murals.

[L 4a.] St. James Church (Roman Catholic), 32 James St., bet. St. James Place and Madison St. E side. 1837. ★

Brownstone Doric Greek Revival. Distyle (2 columns) in antis (between flanking blank walls). Compare it to **Mariners' Temple** below.

[L 4a.] St. James Church (1837)   **[L 13a.]** The Transfiguration RC Church

[L 4c.] Mariners' Temple, Greek Revival with Ionic columns distyle in antis

[L 4b.] First Shearith Israel Graveyard, 55 St. James Place, bet. Oliver and James Sts. S side. 1683–1828. ★

The only people-shaped remnant of Manhattan's 17th century, this bears the remains of **Sephardic Jews** (of Spanish-Portuguese extraction) who emigrated from **Brazil** in the mid 17th century.

[L 4c.] Mariners' Temple (Baptist)/formerly **Oliver Street Church,** 12 Oliver St., NE cor. Henry St. 1844. Isaac Lucas. ★

A stone, **Greek Revival Ionic** temple. Black and Chinese communicants worship in a sailors' church that might well be a **temple to Athena.**

[L 4d.] St. Margaret's House/originally **Robert Dodge residence,** 2 Oliver St., bet. St. James Place and Henry St. E side. 1820. James O'Donnell. 3rd floor added, 1850.

A **Federal** house, now part of adjacent Mariners' Temple's work.

[L 5.] Knickerbocker Village (apartments), Catherine to Market Sts., Monroe to Cherry Sts. 1934. Van Wart & Ackerman.

A **blockbuster,** with **1,600** apartments on 3 acres (New York City public housing averages 80 to 100 units per acre). The central courtyards, reached through gated tunnels, seem a welcome relief by contrast with their dense and massive surroundings. This was the first major housing project even partially aided by public funds. It maintains its reasonably well-kept lower-middle-class air today.

[L 6a.] 51 Market Street/originally **William Clark residence,** bet. Monroe and Madison Sts. W side. 1824. ★

A rare four-story **Federal** house—they were almost always two or three (plus basement and/or dormered attic). Its entranceway is Federal at its most superb.

[L 6b.] Sea and Land Church/The First Chinese Presbyterian Church/originally **Market Street Church,** 61 Henry St., NW cor. Market St. 1819. ★

A **Georgian-Federal** body punched with Gothic Revival windows; of dressed Manhattan schist, with brownstone surrounds (enframement) and trim.

[L 7.] Chinatown Mission/Church of Our Saviour (Episcopal), 48 Henry St., bet. Market and Catherine Sts. S side. 1830.

Two houses saved by churchly missionary needs (as a chapel of **Trinity Church** downtown). The roof balustrade is from a **Georgian** country house; the doorway's elaborate **Federal** carving is encrusted with layers of blurring paint (cut through the rings of paint to tell the age, as you would a tree).

[L 8a.] East Broadway Mall (shopping), under Manhattan Bridge, bet. Market and Forsyth Sts. N side. 1988. T. C. Ho and Jack Eng.

Finally, a use for that gloomy space in the shadow of the bridge.

[L 8b.] 18 East Broadway (offices), NE cor. Catherine St. 1987. T. C. Ho.

Six stories of polished red granite intended to pave the way for a new East Broadway at its western gateway. So far, it seems too glitzy.

[L 9.] Confucius Plaza (apartments) and **Public School 124, Manhattan, The Yung Wing School,** bet. the Bowery, Division St., Chatham Sq., and the Manhattan Bridge approaches. 1976. Horowitz & Chun.

A "dual use" construction of school and housing interlocked. The curved slab is arbitrary but a pleasant skyline form.

[L 10.] Manhattan Bridge, bet. Canal St. and the Bowery in Manhattan and Flatbush Ave. Ext. in Brooklyn. 1905. Gustav Lindenthal, engineer. Pedestrian walk enclosure, 1989, Frank O. Gehry & Assocs. and John Carl Warnecke & Assocs.

Perhaps the most pedestrian design of any of the city's suspension bridges. Gehry's addition may help enliven it.

[L 10a.] Manhattan Bridge Arch and **Colonnade,** at entrance to bridge. 1905. Carrère & Hastings. ★

A regal and monumental horseshoe-shaped colonnade which has somehow overcome all attempts by highway engineers to remove it. Long may it last!

The heart of Chinatown:

[L 11a.] Originally **Citizen's Savings Bank/**now **Manhattan Savings Bank,** 58 Bowery, SW cor. Canal St. 1924. Clarence W. Brazer.

The enormous dome across from the Manhattan Bridge gateway.

[L 11b.] Originally **Edward Mooney residence/**now **Metro Communications Center,** 18 Bowery, SW cor. Pell St. 1785–1789. Alterations, 1807. Restoration, 1971. ★

Built *after* the **Revolution** but *before* Washington's inauguration. This is Manhattan's oldest row house; it combined Georgian elements with the incoming Federal style.

[L 12a.] Bank Central Asia, 4 Chatham Sq., bet. Mott and Doyers St. 1987.

Neo-Chinese neo-Classical neo-Post Modern in white stucco.

[L 12b.] Manhattan Savings Bank branch, 17 Chatham Sq., SW cor. Catherine St. 1977. George W. Clark Assocs.

A virtuoso mock-Chinese temple naively commissioned to serve as a branch bank for Chinatown. Like the rapidly disappearing pagoda telephone booths, it's harmless, amusing kitsch.

Mott Street:

[L 13a.] Church of the Transfiguration (Roman Catholic)/formerly **Zion Episcopal Church,** 25 Mott St., NW cor. Mosco St. 1801. ★

Like **Sea and Land** [see L 6b.], a Georgian church with Gothic windows, although here with Gothic tracery, there with small-paned double-hung windows. Dressed Manhattan schist makes neat building blocks, with brownstone detail. The octagonal tower, copper sheathed, is from the 1860s.

[L 13b.] Eastern Villa Restaurant, 66 Mott St., bet. Bayard and Canal Sts. E side. ca. 1985.

A new restaurant with a new facade of acrylic wonder.

[L 13c.] "Chinese Dragon Restaurant" projecting neon sign, in front of Golden Dragon Restaurant, 73 Mott St., bet. Bayard and Canal Sts. W side. ca. 1935.

Tall, elaborate, multicolored, broken. Few of the neon tubes are intact but some still glow, even though the restaurant bears a new name. A rare survivor: one of the great *two-sided* neon signs to hang over a New York sidewalk. It deserves repair: Friends of Outdoor Neon, where are you?

[L 14a.] Chemical Bank branch, 180 Canal St., SE cor. Mott St. Altered, 1983, Bonsignore, Brignati & Mazzotta.

After years of sporting a refined, black and red, Bauhaus-influenced facade, unlikely in these parts, Chembank updated, for a more traditional (red lacquer) look. It came out just fine.

[L 14b.] Chinese Merchant's Association, 85 Mott St., SW cor. Canal St. 1958.

Grauman's Chinese Theater architecture. On this *both* **Mao** and **Chiang** might have agreed.

[L 14c.] 5th Precinct, N.Y.C. Police Department/originally **6th Precinct,** 19-21 Elizabeth St., bet. Bayard and Canal Sts. W side. 1881. Nathaniel D. Bush.

A dignified Italianate station house. The department's house architect, Bush, was designing *all* of them during this period of rapid constabularial growth.

[L 15.] Hongkong Bank Building (offices)/originally **Golden Pacific National Bank Headquarters,** 241 Canal St., NW cor. Centre St. 1983. Ornament and tiles, from Taiwan artisans.

A red lacquer, polychromed, embellished, Pagoda style, Chinese confection. Not a building: an event.

Entertainments and a full stomach

Mandarin Inn, 14 Mott St., bet. Chatham Sq. and Pell St. E side. and 23 Pell St., bet. Mott and Doyers St. S side.

Cue magazine: "The food at *both* of these restaurants is great. There are [*sic*] a wide selection of dishes from mild to fiery."

Kuan Sing Dumpling House, 9 Pell St., bet. Bowery and Doyers St. S side.

A perfect pick-me-up: **hot and sour soup,** plus an order (or more) of **steamed meat dumplings,** made fresh and served in round bamboo steamer trays. Make your own dip for the dumplings: sugar, soy sauce, vinegar. Or, for a spicier palate, add hot sauce or hot oil. Or have the dumplings boiled or fried, or . . .

Bo-Bo's Restaurant, 20½ Pell St., opp. end of Doyers St. N side.

Unlikely. Disguised as an unattractive commercial storefront, this crowded, popular, reasonably priced restaurant is a mecca for the gastronomically sophisticated but penurious.

"The Bloody Angle": The unexpected sharp turn midway down block-long Doyers Street was named for the *tong* (gang) wars fought there between 1880 and 1926 by the On Leong Tong and the Hip Sing Tong for control of local gambling and opium trafficking.

Nom Wah Tea Parlor, 13 Doyers St., bet. Chatham Sq. and Pell St. W side at "The Bloody Angle."

The real McCoy. Don't ask for a menu; pick your favorite dim sum (varied tiny delights eaten sequentially till there's no room left in your tummy) from trays circulated throughout this old family eatery. These goodies are served on dishes whose size and style are codes to their price. When done, the stack on your table is counted and a check is presented.

Wing Fat Company (retail produce), 33 Mott St., opp. Pell St. W side.

Bok choy, water chestnuts, ginger root, Chinese cabbage, lichee, etc. The tan-and-green-topped white roots that form the nucleus of **Chinese vegetarianism** are featured here, as are seeds and candy to complement. These shops are becoming rare in old Chinatown, as the once highly concentrated ethnic population spreads outward.

Fung Wong Bakery, 30 Mott St., bet. Chatham Sq. and Pell St. E side.

For an after meal snack, order a Chinese **dinner roll** (a sweet delight), **red bean cake** (a sweet delight), a **black bean cake** (a *very* sweet delight), or whatever tempts you. But be assertive, or another customer will beat you to it.

Little Italy:

Canal to Houston Streets, Lafayette Street to the Bowery, is still, in large part, the most important old **Italian** center of New York—but now with **old** Italians, as the newest generation has made the move to suburbia. They return, however, for festivals and family festivities: marriages, funerals, feasts, and holy days. Meanwhile, the **Chinese** have rapidly moved north across the former cultural moat of **Canal Street** and partially share this turf.

[L 16a.] Paolucci's Restaurant/originally **Stephen van Rensselaer residence,** 149 Mulberry St., bet. Hester and Grand Sts. W side. 1816. ★

A **Federal** 2-story, dormered brick house, a surprising remnant in these tenemented streets. The color scheme of black and white signals "Italian Federal."

[L 16b.] Banca Stabile (former bank), 189 Grand St., SW cor. Mulberry St. 1885.

A onetime Italian family bank **totally bypassed by time.** Tin ceilings, terrazzo floors, oscillating electric fans, bare-bulb incandescent fixtures. One of the brass teller's cages still offers steamship tickets (at least that's what the gilt lettering reads). And there are no signs reading "Early withdrawal may result in substantial penalties."

The son of the last owner maintains the relic while conducting a real estate office from the premises, **a personal landmark** according to his neighbors.

[L 16c.] Ferrara's (pastry and coffee shop), 195 Grand St., bet. Mulberry and Mott Sts. S side. Altered, 1980, Sidney P. Gilbert & Assocs.

While the family has been making *dolci* since 1892, this is a new departure, a modern building in which to serve its devoted public. Very different, very flat, a nougat of windows.

[L 16d.] Il Fornaio (restaurant), 132A Mulberry St., bet. Hester and Grand Sts. E side. 1985. Studio Morsa, designers.

An evocation of an old-time Italian restaurant but with no sentimentality, only good design sense.

 [L 17a.] Originally **N.Y.C. Police Headquarters,** 240 Centre St., bet. Grand and Broome Sts., and Centre Market Place. 1909. Hoppin & Koen. ★ Converted to residential, 1988, Ehrenkranz Group & Eckstut.

In the manner of a French *hôtel de ville* (town hall), this is tightly arranged within the city's street system, not isolated palatially (as is City Hall or most any state capitol). Ornate **Renaissance Revival** architecture is laced with bits of **Baroque.** The shape of the building even follows that of the wedge-shaped plot it occupies.

[L 17b.] 165 Grand Street/originally **Odd Fellows Hall,** SE cor. Centre St. 1849. John B. Snook. Extended upward, 1880s. ★

The somewhat bedraggled palace of the **Odd Fellows,** a high rise in brownstone second only to the Cooper Union [V Manhattan/Astor Place A 13.]. **Snook** contributed many cast-iron buildings to the SoHo district to the west.

 [L 18a.] Bowery Savings Bank, 130 Bowery, bet. Grand and Broome Sts. 1894. McKim, Mead & White. ★ **[L 18b.] Grand St. Branch, Citibank,** 124 Bowery, NW cor. Grand St. 1902. York & Sawyer.

Roman pomp wraps around **Renaissance luster** on the Bowery, at the edge of Little Italy. They have served as **architectural and economic anchors** through the Bowery's years of hard times. The interior of the Bowery bank is one of the **great spaces** of New York. *Go in.*

The Feast of San Gennaro fills Mulberry Street from Columbus Park to Spring Streets in the middle of September. Happily, autos are exiled. Arcaded with a filigree of electric lights, the street becomes a vast al fresco restaurant, interspersed with games of chance, for the benefit of this venerable Neapolitan saint. Fried pastries and sausages steam the air, and for one evening you may become part of the gregarious Italian public life (are those vendors really Italian? Greek? Jewish?).

[L 19a.] Engine Company No. 55, N.Y.C. Fire Department, 363 Broome St., bet. Mott and Elizabeth Sts. S side. 1898. R. H. Robertson.

Ornate, eclectic Renaissance Revival.

[L 19b.] 375 Broome Street (tenement), bet. Mott and Mulberry Sts. S side. ca. 1885.

Who is that figure peering out of the deep sheet metal cornice? Jupiter, Michelangelo, Mazzini, Garibaldi—or is it Moses? Note the terra-cotta stars of David (commonly found in turn-of-the-century architectural ornament with no Jewish connection).

[L 19c.] Most Holy Crucifix Church (Roman Catholic), 378 Broome St., bet. Mott and Mulberry Sts. N side. 1926. Robert J. Reiley.

A vest-pocket church, occupying just one lot in this crowded precinct. Everything is arrayed one above the other, as in the adjacent tenements.

Milan Laboratories, 57 Spring St., bet. Mulberry and Lafayette Sts. N side.

The center for vinocultural chemistry, both for ingredients and equipment. Here one can outfit oneself to produce **Chianti in the cellar.** Apparatus and advice are available, as well as spices.

[L 19b.] A well-maintained sheet metal cornice graces 375 Broome St. tenement

[L 20a.] Originally **14th Precinct, N.Y.C. Police Department/**later **Police Department Storehouse/**now **offices,** 205 Mulberry St., bet. Kenmare and Spring Sts. W side. ca. 1870. Nathaniel D. Bush.

An Italianate station house with mansard, somehow spared from both demolition and "modernization." The old "house of detention" is on the left.

[L 20b.] Old St. Patrick's Cathedral (Roman Catholic), 260-264 Mulberry St., bet. Prince and E. Houston Sts. E side. 1815. Joseph Mangin. Restored after fire in 1868. Henry Engelbert. ★

The original **Roman Catholic** cathedral of New York; the present St. Patrick's uptown replaced it after a disastrous fire. Restored, this building was demoted to parish church status. The interior is a grand, murky brown "Gothicized" space, with cast-iron columns supporting a timber roof. The original (prefire) shell is in the Gothic-decorated Georgian tradition of **Sea and Land** or the **Church of the Transfiguration,** both in the Chinatown area.

[L 20c.] Old St. Patrick's Cathedral Rectory, 263 Mulberry St., opp. church.

Very eclectic, very well maintained, very fine ironwork.

[L 20d.] St. Michael's Chapel of Old St. Patrick's Cathedral (Roman Catholic), 266 Mulberry St., bet. Prince and E. Houston Sts. 1859. James Renwick, Jr. and William Rodrigue. ★

Neo-Gothic brownstone and brick, built in a shape and location as if on a tenement lot.

[L 20e.] 282 Mott Street (factory), bet. Prince and E. Houston Sts. E side. ca. 1885.

The unusual **softly rounded corners** along window openings in this brick Romanesque Revival industrial building make for a very different sense of masonry.

[L 21a.] Old St. Patrick's Convent and Girls' School, 32 Prince St., SW cor. Mott St. 1826. ★

A **Georgian-Federal** building with a classy **Federal** entryway. Here the vocabulary of a Federal house was merely inflated to the program requirements of a parish school (originally an orphan asylum).

Chuck Close: On the west lot-line wall of 26 Prince Street, between Mott and Elizabeth, is a portrait by painter Chuck Close done as a giant outdoor mural: a technicolor mosaic of squares arrayed like a halftone.

[L 21b.] Originally **14th Ward Industrial School/Astor Memorial School,** 256-258 Mott St., bet. Prince and E. Houston Sts. E side. 1888. Vaux & Radford. ★

Gothic Revival forms give this somber relic class on an otherwise reserved block. Adaptively reused as a residential co-op.

[L 19a.] Engine Co. No. 55, N.Y.F.D.   **[L 22.]** Severe brick LIRA apartments

[L 22.] 21 Spring Street (apartments), bet. Mott and Elizabeth Sts. N side. 1983. Pasanella + Klein.

A severe, dark red brick monolith but carefully proportioned as to window-masonry relationships and detailing. Sober but satisfying. Sponsored by LIRA, Little Italy Restoration Association, as a Section 8, federally subsidized project, one of the city's last.

[L 23.] Originally **Young Men's Institute, Y.M.C.A.** 222-224 Bowery, bet. Spring and Prince Sts. W side. 1885. Bradford L. Gilbert. Converted to commerce.

A romantic, red brick and Nova Scotia sandstone, Queen Anne minor extravaganza intended to reform by its appearance alone. Library, gymasium, and classrooms are now storage areas for merchandise. Replaced by the Bowery Y [see V Manhattan/East Village E 6a.]

[L 24.] Puck Building (originally **printing plant**), 295-307 Lafayette St., bet. Jersey and E. Houston Sts. E side to Mulberry St. N part, 1886. S addition, 1893. Both by Albert Wagner. Relocated W front to accommodate widened Elm Place (now Lafayette St.), 1899, Albert Wagner and successor, Wagner & Jahn. ★

A colossal **gold-leafed Puck** holds forth from a 3rd-story perch at the corner of Mulberry and Houston; a smaller version welcomes those who enter on Lafayette Street. Built by the publishers and chromoli-

[L 24.] The gold-leafed bust of Puck heralds the printing house of the same name

thographer of the color cartoons that distinguished *Puck,* the **nationally renowned satirical magazine** published in both German- (1876–1896) and English-language (1877–1918) editions, between the publication's founding and its demise. After years of neglect as a marginal structure in the printing trades, the rich red-brick building has now been **resurrected** and **sensitively restored.**

LOWER EAST SIDE

Far more significant historically than architecturally, this area harbors the legions of tenement buildings that **warehoused the** wave of **homeless, tempest-tost** immigrants who arrived from the 1880s up to **World War I.**

Hester Street at the turn of the century: tenements and seething humanity

Chinatown/Little Italy/Lower East Side: see map pp. 4–5   **81**

Six-story masonry blocks covered **90** percent of the lots in question, offering no light and air except at the 90-foot-distant ends of these railroad flats and through minuscule sidewall air shafts. (Rooms strung end to end like railroad cars gave rise to the term "railroad flats.")

On a 25- by 100-foot lot, at 4 families per floor, 24 families (not including boarders, in-laws, and double-ups) living with bathtubs in the kitchen and toilets in the hall were the standard. Post-1930s **reaction against overcrowding** has produced an **unhappy overcompensation.** The density per acre remains the same or greater, but the edges of the Lower East Side have become dominated by high-rise, freestanding structures (it seems the taller and further apart the better). Project dwellers are supposed to **yearn for light and air,** or at least the apparent virtues of light and air. In that cause **they sacrifice the urbanity** that exists, say, in **Brooklyn Heights** or **Greenwich Village** in the name of great sweeping lawns (that you can't touch or cavort upon).

If there is a **significant** building type in this precinct it is **the synagogue.** In the years before World War I, some 500 Jewish houses of worship and *talmud torahs* (religious schools) were built here. Few remain and fewer still are in use. A sampling follows, together with other landmarks of the community.

For our purposes the Lower East Side lies E of The Bowery, NE of the Manhattan Bridge and its approaches, and S of East Houston Street. The area N of Houston and E of The Bowery up to 14th Street is sometimes also referred to as part of the L.E.S. It is covered in the V Manhattan/East Village.

South of Canal Street and Seward Park:

[E 1a.] Intermediate School 131, Manhattan, The Dr. Sun Yat-Sen School, 100 Hester St., SW cor. Eldridge St. at Frank D'Amico Plaza. 1983. Warner, Burns, Toan & Lundy.

Curvilinear, extoverted, expansive—it burst forth and wiped out a block of Forsyth Street's pavement.

[E 1b.] Hester-Allen Turnkey Housing, N.Y.C. Housing Authority, 45 Allen St., NW cor. Hester St. 1973. Edelman & Salzman.

Simple, straightforward concrete and ribbed block housing with some thoughtful detailing at the ground plane.

[E 2a.] St. Barbara Greek Orthodox Church/originally **Congregation Kol Israel Anshe Poland (synagogue),** 27 Forsyth St., S of Canal St. E side. ca. 1895.

A **proud** religious edifice seeing reuse as a church.

[E 2b.] Congregation K'hal Adath Jeshurun (synagogue), 12-16 Eldridge St., bet. Forsyth and Canal Sts. E side. 1887. Herter Bros., architects. ★

Eclectic: **Flamboyant Moorish** embellishment and a Gothic **wheel window** as well. This ornate facade, **the finest** of any of the Lower East Side synagogues, makes the tenements of Eldridge Street look **even more squalid.** Unfortunately, vandalism has taken its toll of the stained glass.

The unfolding of the immigrant experience in the Lower East Side became the focus of an effort, beginning in 1984, to establish a historic/cultural enclave in which that experience could be commemorated and interpreted. The single block of Eldridge Street between Forsyth and Canal, filled as it is with Old Law tenements, the K'hal synagogue, and other remnants of 19th- and early 20th-century life, emerged as the center of the effort by the Lower East Side Historic Conservancy, a private not-for-profit group.

[E 2c.] Originally **Electrical Substation, Manhattan Railway Company,** 100 Division St., NW cor. Allen St. ca. 1892.

The elevated rapid transit ran above city streets because they offered a readily available and **inexpensive right-of-way.** When turns from one narrow thoroughfare into another were required, **private land** had to be purchased over which the viaduct would curve. When electrification came to the els these private sites also became the location for electrical substations, as is this one, skewed to clear the curve of the now-removed viaduct. This facility served the **Second Avenue elevated,** which clattered east out of Chatham Square along Division Street and turned northward into Allen Street (only **50 feet wide** until 1932). Allen Street's **perpetual darkness** and **noise** made it an undesirable place—it was one of the city's most notorious **red-light districts** as a result.

[E 3a.] Originally **S. Jarmulovsky's Bank Building,** 54-58 Canal St., SW cor. Orchard St. ca. 1912.

There are those who consider the domed, columned "temple" atop this building's 12 stories **a local architectural landmark.** But to those who know the saga of this bank, it is **a historical landmark.** Jarmulovsky's was established in 1873 (as the bronze lettering over the entrance still proclaims) as a local bank catering to the growing number of non-English-speaking immigrants being drawn to the area. As assets rose, largely from the working-class depositors' self-denial, **rumors began to spread** about insolvency. With the coming of World War I many wished to withdraw deposits to help relatives caught in Europe. **Runs** on this and other local banks soon developed, and then **actual riots.** For the Lower East Side, **black Tuesday** was August 4, 1914, when this and another bank were ordered closed as being "in an unsound and unsatisfactory condition." Thousands **lost their savings;** the Jarmulovskys received a suspended sentence.

[E 2b.] Cong. K'hal Adath Jeshurun   **[E 3b.]** Orig. Loew's Canal Theatre

[E 3b.] Originally **Loew's Canal Street Theatre,** 31 Canal St., bet. Ludlow and Essex Sts. N side. ca. 1920.

The lobby's ornate glazed terra-cotta and glass facade remains (as does the theater's brick box behind); the marquee is long gone.

[E 4a.] Congregation B'nai Israel Kalwarie (synagogue), 15 Pike St., bet. E. Broadway and Henry St. E side. 1903. ★

A **humble** but lovely house of worship.

[E 4b.] St. Teresa's Roman Catholic Church/originally **First Presbyterian Church of New York,** 16-18 Rutgers St., NW cor. Henry St. 1841.

An ashlar church **in the tradition** of the others nearby, which antedate 1850.

[E 5.] Originally **Forward Building/**now **N.Y. Ling Liang Church,** 175 E. Broadway, bet. Rutgers and Jefferson Sts. S side. 1912. George A. Boehm. ★

The citadel of Yiddish thought and culture (once). Yiddish lettering in polychrome terra-cotta on the roof parapet still reads *Forward* despite the relocation of New York's (and America's) **foremost Jewish language newspaper** to Harper & Row's old space on East 33rd Street. The building's 12 stories housed not only the editorial offices of the newspaper but also the main headquarters of a distinguished social organization, the *Arbiter Ring* (**Workmen's Circle**) which relocated with the *Forward,* and those of many other Jewish social and benevolent organizations (*landsmanshaftn*) and burial societies.

Seward Park: **A bit of green** (3 acres) at the intersection of East Broadway and Canal and Essex Streets **seems less rare today** than it did before urban renewal, when tenements were cleared and towers were placed on lawns. The park was named for Lincoln's secretary of state, **William H. Seward** (1801–1872).

[E 6a.] Recreation Building, in Seward Park. 1939. N.Y.C. Department of Parks & Recreation.

A Greek temple **updated** in the style of the Paris Exposition of 1937. Limestone with an ultramarine blue terra-cotta frieze (and lots of calligraphic grafitti—added later).

[E 6b.] Seward Park Branch, New York Public Library, 192 E. Broadway, opp. Jefferson St. W side. 1909. Babb, Cook & Welch.

A **palazzo for book users** (on the exterior at least). When built, the area was bulging with people and land was scarce, so the roof was planned as an outdoor reading area. Note the balusters and verdigris beginnings of a trellis.

[E 6c.] David Sarnoff Building, Educational Alliance, 197 E. Broadway, SE cor. Jefferson St. 1889. Brunner & Tryon. Remodeled, 1969, David Kenneth Specter.

A **Romanesque Revival** settlement house with its spirit extended by the great new entrance arch.

[E 5.] Orig. (1912) Forward Building   **[E 8.]** Bialystoker Home for Aged

[E 7.] Gouverneur Hospital, N.Y.C. Health and Hospitals Corporation, 227 Madison St., bet. Jefferson and Clinton Sts. N side. 1972. Charles B. Meyers, succeeded by Viola, Bernhard & Philips. Katz, Waisman, Weber & Strauss, architects and engineers; Blumenkranz & Bernhard, consultants.

A **fussy red brick prism** with buff pilasters that reach all the way to the roof. Note how the window's size and placement are **irregular,** reflecting the **complex floor plans** of a modern-day hospital center.

[E 8.] Bialystoker Center Home for the Aged, 228 E. Broadway, E of Clinton St. N side. 1930.

Surviving amid acres of adjacent post-World War II projects, this is an amusing **Moorish Art Deco** product of the **Roaring Twenties.** Two families vying for recognition are represented in *two* cornerstones, at the facade's far ends: Lutenberg (west), and Marcus (east). Shrubbery conceals the rivalry (both).

[E 9a.] Henry Street Settlement/originally **Nurses Settlement,** 263-267 Henry St., bet. Montgomery and Gouverneur Sts. N side. 1827–1834. ★

Greek Revival town houses now happily preserved by a distinguished private social agency, founded by **Lillian Wald** (1867–1940), who is personally memorialized in the public housing bearing her name between East Houston and East 6th Streets on the river. **No. 265** is the star.

[E 9b.] Engine Company No. 15, N.Y.C. Fire Department, 269 Henry St., bet. Montgomery and Gouverneur Sts. 1883.

A **virtuoso facade** of brick over a cast-iron ground floor. Particularly enlivening are the pair of corbeled cornice brackets and marvelous, textured spandrels.

[E 9a.] The Henry St. Settlement row

[E 11.] Orig. the Cong. Poel Zedek

[E 9c.] St. Augustine's Chapel, Trinity Parish (Episcopal)/originally **All Saints' Church,** 290 Henry St., bet. Montgomery and Jackson Sts. S side. 1828. Attributed to John Heath. ★

Georgian body with Gothic Revival windows. Compare Chinatown's **Church of the Transfiguration** or the **Sea and Land Church** [see Chinatown L 13a. and L 6b.]. Built with Manhattan schist and crisp white pediments.

[E 10a.] Land's End I (apartments), 257 Clinton St., bet. Cherry and South Sts. W side. 1977. Edelman & Salzman.

One of a number of housing developments—this one a high rise with precast concrete balconies—that emerged from the Two Bridges Urban Renewal Project. (The two bridges, of course, are the Manhattan and the Williamsburg, between which the project area lay.)

[E 10b.] Formerly **Gouverneur Hospital,** Franklin D. Roosevelt Drive bet. Gouverneur Slips E. and W. N side. 1901. Attributed to McKim, Mead & White.

The tiers of **curved, screened verandas** that jut out toward the Drive are familiar to the thousands of motorists who pass this **old city hospital** every day. Surpassed medically by its modern replacement [E 7.], though its architectural merits remain. Can an adaptive reuse be found? If not, its future is in the **wrecker's ball.**

The Full Stomach

Bernstein-on-Essex-Street (meat restaurant), 135 Essex St., bet. Rivington and Stanton Sts. Kosher; closed Friday through Saturday evenings.

Superbly corned, smoked, and spiced meats in the style of a Jewish delicatessen. But **Kosher Chinese food** as well? No pork, of course, but **beef spareribs** that could fool an expert. And for those whose eating habits are as **eclectic** as their taste for architectural styles, bread and pickles are served with Chinese meals **upon request.** Moderate. Chinese food, however, is considerably more expensive than in an equivalent Chinese restaurant and is only fair. Beer and wine available.

Banana boat piers: With the advent of containerization and its need for enormous backup space, Manhattan in the 1970s and 1980s lost its shorefront piers, docks, and wharves. The last active freight operations were those of the Netumar Line at Piers 35 and 36, East River, at Clinton Street. Until 1987, bananas were offloaded here, giving motorists on the elevated FDR Drive a last glimpse of one of the city's former glories. In writing of the demise in the *New York Times,* Sam Roberts described it as "*the ultimate banana split.*"

Katz's Delicatessen, 205 E. Houston St., SW cor. Ludlow St. Non-Kosher.

Famous and busy but a far cry from the days when its reputation was made.

Guss Pickle Products/L. Hollander & Son, 35 Essex St., bet. Hester and Grand Sts. W side. Kosher. Closed for the sabbath.

They line up on the sidewalk here, alongside the pickle barrels (plastic now—no more wood staves) to buy half-sours, sour tomatoes, sweet red peppers, and sauerkraut. Buy something to munch on as you walk, or buy some to take home . . . jars are available to send you on your way with both pickles *and* their garlic-flavored brine.

Gertel's (bakery and coffee shop), 53 Hester St., W of Essex St. N side. Kosher. Closed for the sabbath.

While primarily a bakeshop there are tables in the rear where you can enjoy a pastry and coffee (or tea). Try some *ruggehlach,* tiny rolled pastries which become more flavorful the more you chew.

Ratner's Dairy Restaurant, 138 Delancey St., bet. Norfolk and Suffolk Sts. N side.

Responsive to the Jewish dietary laws, the foods served here are either dairy or *parveh* (neutral), like fish. The best bets are the ones that risk heartburn: herring in cream sauce, followed by either potato varenickihs (*heavy*), latkihs (heavier), or koogl (**heaviest**), topped by protose steak, a brilliant (but secret) culinary invention that uses no meat but will deceive the most discriminating gastronome.

South of Delancey Street to Grand Street:

[E 11.] Seventh-Day Adventist Church of Union Square/originally **Congregation Poel Zedek Anshe Ileya (synagogue),** 128-130 Forsyth St., SE cor. Delancey St. ca. 1895.

This house of worship is reached by a symmetrical flight of steps on the Forsyth Street sidewalk, thus permitting retail establishments to occupy the ground floor on Delancey Street. The combination of worship (sacred) and business (profane) did well.

Deep down: At Delancey and Eldridge Streets is Shaft 20 of the Catskill Water System, the city's third aqueduct. It is notable in that it is the deepest shaft, 740 feet into the earth's crust.

[E 12.] Originally **dry goods store,** 319-321 Grand St., SW cor. Orchard St. ca. 1870.

Before and after the Civil War, Grand Street east of the Bowery was the city's **center of women's fashions. Lord & Taylor,** at Grand and Chrystie Streets, and **Edward Ridley's,** at Allen Street, were the two **most popular** dry goods stores.

[E 13.] Originally **Eastern Dispensary/**later **Good Samaritan Dispensary,** 75 Essex St., NW cor. Broome St. ca. 1895.

Today, 4 stories of yarn; once the eastern outpost of a dispensary system for Lower Manhattan [see V Manhattan/West Village C 1d.]. Stately golden brown and salmon brick.

[E 14.] Essex Street Market, City of New York (originally **N.Y.C. Department of Markets),** Essex St. bet. Broome, Delancey, Rivington, and Stanton Sts. E side. 1940.

The Department of Markets no longer exists in the City's table of organization (a result no doubt of the preservatives in junk food), but this indoor market does, obligatorily upgraded to the *New* Essex Street Market. **Art Moderne** in red brick, industrial steel sash, and incised lettering which makes no reference to "New." Others of this LaGuardia era genre include First Avenue and East 10th Street, Arthur Avenue in the Bronx, and Thirteenth Avenue and 40th Street in Brooklyn.

[E 15a.] Seward Park Extension (west part), N.Y.C. Housing Authority, 64-66 Essex St., bet. Grand and Broome Sts. E side. 1973. William F. Pedersen & Assocs.

One of 2 tall tan slabs [see E 16a.] whose design is **concentrated** in one **rich, plastic, 3-dimensional, balconied facade,** this one facing south. Adjacent is an outdoor court and a low recreation building. Handsome.

B'nai B'rith: A plaque on the courtyard wall of the public housing calls attention to the birth at that site of B'nai B'rith, the nation's first national service agency, on October 13, 1843.

[E 15b.] Congregation Beth Hamedrash Hagodol (synagogue)/originally **Norfolk Street Baptist Church,** 60-64 Norfolk St., bet. Grand and Broome Sts. E side. 1850. ★

Smooth stuccoing and a cream paint job with brown trim make the facade **a cartoon** of the original Gothic Revival design.

[E 16a.] Seward Park Extension (east part), N.Y.C. Housing Authority, 154-156 Broome St., E of Clinton St. N side. 1973. William F. Pederson & Assocs.

The sibling of 64-66 Essex Street [see E 15a.] but minus a community facility annex. This slab's rich facade faces east to the river.

[E 16b.] St. Mary's RC Ch. (1833)   **[E 16c.]** Comb. Police/Fire stations

[E 16b.] St. Mary's Roman Catholic Church, 438 Grand St., W of Pitt St. N side. 1833. Enlarged, present facade added, 1871, P. C. Keely.

The **oldest** Roman Catholic church structure **in all of the city—** the somber gray ashlar rear portion, that is. The amusing red brick front and its twin spires are by the prolific church architect Patrick Charles Keely.

[E 16c.] 7th Precinct Station House, N.Y.C. Police Department, and Engine Company No. 17, Ladder Company No. 18, N.Y.C. Fire Department, 19½-25 Pitt St., NW cor. Broome St. 1975. William F. Pedersen & Assocs.

Articulated form, each function with its special shape and view, the **antithesis of Mies van der Rohe.** Specific, plastic, slotted, revealed—a unique building for unique uses. Note the use of clinker bricks to develop a subtle texture seen only up close.

[E 17a.] Louis Abrons Arts for Living Center, Henry Street Settlement and Neighborhood Playhouse, 466 Grand St., bet. Pitt St. and Bialystoker Place (formerly Willett St.). N side. 1975. Prentice & Chan, Ohlhausen.

An urban exedra, these buildings make a civic space in this wasteland of amorphous streets. A high moment of architecture that brings a suggestion of urbane Manhattan (cf. **Greenwich Village, Gramercy Park**) to this Rego Park-styled area.

[E 17a.] The Louis Abrons Arts for Living Center, Henry Street Settlement

[E 17b.] Bialystoker Synagogue/originally **Willett Street Methodist Church,** 7-13 Bialystoker Place (formerly Willett St.), bet. Grand and Broome Sts. W side. 1826. ★

Manhattan schist, brownstone, and whitestone. Shifting ethnic populations create changing uses for venerable buildings such as this. Originally a **rural Protestant church,** it now serves the dense Jewish population in this neighborhood.

[E 18a.] Amalgamated Dwellings, 504-520 Grand St., NW cor. Abraham Kazan St. (formerly Columbia St.), to Broome St. 1930. Springsteen & Goldhammer. **[E 18b.] Hillman Housing,** 500, 530, and 550 Grand St., bet. Abraham Kazan Place and Lewis St. 1951. Springsteen & Goldhammer.

Two generations ago, the late **Abraham Kazan,** as president of the **United Housing Foundation,** explored the world of mass housing on behalf of the Amalgamated Clothing Workers, providing, in concert with his architects, these pioneer projects. Times have changed: his **15,500-**unit **Co-op City** in the Bronx is not in the same class of avant-garde thinking as these antecedents.

The pre-Depression project, a hollow rectangular doughnut, was heavily influenced by the work of **Michel de Klerk** (1884–1923), founder of the Amsterdam school, and 1920s public housing, especially Karl Ehn's **Karl Marx Hof** in Vienna. The **parabolic arched opening** from Broome Street offers a view into the fine central courtyard. The post-World War II project begins to reflect the tower on the lawn approach. It comes off poorly in comparison.

[E 18c.] Ritual bathhouse (mikveh)/formerly **Young Men's Benevolent Association,** 313 E. Broadway, W of Grand St. 1904.

This **ornate** facade clads a building now used for the **ritual baths** which Orthodox Jewish women are required to take prior to the marriage ceremony and monthly thereafter. According to the Scriptures, the water must be unadulterated—when possible it is rainwater captured in cisterns.

[E 19.] East River Houses/ILGWU Cooperative Village (International Ladies Garment Workers Union)/originally called **Corlear's Hook Houses,** N and S of Grand St., bet. Lewis and Jackson Sts. to Franklin D. Roosevelt Dr. 1956. Herman Jessor.

Five thousand people dwell in these carven brick monoliths that excel their descendants at **Co-op City** in cost, architecture, and views.

Between Delancey and East Houston Streets:

The marketplace: Ethnically the Lower East Side has changed markedly since the beginning of the century. From what was once an almost entirely Jewish community, a mixed settlement pattern has evolved: Chinese settling along East Broadway and environs, Hispanics moving in north of Delancey Street, and so on. But as these changes occur, one quality remains: that of the citywide marketplace, particularly on Sundays. Most shops are closed between Friday afternoon and Sunday morning in observance of *shabbos,* the Jewish sabbath.

The attraction which brings thousands back to this area to shop: bargains. Don't expect genteel salespeople or elegant displays—this is New York's most exciting bazaar.

[E 20a.] Lower East Side Infill Housing I (apartments), N.Y.C. Housing Authority, Eldridge St. bet. Delancey and Stanton Sts.   Stanton St. SE cor. Forsyth St. 1987. James McCullar.

Long, flat, monotonous 4-story rows of turnkey housing set off by a single 9-story unit, north of Delancey St. The bubble gum pink walls are here relieved by gray inserts of Post Modern ornamental silhouettes—but only two-dimensionally. Grim.

[E 18a.] Amalgamated Dwellings arch   [E 20b.] Orig. the Jassy Congregation

[E 20b.] Originally **Congregation Adath Jeshurun of Jassy (synagogue)**/later **First Warsaw Congregation,** 58-60 Rivington St., bet. Eldridge and Allen Sts. N side. 1903.

A magnificent eclectic facade with bits and pieces from a variety of styles and influences. Damaged by vandalism, so its days may be numbered. **Worth an extra trip** anyway.

[E 20c.] University Settlement House, 184 Eldridge St., SE cor. Rivington St. 1901. Howells & Stokes.

A neighborhood institution by a team of architects better known for their later accomplishments. Howells, son of author William Dean Howells, won the Chicago Tribune Tower competition with Raymond Hood. Stokes wrote the definitive work *The Iconography of Manhattan Island.*

[E 21.] Congregation Shaarai Shomoyim First Roumanian American Congregation (synagogue)/originally **Allen Street Methodist Church,** 83-93 Rivington St., bet. Orchard and Ludlow Sts. S side. ca. 1890.

Solid, stolid Romanesque Revival flattened by paint and soot.

Orchard Street: Wall-to-wall people have for so many years characterized the condition of Orchard Street between Delancey and East Houston (actually no one ever bothers with the "East") that the City fathers finally closed that stretch to vehicular traffic on Sunday, the busiest day. (Saturday finds most of the shops closed—*shomer Shabbos*—in observance of the Jewish sabbath.) The combination of bazaar trading practices, plain pipe rack merchandising, and low prices for brand name goods has given way to some tacky (and some upscale) names and glitzy storefronts: Indulgences, Kids for Less, Klein's of Monticello (now that "Klein's on the Square" is gone). Further north are Opium, Tana, and—despite the long-standing Jewish tradition—Antony, Escala, Trevi, Tobaldi Uomo, and Veetal.

Note: For the 3-block-long Essex Street Market, see [E 14.].

[E 22.] Originally **Congregation Anshe Chesed (synagogue)/later Ohab Zedek/later Anshe Slonim,** 172-176 Norfolk St., bet. Stanton and E. Houston Sts. E side. 1849. Alexander Saeltzer. ★

With the exception of this distinguished house of worship—now in a state of painful disrepair—all Lower East Side Jewish congregations that occupied buildings built before 1850 had purchased and **converted existing churches.** This edifice, the city's **oldest** (and for a time its **largest**) synagogue (and its first Reform temple), was built by an established Jewish community whose members **moved northward,** together with their Christian neighbors, as the area became a refuge for Eastern European immigrants. **Anshe Chesed** is today on the Upper West Side.

Sunday Shopping on Orchard Street   [E 22.] Orig. the Cong. Anshe Chesed

 [E 23.] Intermediate School 25, Manhattan, 145 Stanton St., bet. Norfolk and Suffolk Sts. S side. 1977. David Todd & Assocs.

New Brutalist: a powerful combination of creamy white concrete horizontals with dark red, giant brick infill—all embraced by the strong forms of the stair towers at the corners.

Matzos and wine: Two important industries remain along Rivington Street in the heart of the Lower East Side, Shapiro's Wine Company (No. 126) and Streit's Matzoth Company (No. 150). Both prepare their products for sacramental purposes, although many in the community (and elsewhere) enjoy them throughout the year. Need one add that they are prepared under rabbinical supervision and are kosher?

[E 24.] Public School 160, Manhattan, 107 Suffolk St., SW cor. Rivington St. ca. 1898. C. B. J. Snyder.

What a lift this light-colored neo-Gothic confection must have had upon the impacted Lower East Side when it first opened! Even now, after so many decades of "deferred maintenance," its forms offer refreshing relief.

[E 25a.] Originally **Loew's Apollo Theatre,** 140-146 Delancey St., NW cor. Suffolk St. ca. 1922.

Once an unusually attractive maroon brick box, now capped by a polychrome terra-cotta frieze under a projecting cornice. Today the marquee is gone and the base defaced.

[E 26a.] Originally **Congregation Dukler Mugain Abraham (synagogue),** 87 Attorney St., bet. Delancey and Rivington Sts. W side. ca. 1898.

A humble Roman Revival temple.

[E 26b.] Williamsburg Bridge, from Delancey and Clinton Sts. in Manhattan to Washington Plaza in Brooklyn. 1903. Leffert L. Buck, chief engineer.

To the former **City of Williamsburgh,** now part of Brooklyn. The unusual **(straight)** cables on the land side of the towers result from the fact that support is by truss and pier, rather than pendant cable as in the Brooklyn Bridge. The latter's landside cables hang in a **catenary curve,** in contrast.

[E 26c.] Public School 142, Manhattan, 100 Attorney St., SE cor. Rivington St. 1975. Michael Radoslavitch.

A fashionable form in plan, a banjo, fails to come to life as architecture.

[E 27.] Congregation Chasam Sofer (synagogue)/originally **Congregation Rodeph Sholom,** 8-10 Clinton St., bet. Stanton and E. Houston Sts. E side. 1853.

The second-oldest surviving synagogue in the city [after E 22.]. Rodeph Sholom left these parts in 1886. Today its temple is on West 83rd Street [see W Manhattan/Central Park West C 21.]

[E 28.] Boys Club of New York, Pitt Street Building, 135 Pitt St., SW cor. E. Houston St. N addition, 1985, George Cooper Rudolph III.

The original structure is 1950s institutional blah, but the corner gymnasium addition is a strong architectural statement. The dark blue, glazed brick Houston Street wall creates a stylized "skyline" silhouetted against a "sky" of glass block.

[E 29b.] School of Christian Doctrine   **[E 29a.]** Our Lady of Sorrows Church

[E 29a.] Our Lady of Sorrows Roman Catholic Church, 101 Pitt St., bet. Rivington and Stanton Sts. W side. ca. 1890. **[E 29b.] School of Christian Doctrine,** 219 Stanton St., SW cor. Pitt St. ca. 1890. **[E 29c.] Rectory**/originally **Capuchin Monastery,** 213 Stanton St., bet. Ridge and Pitt Sts. S side. 1890.

Down at the heels, but a spectacular religious complex nonetheless. A particular favorite: the white terra-cotta Virgin Mary sculpture projecting from the 4th floor of the school's Pitt Street facade.

[E 30a.] Hamilton Fish Park Play Center, N.Y.C. Department of Parks & Recreation/originally **Hamilton Fish Park Gymnasium and Public Baths,** in Hamilton Fish Park, 130 Pitt St., bet. Stanton and E. Houston Sts. E side. 1900. Carrère & Hastings. Restored, 1985, John Ciardullo Assocs. ★ Park, 1900, Carrère & Hastings. Park altered, 1903. Swimming pool added, 1936, Aymar Embury II.

The play center's design is a miniaturization of Charles Girault's widely acclaimed Petit Palais in Paris, designed in 1895 for the Paris Exposition of 1900. This is an oompah Beaux Arts pavilion built to serve the recreation and bathing needs of immigrants drawn to this precinct even before the turn of the century. Though monumental in scale, it surely failed to be adequate in size. (Almost immediately after completion, C&H's formal park was totally in ruins "owing, it is said, to the radical defects of the original plan and to the strenuous nature of the youth of the neighborhood"; it was redone in 3 years.)

[E 30b.] Junior High School 22, Manhattan, The Gustave V. E. Straubenmuller School, and **Hamilton Fish Park Branch, New York Public Library,** 111 Columbia St., SE cor. Houston St. 1956. Kelly & Gruzen.

A **square doughnut** on stilts and an adjacent, earthbound library. Its modern materials wore poorly. Stylish in its time, it is now dated.

[E 31.] DeWitt Reformed Church, 280 Rivington St., NE cor. Columbia St. 1957. Edgar Tafel.

A simple brick box that contains a sanctuary faced in reused brick and a cross of tree trunks: **rustic and humane charm** amid overpowering housing.

SOHO

SoHo (or South of Houston), as an acronym, is stretching it, recalling the "Greenwich Village" of London: *Soho.* These 20-odd blocks between Canal and Houston (**How**-stun) Streets, West Broadway and Broadway contain the city's quintessential stock of **cast-iron-fronted buildings,** a high point in urban commercial architectural history. They are, largely, to be noticed not as individual monuments but as parties to whole streets and blocks that, together, make the most glorious urban commercial groupings that New York has ever seen. Mostly **Italianate,** some might be termed **Palladian:** they are surprising precursors of Modern exposed structural expression in another material—concrete—seen at **Kips Bay Plaza** [see M Manhattan/Four Squares E 14.] and the **American Bible Society** [see W Manhattan/Lincoln Center L 2.].

Once these were called **Hell's Hundred Acres** because of the many fires in overcrowded, untended warehouses filled with flammables. Then given over in large part to artists' (and would-be artists') studios and housing, the once-empty streets and buildings became **a lively, urbane place, much tended and loved,** and hence no longer a potential lonely inferno. Huge lofts here give possibility of great space for large paintings or sculptures and equally great space for living. Initially rediscovered by artists, it has since been re-rediscovered by those with "deep pockets." Prices for lofts have skyrocketed.

The richest single street is **Greene,** then **Broome**—but wander throughout. Not only the revived architecture but also shops, stores, galleries, and boutiques of elegance and delight abound.

Confusion: SoHo, being south of Houston, is also south of Manhattan's street grid established by the commissioners' plan of 1811. SoHo is arranged on a grid in which the long blocks stretch *north-south,* their axes exactly perpendicular to those above Houston Street. Similarly, in contrast to Manhattan's main grid, the wide streets in SoHo (except for Broadway, West Broadway, and the much later Sixth Avenue) run *east-west,* and are all called streets, none avenues. Not unsurprisingly, the direction and placement of house numbers vary from thoroughfare to thoroughfare. So watch carefully and make no rash assumptions about SoHo.

SoHo entries appropriately begin south of Houston Street along Broadway (below V Manhattan/Astor Place & Environs). They sequentially snake around, first south, then north, moving generally to the west. Feel free to break the sequence—we did.

[H 1.] SoHo-Cast Iron Historic District, irregular area E of W. Broadway's center line bet. center lines of W. Houston and Canal Sts. to Broadway, and E of Broadway bet. center lines of E. Houston and Howard Sts. to center line of Crosby St. ★

Within the 26 blocks of this Historic District are arrayed, according to the official designation report, "the largest concentration of full and partial cast-iron facades anywhere in the world." Their protection under law in 1973, after having been saved in the late 1960s from destruction for the ill-fated Lower Manhattan Expressway, was a great victory for landmarks preservation activists. Cast iron and other bountiful structures from the city's late 19th-century business boom abound on these streets. Remember, SoHo's festooned fire escapes and its bumpety Belgian block pavements are also part of this wonderfully gritty scene.

SoHo's north edge is bounded by the expressway-scaled Houston Street, which, having been widened for the IND Sixth Avenue Subway, caused the body of SoHo to offer a ragged edge to Greenwich Village on the north. Gas stations, lots, and unkempt buildings' sides are all that SoHo here reveals of its inner splendors. Later roadwork widened the asphalt pavement itself and inserted the slender traffic island down the middle. More recent projects such as the former University Village and N.Y.U.'s sports center [see V Manhattan/Greenwich Village V 16a.] disguise the gash, but the little 2-story polychrome taxpayer between Wooster and West Broadway [see H 27.] emphasizes it by its shallow depth.

Broadway: Between Houston and Prince Streets.

[H 1a.] 600 Broadway (loft building). E side. 1884. Samuel A. Warner. ☆

Corinthian columns of **descending** height for each successively **ascending** floor. The ground-floor alteration still bears scars of "improvements" by local philistines.

The New Museum, 583 Broadway. W side. **Open to the public.** ☆

With the Museum of Modern Art aging, the Whitney becoming self-satisfied, and the Met encyclopedically trying to corner new art as well as all other, it was time for a new museum. Hence, **The New Museum:** serious **avant-**avant-garde exhibitions displayed in one of SoHo's many loft buildings.

Broadway: Between Prince and Spring Streets.

[H 2a.] Singer Building/earlier **Paul Building/**originally **The Singer Manufacturing Company,** 561 Broadway, bet. Prince and Spring Sts. Secondary facade on Prince St. S side. 1904. Ernest Flagg. ☆

"The Little Singer Building," to distinguish it from the now-demolished **Singer Tower** [see Necrology]. Curlicued steel, recessed glass, and textured terra-cotta—all quite advanced for their time. The facade is the forerunner of the curtain wall, that delicate metal-and-glass skin in which much of Manhattan of the 1950s and 1960s is clad—grossly it seems, when compared to this post-turn-of-the-century charmer. Its original name can still be seen cast in iron on the Prince Street store transom of this L-shaped structure.

[H 2b.] Originally **Charles Broadway Rouss Building (lofts),** 555 Broadway. 1889. Alfred Zucker. Attic pediments added, 1900. ☆

A tribute to a debt-ridden Virginian whose name mightily adorns this through-block behemoth. Rouss's construction sign modestly stated, "HE WHO BUILDS, OWNS, AND WILL OCCUPY THIS MARVEL OF BRICK, IRON, AND GRANITE, THIRTEEN YEARS AGO WALKED THESE STREETS PENNILESS AND $50,000 IN DEBT." Also see the annex to this structure on the far side of Mercer, which also bears the Rouss name [H 11b.]

[H 2c.] 547 Broadway (lofts). W side. 1888. O. P. Hatfield. ☆

Brick and stone, bearing tiers of fire escapes of an unusual segmental curved plan.

[H 2d.] 545 Broadway (lofts). W side. 1885. Samuel A. Warner. ☆

Freestanding colonnettes.

[H 2e.] 540 Broadway (lofts). E side. 1867. D. & J. Jardine. ☆

Others of its time were already employing cast iron, but this out-of-the-ordinary facade is very 2-dimensional, of intaglioed sheets of marble.

[H 2f.] 537 Broadway (lofts). W side. 1869. Charles Mettam. ☆

Proud neo-Classical cast iron with colossal windows.

Broadway: Between Spring and Broome Streets.

[H 3a.] 519 Broadway (lofts). W side. 1884. Samuel A. Warner. ☆

Six stories of floriated, polychromed red brick and terra-cotta detail make a magnificent, rich, deeply modeled Queen Anne facade. O, were there only more of these to admire!

St. Nicholas Hotel: Nos. 521-523 Broadway ☆ represents the only remaining part of the much larger 1,000-bed hotel complex (built in 1853 and expanded by 1854) which, together with Astor House, was among Broadway's most prominent hostelries in the 1850s and 1860s. During the Civil War the hotel became the headquarters of the War Department.

[H 3b.] Originally **Loubat Stores (lofts),** 503, 507, 511 Broadway. W side. 1879. J. B. Snook. ☆

A generous composition of 3 warehouses with demure (and grave) cast-iron facades produced at the Cornell Iron Works.

[H 3c.] 502 Broadway (lofts). E side. 1860. John Kellum & Son. ☆

Slender, 2-story arches exquisitely worked, in **stone,** not cast iron. When new, smooth, and pristine white, the tall, graceful columns gave rise to the term **"Sperm Candle Style,"** after those made of whale oil.

[H 3d.] Originally **New Era Building (lofts),** 491 Broadway. W side. 1897. Buchman & Deisler. ☆

An **Art Nouveau** marvel: from the squat street-level Doric columns, fairly bulging from the weight of the masonry walls above, to the colossal multistory verdigris **copper mansard,** 6 floors up.

 [H 3e.] Originally **Haughwout Store (lofts),** 488 Broadway, NE cor. Broome St. 1857. John P. Gaynor. Iron by Badger Iron Works. ★ ☆

Palladio would have been proud of this offspring in cast iron, ever a rich participant (even overcoming its dour overcoat of black paint) in the urban scene. A proud and handsome, but not egocentric, building here proves that quality does not demand originality for its own sake. Built for **Eder V. Haughwout,** a merchant in china, cut glass, silverware, and chandeliers, it also housed the first practical safety elevator, installed by **Elisha Graves Otis,** founder of that ubiquitous elevator company.
The Corinthian columns that flank the arches are sometimes remembered as **Serlian,** after the drawings and writings of **Sebastiano Serlio** (1475–1554), later lifted by **Andrea Palladio** (1508–1580) and most elegantly displayed at the **Basilica in Vicenza.**

Broadway: Between Broome and Grand Streets.

[H 4a.] Formerly **Mechanics & Traders Bank (lofts),** 486 Broadway, SE cor. Broome St. (a.k.a. 437-441 Broome St.) 1883. Lamb & Rich. ☆

The Broome Street facade has long been tatooed with an appliqué of fire escapes. Now this Romanesque and Moorish Revival bank building's half-round brick arches carry newer encrustations of bare neon tubing! Curious.

[H 4b.] Originally **Roosevelt Building (lofts),** 478-482 Broadway. E side. 1874. Richard Morris Hunt. ☆

Filigreed cast iron, with Composite columns on a huge scale, built for the trustees of Roosevelt Hospital. Note particularly the openwork brackets that carry the flat cornice and the curved cast-iron screens at the top of the 4th-floor windows. A very different style of Hunt can be seen at the Metropolitan Museum's Fifth Avenue entrance [see E Manhattan/Met Museum M 12.]. (One bay of the Roosevelt Building continues through the block to become **No. 40** Crosby Street, which carries an abbreviated form of facade.)

[H 2a.] "The Little Singer Building"   [H 3e.] Orig. Haughwout Store (1857)

[H 4b.] The highly refined cast-iron facade of R. M. Hunt's Roosevelt Bldg.

[H 4c.] **459-461 Broadway (lofts),** SW cor. Grand St. (a.k.a. 115-119 Grand St.). 1861. Architect unknown. ☆

A late Italianate temple of commerce whose beautifully weathered stone surfaces are pierced with ranks of finely proportioned round-arched windows.

[H 4d.] 462 Broadway (lofts), NE cor. Grand St. to Crosby St. 1880. John Correja. ☆

This massive cast-iron commercial palace evokes memories of the French Renaissance. The ground floor has been mutilated by suffocation from polished red granite, a malady often reversible in cast-iron buildings. Let's hope. **L'Ecole,** the dining room of the French Culinary Institute, occupies the ground-floor space and offers trendy, pricey fare.

Detour: Crosby Street/Mercer Street

Twin streets in the sense that both reveal the rear of the large structures that line Broadway's originally prestigious flanks. In many respects, from their expanses of poorly maintained Belgian block street pavers to their abundance of fire escapes and loading docks, Mercer and Crosby continue to show a SoHo that predates gentrification.

 [H 4e.] Originally **Roosevelt Building (lofts),** 40 Crosby St., bet. Grand and Broome Sts. 1874. Richard Morris Hunt. ☆

The single-bay rear of [H 4b.].

Note: For Mercer Street, see [H 12.]

Broadway: Between Grand and Howard Streets.

[H 5a.] European-American Bank & Trust Company/originally **Franklin National Bank,** 433 Broadway, NW cor. Howard St. 1967. Eggers & Higgins, architects. Zion & Breen, landscape architects. ☆

A **neo-Georgian** "suburban" bank building provides a tree-canopied plaza. The impulse to provide amenities is commendable, but the result here is strange and inappropriate in this virile cast-iron environment. Incidentally, the **Georges** never used the hexagon for building: that is a later, Greek Revival game.

[H 5b.] 34 Howard Street (lofts), bet. Broadway and Crosby St. N side. 1869. Renwick & Sands. ☆

An unusually distinguished structure—but no surprise since its architects were James Renwick, Jr. and his then partner, Joseph Sands.

Broadway: Between Howard and Canal Streets.

[H 6a.] 429 Broadway (lofts), SW cor. Howard St. 1870. Thomas R. Jackson. ☆

Semicircular arches on black Corinthian cast-iron columns face this lusty, glassy place.

Canal Street:

 [H 6b.] Originally **Arnold Constable & Company (dry goods store),** 307-311 Canal St., NE cor. Mercer St. to Howard St. Corner, No. 309-311, 1856. No. 307, 1862. 5th-story addition, 1862. Architect(s) unknown. ☆

Years of grime and Canal Street's déclassé retail history conceal the lyrical architecture of this once elegant blocklong retail bazaar. *Look this one over carefully.* Success and changing land-use fashions propelled the enterprise to a new location uptown in Ladies Mile [see M Manhattan/Four Squares W 12a.].

Greene Street:

 [H 7.] Greene Street, bet. Canal and Grand Sts. ☆

Nos. 10-14 Greene St. 1869. John B. Snook. Tuscan columns and pilasters. **Nos. 15-17** Greene St. 1895. John A. Warner. Delicate Corinthian pilasters. **Nos. 16-18** Greene St. 1880. Samuel A. Warner. **Nos. 19-21** Greene St. 1872. Henry Fernbach. Bold Tuscan columns by the architect of Central Synagogue [see M Manhattan/Park Avenue P 17a.]. **Nos. 20-26** Greene St. 1880. Samuel A. Warner. Two buildings in grand Corinthian. **Nos. 23-25** Greene St. 1873. Isaac F. Duckworth. Sparsely leaved Corinthian. **Nos. 28-30** Greene St. Blue-painted leafless Corinthian, with a Second Empire roof. **No. 31** Greene St. 1876. George W. DaCunha. Extraordinarily ornate. **No. 32** Greene St. 1873. Charles Wright. Leafless Corinthian. **No. 34** Greene St. 1873. Charles Wright.

Tuscan. **Nos. 83-87** Grand St., SW cor. Greene St. 1872. William Hume. Serene Tuscan over elaborate Corinthian.

[H 8.] Greene Street, bet. Grand and Broome Sts. ☆

No. **33** Greene St., NW cor. Grand St. 1873. Benjamin W. Warner. Composite columns above, Tuscan below. **Nos. 37-43** Greene St. 1884. Richard Berger. Green composite columns over a Corinthian base. **No. 45** Greene St. 1882. J. Morgan Slade. Rusting delicate composite Ionic.

[H 6b.] Orig. Arnold Constable & Company, once a great dry goods emporium

[H 7.] Duckworth's 28–30 Greene St.   **[H 9.]** Duckworth's 72–76 Greene St.

[H 9.] Greene Street, bet. Broome and Spring Sts. ☆

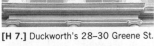

No. **60** Greene St. 1871. Henry Fernbach. Bold Corinthian. **No. 62** Greene St. 1872. Henry Fernbach. Bulky Composite Ionic. **No. 66** Greene St. 1873. John B. Snook. **No. 65** Greene St. 1873. John B. Snook. Bold Tuscan. **Nos. 67, 69, 71, 75, 77, 81** Greene St. 1873. Henry Fernbach. All bold Tuscan. **Nos. 72-76** Greene St. 1873. Isaac F. Duckworth. The creamy king of this block: a magnificently fashioned, projecting-pedimented porch of Corinthian columns and pilasters. **No. 75** Greene St. 1878. Henry Fernbach. **No. 80** Greene St. 1873. Griffith Thomas. Blue-painted Tuscan, its base supports simplicity.

Spring Street:

[H 10a.] 113, 115 Spring Street (lofts), bet. Greene and Mercer Sts. N side. 1878. Henry Fernbach. ☆

A pair of **Tuscan** cast-iron fronts with later strapwork fire escapes that capture the embonpoint of a Victorian dowager.

[H 10b.] 132 A Spring Street (taxpayer), SW cor. Greene St. ca. 1939. ☆

Moderne in red and black, matte-finished brick with subtle modeling and textures.

[H 10c.] 131, 133, 135 Spring Street (lofts), bet. Greene and Wooster Sts. N side. ☆

Rosé pressed brick spruced up with **pink-painted** columns. Sounds awful. Looks great.

Tennessee Mountain (restaurant), 143 Spring St., NW cor. Wooster St. ☆ Extension, 1986, Proposition: Architecture.

An upscale restaurant that does wonderful things for a rare old (1818) brick-fronted/clapboard-sided frame house and an appropriate Wooster Street 2nd-floor extension.

[H 11a.] Greene Street Restaurant, 101 Greene St., bet. Spring and Prince Sts. 1980. Siris/Coombs, architects. Mural, Françoise Schein. ☆

Dark, romantic, popular: a class act.

SoHo Kitchen & Bar, 103 Greene St., bet. Spring and Prince Sts. W side. ☆

Dark, romantic, popular: pizza, pasta, fish.

[H 11b.] Originally Charles Broadway Rouss Annex/now The SoHo Building, 104-110 Greene St. E side (also 125 Mercer St. W side.) bet. Spring and Prince Sts. W side. 1908. William J. Dilthy. ☆

Immediately across Mercer from the rear of the original Charles Broadway Rouss structure [H 2b.] is its annex, **SoHo's tallest building,** a through-block sliver. The 13 stories of brick masonry are distinguished only by the original **cut stone signs** bearing the Rouss name and by the tall, slender Mercer Street fire escape.

Sidewalk subway map: On the east sidewalk of Greene Street in front of the Rouss Annex is "Subway Map Floating on a New York Sidewalk" (1986) by artist Françoise Schein. It is an abstracted map of the interlocking subway systems of Manhattan. Set into a black-on-black matrix, the routes are of stainless steel bars with the individual stations represented by glass roundels of the type once used to illuminate below-the-street sidewalk vaults. Curiously, Schein and colleague Petar Gevremov reversed the design, so the systems are out of sync with Manhattan. That "uptown" is "downtown" on this map is at first difficult to comprehend, since the map shows no other geography: no street grid, no shorelines, no Central Park. Obscurantism.

 [H 11c.] Greene Street, bet. Spring and Prince Sts. ☆

Nos. 93-99 Greene St. 1881. Henry Fernbach. Three buildings sporting Composite Ionic, now spruced up like subtle "painted ladies." **No. 96** Greene St. 1879. Henry Fernbach. Tuscan. **No. 100** Greene St. 1881. Charles Mettam. "Corinthionic!" **No. 105** Greene St. 1879. Henry Fernbach. Modified Corinthian. **No. 112** Greene St. 1884. Henry Fernbach. Seedy brown Ionic. **No. 113** Greene St. Henry Fernbach. In the proper light, its black bottom becomes a Nevelson sculpture. **Nos. 114-120** Greene St. 1882. Henry Fernbach. Two in Composite Ionic with stylized acanthus leaf antefixa atop the cornice.

Mercer Street:

Like Crosby Street on the other side of Broadway, a service thoroughfare.

[H 12.] Originally Firemen's Hall/later Hook & Ladder No. 20, N.Y.C. Fire Department, 155 Mercer St., bet. W. Houston and Prince Sts. 1854. Field & Correja. Altered. ☆

When this building was built, the city's fire laddies were volunteers. Most of the original ornate trim and moldings are gone, but some of its early form is visible in the quoins.

A Photographer's Place (books/antiques/prints), 133 Mercer St., bet. Prince and Spring Sts. ☆

Paradise for those interested in photo memorabilia. Appropriately shaggy on this shaggy street.

Backpages (antiques), 125 Greene St. bet. Prince and Houston Sts. ☆

Juke boxes, Coke dispensers, gas station signs, and other urban-scale graphic ephemera. Fun.

[H 12.] Anglo-Italianate Firemen's Hall, shown intact in this 1866 engraving.

[H 13.] Slade's 109 Prince St. (1889)   **[H 13.]** Berger's 112–114 Prince St.

[H 13.] Prince Street, bet. Greene and Wooster Sts. ☆

No. 109 Prince St., NW cor. Greene St. (a.k.a. 119 Greene St.). 1889. J. Morgan Slade. **Nos. 112-114** Prince St. 1890. Richard Berger. Altered, 1975, Hanford Yang. A City Walls, Inc. photo-realistic painted facade by **Richard Haas** extrapolates rich cast-iron architecture to the side wall. Note the *trompe l'oeil* cat at the "open" window.

Dean & DeLuca (gourmet shop), 121 Prince St. bet. Greene and Wooster Sts. N side. ☆

A beautifully displayed, mouth-watering array of ingredients awaiting *haute cuisine* preparation. In other words, a *goyishe* Zabar's.

[H 14.] Greene Street, bet. Prince and Houston Sts. ☆

No. 121 Greene St. 1883. Henry Fernbach. A cream-colored and classy Corinthian. Savor the monolithic granite sidewalks, self-curbed, an old and disappearing local amenity. **No. 129** Greene St. 1881. Detlef Lienau. Lienau's only work in the district: brick with enormous windows. **Nos. 132-140** Greene St. 1885. Alfred Zucker. Three buildings wear a free-spirited Ionic facade (capitals turned sideways). **No. 135** Greene St. 1883. Henry Fernbach. A delicate Tuscan-ordered building. **No. 139** Greene St. 1825. Architect unknown. A lonely brick Federal holdout. **No. 142** Greene St. 1871. Henry Fernbach. Bulky Tuscan. **No. 148** Greene St. 1884. William Worthen. Magnificent brick and ironwork.

[H 15.] The Chalk & Vermilion Gallery, 141-145 Wooster St., bet. W. Houston and Prince Sts. W side. 1987. Smith-Miller & Hawkinson. Building, 1897, Louis Korn. ☆

Minimalist but with a superb feeling for the materials and detail: etched glass against the original cast iron. *Drop in . . . the interior is even better.*

[H 16a.] Office buildings, 130 Prince St., SW cor. Wooster St. 1988. Lee Manners & Assocs., designer, Walter B. Melvin, associate architect. ☆

A pair of structures: the corner one new, the midblock a former commercial bakery reconfigured. Impressive design.

[H 16b.] Comme des Garçons (men's and women's boutique), 116 Wooster St., bet. Prince and Spring Sts. E side. 1984. Rei Kawakubo, designer. Takao Kawasaki, associate designer. Howard Reitzes, architectural consultant. ☆

Like the world-renowned Japanese fashions that its designer designs, this boutique pursues a goal of total unity, or *ma.* Utilizing a delicious sparseness, it succeeds. (Building, Frederick Fabel, 1908.)

[H 16c.] Knoll International Design Center, 105 Wooster St., bet. Prince and Spring Sts. W side. Lofts, 1892, Charles Behrens. Altered, 1982, Paul Haigh, designer. ☆

Outside, the insertion of a series of half-cylindrical roll-down shutter covers adds a modern look that enriches the original Ohio sandstone and brick structure. Inside, witty games of changing scale are played with the neo-Classical ornament of the cast-iron columns. Superb.

[H 16d.] Originally **Engine Company No. 13, N.Y.C. Fire Department/**now **Stephen Spruce (boutique),** 99 Wooster St., bet. Prince and Spring Sts. W side. 1881. Napoleon LeBrun. ☆ Altered, 1987.

A cast-iron bottom supporting a masonry top. The piers carry shields which once contained the engine company's insignia. Now a "post punk" emporium.

[H 17a.] 84 Wooster Street (warehouse), bet. Spring and Broome Sts. E side. 1896. Albert Wagner. ☆ **[H 17b.] 80 Wooster Street (warehouse).** E side. 1894. G. A. Schellenger. ☆ **[H 17c.] 64 Wooster Street (warehouse),** E side. 1899. E. H. Kendall. ☆

Arches and cornices here creep into these cast-iron precincts: 7- and 8-story Renaissance Revival depositories, **larger and more pretentious** than their neighbors.

[H 18.] 46 Wooster Street (lofts), bet. Broome and Grand Sts. E side. 1895. F. S. Baldwin. ☆

Brick Romanesque Revival, with rock-faced brownstone and cast iron in concert. Here **the attempt is at grandeur,** more than the spartan elegance of cast iron alone.

[H 19a.] 28-30 Wooster Street, SE cor. Grand St., a.k.a. 71 Grand St. Wooster St. brick facade, 1879. Grand St. cast-iron facade, 1888. Both, Mortimer C. Merritt. ☆

Two wonderful facades in different materials, at a different time, but by the same architect.

[H 19b.] 2 Wooster Street, NE cor. Canal St. 1872. W. H. Gaylor. ☆

All of a piece, the **Corinthian** capitals have mostly rusted away.

Canal Street becomes a Casbah between the Avenue of the Americas (Sixth Avenue to everyone) and Centre Street. Here shops spill into the street; their wares—"bargains" real or apparent—abound: VCRs, Swatch watch knock-offs, 9-volt batteries, recycled clothes, plastic shapes, sheet metal—you name it. A great place for the browsing gadgeteer, do-it-yourselfer, or the serious bargain hunter familiar with his or her needs.

Broome Street: From Broadway to West Broadway.

Four blocks of SoHo at its most idiosyncratic. A mixture along the breadth of Broome Street of mostly cast-iron facades in varying states of disarray, decay, and delight. In Paris, these structures might line one of the great boulevards.

[H 20a.] Broome Street, bet. Broadway and Mercer St. ☆

No. 448 Broome Street. 1872. Vaux Withers & Co. An imaginative 5-story cast-iron creation by **Calvert Vaux.** Intricately ornamented.

[H 20b.] Broome Street, bet. Mercer and Greene Sts. ☆

Nos. 453-455 Broome St. 1873. Griffith Thomas. Corinthian. No. 461 Broome St. 1871. Griffith Thomas. Tuscan. No. 467 Broome St. 1873. Isaac F. Duckworth. Tuscan encore.

[H 20c.] Broome Street, bet. Greene and Wooster Sts. ☆

The Gunther Building, No. 469 Broome St., SW cor. Greene St. 1873. Griffith Thomas. Note the rich Corinthian foliage and the elegant curved and glazed corner. Nos. 477-479 Broome St. 1885. Elisha Sniffen. Corinthian. Nos. 476-478 Broome St. 1873. Griffith Thomas. Green-painted Corinthian. No. 480 Broome St. 1885. Richard Berger. Composite Ionic columns.

[H 20d.] Broome Street, bet. Wooster St. and West Broadway. ☆

No. 484 Broome St., NW cor. Wooster St. 1890. Alfred Zucker. Grand Romanesque (in scale) Revival brick and rock-face brownstone. Entwined serpents form corbel arch supports in sandstone. In the 1970s and 1980s it was headquarters of the avant-garde **Kitchen** performance space. Not in cast iron but still one of SoHo's best. Nos. 489-493 Broome St. 1873. J. Morgan Slade. Note the similarity to Griffith Thomas' Gunther Building [above]. Nos. 492-494 Broome St. 1892. Alfred Zucker. While it lost 3 floors in 1938, it didn't lose the foliate ornament up the sides.

West Broadway:

Practically every street in SoHo is a shopping street, but this is **the** shopping street.

Note: In originally designating the SoHo Cast-Iron District, the Landmarks Preservation Commission did not include the west side of West Broadway.

[H 21.] 311-323 West Broadway (apartments), bet. Canal and Grand Sts. E side, through to Wooster St. Uncertain completion date. John Harding. ☆

An intended echo of Ernest Flagg's "Little Singer Building" of deep red brick and green-finished wrought iron. Financing became problematical following Landmarks Preservation Commission approval in 1985.

Kenn's Broome Street Bar (restaurant), 363 West Broadway, SE cor. Broome St. Building, ca. 1825. ☆

A Federal house, advertised with elegant Victorian gilt lettering, is home to a pleasant pseudovintage eating and drinking place. Plants. Ceiling fans. Stained glass.

Broome Street, West of SoHo:

Adorning the seemingly forgotten paved triangle between Broome, Watts, and Thompson Streets is the outdoor display (1972–) of rusted iron delights of welder-sculptor **Robert S. Bolles** (known locally but inaccurately as Bob Steel). Vying for the attention of the thousands of vehicles which pass daily on their way to the Holland Tunnel is the large painted outdoor advertising on 519 Broome Street's east-facing wall.

[H 22a.] Thompson Street Brewery (and **restaurant**), **The Manhattan Brewing Company**/originally **New York Edison Company electrical substation,** 40 Thompson St., SE cor. Watts St. ca. 1920. Altered, 1984, Lemberger Brody Assocs.

Brilliant reuse of a humdrum utilities structure. The projected copper vat through the upper wall is a witty touch. In front one often finds the brewery's Victorian wagon, in the rear its pair of horses stabled in a tin shed.

[H 22b.] Tunnel Garage, 520 Broome St., NW cor. Thompson St. 1922. Hector C. Hamilton.

The allusion to the nearby Holland Tunnel and the very graphic graphics applied to an austere, recessive round-cornered structure are what make this early accommodation to the motor car so special.

West Broadway: Between Broome and Spring Streets.
[H 23a.] 380 West Broadway (lofts). W side. ca. 1870.

Prosperous cast-iron front: a renovation done neatly but without pizzazz.

Name change: Between 1870 and 1899 West Broadway assumed the name South Fifth Avenue (a name change later espoused—unsuccessfully—by Robert Moses), and during that period its house numbers ascended southward from Washington Square to Canal Street. The number 159, cast into the iron pilaster of today's 383 West Broadway, dates from that period.

[H 23b.] D. F. Sanders/originally **Turpan Sanders, Inc. (designer housewares),** 386 West Broadway. W side. Altered, 1981, Craig Logan Jackson, designer.

Knock out the existing ground-floor windows and doors from between the old cast-iron columns, substitute practically invisible sheets of glass, and display the latest in high-tech house- and kitchenwares on a glossy polyurethaned wood floor. It works.

Along Spring Street: On either side of West Broadway.
Spring Street Books, 169 Spring St., bet. West Broadway and Thompson St. N side.

To satisfy that urge to browse among those who are *à la page* in periodicals and more substantial items.

[H 24a.] Metropolitan Lumber & Mill Works/originally **Metropolitan Railway Company electrical substation,** 175 Spring St., bet. West Broadway and Thompson Sts. N side. ca. 1885.

The Sixth Avenue elevated ran up West Broadway before it turned at West 3rd Street to find Sixth Avenue. This robust brick and stone structure served the el's electrical needs after steam propulsion became passé. The mural, in a somewhat different color scheme, dates from 1973, when commissioned by a former occupant, Gem Lumber Company.

Jaap Rietman (art and architecture books), 167 Spring St., bet. West Broadway and Wooster St. ☆

No longer on the corner of West Broadway but just as good a selection of books on the **local** as well as **worldwide** art scene. **And architecture, too.** Only one flight up.

West Broadway: Between Spring and Prince Streets.
[H 24b.] 420 West Broadway (lofts). W side. ca. 1890.

Cut granite over black Tuscan stone: somber elegance containing the art galleries of Sonnabend, Leo Castelli, Charles Cowles.

[H 24c.] Dianne B. (boutique), 426 West Broadway, W side. Store, loft conversion, 1980, Voorsanger & Mills Assocs. Storefronts, building facade, 1980, Voorsanger & Mills Assocs. Richard Haas, artist.

The storefront matches that of Mario Starace, next door, but Dianne B.'s special glamour is within: **Post-Modern opulence.**

[H 25a.] 430, 432, 434 West Broadway (mixed-use complex). W side. 1988. Arpad Baksa & Assocs., architects. Don-Linn Consultant Design Corp.

Five levels of glitz.

Off West Broadway, on Prince Street:

Untitled (postcards, art books), 159 Prince St., bet. West Broadway and Thompson Sts. N side.

New postcards filed by category for compulsives, plus some pulled out for casual shoppers.

[H 25b.] Patisserie Lanciani (pastry/light fare), 177 Prince St., bet. Thompson and Sullivan Sts. N side. 1985. Kevin Walz, interior designer.

Catchy graphics, **shimmering corrugated fiberglass,** select lighting fixtures, black chairs and tables all set off the aromatic pastries.

West Broadway: Between Prince and West Houston Streets.

[H 26a.] Rizzoli (books), 454A West Broadway. W side. 1984. Interior, Michael Barclay, Assocs.

Down a long, Post Modern corridor punched into an innocent building just minding its own business. The real action is up the gentle languorous stairway.

[H 26b.] Artwear (jewelry), 456 West Broadway. W side. 1984. Studio Morsa, designers.

Behind a taut sheet of storefront glass an exquisitely conceived medley of polished granite shards and glass vitrines that display the handcrafted jewelry at its absolute best.

i tre merli (restaurant), 463 West Broadway. E side. 1985. M/NY Design Production, Roberto Brambilia. ☆

Throw three pairs of door open to the crowded sidewalk, hang a banner, celebrate a restaurant. (It translates The Three Blackbirds—or in a more vernacular Italian vein, The Three Jerks.)

Central Falls (restaurant), 478 West Broadway. W side.

One of SoHo's earliest dining spaces; its elegantly striped awning has the tailoring of Saville Row about it.

[H 27.] 65-77 West Houston Street (taxpayer), bet. West Broadway and Wooster St. S side. 1984. Beyer Blinder Belle. ☆

A horizontal sliver building clad in colored tiles. It resembles a large Indian headband, 2 stories high.

Thompson Street: South of West Houston Street.

[H 28a.] Warehouse, 138-144 Thompson St., bet. Prince and W. Houston Sts. E side. 1883. Oscar Seale.

Off the beaten track: tall brick arches worthy of a Roman aqueduct carry a "cornice" of small, windowed spaces. Strangely prescient of Kallmann, McKinnell & Knowles' **Boston City Hall** (1970).

Sullivan Street: South of West Houston Street.

[H 28b.] St. Anthony of Padua Roman Catholic Church, 155 Sullivan St. E side. ca. 1895. **St. Anthony's Pious League,** 151 Thompson St. W side. ca. 1880.

A craggy neo-Baroque church and an even craggier church annex to its east. The side walls of both are here revealed to Houston Street. The parish of the South Village's Italian community.

THE VILLAGES

GREENWICH VILLAGE • WEST VILLAGE • SOUTH VILLAGE
ASTOR PLACE AND ENVIRONS • EAST VILLAGE

GREENWICH VILLAGE

Nonconformist: In its street grids (they differ from each other as well as from those of the rest of Manhattan), in the life-styles it tolerates (or is it nurtures?), and in its remarkable variety of architecture, **Greenwich Village** is a concentration of contrasts in a city of contrasts. But in the **Village's** case, these contrasts have long been synonymous with its identity: **bohemia.** This is less apparent today than when both aspiring and successful artists and writers gravitated to this crooked-streeted, humanely scaled, out-of-the-way, low-rent enclave passed over by the city's growth northward. Actually, today's **Village** encompasses the long-fashionable side streets along **lower Fifth Avenue** as well as those irregular byways to the south and west that are featured in picture postcard views.

Since around 1900 the **Village** has been not only a proving ground for new ideas among its creative residents but also a symbol of the forbidden, the free life—the **closest thing to Paris** that we have in this country. With the opening up of Sixth and Seventh Avenues and the subways beneath them, the area became even more accessible. After the hiatus caused by the **Depression** and **World War II,** the Village once again attracted interest, this time from high-rise housing developers, from smaller entrepreneurs who created little studio apartments with minispaces inversely proportional to their high rents, and from tenants who left the "duller" (meaning the outer) parts of the city to taste **forbidden fruit.** Creators were swept out by observers (middle-class doctors, dentists, cloak and suiters, and other vicarious residents). The people of the visible Village changed—leaving West Village families, such as those written about by urbanist **Jane Jacobs,** and those of the South Village (the Italian community), to go about their own business, largely unnoticed. In the 1950s it was the **beat generation;** since then, after a bout with the drug culture (which has moved easterly) it has returned to beckon yet another younger generation with its special raffishness.

As its nostalgic glamour fades, however, it continues to fulfill a variety of seemingly conflicting roles: a genteel place to live, a fashionable step up the professional ladder, a spawning ground for movements such as feminism and gay liberation, a singles' haven, a place to raise a family, in short, a **perplexing but certainly not colorless** community.

Heritage: Always a village, the first one was an Algonquin community, Sapokanikan. The Dutch, upon their arrival in 1626, quickly kicked out the natives, taking over the fertile rolling farmland for their own profit and pleasure.

Growth was leisurely since the village was completely separated from the bustling community concentrated at the lower tip of the island; but its stature rose suddenly in the 1730s with the land purchases of socially prominent naval **Captain Peter Warren.** When Captain Warren bought a large parcel in **1731,** he was the first of a long line of affluent individuals to settle in the Village. His mansion was soon followed by **Richmond Hill** (owned by Aaron Burr, among others) and the **Brevoort** homestead. **Richmond Hill** was the best known of these homes which, for nearly 100 years, gave the Village an unsurpassed social status.

The city commissioners, having already contemplated the future growth of Manhattan, appointed **John Randel, Jr.,** who from **1808** to **1811** prepared maps and plans for the present gridiron of Manhattan's streets. The Village escaped most of this layout, however, since it was simply too difficult to impose it over the well-established pattern. The commissioners, though, had their way with the hills; **leveling** them all by 1811 and taking with them the grandeur of the old estates. These properties were then easily divisible into small city lots, and by 1822 the community was densely settled, many of the settlers "refugees" from a series of "downtown" epidemics.

Sailors' Snug Harbor and **Trinity Parish** have both had leading roles in the **Village's** growth. The **Harbor** was founded in 1801, when **Captain Robert Richard Randall** deeded in perpetual lease **21 acres of land** (around and north of Washington Square), together with a modest cash grant, for the support of a home for aged seamen. It was moved to **Staten Island in 1833,** and since then has received its income from its leased Village land. Prior to the 1920s, its property had been divided into small lots, rented mainly for individual residences. Since then, **land values have skyrocketed,** and the Harbor understandably sought to increase its income from its holdings. In doing so, however, it leased rather indiscriminately, permitting the demolition of many historic and architectural treasures and their replacement by mediocre works, to the detriment of the area.

Trinity Parish made great contributions to the **development of the West Village** in the 19th century, encouraging respectful care and beautification of its leased land. In 1822 it developed a residential settlement around **St. Luke's Church** which to this day is a positive influence upon the neighborhood.

Residents: Perhaps as important as the architectural heritage are the people the **Village** has attracted; the artists and writers, entertainers, intellectuals, and bohemians who have made their homes alongside long-established but less conspicuous Village families. But the artist in his garret is today more legend than reality. The well-established Hollywood actor, "Madison Avenue gallery" painter, and copywriter have replaced the struggling painter and writer; we find **Dustin Hoffman, Robert Rauschenberg** (perhaps self-serious but certainly "art" motivated), and **Leontyne Price** more typical residents. **Eugene O'Neill** and his group at the Provincetown Playhouse; **Maxwell Bodenheim; Edna St. Vincent Millay;** the delightful, "spirited" **Dylan Thomas** at Hudson Street's White Horse Tavern and quiet **Joe Gould** accumulating material for his "oral history" at the Minetta—these were the ones who once made the Village reputation international. Their forerunners were writers of the 19th century who took up residence here, attracted by modest rents, the leisurely pace, and the delightful streets and houses. They included **Poe** and **Melville, Mark Twain,** and **Henry James.**

Though future "writers in residence" of the **Village** will, more frequently than not, be well-paid copywriters, they will, more than likely, seek out the same **Federal** and **Victorian** row houses and back-alleyed, converted stables that attracted the **Mark Twains** and **E. St. V. Millays** years ago.

The Village, though no longer bohemian, still represents the unconventional, a reputation supported by its winding streets, its tiny houses sandwiched between impersonal behemoths, and its charming shops and eateries.

[V 1.] Greenwich Village Historic District. Irregular boundaries: S of W. 14th St. on the N, S of W. 13th and E. 12th Sts. on the NE, W of

WEST 16TH

WEST 15TH

10TH

9TH

WEST 14TH

Chelsea

11TH

WEST 13TH

Gansevoort Market

STREET

WEST

STREET

4TH

GREENWICH

B9

AVE

STREET

LITTLE WEST 12TH STREET

STREET

BLOOMFIELD STREET

D11

8TH

ST.

STREET

WATER

D15

D16

GANSEVOORT

HORATIO

D10

D14

STREET

D1

JANE

D9

12TH

BLEECKER

D12

D3

WEST

BANK

BETHUNE

D13

West   Village

STREET

D8

WASHINGTON

11TH

D4

D2

WEST

PERRY

D6

D5

C9

GROE

Hudson River

CHARLES

D7

CHARLES

LANE

WEST 10TH

C12

BEDFORD

W HAWKEN

C14

C11

C10

C15

W CHRISTOPHER

C13

C

STREET

BARROW

STREET

STREET

C7

WEST

MORTON

LEROY

CLARKSON

HOUST

WEST

S

N

KING

South

0   500   1000

feet

WASHINGTON

GREENWICH

S

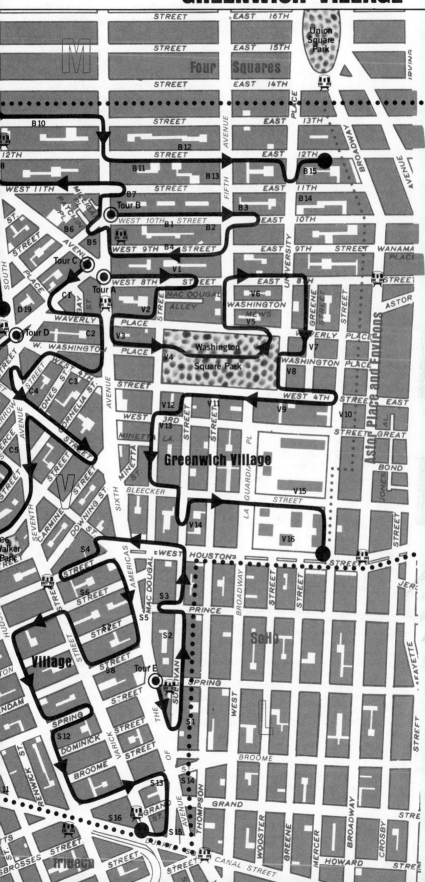

GREENWICH VILLAGE

University Place on the E, N of W. 4th St./Washington Sq. S., N of St. Luke's Place/Leroy St. bet. Hudson St. and Seventh Ave. S. on the S, E of Greenwich St. on the SW, E of Washington St. bet. Horatio and Perry Sts., S of Horatio and Gansevoort Sts. on the NW. ★

It took more than 4 years and 7 public hearings to decide upon one contiguous historic district for the Village—at one point 18 *separate* districts were considered—and the enormous irregular shape of the 100-plus-block area resulted in a two-volume designation report divided into 9 subareas stretching from N.Y.U.'s borders (the university successfully fought inclusion of much of its real estate) to the West Village's Washington Street with its adjacent, then functioning overhead freight line. And, to complicate matters further, there are two *other* official historic districts, another in this section and one in the **South Village** [see V 13e. and S 6.]

Walking Tour A: 8th Street, Washington Square, and N.Y.U. From Village Square, West 8th Street and Sixth Avenue, to West Houston Street and Sixth Avenue. START at Village Square (IND Sixth and Eighth Avenue Lines to West 4th Street Station).

Note: Only some of the entries on this tour lie within the Greenwich Village Historic District; they are marked ☆ .

Walk east along West 8th Street.

West 8th Street may have seen its heyday, for the shops now seem a bit worn and the goods offered between Fifth Avenue and Sixth are more often than not, glitzier, more expensive, poorer variations of what can be found elsewhere in the area.

Frederick J. Kiesler's Film Guild Playhouse (52 West 8th Street ☆) is barely recognizable today, its succession of owners having failed to value the Viennese architect-stage designer's visionary designs, though they were applauded and applied by theater architects throughout the world. Here, in 1928, Kiesler (1892–1965) made provisions for simultaneous slide projections on the side walls and created a main screen where the projection surface area could be altered in size—film projection concepts that are still considered avant-garde. The exterior bears no trace of his hand.

Before taking a right (south) turn into MacDougal Street take a peek farther on toward Fifth Avenue, then return.

Be Bop Café, 28 W. 8th St., bet. Fifth Ave. and MacDougal St. House, 1838. ☆ Redesigned for café, 1984, John Storyk, designer.

Occupying space that was for decades a Village favorite, the **Jumble Shop,** this watering place calls attention to itself via **a sedan impaled** into the floor just behind the show window glass, a subtle contrast to the Hard Rock Café on West 57th Street, whose impaled Cadillac cantilevers out over the sidewalk.

[V 1a.] 24, 26 West 8th Street (residences), bet. MacDougal St. and Fifth Ave. 1838.

Town houses built (together with **No. 28**) as an investment by merchant Joseph W. Alsop, Jr. Their subsequent **conversion into studios** that would enjoy north light has given then distinctive—and not inharmonious—window patterns.

[V 1b.] New York Studio School of Drawing, Painting & Sculpture/ earlier **Whitney Museum of American Art/**earlier **Gertrude Vanderbilt Whitney residence and private art gallery/**originally **8, 10, 12 West 8th Street (residences),** 8 W. 8th St., bet. MacDougal St. and Fifth Ave. Houses, 1838. Converted into residence and gallery, 1931, Auguste L. Noel. Converted into Whitney Museum, 1936, Auguste L. Noel. ☆

The 1930s neo-Classical entranceway remains as **the single hallmark** of the Whitney when it first opened in the middle of the Great Depression. The museum **removed from these parts** for a place next to the Museum of Modern Art garden, and then left for its current Upper East Side digs [see E Manhattan G 54a.].

Now, south on MacDougal Street:

[V 2a.] Tenth Church of Christ, Scientist/originally **factory and store.** 171 MacDougal St., bet. W. 8th St. and Waverly Place. W side. 1891. Renwick, Aspinwall & Russell./Converted to church, 1967, Victor Christ-Janer. ☆

Great corbeled brick openings in an austere facade give this a **monumental scale** in these small streets.

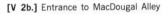

[V 2a.] 10th Ch. of Christ, Scientist   [V 2b.] Entrance to MacDougal Alley

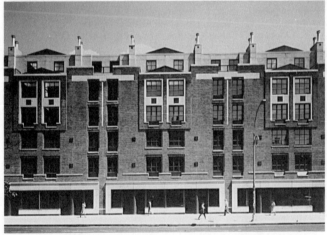

[V 3b.] Washington Court captures Village scale, rhythms, and accretive nature

[V 2b.] MacDougal Alley, off MacDougal St., bet. W. 8th St. and Washington Sq. N. E side. ☆

This charming cul-de-sac (less charming when filled with residents' cars) is **jointly owned** by property holders on Washington Square North and on the south side of 8th Street. The 20-story bulk of No. 2 Fifth Avenue **looms over it,** overwhelming its space and diminishing its small-scaled delight.

Right turn (west) into Waverly Place, and a walk around the block via a left (south) on Sixth Avenue and another left (east) into Washington Place.

[V 3a.] 108 Waverly Place (residence), bet. Sixth Ave. and Washington Sq. W./MacDougal St. S side. 1826. Altered, 1906, Charles C. Haight. Garage entrance removed, 1927. ☆

In this pleasantly Classical street, this eccentric and dour granite house wears crenellations (presumably to protect the skylight against insurrection).

[V 3b.] Washington Court (apartments), Sixth Ave. bet. Waverly and Washington Places. E side. 1986. James Stewart Polshek & Partners. ☆

A brilliantly conceived, designed, detailed, and executed Post Modern apartment house (with stores on Sixth Avenue) that **captures the scale,** the **rhythms,** and something of the **accretive quality** of many a Village street. Yet built only 6 stories high in the rapidly boiling 1980s Manhattan real estate market—chalk up the **low-rise character** to the IND subway running under part of the plot, local **hyperactive** citizen watchdog groups, and a **vigilant** Landmarks Preservation Commission.

Continue east on Washington Place into the park.

[V 4.] Washington Square Park, at the foot of Fifth Ave. Redesigned, 1971. John J. Kassner & Co., engineers. Robert Nichols, landscape architect. Service buildings, 1971. Edgar Tafel & Assocs. Patchwork mosaic plaza, 1971. Cityarts Workshop. ☆ **[V 4a.] Washington Arch,** 1892. McKim, Mead & White. Winged figures, Frederick MacMonnies. West pier, *Washington in Peace,* 1918. A. Stirling Calder. East pier, *Washington in War,* 1916. Herman A. MacNeil. ☆

Originally marshland with **Minetta Brook** meandering through, then a potter's field, and later the site of the hanging gallows; in the 1820s a less sadistic citizenry converted it to a public park and parade ground for the military. With this change, building quickly began on all sides of the park, the north side with its **"Row"** [see V 5.], and the east, which became the site of the first **N.Y.U.** building in **1837.**

The **Memorial Arch** (*1895*) was first erected in wood in **1889** for the centennial celebration of George Washington's inauguration by **McKim, Mead & White.** It was so well liked that pianist **Jan Paderewski** gave a benefit concert to help finance the permanent arch. The statue on the west pier of Washington as a civilian was sculpted by mobile-maker **Alexander Calder**'s father, **Alexander Stirling Calder** (*1870–1945*).

In 1964 local and citywide groups achieved a victory in their battle to keep an underpass from being built beneath the park. They later managed to free the park entirely of vehicular traffic—Fifth Avenue buses had for years used the space around the fountain as a turnaround, idling their engines there between runs. These accomplishments were later escalated into a full-blown redesign of the park, which kept the canopy of trees and added a circular pedestrian plaza ringing the old central fountain, a fresh interpretation of **the European plaza.**

Despite substantial involvement of the community in the redesign, the physical changes have been the subject of great controversy. Some of this is the result of major demographic population shifts in the adjunct community—an outflow of families and an influx of outcasts.

Best seen from the park:

[V 5.] "The Row:" ☆ **[V 5a.] 1-13 Washington Square North (town houses),** bet. University Place and Fifth Ave. 1832–1833. No. 3, new facade added, 1884, J. E. Terhune. Nos. 7-13, converted to apartment house, Fifth Ave. pergola added, 1939, Scott & Prescott. ☆ **[V 5b.] 19-26 Washington Square North (town houses),** bet. Fifth Ave. and MacDougal St. No. 20, 1829; altered, 1880, Henry J. Hardenbergh. Others, 1836-1839. (No. 14, the southern wing of No. 2 Fifth Avenue, 1950, Emery Roth & Sons.) ☆

According to the district's Landmarks Preservation Commission report, **Nos. 1-13** are "the most important and imposing block front of early Nineteenth Century town houses in the City [sic]." **Nos. 19-26,** a Greek Revival group which includes an unusual large town house in the Federal style **(No. 20),** is not far behind. When built, they housed New York's most prominent merchant and banking families and, over time, other distinguished individuals. Architect **Richard Morris Hunt** lived at **No. 2** between 1887 and 1895. Novelist **Henry James,** who was to immortalize the western part of the row in his novel *Washington Square,* paid many visits to his grandmother, Elizabeth Walsh, at **No. 18,** demolished in favor of 2 Fifth Avenue's low wing. In this century **John Dos Passos** wrote *Manhattan Transfer* in **No. 3;** others living there have been **Edward Hopper** and **Rockwell Kent. No. 8** was once the official residence of the mayor.

[V 4.] Washington Sq. Park & Arch

[V 5.] "The Row," Washington Sq. N.

Over the years community pressure and artful illusion have maintained **The Row** in a fairly whole condition. Those from **Nos. 7 to 13,** to the east of Fifth Avenue, retain the shell of their front and side facades only: **Sailors' Snug Harbor** gutted them for multiple-dwelling housing, and entrance to these now N.Y.U.-owned apartments is via a pergola facing Fifth Avenue. On the west side of Fifth, when the huge **No. 2 Fifth Avenue** apartment tower was being planned, citizens put up an outcry, and a **neo-neo-Georgian** wing was designed for the Washington Square frontage, conspicuously lower than the adjacent *real* **Greek Revival** row houses.

Follow Fifth Avenue north for a block, past:

[V 5c.] **Washington Mews,** from University Place to Fifth Ave., bet. E. 8th St. and Washington Sq. N. ☆

A **19th-century mews** lined on its uptown side with converted stables that once served the brownstones on 8th Street and Washington Square and that now, in the case of many, serve **New York University. Nos. 1-10,** on the south side, were built in 1939, and almost all were stuccoed in concert, causing an unfortunate regimentation. A walk through Belgian-block-paved Washington Mews (private, but pedestrians are not discouraged) is the best way to sense this alley's space:

[V 6a.] **1 Fifth Avenue (apartments),** SE cor. E. 8th St. 1929. Helmle, Corbett & Harrison and Sugarman & Berger. ☆

A stepped-back pinnacle of cool brown brick which has been a **visual landmark** on lower Fifth Avenue and Washington Square ever since it was built.

A turn right (east) on East 8th Street.

[V 6b.] **1/5 (1 Fifth Avenue Bar/Restaurant),** 1976. Kiki Kogelnik, designer. ☆

A restaurant and bar outfitted with Art Deco remnants of the Cunard liner SS *Caronia*'s first-class dining room, rescued from her wreckage. Great for Sunday brunch or drinks. Moderate to expensive.

[V 6c.] **4-26 East 8th Street (converted apartments),** bet. University Place and Fifth Ave. 1834–1836. Remodeled, 1916, Harvey Wiley Corbett. ☆

A set of brick houses made picturesque by the addition of bold decorative eaves, brickwork inlaid in a stucco ground, and bits of wrought ironwork. A **stage set,** symbolic of the "village" of a bohemian artist but **not typical** of its Federal/Greek Revival architectural reality.

Continue east on East 8th Street, and turn right (south) into Greene Street.

New York University: N.Y.U.'s avaricious land-grabbing has created an empire larger than the Village holdings of Sailors' Snug Harbor, consisting of **loft buildings, apartment houses, and Greek Revival rows**

on and around Washington Square. Once the bane of Villagers' existence, N.Y.U.'s empire building was tamed in the **1970s** by economic realities. Philip Johnson and Richard Foster had been commissioned to create a unified urban campus where none had existed before. Their plans called for rebuilding and refacing buildings around the east side of Washington Square with the vivid red sandstone visible in the master plan's only fruits: the **Bobst Library,** the **Tisch building,** and the **Meyer physics building.** Happily, the rest of this grandiose scheme has been abandoned.

Sailors' Snug Harbor Headquarters (originally—now apartments) 262 Greene St., bet. E. 8th St. and Waverly Place. The administrative center of a compact real estate empire (within a short walk of this building) funded by Capt. Robert Richard Randall in 1801 to endow a home for aged seamen. The sailors' home for many years [see Staten Island N 15.] an elegant Greek Revival landmark, was vacated by them in 1976 in favor of new facilities in North Carolina.

[V 7.] Kimball Hall, N.Y.U., 246 Greene St., SE cor. Waverly Place. ca. 1890.

The lower 3 floors revel in brick running bond at different scales.

Garvin's (restaurant), 19 Waverly Place, bet. Greene and Mercer Sts.

A warm, welcoming, somewhat pricey place.

The Triangle Shirtwaist Fire: A polite bronze plaque at the northwest corner of Washington Place and Greene Street refers discreetly to "the site" of the Triangle Shirtwaist Company fire, a tragedy which took **146 lives,** mostly those of young women, on the Saturday afternoon of March 25, 1911. The loft building on this corner, originally called the **Asch Building,** is the very building in which the holocaust took place; Triangle occupied the upper three floors of the 10-story building.

[V 8a.] 10 Washington Place Building, N.Y.U./originally **loft building,** bet. Greene and Mercer Sts. 1891. Richard Berger. Facade restored, 1972.

The loss of its cornice has not seriously diminished the delicate character of this loft building's orange terra-cotta, black cast-iron, and granite facade renovated (the original windows were removed) by N.Y.U. upon the advice of master planners Johnson and Foster.

From Greene Street turn right (west) into Washington Place, and walk to Washington Square East.

[V 8b.] Main Building, N.Y.U./earlier **N.Y.U. Law School,** 100 Washington Sq. E., bet. Waverly and Washington Places. 1895. Alfred Zucker.

N.Y.U. originally built this structure to accommodate a paying tenant, American Bank Note Company, on the lower 7 floors (hence the facade division at that point) and the Schools of Commerce, Law, and Pedagogy above. By the end of World War I the increase in students caused a takeover of the entire building for classes.

Grey Art Gallery, N.Y.U. Main Building, 33 Washington Place, E of Washington Sq. E. **Open to the public.**

One of N.Y.U.'s bright spots: an offbeat gallery with high standards of quality. Note the grid of white-painted Doric columns on the interior, around which the exhibitions are arranged.

The Redskins:

[V 9a.] Elmer Holmes Bobst Library, N.Y.U., 70 Washington Sq. S., bet. W. Broadway and Washington Sq. E. S side. 1972. Philip Johnson and Richard Foster.

Johnson is here experimenting with a free neo-Classicism (the "columns" are voids rather than volumes). The redskin facade thus produced is, however, bulky and mannered. Inside, a great atrium brings light and a sense of space to its users, while the outside shades the park. Though Bobst was begun first, in 1968, it took the longest to complete and was beaten to completion by two other bulky works:

[V 9b.] Tisch Hall, N.Y.U., 40 W. 4th St., bet. Washington Sq. E. and Greene St. 1972. **[V 9c.] André and Bella Meyer Physics Hall, N.Y.U.,** 707 Broadway, SW cor. Washington Place. 1971. Both by Philip Johnson and Richard Foster.

Two more "redskins," this time *without* meaningful inner spaces. Note in front of Tisch Hall the Gothic finial from N.Y.U.'s original building on Washington Square. Removed during the demolition in 1894, it had been at N.Y.U.'s Bronx campus [see W Bronx W 24.] until N.Y.U. pulled out in 1974.

For Meyer Hall and other N.Y.U. and related buildings, detour east here to Mercer Street and Broadway beyond. Resume tour at [V 11a.].

[V 10a.] Warren Weaver Hall, N.Y.U., 251 Mercer St., bet. W. 3rd and W. 4th Sts. W side. 1966. Warner, Burns, Toan & Lunde.

An early N.Y.U. attempt at an architectural identity via a new, Modern building—now dated. The Johnson-Foster master plan followed.

[V 8a.] 10 Washington Place Bldg.   **[V 9a.]** Elmer Bobst Library, N.Y.U.

[V 10c.] Mercer St. Res. Hall, N.Y.U.   **[V 10a.]** Warren Weaver Hall, N.Y.U.

[V 10b.] Brookdale Center, Hebrew Union College/Jewish Institute of Religion, 1 W. 4th St., NE cor. Mercer St. to Broadway. 1979. Abramovitz Harris & Kingsland.

Red brick monolith, crystalline, flat, introverted.

[V 10c.] Mercer Street Residence Hall, N.Y.U., 240 Mercer St., SE cor. W. 3rd St. to Broadway. 1981. Benjamin Thompson & Assocs.

Occupying the site of the grand old Second Empire, mansard-roofed Broadway Central Hotel, which collapsed without warning in 1973, this nicely designed beige brick dorm totally lacks any display of awareness of the place it's in. It might look fine in Queens, in a nearby suburb, or even in Cambridge, Mass. But it doesn't look fine here. For a dorm that *does* have a sense of place, see N.Y.U.'s D'Agostino Hall [V 13a.].

From Bobst Library and Tisch Hall walk west along Washington Square South.

[V 11a.] Loeb Student Center, N.Y.U., 566-576 LaGuardia Place, SE cor. Washington Sq. S. 1959. Harrison & Abramovitz, architects. Reuben Nakian, sculptor. **[V 11b.] Holy Trinity Chapel, Generoso Pope Catholic Center at N.Y.U.,** 58 Washington Sq. S., SE cor. Thompson St. 1964. Eggers & Higgins.

Two awkward attempts at "Modern architecture."

[V 11c., d.] Judson Mem. Ch. & Tower   [V 11e.] Hagop Kevorkian Ctr., N.Y.U.

[V 11c.] Judson Memorial Baptist Church, 55 Washington Sq. S., SW cor. Thompson St. 1892. McKim, Mead & White. ★ Stained glass, John LaFarge. Marble relief, S wall of chancel (after Saint-Gaudens' plans), Herbert Adams. **[V 11d.] Judson Hall** and **Tower,** 51-54 Washington Sq. S., bet. Thompson and Sullivan Sts. S side. Tower, Nos. 52-54, 1890–1895, McKim, Mead & White. ★ Hall, No. 51, 1877, John G. Prague. ★

An eclectic **Romanesque Revival** church and tower of yellow roman brick and limestone (in spirit and scale as if built by a Roman) that once dominated Washington Square but is now **dwarfed by many cacophonous neighbors.** Its ornate and pompous detail, en masse, recalls such inflated Roman churches as St. Paul's Outside-the-Walls. *Look inside these walls.* The 10-story campanile and adjacent former tenement are now dormitories.

[V 11e.] Hagop Kevorkian Center for Near Eastern Studies, N.Y.U., 50 Washington Sq. S., SE cor. Sullivan St. 1972. Philip Johnson and Richard Foster.

A classy but overscaled granite building matching in size the adjacent "town house." It would have been a happier neighbor to the Judson complex were it in brick.

As you turn left (south) into Sullivan Street, glance at the N.Y.U. Law School. Walking along this block of Sullivan, you are crossing over the understreet extension of the Law School library (1987).

[V 12.] Vanderbilt Law School, N.Y.U., 40 Washington Sq. S., bet. Sullivan and MacDougal Sts. 1951. Eggers & Higgins.

A blockful of fake Georgian building, trying to be neighborly but succeeding only in being banal.

Turn right (west) into West 3rd Street.

[V 13a.] Filomen D'Agostino Residence Hall, N.Y.U. Law School, 110 W. 3rd St., bet. Sullivan and MacDougal Sts. 1986. Benjamin Thompson & Assocs.

Twelve stories but detailed so as to look in scale with its smaller neighbors. Standard—not jumbo—brick, laid in Flemish bond, like the Law School; deep window reveals and weighty window frames further emphasizing the heft of the masonry walls; substantial ironwork learned from lessons of the past. A fine work.

A left (south) onto MacDougal Street.

MacDougal Street: This street and vicinity between West 3rd and Bleecker was one of the most colorful and magnetic to tourists out for an evening in the Village. With the advent of the drug scene its activities took a turn to the bizarre, and many of its restaurants, coffee houses, jewelry boutiques, and folk song emporia disappeared. Some still remain or have been reincarnated.

A look up MacDougal:

[V 13b.] 127-131 MacDougal Street (row houses), bet. W. 3rd and W. 4th Sts. W side. 1829.

These Federal houses were built for **Aaron Burr.** The pineapple newel posts on the ironwork at **No. 129** are one of the few such pairs remaining in the Village.

[V 14b.] The Atrium Apts. in 1967   **[V 13b.]** 127–131 MacDougal Street

[V 13c.] 130-132 MacDougal Street (row houses), bet. W. 3rd and Bleecker Sts. E side. 1852.

Twin entrances and ironwork portico are uncommon.

Minetta Tavern (restaurant), 113 MacDougal St., SW cor. Minetta Lane.

A **drinking person's museum** of Greenwich Village. The walls are crammed with photographs and other mementoes of the famed characters who claimed the Minetta as a second home during the heyday of the Village. Note especially the **Joe Gould memorabilia.** Italian cooking, moderate prices.

A peek to the right (west) down Minetta Lane, and twisted, one-block Minetta Street.

[V 13d.] Minetta Lane Theatre, 22 Minetta Lane, bet. MacDougal St. and Sixth Ave. N side. Converted, 1984, Larsen-Juster.

Converted from a deserted tin can factory is this modest 415-seat off-Broadway theater with an amusingly developed facade.

[V 13e.] MacDougal-Sullivan Gardens Historic District, bet. MacDougal and Sullivan Sts., W. Houston and Bleecker Sts. ca. 1923. 170-188 Sullivan St., W side. 1850. 74-96 MacDougal St., E side. 1844. Altered, 1921, Arthur C. Holden. ★

The whole-block renovation started with the idea of **William Sloane Coffin** (then a director of the family business, the W. & J. Sloane furniture house) to develop from a slum neighborhood a pleasing residence for middle-income professionals. He formed the **Hearth and Home Corporation,** which bought the block, renovated it, and by 1921, the following year, had rented nearly all the houses. Coffin's dream of a private community garden was realized around 1923; each house has its own low-walled garden that opens onto a central mall with grouped seating for adults and, at one end, a small playground. The garden is for residents only.

Joe's Restaurant, 79 MacDougal St., bet. Bleecker and W. Houston Sts. W side.

Excellent home-cooked Italian meals. Specialties are hot antipasto, shrimp in wine sauce, *zabaglione alla* Joe. Wide price range.

Coffee houses:

Caffè Reggio, 119 MacDougal St., N of Minetta Lane. W side. **Café Borgia,** 185 Bleecker St., NE cor. MacDougal St. **Le Figaro,** 186 Bleecker St., SE cor. MacDougal St. **Caffè Dante,** 81 MacDougal St., S of Bleecker St. W side.

The oldest (since 1927) and most authentic is Reggio with a nickel-plated brass *macchina* spewing forth steamed espresso and various coffee, cocoa, or milk combinations. Dante's special contribution is a giant color photo mural of Florence from **San Miniato.** But all have pastries, hot and cold beverages, and conviviality.

From MacDougal take a left (east) into Bleecker Street. A short detour to the left (north) reveals a Calvert Vaux design.

[V 14a.] Originally **Sullivan Street Industrial School, Childrens Aid Society**/now **Lower West Side Children's Center/Greenwich Village Neighborhood School,** 209-219 Sullivan St., bet. Bleecker and W. 3rd Sts. E side. 1892. Vaux & Radford.

Rich interplay of brick and brownstone (now stucco), solid and void, arches and angles; its details have since been smoothed by less-skilled craftsmen.

Continuing east on Bleecker Street:

[V 14b.] The Atrium (apartments)/originally **Mills House No. 1 (men's residence),** 160 Bleecker St., bet. Sullivan and Thompson Sts. S side. 1896. Ernest Flagg. Converted, 1976.

Reclaimed by the middle class as apartments, the structure was built originally as a hostel for poor "gentlemen" (the room rate was only **20¢** a night, but the expenses were covered by profits on the **10¢** and **25¢** meals). The building was a milestone in concept and plan: **1,500** tiny bedrooms either on the outside or overlooking the two grassed interior courts open to the sky. Eventually the courts were skylighted and paved, and the structure became a seedy hotel, **The Greenwich.** The courts, now neatly rebuilt with access balconies to the apartments which ring them, are the inspiration for the project's new name. In the basement and on street level:

Village Gate (theater nightclub)/Top of the Gate (restaurant). 160 Bleecker St., SW cor. Thompson St.

An ancient (by Village standards) downstairs showplace (1958) with cabaret above and restaurant between, the theater nightclub noted for its avant-garde and traditional entertainment.

[V 15a.] Bleecker Street Playhouse/formerly **Mori's Restaurant,** 146 Bleecker St., bet. LaGuardia Pl. and Thompson St. S side. Restaurant alteration and current facade, 1920, Raymond Hood.

Hood, soon to gain recognition for his firm's winning entry in the *Chicago Tribune* Tower competition, converted a pair of old row houses to one of the Village's best-known Italian restaurants of the period, **Mori's.** He and his wife also lived here briefly in a tiny apartment over the premises.

[V 15b.] Washington Square Village (apartments), W. 3rd to Bleecker Sts., W. Broadway to Mercer St. 1956–1958. S. J. Kessler, architects. Paul Lester Weiner, consultant for design and site planning.

Superbuildings on superblocks. The antithesis of Village scale and charm. The appliqué colors are decorative and not part of the architecture; the self-conscious roof forms were dated the day they were installed.

[V 16.] Originally **University Village,** 100 and 110 Bleecker St., and 505 LaGuardia Pl. Bleecker to W. Houston Sts., bet. Mercer St. and LaGuardia Pl. 1966. I. M. Pei & Partners. Central sculpture, 1970, Pablo Picasso (large-scale concrete translation, Carl Nesjar.).

Three pinwheel-plan apartment **point blocks** visible for miles. What is exceptional for this high-rise housing is that **one can grasp** the size of individual apartments because of their articulated form. Inside, corridors are short—**not the usual labyrinth**—and handsomely lit and carpeted. Outside, the advances in the technology of cast-in-place concrete were remarkable to behold; the smooth surfaces and intricate curved fillets of the deeply formed concrete facade could be achieved despite the vicissitudes of on-site casting. The two **Bleecker Street** units **(Silver Towers)** are N.Y.U. owned; the other is a co-op.

Added later in the center of the project is the 36-foot-high enlargement, in concrete and stone, of **Pablo Picasso's** small cubist sculpture *Portrait of Sylvette.* Despite sensitive craftsmanship, the work loses much in translation.

Turn right (south) into Mercer Street:

[V 16a.] Jerome S. Coles Sports and Recreation Center, N.Y.U., 181 Mercer St., bet. W. Houston and Bleecker Sts. NW cor. Mercer St. 1982. Wank Adams Slavin & Assocs.

A bland, beige box with a running track on its roof.

Note: For Bleecker Court apartments across Mercer Street, see Astor Place and Environs [A 2.].

END of Tour A. The nearest subways are at W. Houston Street and Broadway (IND Sixth Avenue Line, Broadway-Lafayette Station) or Bleecker and Lafayette Streets (IRT Lexington Avenue Line local, Bleecker Street Station).

Walking Tour B: From Jefferson Market Library to East 12th Street near Broadway. START north of Village Square, at West 10th Street and Sixth Avenue (IND Sixth and Eighth Avenue Lines to West 4th Street Station).

Note: Only some of the entries on this tour lie within the Greenwich Village Historic District; they are marked ☆ .

Walk east along West 10th Street.

[B 1a.] 56 West 10th Street (residence), bet. Fifth and Sixth Aves. 1832. ☆

Among the oldest houses in this part of the Village, it has much of its original detail: **pineapple posts** (indicating welcome), with segmented ironwork in mint condition, door with fluted Ionic colonnettes and leaded lights. The cornice and dormer trim came later.

[B 1b.] 50 West 10th Street (originally **stable),** bet. Fifth and Sixth Aves. 1860s–1870s. ☆

The upper stories of this former stable use brick in a bold, straightforward fashion to ornament as well as to support and enclose (in contrast with the smooth nondecorative planes of brickwork elsewhere on the block). This became the residence of playwright Edward Albee.

[B 1c.] "The English Terrace Row" (row houses), 20-38 West 10th St., bet. Fifth and Sixth Aves. 1856–1858. Attributed to James Renwick, Jr. ☆

The first group of row houses in the city to abandon the high, Dutch "stoop," placing the entry floor only 2 or 3 steps up from the street. Being the first builders in Nieuw Amsterdam, the Dutch had followed the home style—stoops high above the canal or street level to protect against periodic flooding—despite no equivalent threat from the waters here.

Terrace does not refer to the handsome balcony that runs the length of these houses; it is the English term for a *row* of houses, such as found in the **Kensington** and **Paddington** districts of London of the **1840s**, **1850s**, and **1860s**. New Yorkers visiting England were impressed with this style and saw good reason to adopt it upon their return.

Sculptor **Frederick MacMonnies** lived in **No. 20** during the 1930s; painters **Louis Bouché** and **Guy Pène du Bois** lived there some years afterward.

[B 1c.] "The English Terrace Row," the city's first to abandon the high, Dutch stoop

[B 1d.] 14 West 10th Street town hse.

[B 3a.] Orig. Lockwood De Forest res.

[B 1d.] 14, 16, and **18 West 10th Street (town houses),** bet. Fifth and Sixth Aves. 1855–1856. ☆

Grand mansions for the small-scaled Village. **No. 14** maintains the crust of its original brownstone detail. **No. 18** is more serene. **No. 16,** in the middle, was neatly stripped.

[B 1e.] 12 West 10th Street (town house), bet. Fifth and Sixth Aves. 1846. Extensive renovations, 1895, Bruce Price. ☆

Breaking from the more popular Italianate town house style, this one is unique. There have been several renovations; one of them was the subdivision into four apartments—one for each daughter—by one owner, architect **Bruce Price.** One of those daughters, **Emily Post,** tells of having President Wilson to Thanksgiving dinner (it is rumored that he proposed to his second wife here).

[B 2.] Church of the Ascension (Episcopal), 36-38 Fifth Ave., NW cor. W. 10th St. 1841. Richard Upjohn. ☆ Interior remodeled, 1885–1889, McKim, Mead & White. Altar mural and stained glass, John La Farge. Altar relief, Augustus Saint-Gaudens. **Parish House,** 12 W. 11th St., bet. Fifth and Sixth Aves. 1844. Altered to present appearance, 1889, McKim, Mead & White. ☆

Random brownstone ashlar in **Gothic Revival** dress. One of the few churches that lights up its stained glass at night, allowing evening strollers on lower Fifth Avenue to enjoy the colors. If you're wondering about the inconsistent quality of the stained glass, you're correct: not all the windows are La Farge's.

[B 3a.] Originally **Lockwood De Forest residence,** 7 E. 10th St., bet. University Place and Fifth Ave. 1887. Van Campen Taylor. ☆
[B 3b.] Apartment house, 9 E. 10th St. 1888. Renwick, Aspinwall & Russell. ☆

Unique in New York is the exotic, unpainted, and intricately carved teakwood bay window which adorns **No. 7.** Its infectious forms influence the other **East Indian** details of this town house as well as those of the apartment building to the east, designed about the same time. Note how the exterior teakwood here has withstood the rigors of the city's atmosphere better than the brownstone of neighboring row houses. De Forest (1850–1932) was an artist who worked in the Middle East and India and founded workshops in Ahmadabad to revive the art of woodcarving.

[B 3c.] The Lancaster (apartments), 39-41 E. 10th St., bet. Broadway and University Place. 1887. Renwick, Aspinwall & Russell. ☆

Like **No. 9,** above, an early apartment house from the era when those who could afford a town house still weren't in a rush to move. Beautiful terra-cotta and a fine Queen Anne entrance.

Retrace your steps to Fifth Avenue, and turn left (south) for a block and then right (west) into West 9th Street.

[B 4a.] The Portsmouth (apartments), 38-44 W. 9th St., bet. Fifth and Sixth Aves. 1882. **[B 4b.] The Hampshire (apartments),** 46-50 W. 9th St. 1883. Both by Ralph Townsend. ☆

Lusty Victorian flats embellished with rich terra-cotta spandrels (and, in the case of The Hampshire, diminished by festoons of fire escapes).

[B 4c.] 54, 56, and **58 West 9th Street (row houses),** bet. Fifth and Sixth Aves. 1853. Reuben R. Wood, builder. ☆

A **distinguished** group: pairs of half-round arched windows set within segmental arched openings.

[B 5.] Jefferson Market Branch, New York Public Library/originally **Third Judicial District (or Jefferson Market) Courthouse,** 425 Sixth Ave., SW cor. W. 10th St. 1877. Vaux & Withers. Exterior restoration, interior remodeling, 1967, Giorgio Cavaglieri. ☆

A mock **Neuschwansteinian assemblage** (after Ludwig II of Bavaria's castle, Neuschwanstein) of leaded glass, steeply sloping roofs, gables, pinnacles, **Venetian Gothic** embellishments, and an intricate tower and clock makes this one of the **city's most remarkable buildings.** Endangered when no use could be found for it—it had remained vacant **since 1945**—local residents went into action. Led by indefatigable **Margot Gayle,** they first **repaired** and **lighted the clock** and eventually persuaded city fathers to **restore the entire structure** as a regional branch library. Budgetary limitations meant the loss of the polychrome slate roof shingles, but the exterior did get a thorough cleaning and repair.

Today's **prominent tower** served originally as a fire lookout, replacing a tall clapboard version, around which the Jefferson Market's sheds, dating from 1833, clustered. In 1877 the courthouse, and its adjoining jail along 10th Street, were completed from Frederick Clarke Withers' designs. In 1883 a **masonry market building** designed by Douglas Smyth filled the remainder of the site, **replacing the market's old sheds.** Both jail and market were demolished in 1927 in favor of the high-rise **Women's House of Detention** (*1931. Sloan & Robertson*), in turn demolished in 1974.

The Jefferson Market's early fire tower   **[B 5.]** Jefferson Market Lib. in 1967

The Jefferson Market Greening, on Greenwich Avenue between Christopher and West 10th Streets, is the official name for the fenced formal park that occupies the site of the old market and of the more recent Women's House of Detention. The greening was started (and is maintained, with help from the Vincent Astor Foundation) by members of the local community. It forms a verdant foreground to the amusing forms of the Jefferson Market Library.

[B 5a.] Bigelow Building (lofts), 412 Sixth Ave., bet. W. 8th and W. 9th Sts. E side. 1902. John E. Nitchie. ☆

Its ground floor still occupied by C. O. Bigelow, Chemists, Inc., this 8-story structure was built for Clarence O. Bigelow. Culture lag is evident here: transitional Romanesque Revival into neo-Classical, more than a decade after it had affected others. ☆

Cross Sixth Avenue and continue briefly on West 10th Street where it has now joined an earlier, diagonal street grid, first to Patchin Place, on your right, and then retracing your steps back, and to the left (north) onto Sixth, Milligan Place.

[B 6a.] Patchin Place, off W. 10th St., bet. Greenwich and Sixth Aves. NW side. 1849. ☆   **[B 6b.] Milligan Place,** Sixth Ave. bet. W. 10th and W. 11th Sts. W side. 1848. ☆

In **1848** and **1852,** respectively, Patchin and Milligan Places were built as second-class boarding houses for the **Basque** waiters and workers at the **old Brevoort House** on Fifth Avenue. Today they are charming not for the quality of their architecture but rather as peaceful pedestrian cul-de-sacs that contrast with the agitated ebb and flow of Village Square crowds only a block to the south.

In the 1920s Patchin Place became famous for its writer residents. Its most renowned tenant was **e. e. cummings,** who lived at **No. 4.** Others: **John Reed, Theodore Dreiser, Padraic Colum, Jane Bowles,** and **Djuna Barnes.**

Follow Sixth one block to West 11th Street, and then cross the wide avenue (east) for a short detour to an ancient cemetery. Do an about-face, cross Sixth again, and continue west on West 11th.

[B 7.] Second Cemetery of the Spanish and Portuguese Synagogue, Shearith Israel, in the City of New York, 72-76 W. 11th St., bet. Fifth and Sixth Aves. 1805–1829. ☆

The original Shearith Israel cemetery is at Chatham Square [see L Manhattan/Chinatown/Little Italy L 4b.]. Burials began here in 1805, in what was a much larger, square plot extending into what now is the street. The commissioners' plan had established the city's grid in 1811, but not until 1830 was West 11th Street cut through, at that time reducing the cemetery to its present tiny triangle. The disturbed plots were moved farther uptown to the **Third Cemetery** on West 21st Street [see M Manhattan/Chelsea H 24b.]. In 1852 City law forbade burial within Manhattan, and subsequent interments have been made in Queens [see Queens C 48.]. West 11th between Sixth and Seventh Avenues is a mixed bag of ridiculous (the institutional) and sublime (the residential) architecture.

Rhinelander Gardens: In 1955, P. S. 41, Manhattan—with its garish yellow-glazed auditorium—on the south side of West 11th Street, just west of Sixth Avenue, replaced James Renwick, Jr.'s, **Rhinelander Gardens.** These were a one-of-a-kind group of 8 wrought-iron balconied row houses, in the manner of New Orleans' Bourbon Street. For nostalgia's sake a bit of the wrought iron was saved and applied to the school's rear facade—barely visible across the bleak asphalt play area from Greenwich Avenue.

Elephant & Castle (restaurant), 68 Greenwich Ave., SE of Seventh Ave. ☆

Omelettes and such. Closely packed tables. Frothy atmosphere. Wine and beer only.

[B 6a.] Patchin Place off W. 10th St.   **[B 9a.]** The IND Electrical Substation

[B 8.] St. Vincent's Hospital & Medical Center of New York, vicinity of Seventh and Greenwich Aves. ☆ **[B 8a.] George Link, Jr. Pavilion,** 165 W. 11th St., NE cor. Seventh Ave. 1984–1987. Ferrenz, Taylor, Clark & Assocs. ☆

The old Elizabeth Bayley Seton Building, by Schickel & Ditmars, was demolished in favor of this, whose lower 11th Street wing is closer in height to its row house neighbors. The cubistic brick architecture, however handsome in its own right, fails to harmonize with the more intricately detailed brownstones, as its taller neighbor's did.

[B 8b.] Materials Handling Center, St. Vincent's Hospital & Medical Center, Seventh Ave. bet. Greenwich Ave. and W. 12th St. W side. 1987. Ferrenz, Taylor, Clark & Assocs. ☆

This triangular site was once that of **Loew's Sheridan,** a vast barn of a movie theater demolished in the 1970s. For a few years it was a charming garden, **The Village Green.** The current collection of brick forms is utilitarian and inoffensive but out of place on this site.

[B 8c.] Edward and Theresa O'Toole Medical Services Building, St. Vincent's Hospital & Medical Center/originally **National Maritime Union of America, AFL-CIO,** 36 Seventh Ave., bet. W. 12th and W. 13th Sts. W side. 1964. Albert C. Ledner & Assocs. Altered, 1977. Ferrenz & Taylor. ☆

In the wake of Frank Lloyd Wright's **Guggenheim Museum** [see E Manhattan/Carnegie Hill C 3.], this huge double-dentured monument is without precedent. It suffered from the same rough concrete work as its **Upper East Side cousin** and so was later veneered with the small white-glazed tesserae which cover the building today. Compare with its **sibling** on West 17th Street. [See M Manhattan/Chelsea H 36.].

Continue across Seventh Avenue to a gentle right onto the diagonal Greenwich Avenue (northwesterly) to West 13th Street.

Jackson Square Area: Greenwich and Eighth Avenues at W. 13th.

[B 9a.] IND Electrical Substation, 253 W. 13th St., NE cor. Greenwich Ave. 1930. ☆

The city's own subway system, the **Independent** (independent at that time of the privately owned **IRT** and **BMT**), arrived on the scene about the time **Art Deco** influences did. Hence utilitarian structures such as this were ornamented in that style. They can be found all over the city.

[B 9b.] The Great Building Crackup/International Headquarters of the First National Church of the Exquisite Panic, Inc./originally **Jackson Square Branch, New York Free Circulating Library/**later **New York Public Library,** 251 West 13th St., bet. Greenwich and Seventh Aves. N side. 1888. Richard Morris Hunt. Altered, 1971, Paul Rudolph. ☆

A benefaction of **George W. Vanderbilt,** this former library building resembles an old **Dutch guildhall.** Its original leaded glass windows, so important in establishing scale, were removed in a conversion to a residence and gallery. Inside the now recessed (and metal-screened) ground floor space is a large plaque worth reading—a mystical statement on the relationship of architect and client. In part, it says

THE GREAT BUILDING CRACKUP IS
AN ACTUAL COLLISION. . . .

SINCE THIS IS AN EVENT AND NOT A
BUILDING IN ACCEPTED NOMENCLATURE,
IT POSSESSES A FLUIDITY WHICH IS
MORE EASILY UNDERSTOOD IF APPRE-
HENDED AS A METAPHOR CONCERNING
MOLECULAR PHYSICS.

IT IS NOT A RECORD OF WHAT HAS
HAPPENED BUT A CONTINUALLY
CHANGING PHENOMENON FUNCTIONING
ON A TIME SCALE WHICH IS NOT
AS RECOGNIZABLE TO HUMAN SENSE
PERCEPTION.

Proceed east on West 13th Street for two blocks.

[B 9c.] Formerly Food and Maritime Trades Vocational High School/earlier **Public School 16, Manhattan,** 208 W. 13th St., bet. Seventh and Greenwich Aves. Center portion, ca. 1869. Extensions, ca. 1879, ca. 1877, ca. 1899. ☆

A fine example of the **Italianate** school buildings built by the city in the third quarter of the **19th** century.

[B 10a.] Portico Place (apartments)/earlier **Village Community Church (Presbyterian)/**originally **13th Street Presbyterian Church,** 143 W. 13th St., bet. Sixth and Seventh Aves. 1847. Attributed to Samuel Thomson. Rebuilt after fires, 1855, 1902. Converted, 1982, Stephen B. Jacobs & Assocs. ☆

Once the *best* **Greek Revival** church in the city, modeled after the **Theseum** in Athens. The columns and pediment resemble stone but are actually wood; the walls are brick and stucco. The porch is most inviting, as was the light and airy interior with its clear glass windows. But, alas, it is no longer a church and the entry porch is now a sham. Converted into duplex and simplex apartments.

Rum, Romanism, and Rebellion: The characterization of Grover Cleveland's Democratic Party as one of rum, Romanism, and rebellion cost Republican candidate James G. Blaine the presidency in 1884. The fiery speech, containing the phrase that antagonized the (Roman) Catholic Irish in New York City, was delivered by Dr. Samuel D. Burchard, long minister of what is today Portico Place. The adjacent row house at 139 West 13th Street was built in 1846 as the manse for Dr. Burchard when he became the church's first rector. ☆

[B 8c.] Edward & Theresa O'Toole Medical Services Building, St. Vincent's Hospital

[B 9b.] The Great Building Crackup   **[B 10a.]** Portico Place apartments

[B 10b.] John and Mary R. Markle Memorial Residence/Evangeline Residence, Salvation Army, 123-131 W. 13th St., bet. Sixth and Seventh Aves. 1929. Voorhees, Gmelin & Walker. ☆

A mildly ornamented Art Deco work, of great charm and understatement.

[B 10c.] 496 Sixth Avenue (tenement), bet. W. 12th and W. 13th Sts. E side. 1889.

Consummate artistry in brickwork and terra-cotta.

At Sixth Avenue zigzag south one block, and continue east on West 12th Street.

[B 11a.] The New School for Social Research, 66 W. 12th St., bet. Fifth and Sixth Aves. 1930. Joseph Urban. ☆ **[B 11b.] Jacob M. Kaplan Building, 11th Street Building,** and **Interior Court,** additions to the W and SW. 1958. Mayer, Whittlesey & Glass; William J. Conklin, associate partner in charge of design. ☆

The **New School** became the "university in exile" for the intelligentsia fleeing Nazi Germany in the 1930s. The original (east) building is a precocious design for New York in its restrained use of strip windows and spandrels whose brick courses set back slightly from the street as they rise. These subtleties make it appear shorter, less imposing, more in scale with the adjacent row house residences on this street. The auditorium within is a dramatic example of Urban's theatrical talents. The school's additions to the south are linked across a rear sculpture court by an impressive glassed-in 2-story-high bridge.

[B 11c.] 59 West 12th Street (apartments), bet. Fifth and Sixth Aves. 1931. Emery Roth. ☆

Art Deco motifs are particularly evident on the elevator and water tank penthouses atop this 14-story box.

[B 12a.] 45 West 12th Street (row house), bet. Fifth and Sixth Aves. 1846. ☆

Look carefully at the east side of this building for the acute angle. The side wall slants back because it originally faced the once above-ground **Minetta Brook.** Frank Lloyd Wright's sister, Mrs. William Pope Barney, owned and lived in the house.

[B 11b.] Interior Court, New School   **[B 12b.]** The Butterfield House apts.

[B 12b.] Butterfield House (apartments), 37 W. 12th St., bet. Fifth and Sixth Aves. 1962. Mayer, Whittlesey & Glass; William J. Conklin, associate partner in charge of design, and James S. Rossant. ☆

The **friendly** neighborhood high rise. On residential 12th Street, this cooperative apartment rises to **only 7 stories;** varied windows, projected bays, and balconies break up the facade and relate it to the prevailing **19th-century residential scale** of the street. A glazed courtyard passage to the north wing shares its neighbors' backyard charm. On 13th Street, though, with numerous lofts and **20th-century** apartment towers, the building's flat wall rises agreeably (and economically) to **13 stories.**

[B 12c.] 35 West 12th Street (residence), bet. Fifth and Sixth Aves. 1840. Altered 1868; right half removed, 1893. ☆

Originally about **25** feet wide; the building of **Nos. 31-33** consumed half of this house, leaving a curious but not unpleasing reminder.

[B 12d.] The Ardea (apartments), 31-33 W. 12th St., bet. Fifth and Sixth Aves. 1895, 1901. J. B. Snook & Sons. ☆

This dark crusty facade, lyrically set off by delicate ironwork balconies, is one of many structures in the city wrongfully attributed to **McKim, Mead & White.** Buildings of great character, like this one, were designed by many distinguished firms. The client here was **George A. Hearn,** the department store magnate, whose dry goods emporium was once a showplace nearby on 14th Street.

[B 12e.] Originally **Macmillan Company Building/**now **Forbes Magazine Building,** 60-62 Fifth Ave., NW cor. W. 12th St. 1925. Carrère & Hastings and Shreve & Lamb. **Galleries open to the public.**

For some four decades, Macmillan conducted its publishing business from this pompous limestone cube whose boring surfaces are embellished here and there with echoes of Rome's glories. Following Macmillan's relocation to an anonymous midtown tower, *Forbes* magazine assumed ownership of the stodgy pile. Malcolm Forbes' various collectibles are on display in the exhibition area within.

[B 12d.] Balconies at The Ardea apts. **[B 13a.]** First Presby. Church House

[B 13.] First Presbyterian Church, 48 Fifth Ave., bet. W. 11th and W. 12th Sts. W side. 1846. Joseph C. Wells. South transept, 1893, McKim, Mead & White. Chancel added, 1919. ☆ **[B 13a.] Church House.** 1960. Edgar Tafel. ☆

A stately, crenellated, coursed, and dressed ashlar **central tower** of brownstone; set well back from Fifth Avenue, this church is identified by its **bold form.** Embellishing the walls of that tall prism is a Gothic Revival tracery of quatrefoils which also forms the motif for the adjacent, properly reticent, church house, built **more than a century** later. Note the handsome fence which rings the site—partly of cast iron and, **surprisingly,** partly of wood.

Boom! For years a tall wooden fence enclosed the property at 18 West 11th Street. Between 1845 and 1970 a Greek Revival row house stood here, similar to its neighbors on either side. On March 5, 1970, the street was rocked by an explosion. When the smoke cleared, little was left of the house—its cellar, it turned out, was being used by a radical group as a bomb manufactory. An attempt soon afterward, by architect Hugh Hardy, to build a contemporary replacement was picked to death by a combination of governmental red tape and rising construction costs. His scheme was later revived for another client (*1978. Hardy Holzman Pfeiffer Assocs.*). ☆

[B 13b.] Salmagundi Club/originally **Irad Hawley residence,** 47 Fifth Ave., bet. E. 11th and E. 12th Sts. E side. 1853. ★ **Periodically open to the public.**

The **Salmagundi Club** is America's oldest artists' club (founded in 1870). This private club moved to Fifth Avenue in 1917; members included **John La Farge, Louis C. Tiffany,** and **Stanford White.** Painting exhibitions open to the public are sometimes installed on the parlor floor, a superbly preserved interior of the period.

Make a short detour south at University Place, and then resume walking east on East 12th Street.

[B 14.] Originally **Hotel Albert/**now **Albert Apartments,** University Place SE cor. E. 11th St. 1883. Henry J. Hardenbergh.

Dark red brick and black-painted wrought-iron trim distinguishes this pre-Dakota Apartments work of architect Hardenbergh.

Bradley's (bar/restaurant), 70 University Place, bet. E. 10th and E. 11th Sts. W side.

A pleasant, quiet place to sip or eat. Moderate prices.

East 12th Street: Between University Place and Broadway

[B 15a.] Youth Aid and Property Clerk Divisions, N.Y.C. Police Department/formerly **Girls' High School/**originally **Public School 47,** 34½ E. 12th St. 1856. Thomas R. Jackson.

Beautifully preserved Italianate painted brownstone and painted brick from an era when most public buildings—whether school, police station, or hospital—were styled the same way. Proper but gloomy. Lydia Wadleigh, for whom the high school (now intermediate school) in Harlem was named, was principal here, where she fought effectively for free education for girls.

[B 15b.] 43 East 12th Street (converted lofts), 1894. Cleverdon & Putzel. **[B 15c.] 42 East 12th Street (converted lofts),** 1894. Cleverdon & Putzel. **[B 15d.] 39 East 12th Street (converted lofts),** 1896. Cleverdon & Putzel. **[B 15e.] 37 E. 12th Street (converted lofts),** 1896. Cleverdon & Putzel. **[B 15f.] 36 East 12th Street (converted lofts),** 1895. Cleverdon & Putzel. **[B 15g.] 35 East 12th Street (converted lofts),** 1897. Albert Wagner.

A big and bold Romanesque Revival row, with each multistory loft outdoing the other. *Look up at the rich stone and brickwork.* Regrettably, the newly added ironwork is not hefty enough and therefore unsympathetic to the buildings' robust nature.

END of Tour B. The nearest subways are two blocks north at Union Square, along East 14th Street, between University Place and Fourth Avenue: 14th Street/Union Square Station (IRT Lexington Avenue Line and BMT Broadway and Canarsie Lines).

WEST VILLAGE

Walking Tour C: The Western West Village. A ramble west of Sixth Avenue to the Hudson River. START at Village Square, Sixth, and Greenwich Avenues (IND Sixth and Eighth Avenue Lines to West 4th Street Station). **See Walking Tour D** for the northern parts of the West Village.

Note: Only some of the entries on this tour lie within the Greenwich Village Historic District; they are marked ☆ .

There are so many early **19th-century houses** in this section of **the Village** that one is tempted to say "when you've seen one, you've seen 'em all." Not so. There are always surprises; some are squashed between 6-story lofts, others are tucked away in backyards, often they are bedecked with nostalgic but destructive wisteria vines. It is this rich texture that makes them such a valuable contribution to **the Village—** take away the contrasts and **the Village** would be a dull place indeed.

Walk southwesterly along Christopher Street, with a peek into little Gay Street.

[C 1a.] 18 and **20 Christopher Street (residences),** bet. Gay St. and Waverly Place. SE side. 1827. Daniel Simonson, builder. Alterations: storefronts. ☆

A **Federal** pair with superdormers.

[C 1b.] 10 Christopher Street (lofts), SE cor. Gay St. 1903. Jardine, Kent & Jardine. Altered, 1939, 1975. ☆

This tall, simple structure contrasts beautifully with the tiny houses around the corner on Gay Street. Its back wall curves to match the bend in the side street.

[C 1c.] Gay Street, bet. Christopher St. and Waverly Place. Houses, 1827–1860. ☆

My Sister Eileen territory. A handful of little **Federal** houses, delightful for being so close to the street. More superdormers.

Turn left (southerly) on Waverly Place, and follow it around as it bends east.

[C 1a.] 18 and 20 Christopher Street   **[C 1c.]** The one-block-long Gay Street

[C 1d.] Northern Dispensary/originally **Northern Dispensary Institute,** 165 Waverly Place, on triangle with Waverly Place and Christopher St. 1831. Henry Bayard, carpenter; John C. Tucker, mason. 3rd floor added, 1854. ☆ Restored, 1977, H. Dickson McKenna.

An austere vernacular **Georgian** building with sheet metal lintels and cornice of a later period. Remarkable for having continuously operated as a public clinic since its founding in **1827**. Edgar Allan Poe was treated here for a head cold in 1837—without charge.

The triangular **Northern Dispensary** is the only building in New York with one side on two streets (Grove and Christopher where they join) and two sides on one street (Waverly Place, where it forks to go off in two directions).

The Lion's Head (restaurant and bar), 59 Christopher St., bet. Waverly Place and Seventh Ave. N side. ☆

Originally a coffeehouse in the West Village, now relocated. A gathering place for younger pols, sports writers, and others of the fifth estate.

[C 2a.] Residence of the Graymore Friars/formerly **St. Joseph's Church Rectory,** 138 Waverly Place, bet. Sixth Ave. and Grove St. S side. 1895. George H. Streeton. ☆

A brick and brownstone **Gothic Revival** outpost in this **mostly Greek Revival** place.

[C 2b.] Pizzeria Uno (chain restaurant), 391 Sixth Ave., bet. Waverly Place and W. 8th St. W side. Converted, 1983, Charles Morris Mount, Inc., designer. ☆

[C 2a.] Residence, Graymore Friars   **[C 2c.]** St. Joseph's RC Church (1834)

More in keeping with the character of the historic district than many of its Sixth Avenue neighbors.

Note: The Washington Court apartments across Sixth Avenue are to be found on Walking Tour A [see V 3b.].

Turn right (south) on Sixth Avenue, past Washington Place:

[C 2c.] St. Joseph's Roman Catholic Church, 365 Sixth Ave., NW cor. Washington Place. 1834. John Doran. ☆

This church is one of the dwindling group of Greek Revival "temples." Its 1980s beige on beige color scheme is very bourgeois.

[C 2d.] St. Joseph's Washington Place School, 111 Washington Place, bet. Sixth Ave. and Grove St. N side. 1897. George H. Streeton. ☆

A 5-story facade embellished by ornament borrowed from **Greek** temples, **Italian** Renaissance palazzi, and **Baroque** country houses.

Turn sharply right (west) on W. 4th St.

[C 3a.] 175-179 West 4th Street (row houses), at Jones St. N side. 1833, 1834. ☆

Three Federal houses whose parlor floors and basements gracefully house elegant shops. Look up at the exquisite dormers—**No. 175** had them too until altered.

[C 3b.] 26, 28, 30 Jones Street (row houses) bet. Bleecker and W. 4th Sts. S side. ca. 1830. Architect unknown. ★

Severely simple, late Greek Revival: 3 stories atop a low basement with low stoops.

Sheridan Square, bounded by Washington Place and West 4th, Barrow, and Grove Streets, used to be the most unused public space in the Village, marked out with a striped asphalt triangle stanchioned with NO PARKING signs. Today that empty space is filled by a magnificent green space (only for the looking) created and maintained by neighborhood volunteers with the cooperation of the City's Department of Transportation—only too happy to show up the Parks Department when it comes to providing verdant amenities. Before this greening the Square was frequently confused with Christopher Park, around the corner, where a statue of Civil War general Philip Sheridan (for whom *this* square is named) happens, in fact, to stand. It caused havoc during emergencies when equipment rushed to the wrong place.

[C 3d.] Sheridan Square Triangle Association Viewing Garden, Sheridan Sq. 1983. Pamela Berdan, landscape designer. David Gurin, planner, N.Y.C. Department of Transportation.

If only the city had more such delights . . .

Turn left (southwest) at Barrow Street and gently left (south) at Seventh Avenue South.

[C 4a.] 15 Barrow Street (originally **stable**), bet. W. 4th St. and Seventh Ave. S. SE side. 1896. H. Hasenstein. ☆

Originally a 4-story stable—note the horse's head protruding from just below the cornice.

[C 4b.] Greenwich House (settlement house), 29 Barrow St., bet. W. 4th St. and Seventh Ave. S. SE side. 1917. Delano & Aldrich. ☆

The building, an ill-kempt Georgian Revival, is most significant for its works: **social reform.** In 1901, when Greenwich House was founded (by **Mary Kingsbury Simkhovitch,** daughter of an old patrician family), Jones Street, a block to the east, was home to 1,400 people—975 to the acre—then the **highest density** in this part of Manhattan. These were first-generation **Italian,** second-generation **Irish,** some **black,** some **French.** From Greenwich House came the **Greenwich Village Improvement Society,** the **first** neighborhood association in the city.

A sharp detour to the right (north) up Seventh Avenue South reveals two interesting restaurants:

[C 4c.] Il Bufalo (restaurant)/formerly **Meridies/**earlier **Buffalo Roadhouse,** 87 Seventh Ave. S., NE cor. Barrow St. Redesigned, 1985, C.M.A. Design Group Ltd., Alfredo Carballude & Michelle H. Morris. ☆

A refreshing reuse—the second time around—of a group of leftover buildings on a difficult triangular site. Serious, imaginative food at appropriate prices.

[C 4d.] The Front (restaurant), 91 Seventh Ave. S., bet. Barrow and Grove Sts. E side. 1980. Richard S. Condon. ☆

Unlike the rash of glassed-in (beyond the building line) clichéd sidewalk cafés, this is a lacy exercise in descriptive geometry resulting in the restaurant's very classy, very glassy greenhouse-storefront.

Reversing direction and walking south on Seventh Avenue south takes you to:

Bleecker Street adventure: Between Seventh Avenue South and Sixth Avenue (Father Demo Square): a colorful Italo-American shopping street.

Vanessa (restaurant)/earlier **Claudio's (restaurant)/**originally **O. Pagani & Bro., Inc.,** 289 Bleecker St., bet. Seventh Ave. S. and Jones St. NE side. Building, ca. 1872. ☆

This elegant "fern-and-frond" spot was, as late as the 1970s, a neighborhood music store. The curvilinear storefront, complete with stained glass and marble, its name set in tiles in the vestibule floor, was how fancy stores were built in the 1920s—even in the Village.

Tavola Calda da Alfredo (restaurant), 285 Bleecker St., near Seventh Ave. S. NE side.

Italian cooking in a light, casual setting, with a standing reputation for good food.

Second Childhood (antique toys), 283 Bleecker St., near Seventh Ave. S. NE side.

Aptly named and disarming, but antiques can be very expensive, even (or especially) antique toys.

John's (Port Alba) Pizza (restaurant), 278 Bleecker St., bet. Seventh Ave. S. and Morton St. SW side.

Claims to be "The Original Brick Oven Pizza" (**original** in Manhattan, perhaps). Although enlarged, still an eating event. Crowded.

Chameleon (vintage clothing), 270 Bleecker St., SE cor. Morton St.

The *new* "vintage" painted signs (ca. 1980) will be notable, once they in fact age.

A. Zito & Sons (bakery), 259 Bleecker St., at Cornelia St. NE side.

Loaves, long, round, sesame-seeded or not, and all crusty. **Mmmm.**

Zampognaro's (food market), 262 Bleecker St., opp. Cornelia St. SW side.

Cheese, quiches, pâtés, and coffee.

Faicco's (sausages), 260 Bleecker St. SW side.

Homemade sausage since 1927. *Tipico italiano.*

Rocco's Pastry Shop, 243 Bleecker St., opp. Leroy St. NE side.

Great Italian ices for a summer stroll. The Italian rum cake (with luscious frosting!) is not to be believed.

Resuming your walk southward on:

Seventh Avenue South, below Bleecker

[C 5.] Formerly **Simo Service Station (Getty)**/originally **Puro Oil Company (gas station** Type A)/now **guest house,** of **Robert Wagonfeld residence** 48 Seventh Ave. S., bet. Commerce and Morton Sts. W side. 1922. Converted, 1982, Joseph Simons. ☆

Occupying a triangle of real estate amputated by the extension of Seventh Avenue is this grimy one-room temple to petroleum left over from the early days of the motor car, an endangered reminder of the not-too-distant past when gas stations only pumped gas. The ill-proportioned-and-detailed brick wall, added to give privacy to the guest house conversion, is regrettable.

[C 5a.] 28 Seventh Avenue South (retail shop/residence), bet. Bedford St. and Leroy St./St. Luke's Place and Bedford St. W side. Building, 1921. Store redesign and residential addition, 1988, Matthew Gotsegen. ☆

Serendipitous architecture for a serendipitous Seventh Avenue South location, an interruption in an earlier, subwayless grid.

Take a right (westerly) into Leroy St./St. Luke's Place.

Changing street names in midstream: St. Luke's Place assumes its name (and a sequential, rather than odd-even, house numbering system) halfway between Seventh Avenue South and Hudson Street—at the bend to be precise. The eastern portion is officially Leroy Street, a lesser thoroughfare to those who are snobbish about such things.

[C 5.] Orig. Puro gas station 1977   **[C 8b.]** Orig. Isaacs-Hendricks res.

[C 6.] Intertwined ironwork, stoops, and trees mark 5–16 St. Luke's Place

[C 6.] 5-16 St. Luke's Place, bet. Leroy and Hudson Sts. N side. 1852–1853. ☆

This impressive row of handsome brick and brownstone Italianate residences seems an eerie stage set in this world of converted industrial lofts visible across **James J. Walker Park**—named for the city's **colorful mayor** who lived at **No. 6.** Fortunately, when the street's two rows of gingko trees green they form a graceful arbor, giving form to a street only **"one-sided"** in winter. Between 1834 and 1898 the land occupied by what was originally called Hudson Park (*Carrère & Hastings, 1898*) was part of Trinity Parish's cemetery until that cemetery was moved up to 155th Street [see U Manhattan U 1a.]. A relic of its previous service is a large marble monument to members of **Eagle Fire Engine Company No. 13,** retained at the St. Luke's Place entrance. The park itself no longer resembles its initial neo-Classical design.

Turn right (northerly) on Hudson Street and right again (east) on Morton (which echoes the Leroy Street/St. Luke's Place bend in the middle).

[C 7.] Morton Street, from Hudson to Bedford Sts. ☆

If there is a typical Village block, this is it. It **bends.** It has a **private court** with its own, out-of-whack numbers (**Nos. 44A, 44B**). It is full of **surprising changes of scale, setbacks, facade** treatments. **No. 66** has a bold bay; **No. 59** has one of the finest Federal doorways in the Village. Old Law tenements interrupt the street, greedily consuming their property, right out to the building line. In them live Italians and Irish, groups that remind their more affluent neighbors of an earlier, less moneyed Village.

Take a sharp left (northwesterly) into narrow Bedford Street.

[C 8a.] "Narrowest house in the Village," 75½ Bedford St., bet. Morton and Commerce Sts. W side. 1873. ☆

It's 9½ feet wide; originally built **to span an alley** to the rear court (where its main entrance is). Though narrow by any standards, it was **wide enough** for the carriages that used to pass through. Unfortunately it has been defaced with a fake brick coating. This is one of several residences of **Edna St. Vincent Millay** which remain in the Village. She lived here in 1923–1924.

Edna St. Vincent Millay (1892–1950): This poet, closely identified with the Village in the 1920s, was given her middle name after St. Vincent's Hospital here, even though she was born in Rockland, Maine. It seems that the hospital had saved the life of a relative.

[C 8b.] Isaacs-Hendricks residence, 77 Bedford St., SW cor. Commerce St. 1799. Alterations, 1836, 1928, 1985. ☆

Significant for its early date; remodeling has altered, and then restored, the original Federal style. The **rebuilt clapboard** walls are visible to the side and rear.

Take a left (southwest) on Commerce Street to see the next pair, and then circle around to the right (northeast) via Barrow Street.

[C 8c.] 39 and **41 Commerce Street,** at Barrow St. E side. 1831 and 1832, respectively. Mansard roofs, 1870s. D. T. Atwood. ☆

This extraordinary **one-of-a-kind pair** proclaims the elegance once surrounding this and neighboring St. Luke's Place. A **local legend holds** that they were built by a **sea captain** for his two daughters—one for each because they could not live together. The **records show** they were actually built for a **milkman,** one Peter Huyler.

The Blue Mill (restaurant), 50 Commerce St., SW cor. Barrow St. Building, 1912, William H. Paine. ☆

A wonderful restaurant, founded in 1941 by the Portuguese-American family of the current proprietor. Simple food (ordered from a portable blackboard that predates all the yuppy clones) is unpretentiously but expertly served "family style." The booths and tables are arrayed around a pair of "mushroom columns" that must have gotten away from Frank Lloyd Wright's Johnson Wax Building.

Having doubled back, take a left (northerly) to resume on Bedford Street.

Chumley's (restaurant), 86 Bedford St., bet. Barrow and Grove Sts. NE side. Building, 1831; altered, 1926. ☆

A famed ex-speakeasy whose reputation still lingers; there is still **no sign or any other outside indication** that this is a pub. Today's side entrance leads to a backyard off Barrow Street called **Pamela Court.** During Prohibition this was the **discreet entry**—the Bedford Street front was disguised as a garage entrance. Its days as a literary rendezvous are recalled by dusty book jackets along the walls. Simple food and drink. Medium prices.

Briefly check out Bedford north of Grove Street, and then take a left (southwest) on Grove.

[C 9a.] Originally **J. Goebel & Company,** 95 Bedford St., bet. Barrow and Grove Sts. W side. 1894. Kurzer & Kohl. ☆

A stable once used by a wine company, as the lettering on the facade clearly indicates; converted into apartments in 1927.

[C 9b.] 17 Grove Street (residence), NE cor. Bedford St. 1822. 3rd floor added, 1870. ☆ **[C 9c.] 100 Bedford Street,** bet. Grove and Christopher Sts. 1833. ☆

William Hyde built this as his house. He was a sash maker and later put up a small building around the corner on Bedford Street for his workshop. His home is the most whole of the few remaining wood-frame houses in the Village. Recent coats of paint seem to hold up the facade.

[C 8c.] 39 and 41 Commerce Street: mansarded twins embracing a green space

[C 9d.] "Twin Peaks," 102 Bedford St.   **[C 11.]** St. Luke-in-the-Fields (1822)

[C 9d.] "Twin Peaks," 102 Bedford St., bet. Grove and Christopher Sts. E side. ca. 1830. Renovation, 1925, Clifford Reed Daily. ☆

The renovation was the work of Daily, a local resident, financed by the wealthy financier and art patron Otto Kahn, whose daughter lived here for some time. Daily considered the surrounding buildings "unfit for inspiring the minds of creative Villagers" and set out to give them this "island growing in a desert of mediocrity." Great fun for the kids—**pure Hansel and Gretel.**

[C 10a.] 14-16 Grove Street (row houses) bet. Bedford and Hudson Sts. S side. 1840. Samuel Winant and John Degraw, builders. ☆

A pair of vine-clad Greek Revival houses in pristine condition. Until altered in 1966, **No. 14** was believed to have been the last completely untouched **Greek Revival** residence in the city.

[C 10b.] Grove Court, viewed bet. 10 and 12 Grove St., bet. Bedford and Hudson Sts. S side. 1853–1854. Alterations. ☆

This charming, pedestrians only, cul-de-sac lined with storybook brick-fronted houses hints at the irregularity of early 19th-century property lines. Evidence of similar holdings can be glimpsed throughout the West Village. These houses were built for workingmen; the court was once known as **Mixed Ale Alley.**

[C 10c.] 4-10 Grove Street (row houses), bet. Bedford and Hudson Sts. S side. 1827–1834. James N. Wells, builder. ☆

An excellent row of houses—brick fronts with clapboard behinds.

Honest and humble. The Federal houses at 4-10 Grove Street represent the prevailing style of the 1820s. Americans had few architects then; instead, the local carpenters and masons copied and adapted plans and details from builders' copybooks. In translation, the detailing is less pretentious, adapting to the needs of American merchant and craftsman clients; nonetheless, there is a faint, pleasant echo of London's Bloomsbury.

Cross Hudson Street for the St. Luke's church complex.

[C 11.] Church of St. Luke-in-the-Fields (Episcopal)/formerly **St. Luke's Episcopal Chapel of Trinity Parish,** 485 Hudson St., bet. Barrow and Christopher Sts. opp. Barrow St. W side. 1822. James N. Wells, builder. Interior remodeling, 1875, 1886. Fire, 1981. Restoration and expansion to W and S, 1986, Hardy Holzman Pfeiffer Assocs. ☆

An austere country church from the time when this was "the country" to New Yorkers living on the tip of Manhattan Island.

The original church was founded independently by local residents, with some **financial help** from the **wealthy, downtown** Trinity Parish. With the influx of immigrants to the area, the **carriage-trade congregation moved uptown** to Convent Avenue to found a St. Luke's there [see H Manhattan/Hamilton Heights T 12b.]. This St. Luke's **reopened** in 1892; it's now under the auspices of downtown Trinity Parish, which had bought the property in the interim.

The additions made following the 1981 fire, which are visible from within the church property, are handsomely conceived, detailed, and executed brick masonry volumes. Emitting rich overtones of the past, they are fresh in spirit, while harmonious to the older structures. *Visit the yard and church interior, too. On leaving St. Luke's, scan the small houses along Hudson and Barrow Streets, and then proceed northward on Hudson.*

[C 11a.] 473-477, 487-491 Hudson Street (row houses), flanking St. Luke's Chapel, bet. Barrow and Christopher Sts. W side. 1825. ☆
[C 11b.] 90-96 Barrow Street (row houses), bet. Hudson and Greenwich Sts. N side. 1827. James N. Wells, builder. ☆

Only 6 houses remain of a total of 14 originally symmetrically arrayed, 7 to the north of the church and 7 to the south. Such planning was made possible because the entire tract of land was developed under a lease from the **Trinity Church Corporation.** The houses are bleak Federal.

Just a glance north of Christopher:

[C 12a.] 510-518 Hudson Street (row houses), bet. Christopher and W. 10th Sts. E side. 1826. Isaac Hatfield, carpenter and builder. ☆

Five **Federal** houses of which **No. 510** (except for its altered ground floor and tasteful paint job) shows the original appearance.

Turn left (southwesterly) on Christopher Street.

[C 12b.] PATH/Port Authority Trans-Hudson Christopher Street station entrance/originally **Hudson & Manhattan Railroad station entrance,** 137 Christopher St., bet. Hudson and Greenwich Sts. 1912. ☆ Restored, 1985, Port Authority of N.Y. & N.J. Architectural Design Team.

A most wonderful restoration of a long-forgotten and sadly neglected amenity. The scene practically transports one—figuratively—to a London tube entrance.

[C 13.] The Archives (mixed use)/originally **U.S. Appraiser's Stores (warehouse)/**then **U.S. Federal Archives Building,** 666 Greenwich St., bet. Christopher and Barrow Sts. to Washington St. 1892–1899. Willoughby J. Edbrooke. William Martin Aiken, James Knox Taylor. ★ Conversion, 1988. Avinash K. Malhotra. Street level and lobby design, Judith Stockman & Assocs., designers.

A huge, **block-filling** 10-story block of smooth brick masonry in the Romanesque Revival style of **H. H. Richardson.** Great brick arches form a virile base, and arched corbel tables march across the cornice against the sky. After many false starts the structure was sold by the feds and converted to a mixed residential-commercial-retail facility, some income from which will **benefit historic preservation activities** in the city via the N. Y. Landmarks Conservancy.

[C 13.] The Federal Archives in 1966   **[C 13a.]** Saint Veronica's RC Church

[C 13a.] St. Veronica's Roman Catholic Church, 153 Christopher St., bet. Greenwich and Washington Sts. N side. 1891.

Here are squat towers worthy of **Prague's Old City.**

[C 13b.] West Village Houses (apartments).

The two groups of **West Village Houses,** along Washington Street's west flank below Christopher Street and above West 10th, are covered on **Tour D.** [See D 6.]

Walk north one block on Washington Street to see an unusual school building, then left (southwesterly) on West 10th, and another left (south) for one last stop on one-block-long Weehawken Street, one of the city's shortest.

[C 14.] Village Community School/originally **Public School 107, Manhattan,** 272 W. 10th St., bet. Greenwich and Washington Sts. 1885.

A five-story schoolhouse from the late 19th century. In a building this height the stairway was important enough to put behind an enormous multistory arched window, which surprises its otherwise symmetric, polychromed brick facade.

[C 15.] 6 Weehawken Street (bar)/originally **George Munson residence,** bet. Christopher and W. 10th Sts. W side. a.k.a. 393 West St. ca. 1849.

Originally the home of a boatbuilder, this little oddity shouldn't be taken seriously as architecture but valued more for the wonder that anything remains of it at all.

Do walk around the block to see the other side of the Weehawken Street building, as well as other vestiges of the area when this was a terminal of the Hoboken ferry. Being so close to the Hudson, do (cautiously) traverse the extraordinary width of West Street to enjoy the river up close from the park strip provided by the City or via the remains of the West 10th or Charles Street piers.

[C 14.] The Village Community School   [C 15.] Venerable 6 Weehawken Street

END of Tour C. The nearest subway stations are quite a distance back, along Seventh Avenue South or Sixth Avenue. A convenient but unusual route to midtown is via the PATH system (uptown to West 33rd Street and Broadway—extra fare to N.Y.C. subway connections—via Sixth Avenue, or to Jersey City, Hoboken, or Newark, N.J.). The PATH Christopher Street Station can be found beneath the marquee on Christopher Street, between Greenwich and Hudson Streets, N side [C 12b.]

Walking Tour D: A loop through the northern West Village and the West Coast. Christopher Street, Westbeth, the West Village, the West Coast, the Gansevoort Market area and back to start. START at what is commonly referred to (though not with great accuracy) as Sheridan Square (IRT Seventh Avenue Line local to the Christopher Street/Sheridan Square Station).

Note: Only some of the entries on this tour lie within the Greenwich Village Historic District; they are marked ☆ .

Proceed southwesterly from Seventh Avenue South along Christopher Street.

Interesting people on Christopher Street: Between West Street and Sheridan Square, Christopher Street is a main drag for gay New Yorkers, especially after dark. The Stonewall Inn, at No. 53, was the scene in June 1969 of a brick- and bottle-throwing rampage following a police raid on the bar. The melee, which sparked the gay lib movement, is commemorated in an annual parade.

[D 1.] St. John's Evangelical Lutheran Church/formerly **St. Matthew's Church (Episcopal)**/originally **The Eighth Presbyterian Church,** 81 Christopher St., bet. Seventh Ave. S. and Bleecker St. N side. 1821. Altered, 1886, Berg & Clark. ☆

Eclectic! A **Federal cupola** over a painted brownstone and sheet metal Romanesque body. The parish house to the west, next door, is stolid brick **Romanesque Revival.**

[D 2.] **95 Christopher Street (apartments),** NW cor. Bleecker St. 1931. H. I. Feldman. ☆

Using a palette of browns, this striped brick Art Deco multiple dwelling is a forceful contrast to the more typical Village scale.

Take a right (north) on Bleecker Street for 3 blocks past all sorts of chic antiqueries and such, and then a right (northeasterly) onto Perry Street for a brief look.

[D 3a.] The Hampton (apartments), 80-82 Perry St., bet. W. 4th and Bleecker Sts. S side. 1887. Thom & Wilson. ☆

A red brick and brownstone supertenement with **Moorish** "keyhole" lintels at the ground floor windows.

[D 3a.] The Hampton apts. entrance   **[D 1.]** St. John's Evan. Luth. Church

A curiosity: "The Dog of the Ilk"   **[D 5a.]** Federal 131 Charles Street

[D 3b.] 70 Perry Street (row house), bet. W. 4th and Bleecker Sts. S side. 1867. Walter Jones, builder. ☆

The architectural gem of this block in a superb state of repair. Tooled brownstone and stately proportions give it a grand scale in the style of the French **Second Empire.** As a result, it seems larger than its neighbors. It isn't.

"Dog of the Ilk": This inscription and a coat of arms embellish the gable of 43 Perry Street, a travertine curiosity altered in (*1967 Simon Zelnik*) from an 1850s stable. ☆

Now, back on Perry southwesterly to Hudson Street, a zig to the left, a zag to the right (southwesterly) onto Charles Street.

[D 4.] Earlier **Sven Bernhard residence,** 121 Charles St., NE cor. Greenwich St. Relocated, 1968, William Shopsin. ☆

This petite white frame mongrel has occupied at least two other sites before stopping in this unlikely spot. Its beginnings are unknown, but it wound up as a backhouse uptown on York Avenue and East 71st Street sometime in the 19th century. When it was threatened with demolition in the 1960s, the Bernhards had it rolled through five miles of city streets to this West Village location. Barely visible in the summers; dense foliage.

[D 5a.] 131 Charles Street (row house), bet. Greenwich and Washington Sts. N side. David Christie, builder. 1834. ★

A beauty of a **Federal** house whose delicate scale contrasts—in a not unpleasant way—with the oompah details of the old police station adjacent. Note the oval window over the second doorway leading to **No. 131½,** a backhouse.

[D 5b.] Le Gendarme (apartments)/originally **9th Precinct, N.Y.C. Police Department,** 135 Charles St., bet. Greenwich and Washington Sts. N side. 1895. John Du Fais. Converted, 1978, Hurley & Farinella.

A **mélange** of many styles, this ungainly 4-story dowager was the Village's police station until 1971, when operations moved to a new, **bland low-rise replacement** at 233 West 10th Street—today's 6th Precinct, truly a visual catastrophe. Now it once again serves as apartments. Revealed by the conversion: PREMIUM VERTUTIS HONIS [sic] (loosely from Cicero's *Philippics*).

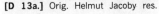

[D 13a.] Orig. Helmut Jacoby res.   **[D 5b.]** Orig. 9th Precinct, N.Y.P.D.

[D 5c.] The Memphis Downtown (apartments), 140 Charles St., SE cor. Washington St. 1986. Rothzeid, Kaiserman, Thomson & Bee.

Out of scale at 20 stories. Most perturbing is that this quite ordinary tall box is glitzed-up with all manner of surface decoration undoubtedly meant to enrich the architecture.

There is also a Memphis Uptown—[see E Manhattan/East of Eden E 2a.]—by other architects.

From Charles Street, turn right (northerly) on Washington Street.

[D 6.] West Village Houses (apartments), along Washington St. bet. W. 10th and Bank Sts., W side. Also along Christopher and Morton Sts. and side streets. 1974. Perkins & Will.

The scene of the **great war** between the **defenders** of **"Greenwich Village scale"** and the **Establishment,** which proposed another high-rise housing project. The David in this case was critic Jane Jacobs; the Goliath, Robert Moses, then the city's urban renewal czar. A **pyrrhic victory** for David: the 5- and 6-story red brick products are dumpy, dull, and for their time, expensive. Scale simply isn't enough!

The Other Side of the Tracks: The old deserted New York Central Railroad freight viaduct (built in 1934) west of Washington Street for all appearances forms the western boundary of the Village. But scattered beyond this gloomy elevated structure are quite a few 19th-century houses—some restored, others decaying—originally built for speculation or in the rush to house those fleeing the epidemics of lower Manhattan. An area to investigate if you have time.

Midblock, turn left into narrow, charming, one-block-long "cobble-stoned" Charles Lane, and then right (northerly) onto West Street, Manhattan's wide Hudsonfront thoroughfare.

The West Coast:

For years this area backing up to the West Street coastline, sandwiched between the gloomy West Side Elevated Highway and the equally gloomy New York Central elevated freight line, had no real name, except perhaps that its uptown part carried the cognomen **Gansevoort Market.** With the demolition of the highway and subsequent gentrification, the area has assumed the name **West Coast**, after an early residential conversion [see D 10b.] with that name.

[D 7a.] 167 Perry Street (apartments), NE cor. West St. 1986. William Monaghan, architect/developer.

A low-rise, neatly detailed, comfy-looking place.

[D 7b.] River's Edge (apartments), 366 W. 11th St., bet. West and Washington Sts. 1986. Architects Design Studio.

Dark red brick and unconvincingly detailed.

At Bank Street, a half-block detour to the right (easterly) will reveal the entrance and light courts of the 13-building Westbeth complex:

[D 8.] Richard Meier's interior court of the Westbeth complex, earlier Bell Labs

[D 8.] Westbeth (artists' housing)/earlier **Bell Labs, American Telephone & Telegraph Company,** 155 Bank St., bet. Washington and West Sts. N side through to Bethune St. ca. 1880–1900. Cyrus W. Eidlitz and others. Converted to housing, 1969, Richard Meier & Assocs.

A **block filler,** reincarnated with major assistance from the **J. M. Kaplan Fund** as **artists' loft housing.** The exterior is a 40-year mélange of loft buildings embracing a bleak entrance court on Bank. The **inner court,** closer to Bethune, is a dark canyon festooned with fire egress balconies.

Continue walking northerly an West Street.

Gulf Coast (bar/restaurant), 489 West St., NE cor. W. 12th St.

The name tells it all (announced by a recycled Gulf gas station sign). The drinks are stiff, the company noisy, the atmosphere out of the Mississippi delta, and they accept cash—only.

Tortilla Flats (bar/restaurant), 767 Washington St., SE cor. W. 12th St.

Same owners and more of the same, but redolent this time of John Steinbeck's Monterey waterfront canneries. Intentionally seedy. THIRSTY? JUST WHISTLE.

All by itself:

[D 9a.] 357-359 West 12th Street (apartments), bet. Washington and Greenwich Sts. 1986.

Note the similarity of this red brick facade to that of Asia Society's red *granite* design [see E Manhattan/Gold Coast G 38a.].

[D 9b.] Jane West Hotel/originally **American Seamen's Friend Society Institute** (shelter), 113 Jane St., NE cor. West St. ca. 1910.

The ships, sailors, longshoremen, wicked women, and gin mills have disappeared from the Hudson's shore. But this reformers' safe haven for merchant mariners sees new life.

Turn right (easterly) on Jane St. and left (northerly) on Washington.

[D 10a.] The West Coast (apartment conversion)/originally **Manhattan Refrigeration Company (warehouse)/Peter J. Carey & Son (printers and publishers),** 95 Horatio St., NW cor. Washington St. to Gansevoort St. Both converted, 1981, Rothzeid, Kaiserman & Thomson, architects. Lebowitz/Gould/Design, Inc., graphics. Mural, Ed Frantz, Sergio Kretschmann.

The 8 once open bays of the 2nd-story arcade of the corner structure, formerly welcomed slow-moving New York Central electric switch engines shunting produce-laden reefers (refrigerator cars) to and fro. It now carries a superrealist mural of the speeding Twentieth Century Limited steam locomotive and its pullman consist, a repaint of history that successfully (if untruthfully) brings drama to a dull surround.

[D 10b.] The West Coast (apartments), 114 Horatio St., SE cor. West St. 1985. Avinash K. Malhotra.

Eight stories of well (if sparsely) detailed brick.

Proceed north on Washington to Gansevoort Street. Note the old industrial structure across the way to the west before reversing direction proceeding easterly on Gansevoort.

Gansevoort Market Area lies roughly between Ninth Avenue and the Hudson River, from Gansevoort Street north to 14th. Busy, chaotic, earthy from before sunrise well into the day . . . empty, eerie, scary at night. From these wholesale meat markets comes the meat for many of Manhattan's restaurants and institutions. Herman Melville (1819–1891) worked here on what was then the Gansevoort Dock as an outdoor customs inspector for 19 years. He came to this job, discouraged and unable to earn a living as a writer. It was during these years that he began *Billy Budd,* his last novel.

[D 11.] Wholesale meat market/formerly **Gansevoort pumping station, High Pressure Fire Service, N.Y.C. Fire Department/**originally **Gansevoort Market House,** 555 West St., NE cor. Gansevoort St. ca. 1900.

Until the LaGuardia era, a **neatly ordered Roman camp** of 10 single-story market buildings, West Washington Market, stretched **west** from **West Street** to what was then Thirteenth Avenue and a pier for the Hudson River **Night** Line.

This clumsily altered Romanesque Revival structure was originally built to serve as a market house to the informal farmers' market stand that then occupied the rest of this block. It was **converted in 1908** to one of two **pumping stations** of Manhattan's new high-pressure water system. Before high-pressure fire trucks were introduced, this system served to increase water-main pressure to a level required to fight fires in vulnerable high-rise structures. **Special fire hydrants** (those large ones with 4 nozzles instead of 2) were installed in an area generally south of 23rd Street on the West Side; south of Houston on the East.

Greenmarket: With remarkable success, architect/planner Barry Benepe reintroduced the idea of urban farmers' markets for New York City in 1976. They have since proliferated in Manhattan and other boroughs. Appropriately, one has been reestablished periodically during the week along Gansevoort Street between Hudson and West.

Frank's Restaurant, 431 W. 14th St., bet. Ninth and Tenth Aves., opp. Washington St.

Don't tell them you knew Frank . . . the founder forgets how the restaurant first was named, but he's certain the founder's name *wasn't* Frank.

Sawdust. Tile floors. Dark woodwork. Tin ceilings. Steaks, chops, etc. In the wee hours it's still frequented by meat market workers. *See for yourself.*

Turn right (south) onto Greenwich Street and, after 4 blocks, at Bethune Street turn right (west) again.

[D 12a.] 19-29 Bethune Street (row houses), bet. Greenwich and Washington Sts. S side. 1837. Henry S. Forman and Alexander Douglass, builders. ☆ **[D 12b.] 24-34 Bethune Street.** 1845. Alexander R. Holden, builder. N side. ☆ **[D 12c.] 36 Bethune Street.** N side. 1837. Altered, 1928.

A block of small-scaled and handsome mongrels. Note the diminutive windows at the 3rd floor (servants' rooms), typical of early **Greek Revival.**

Left (south) at Washington, left (easterly) on Bank Street for a leisurely stroll on this, one of the West Village's most wonderful streets.

[D 13.] 128 and **130 Bank Street (row houses),** bet. Greenwich and Washington Sts. S side. 1837. ☆

Two **Greek Revival** houses, perfect examples in a motley row. Note the windows in the frieze.

[D 13a.] Stephen F. Temmer residence/originally **Helmut Jacoby residence,** 767 Greenwich St., bet. Bank and W. 11th Sts. E side. 1965. Helmut Jacoby, designer. Leonard Feldman, architect. ☆

An individual Modern town house, one of fewer than a dozen in Manhattan. As crisp as a rendering but lacking passion.

Auntie Mame: Beginning in 1927, at 72 Bank Street, Marion Tanner, the self-described "ultimate Greenwich Village eccentric," created a haven and salon for a wide spectrum of **Bohemian types.** Her nephew, Edward Everett Tanner III—under the pen name Patrick Dennis—immortalized her in his best-selling novel *Auntie Mame* (1955), which became a play, then a film, and then a Broadway musical—which resulted in another film. She died nearby in 1985, aged 94, at the Village Nursing Home, 607 Hudson Street.

[D 14a.] 68 Bank Street (row house), bet. W. 4th and Bleecker Sts. S side. 1863. Jacob C. Bogert, builder. ☆ **[D 14b.] 74** and **76 Bank Street (row houses),** 1839–1842. Andrew Lockwood, builder. ☆ **[D 14c.] 55** and **57 Bank Street (row houses),** N side. 1842. Aaron Marsh, builder.

An especially felicitous group of houses.

The Front Porch Restaurant, 253 W. 11th St., NE cor. W. 4th St. ☆

An old drugstore converted to a soup and open-sandwich restaurant. Eat in the company of apothecary fixtures. Tiny, sunny, green with plants—just right for a snack.

[D 15a.] 48 Bank Street (town house)/originally **stable,** bet. Waverly Place and W. 4th St. 1910. Converted, 1969, Claude Samton & Assocs. ☆

Severe brown brick and linseed-oil-brushed copper distinguish this 20th-century town house, a rarity along the Village's **Federal** and **Victorian** blocks.

[D 15b.] 37 Bank Street (row house), bet. Waverly Place and W. 4th St. N side. 1837. ☆

One of the best Greek Revival houses in the Village. The block is striking—despite the curious lintel details **(Nos. 16-34)** and some ghastly refacing across the street.

Ye Waverly Inn, 16 Bank St., SW cor. Waverly Place. ☆

Quaint, New England-style restaurant, tucked away in the basement nooks and crannies of a house dating from 1845. No lunches served on weekends (Sunday brunch only). Liquor available. Moderate prices.

Take a right (southerly) on Waverly Place.

[D 16a.] St. John's-in-the-Village Church (Episcopal), 216-222 W. 11th St., SW cor. Waverly Place. 1974. Edgar Tafel. ☆ **[D 16b.] Parish House/**originally **South Baptist Church,** 224 Waverly Place, bet. Perry and W. 11th Sts. W side. Early 1850s. ☆

An austere red brick box disguised with a pediment and a brow of giant pseudo-Greek details. It replaced **a true Greek Revival temple** destroyed in a fire. A glimpse of its predecessor's style is visible in the parish house.

[D 16a.] St. John's-in-the-Village Ch.   **[D 17b.]** Duane Colglazier residence

Bear right (south) on Seventh Avenue South.

Seventh Avenue South: Before construction of the West Side **IRT** Subway below **Times Square,** around **World War I,** Seventh Avenue began its northward journey at Greenwich Avenue and West 11th Street. The building of the Seventh Avenue subway to connect with Varick Street and the creation of Seventh Avenue South as a surface thoroughfare made **huge scars** through these West Village blocks, leaving the backs and sides of many buildings crudely exposed. Isolated triangles of land once filled with dingy gas stations and parking lots are now seeing reuse as building sites. Seventh Avenue South opened for traffic in 1919.

[D 17a.] 22 Perry Street (apartments), SW cor. Seventh Ave. S. 1987. Architects Design Group. ☆

A "witch's hat" over the rounded acute-angled corner, combined with eyebrow windows in the latter-day mansard, make this a not unappealing novelty—but, because of crude detail and clumsy massing, little more.

 [D 17b.] Duane Colglazier residence, 156 Seventh Avenue S., bet. Perry and Charles Sts. W side. 1983. Smith & Thompson. ☆

An unabashedly personal statement which apes no Greenwich Village sentimentality yet fits surprisingly well in the context of the odd-site-filled Seventh Avenue South corridor. A breath of fresh air.

[D 18a.] 48, 50, 52-54 Charles Street (row houses), bet. Seventh Ave. S. and W. 4th St. 1840. ☆

Among the Village's most riotous and picturesque groupings of brick row houses. What makes them wonderful is the spirited conversion to studios, involving major changes in window size and placement. Remember, a **foolish** consistency can be the hobgoblin of little minds!

[D 18b.] Chez Ma Tante (restaurant), 189 W. 10th St., bet. W. 4th and Bleecker Sts. Converted, 1984, Charles Morris Mount, Inc., designers. ☆

Paired French doors and refreshing graphics evoke a Gallic mood.

Three Lives & Company Ltd. (booksellers), 154 W. 10th St., SW cor. W. 4th St.

A literate, comfy, general bookshop, well stocked in architecture and the arts, located at what first appears to be an unlikely confluence of streets: a Village anomaly.

[D 19.] 59-61 Christopher Street (apartments), NE cor. Seventh Avenue S. 1987. Levien DeLiso White Songer. ☆

A witty essay on contemporary reuse of Federal architecture motifs, built on a very difficult site. Unlike 74 Grove Street, across Columbus Park to the south, or Greenwich House a block or two down [see C 4b.] this exaggerates the historic antecedents instead of simply trying to copy them.

END of Tour D. For the nearest subways and many places to eat, drink, and relax, continue walking south to where the tour began near Sheridan Square (IRT Seventh Avenue Line local to the Christopher Street/ Sheridan Square Station).

SOUTH VILLAGE

Walking Tour E: The South Village. A perambulation through the less well known parts of southern Greenwich Village, ending up near TriBeCa and SoHo. START at Sixth Avenue and Spring Street. The IND subway will take you right to the spot (IND Eighth Avenue Line local, Spring Street Station).

Amble south on Sixth Avenue for one block, and make almost a complete U-turn (north) onto acutely intersecting Sullivan Street. Across the way to the east:

[S 1a.] 57 Sullivan Street (row house), bet. Broome and Spring Sts. E side. 1817. Frederick Youmans, builder. Expanded upward, before 1858.

Once 2 stories with attic, the originally dormered house was increased in height to accommodate a full 3rd floor, so the upper-floor windows are mid 19th-century copies.

[S 1b.] 83 and **85 Sullivan Street (row houses),** bet. Broome and Spring Sts. E side. 1819. Expanded upward. ★

A pair of Greek Revival houses, survivors from a longer row displaced by more recent construction, with cornices added later, on occasion of their upward expansion.

[S 2a.] James S. Rossant residence, 114 Sullivan St., bet. Spring and Prince Sts. ca. 1820. Expanded upward. **[S 2b.] 116 Sullivan Street (row house).** ca. 1820. Expanded upward, 1872. ★

Another pair of wonderful row houses on an otherwise unprepossessing block. Architects of Modern high-rise housing (like Rossant) tend to spend their private lives living in low-rise structures like **No. 114.** According to the landmark designation report, the glory of **No. 116** is the unique enframement of the front door within a simple round-arched masonry opening.

[S 3a.] 203 Prince Street (town house), bet. Sullivan and MacDougal Sts. N side. 1834. Expanded upward, 1888. ★

An overly careful restoration of the facade adds a "restoration village" look to this commercial street's appearance.

*Turn left at West Houston Street, and cross Sixth Avenue to the west side.
A couple of short divertissements; then pick up the tour on the southwest
corner of West Houston and Sixth:*

[S 4a.] 3 Bedford Street (apartments), bet. W. Houston and Downing
Sts. W side. 1987. William Zeph Ginsberg.

This red brick and cast-concrete structure is built in the bed of the
ill-fated western extension of the West Houston superstreet. (Since West
Houston exists as a narrow street that twists to the south, the new one
was to have been called Verrazano Street, as a sop to the Italian community—the bridge was yet to come). Community opposition lasting over
decades made the necessary land condemnation farther west politically
untenable.

[S 4b.] Formerly **Barney Rosset residence,** 196 W. Houston St., bet.
Bedford and Varick Sts. N side. Altered for Rosset, 1969, Eugene
Futterman.

A cool, geometric facade of brown-purple vitreous-tile structural
blocks (like those curved ones used in silos, but flat). One of the few
Modern individual town houses in Manhattan.

[S 5a.] 194 Sixth Avenue in 1977   [S 3a.] 203 Prince Street residence

 [S 4c.] 197-203 West Houston Street (row houses), bet. Bedford and
Varick Sts. S side. ca. 1820.

Four Federal houses in a seedy block. Note the lintels retained over
a picture window intrusion on **No. 201.**

*Return to Sixth Avenue and turn right (south) along Sixth Avenue's
repaved and landscaped flank.*

[S 5.] Avenue of the Americas Improvement, Sixth Ave., bet. Canal and
W. 4th Sts. 1975. N.Y.C. Department of Highways; Frank Rogers, director of urban design.

As Seventh Avenue South was cut through the West Village during
World War I, the extension of Sixth Avenue **below Carmine Street**
(opened in 1930) resulted in more urban surgery. The widenings and
narrowings of the avenue's irregular swath through the South Village's
already confusing grids created a speedway for cars and trucks, a bat-
tlefield for pedestrians. This sensitive municipal improvement, more
than a half century later, places "careful consideration of pedestrian
amenities on a par with the orderly flow of traffic," in the words of the
Municipal Art Society, "turning a no-man's land into a community
resource for sitting, playing, talking, and enjoying the city."

*Across Sixth (Avenue of the Americas, if you insist), just south of Charl-
ton/Prince Streets—the names are different on the two sides of the
avenue:*

[S 5a.] Mid-rise apartment building/earlier **Quartermaster Storehouse, N.Y.C. Police Department**/originally **10th Precinct Station House,** 194 Sixth Ave. (originally 24 MacDougal St.) bet. Prince and Spring Sts. E side. 1893. Nathaniel D. Bush. Converted, 1987, Terrance R. Williams.

Until the City auctioned off this surplus property, the old station house was a stately—if dour—pressed brick and granite structure with great rusticated voussoirs around the arched entrance portal. Now that's about all of the original facade that remains; almost everything above the first floor is new and nowhere near the architectural quality of the original.

Richmond Hill, a country mansion built in 1767, once enjoyed magnificent views from its 100-foot-high mound near today's intersection of Charlton and Varick Streets. George Washington briefly used it as his headquarters during the Revolution; John Adams occupied it as vice-president, later when the city was the nation's capital. In 1797 Aaron Burr acquired the elegant structure to lavish entertainment upon those who might further his political ambitions. It was John Jacob Astor who recognized the value of the surrounding 26 acres. He had them mapped into 25- by 100-foot lots beginning in 1817, after this and other Village hills were leveled by the Commissioners' Plan of 1811 to their present flatness, and saw the development of the row houses still extant in the Charlton-King-Vandam district. Meanwhile the mansion itself, literally knocked off its "pedestal," was moved across the street. After losing its status, it served as a theater and amusement garden and was finally demolished in 1849.

By turning right (west) you have a choice of walking through any (or all) of the three east-west blocks that make up much of the Charlton-King-Vandam Historic District. Choose your route and meet at Varick and King Streets, where the tour resumes.

[S 6., 7.] Charlton Street row houses, Charlton-King-Vandam Historic District

[S 6.] Charlton-King-Vandam Historic District. ★ Early row houses, 1820–1829; later row houses, 1840–1849. From N to S: **[S 6a.] 1–49, 16–54 King Street.** ☆ **[S 7.] 9–43, 20–42 Charlton Street.** ☆ **[S 8.] 9–29 Vandam Street.** ☆ **[S 8a.] 43–51 MacDougal Street.** ☆

This historic district, **minute in size** when compared with that of Greenwich Village to the north, is New York's **greatest display** of Federal style row houses. The two best (and best preserved) examples are **Nos. 37** and **39 Charlton,** whose exquisitely detailed entrances with original doors and leaded glass sidelights convey many of the style's most distinctive qualities. The later Greek Revival rows, like the ones at **Nos. 20, 40, 42, 44 King Street,** almost perfectly preserved, are impressive, too.

Walk west on King Street and, after viewing No. 375 Hudson, turn left (south) on Hudson Street.

 [S 9.] Saatchi & Saatchi D.F.S. Compton World Headquarters, 375 Hudson St., bet. King and W. Houston Sts. W side to Greenwich St. 1987. Fox & Fowle.

The rounded corners of this wraparound, butted-glass-windowed office building conjur a mini-Starrett-Lehigh [see M Manhattan/Chelsea H 13.]—here, however, with ultrarefined details.

Walk south on Hudson Street past industrial behemoths that once housed the city's great printing industry and which were converted for back-office use by the financial industry.

Detour:

At Spring Street, an optional detour west to see three surviving Federal row houses; or proceed south on Hudson, and take a left (east) into Watts Street for the remainder of the tour.

[S 10.] Ear Inn/originally **James Brown residence,** 326 Spring St., bet. Greenwich and Washington Sts. S side. 1817. ★

Gambrel roof, dormers, and Flemish-bonded brick reveal an ill-maintained old Federal house, far better known for the blacked-out lobes of the B in its neon BAR sign—making it recognizable as EAR Inn, an out-of-the-way New York watering spot.

 [S 11.] 502, 504, 506 (John Rohr residence), 508 Canal Street, 480 Greenwich St. All on NW cor. Canal and Greenwich Sts. ca. 1827.

Five Federal row houses built for developer John Rohr, who lived in **No. 506** for its first 20 years. His house remains the most intact.

End of optional detour. A swing left into Spring Street finds:

[S 12a.] N.Y.C. Fire Department Museum/originally **Rescue Company No. 1,** 278 Spring St., bet. Hudson and Varick Sts. S side. **Open to the public.**

A former specialized firehouse now filled with artifacts for fire buffs of all ages and with old equipment, photos, and other goodies.

Continuing south on Hudson:

[S 12b.] 284, 288 Hudson Street (residences), bet. Dominick and Spring Sts. E side. ca. 1820.

Federal remnants, whose forms (simple bodies with pitched roofs and dormer windows) now shelter commercial buildings in which the early American **middle class** once dwelled.

Turn left into Watts Street for a couple of blocks:

 [S 13.] Film Forum 1 & 2 (theaters), 57 Watts St., bet. Sixth Ave. and Varick St. S side. 1981. Design Coalition: Stephen Tilly/Alan Buchsbaum. Outdoor murals, Robert Breer.

Off-the-beaten-track films and motion picture reruns are showcased at this pair of theaters architectonically carved (with consummate style) from a recycled bowstring-trussed commercial garage by Film Forum's indefatigable **Karen Cooper.**

Continuing on Watts on the far side of Sixth—worth the wide crossing—to admire the bas-reliefs up close:

[S 14.] 100 Avenue of the Americas (lofts)/earlier **100 Sixth Avenue/**originally **Green Sixth Avenue Building,** SE cor. Watts St. to Thompson St. 1928. Office of Ely Jacques Kahn.

Three street facades are industrial window-filled Art Deco. Even the fourth, a barren lot-line wall, still lets gobs of sunlight into the building since expected high-rise neighbors to the south never materialized. Particularly note the strongly characterized bas-reliefs of artisans and workers in the 2nd-floor pilasters and the other 2- and 3-dimensional masonry ornament.

Back to the west side of Sixth and continue southward.

Triplet's Roumanian Restaurant, 11-17 Grand St., SW cor. Sixth Ave.

The name refers to three identical triplet brothers separated at birth, individually adopted, raised as "singlets," and reunited accidentally as young adults. The Romanian restaurant that they decided to open serves **Kosher-style** food but not victuals that conform to the slaughtering rituals or dietary rules of Jewish law. Kreplach, kishka, karnatzlack . . . heartburn. And in fancy surroundings, yet.

[S 12b.] 284, 288 Hudson St., 1966   **[S 13.]** Interior of Film Forum 1 & 2

[S 15.] Juan Pablo Duarte (statue), in Juan Pablo Duarte Sq., Sixth Ave. NW cor. Canal St. 1978.

A bearded bronze figure atop a granite plinth who vaguely resembles one of the City's colorful parks commissioners. Duarte (1813–1876) was founder of the Dominican Republic.

A last stop at the enormous traffic intersection of Sixth and Canal, dominated by:

[S 16.] Holland Plaza Building (lofts), 75 Varick St., NW cor. Canal St. to Watts and Hudson Sts. 1930. Office of Ely Jacques Kahn.

A trapezoidal block fully covered by 16 powerful stories of industrial Art Deco, built to serve the needs of the printing trades and other downtown industries.

END of Tour E. If you are ready for more, cross the humongous Canal Street intersection and stroll through TriBeCa, to the south. And to the northeast lies another fascinating area, SoHo. If you're calling it a day, the nearest subways are also here (IRT Seventh Avenue Line local, or IND Eighth Avenue Line local, both at their respective Canal Street Stations (no interchange available).

ASTOR PLACE & ENVIRONS

For one brief generation in the changing fashions of New York, **Lafayette Street** (then Lafayette Place) was its **most wealthy and elegant residential avenue.** Then running only from Great Jones Street to Astor Place, it was a short, treelined boulevard, flanked by town houses of the **Astors, Vanderbilts,** and **Delanos.** Now the trees are gone, and only a piece of **Colonnade Row** (LaGrange Terrace) remains. Although in shoddy condition, its character is so strong that it still suggests the urbane qualities present up until the **Civil War.** Mostly developed in 1832–1833, the street was cut through **Sperry's Botanic Gardens,** later **Vauxhall Gardens,** a summer entertainment enclave, where music and theatrical performances were presented in the open air. **John Lambert,** an English traveler of **1807,** noted it as a "neat plantation . . . the theatrical corps of New York is chiefly engaged at Vauxhall during summer." Only 20 years after this residential development in the 1830s, the street's principal families moved away to Fifth Avenue. At the same time the **Astor Library** (later to become a major part of New York's

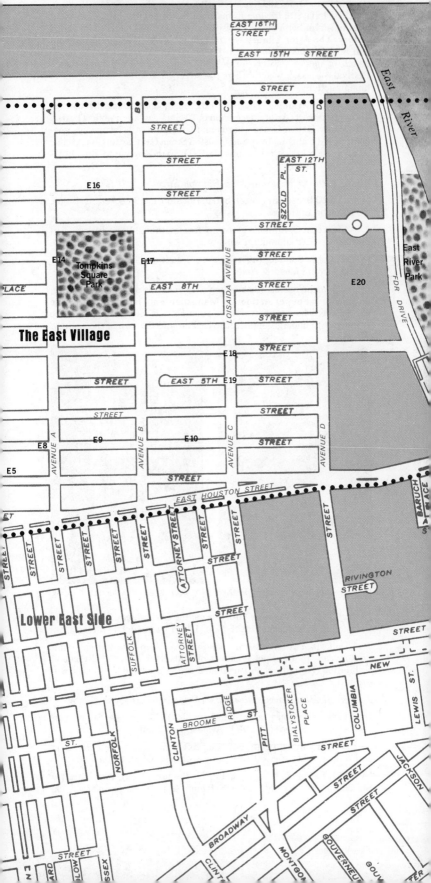

ASTOR PLACE/EAST VILLAGE

EAST 16TH STREET

EAST 15TH STREET

East River

STREET

A   B   C   D

STREET

STREET

E 16

STREET

EAST 12TH ST.

SZOLD PL.

STREET

Tompkins
Square
Park

E 14   E 17

STREET

East
River
Park

FDR DRIVE

LOISAIDA AVENUE

EAST 8TH

STREET

PLACE

STREET

E 20

The East Village

STREET

STREET

E 18

STREET   EAST 5TH E 19   STREET

STREET

STREET

AVENUE A

AVENUE B

E 9   E 10

AVENUE C

STREET

E 8

AVENUE D

E 5

STREET

EAST HOUSTON STREET

ET

STREET

STREET

STREET

STREET

STREET

STREET

ATTORNEY STREET

STREET

STREET

STREET

STREET

BARUCH PLACE

S

RIVINGTON
STREET

Lower East Side

STREET

STREET

SUFFOLK

ATTORNEY STREET

NEW

LEWIS ST.

NORFOLK

CLINTON

RIDGE ST.

BROOME

PITT

BIALYSTOKER PLACE

COLUMBIA

STREET

ST.

STREET

JACKSON STREET

STREET

BROADWAY

CLINT

MONTGO

GOUVERNEU

GOU

ER

N

ARD

LOW

SSEX

Public Library) and the **Cooper Union Foundation Building** were built (started in **1850** and **1853,** respectively), seeding the precinct with different uses: Lafayette became primarily a light-manufacturing and warehousing street, with erratic or isolated physical remnants of its varied history. The **Astor Library** was bought by **HIAS** (Hebrew Immigrant Aid Society), but beginning in the late 1960s it was converted into a clutch of indoor theaters for Joseph Papp's **New York Shakespeare Festival**—a usage which brings the street back to the mainstream of human activity.

Astor Place Walking Tour: **A walk northbound along Broadway/ Lafayette Street/Astor Place/Fourth Avenue** past the **Public Theater, the Cooper Union, Grace Church and lesser, but still intriguing, wonders:** START at Broadway and Houston Street (IRT Lexington Avenue local to Bleecker Street Station or IND Sixth Avenue to Broadway-Lafayette Station).

Amble north on Broadway from Houston Street.

[A 1a.] 620 Broadway (lofts), bet. E. Houston and Bleecker Sts. E side. 1858. John B. Snook.

Vigorous Corinthian cast-iron frames thoughtless, lifeless, flat, bronze-anodized aluminum windows.

[A 1b.] Cable Building (offices), 621 Broadway, NW cor. Houston St. 1894. McKim, Mead & White.

The name reflects the building's original role as **headquarters** for, and one of the **power stations** of, Manhattan's not inconsiderable **cable car empire.** The slots between the running rails later made it possible to convert to underground electric feed around the turn of the century.

[A 1b.] The Cable Building: MM&W   **[A 4a.]** Sullivan's Condict Building

[A 1c.] Originally **The New York Mercantile Exchange,** 628 Broadway, E. Houston and Bleecker Sts. E side. 1882. Herman J. Schwarzmann.

Delicate Tuscan cast-iron columns and deep—very deep—window reveals, by the **chief architect** of Philadelphia's **1876 Centennial Exhibition.** Note the name appliquéd to the 3rd- and 5th-floor spandrels.

Left on Bleecker Street, and then back across Broadway to Crosby:

[A 2.] Bleecker Court (apartment complex), 77 Bleecker St., NE cor. Mercer St. to Broadway. 1981. Avinash K. Malhotra.

A bold joining together of older loft buildings on Bleecker Street and (burned-out) ones on Broadway with new fabric to their rear.

[A 3.] St. Barnabas House (shelter for the homeless), 304 Mulberry St., SE cor. Bleecker St. 1949. Ketchum, Giná & Sharp. Enlarged, ca. 1978.

A modern pioneer in these parts. The expansion from its original 3 stories has deprived it of its specialness.

The Broadway Strip: Beginning in the early 1980s, starting at Astor Place and spreading southward, leaping across Houston and linking to a similar movement coming up Broadway from Canal Street, there sprang up an impressive array of shops and restaurants (and later vibrant sidewalk flea markets) catering to the youth culture, purveying anything from funky jewelry to recycled old clothes to Apache haircuts. The area had previously been devoted to marginal service stores addressing the needs of the textile, garment, and other humdrum wholesale and industrial tenants who occupied the upper floors of Broadway's bulky loft structures. During this period, when the street was hardly fashionable and land prices were understandably depressed, a number of sites on Broadway's west flank between West 3rd Street and Washington Place were purchased and developed by N.Y.U. and Hebrew Union College [see previous section, V 10a., b., c.]. Failing to foresee how Broadway might shift in its use, these institutions of higher learning turned their backs on Broadway and failed to provide for a potentially profitable commercial presence on their side of the street. Regrettable—but seemingly not much of a deterrent to the excitement and success of the rest of The Strip.

[A 4a.] Originally **Condict Building (lofts)**/later **Bayard Building,** 65 Bleecker St., bet. Broadway and Lafayette St., opp. Crosby St. N side. 1898. Louis Sullivan and Lyndon P. Smith. ★

This was a radical building in its time, a direct confrontation with the architectural establishment that had embraced American Renaissance architecture after the **Columbian Exposition** (Chicago World's Fair) of **1893. Sullivan,** the principal philosopher and leading designer of the Chicago School, was the employer and teacher of **Frank Lloyd Wright** (who referred to him romantically as *lieber Meister*). The sextet of angels supporting the cornice was added, over Sullivan's objections but still by his hand, at the request of his client, **Silas Alden Condict.** The building had little influence in New York for, as Carl Condit wondered, "Who would expect an aesthetic experience on Bleecker Street?"

Return to Broadway.

[A 4b.] Originally **Manhattan Savings Institution Building**/now **residential lofts,** 644 Broadway, NE cor. Bleecker St. 1889. Stephen D. Hatch. Restored, 1987.

A great rock-cut brownstone, terra-cotta, and brick heap (with cast-iron trim) finally **recognized for its quality**—and **restored**—after many years of neglect.

The Blue Willow Café, 644 Broadway, NE cor. Bleecker St.

A soigné restaurant that brought confidence back to **No. 644,** long before restoration began.

[A 5a.] **670 Broadway**/originally **Brooks Brothers store,** NE cor. Bond St. 1874. George E. Harney.

A romantic rosé brick and granite commercial structure at the 3rd of 5 **sequential locations** of Brooks Brothers. Eastlakian (after **Charles Eastlake,** one of the 19th century's most ornate designers). The only thing it needs now is the restoration of its ravaged entry.

Turn right on Bond Street.

[A 5b.] **1-5 Bond Street (apartments)**/originally **Robbins & Appleton Building,** SE cor. Shinbone Alley, bet. Broadway and Lafayette St. 1880. Stephen D. Hatch. ★

Capped by a great Second Empire mansard roof and dormers are 5 generous stories of creamy, elegant Corinthian cast iron and glass. The building was originally used for the **manufacture of watch cases.** Mmmm, all that north light.

Turn left onto Lafayette Street. Take a quick detour on Great Jones Street, and then resume your northerly walk on Lafayette.

[A 6.] Engine Company No. 33, N.Y.C. Fire Department, 44 Great Jones St., bet. the Bowery and Lafayette St. N side. 1898. Flagg & Chambers. ★

A huge concave Beaux Arts arch, influenced by **Louis XV's taste** and bearing a cartouche, is the substance of this wonderful Ernest Flagg facade. Once the fire chief's headquarters.

[A 5a.] 670 Bway., once Brooks Bros.   **[A 5b.]** One Bond Street apartments

[A 6.] Engine Co. No. 33, N.Y.F.D.   **[A 7a.]** 376–380 Lafayette in 1966

[A 7a.] 376-380 Lafayette Street (lofts), NW cor. Great Jones St. 1888. Henry J. Hardenbergh.

Designed by the architect of the Dakota and the Plaza Hotel, this **free-swinging** Romanesque Revival work is a rich addition to the area's architecture. From bottom (the polished **granite dwarf columns—** though dimmed by paint) to top (the richly decorative cornice), it's a gem.

[A 7b.] Originally **Mission of the Immaculate Virgin (Roman Catholic),** 381 Lafayette St., bet. Great Jones and E. 4th Sts. E side. ca. 1880.

A composition in red. Note particularly the shell-molded window sills and the **arched corbel table** cornice, rare for its depth on so small a structure.

[A 7c.] Tower Records, 692 Broadway, SE cor. E. 4th St. through to SW cor. Lafayette St. Store, 1983, Buttrick White & Burtis.

After its California parent company had built three dozen units elsewhere in the world, they were ready to brave New York's rigorous competition. As a result of that courageous full-block-deep decision (noise, music, neon, noise) came the establishment (or at least the stabilization) along Broadway below 8th Street of **"the scene"**—the mecca for punk rockers, **Mohawk-topped** young men and **Day-Glo-topped** young women, both the indigenous variety (Manhattan-based) and the regional emigrants from Brooklyn, Queens, and New Jersey, called **Bs & Ts** (Bridges & Tunnels).

Nearby on East 4th Street:

Turn right (east) on East 4th for an interesting detour.

[A 8a.] Old Merchants House of New York, Inc./formerly **Seabury Tredwell residence/**originally **Joseph Brewster residence,** 29 E. 4th St., bet. the Bowery and Lafayette St. 1832. Restored, Joseph Roberto. ★ Interior ★ . **Open to the public—limited hours.**

A relic from New York's Federal past, when blocks surrounding this spot had houses of equal quality. The house and its early interior furnishings derive from Tredwell's daughter who lived here **for 93 years,** until 1933. It has been open to the public since 1936.

[A 8a.] Old Merchants House of N.Y.   **[A 8b.]** Orig. S.T. Skidmore residence

[A 8c.] A tenement at 34 E. 4th: sheet metal cornices, terra-cotta capitals

[A 8b.] Originally **Seabury Tredwell Skidmore residence,** 37 E. 4th St., bet. the Bowery and Lafayette St. 1844. ★

Greek Revival. Those Ionic columns are unequaled in this vintage.

[A 8c.] 34 and **36 East 4th Street (tenements),** bet. the Bowery and Lafayette Sts. ca. 1885.

Twin structures with a **joyful abundance** of 3-dimensional tinplate cornice ornament that's hard to match anywhere in the city.

Back to Lafayette.

Lafayette Street: Between East 4th Street and Astor Place.

[A 9a.] Originally **DeVinne Press Building,** 399 Lafayette St., NE cor. E. 4th St. 1885. Babb, Cook & Willard. ★

Roman brickwork worthy of the Roman Forum's **Basilica of Constantine.** The waterfront of Brooklyn is graced with the poor country cousins (the Empire Stores) of this magnificent pile. Certainly this is a sample of "less is more"—especially when juxtaposed with (and compared to) **No. 376-380** down the block [A 7a.].

[A 9b.] 401 Lafayette Street (lofts). E side. ca. 1885. **[A 9c.]** 400 Lafayette Street (lofts). NW cor. E. 4th St. ca. 1885.

Two different, very wonderful loft structures from the great era of Lafayette Street's expansion.

[A 10b.] Colonnade Row (1966 photo)   [A 9a.] Orig. DeVinne Press in 1966

[A 9d.] 409 Lafayette Street (lofts). E side. 1891. Alfred Zucker. Restored, 1987.

Ornate cast-iron and brick Romanesque Revival. The 3 freestanding columns—interspersed with those engaged—form a virile base.

[A 10a.] Public Theater/formerly **HIAS Hebrew Immigrant Aid Society/**originally **Astor Library,** 425 Lafayette St., bet. E. 4th St. and Astor Place. E side. 1853–1881. South wing, 1853, Alexander Saeltzer. Center section, 1859, Griffith Thomas. North wing, 1881, Thomas Stent. Conversion into theater complex, 1967–1976, Giorgio Cavaglieri. ★

A funky, generously scaled red brick and brownstone building, considered by some to be the finest American example of *Rundbogenstil,* a German variant of Romanesque Revival. **John Jacob Astor** here contributed New York's first free library, later combined with its peers **(Lenox Library,** which was sited where the Frick Collection is today; and the **Tilden Foundation)** to form the central branch of **The New York Public Library** at 42nd Street. These are the theaters of **Joseph Papp,** whose outdoor Shakespeare Festival in Central Park made these its indoor habitat.

[A 10b.] Originally **Colonnade Row/**a.k.a. **LaGrange Terrace,** 428-434 Lafayette St., W side. Attributed to Seth Geer. 1833. ★

Four of nine houses built speculatively by **Seth Geer** in 1833. Five at the south end were demolished for the still existing Wanamaker Annex [see A 14.]. An elegant urban arrangement of private structures subordinated to an imposing Corinthian colonnade (compare the **Rue de Rivoli** or the **Place des Vosges** in Paris). **Delanos, Astors,** and

Vanderbilts lived here, until their game of social musical chairs sent them uptown.

[A 10c.] 440, 442 Lafayette Street (lofts). W side. ca. 1875.

Vigorous architecture of the 19th century's last quarter.

Along Astor Place on the left; then return.

[A 11a.] Originally **Astor Place Building, O. B. Potter Trust,** 444 Lafayette St., SW cor. Astor Place. 1876. Griffith Thomas.

Brick and painted cast-iron **eclectic Eastlake.** Its street floor now houses:

[A 11b.] Astor Wines & Spirits, 12 Astor Place., SW cor. Lafayette St. Store, 1978, Beyer Blinder Belle.

Breathless but appropriate store design for a longtime fixture in this area.

[A 11c.] Conran's (designer home furnishings), 10 Astor Place, bet. Lafayette St. and Broadway. 1982. Gibbons, Heidtmann & Salvador, architects. The Conran Design Group, designers.

One of Terence Conran's worldwide chain of life-style furniture and fittings emporia.

[A 11d.] Originally **Mercantile Library Building**/now **District 65 Building (Distributive Workers of America),** 13 Astor Place, NW cor. Lafayette St. to E. 8th St. 1890. George E. Harney.

Harney's ode to Ruskin at 670 Broadway [see A 5a.], 16 years earlier, is here augmented by establishment Harney.

The District 65 Building rests on the site of the Astor Place Opera House, where in **May 1849** rioting between competing claques of the American actor Edwin Forrest and the English actor William Macready caused the death of 34 stalwarts. The Seventh Regiment National Guard, quartered in an armory then on the present site of Cooper Union's Hewitt building, quelled the passions forcibly.

In the large open space crisscrossed by traffic and frequently the center of a sidewalk flea market:

[A 12a.] "Alamo" (sculpture), on traffic island, Astor Place/E. 8th St./Lafayette St./Fourth Ave. 1966, installed 1967. Bernard "Tony" Rosenthal, sculptor.

Installed as part of a giant but temporary citywide exhibition, "Sculpture in the Environment," *Alamo* was made permanent through a gift to the City by a private donor. A **giant steel cube** "en pointe," it pivots (with some difficulty) and has become **a beloved fixture** in these parts, much as the subway kiosk had been prior to its initial removal [see below].

[A 12b.] Astor Place Subway Station, IRT Lexington Avenue Line, below Lafayette St. and Fourth Ave. at Astor Place. 1904. Heins & La Farge. ★ Restored, 1985, Prentice & Chan, Ohlhausen. Milton Glaser, artist. **[A 12c.] Astor Place subway kiosk.** Replica, 1985, Prentice & Chan, Ohlhausen.

One of the city's best subway station restorations, particularly the integration of new ceramic tiles to **harmonize** with the **glass wall tile** and **mosaic tesserae** of the original. Glaser's abstract murals are **true works of art.** But **best of all** is architect Ohlhausen's new **(yes, brand new!) kiosk** up top, which begins to remedy the Transit Authority's disastrous decision to scrap **all** the IRT kiosks. The new kiosk was cast using new wood patterns developed from Heins & La Farge drawings submitted to the **Hecla Iron Works** in Williamsburg, Brooklyn, the original fabricators. (Both Ohlhausen and Glaser are grads of Cooper Union across the street.)

The Cooper Union for the Advancement of Science and Art

[A 13.] Cooper Union Foundation Building, E. 7th St. to Astor Place, Fourth Ave. to the Bowery, at Cooper Sq. 1859. Frederick A. Peterson. ★ Interior reconstructed, 1975, John Hejduk.

A high-rise brownstone, **Cooper Union** is the oldest extant building framed with steel beams in America. **Peter Cooper,** its founder and a benefactor in the great Victorian paternalistic tradition (he gave presents to Cooper Union on his birthday), was a partner of **Samuel F. B. Morse** in laying the first Atlantic cable and was the builder of the **Tom Thumb steam locomotive;** also an iron maker, he rolled the first steel railroad rails. Such rails were used by Cooper as beams, spanning brick bearing walls. In turn, brick floor arches jumped between rail and rail. The facade is in the **Italianate brownstone** tradition popular at the time with cast-iron designers, but heavier-handed, as it is in masonry except at the ground floor.

The remodeling is almost entirely internal, with simultaneous conservation of **Peterson's** brownstone facade, and fulfillment of **Cooper's** original designs: a round elevator finally rides in his clairvoyantly round shaft.

[A 13.] The steam-powered Third Avenue el clatters past Cooper Union in 1882

[A 13a.] **Peter Cooper monument,** in Cooper Sq. S of E. 7th St. 1897. Augustus Saint-Gaudens, sculptor; Stanford White, architect of the base.

Cooper seated in front of his benefaction.

The Bowery, popularly known as a skid row populated by "bums," is much more complex than that. South from Cooper Square to Canal Street the vista includes the center of commercial kitchen-equipment distribution for New York, and one of the city's principal lighting-fixture sales places. Gentrification is slowly but surely wiping out the street's "hotels" (flophouses to some), resting places of the unwanted, the alcoholic, the derelict. Panhandlers, however, still abound.

East Village: For the area to the east, begining at Third Avenue, including the St. Mark's Place corridor, McSorley's, and Alphabetville, see the next section, East Village.

Resume the northward walk, this time along Fourth Avenue.

[A 14.] Originally **Wanamaker Department Store Annex,** Fourth Ave. bet. E. 8th and E. 9th Sts. to Broadway. 1904. Addition, 1907. Both by D. H. Burnham.

The annex, in this case, was **considerably larger** than the main store, originally A. T. Stewart & Company (*John Kellum, 1862*) on the block to the north: almost as much space in this stolid 15-story monolith as in the 102 floors of the Empire State Building. The main store **occupied a full block** in **Italianate cast iron,** was arranged around a skylighted central court, and offered the most gracious shopping space in New York, very much in the European tradition. The only **Ladies Mile** survivor to continue in business, it finally closed in 1954 and was consumed in a conflagration two years later.

A left on East 10th Street to Broadway, and then a right.

[A 15a.] Pizza Piazza, 785 Broadway, SW cor. E. 10th St. 1982. Charles Boxenbaum.

A particularly personable Post Modern pizza palazzo.

[A 15b.] Grace Church (Episcopal) and **Rectory,** 800, 804 Broadway, at E. 10th St. E side. 1845, 1846, respectively. James Renwick, Jr. Original wood steeple replaced in marble, 1888. ★ Front garden, 1881, Vaux & Co., landscape architects.

A magnificent Gothic Revival church, **designed by an engineer** who studied the copybooks of the **Pugins,** the great English Gothic Revival theorists and detailers. At the bend of Broadway, its tower dominates the vista from the south. One of the city's greatest treasures, together with its related buildings on Broadway and Fourth Avenue.

[A 12c.] Astor Place IRT subway kiosk   **[A 15b.]** Renwick's Grace Ch. (1845)

[A 15c.] "The Renwick" (apartments)/originally **808 Broadway (lofts),** opp. E. 11th St. 1888. Renwick, Aspinwall & Russell. Converted.

A Gothic Revival wall forms a visual backdrop for Grace Church, built 43 years after the church's completion by Renwick's successor firm.

If the Grace Church complex is to your liking you may wish to retrace your steps to Fourth Avenue to see the remainder. The tour continues up Broadway.

[A 15d.] The Grace Church Houses: [A 15e.] The Clergy House, 92 Fourth Ave., bet. E. 10th and E. 12th Sts. W side. 1892. Heins & La Farge. ★ **[A 15f.] Grace Memorial House/Huntington House,** 94-96 Fourth Ave. 1883. James Renwick, Jr. ★ **[A 15g.] Neighborhood House,** 98 Fourth Ave. 1907. Renwick, Aspinwall & Tucker. ★

A trio in the Gothic Revival tradition established by the elder Renwick at Grace Church on the Broadway side of the block. **Endangered** in the 1970s for improvements to the school, the **facades were finally saved.** In this case landmark designation *followed* the threat of loss.

[A 16a.] The Cast Iron Building (apartments)/originally **James McCreery Dry Goods Store,** 67 E. 11th St., NW cor. Broadway. 1868. John Kellum. Converted, 1971, Stephen B. Jacobs. **[A 16b.] 49 East 12th Street (apartments)/**formerly **St. George Hotel,** bet. Broadway and University Place. Converted, 1977, Stephen B. Jacobs.

Two buildings converted to apartments. The old McCreery's cast-iron Corinthian columns and almost endless arches both **enrich** and **discipline** the facade—though concern for historic preservation waned at the upper stories. The old hotel is an interesting array of windows and half-round exit balconies whose reused old brick gives it the look of a slice of salami.

Booksellers' Row:

Fourth Avenue and Broadway from Astor Place to Union Square.

Once upon a time—and well into the 1960s—**both sides** of Fourth Avenue and parts of Broadway and the side streets were lined with used bookshops of all descriptions, beginning at **Bible House** (which occupied the site of Cooper Union's Engineering Building) and stretching almost all the way to **S. Klein's on the Square** (the cut-rate department store whose site is now occupied by Zeckendorf Towers). Books were displayed both within the shops and on racks along the street—a browser's delight, particularly in balmy weather. Alas, the number of shops today is **reduced to a handful,** dominated by giant **Strand Book Store,** at 828 Broadway, on the northeast corner of East 12th Street, where books are displayed on shelves that stretch on street floor and basement (and for aficionados elsewhere) for miles.

[A 17a.] 829-831 Broadway (lofts), bet. E. 12th and E. 13th Sts. ca. 1855.

A truly magnificent pair of Italianate business buildings fashioned in **marble,** patterns for the **later cast-iron** structures that picked up the elegant neo-Renaissance style and details imported from England.

[A 16a.] John Kellum's James McCreery store, an early apartment conversion

[A 17b.] Roosevelt Building (lofts), 841 Broadway, NW cor. E. 13th St. 1893. Stephen D. Hatch.

Despite the mutilated ground floor, the upper parts of the sandstone and brick edifice offer a majestic expression of Romanesque Revival. Named Roosevelt **after Cornelius,** Teddy's grandfather, who lived on the block in midcentury, when Union Square was **The** place to reside.

Turn east on East 13th Street and south on Fourth Avenue to East 11th Street; then left.

East 11th Street between Third and Fourth Avenues

A gold mine of public buildings.

[A 18a.] Originally **Webster Hall**/later **Casa Galicia, O Noso Lar/**and **The Ritz (rock and roll club)** 119 E. 11th St., bet. Third and Fourth Aves. N side. 1886. Charles Rentz.

An 1880s dance hall, turned into a 1930s ballroom, blaring 1980s music. A center of **slam dancing** in the mid 1980s.

[A 18b.] Originally **St. Ann's Parochial School**/later **Delehanty Institute (school),** now **apartments,** 117 E. 11th St., bet. Third and Fourth Aves. N side. 1870.

A dignified dark red brick and terra-cotta institutional building that has seen many uses.

[A 18c.] Originally **N.Y.C. Department of Public Charities & Correction,** 66 Third Ave., NW cor. E. 11th St. 1871.

Look carefully. It's hard to believe this was once a municipal office structure. But the monumental proportions of a one-story building that once carried an impressive one-story mansard roof send out the proper pretentious signals, especially to the residents *in those days* of a poorer part of town.

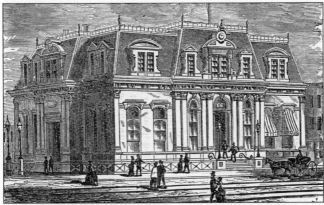

[A 18c.] N.Y.C. Dept. of Public Charities & Correction linked poverty and crime

Left on Third Avenue and left again on East 12th Street.

[A 19a.] St. Ann's Shrine Armenian Catholic Cathedral/originally 12th Street Baptist Church/later Temple Emanu-El (synagogue)/later St. Ann's Roman Catholic Church, 120 E. 12th St., bet. Third and Fourth Aves. ca. 1847.

Yes, this structure exemplified ecumenism long before it became an everyday word. It was Temple Emanu-El between 1856 and 1868.

[A 19b.] Originally **New York Edison Company Building,** 115 E. 12th St., bet. Third and Fourth Aves. 1896. Buchman & Deisler.

From before consolidation, when N.Y. Ed became Con Ed and moved north to 14th. Missing its cornice.

Right on Fourth Avenue.

[A 19c.] Hancock Building, 125 Fourth Ave., bet. E. 12th and E. 13th Sts. E side. 1897. Marsh, Israels & Harder.

Once the home of Hammacher Schlemmer, the gadget store.

Right on East 13th Street.

[A 20a.] Originally **Kearney & Van Tassel Auction Stables,** 130 E. 13th St., bet. Third and Fourth Aves. 1889. D. & J. Jardine. **[A 20b.]** Annex, 128 E. 13th St. 1904. Jardine, Kent & Jardine.

Old horse auction rooms—the ornament makes references. Inside, an enormous space that would hold a blimp.

Look left.

[A 20c.] Variety Photoplays (movie theater), 110-112 Third Ave., bet. E. 13th and E. 14th Sts. W side. ca. 1900.

Some say this is the city's **oldest movie house.** Its marquee of both neon and incandescent lights is a cultural monument of another time and is irreplaceable.

Kiehl's Pharmacy, 109 Third Ave., bet. E. 13th and E. 14th Sts. E side. Building, 1836. Extended upward, 1987.

Everything in homeopathic remedies—short of witchcraft, that is. A fascinating place to visit.

END of Tour. The nearest subways are at Union Square, at East 14th Street, between Fourth Avenue and Broadway: 14th Street/Union Square Station (IRT Lexington Avenue Line and BMT Broadway Line).

EAST VILLAGE

The East Village is an area of **vivid contrasts.** Around St. Mark's-in-the-Bowery Church is evidence of an 18th- and 19th-century aristocracy. But elsewhere the area reveals quite a different social history.

Along St. Mark's Place, 7th, and 6th Sts. is evidence of a 19th-century **German community.** Beginning late in that century, population from the crowded Lower East Side was squeezed northward into the precinct generally lying between East Houston and East 14th Streets, which **also began to assume the name** Lower East Side, like that of the neighborhood to the south. The area became heavy with **eastern European** poulations, **both Jewish and Gentile.** To this day, favored Ukrainian and Polish dishes are still to be found in local restaurants. (On the other hand, most of the kosher delicatessens are gone.) Around First Avenue and East 11th Street the gustatorial remnants of an **Italian community** are evident and are being rediscovered. And McSorley's recalls the day of many other Irish saloons.

In the 1960s the area assumed the name East Village as a result of the incursion of **hippies** and **flower children** from the relatively expensive (and Establishment bohemian) Greenwich Village. The major point of entry was through **the St. Mark's Place corridor,** which led to Tompkins Square Park, to cheap tenement apartments, and to crash pads as far east as **Alphabetville,** where Manhattan's north-south avenues assume letters, rather than numbers.

This area today, between Avenues A and D, is **heavily Hispanic** in population and has been dubbed **Loisaida** (pronounced low-ees-SIDE-ah), the Puerto Rican pronunciation of **Lower East Side.** While this is an area **heavy with poverty,** there is nevertheless evidence that rubble-strewn lots, once packed with tenements, are **being eyed by speculators** as housing in Manhattan becomes ever more scarce.

CBGB (rock and roll club), 315 Bowery, near Bleecker St. E side.

Celebrated in histories of rock as the birthplace of punk. A long dark narrow bar where new rock groups perform. OMFUG.

 [E 1.] Bouwerie Lane Theatre/originally **Atlantic Savings Bank Building/**later **Bond Street Savings Bank Building,** 330 Bowery, NW cor. Bond St. 1874. Henry Engelbert. ★

A more intricate composition of columns than on most cast-iron buildings.

Odds and evens: Here, in these single-digit precincts of Manhattan's grid, the customary placement of odd and even house numbers is reversed. On both 1st and 2nd Streets the even numbers are on the north side; the odd numbers on the south—contrary to the pattern followed elsewhere in the grid.

[E 2a.] New York Marble Cemetery, interior of the block bet. E. 2nd and E. 3rd Sts., Second Ave., and the Bowery. Entrance on Second Ave. bet. E. 2nd and E. 3rd Sts., W side. ★ **Not open to the public.**

One of the earliest sophistications of burial practices, anticipating, and therefore preventing, a marble orchard; the **interred are noted by tablets** inlaid in the perimeter brick wall. [Also see E 3a.]

[E 2b.] Church of the Nativity (Roman Catholic), 46 Second Ave., bet. E. 2nd and E. 3rd Sts. E side. 1970.

A **modern architectural cartoon exhibiting a gross** idea without detail. It replaces an elegant 1832 Greek Revival building by Town & Davis that was demolished in 1970. Security grilles further detract.

[E 2c.] Provenzano Lanza Funeral Home/originally **Engel Building (lofts),** 43 Second Ave., bet. E. 2nd and E. 3rd Sts. ca. 1925.

Distinguished by its slender form and the tiers of industrial steel sash windows that rise up from Second Avenue.

[E 3a.] New York City Marble Cemetery, 52-74 E. 2nd St., bet. First and Second Aves. N side. 1832. ★ **Not open to the public.**

President **James Monroe** was briefly interred in this, one of two remaining cemeteries (also interred: Mayor Isaac Varian, shipping merchant Preserved Fish, financier Moses Taylor, book collector James Lenox, and James Henry Roosevelt, founder of Roosevelt Hospital) in a part of town that contained many cemeteries in the 1830s and 1840s. [See also E 2a.]

[E 3b.] Protection of the Holy Virgin Cathedral (Russian Orthodox Church in America)/originally **Mt. Olivet Memorial Church,** 59 E. 2nd St., bet. First and Second Aves. S side.

Russian Orthodox only since 1943. Mushy rock-cut limestone.

[E 3c.] The 63 East 2nd Street apts.   **[E 1.]** Bouwerie Lane Theatre in 1966

[E 3c.] 63 East 2nd Street (apartments), bet. First and Second Aves. S side. ca. 1860.

Mt. Olivet's Italianate church rectory now converted to apartments. The generously curvilear wrought-iron fire escapes echo the generous proportions of Victorian matrons.

[E 4.] Originally Public School 79, Manhattan, 38 E. 1st St., bet. First and Second Aves. N side. ca. 1886.

Like so many of the nearby tenements whose occupants it once served (it is no longer a school) this is an ornamented red brick and terra-cotta "high-rise" walk-up. Our legs hurt.

[E 5.] Originally Rectory, St. Nicholas Roman Catholic Church/now **apartments,** 135 E. 2nd St., bet. First Ave. and Avenue A. 1867.

An essay in late Gothic Revival mannerism. Swell stone trim around the tiers of pointed arch windows. Note the silhouette of the demolished church on the old rectory's west wall. Palimpsest.

[E 6a.] Originally Bowery Branch, YMCA/now **N.Y.C. Men's Shelter,** 6-20 E. 3rd St., bet. the Bowery and Second Ave. ca. 1915.

Opened to relieve the pressure on the earlier Bowery outpost at the Young Men's Institute [see L Manhattan/Chinatown-Little Italy L 23]. Now an ill-maintained municipal shelter for homeless men.

[E 6b.] Formerly **New York Turn Verein**/originally **Primary School No. 6,** 15 E. 3rd St., bet. the Bowery and Second Ave. ca. 1875.

Vacant, but the sign of this German-American gymnasts' organization is still legible. Note the deeply modeled hood molds over the windows.

[E 6c.] **30-38 East 3rd Street (row houses),** SW cor. Second Ave. ca. 1830.

Five wonderful relics, particularly **No. 36.**

[E 7.] **67 East 3rd Street (apartments),** bet. First and Second Aves. 1987. Ted Reeds Assocs.

Clear Post Modern evidence of gentrification in these poorer parts. (This is the Hell's Angels' block, incidentally.)

[E 8a.] **Ageloff Towers (apartments),** 141 E. 3rd St., NW cor. Avenue A. 180 East 4th St. SW cor. Avenue A. 1929. Shampan & Shampan.

The massive size of this apartment pair offers some indication that developers thought the Roaring Twenties would make a silk purse even out of the Lower East Side. Needless to say, it didn't. Some charming sculptural detail remains.

[E 8b.] **First Houses, N.Y.C. Housing Authority,** 29-41 Avenue A, SW cor. E. 3rd St., 112-138 E. 3rd St., bet. First Ave. and Avenue A. Reconstructed into public housing, 1935, Frederick L. Ackerman. ★

The first houses built, or rather **rebuilt** in this instance, by the City's housing authority. In a block of tenements every third was demolished, allowing the remaining pairs light and air on three sides. This, as a remodeling, and **Williamsburg Houses** [see N Brooklyn W 24.], as new construction, are still the brightest lights in the history of this city's **early** public housing. Walk through the urbane cobbled and tree-filled space behind.

[E 9.] **Most Holy Reedemer Roman Catholic Church and Rectory,** 161-165 E. 3rd St., bet. Avenue A and Avenue B. ca. 1905.

A stiff, high-collared limestone edifice which is among the tallest structures (except for the **"projects"**) in the community.

[E 10.] **NENA Comprehensive Health Service Center, Northeast Neighborhood Association,** 279 E. 3rd St., bet. Avenue C and Avenue D. 1976. Edelman & Salzman.

The facade of this multistory health center enjoys the monumentality once reserved for cathedrals. Within, the spaces (and the muted color scheme) establish a scale more **appropriate to community health care.**

Note that the picture windows are "glazed" in transparent polycarbonate plastic sheets (which have high impact resistance to vandals' missiles). Ordinary glass in adjacent tenements fares considerably less well.

Forming the "International": Tinned-over windows and a storefront glued together with handbills and posters conceal the history of the former Labor Lyceum, at 64 East 4th Street, between the Bowery and Second Avenue. It was here on June 3, 1900, that the United Brotherhood of Cloakmakers of New York and Vicinity convened with their far-flung brethren (from Philadelphia, Baltimore, Newark, and Brownsville) to form the International Ladies' Garment Workers Union.

[E 11.] Formerly **Industrial National Bank Building,** 72 Second Ave., NE cor. E. 4th St. ca. 1926.

Polychromed Art Deco terra-cotta walls and original name still evident atop the south wall.

[E 12a.] Formerly **Isaac T. Hopper residence,** 110 Second Ave., bet. E. 6th and E. 7th Sts. E side. 1839.

A very grand Greek Revival town house. The **"wayward" girls** (as **Horatio Alger** would have called them) are no longer behind the Italianate door. (They tend, rather, to be found on the outside, in this marginal area trying to cope with a significant drug scene.)

[E 12b.] Middle Collegiate Church (Reform), 112-114 Second Ave., bet. E 6th and E 7th Sts. E side. 1892. S. B. Reed. **[E 12c.]** Originally **Middle Collegiate Church, Church House,** 50 E. 7th St., bet. First and Second Aves. ca. 1910.

The church is rock-faced granite dressed with smooth, from the **sidewalk** to the **very tip of the spire.** All windows are by Tiffany. The old church house is neo-Romanesque.

[E 13.] Community Synagogue, Max D. Raiskin Center/originally **St. Mark's Lutheran Evangelical Church,** 323 E. 6th St., bet. 1st and 2nd Aves. 1848.

It was the German immigrant parishioners of St. Mark's who boarded the *General Slocum,* in June 1904 for that ill-fated excursion which **cost over 1,000 lives,** as the ship caught fire just after passing through the Hell Gate. It has been a synagogue **since 1940.**

Indo-Pak restaurant row: Between First and Second Avenues, the south side of East 6th Street is lined with a phalanx of restaurants serving different versions of the cuisine of the Indian subcontinent. Reading from W to E: Passage to India, Taj, Rose of India, Balaka, Bombay Dining, Ronana, Calcutta, Kismoth, Sonali, Shah Bagh (the first to take up residence), Panna, Nishan, Mitali East, AnarBagh, Ganges, Prince of India. (Some say that despite the 16 entrances there's only *one* kitchen.)

Leshko Coffee Shop (restaurant), 111 Avenue A, NW cor. E. 7th St.

Polish cooking in a formica setting. Try the *pierogi,* available either boiled or fried, filled with meat, potatoes, or sauerkraut.

[E 14.] Tompkins Square Park/originally **Tompkins Square,** E. 7th to E. 10th Sts., Avenue A to Avenue B. 1834.

Another **English** (Bloomsbury) park surrounded by high-density, low-rise housing. Sixteen blessed acres in these tight and dense streets. One day, when this area is rebuilt, this mature park will be a godsend.

[E 14a.] St. Nicholas Carpatho-Russian Orthodox Greek Catholic Church/originally **St. Mark's Memorial Chapel,** 288 E. 10th St., SW cor. Avenue A. 1883. James Renwick, Jr. and W. H. Russell.

Gothic Revival in exuberant red brick and matching terra-cotta.

[E 15.] 171 First Avenue (lofts), bet. E. 10th and E. 11th Sts. W side. ca. 1880.

Outcast 4-story cast iron. A wonderful surprise.

[E 16.] Evangelical Christian Church/originally **People's Home Church and Settlement (Methodist Episcopal),** 545 E. 11th St., bet Avenues A and B. 1868.

Italianate brick, simple but with great oversize details.

[E 17a.] Originally **Christodora House (settlement house)**/now **Christodora House (apartments),** 1 Tompkins Sq. a.k.a. 145 Avenue B, NE cor. E. 9th St. 1928. Henry C. Pelton. Conversion, 1987, John T. Fifeld Assocs.

Peering over the **low-rise** East Village is this **brooding tower** that has seen almost as many lives as the proverbial cat. In its original 3rd-floor concert hall **George Gershwin** gave his first public recital. **Beautifully detailed** brick and stone in a transition between neo-Classical and Art Deco.

[E 17b.] Originally **Tompkins Square Lodging House for Boys and Industrial School, Children's Aid Society a.k.a. Newsboys' and Bootblacks' Lodging House**/later **Talmud Torah Darch Moam**/now **apartments,** 127 Avenue B, NE cor. E. 8th Sts. a.k.a. 295 E. 8th St. 1887.

Vaux & Radford. **[E 18a.]** Originally **6th Street Industrial School, Children's Aid Society/**later **Sloane Children's Center/**now **Trinity Lower East Side Parish and Shelter (Lutheran),** 630 E. 6th St., bet. Avenues B and C. 1890. Vaux & Radford.

Two of a series of industrial schools/lodging houses to which **Calvert Vaux** turned his **attention** and **considerable talent** after his Central Park–Prospect Park days were behind him.

Pyramid (rock and roll club), 101 Avenue A, bet. 6th and 7th Sts. W side.

What CBGB once was.

[E 18b.] Originally **Congregation Ahavath Yeshurun Shara Torah (Love of Israel, Gates of the Torah)/**later **Iglesia de Dios,** 638 E. 6th St., bet. Avenues B and C. 1898. **[E 18c.] Stone House in Lower Manhattan (apartments)/**originally **Congregation Beth Hamedrash Hagodol Anshe Ungarn (Great House of Study of the People of Hungary),** 242 E. 7th St., bet. Avenues C and D. 1905. Converted, 1986.

Built as *shtiblech,* tiny synagogues, their embellished exteriors remain as a reminder of what once was.

[E 19.] Lower East Side Infill Housing II (apartments), N.Y.C. Housing Authority, along parts of E. 4th, E. 5th, and E. 6th Sts., bet. Avenues B, C, and D. 1987. Vitto & Oaklander.

Pink, bubble gum-colored, 3-story **turnkey housing** that was meant to help relieve the severe housing shortage for low-income families. It makes the surviving tenements nearby look better and better—at least as far as the quality of their facades is concerned.

 [E 20.] Riis Houses Plaza, within **Jacob Riis Houses, N.Y.C. Housing Authority,** E. 6th to E. 10th Sts., Avenue D to Franklin D. Roosevelt Dr. Plaza, 1966. Pomerance & Breines, architects. M. Paul Friedberg, landscape architect. (Housing, 1949.)

This is well worth the trip. Public space, between buildings, is usually filled with either traffic or parked cars, or is grassed and fenced off from the pedestrian. Here space is made available in a construction to delight all ages: pyramids to climb on for the small, an amphitheater that accommodates all age groups, places to **sit, stand, walk, talk, hop, skip, scoot,** and **tag.** Given an asphalt street down the block from a local park, kids will most frequently pick the street to play. Planned as an alternate to streets, Riis is where the action is, in these parts, these days. **A great place.**

Loisaida, pronounced low-ees-**SIDE**-ah, is the term used by the predominantly Puerto Rican community for the real estate lying between Houston and 14th Streets from Avenue A eastward. The term dates from the mid 1970s, and its origin is generally credited to Bimbo Rivas, a local poet and playwright. In 1986, Avenue C was officially given an additional name, Loisaida Avenue. So far, its earlier name has *not* been changed to Avenue Sí.

[E 20a.] San Isidro y San Leandro Orthodox Catholic Church of the Hispanic Rite/originally **Russian Orthodox church,** 345 E. 4th St., bet. Avenues C and D. ca. 1895.

Even more interesting than the corpus of the church building itself are the recent embellishments in a **folk art** idiom: the steeple, the adjacent vacant lot, the **photo-realism mural** skillfully painted on the west wall of **No. 353,** and the rear of the church (visible from East 5th Street's vacant lots).

The St. Marks's Place corridor:

Starting near and along East 7th Street:

[E 21a.] 69 Cooper Square (apartments), on Third Ave. bet. E. 7th St. and St. Mark's Place. E side. 1985. Kudroff Rycar Assocs.

The tiers of fire balconies and dark brick make this an acceptable 6-story neighbor.

[E 21b.] Cooper Square Assembly of God/originally **The Metropolitan Savings Bank,** 59 Third Ave., NE cor. E. 7th St. 1867. Carl Pfeiffer. ★

Marble parallel to the then-current cast-iron world: such material denoted class (cast iron was used to gain elaboration inexpensively). The church use is a happy solution to the problem of preserving a grand old neighborhood friend. Not too old, however: **McSorley's (wonderful) Saloon** down the block is **13** years its senior.

[E 21c.] St. George's Ukrainian Catholic Church, 16-20 E. 7th St., SE cor. Taras Shevchenko Place. 1977. Apollinaire Osadca.

A domed polychromed symbol of the parish's wealth and burgeoning membership: **Atlantic City on 7th Street.** It replaced the real thing—the humbler Greek Revival style St. George's Ruthenian Greek Church, now a parking lot at **Nos. 24-28.**

[E 17a.] The Christadora House apts.   **[E 20a.]** San Isidro y San Leandro

McSorley's Old Ale House/formerly **McSorley's Saloon,** 15 E. 7th St., bet. Cooper Sq. and Second Ave.

Opened in **1854,** the year after construction on **Cooper Union** started, it was made famous by painter **John Sloan** and the *New Yorker* stories by **Joseph Mitchell.** Ale, brewed to their own formula, is sold in pairs of steins. The unisex toilet facilities date back to when this was a male-only retreat. Now co-ed and a college hangout.

The Surma Book and Music Company, 11 E. 7th St., bet. Cooper Sq. and Second Ave.

A fascinating **Ukrainian** store (books, records, decorated Easter eggs) retains the flavor of this old neighborhood's **eastern European society.**

St. Mark's Place, although the standard width (60 feet between building lines) in theory, is actually wider, as most of the buildings are built back from their respective property lines (unusual for Manhattan). Cast-iron stairs once modulated the space, jumping from street to parlor floors as matter-of-fact pop sculpture; scarcely any remain, except for those at **No. 7.** Basement shops of considerable design elegance now line both sides of the street, including those for **dresses, jewelry, beads, buttons,** and **posters.**

[E 22a.] Deutsch-Amerikanische Schuetzen Gesellschaft, 12 St. Mark's Place, bet. Second and Third Aves. 1885. William C. Frohne.

A **German marksmen's club** reveled here and shot elsewhere.

[E 22b.] Originally **Daniel LeRoy residence,** 20 St. Mark's Place, bet. Second and Third Aves. 1832. ★

Greek Revival swings again as the Grassroots Tavern.

[E 23a.] Ottendorfer Branch, New York Public Library/originally **Freie Bibliothek und Lesehalle,** 135 Second Ave., bet. St. Mark's Place and E. 9th St. W side. 1884. William Schickel. ★

Built as a free German public library during the period of heavy German immigration to the surrounding streets. **An architectural confection.**

[E 23b.] Stuyvesant Polyclinic Hospital/formerly **German Poliklinik,** 137 Second Ave., bet. St. Mark's Place and E. 9th St. W side. 1884. William Schickel. ★

Originally the downtown dispensary of the German Hospital (today's Lenox Hill) at Park Avenue and 77th. (It lost its "German" appellation as a result of rampant anti-German feelings during World War I.) The ornate facade of this building has been scrubbed clean of its white paint, revealing a symphony of red masonry.

St. Mark's-in-the-Bowery and northward:

[E 24.] Undergraduate Dormitory, N. Y. U., 33 Third Ave., NE cor. E. 9th St. 1986. Voorsanger & Mills Assocs.

While the tower of the 16-story dorm steps back from a base the height of adjacent 5-story tenements, its **3 colors of brick,** bold square windows, timid cornices, and lack of any small-scale detail (the windows are large and single-paned) make this look like the bully on the block. Will the curved, roofed "aerodrome" that hovers atop the tower become a beloved Third Avenue landmark?

[E 24.] Undergraduate Dorm., N.Y.U.   **[E 25d.]** Orig. Stuyvesant-Fish res.

[E 25.] St. Mark's Historic District and Extension, 21-35 and 42-46 Stuyvesant St., 102-128 and 109-129 E. 10th St., 232 E. 11th St. and St. Mark's-in-the-Bowery Church. ★

This historic district, subdivided and partly developed by Governor Peter Stuyvesant's grandson, includes two landmarks established earlier, St. Mark's and the Stuyvesant-Fish house, as well as the "Renwick" Triangle.

[E 25a.] "Renwick" Triangle, 114-128 E. 10th St., 23-35 Stuyvesant St., bet. Second and Third Aves. 1861. Attributed to James Renwick, Jr. ☆

Buildings with differing plans but uniform facades (within, buildings vary in depth from **16** to **48** feet, in width from **16** to **32** feet) make a handsome grouping, carefully restored by new owners as 1- and 2-family houses. **Stanford White** once lived on the site of **No. 118** in an earlier building (No. 110).

[E 25b.] St. Mark's-in-the-Bowery Church (Episcopal), Second Ave. NW cor. E. 10th St. 1799. Steeple, 1828. Ithiel Town. Cast-iron portico, 1858. ★ ☆ Restored, 1975–1978, The Edelman Partnership. Fire, 1978. Restored, 1978–1984, The Edelman Partnership.

This **Federal** body, **Greek Revival** steeple, and pre-**Civil War** portico stand on the site of a garden chapel of **Peter Stuyvesant's** estate.

The graveyard, containing Stuyvesant's vault, is now remodeled in undulating cobblestones for play purposes.

Frank Lloyd Wright in 1929 produced a design for a group of three apartment towers (one at 18 stories, two at 14 stories) that presaged his later Price Tower in Oklahoma. Commissioned by the rector of St. Mark's-in-the-Bowery, they were to have been shoehorned into the space on either side of and behind the diminutive church—and would have totally overwhelmed it. The onset of the Great Depression scuttled the project . . . thankfully.

[E 25c.] Rectory, St. Mark's-in-the-Bowery Church, 232 E. 11th St., bet. Second and Third Aves. 1900. Ernest Flagg. ☆

A lesser known work of a great architect. Note the cast-iron entrance stair.

[E 25a., b.] "Renwick Triangle," with St. Mark's-in-the-Bowery Ch. in background

---

Governor Peter (Petrus) Stuyvesant's country house sat roughly at the intersection of Tenth and Stuyvesant Streets, just west of Second Avenue. The Bowery was then the Bouwerie (Dutch for "plantation") Road, bounding the southwest flank of the Stuyvesant estate (which extended north to 23rd Street, east to Avenue C, and south to 3rd Street). Stuyvesant Street was the driveway from the Bouwerie Road to the ex-governor's mansion, which was destroyed by fire in 1778.

[E 25d.] Stuyvesant-Fish residence, 21 Stuyvesant St., bet. Second and Third Aves. NW side. 1804. ★ ☆

A fat Federal house, of width unusual for its time, only 5 years younger than the body of St. Mark's down the block. The house was built by Governor Stuyvesant's great-grandson as a wedding gift for his daughter, who was to marry Nicholas Fish—hence its hyphenated name. It suffers from "overrestoration," giving it a bland cast.

Entertainment, Stimuli, and the Full Stomach

To appreciate the buildings and urban design of this—or any—area, the local cuisine and/or artifacts add greatly:

Di Roberti's Pasticceria, 176 First Ave., bet. E. 10th and E. 11th Sts. E side.

A coffeehouse from the Old World. Its interior is surfaced with mosaic tiles worthy of Ravenna. The cappuccino is frothy, the homemade ices are flavorful.

Veniero's Café & Pasticceria, 342 E. 11th St., bet. First and Second Aves.

Only the Italian pastries date from 1894, not the gentrified addition.

The shvitz: Yiddish slang for a steam bath is *shvitz,* literally "sweat." Once the Lower East Side stretching up to 14th Street was home to dozens of traditional Russian-Turkish steam baths. Now there is only one in all five boroughs: the venerable 10th Street Baths at **No. 268.** As much as the steam treatment is a health activity, it is also a night out with the guys, a male bonding event. The ultimate in shvitzing, incidentally, is the platzka, a vigorous soapy scrubbing with a handbrush of oak leaves—"Jewish acupuncture," someone once called it.

[E 26.] Originally **The Yiddish Art Theatre/**later **The Phoenix/**now **Entermedia,** 189 Second Ave., SW cor. E. 12th St. 1926. Harrison G. Wiseman.

This part of Second Avenue was known as "the **Jewish Rialto,** with **close to 20 theaters** staging performances **in Yiddish** in the mid 1920s, when developer Louis N. Jaffe, a devotee of actor Maurice Schwartz, **"Mr. Second Avenue,"** built this theater for him. Like many a synagogue of that era searching for an architectural style, the house is a **neo-Moorish adaptation.** In 1932 I. J. Singer's *Yoshe Kalb* ran for a record 300 performances.

[E 27.] Undergraduate Dormitory, N. Y. U., 77 Third Ave., bet. E. 11th and E. 12th Sts. 1987. Voorsanger & Mills Assocs.

Three connected 14-story towers astride a low base that supposedly strives to simulate the height of adjoining town houses. The desire to fit in is there, but somehow the gray brick composition doesn't quite achieve the goal.

Café Royal, on the SE corner of Second Avenue and East 12th Street, until it closed in 1953, was, according to the *New York Times*'s Richard F. Shepard, "the uncontested artistic and intellectual center of the Yiddish-speaking world in America . . . an enclave where artists, actors and writers came to debate, over endless glasses of tea, the great questions of art that have gone unanswered in every civilized language." It is now a dry cleaner's.

[E 27a.] 201 East 12th Street (apartments), bet. Second and Third Aves. ca. 1880. Converted, 1981, Mullen Palandrani Grossberg.

A beautifully detailed brick mill building (catch the decorative brick arched lintels) today updated with wit for residential uses.

[A 28a.] Formerly **Karl Bitter studio,** 249½ E. 13th St., bet. Second and Third Aves.

Bitter (1867–1915) was sculptor of the figures of *Architecture, Sculpture, Painting, Music* on the Metropolitan Museum entrance, among many well known works. Note his (and a partner's) name carved in stone:

BITTER & MORETTI SCULPTORS

[E 28b.] New York Eye and Ear Infirmary, 218-222 Second Ave., NE cor E. 13th St. 1893. R. W. Gibson.

Careful perusal of the pallid Romanesque Revival building's top will reveal a plaque with date A.D. **1893.** The bottom has been poorly treated by the infirmary and time.

Butch Cassidy of Same & Sundance Kid fame lived (1901) in a boardinghouse run by Mrs. Catherine Taylor at 234 East 12th Street, between Second and Third Avenues.

MIDTOWN MANHATTAN

CHELSEA • FOUR SQUARES • HERALD SQUARE AND WEST
MURRAY HILL • CLINTON • TIMES SQUARE AREA
BRYANT PARK AREA • GRAND CENTRAL/PARK AVENUE
UNITED NATIONS–TURTLE BAY • FIFTH AVENUE
ROCKEFELLER CENTER AREA • CENTRAL PARK SOUTH
THE PLAZA SUITE • EAST 57TH STREET

If Manhattan is **the center of the city,** midtown is **the center of the center.** Here are most of the elements one expects to find in a city core: the **major** railroad and bus stations, the **vast majority** of hotel rooms, the **biggest** stores, the **main** public library and post office. Of the **four principal activities** that have traditionally sustained New York, two— nationwide corporations and the garment industry—are concentrated in midtown. Another of the four, shipping—also historically centered in Midtown—has declined to a point where freight, largely in the form of container shipping, has sought available space elsewhere, in Staten Island and Brooklyn. Transatlantic passenger travel, once cause of **grand experiences of arrival and departure** on West Side piers, has become **almost extinct;** and the new West Side passenger terminal is now a place for catching cruises, rather than a ride to Europe on the *France* or *Michelangelo.* But the **QE2** still stops in occasionally. Only **one** of Manhattan's major commercial activities—the financial center— is concentrated on another part of the island.

Social status in midtown once followed a clear-cut pattern: all the fashionable shops and living quarters ran **up a central spine** along Fifth and Park Avenues and Broadway. But Central Park, by **driving a cleft** between this spine and the Upper West Side, **diverted** fashionable Manhattan **a bit to the east,** and the purposeful development of Park Avenue in the 1920s shifted the weight a bit further, encouraging some colonies of high society to move far to the east, particularly after the demolition of that psychological barrier, the **Third Avenue el,** in 1956. With the construction of the United Nations Headquarters on the East River and its many ancillary and quasi-official satellites and delegations' structures, **a whole new profile** took shape.

CHELSEA

A century and a half of ups and downs has left Chelsea a **patchwork** of town houses, tenements, factories, and housing projects. The name was originally given by **Captain Thomas Clarke** to his estate, staked out in 1750, which extended roughly from the present 19th to 28th Streets, from Eighth Avenue west to the Hudson. The modern place-name covers approximately the same area, with its eastern boundary at Seventh Avenue and its southern one at 14th Street.

Captain Clarke's grandson, **Clement Clarke Moore** (1779–1863), who grew up in the family mansion near the present 23rd Street west of Ninth Avenue, **divided the estate** into lots about 1830. Moore, noted in his time as a **scholar of languages,** is remembered now mainly for his poem "A Visit from Saint Nicholas," which sealed the unscholarly but indestructible **connection** between Saint Nick and Christmas. Moore donated one choice block for the General Theological Seminary, which is still there, and the surrounding blocks prospered as **a desirable suburb.** Then the **Hudson River Railroad** opened along Eleventh Avenue in 1851, attracting slaughterhouses, breweries, and so on, followed quickly by the shanties and tenements of workers.

In 1871 the dignity of town house blocks still unaffected by the railroad was shattered by the steam locomotives of New York's **first**

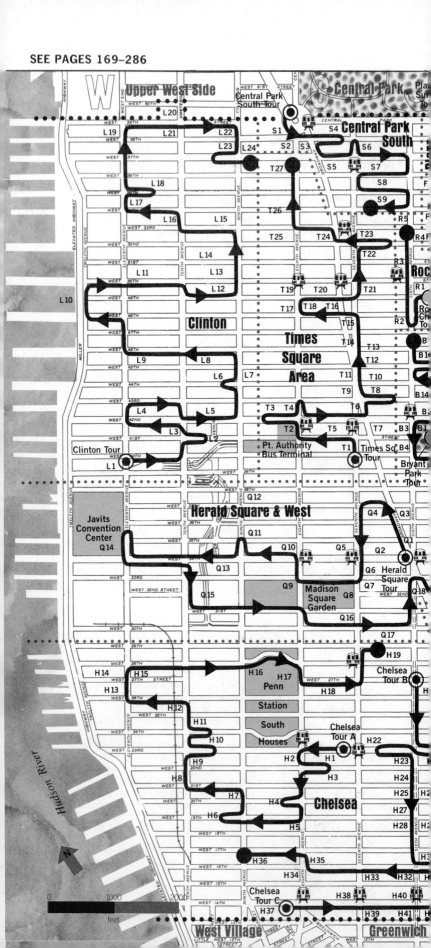

MIDTOWN MANHATTAN

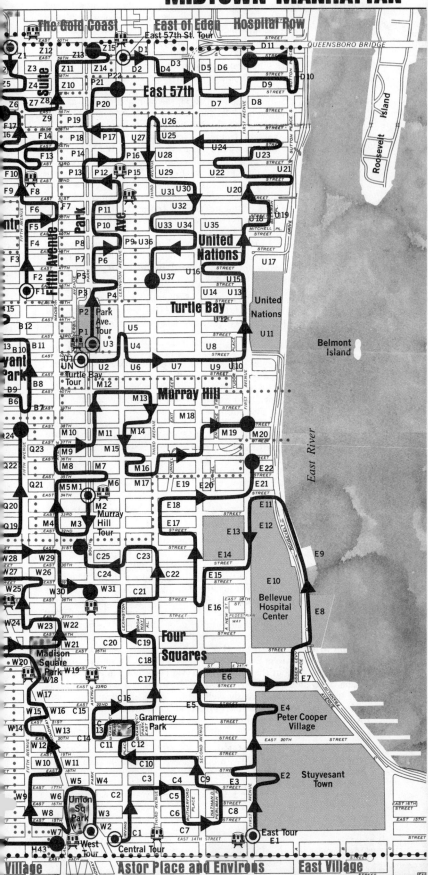

elevated railroad, which ran up **Ninth Avenue.** In the 1870s a declining Chelsea was brightened by the blossoming of the city's **theater district** along West 23rd Street. For a decade or so, these blocks were **ideally convenient** to both the **high society** of Madison Square and the **flourishing vice district** along Sixth Avenue in the upper 20s and 30s. When the theater world moved uptown, artists and literati stayed on to make Chelsea New York's **bohemia;** early in this century bohemia moved south to **Greenwich Village,** but the writers never quite deserted 23rd Street.

Around 1905–1915 a **new art form,** the **motion picture,** was centered in Chelsea, whose old lofts and theaters made economical studios until the sunshine of **Hollywood** lured the industry away. In the 1920s and 1930s Chelsea got a lift from some **impressive new industrial buildings** near the piers and some luxury apartments inland. But the greatest improvements were on the grade-level freight line, long since part of the New York Central, which ran along Eleventh Avenue (there was a Death Avenue Cowboy on horseback, carrying a red flag of warning ahead of each train); it was replaced in 1934 by an inconspicuous **through-the-block** elevated line just west of Tenth Avenue. Just prior to World War II the rattling Ninth Avenue el, the city's first **above-the-streets rapid transit** line, was torn down.

In the 1950s and 1960s public housing and urban renewal **uprooted** large chunks of slum housing, and rehabilitation of Chelsea's many fine town houses followed **a slow upward trend.** By the 1980s **gentrification** had reclaimed almost all the brick and brownstone town houses.

Chelsea Walking Tour A: The heart of Chelsea. START at West 23rd Street W of Seventh Avenue. (Take the the IRT Seventh Avenue Line local or the IND Eighth Avenue Line local to their respective 23rd Street Stations.)

The Grand Opera House stood on the northwest corner of 23rd Street and Eighth Avenue until 1960, when land was cleared for the surrounding Penn Station South. Bought by the notorious financier, impresario, and bon vivant "Jubilee" Jim Fisk in the late 1860s, it did double service as head office of his Erie Railroad. It withstood repeated assaults by irate Erie stockholders (with steel doors reputedly 12 inches thick) and was the scene of Fisk's funeral in 1872, after he was shot by Edward S. Stokes, hot-blooded third party of a triangle whose apex was the famous actress Josie Mansfield, Fisk's onetime mistress. Fisk's demise was a preview of a similar tragedy in the assassination of Stanford White 34 years later [see Four Squares W 22.].

 [H 1.] Chelsea Hotel, 222 W. 23rd St., bet. Seventh and Eighth Aves. 1884. Hubert, Pirsson & Co. ★

Built as one of the city's first cooperative apartment houses, the Chelsea became a hotel in 1905 but has a high ratio of permanent tenants even today. The 12-story brick **bearing-wall** structure has been called Victorian Gothic, but its style is hard to pin down. The most prominent exterior features are the delicate iron balconies (made by J. B. and J. M. Cornell) that screen the hefty brickwork. Plaques at the entrance honor writers who have lived here: **Thomas Wolfe, Dylan Thomas,** and **Brendan Behan,** three of a long list that runs from **Mark Twain** and **O. Henry** to **Tennessee Williams, Yevgeni Yevtushenko,** and **Arthur Miller.** Guests from other arts have included **Sarah Bernhardt, Virgil Thomson, John Sloan,** and **Jackson Pollock. Edgar Lee Masters** wrote a poem about the Chelsea, and **Andy Warhol** made it the scene of his 1966 movie *The Chelsea Girls.* The lobby is a bit of a letdown, but the rooms are reportedly well kept and full of Edwardian atmosphere—and quite reasonable in price, at least by midtown standards. Now refreshed and repainted.

Name change: Philip G. Hubert (1830–1911), partner in the firm of Hubert, Pirsson & Company, was the son of Charles Antoine Colomb Gengembre, whose children adopted the surname of their mother, Hubert, since their father's was so difficult for Americans to pronounce.

J. B. & J. M. CORNELL,

I
R
O
N

Buildings.
Bridges.
Roofs.
Fronts.
Girders.
Beams.
Stairs.
Columns.
Etc.

141 Centre Street, N.Y.

[H 1.] Chelsea Hotel detail of balcony railings cast by J. B. and J. M. Cornell

[H 2.] Chelsea Historic District, generally bet. W. 20th and W. 22nd Sts. bet. Ninth and Tenth Aves. with irregular legs E of Ninth Ave. ★ **Chelsea Historic District Extension,** includes W. 22nd St. almost to Eighth Ave. and the S side of W. 23rd St. bet. Ninth and Tenth Aves. ★

This historic district and its extension are a condensation of **the best qualities of Chelsea** with architecture from all its periods: Greek and Gothic Revival, Italianate, and 1890s apartment buildings by such firms as **C. P. H. Gilbert** and **Neville & Bagge.**

[H 2a.] 305-313 West 22nd Street (apartments), bet. Eighth and Ninth Aves. 1873. Extended and altered upward, 1986, Weinberg, Kirschenbaum & Tambasco, with Jay Almour Assocs. ☆

Here venerable mansard roofs crested with **cast iron** are beautifully restored, and a modern entry tower at the west end gracefully stands in the background.

[H 3.] 260 West 22nd Street (apartments), bet. Seventh and Eighth Aves. Converted, 1969. Robert Ostrow.

The owner-architect rebuilt this row house with **wit and imagination.** His rich exterior modeling of dark brick, glass, and ribbed metal roofing reflects equally intricate interior spaces. After completing this and his other Chelsea gem on 19th Street [see H 5b.], he became fed up with the city and moved to Stateline, **Nevada.**

[H 4a.] St. Peter's Church (Episcopal), 344 W. 20th St., bet. Eighth and Ninth Aves. 1836–1838. James W. Smith, builder, after designs by Clement Clarke Moore. ☆ **[H 4b.] Rectory.** 1832. ☆ **[H 4c.] Apple Corps Theater** ☆

These buildings form **a remarkable study** in the **popular adaptation** of styles. The rectory, which apparently served first as the church, is in a very stripped-down Greek Revival style, but its fine proportions give it dignity. By the time the much larger church was built, the congregation was ready to make it one of New York's **earliest ventures** into the Gothic Revival. Its massively buttressed fieldstone walls, with spare trim of cut granite, give it a military look.

The third building in the group, the hall east of the church, is an example of later **common brick Gothic;** it was started in 1854 and given its strangely churchlike front in 1871. Now the **Apple Corps Theater** lives here. The wrought-iron fence along the street is older than any of the buildings. It dates from about 1790 and was a **hand-me-down** from venerable Trinity Church, which was putting up its 3rd edifice in the 1830s.

[H 5a.] Joyce Theatre/originally **Elgin (movie theater),** 175 Eighth Ave., SW cor. W. 19th St. 1942. Simon Zelnik. Converted to dance theater, 1982, Hardy Holzman Pfeiffer Assocs.

A onetime neighborhood movie house, then a revival showcase, now lovingly updated to honor its Art Moderne beginnings.

[H 5a.] The Art Moderne Joyce Theatre reincarnated from the Elgin (movies)

[H 5b.] 365 West 19th Street (apartments), bet. Eighth and Ninth Aves. Converted, 1970, Robert Ostrow.

Another special event among Chelsea's converted row houses [also see H 3.] by a talented architect who followed Horace Greeley's (much earlier) advice: he went west.

Cuban Chinese Restaurants: hereabouts lies one of the several major enclaves of Cuban Chinese expatriated in the 1960s—others are on the Upper West Side and on Hamilton Heights near the City College campus. Here the *comidas china y criolla* can be ordered from a menu on which *ropa vieja* shares space with egg foo yung; *pernil asado* with *moo goo gai pan.*

[H 6.] 435 West 19th Street (converted lofts), bet. Ninth and Tenth Aves. Converted, 1987.

A Post Modern conversion of a brick building into condominiums.

[H 7.] General Theological Seminary, Ninth Ave., bet. W. 20th and W. 21st Sts., to Tenth Ave. **Main buildings,** 1883–1900. Charles C. Haight. **[H 7a.] West Building,** Nos. 5 and 6 Chelsea Sq., W. 20th St., bet. Ninth and Tenth Aves. N side. 1836. ☆

The stoutly fenced, full city block of the seminary is accessible through the building (*1960. O'Connor & Kilham*) on the Ninth Avenue front, but the major buildings can be seen from West 20th Street. The **West Building,** one of the city's oldest examples of Gothic Revival, was modeled after an even earlier, matching **East Building** (built 1827; razed 1892). Haight's surrounding dour red brick and brownstone structures are, for their period, quite simple in massing and ornament.

[H 7b.] The Cushman Row (row houses), 406-418 W. 20th St.; bet. Ninth and Tenth Aves. 1840. ☆

Built by dry goods merchant **Don Alonzo Cushman** (Don was his first name), a friend of Clement Moore's who became a millionaire developing Chelsea. The fine Greek Revival detail, except for losses here and there, is intact: tiny, **wreath-encircled** attic windows; **deeply recessed** doorways with brownstone frames; **handsome** iron balustrades, newels, and fences. The dormers are a later addition.

[H 7c.] 446-450 West 20th Street, bet. Ninth and Tenth Aves. 1855. **[H 7d.] 465-473 West 21st Street,** NE cor. Tenth Ave. 1853. ☆

Eight exceptional **Italianate** houses facing, respectively, the austere side walls (West 21st Street) and the gardens (West 20th Street) of the seminary across the streets.

[H 8.] Church of the Guardian Angel (Roman Catholic), 193 Tenth Ave., NW cor. W. 21st St. 1930. John Van Pelt.

Its simple brick and limestone southern **Sicilian Romanesque** facade merges with the **Tuscan village forms** of auxiliary buildings to the north in a well-related group.

[H 9a.] Clement Clarke Moore Park, W. 22nd St. SE cor. Tenth Ave. 1968. Coffey, Levine & Blumberg, architects/landscape architects. ☆

A friendly, understated canopy of trees is an adjunct to this row house district.

[H 8.] Church of the Guardian Angel   **[H 13.]** The Starrett-Lehigh Building

[H 9b.] The sleekly classic Art Moderne Empire Diner serves very trendy fare

[H 9b.] Empire Diner, 210 Tenth Ave., NE cor. W. 22nd St. 1943. Altered, 1976, Carl Laanes, designer. ☆

The reincarnation of, and ultimate homage to, the **American diner.** Stainless steel never looked better, set off by black and chrome furnishings.

[H 10a.] 428-450 West 23rd Street (row houses), bet. Ninth and Tenth Aves. ca. 1860. ☆

A phalanx of **Anglo-Italianate** brownstones opposite the bulk of London Terrace. Here is a "terrace" remnant that gives a taste of what were once almost endless and uniform blocks.

[H 10b.] London Terrace (apartments), W. 23rd to W. 24th Sts., Ninth to Tenth Aves. 1930. Farrar & Watmaugh.

This vast brick pile, in **proto-Modern planar style** with faintly Gothic verticality, is actually 2 rows of connected apartment buildings enclosing a blocklong private garden, invisible from the street. All in all it contains 1,670 units, with swimming pool, solarium, and shops and banks in the avenue fronts. The name comes from a row (*terrace* is what the English call it) of 4-story houses that once stretched along the same West 23rd Street frontage, facing the **18th-century Clarke mansion.** When the present complex was new, doormen were dressed as London bobbies to play the game.

For the home: An old standby occupies a rebuilt old building across Tenth Avenue. The original Pottery Barn (No. 231) sells all manner of first- and second-quality wineglasses, china, enameled pots and what-have-you.

[H 11a.] 437-459 West 24th Street (row houses), bet. Ninth and Tenth Aves. 1850. Philo Beebe, builder. ★

A row of late Italianate brick houses unusual in their large setback from the street. **No. 461** next door is an earlier Federal house. The front gardens are a refreshing pause in the streetscape.

[H 11b.] 242-258 Tenth Avenue (row houses), bet. W. 24th and W. 25th Sts. E side.

An **Italianate** commercial row.

[H 12.] Originally **H. Wolff Book Bindery,** 259-273 Tenth Ave., bet. W. 25th and W. 26th Sts. W side. ca. 1900. Addition, 1926, Frank Parker.

Notable for its technology—not its aesthetics: here was an early poured-in-place (**in situ**) building, an industrial monument.

Famous Players in Famous Plays: Adolph Zukor, who originated this title, produced a number of old films in Chelsea. Nor was his the only studio, others being Kalem, Charles O. Bauman & Adam Kessel Films, Reliance, Majestic, etc. The Famous Players Studios was at 221 West 26th Street; its roster of stars contained such names as Mary Pickford and John Barrymore.

 [H 13.] Starrett-Lehigh Building (lofts), W. 26th to W. 27th Sts., Eleventh to Twelfth Aves. 1931. Russell G. and Walter M. Cory. Yasuo Matsui, associated architect. ★

About **9 miles** of strip windows, with their brick-banded spandrels, streaking and swerving around this block-square, 19-story factory-warehouse structure have made it **a landmark of modern architecture** ever since it rose in the air rights of the former Lehigh Valley Railroad freight terminal.

[H 14.] Originally **Central Stores, Terminal Warehouse Company,** W. 27th to W. 28th Sts., Eleventh to Twelfth Aves. 1891. Walter Katté, chief engineer.

Twenty-four acres of warehousing within a brick fortress composing 25 separate buildings crowned with Tuscan detail. The inevitable gentrification into condominium apartments will strike here next.

Tunnel, 220 Twelfth Avenue, a mid-1980s dance club, occupies the lowest level of the Terminal Warehouse Company and milks the magic and mystery of the onetime warehouse for all it's worth. From the disco's publicity: "Opulence inside a stone fortress. Golden chambers and heavy machinery. Dungeons below ivory towers." Hype.

[H 15.] Michael Dezer Classic Motors, 270 Eleventh Ave., bet. W. 27th and W. 28th Sts. E side. 1985. Michael Dezer, owner-designer.

Here a giant sculpted concrete frieze, punctuated by glass block, displays vintage cars symbolically, while below and within are the real things. It is **Hollywood-Times Square Art Moderne.** The cars inside are the most convincing "architectural" relics. The future: a **Hotrod** diner and bar within and, eventually, **"Dezerland,"** where 1950s movies will be screened for viewers from cars on an **indoor-outdoor** screen (! ?).

[H 16.] Church of the Holy Apostles (Episcopal), 300 Ninth Ave., SE cor. W. 28th St. 1848. Minard Lafever. Transepts, 1858. Richard Upjohn & Son. ★

This **remarkably independent work** fits into no stylistic slot. It has been called an early effort at Romanesque Revival, but its brick details, bracketed eaves, and unique bronze and slate spire—completely dominating the low nave—mark it as an equally early appearance of the Italianate style, rarely seen in churches. The interior has the simple barrel-vaulted geometry of early Italian Renaissance, without the classical details. The windows, by **William Jay Bolton,** are as unusual as the building, if less vigorous; each is composed of square panels in a colorful abstract design, with central medallions painted in a delicate monochromatic and realistic style. Here also is the largest soup kitchen in Manhattan.

[H 17.] Penn Station South (apartment complex), W. 23rd to W. 29th Sts., Eighth to Ninth Aves. 1962. Herman Jessor.

This **2,820**-unit urban renewal development is a cooperative sponsored by the **International Ladies' Garment Workers Union** ("ladies" here refers to the **garments**), conveniently located at the southwest corner of the **Garment District** (which extends north to West 40th Street and east to Sixth Avenue).

[H 18.] Fashion Institute of Technology, W. 26th to W. 28th Sts., bet. Seventh and Eighth Aves. **[H 18a.] Administration and Technology Building,** and **[H 18b.] Morris W. & Fannie B. Haft Auditorium,** both on W. 27th St. N Side. 1958. **[H 18c.] Nagler Hall (dormitory),** W. 27th St. S side. 1962. **[H 18d.] Shirley Goodman Resource Center,** Seventh Ave., bet. W. 26th and W. 27th Sts. W side. 1977. **[H 18e.] Arts and Design Center,** Seventh Ave., bet. W. 27th and W. 28th Sts. W side. 1977. **[H 18f.] David Dubinsky Student Center,** Eighth Ave., bet. W. 27th and W. 28th Sts. E side. 1977. All by DeYoung & Moscowitz. **[H 18g.] New Dormitories,** W. 27th St. S side. 1988. Henry George Greene.

This complex was planned as the training ground for acolytes to New York's garment industry. In dresses, coats, and suits, fashions change every season, as did the style of the architecture over the years this campus took to complete.

The Ballroom, theater/cabaret/restaurant, 253 W. 28th St., bet. Seventh and Eighth Aves. It emigrated from SoHo to more generous quarters, where one can **nosh** at the bar on Chef Rojas-Lombardi's 16- to 20-bowl **tapas,** or eat and drink while watching a show, at night, listening to classical guitar at lunch.

[H 19.] 142 West 29th Street (storefront), bet. Sixth and Seventh Aves. ca. 1929.

Seagram Building look out! An antecedent in straight-edged Sullivanesque patterning.

END of Chelsea Tour A.

Chelsea Walking Tour B: From West 29th Street and Sixth Avenue (Avenue of the Americas) south to West 14th Street. (Take the Sixth Avenue Subway to the 23rd Street station.)

Sixth Avenue Magasins: The old **Stern's** dry goods store on West 23rd Street and the other blocklong ghosts lining what is officially **Avenue of the Americas** recall the latter part of the 19th century, when this was the turf termed Fashion Row. Though now mostly used for loft and office space, their splendor is still quite evident, and reincarnations are slowly making their long-seedy skeletons glisten once again. In their heyday, it was quite a different avenue, with the clatter of the Sixth Avenue el bringing the middle class to this segment of what came to be a far-ranging, ready to wear clothing district.

[H 20.] Coogan Building/originally **Racket Court Club,** 776 Sixth Ave., NE cor. W. 26th St. 1876. Alfred H. Thorp.

Here is an eclectic Romanesque Revival building whose cornice is supported by a set of filigreed iron brackets. Coogan, incidentally, is the same Coogan as Coogan's Bluff, the escarpment that overlooked the New York Giants' Polo Grounds in U Manhattan.

[H 21.] Originally **Stern's Dry Goods Store,** 32-36 W. 23rd St., bet. Fifth and Sixth Aves. 1878. Henry Fernbach. 38-46 W. 23rd St. 1892. William Schickel. Altered, 1986, Rothzeid, Kaiserman, Thompson & Bee.

A **resplendent** cast-iron emporium for "New York's first merchandising family." It reeks of **Birthday Cake** with vanilla icing. A new glass and iron canopy adds a note of elegant entry, but the added floors atop 32-36 are out of context.

Edith Wharton, author of such revealing New York novels as *The Age of Innocence,* was born in 1862 at 14 West 23rd Street, in a 3-story brownstone altered into a store by H. J. Hardenbergh in 1882. The cast-iron columns date from yet another alteration in 1892. As a signal of the migrating social geography of her own early years, Mrs. Wharton noted that her hero, Newland Archer, in reflecting on his father-in-law to be, "knew that he already had his eye on a newly built house in East Thirty-ninth Street. The neighborhood was thought remote, and the house was built in a ghastly greenish-yellow stone that the younger architects were beginning to employ as a protest against the brownstone of which the uniform hue coated New York like a cold chocolate sauce; but the plumbing was perfect."

[H 22a.] The Milan (apartments), 118-122 W. 23rd St., bet. Sixth and Seventh Aves. 1988. Der Scutt.

This Post Modern tan brick construction, with its deeply sculpted balconies, adds its vigorous presence to this noisy street. The **gables** are a cliché; nevertheless this is a welcome addition to the block.

[H 22b.] 167 West 23rd Street (commercial building), bet. Sixth and Seventh Aves. Altered, 1898, P. F. Brogan.

Sheet metal and cast iron make its unusual facade. Savor the small, pyramidal tower.

[H 23.] Originally **Ehrich Brothers Emporium,** 695-709 Sixth Ave., bet. W. 22nd and W. 23rd Sts. W side. 1889. William Schickel.

An **elegant** cast-iron facade, sadly ill-kempt.

[H 24a.] Originally **Adams Dry Goods Store/**now **Mattel Toys,** 675-691 Sixth Ave., bet. W. 21st and W. 22nd Sts. W side. 1900. DeLemos & Cordes.

A late arrival to retail row. Note the **ADG monograms** among the ornament.

[H 24b.] Third Cemetery of the Spanish-Portuguese Synagogue, Shearith Israel, 98-110 W. 21st St., bet. Sixth and Seventh Aves. 1829–1851.

Contained by painted brick loft buildings on 3 sides, this is a handsome private haven graced with a venerable ailanthus tree. This cemetery is the youngest of **three** on Manhattan Island.

The others are just south of Chatham Square (Chinatown) and in Greenwich Village.

[H 24c.] Lox Around the Clock (restaurant), 676 Sixth Ave., NE cor. 21st St. 1986. Sam Lopata, designer.

For those in need of a **designer deli** at all hours, this offbeat and off-located center of smoked and salted salmon is an oasis. Other wonders include the balance of its repertoire, from **herring in sour cream** to **pastrami.** A favorite of the local arts scene.

[H 24d.] Private Eyes (disco/nightclub), 12 W. 21st St., bet. Fifth and Sixth Aves. 1984. Sam Lopata, designer.

For swingers not content with food alone.

[H 25.] Originally **Hugh O'Neill Dry Goods Store,** 655-671 Sixth Ave., bet. W. 20th and W. 21st Sts. W side. 1875. Mortimer C. Merritt.

The cast-iron **Corinthian** columned and pilastered facade, with almost full cylindrical towers, was once crowned with domes interlocked at its two corners. The name remains clearly visible in relief at the pediment.

[H 25.] The cast-iron and Corinthian-columned Hugh O'Neill Department Store

[H 22a.] 23rd Street's Milan apts.   **[H 26.]** Limelight Disco (Episcopal?)

[H 26.] Originally **Church of the Holy Communion (Episcopal)/**now **Limelight Disco,** 49 W. 20th St., NE cor. Sixth Ave. 1846. Richard Upjohn. ★ **Rectory,** 1850. **Chapel,** 1879.

More notable because Upjohn **did** it than because of its intrinsic architectural quality. Now a stylish disco. Churches seem to become lustily secular in this city when religion has abandoned them.

[H 27.] Originally **Simpson Crawford & Simpson/later Simpson Crawford (dry goods store),** 641 Sixth Ave., bet. W. 19th and W. 20th Sts. W side. 1900. William H. Hume & Son.

Seven stories of limestone, a sober work of architecture. The technical school at the corner thinks of itself as a 1950s **sub**-urb, ignoring the architecture of the "urb" of which it is a part.

Witches and warlocks: The Magickal Childe, at 35 West 19th Street, vends amulets, talismans, herbs, roots, and spices, ostensibly to bring protection, good luck, and/or love.

[H 28.] Originally **B. Altman Dry Goods Store,** 621 Sixth Ave., bet. W. 18th and W. 19th Sts. W side. 1877. D. & J. Jardine. Addition to S, 1887, William H. Hume. Addition on W. 18th St., 1910, Buchman & Fox.

B. Altman's (or **Baltman's** to some) forsook this cast-iron emporium in 1906 for its imposing stone edifice at Fifth Avenue and 34th Street. Now converted to offices and a small shopping mall.

[H 29.] Originally **Siegel-Cooper Dry Goods Store,** 616-632 Sixth Ave., bet. W. 18th and W. 19th Sts. E side. 1896. DeLemos & Cordes.

Fifteen-and-a-half acres of space are contained in this latecomer to the area. Elaborately embellished in glazed terra-cotta, it clearly bears the stamp of the **Chicago World's Fair of 1893.** At one time it was a favored meeting place, the phrase "Meet you at the fountain!" referring to the jet of water graced by the figure of the *Republic* by **Daniel Chester French** (now reposing at California's Forest Lawn Cemetery). After a brief but turbulent retailing history, it was converted to a military hospital during World War I.

Waiting for **Godot,** the gentrifier.

[H 29.] Siegel-Cooper Dry Goods Store   **[H 31a.]** 31 West 16th Street house

[H 30.] New York Foundling Hospital, Sixth Ave. SE cor. W. 17th St. 1988. Perkins Geddis Eastman.

A modestly articulated brick **haven** for those babies who once were ensconced in the former foundling home at Third Avenue and East 68th Street. Upper East Side real estate escalation paid for a newer and grander facility in this more economical neighborhood.

West 16th Street between Fifth and Sixth Avenues.

A wealth of architectural styles and building types.

[H 31a.] 31 West 16th Street (row house). Altered, 1971, Stephen B. Jacobs.

Syncopated rhythms mark the window placement in this altered row house.

[H 31b.] Originally **IRT Electrical Substation No. 41,** 27-29 W. 16th St. 1917.

A chaste tapestry of brick embellished by an intricate verdigris cornice.

[H 31c.] 17 West 16th Street (row house)/now **apartments,** ca. 1846. ★

A **Greek Revival** residence to which Margaret Sanger moved her Birth Control Clinical Research Bureau in 1930–1973. Its bow-front (and those of its neighbors at **Nos. 5-9**) was a common characteristic of **Boston's Greek Revival** (as around Louisburg Square) but was rare in New York.

[H 31d.] Church of St. Francis Xavier (Roman Catholic), 30 W. 16th St. 1882. P. C. Keely.

The monumental porch of this **neo-Baroque** church spills onto the sidewalk. Inside is an equally monumental **Baroque** space.

 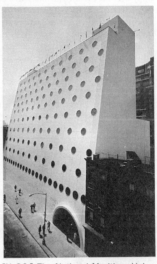

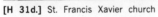
[H 31d.] St. Francis Xavier church   **[H 36.]** The National Maritime Union

[H 32a.] Originally **New York House and School of Industry,** 120 W. 16th St., bet. Sixth and Seventh Aves. 1878. Sidney V. Stratton.

Red brick Queen Anne eclectic, with a strong personality. The picturesque was just coming into full bloom, abetted by the romantic landscapes and architecture of recently completed Central Park. This institution was founded in 1851 to teach poor women "plain and fine" sewing.

[H 32b.] French Evangelical Church/originally **Catholic Apostolic Church/**later Eglise Evangélique Française de New-York, 126 W. 16th St., bet. Sixth and Seventh Aves. ca. 1835. Current facade, 1886, Alfred D. F. Hamlin.

A robust example of what the Germans called *Rundbogenstil.*

[H 33.] Originally **Liggett & Meyers Tobacco Company,** 91-97 Seventh Ave., SE cor. W. 16th St. ca. 1885.

Historically interesting for its role for the **smokers** of America, but architecturally merely a bland **Romanesque Revival.** Would that the effects of smoking were equally bland.

[H 34.] Originally **Port of New York Authority Commerce Building/ Union Inland Terminal No. 1,** 111 Eighth Ave., bet. W. 15th and W. 16th Sts. to Ninth Ave. 1932. Abbott, Merkt & Co., Lusby Simpson, designer.

An **enormous** inner-city warehousing facility occupying a full city block, **a whale of a structure** but only **a little brother** to **Starrett-Lehigh** [see H 13.]. Before occupying space in its World Trade Center, this was the headquarters of the Port of New York Authority (today, Port Authority of New York and New Jersey).

[H 35.] Apartments, Eighth Ave., bet. W. 16th and W. 17th Sts., E side. 1988. James Stewart Polshek & Partners.

New condominium units to fill the ever-soaring demand for a niche in Greenwich Village **"and vicinity."** Polshek's **Washington Court** at Sixth Avenue and Waverly Place [see Greenwich Village V 36.] is a handsome predecessor of this project.

[H 36.] Originally **National Maritime Union of America, Joseph Curran Annex,** 346 W. 17th St., bet. Eighth and Ninth Aves. 1966. **[H 36a.]** Originally **Joseph Curran Plaza,** 100 Ninth Ave., bet. W. 16th and W. 17th Sts. Both by Albert C. Ledner & Assocs.

A startling white tile-faced, porthole-pierced front wall sloping 8½ degrees from vertical was the architect's way of meeting the setback requirements of the 1961 zoning resolution: the 20-foot setback required above 85 feet from the sidewalk is here so accommodated. As novel on the exterior as the union's former main building [see V Manhattan/ Greenwich Village B 8c.], it is efficiently laid out inside to accommodate medical and recreational facilities for union members.

The Kitchen, the media center at 512 West 19th Street, began as a reuse of the old Broadway Central Hotel's food preparation area (hence its name). For years it occupied space in SoHo [see L Manhattan/SoHo H 20d.], but rising rents made it an expatriate to Chelsea's west edge. The place for avant-garde video, music, dance, performance, and film. And at 169 Eighth Avenue also at 19th Street, part of the Eiffel Tower's old spiral stairs gives access to the restrooms of Man Ray (restaurant).

END of Chelsea Tour B. The nearest subway is the 14th Street Station of the IND Eighth Avenue Line and the BMT Canarsie Line, which slowly rambles crosstown under 14th Street to connect with the IND at Sixth Avenue, and the BMT Broadway Line and IRT Lexington Avenue Line at Union Square.

Chelsea Walking Tour C: The 14th Street Corridor. START at West 14th Street between Eighth Avenue and Hudson Street. (Take the IND Eighth Avenue Line, or the IRT Broadway-Seventh Avenue Line to their 14th Street Station or the BMT 14th Street-Canarsie Line to the Eighth Avenue Station.)

West as well as east, 14th Street has seen better days, when the magnetism of Wanamaker's department store radiated from Broadway and East 9th Street throughout the area. Today, much of the street from Seventh Avenue to Union Square is crowded with shoppers bargaining for the cheap merchandise which spills out onto the wide sidewalks from a variety of small shops. Above the bustle are the great facades from an earlier era, well worth considering and enjoying.

[H 37a.] The Church of St. Bernard (Roman Catholic), 330 W. 14th St., bet. Eighth and Ninth Aves. 1875. P. C. Keely.

Two-tone brownstone **Ruskinian Gothic Revival,** with a wheel window overlooking 14th Street.

[H 37b.] Manufacturers Hanover Trust Company branch/originally **New York County National Bank,** 75-79 Eighth Ave., SW cor. W. 14th St. 1907. DeLemos & Cordes, succeeded by Rudolph L. Daus. Later addition to S. **[H 37c.]** Originally **The New York Bank for Savings headquarters/**later **Goldome bank branch,** 81 Eighth Ave., NW cor. W. 14th St. 1897. R. H. Robertson.

A rare occurence for this city: a **pair** of classically inspired sentinels guarding the western corridor of 14th Street.

[H 38a.] Originally **Andrew Norwood residence,** 241 W. 14th St., bet. Seventh and Eighth Aves. 1847. ★

An Italianate brownstone with **late Greek Revival** detail. It, and two defaced neighbors, were the first masonry houses between Seventh and Eighth Avenues.

[H 38b.] The Sequoia (apartments), 222 W. 14th St., bet. Seventh and Eighth Aves. 1987. Ted Reeds Assocs.

A Post Modern apartment house displaying too many materials, but with remarkable cornices at the 7th floor.

[H 38c.] Iglesia Católica Guadalupe (Roman Catholic), 229 W. 14th St., bet. Seventh and Eighth Aves.

An extraordinary brownstone conversion from row house to humble Spanish Catholic church. Its Iberian ancestry is expressed both in the language of its services and in its New World **Spanish Baroque** facade.

[H 39a.] 154-160 West 14th Street (lofts), SE cor. Seventh Ave. 1913. Herman Lee Meader.

A rich display of glazed and colored terra-cotta decoration with some flavor of the older Art Nouveau (the frieze at the 2nd floor) and yet anticipating the later Art Deco at its cornice. [Also see Cliff Dwellers' Apartments, W Manhattan/Riverside Drive R 19.]

[H 39a.] 154–160 West 14th Street   **[H 42b.]** Painting Ind. Welfare Bldg.

[H 39b.] 138-146 West 14th Street (lofts), bet. Sixth and Seventh Aves. ca. 1899.

Roman Revival encrusted with elaborate terra-cotta detail; inspired by the **World's Columbian Exposition** of 1893.

[H 40.] 42nd Division Armory N.Y. National Guard, 125 W. 14th St., bet. Sixth and Seventh Aves. 1971. N.Y.S. General Services Administration, Charles S. Kawecki, State Architect.

A gross and overbearing modern drill hall that replaced a 19th-century fantasy fort of rich detail.

[H 41a.] Salvation Army Centennial Memorial Temple and Executive Offices, 120 W. 14th St., bet. Sixth and Seventh Aves. 1930. **[H 41b.] John and Mary R. Markle Memorial Residence/Evangeline Residence, Salvation Army,** 123-131 W. 13th St. 1929. All by Voorhees, Gmelin & Walker.

Art Deco on a monumental scale gives entrance to the Centennial Memorial Temple. The interior is as splashy. To the west and south (on 13th Street) are related but more subdued adjuncts.

[H 42a.] 56 West 14th Street/once **Macy's Drygoods Store,** bet. Fifth and Sixth Aves. ca. 1894.

This 9-story sliver, pompously laden with Beaux Arts eclectic detail, was once part of **R. H. Macy's many holdings** in the vicinity of 14th Street and Sixth Avenue before the store consolidated at Herald Square. Dimly visible under years of grime is the **Macy's logo and red star,** now overwhelmed by the signs of current retail occupants, an odd juxtaposition of a once-elegant past and today's aging honky-tonk.

 [H 42b.] Painting Industry Welfare Building, 45 W. 14th St., bet. Fifth and Sixth Aves. 1960. Mayer, Whittlesey & Glass, William J. Conklin, associate partner in charge.

Bronze and glass, paper and trash.

In 1967, the *AIA Guide* said: "Hopefully, this witty and elegant refacing of a tired facade will inspire its neighbors to follow." They didn't.

[H 42c.] Originally **Ludwig Brothers Dry Goods Store,** 34-42 W. 14th St., bet. Fifth and Sixth Aves. 1878. W. Wheeler Smith. Enlarged, 1899, Louis Korn.

A subdued cast-iron building above with cheap stores below.

[H 43a.] Originally **Le Boutillier Brothers (dry goods),** 12-16 E. 14th St. 1891. D'Oench & Simon.

A pioneering retailer in women's fashions. The **pomp of the original facade** is evident above the street-level storefront.

[H 43b.] Originally **Baumann's Carpet Store,** 22-26 E. 14th St., bet. Fifth Ave. and University Place. 1880. D. & J. Jardine.

A rich embroidery of cast iron—Composite columns, anthemia, garlands, festoons, floral bas-reliefs—embraces 4 tiers of enormous double-hung windows. The economics of keeping 14th Street green (with money) has erased the results of the patternmaker's craft at street level in favor of a retail emporium.

END of 14th Street Tour: The IRT Lexington Avenue Line and the BMT Broadway and 14th Street-Canarsie Line subways are at Union Square.

FOUR SQUARES

The laying out of **Union, Gramercy, Stuyvesant,** and **Madison Squares** in the 1830s and 1840s gave promise of urbane residential precincts for wealthy New Yorkers. All four squares were speculative developments in the spirit of **London's Bloomsbury** and Covent Garden (where the Dukes of Bedford had developed farmland into a grand neighborhood of Georgian architecture and garden squares).

*Note: The entries that follow are arranged in three corridors: the **Western,** from Union Square northward to Madison Square and beyond; the **Central,** Irving Place, Stuyvesant Square, Gramercy Park, and the area of the armory; and the **Eastern,** east to Stuyvesant Town, Peter Cooper Village, Kips Bay, and the East River.*

West Corridor

Four Squares West Walking Tour. A northward ramble up **Ladies Mile** from Union Square, eventually to 28th Street and Park Avenue South. START at Union Square. (Take the IRT Lexington Avenue Line, the BMT Broadway Line, or the 14th Street-Canarsie Line to the Union Square/14th Street Station.)

Union Square: First named **Union Place,** it served as the crotch of Broadway from the southwest and the **Bowery** (Fourth Avenue at this point) from the southeast—its nickname then was The Forks. Before the Civil War it was a grand residential square, with an iron-fenced public park, primarily for the fashionable town house residents surrounding it, much as Gramercy Park (fenced *and locked*) still is today. In 1854 it blossomed as a new **"uptown"** theatrical district with the opening of the **Academy of Music.** That venerable house was on the site of the present Con Edison building, opposite its later, namesake **Academy** (now the **Palladium**).

Union Square later became the center of the political left: here, in August 1927, protestors awaited news of the execution of **Sacco and Vanzetti. May Day,** the annual celebration of **socialism,** brought a million to this mecca where the **Daily Worker** and many other radical publications and organizations abounded.

[W 1a.] Union Square Park, E. 14th to E. 17th Sts., Union Sq. W. to Union Sq. E. Laid out, 1830. Opened to public, 1839. Rebuilt, 1986. Bronson Binger, architect; Hui Mei Grove, landscape architect; N.Y.C. Department of Parks & Recreation, Capital Projects Division. **Newsstand,** Union Sq. E. opp. E. 15th St. 1986. Kuo Ming Tsu.

The park's raised posture is a latter-day event, allowing the subway to snake through its underworld: the original street-level park with romantically curving pathways was then totally rebuilt as a more formal public place. In those early subway times crowds gathered around their favorite debater to heckle, support, or berate him or her. This was **New York's Speakers' Corner;** it became a sacred precinct for soapbox orators and other agitators after police excesses in repressing unemployment rallies in the 1930s.

Drug traffickers in the 1960s and 1970s controlled the scene, but the 1986 renovation removed the perimeter screens of green, making all activities within visible and returning the park to a civilized population. (The druggies, of course, merely emigrated to new turf).

The renovation, designed by the Parks Department's own staff, is the best in anyone's memory: bold replanning of the entry areas, generous stone detailing, railings in scale (for once!) with a public place (using bulbous malleable iron fittings at joints), punctuated with built-up steel and glass kiosks over the subway entrances and for the newsstand, and lighted with ornate multiglobed lamps. Why not the same verve and skill to enhance Madison and Bryant Parks, and Greeley and Herald Squares!

The park abounds in sculpture: *Washington* (Henry Kirke Brown, sculptor), a copy of Houdon's original horseback eulogy, arrived in 1856. **Brown** also contributed *Lincoln* in **1866.** In 1876 **Bartholdi,** sculptor of the **Statue of Liberty,** left *Lafayette* as a token of Franco-American relations at a point early in his unceasing campaign to raise funds for the **base** of *Liberty*. The flagpole base is by **Anthony de Francisi,** sculptor.

[W 1b.] Union Square farmers' market, along W. 17th St. bet. Broadway and Park Ave. S. at the N edge of Union Sq. Gateways, 1987, Roy Strickland and Carson & Stillman.

The ephemeral Green Market, an idea of architect-planner **Barry Benepe,** is the serious architecture of cheese, tomatoes, legumes, and other edibles. The structures are confined to two rather pretentious but sad metallic gateways at the northwest and northeast corners.

[W 2.] Zeckendorf Towers (mixed use), 1 Irving Place, bet. W. 14th and W. 15th Sts. to Union Sq. E. 1987. Davis, Brody & Assocs.

Four finials, each with an illuminated, levitating, pyramidal yarmulka, crown a massive commercial bottom: each finial is a separate apartment tower. This is a **colossal** project that largely blocks the once familiar view of Con Edison's clock tower for users of the park.

From 1921 until they were demolished in 1985 this was the site of a clutch of small 19th-century buildings that were the home of **S. Klein's on the Square,** the original discount department store. Above them stood a Times Square-scale neon sign that advertised Klein's name to hordes of women shoppers. The modest budget was served there not only with bargains but also **occasional high style . . .** the latter for those stalwarts with energy and sharp eyes who combed the sea of clothes racks with vigor. (Klein's closed in August, 1975.)

At the southeast corner of 15th Street and Fourth Avenue, later to be included in Sam Klein's empire, stood the original Union Square Hotel. The **single-tax economist** Henry George died here on October 29, 1897. George sought simplification of the maze of taxes that were then only in their infancy. His mind would have boggled at today's **Byzantium** imposed by federal, state, city, and other taxes.

[W 3.] American Savings Bank/originally **Union Square Savings Bank,** 20 Union Sq. E., NE cor. E. 15th St. 1924. Henry Bacon.

A classy **Corinthian colonnade** is somewhat forlorn in these precincts. **Bacon's** best remembrance is the **Lincoln Memorial.**

 [W 4a.] Guardian Life Insurance Company/originally **Germania Life Insurance Company,** 201 Park Ave. S., NE cor. E. 17th St. 1911. D'Oench & Yost. **[W 4b.]** Annex, 105 E. 17th St., bet. Park Ave. S. and Irving Place. 1961. Skidmore, Owings & Merrill.

The mansarded bulk of this Renaissance Revival marvel is best seen from a distance, down 17th Street or from the adjacent Union Square Park. **Germania Life** was a name that became an onerous millstone at the advent of World War I. The board of directors agreed to rename it, picking a name with the largest number of reusable letters that they could find. **Guardian** still crowns the roof against its mansard backdrop.

Next door is the sleek annex, a simple grid of aluminum and glass infilled behind with white vertical blinds. As an accessory, it is a graceful annex to the proud parent, unabashedly "modern," an articulated annex.

[W 2.] Zeckendorf Towers (apts.)   **[W 5.]** Century Building at Union Sq.

 [W 5.] Originally **The Century Building,** 33 E. 17th St., bet. Park Ave. S. and Broadway to W. 18th St. 1881. William Schickel. ★

This red brick and whitestone charmer is where the popular **Century** magazine (for grown-ups) and **St. Nicholas** (for boys and girls) were published before the century turned.

[W 6.] 31 Union Square West/originally **Bank of the Metropolis Building,** NW cor. 16th St. 1903. Bruce Price.

An early and unwitting **sliver building,** this neo-Renaissance slab now houses a restaurant in its original banking rooms, a place for **SUPERMAN'S** lunch.

[W 7.] Originally **Lincoln Building,** 1 Union Sq. W., NW cor. E. 14th St. 1890. R. H. Robertson

Romanesque Revival granite crowned with a cornice of **40** little windows with interstitial paired columns.

[W 8.] Originally **YWCA (Young Women's Christian Association)**/formerly **Rand School,** 7 E. 15th St., bet. Union Sq. W. and Fifth Ave. ca. 1889. R. H. Robertson.

Romanesque Revival in granite, brick, and brownstone. The grand bay windows give the entrance portal a stronger stature.

 [W 9a.] Sidney Hillman Health Center/originally **Margaret Louisa Home, YWCA (lodging house),** 16 E. 16th St., bet. Union Sq. W. and Fifth Ave. 1890. R. H. Robertson.

Rock-face brownstone in Romanesque Revival, with a charming colonnade at the top floor. A benefaction of Mrs. Elliott F. Shepard, Cornelius Vanderbilt's eldest daughter.

[W 9b.] 9 East 16th Street (lofts), bet. Union Sq. W. and Fifth Ave. ca. 1890.

Sullivanesque limestone for the first 2 floors and then **terra-cotta candy cane** above.

[W 9c.] Originally **Judge Building,** 110 Fifth Ave., NW cor. W. 16th St. 1888. McKim, Mead & White. Altered, 1988, Davis, Brody & Assocs.

Built for Mrs. Frank Leslie (of **Frank Leslie's Illustrated Weekly**), this is a gutsy brick and granite **Roman Revival** monolith, now happily restored, even up to the cornice. Early M M & W.

[W 9d.] 91 Fifth Avenue (lofts), bet. E. 16th and E. 17th Sts., E side. 1894. Louis Korn.

Six busty caryatids bearing up under the weight of four Corinthian columns and two matching pilasters.

[W 10.] America (restaurant), 9 E. 18th St., bet. Broadway and Fifth Ave. 1985. MGS Architects.

A grand space with a raised and skylit bar that is a stage for the restaurant-tabled audience. Here architecture is space, rather than form. Neon lances itself across the restaurant sky, a colored vibrant sculptured **heaven** over the pedestrian world below.

Ladies Mile

Between Union and Madison Squares:

The remnants of **Ladies Mile** are congregated in this area of Broadway. Here the elite shopped, and hence this was a precinct of the **carriage trade**—a shopping strip of somewhat more elevated snobbery than that enjoyed by Fashion Row, the great Sixth Avenue emporiums in the shadows of the el. The latter might be termed, in contrast, the **transit trade,** serving in vast department stoves great hordes of the middle class. Here along Broadway the shined hooves of curried horses drew the glistening black enamel and leather carriages of Society, traveling from their town houses nearby, past Lord & Taylor, W. & J. Sloane, and their equals, from Union Square to Madison Square. Sadly, these once participants in elegance show their ill-cared-for forms only above the street, where "modern" alterations have defaced what were once grand doorman-guarded entries.

[W 11.] McIntyre Building (lofts), 874 Broadway, NE cor. E. 18th St. 1892. R. H. Robertson.

Unspeakable eclectic: a murmuration of Byzantine columns, Romanesque arches, Gothic finials and crockets—the designer used the whole arsenal of history in one shot.

[W 12a.] Originally **Arnold Constable Dry Goods Store,** 881-887 Broadway, SW cor. E. 19th St., through to Fifth Ave. with a later entry and address at 115 Fifth Ave. 1869. Extended, 1873, 1877. All by Griffith Thomas.

Lovers of marble walls, cast-iron facades, and mansard roofs, rejoice! There is something here for each of you. The Broadway facade, the oldest, is of marble. The extension to Fifth Avenue, the youngest, is of cast iron, an economical simulation of its adjacent parent. In between, the 2-story **miraculous mansard crown** rises over the original body and the Fifth Avenue extension. It now houses publishers' offices and menswear outlets.

[W 12b.] Originally **W. & J. Sloane Store,** 884 Broadway, SE cor. E. 19th St. 1881. W. Wheeler Smith.

Located on Broadway opposite City Hall since 1843, Sloane's moved here (temporarily) before settling on Fifth Avenue and 45th Street. In this substantial structure the firm sold carpeting, Oriental rugs, lace curtains and upholstery fabric. They later expanded to furniture.

[W 12c.] Originally **Gorham Manufacturing Company Building/**now **cooperative apartments,** 889-891 Broadway, NW cor. E. 19th St. 1884. Edward H. Kendall. ★

The skyline labors desperately to achieve a varying picturesque profile, as bits and pieces of roof interlock at random with the brick facade. Gorham, of course, manufactured silverware.

[W 13a.] Originally **Lord & Taylor Dry Goods Store,** 901 Broadway, SW cor. E. 20th St. 1867. James H. Giles. ★

An **exuberant** cast-iron facade, capped with a dormered mansard roof. The corner pavilion is reminiscent of the Renaissance architecture of **Prague.** The ground floor has been remodeled for selfish commercial purposes that have no respect for their uppers. Soon, one hopes the tide of gentrification will restore style to the streetfronts.

[W 13b.] Originally **Goelet Building (lofts),** 900 Broadway, SE cor. E. 20th St. 1887. McKim, Mead & White.

Here were bricksmiths: limestone below supports a great set of polychromatic arches. Vandals have removed the cornice and defaced the ground floor for dubious commercial enterprises.

[W 13c.] **Theodore Roosevelt Birthplace, U.S. National Park Service,** 28 E. 20th St., bet. Broadway and Park Ave. S. Original building, 1848, demolished. Replicated, 1923, Theodate Pope Riddle. ★ **Open to the public.**

After the property was recaptured by the **Theodore Roosevelt Association,** this structure was **built to reproduce the one** Roosevelt knew (he was born here in 1858 and died elsewhere in 1919).

[W 14a.] Originally **The Methodist Book Concern (lofts),** 150 Fifth Ave., SW cor. W. 20th St. 1889. E. H. Kendall.

Romanesque Revival in brick: the ground-floor entrance has been modernized with misunderstanding. Nevertheless, the brick on top still rests on a rock-face granite podium.

[W 14b.] Originally **Presbyterian Building (lofts),** 154-158 Fifth Ave., NW cor. W. 20th St. 1894. James B. Baker.

Baker created this Sullivanesque building while a neo-Classical counterrevolution was gathering steam at the Chicago World's Fair of 1893. He hopped on board that American Renaissance express and later produced the wondrous Chamber of Commerce of the State of New York [see L Manhattan/Broadway-Nassau N 76.] in 1901. Baker's grandnephew and namesake practices in New York.

[W 14c.] **Merchants' Bank/**Originally **Mohawk Building,** 160 Fifth Ave., SW cor. W. 21st St. 1891. R. H. Robertson.

This Renaissance Revival pile becomes increasingly complex as it approaches its domical corner tower. Nicely cleaned and restored.

[W 14d.] **Spero Building (lofts),** 19 W. 21st St., bet. Fifth and Sixth Aves. N side. 1908. Robert Kohn.

A strong-scaled **Art Nouveau** brick pile.

[W 15.] **The United Synagogue of America Building/**originally **Scribner Building,** 153-157 Fifth Ave., bet. E. 21st and E. 22nd Sts. E side. 1894. Ernest Flagg. ★

The **first** headquarters built for publishers Charles Scribner's Sons by an architect and relative who would later build them a bookstore and headquarters uptown, a printing plant, and a family residence. This chaste facade once **sported** a broad, semiellipsoidal cast-iron and glass canopy, in the **Parisian mode.**

[W 16a.] **Just Bulbs (shop)/**originally (1884-1915) **Brooks Brothers store,** 938 Broadway, SE cor. E. 22nd St. ca. 1884. Building remodeled, 1935, Office of Ely Jacques Kahn. Shop, 1984, Conklin & Rossant. Balance of building redesigned, 1987, Conklin & Rossant.

Neo-Art Moderne updates an earlier **Art Moderne** remodeling. The Brooks Brothers would shudder at this "trendy" styling. Inside one can find those spots, floods, tubes, and other exotic bulbs (engineers call them **lamps**) that can enhance or romance your pad.

[W 16b.] Originally **Hotel 21,** 21 E. 21st St., bet. Broadway and Park Ave. S. 1878. Bruce Price.

A socialite architect, **Price** planned the wealthy suburban private community of Tuxedo Park, N.Y., and designed many of its **Shingle Style** houses. His daughter, **Emily Post,** dictated social manners to the flock that wanted to join the elite. **No. 21,** now a seedy example of American **Queen Anne,** is a picturesque composition ornamented with its original metalwork. Note the finial at its gable.

[W 17a.] Albert Building/originally **Glenham Hotel,** 935 Broadway, SW cor. E. 22nd St. to Fifth Ave. 1861.

A dignified neo-Renaissance structure despite the ravages of retail commercialism in its storefronts. Remnants of gilded wood letters that once spelled ALBERT, and the projecting clock (stopped) are noteworthy mementos of past gentility.

[W 12a.] Originally Arnold Constable   **[W 17b.]** Flatiron, orig. Fuller Bldg.

[W 17b.] Flatiron Building/originally **Fuller Building,** 175 Fifth Ave., E. 22nd St. to E. 23rd St., Fifth Ave. to Broadway. 1902. Daniel H. Burnham & Co. ★

The diagonal line of Broadway formed important triangular buildings here and at Times Square. Burnham was master of architectural ceremonies at the **World's Columbian Exposition** in 1893, which changed the course of **civic architecture** for a generation (its canons are now reappearing in **Post Modern** dress). In those earlier years Roman and Renaissance Revival architecture gave a face of pomp to commercial and government buildings.

Here rusticated limestone is uniformly detailed from ground to sky, in the manner of an elevatored palazzo. The acutely angled corners give it an exaggerated and dramatic perspective.

Sometimes incorrectly thought to be the **first** (or at least an early sample) steel-skeletoned skyscraper; dozens of New York commercial buildings had been steel-framed in the 1890s, the decade before, including the tallest at the time, the Park Row Building [see L Manhattan/ Civic Center C 6a.].

[W 17c.] Originally **Western Union Telegraph Building,** 186 Fifth Ave., SW cor. W. 23rd St. 1884. Henry J. Hardenbergh.

An amazing holdover from Hardenbergh's **Dakota** period, completed that same year. This is one of Fifth Avenue's earliest commercial buildings, from a time when the fashionable were fleeing to residences further north.

Madison Square and Environs

[W 18.] Madison Square Park/earlier **Madison Square/**formerly part of **The Parade/**originally a **potter's field,** Fifth to Madison Aves., E. 23rd to E. 26th Sts. Opened, 1847.

The city crept past this point just prior to the **Civil War.** Madison Avenue springs from 23rd Street on the east flank of the square, bisecting the block from Fifth to Fourth (or Park Avenue South in its 1959 renaming). The **commissioners' plan of 1811** had shown a **Parade** from Third to Seventh Avenues, 23rd to 34th Streets, a pleasant void in the surveyor's grid. The present space is all that remains of that intention, replaced in scale by **Central Park,** (which had **never** been a part of the **commissioners'** scheme).

Statuary: *Chester Allen Arthur,* 1898. George Bissell. *Admiral David G. Farragut,* 1880. Augustus Saint-Gaudens, sculptor. Stanford White, architect. A great and melancholy **art nouveau** memorial. *Roscoe Conkling,* 1893. John Quincy Adams Ward. Republican political leader. *William H. Seward,* 1876. Randolph Rogers. Lincoln's secretary of state. Here, owing to unsuccessful fund raising, the sculpted body is one that Rogers modeled of Lincoln. With Seward's head attached, it holds the Emancipation Proclamation. *The Eternal Light* flagpole is the work of Carrère & Hastings.

[W 18a.] Sidewalk clock, in front of 200 Fifth Ave., bet. W. 23rd and W. 24th Sts. W side. ★

A shopper's clock from the era when these blocks marked the end of Ladies Mile, an area of mercantile elegance.

[W 19a.] Metropolitan Life Insurance Company, Main Building, 1 Madison Ave. in NE cor. E. 23rd St. to Park Ave. S. 1893. Altered. **[W 19b.] Tower,** SE cor. E. 24th St. 1909. Both by Napoleon LeBrun & Sons. Tower altered, 1964, Lloyd Morgan. **[W 19c.] North Building,** 11-25 Madison Ave., bet. E. 24th and E. 25th Sts. E side. 1932. Harvey Wiley Corbett and D. Everett Waid.

The tower was retained as a symbol after its adjacent base was rebuilt; stripped of its ornament, it was, for a long time, used as a warehouse for the company's records—in effect the **insured world's attic:** now rental offices. At the **North Building,** note the polygonal modeling of the upper bulk to allow it more grace—a search for form by Harvey Wiley Corbett in the early modern architecture—and the wondrous vaulted entrance spaces at each of the 4 corners.

The Gilded Age: Evelyn Nesbit was sixteen and a chorus girl in *Floradora* when a colleague in the show first brought her to lunch at Stanford White's favorite hideaway, camouflaged behind the nondescript facade of 22 West 24th Street. A few months later she returned for a champagne supper—for two. Afterward, the 48-year-old architect showed her the tiny room with the immense green velvet couch, where mirrored walls and ceiling glimmered warmly in the glow of hidden lights. In another room a swing hung from the ceiling on red velvet ropes, green smilax trailing from its velvet seat. What dizzying fun it was, she later related in her memoirs, to swing higher and higher across the floor, her feet piercing a huge Japanese paper parasol suspended from the ceiling. In another, velvet-lined room was a four-poster bed with a mirrored canopy lit indirectly by tiny multicolored bulbs. "It's all over, kittens. Don't cry," White begged her when she awoke. "Now you belong to me."

[W 20a.] Serbian Orthodox Cathedral of St. Sava/originally **Trinity Chapel,** 15 W. 25th St., bet. Fifth and Sixth Aves. 1855. ★ **[W 20b.] Clergy House,** 16 W. 26th St. 1855. Both by Richard Upjohn. ★ **[W 20c.] Parish House/**originally **Trinity Chapel School,** 13 W. 25th St. 1860. J. Wrey Mould. ★ In the church: Swope Memorial reredos, 1892, and altar, 1897. Both by Frederick Clarke Withers.

This complicated midblock complex presents a somber brownstone church and clergy house joining a **playful Ruskinian Gothic** polychromatic parish house to the east and resulting in an unexpected pedestrian **shortcut** from 25th to 26th Streets. A century of grime conceals the detailing and multicolor of the ensemble.

A statue of **Michael Pupin** (*1858–1935*), a noted physicist of Serbian background, stands in the walkway. Pupin Hall at Columbia University is named for him.

[W 20d.] Worth Monument, W. 25th to W. 26th Sts., Fifth Ave. to Broadway. 1857. James G. Batterson.

General **William J. Worth,** hero of the **Seminole** and **Mexican wars,** is buried here, one of the city's few interments that is actually **under** the memorial monument (General Grant is entombed in his own mausoleum as well). Here one noted for subduing native and Hispanic Americans rests under a Renaissance Revival obelisk. Worth Street in Lower Manhattan is named for him.

[W 20e.] Originally **Cross Chambers (lofts),** 210 Fifth Ave., bet. W. 25th and W. 26th Sts. W side. ca. 1895.

A **Belle Epoque** extravagance with balconies and bay windows. *Look up,* the riches are on high.

[W 21a.] Appellate Division, N.Y.S. Supreme Court, 35 E. 25th St., NE cor. Madison Ave. 1900. James Brown Lord. ★ Interior ★.

This small marble palace is the **reincarnation** of an English 18th-century country house. *Wisdom* and *Force* by Frederick Ruckstuhl flank the portal; *Peace* by Karl Bitter is the central figure on the balustrade facing the Square. *Justice* (fourth from left on 25th Street) is by Daniel Chester French, whose seated Lincoln chairs the Lincoln Memorial.

[W 19a.] Metropolitan Life Buildings   **[W 23.]** Originally A.S.P.C.A. Bldg.

[W 21b.] Provident Loan Society of New York, 346 Park Ave. S., NW cor. E. 25th St. 1909.

Three stories of limestone atop a granite base: an English club dispensing credit. It followed in the footsteps of MM&W's nearby bank [see **W 25a.**].

North of Madison Square

[W 22.] New York Life Insurance Company, 51 Madison Ave., E. 26th to E. 27th St., Madison to Park Ave. S. 1928. Cass Gilbert.

Limestone Renaissance at the bottom, **birthday cake** at the top. Gilbert was obsessed with pyramidal hats for his buildings: compare the **Woolworth Building** (1913) and the **Federal Courthouse** at Foley Square (1936). Among Gilbert's iconic heirs, Helmut Jahn is today crowning many towers with fancy hats all over the island.

This site has a rich history. It was originally occupied by the Union Depot, the New York terminal of the **New York and Harlem Railroad.** After 1871, when the **first** Grand Central Station opened at 42nd Street, the Depot was converted to house **Gilmore's Garden** and then P. T. Barnum's **Hippodrome;** it was later refinanced and renamed (1879) **Madison Square Garden.** Stanford White then designed a lavish replacement, complete with a tower copied from the **Giralda** in Seville, which opened in 1892. White was shot on its roof garden in **1906** by Harry Thaw, whose wife, the actress Evelyn Nesbit, had reputedly been White's mistress before her marriage. One added irony: Madison Square Garden's quarters (two buildings later and preparing to move once more) are on the site of the demolished Pennsylvania Station, McKim, Mead & White's *greatest* New York work.

[W 23.] Originally **American Society for the Prevention of Cruelty to Animals (offices),** 50 Madison Ave., NW cor. E. 26th St. 1896. Renwick, Aspinwall & Owen.

A proper **London club** in delicately tooled limestone. Note the elaborately tooled cornice. Even stray mongrels and alley cats deserved distinguished architecture in the 1890s.

[W 24a.] Originally **Croisic Building (offices),** 220 Fifth Ave., NW cor. W. 26th St. 1912. Frederick C. Browne. Rudolph H. Almiroty, associate architect.

At the top a richly ornamented confection—watch those architectural calories. It stands on the site of the earlier Croisic apartment hotel (*1887. August O. Hoddick/Hubert Pirsson & Co.*).

[W 24b.] 224 Fifth Avenue (lofts), bet. W. 26th and W. 27th Sts. W side. New facade, 1985.

Granite and glass, with anodized aluminum: **modern,** as a word, was invented for moments like these, concerned more with dates than with any substantial quality.

[W 24c.] 242 Fifth Avenue (lofts), bet. W. 27th and W. 28th Sts. W side. ca. 1892.

A triumphant pediment crowns this glassy precursor of the post-World War II curtain wall. The ground floor succumbed to "renovation."

[W 25a.] Citibank branch/originally **Second National Bank/**then **National City Bank of New York branch,** 250 Fifth Avenue, NW cor. W. 28th St. 1908. W. S. Richardson of McKim, Mead & White.

One of the few McKim, Mead & White small banking buildings (compare with the one at 55 Wall Street [L Manhattan F 10b.]. No great shakes, it is in awkwardly proportioned limestone. White, of course, had been assassinated in 1906.

[W 25b.] Baudouine Building (lofts), 1181 Broadway, SW cor. W. 28th St. 1896. Alfred Zucker.

A sliver with a temple on top. *Peer upwards.*

[W 25c.] 256 Fifth Avenue (lofts), bet. W. 28th and W. 29th Sts. W side. ca. 1892.

Terra-cotta virtuosity maximized in a **neo-Venetian neo-Gothic,** somewhat **Moorish** phantasmagoria, mostly **above** the commercialized ground floor.

[W 26.] Church of the Transfiguration (Episcopal)/"The Little Church Around the Corner" (Episcopal), 1 E. 29th St., bet. Fifth and Madison Aves. **Church, Rectory, Guildhall,** 1849–1861. **Lich Gate,** 1896. Frederick Clarke Withers. **Lady Chapel, Mortuary Chapel,** 1908. All ★.

Its notorious nickname has stuck since 1870, when a fashionable local pastor declined to officiate at the funeral of George Holland, an actor, and suggested that the obsequies be held at the "little church around the corner." It has been a church for those in the theater ever since. It has a charming small scale, with a delightful garden.

[W 27a.] Marble Collegiate Church (Dutch Reformed), 1 W. 29th St., NW cor. Fifth Ave. 1854. Samuel A. Warner. ★

Sharp-edged limestone Gothic Revival, contemporary with Grace and Trinity Churches. Clean planes give elegant shade and shadow to the street. Architecturally modest, Marble Collegiate is most remembered for its former pastor, **Norman Vincent Peale,** whose many books have tried to meld popular religion with popular psychology. **Richard Nixon** attended this church in his lawyer days, between his roles as vice-president and president.

Holland House: The adjacent loft building at the southwest corner of Fifth Avenue and West 30th Street is the old and famous Holland House Hotel, spruced up in the early 1920s for use as a mercantile establishment. In its original incarnation (*1891. Harding & Gooch*) its opulent interior was adorned with marble, brocade, and lace, and the hotel was considered the peer of any in the world. Its suites were patterned on those of Lord Holland's mansion in London.

[W 27b.] Originally **Gilsey House (hotel)**/now **apartments,** 1200 Broadway, NE cor. W. 29th St. 1871. Stephen D. Hatch. ★

Here is a **General Grant** Second Empire eclectic extravaganza, columned and mansarded, with the vigor that only the waning years of the 19th century could muster. Cast iron and stone . . . but in brown?

[W 27a.] The Marble Collegiate Church   **[W 27b.]** The Gilsey House apartments

[W 28a.] Originally **Grand Hotel,** 1232 Broadway, SE cor. W. 31st St. 1868. Henry Engelbert. ★

Two blocks from Gilsey, this tired remnant is simpler and less cared for, but its mansarded hat gives it a strong posture on this street.

[W 28b.] **Hotel Clinton**/originally **Life Building,** 19 W. 31st St., bet. Fifth Ave. and Broadway. 1894. Carrère & Hastings.

This ornate Classical facade once enclosed the offices of the very literate humor magazine *Life* (from which the present Time-Life organization bought the name in 1936). Visible mementos include the inscriptions **"wit"** and **"humor"** and a pattern of *L*'s back to back on handsome iron balconies. Literate **putti** above the door.

[W 28c.] **Wolcott Hotel,** 4-10 W. 31st St., bet. Fifth Avenue and Broadway. 1904. John Duncan.

An **extravagant** French Empire bay-windowed facade—carved, corniced, and mansard-roofed; the style conceals a white and gilt lobby that is both flamboyant and sad at the same time.

[W 28d.] **Wilbraham Building** (originally **apartments),** 284 Fifth Ave., NW cor. W. 30th St. 1890. D. & J. Jardine.

Brownstone and brick **Belle Epoque** crowned with a verdigris-copper roof—one of the earliest settlers on Fifth Avenue. Here the

Brown Decades that preceded the **Great White City** of the 1893 Chicago World's Fair were still exuding their murky medievalism.

[W 29a.] 22 East 31st Street (row house), bet. Fifth and Madison Aves. 1914. Israels & Harder.

A very mannered Georgian Revival town house with—surprise!—7 stories.

[W 29b.] Madison Avenue Baptist Church Parish House, 30 E. 31st St., bet. Madison Ave. and Park Ave. S. 1906.

An offbeat gem in brick and limestone. **Middle Eastern** motifs decorate a Romanesque Revival body. Atop it all is a verdigris copper cornice in the form of an overhanging eave supported by exotic brackets.

[W 29c.] American Academy of Dramatic Arts/originally **The Colony Club,** 120 Madison Ave., bet. E. 30th and E. 31st Sts. W side. 1905. McKim, Mead & White. ★ Original interiors, Elsie de Wolfe, designer.

Georgian-Federal Revival seems appropriate not-so-fancy dress for venerably connected and socially prominent ladies. The brickwork is unusual, with the headers (short ends) facing out. The false balcony is an irritating mannerism from a firm of talent. **Stanford White,** its designer, succumbed to an assassin a year after this opened—and only 3 blocks away.

[W 29d.] 121 Madison Avenue (apartments)/originally **Hubert Home Club,** NE cor. E. 30th St. 1883. Hubert, Pirsson & Co. Altered, 1940, Mayers, Murray & Philip.

Pre-World War II alterations to this relative of the **Chelsea Hotel** disguised its picturesque skyline. Although now seedy, it is distinguished by its bulk, red color, and remnants of its original detail.

[W 30.] Emmet Building (offices), 89-95 Madison Ave., SE cor. E. 29th St. 1912. J. Stewart Barney and Stockton B. Colt, associated architects.

A terra-cotta neo-Renaissance confection, in the spirit of the **Woolworth Building.** Note particularly the canopied cavaliers and courtesans atop the first floor.

[W 31.] Bowker Building (offices), 415 Park Ave. S., SE cor. E. 29th St. ca. 1929. Office of Ely Jacques Kahn.

A strange multihued, almost phosphorescent, terra-cotta-clad building. Its polychromy suggests an unknown **Islamic Industrial** style.

END of Four Squares West Tour. The closest subway is the IRT 28th Street Station on Park Avenue South.

Central Corridor

Four Squares Central Walking Tour. A saunter through Stuyvesant Square, Gramercy Park, and further uptown. START at 14th Street and Irving Place, a block east of Union Square. (Take the IRT Lexington Avenue Line, BMT Broadway Line, or the BMT 14th Street-Canarsie Line to the Union Square/14th Street Station.)

Irving Place to Stuyvesant Square

[C 1.] Consolidated Edison Company Building/originally **Consolidated Gas Company Building,** 4 Irving Place, NE cor. E. 14th St. 1915. Henry J. Hardenbergh. **[C 1a.] Tower,** 1926. Warren & Wetmore.

Hardenbergh, who gave us the **Dakota,** the **Plaza Hotel,** and the **Art Students League,** here delivered a very dull swan song for an establishment client—profitable no doubt but a far cry from his earlier glories. A landmark clock tops this, Con Ed's **GHQ,** on the site of the **original Academy of Music.** The academy's namesake, an aging movie palace, is now **The Palladium,** across the street. Their nominal affiliation is enhanced by night, when both Con Ed's tower and The Palladium facade are illuminated.

[C 1b.] The Palladium (disco)/originally **Academy of Music (movie theater),** 126 E. 14th St., bet. Third and Fourth Aves., opp. Irving Place.

1926. William Fried. Altered into discotheque, 1985, Arata Isozaki, design architect. Bloch Hesse & Shalat, architects. Andree Putman, interior design consultant. Kenny Scharf, lower lounge. Keith Haring, stage rear wall mural. Francesco Clemente, vestibule ceiling fresco.

The American debut of the talented **Japanese** architect Arata Isozaki, who subsequently produced the Los Angeles Museum of Contemporary Art and won (with associate James Stewart Polshek) the competition for the Brooklyn Museum's vast expansion program.

Built within the shell of a grandiose, 1920s movie-vaudeville palace, **Isosaki's** addition is itself an enormous stage set that has moved out of the traditional confines of the stage to modulate and animate the existing ornament, as well as the undulating dancers and spectators in the auditorium proper. The new high-tech double staircase, whose floor is **2,400 round lights** set in glass block, is wondrous to behold—particularly if under the influence . . . *any* influence. Well worth the price of admission.

[C 1c.] Originally **Lüchow's Restaurant Building,** 110 E. 14th St., bet. Third and Fourth Aves. 1914. Frank Wennemer.

A sorry shell, once the grazing ground of great gourmands and sometime gourmets. Aged and mellowed mahogany, cut-glass mirrors, and stained-glass skylights once enriched vast spaces within. The innards and their related cooking are now below street level at Broadway and 51st Street, a move of permanent stage sets analogous to opening **Lohengrin** at **Roseland** and staying on stage forever.

[C 2.] **"Washington Irving House,"** 122 E. 17th St., SW cor. Irving Place. 1845.

Irving's connection with this house is the wishful thinking of an ancient owner; this is one **Washington** who **never slept here.** In the real world, **Elsie de Wolfe** and **Elisabeth Marbury** lived here from **1894** to **1911.** They maintained a salon where notables from all walks of life gathered amid Elsie's "white decor," the stylistic statement that launched her career as America's first paid (and **highly** paid) interior decorator. Later, as **Lady Mendl,** she gave parties with as much élan as her decor.

Where TIME began: In an upstairs room at 141 East 17th Street in 1922 Briton Hadden and Henry Luce wrote the prospectus for what was to become TIME magazine. The rent was $55 a month.

[C 3.] **Tuesday's Restaurant and Fat Tuesday's Jazz Club**/formerly **Joe King's Rathskeller,** or **The German-American**/originally **Scheffel Hall,** 190 Third Ave., bet. E. 17th and E. 18th Sts. W side. 1894. Weber & Drosser.

German-American eclectic Renaissance Revival. The jazz is cool downstairs, where collegians of an earlier generation merely drank beer and made out. Now youth of all ages can do both—to jazz rhythms. Once upon a time the massive local immigrant German population centered its recreation here.

[C 4.] **Stuyvesant Square Historic District,** generally including the Square, its entire frontage on Rutherford Place, partial frontages on E. 15th and E. 17th Sts., and parts of E. 15th, E. 16th, E. 17th, and E. 18th Sts. bet. Second and Third Aves. ★

A complex area of widely mixed uses: the side streets are graced with groups of homogeneous row houses, the blocks facing the square bear religious buildings and, outside the district, hospitals. Third Avenue, to which the district barely extends, is the neighborhood shopping strip.

[C 4a.] **Stuyvesant Square Park**/originally **Stuyvesant Square,** Second Ave. bet. E. 15th and E. 17th Sts., Rutherford and Nathan D. Perlman Places. 1836. Reconstructed, 1936, N.Y.C. Department of Parks. ☆

This pair of parks bisected by Second Avenue brings the English tradition to what was once a strictly residential neighborhood. Squares in London are fenced green areas unlike the paved *piazze, plazas, Plätze,* or *places* of continental Europe. This duo, a gift of Peter G. Stuyvesant, benefited the city as well as owners of the surrounding land: the first in urban grace, the latter in future profits. Statuary: *Peter G. Stuyvesant* (1936. Gertrude Vanderbilt Whitney).

[C 4b.] Salvation Army/originally **St. John the Baptist House,** 231-235 E. 17th St., bet. Second and Third Aves. E part, 1877, Emlen T. Littel. W part, 1883, Charles C. Haight. ☆

Picturesque, asymmetrical Victorian Gothic.

[C 4c.] David B. Kriser Psychiatric Day Treatment Program/originally **Sidney Webster residence,** 245 E. 17th St., bet. Second and Third Aves. 1883. Richard Morris Hunt. ☆

A brick and brownstone updating of the French Renaissance.

[C 3.] Former Joe King's (1967 photo)   [C 5a.] St. George's Parish House

[C 5.] St. George's Church (Episcopal), Rutherford Place, NW cor. E. 16th St., facing Stuyvesant Sq. 1856. Blesch & Eidlitz. ★ ☆ **[C 5a.] Parish House,** 207 E. 16th St. 1888. Cyrus L. W. Eidlitz. ☆ **[C 5b.] Chapel,** 4 Rutherford Place. 1911. Matthew Lansing Emery and Henry George Emery. ☆ **[C 5c.] Henry Hill Pierce House**/originally **Rectory,** 209 E. 16th St. Early 1850s. Leopold Eidlitz. ☆

J. P. Morgan's church: stolid brownstone, cut and dressed. The chapel is not in the same bald and bold class as its parent; it is **overdressed,** in a **Byzantine-Romanesque Revival** fashion. The parish house bears a rock-face brownstone facade, a towered **Gothic Revival.**

[C 6.] Friends Meeting House and **Seminary,** 221 E. 15th St., NW cor. Rutherford Place, facing Stuyvesant Sq. 1860. Charles T. Bunting. ★ ☆

Appropriately plain Quaker architecture. Such spartan buildings spoke well to the era of austere modern architecture. Here it is packaged in red brick, brownstone quoins, and white trim.

[C 7.] St. Mary's Catholic Church of the Byzantine Rite, 246 E. 15th St., SW cor. Second Ave. 1964. Brother Cajetan J. B. Baumann.

A concrete and stained-glass box that glows polychromatically on the nights it is lit within.

[C 8.] Originally **New York Infirmary**/now **New York Infirmary-Beekman Downtown Hospital,** Nathan D. Perlman Place, bet. E. 15th and E. 16th Sts. E side. 1950. Skidmore, Owings & Merrill.

One fault of "modern" architecture is that it can become dated more rapidly than that of any other period. Here the bold modernism of 1950 seems a bore in retrospect. Alterations, of course, have dimmed its elegant detailing: clunky windows have replaced those of considerable style.

[C 9.] Apartments and offices/originally **Lying-In Hospital,** 305 Second Ave., bet. E. 17th and E. 18th Sts. W side. 1902. R. H. Robertson. Converted, 1985, Beyer Blinder Belle.

Swaddled babies lurk in laurel wreaths in the spandrels. Otherwise this bland neo-Renaissance block is boring until one reaches the top, where a **Palladian crown** surmounts it all. Architects of the turn of the 20th century, concerned about the idea of a New York skyline, occasionally neglected the pedestrian, spending all their efforts—and money—against the sky.

Gramercy Park and Environs

[C 10.] Gramercy Park Historic District, an irregular area including the park, its west and south frontages, and part of that to the east; also much of the north side of E. 18th St., and both sides of E. 19th St. bet. Irving Place and Third Ave., including Calvary Church. ★

[C 10a.] The Block Beautiful, E. 19th St. bet. Irving Place and Third Ave. Remodeled as a group, ca. 1920s, Frederick J. Sterner. ☆

A handsome, picturesque, architectural unit, notable more for the sum than the parts. No single building is of great distinction; still, it is one of best places in New York. Treelined, with limited traffic, it is quiet, serene, urbane.

Pete's Tavern/once **Portman Hotel/**later **Tom Healy's,** 129 E. 18th St., NE cor. Irving Place. 1829.

A **social landmark** since 1903 in a corner bar that has the patina of age. A shallow sidewalk café bounds two sides, and bare brick brings a vintage experience: good Itálian food and burgers. O. Henry wrote "The Gift of the Magi" in the **second booth.**

Paul and Jimmy's Place (restaurant), 123 E. 18th St., bet. Park Ave. S. and Irving Place.

Formerly on **Irving Place** proper, it has moved around the corner. Superb southern Italian cooking in a small, popular restaurant, with a bar up front.

[C 11.] Gramercy Park, Gramercy Park E. and W., Gramercy Park N. and S., with axis on Lexington Ave. to the N, Irving Place to the S. 1831. Samuel Ruggles. ☆

Enlightened self-interest graced this neighborhood with a park. Although private and restricted to the tenants occupying the original surrounding plots, it is a handsome space for all strollers to enjoy. It was built with the same principle the **Dukes of Bedford** employed in London, where the speculative housing precincts of **Bloomsbury** and **Covent Garden** were made not only more delightful but also more profitable by the addition of parks and squares, and by consistent architectural quality control. **Union Square** originally had a similar role with its surrounding private mansions.

Edwin Booth, brother of Lincoln assassin John Wilkes, lived at 16 Gramercy Park South. His statue stands in the park as placed by sculptor **Edmond T. Quinn** in 1916.

[C 11a.] The Players, 16 Gramercy Park S., bet. Park Ave. S. and Irving Place. S side. 1845. Remodeled, 1888, Stanford White. ★ ☆

Edwin Booth bought this house to found a club for those in the theater (as loosely defined). He was a star in a sense not easily conceivable today, when stars are not so rare. A **super** brownstone, with a 2-story Tuscan porch bracketed by great wrought-iron lanterns.

[C 11b.] National Arts Club, 15 Gramercy Park S., bet. Park Ave. S. and Irving Place S side. 1884. Calvert Vaux. ★ ☆

Here the **Vaux** (say "Vawx") of **Olmsted & Vaux** reverted to a single architectural commission for **Samuel J. Tilden,** outspoken opponent of the Tweed Ring who was elected governor of New York in **1874.** In 1876 **Tilden** ran for president against **Rutherford B. Hayes;** he won the popular vote by almost 250,000 but lost in the electoral college. Fearful of his personal security in a time of riots, **Tilden** had rolling steel doors built into the Gramercy Park facade (behind the windows), and a tunnel to 19th Street for a speedy exit in case the doors failed. Gothic Revival in the manner of **John Ruskin.** Brownstone and polished black granite trim. Recently restored.

[C 12a.] Evyan House/formerly **Benjamin Sonnenberg residence/** formerly **Stuyvesant Fish residence,** 19 Gramercy Park S., SE cor. Irving Place. 1845. Altered. ☆

John Barrymore lived here while working on Broadway. Ben Sonnenberg was an oldtime publicist as renowned as **Ivy Lee & T. J. Ross,** or **Edward L. Bernays.** Bernays was the advisor to John D. Rockefeller, who recommended that Rockefeller give away dimes prolifically to little kids.

[C 12b.] The Brotherhood Synagogue/originally **Friends Meeting House,** 28 Gramercy Park S., bet. Irving Place and Third Ave. S side. 1859. King & Kellum. ★ Remodeled as synagogue, 1975, James Stewart Polshek & Partners. ☆

An appropriately **spartan** brownstone box built for the Quakers and now used by another religious group.

[C 12c.] Originally **Gramercy Park Hotel,** 34 Gramercy Park E., NE cor. E. 20th St. 1883. G. W. da Cunha. ☆

A craggy, mysterious red brick and red terra-cotta pile whose Queen Anne forms are among the city's most spectacular.

[C 12d.] 36 Gramercy Park East (apartments), bet. E. 20th and E. 21st Sts. E side. 1910. James Riely Gordon.

The uptown brethren of this neo-Gothic, white terra-cotta, bay-windowed apartment house have been mostly demolished to build apartments with more floors and lower ceilings.

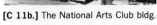
[C 11b.] The National Arts Club bldg.   **[C 13.]** 3 and 4 Gramercy Park West

[C 13.] 3 and **4 Gramercy Park West,** bet. E. 20th and E. 21st Sts. W side. 1846. Alexander Jackson Davis.

The ironwork is notable here, over plain brick bodies. Davis was one of America's most versatile 19th-century architects.

 [C 14a.] Hastings (tile and block showroom), 230 Park Ave. S., SW cor. E. 19th St. Showroom, 1987, Studio Morsa, designers.

Lots of slick tempered glass held together by bold clips . . . but then, set in the entrance floor some old tesserae, as though from Pompeii. Magnificent.

[C 14b.] Entry, 233 Park Avenue South (lofts), SW cor. E. 19th St. Entrance redesigned, 1986, Peter Pran and Carlos Zapata, design. Russo+Sonder, architects.

A svelte Post Modern entry to a typical Fourth Avenue (old name) loft.

[C 14c.] Positano (restaurant), 250 Park Ave. S., SW cor. E. 20th St. 1985. Randolph Croxton.

A cool, classic, elegant dining salon, in understated cream, white, and tan. Restaurateurs usually choose a single level for kitchen and dining, providing maximum efficiency for the aching legs of waiters and waitresses. Here, however, **spry thighs** deliver goodies on multiple elevations, a kinetic event that gives 3 dimensions to this restaurant world.

[C 15a.] Calvary Church (Episcopal), 273 Park Ave. S., NE cor. E. 21st St. 1848. James Renwick, Jr. **[C 15b.] The Sunday School Building,** to N on Park Ave. S. 1867. James Renwick, Jr. ☆

Second-rate Renwick; its wooden towers long since removed because of deterioration. The adjacent Sunday school pavilion is now rented as offices.

[C 15c.] Protestant Welfare Agencies Building/originally **Church Missions' House,** 281 Park Ave. S., SE cor. E. 22nd St. 1894. R. W. Gibson and E. J. N. Stent. ★

A glassy, articulated stone office building worthy of commercial buildings of the Flemish and **Dutch Renaissance.** Lovely. It provides generous light and a sleek glass wall to the street.

[C 15d.] Gramercy Place (apartments)/originally **New York Bank for Savings,** 280 Park Ave. S., SW cor E. 22nd St. 1894. C. L. W. Eidlitz. Alterations to bank building and new apartment tower, 1987, Beyer Blinder Belle.

The shell of the old **Bank for Savings** presents a historical entrance to an otherwise ordinary apartment tower. The streetfronted corner maintains a link with lower Fourth Avenue history.

[C 15e.] Originally **United Charities Building,** 287 Park Avenue S., NE cor. E. 22nd St. 1891. R. H. Robertson and Rowe & Baker.

Though ornamented, a bulky and boring work. Even Robertson could occasionally produce a bland product.

[C 16a.] Gramercy Towers (apartments)/originally **Russell Sage Foundation,** 4 Lexington Ave., SW cor. E. 22nd St. ca. 1914. Grosvenor Atterbury. Tower added, ca. 1919. Converted to apartments, 1975.

Now housing people instead of offices, this lovingly detailed Renaissance Revival building continues to bear traces of its beginnings, e.g., the frieze: FOR THE IMPROVEMENT OF SOCIAL AND LIVING CONDITIONS. Among the early works of the philanthropic foundation was Forest Hills Gardens [see C Queens C 53.].

[C 16b.] Mabel Dean Bacon Vocational High School/originally **Manhattan Trade School For Girls,** 129 E. 22nd St., NW cor. Lexington Ave. 1919. C. B. J. Snyder.

No nonsense here: 10 stories of loft space for vocational education. The exterior does have some handsome terra-cotta detailing.

[C 16c.] 134 East 22nd Street (apartments), bet. Lexington and Third Aves. Converted to apartments, 1975, William B. Gleckman.

A stylish 7-story brown brick apartment house that might be at home in Milan. The crossover balconies (for fire exits from the duplexes) provide large-scaled architectural form.

[C 16d.] 150 East 22nd Street (carriage house), bet. Lexington and Third Aves. 1893. S. V. Stratton.

Buildings for our 4-footed friends often exceed in visual quality those meant for the biped variety. This Dutch-gabled specimen is a case in point.

[C 17.] Madison Square Station, U. S. Post Office, 149 E. 23rd St., bet. Lexington and Third Aves. 1937. Lorimer Rich, architect. Louis A. Simon, Supervising Architect of the Treasury.

A cool, stripped Classical building in polished dark red granite, that could, surprisingly, be in the idiom of 1930s Washington, Albert Speer's Berlin, or the mortuary temple of **Queen Hatshepsut** at Dayr al-Bahri (1500 B.C.). Plus ça change . . .

Armory Sector
From 23rd to 34th Streets; Lexington to Second Aves.

[C 18.] Originally **Fiss Doerr & Carroll Horse Company (stables),** 151 E. 24th St., bet. Lexington and Third Aves. 1906. Horgan & Slattery.

One of two great barrel-vaulted riding stables, separated by a new-comer. This, the eastern one, is decorated with horse's heads. The architects are best known for their **Surrogate's Court/Hall of Records** across from City Hall [see L Manhattan/Civic Center C 14a.]. The western one, at **No. 139** is **H. Kauffman & Sons,** purveyors of riding equipment . . . since 1875.

Presidential inauguration: Such ceremonies normally take place in Washington. But on September 20, 1881, Chester A. Arthur was sworn in as president in the front parlor of his home at 123 Lexington Avenue, north of East 28th Street, by Judge John Brady of the New York State Supreme Court. The assassination of James A. Garfield had unexpectedly promoted Vice-President Arthur to the post.

 [C 19.] Originally **"I Love You Kathy" (apartments),** 160 E. 26th St., SW cor. Third Ave. Altered, 1975, Stephen B. Jacobs.

An unusual solution to fire escapes when altering an old tenement. The 26th Street facade is a stuccoed sculpture. (The building's name refers to the developer's emotional life.)

[C 18.] Morgan & Slattery's great bow-string-trussed former riding stables

Caliban (bar and restaurant), 360 Third Ave., bet. E. 26th and E. 27th Sts. W side. 1966. Haroutiun Derderian.

An elegant modern bar: its exposed brick in counterpoint with a rich Victorian bar-counter. Spacious, richly austere. The wine list is extensive.

Newsstand, E. 29th St., SE cor. Third Ave.

A rare holdout. This one is *not* at a subway entrance and is *not* a minuscule "doghouse" at the curb. Large and boldly occupying globs of sidewalk space, it leans against the brick wall of the building, its prime means of (physical) support. Economic support is provided by the purchasers of the magazines and newspapers which **plummet forth** from all directions. It doesn't offer much of a living so its days are numbered—unless Hollywood preserves it for its upcoming **nostalgia** films about Gotham: one of a dying breed.

[C 20.] Originally **69th Regiment Armory, N. Y. National Guard,** 68 Lexington Ave., bet. E. 25th and E. 26th Sts. W side. 1906. Hunt & Hunt. ★

The armory of the **Armory Show** of 1913, the bombshell entry of cubist painting to America. A brick, mansarded palace with **gun bays surveying Lexington.** The drill hall behind the Lexington Avenue facade shows its barrel form to the street, ribbed and buttressed with an exposed, articulated structure.

[C 21.] St. Stephen's Catholic Church   **[C 20.]** The 69th Regiment Armory

[C 21.] St. Stephen's Church (Roman Catholic), 149 E. 28th St. bet. Lexington and Third Aves. 1854. James Renwick, Jr. Extended to N, 1865, P. C. Keely. Restored, 1949. School, ca. 1902, Elliott Lynch.

Brownstone Romanesque Revival: an airy hall. Its slender cast-iron (plaster encased) columns with elaborate foliated capitals support multiribbed vaulting. The transepts have unusual galleries overseeing the nave. Interior mural by Constantino Brumidi, "decorator" of the Capitol in Washington. Unfortunately, the whole has been smoothed over in brownstone-colored stucco. The extension onto East 29th Street is more tempestuous and in the original brick and stone.

[C 22.] 203 East 29th Street (residence), bet. Second and Third Aves. 1790 (carriage house). 1870 (house). James Cali, architect. John Sanguiliano, restoration architect.

It is a rarity to find a **wood frame** building in Manhattan, particularly right on the street and not hidden in some out-of-the-way backyard. Here it is! Lovingly restored. Too lovingly?

[C 23.] Kips Bay Branch, New York Public Library, 446 Third Ave., SW cor. E. 31st St. 1971. Giorgio Cavaglieri.

A sculptured corner-turner along Third Avenue. Just enough of a widened sidewalk to invite its users to enter.

A touch of India: The area around 28th Street, between Madison and Third Avenues, is a minibazaar of foods, fabrics, and other delicacies from the Indian subcontinent. **Spice & Sweet Mahal** (135 Lexington Ave., cor. E. 29th St.), for example, purveys freshly prepared snacks and desserts for sidewalk feasting, as well as the normal stock of canned and packaged foods. Diaphanous fabrics for saris are available elsewhere in this area, as well as oriental rugs.

Old Print Shop, 150 Lexington Ave., bet. E. 29th and E. 30th Sts. W side.

Appropriately humble, like the rich wearing old clothes, it is a mine of maps and prints, from modest to very expensive.

[C 24a.] First Moravian Church/originally **Church of the Mediator (Baptist)**, 154 Lexington Ave., SW cor. E. 30th St. ca. 1845.

A plain brick box with gabled roof and tall, narrow, half-round arched windows. A modest gem. Lombardian Romanesque.

 [C 24b.] Vocational Rehabilitation Agency/originally **New York School of Applied Design for Women**, 160 Lexington Ave., NW cor. E. 30th St. 1909. Pell & Corbett. ★

A great tour de force of neo-Grecian design: a veritable 20th-century **temple to the arts.** Note the witty, single polished gray marble column (in antis) on the Lexington Avenue facade. It is said that designer Harvey Wiley Corbett's atelier of fledgling architects worked on the drawings.

 [C 25.] Raymond R. Corbett Building/originally **Iron Workers Security Funds (offices)**, 451 Park Ave. S., bet. E. 30th and E. 31st Sts. E side. Altered, 1978. 7-story addition, 1988, Wank, Adams, Slavin & Assocs.

This "cor-ten" building (rusty steel **meant** to be rusty) expanded upward, with a new facade worthy of the union leader for whom it was renamed.

Baseball's beginnings: A plaque once affixed at the southeast corner of Lexington Avenue and 34th Street states that at this site Alexander Joy Cartwright, Jr. organized the first baseball game played in America using most of the rules governing today.

END of Central Tour. Nearest subway is the IRT Lexington Avenue Line local at the 33rd Street Station, Park Avenue at East 33rd.

East Corridor

Four Squares East Walking Tour: A ramble along Stuyvesant Town, Peter Cooper Village, and the hospital complexes to the north. **START** at 14th Street and First Avenue and walk uptown along First. The nearest subway is the First Avenue Station of the infrequent BMT 14th Street-Canarsie Line, which does offer free connections at Union Square, Sixth Avenue, and Eighth Avenue to IRT Lexington Avenue, BMT Broadway, and IND Sixth and Eighth Avenue trains.

[E 1.] Immaculate Conception Church (Roman Catholic)/originally **Grace Chapel and Dispensary (Episcopal)**, 406-412 E. 14th St., bet. First Ave. and Avenue A. 1894. Barney & Chapman. ★

These **François I**-style buildings were built as an outpost of Grace Church and were purchased by the Roman Catholic archdiocese in 1943. Their picturesque forms might be found in the **Loire Valley,** as might those of their uptown descendant, Holy Trinity, in Yorkville.

[E 2.] Stuyvesant Town (apartment complex), E. 14th to E. 20th Sts., First Ave. to FDR Drive/Avenue C. 1947. Irwin Clavan and Gilmore Clarke.

Tax abatement allowed this Metropolitan Life Insurance Company project to supply middle-income housing to servicemen returning from World War II. The early brutality of this huge, dense (8,755 families) project is now softened by trees.

[E 3.] 326, 328, and 330 East 18th Street (row houses), bet. First and Second Aves. 1853. ★

Deep front yards have caused this tiny trio to be overlooked but certainly not neglected; the charming original cast-iron work is reminiscent of New Orleans. An early development for land east of Third Avenue here leased from Cornelia Stuyvesant Ten Broeck.

[E 4.] Peter Cooper Village (apartment complex), E. 20th to E. 23rd Sts., First Ave. to FDR Drive. 1947. Irwin Clavan and Gilmore Clarke.

More space and more rent make this the **rich stepbrother** of Stuyvesant Town.

[E 5a.] Church of the Epiphany (Roman Catholic), 373 Second Ave., bet. E. 21st and E. 22nd Sts. W side. 1967. Belfatto & Pavarini.

Highly styled brown brick: this is the **phoenix** of a 19th-century church on this site destroyed by fire. It is the most positive modern religious statement on **Manhattan Island** to date.

[E 5b.] 220 East 22nd Street (apartments), bet. Second and Third Aves.

A conversion similar to that at **134 East 22nd** [C 16c.].

[E 5a.] R.C. Church of the Epiphany   **[E 3.]** 326-330 E. 18th Street houses

[E 5c.] 235 East 22nd Street apts.   **[E 5b.]** 220 East 22nd Street apts.

[E 5c.] 235 East 22nd Street (apartments), NW cor. Second Ave. 1928. George & Edward Blum.

An Art Deco frieze bands this early Modern apartment house in glazed terra-cotta. The most interesting thing here is the precocious date. [For another, see E Manhattan/East of Eden E 15.]

Kips Bay and Environs

From 23rd to 34th Streets between Second Avenue and the East River.

[E 6.] East Midtown Plaza (apartment complex), E. 23rd to E. 25th Sts., bet. First and Second Aves. 1972, 1974. All by Davis, Brody & Assocs.

Brown brick, **cut, carved, notched and molded:** the "balconies" are architectural spaces and forms, not paste-ons. Urbane street architecture, with the terraces of Babylon; this is **an ode to brick.**

[E 7.] Public Baths, City of New York, E. 23rd St., NE cor. Asser Levy Place, bet. First Ave. and FDR Drive. 1906. Arnold W. Brunner and William Martin Aiken. ★

Roman pomp was particularly appropriate for a public bath, a Roman building type we reproduced indiscriminately for other functions (cf. the now demolished Pennsylvania Station modeled on the **Baths of Caracalla**). These public baths are, in that sense, our **Baths of Roosevelt** (Teddy) or, on a local level, the **Baths of McClellan** (mayor of New York).

[E 8a.] United Nations International School, 2450 FDR Drive, opp. E. 25th St. S of Waterside. 1973. Harrison, Abramovitz & Harris.

A bulky, white precast-concrete block hugging the East River shore and **Waterside; an illogical site** for students in need of public transportation at a large volume.

[E 8b.] Waterside apartment complex   **[E 6.]** East Midtown Plaza apartments

[E 8b.] Waterside (apartment complex), FDR Drive bet. E. 25th and E. 30th Sts. E side. 1974. Davis, Brody & Assocs.

Brown towers of a **cut and carved cubism** mounted on a platform tucked in a notch of the East River. Sixteen hundred units, shopping, restaurants, and pedestrian plazas give a share of Manhattan's glorious waterfront **back to the people.** *Wander about, and to the water's edge. Try not to notice the bleakness of the barren, relentlessly paved central space.*

[E 9.] The Water Club (restaurant), 500 E. 30th St. at the East River. 1982. Michael O'Keeffe, owner-designer; Clement J. Benvenga and Mullen Palandrani, architects; M. Paul Friedberg, landscape architect.

A Post Modern structure using the traditional bent metal materials from which its wharf predecessors—alas, largely demolished—were often crafted. Popular with the "enjoy dinner with a view of Newtown Creek across the river" set. Drop in for a drink.

[E 10.] Bellevue Hospital Center, E. 25th to E. 30th Sts., First Ave. to FDR Drive. 1908–1939. McKim, Mead & White. **[E 10a.] Psychiatric Hospital,** Charles B. Meyers and Thompson, Holmes & Converse.

Its old brick hulk is now squeezed between the parking garage addition on First Avenue and a giant 22-story "wing" facing the river. The top floors and roof contain the only serious architectural embellishments: Roman brick Corinthian columns and pitched tile roofs. **"Belle Vue"** was the name of Peter Keteltas' farm, which occupied this site in the 18th century.

[E 10b.] New Building, Bellevue Hospital, E. 27th to E. 28th Sts. 1974. Katz, Waisman, Weber, Strauss; Joseph Blumenkranz; Pomerance & Breines; Feld & Timoney. Parking garage, 1965.

A behemoth. Each floor is 1½ acres of loft space served by 20 elevators. It's the tall beige cube you pass on the FDR Drive.

[E 11.] Jesse Stanton Developmental Playground for Preschool Handicapped Children, Howard A. Rusk Institute of Rehabilitation Medicine, N.Y.U.-Bellevue Medical Center, 400 E. 34th St., bet. First Ave. and FDR Drive. 1971. Richard Dattner & Assocs.

A specially designed playground for the handicapped, just barely visible on tall tiptoes from the sidewalk.

[E 12a.] N.Y.U.-Bellevue Medical Center, 550 and 560 First Ave., bet. E. 30th and E. 34th Sts. E side to FDR Drive. 1950. Skidmore, Owings & Merrill. Additions through 1977.

A teaching hospital can attract staff and faculty of the highest stature. They are provided for here in a facility complementing **Bellevue Hospital,** designed in a single master plan by **SOM** and constructed over more than 25 years. White glazed brick and aluminum sash.

[E 13.] N.Y.U. Medical School (housing), 545 First Ave. bet. E. 31st and E. 32nd Sts. W side. 1986. Pomerance & Breines.

Elegant detailing sings of architecture, although the form (a simple slab) is nothing special; but why should it be? Gray brick, with subtle limestone bandings, is **exuberantly** enhanced with showstopping vermillion window frames.

[E 14.] The vast concrete grillage of one of the paired Kips Bay Plaza apartments

[E 14.] Kips Bay Plaza (apartment complex), E. 30th to E. 33rd Sts., First to Second Aves. S Building, 1960. N Building, 1965. I. M. Pei & Assocs. and S. J. Kessler.

New York's **first** exposed concrete apartment houses, joined soon after by **Chatham Towers** (*1965, Kelly & Gruzen*) and Pei's own **University Plaza** (1966). No longer either fashionable or economically feasible, concrete has been replaced by stone, usually granite, in the buildings of the 1980s. New technology allows **ultrathin** stone, mounted on a steel frame, to both veneer solid form and create lithic tents, as at the E. F. Hutton Building [Fifth Avenue F 11a.]

The vast open space tries to compensate for the huge 21-story building slabs. These are stepchildren of Le Corbusier's **Marseilles Block,** the giant and beautifully detailed concrete building in a park. Here, the **city planning decision** is more important than architectural detail (although the latter is careful but boring). Do buildings define urban pedestrian space—streets, boulevards and plazas—or shall they be freestanding objects in a park? In 1960 the latter proposition seemed to be gaining currency; these days **the streets are winning** again.

[E 15a.] Pinkerton Environmental Center, Madison Square Boys & Girls Club, 524-528 Second Ave., NE cor. E. 29th St. 1979. Wank, Adams & Slavin, architects. Zion & Breen, landscape architects.

The club describes this as "a community garden and nature education center." Go in—it's a lovely oasis.

[E 15b.] Madison Square Boys and Girls Club, 301 E. 29th St., bet. First and Second Aves. 1940. Holden, McLaughlin & Assocs.

A handsome, no-nonsense **early Modern** building in salmon brick, with a dado of shining black glazed tile.

[E 16.] Phipps Plaza (apartment complex), Second Ave. bet. E. 26th and E. 29th Sts. E side. 1976. Frost Assocs.

High-rise red brick that caught some styling from East Midtown Plaza to the south [see E 6.]. **Polygonal diagonal.** But it fails to honor **any street** as does East Midtown's glorious bow to 23rd.

[E 17.] Milton Glaser, Inc. (design studio)/earlier **Push Pin Studios/** earlier **New York Magazine/**originally **4th District Municipal Courthouse** a.k.a. **Yorkville Municipal Courthouse,** 207 E. 32nd St., bet. Second and Third Aves. ca. 1910.

Beaux Arts pomp and circumstance orphaned when its row house neighbors were removed for an apartment house plaza and a school yard. Its adaptive reuses reveal a studied appreciation of its visual values by a prestigious list of occupants.

 [E 18.] Public School 116, Manhattan, 220 E. 33rd St., bet. Second and Third Aves. 1925. William H. Gompert.

Neo-Romanesque brick, terra-cotta, and limestone. Whimsical figures support arches over the "Boy's" and "Girl's" entrances.

 [E 19.] Originally **Civic Club/**now **Estonian House,** 243 E. 34th St., bet. Second and Third Aves. 1899. Thomas A. Gray. ★

A lonely limestone **Beaux Arts** town house commissioned by philanthropist **F. Norton Goddard.**

[E 20.] St. Vartan Cathedral of the Armenian Orthodox Church in America, 620 Second Ave., bet. E. 34th and E. 35th Sts. E side. 1967. Steinmann & Cain.

A huge (to accommodate cathedral-sized congregations) version of early **Romanesque Armenian** churches in Asia Minor. Note the corner crucifix dovetailings.

[E 21.] Rivergate apartments Ice Skating Rink, 401 E. 34th St., NE cor. First Ave.

A public amenity that allowed a bonus in floor area for the stepped-back apartment tower that occupies the site of what was once a 2-story Coca-Cola bottling plant. As required by the City Planning Department a permanent inventory of the amenity is properly affixed: **1** skating rink, **24 4″** caliper trees, **790** linear feet of seating (**79** linear feet with backs), **48** bicycle spaces, **1** drinking fountain. These and the delicately fashioned space-frame ornaments somehow **do not** an amenity make.

[E 22.] Manhattan Place (apartments), 630 First Ave., bet. E. 36th and E. 37th St. E side. 1984. Costas Kondylis of Philip Birnbaum & Assocs. **Plaza,** 1984, Thomas Balsley Assocs., landscape architects.

A long, tall bay-windowed brick mass forcefully turned on the bias, creating a triangular plaza with fountain. Glitzy polished brass adorns the first few floors; dark anodized aluminum clads the penthouse level (as though the budget for glitz ran out).

END of Four Squares East Tour. The nearest subway is at the 33rd Street Station of the IRT Lexington Avenue Line local.

HERALD SQUARE AND WEST

In the **1870s** and **1880s** the whole area between the respectability of Fifth Avenue and the slums of **Hell's Kitchen** (west of Seventh Avenue), from the 20s through the 30s, was New York's **Tenderloin.** The present Herald Square was right in the middle of it. Dance halls and cafés were lined up under the el' along Sixth Avenue, with bordellos on the shady side streets, all flourishing under the Tammany Hall political machine. A brief period of reform in the 1890s **dimmed the gaiety** of the Tenderloin, and it slowly faded away. Both the theater and the press (such as **James Gordon Bennett's** *New York Herald*) made brief stops at Herald Square in the 1890s on their way north—leaving behind one of two squares with newspaper names.

In 1904 the Pennsylvania Railroad **opened its tunnel** under the Hudson and cut a broad swath to its monumental 2-block-square station (opened 1910), erasing some of the **Hell's Kitchen tenements.** (In the 1930s Lincoln Tunnel approaches cut down more.) The **new station** quickly attracted the equally monumental General Post Office, some major hotels, and a cluster of middle-class department stores, which found the square an ideally convenient goal for **their march up Sixth Avenue** from 14th Street. By the 1920s garment manufacturing had moved from the Lower East Side into the streets surrounding these pivot points. Today's garment industry is concentrated in the West 30s and 40s between Sixth and Eighth Avenues, with suppliers of fabrics, trimmings, and such located to the east as far as Madison Avenue.

In the 1980s the precinct was reactivated, with, most prominently, the **Javits Center** as its economic if not spiritual leader. In the meantime the faded hulk of old Gimbel's was renovated for a new **A&S** (Abraham & Straus), joined with a clutch of appropriate commercial bedfellows. Commerce, which seemed to *be* **MACY'S,** and once **GIMBEL'S** and **SAKS,** is still centered around this most redolent place, a juncture of transportation and merchandising.

Herald Square Walking Tour: From Macy's through part of the Garment Center, west to the Javits Convention Center, and then back to the Empire State Building and up a bit of Fifth Avenue. Put on your walking shoes. (Take a subway to the underground ganglion that stretches between Herald and Greeley Squares: the BMT Broadway Line and the IND Sixth Avenue Line to the 34th Street Station, and the PATH service from Greenwich Village and New Jersey to the 33rd Street Station.)

[Q 1.] Herald Square, intersection of Sixth Ave. and Broadway bet. W. 34th and W. 35th Sts. *Minerva, the Bellringers, and Owls,* 1895. Antonin Jean Carles, sculptor. Plaza, 1940, Aymar Embury II.

Namesake of the *New York Herald,* whose 2-story palazzo (*1893, McKim, Mead & White*) stood just to the north, this small triangular park is dominated by the newspaper's once crowning clock. Every hour **Stuff and Guff,** the bronze mannequins, pretend to strike the big bell as **Minerva** supervises from above. **Don't confuse** this square with **Greeley Square** to the south [see Q 18.].

[Q 1a.] Alpine Tavern/originally **Marine Grill, McAlpin Hotel,** 50 W. 34th St., SE cor. Sixth Ave. Lower level, 1913. F. M. Andrews.

In the bowels of a onetime hotel a vaulted, tiled, faience-embellished wonderment. On the walls are spirited ceramic scenes of New York Harbor's evolution. Simple fare down an uninspired flight of stairs.

[Q 2.] Macy's Department Store, W. 34th to W. 35th Sts., Broadway to Seventh Aves. Original (Broadway) building, 1902, De Lemos & Cordes. Successive additions to W, 1924, 1928, 1931. All by Robert D. Kohn.

The oldest (eastern) part of **"the world's largest store"** is sheathed in a dignified **Palladian facade.** The newer (western) parts grew increasingly **Art Deco** in style. At the southeast corner of the block there appears to be the **world's busiest hot dog stand** with a MACY'S sign on top. It's actually a 5-story 19th-century building bought at the turn of the century for an outrageous $375,000 by Robert S. Smith, Macy's neighbor at its old locations at 14th and Sixth [see Chelsea H 42a.]. Smith was thought to be acting as a spoiler on behalf of the owners of Siegel-Cooper [see Chelsea H 29.] who had completed what *they* believed to be the world's largest store in 1896. Macy's imperiously built around the corner holdout by creating a right-angled arcade so its window shoppers could traverse the department store's perimeter without passing Smith's frontage. The arcade is gone and Macy's went on to negotiate a rooftop site for its sign with Smith's heirs and their successors, the Kaufman (real estate) family.

The Broadway entrance and show windows have been remodeled, but the 34th Street side shows the handsome original details; note the **canopy, clock,** and the **hefty turn-of-the-century lettering.** The main floor has succumbed to a neo-**Art Deco** renovation. However, a quartet of older caryatids guards the 34th Street entrance.

Keens Chop House, 72 West 36th Street, just east of Sixth Avenue. Founded in 1878. A fixture in this area, dating back to its Tenderloin days. Known for its mutton chops (hard to find in the city's restaurants) and a display of thousands of clay pipes, each numbered and keyed to a master list, smoked by its many satisfied customers. The pipes are arrayed on the dining room's ceilings!

[Q 3.] Originally Greenwich Savings Bank/now **CrossLand Savings Bank,** 1356 Broadway, NE cor. W. 36th St. a.k.a. 985 Sixth Ave. 1924. York & Sawyer.

Giant Corinthian columns **march around 3 sides** of this templelike bank, interrupted only by columnar signs on 2 facades that almost undo the effect. Inside, more columns define a **grand oval rotunda** with a central skylight.

[Q 4a.] Church of the Holy Innocents (Roman Catholic), 128 W. 37th St., bet. Seventh Ave. and Broadway. S side. 1870. P. C. Keeley.

Light sandstone and darker brownstone intermingle in this Gothic Revival church, more elegantly detailed than the prolific Keeley's usual red brick models. Savor the ceiling within.

[Q 4b.] Woods 37th (restaurant), 148 W. 37th St., bet. Broadway and Seventh Ave. 1980. Charles Boxenbaum and James D'Auria.

Reserved, beautifully detailed, and an unusually civilized dining spot for the Garment Center. Deluxe.

The Garment Center: The West 30s have been the center of sewing, fabrics, ruffles, and lace since entrepreneurs discovered the wealth of labor in vast pools of urban immigrants—once eastern European, now sometimes Hispanic, sometimes Oriental. Fashion designers still hover around these needle-trade blocks, where the hand-hewer still vies with the machining needle. Nowadays, however, uptowners in other businesses (architects, lawyers, for example) have moved in, and condominium residences are rife. Constant threats of removal to distant pools of "more economic" labor surface, but where is this breed of economics reborn, and re-reborn again: Nueva York.

[Q 5.] Nelson Tower (offices), 450 Seventh Ave., bet. W. 34th and W. 35th Sts. W side. 1931. H. Craig Severance.

That slim, mysterious office tower with a rich **Art Deco** bas-relief at its crown, mostly savored from afar.

[Q 6.] J. J. Applebaum's Deli Company (restaurant), 431 Seventh Ave., bet. W. 33rd and W. 34th Sts. E side. 1980. Charles Morris Mount, Inc., designers.

A 4-story Kosher-style deli, skylit over its stacked stairs. It is surprising to find an architectural attempt among the litter of fast-food restaurants. Lesser neighbors include **Sbarro, King of China, Sushi King,** and **Gyro II,** demonstrating that any ethnic group can join the world of fast foods.

Here the corn is as ripe as the corned beef, from a **Rye Not** sandwich to one titled **Reuben' Elbows.**

[Q 7.] New York Penta (hotel)/originally **Hotel Pennsylvania,** 401 Seventh Ave., bet. W. 32nd and W. 33rd Sts. W side. 1918. McKim, Mead & White.

Like its neighbor to the south, the former **Equitable Building**—not to be confused with its downtown namesake [see L Manhattan/Broadway Nassau N 9.], this Classical block is set back 15 feet from the building line in response to the old **Pennsylvania Station** colonnade that faced it. It was a center for the big bands of the 1930s, and Glenn Miller wrote a tune called "PEnnsylvania 6-5000," still the hotel's phone number, now converted to all digits.

[Q 8.] Madison Square Garden Center, W. 31st to W. 33rd St., Seventh to Eighth Aves. 1968. Charles Luckman Assocs.

Anybody who remembers the **vast** Roman Revival **waiting room** and **even vaster iron-and-glass train shed** of McKim, Mead & White's 1910 Penn Station **will feel bereaved** here.

The **replacement entertainment and office complex** covering two blocks includes a 20,000-seat "garden," a 1,000-seat "forum," a 500-seat cinema, a 48-lane bowling center, a 29-story office building, an exposition "rotunda," an art gallery, and the usual dining, drinking, and shopping areas—all above the railroad station, which was underground to begin with but had a ceiling 150 feet high. The present "garden," the third one and closer to Madison Square than the second, is housed in a **precast-concrete-clad cylinder** and roofed by a 425-foot-diameter cable structure which **only physically replaces** its grand and beautiful noble predecessor. To be **demolished** and moved two blocks west to make room for a high-rise office tower with a **form of a fish** by Los Angeles architect **Frank Gehry.**

McKim, Mead & White's great steel and glass train shed for Penn Station in 1962

Pennsylvania Station: It's still called that, but today it's little more than the Amtrak/LIRR rabbit warren under the 2-square-block Penn Plaza office building and sports arena. It was on August 2, 1962, that a band of stalwart architects picketed—alas, unsuccessfully—against the demolition of the *real* Penn Station, by McKim, Mead & White (see Necrology). The demonstration was organized by AGBANY, the Action Group for Better Architecture in New York, a group of young New York architects led by Norval White. Jim Burns, Jordan Gruzen, Norman Jaffe, Diana Kirsch, Jan Rowan, Peter Samton, and Elliot Willensky, among others, picketed with posters prepared by students at all of the city's architectural schools. Among the architectural notables it attracted for picketing and television interviews were Philip Johnson, Peter Blake, Aline Saarinen, John Johansen, and board members of the Museum of Modern Art.

[Q 9.] General Post Office, Eighth Ave. bet. W. 31st and W. 33rd Sts. W side. 1913. McKim, Mead & White. Annex to W, 1935. ★

The 2-block row of 53-foot Corinthian columns, and what is probably **the world's longest inscription,** once faced the equally long, somewhat stubbier row of Penn Station's Doric columns.

[Q 3.] The Greenwich Savings Bank   [Q 9.] New York's General Post Office

[Q 10a.] Originally **New Yorker Hotel,** 481 Eighth Avenue, bet. W. 34th and W. 35th Sts. W side. 1930. Sugarman & Berger.

An Art Deco relic, once a popular economy-priced hotel. In its heyday it boasted **2,500 rooms,** 92 **"telephone girls"** at the 41st-floor switchboards, and a **42-chair barber shop** with 20 manicurists. In 1976 it became a facility of Rev. Sun Myung Moon's **World Unification Church,** as did Manhattan Center, next door:

[Q 10b.] Formerly **Manhattan Center/**originally **Manhattan Opera House,** 311 W. 34th St., bet. Eighth and Ninth Aves. 1906. Altered.

A traditional gathering place for union contract debate and votes. An annex to [Q 10a.] above.

Sound films were still experimental when Warner Brothers, collaborating with Bell Laboratories, exhibited them at the Manhattan Center in 1926, when it was still known as the Manhattan Opera House. Warner created elsewhere, but here was a vast auditorium that preceded by several years Radio City, the Roxy, and other mass places of mesmerization.

[Q 11.] Midtown South Precinct, N.Y.C. Police Department, 357 W. 35th St., bet. Eighth and Ninth Aves. 1970. Frost Assocs.

A freestanding temple to incarceration; its dark brown brick adds to the gloom of this loft-shadowed side street.

For the Hungry:

[Q 12.] Manganaro's Grosseria/originally **Ernest Petrucci's (food shop/restaurant),** 488 Ninth Ave., bet. W. 37th and W. 38th Sts. E side. 1893.

The architecture of food: pendant, stacked, glazed, bottled, canned—a symphony of color, texture, patina, and aroma. If you pass through, you will reach the Old World (self-service) restaurant. A special place.

Paddy's Market: A stretch of Ninth Avenue, between 36th and 42nd Streets, was for almost 50 years full of pushcart food venders, banished by Mayor La Guardia in the late 1930s. The market soon revived, however, as indoor shops with big outdoor displays featuring fresh fruit and vegetables, Italian, Greek, Polish, Spanish, and Philippine products.

[Q 13a.] St. Michael's Church, 424 W. 34th St., bet. Ninth and Tenth Aves. 1892. **Rectory,** 1906.

Romanesque Revival limestone church, the wall in rock-face ashlar, the arches and details smoothly contrasting.

[Q 13b.] Spearin Preston & Burrows, Inc. (offices), 446 W. 34th St., bet. Ninth and Tenth Aves. 1967. Edelman & Salzman.

A diminutive office block occupying a sliver of land left over after the approaches to the third tube of the Lincoln Tunnel were cut through.

[Q 14.] The J. K. Javits Center: shiny multifaceted set of obsidian glass forms

[Q 14.] Jacob Javits Convention Center, Eleventh to Twelfth Aves., bet. W. 34th and W. 37th Sts. 1986. James Ingo Freed of I. M. Pei & Partners. Lewis Turner Assocs., associate architects.

Aspiring to be the **Crystal Palace** of our generation, this shiny black multifaceted set of forms conjures thoughts of **geodes,** those geological broken remnants that are wondrous but opaque. The ball-jointed space frames within are impressive, a complex world of filigrees against the glass-shielded sky. The first pavilion of this ilk was that of the great London exhibition of 1851, gardener Joseph Paxton's fantastically inflated greenhouse, which housed Prince Albert's attempts to display Britain's industrial revolution to the world. Here the events are more mundane: those of conventioneers both professional and commercial, presenting ideas or products.

At night, the glowing lights within give a sense of the Center's potential transparency; by day the building might just as well be a set of opaque obsidian prisms.

[Q 14a.] Hudson River Center (mixed use), Twelfth Ave. bet. W. 34th and W. 37th Sts. W side. 1992? Gruzen Samton Steinglass.

Behind the Javits Center and mingling with the Hudson's waters is a project that will combine a little bit—or a lot—of many uses. Fluid: the program, the design, the cost, the river's waters.

[Q 15a.] Originally **Westyard Distribution Center,** Tenth Ave. bet. W. 31st and W. 33rd Sts. E side. 1970. Davis, Brody & Assocs.

A gutsy concrete structure that spans the Penn-Central tracks below. Its penthouse shelters an ice skating place, **Sky Rink** (450 West 33rd Street): crowded, with no windows—and *no* views.

[Q 15b.] **"The Ninth Avenue Tower"** and **Plaza,** 375 Ninth Ave., NW cor. W. 31st St. 1990? Both by Kohn Pedersen Fox Assocs. **[Q 15c.]** **"The Tower at Ninth Avenue,"** 401 Ninth Ave., SW cor. W. 33rd St. 1991? Gwathmey Siegel & Assocs.

A pair of office towers planned at the end of the 1980s construction boom facing each other across a plaza built atop the sunken Amtrak/LIRR tracks.

[Q 16a.] **St. John the Baptist Church (Roman Catholic),** 211 W. 30th St., bet. Seventh and Eighth Aves. 1872. Napoleon LeBrun. **[Q 16b.]** **Capuchin-Franciscan Friary,** 210 W. 31st St. 1975. Genovese & Maddalene.

Lost in the Fur District is this **exquisite** single-spired brownstone church, a **Roman Catholic** midtown **Trinity.** The interior, of white marble, radiates light. Worth a special visit. The friary is a properly modest new work on the opposite blockfront.

[Q 17a.] Originally **23rd Precinct, N.Y.C. Police Department/**now **Manhattan Traffic Unit B,** 134 W. 30th St., bet. Sixth and Seventh Aves. 1907. R. Thomas Short.

Battlements, merlons, embrasures, crenellations—**a fortress out of place** among loft buildings but serving the area by the contribution of its wit to a midtown canyon.

[Q 17b.] **The S.J.M. Building (lofts),** 130 W. 30th St., bet. Sixth and Seventh Aves. 1927. Cass Gilbert, Inc.

Assyrian Revival. An early bronze and glass curtain wall embraced by a pair of masonry elevator towers. Figures in **Mesopotamian friezes** race around the walls of the building at each setback. And over the two entrances stylized symmetrical lions glare in polychromed terra-cotta bas-relief.

[Q 18.] **Greeley Square,** intersection of Sixth Ave. and Broadway, bet. W. 32nd and W. 33rd Sts. Designated, 1894.

Horace Greeley, founder of the *New York Tribune,* is remembered by this triangle and a statue (*1890. Alexander Doyle*).

[Q 18a.] **A & S Greeley Square Plaza/**originally **Gimbel Brothers Department Store,** 1275 Broadway, bet. W. 32nd and W. 33rd Sts. opp. Greeley Sq. W side. 1912. D. H. Burnham & Co. Converted to mall, 1988, RTKL Assocs. Office tower addition, 1989, Emery Roth & Sons.

A neo-Classical box by Chicago's Burnham hollowed out into a Post Modern galleria by Baltimore's RTKL for primary tenancy by Brooklyn's A & S.

High above 32nd Street, the multistory connecting bridge (*look up!*) is a copper-clad Art Deco sleeper by Shreve, Lamb & Harmon, of Empire State Building fame. Another bridge of sighs, closer to the street, connected the old Gimbel's to its sister store across 33rd Street, first called Saks; when Saks opened on **Fifth Avenue** [see Fifth Avenue F 5a.] it changed its name to **Saks-34th.** This bridge was demolished with its conversion to a Korvette's discount department store, reconstructed again to:

[Q 18b.] **Herald Center/**originally **Saks & Company (department store)** later **Saks-34th Street,** 1911-1233 Broadway, bet. W. 33rd and W. 34th Sts. 1902. Buchman & Fox. Redesigned, 1985, Copeland, Novak, Israel & Simmon.

A bulbous blue whale with a demure—too demure—identification sign and—a first for New York—glassed-in elevators that twinkle their way upward at the 34th Street corner.

[Q 18c.] **Hotel Martinique,** 53 W. 32nd St., NE cor. Broadway. 1897. Annex, 1910. Both by Henry J. Hardenbergh.

An **opulent French Renaissance pile, topped** with several stories of mansards; the south facade is the real front. For years a notorious shelter for the homeless.

[Q 15a.] Orig. Westyard Distrib. Ctr. [Q 20a.] The Empire State Building

[Q 19.] **Kaskel & Kaskel Building,** 316 Fifth Ave., SW cor. W. 32nd St. 1903. Charles I. Berg.

A wonderful and crusty old **Beaux Arts** building, in the process of being devoured by its crummy commercial occupants.

The outsized pair of scissors projecting from the storefront announces in a time-honored way the scissors, shears, and leather-tools shop of Henry Westpfal & Company at 4 East 32nd Street, established in 1874 and looking very ancient within. Fun to browse.

[Q 20a.] **Empire State Building,** 350 Fifth Ave., bet. W. 33rd and W. 34th Sts. W side. 1931. Shreve, Lamb & Harmon. ★ Partial interior ★.

Once the world's tallest building, originally 1,250 feet high to the top of its mooring mast for apocryphal dirigibles. That height remained unequaled until completion of the **World Trade Center** towers, a record since surpassed only by the **Sears Tower** in Chicago. Planned during the booming 1920s, it went up during the Depression. Largely vacant in its early years, it was said that the building relied on the stream of sightseers to the observation decks to pay its taxes.

The monumental Fifth Avenue entrance is less interesting than the modernistic stainless steel canopies of the two sidestreet entrances. All of them lead to 2-story-high corridors around the elevator core (with 67 elevators in it), which is crossed here and there by stainless steel and glass-enclosed bridges.

[Q 20b.] Originally **Spear & Company (furniture store)/**now **retail stores and offices,** 22 W. 34th St., bet. Fifth and Sixth Aves. 1934. De Young & Moscowitz.

A startling Modern work for Midtown when completed during the Great Depression. Its antecedents in the work of **Willem Dudok** in the Netherlands and in Great Britain's cinema designs of the 1930s are evident (if you take the trouble to look beneath the retail camouflage that tattoos its facade today).

Empire State site: This pivotal spot has been occupied by two previous sets of landmarks. From 1857 to 1893 it was the site of two mansions belonging to the Astor family. Mrs. William Astor's place, on the corner of 34th Street, was for years the undisputed center of New York social life, and the capacity of her ballroom gave the name **The 400** to the city's elite. But in the early 1890s a feud developed between Mrs. Astor and her nephew, William Waldorf Astor, who had the house across the garden, on 33rd Street. He and his wife moved to Europe and had an 11-story hotel built on his property, naming it the **Waldorf** (the first John Jacob Astor's native village in Germany). Within a year after it opened in 1893, Mrs. Astor wisely decided to move out of its ominous shadow (up to 65th Street and Fifth Avenue) and put a connecting hotel, the **Astoria,** on her property. When the 16-story structure was completed in 1897, the hyphenated hotel immediately became a social mecca. The requirement of full formal dress (tails) in the Palm Room created a sensation even then, but made it the place to be seen. Successful as it was, the old Waldorf-Astoria operated under a curious agreement that the elder Mrs. Astor could have all connections between the buildings walled up at any time on demand.

 [Q 21.] B. Altman & Company (department store), 361 Fifth Ave., bet. E. 34th and E. 35th Sts. E side. 1906, extended 1914. Trowbridge & Livingston. ★ **Altman Midtown Centre,** office tower addition along Madison Ave., 1990, Hardy Holzman Pfeiffer Assocs.

Even after the first Waldorf-Astoria opened in 1897, Fifth Avenue from the 30s north remained **solidly residential.** Benjamin Altman made a prophetic breach by **moving his department store** from Sixth Avenue and 18th Street to this corner. To make the change less painful, it was designed (on its Fifth Avenue frontage) as a dignified 8-story Renaissance Revival block; the Fifth Avenue entrance shows the **atmosphere** Altman was trying for. Altman's set off a rush of fashionable stores to Fifth Avenue above 34th Street. Many of them made a **second** jump, to the 50s, leaving Altman's behind and, ironically, isolated.

[Q 22.] Originally Gorham Building   **[M 3d.]** Originally the Grolier Club

 [Q 22.] 390 Fifth Avenue/formerly **Russek's Furs**/originally **Gorham Building,** SW cor. W. 36th St. 1906. McKim, Mead & White. Alterations.

When Altman's opened at 34th Street, Gorham's, **the famous jewelers,** had just completed its Italian Renaissance **palace.** Russek's kept the fine architecture largely intact. The lower floors have been grossly altered, but the original columns and arches are visible on the 36th Street side. Above is a superb crowning cornice.

 [Q 23.] 409 Fifth Avenue (offices)/originally **Tiffany's,** SE cor. E. 37th St. 1906. McKim, Mead & White. Altered.

Finished only a year after the Gorham Building by the same architects, this more massive structure was modeled after the **Palazzo Grimani** in Venice. The 37th Street side retains the original motif of three ranks of giant paired Corinthian columns shouldering a broad cornice.

[Q 24a.] Once **W. & J. Sloane (furniture)**/formerly **Franklin Simon & Company (women's wear),** 414 Fifth Ave., SW cor. W. 38th St. 1922.
[Q 24b.]Lord & Taylor, 424-434 Fifth Ave., NW cor. W. 38th St. 1914. Starrett & Van Vleck.

These two buildings were the first along the avenue to dispense with colonnades and look frankly commercial. They are **pleasantly uncomplicated** in the middle floors but have vestiges of the palazzo at top and bottom.

A few notions: The side streets between Fifth and Sixth Avenues in the upper 30s are full of suppliers of trimmings for garments and millinery, and their windows are a great show. Beads, rhinestones, spangles, and laces predominate on West 37th Street; milliners' flowers and feathers, on West 38th.

END of Herald Square Walking Tour: Fifth Avenue buses downtown, Sixth and Madison Avenue buses uptown. Subways along 42nd Street at Fifth Avenue, Grand Central, or Times Square.

MURRAY HILL

The country home of **Robert Murray** once stood near where East 37th Street now crosses Park Avenue; it was here that **Murray's wife** is said to have entertained **General Howe** and his staff while the Revolutionary troops escaped to the northwest. In the late 19th century, social status on the fashionable hill was highest near the great mansions of Fifth Avenue, dropping off toward the east, where carriage houses gave way to tenements at **el-shaded** Third Avenue. When commerce moved up Fifth Avenue in the early 1900s, Murray Hill became an isolated but **vigorous patch of elegance,** centered about Park Avenue, where through traffic (first horsecars, then trolleys, now cars) was diverted into the old railroad tunnel from 33rd to 40th Streets. Fashionable Murray Hill has gradually **shifted to the east,** where carriage houses have become residences, and **commerce** has made **slow but steady inroads** on the other three sides.

Murray Hill Walking Tour: Park Avenue and East 34th Street (IRT Lexington Avenue Line, 33rd Street Station) to Park Avenue and East 42nd Street.

[M 1.] 10 Park Avenue (apartments), NW cor. E. 34th St. 1931. Helmle, Corbett & Harrison.

The massing of this apartment hotel resembles a larger-than-life **crystalline outcropping** of some exotic mineral. Its golden-hued brick and expansive windows (divided into tiny panes) foretell an appropriate domestic scale. Terrific within.

[M 2a.] 3 Park Avenue (office building) and **Norman Thomas High School,** bet. E. 33rd and E. 34th Sts. E side. 1976. Shreve, Lamb & Harmon Assocs., architects. *Obelisk for Peace.* Irving Marantz, sculptor.

An **architectural and fiscal amalgam** developed by the Educational Construction Fund. The 42-story sorrel brick tower, turned **diagonally** to the school and street grid below, springs above its neighbors and is further accentuated at night when its top is bathed in orange light.

In memory of an armory: Though the picturesque 71st Regiment Armory (1905. Clinton & Russell) was demolished to build 3 Park Avenue, its bronze plaque, polished up, graces the terrace wall at East 33rd Street.

[M 2b.] Originally **Vanderbilt Hotel**/now **offices,** 4 Park Ave., bet. E. 33rd and E. 34th St. W side. 1912. Warren & Wetmore.

The reconstruction of the lower-floor facades has robbed the building of any great street presence, but under a low vaulted tile ceiling cocooned over the years by acoustic ceilings emerged:

Fiori Restaurant, 4 Park Ave. NE cor. E. 33rd St.

The old Vanderbilt Hotel's vaulted crypt shelters what might be termed an Italian rathskeller.

[M 2c.] 33rd Street (subway) Station under Park Ave. 1904. Heins & La Farge. ★

A venerable, if not beautiful stop on August Belmont's original IRT (Interborough Rapid Transit) line.

[M 3a.] 475 Park Avenue South (offices), SE cor. E. 32nd St. 1970. Shreve, Lamb & Harmon Assocs., architects. *Triad.* Irving Marantz, sculptor.

Prismatic forms associated with 1960s skyscrapers here have cut corners—intricately detailed in brick, dark metal, and glass. It became quickly dated.

[M 3b.] 2 Park Avenue (offices), bet. E. 32nd and E. 33rd Sts. W side. 1927. Office of Ely Jacques Kahn.

A very neat pier-and-spandrel pattern on the walls of this office block bursts into Art Deco **angular terra-cotta decoration** in primary colors at the top.

[M 3c.] Ritz Café, in 2 Park Avenue Building (entrance on E. 32nd St.) 1985. Sam Duvall, owner-designer.

Neo-Art Deco envelops New Orleans-style cuisine. In another very different guise it was La Cupole (*1983. Adam D. Tihany*).

[M 3d.] Formerly **Gilbert Kiamie residence**/originally **Grolier Club,** 29 E. 32nd St., bet. Madison and Park Aves. 1895. Charles W. Romeyn & Co. ★

Superb Richardsonian Romanesque with brownstone—smooth, rough, and carved. An unlikely specimen in a street of loft buildings.

[M 4a.] Remsen Building, 148-150 Madison Ave., SW cor. E. 32nd St. 1917. Altered ca. 1930, Frank Goodwillie.

A pleasant pattern of **Art Moderne** terra-cotta at the base, interspersed with strangely contrasting **Gothic** niches.

[M 4b.] The Factory (Andy Warhol's place)/originally **New York Edison Company substation,** 19 E. 32nd St., 22 E. 33rd St., bet. Fifth and Madison Aves. 158 Madison Ave., bet. E. 32nd and E. 33rd Sts. W side. Remodeled, 1983, Proposition: Architecture.

Here were the offices, studio space, and magazine production facilities for the late **Andy Warhol,** who will, perhaps, have had more a philosophical impact on art than his **Campbell's Soup Can** paintings suggest. As a former Con Ed electrical transformer station, its exterior is properly noted more for its former occupant than its dress.

The Complete Traveller (bookshop), at 199 Madison Avenue. Travelers and tourists—and otherwise serious people—should mine this lode of guidebooks, maps, and other nuggets for those of the wandering bent. In addition to a clutch of New Yorkiana, those more brave will discover literature on Mongolia, Montparnasse, and even Montana.

[M 5.] Collectors' Club/originally **Thomas B. Clarke residence,** 22 E. 35th St., bet. Madison and Park Aves. 1902. McKim, Mead & White. ★

A neo-Georgian town house with extravagant small-paned bay windows, reminiscent of the late 19th-century avant-garde work of the talented Briton, Richard Norman Shaw. The composite-columned portal is elegant.

[M 6a.] The New Church (Swedenborgian), 112 E. 35th St., bet. Park and Lexington Aves. 1858.

A small-scale whitewashed Italianate structure that adds a bit of open space to a block of good town houses.

[M 6b.] Originally **James F. D. Lanier residence,** 123 E. 35th St., bet. Park and Lexington Aves. 1903. Hoppin & Koen. ★

All intact, inside and out, this Composite-pilastered Beaux Arts town house is the tiara on a block of brownstones. Note the copper roof and dormers.

[M 7.] Apartments/formerly **Advertising Club of New York**/originally **J. Hampton Robb residence,** 23 Park Ave., NE cor. E. 35th St. 1898. McKim, Mead & White.

A brown brick/brownstone Italian Renaissance palazzo. Stately. Once an appropriate disguise for flamboyant advertising account executives. Now merely condominiums for the more than affluent.

[M 10a.] The Polish Consulate General   **[M 4b.]** The Factory of Andy Warhol

[M 8a.] Church of the Incarnation (Episcopal), 205 Madison Ave., NE cor. E. 35th St. 1864. Emlen T. Littel. Enlarged, 1882 ★ **[M 8b.]** The H. Percy Silver Parish House, 209 Madison Ave., bet. E. 35th and E. 36th Sts. E side. 1868. Robert Mook. Altered, ca. 1905, Edward P. Casey ★

Two **orphans** from Madison Avenue's **earlier elite years:** a dour Gothic church and a Renaissance Revival town house named for a rector of the adjacent church. Murals by John La Farge, stained glass by Tiffany Studios.

[M 8c.] Morgan Court (apartments), 211 Madison Ave., bet. E. 35th and E. 36th Sts. E side. 1985. Liebman Liebman & Assocs.

The sliver for J. P. Morgan's onetime carriage house.

[M 9a.] Pierpont Morgan Library, 33 E. 36th St., bet. Madison and Park Aves. 1906. McKim, Mead & White. Addition at 29 E. 36th St., NE cor. Madison Ave. 1928. Benjamin W. Morris. ★ Interior ★. **Open to the public.**

Brunelleschi would be pleased by this, his offspring. The addition, built on the site of the J. Pierpont Morgan, **Sr.** mansion after his death, modestly defers to the older part. The **interior is notable** not only for its exhibits of rare prints and manuscripts, but also for Morgan's **opulent** private library, maintained just as he left it. The best place in New York to look at drawings (**15th** to **19th** century). Whitestone, brownstone, bronze, wrought iron.

[M 9b.] Lutheran Church in America/originally **Isaac N. Phelps residence**/later **Anson Phelps Stokes residence**/formerly (1904–1943) **J. P. Morgan, Jr. residence,** 231 Madison Ave., SE cor. E. 37th St. 1853.

A Classical block that has suffered from additions to and restoration of its brownstone. The sinuous iron balustrades on the entry stoop first-floor windows are outstanding. The church **successfully contested** its official landmark designation in the courts: money is more important than history, even to Luther's heirs, who foresaw commercial development possibilities on this prime site. Here is a literally **antebellum** residence of grandeur that **must** be saved for its roles both in **architectural** and in **social** history.

[M 10a.] Consulate General of the Polish People's Republic/originally **Joseph R. DeLamar residence,** 233 Madison Ave., NE cor. E. 37th St. 1905. C. P. H. Gilbert. ★

The interiors are as opulent as the exterior, and largely intact. At one time it housed the National Democratic Club. Note the **putti** over the entry. DeLamar was a Dutch-born merchant seaman who made his fortune in mining and metallurgy.

[M 10b.] Morgan's (restaurant), in **Morgan's (hotel)/**originally **Duane Hotel,** 237 Madison Ave., bet. E. 37th and E. 38th Sts. E side. 1926. Andrew J. Thomas. Converted, 1985, Haigh Space Ltd. and Andrée Putman, designers.

Black, black, black, black: beautiful interiors redo a small hotel/restaurant.

[M 10c.] 19 and **21 East 37th Street,** bet. Madison and Park Aves. ca. 1900.

Remnant town houses. Note the Composite—capitalled porch of **No. 19** (ca. 1900), the doorway and iron balustrades of **No. 21** (ca. 1885).

Union League Club: The effete and bland neo-Georgian pile at the southwest corner of East 37th Street and Park Avenue (*1931. Morris & O'Connor*) is the red brick home of a club founded by Republicans who left the Union Club in 1863, incensed by its failure to expel Confederate sympathizers.

[M 11a.] 52 Park Avenue (apartments), bet. E. 37th and E. 38th Sts. W side. 1986. David Kenneth Specter.

A silver apartment project on the site of what was, originally, a single town house (cf. the former Douglas residence below). The huge blaaah side wall brutally detracts from the glossily detailed narrow Park Avenue facade. For more—and better—Specter, see The Galleria [Park Avenue P 22a.] and 245 East 50th Street [UN–Turtle Bay U 32.].

[M 11b.] Originally **Adelaide E. Douglas residence/**now **Guatemalan Mission to the United Nations,** 57 Park Ave., bet. E. 37th and E. 38th Sts. E side. 1911. Horace Trumbauer. ★

More limestone Beaux Arts, now used by a Central American mission that can **more lustily savor its ebullience** than could its original Protestant tenant.

[M 11c.] Church of Our Saviour (Roman Catholic), 59 Park Ave., SE cor. E. 38th St. 1959. Paul W. Reilly.

Apparently correct **Gothic Romanesque** archaeology. Among its inconsistencies, however, is **air conditioning equipment** where, in a true Romanesque church, a **carillon** would be. Look up within at the neo-Baroque ceiling. Outside, the carved Gallery of Kings has all the expression of a flock of **"Barbie Dolls."**

[M 11d.] The Town House (apartments), 108 E. 38th St., bet. Park and Lexington Aves. S side. 1930. Bowden & Russell.

An unsung **Art Moderne** apartment house in a reddish-black brick that sports rippling spandrels, also in brick. The cubistic composition is crowned with **brilliant** glazed terra-cotta panels in a broad and wondrous spectrum that can be enjoyed as a special colorful cresting from a distant skyline view.

[M 12.] 101 Park Avenue (offices), NE cor. E. 40th St. 1985. Eli Attia.

A **prismatic** glass form skewed to the Manhattan grid here replaces the **Architects Building** (*1912. Ewing & Chappell and La Farge & Morris*). The corner plaza is small and uncomplicated enough not to detract from the grace of Park Avenue. This is, however, one of the first buildings to **challenge the grid** with new geometry and the skyline with new profiles. It is banal, an ego event among more modest neighbors.

[M 13.] 148 East 40th Street (carriage house), bet. Lexington and Third Aves. ca. 1875.

Lonely and lovely, complete with center doors, now languishing amid characterless high rises on all sides. **Outstanding Second Empire detailing.**

La Maison Japonaise (restaurant), 125 E. 39th St., bet. Park and Lexington Aves.

"French cooking with an oriental accent," the menu says, or to put it another way, *sukiyaki bourguignon.* Lunch and dinner. Moderate. It moved half a block from its previous corner.

[M 14a.] 152 East 38th Street (residence), bet. Lexington and Third Aves. 1858. Remodeled, 1935. Robertson Ward. ★

The front garden is a happy urban design gift for this block.

[M 14b.] E. 38th St. carriage house **[M 13.]** E. 40th St. carriage house

[M 14b.] 149 East 38th Street (carriage house), bet. Lexington and Third Aves. 1902.

Dutch Renaissance with carved heads of bulldogs and wreathed horses.

[M 14c.] 125 East 38th Street (residence), NW cor. Lexington Ave.

A large house redone in **Old Charleston** style.

[M 15.] 130 East 37th Street (residence), SW cor. Lexington Ave.

A colorful example of 1920s-style remodeled houses, Latin variety.

[M 16.] Sniffen Court Historic District, 150-158 E. 36th St., bet. Lexington and Third Aves. ca. 1850–1860. ★

Ten Romanesque Revival brick carriage houses make a mews, a **tasteful oasis,** and an urbane lesson for those developing dense streets. Here urban style could be replicated with whole blocks of such mews at intervals in the cityscape.

[M 17.] 157 and **159 East 35th Street (carriage houses),** bet. Lexington and Third Aves. ca. 1890.

Two conversions to modern use. **No. 157** is restrained and successful. **No. 159, I Am Temple,** which was the more ebullient architectural statement (note the terra-cotta garlands at the cornice), suffers from a stuffy ground-floor reconstruction.

[M 18a.] Originally **J. Christopher G. Hupfel Brewing Corporation,** 233-235 E. 38th St., bet. Second and Third Aves. 1910.

The remnant of a midblock brewery that once extended all the way to East 37th.

 [M 18b.] The Whitney (apartments), 311 E. 38th St., bet. Second Ave. and the Queens-Midtown Tunnel access road. 1986. Liebman Liebman Assoc.

Smoothly **syncopated** balconies with alternating curved and straight edges give this yellow brick slab considerable style.

[M 18b.] The Whitney/311 E. 38th St.   **[M 19.]** The Corinthian's fluted tower

 [M 19.] The Corinthian (apartments), 645 First Ave., bet. E. 37th and E. 38th Sts. W side. 1987. Der Scutt, design architect. Michael Schimenti, architect.

A high-style fluted tower presents myriad round bay windows. This is **reminiscent** in detail, but not in urban posture, of the Rockefeller Apartments of Harrison & Fouilhoux [see F 15f.], perhaps one of the city's few modern apartment buildings of distinction. Many included are stylish, but the Rockefeller plan and profile are gorgeous. Here Scutt has excelled—his best building by far.

[M 20a.] Originally **Kips Bay Brewing Company,** 660 First Ave., bet. E. 37th and E. 38th Sts. E side. ca. 1895. Additions.

Lager beer, ales, and porter, its colorful posters once boasted. They also featured this fortress of a building with curious mansarded cupolas at opposite corners of the roof. Brewing has disappeared here; substantial floors once meant for **mash cookers** and **brew kettles** now serve the needs of picture services, relief organizations, and an architect whose rear-wall picture window enjoys **East River** views. The roof is a display center of cast-iron furniture, used demurely by the tenants below as an entertainment terrace.

[M 20b.] The Horizon (apartments), 415 E. 37th St., bet. First Ave. and FDR Drive, to E. 38th St. 1988. Costas Kondylis of Philip Birnbaum & Assocs.

A mild echo of The Corinthian [see above] but even closer to the river.

END of Murray Hill Tour: Grand Central at East 42nd Street and Park Avenue offers a variety of rapid transit and commuter connections.

CLINTON

From Ninth Avenue westward to the Hudson, roughly **opposite the Times Square theater district,** lies the area known since the 1970s as Clinton, after DeWitt Clinton Park (*1905*) at its western edge between West 52nd and West 54th Streets. Like Cobble Hill, Carroll Gardens, and Boerum Hill in Brooklyn, **Clinton** is a new moniker for a community trying to live down its infamous past. From the Civil War to World War II the area south to about West 30th Street was better known as **Hell's Kitchen,** one of the city's **most notorious precincts.** Gangster rule in its early years and the abundance of slaughterhouses, freight yards, factories, and tenements (to house those whose meager livings these industries provided) established the area's physical character. It is a quality the current inhabitants **wish to upgrade,** and the area boasts a few improvements toward that end. But the ubiquitous lofts, repair shops, and taxi garages and the disappearance of pier activity (as well as piers) have made this stretch unfamiliar to all except those who live, work, or play here. It remains **an enigma** why Clinton, **so close to the heart** of Manhattan's central business district, is still **a backwater.**

Another festive activity of the district was once **the sailing of ocean liners.** Most of the big ones docked along the Hudson between 42nd and 52nd Streets; now all but extinct, their occasional cruise ship successors stop at the three-fingered terminal between 48th and 52nd Streets. The **QE 2** also calls from time to time. **Clinton** is the place where *West Side Story, Slaughter on Tenth Avenue,* and other vital cultural remembrances enriched the **West Side.**

Clinton Walking Tour: The nearest subways are not too close, which helps to explain Clinton's sluggishness in being redeveloped. (Take the IND Eighth Avenue Line, the closest, to the 42nd Street Station.)

[L 1.] Originally **New York Butchers' Dressed Meat Company (slaughter house),** 495-511 Eleventh Ave., bet. W. 39th and W. 40th Sts. W side. S wing, 1905, Horgan & Slattery. N wing, 1919.

A vertical abattoir, the interior designed to be a mass production, urban slaughtering facility. **Rams' and steers' heads** provide visual relief on the exterior.

[L 2a.] Covenant House/formerly **Manhattan Community Rehabilitation Center, N.Y.S. Office of Drug Abuse Services,** 460 W. 41st St., bet. Ninth and Tenth Aves. and 550 Tenth Ave., NE cor. W. 40th St. Conversion for N.Y.S., 1970, Gueron, Lepp & Assocs.

A west of Times-Square motel and a public library branch, both emptied by changing patterns of city living. They were converted to a drug addicts' rehabilitation center by adding **a handsome board-framed concrete and brown brick reception center** the scale of which is crushed by its neighbors. Tilted louvers shield the tenants of the former motel from view.

[L 2b.] Univision/formerly **Spanish International Communications Corporation,** atop the old West Side Airlines Terminal, 460 W. 42nd St., SE cor. Tenth Ave. 1986. Hardy Holzman Pfeiffer Assocs.

From afar (and you can see it *only* from afar) it looks like a green spaceship atop this bland white brick building—or perhaps a Martian monster in person. It certainly enlivens the low streetscape of this neighborhood. At night the neon east wall controls.

[L 3.] Model Tenements for **New York Fireproof Tenement Association,** 500-506 W. 42nd St., SW cor. Tenth Ave. and 569 Tenth Ave., bet. W. 41st and W. 42nd Sts. ca. 1900. Ernest Flagg.

Their fireproof qualities may have been a step forward for tenements, but having lost their ironwork embellishments, they are grim, very grim, in appearance.

[L 4a.] Riverbank West (apartments), 555 W. 42nd St., NE cor. Eleventh Ave. 1987. Hardy Holzman Pfeiffer Assocs., design architects. Schuman, Lichtenstein, Claman & Efron, architects.

Polychromatic brickwork and staggered balconies make a lively if not graceful facade.

[L 4b.] Rescue Company No. 1, N.Y.C. Fire Department, 530 W. 43rd St., bet. Tenth and Eleventh Aves. 1988. The Stein Partnership.

A substitute for—can you believe it?—a firehouse that burned down.

[L 5.] Manhattan Plaza (apartment complex), W. 42nd to W. 43rd Sts., Ninth to Tenth Aves. 1977. David Todd & Assocs.

Two 45-story red brick balconied towers anchor this block-square amalgam intended to **spur redevelopment** of the Clinton community. Between the towers, on the garage deck, are all sorts of recreational activities for the residents of the 1,688 apartments.

[L 6.] Actors Studio/originally **Seventh Associate Presbyterian Church,** 432 W. 44th St., bet. Ninth and Tenth Aves. 1859.

Lee Strasberg held forth in this simple, late Greek Revival, painted brick church. Here was the cradle of thespians such as **Marlon Brando.**

[L 7a.] Film Center Building, 630 Ninth Ave., bet. W. 44th and W. 45th Sts. E side. 1929. Buchman & Kahn. Lobby interior ★.

Typical of 1920s Art Deco-influenced loft buildings whose designs are just skin deep. This one, however, has a gem of a **polychromed elevator lobby** (and an asymmetric, Moderne bronze tenants' directory).

[L 7b.] Film Center Café, 635 Ninth Ave., bet. W. 44th and W. 45th Sts. W side.

A small and stylish **Art Moderne** café frequented by the movie/video clan that works across the street in the Film Center.

---

428 West 44th Street, the former home of actress June Havoc, is also the scene of mysterious tapping sounds. Perhaps its resident tapper was a friend of Peter Stuyvesant and afforded him temporary digs during the 1978 fire that gutted his home. Séances have been conducted to determine who the noisy ghost is. Two spirits are said to have been contacted so far.

[L 8a.] Playground, N.Y.C. Department of Parks & Recreation, W. 45th to W. 46th Sts., midblock bet. Ninth and Tenth Aves. Reconstructed, 1977, Michael J. Altschuler, architect. Outdoor mural, 1973, Arnold Belkin, Cityarts Workshop. Mosaics, 1974, Philip Danzig, with community participants.

An unusual reconstruction of the ubiquitous city playground: community-crafted mosaics on the walls, reflections and distortions from polished stainless steel mirrors, all beneath a Mexican-inspired outdoor mural of social commentary. No picturesque charmer this, but **a response to diverse user needs.**

[L 8b.] Clinton Court (residential group), 420 W. 46th St., bet. Ninth and Tenth Aves.

A charming backwater only partially visible through a locked gate.

[L 8c.] St. Clement's Church (Episcopal)/formerly **St. Cornelius Church**/originally **Faith Chapel, West Presbyterian Church,** 423 W. 46th St., bet. Ninth and Tenth Aves. Edward D. Lindsey. 1870. Altered 1882.

A most **unusual and picturesque** parish church. Victorian brickwork, fish-scale slate shingles, and very pointed Gothic Revival arched windows. For years the church has also served as the home of **Playhouse 46** and for many noteworthy dance and dramatic productions.

[L 8d.] The Piano Factory (apartments)/originally **Wessell, Nickel & Gross Company,** 452-458 W. 46th St., bet. Ninth and Tenth Aves. 1888. Converted, 1980.

A **New England-style mill** building (complete with mill yard entered through robust iron arched openings) squeezed onto an urban site. The factory made the innards for pianos.

Landmark Tavern, 626 Eleventh Ave., SE cor. W. 46th St.

It dates from 1868 and looks every minute of it: dark wood, dusty mirrors, floors of two-bit-sized round white tiles, and Franklin stoves for heat on cold days. There's even a **paneled** and **stained glass** "Gentlemen's" off the bar. Go for the atmosphere—the pub food is just okay. Moderate.

[L 9.] Salvation Army Thrift Store/originally **Acker, Merrall & Condit Company,** 536 W. 46th St., bet. Tenth and Eleventh Aves. ca. 1910.

A stately baronial warehouse of tapestry brick and expansive neo-Roman arches. But here are bargains of a practical, eccentric, or stylish ilk.

[L 7a.] Film Center Building lobby   **[L 14.]** Sacred Heart of Jesus Church

[L 10.] N.Y.C. Passenger Ship Terminal, Port Authority of New York and New Jersey, Hudson River at W. 48th, W. 50th, and W. 52nd Sts. along Twelfth Ave. W side. 1976. Port Authority of N.Y. & N.J. Architectural Design Team.

When the *Liberté, Queen Mary, United States,* or *Andrea Doria* were still plying the oceans, it was said that what New York City needed to dignify transatlantic arrivals and departures was modern superliner piers. The **piers were finally built;** the **superliners,** however, **were scrapped:** the Queen Elizabeth 2 (**QE 2**) still visits, mostly for those superaffluent who relish the luxurious ride one way—and take the **Concorde** back.

The Intrepid, a World War II aircraft carrier, is moored at Pier 86 at the foot of West 46th Street (officially at the impossible-to-locate 1 Intrepid Plaza). It is a floating museum of carriers and aircraft where one can climb into the cockpit of a torpedo bomber, or see films of fighting in the forties. It is a giant hulk of floating architecture, action within, and at the top. (All the public spaces are heated by electricity, making the Intrepid one of Con Ed's most valued customers in cold weather.) **Open to the public.**

[L 11a.] Park West High School, 525 W. 50th St., bet. Tenth and Eleventh Aves. to W. 51st St. 1977. **[L 11b.] 747 Tenth Avenue (apartment complex),** SW cor. 1976. Both by Max O. Urbahn Assocs.

The school's West 50th Street facade's powerful forms, raw concrete and striated block, evoke a landlubber's image of a World War II aircraft carrier. The West 51st Street facade, on the other hand, is disconcertingly placid. The high-rise apartment tower at the corner is banal. An honorable economic trick allowed the housing to pay for the school.

[L 12.] High School of Graphic Communication Arts/originally **High School of Printing,** 439 W. 49th and W. 50th Sts., bet. Ninth and Tenth Aves. 1959. Kelly & Gruzen.

In retrospect, one of the most vigorous **International Style** buildings in town, overlooked in its isolation in the west reaches of Clinton. Here glass block presents a facade of style, with a sinuous articulated auditorium umbilically connected as a specially shaped form. The interior sports escalators, the first to be used in a local high school.

[L 13.] Originally **New York Telephone Company (offices)** now **AT&T Company,** 425-437 W. 50th St., and 430 W. 51st St. bet. Ninth and Tenth Aves. 1930. Voorhees, Gmelin & Walker.

A telephone building from the era when people were still needed to complete your phone call (thus requiring windows) and the **image of a building** in the community **was a high priority** (thus justifying the willow leaf Art Deco and Art Moderne ornament).

[L 14.] Sacred Heart of Jesus Church (Roman Catholic), 457 W. 51st St., bet. Ninth and Tenth Aves. 1884. Napoleon LeBrun & Sons. **Rectory,** 1881, Arthur Crooks.

A **symmetric confection** of deep red brick and matching terra-cotta frosted with light-colored stone arches, band courses, and copings: **Victorian Romanesque.**

[L 15.] 410 West 53rd Street (apartments), bet. Ninth and Tenth Aves. 1987. Avinash K. Malhotra.

A **low-key, low-**profile, **low-rise, good** neighbor in these Clinton streets. This is the kind of background architecture that can allow space and posture to scattered monuments, a bit like Broadway's nearby **Chorus Line,** where individuals stand back to jointly create a context of quality in which an occasional star might shine.

[L 16.] Originally **Switching Center, New York Telephone Company/ American Telephone & Telegraph Company,** 811 Tenth Ave., bet. W. 53rd and W. 54th Sts. W side. 1964. Exterior, Kahn & Jacobs. Interior, Smith, Smith, Haines, Lundberg & Waehler.

A tall windowless monster which looks, from a distance, as though it's covered with glistening mattress ticking. No long distance operators here—only the electronic robotry that has yet to enjoy a windowed vista.

[L 17.] Clinton Tower (apartments), 790 Eleventh Ave., NE cor. W. 54th St., and 590 W. 55th St., SE cor. Eleventh Ave. 1975. Hoberman & Wasserman.

The high-rise tower and its low-rise leg on West 55th Street are clad in a combination of smooth and striated pink concrete block. They embrace a courtyard and play area that gather the noonday sun.

[L 18.] Harbor View Terrace, N.Y.C. Housing Authority, W. 54th and W. 55th, and W. 55th and W. 56th Sts., bet. Tenth and Eleventh Aves. 1977. Herbert L. Mandel.

The height of midblock housing can be limited by zoning, which explains why these are **in scale** with the adjacent mixed-use community. The combination of cast-in-place concrete and deep-terra-cotta-colored giant brick for walls and bronze anodized aluminum for balcony railings **furthers the domesticity** of the design, the **Authority**'s best in Manhattan (The project is built over the air rights of the depressed West Side freight line.).

[L 19.] Originally **Interborough Rapid Transit Company (IRT) Powerhouse/**now **Consolidated Edison,** W. 58th to W. 59th Sts., bet. Eleventh and Twelfth Aves. 1904. McKim, Mead & White.

A brick and terra-cotta **temple to power** with a Stanford White exterior, that **once boasted** 6 tall smokestacks **belching smoke** from enormous coal furnaces. The coal was received at an adjacent dock on the Hudson and transported to bunkers in electric conveyor belts; ashes were removed the same way. All the electricity for the original IRT subway, opened in 1904, was generated here.

[L 20.] Church of St. Paul the Apostle (Roman Catholic), Columbus Ave., SW cor. W. 60th St. 1876, 1885. Jeremiah O'Rourke. Altar and baldachin, 1890. Stanford White. Ceiling and windows, John La Farge.

An unadorned fort on the outside, except for one awkward bas-relief mural over the entrance, it turns into **a Roman basilica** inside, embellished with the works of such as **Augustus Saint-Gaudens, Frederick MacMonnies,** and **John La Farge,** with the advice of **Stanford White** and **Bertram Goodhue.** All of their efforts are lost in the thick atmosphere. The largest un-cathedral in America. O'Rourke died before the plans were complete. Paulist Father George Deshon, U.S. Grant's roommate at the U.S. Military Academy, took over.

[L 21.] The Metropolis film studios   **[L 19.]** Originally an IRT powerhouse

[L 21.] The Metropolis Project/formerly **Haaren High School**/originally **DeWitt Clinton High School,** 899 Tenth Ave., bet. W. 58th and W. 59th Sts. 1906. C. B. J. Snyder. Rebuilt and expanded, 1988, Rafael Viñoly.

Flemish Renaissance Revival **encrustations** enliven the facades of this old high school, now evolving into film studios.

[L 22.] Outpatient Psychiatric Clinic/originally **William J. Syms Operating Theater, Roosevelt Hospital,** W. 59th St., SW cor. Ninth Ave. 1892. W. Wheeler Smith.

The oldest member of this constantly regrowing complex: **a teaching amphitheater,** where spectators, on concentric, stepped seating rings oversaw the master surgeons at work.

[L 22a.] St. Luke's/Roosevelt Hospital Center, Tenth Ave. bet. W. 58th and W. 59th Sts., E side. 1990. Skidmore, Owings & Merrill.

A 13-story cube that will bring the old Roosevelt block into the late 20th century. A technological set of tubes, wires, computers, and other hard assets that are encapsulated in some bland external fancy dress.

[L 23.] Catholic Apostolic Church, 417 W. 57th St., bet. Ninth and Tenth Aves. 1895. Francis H. Kimball.

A **superior work** of urban architecture, **three-dimensional**—not merely a facade—now almost forgotten because of bulky nonentities that squeeze against but fail to conceal it. Its **restrained coloring** of russet brick and terra-cotta adds to its power.

[L 24.] Formerly **Henry Hudson Hotel**/originally **Clubhouse, American Women's Association,** 353 W. 57th St., bet. Eighth and Ninth Aves. 1929. Benjamin Wistar Morris.

A landmark on San Juan Hill, it began as **a club for young women,** served as bachelor officers' quarters in World War II, and since 1975 has housed WNET, the city's public television outlet. Note **the bridge in the sky** connecting the roof gardens of the two wings.

San Juan Hill: The rise in topography near Ninth Avenue and West 57th Street was, around 1900, a black community dubbed San Juan Hill after the heroic exploits of a black unit in the Spanish-American War. This stretch of West 57th Street between Eighth and Ninth Avenues bears a curiously European look in its architectural scale.

END of Clinton Tour: The nearest subways are along Eighth Avenue between 57th Street and Columbus Circle: the IND Sixth and Eighth Avenue Lines and the IRT Broadway-Seventh Avenue local.

TIMES SQUARE AREA

Up to the 1890s, much of the 40s and 50s west of Seventh Avenue were written off as **Hell's Kitchen,** a seething mixture of factories and tenements where **even the cops moved in pairs.** The rich ventured in only as far west as Broadway in the upper 40s, an area of carriage shops for the horsey set called **Long Acre,** after a **similar district** in London. In 1883 the Metropolitan Opera House opened on Broadway between 39th and 40th Streets. Some said the 3,700-seat theater looked like a **yellow brick brewery** on the outside, but **inside** the city's nouveaux riches could observe each other in red and gold-encrusted splendor. They had built their very own opera house when the Old Guard denied them boxes in **their** Academy of Music downtown. The tide turned quickly as the moneyed classes soon flocked **uptown,** and three years later the Academy closed. The whole center of social gravity had now shifted to the 50s on Fifth Avenue, from points south.

Then big things happened quickly. **Charles Frohman** ventured to open his Empire Theatre, directly across Broadway from the Metropolitan Opera, in 1893; **Oscar Hammerstein I** did him one better in 1895 by opening the Olympia, a blocklong palace on Broadway between 44th and 45th Streets (then a muddy stretch) with a concert hall, a music hall, a theater, and a roof garden. Soon lavish restaurants like Rector's, Shanley's, and Café de l'Opéra were dispensing lobster and champagne to **Diamond Jim Brady, "Bet a Million" Gates, George M. Cohan,** and other luminaries of the theater, financial, and sporting world. When the city decided to route its first subway west from Grand Central along 42nd Street, then north on Broadway, *New York Times* publisher **Adolph Ochs** saw a chance to outdo his competitors by erecting an imposing tower at Broadway and 42nd. He got the station there officially named **Times Square** in April 1904.

By then the area was becoming established as the theater district, and the evening crowds and broad vistas attracted **the early electric sign makers;** the 1916 Zoning Resolution made specific allowances for vast signs in the area. In the 1920s, **neon and movies** took over. In Hollywood's heyday, movie and variety palaces preempted the valuable Broadway frontier, and legitimate theater retreated to the side streets. The signs got bigger as the crowds got bigger, and began to feature things like **rooftop waterfalls** and **real smoke rings.** As bigtime movies waned in the 1950s and 1960s, most of the **palatial movie theaters** were razed, and Times Square was **on the verge** of an office-building boom.

In the 1970s some glassy office blocks arrived, and so did an enormous **explosion in pornography** and the sale of live sex on the streets and in "massage" parlors. Now there is a vast boom of **Post Modern** office and hotel buildings that threatens the vitality of the Square, bringing **exotic skyline profiles** but **little excitement** to the street.

Times Square Area Walking Tour: Encompassing Times Square and its immediate environs almost up to Columbus Circle. START just to Times Square's south at Seventh Avenue and West 40th. (Take IRT Broadway-Seventh Avenue Line, Flushing Line, or Shuttle from Grand Central, or the BMT Broadway Line to the interconnected Times Square Station.)

[T 1.] Originally **Brotherhood in Action Building**/now **Parsons Fashion Education Center,** 560 Seventh Ave., NW cor. W. 40th St. 1950s. William Lescaze.

Lescaze's elegant early Modern house on East 48th Street is vintage Lescaze—here his later work is much less suave.

[T 2.] Port Authority Bus Terminal, W. 40th to W. 41st Sts., bet. Eighth and Ninth Aves. 1950. Decks added, 1963. Expansion to W. 42nd St. 1980. All by Port Authority of N.Y. & N.J. Architectural Design Team

Glorious Pennsylvania Station **is only a memory;** Grand Central Terminal basks in **rediscovery** and freshening up. The Port Authority Bus Terminal only **grows in popularity** as the city's vomitory for commuters and for those reduced to using long-distance buses. The new and upgraded spaces are, happily, remarkably civilized.

[T 3a.] Formerly **GHI Building (Group Health Insurance)/**originally **McGraw-Hill Building,** 330 W. 42nd St., bet. Eighth and Ninth Aves. 1931. Raymond Hood, Godley & Fouilhoux. ★

Hood designed this tower with continuous horizontal bands of blue-green terra-cotta at the time his vertically striped **News Building** [see U 7b.] was going up at the other end of 42nd Street. This was the **only New York** building shown in Hitchcock and Johnson's epoch-making book *The International Style* in 1932. However, the detail is Art Deco/Art Moderne: the lobby is an extraordinary remembrance of Carrera (opaque) glass, stainless steel, and elegant lights.

[T 3b.] Holy Cross Church (Roman Catholic), 333 W. 42nd St., bet. Eighth and Ninth Aves. 1870. Henry Engelbert. **[T 3c.] Holy Cross School,** 332 W. 43rd St. 1887. Lawrence J. O'Connor.

Identified as being in the **"Byzantine style"** when built, the brick facade conceals the verdigris-clad construction over the crossing, octagonal drum, dome, lantern, and crucifix (148 feet to the top). This was the parish church of **Father Duffy** of World War I fame [see his statue at Duffy Square]. The school, on West 43rd Street, has a rich **Romanesque Revival** facade of red brick and matching terra-cotta.

[T 4a.] American Savings Bank/originally **Franklin Savings Bank,** 661 Eighth Ave., NW cor. W. 42nd St. 1974. Poor, Swanke, Hayden & Connell.

A one-story orange brick and concrete bank that is a far cry from its Beaux Arts predecessor, once diagonally across the intersection. (For one thing, **it lacks the spinning clock** that once hung out over the sidewalk.) Nevertheless, the brick and concrete interior is **a refuge** from the **flesh circus** constantly underway outside. The zebra stripes painted on the reentrant walls of the bank's L-shaped high-rise neighbor fail to control the chaotic scene.

[T 4b.] Originally **Charles Scribner's Sons printing plant,** 311 W. 43rd St., bet. Eighth and Ninth Aves. 1907. Ernest Flagg.

Flagg, architect of Scribner's headquarters, stores, and town houses, was, predictably, also architect for this straightforward industrial facility. Its iron curtain wall is marred by a thoughtless ground-floor "improvement and replacement of the gutsy, industrial steel, sash windows." See the faded **"Scribner's"** on the west wall.

Eighth Avenue to Broadway:

"Sin Street," this lurid block between Eighth Avenue and Broadway, has had a sophisticated past and holds promise of renaissance in a vast effort organized by **The 42nd Street Development Corporation.** New buildings at Times Square are discussed under **Behemoths** below, but a return of the "legitimate" stage to some of these now gaudy playhouses will give opportunity to uncover the soberer early 20th-century architecture underneath.

The **sex shops** will probably move to another precinct, and then a natural influx of shopping and restaurants will make a more bourgeois, but certainly **less lively,** street.

[T 5a.] Candler Building (offices), 220 W. 42nd St., bet. Seventh and Eighth Aves. 1914. Willauer, Shape & Bready.

The nationwide success of **Coca-Cola** persuaded **Asa Candler,** its supersalesman, to build this gleaming white terra-cotta-clad tower off Times Square. Its skin, like that of the buildings around it, is begrimed. *Look up.*

[T 5b.] New Amsterdam Theatre, 214 W. 42nd St., bet. Seventh and Eighth Ave. 1903. Herts & Tallant. ★ Interior ★. **[T 5c.] New Amsterdam Roof Theatre**/originally **New Amsterdam Aerial Gardens.** 1904. Herts & Tallant.

The Renaissance Revival sliver office tower entered on 42nd Street is an excuse to build a lobby that leads to the theater in the rear, on 41st. Rare for New York: Art Nouveau.

Times Square

A **state of mind** as much as a physical location, this is the center of circulation to a much larger area of theaters and restaurants—**a vast vestibule** to entertainment. Gaudy signs are its nighttime architecture, their exuberant vulgarity the marquee that proclaims the theatrical wonders in the surrounding streets.

Times Square's untidy and gaudy signs expressed exuberant vulgarity in 1959

[T 6a.] 1 Times Square/formerly **Allied Chemical Tower**/originally **Times Tower,** W. 42nd St. bet. Broadway and Seventh Ave., N to W. 43rd St. 1904. Eidlitz & MacKenzie. Remodeled, 1966, Smith, Smith, Haines, Lundberg & Waehler.

The *New York Times* moved into its 25-story tower with **dramatic timing** on December 31, 1904, marking the occasion with a fireworks display at midnight that made Times Square **the place to see in the New Year** ever since. The paper moved out in a couple of decades to larger quarters on West 43rd Street, but the name remained. New owners stripped off the original Italian Renaissance terra-cotta skin and replaced it with **Miami Beach marble.** Times Square "renewal" augurs its demolition.

World's first "moving" sign: First to electrify passers-by along the Great White Way were the election returns of 1928 delivered along the Motogram, a 5-foot-high, 360-foot-long sign flasher that wrapped around the old Times Tower's 4 sides and utilized 14,800 lamps to convey its constantly changing messages. The tower has changed its face; a revised and restored Motogram remains.

[T 6b.] The Crossroads Building site, W. 42nd St. bet. Broadway and Seventh Ave., S to W. 41st St. 1986. T. M. Prentice, Jr. and Prentice & Chan, Ohlhausen.

Temporary support for tourists is housed in a witty **false-fronted clutch** of "mobile homes": Visitors, Travelers, and Information Center and Police. It occupies the site of the old Crossroads Building, whose windowless tower was more the vehicle for a giant wall painting by Richard Haas in the 1980s than any substantial rentable space.

 [T 7.] 1466 Broadway (mixed use)/formerly **Newsweek Building**/originally **Knickerbocker Hotel,** SE cor. Broadway. 1906 Marvin & Vavis, architects. Bruce Price, consultant. Altered, 1980, Libby, Ross & Whitehouse.

A mix of condominium uses now fill the Classical, mansard-topped shell of a hotel—originally commissioned by **Col. John Jacob Astor**—where **Enrico Caruso** and **George M. Cohan** once lived. It had a gold service for sixty and a bar so fashionable in its heyday that it was known as the 42nd Street Country Club. A mural from this bar now sets the theme for the **King Cole** restaurant at the **St. Regis-Sheraton Hotel** [see Fifth Avenue F 16.].

Behemoths: On the corners of 42nd Street, Seventh Avenue, and Broadway 4 planned giant buildings (Times Square Center) promise to have a "sobering effect" on the neighborhood. Will they sterilize this lively urban sector, replacing its septic vitality with Avenue of the Americas dullness? Let's hope that its architects (John Burgee with Philip Johnson) will yet apply some genuine architectural wit comparable to Johnson's famed verbal entertainments.

[T 8.] Town Hall, 113-123 W. 43rd St., bet. Sixth Ave. and Broadway. 1921. McKim, Mead & White. ★ Interior ★.

Bland **Georgian Revival** on the outside shelters a large, but intimate, acoustically successful concert hall within.

[T 9.] Originally **Paramount Theatre Building,** 1501 Broadway, bet. W. 43rd and W. 44th Sts. W side. 1926. C. W. Rapp & George L. Rapp.

The tower, clocks, and globe (once illuminated) are sensational. In the early days there was even an observation deck . . . and a theater.

[T 10a.] Originally **The Lambs Club**/now **Lambs Theater** and **Manhattan Church of the Nazarene,** 130 W. 44th St., bet. Sixth Ave. and Broadway. 1905. Stanford White of McKim, Mead & White. Addition, 1915, George A. Freeman. ★

A **neo-Federal** clubhouse built for a still-lively actors' group. The group has moved elsewhere. "Floreant Agni 1874–1904." McKim, Mead & White were all members of the **Lambs.**

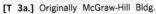
[T 3a.] Originally McGraw-Hill Bldg.   **[T 10b.]** 1-2-3 Hotel, 123 W. 44th St.

[T 10b.] 1-2-3 Hotel/originally **Hotel Girard,** 123 W. 44th St., bet. Sixth Ave. and Broadway. 1894. George Keister. ★

A tan and limestone pile—one of many which once filled Times Square's side streets—**extravagantly decked out** with German Renaissance gables and dormers, undulating bow windows (beaux bows) and the **Café Un-Deux-Trois.** *Look up* and *further up.*

[T 11a.] Astor Plaza, 1515 Broadway, bet. W. 44th and W. 45th Sts. W side. 1969. Kahn & Jacobs.

A 50-story office tower that **replaced** one of Times Square's long-time landmarks, **the Astor Hotel.** From afar its finial fins look like the tail of an impaled spaceship.

This was the first building to exploit the special Times Square Theater District **zoning bonuses** that allowed developers to erect buildings of greater than normal bulk in return for constructing a new legitimate theater.

[T 11b.] Shubert Alley, from W. 44th St. to W. 45th St., bet. Broadway and Eighth Aves.

Now a convenience for theatergoers, this private alley was once a magnet for aspiring actors, who gathered in front of the offices of **J. J.** and **Lee Shubert** when plays were being cast.

[T 11c.] Sam S. Shubert Theatre, 221 W. 44th St., bet. Broadway and Eighth Ave. at Shubert Alley. 1913. Henry B. Herts. ★. Interior ★.
[T 11d.] Booth Theatre, 222 W. 45th St. 1913. Henry B. Herts. ★. Interior ★.

The pair of **richly ornamented** theaters—the large Shubert and the smaller Booth—that forms the west "wall" of Shubert Alley.

Sardi's: The restaurant at 234 West 44th Street, strategically located among theaters and at the back door to the *New York Times,* has for decades been the place for actors to be seen—except during performance hours.

[T 11e.] Marriott Marquis Hotel, 1531-1549 Broadway, bet. W. 45th and W. 46th Sts. W side. 1985. John Portman.

A spectacular lobby with glassed-in rocket ship elevators starts at the 8th floor, a superatrium here squeezed into Broadway real estate (Portman's earlier attempts in Atlanta, Chicago, and San Francisco allowed for more horizontal dimension). On its inside it is **glitzy** in a way its developers thought appropriate to Broadway. The exterior is bleak, with an illuminated advertising sign that bows to the need for a bit of vulgar sparkle but that fails in the end to capture the many-lighted Broadway spirit. The price for this site: 3 Broadway theaters. Perhaps this is their tombstone.

[T 11e.] The Marriott Marquis Hotel   **[T 12a.]** Neo-Baroque Lyceum Theatre

[T 12a.] Lyceum Theatre, 149 W. 45th St., bet. Sixth Ave. and Broadway. 1903. Herts & Tallant. ★   Interior ★.

Powerful neo-Baroque columns predominate. Saved from demolition in 1939, it survived to become **the oldest New York theater** still used for legitimate productions and **the first to be landmarked.**

[T 12b.] The Eichner Hotel, Seventh Ave. bet. E. 45th and E. 46th Sts. E side. 1989. Murphy/Jahn.

Helmut Jahn is one of the most prolific architects of New York's late 1980s towers. All of them have exotic colors and materials, as well as finials or crowns that interweave in the skyline.

[T 13a.] Church of St. Mary the Virgin Rectory, Clergy House, Mission House, 145 W. 46th St., bet. Sixth and Seventh Aves. 1895. Napoleon Le Brun & Sons.

A rich liturgical oasis in this precinct of **Mammon, booze,** and **pornography**—incense and liturgy here exceed that of the Catholic Counter-Reformation. The first church in the world to be erected on a **steel** frame (many before, particularly in France, were of **cast**-iron and **wrought** iron).

[T 13b.] Formerly **Public School 67, Manhattan**/later **High School of the Performing Arts**/now **Liberty High School,** 120 W. 46th St., bet. Sixth and Seventh Aves. 1894. C. B. J. Snyder. ★

Brick and brownstone **Romanesque Revival:** a sober "Protestant" foil to St. Mary's quasi-Catholic facade opposite.

Great women of the theater are honored in sculpture on the facade of the former I. Miller Building (West 46th Street, northeast corner of Seventh Avenue): Mary Pickford, Rosa Ponselle, Ethel Barrymore, and Marilyn Miller. They are all by A. Stirling Calder, father of the late, famed inventor of mobiles, Alexander Calder. 1929.

Duffy Square: The northern triangle of Times Square is dedicated to **Father Francis P. Duffy** (1871–1932), a national hero in World War I as "Fighting Chaplain" of New York's 69th Regiment, later a friend of actors, writers, and mayors as pastor of **Holy Cross Church** on West 42nd Street. His statue (*1937. Charles Keck.*) faces the back of one representing **George M. Cohan** (1878–1942), another Times Square hero (*1959. George Lober*).

A line to the elegant **tkts** structure forms around and behind Father Duffy

[T 14a.] tkts, W. 47th St., bet. Seventh Ave. and Broadway. S side. 1973. Mayers & Schiff.

The uptown half of Duffy Square is occupied by the Times Square Theatre Center [**tkts**], an elegant pipe-and-canvas structure where **half-price ducats** are available just before showtime.

BROADWAY THEATERS

Theater(s)	Location	Architect	Opened
Ambassador	215 W. 49th St.	Herbert J. Krapp	1921 Interior only ★
Belasco originally Belasco's Stuyvesant	111 W. 44th St.	George Keister	1905 ★ Interior ★
Biltmore	261 W. 47th St.	Herbert J. Krapp	1926 Interior only ★
Booth	222 W. 45th St.	Henry B. Herts	1913 ★ Interior ★
Broadhurst	235 W. 44th St.	Herbert J. Krapp	1917 ★ Interior ★
Broadway originally B. S. Moss's Colony	1681 Broadway	Eugene De Rosa	1924
Brooks Atkinson originally Mansfield	256 W. 47th St.	Herbert J. Krapp	1926 ★ Interior ★
Century originally Billy Rose's Diamond Horseshoe	235 W. 46th St. (in Paramount Hotel)	Thomas W. Lamb	1928
Cort	138 W. 48th St.	Thomas W. Lamb	1913 ★ Interior ★
Ed Sullivan originally Hammerstein's later Manhattan Music Hall, Billy Rose Music Hall	1697 Broadway	Herbert J. Krapp	1927 Interior only ★
Embassy I originally Embassy	1560 Broadway	Thomas W. Lamb	1925 Interior only ★
Empire originally Eltinge	236 W. 42nd St.	Thomas W. Lamb	1913
Ethel Barrymore	243 W. 47th St.	Herbert J. Krapp	1927 ★ Interior ★
Eugene O'Neill originally Forrest later Coronet	230 W. 49th St.	Herbert J. Krapp	1925 Interior only ★
Forty-sixth Street originally Chanin's Forty-sixth Street	226 W. 46th St.	Herbert J. Krapp	1924 ★ Interior ★
Golden originally Theatre Masque	252 W. 45th St.	Herbert J. Krapp	1927 ★ Interior ★
Harris originally Candler later Cohan & Harris, Sam H. Harris	226 W. 42nd St.	Thomas W. Lamb	1914
Helen Hayes originally Little/ then Anne Nichol's Little, Times Hall, Winthrop Ames	240 W. 44th St.	Ingalls & Hoffman Interior rebuilt, Herbert J. Krapp	1912 ★ Interior, 1917 ★
Henry Miller's a.k.a. Xenon (disco)	124–130 W. 43rd St.	Allen, Ingalls & Hoffman	1918 ★
Hudson formerly Savoy	139–141 W. 44th St.	J. B. McElfratrick & Company Israels & Harder	1903 ★ Interior ★
Imperial	249 W. 45th St.	Herbert J. Krapp	1923 Interior only ★
Liberty	234 W. 42nd St.	Herts & Tallant	1904

Theater(s)	Location	Architect	Opened
Longacre	220 W. 48th St.	Henry B. Herts	1913 ★ Interior ★
Lunt-Fontanne originally Globe	205 W. 46th St.	Carrère & Hastings	1910 ★
Lyceum orig. New Lyceum	149 W. 45th St.	Herts & Tallant	1903 ★ Interior ★
Lyric	213 W. 42nd St. 214 W. 43rd St.	V. Hugo Koehler	1903
Majestic	245 W. 44th St.	Herbert J. Krapp	1927 ★ Interior ★
Mark Hellinger originally Hollywood, Fifty-first Street	237 W. 51st St.	Thomas W. Lamb	1929 ★ Interior ★
Martin Beck	302 W. 45th St.	G. Albert Lansburgh	1924 ★ Interior ★
Music Box	239 W. 45th St.	C. Howard Crane	1920 ★ Interior ★
Nederlander orig. sports arena/ later National, Billy Rose	208 W. 41st St.	William N. Smith	Converted to theater, 1920
Neil Simon originally Alvin	244–254 W. 52nd St.	Herbert J. Krapp	1927 ★ Interior ★
New Amsterdam	214 W. 42nd St.	Herts & Tallant	1903 ★ Interior ★
New Amsterdam **Roof** originally New Amsterdam Aerial Gardens	214 W. 42nd St.	Herts & Tallant	1904
New Apollo originally Bryant/ later Apollo	215 W. 42nd St., 230 W. 43rd St.	De Rosa & Pereira	1920
Palace formerly R.K.O. Palace	1564 Broadway	Kirchoff & Rose	1913 Interior only ★
Plymouth	236 W. 45th St.	Herbert J. Krapp	1917 ★ Interior ★
Rialto originally Victoria	1481 Broadway	J. B. McElfatrick & Co. Altered, 1915, 1935, Herbert J. Krapp	1899
Ritz	225 W. 48th St.	Herbert J. Krapp	1920
Royale formerly Golden	242 W. 45th St.	Herbert J. Krapp Interior, Roman Melzer	1927 ★ Interior ★
St. James originally Erlanger	246 W. 44th St.	Warren & Wetmore	1927 ★ Interior ★
Sam S. Shubert	221 W. 44th St.	Henry B. Herts	1913 ★ Interior ★
Selwyn	229 W. 42nd St.	George Keister	1918
Studio 54 (disco) originally Gallo/ later New Yorker	254 W. 54th St.	Eugene De Rosa	1927
Times Square	219 W. 42nd St.	De Rosa & Pereira	1920
Victory originally Republic/ later Belasco	207 W. 42nd St.	Albert Westover Altered, J. B. McElfatrick & Co.	1899
Virginia formerly ANTA/ originally Theatre Guild	245 W. 52nd St.	Crane & Franzheim	1924 Interior only ★
Winter Garden	1634 Broadway	William A. Swasey Renovated, 1923, Herbert J. Krapp	1911 Interior only ★

[T 14b.] Palace Theatre, 1564 Broadway, bet. W. 46th and W. 47th Sts. E side. 1913. Kirchoff & Rose. Interior ★. To be absorbed into a new building, 1989, Fox & Fowle.

The old building, the **Carnegie Hall of vaudeville,** was another vehicle for signs that obliterated any architectural character underneath. Its successor promises to integrate architecture and signage as a joint venture.

[T 15a.] 1580 Broadway (offices), on the island at Times Square's north end, between W. 47th and W. 48th Sts., Broadway to Seventh Ave. 1989. Mayers & Schiff.

Here a building is meant as much as a carriage for signs as it is a useful office tower. The model promises something of the busy, sparkling complexity of the old Times Square, a grown-up version of their simple **tkts** pavilion at its feet. But it may be difficult to capture the serendipity of yore.

[T 15b.] 49th Street BMT subway station, below Seventh Ave. bet. W. 47th and W. 49th Sts. 1919. Renovated, 1973, Johnson/Burgêe.

Brilliant **glazed** vermillion brick sets the tone for a reconstructed subway station, one of the few in the entire city that can be called a fully satisfying environment. All surfaces, as well as lighting and graphics, were redone. Even the roar of passing express trains was reduced by installing welded track and half-height, sound-absorbing hollow masonry walls. Now for the Transit Authority to redo **all** the remaining stations . . .

[T 15c.] 1585 Broadway (offices), SW cor. W. 48th St. 1989. Gwathmey Siegel Assocs., design architects. Emergy Roth & Sons, architects.

Here a firm of considerable talent has designed its first major office building—a jump in scale difficult for all, no matter how talented. See, however, their elegant dormitory at Columbia.

[T 16.] Crowne Plaza Hotel, 1601 Broadway, bet. W. 48th and W. 49th Sts. W side. 1989. Alan Lapidus & Assocs.

The Marriott opened the door for the return of hotels to Times Square. Alan Lapidus, son and sometime partner of his father, Morris (who created the Miami Beach hotel architecture of the 1940s and 1950s), brings a second dollop of glitz to this precinct.

[T 17.] B. Smith's Restaurant, 771 Eighth Ave., NW cor. W. 47th St. 1986. Anderson/Schwartz.

A **supersleek Italo-new wave** restaurant, topped with a penthouse of corrugated steel in the fashion of California architect Frank Gehry. The painted stucco and simple detailing of the exterior give way to elegance inside. **Gold chains** brighten the terrazzo within, while **bottle caps** inlay the asphalt street without.

[T 18.] Engine Company No. 54, Ladder Company No. 4, Battalion 9, N.Y.C. Fire Department, 782 Eighth Ave., SE cor. W. 48th St. 1974. Department of Public Works.

Even the city's avenue of streetwalkers needs fire protection. This muted brown brick cubist exercise provides it. Congratulations to the D.P.W.

[T 19.] Worldwide Plaza (mixed use), Eighth to Ninth Aves., W. 49th to W. 50th Sts. Apartment towers, 1989, Frank Williams. Office tower, 1989, Skidmore, Owings & Merrill.

This giant complex occupies the site of the **second** Madison Square Garden (1925–1966), which was replaced by the **present** Garden between 31st and 33rd Streets, Seventh and Eighth Avenues. Zoning changes have encouraged this **western migration** of both offices and residences, by allowing more construction here than can now be erected in East Midtown.

 [T 20.] St. Malachy's Roman Catholic Church, 239-245 W. 49th St., bet. Broadway and Eighth Ave. 1903. Joseph H. McGuire.

Brick and limestone **neo-Gothic,** best known as Broadway's chapel for **Catholic actors,** where a mass could be interwoven with their matinee and evening schedules.

[T 21a.] 750 Seventh Avenue (offices), bet. W. 49th and W. 50th Sts., Broadway and Seventh Ave. 1989. Kevin Roche John Dinkleloo & Assocs.

Here the heirs of **Eero Saavinen** bring high style to the blocks north of Times Square proper. Elsewhere see their **Morgan Bank Headquarters** at 60 Wall Street, the **new Central Park Zoo,** and **United Nations Plaza, Nos. 1, 2, and 3.**

[T 21b.] Originally **Earl Carroll Theater/**later **Casa Mañana,** 154-158 W. 50th St., SE cor. Seventh Ave. 1931. George Keister, architect. Joseph J. Babolnay, designer. Lower facade altered, 1977.

This Art Deco polychromed-brick showplace is now sadly desecrated by bronze anodized aluminum and lots of signs. It replaced an earlier Earl Carroll temple to pulchritude that had edified the showman's boast, **"Through these portals pass the most beautiful girls in the world."** After Carroll vacated, Billy Rose opened a short-lived nightclub, Casa Mañana, in 1938.

Women, in early Broadway memories, were honored, revered, prostituted, loved, and made symbols of an earlier male chauvinism. The showgirl who made it to the top was the exceptional female of upward mobility, and a few were those that Billy Rose helped to rise (c.f. Eleanor Holm, who became his wife).

[T 22.] Equitable Center (offices), 787 Seventh Ave., bet. W. 51st and W. 52nd St. E side. 1986. Edward Larabee Barnes Assocs.

This replaced the Skidmore, Owings & Merrill-designed building to the east as the Equitable headquarters. Here a great atrium and **through-block galleria** (note the Barry Flanagan **elephant**) modulate the bulk of polished rose granite. The atrium is open to the public except on Sundays and Holidays.

From afar one can see the great arch of Equitable's boardroom at the top, but up close the building skin is bland and smooth, without articulated detail, a kind of Asia Society times ten [see E Manhattan/Gold Coast E 38a.].

Within the ground floor are two symmetrical Whitney Museum spaces at the northwest and southwest corners. Flanking them, in turn, are two tiny shops, field representatives of the Cathedral of St. John the Divine for obvious fund-raising purposes. (*1986. Hardy Holzman Pfeiffer Assocs.*)

Roy Lichtenstein's great mural dominates the lobby's central atrium space.

[T 23a.] Sheraton Centre/originally **Americana Hotel,** Seventh Ave. bet. W. 52nd and W. 53rd Sts. E side. 1962. Morris Lapidus & Assocs.

A sleek supermotel that offers characterless but efficient quarters for the traveler. For character and class go to the Plaza or St. Regis.

Here is a point to look back and savor the clocks and great metalwork globe atop the old Paramount Building to the south.

[T 23b.] The Manhattan (apartments and offices), 131 W. 52nd St., bet. Sixth and Seventh Aves. 1987. Rafael Viñoly & Assocs.

A handsome cubistic, neo-1930s multiple-use building, where the play of glazing subdivisions (squares) is in the popular **PoMo** (Post Modern) vocabulary. Precast concrete—some rough, some smooth—in differing shades of gray gives a base to the glassy construction overhead. The modeling of the upper floors is both subtle and elegant. A pedestrian allée connects with 53rd Street.

Gallagher's Restaurant: 228 West 52nd Street. Slaughterhouse on Seventh Avenue, its windows a refrigerator displaying meat that is an encyclopedia of beef's possibilities. The restaurant within offers a sauce that makes the simplest sliced steak a mouth-watering proposition.

[T 24.] 1675 Broadway (offices and theater), NW cor. W 52nd St. 1989. Fox & Fowle.

A green granite slab reminiscent in its modeling of the RCA Building in Rockefeller Center. It yearns for a solidity of masonry that 1950s and 1960s modern rejected in favor of glass (but daytime glass is visually solid, and nighttime glass a see-through negligee).

Dining and dancing, Times Square style: With venerable Lindy's gone from Times Square, **Jewish-American** delicatessen-style food, long-favored by entertainers, reaches its peak at the **Stage Delicatessen,** a small, crowded place at 834 Seventh Avenue between West 53rd and West 54th Streets, and the **Carnegie Delicatessen,** a block north at **No. 854.** Each has partisans who claim **theirs is better.** Try both and decide. Big dance halls, once common around the square, survive only in the sedate **Roseland,** in a former ice skating palace at 239 West 52nd Street (between Broadway and Eighth Avenue).

[T 25.] St. Benedict's Church (Roman Catholic)/formerly **Church of St. Benedict, the Moor,** 342 W. 53rd St., bet. Eighth and Ninth Aves. 1869. R. C. McLane & Sons.

This church for **black Catholics** was founded in 1883 at 210 Bleecker Street. In the mid 1890s the congregation moved to this **Italianate** building, built by an earlier Protestant Evangelical congregation, at the edge of what was then a **middle-class** black community.

[T 22.] The Equitable Center offices   **[T 25.]** St. Benedict, the Moor, Ch.

[T 26a.] Midtown North Precinct, N.Y.C. Police Department/originally **18th Precinct,** 306 W. 54th St. 1939. Department of Public Works.

A serene limestone cube contrasts with the chaos of entertainment-district police business flowing into and out of its doors. Note the freestanding **Art Moderne lanterns** of stainless steel that flank the entrances, and the moss growing under the air conditioners.

[T 26b.] St. George Tropoforos Hellenic Orthodox Church/formerly **New Amsterdam Building,** 307 W. 54th St. 1886.

This **Romanesque Revival** building began as a small office building and now, in sandblasted natural brick, serves as a church. The joyous ornament is still evident.

[T 26c.] American Theater of Actors and **Children's Museum of Manhattan/**originally **11th Judicial District Court,** 314 W. 54th St., bet. Eighth and Ninth Aves. 1896. John H. Duncan. Altered, 1970. James Stewart Polshek & Assocs. and Walfredo Toscanini.

Archways, entrance doors, and ventilators painted primary red, yellow, and blue **announce arrival** at this limestone Beaux Arts courthouse, now converted. Next door, the Depression-era police station continues to perform.

[T 27.] Originally **International Magazine Building**/now **Hearst Magazine Building,** 959 Eighth Ave., bet. W. 56th and W. 57th Sts. W side. 1928. Joseph Urban and George B. Post & Sons.

Shades of the Austrian **Secession movement,** this sculptured extravaganza was commissioned by the William Randolph Hearst publishing empire. It was a base for a skyscraper aborted due to the Depression. The foundations are still there, waiting . . .

[T 27.] The Hearst Magazine Building: plinth for an office tower never built

END of Times Square Area Tour: The nearest subways are along Eighth Avenue; the IND Sixth and Eighth Avenue Lines and the IRT Seventh Avenue Line local, all available at the 59th Street/Columbus Circle Station.

BRYANT PARK AREA

The land of **Bryant Park** and the **Public Library** was set aside in **1823** by the City as a potter's field. The Egyptian-style **Croton Reservoir,** with walls 50 feet high and 25 feet thick around a 4-acre lake, was completed on the Fifth Avenue side (site of The New York Public Library) in 1842. The locale was still at the northern fringe of the city in 1853 when New York's imitation of London's **Crystal Palace** opened on the park site; it burned down in 1858. The park was established in 1871 and in 1884 was named for **William Cullen Bryant,** well-known poet and journalist; in 1899–1901 the reservoir was razed to make way for the library.

Bryant Park Area Walking Tour: West 42nd Street between Fifth and Sixth Avenues (IRT Flushing Line to the Fifth Avenue Station; IND Sixth Avenue Line to the 42nd Street Station) to Fifth Avenue and 46th Street. The tour passes through one building open during weekday business hours: the Bar Association Building (37 West 43rd Street; 42 West 44th Street).

[B 1.] Bryant Park/originally **Reservoir Square,** Sixth Ave., bet. W. 40th and W. 42nd Sts. E side. 1871. Present design, 1934, Lusby Simpson. Scenic landmark ★. Library stacks extended beneath park, 1989, Davis, Brody & Assocs. Surface reconfigured, 1989, Hanna/Olin, landscape architects; kiosks, Hardy Holzman Pfeiffer Assocs.

Midtown's only large greenspace. A serene and formal garden redesigned through a competition among unemployed architects. Ringed by allées of trees and filled with statues of **William Cullen Bryant** (*1911. Herbert Adams*), Phelps-Dodge copper magnate **William E. Dodge** (*1885. J. Q. A. Ward*), **Goethe** (*1932. Karl Fischer*), and **José de Andrada,** father of Brazil's independence (*1954. José Lima*), and, formerly, a convention of drug pushers. The druggers move as the middle class regains its turf, a step behind this version of landscape gentrification—but the coke and pot will no doubt reappear, not very far away.

 [B 2a.] City University Graduate Center, CUNY/originally **Aeolian Hall,** 33 W. 42nd St., bet. Fifth and Sixth Aves. 1912. Warren & Wetmore. Redesigned, 1970, Carl J. Petrilli & Assocs.

What was once a concert hall and then a five-and-ten is now a bluestone-floored pedestrian arcade forming an **elegant shortcut** between 42nd and 43rd Streets. It also affords access to the graduate school's spaces above and library and auditorium below, as well as a pass-through gallery for exhibitions of art and design. The top floor is an equally inviting "buffeteria" open to all (nonuniversity people must pay a minimum). George Gershwin introduced **Rhapsody in Blue** in Aeolian Hall with Paul Whiteman's orchestra in 1924.

[B 2b.] W. R. Grace Building (offices), 1114 Avenue of the Americas, SE cor. W. 43rd St., a.k.a. 41 W. 42nd St., bet. Fifth and Sixth Aves. 1974. Skidmore, Owings & Merrill.

A disgrace to the street. Bowing to that era's zoning requirements for setbacks was merely an excuse to develop the flashy swooping form that interrupted the street wall containing Bryant Park. The plaza behind is a bore. Benches, fences, planters, trees, and sculpture [see Necrology] have been added over time—and, in some cases, removed—but the space remains a dark, uninviting backwater.

[B 2c.] Home Box Office Inc. (offices)/originally **Bryant Park Building,** 1100 Avenue of the Americas, NE cor. W. 42nd St. ca. 1912. Converted for HBO, 1985, Kohn Pedersen Fox Assocs.

A scintillating mirrored curtain wall sitting atop a thermal granite base that tames the excesses of 42nd Street's other tawdry retail shops into a coherent whole. Cecil B. De Mille would have been proud of the romantic lobby. But all that square-gridded glass is part of the demise of such curtain walls, originally reflecting an older, stone city and now reflecting merely other glassy neighbors.

Subway passage: Connecting the 42nd Street Station of the Sixth Avenue IND and the Fifth Avenue Station of the IRT Flushing Line is an underground passageway (*1975. N.Y.C. Transit Authority architecture staff.*) that is rare for the city: It is well lighted, lined with dapper, leather-colored structural tile blocks, and enhanced by a group of bold photographic enlargements of nearby street scenes, old and new, transferred to porcelain enamel panels. Among the views are those of today's Bryant Park when it was the site of New York's Crystal Palace, the Latting Observatory tower, and the old Croton Reservoir.

[B 3a.] New York Telephone Company (offices), 1095 Avenue of the Americas, bet. W. 41st and W. 42nd Sts. W side. 1970. Kahn & Jacobs.

Prominently sited, tall, and carrying a curiously modulated curtain wall that changes scale as it rises from Sixth Avenue's sidewalk. Ho-hum.

[B 3b.] Originally Bush Tower (offices), 132 W. 42nd St., bet. Sixth Avenue and Broadway. 1918. Helmle & Corbett.

This building rises **480** feet from a base only **50** by **200** feet, built by the developers of Brooklyn's vast industrial complex, **Bush Terminal.** Note the *trompe l'oeil* brickwork on its east flank. The **"Terminal"** is a set of immense warehouses along Brooklyn's waterfront, a staggering concept, the administration of which was operated from these **eyries.**

[B 4.] World's Tower Building, 110 W. 40th St., bet. Sixth Ave. and Broadway. 1915. Buchman & Fox.

An elaborate and **unique** terra-cotta prism in the Beaux Arts mode. Although sandwiched between two lower adjacent buildings, it presents **4** ornate facades. One of Edward West Browning's terra-cotta clad developments.

[B 5a.] Bryant Park Studios/originally **Beaux Arts Studios,** 80 W. 40th St., SE cor. Sixth Ave. 1901. Charles A. Rich.

A Beaux Arts extravaganza. Double-height studios gather north light from across Bryant Park via double-height windows.

[B 5b.] Originally **Republican Club**/now **Daytop Village,** 54-56 W. 40th St., bet. Fifth and Sixth Aves. 1904. York & Sawyer.

Monumental **Tuscan** columns ennoble the grand portal of this rehabilitation center.

[B 5c.] American Standard Building/originally **American Radiator Building,** 40 W. 40th St., bet. Fifth and Sixth Aves. 1924. Hood & Fouilhoux. Addition, 1937, André Fouilhoux. ★

The centerpiece in a row of **Renaissance** club facades is designer Hood's black brick and gold terra-cotta, Gothic-inspired tower. The first-floor facade, of bronze and polished black granite, and the black marble and mirror-clad lobby are worth a close look. The plumbing fixture showroom is a later addition.

[B 5d.] The Columns (apartments)/originally **The Engineers Club,** 32 W. 40th St., bet. Fifth and Sixth Aves. 1906. Whitfield & King.

Brick and limestone **Georgian** and **Renaissance Revival.** Giant Corinthian pilasters give this a scale appropriate to the New York Public Library opposite.

[B 6a.] Republic National Bank Tower, incorporating the former **Knox Hat Building,** 452 Fifth Ave. bet. W. 39th and W. 40th Sts. W side. 1986. Attia & Perkins. **[B 6b.]** Formerly **Republic National Bank Building**/originally **Knox Hat Building,** 452 Fifth Ave., SW cor. W. 40th St. 1902. John H. Duncan. ★

Overhead a **digital tidal wave** swells over the old Knox Building, built as an **exuberant Classical showcase** for Col. Edward M. Knox, hatter to presidents.

[B 7.] 4 East 39th Street, bet. Fifth and Madison Aves. 1905. George B. Post & Sons.

The gargoyles on this small side-street building's cornice will watch you intently as you examine the sculpted heads of Whistler and Rembrandt.

[B 8.] 461 Fifth Avenue (offices), NE cor. E. 40th St. 1988. Skidmore, Owings & Merrill.

The conservative Modernists who brought us Lever House have switched here to **Post Modern** (technological division), with exposed, pedimented trusswork for wind bracing decorating the building form. Atop it all is a fancy hat added to the stylish ones already filling the skyline. The innovative and ultrarefined precast-concrete curtain wall, evoking memories of bent metal office cubicles (and clerks with green eyeshades), is a refreshing note.

[B 9.] The New York Public Library, Fifth Ave. bet. W. 40th and W. 42nd Sts. W side. 1911. Carrère & Hastings. Lions, E. C. Potter, sculptor. Figures over fountains, Frederick MacMonnies, sculptor. ★ Partial interior ★. Restoration and renovations: **Periodicals Reading Rooms,** 1985, Giorgio Cavaglieri and Davis, Brody & Assocs. Murals, Richard Haas. **Gottesman Exhibition Hall,** 1986; **Celeste Bartos Forum,** 1987; and other spaces, all by Davis, Brody & Assocs. **Open to the public.**

The **apogee of Beaux Arts** for New York, a white marble "temple" magnificently detailed inside and out, entered over extravagant terraces, imposing stairs and post-flamboyant fountains, all now happily restored. Here knowledge is stored in a place worthy of aspiration—a far cry from one's local library-supermarket.

The Roman Renaissance detailing is superb.

The 1980s restorations gave back public spaces claimed by library-dom's bureaucracy. Some are breathtaking; others, divorced from posters, prints, and paintings on the walls, produce a shadowless **Last Year at Marienbad** surrealism.

[B 9.] An apogee of Beaux Arts for New York: The New York Public Library

[B 5c.] American Standard Building   **[B 9.]** Celeste Bartos Forum, N.Y.P.L.

[B 9a.] The Kiosks, New York Public Library, Fifth Ave. terrace bet. W. 40th and W. 42nd Sts. W side. 1987. Hardy Holzman Pfeiffer Assocs.

A symmetrical pair of movable "neo-Renaissance" country cottages give food and solace to the warm weather lunchtime crowd. In the winter they are removed to space within.

[B 10a.] 500 Fifth Avenue (offices), NW cor. W. 42nd St. 1931. Shreve, Lamb & Harmon.

A 699-foot-high phallic pivot that once balanced a great tin can marked "500," and now simply supports an unadorned cooling tower.

[B 10b.] Manufacturers Hanover Trust Company branch/originally **Manufacturers Trust Company,** 510 Fifth Ave., SW cor. W. 43rd St. 1954. Skidmore, Owings & Merrill.

This building led the banking profession out of the cellar and onto the street; a glass-sheathed **supermarket of dollars.** The safe in the window is a symbolic descendent of Edgar Allan Poe's **purloined letter.**

[B 11.] Israel Discount Bank/originally **Postal Life Insurance Building,** 511 Fifth Ave., SE cor. E. 43rd St. 1917. York & Sawyer. Remodeled, 1962, Luss, Kaplan & Assocs., Ltd., designer.

Superb renovation of a Renaissance Revival bank interior. All the **old** fittings that could be kept have been; everything added is clearly **new.**

[B 12.] Sidewalk clock, in front of 522 Fifth Ave., SW cor. W. 44th St. ★

As the European church signaled the **hour** to the town dweller, here the **minutes** are displayed for the more time-conscious American. The pair of harmonizing bollards are happy post-landmark designation additions.

[B 13a.] Unification Church Headquarters/formerly **Columbia University Club/**originally **Hotel Renaissance,** 4 W. 43rd St., bet. Fifth and Sixth Aves. 1900. Howard, Cauldwell & Morgan, with Bruce Price.

A simplified **Renaissance Revival** palazzo, less elegant than the **Century** across the street—and inflated. John Galen Howard eventually became the architect of the University of California at Berkeley.

[B 13b.] The Century Association, 7 W. 43rd St., bet. Fifth and Sixth Aves. 1891. William Kendall of McKim, Mead & White. ★

A **delicate Palladian facade** for a club of artists, professionals, and intellectuals. The large window above the entrance was originally an open loggia.

[B 14a.] Association of the Bar of the City of New York, 37 W. 43rd St. and 42 W. 44th St., bet. Fifth and Sixth Aves. 1895. Cyrus L. W. Eidlitz. ★

A Classical limestone structure with the **massive sobriety** of the law. Doric, Ionic, and Corinthian orders are all there. But as an ensemble, it has the austere elegance of **Greek architecture** of the 5th century B.C.

[B 14b.] Originally Army & Navy Club of America/now **Touro College,** 30 W. 44th St., bet. Fifth and Sixth Aves. 1900. Tracy & Swartwout.

A neo-Georgian brick and limestone clubhouse.

[B 10b.] Manufacturers Hanover Trust, the original supermarket of dollars

[B 14c.] General Society of Mechanics and Tradesmen (Building)/originally **Berkeley Preparatory School,** 20 W. 44th St., bet. Fifth and Sixth Aves. 1891. Lamb & Rich. Extension, 1909, Ralph Townsend. **Open to the public.**

A free, evening technical school founded in 1820 is housed in this dour Classical structure. The interior is a surprise: **a 3-story gallery-ringed drill hall** housing a library and exhibits of old locks, the **John H. Mossmann Collection.** Savor particularly "A Very Complicated Lock."

[B 15a.] Harvard Club, 27 W. 44th St., bet. Fifth and Sixth Aves. 1894. Major additions, 1905, 1915. All by McKim, Mead & White. ★ Addition, 1989, Edward Larrabee Barnes Assocs.

Behind the modest neo-Georgian exterior are some imposing spaces; their large scale can be seen on the 45th Street rear facade.

Barnes has designed an addition that enhances the **facilities** without competing with **MM&W.** It is rumored that sometimes applicants seek Harvard admission just for the future opportunity of joining here.

[B 15b.] New York Yacht Club, 37 W. 44th St., bet. Fifth and Sixth Aves. 1900. Warren & Wetmore. ★

A fanciful example of Beaux Arts design with windows that bear the sterns of old ships, worked in among the columns. The **"America's Cup"** was born here.

[B 13b.] The Century Association   [B 15b.] The New York Yacht Club

[B 15c.] Algonquin Hotel/originally **The Puritan Hotel,** 59 W. 44th St., bet. Fifth and Sixth Aves. 1902. Goldwin Starrett.

The hotel/restaurant has a 1902 neo-Renaissance facade like many others, but it has long been a rendezvous for theater and literary figures. In the 1920s its Oak Room housed America's most famous luncheon club, the **Round Table,** at which **F. P. Adams, Robert Benchley, Harold Ross, Dorothy Parker,** and others sat. Stop for refreshment in the closet-sized Blue Bar, or relax on one of the easy chairs in the lobby.

1903 prices: sitting room, library, dining room, 3 bedrooms, 3 baths, private hall—$10.00/day. Bedroom and bath—$2.00/day.

[B 16a.] Hotel Webster/originally **Webster Apartments,** 38-42 W. 45th St., bet. Fifth and Sixth Aves. 1904. Tracy & Swartwout.

A wonderful rusticated base supports a simple brick body.

[B 16b.] 1166 Avenue of the Americas (offices), bet. W. 45th and W. 46th Sts. E side. 1973. Skidmore, Owings & Merrill.

A black **Saran Wrap** lemon—but only fiscally—when the bottom dropped out of the city's 1970s real estate boom, making it impossible to find a tenant. Finally, in 1977, it became a commercial condominium. Sleek and restrained, it is now **vigorously** occupied. Its midblock plaza is a very popular lunchtime picnic spot for nearby office workers.

ICP/MIDTOWN: The International Center of Photography's central business-district branch is located off the 45th side of 1166's plaza. A fine street-level display of photographic exhibitions that change regularly and also a source of selected books on photography. This is an adjunct of ICP's main exhibition space at 1130 Fifth Avenue [see E Manhattan/Carnegie Hill C 19a.]. **Open to the public.**

[B 17.] 1180 Avenue of the Americas/originally **Phoenix Building,** NE cor. W. 46th St. 1963. Altered and reskinned, 1985. All by Emery Roth & Sons.

It was perhaps the **finest** handling of an office tower within the maximum envelope of the 1916 Zoning Resolution. The syncopated setbacks and the carefully studied detailing of the strip windows and tiers of continuous brick spandrels made this a fine work. The current owners have upgraded its stylish wall to one even more stylish.

END of Bryant Park Area Tour: The closest subways are at 47th-50th Street/Rockefeller Center Station of the IND Sixth Avenue Line.

GRAND CENTRAL/PARK AVENUE

Grand Central Terminal to East 57th Street:

"As a bullet seeks its target, shining rails in every part of our great country are aimed at Grand Central Station, heart of the nation's greatest city. Drawn by the magnetic force of the fantastic metropolis, day and night great trains rush toward the Hudson River, sweep down its eastern bank for 140 miles, flash briefly by the long red row of tenement houses south of 125th Street, dive with a roar into the 2½-mile tunnel which burrows beneath the glitter and swank of Park Avenue and then . . . Grand Central Station! Crossroads of a million private lives! Gigantic stage on which are played a thousand dramas daily."
—**Opening from "Grand Central Station,"** broadcast over the NBC Radio Blue Network, beginning 1937.

The one-mile stretch from Grand Central Terminal to East 59th Street—the busiest portion of Park Avenue—is **a uniquely successful integration** of railroad and city. The avenue itself is built over the old New York Central lines (also used by the old New York, New Haven & Hartford), and up to 50th Street the buildings along it are built over the fan-shaped yards.

The railroad's **right-of-way,** down what was originally Fourth Avenue, dates back to 1832, when the **New York and Harlem Railroad** terminated at Chambers Street. The **smoke and noise** of locomotives were later banned below 23rd Street, then 42nd Street, as the **socially prominent** residential areas **moved north.** At 42nd Street the original, cupolaed **Grand Central Depot,** with **a vast iron-and-glass train shed,** was opened in 1871 (*J. B. Snook, architect; R. G. Hatfield, shed engineer. Remodeled, 1892, Bradford L. Gilbert*).

In the early 1900s, when electric locomotives were introduced, the railroad took **audacious steps** that not only **increased the value of its property** many times over but also gave the city a three-dimensional composition that was a major achievement of **the City Beautiful era.** The terminal itself was made more efficient and compact by dividing its 67 tracks between two subterranean levels, and Park Avenue north and south of the terminal was joined in 1919 by a system of automobile viaducts wrapping around the station.

New engineering techniques for shielding tall buildings from railroad vibrations made possible **a complex of offices and hotels** around the station and extending north above the yards and tracks. By the onset of the Great Depression the avenue through the 50s was lined with **remarkably uniform rows** of apartments and hotels, all solid blocks about 12 to 16 stories high, punctuated by the divergent form of a church or club. Although some of the buildings had **handsome central courtyards,** their dense ground coverage must have made **summer living unbearable** in pre-air-conditioning times—but, then, people who lived here **never summered in the city.**

Firm as these palaces appeared, most of them lasted only a few decades. Their loss, as a result of the office building boom of the 1950s and 1960s ("convenient to Grand Central") eliminated the avenue's air of elegance. Today only one apartment building survives below 59th Street, **No. 417** Park Avenue, at 55th.

Park Avenue Walking Tour: From Grand Central Terminal to 57th Street. (Take a subway to the terminal itself: the IRT Lexington Avenue Line, the IRT Flushing Line, or the IRT Shuttle from Times Square.)

[P 1.] Grand Central Terminal, E. 42nd St. at Park Ave. N side. 1903–1913. Reed & Stem and Warren & Wetmore. ★ Painted ceiling over main concourse, Whitney Warren with Paul Helleu and Charles Basing. Partial interior ★. **[P 1a.] Pershing Square Viaduct**, 1919. ★

The remarkably functional scheme of the terminal and its approaches is housed in an imposing Beaux Arts Classical structure. The main facade, facing south down Park Avenue, is a fine symmetrical composition of triumphal arches, filled in with steel and glass, and surmounted by **a colossal clock and sculpture group** (by Jules Coutan) in which **Roman deities fraternize** with an American eagle. The symbolism may be confusing, but the scale and composition are most imposing.

The main room inside is unexpectedly spare in detail, a virtue now obscured by advertising displays, particularly that colossal Kodak transparency and its surrounds that **must go** in any intelligent refurbishing. The simple ceiling vault, 125 feet across, decorated with the **constellations** of the zodiac, is actually hung from steel trusses. Smaller spaces are structurally spanned by **Guastavino tile vaulting** left exposed, with handsome effect, in parts of the lower level, as at the **Oyster Bar.**

Grand Central Oyster Bar: This restaurant has been world-renowned for its shellfish stews and pan roasts. The oyster bar and its equipment are worth seeing under exposed tan tile vaulting low enough to touch.

[P 2.] Pan Am Building (office complex), 200 Park Ave. 1963. Emery Roth & Sons, Pietro Belluschi, and Walter Gropius. Lobby alterations, 1987, Warren Platner.

This **latter-day addition** to the Grand Central complex was purely a speculative venture. The building **aroused protest** both for its enormous volume of office space—2.4 million square feet, **the most** in any single commercial office building at the time—and for **blocking the vista** up and down Park Avenue, previously **punctuated but not stopped** by the Helmsley (originally New York Central) Building tower [see P 3.]. The precast concrete curtain wall was one of the first in New York. **68** elevators! The lobby remodeling is again an owner's recollection of what sells in Miami and Houston: sinuous, out-of-scale, pretentious. If it were a stage set it could at least be knocked down at the end of the performance.

Note the staid, neo-Classical **Yale Club** (identified in letters only one inch high) across Vanderbilt Avenue from the Pan Am at East 44th Street (*1901. Tracy & Swartwout.*) It was once part of a group, severely compromised with the closing and recladding of the Biltmore Hotel, between 43rd and 44th.

Pan Am restaurants: The east side of the Pan Am lobby, at street level, has a row of three eateries with lively decoration representing three nations: **Charlie Brown's (would-be** Edwardian English club), the **Trattoria** (attempt jet-age Italian), and **Zum Zum** (*Wursthaus* German).

[P 2a.] Zum Zum, Pan Am Building lobby. 1964. George Thiele and Harper & George, designers. Expanded, 1987.

The **prototype** Zum Zum from which all others (in a now decimated empire) descended.

[P 2b.] Pan American World Airways ticket office, 60 E. 45th St., SE cor. Vanderbilt Ave. 1963. Edward Larrabee Barnes Assocs. and Charles Forberg.

The major tenants gave the Pan Am Building its **most noteworthy** public space. The arrangement of freestanding curvilinear elements against a brightly lit, undulating white wall is especially effective when seen from outside.

 [P 3.] Helmsley Building (offices). Originally **New York Central Building**/later **New York General Building,** 230 Park Ave., bet. E. 45th and E. 46th Sts. 1929. Warren & Wetmore. ★ Partial interior ★.

This office tower, **symbol** of the then-prosperous railroad, was once **visible for miles** along Park Avenue. Its fanciful cupola and opulent but impeccably detailed lobby **departed from the sobriety** of the terminal and the surrounding buildings.

The north facade, once a remarkably successful molding of urban space, maintained the cornice line of buildings flanking the avenue to the north, carrying it around **in small curves** to create **an apse of grand proportions,** crowned by the tower. Only a fragment of the original composition remains, in the relation of the building to 250 Park Avenue. Carved into this facade are two **tall portals for automobile traffic,** clearly differentiated from the central lobby entrance and the open pedestrian passages to the east and west. The **renaming** from **Central to General** required only the filling and recutting of two letters over the auto portals; **Helmsley** was another matter.

The Helmsley ownership accounts for the gilding of the ornament and the spectacular nighttime illumination of the building's crown.

[P 1.] The great Beaux Arts Grand Central Terminal building at 42nd Street

[P 2.] The Pan Am Building (offices)

[P 7.] The Mfrs. Hanover Trust Tower

[P 4.] Originally **Postum Building (offices),** 250 Park Ave., bet. E. 46th and E. 47th Sts. W side to Vanderbilt Ave. 1925. Cross & Cross, architects, Phelps Barnum, assoc. architect. **[P 4a.] Banco di Sicilia,** E. 47th St. side. Altered, 1978, Shreve, Lamb & Harmon.

Saved miraculously (by its small full-block site) from being demolished and replaced by a grotesquely larger occupant, **No. 250** is one of Park Avenue's few 'tween the wars neo-Classical office structures that revere the idea of Warren & Wetmore to create a Terminal City to surround—and enhance—their Grand Central Terminal complex. **Banco di Sicilia** is a Modern latter-day insertion with verve.

[P 5.] Park Avenue Atrium (offices), 466 Lexington Ave. bet. E. 45th and E. 46th Sts. E side. 1984. Edward Durrell Stone Assocs. Atrium sculpture, Richard Lippold.

Here one block of the original Grand Central Station complex was reincarnated and reclad. More interesting is the inner courtyard, originally open to the sky and now a glass-roofed atrium. In the manner of John Portman's various hotel atriums (but here more in the spirit of a small-town Marriott), **rocket ship elevators** float up and down the side of this huge space.

[P 6.] Chemcourt at the Chemical Bank Building, 277 Park Ave., bet E. 47th and E. 48th Sts. E side. Building, 1962, Emery Roth & Sons. Chemcourt addition, 1982, Haines Lundberg Waehler.

An unutilized and barren plaza upgraded into a greenhouse lobby. It's a bit clunky but more appropriate urbanistically than a small paved area in this frequently cool climate.

[P 7.] Manufacturers Hanover Trust Company Headquarters/originally **Union Carbide Building (offices),** 270 Park Ave., bet. E. 47th and E. 48th Sts. W side to Madison Ave. 1960. Remodeled, 1983. All by Skidmore, Owings & Merrill.

The 53-story **sheer** tower is **articulated** with bright stainless steel mullions against a background of gray glass and black matte-finished steel panels. The 13-story wing to the rear (well related in scale to Madison Avenue) is linked to the tower by a **narrow transparent bridge,** dramatically placed at the north end of Vanderbilt Avenue. The site of the building over railroad yards made it necessary to start elevators at the **second floor,** reached by escalators. In charge was **SOM**'s Natalie DuBois, one of Modern architecture's early prominent women. The emigration of Union Carbide to the suburbs removed the outlandish pink terrazzo sidewalks and substituted tame planters instead.

[P 8.] Bankers Trust Building, 280 Park Ave., bet. E. 48th and E. 49th Sts. W side. 1963. Emery Roth & Sons. Henry Dreyfuss, designer. Addition to W, 1971, Emery Roth & Sons. Oppenheimer, Brady & Lehrecke, associated architects. **[P 8a.] Aurora (restaurant),** 60 E. 49th St., in addition. 1986. Milton Glaser, designer.

A rare example of an industrial designer (Dreyfuss) playing a major role in the design of a large building, most obvious in the very neat concrete curtain wall. The effort to fit into the 1916 Zoning Resolution envelope without producing the stepped-back wedding-cake silhouette has produced two rectangular masses that simply coexist. **Aurora's** facade is so reserved it only adds to the bleakness of the sidestreet plaza.

[P 8b.] CAAC, National Airline, People's Republic of China/originally **addo-x (showroom)/**later **AEROFLOT,** 45 E. 49th St., bet. Madison and Park Aves. 1957. Batir Design Assocs.: Hans Lindblom, Oskar Nitzcke, designers.

An exquisitely designed building, shoehorned into its site.

[P 9a.] Hotel Inter-Continental/originally **Barclay Hotel,** 111 E. 48th St., NW cor. Lexington Ave. 1927. Cross & Cross.

An elegant survivor of the Park Avenue development of the 1920s. Cocktails are served on the terrace overlooking the lobby, the centerpiece of which is a large gilded birdcage.

[P 9b.] Halloran House/originally **Shelton Towers Hotel,** 525 Lexington Ave., bet. E. 48th and E. 49th Sts. 1924. Arthur Loomis Harmon.

A 34-story experiment in the then-new **1916 Zoning Resolution,** that modeled the required setbacks for light and air into a cubistic brick composition. A powerful influence on architects and artists in the 1920s, it is embellished with a **Romanesque Revival fillip** here and there.

[P 10.] Waldorf-Astoria Hotel, 301 Park Ave., bet. E. 49th and E. 50th Sts. E side. 1931. Schultze & Weaver.

When this **world-famous institution** moved from its original site (where the Empire State Building now rises), it chose to build in **a sedate**

version of the Art Deco style. The facades and lobbies were once a picture of 1930s chic, but in the early 1960s the management tried to turn back the clock to the Edwardian period; whatever couldn't be replaced was gilded. Cooler heads have since prevailed, and its Art Deco has been revived. The 625-foot towers, which have a separate entrance on East 50th Street, have been temporary home to such notables as **President Hoover, General MacArthur,** the **Duke of Windsor, Secretary of State Henry Kissinger,** and **John F. Kennedy.**

[P 11a.] St. Bartholomew's Church (Episcopal), Park Ave. bet. E. 50th and E. 51st Sts. E side. 1919. Bertram G. Goodhue. Entrances relocated from old St. Bartholomew's, Madison Ave. SW cor. E. 24th St., 1902. ★ McKim, Mead & White. **Community House,** 109 E. 50th St., bet. Park and Lexington Aves. 1927. Bertram G. Goodhue Assocs. and Mayers, Murray & Philip. ★ **Sallie Franklin Cheatham Memorial Garden,** 1971. Hamby, Kennerly, Slomanson & Smith, architects. Paschall Campbell, landscape architect.

St. Bartholomew's and the buildings behind it gave the old Park Avenue what it desperately needed: open space, color, variety of form and detail. Around its open terrace at the 50th Street corner are arrayed picturesque polychrome forms that rise to the **ample dome** of the church, dip, and then soar to the **570-foot pinnacles** of the General Electric tower.

In 1983 an effort was begun by the church to obtain permission from the Landmarks Preservation Commission to demolish the Community House and Cheatham Garden in favor of a high-rise office tower. Twice turned back by the commission, the matter made its way to the U.S. Supreme Court. Please hold your breath.

[P 11a.] The relocated McKim, Mead & White portal of St. Bartholomew's Church

[P 11b.] General Electric Building/originally **RCA Victor Building,** 570 Lexington Ave., SW cor. E. 51st St. 1931. Cross & Cross. ★

Built to be **contextual to St. Bart's,** its neighbor, long before that word entered the city's development vocabulary. The detailing at both bottom and top is sumptuous.

[P 11c.] 560 Lexington Avenue (offices), NW cor. E. 50th St. 1981. The Eggers Group. Brick sculpture, Aleksandra Kasuba.

A latter-day addition to the St. Bart's block, this reserved tower attempted consciously (with Landmarks Preservation Commission prodding) to integrate itself into the total composition. The entrance to the subway, which also leads to the Cathedral Branch of The New York Public Library, is notable, too.

[P 11d.] 51st Street Station, IRT Lexington Avenue Line. 1918. Redesigned, 1988, Mayers & Schiff.

A Post Modern remake of an ordinary local stop. It's no longer ordinary.

Fire down below. What lies beneath New York's streets is often as intriguing as the buildings and monuments that adorn them—at least for Hollywood. In the 1946 fantasy *Angel on My Shoulder,* set in New York, Claude Rains as the devil commuted between his world and ours via a rising sidewalk freight elevator. Marilyn Monroe, in *The Seven Year Itch,* enjoyed a world-famous burst of subway-blown air, raising Tom Ewell's eyebrows (and hopes) as her skirt billowed over an IRT subway grating. The grating is still there, in Lexington Avenue's west sidewalk, just south of 52nd Street—the buildings have changed.

 [P 12.] Seagram Building (offices), 375 Park Ave., bet. E. 52nd and E. 53rd Sts. E side. 1958. Ludwig Mies van der Rohe with Philip Johnson, design architects. Kahn & Jacobs, associate architects.

The bronze and bronze-glass tower that reintroduced **the idea of plaza** to New York. **Mies van der Rohe** brought here and to reality the **fantasies he proposed for Berlin** in the 1920s; **Philip Johnson,** his biographer and acolyte (then, not now) designed its interiors. **Phyllis Lambert,** daughter of the Seagram board chairman, the late Samuel Bronfman, was the catalyst for it all, bringing architectural standards learned at Vassar. A father's love and respect for his daughter here allowed **a modern monument.**

The plaza, daring in that it was proposed at all (considering real estate values), is a bit of a bore; but at Christmastime the trees and lights are like a great piling of bridal veil—a delight.

 [P 12a.] The Four Seasons (restaurant), 99 E. 52nd St. (in the Seagram Building), bet. Park and Lexington Aves. 1959. Philip Johnson & Assocs.

An entrance dominated by Picasso's backdrop for the ballet *The Three-Cornered Hat* (1919) leads from the Seagram lobby into the restaurant (to the north) and the bar (to the south). The walnut-paneled dining room is laid out around a square pool, the other room around the square bar, over which is a quivering brass rod sculpture by **Richard Lippold.** Both rooms are impeccably designed down to the last napkin, with tableware by **L. Garth Huxtable.** A stair connects the bar with the East 52nd Street lobby, one floor below, adorned with modern paintings. At this entrance, planting boxes and doormen's uniforms **are changed quarterly to mark the seasons.**

Dining at The Four Seasons is elegant and expensive. Sightseers are not generally welcome, but during the afternoon lull (around 4 P.M.) the management may be more permissive.

Brasserie: The Seagram Building's other restaurant, less lavish but well designed, is entered at 100 East 53rd Street. Its menu is eclectic, but you can have anything from a beer or a sundae to a full-course dinner. The Brasserie also makes up picnic baskets. Open 24 hours.

 [P 13a.] Racquet and Tennis Club, 370 Park Ave., bet. E. 52nd and E. 53rd Sts. W side. 1918. McKim, Mead & White. ★

An **elegant Brunelleschian foil** for the Seagram's plaza, this Florentine Renaissance palazzo is a wealthy male chauvinist's club housing **squash** (both lemon and racquets) and one of the few extant **court tennis** courts (the game of Louis XIV).

[P 13b.] Park Avenue Plaza (offices), E. 52nd to E. 53rd St., bet. Madison and Park Aves. 1981. Skidmore, Owings & Merrill.

A bulky glass prism lurking behind the **Racquet and Tennis Club,** which sold its **air rights** so that the "Plaza" might enjoy a greater bulk. The Club, in turn, will in all likelihood remain unchanged forever by virtue of its landmark designation and the impossibility of replacing it with something bigger.

The atrium within has a subtle waterfall and restaurant service, but feel free to sit there without ordering—mandated by the zoning concessions obtained. It is a **public** place and has remarkably clean public toilets!

[P 14.] Lever House (offices), 390 Park Ave., bet. E. 53rd and E. 54th Sts. W side. 1952. Skidmore, Owings & Merrill. ★

Where the glassy curtain wall began.

These prismatic forms, now small-scaled for Park Avenue, were the **avant-garde** of the metal and glass curtain wall, first receiving the reflections of ornate neo-Renaissance stonework from the **Racquet Club** to the south, and **assorted classy apartments** to the north and east. Glass has been reflecting **other glass** almost everywhere, a phase happily almost over, now that **Post Modernism** brings back solid form—a paradox in that there is something else to reflect again.

[P 12.] Seagram Building and Plaza   [P 14.] Lever House: Modern classic

[P 15.] 599 Lexington Avenue (offices), SE cor. E. 53rd St. 1987. Edward Larrabee Barnes Assocs.

The corner idea, chamfered here, overhung elsewhere (IBM). The glassy subway kiosk is a new and pleasant entrance to the IND Lexington Avenue Station and the IRT 51st Street Station, connected as part of a zoning bonus that gave the tower more bulk. This might be classed as **Son of Citicorp** (see below), a sleek metal relative but by a different architect.

[P 16.] Citicorp Center, Lexington Ave. bet. E. 53rd and E. 54th Sts. E side. 1978. Hugh Stubbins & Assocs., design architects. Emery Roth & Sons, architects. **[P 16a.] St. Peter's Church (Lutheran).** 1977. Hugh Stubbins & Assocs. Erol Beker Chapel of the Good Shepherd. Louise Nevelson, designer-sculptor. Interior, Massimo Vignelli, designer.

A **tour de force** for the skyline as a stylish silhouette and, for the pedestrian, a hovering cantilevered hulk under which **nests** St. Peter's Church. The **smooth aluminum facade** lacks the rich austerity of 140 Broadway (its flush, but black, predecessor). The raked profile at its crest was a gesture to the idea of a sloping sun collector but now is just a vestigial form, like the Mercedes-Benz radiator cap and symbol.

For the "Lipstick Building," across Third Avenue, see United Nations–Turtle Bay [U 28.].

[P 17a.] Central Synagogue (Congregation Ahawath Chesed Shaar Hashomayim), 652 Lexington Ave., SW cor. E. 55th St. 1872. Henry Fernbach. ★

The oldest building **in continuous use** as a synagogue in New York, this one represents the roughhewn Moorish style considered appropriate in the late 1800s. Although dour on the exterior, except for the **star-studded** bronze cupolas, the synagogue has an interior **gaily stenciled** with rich blues, earthy reds, ocher, and gilt—Moorish but distinctly American 19th century. Fernbach was America's first prominent Jewish architect.

[P 17b.] 116, 120, 122, 124 East 55th Street (former town houses), bet. Park and Lexington Aves.

A remarkable row of holdouts from the era when this block was residential.

[P 17c.] Fifty-fifth Plaza (offices), 110 E. 55th St., bet. Park and Lexington Aves. 1987. The Eggers Group.

An offbeat brick tower that looms over this once modestly scaled street of elegant town houses. Its form, narrow and tall, is difficult to reflect upon: street trees fortunately mute it all. At the base a glass pediment states baldly that **we too** are Post Modern.

[P 18a.] Chase Manhattan Bank branch, 410 Park Ave., SW cor. E. 55th St. 1959. Skidmore, Owings & Merrill (bank and curtain wall). Emery Roth & Sons (building).

A building of wedding cake form, common in its time, with a **better than usual** metal and glass curtain wall, designed to meet the needs of the bank on the lower two floors. The bank interior has unusually refined details. The high 2nd-floor banking room is an impressive setting for an **Alexander Calder** mobile.

[P 17a.] The 1872 Central Synagogue   [P 18b.] The Heron Tower (offices)

 [P 18b.] Heron Tower (offices), 70 E. 55th St., bet. Madison and Park Aves. 1987. Kohn Pedersen Fox.

A neo-1930s tower reminiscent of the style—if not the detail—of the Empire State Building: honed gray granite with **rock-face** blocks punctuating the facade. It all brings back thoughts of a possible 1930s movie that might have been termed *Prince Kong.* Take in the lobby!

 [P 19a.] Park Avenue Tower (offices), 65 E. 55th St., bet. Madison and Park Aves., through to E. 56th St. 1987. Murphy/Jahn.

Sleek and sassy, the skin below is warped in planes, then articulated with stainless steel tori: half-round horizontal projections typical in Renaissance architecture. Although this would generally be classified as **Post Modern,** it has many early modern mannerisms.

[P 19b.] Le Cygne (restaurant), 53 E. 55th St., bet. Madison and Park Aves. 1982. Voorsanger & Mills.

Architecture of quality outside and in makes inroads on an equal cuisine, a rare conjuncture of two practical arts.

[P 19c.] Mercedes-Benz showroom/originally **Jaguar showroom,** 430 Park Ave., SW cor. E. 56th St. 1955. Frank Lloyd Wright. Altered, 1982, Taliesin Associated Architects.

In the master's first New York City work, his creativity seems to have been smothered by the cramped space. More notable in that **he** did it, rather than for **what** he did.

[P 20.] Universal Pictures Building, 445 Park Ave., bet. E. 56th and E. 57th Sts. E side. 1947. Kahn & Jacobs.

The first office building built on this once-residential portion of Park Avenue, it achieved **a prismatic distinction** as the first evenly stepped back "wedding cake" form—precisely prescribed by the zoning law.

[P 19a.] Park Avenue Tower (offices)   **[P 19b.]** Le Cygne (French restaurant)

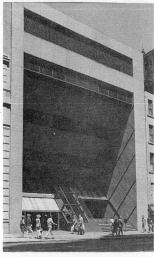

[P 22a.] The Galleria (apartments)   **[P 22b.]** 135 East 57th St. building

[P 21.] Ritz Tower (apartment hotel), 109 E. 57th St., NE cor. Park Ave. 1925. Emery Roth and Carrère & Hastings.

A 42-story tower, a stepped obelisk, **conspicuous on the skyline.** Rich details around the street-level walls are matched only by the opulent enterprises behind them, such as the First Women's Bank.

At 111 East 57th Street (in the side flank of the Ritz Tower) stood France's greatest restaurant in America, Le Pavillon, founded by Henri Soulé at the New York World's Fair of 1939, then moved here to fulfill the wildest dreams of both gourmands and gourmets. Now defunct (Soulé died in 1966), it is currently the home of the First Women's Bank (1975. Stockman & Manners Assocs., designers).

[P 22a.] The Galleria (apartments), 119 E. 57th St., bet. Park and Lexington Aves. 1975. David Kenneth Specter, design architect. Philip Birnbaum, associated architect.

Luxury apartments stacked over offices and a club, embracing a balconied 7-story public galleria (cf. **La Galleria, Milan**). The skylit balconied space penetrates the block to **58th** Street, affording pedestrians delight in passing through. Pretentious, but it has some grounds to be so.

 [P 22b.] 135 East 57th Street (mixed use), NW cor. Lexington Ave. 1987. Kohn Pedersen Fox Assocs.

New York's response to the French architecture of Spaniard **Ricardo Bofill** and his arcuated housing for Paris. Here the corner is king, an **exedra** opening the intersection of Lexington and 57th. And within that space stands a **tempietto** marking what the sponsors term the **Place des Antiquaires.**

END of Park Avenue Walking Tour: The nearest subways are at 59th and Lexington: the IRT Lexington Avenue local (59th Street Station) or the BMT Broadway Line (Lexington Avenue Station).

UNITED NATIONS–TURTLE BAY

The tract known by the mid 18th century as **Turtle Bay Farm** extended roughly from East 40th to East 48th Streets, from Third Avenue to the East River. The **little cove** that gave it its name is now covered by the gardens on the northern half of the United Nations grounds. **Bucolic** in the early 19th century, the area was **invaded** around 1850 **by riverfront industry,** with shantytowns inland that were replaced by tenements. By 1880, el trains were rumbling along both Second and Third Avenues. Town houses on the Beekman tract along the river around East 50th Street remained respectable (due to deed restrictions against industry) until about 1900 and were among the first in the area to be rehabilitated. There was much **ambitious building and renovation** in the 1920s, but it was not until six city blocks of slaughterhouses along the river were razed in 1946 for the United Nations, and the Third Avenue el (the last one to operate in Manhattan) closed down in 1955, that Turtle Bay was ready for thorough rehabilitation.

United Nations–Turtle Bay Walking Tour: Across 42nd Street to the United Nations, through the Second and Third Avenue high-rise development areas, and past some 1930s Modern and older row housing like Turtle Bay Gardens. START at Grand Central, where the IRT subways abound.

 [U 1.] Philip Morris Headquarters (offices) and **Whitney Museum Branch,** 120 Park Ave., SW cor. E. 42nd St. (Pershing Sq.). 1982. Ulrich Franzen & Assocs.

A **sober** granite slab, somewhat schizophrenic in its elevations, it houses a branch of the wondrous Whitney Museum. This oasis not only allows contemplation of the art but also provides a dry and warm resting-place for the harried midtown traveler: a small café offers hot chocolate, coffee, and spiced cider.

 [U 2a.] Bowery Savings Bank, 110 E. 42nd St., bet. Park and Lexington Aves. 1923. York & Sawyer.

Monumental in its arched entrance; even more so in its great and richly detailed banking room. One of the great spaces of New York.

 [U 2b.] Chanin Building (offices), 122 E. 42nd St., SW cor. Lexington Ave. to E. 41st St. 1929. Sloan & Robertson. ★ Lobby, Jacques Delamarre.

Surprising combinations of angular and floral decoration—even Gothic buttresses—sprout on this **exuberant** office tower. See the lobby, especially the extraordinary convector grilles; outside, the Art Deco bas-relief runs around the facades by Edward Trumbull, designer. The Chanin brothers got their start in Brooklyn and went on to develop the Times Square theater district, Central Park West, and this, among many projects. Look back on such a distinguished evolution, Mr. Trump.

[U 3.] Grand Hyatt Hotel/originally **Commodore Hotel,** 125 E. 42nd St., NW cor. Lexington Ave. 1920. Warren & Wetmore. Rebuilt, 1980, Gruzen & Partners and Der Scutt.

A dowager hotel building reoutfitted in a somewhat rumpled reflective glass dress. Within, past the 3D lobby, old walls lurk behind all that **glitter.**

[U 4.] Chrysler Building (offices), 405 Lexington Ave., NE cor. E. 42nd St. 1930. William Van Alen. ★ Partial interior ★. Lobby restoration, 1978, JCS Design Assocs., designers, and Joseph Pell Lombardi.

The tallest building in the world **for a few months,** before completion of the Empire State Building [see Q 20a.]: 1,048 feet to the top of its spire. One of the first uses of stainless steel over a large exposed building surface. The decorative treatment of the masonry walls below changes with every setback and includes story-high **basket-weave** designs, gargantuan **radiator cap gargoyles,** and a band of **abstract automobiles.** The lobby is an Art Deco composition of African marble and chrome steel. A **fluorescent lancet crown** decorates the skyline at night.

[U 2b.] Chanin Building bas-reliefs   **[U 4.]** The Art Deco Chrysler Building

[U 5a.] 425 Lexington Avenue (offices), bet. E. 43rd and E. 44th Sts. E side. 1988. Murphy/Jahn.

A **flamboyant** skyline building, it **grows outward** as it reaches the top. As the new and **seemingly stunted** neighbor of the Chrysler Building, it seems **more of Disneyland** than solid stuff.

[U 5b.] St. Agnes Church (Roman Catholic), 145 E. 43rd St., bet. Lexington and Third Aves. 1876. Lawrence J. O'Connor.

This was the church of **Bishop Fulton J. Sheen,** popular television priest and converter to Roman Catholicism of such notables as **Claire Booth Luce,** author of *The Women,* wife of *Time* magazine founder Henry Luce, and sometime ambassador to Italy.

Bus shelters: Patterned after Parisian bus shelters (the Gallic versions have three legs, not four, and other differences), a host of elegant brown-painted steel and tempered glass pergolas began to proliferate on the city's street corners in 1975. Even the full-color advertising, which supplies light (and income to the entrepreneurs), is good-looking. Architects: Holden, Yang, Raemsch & Terjesen.

[U 6.] Mobil Building/originally **Socony Mobil Building,** 150 E. 42nd St. bet. Lexington and Third Aves. 1955. Harrison & Abramovitz.

A 1.6 million-square-foot building sheathed with embossed stainless steel panels. A clever bore, it is now banal and tawdry, the ultimate architectural tin can.

[U 7a.] New York Helmsley Hotel/originally **Harley Hotel of New York,** 212 E. 42nd St., bet. Second and Third Aves. 1981. Emery Roth & Sons.

Originally named for Harry (Har-) and Leona (-ley) Helmsley, the husband-and-wife real estate team. Its greatest significance is that it competes, in height only, with its neighbor to the east, one of New York's first Modern skyscrapers:

The world's last Automat reposes at 200 East 42nd Street, in the office building at the southeast corner of Third Avenue. A cafeteria in which food is dispensed from little glass compartments, in individual portions, the Automat was born just before World War I, when technology was believed capable of solving all ills. Most of its siblings elsewhere were also housed in 1930s architecture, most spectacularly at what is now the New York Deli, 104 West 57th Street. A thousand little glass doors display the goodies within (baked beans, macaroni en casserole), and open to the magic of your coins. Once upon a time a nickel or two could buy almost anything in the Automat; today special tokens are required.

 [U 7b.] The News Building (offices and printing plant), 220 E. 42nd St., bet. Second and Third Aves. 1930. Howells & Hood. ★ Addition, SW cor. Second Ave. 1958. Harrison & Abramovitz.

Howells and Hood abandoned the Gothic sources with which they won the *Chicago Tribune* tower competition in 1922, and here used **a bold, striped verticality:** patterned red and black brick spandrels and russet window shades alternating with white brick piers—the whole effect to minimize the appearance of windows in the prism. The 1958 addition **wisely repeated** the same stripes, but in different proportions, to yield wider windows. The street floor, outside and in, is ornamented in Art Deco abstractions. See the **enormous revolving globe** and **weather instruments** in the (mostly) original old lobby.

[U 7c.] Extra! Extra! (restaurant), in The News Building, entrance on Second Ave. bet. E. 41st and E. 42nd Sts. W side. 1987. Sam Lopata, designer.

"What's black and white and red all over?" A newspaper (red-read), dummy! And so is this restaurant that takes its cue from the *News:* bare bulbs, giant stats, cartoons, a fun atmosphere.

[U 8.] Ford Foundation's indoor garden   **[U 8.]** The Ford Foundation Building

 [U 8.] Ford Foundation Building, 321 E. 42nd St., bet. First and Second Aves. to E. 43rd St. 1967. Kevin Roche John Dinkeloo & Assocs.

People and plants share a world **worthy of Kew,** elegantly contained in masses of brick and stretches of glass. Among the city's finest works of architecture.

[U 9.] United Presbyterian Church of the Covenant, 310 E. 42nd St., bet. First and Second Aves. 1871. J. C. Cady.

In its present context, sandwiched between the bluff of Tudor City and a building to the west, it shows its history as a lonely leftover from other times, almost like a piece of **Tudor Scarsdale** floated into town.

[U 10.] Tudor City, E. 40th St. to E. 43rd St., bet. First and Second Aves. 1925–1928. Fred F. French Co., H. Douglas Ives.

An **ambitious private renewal effort** that included 12 buildings, with 3,000 apartments and 600 hotel rooms **along its own street** (Tudor City Place), hovering on abutments over First Avenue. Restaurants, private parks, shops, and a post office round out the little city, all in Tudor style. Everything faced in, **toward** the private open space and **away from** the surrounding tenements, slaughterhouses, and generating plants. As a result, **almost windowless walls** now face the United Nations.

La Bibliothèque (restaurant), 341 E. 43rd St., E of Tudor City Place. Glasshouse extension, 1979, Ira Grandberg & Lawrence Marek.

At the head of a monumental stair overlooking the United Nations, this pleasant restaurant offers an overseeing outdoor cafe. Expensive.

Walk down the steps at 43rd Street to Ralph Bunche Park, across from the United Nations.

[U 11.] United Nations Headquarters, United Nations Plaza (First Ave.), bet. E. 42nd and E. 48th Sts. E side. 1947–1953. International Committee of Architects, Wallace K. Harrison, chairman. **Partially open to the public. [U 11a.]** Library addition, NE cor. E. 42nd St. 1963. Harrison, Abramovitz & Harris.

John D. Rockefeller Jr.'s donation of the $8.5 million site, already assembled by **real estate tyro William Zeckendorf** for a private development, decided the location of the headquarters. The team of architects included **LeCorbusier** of France, **Oscar Niemeyer** of Brazil, and **Sven Markelius** of Sweden, and representatives from ten other countries. The whole scheme is clearly a LeCorbusier concept (seconded by Niemeyer), but the details are largely Harrison's.

The 544-foot-high slab of the Secretariat (only 72 feet thick) domi-

[U 11.] The United Nations complex seen from across the East River (1950s)

nates the group, with the Library to the south, the General Assembly to the north—its form played against the Secretariat's size—and the Conference Building extending to the east over Franklin D. Roosevelt Drive, out of sight from U.N. Plaza. Every major nation **has donated some work of art** to the headquarters. Immediately noticeable is England's gift, a **Barbara Hepworth** sculpture standing in the pool (a gift from U.S. schoolchildren) in front of the Secretariat. Probably the most interesting are the **three Council Chambers** donated by three Scandinavian countries.

The city, under **Robert Moses'** direction, made way for the U.N. by diverting First Avenue's through traffic into a tunnel under United Nations Plaza and opening up a half-block-wide landscaped park, Dag Hammarskjold Plaza, along East 47th Street—**a meager space** in the shadow of tall buildings, with no view at all of the U.N. Headquarters. The General Assembly lobby and gardens are open to the public and tours of the conference spaces are available. **Enter at East 46th Street.**

Dining: At the coffee shop, lower level (ordinary), or lunch weekdays at the Delegates' Dining Room (elegant).

[U 12a.] 1 and **2 United Nations Plaza (offices/hotel),** NW cor. E. 44th St. 1976 and 1983. All by Kevin Roche John Dinkeloo & Assocs.

Folded graph paper—elegant scaleless envelopes of aluminum and glass, one form sliced at its corner and sheltering the pedestrian at the street with an overhead glass apron. The public spaces within are some of the best in New York's modern architecture.

The buildings are more popular than distinguished, **a passing bit of superstyle.**

Try the **Ambassador Grill's** mirrored-ceiling bar, where optical illusions tend to intensify the alcohol's proof.

[U 12a.] 1 & 2 United Nations Plaza   [U 12b.] UNICEF Building, 3 U.N. Plaza

[U 12b.] UNICEF (United Nations International Children's Emergency Fund) Building, 3 United Nations Plaza (E. 44th St. S side.), bet. First and Second Aves. 1987. Kevin Roche John Dinkleloo & Assocs.

Two tones of granite clad this architectural cousin of the **E. F. Hutton Building** [see Fifth Avenue F 11a.] Here the columns are more restrained, and the building fits more serenely into its blockfront.

[U 12c.] Kuwait Mission to the United Nations, 321 E. 44th St., bet. First and Second Aves. 1986. Swanke Hayden Connell.

A mélange of Gulf States fantasies and New York State Post Modern.

[U 12d.] Beaux Arts Apartment Hotel, 307 and 310 E. 44th St., between First and Second Aves. 1930. Kenneth Murchison and Raymond Hood, Godley & Fouilhoux.

Named for the adjacent Beaux Arts Institute building, this pair of **cubistic compositions** in light and dark tan brick faces each other across the side street.

[U 12e.] Originally **Beaux Arts Institute of Design,** 304 E. 44th St., between First and Second Aves. 1928. Dennison & Hirons.

The fantasies of Beaux Arts architectural education in this country (heavily influenced by the techniques of the École des Beaux-Arts in Paris) are incorporated in this structure, built when the system was already on the wane. The style is, of course, Art Deco, now reloved by the profession that despised and rejected it for so long.

[U 13.] United States Mission to the United Nations, 799 United Nations Plaza, bet. E. 44th and E. 45th Sts. W side. 1961. Kelly & Gruzen and Kahn & Jacobs.

A grimy **precast concrete eggcrate sunscreen** veneers this governmental office block. (Its design, of course, caters **not at all** to sun control—facing, as it does, east and north.)

On opposite sides of Second Avenue between East 44th and East 45th Streets are two classic and venerable steak restaurants providing elegant meats in simple surroundings: **The Palm** at **No. 837** and **The Palm Too** at **No. 840**. Expensive.

[U 14a.] Institute of International Education, 809 United Nations Plaza, bet. E. 45th and E. 46th Sts. W side. 1964. Harrison, Abramovitz & Harris.   212 · 883 · 8200

Important for an interior space—the penthouse **Edgar J. Kaufmann Conference Rooms,** one of only two U.S. works of the Finnish architect **Alvar Aalto.**

[U 14b.] Turtle Bay Towers (apartments), 310 E. 46th St., bet. First and Second Aves. Conversion, 1978, Bernard Rothzeid & Partners.

A major gas explosion blew out the east wall of this loft building, giving its owners the opportunity to convert it to residential use. The zoning setbacks allowed placement of greenhouses for its new residents.

[U 15a.] Carnegie Endowment International Center (offices), 345 E. 46th St., NW cor. United Nations Plaza. 1953. Harrison & Abramovitz.
[U 15b.] United Engineering Center (offices and library), 345 E. 47th St., NW cor. United Nations Plaza. 1961. Shreve, Lamb & Harmon.

A pair of institutional structures not quite equal in design to their auspicious setting.

[U 16a.] Dag Hammarskjold Plaza (offices), E. 47th St., SE cor. Second Ave. 1971. Raymond & Rado.

A **demure** curtain-walled office tower set on an elevated terrace designed to display outdoor sculpture. **Changing exhibits** all year round just a few steps up from Second Avenue.

[U 16b.] Dag Hammarskjold Tower (apartments), 240 E. 47th St., SW cor. Second Ave. to E. 46th St. 1984. Gruzen & Partners.

An understated tower with simple, faceted balconies, all built of preassembled brick panels, the joints of which give another design rhythm to the facade.

[U 16c.] Japan House, 333 E. 47th St., bet. First and Second Aves. 1971. Junzo Yoshimura and George Shimamoto of Gruzen & Partners. **Open to the public.**

Japan's **public architectural emissary** to the City of New York. Delicately detailed, inside and out, it stages cultural exhibitions often worth seeing. A somber black building with delicate sun grilles.

[U 17.] 860 and **870 United Nations Plaza (apartments),** bet. E. 48th and E. 49th Sts. E side. 1966. Harrison, Abramovitz & Harris.

Desirable for views and its ostensible social snobbery, not for its architecture.

[U 18.] Beekman Tower (apartments)/originally **Panhellenic Hotel,** 3 Mitchell Pl. (E. 49th St.), NE cor. First Ave. 1928. John Mead Howells.

A miniature reprise to Eliel Saarinen's second-prize **"styleless"** design in the 1922 *Chicago Tribune* tower competition. Howells (with Raymond Hood as partner) took first prize with a free neo-Gothic entry. Originally a hotel for women members of **Greek letter societies** (sororities).

A walk along FDR Drive: At the east end of East 51st Street, steps lead down to a small park and a footbridge over the Franklin D. Roosevelt Drive. **Cross the bridge** for a back view of Beekman Place and a view of the drive disappearing at East 52nd Street under a Sutton Place South apartment house. From the walk along the river there is a good view of the waterside of Beekman Place, one of those affluent bluffs that defied industrial expansion at the commercial waterfronted edge of the city:

Beekman Place:

Along with Sutton Place and, to an extent, Gracie Square, an elegant social enclave atop a river-fronted bluff. Here, on two blocks, are the town houses and **understated** apartment houses of **WASPS,** diplomats, movie stars, and others who savor low-key luxury. Among them is the home of an architectural hero of the 1950s and 1960s, one time dean of Yale School of Architecture and its controversial architect:

[U 19.] Paul Rudolph residence, 23 Beekman Place, bet. E. 50th and E. 51st Sts. E side. 1983–1987. Paul Rudolph.

The egocentric effort of a very talented architect of the Modern movement. Behind is a steel-framed cage of balconies that give a stronger radical presence to the river.

[U 20.] Formerly **Public School 135, Manhattan**/later **United Nations School,** 931 First Ave., NW cor. E. 51st St. 1892. George W. Debevoise. Conversion, 1989. Conklin & Rossant.

Brick and brownstone **Romanesque Revival** multistory schoolhouse, now converting to condominiums.

[U 21.] River House, 435 E. 52nd St., E of First Ave. 1931. Bottomley, Wagner & White.

A palatial 26-story cooperative apartment house with a gated, cobbled entrance court. The River Club, on its lower floors, includes squash and tennis courts, a swimming pool, and a ballroom. Prior to construction of the FDR Drive, there was even **a private dock where the best yachts tied up.**

[U 22.] A pair of Second Empire-inspired town houses: 312 and 314 E. 53rd St.

[U 22.] 312 and **314 East 53rd Street (residences),** bet. First and Second Aves. 1866. **No. 312** ★.

A pair of wood town houses of Second Empire inspiration with interesting **corbeled** entrance hoods and **round-topped** dormers.

[U 23a.] Rivertower (apartments), 420 E. 54th St., E of First Ave. 1981. Schuman, Lichtenstein, Claman & Efron. Rudolph de Harak, designer.

This building's sole distinction is in its **skewed axis** to the street grid. Atop it all is a crenellated hat of stepping apartments.

[U 23b.] St. James Tower (apartments), 415 E. 54th St., bet. First Ave. and Sutton Place S. 1983. Emery Roth & Sons.

A smooth purplish-brown iron-speckled brick gives this austere building a sleek countenance.

[U 24.] Recreation Center and Indoor Pool, N.Y.C. Department of Parks & Recreation/originally **54th Street Public Bath and Gymnasium,** 348 E. 54th St., bet. First and Second Aves. 1906. Werner & Windolph.

A **minor** building with a **major** facade. For once the screened roof space is part of the overall design, heralded by 4 **supermonumental** Classical columns.

[U 25.] 909 Third Avenue (offices), and **Franklin D. Roosevelt Station, U.S. Post Office,** bet. E. 54th and E. 55th Sts. E side. 1967. Max O. Urbahn & Assocs.

The tower's **deeply coffered,** cast-concrete **window walls** prove that three-dimensionality *per se* does not necessarily make a building gutsy. The podium is **New York 10022's** mail-handling factory.

[U 16b.] Dag Hammarskjold Tower   [U 28.] 885 Third: "The Lipstick"

[U 26.] 919 Third Avenue (offices), bet. E. 55th and E. 56th Sts. E side. 1970. Skidmore, Owings & Merrill.

A smooth black metal and glass monumental curtain wall that has P. J. Clarke's as a foil:

P. J.'s: This characteristic 19th-century relic (at 915 Third Avenue, northeast corner of East 55th Street), with a dining room in the rear, has always been known officially as Clarke's Bar. But to generations of collegians it has been **P. J.'s,** and it is partly responsible for the rash of other places called P. J. "Something." Seen by millions as the set for the 1945 movie *Lost Weekend,* it has lots of real stained glass and mahogany, and one of New York's most lavish old-fashioned men's rooms. Clarke's is so economically successful that everything on the block except the first 2 of its original 4 floors was demolished for **No. 919.**

[U 27.] 900 Third Avenue (offices), NW cor. E. 54th St. 1983. Cesar Pelli and Rafael Viñoly, design architects. Emery Roth & Sons, associate architects.

Another sleek shaft in the manner of Citicorp for the Argentine developer **Jacobo Finkielstain.**

[U 28.] 885 Third Avenue (offices), bet. E. 53rd and E. 54th Sts. E side. 1986. John Burgee with Philip Johnson.

A bumpy ellipse (in plan) of red-brown and pink, this acquired the sobriquet **Lipstick Building** because of its telescoping tiers. Columns with **Turkish** hats saunter around its grand ground floor. A connection to what is becoming one of the more complex (and yet convenient) subway concourses, the IND Lexington Avenue Station, is here provided.

[U 28a.] Toscana Ristorante, 200 E. 54th St., in 885 Third Avenue building, SE cor. Third Ave. 1987. Piero Sartogo and Nathalie Grenon, architects. Vignelli Assocs., graphic designers.

Time-honored materials used in a fresh Modern way.

[U 29.] 875 Third Avenue (offices), bet. E. 52nd and E. 53rd Sts. 1982. Skidmore, Owings & Merrill (Chicago).

The ghost of the Mies Van Der Rohe grid appears in this Windy City octapod invention that is about as much New York as pan pizza, or cherry phosphate. **Poor Mies . . .**

[U 30a.] The Enclave (apartments), 224 E. 52nd St., bet. Second and Third Aves. 1985. Marvin H. Meltzer.

A modern eccentric, in glass block and pink stucco, with curved balconies.

[U 30b.] Originally **Museum of Modern Art guesthouse,** 242 E. 52nd St., bet. Second and Third Aves. 1950. Philip Johnson & Assocs.

Roman brick and painted steel front a house built for guests of the Rockefeller Brothers (John D., Jr., David, Nelson, and Winthrop), who later gave it for similar guest purposes to the Museum of Modern Art. Johnson, its architect, later bought it for his house in town: now, however, he has removed his residence elsewhere.

[U 30c.] 301 East 52nd Street (apartments)/originally **Kips Bay Boys Club,** bet. First and Second Aves. 1931. Delano & Aldrich. Converted, 1978.

A handsome, low-key conversion. Note the segmental arched windows and brickwork with alternating headers and stretchers.

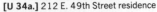

[U 34a.] 212 E. 49th Street residence   **[U 30b.]** Originally MOMA guesthouse

[U 31.] Greenacre Park, 217-221 E. 51st St., bet. Second and Third Aves. 1971. Sasaki, Dawson, DeMay Assocs., landscape architects. Goldstone, Dearborn & Hinz, consulting architects.

A gift to the city by the daughter of John D. Rockefeller, Jr., Mrs. Jean Mauzé. It is larger and fussier than its predecessor. Paley Park [see Fifth Avenue F 13b.].

[U 32.] 245 East 50th Street (apartments), bet. Second and Third Aves. 1980. David Kenneth Specter & Assocs.

A modest 8-story modern apartment house with flower-crested balconies. Look up; the bay windows look down.

[U 33a.] Crystal Pavilion (offices), 805 Third Ave., SE cor. E. 50th St. 1982. Emery Roth & Sons.

A bulky, mirrored, round-cornered vertical tub—hardly a crystal. Utilizes development rights from the adjacent restaurant and Amster Yard [see below].

Smith & Wollensky's (restaurant)/earlier **Manny Wolf's Chap House,** 201 E. 49th St., NE cor. Third Ave. Altered, 1977, Arnold Syrop.

This 2-story steak house has its low-rise longevity ensured by the sale of its air rights to its uptown neighbor.

[U 33b.] Amster Yard, 211-215 E. 49th St., bet. Second and Third Aves. 1870. Remodeled, 1945, Harold Sterner. ★

The vagaries of **early property transfers** created this inside-the-block space. A passage with a slate floor and iron settees leads into a garden, from which the office of **James Amster Associates,** other interior designers, and a few shops can be reached. Look carefully for the mirror at the end of the garden vista. Sculptor **Isamu Noguchi** once did his work in this yard, before discovering Ravenswood [see W Queens 15c.]

[U 34a.] 212 East 49th Street (residence), bet. Second and Third Aves. 1986. Mitchell-Giurgola.

An elegant and successful Post Modern town house, with marble, granite, and limestone mingling in exquisite detail. The adjacent buildings to the west, with false shutters, and to the east, in a heavy-handed Modern, seem gross by comparison.

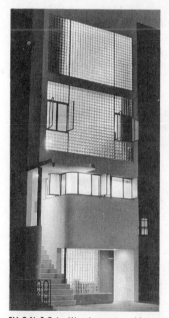

[U 34b.] Orig. Wm. Lescaze residence   **[U 34c.]** 219 East 49th Street res.

[U 34b.] Originally William Lescaze residence, 211 E. 48th St., bet. Second and Third Aves. 1934. William Lescaze. ★

A **pioneering Modern town house** by and for a **pioneering Modern architect,** protected from city atmosphere by glass block and air conditioning. The office was at the bottom, the house above, with a living room occupying the whole top floor.

[U 34c.] 219 East 49th Street (residence), between Second and Third Aves. 1935. Morris Sanders.

A ground-floor office and 2 duplexes, all clearly expressed on the facade in the Art Moderne style of the 1930s. Dark glazed brick was used to fend off soot; balconies control sunlight.

[U 34d.] Turtle Bay Gardens Historic District, 226-246 E. 49th St., bet. Second and Third Aves. and 227-247 E. 48th St. Remodeled, 1920, E. C. Dean and William Lawrence Bottomley. ★

Two rows of 10 houses each, back to back, assembled by Mrs. Walton Martin. A 6-foot strip was taken from the backyard of each house to form **a common path and garden.** Near a very old willow tree at the center of the group is a fountain copied from the **Villa Medici.** Low walls and planting mark off the private yards. House interiors were remodeled with living rooms opening to the yard, lowered front doors in pastel-painted stucco fronts. Such notables as **Katharine Hepburn, Leopold Stokowski, E. B. White, Stephen Sondheim, Garson Kanin, Maggie Smith,** and **Tyrone Power** have lived here. White memorialized the block in his marvelous anthology *The Second Tree from the Corner.*

[U 34e.] Sterling Plaza (apartments), 255 E. 49th St., NW cor. Second Ave. 1985. Schuman, Lichtenstein, Claman & Efron, architects. Arquitectonica, design consultants.

The fins on top are styling added to an otherwise ordinary apartment building. Arquitectonica's normal turf is Miami, where they have created numerous flamboyant structures.

[U 35.] 303-309 East 49th Street (apartments), bet. First and Second Aves. 1984. Architects Design Group.

The sliver wing on Second Avenue is attached to a slab on 49th—all in smooth and striated **contrasting concrete block.** The curved masonry balcony parapets give a **strong modulation** to the facade; but they are low enough, with railings atop, to allow those seated to enjoy the view.

Note: Turtle Bay Gardens Historic District addresses on East 48th Street are covered in [U 34d.].

[U 36a.] The Wang Building (offices), 780 Third Ave. bet. E. 48th and E. 49th Sts. W side. 1984. Skidmore, Owings & Merrill.

There is an implicit indication of structure in this red granite monolith: the omitted windows draw blank diagonal lines across the facade where **wind bracing** lurks.

[U 36b.] The Cosmopolitan (apartments), 145 E. 48th St., bet. Lexington and Third Aves. 1987. Gruzen Samton Steinglass.

A modestly **Post Modern** brick building, enhanced with a curve here, a bay window there.

[U 37.] 767 Third Ave. brick ribbons   **[U 37a.]** 747 Third Ave. streetscape

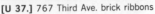

[U 37.] 767 Third Avenue (offices), SE cor. E. 48th St. 1980. Fox & Fowle.

Brick ribbons wrap around a sinuous and stylish form. At the base is a "Japanese" Post Modern wood grillage (catercorner to the building of a Chinese computer company).

[U 37a.] Streetscape, around 747 Third Avenue Building, SE cor. E. 47th St. to E. 46th St. 1971. Pamela Waters, designer.

While the aluminum and glass, curtain-walled speculative office tower at **No. 747** is more of the same, the sidewalk treatment is certainly unusual, its **convoluted surface** resembling the aftereffects of an earthquake without the earthquake. Developer **Mel Kaufman** commissioned it, as he did at his downtown efforts, 77 Water Street and 127 John Street [see L Manhattan/Water Street W 7c., W 10d.].

END of United Nations–Turtle Bay Walking Tour: There is a choice of closest subways. A few blocks uptown is the combined IRT Lexington Line local's 51st Street Station/IND Lexington Avenue Station. A few blocks downtown, at 42nd Street, is the major IRT interchange at Grand Central Station.

FIFTH AVENUE

East 45th to East 57th Streets:

This stretch of the avenue, where fashionable shops were **concentrated** since the 1920s, had been a solid line of mansions, churches, and clubs two decades before. **Two factors** sustained the elegance of Fifth Avenue as stores moved north along it: the **Fifth Avenue Association** (whose members had fought off billboards, bootblacks, parking lots, projecting signs—even funeral parlors), and **the absence of els or subways.** To provide **a genteel alternative** for rapid transit, the Fifth Avenue Transportation Company was established in 1885, using horse-drawn omnibuses until 1907, followed by the fondly remembered open-top (until 1936) double-deck buses.

Now these once staid and conservative blocks have slowly (and mostly) given way to impostors of style, "discount houses" vending electronics and lace, and merchants scrambling to revive (or attempt to revive) some continuing vestiges of what it all was. The peddlers, now frequently temporaries from Senegal, offer their not-so-magic carpets on the streetscape. Certainly in-between there is **Cartier's, St. Patrick's,** the **University Club,** and even the **St. Regis.** But the surrounds have succumbed in part to that commercial deterioration that afflicts many downtowns.

Once upon a time even the traffic lights were special: bronze standards with a neo-Grec **Mercury** atop, subsidized by the **Fifth Avenue Association** concerned with style and that successfully banned trucks and other commercial traffic for a time. But the 1980s have lost control for this softening as well.

One can still go to Cartier's for an occasional diamond or to the St. Regis' **King Cole Restaurant** for an elegant remembering dinner dance; but much of the **Fifth Avenue style** has gone.

Fifth Avenue Walking Tour: From 45th to 56th Streets. **Fat**—or merely **avaricious—cats** abound hereabouts, although the best work was done by the enlightened self-interest of old-line, hard-nosed capitalists, best exampled in the next section, **Rockefeller Center.** But even without the **John D.** (Jr. and Sr.) this precinct enjoyed **Scribner, Saks, Villard, Onassis, Heckscher,** and others more modest, who gave some wonderful moments of class through buildings and shops to this sequence of blocks. Here **looking up** is as important as **looking in;** for above the luxurious, or interesting, or even sometimes tawdry shopfront merchandise rises architecture of consequence. Even those **"Going Out of Business"** stores are often languishing within a **neo-Renaissance** relic of distinction.

(The closest subway is the IRT Flushing Line Fifth Avenue Station at West 42nd Street at The New York Public Library's north entrance. But a more accessible stop is the IRT Grand Central Station with Lexington Avenue, Flushing Line, and 42nd Street Shuttle access.)

[F 1.] Fred F. French Building, 551 Fifth Ave., NE cor. 45th St. 1927. Fred F. French Co., H. Douglas Ives and Sloan & Robertson. ★ Partial interior ★.

The headquarters of the prosperous designer-builder company have **strange multicolored faience** at the upper floor setbacks and a well-preserved ornate lobby. From the days when even the greediest developer owed serious and intricate architectural detail and materials to the **public,** not to mention the **client.**

Gotham Book Mart, at 41 West 47th Street, in the heart of the city's jewelry district, is a great, though cramped and cluttered, bookshop. Its strengths are literature, poetry, dance, and esoterica. Its loyal customers are the literati of the city and the world. Upstairs, in the gallery (clubhouse for the James Joyce Society), are changing exhibitions including—in the summer—those on postcards, its owner's passion. Go in with the spirit of the sign: "WISE MEN FISH HERE."

[F 2.] 575 Fifth Avenue (office building and arcade), SE cor. E. 47th St. 1985. Emery Roth & Sons.

This 40-story building is a reconstruction of the old **W. & J. Sloane Store** (home furnishings), which was later converted into **Korvette's** discount operations with an added exterior skin. All of that is gone now in favor of a mild but stylish stone veneer facade with a multilevel shopping galleria within.

[F 3.] National Westminster Bank, USA, branch/earlier, **National Bank of North America/**originally **Black, Starr & Frost (jewelers),** 592 Fifth Ave., SW cor. W. 48th St. Carrère & Hastings. 1912. Totally reclad, 1964, Hausman & Rosenberg.

Elongated **black portholes** serve as windows for this stark white marble-veneered prism. The C & H neo-Classical facade was considered "old-fashioned" by its owners in the early 1960s, and so it was was "modernized." (N.B. Penn Station came down in early 1963; the Landmarks Preservation Commission was established under law in 1965.)

[F 4a.] Within is the almost basilican space of Charles Scribner's Sons bookshop

[F 4a.] Charles Scribner's Sons (bookstore/offices), 597 Fifth Ave., bet. E. 48th and E. 49th Sts. E side. 1913. Ernest Flagg. ★

An ornate black iron and glass storefront opening to a grand, 2-story, plaster-vaulted mezzanined space: an almost-basilica. The south side (lot-line) wall carries the original advertising. [Also see the earlier Scribner's, Four Squares W 15.].

[F 4b.] Benetton (women's wear), 601 Fifth Ave., bet. E. 48th and E. 49th Sts. E side. 1979. Afra & Tobia Scarpa.

The epidemic of Benettons in America began here. Their proliferation results from management's belief that advertising dollars are better spent on a shop in every block than on ephemeral ads.

[F 4c.] Originally **Child's Restaurant Building,** 604 Fifth Ave., bet. W. 48th and W. 49 Sts. W side. 1925. William Van Alen.

A lesser work by the Chrysler Building's architect. A now-demolished church to the south explains the structure's rounded downtown corner.

[F 4d.] Goelet Building/Swiss Center (offices), 608 Fifth Ave., SW cor. W. 49th St. 1932. E. H. Faile & Co. with Victor L. F. Hafner. Lower floors altered, 1966, Lester Tichy & Assocs.

Above the new base, the crisp original cubist office building with rich geometry of contrasting materials.

[F 6.] St. Patrick's Cathedral (R.C.)   **[F 4d.]** Goelet Building/Swiss Center

[F 4e.] La Réserve (restaurant)/originally **Swiss Pavilion,** 4 W. 49th St., bet. Fifth Ave. and Rockefeller Plaza, in Swiss Center. 1969. Interior Concepts, Inc., designers. Altered.

Understated stucco walls contrasted with a vermillion enameled cylinder on the outside. The detailing inside is equally elegant.

*Note: The **Rockefeller Center** area is covered in the next section.*

[F 4f.] Pearl's (Chinese restaurant), 38 W. 48th St., bet. Fifth and Sixth Aves. 1973. Gwathmey Siegel & Assocs.

Across from Rockefeller Center, a subdued design **unlike any other** Chinese restaurant. **Sophisticated,** and pricey.

[F 5a.] Saks Fifth Avenue (department store), 611 Fifth Ave., bet. W. 49th and W. 50th Sts. E side. 1924. Starrett & Van Vleck. ★

A stately department store that acts as a low-key foil to **St. Patrick's** to the north and the RCA Building, visible on axis through the Channel Gardens, to the west [see R 1.]. It is a **landmark** more for its role in **not** competing while nevertheless presenting a facade of style.

[F 5b.] Swiss Bank Tower (offices), 12 E. 50th St., bet. Fifth and Madison Aves. through to E. 49th St. 1989. Lee Harris Pomeroy Assocs. and Abramovitz Kingsland Schiff.

A midblock event, using the **air rights** of the landmark **Saks** store. One of the successors to a firm that shared creation of Rockefeller Center (Abramovitz was the latter-day partner of Wallace Harrison, who was in on the Center's creation) is joined here to a newer talent, Lee Pomeroy.

[F 6.] St. Patrick's Cathedral (Roman Catholic), E. 50th to E. 51st Sts., bet. Fifth and Madison Aves. 1878. Towers, 1888, James Renwick, Jr., and William Rodrigue. ★ **[F 6a.] Archbishop's (Cardinal's) Residence,** 452 Madison Ave., NW cor. E. 50th St. and **Rectory,** 460 Madison Ave., SW cor. E. 51st St. 1880. Both by James Renwick, Jr. ★ **[F 6b.] Lady Chapel,** 1906, Charles T. Mathews. ★

Renwick's adaptation of French Gothic was weakened by his use of unyielding granite and his deletion of the flying buttresses (without deleting their pinnacle counterweights). But the cathedral, with its twin 330-foot towers, is **a richly carved counterfoil** to Rockefeller Center, across Fifth Avenue. *Go in.* The **Lady Chapel,** added behind the altar, is in **more academically correct** French Gothic.

[F 7a.] Originally **Villard Houses,** 451-455 Madison Ave., bet. E. 50th and E. 51st Sts. E side. 1884. McKim, Mead & White. ★ Restoration, 1981, James Rhodes, restoration architect. **[F 7b.] Helmsley Palace Hotel** (behind), 1980. Emery Roth & Sons.

Once there were five brownstone mansions, built as if they were a single great Renaissance **palazzo:** two of them—and parts of the third, fourth, and fifth—were severed from the grand Madison Avenue forecourt to create the Palace Hotel. That tall, bulky, but essentially **innocuous** structure can be entered grandly through the courtyard, or banally under its glitzy 50th or 51st Street canopies. The price for preservation was greater height and bulk for the hotel.

Journalist, railway promoter, and financier **Henry Villard** built the surviving Madison Avenue remnants first; they were extended down the side streets immediately thereafter. The hotel occupies the south wing, preserving the **Gold Room** as a cocktail lounge. The north wing is the **Urban Center:**

[F 7c.] The Urban Center, 457 Madison Ave., SE cor. E. 51st St. entry through the Helmsley Palace Madison Ave. forecourt. 1980. **Open to the public. [F 7d.] The Urban Center Bookstore,** 1980. **[F 7e.] New York Chapter, American Institute of Architects,** 2nd floor. 1983. Voorsanger & Mills Assocs. **Open to the public.**

The **Municipal Art Society** negotiated a lease for the Villard mansion's north wing, creating space for a cluster of concerned professional organizations in addition to itself, a venerable and sometimes feisty civic organization with a largely lay membership. The **Architectural League of N.Y.,** the N.Y. Chapter, **American Society of Landscape Architects,** and the **Urban Center Bookstore** share common exhibition and lecture facilities with the Society and the A.I.A. Chapter. The Bookstore is a great source of books and periodicals on architecture, planning, and urban history.

The Chapter's suite of offices are often the site of exhibitions held in its dark wood-paneled Georgian/Post Modern spaces.

[F 8a.] Olympic Tower (mixed use), 645 Fifth Avenue, NE cor. 51st St. 1976. Skidmore, Owings & Merrill. **Olympic Place,** from E. 51st to E. 52nd Sts. 1977. Chermayeff, Geismar & Assocs.; Zion & Breen, designers. Levien, Deliso & White, architects. Abel & Bainnson, landscape architects.

An **elegant urban idea** for multiple uses (apartments over offices over shops) in a sleek but dull skin. To the pedestrian its graces are its elegant shops but especially the arcade, Olympic Place, that **penetrates the building midblock,** from St. Patrick's to 52nd Street, with a skylit, treed, and waterfalled public space of gray granite. Its dedication to public use allowed the owner to build a bigger building than normally permitted.

[F 8b.] Olympic Airways (ticket office)/originally **George W. Vanderbilt residence,** 647 Fifth Ave., bet. E. 51st and E. 52nd Sts. E side. 1905. Hunt & Hunt. Converted. ★ **[F 8c.] Cartier, Inc./**originally **Morton F. Plant residence,** 651 Fifth Ave., SE cor. E. 52nd St. 1905. Robert W. Gibson. Converted to shop, 1917, William Welles Bosworth. ★ **[F 8d.] Cartier, Inc. extension/**originally **N wing of Morton F. Plant residence,** 4 E. 52nd St., bet. Fifth and Madison Aves. C. P. H. Gilbert. 1905. ★

Mansions from the era when Fifth Avenue housed the Astors, Goulds, Belmonts, Vanderbilts, and the original owners of these three, now converted to retail purposes.

[F 9.] Piaget Building (offices), 650 Fifth Ave., SW cor. W. 52nd St. 1978. John Carl Warnecke & Assocs.

Horizontal bands of strip windows alternate with spandrels of reddish brown granite. The setback and public mall are a result of the **Fifth Avenue Special Zoning District** requirements. Originally sponsored by the **Pahlavi Foundation,** a work of the late Shah of Iran, and long vacant before finding an occupant.

---

21 Club: "Jack and Charlie's place" at 21 West 52nd Street (*1872. Duggin & Crossman*) was only one of several Prohibition-era clubs on its block that became fashionable in the 1930s. But it alone remains, having become successor to Delmonico's and Sherry's as café society's dining room. Sometimes termed the "61 and Over" Club.

[F 10a.] Museum of Broadcasting, 23 W. 52nd St., bet. Fifth and Sixth Aves. 1989. John Burgee with Philip Johnson. **Open to the public.**

William S. Paley [see Paley Park F 13b.], chairman of the museum, contributed land for this new facility, to replace the one at 1 East 53rd Street (*1976. Beyer Blinder Belle*). **Is it possible** that there is to be an expansion of the wonderful Paley Park?

The museum collects recordings, films, and videotapes of radio programs, and television, which are shown in its main theater, study centers, and informal **videothèques.** Exhibitions and seminars are also presented.

[F 7e.] The New York Chapter, A.I.A.   **[F 8c.]** Orig. Morton Plant residence

[F 10b.] 666 Fifth Avenue (offices), bet. W. 52nd and W. 53rd Sts. W side. 1957. Carson & Lundin.

A million square feet of office space wrapped in embossed aluminum. Note the sculpted arcade waterfall and the lobby's sinuous ceiling by sculptor **Isamu Noguchi.**

[F 11a.] E. F. Hutton Building (offices), 31 W. 52nd St., bet. Fifth and Sixth Aves., through to W. 53rd St. 1987. Kevin Roche John Dinkleloo & Assocs. **[F 11b.] American Craft Museum,** 44 W. 53rd St. 1987. Fox & Fowle.

Polygonal granite **neo-Assyrian** columns form an allée through the block, leaving a small plaza between this and the adjacent **CBS building.** Atop it all, against the skyline, is a Halloween crazy hat, cut and serrated. The granite detailing is a thin skin, **a granite balloon** over a steel armature.

The **American Craft Museum** (once located in a former row house on the site) is a noble venture but one that gives form to the concept that to house a museum as patron is to **possess** culture.

[F 12a.] Museum Tower (apartments), 21 W. 53rd St., bet. Fifth and Sixth Aves. 1985. Cesar Pelli & Assocs.

Many distinguished minds and talented pencils participated in the basic planning of this condominium tower and the replanning and expansion of the adjacent Museum: planner Lord Llewellyn Davies; architect and educator Jaquelin Robertson; and Gruen Associates. But the task of converting ideas into three-dimensional building fell to Cesar Pelli.

The tower is sleek and subtly polychromatic, leaving architectural histrionics to the **E. F. Hutton Building** down the block.

[F 12b.] Museum of Modern Art in '39   [F 12b.] MOMA's sculpture garden

[F 12b.] Museum of Modern Art, 11 W. 53rd St., bet. Fifth and Sixth Aves. 1939. Philip Goodwin and Edward Durrell Stone. Additions and alterations, 1951 and 1964. Philip Johnson Assocs., architects, and James Fanning, landscape architect. Further additions and alterations, 1985, Cesar Pelli & Assocs., design architects. Edward Durrell Stone Assocs., associate architects. **Open to the public.**

The **history of modern art,** more than its **current events,** is here enshrined. The 1939 building was **a catechism** of the International Style (so dubbed by MOMA's 1932 exhibition, presented by Henry-Russell Hitchcock and Philip Johnson): an austere streetfront of marble veneer, tile, and opaque and transparent glass, with a pleasant rooftop garden worthy of **a Le Corbusier acolyte.** Johnson's east wing (extant) departs radically from the original flat **International Style** surfaces, with **deeply three-dimensional** grids of painted steel standing free of the wall.

Johnson's finest contribution is the 1964 garden along 54th Street. Here elegant stone, plantings, pools, and fountains have been composed into a serene and urbane oasis, **one of the great** urban gardens.

The guts of the museum have been vastly altered and expanded (in part into Johnson's garden) by Cesar Pelli. The multileveled galleried and escalated interior seems more like **a shopping center** of packaged aesthetics than a true museum, where the visitor can selectively savor the **history of modern art.**

[F 12c.] St. Thomas' Church and **Parish House (Episcopal),** 1 W. 53rd St., NW cor. Fifth Ave. 1914. Cram, Goodhue & Ferguson. Reredos, Bertram G. Goodhue, architect; Lee Lawrie, sculptor. ★

One of Goodhue's **finest essays** in picturesque massing and detail, built on a constricted corner. Note the play of dense detail against big plain surfaces. The powerful French Gothic interior **culminates** in the shimmering white, richly carved reredos behind the altar. Windows by **Whitefriars** of London.

[F 13a.] Fifth Avenue Station IND Subway Line, below W. 53rd St. bet. Madison and Fifth Aves. 1933. Renovated, 1987, Lee Harris Pomeroy Assocs., architects. Pentagram Design, graphic designers.

Here, lacing together **the Museum of Modern Art, the American Craft Museum,** the **Museum of Broadcasting,** and other, street-level events is a handsome redesign of this barrel-vaulted space. Graphics of local institutions adorn its walls.

[F 13b.] Samuel Paley Plaza a.k.a. **Paley Park,** 3 E. 53rd St., bet. Fifth and Madison Aves. 1967. Zion & Breen, landscape architects. Albert Preston Moore, consulting architect.

A parklet on the former site of the **Stork Club** contributed by **William S. Paley,** founder of CBS, and named for his father (1875–1963). A **great oasis** in good weather to refresh in the spray of the waterfall, and to lightly snack. The fall's **white noise** masks the cacophony of the city.

[F 13c.] Harper & Row Bookstore, 10 E. 53rd St., bet. Fifth and Madison Aves. 1973. Smotrich & Platt, architects. Chermayeff & Geismar, designers. Altered 1979. Soloway & Lorand.

The midblock headquarters of the publishing firm are announced by **mirror-finished cylinders** at the sidewalk. The reflective surfaces are echoed in the **high-style bookshop:** on 4 double-height display columns are displayed eye-catching multiples of new editions' dust jackets. **Don't miss the exhibition** on the history of Harper's, on the mezzanine up the stair to the left.

Opposite in the arcade is a good map store: Rand McNally.

[F 11b.] The American Craft Museum   **[F 12c.]** St. Thomas' Episcopal Church

[F 14a.] Sarinah Indonesian (store)/originally **William H. Moore residence,** 4 E. 54th St., bet. Fifth and Madison Aves. 1900. McKim, Mead & White. ★

When Fifth Avenue's flanks were lined with residential palaces, fortresses, and châteaux, the side streets were lined with such as this.

[F 14b.] Alpha Garage, 15 W. 54th St., bet. Fifth and Madison Aves. 1965. William Gleckman.

The white cast-in-place concrete frames (can you believe it?) which constitute its wall to the street make this garage **a welcome neighbor.** (The original developer was in the concrete business and considered this project to be **free advertising.**)

[F 14c.] Continental Illinois Center (offices), 520 Madison Ave., bet. E. 53rd and E. 54th Sts. W side. 1981. Swanke Hayden Connell.

Polished red granite veneers a pretentious piece of architectural geometry with ski slope sides at the bottom, transitioning to the more familiar rectangular prism up top. A holdout site occupant, **Reidy's Restaurant** at 22 East 54th (sporting its original front), courageously served all during the tower's construction, which explains the interruption in the tower's north slope. Note *new* sidewalk clock.

[F 14d.] 527 Madison Avenue (offices), SE cor. E. 54th St. 1987. Fox & Fowle.

Pleated glass and two-toned granite modulate an otherwise simple Madison Avenue facade. Along 54th Street stretches a great glass-sheeted skylight to its entrance atrium, tilted assuredly to make **Continental Illinois,** across Madison, feel less out of place.

[F 14e.] 535 Madison Avenue (offices), NE cor. 54th St. 1986. Edward Larabee Barnes Assocs.

A distant relative of **Citicorp Center** [see Grand Central/Park Avenue P 16.] As he did at IBM [see Plaza Suite Z 8.] Barnes again overpowers the pedestrian. Here, however, the giant cantilever is supported by a **Brobdignagian** column.

[F 15a.] University Club, 1 W. 54th St., NW cor. Fifth Ave. 1899. McKim, Mead & White. ★

A super palazzo **beyond** the Medicis' wildest dreams.

[F 15a.] MM & W's University Club   **[F 15f.]** The Rockefeller Apartments

[F 15b.] Originally **Philip Lehman residence,** 7 W. 54th St., bet. Fifth and Sixth Aves. 1900. John H. Duncan.

Not only has Robert Lehman's fine private collection of paintings been removed to the Metropolitan's **Lehman Wing,** so have his town house's original interiors. [See E Manhattan/Met Museum M 12.]

[F 15c.] U.S. Trust Company/originally **James J. Goodwin residence,** 9-11 W. 54th St., bet. Fifth and Sixth Aves. 1898. McKim, Mead & White. ★ Haines Lundberg Waehler, restoration architects. **[F 15d.] 13-15 West 54th Street (row houses),** bet. Fifth and Sixth Aves. 1897. Henry J. Hardenbergh. ★ **[F 15e.] Privatbanken Building,** 20 West 55th Street, bet. Fifth and Sixth Aves. Emery Roth & Sons and Hobart Betts.

Nelson Rockefeller maintained his private offices at **No. 13** and died there on January 26, 1979. Behind, facing West 55th Street **(No. 20),** is an office building sharing the zoning lot: the Bank of Denmark.

[F 15f.] Rockefeller Apartments, 17 W. 54th St., bet. Fifth and Sixth Aves. 1936. Harrison & Fouilhoux. ★ Interior alterations, 1982, Hobart Betts.

Elegant **cylindrical bay windows** overview the Museum of Modern Art Garden—on part of a midblock strip of land **acquired by the Rockefellers** when their Center was assembled. The leftovers include the **Donnell Library** on West 53rd Street, the **Museum of Modern Art,** and **this urbane place.** The garden within is a pleasant private oasis.

[F 15g.] **35 West 54th Street (row house),** bet. Fifth and Sixth Aves. 1878. James G. Lynd. New facade, 1905, Foster, Gade & Graham.

Face-lifting was not uncommon in the early 20th century. To be "modern" was the goal of many a parvenu, for whom "Modern" came mostly in some form of **Classical Revival.**

[F 15h.] **41 West 54th Street (row house),** bet. Fifth and Sixth Aves. 1878. James G. Lynd. New facade, 1909, Foster, Gade & Graham.

The second face-lift on the block by the same team veneering the work of the same original architect.

[F 16.] St. Regis-Sheraton Hotel, 2 E. 55th St., SE cor. Fifth Ave. 1904. Trowbridge & Livingston. Addition to E, 1925.

A richly decorated Beaux Arts mass that gets **better toward the top.** Second only to the Plaza in number of prominent guests, the hotel is especially popular with foreign diplomats. The King Cole Restaurant is designed around a **Maxfield Parrish** mural that once graced Times Square's old Knickerbocker Hotel bar [see Times Square T 7.] The brass-and-glass doorman's station is a **gem.**

[F 17a.] Hotel Maxim's de Paris/originally **Gotham Hotel,** 2 W. 55th St., SW cor. Fifth Ave. 1905. Hiss & Weeks. Partly altered, 1984, Stephen B. Jacobs & Assocs. Altered, 1987, Hirsch/Bender, designers; AiGroup Architects, architects.

The **mate of the St. Regis** across the street, a little more angular but just as ornate. Closed for years and altered for Nova Park, it finally opened for new owners with Belle Epoque styling, trying to emulate the original.

[F 16.] The St. Regis-Sheraton Hotel   **[F 17a.]** Hotel Maxim's de Paris

[F 17b.] Fifth Avenue Presbyterian Church, 705 Fifth Ave., NW cor. W. 55th St. 1875. Carl Pfeiffer.

A somber brownstone **neo-Gothic** remnant of early days on Fifth Avenue, long before it became a boulevard of fashionable mansions.

[F 17c.] Formerly **Rizzoli Building,** 712 Fifth Ave., bet. W. 55th and W. 56th Sts. W side. 1908. Adolf S. Gottlieb. ★ **[F 17d.]** Formerly **Coty Building,** 714 Fifth Ave., bet. W. 55th and W. 56th Sts. 1909. Woodruff Leeming. 1912. Window glass by René Lalique. ★ **[F 17e.] Office Building,** behind. 1989. Kohn Pederson Fox Assocs. Restored and redesigned, Rizzoli and Coty, 1989. Beyer Blinder Belle.

Here two early (first growth) commercial buildings replaced town mansions of the latter 19th century. Threatened by demolition, they were belatedly landmarked and serve as the historical entry to an office tower behind.

[F 18a.] Originally **Birdsall Otis Edey residence,** 10 W. 56th St., bet. Fifth and Sixth Aves. 1901. Warren & Wetmore.

An exuberant **Beaux Arts** town house with a grand Palladian window over the ground floor.

[F 18b.] Originally **Harry B. Hollins residence**/now **Consulate of Argentina,** 12-14 W. 56th St., bet. Fifth and Sixth Aves. 1901. Stanford White of McKim, Mead & White. ★

A **neo-Georgian town house** bearing wreathed eagles above the ground floor.

[F 18c.] Omo Norma Kamali (boutique), 11 W. 56th St., bet. Fifth and Sixth Aves. 1978. Rothzeid Kaiserman Thompson & Bee, architects. Peter Marino, designer.

A stuccoed facade presents a somewhat **fortified** appearance: its squinting windows seem like slots for defensive surveillance of the street.

Eat Street: That was the late columnist Earl Wilson's name for West 56th Street between Fifth and Sixth Avenues. It held the record for a single block, with about two dozen restaurants—from French and Italian to Japanese and Korean. Above the close ranks of canopies are some interesting old house fronts.

ROCKEFELLER CENTER AREA

The waves of elegant construction that rolled up Fifth Avenue never reached as far west as Sixth. Rockefeller Center was expected **to trigger renewal** in the 1930s, but the Sixth Avenue el, rumbling up to 53rd Street until 1938, was too grim an obstacle. It was not until an enormous new **Time & Life Building** went up at West 50th Street in 1959 that a Sixth Avenue building boom started, resulting in the glitzy canyon we see today. All these blocks were formerly, and almost uniformly, seas of brownstones before the glitz: middle-class dwellings that declined in elegance and opulence with each increment of their distance from Fifth Avenue. Rockefeller Center proper had erased hundreds of them; but its 1947–1973 annexes, and the other commercial development they inspired, were the crowning blows.

Rockefeller Center Area Walking Tour: Through the office and entertainment complex and to the north. (Take the IND Sixth Avenue Line to the 47th-50th Street/Rockefeller Center Station, accessible underground to all the Center's buildings.)

 [R 1.] Rockefeller Center (office/entertainment/retail complex), Originally W. 48th to W. 51st Sts. bet. Fifth and Sixth Aves. 1932–1940. The Associated Architects: Reinhard & Hofmeister; Corbett, Harrison & MacMurray; Raymond Hood, Godley & Fo5ilhoux. ★ Expanded 1947–1973. **[R 1a.] 1270 Avenue of the Americas Building**/originally **RKO Building.** 1932. ★ **[R 1b.] Radio City Music Hall.** 1932. (Edward Durrell Stone, design architect; Donald Deskey interior design coordinator.) ★ Interior ★. **[R 1c.] RCA Building.** 1933. ★ Partial interior ★. **[R 1d.] British Empire Building, Channel Gardens, La Maison Française.** 1933. ★ **[R 1e.] Palazzo d'Italia.** 1935. ★ **[R 1f.] International Building.** 1935. ★ Partial interior ★. **[R 1g.] 1 Rockefeller Plaza**/originally **Time & Life Building.** 1937. ★ **[R 1h.] The Associated Press Building.** 1938. ★ **[R 1i.] 10 Rockefeller Plaza**/originally **Eastern Airlines Building.** 1939. ★ **[R 1j.] Simon & Schuster Building**/originally **U.S. Rubber Company Building** and **addition** (on site of **Center Theater).** 1940. ★ All by Associated Architects. Additions since the original: **[R 2.] Warner Communications Building**/originally **Esso Building,** 15 W. 51st St., bet. Fifth and Sixth Aves. to W. 52nd St. 1947. Carson & Lundin. ★ **[R 3.] 600 Fifth Avenue Building**/originally **Sinclair Oil Building,** NW cor. W. 48th St.

(purchased by Rockefeller Center, 1963). 1952. Carson & Lundin. ★ **[R 4a.] Celanese Building,** 1211 Sixth Ave., bet. W. 47th and W. 48th Sts. W side. 1973. Harrison, Abramovitz & Harris. **[R 4b.] McGraw-Hill Building,** 1221 Sixth Ave., bet. W. 48th and W. 49th Sts. W side. 1972. Harrison, Abramovitz & Harris. **[R 4c.] Exxon Building,** 1251 Sixth Ave., bet. W. 49th and W. 50th Sts. W side. 1971. Harrison, Abramovitz & Harris. **[R 4d.] Time & Life Building,** 1271 Sixth Ave., bet. W. 50th and W. 51st Sts. W side. 1959. Harrison & Abramovitz. **[R 5.] Sperry Corporation Building/**originally **Sperry Rand Building,** 1290 Sixth Ave., bet. W. 51st and W. 52nd Sts. E side. 1961. Emery Roth & Sons.

An island of **architectural excellence,** this is the greatest urban complex of the 20th century: an understated and urbane place that has become a classic lesson in the point and counterpoint of space, form, and circulation. Its **campanile** is the **RCA Building,** a slender, stepped slab **rising precipitously** from Rockefeller Plaza proper, that **many-leveled** pedestrian space surrounding and overlooking the **ice skating rink** in winter, outdoor cafés in summer, all overseen by *Prometheus* (1934, Paul Manship). Opposite, **Channel Gardens** rises on a flower-boxed slope to Fifth Avenue between the low-scaled French and British Pavilions; the foliage here is changed with the seasons.

Limestone, now-grayed cast aluminum, and glass clad these towers and their low-scaled neighbors. The skin is straightforward, modern, and **unencumbered by the need for stylishness**—but nevertheless **of great style,** elegant, and perhaps the most undated modern monument that New York enjoys.

[F 17c.,d.] The two early (first growth) office buildings for Coty and Rizzoli

The **assorted annexes** to the Center along the Avenue of the Americas (Sixth Avenue) **are of lesser stuff:** posturing, bulbous boxes built in the 1960s and 1970s, grabbing onto the Rockefeller Center name, organization, and underground passages but sorry neighbors to their parent buildings. Included here are the **Time & Life,** the old **Sperry-Rand, McGraw-Hill, Exxon, Celanese** buildings and others. In concert with the Zoning Resolution of 1961, they brought **barren plazas** to the Avenue of the Americas: good intentions misdirected those present lifeless places without the people who would populate an Italian piazza, wind-swept and dull. The midblock **open-air arcades to the west** of the three southernmost towers fail equally to become animated.

The Channel Gardens: The gently sloped and fountained space, which takes you from Fifth Avenue to the stairway leading into the sunken plaza, is called Channel Gardens since it is, like the **English Channel,** the separation between France (**La Maison Française** to the south) and the United Kingdom (the **British Empire Building** to the north).

[R 1.] Rockefeller Center, greatest 20th-century urban complex (1967 ph.)

The New York Experience, deep in the lower levels of the McGraw-Hill Building, 1221 Sixth Avenue, is a multiscreen spectacular featuring 45 projectors, 16 screens, and more—for those who want their exposure made easy, preferring fantasy to the reality of the first-hand city.

 [R 6a.] **Seamen's Bank for Savings,** 127 W. 50th St., bet. Sixth and Seventh Aves. in Time & Life Building. 1971. Carson, Lundin & Shaw.

A ribbon of veined, dark green polished marble forms a sinuous wall, into which are cut elongated portholes that contain masterpieces of sailing ship modeling (and, incidentally, the bank's tellers). The bank is a masterpiece, too.

[R 6b.] **Uncle Sam's Steakhouse (restaurant),** 120 W. 51st St., between Sixth and Seventh Aves. in Time & Life Building. 1975. Gwathmey Siegel, architects. George Lois, graphic designer. Altered, 1976, Stockman & Manners Assocs., designers.

An American steak house in a dark, elegant **high-style** setting. Moderate to expensive. Have a drink at the handsome bar.

 [R 7.] **CBS Building (Columbia Broadcasting System),** 51 W. 52nd St., NE cor. Sixth Ave. 1965. Eero Saarinen & Assocs. Interior architects, office floors: Carson, Lundin & Shaw. Interior designers, office floors: Knoll Planning Unit.

"Black Rock," Saarinen's **only high-rise building** is a sheer, free-standing 38-story, concrete-framed tower clad in dark gray honed granite: a **somber** and **striking** understatement.

One of several buildings of its time to depart from established post-and-beam framing, CBS supports its floors instead on its central core and a dense grid—in effect a bearing wall—at the exterior.

Here the lawyers and money managers sit in splendor, while creativity is rampant in considerably lesser facilities elsewhere.

[R 8.] New York Hilton, 1335 Avenue of the Americas, bet. W. 53rd and W. 54th Sts. 1963. William B. Tabler.

Clearly designed for conventions, this 2,200-room hotel has a **low, horizontal box** of public spaces hovering above deeply recessed entrances; rising from it is **a thin vertical slab** of guest rooms. The **rickrack blue glass walls** of the slab give each room a bay window and have a pleasing crystalline look when seen at an angle. The clarity of the exterior volumes is not reflected in the interior.

END of Rockefeller Center Area Walking Tour: A choice of subways: the IND Sixth or Eighth Avenue Lines at the Fifth Avenue Station along West 53rd Street, or the IND Sixth Avenue Line at Rockefeller Center.

CENTRAL PARK SOUTH

A transition, a zone between Times Square **honky-tonk** and Central Park **gentility,** with Fifth Avenue's **elegance percolating west** through it into Clinton, now just **starting to emerge** from years of shabbiness. The wall of affluent residence along the park is like a dogleg of Fifth Avenue fashion carried across to Columbus Circle, stretching from The Plaza past elegant hotels with a European flavor to the old Coliseum site. But to the south, commerce and culture take over: the former in the shape of the old General Motors Building, the latter ranging from the Hard Rock Café and St. Thomas' Choir School to Carnegie Hall and the City Center. Here music resounds in a much richer and more eclectic way than at the sterile halls of Lincoln Center.

Central Park South Walking Tour: START at Columbus Circle's intersection of the IND and IRT subways. Then move southward, eventually returning to the Circle's stations, but alternately reaching the IND once more at its Seventh Avenue Station, at West 53rd Street, east of Broadway.

[S 1.] Columbus Circle, Broadway/Eighth Ave./Central Park W./Central Park S.

This focal point, where Broadway glances the corner of Central Park, was the **obvious** place for **monumental treatment,** but it resulted only in a **few sculptures** in a **tangle of traffic.** Gaetano Russo's statue of *Columbus* (1892) is at the hub: architect H. Van Buren Magonigle's *Maine Memorial* (1913) wallows in from the park corner, with a boatload of figures by sculptor Attilio Piccirilli.

[S 1a.] Columbus Center (mixed use), Columbus Circle W., 58th to W. 60th Sts. W side. ca. 1990.

In the first round of this **fantasy-proposal,** the old **Coliseum** would have given way to a dual set of enormous towers (*Moshe Safdie, architect*), a new colossus that threatened to throw an elongated shadow across the lawns of Central Park while exacerbating the traffic volume at this node in the Broadway corridor. Round two was initiated by the **pull-out of a key tenant** and the **winning of a lawsuit brought against the City** and the Triborough Bridge and Tunnel Authority by the **Municipal Art Society and allied groups,** who charged double-dealing. The resultant rethinking of the project considered a milder intensity of development with a new architect (*David Childs of Skidmore, Owings & Merrill*). Round three . . . ?

[S 1b.] Columbus Circle Station, IRT Seventh Avenue Line subway, below Broadway, Eighth Ave., and Central Park W. and Central Park S. 1904. Heins & La Farge. ★ Altered.

One of the original IRT subway's architectural relics, now much tampered with as a result of its joining with the IND Line.

[S 2.] 1 Central Park Place (apartments) NW cor. W. 57th St. and Eighth Ave. 1988. Davis, Brody & Assocs.

A very tall, very slender luxury tower by the architects who gave us the city's most distinguished publically assisted housing. It seems sad that Manhattan's **tower mania** has so subverted the attitudes of developers that the firm that produced **East Midtown Plaza** [see E 6.] finally had to play the 1980s urban finial game.

[S 3a.] N.Y.C. Department of Cultural Affairs (offices and gallery)/ formerly **New York Cultural Center**/originally **Gallery of Modern Art,** 2 Columbus Circle, bet. Broadway and Eighth Ave. to W. 58th St. 1965. Edward Durell Stone.

A compact white marble confection with vaguely Middle Eastern motifs, commissioned by A & P's **Huntington Hartford** and shaped to the constricted site. It shows off well when seen from the north, on Broadway, gleaming among larger, darker structures. This may have persuaded **Gulf + Western,** its neighbor across Columbus Circle, to purchase it and present it to the city as headquarters for the **Department of Cultural Affairs** and center for the New York Convention and Visitors Bureau.

[S 3b.] 240 Central Park South (apartments), SE cor. Broadway. 1941. Mayer & Whittlesey.

Two apartment towers in a cubistic modeling, rising from a one-story, **garden-topped podium,** give all the big windows and balconies a good view. There are some problems of form in the ziggurat top, but the detailing is fine. Note the **zigzag storefronts** on Broadway.

[S 3b.] 240 Central Park S. (apts.)   **[S 4c.]** The St. Thomas Choir School

Central Park South east of **No. 240** is an impressive cliff, including luxury hotels and apartments, but except for the careful decoration on the old **Gainsborough Studios,** at **No. 222,** there is little that calls for a close look. (*1908. C.W. Buckham, architect. Frieze, Isidore Konti.*) **Essex House, Hampshire House,** the **New York Athletic Club,** and the **St. Moritz** are all distinguished by their opulence and opulent residents. Architecturally they form a bland wall (perhaps appropriately) for the lush parkland opposite.

[S 4a.] Originally **Helen Miller Gould stables,** 213 W. 58th St., bet. Seventh Ave. and Broadway. 1902. York & Sawyer.

This limestone stable bears hitching rings carved from the stone itself.

[S 4b.] Engine Company No. 23, N.Y.C. Fire Department, 215 W. 58th St., bet. Seventh Ave and Broadway. 1905. Alexander H. Stevens.

A handsome fraternal twin to **No. 213.**

[S 4c.] St. Thomas Choir School, 202 W. 58th St., bet. Seventh and Eighth Aves. 1987. Buttrick, White & Burtis.

Boy sopranos here study, dwell, and sing in preparation for magnificent Bach at the parent St. Thomas Church [see F 12c.].

[S 5a.] Originally **General Motors Company (offices)**/now **Argonaut Building,** 224 W. 57th St., SE cor. Broadway, 1910. Kimball & Thompson.

The east lot-line wall still carries the original advertising sign although GM long ago vacated this terra-cotta-clad structure, first to the one diagonally across Broadway (with an enormous illuminated rooftop sign facing Central Park) and then to the Plaza [see Z 1.]

[S 5b.] Hard Rock Café, 221 W. 57th St., bet. Seventh Ave. and Broadway. 1983.

Here an impaled 1959 Cadillac serves as its canopy, a pop insert in the context of this sober street. The lines to buy its T-shirts and other memorabilia are even longer than the lines to savor the experience firsthand.

[S 5b.] The Hard Rock Café canopy   **[S 5c.]** Art Students League building

[S 5c.] Art Students League/originally **American Fine Arts Society,** 215 W. 57th St., bet. Seventh Ave. and Broadway. 1892. Henry J. Hardenbergh, with W. C. Hunting & J. C. Jacobsen. ★

A stately French Renaissance structure, originally built for an organization that included the **Architectural League,** is now an art school.

[S 5d.] The Osborne Apartments, 205 W. 57th St., NW cor. Seventh Ave. 1885. James E. Ware. Extension, 1906, Alfred S. G. Taylor.

The **crazy-quilt** exterior of Classical and Chicago school stonework and glassy storefronts hides elegant interiors, hinted at in the extravagant marble vestibule and lobby. In the manner of a Florentine palazzo, it is stark and dour without, lush and luxurious within.

[S 6a.] Alwyn Court Apartments, 180 W. 58th St., SE cor. Seventh Ave. 1909. Harde & Short. ★   Restoration, 1985, Beyer Blinder Belle; murals by Richard Haas.

A French Renaissance exterior, every square foot of which is **literally encrusted** with terra-cotta decorations: crowns and dragons everywhere. Within the courtyard is a painted architectural facade by **Richard Haas.** Fantastic!

[S 6b.] CAMI Building/originally **Louis H. Chalif's School of Dancing,** 165 W. 57th St., bet. Sixth and Seventh Aves. 1917. G. A. and H. Boehm.

Italian mannerist with Tuscan overtones that make it a fine neighbor to Carnegie Hall across 57th.

[S 6c.] Row houses, 147–153 W. 57th St., bet. Sixth and Seventh Aves. ca. 1885.

"Only 6 minutes and 23 seconds from Lincoln Center and slightly to the left of Carnegie Hall," boasts the Russian Tea Room **radio commercial.** Now just turn around and discover these hearty survivors from 57th Street's Queen Anne past.

[S 6a.] The Alwyn Court Apartments   **[S 7a.]** Carnegie Hall/new marquee

[S 7a.] Carnegie Hall, 156 W. 57th St., SE cor. Seventh Ave. to W. 56th St. 1891. William B. Tuthill. Richard Morris Hunt, Dankmar Adler, consultants. ★ Redesigned and restored, 1986. James Stewart Polshek & Partners.

The caramel block of the hall itself is **engulfed** in the bristling offices and studios above and around it. The hall, **noted more for its sound** than its appearance, was **almost lost** in the early 1960s when Philharmonic Hall went up, but is now constantly booked. The building also houses a fine recital hall and a cinema. Now lovingly restored, it is grander than ever. One can even enter at grade. The commercial corner has been returned to Carnegie's service within, with a concomitant **Viollet-le-Duc** exterior restoration without.

[S 7b.] Carnegie Hall Tower (mixed use), 152 W. 57th St., bet. Sixth and Seventh Aves. 1990. Cesar Pelli & Assocs.

In the venerable void between Carnegie Hall and the **Russian Tea Room,** just to the left of Carnegie Hall, rises **a slender tower** that defers to the Renaissance Revival architecture of its parent next door.

The Russian Tea Room (restaurant), 150 West 57th Street, squeezed between the preceeding and the following.

[S 7c.] Metropolitan Tower (mixed use), 140 W. 57th St., bet. Sixth and Seventh Aves. 1987. Schuman, Lichtenstein, Claman & Efron.

Harry Macklowe, the developer, says that he designed this himself. If so, he can take the blame for a gross and insensitive intrusion into these blocks. Its **knife-edged** glass form is impressive but inappropriate. But the rock star tenants and their peers will savor its **nouveau riche glitz.**

[S 7d.] Hotel Parker Meridien, 118 W. 57th St., bet. Sixth and Seventh Aves. 1981. Office of Philip Birnbaum.

A 2-story vaulted colonnade of **Tuscan** columns leads to a skylit colonnaded **atrium.** One can't help wondering whether the architect finds this serious or a Post Modern jest.

[S 7e.] Manhattan Life Insurance Building/originally **Steinway Hall,** 111 W. 57th St., bet. Sixth and Seventh Aves. 1925. Warren & Wetmore.

A sober Classical tower built by one of the many music concerns clustered around Carnegie Hall. The change of ownership has not changed the colorful street-floor piano showroom.

[S 7f.] New York Delicatessen/originally **Horn & Hardart's Automat,** 104 W. 57th St., bet. Sixth and Seventh Aves. 1938. Ralph B. Bencker. Remodeled, 1983, Hochheiser-Elias Design Group, Inc.

Hollywood Deco, a bit of a **Busby Berkeley movie set,** and a touch of Radio City Music Hall.

[S 8a.] CitySpire (mixed use), 150 W. 56th St. through to W. 55th St., bet. Sixth and Seventh Aves. 1987. Murphy/Jahn.

A dull podium and a 69-story Helmut Jahn lurid skyline are made possible by the transfer of **City Center's** air rights. Cityspire's phallic domical hat apes the City Center's own dome below, a behind *en* bustle.

Like Carnegie Hall Tower and Metropolitan Tower, its neighbors across the street with equally overactive thyroids, the lower part is devoted to commercial uses and the upper, the part in the clouds, to lavish apartment living.

Patelson's, at 160 East 56th Street, is an emporium of sheet music, books, and oddments sought out by serious musicians from all over the world. Here each instrumentalist can find his or her score of Bach, Beethoven, or Bartok.

[S 8b.] City Center of Music and Drama/originally **Mecca Temple (Masonic),** 135 W. 55th St., bet. Sixth and Seventh Aves. 1924. Harry P. Knowles, succeeded by Clinton & Russell. ★

Saved from destruction by **Mayor LaGuardia,** this **Spanish tile-domed** multitiered theater has served for decades as a performing arts center. The architecture is delightfully absurd, as might be expected from members of the **Ancient and Accepted Order of the Mystic Shrine,** its original builders.

[S 8c.] 154 West 55th Street/formerly **55th Street Playhouse,** bet. Sixth and Seventh Aves. 1888. Bassett Jones.

A Romanesque Revival stable that became a movie theater.

[S 9.] Hotel Royal Concordia, 154 W. 54th St., bet. Sixth and Seventh Aves. N side. 1989. Frank Williams & Assocs.

Williams is credited with designing two of the Upper West Side's most interesting high-rise apartment buildings, the Columbia and the Park Belvedere.

END of Central Park South Walking Tour: A choice of subways: the BMT Broadway Line's 57th Street Station (with access at both West 55th and West 57th and Seventh Avenue) or the IND Sixth and Eighth Avenue Lines at the Seventh Avenue Station, at West 53rd Street, east of Broadway.

THE PLAZA SUITE

The Plaza and its namesake hotel are the joint between Midtown and the Upper East Side. Hereabouts, rising from the south, end the phalanxes of Midtown office buildings. Here also commences the wall of luxury apartment buildings that sail up into the East 90s; to west is the apartment and hotel opulence of Central Park South.

Plaza Suite Walking Tour: A short spin radiating out from the Plaza for only a few blocks. (BMT Broadway Line to the Fifth Avenue Station.)

[Z 1.] The Plaza/officially **Grand Army Plaza,** Fifth Ave. bet. W. 58th and W. 60th Sts. W side. Central Park, 1912. Thomas Hastings of Carrère & Hastings. ★

Formally called **Grand Army Plaza,** this is **The Plaza** to New Yorkers; until 1973 it was New York's only public urban plaza for people. The Police Plaza is number two (chronologically). Plazas at Rockefeller and Lincoln Centers, and at the World Trade Center and at the World Financial Center, are parts of private building complexes;

but here, in the European tradition, is an outdoor room contained by buildings of varied architecture and function, an island of urbane repose. The more significant half (the area is bisected by 59th Street) to the south is centered on the **Plaza Hotel** on the west and the **General Motors Building** across Fifth Avenue.

The **Plaza** is ornamented by varied paving and trees enclosing the **Pulitzer Fountain,** surmounted by *Pomona,* a lithe lady by **Karl Bitter** on a cascade of pools by Carrère and Hastings.

South are the buildings of **Bergdorf Goodman** (*1928. Buchman & Kahn*) and the **Paris Theater** (*1948. Emery Roth & Sons, with interiors by Warner-Leeds Assocs.*). Looming high in the local skyline is **9 West 57th Street** [see Z 5a.].

General Sherman occupies the **Plaza's** northern half, which is more of a traffic turnaround than a pedestrian enclave. **The General** (**William Tecumseh**) is here marching, not through **Georgia** but, rather, in allegory. **Augustus Saint-Gaudens** presented this casting at the **Paris Exposition** of **1900,** and the good General mounted his present pedestal in **1903.** Now the oldest resident of this place, he antedates the **Plaza Hotel** by four years.

 [Z 2.] The Plaza Hotel, W. 58th to W. 59th Sts. facing Grand Army Plaza. 1907. Henry J. Hardenbergh. ★

A vestige of **Edwardian** elegance. **Hardenbergh,** its designer, graced **New York** with another, and equal, social and architectural monument: **The Dakota** (apartment house). The white glazed brick and the verdigris copper and slate mansard roof have been returned to their pristine splendor. One of the most exciting views of **New York** (Eloise-style) is from any room on the north side, from the third to the fifth floors. From there eyes can skim the trees in a dramatic perspective of **Central Park** and **Fifth Avenue. Frank Lloyd Wright** was a devotee of the **Plaza** and used it as his New York headquarters.

[Z 2.] Hardenbergh's Plaza Hotel   **[Z 7.]** Der Scutt's glassy Trump Tower

 **[Z 2a.] Shezan Restaurant,** 8 W. 58th St., bet. Fifth and Sixth Aves. 1976. Gwathmey Siegel.

An elegant below-street-level place of "light and illusion" (Gwathmey's words). Expensive Indian and Pakistani food that has nothing to do with Captain Marvel.

Note: For the Sherry-Netherland Hotel, see E Manhattan/Goldcoast [G 1a.].

[Z 3.] General Motors Building, 767 Fifth Ave., bet. E. 58th and E. 59th Sts. to Madison Ave. 1968. Edward Durell Stone, Emery Roth & Sons, associated architects.

Here lay the **Savoy Plaza** (Hotel) and a miscellany of others, none particularly distinguished. The hue and cry over the new **tower** was based not on architecture but on the sacrifice of elegant shopping amenities to automobile salesmanship. (An auto showroom is particularly galling at the spot in New York that most honors the pedestrian). And who needs a plaza on a plaza?

In the sunken central space Vidal Sassoon's shop is a lurking star (*1976. Gwathmey Siegel*).

[Z 3a.] Hongkong and Shanghai Banking Corporation/formerly **Playboy Club,** 5 E. 59th St., bet. Fifth and Madison Aves. Altered, 1984, Der Scutt.

This modest building has passed through serial incarnations. Once the Savoy Art Galleries, it was remodeled into the **Playboy Club** (*1962. Oppenheimer, Brady & Lehrecke*) and, later, remodeled again (*1976. Paul K. Y. Chen*). Now sexy dining has been replaced by sexy banking.

[Z 3b.] 745 Fifth Avenue (offices), SE cor. E. 58th St. 1931. Office of Ely Jacques Kahn. Upgraded, 1988, Hammond, Beebe & Babka.

The longtime home of that inimitable toy store, F.A.O. Schwarz, now removed to more sumptuous quarters at General Motors.

[Z 1.] New York's original plaza anchors the SE corner of Central Park (1908)

[Z 4.] Originally **New York Trust Company Building (offices)**/now **Manufacturers Hanover Trust Company,** 1 E. 57th St., NE cor. Fifth Ave. 1930. Cross & Cross. Bank conversion, 1966, Skidmore, Owings & Merrill.

A subtle and elegant update of the first 2 floors of a **neo-Classic** building.

[Z 5a.] 9 West 57th Street (offices), bet. Fifth and Sixth Aves. to E. 58th St. Skidmore, Owings & Merrill.

A black-and-white swooping form, as destructive to the street wall as its sibling overlooking Bryant Park [see B 2b.]. Wind bracing here is proudly displayed like a pair of new suspenders.

[Z 5b.] Originally **Ampico Building**/later **Curtiss-Wright Building (offices/galleries),** 29 W. 57th St., bet. Fifth and Sixth Aves. 1923. Cross & Cross.

One of 57th Street's midblock office/gallery structures that represents the "old culture" of pianos and easel paintings. The ornate star on the east lot-line wall was the symbol of the American Piano Company.

[Z 5c.] Rizzoli Bookshop, 31 W. 57th St., bet. Fifth and Sixth Aves. ca. 1905. Restored, 1986, Hardy Holzman Pfeiffer Assocs.

A bookshop that *feels* like a library in a baronial mansion, designed by the multitalented firm that restored the Carnegie mansion for use as the Cooper-Hewitt Museum.

[Z 6a.] The Crown Building (offices)/ formerly **Genesco Building/** originally **Heckscher Building,** 730 Fifth Ave., SW cor W. 57th St. 1921. Warren & Wetmore.

The first office building erected after passage of the city's 1916 Zoning Resolution. Surprisingly, because of eclectic detailing (such as the rooster that once topped its water tank enclosure), it reveals no radical departure from old ways. The Museum of Modern Art's **first gallery** opened here on the 12th floor in November 1929.

[Z 6b.] I. Miller shoe salon, 730 Fifth Ave., SW cor. W. 57th St., in the Crown Building. 1961. Victor Lundy.

Treelike wood-clad columns in this 2-story space spread at the ceiling with **cathedral-like effect.** The original muted colors have been livened up by the owners. Washing the inside of the plate glass windows, screened by the wood, seems a perpetual problem.

Tiffany's: One of the world's oldest and most famous jewelers came to the corner of Fifth Avenue and 57th Street in 1940. The show windows in the massive polished granite facade (727 Fifth Avenue) are famous for their miniature stage-setting displays. See their original palace at 409 Fifth Avenue [Herald Square Q 23.].

[Z 7.] Trump Tower (mixed use), 725 Fifth Ave., NE cor. 56th St. 1983. Der Scutt, design architect, and Swanke Hayden Connell.

A simplistic folded glass tower conceals a fantasyland for the affluent shopper. Within, the multilevel space houses a café with waterfalls and moving stairways to shoppers' heaven. It is flamboyant, exciting, and emblematic of the **American Dream.**

Donald Trump entered the imagination of New Yorkers here and has since produced **Trump Plaza, Trump Parc,** casinos in Atlantic City, and the skating rink in Central Park that the City could never finish. His aesthetics, however, are more akin to wine coolers than to Veuve Cliquot.

[Z 8.] IBM Building (offices and atrium), 590 Madison Ave., bet. E. 56th and E. 57th Sts. W side. 1983. Edward Larrabee Barnes Assocs. **IBM Gallery,** basement: **Open to the public.**

This polished black granite monolith is a cut prism, its faceted form skewing the street. Most obvious to the pedestrian is the looming cantilevered corner at 57th and Madison. Attached at the south is its atrium, a bamboo-forested greenhouse, a restful garden, where one can gain access to a snack, the **IBM Gallery,** the **New York Botanical Garden** sales shop, and even to **Bonwit Teller** and **Trump Tower** next door.

[Z 9.] AT&T Headquarters, (offices), 550 Madison Ave., bet. E. 55th and E. 56th Sts. W side. 1984. Philip Johnson/John Burgee.

Known to many as the **Chippendale skyscraper,** this granite hulk turned the market around among developers in New York. **Glass Modern** now became replaced with **stone Post Modern,** and a building's profile against the sky became a game of who could create that which was the most bizarre.

The **galleria** is smashing, its quarter-arched glass roof truly reminiscent in scale of that ancestral **Galleria,** by Giuseppe Mengoni, in Milan. But the underspace below the office tower proper is a street-level subway station, a circumstance that the cast-iron garden furniture cannot do much to improve.

[Z 10.] Fuller Building (offices), 41 E. 57th St., NE cor. Madison Ave. 1929. Walker & Gillette, architects. Elie Nadelman, sculptor. ★ Interior. ★

The Brooks Brothers of Art Deco: black, gray, and white.

[Z 11.] 625 Madison Avenue (offices)/originally **Plaza Building,** bet. E. 58th and E. 59th Sts. E side. 1930. Sloan & Robertson. Expanded, 1956, Sylvan Bien. Reclad, 1987, Der Scutt.

It has never looked better: glistening mauve, bronze, and black panels sheath a building formerly clad with a banal 1950s curtain wall, installed when it was enlarged from 12 to 17 stories.

[Z 12.] 650 Madison Avenue (offices)/originally **C.I.T. Building,** bet. E. 59th and E. 60th Sts. W side. 1957. Harrison & Abramovitz. Reclad and tower added, 1987, Fox & Fowle.

The original black granite and stainless steel 8-story building has been overcome by its new tower and skin. The crowning floors are the most impressive sight, with a stainless steel logo against the sky. In between are incessant panels of green glass.

[Z 13a.] Delmonico Plaza (offices), 55 E. 59th St., bet. Madison and Park Aves. 1986. Davis, Brody & Assocs.

Slate and granite. The ground-floor colonnade is a pleasant break in the streetfront architecture, and its matte finish contrasts well with the glitter opposite.

[Z 8.] Edward L. Barnes' IBM building   **[Z 9.]** AT&T: Chippendale skyscraper

[Z 15a.] Lighthouse building/plaza   **[Z 15b.]** The former Aramco Building

[Z 13b.] 500 Park Avenue Tower (apartments), annexed to the Amro Bank Building, on E. 59th St., bet. Madison and Park Aves. 1986. James Stewart Polshek & Partners, design architects. Schuman, Lichtenstein, Claman & Efron, associated architects.

A residential condominium annexed both legally and architecturally to the **elegant heirs** of Pepsi-Cola. At the lower levels and on top it matches Pepsi's sleekness. In between, deeply incised granite openings provide a strong and handsome foil. As for the old Pepsi:

[Z 13c.] Amro Bank Building/formerly **Olivetti Building**/originally **Pepsi-Cola Building (offices),** 500 Park Ave., SW cor. E. 59th St. 1960. Skidmore, Owings & Merrill.

An **understated elegance** that bows to the scale of its Park Avenue neighbors rather than advertising itself as the newest (of its time) local modern monument. Large bays of glass are enlivened by the seemingly random arrangements of partitions (that **kiss the glass** with rubber gaskets) and vertical blinds.

Built for Pepsi-Cola (which withdrew to the suburbs), it was bought by **Olivetti**, the **world's foremost patron** of architecture, planning, and good design. Now Amro Bank enjoys its elegance, permanently secured by the sale of air rights to the 500 Park Avenue Tower next door.

 [Z 14a.] Banque de Paris Building (offices), 499 Park Ave., SE cor. E. 59th St. 1984. I. M. Pei & Partners.

This **obsidian** prism, blackly marking its Park Avenue corner, is so subtle externally as to be boring. Its lobby, however, presents a wondrous—and wondrously lit—tree to the passer-through (diagonally, from Park to 59th, and vice versa).

[Z 14b.] 110 East 59th Street (offices), bet. Park and Lexington Aves. 1968, William Lescaze.

This simple, understated, and unpretentious tower is a notch above its speculative competition. The sculpture (*1973. Tony Rosenthal*) in the south plaza (on 58th Street) is a rich, carved piece of a bronze cylinder.

[Z 14c.] Argosy Print and Book Store, 115 E. 59th St., bet. Park and Lexington Aves. 1966. Kramer & Kramer.

An elegant shop that replaces the long-gone street stands along this block; used books, maps, and prints filled the sidewalk to the delight of browsers, as on the **Left Bank** of the **Seine.** Upstairs (by elevator) are floors devoted to old prints, painting, and specialized books. Perhaps too elegant, too stylish, too neat for such a bookstore, **Argosy** is the current uptown outpost of a trade that once flourished on the flanks of Fourth Avenue, in dusty storefronts between **Astor Place** and **14th Street.**

[Z 15a.] The Lighthouse: New York Association for the Blind, 111 E. 59th St., bet. Park and Lexington Aves. 1964. Kahn & Jacobs.

A simple limestone facade with tall, color-anodized, aluminum-framed windows. Its placement forms a tiny plaza with the wall of the corner building. The 4 stacks release air conditioning exhaust without subjecting passersby to blasts of warm, stale "air." The handcrafted delights of the ground-floor shop are worthy.

[Z 15b.] 505 Park Avenue/originally **Aramco Building (offices),** NE cor. E. 59th St. 1948. Emery Roth & Sons. Ground-floor facade alterations, 1987. Der Scutt.

A supreme stylist, Der Scutt provides a face-lift of banded glitz in black and gold.

END of Plaza Suite Walking Tour: The closest subways are at Bloomingdale's: IRT Lexington Avenue Line's 59th Street Station and the BMT Broadway Line's Lexington Avenue Station.

EAST 57TH STREET

From Lexington Avenue east to Sutton Place and the East River, this Midtown precinct offers the turbulence of shopping at Bloomingdale's and Alexander's and the serenity of river views redolent of 1930s Hollywood leading men in smoking jackets stepping out on terraces to view the sparkling form of the Queensboro Bridge.

East 57th Street Walking Tour: Encompasses the consumer jungle of Lexington around 59th, the svelte 57th Street corridor eastward to exclusive Sutton Place, and ends beneath the powerful form of the Queensboro Bridge. (Take the IRT Lexington Avenue Line to the 59th Street Station or the BMT Broadway Line to the Lexington Avenue Station.)

[D 1.] Bloomingdale's (department store)/originally **Bloomingdale Brothers,** E. 59th to E. 60th Sts. bet. Lexington and Third Aves. **Main**

Lexington Avenue Building, 740 Lexington Ave. 1930. Starrett & Van Vleck.

An aggregation of Victorian and Art Deco structures, completely interlocking on the interior, houses one of America's most comprehensive and sophisticated stores.

Demolition of the Third Avenue el and the 1960s renaissance of that saloon-bespotted boulevard inspired **Bloomie's** to shed its **bargain basement** image. The castle of consumerism that emerged became, for many, the source from which all **upscale, total life-style statements** flow.

[D 1a.] 750 Lexington Avenue (offices), bet. E. 59th and E. 60th Sts. W side. 1988. Murphy/Jahn.

Chicago's Helmut Jahn is providing New York with its most prolific **skyline** elements since those slender finialed towers of the 1930s—from the **Chrysler Building** to the **Canadian Imperial Bank of Commerce.** The catch is that these new vast office structures have the waistline of a Dutch burgher rather than a Chanel model. Air conditioning, nonexistent in the 1930s, now allows buildings to be deep and mechanically ventilated. The Chrysler Building's air conditioning (and light) was provided by windows.

[D 2.] Alexander's (department store), 731 Lexington Ave., NE cor. E. 58th St. to Third Ave. 1965. Emery Roth & Sons.

The modestly designed, and modestly priced, contents are what is important here. The container is innocuous commercial modern pretending to be more. Designed along a module with intentions of expansion to fill the entire block, Alexander's may be in danger of replacement by a high rise, reflecting the enormous desire for space in this area.

[D 2.] The endangered Alexander's store, ripe for a high-rise replacement

[D 3a.] Cinema I and Cinema II, 1001 Third Ave., bet. E. 59th and E. 60th Sts. 1962. Abraham W. Geller & Assocs.

A piggyback pair of great architectural **quality. Geller** and his wife, who did the interiors, have produced a simple elegance with counterpoints of rich paintings and graphics. Instead of escapist entertainment in escapist environments (as in a 1920s movie "palace"), movies here are serious business.

[D 3b.] Manhattan 1 and 2 (movie theaters), 220 E. 59th St. bet. Second and Third Aves. 1980. Richard Dattner.

A squat pair of movie houses presents a broken **Post Modern** pediment to the street.

[D 4.] Decoration and Design Building, 979 Third Ave., NE cor. E. 58th St. 1965. David & Earl Levy.

The zigguratted New York zoning envelope is capitalized into a positive architectural statement (*if you look skyward*).

[D 5.] 311 and **313 East 58th Street (residences),** bet. Second Ave. and the Queensboro Bridge access ramp. 1857. ★

The new approaches (1930) to the bridge have partially submerged these modest dwellings, built in an era when this part of town was a semisuburb.

[D 6.] Originally **Gnome Bakery,** 316 E. 59th St., SE cor. Queensboro Bridge approach. Converted, 1933, Adams & Prentice.

A Hansel and Gretel cottage visible from East 58th Street, built to serve the needs of a 1930s bakery. A curiosity.

[D 7.] 322 East 57th Street (studios) bet. First and Second Aves. 1930. Harry M. Clawson of Caughey & Evans.

A simple **Park Avenue facade,** rusticated at the base, houses studios with dramatic 2-story windows.

[D 8.] 400 East 57th Street (apartments), SE cor. First Ave. to E. 56th St. 1931. Roger H. Bullard, Philip L. Goodwin, and Kenneth Franzheim.

An Art Moderne apartment building in the style of Central Park West's **Century** and **Majestic,** but monotowered.

[D 9.] The Eastsider (apartments), 420 E. 58th St., bet. First and York Aves. 1987. Gatje, Papachristou & Smith.

Two-toned brick with bay windows and balconies from these the heirs of Bauhaus designer Marcel Breuer. Another reminder that architects can't solve the urban design problems of streets—the joint essence of the city—by merely exterior decoration. This tower clearly violates the streetscape.

Sutton Place

[D 10.] Sutton Place town houses, Sutton Place bet. E. 57th and E. 58th Sts. E side, Sutton Sq. (E. 58th St.), and Riverview Terr. (a private street bet. Sutton Sq. and E. 59th St.).

This became an enclave of wealth and elegance in the early 1920s, when factories and tenements largely shared the banks of the East River. The **Dead End Kids** were the denizens of these blocks, **which dead-ended into piers** at the river and where summer fun included diving into that not yet fetid tidal waterway. (Construction of the East River Drive and the **toiletization of the river** itself ended all that.)

This group was started as an experimental enclave of private houses at a time when most of those who could afford a private house were moving to (or already living in) Park and Fifth Avenue apartments. Architects here included **Mott Schmidt** (Nos. 1, 3, 13, and 17 Sutton Place), **H. Page Cross** (No. 9), **William Lescaze** (No. 21), **Delano & Aldrich** (No. 12 Sutton Square), and **Ely Jacques Kahn** (6 Riverview Terrace). Nothing is spectacular in itself, but the whole is an intact block and a half, with riverfront private gardens that jointly provide an urbane architectural grouping. Prominent residents included **Mrs. William K. Vanderbilt** (No. 1 Sutton Place) and **Robert W. Goelet** (No. 9).

[D 11.] Bridgemarket, under the Queensboro Bridge, along E. 59th St. to E. 60th St., E of First Ave. 1988. Hardy Holzman Pfeiffer Assocs.

Here great groin-vaulted space is converted for use as an elegant marketplace. It is one of the grand **found spaces** formerly wasted on pedestrian storage by City agencies. Others that should be recaptured include the vast volume under the Riverside Drive viaduct in the West 150s and those beneath the Brooklyn Bridge.

END of East 57th Street Walking Tour: The nearest subways, at Bloomingdale's, are centered on Lexington Avenue and 59th Street.

UPPER WEST SIDE

LINCOLN CENTER • RIVERSIDE DRIVE/WEST END AVENUE
BROADWAY AND ENVIRONS
CENTRAL PARK WEST/THE PARK BLOCKS
WEST SIDE URBAN RENEWAL AREA • MANHATTAN VALLEY

In a way the **Upper West Side** is as much a state of mind as a place to live: a successor to **Greenwich Village** as a magnet for those in the vanguard of cultural or social action and also—particularly today— political action.

Early Manhattan's development was confined mostly below and to the east of Central Park; the latecomer **West** blossomed during a period of substantial immigration of urbane Europeans. That population, culturally crossbred with adventurous local migrants, and served by equally adventurous developers, created a mix of people and buildings with a flavor distinct from that of the **East.** The **West** owes as much to the imported culture of Vienna, Berlin, and Budapest as to the enterprising patronage of those such as Singer Sewing Machine heir **Edward Severin Clark.** His Dakota Apartments at 72nd Street became a social outpost so remote from **The 400** that it was considered the geographical equivalent—in New York City terms—of the **Dakota Territory.**

Whereas **Greenwich Village** became a Bohemian haven and a crucible for the **individual** painter, sculptor, writer, or poet—a place of rebellion and artistic creativity—the **West Side** is a nexus of **group** art: concerts, opera, theater, film—the cultural mecca for national as well as New York audiences. Here live a major portion of those who fill those many stages, intermingled with a locally passionate audience. Perhaps passion is a local character trait, not only of those who perform or savor performance but also of a vast group of political activists who voice their community and national concerns with a vigor unequaled elsewhere in the city.

But how did it all begin?

After the English "conquest" of New Amsterdam in 1664, Richard Nicolls was appointed governor by the Duke of York to oversee his new proprietary colony. Nicolls not only honored Dutch property owners and landlords already in place but also granted vast tracts to new **patentees.** The **Thousand Acre Tract,** bounded by the Hudson and (roughly) modern 50th Street, 89th Street, and Sixth Avenue, now the heart of the Upper West Side, was divided into ten lots and granted to four Dutchmen and one Englishman.

In its original verdant state the area was known as Bloomingdale, honored by its nominal association with a flower-growing region near Haarlem named **Bloemendael.** The Bloomingdale Road followed a serpentine Indian trail that also produced the meandering alignment of much of Broadway. As a northern extension of Lower Manhattan's principal street, it was the road to Albany, a commercial route whose scale after widening (1868–1871) allowed its ultimate potential to be planned. And so, it was briefly renamed **The Boulevard** until 1899, when buildings such as **The Ansonia, The Belnord, The Apthorp,** and **The Belleclaire** would begin to fulfill these plans.

It was not until public transportation had penetrated these precincts that serious development occurred. Although horsecars had reached West 84th Street by 1864, the Ninth Avenue elevated did not arrive until 1879, with stations at 72nd, 81st, 93rd, and 104th Streets (others were added later). Clark's almost simultaneous construction of the Dakota (1880–1884) was an equal inspiration and stimulus. New buildings centered on these nodes at first, with builders uncertain about the city's intentions to level and grade the streets and to evict squatters

Upper West Side: see map p. 288

UPPER WEST SIDE/CENTRAL PARK

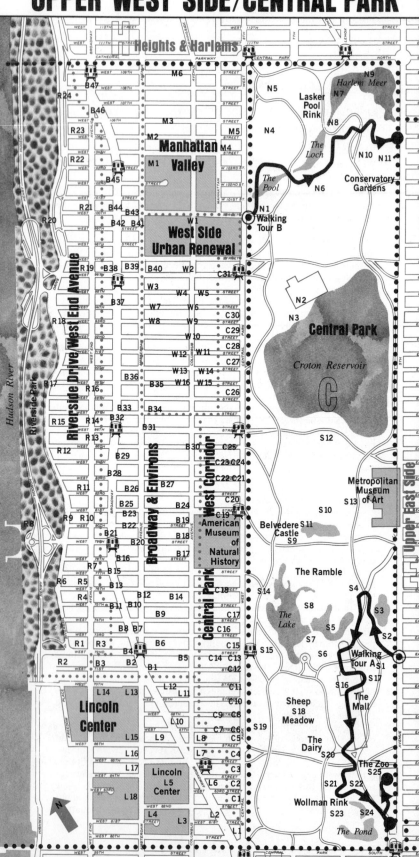

Heights & Harlems

N9 Harlem Meer
N5
Lasker Pool Rink
N7
N8
N4
N10 N11
The Loch
M6
N6
M3
Conservatory Gardens
M2
M5
M4

Manhattan Valley

M1
The Pool

W1

West Side Urban Renewal

N1 Walking Tour B
B47
B46
R24
R23
R22
B45
R21 B44 B43
B42 B41
R20 B40 W2

C31
W3
N2
W4 W5
B39 B38 R19
N3
W7 W6
B37 W8 W9
R18 W10 C30

Central Park

W12 W11 C29
C28
B36 W13 W14
C27
B35 W16 W15
R16 C26
B33 B34
R15 B32 R14
R13 B31

Croton Reservoir
C

S12

C25
B30 C23 C24
R12 C22 C21
B29
B28 C20
R11 B26 B27
Metropolitan Museum of Art
S13
B25 C19
R9 R10 B23 B24
R8 B22
American Museum of Natural History
S10
Belvedere Castle S11
S9
B21 B19
B20 B18
R7 B16 B17
The Ramble
S4
R6 R5 B15
S8
S3
R4 B13
B12 B14
S14
C18
S2
B11 B10
The Lake
S5
B9 C17
S7
S6
B8 B7 C16
Walking Tour A S1
R1 R3 B4 B6 C15
S15
R2 B3 B2 C14 C13
B1 B5 C12
S16 S17

Lincoln Center

L14 L13
L12 L11
C11
C10
L10 C9 C8
The Mall
L9 C7 C6
Sheep Meadow S18
L15 L8 C5
L16 L7 C4
S19
L17 Lincoln L5 Center C3
The Dairy
S20
L18 L6 C2
The Zoo S25
L4 L3 C1
S21 S22
L2
Wollman Rink
L1
S23 S24
The Pond

Hudson River

Riverside Park

Riverside Drive/West End Avenue

Broadway & Environs

West Corridor

Central Park West

Upper East Side

0 1000 2000 3000
feet

Midtown

The Plaza

and shanty owners. But by 1886, a **boom** had occurred, as related grandiloquently in the **Times:**

"The West side of the city presents just now a scene of building activity such as was never before witnessed in that section, and which gives promise of the speedy disappearance of all the shanties in the neighborhood and the rapid population of this long neglected part of New York. The huge masses of rock which formerly met the eye, usually crowned by a rickety shanty and a browsing goat, are being blasted out of existence. Streets are being graded, and thousands of carpenters and masons are engaged in rearing substantial buildings where a year ago nothing was to be seen but market gardens or barren rocky fields."

For the purposes of this guide we have divided the Upper West Side's 2 square miles into precincts: **Lincoln Center, Riverside Drive, Central Park West,** the **West Side Urban Renewal Area,** and **Manhattan Valley.** The vital center, loosely termed **Broadway and Environs,** embraces the powerful diagonal thoroughfare where a dual necklace of shops attempts to emulate, admittedly somewhat crassly, the **boulevards of Paris.** With one exception, the Urban Renewal Area, each precinct is described in an **uptown** sequence, moving away from the central business district. The Renewal Area, **constructed** sequentially from north to south, is also **described** in that direction.

LINCOLN CENTER

The southern part of the Upper West Side developed quickly in the 1880s along Columbus Avenue, the route of **the Ninth Avenue el,** which intersected Lincoln Square at Broadway and 65th Street. The area was never fashionable except along Central Park. By the late 1940s that part west of Broadway was **a slum,** fostered by its **proximity to** the New York Central **railroad yards** lying between West End Avenue and the river. This latter area was the subject first of low-rent subsidized apartments and then of a 12-block **urban renewal project** that cleared the tenements and is now the site of Lincoln Center, Lincoln Towers apartments, and Fordham University's in-town campus, as well as many other public and institutional buildings. The old railroad yards have proven to be more difficult to recycle.

The area described below lies between West 60th and West 70th Streets from Broadway to the Hudson River.

[L 1.] Gulf + Western Plaza (office building), Columbus Circle bet. Central Park W., Broadway, and W. 61st St. 1969. Thomas E. Stanley.

This **flatiron-shaped site** did not produce a flatiron-shaped building, just a **rectangular slab** plus the bronze-anodized aluminum and glass Paramount Theater "hatbox" which fills the space left over on the Broadway side. The movie theater—not to be confused with the grandiose but now-removed Paramount in Times Square—lies below the podium.

[L 2.] American Bible Society Building, 1865 Broadway, NW cor. W. 61st St. 1966. Skidmore, Owings & Merrill.

The neatly cast-in-place concrete of this burly building is exposed: its bridge-sized beams make **a giant ladder** of the Broadway end.

[L 3.] Fordham University, Lincoln Center Campus, W. 60th St. NW cor. Columbus Ave. **[L 3a.] Fordham Law School (South Building),** 1962. Voorhees, Walker, Smith, Smith & Haines. **[L 3b.] Leon Lowenstein Center (North Building),** 1969. Slingerland & Booss.

Part of the same urban renewal package as Lincoln Center's performing arts spaces, these buildings fortunately don't attempt to join the overuse of travertine. Nevertheless their **bleached surfaces** are very white and very monotonous.

[L 4a.] 43 West 61st Street (apartments)/formerly **Sofia Brothers, Inc. (storage warehouse)/**originally **Kent Garage,** NE cor. Columbus Ave. to W. 62nd St. 1930. Jardine, Hill & Murdock. ★ Converted to apartments, 1985, Alan Lapidus Assocs.

A midblock **Art Deco delight.** All walls, even those on lot lines that might one day have been masked by tall neighbors (such as Lincoln

Plaza Tower, for example), were embellished with some (two-dimensional) ornament. Curiously enough, this structure was built as **an early "automatic" (meaning elevatored) garage;** its fortresslike walls were fenestrated during conversion to human occupancy.

[L 2.] American Bible Society Bldg.   [L 4b.] Lincoln Plaza Tower (1967)

[L 4b.] Lincoln Plaza Tower (apartments), 44 W. 62nd St., SE cor. Columbus Ave. 1973. Horace Ginsbern & Assocs.

A pleasing 30-story stack of **bay windows** and **dish-shaped balconies** caught in an embrace of cylindrical columns.

Lincoln Center

[L 5.] Lincoln Center for the Performing Arts, W. 62nd to W. 66th Sts. Columbus to Amsterdam Aves. 1962–1968. Wallace K. Harrison, director of board of architects (composed of architects of individual buildings).

This **travertine acropolis** of music and theater represents an initial investment of more than $165 million of early 1960s dollars—mostly in private contributions—along with federal aid in acquiring the site and a State contribution to the New York State Theater.

The project **aroused dissent** on both urbanistic and architectural grounds. The congestion caused by the location of so many large theaters in one cluster (with only meager public transportation) has been an obvious problem, left unsolved by the vast underground garage beneath the project. Making **a single impressive group** out of structures with such demanding interior requirements has **imposed inhibitions** on the individual buildings. As a result, former *New York Times* architecture critic Ada Louise Huxtable wrote, "Philharmonic Hall, the State Theater, and the Metropolitan Opera are lushly decorated, conservative structures that the public finds pleasing and most professionals consider a failure of nerve, imagination and talent."

"Fortunately," she continued, "the scale and relationship of the plazas are good, and they can be enjoyed as pedestrian open spaces."

[L 5a.] New York State Theater, SE cor. Lincoln Center, Columbus Ave., bet. W. 62nd and W. 63rd Sts. W side. 1964. Philip C. Johnson and Richard Foster. Reconstructed, 1982.

This 2,737-seat hall, designed mainly for ballet and musical theater, also includes a vast 4-story foyer suitable for receptions and balls. It is the **most frankly Classical building** in the group. The plaza-level lobby is a Baroque space that seems to have been carved from the enveloping travertine. The **grand foyer** above it, by contrast, is bounded by tiers of busy metal balcony railings, gold-colored chain drapery, and a gold velvet ceiling. It is dominated by two **wonderful white marble sculptures,** enlargements of earlier **Elie Nadelman** works. The **Delancey Street rhinestone** lights and chandeliers, inside and out, are a false note.

[L 5b.] Damrosch Park, [L 5c.] Guggenheim Band Shell, SW cor. Lincoln Center, W. 62nd St. NE cor. Amsterdam Ave. 1969. Eggers & Higgins.

Planned as a space for free outdoor concerts, this park surrounds a flat, **intricately paved** center section with an edge of verdant formal landscaping. The band shell, hugging Amsterdam Avenue on the west, seems to derive its form from **Middle Eastern antecedents,** thus adding yet another curious dimension to the already **eclectic** Lincoln Center scene.

[L 5a.] Philip Johnson's New York State Theater at Lincoln Center, in 1967

[L 5d.] Metropolitan Opera House, W side of Lincoln Center, bet. W. 63rd and W. 64th Sts. 1966. Wallace K. Harrison of Harrison & Abramovitz. Lobby paintings facing the plaza, Marc Chagall.

After years of trying to remove itself from its garment center location on Broadway between 39th and 40th Streets—negotiating at one point to occupy what eventually became the site of Rockefeller Center's RCA Building—the Met finally came here, to Lincoln Center. It is the **focal building** of the complex and its largest hall. It is also **a schmaltzy pastiche of forms,** materials (mostly travertine), and effects beginning with self-consciously **sensuous red-carpeted stairs** (which wind around themselves at the entrance) and ending with **brilliant Austrian crystal chandeliers** (which hang in the tall lobby space, as they do in the hall itself until, at the start of a performance, they silently rise to the gold-leafed ceiling). The café at the top of the lobby offers a **dazzling view down** into the entry area and out across the plaza.

[L 5e.] Vivian Beaumont Theater, NW cor. Lincoln Center, 150 W. 65th St., SE cor. Amsterdam Ave. 1965. Eero Saarinen & Assocs. **[L 5f.] Library and Museum of the Performing Arts, The New York Public Library,** 111 Amsterdam Ave. 1965, Skidmore, Owings & Merrill. Pool sculpture in plaza, *Reclining Figure,* Henry Moore.

An **unusual collaboration** of both **architects and architecture.** The library fills the massive, travertine-clad attic story which cantilevers over the 1,000 seat theater at plaza level. The building forms a **handsome backdrop** for the **reflecting pool** and its **modern sculpture,** especially when the glass-enclosed, split-level lobby is lighted and populated. In the main theater—there is a smaller one below—neutral, dark interior surfaces do not compete with the **colorful tiered seating** or the action on the **highly flexible stage.**

The library-museum, best entered through the link connecting it to the opera house, has typically meticulous SOM details, **a fun-to-shop-in boutique** specializing in performing arts books and memorabilia, and always some lively exhibits arranged by its **Shelby Cullom Davis Museum.** The lowest entrance from Amsterdam Avenue opens upon both a small lecture hall and a charming exhibit space given over to theater-related shows.

[L 5e.] Eero Saarinen's Vivian Beaumont Theater at Lincoln Center, in 1967

[L 5g.] Avery Fisher Hall/originally **Philharmonic Hall,** NE cor. Lincoln Center, Columbus Ave. SW cor. W. 65th St. 1962. Max Abramovitz of Harrison & Abramovitz. Reconstructed, 1976, Johnson/Burgee, architects. Cyril Harris, acoustical engineer. Stabile suspended from lobby ceiling, 1962, Richard Lippold, sculptor.

The many-tiered lobby of this concert hall has a clear glass enclosure set inside an arcade defined by tall, crisply tapered travertine columns. It is the most controversial of the performing arts center's buildings, and its hall has been **rebuilt a number of times** in attempts to solve its well-publicized acoustical deficiencies. The most elaborate change, in 1976, converted the hall into **a classic European rectangle** (and redesigned the public lobby spaces as well) to **wide acclaim** from both acoustical and architectural critics.

[L 5h.] Juilliard School of Music, 144 W. 66th St., bet. Broadway and Amsterdam Ave. 1968. Pietro Belluschi, with Eduardo Catalano and Westermann & Miller.

Connected to the superblock of Lincoln Center proper by a bridge over West 65th Street, this is the youngest of the Center's buildings. **Monolithic in appearance,** it is as if carved from travertine. It makes the best of an irregular site caused by Broadway's diagonal slash.

Lincoln Center Mall: Late in 1966 an ill-advised plan was announced to create a landscaped mall that would link Lincoln Center's Plaza with Central Park, a long city block away. The plan called for demolishing the West Side YMCA (*1930. Dwight James Baum*) and the meetinghouse of the New York Society for Ethical Culture along with other structures between West 63rd and West 64th Streets—the Broadway frontage was by then an enormous parking lot. Additionally, a block-sized underground parking area was envisioned beneath the proposed greenery. The plan lost and the threatened institutions remain. From the parking lot, however, grew the ASCAP Building, a spastic work that seems unable to respect either the rectangular street grid or Broadway's diagonal. Some decades **everything goes wrong.**

[L 5i.] Lincoln Center North (mixed use), W. 65th St. NE cor. Amsterdam Ave. 1989. Davis, Brody & Assocs. and Abramovitz Kingsland Schiff.

This multiuse annex to Lincoln Center proper provides in the base an auditorium and rehearsal spaces for the Juilliard School and dormitory space and apartments in the tower.

Eating near Lincoln Center

O'Neal's Baloon, (restaurant), 48 W. 63rd St. at Columbus Ave.

This pub *cum* enclosed sidewalk café was to have been called O'Neal's Saloon. But saloons are a holdover **temperance union no-no;** hence, Baloon—the story goes—which meant changing only one letter in the sign. Draws a big crowd at performance times.

Fiorello's (restaurant), 1900 Broadway, bet. W. 63rd and W. 64th Sts. Charles Morris Mount, Inc., designer.

Looking for an off-the-beaten-track candlelit Italian trattoria with checkered tablecloths? This isn't it. It's on Lincoln Center's doorstep, brightly lit, well designed, and good for a quick Italian meal. A sidewalk café operates in warm weather.

Columbus Avenue north of Lincoln Square also has many places to eat, snack, and nosh.

[L 6.] Dante Park, W. 63rd to W. 64th Sts., bet. Broadway and Columbus Ave. *Dante,* 1920, Ettore Ximenes, sculptor.

Here Dante holds the **Commedia,** a hard act for all of Lincoln Center's halls to follow.

[L 6a.] Originally **Liberty Warehouse,** 43 W. 64th St., bet. Central Park W. and Columbus Ave.

A 55-foot replica of the **Statue of Liberty** has **crowned the storage warehouse** of the same name since 1902—she lost the torch in a windstorm long ago. The ground floor of the warehouse (and a mezzanine) have, as a result of Lincoln Center, seen some successful **adaptive reuse** as a chic restaurant annexed to the Ginger Man Café.

[L 6b.] Maestro Café, 58 W. 65th St., bet. Central Park W. and Broadway. 1982. Grandberg/Marek.

An elegant place to drink or dine before a concert at Lincoln Center down the block. **High style.**

[L 6c.] West Side YMCA, 5 West 63rd St., bet. Central Park W. and Broadway. 1930. Dwight J. Baum. Adjacent **apartment tower,** 1989, Beyer Blinder Belle.

A center of cultural athletics, this **Y** is one of two remnants from a time when young urban immigrants were merely housed in Christian or Hebrew hostels (the other is the **YMHA** at East 92nd Street). Here and there housing still exists, but the **Ys** are known more for their cultural and athletic possibilities than their service as caravansaries.

The **West Side Y** is a neo-Romanesque pile, in limestone and brick, complete with **machicolations, arched corbel tables,** and other medieval encrustations.

[L 6d.] ASCAP Building (mixed use), 1 Lincoln Plaza, bet. W. 63rd and W. 64th Sts., E side of Broadway. a.k.a. 20 W. 64th St. 1971. Philip Birnbaum.

Another **behemoth** from the Lincoln Center syndrome. To pay for this vast sector of 1960s urban renewal, one must seat the densest population of New York at culture's flanks. **ASCAP,** the noted **American Society of Composers, Authors and Publishers,** is housed at the base in this geographically appropriate place, **but** the overwhelming skewed prism has no redeeming social significance. The public arcade only allowed it to be bigger—what an urbanistic mistake!

[L 7.] Mormon Visitors' Center, a.k.a. **Church of Jesus Christ of Latter-day Saints,** 2 Lincoln Sq., Columbus Ave. bet. W. 65th and W. 66th Sts. E side. 1975. Schuman, Lichtenstein & Claman.

Another **vapid behemoth** houses this proselytizing passion. Within, the **Mormons** convert the heathen in an appropriately Broadway fashion.

[L 7a.] Bank Leumi branch/originally **Bankers Trust Company branch,** 1960 Broadway, NE cor. W. 66th St. to Columbus Ave. 1963. Oppenheimer, Brady & Lehrecke.

A neat and tautly detailed bank in the spirit of Mies van der Rohe. Unfortunately, black anodized aluminum fails to fulfill the lusty spirit of painted steel. It seems a charade.

American Broadcasting Company

[L 7b.] Originally **First Battery Armory, N. Y. National Guard**/then **102nd Medical Battalion Armory**/now **American Broadcasting Company (television studios),** 56 W. 66th St., bet. Central Park W. and

Columbus Ave. 1901. Horgan & Slattery. Altered, 1978, Kohn Peder-son Fox Assocs.

Lots of **stylistic bravado** here but only **in the front ranks** (as a sidelong glance from the east will reveal). The reserves are utilitarian and dull (never having been meant to be seen), in contrast with the **elegantly attired architectural forces** leading the march. The fun-filled facade might as well be one of those intricate European cardboard scale models. Nevertheless, a delight!

[L 7c.] American Broadcasting Company (television studios), 47 W. 66th St., bet. Central Park W. and Columbus Ave. 1985. Kohn Pedersen Fox Assocs.

Stacked studios, each at a 2-story scale. The entry is mono-chromatic **Post Modern,** has somewhat heavy-handed detail.

[L 7d.] Capital Cities/ABC Incorporated headquarters, 55 W. 66th St., bet. Central Park W. and Columbus Aves. 1988. Kohn Pedersen Fox Assocs.

The corporate headquarters, at 23 stories, is mature Post Modern, but most important—especially to its shadowed neighbors to the north—is the arrogance of the midblock tower's height and bulk.

[L 8a.] WABC Channel 7 Building, 149-155 Columbus Ave., SE cor. W. 67th St. 1981. Kohn Pedersen Fox Assocs.

The Channel 7 studios are a remarkably fresh and direct complex, rich in their counterpoint of glass and brick, and without any trite mannerisms. Hooray!

[L 7b.] Orig. 1st Battery Armory   [L 7c.] Amer. Broadcasting Co. Studios

[L 8b.] 45 West 67th Street (apartments), NE cor. Columbus Ave. 1983. Buck/Cane, design architects. Schuman, Lichtenstein, Claman & Efron, architects.

A 31-story residential tower that rises from a limestone-clad base recalling Classical motifs.

[L 9.] Abraham Goodman House/Merkin Concert Hall, 129 W. 67th St., bet. Broadway and Amsterdam Ave. 1978. Johansen & Bhavnani.

A **constructivist** histrionic facade redolent of Soviet architecture of the early 1930s. Its **intricate convolutions** are not, unfortunately, **wearing well** in the New York climate.

[L 10.] The Copley (apartments), 2000 Broadway, NE cor. W. 68th St. 1987. Davis, Brody & Assocs.

A sleek, smooth, modest, understated, rounded tower among the mess of Broadway. One of the best new buildings on the old **Boulevard.**

[L 10a.] 1991 Broadway, (apartments), bet. W. 68th and W. 69th Sts. W side. 1986. John Harding.

Public space, officially given to the street, has been usurped here by a café that flaunts its wares. Zoning **freebies** required the space to be free and accessible but produced instead a further opportunity to hawk empty condos.

[L 10b.] Hotel Embassy/originally **The Ormonde,** 154 W. 70th St., SE cor. Broadway. 1900. Robert Maynicke.

A soldier in the battle of Broadway, bringing substance and scale to the boulevard. This bland brick and limestone blockfront shares space with the former Hotel Seminole to the south, a pair of modest urban twins that match the understated streetscape of Park Avenue.

[L 9.] The Abraham Goodman House

[L 10.] The sleek, smooth Copley apts.

[L 11a.] Levana Restaurant, 141 W. 69th St., bet. Columbus Ave. and Broadway. 1981. Rodolfo Imas.

Triangulated green slate piers articulate this simple modern facade; **New American** and **Continental** cuisine is served behind it.

[L 11b.] Christ and St. Stephen's Church (Episcopal)/formerly **St. Stephen's Church**/originally **Chapel of the Transfiguration,** 120 W. 69th St., bet. Columbus Ave. and Broadway. 1880. William H. Day. Altered, 1897.

Predating the Dakota and therefore left over from when the West Side was among the city's **great open spaces.** Its green front yard is **a small-scale oasis** in this dense precinct. It began as a chapel for the Church of the Transfiguration on East 29th Street.

Eating on Columbus: Columbus Avenue and its surroundings have attracted a wide variety of restaurants, mostly expensive, since gentrification began in the 1970s. Among those with panache, a bit of style, and imaginative food are: Lenge at **No. 202** and **Rikyu** at **No. 210,** favorite Japanese restaurants of sushi aficionados. **Victor's (Cuban)** at **No. 240.** The bas-, or not-so-bas, relief is extravagant. **Ruppert's** at **No. 269. Indian Oven** at **No. 285,** where the **Tandoori** is wondrous. **Dobson's** at **No. 341. Museum Café** at **No. 366,** an early outpost.

[L 12.] Originally **Pythian Temple**/now **Pythian Condominium,** 135 W. 70th St., bet. Columbus Ave. and Broadway. 1927. Thomas W. Lamb. Renovated, 1986, David Gura.

Hollywood may have had its Grauman's Chinese, but New York has its Pythian Temple! Hidden on an anonymous side street, this **opium-smoker's dream** is best seen from across the street—or better still, from someone's upper-floor apartment to the south.

[L 13.] Lincoln Square Synagogue, 200 Amsterdam Ave., NW cor. W. 69th St. 1970. Hausman & Rosenberg.

The theaters of nearby Lincoln Center set the travertine tone for the area, and this mannered, curvy, articulated synagogue picks up the cue. The travertine bank to the north actually came first, but the two together seem to be making an **inadvertent comment** about money changers at the temple.

Lincoln Center: see map p. 288   **295**

[L 14.] Public School 199, Manhattan, 270 W. 70th St., bet. Amsterdam and West End Aves. 1963. Edward Durell Stone & Assocs.

Notable mostly as an **early example** of an urban public school designed by a prominent architect. It was built in connection with the **red brick megaslabs** of the 2,000-odd-unit Lincoln Towers urban renewal project around it.

The back lot: Exterior scenes in Hollywood productions are often filmed in studio back lots, expansive outdoor spaces in which mock-ups of the necessary scenery are concocted at considerable expense. For the filming of *West Side Story,* what better (and cheaper) substitute for Hollywood artifice than the real thing? The vacating of the Lincoln Square Urban Renewal Area in the late 1950s provided just such an opportunity for its tenements to have their day on film before they came crashing down.

[L 15.] Gladys and Roland Harriman Building, American Red Cross, 150 Amsterdam Ave., bet. W. 66th and W. 67th Sts. W side. 1964. Skidmore, Owings & Merrill.

A temple built with a firm but perhaps **naive commitment** to the **less is more** principle. Surveying traffic-choked Amsterdam Avenue, its low podium is hardly an acropolis.

[L 16.] Martin Luther King, Jr., High School, 122 Amsterdam Ave., bet. W. 65th and W. 66th Sts. W side. 1975. Frost Assocs., architects. William Tarr, sculptor.

A glass box of enormous size and scale sits proudly on the busy avenue. A **self-weathering steel,** Mayari R, was employed in both the school's carefully detailed curtain wall and in the **boldly fashioned memorial sculpture** to the slain civil rights leader that towers over the sidewalk.

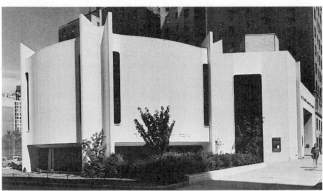

[L 13.] The creamy, curvy, articulated, travertine-clad Lincoln Square Synagogue

[L 16a.] American Broadcasting Company Studios 23/24, 320 W. 66th St., W of West End Ave. opp. Freedom Place. 1984. Kohn Pedersen Fox Assocs.

A magnificent brick box, made largely opaque to serve the needs of media production, and then enlivened with ebullient brick ornamentation (reminiscent of the work of Modernist Dutch architects) to satisfy its urbanistic responsibilities.

The full impact of this structure's bold silhouette is best achieved from the west, from the West Side elevated viaduct, from ships on the Hudson River, and from the heights of Jersey.

From both far and near, it is a gem.

[L 17.] Fiorello H. LaGuardia High School, 108 Amsterdam Ave., bet. W. 64th and W. 65th Sts. W side. 1985. Eduardo Catalano.

A strongly articulated, poured-in-place concrete building typical of the best of **1960s** construction. The cost of achieving such quality in New York soon became prohibitive, and architects switched to mostly brick and metal assemblies. This exception resulted from the halt of all school construction during the City's financial crisis and completion of the original plans many years later.

Trump City: Stretching inland from the Hudson River shore between 59th and 72nd Streets and fostering the slums that gave rise to Lincoln Center's redevelopment plan was the former freight yard of the New York Central Railroad (and of the Hudson River Rail Road before that), a dead-flat expanse worthy of Chicago. The noisy, dusty scene included thousands of freight cars shunted day and night along scores of parallel ladder tracks, some leading to a waterfront grain elevator, others to wharves projecting diagonally into the river—like half chevrons—accomodating the ships and barges that helped interchange freight all over the waters of the Port of New York. It even has a locomotive roundhouse and turntable. The fallow site, long abandoned by the railroad but traversed by the elevated West Side Highway viaduct, continues to separate the precinct from its nearby Hudson River shoreline. Since the railroad activities began to wind down in the 1950s the 76-acre waterfront site had been the subject of a number of ill-fated redevelopment proposals [see Necrology] until purchased for $95 million in 1983 by Donald J. Trump, heir to the Brooklyn residential development fortune accumulated by his father and grandfather. It is on these idle acres that young Trump proposed to erect a 150-story tower—the world's tallest—again worthy of Chicago, as well as 7,600 units of housing and a major shopping development, using the skills of a Chicago architect, Helmut Jahn. Trump's dream of a relocated NBC media empire (and its attendant city subsidies) evaporated in 1987, as did Jahn. Alexander Cooper & Assocs. then took on the challenge, which includes negotiating with a feisty Upper West Side community that just loves to fight.

[L 18a.] Amsterdam Houses Addition, N.Y.C. Housing Authority, 240 W. 65th St., bet. Amsterdam and West End Aves. 1974. Oppenheimer, Brady & Lehrecke.

Change does not come easily. Overly self-conscious concern for design, to achieve a break with the dead public-housing hand of the past, can be forgiven in this structure. Its designers' **expressionistic use of angles** and exposed concrete **gives character** (and triangular bay windows) to the project.

[L 12.] Originally the Pythian Temple   **[L 16.]** Martin Luther King, Jr., H.S.

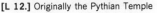

[L 18b.] Lincoln-Amsterdam House (apartments), 110 West End Ave., bet. W. 64th and W. 65th Sts. E side. 1976. David Todd & Assocs.

Multistory housing is treated here almost as **heroic,** nonrepresentational **sculpture in the round.** The arrangement of apartments ensures different plastic qualities for each facade within a strong, unified composition of cast concrete and large orange brick. The **views across the Hudson** understandably draw out the richest qualities in the design, the west facade.

[L 19.] Former **Phipps Houses (apartments),** 235, 239, 243, 247 W. 63rd St., E of West End Ave. (cul-de-sac). 1907. 236, 240, 244, 248 W. 64th St., bet. Amsterdam and West End Aves. 1911. Both by Whitfield & King.

Slum clearance efforts west of Lincoln Center made a thorough sweep between the late 1940s (Amsterdam Houses) and the urban renewal projects of the 1960s. The only residential buildings which remain from the early 20th century are these, billed as **model tenement houses** by Henry Phipps's pioneering housing society. They offer **little as urban design,** but their interior planning was **an esteemed prototype** for efforts to improve working-class housing.

RIVERSIDE DRIVE/WEST END AVENUE

Terrain that slopes steeply west to the banks of the river, **a roller coaster** of north-south gradients, **the water level route** of the smoke-belching New York Central and Hudson River Railroad, and the Palisades **across the flowing Hudson River** currents—such contrasts made the planning of "the Riverside Park and Avenue" **a powerful challenge** to landscape architect Frederick Law Olmsted. Between 1873 and 1910 Olmsted, and his associates and successors, developed **a great green waterside edge** for the West Side, as he and Calvert Vaux had earlier created "the Central Park" on the inland site. The style was in the tradition of English landscape architecture: **naturalistic and picturesque.** Development along Riverside Drive (and **straight as an arrow** West End Avenue behind it) resulted **from the magnetism** of this great urban design.

In the 1930s the Henry Hudson Parkway Authority, using WPA funds, added a four-lane highway to the park area (since expanded to six) and a host of recreational amenities—essentially the **amalgam of asphalt and greenery** we see today. This change accomplished two other important results: it **covered** the freight line, and it **built** the highway in part on landfill.

[R 1a.] Originally **Frederick C. Prentiss residence,** 1 Riverside Dr., NE cor. W. 72nd St. 1901. C. P. H. Gilbert. **[R 1b.]** Originally **John S. Sutphen, Jr. residence** 311 West 72nd St., bet. West End Ave. and Riverside Dr. 1902. C. P. H. Gilbert.

Two **self-satisfied** town houses that herald the start of Riverside Drive's limestone lane.

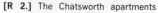

[R 2.] The Chatsworth apartments   **[R 6.]** Some Clarence F. True houses

[R 2.] The Chatsworth (apartments), 344 W. 72nd St., SE cor. Henry Hudson Pkwy. and 353 W. 71st St., W end of W. 71st St. 1904. ★ **Annex,** 340 W. 72nd St. 1906. Both by John E. Scharsmith. ★

The Chatsworth is actually **3 towers.** The **2 main buildings** are on West 72nd and West 71st Streets, gracious russet-colored brick apartment blocks embellished with lavish limestone trim. **The annex to the** east on West 72nd is lower and all limestone. The main towers are in the West Side tradition of the Kenilworth and Rossleigh Court/Orwell House.

[R 3.] Originally **Spencer Aldrich residence,** 271 W. 72nd St., NE cor. West End Ave. 1897. Gilbert A. Schellenger. Altered.

The mercantile uses to which the lower floors have **thoughtlessly been converted** serve only to point up the richness of what remains: the sprightly forms of the upper floors and roof.

Schwab House: A rare Gallic composition of pinnacles, spires, chimneys, and steeply sloping roofs once embellished the Drive's skyline between West 73rd and West 74th Streets. Consciously seeking to bring the joys of the French château to the banks of the Hudson, architect Maurice Hebert adapted the facades of three—Blois, Chenonceaux, and Azay-le-Rideau—to the needs of Charles M. Schwab, Andrew Carnegie's associate. The enormous Schwab residence was not only freestanding, but it occupied, with its surrounding gardens, an entire city block (it had formerly been the New York Orphan Asylum). Schwab could afford it since he was reputed to earn, in the days before income taxes, an annual salary of $1 million. Unfortunately the mansion was not to survive New York's post-World War II building boom. Completed in 1906, it was demolished in 1948 and replaced by another Schwab House, this time a 16-story red brick human hive of a type more familiar to New Yorkers.

[R 4.] West End-Collegiate Historic District generally bet. Riverside Dr. and Broadway, W. 75th to W. 77th Sts., with irregular extensions. ★

A full palette of materials and styles, bow and bay windows, copper-clad cornices and dormers—rich and wonderful. Architects include **Clinton & Russell, C. P. H. Gilbert, Lamb & Rich, Neville & Bagge,** and the endless and marvelous houses of **Clarence F. True.**

[R 5.] Row houses, 301-305 W. 76th St., 341-357 West End Ave., W side, and 302-306 W. 77th St. 1891. Lamb & Rich. ☆

A varied and witty row which enlivens a whole blockfront of West End Avenue. Long may they reign. Eberhard Faber, the **pencil king,** lived at **No. 341.**

Clarence F. True

Lower Riverside Drive, as the earliest area opened to improvement, was **slated to be filled with flats,** according to an 1899 account by a local architect and land developer Clarence F. True. It was he, he stated, who recognized **the higher potential** of the area by **buying up** all available Driveside parcels below West 84th Street and **covering them** "with beautiful dwellings" of his own design. **Hardly typical** row houses (though built speculatively and employing party walls), **many** of these elegant mansion-residences **have survived.** They are highly idiosyncratic and readily identified as being in **the True style** (characterized at the time as Elizabethan Renaissance): ornate roof lines, crow-stepped gables, bay, bow, and three-quarter-round oriels, and so on. Most are concentrated in these groupings:

[R 6.] True houses: [R 6a.] ☆ 40-46 Riverside Drive, 337 W. 76th St., 334-338 W. 77th St. **[R 6b.]** ☆ 74-77 Riverside Drive, 320-326 W. 80th St. **[R 6c.]** ☆ 81-89 Riverside Drive, 307-323 W. 80th St., 316-320 W. 81st St. **[R 6d.]** ☆ 105-107 Riverside Drive, 332 W. 83rd St. All 1890s. All by Clarence F. True in two adjacent historic districts.

[R 7a.] West End Collegiate Church and School, West End Ave., NE cor. W. 77th St. 1893. Robert W. Gibson. ★

It's easy to understand the generous use of **Dutch stepped gables** on this church's facade, since the **roots** of the Reformed Church in America **lie in the Netherlands.** But don't draw hasty conclusions about the reintroduction of a style missing since the days of New Amsterdam. Here, along West End Avenue, McKim, Mead & White **had already built** such a Dutch-inspired house **as early as 1885** (demolished); another one predating the church (not by M, M & W) **still remains** at the northwest corner of West 78th Street.

Entered from the next block north is a new addition to the old school building:

[R 7b.] The Collegiate School (annex), 260 W. 78th St., bet. Broadway and West End Ave. 1968. Ballard, Todd & Assocs.

A highly disciplined facade that, because it faces north, rarely receives the sunlight necessary to show it off to best advantage. The student-designed mural that later **superimposed a sunrise** over the ground-floor limestone wall also fails to provide the needed light.

[R 7a.] The Dutch stepped-gabled West End Collegiate Church and School

[R 7c.] Row houses, 301-307 W. 78th St. and 383-389 West End Ave. 1886. Fredrick B. White.

Individualistic houses by an architect who died, shortly after their completion, at the untimely age of 24.

[R 8.] Riverside Park, Riverside Dr. to the Hudson River bet. W. 72nd and W. 153rd Sts. 1873–1910. Original design, Frederick Law Olmsted. New work, 1888. Calvert Vaux and Samuel Parsons, Jr. Completion, Frederick Law Olmsted, Jr. Reconstruction for Henry Hudson Parkway, 1937. Clinton F. Loyd. ★

To the endless relief of stifled West Siders, this green ribbon of hills and hollows, monuments, playgrounds, and sports facilities **fringes some 70 blocks** of winding Riverside Drive, all the while **covering the abandoned rail line** in a tunnel below. One of its most complex parts is the **three-level structure** at West 79th Street: traffic circle at the top; masonry arcade and pedestrian paths surrounding a splendid, circular, single-jet fountain at the middle level; and, at the bottom, parking space for frequenters of the **79th Street Boat Basin.**

[R 9a.] Riverside Drive–West 80th Street Historic District, Riverside Dr. to a line north-south midblock bet. Riverside Dr. and West End Ave., including the S side of W. 81st St. and both sides of W. 80th St. ★

A group of 32 row houses built between 1892 and 1899 by architects Charles H. Israels and Clarence F. True. For more on the True houses, see [R 6.]

[R 9b.] 411 West End Avenue (apartments), SW cor. W. 80th St. 1936. George F. Pelham II.

Art Deco with touches of Corbusier-inspired ships' railings on the balconies and terraces near the top. Note how "drapes" of ornament cascade from some of the parapets (in stainless steel) and over the entrance (in cut stone).

[R 9c.] 307-317 West 80th Street (row houses), bet. West End Ave. and Riverside Dr. ca. 1890.

Gothickesque—neither the Gothic Revival of earlier years nor the Collegiate Gothic of the 1920s—and **picturesque** too. Note the stained glass over the doors and windows (except for **No. 317,** which has also been painted). These houses are in handsome company on both sides of the street.

[R 10.] The Calhoun School Learning Center, 433 West End Ave., SW cor. W. 81st St. 1975. Costas Machlouzarides.

A modern-day Gulliver must have been here and left behind his giant-sized TV. And if one picture tube (along West End Avenue) isn't enough, another (along West 81st Street) has been provided **as a spare.** A more unsubtle and out-of-scale response to this urban design challenge is hard to imagine. Fortunately (in the warm weather months at least) maples provide **a green screen.**

[R 11.] 309-315 and **317-325 West 82nd Street (row houses),** bet. West End Ave. and Riverside Dr. ca. 1892.

Two groups of Roman brick plus brownstone-trimmed residences, **the first rich** in intricately formed roofs, dormers, chimney pots, finials, colonnettes; **the second more restrained** with handsome verdigris-colored cornices.

[R 12a.] The Red House apartments   **[R 7c.]** 307 West 78th St. row house

[R 12a.] The Red House (apartments), 350 W. 85th St., bet. West End Ave. and Riverside Dr. 1904. Harde & Short. ★

A romantic 6-story masterpiece. Note the **dragon and crown** cartouche set up high into the brickwork. These talented architects **also designed** the **Studio Building** on West 77th Street and the **Alwyn Court Apartments** on West 58th Street.

[R 12b.] 316-326 West 85th Street (row houses), bet. West End Ave. and Riverside Dr. ca. 1895. Clarence F. True.

This group of 6 was designed as a unit. The stoop railings are only **one voluptuous example** of fine stone carving **everywhere abundant.**

[R 12c.] 520 West End Avenue (apartments), NE cor. W. 85th St. 1892. Clarence F. True. ★

A rock-faced brick and brownstone many-gabled former town house. A **daring developer** proposed to hover an apartment structure on legs above it all (*1987. William Gleckman*); the bizarre thought met with thunderous opposition from the neighborhood.

[R 13a.] 530 West End Avenue (apartments), SE cor. W. 86th St. 1912. Mulliken & Moeller.

A representative West End Avenue example of the Renaissance palazzo adapted to high-rise living. **Fine masonry craftsmanship** in the early tradition.

[R 13b.] Church of St. Paul and St. Andrew (United Methodist)/ originally **Church of St. Paul (Methodist Episcopal),** 540 West End Ave., NE cor. W. 86th St. 1897. R. H. Robertson. ★

A startling work for the West Side—or for anywhere in the city for that matter. While other architects (including Robertson himself) were pursuing more or less faithful revival-style churches, this work is in the imaginative vein of the French neo-Classicist architects **Claude Nicolas Ledoux** or **Étienne Louis Boullée.** The octagonal corner tower is reminiscent of the fire tower which was once part of the **Jefferson Market.** St. Andrew's Church was on West 76th Street until 1937, when it merged with St. Paul's [see Broadway B 13b.]

[R 14a.] St. Ignatius Church (Episcopal), 552 West End Ave., SE cor. W. 87th St. 1902. Charles C. Haight. **Shrine** (inside), 1926. Cram & Ferguson.

One of Haight's less inspired works. Perhaps he decided that this site, adjacent to its already completed West 86th Street neighbor, demanded a piece of background architecture. Fortunately, these **churches and the remaining row houses** in the vicinity **combine** to keep West End Avenue from being **a monotonous apartment house canyon.**

[R 14b.] Cathedral Preparatory Seminary (Roman Catholic)/formerly **McCaddin-McQuick Memorial, Cathedral College**/originally **St. Agatha's School,** 555 West End Ave., SW cor. W. 87th St. 1908. Boring & Tilton.

Dignity personified in red brick and limestone by the architects of **Ellis Island** and the Brooklyn Heights (Tennis) **Casino.**

[R 14c.] 560 West End Avenue (town house), NE cor. W. 87th St. 1890. Joseph H. Taft.

This house once had **nine similar neighbors** to the north. These were among the many West Side projects of W. E. D. Stokes, developer of the Ansonia Hotel.

 [R 14d.] 565 West End Avenue (apartments), NW cor. W. 87th St. 1937. H. I. Feldman.

The **vocabulary** of the neo-Renaissance **expressed in Art Deco terms:** brick replaces stone; corner windows substitute for quoins; dark banded brick around the base is the translation of the shadows which a rusticated plinth would have cast. And as for the pediment at the entrance, its 1930's stand-in is a small, streamlined, stainless steel cornice. The canvas and pipe canopy in this apartment, as in too many others, is a practical but unrelated afterthought.

[R 14e.] 562 West End Avenue (apartments), bet. W. 87th and W. 88th Sts. E side. 1913. Walter Haefeli.

An effective use (or reuse) of Doric columns to flank the entrance.

 [R 15.] The Normandy (apartments), 140 Riverside Drive, NE cor. W. 86th St. 1939. Emery Roth. ★

A sleek Art Moderne streamlined cornering of this prominent 86th Street intersection. Its **sensuous curves** and prominent horizontal fluting at the base are notable.

[R 16a.] Congregation B'nai Jeshurun, 257 W. 88th St., bet. Broadway and West End Ave. 1918. Henry B. Herts and Walter Schneider. **[R 16b.] Community Center,** 270 W. 89th St. 1928. Henry B. Herts. Louis Allan Abramson, associate.

The synagogue's facade is **a Moorish fantasy** from the waning days of an era when important Jewish houses of worship were designed in an exotic Byzantine/Romanesque mode. The community center one block north is considerably more restrained.

[R 17a.] Yeshiva Chofetz Chaim/originally **Isaac L. Rice residence, "Villa Julia"**/then **Solomon Schinasi residence,** 346 W. 89th St., SE cor. Riverside Drive. 1901. Herts & Tallant. Additions and alterations, 1906–1948. ★

Though the Drive was once lined with **freestanding mansions,** only this maroon brick villa and one other survive. Isaac L. Rice, a successful **industrial pioneer** in the field of electric storage batteries commissioned this residence and named it Villa Julia **for his wife,** the prescient founder of the **Society for the Suppression of Unnecessary Noise.** In 1907 the building was sold to **Solomon Schinasi,** a member of the well-known **cigarette manufacturing firm** of Schinasi Brothers. That same year Schinasi's brother, Morris, was awaiting completion of *his* freestanding mansion on the Drive, at West 107th Street. Curiously **it is these two** Schinasi mansions **that survive** [see R 24a.]

[R 17b.] Soldiers' and Sailors' Monument, in Riverside Park, Riverside Dr. at W. 89th St. 1902. Stoughton & Stoughton, Paul E. M. Duboy. ★

A marble monument to the Civil War dead modeled on the **choragic monument of Lysicrates** (335 B.C.) in Athens (a favorite question on history of architecture quizzes). Duboy was the architect of that other West Side monument, the Ansonia Hotel.

[R 13b.] Ch. of SS. Paul & Andrew   **[R 17b.]** Soldiers'/Sailors' Monument

 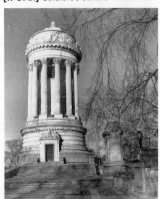

[R 18.] The Joan of Arc Statue: the "Maid of Orleans," advancing in full armor

[R 18.] Joan of Arc Statue, in Joan of Arc Park, Riverside Dr. at W. 93rd St. 1915. Anna Vaughn Hyatt Huntington, sculptor. John V. Van Pelt, architect.

The Maid of Orleans **in full armor** stands in her marching steed's stirrups, looking heavenward **with sword held high.** The bronze equestrian sculpture sits atop a granite pedestal containing **stones from**

Rheims Cathedral and from the old tower at Rouen in which Joan was imprisoned and tried. The 1.6 acre space straddled by the Drive is officially Joan of Arc Park.

No doubt this statue and its park influenced the naming of the junior high school built a quarter of a century later, to the east.

 [R 19.] Cliff Dwellers' Apartments, 243 Riverside Dr., NE cor. W. 96th St. 1914. Herman Lee Meader.

An **odd building** predating the **Art Deco interest in Mayan motifs.** It is known primarily for the **naturalistic frieze** of mountain lions, rattlesnakes, and buffalo skulls. They symbolize the life of the Arizona cliff dwellers and serve to tie these prehistoric people to **Manhattan's modern cliff dwellers.** All in all, **an underrated facade.**

Woodman, Spare That Tree: In 1837 an old elm on the property of the Stryker's Bay Mansion—which then stood on a hill northeast of the 96th Street viaduct—was to be cut down. George Pope Morris, journalist and poet (1802–1864), was inspired to pen the poetic exhortation which saved the tree.

[R 20a.] Carrère Memorial, Riverside Park at W. 99th St. 1916. Thomas Hastings.

A small granite-balustered terrace at a lower level of the park entrance contains a graffitied, **barely noticeable** memorial tablet to one of New York's **great architects:** John Merven Carrère (of Carrère & Hastings), killed in an automobile accident in 1911.

[R 20b.] Firemen's Memorial, Riverside Dr. at W. 100th St. 1913. Attilio Piccirilli, sculptor. H. Van Buren Magonigle, architect.

Courage and *Duty* guard this large pink marble monument to SOLDIERS IN A WAR THAT NEVER ENDS. Embedded in the plaza is a bronze tablet to the firehorses who also served in that "war."

[R 21a.] 838 West End Avenue (apartments), SE cor. W. 101st St. 1914. George & Edward Blum.

Intricate vinelike forms make large terra-cotta tiles into damask, thus embellishing this building and recalling a **Sullivanesque** approach to ornament.

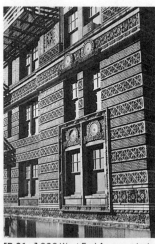 

[R 21a.] 838 West End Ave. apartmts.   **[R 22.]** Master Apartments, 103rd St.

[R 21b.] Originally **William Ditmars residence,** 294 Riverside Drive., bet. W. 101st and W. 102nd Sts. 1901. Schickel & Ditmars.

Beaux Arts limestone mansion with a remarkable **Art Nouveau** window guard at the first floor.

 [R22.] Master Apartments/formerly **Master Institute of United Arts and Riverside Museum/**formerly **Roerich Museum,** 310 Riverside Dr., NE cor. W. 103rd St. 1929. Helmle, Corbett & Harrison and Sugarman & Berger.

Built to house a school, museum, auditorium, and restaurant in a residential hotel. Artist **Nicholas Roerich,** whose museum [see R 23d.] was once located within the building seems to have been responsible for the idea of **shading the building's brickwork** from a purpled base to a pale yellow top. Wind-borne soot has all but eradicated the color change, but a similar color palette is still visible elsewhere on the West Side [see Central Park West C 4c.].

[R 23.] Riverside-West 105th Street Historic District, generally along Riverside Dr. bet. W. 105th and W. 106th Sts., plus some of both sides of W. 105th St. bet. West End Ave. and Riverside Dr. ★

Paris o'er the Hudson. Enjoying a magnificent setting overlooking the city's great river is this **enclave** of French Beaux Arts town houses. Executed between 1899 and 1902, they were designed by Janes & Leo, Mowbray & Uffinger, Hoppin & Koen, and Robert D. Kohn. Of special interest is:

[R 23a.] River Mansion, 330 Riverside Dr., NE cor. W. 105th St., 1902. Janes & Leo. ☆

A Beaux Arts corner house enjoying a fine view of both river and drive.

[R 23b.] New York Buddhist Church and American Buddhist Academy, 331-332 Riverside Dr., bet. W. 105th and W. 106th Sts. **No. 331,** formerly **Marion Davies residence,** 1902. Janes & Leo. **No. 332,** 1963. Kelly & Gruzen. Included within the historic district. ☆

The heroic-size bronze statue of **Shinran-Shonin** (1173–1262), founder of a Buddhist sect, became a **local** landmark before the City designated it an **official** landmark. A church and social center occupy the two buildings.

[R 23c.] Statue of Franz Sigel, Riverside Dr. at W. 106th St. 1907. Karl Bitter, sculptor. W. Welles Bosworth, architect of base.

A placid equestrian statute of a commander of the Union Army during the Civil War. In the **iconography of equestrian sculpture** the steed's four legs touching terra firma mean the hero died a peaceful death: in the case of Sigel (1824–1902) he resigned his military commission in 1865 and then published and edited a German-language newspaper.

[R 23d.] Nicholas Roerich Museum, 319 W. 107th St., bet. Riverside Dr. and Broadway. 1898. Clarence F. True.

Permanent collection of the work of Nicholas Roerich, prolific artist, designer, explorer, philosopher, and collaborator of Stravinsky and Diaghilev. Architectural landmarks of his native Russia were the subjects of many of Roerich's early paintings, and he contributed to the design of 310 Riverside Drive.

[R 24a.] The Children's Mansion (school)/originally **Morris Schinasi residence,** 351 Riverside Dr., NE cor. W. 107th St. 1909. William B. Tuthill. ★

A marble freestanding château by **the architect of Carnegie Hall.** A Schinasi also owned the other remaining freestanding mansion on the Drive [see R 17a.].

[R 24b.] Assumptionist Provincial House/formerly **America Press Building,** 329 W. 108th St., bet. Broadway and Riverside Dr. ca. 1900. Thomas Graham. Altered, 1902, Horgan & Slattery.

Actually 2 double-width row houses joined to form an internally interlocked residence for a Roman Catholic order. **Spiffy from bottom to top:** ornate limestone carving, a fine cool-red brick, and verdigris copper detail. The dormers of the mansard roof have been replaced by an incongruous **hat.**

BROADWAY AND ENVIRONS

From 70th Street to Cathedral Parkway (110th Street)

Broadway's route in this area dates from the laying out in 1703 of the **Bloomingdale Road.** The road initially measured only about 33 feet across, but as its popularity increased, so did its width. By 1868 it was

150 feet wide, its course was being straightened between 59th and 155th Streets, and it was renamed **The Boulevard.** In 1899 it was given the name **Broadway.**

Tucked into a modest side-street brownstone is a northern outpost of Greenwich Village from another era. **Café La Fortuna** at 69 West 71st Street offers the ambience (and coffee) from a time when coffeehouses were centers of intellectual and social life. Social, one suspects, is the dominant factor today.

[B 1a.] The Dorilton (apartments), 171 W. 71st St., NE cor. Broadway. 1900. Janes & Leo. ★

If you are walking uptown along Broadway this robust mansarded Beaux Arts masterpiece **will begin to prepare you** for the even greater Ansonia a few blocks north: here a **cornice-copia.** *Look up at the frolicking freestanding amazons.*

[B 1b.] Blessed Sacrament Church (Roman Catholic), 150 W. 71st St., bet. Columbus Ave. and Broadway. 1921. Gustave Steinback.

The facades of sanctuary and rectory are brilliantly modeled to exploit this **difficult midblock site** into which the church **has been squeezed.** Though the stonework is **not heavily tooled,** the **vigorous interplay** of volume, void, and silhouette is just enough for the **shallow viewing space** of a typically narrow 60 foot-wide side street. The rose window is in striking reds and blues. See Steinback's other churches, too.

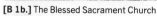
[B 1b.] The Blessed Sacrament Church   **[B 2b.]** Orig. The Godmothers League

[B 2a.] Originally **Christ Church Rectory,** 213 W. 71st. St., bet. Broadway and West End Ave.

A handsome remembrance of the church that **was** next door.

[B 2b.] Originally **The Godmothers League/**now **The Children's Day Treatment Center and School,** 255 W. 71st St., bet. Amsterdam and West End Aves. 1950. Sylvan Bien.

Architects had come to realize that the **International Style was victor** in the post-World War II **battle of styles** but for some it was difficult to adjust to that new vision. This modest work **reflects the struggle.** The Godmothers League began in 1918 as an agency helping to serve the children of doughboys and working mothers; today its efforts are directed to the needs of emotionally disturbed children with learning problems. A pleasant indentation in the block.

[B 3a.] 274, 276 West 71st Street (row houses), bet. Amsterdam and West End Aves. ca. 1890.

Shades of Philadelphia architect **Frank Furness's excesses** are visible in the window projected over the entrance of this **Queen Anne maverick.**

[B 3b.] Originally **Forrest Lawther residence**/later **Abraham Erlanger residence,** 232 West End Ave., bet. W. 70th and W. 71st Sts. E side. 1887. E. L. Angell. Altered for Erlanger, 1904, Herts & Tallant.

A robust Beaux Arts facade glued to an earlier structure at the behest of Broadway producer Erlanger.

The lack of a projecting stoop on West End Avenue's narrow sidewalk failed, in this unusual case, to cheat the residents of the **ceremony of ascending** its steps to wave a parting greeting. The alteration is **stylistically reminiscent** of the architects' Aguilar Branch Library.

Let them eat cake: Named for the family who settled it, the hamlet of Harsenville was one of several strung along what is now upper Broadway. Its rustic charm attracted a number of French émigrés fleeing their revolution's Reign of Terror. The statesman Charles Maurice de Talleyrand-Périgord sought refuge here in 1795 while heads rolled at home, and the duc d'Orléans—later to become King Louis Philippe—came here two years later. While on an extended visit he toured much of the newborn republic from Maine to Louisiana, supplementing his meager financial resources by teaching French at the Somerindijk farmhouse, located at what is now the northwest corner of Broadway and West 75th Street. Does his ghost hover nearby, savoring the croissants, brioches, and other *patisseries françaises* purveyed by Beaudésir, the site's present occupant? *Allons, enfants . . .*

[B 4a.] **72nd Street IRT subway entrance,** Broadway and Amsterdam Ave. S of W. 72nd St. 1904. Heins & La Farge. ★

While their black-painted cast-iron and glass **subway kiosks are all gone,** although **one** has been **revived** at Astor Place, this and a few **other masonry structures** by these architects **still remain.** Clearly the number of subway riders who use this entrance today exceeds its designers' modest expectations. Development rights for the vast train yards to the west will include the total rebuilding of this station.

[B 3b.] 232 West End Ave. residence   **[B 4a.]** 72nd Street IRT entry in 1907

[B 4b.] **Verdi Square,** Broadway, Amsterdam Ave., and W. 73rd St. 1906. *Giuseppe Verdi,* Pasquale Civiletti, sculptor. Scenic landmark. ★

This small green honors the great Italian composer. At the base of the marble statue are **life-size figures** of characters from Verdi's *Aïda, Falstaff, Otello,* and *La Forza del Destino.*

Full Stomach, Light Feet, and Entertainment:

Gray's papaya: a local landmark famed for its **50 cent** hot dogs. Here the mustard is **Dijon** (Gulden's out of gallon containers). Wash it down with a glass of papaya juice, piña colada, or fresh squeezed oranges. It's all good and based on quality served in great volume.

Around the corner, wedged into the shell of the old 72nd Street **Automat** (*1931. F. P. Platt & Bros.*), are **Popeye's** fast food and the **Athlete's Foot,** looking a bit uncomfortable in that **Art Moderne** not-so-fancy dress.

The **Eclair Restaurant** (141 West 72nd St.) brought Viennese pastry and schnitzel to the Jewish expatriates who flooded these West Side streets before and after World War II. Today it serves patrons of many persuasions.

And for movies try the venerable **Embassy Cinema** on Broadway just north of 72nd Street: always a pair (in separate screening rooms) of first-run foreign films. Newsreels were once screened here, until television made *The March of Time* a journalistic dinosaur.

 [B 5a.] Originally **Park & Tilford Building (offices),** 100 W. 72nd St., SW cor. Columbus Ave. 1892. McKim, Mead & White.

An MM&W rusticated limestone and brick background building, not very noticeable but a nice neighbor. Next door, to the west, is a humdinger:

[B 5b.] Originally **Hotel Hargrave,** 110 W. 72nd St., bet. Columbus Ave. and Broadway. 1907. Frederick C. Browne.

Belle Epoque bay windows give a rich modulation to this rusticated limestone and brick facade. Atop it all is a double-dormered mansard roof. All of it is redolent of Paris, except its inflated height. In Paris, mansards and all, it would never total more than 8 floors. Here there are 12.

[B 5c.] Originally **The Earlton (studios),** 118 W. 72nd St., bet. Columbus and Amsterdam Aves. 1915. Buchman & Fox.

One of several white glazed terra-cotta studio buildings, tall and on narrow lots (the space of one former town house), these were developed by builder **Edward West Browning,** whose **initials** are entwined in the facade above the second floor.

Mr. Browning is remembered more for his social life than his contribution to architecture. A wealthy real estate man, he advertised in the *Herald Tribune* in 1925 to adopt a "pretty, refined fourteen-year-old." His subsequent trials and tribulations with the winner, 15-year-old Frances (**"Peaches"**) Heenan, made headlines for months.

[B 6a.] **126 West 73rd Street (studios),** bet. Columbus and Amsterdam Aves. 1915. Buchman & Fox.

Déjà vu? No, this is **another** of those slender white West Side ghosts, as in [B 5c.] above.

[B 6b.] **Sherman Square Studios,** 160 W. 73rd St., bet. Columbus and Amsterdam Aves. 1929. Tillion & Tillion.

Casement-windowed apartments specially soundproofed for professional musicians, long before Lincoln Center became a neighbor. Though weathered by time, the architects' names can be found **on the cornerstone** to the west. Neo-Gothic brick and sandstone.

 [B 7.] **Apple Bank for Savings**/originally **Central Savings Bank,** 2100 Broadway, NE cor. 73rd St. 1928. York & Sawyer, architects. Decorative ironwork, Samuel Yellin Studio. ★ Interior. ★

Founded in 1859 as the German Savings Bank in the City of New York, a name dispensed with during the anti-German period of World War I. The original bank's board members **chose the architects of the Federal Reserve Bank** to create its new West Side office. The **miniature Federal Reserve** that resulted is one of the West Side's **noblest and most imposing** edifices.

[B 8a.] **Ansonia Hotel,** 2109 Broadway, bet. W. 73rd and W. 74th Sts. W side. 1904. Graves & Duboy. ★

In the words of the Landmarks Preservation Commission, the Ansonia's effect is one of **"joyous exuberance profiled against the sky."** The collaboration between a demanding developer, **W. E. D. Stokes**—he was descended from **Phelps Dodge** on his paternal side and **Ansonia Brass & Copper** on his maternal—and an architect steeped in the forms of Parisian apartment buildings, Paul E. M. Duboy, seems to have had

a magic result. The Ansonia is one of New York's architectural gems. Judging from the "guest list" of this apartment hotel, **a galaxy of important figures** thought so too: Arturo Toscanini, Lily Pons, Florenz Ziegfeld, Theodore Dreiser, Sol Hurok, and Igor Stravinsky, to name but a few.

[B 8b.] Originally **The Level Club (of the Masonic order)**/then **Hotel Riverside Plaza**/now **condominium apartments,** 253 W. 73rd St., bet. Broadway and West End Ave. 1926. Clinton & Russell.

This neo-Romanesque verging upon Art Deco facade retains the **secret signs and symbols** required by the original client, a **Masonic** organization. Savor the **Composite columns** with bronze filigreed globes atop.

[B 7.] Central Savings Bank, in 1967   **[B 8a.]** 1904 Ansonia Hotel, in 1967

[B 9a.] 161-169 **West 74th Street** and 301-309 **Amsterdam Avenue,** NE cor. W. 74th St. 1886. Lamb & Rich.

Early West Side row housing which, happily restored at the corner, conveys a clear sense of the area's initial development. **No. 161** has been **least touched** by change.

[B 9b.] 153, 155, 157, 159 **West 74th Street,** bet. Columbus and Amsterdam Aves. 1887. James Brown Lord.

More early development. **No. 153** has been **surgically separated** from its **Siamese twin**—note the half remainder of its foliate cartouche. **No. 159** winds up, after alteration, with two stoops: the original used as a planting bed, and a new one which makes **a floral semicircle** out of the original wall ornament.

[B 10a.] **Beacon Theater,** 2124 Broadway, bet. W. 74th and W. 75th Sts. E side. 1928. Walter Ahlschlager. Partial interior. ★

Skip the exterior. It's the **opulent interior,** second only to that of Radio City Music Hall, that counts. **Go in,** even if you must attend a concert that deafens you—the interior is **Greco-Deco-Empire** with a **Tudor** palette.

[B 10b.] **Astor Apartments,** 2141-2157 Broadway, bet. W. 75th and W. 76th Sts. W side. 1905. Clinton & Russell. Addition to N, 1914, Peabody, Wilson & Brown.

One of William Waldorf Astor's apartment developments. He was a major landowner in this community. Bland. More interesting socially than architecturally.

[B 11.] 254 **West 75th Street,** bet. Broadway and West End Ave. ca. 1885.

Three arches make this an extra special row house with great brick-, stone-, and ironwork. The blocks between Broadway and West End in the 70s hold **many surprises.** Take a stroll and keep your eyes peeled.

[B 12a.] Berkley Garage/originally **The New York Cab Company (stables)**, 201 W. 75th St., NW cor. Amsterdam Ave. ca. 1889. C. Abbott French.

Three great Romanesque Revival half-round arches on 75th Street **trumpeted entrance** to the horses and drivers using this onetime multistory stable. Its visual links to the long-gone Marshall Field Wholesale Store (*1887. H. H. Richardson*) in Chicago are clear.

[B 12b.] Riverside Memorial Chapel (funeral home), 331 Amsterdam Ave., SE cor. W. 76th St. 1925. Joseph J. Furman and Ralph Segal.

Designed using a **limited palette** of browns and dull reds. It is **a soothing result,** executed in tapestry brick, matte terra-cotta, stucco, and a gray slate roof. Gothic windows reveal the chapel proper.

[B 12b.] Tapestry brick and matte terra-cotta enrich Riverside Chapel's facade.

[B 13.] Hotel Churchill, 252 W. 76th St., bet. Broadway and West End Ave. 1903. Ralph Townsend.

One of many **Beaux Arts** hotels that flock around Broadway and West End, this one is in superb condition. Note the wonderful **mannerist** window detailing.

[B 14.] West Side Institutional Synagogue/originally **St. Andrew's Methodist Episcopal Church,** 120 W. 76th St., bet. Columbus and Amsterdam Aves. 1889. Josiah Cleveland Cady. Altered, 1958.

One approach to converting a church to a new use following a severe fire. The only part recommended is **what remains of the original.** St. Andrew's merged with St. Paul's on West 86th and West End in 1937. Here the body has been desteepled and deroofed.

[B 14a.] La Rochelle (apartments), 57 W. 75th St., NE cor. Columbus Ave. 1896. Lamb & Rich.

Here is a grand entry portal worthy of an English Renaissance town house (but with a French name). The powerful columns are repeated in the storefront enframement along the avenue as well. Such architectural strength is welcome: most buildings, good or bad, are mutilated along their commercial streetfronts.

[B 14b.] The Hartford (apartments), 60 W. 75th St., SE cor. Columbus Ave. 1890. Frederick T. Camp.

Construction of these French flats spanned the **name change** from Ninth to Columbus Avenue. The pedimented **stone insert** at the 3rd-floor corner preserves the old name.

[B 14c.] The Aylsmere (apartments), 60 W. 76th St., SE cor. Columbus Ave. ca. 1893.

French flats from the **Brown decades** of picturesque architecture, but here with some growing neo-Classical influences. The verdigris bronze letters are a charming detail.

[B 15a.] Sports (restaurant), 2182 Broadway, bet. W. 77th and W. 78th Sts. E side. 1986. Patricia Sapinsley, Sapinsley Architecture.

Video sports for a bar and bleachers. A dark, austere place, reminiscent of avant-garde 1920s **Mitteleuropa.**

Columbus Avenue's gentrification in the 1970s and 1980s has not only brought yuppies galore to this pulsating strip, with a supporting cast of restaurants serving every eccentric taste from Buffalo chicken wings to Rocky Mountain oysters. It has also created the need for the offbeat, sometimes eccentric shop, mostly of inedibles:

The Silver Palate at **No. 274.** Though its cookbook is better known than the store, the goods purveyed within are a noble contribution to **take-home** gastronomy.

The Last Wound-Up at **No. 290** stocks windup toys that range from crawling strawberries to berserk inanimate legs that rush around the floor with unnerving vitality.

Think Big! at **No. 313,** provides the Lilliputian with everything from a four-foot crayon to a giant lamp.

Mythology Unlimited at **No. 370,** offers eccentric stationery and novelties.

Maxilla & Mandible, at **No. 453** sells skeletons, antlers, and carapaces of all creatures, human and otherwise. Most fetching, perhaps, is a tortoise carapace, with its skeletal head floating in front of the shell.

[B 15b.] Hotel Belleclaire, 250 W. 77th St., SW cor. Broadway. 1901. Stein, Cohen & Roth. ★

Belle Epoque with bay windows, typical of a dozen similar exiles from the Rue Réaumur in Paris built hereabouts. Within its Beaux Arts body are inserted unusual **Art Nouveau** pilasters. While in New York to raise funds for the bolsheviks, Maxim Gorky and his mistress stayed here briefly in 1906. They were asked to leave when word got out that **"Mme. Gorky"** was not only **not his wife** (horrors!) but an actress (shudder!) with whom he had been living for three years.

[B 15c.] Pyramid Garage/originally **Dakota Stables,** 348-354 Amsterdam Ave., SW cor. W. 77th St. 1984. Bradford W. Gilbert.

A "high rise," originally for horses and carriages, comprised along the ground floor for reuse by automobiles.

[B 16.] Apthorp Apartments, grand & block-encompassing by Clinton & Russell

[B 16.] The Apthorp Apartments, 2211 Broadway to West End Ave., W. 78th to W. 79th Sts. 1908. Clinton & Russell. ★

This unusually grand, handsome, richly ornamented limestone Renaissance Revival building occupies an entire block. The individual entrances are reached through **high vaulted tunnels** and **a large interior court** with a fountain in its center. Probably the best of the surviving Astor apartments in New York.

[B 16a.] West 78th Street, bet. Amsterdam Avenue and Broadway.

Here is what might be considered, in this short block, an architectural exhibit of stylistic sources—or is it a montage of Hollywood stage sets? Some watered-down **Tudor England** hangs out at **No. 210.** A bit of **1890s Chicago** fronts **No. 215.** Sedate **19th-century Boston** occupies **No. 226.** At **Nos. 219-223** local row house talents left their own New York West Side marks. It's bizarre but fortunately the West Side is generally more orderly. One block of such display is a permissible and amusing relief.

[B 17a.] The Evelyn (apartments), 101 W. 78th St., NW cor. Columbus Ave. 1886. Emile Gruwé.

A big, bold symphony in reds: brick with all kinds of wonderful unglazed terra-cotta flourishes.

[B 17b.] West 78th Street, bet. Columbus and Amsterdam Aves. ca. 1885–1890.

A modern public school and other regrettable "improvements" have emasculated what was once **one of the** most **vigorous and spirited streetscapes** of the Upper West Side. The spirit was due in part to the works of **Rafael Guastavino,** who designed the **fun-filled** red and white quintet, **Nos. 121-131** and **Nos. 118-134** across the way (all completed in 1886). The client for these rows, Bernard S. Levy, allowed Guastavino, then a recent emigrant from Catalonia, to introduce his system of **"cohesive construction"** in **No. 122** making it an entirely fireproof row house. (Levy himself lived at **No. 121** between 1886 and 1904.) Don't fail to look at the **curious stepped balusters** along the stoops in front of **Nos. 157-167.** Their unusual forms and shadows are a favorite among architectural photography buffs.

[B 15b.] The Belle Epoque Belleclaire   [B 17b.] 123-129 West 78th Street

[B 18.] Park Belvedere (apartments), 101 W. 79th St., NW cor. Columbus Ave. 1985. Frank Williams & Assocs.

A finial-fingered pencil tower that dominates the Columbus Avenue vista. Ruddy brown, it has some wonderful cubism at its crown.

[B 18a.] Andrew Marc (boutique), 404 Columbus Ave., bet. W. 79th and W. 80th Sts. W side. 1987. Arquitectonica.

Leather, furs, men's and women's outer- and sportswear purveyed in an elegantly evolved container.

[B 19.] 100 West 81st Street (apartments), SW cor. Columbus Ave. 1981. Marvin Meltzer.

A brick and stucco conversion that is schizophrenic: the body is **Miami Beach;** its coloring is Germanic. Shade and shadow count for little with such a dark palette.

[B 20a.] Hotel Lucerne, 201 W. 79th St., NW cor. Amsterdam Ave. 1904. Harry B. Mulliken.

Distinguished detailing in **plum-colored brownstone** and brick. The deeply modeled, banded entrance columns, adopted from the Baroque, are great. Now gloriously restored as a condominium—an extravagant palace for its cooperators.

[B 20b.] Baci (restaurant), 412 Amsterdam Ave., bet. W. 79th and W. 80th Sts. W side.

A graceful small pastry and coffee shop whose logo is **Baci** (Kisses) on a silhouette of Sicily. The terrazzo tabletops are made of **glass shards** rather than marble chips. This is a stylish example of Italian Modern.

[B 18.] Park Belvedere apartments   **[B 19.]** 100 West 81st St. apartments

[B 21.] Keister's 1st Baptist Church   **[B 22.]** W. 80th St. Cmty. Ctr. in 1972

[B 21.] First Baptist Church, 265 W. 79th St., NW cor. Broadway. 1894. George Keister.

Like the life that swirls past it on this busy Broadway corner, this church's eclectic facade is **busy, restless,** and **polyglot.**

The 79th Street Restaurant at 2231 Broadway, just north of the First Baptist Church, is a stage set from a 1940s movie, but you won't find Joan Blondell slinging hash behind the counter. This is for West Siders ripe in age and experience, where potatoes and gravy are still on the blue plate special. A fly in amber, it advertises with a neon sign that could soon be part of the historical graphics collection at the Museum of Modern Art.

[B 22.] West 80th Street Community Child Day Care Center, 223 W. 80th St., bet. Amsterdam Ave. and Broadway. 1972. Kaminsky & Shiffer.

The hoped-for **creative plaything** on the scale of side-street architecture didn't **make it despite good intentions.** Now abandoned, it deserves a renaissance.

[B 23.] The Broadway (apartments), 2250 Broadway, SE cor. W. 81st St. 1987. Beyer Blinder Belle, behind **[B 23a.] Conran's (home furnishings)**/formerly **Reeves Television Studios**/originally **RKO 81st Street Theatre.** 1914. Thomas W. Lamb. Converted, 1988, Beyer Blinder Belle, architects. Conran Design Group, designers.

A wonderful glazed white terra-cotta neo-Palladian theater building is the landmark frontispiece of this blank brown brick tower. Somehow what should have been architectural consonance and context here misfired.

Broadway is the quintessential New York street, providing the entire gamut of quality food shopping. Without the pretentious precincts and prices of the East Side (say upper Madison Avenue) one can find superior fruit and vegetables at **Fairway** (market) between 74th and 75th Streets, fresh seafood at **Citarella** at the southwest corner of 76th Street, and just about anything at **Zabar's** (see below). Elaborate cooking is an everyday matter in this cosmopolitan neighborhood, and the raw, canned, pickled, smoked, or whatever materials are conveniently at hand.

Zabar's, 2245 Broadway, bet. W. 80th and W. 81st Sts. W side.

Larger-than-life horn of plenty: wall-to-wall food and, on weekends, wall-to-wall people as well. What makes Zabar's remarkable is its phenomenal variety of foodstuffs from all over the world. It combines the delights of the Jewish **appetizing store** with charcuterie, salumeria, and Wurstgeschäft, adds an array of cheeses, coffees, and breads, and offers a selection of cooking utensils and cookbooks, too.

[B 23a.] The Broadway apartments   **[B 24c.]** A Po Mo palazzo newsstand

The Gryphon Bookshop, 2246 Broadway, bet. W. 80th and W. 81st Sts. E side.

A **musty** and **lovable** bookstore that offers used books at both ground floor and mezzanine.

[B 23b.] Sarabeth's Kitchen (restaurant), 423 Amsterdam Ave., bet. W. 80th and W. 81st Sts. 1986. Ira Grandberg.

The almost New England exterior (except for the penthouse) would do honor to Beacon Hill, but the vaulted central space inside is supported by **Post Modern** Tuscan columns. Back off and you will see farther up an even farther-out penthouse.

[B 24a.] Formerly **Hotel Endicott**/now **apartments,** Columbus Ave. bet. W. 81st and W. 82nd Sts. W. side. 1889. Edward L. Angell. Converted, 1984, Stephen B. Jacobs & Assocs.

The durability of red brick and matching terra-cotta ornament still preserves **a sense** of what this hotel once was—both a fashionable and a comfortable place to stay. Lovingly restored as a condominium; at the ground floor are elegant shops framed in understated oak.

[B 24b.] West 81st Street, bet. Columbus and Amsterdam Aves. ca. 1888–1892.

Not the most stylish of West Side streets anymore but filled with **a rich assortment** of facade detail that will reward neck-craners. **Blast those landlords** who think a coat of gray deck paint can erase the excesses of another era. It merely **dulls the delight.**

[B 24c.] Newsstand, NE cor. W. 81st St. and Columbus Ave. 1986. Wayne Turrett.

The world's smallest **Po Mo** palazzo, designed and owned by an architect and his wife who knew how to make their mark on civilization.

[B 25.] Marvin Gardens (restaurant), 2270 Broadway, bet. W. 81st and W. 82nd Sts. 1975. Haroutiun Derderian.

A crisply designed restaurant with a popular bar. Though the name derives from the game of **Monopoly,** the design is too cool to carry the connection any further.

[B 26.] Holy Trinity Roman Catholic Church, 213 W. 82nd St., bet. Amsterdam Ave. and Broadway. 1900. J. H. McGuire. **Rectory,** 1928, Thomas Dunn.

Drawing on many stylistic influences and bearing a dome upon a band of **clerestory oculi windows,** this modestly located church—it doesn't occupy a corner site—has intricate brickwork and white-glazed terra-cotta. Two choragic monuments of Lysicrates crown it all.

[B 27.] Engine Company No. 74, N.Y.C. Fire Department, 120 W. 83rd St., bet. Columbus and Amsterdam Aves. 1888. Napoleon LeBrun & Sons.

Can't you see the horses **charging out of the doorway** pulling a bright red and polished brass fire engine **billowing white clouds** of water vapor? The horses and steam engine are gone, but the iron jib **for hoisting hay** is very much in evidence overhead. Rock-face brownstone and brick. House-scaled.

[B 28a.] Kondylis' Bromley apartmts   **[B 29.]** Boxenbaum's Patzo's rstrnt.

[B 28a.] The Bromley (apartments), 225 W. 83rd St., NE cor. Broadway to W. 84th St. 1987. Costas Kondylis of Philip Birnbaum & Assocs.

A chunky filler of Broadway's belly. Post Modern green glazing with limestone gives a graceful edge to West 83rd St. and a serrated neo-Dutch profile. The old Loew's 84th Street fills the northern corner, enveloped by the towering building surrounding it.

[B 28b.] Broadway Fashion Building (offices), 2315 Broadway, SW cor. W. 84th St. 1931. Sugarman & Berger.

Long before the curtain walls of metal and glass descended upon midtown, this curtain wall of metal and glass *and* **glazed terra-cotta** came to grace Broadway. The retail signs at street level are a disgrace.

Nevermore: Notwithstanding the two plaques affixed to upscale apartment buildings along West 84th Street, *both* claiming to be *the* site where Edgar Allan Poe put the finishing touches to "The Raven," the tenement at No. 206 just west of Amsterdam Avenue is the rightful claimant to that distinction. It was here in "the bleak December" of 1844 that Poe and his ailing wife boarded at Patrick and Mary Brennan's farmhouse, which surmounted a promontory dynamited when the site was graded. Poe would often stroll down the hill to the immense rock outcropping west of Riverside Drive near West 83rd Street that he named Mount Tom after the Brennans' young son. There he would sit alone for hours, gazing across the river. In more sociable moments he would amble up the sylvan Bloomingdale Road to the Striker's Bay Tavern, located northeast of today's Riverside Drive viaduct over 96th Street. Only one remnant survives from the "home by horror haunted": the mantel upon which Poe scratched his name, now preserved at Columbia University.

 [B 29.] Patzo's (restaurant)/originally **Ancora,** 2330 Broadway, SE cor. W. 85th St. 1985. Charles Boxenbaum.

Hispanic **Po Mo** that combines a stuccoed semi-neo-Renaissance profile with teak woodwork. One of the few New York restaurants that dares to bring its architecture **outside.**

 [B 30a.] 74, 76, and **78 West 85th Street (apartments),** SE cor. Columbus Ave. 1895.

The facades of this trio are ordinary for this period. But the foliate carving in the entrances—particularly SUDELEY at **No. 76**—is exquisite and intact. **Try to make out the letters** incised over **No. 74.** Are they a Roman numeral? Do they spell CLIIION? Is the word CLIFTON? Or is this a rare example of a poor **speller** turned fine **stonecutter?**

[B 30a.] The Sudeley, 76 W. 78th St.   **[B 30b.]** The Brockholst apartments

[B 30b.] The Brockholst (apartments), 101 W. 85th St., NW cor. Columbus Ave. 1890. John G. Prague.

Endearingly dark and craggy for rock-face stone and brick, these French flats are **laced with delicate ironwork** fire escapes. It announces its name in floral terra-cotta relief.

 [B 30c.] Mannes College of Music/originally **United Order of True Sisters,** 150 W. 85th St., bet. Columbus and Amsterdam Aves. 1928.

A simple and austere neo-Georgian brick and limestone house for music, with a verdigris copper mansard roof and a mildly Palladian window over its portal.

 [B 31.] West-Park Presbyterian Church/originally **Park Presbyterian Church,** Amsterdam Ave., NE cor. W. 86th St. 1890. Henry F. Kilburn.

A fine Romanesque Revival edifice in brownstone. Were it and its tower not overwhelmed by the grim apartment building to the north, it would be one of the West Side's loveliest landmarks.

[B 31a.] The Packard (apartments), 176 W. 86th St., SE cor. Amsterdam Ave. 1987. Ted Reeds Assocs.

East Side apartment developers have exhausted the list of painters with the **Van Gogh,** the **Picasso,** the **Gauguin,** and so forth. But class here is instantly implied by expensive cars: today we see the **Packard,** but in the interest of historical class, will we shortly be enjoying the **Pierce-Arrow,** the **Hispano-Suiza,** and the **Duesenberg?** The building is a modest attempt at style of some sort, but did the builder run out of quoins?

[B 32.] Belnord Apartments, 225 W. 86th St., Amsterdam Ave. to Broadway, W. 86th to W. 87th Sts. 1908. H. Hobart Weekes. ★

Like its smaller cousin the Apthorp, this block-square Renaissance Revival structure is built around a garden court. Brilliant but boring.

[B 32a.] The Boulevard (apartments), 2373 Broadway, bet. W. 86th and W. 87th Sts., W side. 1988. Voorsanger & Mills Assocs.

Neo-Ruskinian polychromatic brickwork clads this stylish new apartment block. Here a firm of architects concerned with high design leaves its mark on the Broadway corridor.

Signs of the times: The Broadway Butcher, at 2446 Broadway, between 90th and 91st Streets, heralds the arrival of stylish shopping on upper Broadway. An elegant shopfront and a sea of marble-fatted meats meet the passing eye; conspicuous consumption conjoined to cholesterol. Now a small outpost of affluence, it will soon be the old boy in this fast-supergentrifying sector.

[B 33a.] The Montana (apartments), 247 W. 87th St., NE cor. Broadway to W. 88th St. 1986. The Gruzen Partnership.

A hopefully named grandchild of the **Dakota** whose patron, Stephen Clark, honored the Upper West Side with both architecture and a sense of the Wild West. Here the grandeur of the Dakota is reduced to merely affluent unadorned apartments, and the pioneers' verve that brought settlers to the Dakota merely brings endless yuppies ever northward.

Nevertheless it is a blandly handsome place, its twin towers signaling adherence to a West Side icon.

[B 33b.] Boulevard (restaurant), 248 W. 88th St., SE cor. Broadway. 1987. Charles Morris Mount, Inc., designer.

A sleek, straightforward Modern restaurant within Montana's embrace.

[B 34a.] Glenn Gardens (apartments), 175 W. 87th St., NE cor. Amsterdam Ave. 1975. Seymour Joseph.

Two wings form this **housing complex.** The tall one on the avenue is banal, but the lower slab on West 88th Street is interesting.

[B 34b.] West 87th Street, bet. Columbus and Amsterdam Aves.

Some **fine row houses** in this block: **Nos. 133** and **147** look as though different architects designed the successive tiers; **Nos. 137** and **139** make an intriguing combination; **No. 159** has a black, weathered cornice that might **almost be a Louise Nevelson** sculpture.

[B 35a.] Public School 166, Manhattan, 140 W. 89th St., bet. Columbus and Amsterdam Aves. 1899. C. B. J. Snyder.

A limestone **neo-Gothic** school by this prolific architect of schools of the 1890s.

[B 35b.] Playground, Public School 166, Manhattan, E of school, 132 W. 89th St., bet. Columbus and Amsterdam Aves. 1967. M. Paul Friedberg & Assocs., landscape architects.

A playground jointly operated by the Board of Education and the city's Department of Parks & Recreation, it was commissioned by the **Vincent Astor Foundation** as a radical departure in playground design.

[B 35c.] Claremont Riding Academy, 175 W. 89th St., bet. Columbus and Amsterdam Aves. 1892. Frank A. Rooke.

These **high-rise stables** owe their survival to their use as domicile for horses used on **Central Park's bridle paths.** Riding a steed from here to the park offers a special architectural experience: **looking** at the row house facades **from a horse's back,** a vantage point more commonly available to 19th-century viewers. **It makes a difference.**

In the late 1960s it was proposed that the stable be removed to make way for urban renewal, a replacement to be made available as part of **an enormous new mounted police complex** to be built within Central Park. Park preservationists **raised an outcry** against tampering with the park; others pointed out that horses had always been a **part of that scene.** The preservationists prevailed, thus canceling the park project; the forces of urban renewal ran out of money, thus extending the life of these stables. Rent a horse.

[B 35d.] Ballet Hispanica (dance school), 167 W. 89th St., bet. Columbus and Amsterdam Aves. ca. 1890.

One of a series of carriage houses that served the grand mansions nearer and on Central Park West.

[B 35c.] Claremont Riding Academy   [B 36.] Ichabod's Restaurant & Bar

[B 36.] Ichabod's (restaurant/bar), 2420 Broadway, NE cor. W. 89th St. 1985. Ralph P. Albanese.

An elegant, but strong understatement. The neon-articulated column with its Ionic flourishes is a powerful centerpiece to this clean and lively bar and restaurant.

The night shift: Soon after her first arrest as a procuress, Polly Adler decided to go legit. With $6,000 in savings she and a friend opened a lingerie shop in 1922 at 2487 Broadway near West 92nd Street. Within a year the shop was out of business—and Adler was back to business as usual.

[B 37a.] At Our Place (restaurant)/originally **Cleopatra,** 2527 Broadway, near W. 95th St. W side. 1970. Gamal El Zoghby.

An ultrasophisticated earth-colored and dark blue exterior is left behind as you enter a stepped, mirrored, carefully modulated (and somewhat claustrophobic) interior full of architectural and culinary surprises. When the restaurant changed names it was decided to reuse as many of the bold sans-serif sign letters as possible in the new name. Hence the one chosen—it required only the fabrication of a new **"U."**

[B 37b.] Pomander Walk (apartment complex), 261-267 W. 94th St. and 260-266 W. 95th St. bet. Broadway and West End Ave. 1922. King & Campbell. ★

Pomander Walk first came to New York as the name of a stage play. This charming **double row** of small town houses arrayed along a

private pedestrian byway is **modeled after the stage sets** used in the New York production. Note the metalwork over the entrance.

[B 37c.] Originally **Astor Market/**later converted to include: **Symphony Theatre/**now **Symphony Space,** 2537 Broadway, bet. W. 94th and W. 95th Sts. W side. **Thalia Theatre,** 258 W. 95th St. Building, 1915. Altered into theaters, 1917, 1931. Ben Schlanger and R. Irrera.

Astor built a street-level produce market and underneath, in the space that later became the Thalia Theatre, a **fish market**—perhaps on the theory that most mammals ride high, while the fish swim below.

More recent events have suggested that this will become another high-rise condominium. The varied owners of fee, leasehold, and other, more substantial, property are quarreling about it.

[B 37b.] Pomander Walk apartments   **[B 38.]** The Columbia apartments

[B 38.] The Columbia (apartments), 275 W. 96th St., NW cor. Broadway to W. 97th St. 1984. Liebman Williams & Ellis.

Here was the site of a battle between community and commerce. Gimbel's, based at Herald Square, had an East Side beachhead at 86th St. and Lexington Avenue; an equivalent West Side outpost was to have been here. Commerce lost the battle here and, ironically, lost it on the East Side too. (Alexander's had sought this West Side outpost.)

This towering bulk is the earliest adventure in sophisticated modern housing on the Upper West Side. A bit brash, it evokes the cubistic dreams of **Walter Gropius** in his wonderful but losing scheme for the Chicago Tribune Tower. For more Williams' work, see the **Park Belvedere** [see B 18.].

[B 38a.] Caramba!!! (restaurant), 2567 Broadway, bet. W. 96th and W. 97th Sts. W side. 1985. Paul Seaman, designer.

A sleek, multilevel Mexican restaurant, the third (count the exclamation points) of a proliferating chain. The margaritas are renowned.

[B 39.] Holy Name of Jesus Church (Roman Catholic), Amsterdam Ave., NW cor. W. 96th St. 1891. T. H. Poole.

This **tight-chested ungiving German Gothic-influenced fácade** is forbidding. **Enter** for a more pleasing architectural experience—particularly the **hammer-beamed** ceiling and roof.

[B 40.] East River Savings Bank, 743 Amsterdam Ave., NE cor. W. 96th St. 1927. Expanded to N. Both by Walker & Gillette.

A Classical temple inscribed with **exhortations to the thrifty.** Note how the Ionic columns come down to the sidewalk in the Greek fashion, without pedestals.

[B 41.] St. Michael's Church (Episcopal), 225 W. 99th St., NW cor. Amsterdam Ave. 1891. Robert W. Gibson.

A church complex: tall tower, rounded apse, arcades, parish house, rectory, and a quiet garden. Inside are mosaics and Tiffany glass.

[B 42.] Metro Theater/originally **Midtown Theatre,** 2626 Broadway, bet. W. 99th and W. 100th Sts. E side. 1933. Boak & Paris.

A design **more appropriate to a 1930s interior** was made into a weatherproof facade through the imperviousness of glazed terra-cotta. Art Deco.

[B 43.] Ukrainian Academy of Arts and Sciences/originally **New York Free Circulating Library,** 206 W. 100th St., bet. Amsterdam Ave. and Broadway. 1898. James Brown Lord.

Beaux Arts Ionic above, Tuscan columns below. Libraries were obviously intended as **temples of learning** in the 1890s, rather than supermarkets for checking out books.

 [B 44.] 2641 Broadway and **225 West 100th Street,** NW cor. Broadway. 1871. Addition to W, 1900.

Amid the masonry canyons of Broadway, West End Avenue, and the side streets stands this **wood frame holdout** from the West Side's **frontier days.** Once a saloon, it now offers more substantial provender.

 [B 45.] Originally **Hotel Marseilles/**now **apartments,** 2689 Broadway, SW cor. W. 103rd St. 1905. Harry Allan Jacobs.

Another Renaissance Revival Broadway hotel, here with banded and fluted Tuscan columns and fruit-filled friezes.

[B 45a.] Columbia Cinema/formerly **Edison Theatre/**originally **Broadway Theatre,** 2706 Broadway, bet. W. 103rd and W. 104th Sts. E side. 1913.

One of the city's **oldest movie theaters,** renovated after a long run showing Spanish-language films, to reflect upscale tastes—and prices.

[B 45b.] Formerly **Horn & Hardart Automat/**now **Sloan's** (supermarket), 2712 Broadway, SE cor. W. 104th St. 1920. Altered, 1928.

A limestone and glazed terra-cotta **memory is recycled** as an Art Deco supermarket.

[B 46.] Straus Park and **Memorial Fountain/**originally **Schuyler Square** (1895–1907)/later **Bloomingdale Square,** Broadway and West End Ave., at W. 106th St. N side. 1919. H. Augustus Lukeman, sculptor. Evarts Tracy, architect.

Named Bloomingdale in 1907 not for the midtown department store (pure coincidence) but for the old settlement here of **Bloemendael** (flower valley in Dutch). The *Titanic* disaster in 1912 claimed the lives of **Macy's owners** Isidor and Ida Straus whose house, across the street at 2745 Broadway, overlooked the triangle. The park was **renamed in their honor** when the monument was completed two years later.

[B 46a.] Ivy Court (apartments), 210, 220, and 230 West 107th St., bet. Amsterdam Ave. and Broadway. 1903. William C. Hazlett.

This apartment house trio imparts **a town house scale and feel** by use of streetfront courtyards. The wrought iron is of interest.

 [B 46b.] Church of the Ascension (Roman Catholic), 221 W. 107th St., bet. Amsterdam Ave. and Broadway. 1897.

A Romanesque Revival surprise—and a pleasant one. *Go inside.*

[B 47.] The Manhasset (apartments), 301 W. 108th St. and 300 W. 109th St. along Broadway, W. side. 1904. Joseph Wolf and Janes & Leo.

Crass commercialism has **concealed the elegance** of the original stores but up above, **oh what attention to detail!** As if unable to control their creativity the architects topped their building off with a story-high banded brick ribbon, then a **hefty cornice,** and above that a smooth light-colored brick expanse with a 2-story mansard above that. Imagine Broadway's appearance **if it had more** of these flanking it.

CENTRAL PARK WEST/THE PARK BLOCKS

While the Upper West Side is a place of contrasts and **in constant flux,** Central Park West, if not the so-called "park blocks," has generally retained its **unflaggingly fashionable quality**—at least up through 96th

Street. The park blocks began to be converted into rooming houses following World War II, a pattern turned around somewhat by **the rising desirability of brownstone living** among upwardly mobile middle-class families and by the "singles" of the West Side. In the northern stretch the Urban Renewal Act **helped save its row house stock** on the park blocks above 86th Street; their health can be seen to fall off the greater their distance from Central Park. Olmsted and Vaux's **great green space,** one of the **major attractions** in the settlement of the West Side, still acts as an important **touchstone.**

This precinct begins above Columbus Circle and includes Central Park West up to 96th Street and the park block corridor up to 86th Street. North of 86th Street lies the West Side Urban Renewal Area.

[C 1.] Century Apartments, 25 Central Park W., bet. W. 62nd and W. 63rd Sts. 1931. Office of Irwin S. Chanin; Jacques Delamarre, architectural director. ★

Like the Majestic by the same architects, it makes some **pleasant gestures toward Modern style.** The name recalls a lavish and unprofitable **Century Theater,** designed by Carrère & Hastings, which stood on the site from 1909 until razed for the apartments.

[C 1.] Chanin's Century Apartments   **[C 2b.]** 1903 Ethical Culture School

[C 2a.] New York Society for Ethical Culture, 2 W. 64th St., SW cor. Central Park W. 1910. Robert D. Kohn, architect. Estelle Rumbold Kohn, sculptor. ★ **[C 2b.] Ethical Culture School,** 33 Central Park W., NW cor. W. 63rd St. 1903. Carrère & Hastings and Robert D. Kohn.

Considered in the architectural press of its time to be quite the best piece of Art Nouveau architecture yet designed in this century, it has lost prestige since then. **Warning:** It is not as exuberant as Hector Guimard's Parisian efforts or those in Brussels by Victor Horta, nor does it match the quality of Otto Wagner's or Josef Hoffmann's Viennese works. It is, however, **a clear departure** from the Beaux Arts.

[C 3.] The Prasada (apartments), 50 Central Park W., SW cor. W. 65 St. 1907. Charles W. Romeyn and Henry R. Wynne.

Banded limestone columns, monumental in scale, and other freely interpreted Classical ornaments **embellish but do not quite animate** this bulky apartment facade.

[C 4a.] Holy Trinity Lutheran Church, Central Park W., NW cor. W. 65th St. 1903.

A **refreshing break** in Central Park West's phalanx of boxy apartment blocks. The kaleidoscopelike rose window and the **delicate flèche** over the crossing are notable.

[C 4b.] Estelle R. Newman City Center, Jewish Guild for the Blind, 15 W. 65th St., bet. Central Park W. and Columbus Ave. 1971. Matthew J. Warshauer.

A **horizontally striped box** (dark glass and metal strip windows alternating with cream-colored precast concrete spandrels) projects from an orange salt-and-pepper glazed-brick utility core.

[C 4c.] 55 Central Park West (apartments), SW cor. W. 66th St. 1930. Schwartz & Gross.

Art Deco evolved through a carefully studied **modulation of brick planes** and boldly fluted ornament. If the sun seems brighter at top than at bottom, look more carefully at the brick color. It changes subtly.

[C 5.] Congregation Habonim (synagogue), 44 W. 66th St., bet. Central Park W. and Columbus Ave. 1957. Stanley Prowler and Frank Faillance.

A stained-glass cube set 45 degrees to itself and its neighbors along the street. Its setback permits a better understanding of the old armory next door.

For the American Broadcasting Company buildings, see Lincoln Center [L 7b.–L 8.].

Studio Street: The park block of West 67th Street is a haven for those who like studio living or living among artists: there are no fewer than six studio buildings on the block. Among them:

[C 6.] 70 Central Park West (apartments), SW cor. W. 67th St. 1916. Rich & Mathesius.

A 15-story studio building. The 2-story industrial sash that illuminates the duplex apartments is spectacular.

[C 7a.] Hotel des Artistes (apartments), 1 W. 67th St., bet. Central Park W. and Columbus Ave. 1918. George Mort Pollard. Café redecorated, 1979, Judith Stockman & Assocs.

The **fanciful facade** clearly shows the balconied studios behind it. An early tenant, Howard Chandler Christy, painted a pinup girl (his specialty) to decorate the cozy **Café des Artistes** on the first floor. An **all-time roster** of tenants of the elaborate (and lavish) spaces would also include Isadora Duncan, Norman Rockwell, Alexander Woollcott, Noel Coward, Fannie Hurst, and former mayor John V. Lindsay.

[C 7b.] Central Park Studios, 15 West 67th Street, bet. Central Park W. and Columbus Ave. 1906. B. H. Simonson and Pollard & Steinam.

Note the neo-Gothic lobby.

[C 7c.] 67th Street Atelier Building (apartments), 33 W. 67th St., bet. Central Park W. and Columbus Ave. 1906. B. H. Simonson and Pollard & Steinam.

Reputedly the first co-op building built as such in New York City. The studio appellation is apparently only a fashion: studios historically were apartments with 2-story living rooms.

[C 7d.] Swiss Home of the Swiss Benevolent Society, 35 W. 67th St., bet. Central Park W. and Columbus Ave. 1905. John E. Schlarsmith.

The scale of the red and white parts to the whole is harmonious. The forms **calm your anxiety** about being a stranger in a far-off land.

[C 7e.] 39-41 West 67th Street (studios), bet. Central Park W. and Columbus Ave. 1907. Pollard & Steinam.

Four stacks of bay windows **zip up the street facade** of this tall narrow studio building. They are of sheet metal, not masonry—a kind of early curtain wall.

Tavern on the Green: The entrance to this chronically remodeled eating-drinking-dancing spot, built around Central Park's 1870 sheepfold, is at 67th Street and Central Park West. Expensive. (At night the trees, wrapped to their roots in minilights, look like the invasion of the bulb people.)

[C 8a.] Second Church of Christ, Scientist, 77 Central Park W., SW cor. W. 68th St. 1900. Frederick R. Comstock.

Boring except for its **green domes,** best seen from edge of park.

[C 8b.] 14 West 68th Street (apartments), bet. Central Park W. and Columbus Ave. 1895. Louis Thouvard.

A **somber brownstone box** whose entrance is from an adjacent and **compensating green space** open to the street. Imagine when the house had a view clear into Central Park. . .

[C 9.] Hebrew Union College–Jewish Institute of Religion/originally **The Free Synagogue,** 40 W. 68th St., bet. Central Park W. and Columbus Ave. 1923. S. B. Eisendrath & B. Horowitz. **[C 9a.] Stephen Wise Free Synagogue,** 30 W. 68th St. 1941. Bloch & Hesse.

Somber and unobtrusive. Today's college building was the sanctuary until the new one was begotten in 1941. An **important center** of the Reform Jewish movement.

[C 10.] The Brentmore (apartments), 88 Central Park W., SW cor. W. 69th St. 1909. Schwartz & Gross.

A prim Edwardian block, with a strong bracketed **verdigris copper** cornice.

[C 11.] Congregation Shearith Israel (synagogue), 99 Central Park W., SW cor. W. 70th St. 1897. Brunner & Tryon. ★

The newest home of New York's **oldest Jewish congregation,** founded downtown in what was then New Amsterdam by Spanish and Portuguese immigrants in 1655. A connected **Little Synagogue** reproduces the Georgian style of the congregation's first real synagogue, built in 1730; it contains many furnishings used in that building.

It is unclear why the congregation settled for this stuffy design back in 1897. Perhaps it was **a compromise** between the **glittering White City** architecture of the 1893 Chicago World's Fair and the **dignified needs** of a religious building. The 3 venerable Shearith Israel cemeteries which resist the march of progress in Manhattan belong to this congregation [see index].

[C 11.] Congregation Shearith Israel   **[C 17.]** Emery Roth's San Remo Apts.

[C 12a.] Row houses, W. 71st St., bet. Central Park W. and Columbus Ave. 1890s.

What a **terrific selection! No. 24** is especially fine with its unusual stoop, cupids at its cornice, and concave shell-molded lintels over the topmost windows. **Nos. 26, 28,** and **30** show that handsome houses **come in threes:** an elegant russet color scheme (brick, stone, terra-cotta, and the cartouches) and wide doors that must certainly have encouraged the purchase of expansive furnishings. Note how the imitation cement plaster "stonework" **has been tooled to disguise** the removal of **No. 30's** stoop. On the stoops of **Nos. 32-40** a gentle separation of the balusters as they reach the sidewalk **subtly signals you** to enter. Across the street **Nos. 33-39** offer both **hungry** and **satiated** lion's-heads to decorate the doorway keystones. An architectural feast.

[C 12b.] Originally **Parkside Hotel/**later **The Bromley (studios),** 31 W. 71st St., bet. Central Park W. and Columbus Ave. 1916. Robert L. Lyons.

A tall studio building faced on its narrow street frontage by white glazed terra-cotta. One of a West Side breed.

 [C 13.] Majestic Apartments, 115 Central Park W., bet. W. 71st and W. 72nd Sts. 1930. Office of Irwin S. Chanin; Jacques Delamarre, director of architecture. ★

One of 5 twin-towered apartment buildings—if you include The Beresford [C 20a.]—that make the skyline along Central Park West a unique visual treat. This **streamlined building** has wide banks of windows that extend around its sides. The much-copied brickwork patterns and futurist forms were designed by **sculptor René Chambellan.**

[C 14.] 42 West 72nd Street (studios), bet. Central Park W. and Columbus Ave. 1915. Buchman & Fox.

Another lanky white studio tower by developer **Daddy Browning** [see Broadway and Environs B 5c.].

[C 15.] Dakota Apartments, 1 W. 72nd St., NW cor. Central Park W. to W. 73rd St. 1884. Henry J. Hardenbergh. ★

The city's first luxury apartment house. Designed for **Singer Sewing Machine heir** Edward S. Clark, it dominated Central Park before the park drives were paved. **A prestige address,** particularly for those in the arts, since the days when this part of the city was thought to be as remote as the Dakota Territory. Note the railings with **griffins and zeuses.**

[C 16.] Central Park West–W. 73rd Street–W. 74th Street Historic District, the whole block between W. 73rd and W. 74th Sts., Central Park W. and Columbus Ave. ★

A wonderful intermixture of town houses and apartments, including:

[C 16a.] 15A-19 and **41-65 West 73rd Street (row houses),** bet. Central Park W. and Columbus Ave. 1885. ☆ **[C 16b.] 101** and **103 West 73rd Street (apartments and row house),** NW cor. Columbus Ave. 1879. All by Henry J. Hardenbergh. ☆

These houses are another product of the collaboration of the **client** (Clark) and the **architect** (Hardenbergh) of the Dakota Apartments. (Regrettably their **delicate beauty** is **overwhelmed** by midblock apartment houses.) Originally there were two long rows bracketing Columbus Avenue, with larger flats at the corners. Only the one to the west remains, from an era prior to the Dakota's construction.

 [C 16c.] The Langham (apartments), 135 Central Park W. bet. W. 73rd and W. 74th Sts. 1905. Clinton & Russell. ☆

A **ponderous prism** till you look at the roofline, where a simple cornice has been so elaborated with ornament and ornate dormers that **it sparkles with light.**

 [C 16d.] 18-52 West 74th Street (row houses), bet. Central Park W. and Columbus Ave. 1904. Percy Griffin. ☆

A **phalanx of 18** neo-Georgian row houses fills the block's south side and bears such names as Park Terrace, Riverside, and Hayden Manor. **Built to compete with apartment buildings,** which were growing in popularity, these 25-foot-wide, 17- to 19-room houses **each boasted** four or **five bathrooms** and an electric elevator. It is easy to understand their conversion to school and other institutional uses. The architect also designed the **O-Te-Sa-Ga Hotel** in Cooperstown, N.Y.

[C 17.] San Remo Apartments, 145-146 Central Park W., bet. W. 74th and W. 75th Sts. 1930. Emery Roth. ★

The twin-towered silhouette shows **finialed Roman temples against the sky.**

[C 18.] Central Park West–76th Street Historic District, Central Park W. bet. W. 75th and W. 77th Sts., including W. 76th St. W to Nos. 51 and 56, and 44 W. 77th St. ★

In addition to the buildings on Central Park West and West 77th Street, covered below, the Historic District encompasses a **variety of row housing** along West 76th Street dating from 1889 to 1900. The earliest, **Nos. 21-31,** is by architect **George M. Walgrove,** who used neo-Grec trim and a newly fashionable rock-faced surface treatment. The most recent, **Nos. 8-10,** is Upper East Side-like in its neo-Baroque **town house flamboyance** by **John H. Duncan,** designer of Grant's Tomb and Brooklyn's Soldiers' and Sailors' Memorial Arch. Works by other architects fill in both sides of the block: **Gilbert A. Schellenger, Schickel & Ditmars,** and **Cleverdon & Putzel.** The architecture is decorative, the designation abounding with references to garlanded brackets, Herculean heads, elegant cartouches, and spiral colonnettes.

[C 18a.] The Kenilworth (apartments), 151 Central Park W., NW cor. W. 75th St. 1908. Townsend, Steinle & Haskell. ☆

A cubical russet-brick **wedding cake** topped by a grand convex mansard roof. The whipped-cream efforts are executed in limestone in the interests of posterity.

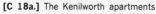

[C 18a.] The Kenilworth apartments   [C 18b.] Universalist Church of N.Y.

[C 18b.] Universalist Church of New York and Parish House/formerly **Church of the Divine Paternity**/originally **Fourth Universalist Society,** 4 W. 76th St., SW cor. Central Park W. 1898. William A. Potter. ☆

Oxford University on Central Park West: this church sports a neo-Gothic tower reminiscent of **Oxford's Magdalen College.** In its early years **Andrew Carnegie** attended church here, along with other prominent New Yorkers.

[C 18c.] New-York Historical Society, 170 Central Park W., bet. W. 76th and W. 77th Sts. Central portion, 1908. York & Sawyer. N and S wings, 1938. Walker & Gillette. ☆ ★

Resembling a Parisian bibliothèque, this is both an **important museum** and **a research library for American and local history.** It is almost certain that **a witty and informative exhibition** on some aspect of the city's history will be on display when you visit. Among the library's vast holdings are the McKim, Mead & White files and the 432 original watercolors of John James Audubon's *Birds of America,* usually remembered in the **Havell** engravings or reproductions thereof.

[C 18d.] The Studio Building, 44 W. 77th St., bet. Central Park W. and Columbus Ave. 1909. Harde & Short. ☆

Several of the adjacent apartments along West 77th Street replaced row housing when the **abundant and unobstructed north light** encouraged redevelopment. Though a great deal of terra-cotta was removed in 1944, the **lacy tapestry** of the neo-Gothic facade is still **breathtaking.**

[C 19a.] American Museum of Natural History, Manhattan Sq., Central Park W. to Columbus Ave., W. 77th to W. 81st St. General plan and first wing, 1872–1877. Calvert Vaux and J. Wrey Mould. W. 77th Street wings, 1892–1898, J. C. Cady & Co., and 1899, Cady, Berg & See. Columbus Avenue wing and powerhouse, 1908. Charles Volz. Additions, 1924, 1926, 1933. Trowbridge & Livingston. **Theodore Roosevelt Memorial,** Central Park W., 1936. John Russell Pope, architect. Roosevelt statue and heroic figures on attic. James Earle Fraser, sculptor. Animal relief, James L. Clark, sculptor. ★

Conceived by Vaux and Mould, "Architects of the Department of Public Parks," to be **the largest building on the continent.** The museum trustees had other thoughts, and V&M's wing (the first) is now **only barely visible** from Columbus Avenue. The best parts of the building are Cady's Romanesque Revival efforts on West 77th Street—though Pope's pompous Central Park West facade, the Roosevelt Memorial, gets the publicity photos and therefore **seems** important. Exhibits range from ponderous to exhilarating. See the **Hall of Minerals and Gems,** 1976, and **The People Center,** 1973. A complex of 22 interconnected buildings.

[C 19a.] The American Museum of Natural History's Roosevelt Memorial wing

[C 20a.] 1929 Beresford apartments   **[C 18d.]** 44 W. 77th St. Studio Bldg.

[C 19b.] Hayden Planetarium, American Museum of Natural History, W. 81st St., bet. Central Park W. and Columbus Ave. S side. 1935. Trowbridge & Livingston.

This verdigris copper dome perched on a brick box combines a clear expression of the **astronomical sky theater** inside with **an ambiguity of forms** which have come to be associated with **the mysteries of Middle Eastern theology.** For program title, performance times, ticket prices, call.

[C 20a.] The Beresford (apartments), 1 and 7 W. 81st St. and 211 Central Park W., NW cor. 1929. Emery Roth. ★

Named for the hotel it replaced, the Beresford is another of Central Park West's twin-towered luxury apartment buildings **but with a plus:** it has a twin-towered silhouette not only from the **east** but also from the **south,** a result of **three** Baroquoid projections above its roof.

[C 20b.] Hayden House (apartments), 11 W. 81st St., bet. Central Park W. and Columbus Ave. 1908. Schickel & Ditmars.

Here cast-iron balconies modulate the facade, all topped with a mansard roof and dormer windows.

[C 21a.] Congregation Rodeph Sholom (synagogue), 7 W. 83rd St., bet. Central Park W. and Columbus Ave. 1930. Charles B. Meyers.
[C 21b.] Day School, 12 W. 84th St. 1976. Michael Rabin Assocs.

The synagogue is an inflated but restrained facade in the neo-Romanesque style. The school, reflecting a 1970s fad of deeply recessed windows and sloped brick reveals, is a reconstruction of an earlier group of row houses.

[C 22.] 65, 67, and **69 West 83rd Street (row houses),** and **71 West 83rd Street (apartments),** bet. Central Park W. and Columbus Ave.

These exuberant Queen Anne row houses were planned so that **No. 69** carries their recessed facades out to the building line, where **the group curtsies** to **No. 71,** a restrained and **exquisitely detailed** apartment house. Note the bronze balcony railings and the curious angle that the west wall makes with the street—the result of **a rambling property line** from the West Side's earliest farming era. Copper bas-reliefs infill curved window heads.

[C 23.] Church of St. Matthew and St. Timothy (Episcopal), 26 W. 84th St., bet. Central Park W. and Columbus Ave. 1970. Victor Christ-Janer.

Following a disastrous fire in 1965, this **radical, cast-in-place concrete edifice** was substituted. The bold simplicity of the exterior does not prepare you for **the carefully modulated circumambulatory entry** and what you find within: a rich combination of white (plaster) and gray (concrete) surfaces set off by warm natural wood pews, metallic organ pipes, and a richly colored mosaic crucifix and fabric hangings. **A fine work.**

[C 24.] 241 Central Park West (apartments), NW cor. W. 84th St. 1930. Schwartz & Gross.

Subtly colored glazed terra-cotta ears of corn **sprout** (literally) from the brickwork of this Art Deco structure. The West 84th Street side is beautifully modeled at street level.

[C 25a.] 53-75 West 85th Street (row houses), bet. Central Park W. and Columbus Ave. ca. 1885.

This long row conceals none of its charming red and white Queen Anne style excesses, except for **Nos. 69** and **71,** which were covered over by a 9-foot-deep olive-green glazed brick addition which is **truly an affront** to all sensibilities.

Renewal area: Central Park West's frontages between West 87th and 97th Streets and the park blocks in that stretch all lie within the official boundaries of the West Side Urban Renewal Area. CPW's apartment buildings (with the exception of **No. 325**) did not directly benefit from the designation; but many of the side-street brownstones, converted into single-room occupancy and rooming houses, did. (**No. 235,** slated to be demolished, was saved, upgraded, and turned into a co-op.) [For the side streets, therefore, see the precinct called West Side Urban Renewal Area; for the continuation of CPW's buildings uptown to West 97th, see below.]

[C 25b.] Rossleigh Court, 1 W. 85th St., NW cor. Central Park W. 1906. **[C 25c.] Orwell House/**formerly **Hotel Peter Stuyvesant/**originally **Central Park View,** 257 Central Park W., SW cor. W. 86th St. 1905. Both by Mulliken & Moeller.

Twin apartment buildings occupying the full Central Park West blockfront. They are of **a disarming and cheery purple brick** set off to advantage by limestone trim.

[C 26a.] The Walden School/Andrew Goodman Building, 11-15 W. 88th St., bet. Central Park W. and Columbus Ave. 1974. Edgar Tafel.

The **desire to relate** the addition's facade to that of the now-demolished **Progress Club,** the school's Classical revival original building, **is commendable.** The result, on the other hand, misses the mark. The parent building (*1904. Louis Korn*) had almost a **Post Modern** look, with its hefty columns supporting thin air.

Moses King, author and publisher of the incomparable *King's Handbooks* and *King's Views of New York City* (and the cities of Brooklyn and Boston and even of the United States) lived in **The Minnewaska,** an 8-story apartment house which once stood at 2 West 88th Street. He died there on June 12, 1909.

[C 26b.] The St. Urban (apartments), 285 Central Park W., SW cor. W. 89th St. 1905. Robert S. Lyons.

CPW's only **single-towered** apartment building. Its tower is splendidly crowned by dome and cupola, gray shingles and verdigris trim. And all is festooned with **16** broken-pediment dormers.

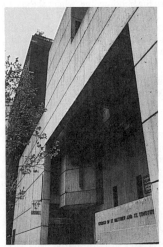

[C 23.] SS. Matthew & Timothy Church   [C 26b.] The St. Urban apartments

[C 27.] The Eldorado (apartments), 300 Central Park W., W. 90th to W. 91st Sts. 1931. Margon & Holder, architect. Emery Roth, consultant. ★

The northernmost of CPW's twin-towered apartment houses. Art Deco metalwork embellishes **the base** (subtle bronze reliefs) and **the towers** (Flash Gordon finials).

[C 28a.] 5 West 91st Street (apartments), bet. Central Park W. and Columbus Ave. 1972. Horace Ginsbern & Assocs.

A modest 6-story work which evidences in the development of its facade a clear desire **to enrich the streetscape without heroic efforts** or **lavish budget.** It does.

[C 28b.] The Ardsley (apartments), 320 Central Park W., SW cor. W. 92nd St. 1931. Emery Roth.

Mayan influences appear in this Art Deco apartment building, particularly in the modeling of the upper stories. In addition, there is a quality almost like that of **inlaid furniture** in the ribbons of contrasting brick which enrich the surfaces of the upper facades. And at the street level, closest to the eye, are precast exposed-aggregate terrazzo reliefs in subtle colors and forms. Compare this with the San Remo, completed by the same firm the previous year. And note the subtle detailing on the incised, mauve marble doctors' doorways.

[C 29.] The Raleigh (apartments), 7 W. 92nd St., bet. Central Park W. and Columbus Ave. 1898. Gilbert A. Schellenger.

A magnificent **tenement** that displays mannered rustication at its lower floors.

[C 30a.] Columbia Grammar and Preparatory School, 5 W. 93rd St., bet. Central Park W. and Columbus Ave. 1907.

What's interesting here is the neo-Classical frieze adorning this building below its **surprisingly modern-looking** deep, flat cornice.

[C 28b.] The "Mayan" Ardsley apts.   **[C 29.]** A magnificent 1898 tenement

[C 30b.] Columbia Grammar School   **[C 31b.]** 1st Church/Christ, Scientist

[C 30b.] New building, Columbia Grammar and Preparatory School, 4 W. 93rd St., bet. Central Park W. and Columbus Ave. 1986. Pasanella + Klein.

A handsome modern building, happily scaled for the block. Its crossed green mullions are lively and elegant. A welcome Modern outpost in these northern blocks.

[C 30c.] The Turin (apartments), 333 Central Park W., NW cor. 93rd St. 1910. Albert J. Bodker.

Study the **Roman coin** medallions in the spandrels.

[C 30d.] 336 Central Park West (apartments), SW cor. W. 94th St. 1929. Schwartz & Gross.

This 16-story apartment house is **crowned with terra-cotta reminiscences** of Egyptian-styled **papyrus stalks** (don't confuse this with the 19th-century Egyptian Revival style, of which very few examples remain in the city). The tapestry brick enriches the viewer's experience closer to eye level.

The West 95th Street park block, a diverting detour, is described in West Side Urban Renewal Area.

[C 31a.] 351-355 Central Park West (row houses), NW cor. W. 95th St. 1893. Gilbert A. Schellenger. ★ Porch added to No. 351, 1906. ★

Five early West Side speculative houses that look as though they **belong on a side street,** from the era **when no one believed** Central Park West would be anything else. Cigarette baron **Solomon Schinasi** bought **No. 351** in 1906, before buying the Rice residence on Riverside Drive [see R 17a.].

[C 31b.] First Church of Christ, Scientist, 1 W. 96th St., NW cor. Central Park W. 1903. Carrère & Hastings. ★

The architects of the Beaux Arts-style New York Public Library at Fifth Avenue and 42nd Street flirt here with the forms of **Nicholas Hawksmoor's** great Baroque churches in London. **Exciting.**

WEST SIDE URBAN RENEWAL AREA

The blocks between West 87th and West 97th Streets, from Amsterdam Avenue to Central Park West, sheltered 40,000 residents in 1956, when this area's **acute social and physical decline** indicated **a need for public action.** In a series of moves the district, one of the nation's **most densely populated,** was designated the West Side Urban Renewal Area, and plans were drawn for change.

The concepts that emerged were **radically different** from those of earlier renewal efforts. Exploitation of the highest possible rental scales was abandoned. **Clearance and rebuilding** from scratch, once the *only* redevelopment tools, were combined with **rehabilitation and renovation,** particularly of the basically sound side-street brownstone row houses. Steps were taken to ensure an economic and social mix within the district by providing not only **separate** low-rent projects but also low-rent families **within** middle-income developments. Finally, the plan provided for **phased development** from West 97th Street south to encourage the relocation of on-site tenants. The plan as amended called for 2,500 low-income units, 5,421 middle-income units, and 151 luxury units. In addition, 485 **brownstones were to be saved** and renovated.

The results are most visible architecturally along Columbus Avenue, which is lined with high-rise construction. The side streets have been **more subtly upgraded:** behind the facades, in backyards, and with added street trees or street embellishment, as on West 94th Street.

One thing is clear. The renewal effort, **though not without its critics,** has done much **to reverse the decline** of this part of the West Side. Unlike other West Side precincts in this guide, this one proceeds from north to south to reflect the phasing of the redevelopment plan. Although the first project, Park West Village, actually **predates** these plans (it is within another urban renewal area, West Park), we include it first, both as **a logical part** of the urban renewal story and as an example of the techniques **which had been abandoned.** Start at West 96th Street and Amsterdam; then continue over to Columbus and proceed south.

[W 1.] Park West Village (apartment complex), Central Park W., to Amsterdam Ave. W. 97th to W. 100th Sts.

This large and banal housing development was built in the aftermath of the 1957 Manhattantown **urban renewal scandal.** Developers had acquired six blocks of tenements at **a reduced price** from the City under the federal urban renewal program. Instead of developing the site they sat tight for five years, collecting rents, neglecting repairs, and inventing ingenious schemes **to exploit their unhappy tenants.** Some say these disclosures marked the beginning of N.Y.C. construction czar Robert Moses' loss of power.

West Side Urban Renewal Area

[W 2.] Key West (apartments), 750 Columbus Ave., bet. W. 96th and W. 97th Sts. W side. 1987. Schuman, Lichtenstein, Claman & Efron.

An 11-story apartment house that **steps down** along 96th Street to form a happier relationship with the community than do many of the architecturally self-conscious towers of the original urban renewal work.

[W 3a.] RNA House (apartments), 150-160 W. 96th St., bet. Columbus and Amsterdam Aves. 1967. Edelbaum & Webster.

A concrete beehive of a facade: **oppressive.**

[W 3b.] New Amsterdam (apartments), 733 Amsterdam Ave., bet. W. 95th and W. 96th Sts. E side. 1971. Gruzen & Partners.

Buff brick, used here in profusion, seems always to be an architectural bugaboo—very difficult, because of its blandness, to use well. This is **a striking exception.** The concrete balconies, made private by tall side walls, exposed concrete floor slabs, and floor-to-floor window modules, make for a strongly designed tower. Unfortunately, too much is going on at street level.

[W 4a.] Columbus House (apartments), 75 W. 95th St., NE cor. Columbus Ave. to W. 96th Sts. E side. 1970. Horace Ginsbern & Assocs.

A **highly articulated** concrete structure with expansive balconies sandwiched between deep protruding columns. (Note that the balconies don't begin until the 9th floor.)

[W 4b.] West 95th Street, bet. Columbus and Amsterdam Aves.

Potentially one of the West Side's finest streets, certainly from an urban design viewpoint. It is good to see **restoration underway and completed** but depressing to find it temporarily halted. Of particular interest is **No. 143:**

[W 4c.] 143 West 95th Street (residence), bet. Columbus and Amsterdam Aves. 1889. James Cole.

Exuberant neo-Gothicism as if done in the Renaissance fashion by a student trained at the École des Beaux-Arts. It is a grand presence on this handsome block.

[W 4d.] West Side Manor, 70 W. 95th St., SE cor. Columbus Ave. to W. 94th St. 1968. Gruzen & Partners.

A long prism perpendicular to Columbus Avenue. The avenue side is buff brick and bland; the side-street facades are recessed balconies and bland.

[W 4e.] Congregation Ohab Zedek (synagogue), 118 W. 95th St., bet. Columbus and Amsterdam Aves. 1926. Charles B. Meyers.

Inticate terra-cotta ornament enriches the tall Byzantine arch which **sums up** this synagogue's facade.

[W 5.] West 95th Street, bet. Central Park W. and Columbus Ave.

Diversely styled row houses, luxuriant trees, and lots of care make this **one of the loveliest** of the **park blocks.** A leisurely walk will reveal delightful touches: sculpted griffins and cherubs, fine lanterns, simply designed metal guards around the street-tree pits, the fussy concern (competition?) with appliqué house numbers. The **rhapsodic** architectural **exercise in circles and arcs** at the entrances, balconies, and stoops of **Nos. 6** and **8** is a small delight. The quality of this block is attributable in many respects to the influence of the West Side Urban Renewal Area in which it is included.

[W 6.] Jefferson Towers (apartments), 700 Columbus Ave., bet. W. 94th and W. 95th Sts. W side. 1968. Horace Ginsbern & Assocs.

Alternating the arrangement of balconies—separated on odd floors and joined on even floors—creates **a powerful rhythm** in the facade—**too powerful.**

Experimental street improvements: West 94th Street between Central Park West and Amsterdam Avenue is the site of an early 1970s experiment in modulating the width of city side streets. Here the endless rows of parked cars were interrupted with brick paved projections, suitably greened with trees or shrubs, that neck the asphalt roadway width appreciably.

[W 7.] Gottesman Playground, W. 94th St. bet. Columbus and Amsterdam Aves. N side. 1970. M. Paul Friedberg & Assocs., landscape architects.

Imaginative design is only one of many ingredients for the success of an urban playground. **Time** and boredom weigh heavily on young lives and can translate into destructive behavior in an unsupervised outdoor space like this—unsupervised because, as a privately sponsored facility, it was to have been the ward of the adjacent cooperative apartment corporation. Maintenance and supervision proved to be too expensive, hence a bombed-out playground.

[W 7.] The Gottesman Playground, an Upper West Side "bombed out" relic

[W 8a.] 125-139 and **151-159 West 93rd Street (row houses),** bet. Columbus and Amsterdam Aves. ca. 1890.

Two groups of Queen Anne facades in red and gray. Curiously restrained for this style.

[W 8b.] Junior High School 118, Manhattan, Joan of Arc Junior High School, 154 W. 93rd St., bet. Columbus and Amsterdam Aves. 1941. Eric Kebbon.

Reflecting relatively high land values, this school was built upward rather than laterally. Almost mimicking in limestone relief the high-rise character of the building is **a luxuriant mythic beanstalk** emerging from an urn; it "grows" between the entrance doors.

[W 8c.] Templo Adventista del Septimo Dia/originally **The Nippon Club,** 161 W. 93rd St., bet. Columbus and Amsterdam Aves. 1912. John Van Pelt.

A **serene facade** in a curiously different style, perhaps influenced by the work of the Chicago School. The deep overhanging cornice on crisply modeled console brackets gives the facade **a convincing terminus** against the sky.

[W 9a.] Strykers Bay Houses (apartments), 689 Columbus Ave., bet. W. 93rd and W. 94th Sts. E side. 1967. Holden, Egan, Wilson & Corser.

Red brick, corner windows, and rounded brick penthouses enclosing elevator machinery and a water tank: it resembles the best of public housing of the 1940s and 1950s rather than urban design of the 1970s. The smaller building on West 94th Street, almost square in plan, has more satisfying proportions.

[W 9b.] Columbus Park Towers (apartments), 100 W. 94th St., SW cor. Columbus Ave. to W. 93rd St. 1967. Ballard, Todd & Snibbe.

Rough board-formed concrete balcony balustrades add whatever design distinguishes this brownish brick slab.

[W 10a.] Columbus Manor (apartments), 70 W. 93rd St., SE cor. Columbus Ave. to W. 92nd St. 1971. Liebman & Liebman.

A tall **Buffter** Keaton, pork pie hat and all.

[W 10b.] Leader House (apartments), 100 W. 93rd St., SW cor. Columbus Ave. to W. 92nd St. 1972. Dominick Salvati.

Perhaps the sponsors believed that this tower's severe appearance would automatically **lead to economical monthly rents.** It doesn't. This buff brick and reinforced concrete building looks as if the brick walls hold up the exposed concrete—actually **it's just the other way.** What a **civic bore!**

[W 10c.] 180 West 93rd Street (apartments), SE cor. Amsterdam Ave. ca. 1940.

An elegant **Art Moderne** brick apartment block. Though seemingly just a background building, its detail is redolent of the best of those years between the world wars. A symmetrical entrance gives its alternate address as **175 West 92nd Street.**

[W 11.] 74 West 92nd Street (apartments), N.Y.C. Housing Authority and **Goddard Riverside (New) Community Center,** 647 Columbus Ave., bet. W. 91st and W. 92nd Sts. E side. 1965.

A lackluster Housing Authority building in an out-of-the-ordinary (but not **buff**) dark **brown** brick.

[W 12a.] Trinity School, Main Building, 139 W. 91st St., bet. Columbus and Amsterdam Aves. 1894. Charles C. Haight. **[W 12b.] East Building**/originally **Parish House, St. Agnes Chapel (Episcopal). [W 12c.]** 1892. William A. Potter.

Founded in 1709. Among the many interlocked buildings that this school occupies are the Anglo-Italianate brownstone Main Building, the **wonderful Romanesque Revival remnant** of an otherwise demolished Trinity Parish outpost (St. Agnes Chapel), and the podium of Trinity House.

[W 12c.] Trinity House (apartments) and Trinity School addition (mixed use), 100 W. 92nd St., SW cor. Columbus Ave. to W. 91st St. 1969. Brown, Guenther, Battaglia, Seckler.

At grade an extension of adjacent Trinity School; neatly stacked apartments in a tower above. The intricately fashioned facade reminds you of a **Chinese wood-block puzzle:** pull out the magic piece and the whole thing will come apart.

[W 13a.] Play area, Stephen Wise Towers, N.Y.C. Housing Authority, W. 90th to W. 91st Sts., midblock bet. Columbus and Amsterdam Aves. Play area only. Richard G. Stein & Assocs., architects. Constantino Nivola, sculptor.

A modern horse fair for West Side cowchildren is the feature of this play area, subsidized by the J. M. Kaplan Fund to enliven otherwise pedestrian public housing. It sees some heavy use but, alas, there is no ASPCA to protect **concrete** horses.

[W 13b.] Heywood Tower (apartments)/originally **Heywood Broun Plaza,** 175 W. 90th St., NE cor. Amsterdam Ave. to W. 91st St. 1974. Gerald Karlan.

Monotonous.

[W 14.] St. Martin's Tower (apartments), 65 W. 90th St. (a.k.a. Henry J. Browne Blvd.), NE cor. Columbus Ave. to W. 91st St. 1971. Ifill Johnson Hanchard.

Design through the arrangement of balconies, this time in repetitive groups of four: two pairs, one above the other, and then a space—a kind of **architectural square dance,** but the massing of the building is clunky. The sculptural concrete element at the West 90th Street corner is refreshing until you realize it conceals (not too well) a ventilation grille from the cellar.

[W 15.] Turin House (apartments), 609 Columbus Ave., bet. W. 89th and W. 90th Sts. E side. 1972. Holden, Yang, Raemsch & Corser.

Sandy concrete block walls (the construction dollar bought less in the 1970s than in the 1960s) instead of brick give this spartan building a deceiving scale. So do the 2-story fenced-in "sky lobbies" on the side-street facades. The barred cages on the avenue facade are fire exits between adjacent duplex apartments, the building code's substitute for the more traditional fire escape.

 [W 16a.] 600 Columbus Avenue (apartments), bet. W. 89th and W. 90th Sts. W side. 1987. **[W 16b.] 103-105 West 89th Street ("town houses"),** bet. Columbus and Amsterdam Aves. 1987. **[W 16c.] community garden,** bet. W. 89th and W. 90th St. behind 600 Columbus Ave. 1988. All by Hoberman & Wasserman, architects. The Schnadelbach Partnership, landscape architect.

The greenhouses along Columbus Avenue make a graceful transition from the setback slab and the streetfront stores below. The "town houses" are a pleasant bow to the tradition of the sidestreeted West Side. But whereas most of the West Side was originally composed of **single-family houses,** these were built to be apartment units from the start.

[W 14.] St. Martin's Tower apartmts.   **[W 16b.]** 103-105 West 89th Street

MANHATTAN VALLEY

A new event in Manhattan's **usually predictable** gridiron plan occurs at West 100th Street. It is here, between Central Park West and Columbus Avenue, that a new north-south thoroughfare is born: **Manhattan Avenue,** which strikes out northward across Cathedral Parkway into Harlem. As it moves north, the topography it covers **begins to drop** (as does the economic level of the community), and this descent of the terrain has given rise to the area's unofficial name: Manhattan Valley. We define it in this guide as bordered by West 100th Street and Cathedral Parkway (West 110th Street) and by Central Park West and Amsterdam Avenue.

[M 1.] Originally **Association for the Relief of Respectable Aged Indigent Females,** 891 Amsterdam Ave., bet. W. 103rd and W. 104th Sts. E side. 1881. Richard Morris Hunt. ★

Vacated in 1975, this institution, once open only to women who had not "lived as servants," **may be demolished** if an alternate use (and budget) are not found. Its red brick forms and its busy, dormered and gabled roof lines are **a visual asset** to the neighborhood.

 [M 2.] West End Presbyterian Church, 325 Amsterdam Ave., NE cor. W. 105th St. 1891. Henry Kilburn.

Romanesque Revival but restrained—not Richardsonian at all. The tall, delicately striped brick corner tower marks the intersection well. Note the **refined ornament** to which terra-cotta lent itself—almost damask but of a scale demanded of architecture.

[M 3a.] Public School 145, Manhattan, The Bloomingdale School, 150 W. 105th St., bet. Columbus and Amsterdam Aves. 1961. Unger & Unger.

Bright vermillion column caps, and a concrete entrance canopy reminiscent of **an angel's wings,** highlight this school's facade.

[M 3b.] St. Gerasimos Greek Orthodox Church, 155 W. 105th St., bet. Columbus and Amsterdam Aves. 1951. Kokkins & Lyons.

A design which **refuses to abandon old traditions** but arrives nevertheless at a strong composition in limestone and orange brick.

[M 4.] Manhattan Valley Town Houses, Manhattan Ave. bet. W. 104th and W. 105th Sts. E side. 1986. Rosenblum/Harb.

A **reductionist** row that pales in comparison to the richly detailed 1888 houses across Manhattan Avenue.

[M 4.] Rosenblum/Harb's reductionist town house row in Manhattan Valley

[M 5.] Old N.Y. Cancer Hospital in '66   **[M 6.]** The Cathedral Parkway Houses

[M 5.] Originally **New York Cancer Hospital/**later **Towers Nursing Home/**now **apartments,** 2 W. 106th St., SW cor. Central Park W. 1887. Charles C. Haight. ★ Remodeled and adjacent residential tower added, 1989, John Harding and Victor Caliandro.

This **castellated émigré** from the Loire Valley has charmed the Upper West Side for more than a century. The first American hospital devoted exclusively to cancer patients, it served as a nursing home and may yet ennoble the looming **Tyrannosaurus Rex** behind.

[M 5a.] Originally **Edison Company substation,** 171-173 W. 107th St., bet. Columbus and Amsterdam Aves. ca. 1916.

Even **dynamos** were once housed in utilitarian structures of architectural interest.

[M 6.] Cathedral Parkway Houses (apartments), 125 W. 109th St., bet. Columbus and Amsterdam Aves. to Cathedral Pkwy. 1975. Davis, Brody & Assocs. and Roger Glasgow.

Two enormous **zigzag** towers occupy opposite corners of this hilly midblock site; between them a private, terraced, open space leaps from level to level, street to street. The towers, **cousins** to Davis, Brody's **Waterside, Yorkville and Ruppert,** and **Riverpark** in the Bronx, are here more self-consciously articulated in plan and massing to **minimize their impact upon the adjacent smaller-scale** community. The site was formerly occupied by **Woman's Hospital.**

[M 6a.] West 110th Street substation, Con Edison, 464 W. 110th St., SE cor. Amsterdam Ave. to W. 109th St. 1964. Con Edison architectural staff.

Albert Speer might have liked this **forbidding mausoleum,** which takes far too much for granite.

CENTRAL PARK

This great work of art, the **granddaddy** of America's naturally landscaped parks, was named a **National Historic Landmark** in **1965.** Better still, for the sake of its eternal preservation, it is now a "scenic landmark," so designated by the **New York City Landmarks Preservation Commission.** This latter designation, happily, has teeth (whereas the national one is largely honorific and hopeful). Many believe that this park, **Prospect Park,** and the **Brooklyn Bridge** are the three greatest creations in New York City.

But who made this 840-acre (larger than Monaco) masterpiece possible in the center of New York City? One of the first was the poet and newspaper editor **William Cullen Bryant,** who in 1844 called for a large, public pleasure ground (at that time Washington Square was considered uptown). After landscape architect **Andrew Jackson Downing** appealed for a park, the idea caught on, and both mayoralty contestants made it a promise in the 1850 campaign. The winner, Ambrose C. Kingsland, kept his word, and the Common Council took action.

The site was then physically unprepossessing: "A pestilential spot where miasmic odors taint every breath of air," one report concluded. But it was available. Land was acquired (*1856*) for $5.5 million and surveyed by **Egbert L. Viele.** Clearing began the next year: squatters and hogs were forcibly removed, often with the aid of the police; bone-boiling works and swill mills were torn down, swamps were drained, and the omnipresent Manhattan schist was blasted.

The first **Board of Park Commissioners,** helped by a committee including **Bryant** and the writer **Washington Irving,** decided in 1857 that an open competition should determine the park's design.

Greensward, so named by contestants **Frederick Law Olmsted** and **Calvert Vaux,** won out among the **33 designs submitted.** It was a simple, uncluttered plan, calling for a picturesque landscape: glade, copse, water, and rock outcroppings. Bridges (each individually designed by Vaux) separated footpaths, bridle paths, and the carriage drives— which were curved to prevent racing. The four sunken transverse roads for crosstown traffic were revolutionary.

Ten million cartloads of stone, earth, and topsoil were moved in or out of the site as **Greensward** became an actuality. It took nearly 20 years but, long before completion, the park became the place for rich and poor alike to promenade, to see and be seen. Today it is even more the playground for New Yorkers: for some a place to enjoy nature, for many the only "country" they have ever seen, for others a magnificently designed **Garden of Eden** to ease the strains of city living, and most recently a place of amateur gambling, gamboling, and beer drinking for residents of all boroughs.

Central Park is the **forecourt** and **front garden** to the residential slabs and towers of Central Park **South,** Central Park **West,** Central Park **North,** and **Fifth Avenue** (otherwise Central Park East). At the southeast corner the surrounding towers cast romantic reflections in its waters (for the postcard maker) and enjoy the Plaza's great space, a happy symbiosis for both.

Venerable trees, planted at Olmsted & Vaux's direction, shade the wooded paths

Invasions: Despite continuing threats of preposterous intrusions, the original plan was closely followed until the advent of the automobile and active sports. In 1912 the gravel drives were paved with asphalt, and two new entrances were cut through on Central Park South. Permanent tennis courts were then constructed. The first paved playground, the **Heckscher,** appeared in 1926. By the 1950s large structures had sprung up, all partially financed by philanthropists: the **Wollman Memorial Rink,** the **Delacorte Theater,** the **Children's Zoo,** and the **Lasker Pool-Rink:** some worthy additions, others vulgar and ugly intruders. The establishment of the **Central Park Conservancy** offers an opportunity to reconstruct the park in an Olmstedian vision adapted to current needs . . . but only if the well-meaning gifts can be directed toward thoughtful goals.

South and North:

By topography and design the park falls into two sections. The large "pastoral" south is by far the more familiar; but the mostly neglected north is well worth a visit for its contrasting wild picturesqueness—a worthiness best savored in groups by day (avoided totally by dusk or dark) for personal security. The following two tours are meant to serve only as an introduction to these sections.

Walking Tour A, The South: Conservatory Water (at East 72nd Street and Fifth Avenue) to Grand Army Plaza (59th Street and Fifth Avenue) or the Zoo. Arrive via 68th Street Station of the Lexington Avenue IRT subway; Madison or Fifth Avenue buses.

START at Fifth Avenue and 72nd Street (this is **Inventors' Gate,** one of Vaux's 18 named gates piercing the park's wall). Detour to the south to view the delightful **East 72nd Street Playground** *(1970. Richard Dattner & Assocs.)* **[S 1.].** Turn back north, crossing the park drive, and bear left past the **Pilgrim Memorial** *(1885. John Quincy Adams Ward, sculptor)* **[S 2.].** Note the pilgrim's spectacular bronze boots. Descend **Pilgrim Hill** to the **Conservatory Water [S 3a.],** a formal neo-Renaissance concrete basin, named for the conservatory (greenhouse) promised but unbuilt on its eastern shore. Model and toy boats, some of which are stored at the **Alice H. and Edward A. Kerbs Memorial Boathouse** *(1954)* **[S 3b.],** are usually sailing here (races April through October mornings). Two statues overlook this water: **Alice in Wonderland Margarita Delacorte Memorial** *(Jose de Creeft, sculptor)* and **Hans**

Christian Andersen *(1956. George J. Lober, sculptor. Otto F. Langmann, architect.).* Neither is of any great artistic merit, but both are beloved by swarming children (storytelling at Andersen, Saturday mornings, May-September). From here look across the water to enjoy a view of Fifth Avenue through a filigree of branches and/or leaves.

Continue around the western shore to the path leading west to **Trefoil Arch [S 4.]** *(restored, 1985, Beyer Blinder Belle)* a brownstone tunnel with a wood ceiling, and pass under the **East Drive** to reach the shore of **The Lake [S 5.],** where a gondola and a circuiting public launch once accompanied the flotilla of rowboats. The **72nd Street Boathouse** *(1954)* **[S 5a.]** is in the brick neo-Victorian style favored by one time Parks Commissioner **Robert Moses.** Note the rowboat sculpture, from a fudgy clay, cast into bronze, in the front court *(1967. Irwin Glusker, sculptor).* The boathouse has a restaurant and a pleasant terrace overlooking The Lake. The bicycle concession to the right is jammed, particularly on those days and evenings when the park drives, closed to traffic, become the cyclist's province.

The path along the south shore reaches the **Bethesda Terrace [S 6.].** *(Restored, 1987, The Ehrenkrantz Group & Eckstut, architects; Philip Winslow, landscape architect),* the only formal architectural element of the **Greensward Plan.** Jacob Wrey Mould detailed the stonework, but Vaux was the conceptual designer. **Bethesda Fountain** *(1870. Emma Stebbins, sculptor. Calvert Vaux, architect)* is the centerpiece, with a bronze winged **Angel of the Waters** crowning vigorous chubby cherubs (Purity, Health, Peace, and Temperance). The terrace is a faded elegance of brick paving, sandstone bordered, walled, and crowned.

Side trips: Southwest of **The Terrace** stands **Bow Bridge [S 7.]** *(1860. Calvert Vaux. Restored, 1974),* a cast-iron elegance spanning the Lake to the Ramble. The bosky **Ramble [S 8.],** where even vigilant bird watchers have been known to lose their way on the mazelike paths, contains meandering streams, exotic trees and shrubs, and small, hidden lawns. At its north the Ramble ascends to **Vista Rock,** topped by **Belvedere Castle [S 9.],** former home of the city's weather station. *(Restored, 1978, James Lamantia).* Below the Castle is **Belvedere Lake,** last vestige of the old reservoir drained in 1929. The reservoir's dry bed was used by squatters during the Depression, then filled in, becoming the **Great Lawn [S 10.],** today's favored spot for touch football, soccer, and softball. The **Delacorte Theater [S 11.],** with summer Shakespeare, hovers over the new lake's western flank. The **Central Park Precinct, N.Y.C. Police Department [S 12.],** on the 85th/86th Street Transverse Road, is another Calvert Vaux building *(1871).* East, behind the Metropolitan Museum of Art [see E Manhattan/Met Museum M12.], rises the **Obelisk [S 13.]** from the reign of Thutmose III (ca. 1450 B.C.). A gift from the khedive of Egypt, it was erected in the park in 1881. Resting on on a promontory on the west side of the Lake (near the West 77th Street park entrance) is **The Ladies Pavilion [S 14.]** *(1871. Vaux & Mould).* It was purportedly moved there from its original location on the edge of the park at Columbus Circle, where it had sheltered ladies awaiting streetcars, and was later bumped for the erection of The Maine Monument. Vandalized and ruined at the lake shore, it was reincarnated through the efforts of the Parks Department monuments officer, Joseph Bresnan, and is now a lacy cast-iron Victorian delight. To its south, near the West 72nd Street park entrance, is the Italian mosaic spelling out **"Imagine"** set in the paving of **Strawberry Fields [S 15.]** *(1983. Bruce Kelly, landscape architect),* a gift from **John Lennon**'s widow, Yoko Ono, in memory of the legendary **Beatle** killed in front of the Dakota, which overlooks the site. *Resume tour.*

The Mall [S 16.], the Park's grand promenade, lies south of the Terrace Arcade. Pass through, noting the glazed and decorated tile ceiling. The Mall's axis points to the Belvedere Castle, deliberately kept small by architect Vaux to lengthen the perspective. Full-grown trees have almost obliterated the vista. Behind the intrusive limestone half-hemispherical vaulted **Naumburg Bandshell [S 17a.]** is **The Pergola [S 17b.].** *(Rebuilt, 1987, Laura Starr, landscape architect),* a low, light-filtered wood trellis, one of the park's few wisteria-covered arbors. Behind it is **Rumsey Playground [S 17c.].** *(Redesigned, 1986, Philip Winslow).* **The Mall,** in recent years, has been a place for action, rather than strolling: juggling, guitar playing, drug dealing, beer drinking, gambling, hamburger eating, and so forth.

On The Mall are several statues: **Fitzgreene Halleck** *(1877. J. Wilson MacDonald).* A prissy and pretentious bronze of a self-styled poet. **Walter Scott** *(1872. John Steell).* The 100th anniversary of Scott's birth is memorialized by this dour bronze, a copy of Steell's original in the Scott Memorial in Edinburgh. **Robert Burns** *(1880. John Steell)* is represented as a faraway and saccharine romantic. **Columbus** *(1894. Jeronimo Suñol):* an entranced religious maniac. **Shakespeare** *(1870. John Quincy Adams Ward):* the thoughtful bard in pantaloons.

[S 6.] Bethesda Fountain and Terrace   **[S 9.]** Vaux's Belvedere Castle in 1909

Side trip: West of The Mall, past the park's closed Center Drive, stretches the **Sheep Meadow [S 18.]**, a sweeping lawn where sheep could safely graze until banished in 1934 (they lived in the nearby **Sheepfold** now converted to the Tavern-on-the-Green). From the north end is a splendid view of skyscrapers. To the southwest, along Central Park West, stands the **Tavern-on-the-Green [S 19.]**, periodically renovated for glitzy greenhouse and terrace dining. Nearby, overlooking West 68th Street, is Central Park's first **Adventure Playground [S 19a.]** *(1966. Richard Dattner & Assocs.). Resume tour.*

Continue at the **southern end** of The Mall cross the drive, and don't blame Olmsted for not providing an underground passage here: the Marble Arch, the park's most famous bridge, was removed in the 1930s. Take the southeast path along the drive, and while crossing over the 65th Street Transverse Road, notice how little the sunken drive intrudes into the park. To the right, a path leads past **The Dairy [S 20.]**, a sturdy Gothic Revival building delivered once again its original porch *(Restored, 1979, James Lamantia with Weisberg Castro Assocs.).* Note Manhattan schist and sandstone neo-Gothic colonnettes. **Vaux designed it.**

Another side trip: Head west, to the north of the hillsite of the **Kinderberg**, once a large arbor. It's now replaced by the squat **Chess and Checkers House [S 21.]**, a gift of financier Bernard Baruch, a red and beige brick neo-Ruskinian *cum* Moses (Robert, that is) octagonal lump. Continue west, under **Playmates Arch** beneath the drive to the **Michael Friedsam Memorial Carousel** *(1951),* another beige and red brick octagon replacing an earlier one, destroyed by fire. *Resume tour.*

From **The Dairy**, after dropping down to the left, the path passes east of the Chess and Checkers site. Skirt southeast around the **Wollman Memorial Rink [S 22.]** and go up the hill along the fence enclosing the **Bird Sanctuary [S 23.]. Gapstow Bridge**, crossing the Pond **[S 24.]**, is a good place to admire the reflections of the city's towers in the water below. A few swans and many ducks are usually swimming around. Swan boats, the same as those still in Boston Public Garden, sailed here until 1924. Leave the park by the gate across from Sherman's statue or, if you want to visit **the Zoo,** go, via **Inscope Arch** under the East Drive, northeast of the Pond.

END of tour: Nearest transit is the BMT Broadway Line Fifth Avenue Station at East 60th Street or Fifth or Madison Avenue buses.

Side trip: The Zoo [S 25.], off Fifth Avenue at 64th Street, is a favorite haunt of New Yorkers. It is a formal plaza once surrounded by WPA-built red brick arched buildings now totally redesigned *(1988. Kevin Roche John Dinkeloo & Assocs.)* to provide glazed arcades and more professional operation by the New York Zoological Garden staff. A constant is the centrally located and much beloved sea lion pool. **The Arsenal** [see E Manhattan/The Gold Coast G 12.] is a participant in the Zoo plaza by default.

[S 19a.] First Adventure Playground   The Spector Playground at W. 86th St.

Walking Tour B, The North: The Pool to Conservatory Garden. (IND Eighth Avenue subway to 96th Street Station.) **Start** at Central Park West and West 100th Street.

The Boys' Gate gives access to a path descending to **The Pool [N 1.].** It is the start of the waterway which flows east to **Harlem Meer** and was once the course of Montayne's Rivulet, which led to the East River. Across the **West Drive** and to the south of the **96th Street Transverse** are a group of tennis courts popular with the public but an intrusion into the Olmsted & Vaux vision. In 1987 plans were offered by the Central Park Conservancy to replace the 1930 **Tennis House [N 2.]** with a new structure at a higher elevation *(1989. Buttrick, White & Burtis).* This area of the park is also the home of cast-iron **Bridge No. 28 [N 3.]** *(1861. Calvert Vaux with E. C. Miller),* a Gothic Revival masterpiece.

Side trip: North of the Pool is the **Great Hill [N 4.],** where picnickers once enjoyed an unobstructed view of the Hudson and East Rivers. Perched on a cliff to the northeast is a lonely **Blockhouse [N 5.],** a remnant of the fortifications built during the War of 1812 when the British threatened the city. *Resume tour.*

At the eastern end of **The Pool,** the **Glen Span** carries the West Drive over **The Ravine.** On the other side flows **The Loch,** formerly an abundant body of water, now a trickle. This is very picturesque and completely cut off from the city.

Side trip: To the south, behind the slope, is the **North Meadow [N 6.],** scene of hotly contested baseball games: to get there, take **Springbanks Arch.** *Resume tour.*

In wet weather the Loch cascades down before disappearing under the East Drive at **Huddlestone Bridge.** Through the arch in front of Harlem Meer [N 7.] you can see the park's most disastrous "improvement," the **Loula D. Lasker Pool-Rink [N 8.].** New Yorkers have always tried to give things—especially buildings—to their park. Few succeeded until recent generations of park administrators misguidedly began again to encourage large philanthropic bequests.

Across Harlem Meer, backing onto Central Park North, is a **Central Park Conservancy** project to provide quality food service and such amenities as boat rentals to an arriving upscale community through a new **Restaurant/Boathouse [N 9.]** *(1990. Buttrick, White & Burtis).*

To the right of The Loch find **Lamppost No. 0554.** (All the older lampposts, designed by Henry Bacon in 1907, bear a street-designating plaque; here, the first two digits indicate that this one stands at 105th Street.) A path goes sharply uphill and then turns east, crossing the East Drive below **McGown's Pass,** which was fortified by the British during the Revolutionary War. **The Mount [N 10.],** to the right, was for many years the site of a tavern; its chief ornament today is the park's mulch pile.

The path descends to **Conservatory Garden [N 11.],** designed by Thomas D. Price in 1936. The **Greensward Plan** called for a large arboretum of native trees and shrubs to be planted here. Instead, a conservatory was built at the turn of the century but torn down in 1934. On the east side the **Vanderbilt Gate** opens on Fifth Avenue. Nearby is the **Museum of the City of New York,** where historical material about the park is on display [see E Manhattan/Carnegie Hill C 29c.]

END of tour: Transportation: IRT Lexington Avenue subway at East 96th Street, and Fifth or Madison Avenue buses.

Other playgrounds: Playgrounds were not part of Olmsted & Vaux's original scheme. Those **around the park's perimeter,** intended for the children of those who later populated the desirable communities adjoining the park, were added during the regime of Mayor La Guardia (1934–1945) and his agile parks commissioner, Robert Moses, and were designed in their **inimitable bunker style.** Beginning in the 1960s they were redesigned, often with the financial assistance of local community groups and special donors. In addition to those already mentioned are these along Fifth Avenue: **East 68th Street Playground** *(1987. M. Paul Friedberg & Partners);* **Sophie Loeb Playground,** between East 77th and 78th Streets *(1987. Bruce Kelly, landscape architect);* **Ancient Play Garden** between East 85th and 86th Streets *(1972. Richard Dattner & Assocs.);* and **East 96th Street Playground** *(1987. Lois Scherr, landscape architect).* Along Central Park West are **Diana Ross Playground,** at West 81st Street *(1986. John Lesniak);* **Spector Playground,** at West 86th Street *(1976. Abraham Rothenberg Assocs.);* and, at the southern end of the park, the **Water Playground** section of the Heckscher Playground *(1972. Richard Dattner & Assocs.).*

All are havens for the adventurous child-explorer, renouncing the rigid predictability of New York streets for a **realm of fantasy and physical challenge:** incidentally handsome, sculptural places with rich materials and textures.

UPPER EAST SIDE

THE GOLD COAST • METROPOLITAN MUSEUM VICINITY
CARNEGIE HILL AND BEYOND • EAST OF EDEN • HOSPITAL ROW
YORKVILLE • GRACIE SQUARE AND ENVIRONS

The area's **first development** was not residential but, rather, recreational: **Central Park.** Toward the middle of the last century, the tremendous influx of Irish and German immigrants, dislocated by economic and political turmoil in their homeland, was straining the City's resources. Reformers were pressuring for a **great public park** to serve a

UPPER EAST SIDE

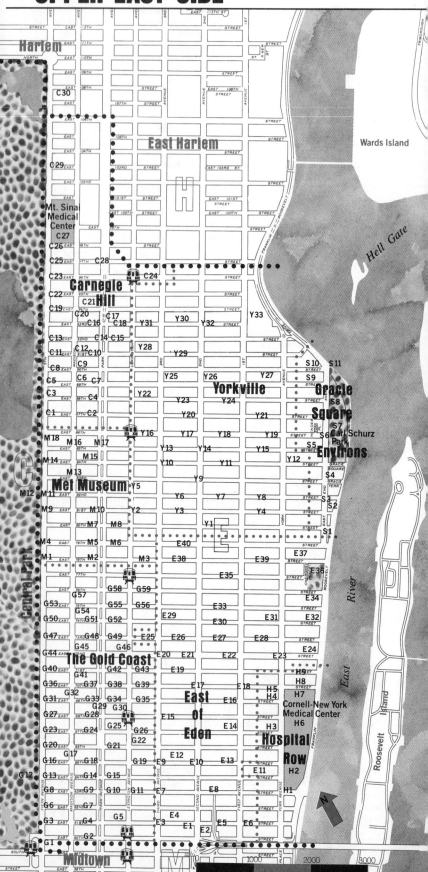

population expected to grow even further. In the 1850s Mayor Fernando Wood and his Tammany Hall cronies foresaw the construction of the park as an opportunity to create enormous numbers of **patronage positions** among the new electorate. And the park's central site would neatly divide upper Manhattan into twin development opportunities: the rough terrain of the West Side (to be reserved for later) and the relatively flat East Side. The latter was made more accessible from downtown by **cutting through** Madison and Lexington Avenues as **additions to the original** gridiron street plan of 1811.

The first **transit connections** from downtown were **horsecar lines** along Second, Third, and Madison Avenues and steam trains (including local service) along today's Park Avenue. Not surprisingly, the first row house development, during the 1860s and until the Panic of 1873, followed these **routes of opportunity.** The late 1870s brought the Second and Third Avenue **elevated lines** from downtown—*mass* transit. With it came the masses, housed in an explosive development of tenements— many of which remain—in the area's eastern flank.

The elegant associations with the term **Upper East Side** are relatively recent. To those who could afford them, Park Avenue's steam trains provided accessibility but also brought **smoke and noise,** thus creating an **"other side of the tracks"** opportunity. Between Park Avenue and the park, Central, a corridor formed, beginning in the 1890s, that attracted **capitalists from downtown** residential enclaves, such as lower Fifth Avenue and Gramercy Park, to costly sites along Fifth Avenue—**the Gold Coast**—and to lesser ones along the side streets and brownstone-lined Madison Avenue. East of Park Avenue huddled a mixture of row houses, stables, and carriage houses—truly the other side of the tracks.

Most of the mansions built at the turn of the century along Fifth (save those now used largely as museums) were demolished in **two waves of high-rise** luxury apartment development, the first in the Roaring Twenties, the second following World War II. In response to the first building boom, Madison Avenue's **brownstones were altered** to provide neighborhood shops and services for an expanding number of **affluent apartment dwellers.** Gracie Square and parts of East End Avenue also saw apartment development then.

Mrs. Astor's Fifth Avenue mansion at E. 65th Street (site of Temple Emanu-El)

The post-World War II boom, (to the east signaled by the 1956 demolition of the grim Third Avenue el structure) extended—with gasps for air—well into the 1980s. It transformed practically every Upper East Side development site into a **pot of gold** and turned Madison Avenue into the **ultrachic shopping street** for wealthy Americans—and internationals as well.

Note: The listings in the Upper East Side run generally eastward from Central Park, block by block, working their way uptown, northward.

THE GOLD COAST

Borrowing a term initially used to denote Fifth Avenue along Central Park, together with its park blocks, the area included below is bounded by Fifth and Lexington Avenues, from just above 59th Street to 78th. Much—but not all—is officially designated as the Upper East Side Historic District. The upper reaches of Fifth Avenue are covered in precincts called **Metropolitan Museum Vicinity** and **Carnegie Hill.**

[G 1.] Upper East Side Historic District ★

In 1981, sixteen years after the passage of the city's landmarks law, **the unachievable was achieved**: the establishment, under Chairman Kent L. Barwick, of a historic district that stretches along Fifth Avenue's gold coast from 59th to 78th Streets—where it abuts the Metropolitan Museum Historic District [see M 1.]—and reaches inland in a leg that wraps up to 79th and Park. In between, its boundaries irregularly encompass properties beyond Madison and Park Avenues to the east, **even crossing Lexington** from 69th and 71st. Upper East Side Historic District properties in **the Gold Coast area** are identified ☆.

[G 1a.] Sherry Netherland Hotel, 781 Fifth Ave., NE cor. E. 59th St. 1927. Schulze & Weaver. ☆

A tower fit for a *muezzin* crowns its peaked and finialed roof. The bar along Fifth Avenue is one of New York's greatest: venerable elegance. **A la Vieille Russie** vends wares of czarist opulence.

[G 1b.] Diane von Furstenberg Fifth Avenue (boutique), 783 Fifth Ave. (in the Sherry Netherland Hotel), bet. E. 59th and E. 60th Sts. 1984. Michael Graves. ☆

A boutique bearing the razzle-dazzle and craftsmanship last seen on Fifth Avenue in the heyday of the Roaring Twenties.

[G 1c.] Sidewalk clock, in front of 783 Fifth Ave., bet. E. 59th and E. 60th Sts. E side. ★

General Sherman's timepiece as he gallops through history in The Plaza [see M Manhattan/Plaza Suite Z 1.]

[G 1d.] The Metropolitan Club, 1 E. 60th St., bet. Fifth and Madison Aves. 1893. McKim, Mead & White. E wing, 1912, Ogden Codman, Jr. All ★ ☆.

J. P. Morgan organized this club, primarily for his friends who were not accepted in others. An Italian palazzo is crossed with a proper English carriage entrance and courtyard. For those able to enter, the interior is an extravaganza of space, marble coffers, and gilt: Corinthian columns, velvet ropes, and scarlet carpeting.

Plans to add a 37-story residential tower (James Stewart Polshek & Partners) atop the east wing (occupied by the **The Canadian Club**) and its connecting link were nixed by the Landmarks Preservation Commission in 1987.

[G 1e.] The Harmonie Club, 4 E. 60th St., bet. Fifth and Madison Aves. 1906. McKim, Mead & White. ☆

A high-rise Renaissance palace, the second home of the club founded by members of the crowd chronicled in *Our Crowd.*

Copacabana, 10 E. 60th St. (in the former **Hotel Fourteen,** 1902, addition 1905, Raleigh C. Gildersleeve.) ☆

A huge nightclub by contemporary standards, from the era of **big bands** and **big shows,** à la Ziegfeld. Now a double-deck disco.

Note: For the **650 Madison Avenue** office tower, see [M Manhattan/ Plaza Suite Z 12.]

[G 2a.] The Grolier Club, 47 E. 60th St., bet. Madison and Park Aves. 1917. Bertram G. Goodhue. [Outside Upper East Side Historic District.]

Named for the 16th-century French bibliophile **Jean Grolier,** this club is for those devoted to the bookmaking crafts. In the 1960s poor Grolier's name was taken in vain for the gold skyscraper at the northeast corner of 51st and Lex. See also the club's original home [see M Manhattan/Murray Hill M 3d.].

[G 2b.] Christ Church (Methodist), 520 Park Ave., NW cor. E. 60th St. 1932. Ralph Adams Cram. [Outside Upper East Side Historic District.]

A church designed to *appear* aged: the random limestone and brick is intended to look like a sophisticated patch job, centuries old. Similarly, the marble and granite columns appear to be, in the **Romanesque** and **Byzantine** manner, pillage from **Roman** temples. Handsome, and of impeccable taste, it is an archaeological and eclectic stage set for well-to-do parishioners. *Look at the mosaic ceiling, especially when lit by blue bulbs.*

[G 3a.] Hotel Pierre, 795 Fifth Ave., SE cor. E. 61st St. 1929. Schultze & Weaver. ☆

A tall, slender, romantic hotel-apartment house with a mansard roof tower silhouette. Founded by **celebrated chef** Charles Pierre, whose restaurant had been at 230 Park Avenue.

[G 3b.] 800 Fifth Avenue (apartments), NE cor. E. 61st St. 1978. Ulrich Franzen & Assocs., design architects; Wechsler & Schimenti, associate architects. ☆

Here, until 1977, stood the shuttered town house of **Mrs. Marcellus Hartley Dodge,** the seldom used, seemingly abandoned home of a Rockefeller kin. Its replacement is a high-rise structure with a **split personality**: on the avenue it is set behind a pretentious 3-story limestone-clad false wall; on the side street it reveals a **refreshing facade** of brick syncopated by tiers of curved balconies. The limestone screen responds literally to the Fifth Avenue Special Zoning District's demands and matches in height—but not in ambience—the Knickerbocker Club to the north.

East 61st Street, between Madison and Park Avenues:

[G 4a.] 667 Madison Avenue (offices), SE cor. E. 61st St. 1987. David Paul Helpern. [Outside Upper East Side Historic District.]

This office tower, the architect's first in Manhattan, is a vigorous yet carefully controlled design that **gracefully turns a corner** within the complex rules of the Zoning Resolution while displaying a rare and masterful command (in these times) of a traditional cladding material: stone. *Don't fail to marvel at the lobby's chandeliers, too.* Built on the site of a 1900 Horgan & Slattery structure—a very worthwhile trade-off.

[G 4b.] Columbia Presbyterian Medical Associates, East Side, 38 E. 61st St./**40 East 61st Street (apartments)**/originally **LeRoy Hospital,** 1927. Alteration and additions, 1983, Rothzeid, Kaiserman & Thompson and Paul Segal Assocs. [Outside Upper East Side Historic District.]

An extremely thoughtful—and successful—addition, laterally *and* vertically, to an older Art Deco structure where entertainment personalities such as **Judy Garland** and **Nat King Cole** came for medical care. The new structure echoes and amplifies—but doesn't ape—the forms of the old.

[G 5.] Weyhe's Bookstore and Gallery, 794 Lexington Ave., bet. E. 61st and E. 62nd Sts. 1923. Henry Churchill. [Outside Upper East Side Historic District.]

Behind the tiled front, a non-American experience of great charm is in store here. A source of new and old art and architecture books, this delightful shop is packed with stock of all vintages. Upstairs (by a flight immediately inside the shop door) is a small gallery of etchings, engravings, silk-screens, and lithographs.

East 62nd Street, between Fifth and Madison Avenues:

[G 6a.] The Knickerbocker Club, 2 E. 62nd St., SE cor. Fifth Ave. 1915. Delano & Aldrich. ★ ☆

Elegant neo-Federal with classy limestone and brick detailing.

[G 4a.] 667 Madison Avenue building   [G 6b.] The Curzon House apartments

[G 6b.] Curzon House (apartments): Combination of 4 E. 62nd St. 1880. Breen & Nason. Present facade, 1898, Clinton & Russell. Formerly 6 E. 62nd St. 1901. Welch, Smith & Provot. General renovations and **addition** to W of former 4 E. 62nd St., 1985, Stephen B. Jacobs & Assocs. ☆

Since 1931 **old Nos. 4 and 6** had been the former York Club. In the superheated 1980s luxury housing boom, when it became clear that the Landmarks Preservation Commission **would not permit the demolition** of the two town houses for a high-rise replacement, they were converted to condos and expanded westward to fill the gap next to the Knickerbocker Club. The **infill** addition is **quite respectable** except for heavy-handed window framing. *Particularly note the witty see-through dormers.*

[G 6c.] The Fifth Avenue Synagogue, 5 E. 62nd St. 1956. Percival Goodman. ☆

An urban temple. Clad in finely striated cream-colored stone, with sharply incised, cat's-eye windows filled with stained glass. In daylight they read as black cat's eyes; after dark they glow once the interior is lit.

[G 6d.] The Fleming School/originally **Edmund L. Baylies residence,** 10 E. 62nd St. 1906. Hoppin, Koen & Huntington. ☆

The floors above the parlor level decrease in height as they increase in intricacy. Oh, for an entire block of such visual delight!

[G 6e.] Johnson O'Connor Research Foundation/originally **Mr. & Mrs. Ernesto Fabbri residence,** 11 E. 62nd St. 1900. Haydel & Shepard. ☆

Carefully detailed (note the fillets in the French door frames), exuberant limestone and pale-toned brick Beaux Arts town house commissioned by William H. Vanderbilt's eldest daughter **Margaret Louisa Vanderbilt Shepard.** Upon completion she **presented it to her daughter** (née Edith Shepard) and son-in-law, the Fabbris. In 1916 the Fabbris moved to their new house at 7 East 95th [see Carnegie Hill C 22.].

East 62nd Street, between Madison and Park Avenues:

[G 7a.] The Limited (women's apparel)/originally **Louis Sherry's restaurant/**later **assorted shops,** 695 Madison Ave., NE cor. E. 62nd St. 1928. McKim, Mead & White. ☆ Altered into stores, 1950. Redesigned for The Limited, 1986, Beyer Binder Belle.

A late MM&W neo-Classical/Art Deco ho-hum candy box now metamorphosed (and gilded) with **spectacular success** as the flagship for the supernova Indianapolis-based national womenswear chain. The **new boxy skylight** gives the building dignity and **adds the bulk it needs** to effectively compete—architecturally—on Madison Avenue. A magnificent renovation.

[G 7b.] Originally **The Studio Club/**now part of **The Fleming School,** 35 E. 62nd St. 1905. George Keller. ☆

Seven floors, six openings per floor, three at street level: a fugue of form and ornament. This facade is **frozen music.**

[G 7a.] The Limited/once Sherry's

[G 7d.] Neo-Tudor 40 East 62nd St.

[G 7c.] The Links Club/originally **Lillian W. Porter residence,** 36 E. 62nd St. 1902. Trowbridge & Livingston. Present facade, Cross & Cross, 1916. ☆

Creamy travertine frames rose-red Flemish bond brickwork, making a neo-Georgian swell-fronted facade **worthy of the real thing.** If God is in the details then this warm, evocative, exquisitely realized town house confirms His existence. Compare with the Assisium School on East 63rd [G 9d.]

[G 7d.] 40 East 62nd Street (apartments), 1910. Albert Joseph Bodker. ☆

An 8-floor studio building utilizing medieval forms: tier upon tier of multipaned casemented bay windows tucked *into* the facade atop a 2-story terra-cotta embellished base. Nifty.

[G 7e.] The Colony Club, 564 Park Ave., NW cor. E. 62nd St. a.k.a. 51 E. 62nd St. 1916. Delano & Aldrich. ☆

Female social leadership is split between the Colony and the Cosmopolitan, the former oriented more to *grandes dames,* the latter to activists. The Colony was founded in 1903 by the wives of Those Who Mattered. This prissy neo-Georgian town palace replaced the original on lower Madison Avenue [see M Manhattan/Four Squares W 29c.].

East 63rd Street, between Fifth and Madison Avenues:

[G 8a.] 817 Fifth Avenue (apartments), SE cor. E. 63rd St. 1925. George B. Post & Sons. ☆ **[G 8b.] 820 Fifth Avenue (apartments),** NE cor. E. 63rd St. 1916. Starrett & Van Vleck. ☆

High-rise palazzi of copper-corniced limestone, these are two of the great eclectic apartment houses of New York.

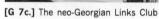

[G 7c.] The neo-Georgian Links Club   **[G 8c.]** Orig. William Ziegler, Jr. res.

[G 8c.] The New York Academy of Sciences/originally **Mr. & Mrs. William Ziegler, Jr. residence,** 2 E. 63rd St. 1920. Sterner & Wolfe. ☆

A pasty palace, large but not quite elegant, commissioned by the president of the Royal Baking Powder Company, which had been founded by his father's half brother. The house was later purchased by **Norman Bailey Woolworth,** of the **5 & 10 family,** who gave it to the academy. The colossal iron fence is a lesson in how something necessarily large can be detailed to be in scale with its surroundings. *Imagine the look of a chain link fence this high.*

[G 8d.] 14 East 63rd Street (row house), 1873. J. G. and R. B. Lynd. ☆ **[G 8e.] 16, 18 East 63rd Street (row houses),** 1876. Gage Inslee. ☆ **[G 8f.] 15 East 63rd Street (row house),** 1901. John H. Duncan. ☆ **[G 8g.] 17 East 63rd Street (row house),** 1901. Welch, Smith & Provot. ☆

In **Nos. 14, 16, 18** the brownstone is elevated to mansion status, unlike the endless rows east of Park Avenue; the Composite-columned porches on **Nos. 16 and 18** are grand for their time. **Nos. 15 and 17,** in milky limestone across the street, are newer and more pretentious—but grand—**nouveau riche** neighbors: **No. 15** was built for stockbroker Elias Asiel, whose daughter Irma became Mrs. Lyman G. Bloomingdale, a founder of the nearby department store. They lived in the town house that Bloomingdale commissioned next door—forgive its 1979 mutilation—at **No. 21** (*1900, Buchman & Fox*). ☆ **No. 17** was the home of Brooklyn brewer Joseph Huber between 1911 and 1945.

[G 8h.] The Bank of New York, 63rd Street Office, 706 Madison Ave., SW cor. E 63rd St. 1922. Frank Easton Newman. ☆

Over the rear side street entry is incised the true tale of this tiny neo-Federal charmer:

· THIS · BVILDING · WAS · ERECT ·
· ED · BY · THE · NEW · YORK · LIFE ·
· INSURANCE · AND · TRUST ·
· COMPANY · A · D · 1922 ·

[G 9a.] Fausto Santini (boutique)/originally **Santini e Dominici,** 697 Madison Ave., bet. E. 63rd and E. 64th Sts. E side. ☆ 1981. Fausto Santini, designer.

The spectrum of stripes says it all. A sporty Continental understatement.

[G 9b.] Le Relais (restaurant), 712 Madison Ave., bet. E. 63rd and E. 64th Sts. 1977. François Marchand, designer. W side. ☆

Looks just like many in Gay Paree—but on Madison it's a genuine treat.

[G 9c.] The Lowell (apartment hotel), 28 E. 63rd St., bet. Madison and Park Aves. 1926. Henry Churchill and Herbert Lippman. Entrance mosaic, Bertram Hartman. ☆

Tapestry brick and a totally unexpected glazed terra-cotta entry in an Art Deco mode.

[G 9d.] Assisium School, Missionary Sisters of the Third Order of St. Francis/ originally **The Hangar Club,** 36 E. 63rd St. bet. Madison and Park Aves. 1930. Cross & Cross. ☆

The bowfront central bay of brick and real travertine is set against the flat plane of the structure's remainder, much like the same architects' Links Club on East 62nd [see G 7c.]. A neo-Georgian composition of contrasting colors and textures. Simply wonderful.

Kenneth Murchison (1872–1938), architect of such works as the railroad and ferry terminal in Hoboken (1906, extant), lived at 49 East 63rd Street between 1909 and 1926—prior to the Mediterraneanization of its facade (in 1930). In those days it still looked like **No. 47,** which bears the original 1884 neo-Grec brownstone front by Thom & Wilson. In the latter part of his career Murchison joined Raymond Hood, Godley & Fouilhoux, architects of the old McGraw-Hill Building and associates in the design of Rockefeller Center.

[G 10a.] Third Church of Christ, Scientist, 585 Park Ave., NE cor. E. 63rd St. 1923. Delano & Aldrich. ☆

Lantern over a flat dome; mild neo-Georgian.

[G 10b.] Originally **Alexander Hirsch residence/**now **Roy H. Frowick (Halston) residence,** 101 E. 63rd St., bet. Park and Lexington Aves. 1968. Paul Rudolph. ☆

A somber brown steel and dark glass grid gives an **understated face** to a gracious set of domestic spaces within. Recast from a former stable-garage built in 1881.

[G 11a.] Barbizon Hotel/originally **Barbizon Hotel for Women,** 140 E. 63rd St., SE cor. Lexington Ave. 1927. Murgatroyd & Ogden. Lobby, restaurants, public spaces altered, 1986, Judith Stockman & Assocs., designers.

A romantic, neo-Gothic tawny brick charmer, lovingly restored in the 1980s.

[G 11b.] Barbara Rutherford Hatch residence, 153 E. 63rd St., bet. Lexington and Third Aves. 1919. Frederick J. Sterner. ★

A **picturesque loner** in well-crafted stucco by the designer of the

"Block Beautiful" [see M Manhattan/Four Squares C 10a.]. **Interesting owners:** Mrs. Hatch, daughter of Mrs. William K. Vanderbilt; Broadway producer Charles B. Dillingham; ecdysiast Gypsy Rose Lee.

[G 12.] The Arsenal, N.Y.C. Department of Parks & Recreation headquarters, 821 Fifth Ave., in Central Park opp. E. 64th St. 1848. Martin E. Thompson. Altered, 1860, Richard Morris Hunt. **Gallery open to the public.**

The "fortified" retreat of New York City's parks commissioner, located 4 miles from the seat of municipal power at City Hall. It has been said that the quality of maintenance of any city park diminishes in direct proportion to its distance from this central point in that empire. Originally the main cache of **military explosives** in the state, it became city property within nine years and then the beginnings of the American Museum of Natural History. The pyramidal roofs that once topped its octagonal towers, evident in early photos, are now gone. [For the Central Park Zoo, behind the Arsenal, see Central Park S 25.]

[G 13a.] Originally **Edward J. Berwind residence**/later **Institute of Aeronautical Sciences,** 2 E. 64th St., SE cor. Fifth Ave. 1896. Nicholas Clark Mellen. Dormers, 1902, Horace Trombauer. ☆

Berwind built this house for "town" and The Elms in Newport, R.I., for "country." Then the world's largest owner of coal mines, **Berwind fueled the U.S. Navy** throughout World War I. Note the richly modeled railings that surround the "moat." After use as institutional HQs, it was penthoused and converted to apartments in the late 1970s.

[G 13b.] New India House/originally **Marshall Orme Wilson residence,** 3 E. 64th St., bet. Fifth and Madison Aves. 1903. Warren & Wetmore. ☆ Interior altered for Government of India, 1952, William Lescaze.

Powerful, molded limestone, but **the guts are at the sky:** slate and copper mansarded attic, grand dormers, and oval windows. Mrs. Wilson was Caroline Astor, daughter of **The** Mrs. Astor of "400" fame. Mamma lived around the corner in a mansion on the site of today's Temple Emanu-El.

[G 13c.] Wildenstein & Company (art gallery), 19 E. 64th St., bet. Fifth and Madison Aves. 1932. Horace Trombauer. ☆

Travertine within and without: an art palace (never a house) that marked, with a ribbon, the end of Trombauer's rich, eclectic career. **Beautiful in proportion and patina.** Founded in Paris in 1875, the art house had previously been at 647 Fifth Avenue.

[G 13d.] Originally **Bank of the Manhattan Company branch**/now **Chase Manhattan Bank,** 726 Madison Ave., SW cor. E. 64th St. 1932. Morrell Smith. ☆

Charming neo-Georgian fairy tale architecture.

[G 14a.] The Verona (apartments), 32 E. 64th St., SE cor. Madison Ave. 1908. William E. Mowbray. ☆

Names were once just as important as addresses. The entrance to this magnificent high-rise Venetian Renaissance throwback is **elegantly flanked** by bronze lamp standards.

[G 14b.] Near East Foundation/originally **Robert I. Jenks residence,** 54 E. 64th St., bet. Madison and Park Aves. 1907. Flagg & Chambers. ☆

Four stories of delicate neo-Federal detail, complete with Flemish-bond brick.

[G 14c.] Originally **Jonathan Buckley residence,** 600 Park Ave., NW cor. E. 64th St. 1911. James Gamble Rogers. ☆

A proper palace in neo-English Renaissance garb, for an American paper manufacturer.

[G 15a.] Originally **Mrs. Emilia Howell residence,** 603 Park Ave., NE cor. E. 64th St. 1920. Walter Lund and Julius F. Gayler. ☆

Stupendous neo-Federal as though, like Popeye, it had feasted on cans and cans of spinach! Best from the modillioned cornice up.

[G 15b.] Central Presbyterian Church/originally **Park Avenue Baptist Church,** 593 Park Ave., SE cor. E. 64th St. 1922. Henry C. Pelton and Allen & Collens. ☆

The original Baptist congregation (previously Norfolk Street Baptist Church and later Fifth Avenue Baptist Church, **where the Rockefellers worshipped**) left here to build its true monument, Riverside Church, with the **same architects** and **JDR's money.** A church in a vigorous crystalline sand castle form.

[G 9d.] Assisium School, once a club   **[G 15b.]** Central Presbyterian Church

[G 15d.] Originally Asia House gallery   **[G 15e.]** The Edward Durell Stone res.

[G 15c.] 110 East 64th Street (town house), bet. Park and Lexington Aves. 1988. Agrest & Gandelsonas. ☆

Captured in conversation between a stony church and a glassy box [see next], as though at tea. This very very very high-style urban single house **toasts its neighbors** while demurely lifting its chin and preening, just a very very very little bit, too.

[G 15d.] Originally **Asia House/**now **Russell Sage Foundation/Robert Sterling Clark Foundation,** 112 E. 64th St., bet. Park and Lexington Aves. 1959. Philip Johnson & Assocs. ☆

A **decorous curtain** of dark glass suspended in a **gossamer grid** of thin, white-painted steel makes a street wall that "works" in this varied block. The sometimes disturbing opacity of the glass, mirroring the street's opposite side, disappears at night, revealing the volume of interior spaces behind the wall.

[G 15e.] Formerly **Edward Durell Stone residence,** 130 E. 64th St., bet. Park and Lexington Aves. 1878. James E. Ware. Front addition, 1956, Edward Durell Stone. ☆

Originally one of a row of 4, similar in appearance to today's **No. 128.** In 1956 architect-owner **Stone extended the facade,** and hence volume, of the structure, to the permissible building line. The precast terrazzo grillage echoes the design of his **American Embassy in New Delhi,** widely acclaimed when it was built.

[G 15f.] Originally **First of August (boutique)**/now **Pino Fiori,** 860 Lexington Ave., bet. E. 64th and E. 65th Sts. W side. 1978. George Ranalli.

A storefront of glass squares set within mini-monkey bars (as in a city playground) that crawl up an old brownstone (as ivy crawls up brick walls). Ivy is preferable.

East 65th Street, from Fifth to Madison Avenues:

[G 16a.] **Union of American Hebrew Congregations,** 838 Fifth Ave., SE cor. E. 65th St. 1950. Harry M. Prince. ☆

The flatness of this structure's limestone facade makes it ideal to study the effects of weather upon buildings, resulting from its location opposite Central Park's openness and the deflections caused by the proximity of much larger Temple Emanu-El. The **interplay of wind, rain, and soot** are here revealed on the side wall, almost if the deity meant to show His presence thereby.

[G 16b.] **Temple Emanu-El (synagogue),** 840 Fifth Ave., NE cor. E. 65th St. 1929. Robert D. Kohn, Charles Butler, Clarence Stein, and Mayers, Murray & Philip, associated architects. ☆

The **joining in 1927** of this congregation with that of **Temple Beth-El** (whose sanctuary then stood at the southeast corner of Fifth and 67th) paved the way for construction of this large, bearing-wall sanctuary on the **former site** of Richard Morris Hunt's double mansion for Mrs. Caroline Schermerhorn Astor, **The Mrs. Astor.** North of the main space, and set back from the avenue, is the Beth-El Chapel, built in memory of the other congregation's structure (*1891. Brunner & Tryon.*), which was then demolished.

[G 16e., f.] The Kosciuszko Foundation (left) and French & Company (right)

[G 16c.] **6, 8 East 65th Street (town houses),** 1902. Hiss & Weeks. ☆ **[G 16d.]** **12 East 65th Street (town house),** 1909. Walter B. Chambers. ☆

Two Beaux Arts gems, both commissioned by Mrs. William H. Bliss. No. 8, now the **Permanent Mission to the United Nations of the Republic of Pakistan,** is an exceptionally wide (43-foot) structure with a generous 2-story mansard pierced by bull's-eye dormers. It is visually linked to its neighbor **No. 6** by a common 2nd-floor balcony and roof cornice. **No. 12,** now Pakistan House, also harmonizes.

[G 16e.] Kosciuszko Foundation/originally **James J. Van Alen residence,** 15 E. 65th St. 1917. Harry Allan Jacobs. ☆

Soigné limestone with an inset pink marble Palladian window. Original owner Van Alen, a socialite, was The Mrs. Astor's son-in-law. He sold the house in 1919 and moved to Europe in protest over impending Prohibition. The foundation has held it since 1945.

[G 16f.] French & Company/originally **Sherman M. Fairchild residence,** 17 E. 65th St. 1941. George Nelson and William Hamby. New facade, 1981, Milton Klein. ☆

A revolutionary plan and facade in its day: 2 separate functional elements at the front and rear of lot, **separated by an open garden court** over which glass ramps sprang, linking living/dining/kitchen (front) with bedrooms (rear). The 1941 facade was a series of **motor-operated wood louvers** to control sunlight—Fairchild was the aircraft manufacturer. Klein's new facade is a **carefully studied cubistic composition** of fired (rough) and highly polished red granite veneer, set off by a polished stainless steel ship's railing, and a lone gingko tree.

Madison Avenue, between East 65th and East 66th Streets:

[G 17a.] Originally **Frederic H. Betts residence,** 750 Madison Ave. a.k.a. 22 E. 65th St., SW cor. Madison Ave. 1897. Grosvenor Atterbury. Stores added, 1915, 1936. **[G 17b.] Andrea Carrano (shoe boutique).** 1979. Andrea Carrano, owner-designer. ☆

Time has had a schizophrenic effect on this corner town house: on Madison **it has become a proscenium** for a succession of shops, currently Carrano with a witty sign of wrought-metal spaghetti **(No. 2).** On 65th the original character is largely retained.

[G 17c.] New Man (men's boutique), 755 Madison Ave., bet. E. 65th and E. 66th Sts. E side. 1981. ☆

Simple shop, great graphics!

[G 17d.] Bruno Dessange (boutique), 760 Madison Ave., bet. E. 65th and E. 66th Sts. W side. 1983. Fred Perkey, designer. ☆

When the design is strong enough, even a 2nd-floor location and sheets of plate glass cannot diminish it.

[G 17e.] Troa Cho (boutique), 22 E. 66th St., bet. Fifth and Madison Aves. 1982. Alfredo De Vido Assocs., architect. Muir Cornelius Moore, graphic designer. ☆

Freely interpreted Classical columns become vitrines displaying high-style women's apparel and accessories in this airy, high-style shop whose architecture **without** remains architecture **within.**

Paris Rome Express (costume jewelry), 770 Madison Ave., SW cor. E. 66th Sts. W side. ☆

A fun design approach for a shop that specializes in baubles.

East 65th Street, between Madison and Park Avenues:

[G 18a.] American Federation of the Arts/originally **Benson Bennett Sloan residence,** 41 E. 65th St. 1910. Trowbridge & Livingston. ☆ Interior remodeling, 1960, Edward Durell Stone. **Galleries open to the public.**

The galleries within shelter traveling exhibitions gathered and circulated by the federation.

[G 18b.] Institute for Rational Living/originally **John M. Bowers residence,** 45 E. 65th St. 1910. Hoppin & Koen. ☆

An irrationally wonderful neo-Georgian limestone and rosé-colored brick town house.

[G 18c.] Sara Delano Roosevelt Memorial House, Hunter College CUNY/originally **Mrs. James (Sara Delano) Roosevelt residence,** 47-49 E. 65th St. 1908. Charles A. Platt. ★ ☆

Built as a double town house (with a single entry) by **FDR's mother:** she lived in **No. 47** while **Franklin and Eleanor** lived in **No. 49.**

It was here, in a 4th-floor bedroom, that the president-to-be convalesced from his bout with polio in 1921–1922. The structure was purchased by Hunter in 1942, and the divisions were subsequently removed.

[G 18d.] 55 East 65th Street (apartments). 1892. Thom & Wilson. ☆

An early flathouse of roman brick and brownstone for 13 families, now happily saved by remodeling into co-ops. The sheet-metal fire escape covers (added later) were a Bauhaus-inspired attempt to sterilize the late 19th-century vigor.

The IRT, the city's first subway system, invariably linked to the name of its financier, August Belmont, the son (1853–1924), was actually planned and constructed under the supervision of engineer William Barclay Parsons. Parsons commissioned the double-width, double-scaled neo-Federal house at 121 East 65th Street from architects Welles Bosworth and E. E. Piderson. It was completed in 1923. ☆

[G 19a.] The Parge House, 130½ E. 65th St., SW cor. Lexington Ave., Altered, 1922, Frederick J. Sterner. Altered since.

Though compromised by the addition of a Lexington Avenue shop, this picturesque conversion of a row house into architect Sterner's office and apartments remains an unusual work. *Note the decorative stucco relief.*

[G 19b.] Originally **Michael and John Davis residence,** 135 E. 65th St., NW cor. Lexington Ave. a.k.a. 868 Lexington Ave. 1904. Edwin Outwater. ☆

Get a load of that 3rd-floor limestone oriel, dramatically bracketed out over the sidewalk.

East 65th Street, between Lexington and Third Avenues:

 [G 19c.] Church of St. Vincent Ferrer (Roman Catholic), Lexington Ave. SE cor. E. 66th St. 1918. Bertram G. Goodhue. ★ **[G 19d.] Priory, Dominican Fathers/**originally **Convent,** 869 Lexington Ave., NE cor. E. 65th St. 1881. William Schickel. ★ **[G 19e.] Holy Name Society Building,** 141 E. 65th St. 1930. Wilfrid E. Anthony. **[G 19f.] St. Vincent Ferrer School,** 151 E. 65th St. 1948. Elliot L. Chisling of Ferrenz & Taylor.

A **fashionable parish church complex** built by the Dominican Order (and therefore not under the control of the New York Archdiocese). The Goodhue-designed church, in rock-face granite with limestone trim, detailing, and sculpture, is **academically correct and precise** but suffers from something of a **"manufactured"** quality. A planned 150-foot steeple was never built. Well worth a visit within.

While the Priory is an older, quite picturesque relic, the two newer structures along 65th Street pale in comparison to their Lexington Avenue cousins. (The incised Old English inscription on the new school gives its date as 1954; the Buildings Department dates it 1948.)

Across 65th Street from the St. Vincent Ferrer Church complex is a picturesque set of row houses, **Nos. 132-156,** of varying quality but united by trees, ivy, and ironwork that peters out as it approaches Third Avenue. Among the houses is:

[G 19g.] Formerly **Richard M. Nixon residence/**originally **Charles C. Pope residence,** 142 E. 65th St. 1871. Frederick S. Barus. Altered, 1961, Casale & Nowell.

Between 1963 and his relocation to the White House, Richard Nixon and his family had a generous apartment at 810 Fifth Avenue. Following his resignation as president and his unsuccessful attempt to buy a co-op **apartment,** Nixon settled for this row house in 1979. Federal Judge Learned Hand had lived here from 1906 until his death in 1961.

From Fifth Avenue along East 66th Street to Madison Avenue:

[G 20a.] Federal People's Republic of Yugoslavia Mission to the United Nations/originally **R. Livingston Beekman residence,** 854 Fifth Ave., bet. E. 66th and E. 67th St. 1905. Warren & Wetmore. ★ ☆

It would seem that Communists savor splendor as much as capitalists.

Two neighbors:

[G 20b.] The Lotos Club/originally **Margaret Vanderbilt Shepard residence**/later **Mr. & Mrs. William J. Schiefflin residence,** 5 E. 66th St. 1900. Richard Howland Hunt. ☆

Rosé-colored brick and limestone Beaux Arts *Schlag*. Built for William H. Vanderbilt's eldest daughter, Margaret, the house was presented to her daughter and son-in-law, William J. Schieffelin, of the wholesale drug firm of Schieffelin & Company. He was also president of Citizen's Union for 32 years. The Deutscher Verein took possession briefly in 1925; the Lotos in 1946.

[G 19c.] Priory of the Dominican Fathers, St. Vincent Ferrer church complex

[G 20a.] Yugoslav Mission to the UN   [G 20b.] Lotos Club, once Vanderbilt's

[G 20c.] Permanent Mission of the Polish People's Republic to the United Nations/originally **Charles Scribner, Jr. residence,** 9 E. 66th St. 1912. Ernest Flagg. ☆

An airy and masterful facade with so much glass that it presages (visually) curtain walls by a half century. Flagg also did the Scribner commercial buildings at **Nos. 153-157** and **597 Fifth Avenue.** (He had married into the family of the publishing house's founder.)

[G 20d.] Consular Residence, Republic of the Philippines/originally **Harris Fahnestock residence,** 15 E. 66th St. 1918. Hoppin & Koen. ☆

The architects' *chef d'oeuvre* was the old Police Headquarters [see L Manhattan/Chinatown-Little Italy L 17a.]. This house was rumored to be one of the many shoe storehouses of former Philippine first lady Imelda Marcos.

[G 20e.] 45 East 66th Street (apartments), NE cor. Madison Ave. 1908. Harde & Short. ★ ☆

They hoped for Perpendicular Gothic. Two glassy 10-story walls of 12 over 12 double-hung windows intersect in a magnificent cylinder of even more windows, making this **one of the city's grandest facades.** Forgiven is the destruction of the Church of the Holy Spirit (later All Souls' Episcopal Church), on whose site this was built.

East 66th Street, between Park and Lexington Avenues:

[G 21a.] 7th Regiment Armory, N.Y. National Guard, Park to Lexington Aves. bet. E. 66th and E. 67th Sts. 1880. Charles W. Clinton. Tower removed, Park Ave. facade. ★ ☆ Interiors, Park Ave. wing, Louis Comfort Tiffany.

A friendly brick fortress. New York armories were composed of two distinct elements: a 3- or 4-story collection of office, meeting, and socializing spaces (Park Avenue) and a vast drill hall (Lexington). The latter, 187 × 270 feet of clear space, is sufficient for maneuvering modern military vehicles—not to mention its adequacy for tennis practice and antiques expositions. Also see the regimental monument along Central Park's wall [G 23a.].

***

The Armory was, in large part, furnished and detailed on the interior by Louis Comfort Tiffany, son of Charles, founder and owner of Fifth Avenue's Tiffany & Company. Louis rejected the business world for that of the applied arts. His studios eventually specialized in decorative crafts ranging from the stained glass for which he is best remembered to stone-carving, metalworking, and casting of bronze—crafts complementing the ornate Late Victorian architecture of his architect-clients. In this case some tables were turned: Stanford White worked under Tiffany's direction on this interior work, rather than the later, and more obvious, reversed relationship.

[G 20d.] Republic of the Philippines   [G 21c.] The John Hay Whitney garage

[G 21b.] The Cosmopolitan Club, 122 E. 66th St., 1932. Thomas Harlan Elett. ☆

One of the northernmost outposts of **"New Orleans" cast iron.** Organized as a club for women professionals and semiprofessionals, the Cosmo contrasts with the Colony Club [see G 7e.]. As the Colony's architecture was prissy, the Cosmo's was frivolous.

[G 21c.] John Hay Whitney garage/originally **Henry O. Havemeyer stable, coach house, coachman's residence/**later **Oliver H. Payne stable, etc.,** 126 E. 66th St. 1895. W. J. Wallace and S. E. Gage. ☆

A handsome brick arch is portal for 9 Whitney cars—rarely does even consciously monumental architecture achieve such power. **The archivolt is breathtaking.** [For the **St. Vincent Ferrer Church complex,** see G 19c., d., e., f.]

[G 22a.] 131-135 East 66th Street (apartments), NE cor. Lexington Ave. 1906. Charles A. Platt of Pollard & Steinam. **[G 22b.] 130-134 East 67th Street (apartments),** SE cor. Lexington Ave. 1907. Charles A. Platt of Rossiter & Wright. ★

Two **adjacent apartment blocks** in the neo-Italian Renaissance style for a developer of studio buildings on West 67th Street. Though designed by two different architects of record, the **driving force** for both was Platt, who **left one firm to join the other** so that he could design **a complement to his first work.**

From Fifth Avenue along East 67th Street to Madison Avenue:

[G 23a.] 7th Regiment Monument, N.Y. National Guard Fifth Ave. at E. 67th St. W side, fronting Central Park. 1927. Karl Illava, sculptor. ★

Dynamic bronze; seething bayonets.

[G 21a.] The 7th Regiment Armory   **[G 22a.]** 131-135 E. 66th Street apts.

[G 23a.] Memorial to the heroism of the 7th Regiment, N.Y. National Guard

[G 23b.] Residence of the Consul General of Japan/originally **Henri P. Wertheim residence,** 4 E. 67th St. 1902. John H. Duncan. ☆

A brick and limestone Beaux Arts mansion.

[G 23c.] Originally **Samuel H. Valentine residence,** 5 E. 67th St. 1909. Carrère & Hastings. ☆

This neo-Classical facade is set off by an ornately ornamented 2-story rounded oriel.

[G 23d.] Originally **Charles C. Stillman residence,** 9 E. 67th St. 1882. Thom & Wilson. Current facade, 1912, Hiss & Weeks. ☆

Inspired by Renaissance forms as they were employed in France.

 [G 23e.] Formerly **Jules S. Bache residence,** 10 E. 67th St. 1881. James E. Ware. Altered for Bache, 1899, C. P. H. Gilbert. ☆

A fashionable neo-Classical front replaced the original—but by then old-fashioned—Queen Anne facade, per banker Bache's instructions.

[G 23f.] Originally **Martin Beck residence,** 13 E. 67th St. 1921. Harry Allan Jacobs. ☆

Martin Beck was a prominent New York theatrical figure who built the Martin Beck and Palace theaters. The Serlian arch, at the 2nd floor, is named after Italian architect-author Sebastiano Serlio; it is also called a Palladian window, after Andrea Palladio. *Note the incised* XIII.

[G 23c., d., f., h.] Elegant limestone town houses line 67th St. E of Fifth Avenue

[G 23g.] Formerly **Jeremiah Milbank residence,** 14-16 E. 67th St. (combined residences). **No. 14,** 1879, Lamb & Wheeler; altered, 1920, Dodge & Morrison. **No. 16,** 1905, John H. Duncan. ☆

Separate structures, linked within and harmonized without, all for Mr. Milbank in 1920.

 [G 23h.] The Regency Whist Club/originally **Cortlandt F. Bishop residence,** 15 E. 67th St. 1907. Ernest Flagg. ☆

A turn-of-the-century Paris town house. The shallow "French" balconies, in front of the French doors, for (mostly psychological) security enliven the facade. Bishop was the first to receive a permit to drive a car in Central Park.

[G 23i.] Formerly **R. Fulton Cutting residence,** 22 E. 67th St. 1879. Lamb & Wheeler. Altered for Cutting, 1908, Harry Allan Jacobs. ☆

Robert Fulton Cutting (1852–1934) was known in his time as the **"first citizen of New York"** for his leadership of such groups as the Association for Improving the Condition of the Poor, the City and Suburban Homes Company, and the Cooper Union. He was Citizens Union's first president. A reserved facade, as befits a brahmin.

[G 23j.] D. Cenci (boutique), 801 Madison Ave., bet. E. 67th and E. 68th Sts. E side. 1985. Giorgio Cavaglieri.

Reserved. A far cry from the radical facade of the former occupant, **Valentino** [see Necrology]. ☆

East 67th Street, between Madison and Park Avenues:

[G 24a.] Histadruth Foundation/ originally **Hugh D. Auchincloss residence,** 33 E. 67th St. 1903. Robertson & Potter. ☆   **[G 24b.] Egyptian Mission to the United Nations/**originally **Elizabeth and Mary**

Thompson residence, 36-38 E. 67th St. 1906. Henry Bacon. ☆
[G 24c.] Originally **Arthur H. Scribner residence**/now **N.Y.S. Pharmaceutical Association,** 39 E. 67th St. 1877. D. & J. Jardine. Present facade, 1904, Ernest Flagg. ☆ **[G 24d.]** Originally **James R. Sheffield residence**/later (1964–1973) **Gloria Vanderbilt Cooper residence,** 45 E. 67th St. 1913. Walter B. Chambers. ☆ **[G 24e.] 51, 53 East 67th Street (row houses),** 1879. D. & J. Jardine. ☆

Before the rise of Fifth and Park Avenues these neo-Grec examples were the **houses of the well-to-do.** Now they seem dull ancestors of the grandeur that surrounds them. **No. 39's** Scribner owner was president of the publishing house from 1928 to 1932. The Scribners and architect Flagg were a team—and also brothers-in-law. [See G 20c.].

East 67th Street, between Park and Lexington Avenues:

[G 25.] Milan House (apartments), 115 E. 67th St., and 116 E. 68th St. 1931. Andrew J. Thomas. ☆

Two 11-story gems in the neo-Romanesque style, complete with carved **monsters, grotesques, and florid capitals** atop colonnettes and wonderful multipaned casements—all maintained in immaculate condition by a zealous co-op board (thank God!) that recognizes how wonderful the 67th Street (and the similar 68th Street) facade is. Architect Thomas was an important designer of enlightened apartment developments. The **midblock Italian garden court** between the wings, barely visible through the entry doors, is a dream.

East 67th Street, between Lexington and Third Aves:

[G 26a.] Kennedy Child Study Center/originally **Mt. Sinai Dispensary,** 151 E. 67th St. 1890. Buchman & Deisler and Brunner & Tryon. ★

Built as an adjunct to an **earlier** Mt. Sinai Hospital (*1872. Griffith Thomas*) that occupied the south side of this 67th Street block: dignified neo-Italian Renaissance styling that required the collaboration of two distinguished partnerships of architects.

[G 26b.] 19th Precinct, N.Y.C. Police Department/originally **25th Precinct,** 153 E. 67th St. 1887. Nathaniel D. Bush. Altered, 1988, The Stein Partnership.

Limestone Florentine palace architecture; a rusticated base supports a turgid Victorian body. A complicated 1980s restoration-reconstruction links it to:

[G 26c.] Originally **N.Y.C. Fire Department Headquarters**/later **Engine Company No. 39, Ladder Company No. 15,** 157 E. 67th St. 1886. Napoleon Le Brun & Sons. Altered, 1988, The Stein Partnership.

A hearty exercise in Romanesque Revival, clad in brownstone and brick.

[G 26d.] Park East Synagogue/Congregation Zichron Ephraim, 163 E. 67th St. 1890. Schneider & Herter. ★

Inside, a Victorian preaching space, nominally **made Jewish through Saracenic detail.** Stripped to its essentials it could be Civil War period Catholic or Congregational. Outside, it is a confection that might have been conceived in a Moorish trip on **LSD:** a wild, vigorous extravaganza.

East 68th Street, between Fifth and Madison Avenues:

[G 27a.] Republic of Indonesia Delegation to the United Nations/ originally **John J. Emery residence,** 5 E. 68th St. 1896. Peabody & Stearns. ☆

A mansion without good proportions, scale, or style. It may impress at first glance, *but take a closer look.*

[G 27b.] 6 East 68th Street (residence), 1881. John G. Prague. **8, 10 East 68th Street (residences),** 1882. Lamb & Wheeler. Linked and altered, 1920, Harry Allan Jacobs. ☆

This **classy trio** of now-interlinked mansions was owned, in varying combinations, by family members of the Lehman Brothers and Kuhn, Loeb & Company banking firms, including arts patron Otto H.

Kahn, who lived at **No. 8** until he moved into the somewhat larger quarters he commissioned at 1 East 91st Street [see C 11b.].

[G 27c.] Center for Marital and Family Therapy/originally **Mrs. George T. Bliss residence**, 9 E. 68th St. 1907. Heins & La Farge. ☆

Sir John Soane, revived a century later. Soane is known for the magic of his architecture: his mansion (now a museum), at Lincoln's Inn Fields, and his Dulwich College Picture Gallery, both in London. Great Ionic columns here support the sky but, with the salmon brick, make a smashing work!

[G 26d.] Park East Synagogue/Cong. Zichron Ephraim: vigorous extravaganza

[G 27d.] The Marquand (apartments), 11 E. 68th St., NW cor. Madison Ave. 1913. Herbert Lucas. ☆

The brick, bow-bay upper floors of this 11-story apartment rest atop a handsome pillowed-rusticated limestone base. The structure occupies the **site of 3 brownstones** designed by Richard Morris Hunt for **Henry G. Marquand** in 1880. Note **the incised M** at various points in the facade.

[G 27e.] Originally **Henry T. Sloane residence**, 18 E. 68th St. 1905. C. P. H. Gilbert. ☆

Don't confuse this Beaux Arts Sloane residence with the one at 9 East 72nd [see G 44b.] where Sloane (1845–1937), of the W. & J. Sloane store, lived with the **first** Mrs. Sloane. After his divorce, he built this gem.

[G 27f.] Giorgio Armani (boutique)/formerly **antique furniture store,** 815 Madison Ave., bet. E. 68th and E. 69th Sts. E side. 1882. Altered into store, Walter B. Chambers, 1926. Altered for Armani, 1985, Weisberg Castro Assocs. ☆

One great big neo-Georgian multipaned arch, now with a ground-floor recess to satisfy current merchandising fads.

[G 27c.] Heins & La Farge's 9 E. 68th   [G 27a.] Indonesian UN Delegation

[G 27g.] Originally **Dr. Christian A. Herter residence,** 817-819 Madison Ave., bet. E. 68th and E. 69th Sts. E side. 1892. Carrère & Hastings. Storefronts added, 1922, Carrère & Hastings.

One of two mansions remaining on this stretch of Madison Avenue [see G 17a.], this one is severely compromised by fire escape regulations and the needs of commerce. Nevertheless, the surprise of discovering this **monumental survivor** above the commercial fronts offers a delicious sensation. ☆

East 68th Street, between Madison and Park Avenues:

[G 28a.] Originally **Mary D. Dunham residence,** 35 E. 68th St. 1901. Carrère & Hastings. ☆

Extravagant ornament on a cut-rate Carrère & Hastings palace.

[G 28b.] Formerly **John D. Crimmins residence,** 40-42 E. 68th St. **No. 40,** 1879, William Schickel. **No. 42,** 1878, architect unknown. Joined, 1898, Schickel & Ditmars. ☆

The joining of 2 row houses resulted in a **monumental Beaux Arts facade** of bay window and bold mansard roof. Crimmins was the contractor for some of the City's largest 19th-century public works.

[G 28c.] Dominican Academy/originally **Michael Friedsam residence,** 44 E. 68th St. 1922. Frederick G. Frost. ☆

Noted for its historical associations rather than its architecture. Businessman, philanthropist, art collector, and civic leader Friedsam **succeeded Benjamin Altman** as the department store's president.

[G 28d.] Originally **Ruth Hill Beard residence,** 47 E. 68th St. 1907. Adams & Warren. ☆

Good but not great. Bold Italian Renaissance detail.

[G 28e.] Formerly **Automation House**/originally **Mrs. J. William Clark residence,** 49 E. 68th St. 1914. Trowbridge & Livingston. Altered, 1970, Lehrecke & Tonetti. ★ ☆

The sheer glass replacement windows of 1970 give the facade of this row house the appearance of having **eyes that cannot see.** Without window divisions, the structure's scale appears eerie.

[G 28f.] Council on Foreign Relations/originally **Harold I. Pratt residence,** 60 E. 68th St., SW cor. Park Ave. 1919. Delano & Aldrich. ☆ Addition to W, 1954, Wyeth & King.

Harold was the youngest son of Brooklyn's 19th-century industrialist **Charles Pratt,** kerosene magnate and later major shareholder in the Standard Oil trust. Four of the youngest sons **built minor palaces** along Brooklyn's Clinton Avenue (3 still stand) near their dad's mansion [see

WC Brooklyn/Ft. Greene Clinton Hill L 9a., b., c., L 8.] When Harold's turn came, he was **swept by changing fashions** to Manhattan's Park Avenue—hence this limestone neo-Renaissance marvel.

[G 29.] Park Avenue, W blockfront between E. 68th and E. 69th Sts. ☆

The parts of this ensemble are not in themselves important. Georgian architecture's greatest contribution is not the style of individual structures but **a comprehensive attitude** toward urban design. Buildings of character, quality, and refinement were **subordinated to a larger system** of designing cities, which applies here in this neo-Georgian row: the whole is greater than the sum of its parts.

[G 29.] Park Avenue blockfront: parts less important than the neo-Georgian whole

[G 28f.] Council on Foreign Relations/originally Harold I. Pratt residence in 1966

[G 29a.] Center for Inter-American Relations/formerly **U.S.S.R. Delegation to the United Nations/**originally **Percy Pyne residence,** 680 Park Ave., NW cor E. 68th St. 1911. William Kendall of McKim, Mead & White. ★ ☆

Client Percy R. Pyne (1857–1929) was a New York financier and philanthropist. It was here that Prime Minister Khrushchev held forth from the 2nd-floor window in 1960.

[G 29b.] Spanish Institute/originally **Oliver D. Filley residence,** 684 Park Ave. 1926. McKim, Mead & White. ★ ☆

Built by Percy Pyne next door for his daughter and her husband, the Filleys.

[G 29c.] Istituto Italiano di Cultura/originally **William Sloane residence,** 686 Park Ave. 1919. Delano & Aldrich. ★ ☆

Another Sloane (1873–1922) of the W. & J. Sloane clan.

[G 29d.] Consulate General of Italy/originally **Henry P. Davison residence,** 690 Park Ave., SW cor. E. 69th St. 1916. Walker & Gillette. ★ ☆

Henry P. Davison was a J. P. Morgan partner, among other things.

Marquesa de Cuevas (a Rockefeller gone Spanish) received wide praise in 1965 for buying the endangered structures at 680 and 684 Park Avenue to save them from demolition; she then presented them (and later her own residence, 52-54 East 68th Street) to her favorite charities. The Marquesa was the former Margaret Rockefeller Strong, married to the eighth Marqués de Piedrablanca de Guana Cuevas.

Hunter College

Note: Hunter College's buildings straddle the boundary of the Upper East Side Historic District. Those within the district are, like others so protected, identified ☆.

[G 30a.] Hunter College, CUNY, 695 Park Ave., bet. E. 68th and E. 69th Sts. E side. 1940. Shreve, Lamb & Harmon, Harrison & Fouilhoux, associated architects. ☆

An interruption in the pace of Park Avenue. Hunter is not only modern and glistening with glass; it is also set back 10 feet from the lot line. A proud self-confident monument of the city's early Modern.

[G 30b.] Old Building, Hunter College   **[G 30c.]** New Bldgs., Hunter College

[G 30b.] Old Building, Hunter College, CUNY/briefly **Hunter College High School,** 930 Lexington Ave., bet. E. 68th and E. 69th Sts. W side 1913. C. B. J. Snyder. ☆

The last gasp of John Ruskin here housed quality education in an "English Gothic" shell. The prestigious Hunter High, part of the public school system, enrolled talented girls from throughout the city through a competitive examination program. Hunter High (now co-ed) later moved to the fortlike former I.S. 29, Manhattan building. [See Carnegie Hill C 21b.]

[G 30c.] South Building and **East Building, Hunter College, CUNY,** E. 68th St. SW cor. and SE cor. Lexington Ave. Designed 1980, completed 1986 (delayed by City fiscal crisis). Ulrich Franzen & Assocs.

Resplendent, beautifully detailed Modern towers, delayed by the City's near-bankruptcy, are now **superb additions to the cityscape.** The **enclosed glassy overpasses** on the 3rd and 8th floors over Lexington Avenue, and the lower connection over 68th Street to old Hunter High, are unique and still extremely controversial for the interruptions they make in the city's endless street vistas. The open-air subway entrances (and redesigned subway mezzanine) are **rare but welcome design amenities,** acknowledgments of those who *must* ride under ground.

[G 30d.] Sam and Esther Minskoff Cultural Center, Park East Day School, 164 E. 68th St., bet. Lexington and Third Aves. 1974. John Carl Warnecke & Assocs.

Creamy brick articulated with granite. A throwback to the curvilinear streamlined architecture of the early 1930s.

[G 31.] East 69th Street, Fifth to Madison Aves.

Roll call: No. 7: (*1986, Hobart Betts*) ☆, Infill: difficult problem; interesting solution. No. 9: (*1917, Grosvenor Atterbury*) ☆, No. 11: **American Friends of Hebrew University** (*1924, Delano & Aldrich*) ☆, No. 12: (*1884; altered, 1913, William Welles Bosworth*) ☆ are interesting as lesser comparative works of good architects. No. 16, **English-Speaking Union** (*1882; altered, 1930, A. Wallace McCrea*) ☆ is in proper neo-Georgian dress for these hands-across-the-sea.

[G 28d.] Orig. Ruth Beard residence   [G 38b.] Visiting Nurse Service of N.Y.

[G 32a.] Sointu (modern design shop), 20 E. 69th St., bet. Fifth and Madison Aves. 1981. Tod Williams & Assocs. ☆

A trio of crisp, **tented awnings** marks this rarefied shop, evoking the qualities of a crystalline museum gallery.

[G 32b.] Kenzo Paris (boutique), 824 Madison Ave., SW cor. E. 69th St. ☆   1987.

Minimalist fun.

[G 32c.] Pratesi (linens), 829 Madison Ave., bet. E. 69th and E. 70th Sts. E side. 1972. Expanded, 1985. All by Louis Leoni. ☆

A suave, masterful **twist of metal** into facade, as though it were itself a magician's cape: presto!

[G 32d.] Originally Isaac and Virginia Stern residence, 835 Madison Ave., bet. E. 69th and E. 70th Sts. 1885. William Schickel. Storefronts added, 1921; altered 1930, and since. ☆

There's **great satisfaction** in discovering a weather-beaten but **largely intact Queen Anne** masonry row house atop the ubiquitous Madison Avenue storefronts.

[G 33.] East 69th Street, Madison to Park Aves.

A **rich and changing block** of varied architectural styles, all of human scale, and greater than the sum of its parts. **Roll call:** No. 27: formerly Lucretia Lord Strauss (*1886; altered, 1922, York & Sawyer*) ☆, an altered facade in neo-Tudor, No. 31: **Consulate General of Austria**/originally **Augustus G. Paine, Jr. residence** (*1918, C. P. H. Gilbert*) ☆, No. 33 (*1912, Howells & Stokes*) ☆, No. 35: (*1911, Walker &*

Gilette) ☆, No. 36: (*ca. 1875; altered 1903, Jardine, Kent & Jardine; altered 1923, Carrère & Hastings*) ☆. Lesser works by name architects: No. 42: **Jewish National Fund** (*1921, C. P. H. Gilbert*) ☆, for Arthur and Alice G. Sachs, descendants of the founders of the Goldman, Sachs & Company investment banking firm, No. 50: (*1918, Henry C. Pelton*) ☆, a grand house.

[G 34.] The Union Club of New York, 701 Park Ave., NE cor. E. 69th St. a.k.a. 101 E. 69th St. 1932. Delano & Aldrich. ☆

New York City's oldest social club (founded in 1836) is housed in the style of the English 18th century: limestone and granite with a slate mansard roof.

[G 35.] East 69th Street, Lexington to Third Aves.

Stable/carriage house/garage roll call: No. 147 (*1880. John Correja. Present facade, 1913, Barney & Colt*). No. 149: for London subway financier **Charles T. Yerkes**/later **Thomas Fortune Ryan** (*1896. Frank Drischler*) ☆, No. 153 (*1884. William Schickel*) ☆, No. 159: for W. & J. Sloane's **John Sloane** (*1882. Charles W. Romeyn*) ☆, No. 161: for William Bruce-Brown (*1916. Frederick B. Loney.*) Note BB in keystone. ☆, No. 163: for printing-press magnate **Richard M. Hoe** [see G 40c.] (*1909. Albro & Lindeberg.*) now **Congregation Zichron Ephraim.** No. 167: for the Museum of the American Indian's founder, **George G. Heye** (*1909. Charles E. Birge*) now **The Sculpture Center.** A diverse collection of 19th century necessities.

[G 35.] East 69th St. carriage houses   **[G 35.]** 153-157 East 69th Street

[G 36a.] Richard Morris Hunt Memorial, E. 70th St. at Fifth Ave., W side, fronting Central Park, ★ . 1898. Daniel Chester French, sculptor. Bruce Price, architect.

A monument to the first American architect trained at the **Ecole des Beaux-Arts** in Paris and the founding president of the **American Institute of Architects.** Appropriately located here opposite the site of Hunt's **Lenox Library,** built between 1869 and 1877. The Lenox site is now occupied by:

East 70th Street, between Fifth and Madison Avenues:

The north side of this block, through to 71st Street, was developed early in the 20th century, following the demolition of the Lenox Library, which occupied the Fifth Avenue frontage. The library's holdings were transferred to The New York Public Library's Astor, Lenox & Tilden Collections at 42nd Street prior to the building's opening in 1911.

[G 36b.] Frick Collection/originally **Henry Clay Frick residence,** 1 E. 70th St., NE cor. Fifth Ave. to E. 71st St. 1914. Carrère & Hastings. Altered as a public museum, 1935, John Russell Pope. ★ ☆ Addition to E, 1977, Harry Van Dyke and John Barrington Bayley, architects; Russell Paige, landscape architect. ★ ☆ **Museum open to the public.** [For the Frick Art Reference Library, see G 40b.]

The Collection's garden and open, balustraded stone railing provide **a welcome break** in the otherwise largely unbroken wall of high rises along Fifth Avenue's east side.

Bland, sometimes fussy, frequently indecisive, the exterior belies **a rich interior,** both in architecture and contents. The **glass-roofed courtyard,** entered almost directly, is a delightful **transition** from the noisy activity of the street. The soothing sound of water from a **central fountain** makes this is a place for pause, utterly relaxing—not surprising in the work of Pope, who created similar **islands of light, sound, and repose** at the National Gallery in Washington.

The eastern addition is a conscious anachronism for these times: **a garden court in a Beaux Arts embrace** atop a world of underground services.

[G 36c.] East 70th Street, Fifth to Madison Aves.

Roll call: No. 11: formerly **Consuelo Vanderbilt Smith residence** (*1910. John Duncan.*) ★ ☆. No. 15: (*1910. Charles I. Berg.*) ★ ☆, and No. 17: (*1911. Arthur C. Jackson of Heins & La Farge.*) ★ ☆ are interesting more for their survival as a group than for individual merits. No. 19: **Knoedler Gallery** (*1910. Thornton Chard.*) ★ ☆ is distinguished by 3 elegant arches springing from Tuscan columns. No. 21: **Hirschl & Adler Galleries** (*1919. William J. Rogers.*) ★ ☆. Finicky.

East 70th Street, Madison to Park Aves:

La Goulue (restaurant), 28 E. 70th St. ☆

Plucked from a back street in Paris and deposited here, it has powerful visual overtones of the real thing. *Cuisine française,* of course.

[G 37a.] Originally **Laura K. Bayer residence**/then **Clendenin Ryan residence**/then **Clendenin Ryan, Jr. residence,** 32 E. 70th St. 1911. Taylor & Levi. ☆

The Ryans were the son and grandson of financier Thomas Fortune Ryan. Curiously, both Clendenin and his son committed suicide in this limestone, mansarded house, in 1939 and 1957, respectively.

[G 37b.] James P. Warburg residence, 36 E. 70th St. 1885. Altered, 1924, William Lawrence Bottomley. ☆

A green-shuttered, double-width, eclectic house.

James, a banker and author, is the son of Paul M. Warburg, whose father, Felix M., conveyed the family's 92nd Street mansion to form part of the Jewish Museum [see C 13b.]

[G 37c.] 40 East 70th Street (garage)/originally **Augustus G. Paine, Jr. garage.** 1918. C. P. H. Gilbert. ☆

This charmingly designed neo-Georgian garage, topped by a wood-trellised terrace, was originally an adjunct to the town house of paper-maker Paine at **No. 31 East 69th Street** [see G 33.].

[G 37d.] Originally **Mr. & Mrs. Walter N. Rothschild residence**/now **Twentieth Century Fund,** 41 E. 70th St. 1929. Aymar Embury II. ☆ *Column with Objects,* 1969. Gonzalo Fonseca, sculptor.

An austerely facaded house (now set off by a wonderful freestanding sculpture) built for the chairman of the board of Abraham & Straus department store; his wife was Carola Warburg, daughter of Felix M. Warburg.

[G 37e.] Formerly **Maurice Wertheim residence,** 43 E. 70th St. 1929. Mott B. Schmidt. ☆

In the warm, pocked texture of travertine.

[G 37f.] Originally **Arthur S. Lehman residence**/now **Joseph and Estée Lauder residence,** 45 E. 70th St. 1929. Aymar Embury II. ☆

The original owner of this bland town house, a senior partner in Lehman Brothers investment bankers, was Governor Herbert H. Lehman's brother. The Lauders make cosmetics.

[G 37g.] Lowell Thomas Building, Explorers' Club/originally **Stephen C. Clark residence,** 46 E. 70th St. 1912. Frederick J. Sterner. ☆

An unusual, richly ornamented neo-Jacobean work commissioned by a member of the Singer Sewing Machine Clarks.

[G 38a.] The Asia Society Gallery, 725 Park Ave., NE cor. E. 70th St. 1981. Edward Larabee Barnes Assocs. ☆ **Open to the public.**

An awkward, fussy, severe (but not serene) polished brown granite prism that turns its back on all around it. Only when it flies colorful multistory banners above its Park Avenue entry does it extend a welcome to those who visit its fine exhibitions of Asian art.

East 70th Street, between Park and Lexington Avenues:

A block as diverse, friendly, inviting, tactile, dappled, intricate, and surprising as anyone might wish. A masterpiece of the culture rather than of narrow architectural or planning decisions.

[G 38b.] The Visiting Nurse Service of New York/originally **Thomas**
W. Lamont residence, 107 E. 70th St. 1921. Walker & Gillette. ☆

English Gothic—or Tudor Revival, if you wish—for the **taste of the country parson's son** who became head of J. P. Morgan & Company, Inc. The ashlar and cut stone, gable-roofed facade is an unexpected—and welcome—break in the rhythms of this block.

Lamont, also founder of the *Saturday Review,* was associated with many philanthropies, as well as with Columbia University's Lamont-Doherty Geological observatory at Palisades, N.Y.

[G 38c.] 112-114 East 70th Street (residences), 1869. James Santon. ☆

Two late Italianate brownstone survivors of a matching row of 5, with English basements. **No. 112** retains its original double-hung window pattern and detail; **No. 114** has been "modernized," its window openings refitted (before landmarks designation) with single sheets of glass. *Which do you prefer?*

[G 38d.] Originally **I. Townsend Burden residence,** 115 E. 70th St.
1922. Patrick J. Murray. Mansard added, 1935. ☆

Bold neo-Georgian at the larger scale of an Italian Renaissance palace for the cousin of iron and steel magnate James A. Burden [see C 11c.].

[G 38e.] Originally **Edward A. Norman residence,** 124 E. 70th St.
1941. William Lescaze. ☆

A dated Modern house that seems, on this block, to shout "look at me!" It was included in the Museum of Modern Art's Built in USA, 1932–1944 exhibition, undoubtedly because it did thumb its nose at its historicist neighbors.

[G 38f.] Paul Mellon residence, 125 E. 70th St. 1965. Mazza & Seccia. ☆

Replacing 2 row houses of the 1860s, this is one of the few row houses built in Manhattan after World War II. Anachronistic: **a charming stuccoed confection** of "French Provincial" that France itself never experienced.

[G 38g.] Originally **James and Helen Geddes residence,** 129 E. 70th St. 1863. Architect unknown. Stoop removed, 1940. ☆

The **oldest** survivor in the Upper East Side Historic District, speculatively built as one of five: **Nos. 121–129.** (The "white" stone is actually *painted* brownstone.)

[G 38h.] Formerly **Mr. & Mrs. Charles Larned Atterbury residence,** 131 E. 70th St. ca. 1871. Altered and extended, 1911, Grosvenor Atterbury. Store, 1940. ☆

A picturesque extravaganza fashioned from an earlier structure by Atterbury for his parents—sometimes it pays to send your son to architecture school.

East 70th Street, between Lexington and Third Avenues:

[G 39a.] Originally **Stephen H. Brown residence/**now part of **The Lenox School,** 154 E. 70th St. 1907. Edward P. Casey. ☆

This double-width Tudor Revival house was built for a family known as collectors of medieval art. Since 1932 it has served a series of private educational institutions.

[G 39b.] Originally **Jules S. Bache stable**/later **John D. Rockefeller garage,** 163 E. 70th St. 1902. C. P. H. Gilbert. ☆ **[G 39c.]** Originally **Henri P. Wertheim stable**/later **Stephen C. Clark garage**/now **Paul Mellon garage,** 165 E. 70th St. 1902. C. P. H. Gilbert. ☆

Supergrand carriage houses with mansard roofs, used by a series of superrich owners. **No. 163** (and therefore the entire street) is compromised by the substitution for the originals of bland single-light windows.

[G 38f.] The Paul Mellon residence   **[G 39b., c.]** Two stables into garages

[G 39d.] Lenox School/originally **Daniel G. Reid stable and groom's apartments,** 170 E. 70th St. 1902. C. P. H. Gilbert. Converted to school, 1925, Bradley Delehanty. Expanded upward, 1939, 1963. ☆

The original structure is of finely worked limestone in the Renaissance Revival mode, with a rich, arched entrance.

East 71st Street, between Fifth and Madison Avenues:

The south side of this block, through to East 70th, was developed after the death (1880) of James Lenox, whose Lenox Library had occupied part of it.

[G 40a.] Birch Wathen School/originally **Herbert N. Straus residence,** 9 E. 71st St. 1932. Horace Trombauer. Roof addition, 1977. ☆

Straus, of the Macy's Strauses, never occupied this mansarded house; work was stopped shortly before his death in 1933.

[G 40b.] Frick Art Reference Library, 10 E. 71st St. 1935. John Russell Pope. ★ ☆ **Open to researchers by appointment.**

Tall and bland, **the verbal annex to the visual Frick.** The tallest object in this otherwise low-rise full block.

[G 40c.] Originally **Mr. & Mrs. Richard M. Hoe residence,** 11 E. 71st St. 1892. Carrère & Hastings. ☆

An Upper East Side town house for the owner of the multiblock printing press and saw works that once occupied the site at **504 Grand Street** in the Lower East Side. Note the portico in veined marble set off by the even-toned limestone everywhere else.

[G 40d.] Originally **William A. Cook residence,** 14 E. 71st St. 1913. York & Sawyer. ☆

Magnificent bronze gates. A great overhanging cornice shelters a Guastavino-vaulted penthouse balcony. The limestone is subtly worked, as though it were tooled leather.

[G 40e.] 16, 18 East 71st Street (originally **residences**). 1911. John H. Duncan. ☆

Early 20th-century Plain Janes which, over the years, have served as town houses, apartments, private hospitals, and private schools.

[G 40f.] Originally **Julius Forstmann residence/**later **Catholic Center for the Blind,** 22 E. 71st St. 1923. C. P. H. Gilbert. Altered, 1942, Robert J. Reiley. ☆

Smashing: a wider-than-usual limestone house with well-heeled proportions that comfortably fit its **wider-than-usual facade.** The result is a contented, self-satisfied appearance. Forstmann was a well-known manufacturer of wool fabrics.

[G 41a.] St. James Episcopal Church, 861–863 Madison Ave., NE cor. E. 71st St. 1884. R. H. Robertson. Rebuilt, 1924, Ralph Adams Cram. Original tower, 1926, Ralph Adams Cram; replacement (smaller) tower, 1950, Richard Kimball. ☆

Crisp brownstone and steel produce Modern overtones on the reworked neo-Gothic body whose **intended tower** (had it been built) would have been more than **twice the height** of the main roof peak. The stonework of Cram's more modest tower of 1926 began to crumble, but today's basketweave-ornamented replacement is a regrettable addition.

[G 41b.] St. James Parish House, 865 Madison Ave., bet. E. 71st and E. 72nd St. E side. 1937. Grosvenor Atterbury. ☆

A late Atterbury work in the neo-Gothic, designed to substitute for a brownstone purchased by the church in 1920 and subsequently outgrown.

East of Madison Avenue:

[G 42a.] Viscaya (apartments)/formerly **New York Society for the Prevention of Cruelty to Children,** 110 E. 71st St., bet. Park and Lexington Aves. 1917. Hill & Stout. Expanded upward, 1982, Architects Design Group. ☆

A **round-cornered 16-story sliver** pokes through—and dramatically cantilevers over—the midsection of a dignified 5-story neo-Georgian town house. New Yorkers have "never seen anything like the Tower on top of the Brownstone," said the ads. True enough. *Cross Park Avenue for the total effect.*

[G 42b.] Formerly **Elsie de Wolfe residence,** 131 E. 71st St., bet. Park and Lexington Aves. 1867. Architect unknown. New facade, 1910, Ogden Codman, Jr., architect. Elsie de Wolfe, designer. ☆

The original de-stooped house. Miss de Wolfe, the original "lady decorator" (later Lady Mendl, the almost-original great party giver), set the pace for brownstone conversions throughout Manhattan's Upper East Side. The few remaining stoops are, in reaction, nostalgically embraced and protected.

[G 43.] Formerly **Mildred Phelps Stokes Hooker residence,** 173–175 E. 71st St., bet. Third and Lexington Aves. 1869. James Fee. Current facade, 1911, S. E. Gage. Altered within, 1920, 1944. ☆

A romantic neo-Gothic redesign of what was once a pair of straightforward row houses. The owner from 1910 to 1946 was the sister of Isaac Newton Phelps Stokes, architect and author of the invaluable *Iconography of Manhattan Island,* who died in this house.

East 72nd Street, between Fifth and Madison Avenues:

[G 44a.] Lycée Français de New York/originally **Oliver Gould Jennings residence,** 7 E. 72nd St. 1899. Flagg & Chambers. ★ ☆

The rich opulence of **Napoleon III's Paris.** Vermiculated stonework. This and its neighbor (see below) are among the city's finest town houses.

[G 44b.] Lycée Français de New York/originally **Henry T. Sloane residence/**later **James Stillman residence,** 9 E. 72nd St. 1896. Carrère & Hastings. ★ ☆

New York's French have occupied their own image, an *architectural* home away from home. A superior facade.

[G 44c.] The Pace Collection (art gallery), 888 Madison Ave., SW cor. E. 72nd St. 1985. Stephen Holl. ☆

An exquisitely crafted metal and glass storefront to purvey equally exquisitely crafted objets d'art. *Note the jaunty yellow awning.*

[G 44d.] 19 East 72nd Street (apartments), NW cor. Madison Ave. 1936. Rosario Candela with Mott B. Schmidt. Entrance enframement, C. Paul Jennewein, sculptor. ☆

A **timid Moderne apartment house** which replaced Charles Tiffany's **robust Romanesque Revival mansion** (an early McKim, Mead & White masterpiece), later decorated and occupied by his son, Louis Comfort Tiffany.

[G 45a.] Ralph Lauren (boutique)/formerly **Olivotti Building/**originally **Gertrude Rhinelander Waldo residence,** 867 Madison Ave., SE cor. E. 72nd St. 1898. Kimball & Thompson. Altered for shops, 1921. ★ ☆

Every part of this building **exudes personality:** oriels, a steep tile-covered mansard, a roof line bristling with dormers and chimneys. The extraordinarily ornamented neo-French Renaissance limestone palace has **captured the imagination of the commercial world** since 1921, when it was first occupied by an antiques firm. It has subsequently housed interior decorators, auction houses like Christie's of London, the Zabar family's East Side outpost E.A.T., and now fashion designer Ralph Lauren's flagship retail outlet.

[G 44a.] Flagg & Chambers' 7 E. 72nd   **[G 44b.]** Carrère & Hastings' 9 E. 72

[G 45b.] August and Company/formerly **Lambert's Pasta & Cheese/** originally **Pasta & Cheese, (gourmet shop),** 31 E. 72nd St., NE cor. Madison Ave. 1978. Martin Nystrom, architect; Sue Gould, graphic design. Altered, 1987, Lebowitz/Gould, designers ☆

One of a chain of well-designed food shops and restaurants, earlier known as **Pasta & Cheese,** catering to the "high end" market, given a new cognomen (using founder Henry August Lambert's middle name) and a spiffy new logo.

[G 45c.] Sisley (men's boutique), 905 Madison Ave., bet. E. 72nd and E. 73rd Sts. E side. 1986. Afra & Tobia Scarpa. ☆

A very idiosyncratic understated design in wood, glass, and colored acrylic. Real class from the designers of all those Benetton shops.

[G 45d.] Pasárgada (women's boutique), 902 Madison Ave., bet. E. 72nd and E. 73rd Sts. W side. 1987. Stephen Schwartz. ☆

A "water white" transparent glass front revealing a simple Post Modern interior.

[G 45e.] Giada (boutique), 904 Madison Ave., bet. E. 72nd and E. 73rd Sts. W side. 1987. Stephen Holl. ☆

Crafted of copper, clear acrylic, and glass, this impressive storefront (and interior) is a consummate work of pure sculpture.

[G 45f.] Manufacturers Hanover Trust Company branch, 35 E. 72nd St., bet. Madison and Park Aves. 1931. Cross & Cross. ☆

A bank, of all things, in the manner of the **Brothers Adam,** who worked in 18th-century London and Edinburgh.

[G 45g.] Claremont House (apartments), 52–54 E. 72nd St., bet. Madison and Park Aves. 1987. Norval White, design architect. Goldhammer, Wittenstein & Good, architects. ☆

A large infill apartment structure intended as background in the district, blending in with its neighbors along 72nd Street.

[G 45h.] 750 Park Avenue (apartments), SW cor. E. 72nd St. 1951. Horace Ginsbern & Assocs. ☆

A strong statement of white balconies and red brick in the relatively bland, older wall of Park Avenue.

[G 45h.] 750 Park Avenue apartments   [G 49a.] The Buckley School addition

[G 46.] Word of Mouth (catering and delicacies), 1012 Lexington Ave., bet. E. 72nd and E. 73rd Sts. W side. 1979. Alfredo De Vido Assocs., architect. Roger Whitehouse, graphic designer.

Inside the briefly fashionable, black, graphpaper-framed glass grid is the long narrow space of this gourmet shop, ending in **a gleaming kitchen** where the chefs' every ingredient and every process are revealed to the customers' view. The Kodalith mouth logo—and the rest—are terrific.

East 73rd Street, between Fifth and Madison Avenues:

[G 47a.] 5 East 73rd Street (town house). 1901. Buchman & Fox. ☆

Beaux Arts set off and made grander by the garden next door at **No. 11.**

[G 47b.] Originally **Joseph Pulitzer residence**/now **apartments,** 11 E. 73rd St. 1903. McKim, Mead & White. Rear extension, 1904, Foster, Gade & Graham. Converted to apartments, 1934, James E. Casale. ☆

It would be happy on the Grand Canal in Venice like Palazzo Pesaro, Rezzonico, or Labia: here, paired Ionic composite columns frame a glassy body. Also note the **marshmallow rustications** at the ground floor columns. The **Pulitzer Prize in architecture**—alas, a sad omission from that set of annual awards—should be given, retroactively, to this building.

[G 47c.] Originally **Albert Blum residence,** 20 E. 73rd St. 1911. George and Edward Blum. ☆

The best in the row from **No. 8** to **No. 26** ☆, inclusive. The other facades (1897–1923) are by such architects as Donn Barber (*No. 8*),

Harry Allan Jacobs (*Nos. 10, 12*), William A. Boring (*No. 14*), William Lawrence Bottomley (*No. 18*), and Alexander M. Welch (*Nos. 24, 26*).

[G 48a.] Madison Avenue Presbyterian Church, 917 Madison Ave., NE cor. E. 73rd St. 1899. James E. Ware & Sons. Madison Ave. entrance altered, 1960, Adams & Woodbridge. ☆ **[G 48b.] Parish House,** 921–923 Madison Ave., bet. E. 73rd and E. 74th Sts. E side. 1917. James Gamble Rogers. ☆

The plainness of the church's walls contrasts sharply with its ornate detail, making the normal neo-Gothic carving appear extra ornate. The 9-story parish house is a regal neo-Renaissance neighbor with Venetian overtones.

[G 48c.] James Lenox House (apartments), 49 E. 73rd St., bet. Madison and Park Aves. 1976. Rogers, Butler, Burgun & Bradbury. ☆

A spare and inelegant **replacement** to the **old Presbyterian Home** [see Necrology], a marvelous Victorian monstrosity that occupied land donated by James Lenox. Social values prevailed, without architecture in concert.

[G 49a.] The Buckley School addition/originally **Mr. and Mrs. Arthur C. Train residence,** 113 E. 73rd St., bet. Park and Lexington Aves. 1908. George B. Post & Sons. Converted, new facade added, 1962, Brown, Lawford & Forbes. ☆

A simple, well-scaled facade for an extension through the block from 74th Street for a venerable boys' private primary school.

[G 49b.] Originally **Charles Dana Gibson residence/**now **The American-Scandinavian Foundation,** 127 E. 73rd St., bet. Park and Lexington Aves. 1903. McKim, Mead & White. ☆

Commissioned of Stanford White by his friend, the artist who created the **Gibson Girl.**

Succès La Côte Basque/originally **Délices La Côte Basque, (patisserie),** 1032 Lexington Ave., bet. E. 73rd and E. 74th Sts. E side.

Délicieuse French pastry.

[G 50a.] Formerly **Mary E. W. Terrell residence,** 925 Fifth Ave., bet. E. 73rd and E. 74th Sts. ☆ **[G 50b.]** Originally **John W. Simpson residence,** 926 Fifth Ave., bet. E. 73rd and E. 74th Sts. ☆ Both 1899. Both by C. P. H. Gilbert.

A pair of Beaux Arts 5-story town houses (both built for Simpson) that represent the *more modest* Fifth Avenue residences of the turn of the century. Of the elaborate ones only those that are museums or institutions (the Frick, Stuyvesant, Vanderbilt, Carnegie, Warburg, Straight mansions) remain.

[G 50c.] 927 Fifth Avenue (apartments), SE cor. E. 74th St. 1917. Warren & Wetmore. ☆

A modest—in facade, not rent—neo-Italian Renaissance apartment house.

[G 50d.] East 74th Street, Fifth to Madison Aves. ☆

Lined with unpresuming rows of brownstones, many refaced, dating from ca. 1869–1871, when the area was seeing its earliest development. An exception is **No. 4** (*1899, Alexander M. Welch*), a Beaux Arts beauty for the prolific local developers, W. W. and T. M. Hall. Its first occupant was hat maker Stephen L. Stetson.

[G 51.] Originally **Raymond C. Kramer residence,** 32 E. 74th St., bet. Madison and Park Aves. 1935. William Lescaze. ☆

A handcrafted version of the machine aesthetic common to most Bauhaus-inspired design and architecture: that the idea of the machine or machinemade product is more important than that it is made by a machine. Its original composition of glass, glass block, and white stucco must have startled its neighbors in the 1930s.

[G 52.] Church of the Resurrection (Episcopal)/originally **Church of the Holy Sepulchre (Episcopal),** 115 E. 74th St., bet. Park and Lexington Aves. 1869. Renwick & Sands. ☆

A shy, retiring, side-street edifice of random ashlar bluestone with a steep polychrome slate roof. **An ecclesiastical sleeper.**

From Fifth Avenue and 74th Street to 75th and Madison:

[G 53a.] French Consulate/originally **Charles E. Mitchell residence,** 934 Fifth Ave., bet. E. 74th and E. 75th Sts. 1926. Walker & Gillette.

A timidly scaled neo-Renaissance building.

[G 53b.] The Commonwealth Fund/originally **Edward S. Harkness residence,** 1 E. 75th St., NE cor. Fifth Ave. 1907. Hale & Rogers. ★ ☆

A classy palace guarded by an intricate wrought-iron fence.

[G 53c.] Formerly **Harkness House for Ballet Arts**/originally **Nathaniel L. McCready residence**/later **Thomas J. Watson, Jr. residence,** (IBM), 4 E. 75th St., bet. Fifth and Madison Aves. 1896. Trowbridge, Colt & Livingston. Renovated for William Hale Harkness Foundation, 1965, Rogers, Butler & Burgun. ☆

Standard Oil heiress Rebekah Harkness transformed this chaste neo-French Renaissance double house into an opulent **temple of Terpsichore,** as the home of her very own ballet company. Ten years and $20 million later, she changed her mind and terminated the company. *Sic transit . . .*

[G 53d.] 5 and **7 East 75th Street,** bet. Fifth and Madison Aves. 1902. Welch, Smith & Provot. ☆

Tooled and rusticated limestone, in the Beaux Arts mode.

[G 53e.] 964 Madison Avenue (stores and offices), NW cor. E. 75th St. a.k.a. 21–27 E. 75th St. 1925. George F. Pelham. Altered, ca. 1985. ☆

Three stories of white-glazed neo-Classical terra-cotta ornament **do** a commercial temple make.

[G 54a.] Whitney Museum of American Art, 945 Madison Ave., SE cor. E. 75th St. 1966. Marcel Breuer & Assocs./Hamilton Smith. ☆

Almost as startling on the city street as the **Guggenheim,** it boasts its wares with a vengeance. Reinforced concrete clad in granite, moated, bridged, cantilevered in progressive steps overshadowing the mere patron, it is a forceful place and series of spaces. The cantilevered floors recall the machicolations of **Carcassonne**—beware of boiling oil! The Whitney, nevertheless, is at the top of the list of must-be-seen modern objects in New York.

Whitney Museum addition: In the spirit of MOMA's residential tower, the Whitney trustees in 1978 considered building a high-tech, high-rise, 35-story mixed-use tower to the south of the Breuer building by a collaboration of British architects **Foster Associates** and **Derek Walker Associates.** This plan was canceled in favor of an expansion to the museum itself, first proposed in 1986 by **Michael Graves.**

Books, Inc. 941 Madison Ave., bet. E. 74th and E. 75th Sts. E side.

A **friendly and knowledgeable** bookshop whose range of specialties is **a happy one,** as is its location in the shadow of the Whitney (its landlord).

[G 54b.] 980 Madison Avenue (galleries)/originally **Parke-Bernet Galleries**/later **Sotheby, Parke-Bernet,** bet. E. 75th and E. 76th Sts. W side. 1950. Walker & Poor, architects. Wheeler Williams, sculptor. Addition upward, 1987, Weisberg Castro Assocs.

Parke-Bernet has understood and **catered to America's cultural starvation:** buy history or at least live vicariously with its remnants. Unfortunately, Parke-Bernet's "house" is an insipid box unrelated to any cultural values. The Wheeler Williams sculpture pinned on the facade is a dreary gatekeeper, meaningless art at the portal of "art is money." The Parke-Bernet descendants have removed elsewhere, perhaps realizing the error of their ancestors' ways. [See E 23c.]

THE GUGGNEY   THE WHITENHEIM

[G 54a.] T. M. Prentice, Jr. solves Whitney and Guggenheim expansion problems

[G 54a.] Whitney Museum of Amer. Art

[G 57c.] Form. Leonard N. Stern res.

[G 54c.] **Miss Hewitt's Classes**/originally **Dr. Ernest Stillman residence,** 45 E. 75th St., bet. Madison and Park Aves. 1925. Cross & Cross. ☆

A late neo-Georgian town house. **Dr. Stillman** was an amateur fire buff (as was Mayor La Guardia) and had installed an alarm system that would tell him where any current fire was located. He often served, unpaid, those needing medical care.

[G 54d.] **57 East 75th Street (residence),** bet. Madison and Park Aves. 1979. William B. Gleckman. ☆

This curious row house revision, an unfelicitous intrusion, remained an incomplete construction project for an extremely long time. During that dusty period neighbors fantasized it would go away. It didn't.

[G 55a.] **823** and **829 Park Avenue (apartments),** bet. E. 75th and E. 76th Sts. E side. 1911. Pickering & Walker. ☆

Floral pilasters bracket windows in gently projecting central bays in these (almost) matching midblock and corner apartment blocks. A lovely touch.

[G 55b.] **Temple Israel (synagogue),** 112 E. 75th St., bet. Park and Lexington Aves. 1966. Schuman & Lichtenstein.

Overpowering and austere.

[G 56.] **168, 170, 172, 174, 176 East 75th Street (carriage houses),** bet. Lexington and Third Aves. ca. 1900.

A clinker brick complex of stables with a very complex and pictur-esque roof line. A **happy punctuation** in the blockscape.

[G 57a.] 32 East 76th Street (apartments), bet. Madison and Park Aves. a.k.a. 969 Madison Ave. 1983. Stephen B. Jacobs & Assocs. ☆

A stylish residential high rise on an L-shaped plot that wraps around to Madison, where it embraces the **Zitomer Pharmacy,** a chic, glitzy drugstore for the carriage trade.

[G 57b.] Hotel Carlyle, 35 E. 76th St., NE cor. Madison Ave. to E. 77 St. 1929. Bien & Prince.

One of the last gasps of the Great Boom, this became, in its latter years, New York headquarters for both Presidents Truman and Kennedy, who usually stayed here when visiting the city. **Ludwig Be-melmans** was unleashed with delightful success in the bar; even the ceiling was not spared his whimsical brush as airplanes and birds float overhead.

[G 57c.] Formerly **Leonard N. Stern residence,** 870 Park Ave., bet. E. 76th and E. 77th Sts. W side. 1898. Altered, 1976, Robert A. M. Stern and John S. Hagman. ☆

An altered stable, this bow-fronted faux-limestone early-Post Mod-ern town house is an asset to Park Avenue.

[G 58.] Percy and Harold D. Uris Pavilion, Lenox Hill Hospital, Park Ave. NE cor. E. 76th St. 1975. Rogers, Butler, Burgun & Bradbury.

A handsome carved-brick monolith, a stylish contrast to the same firm's banal pink metal and glass curtain wall to the north.

[G 59.] St. Jean Baptiste Church (Roman Catholic), 1067-1071 Lex-ington Ave., SE cor. E. 76th St. 1913. Nicholas Serracino. ★

Pomp but not pompous. Various Roman parts are clustered about a nave and transepts, unfortunately with a pasty result. It seems more **stage architecture** than the stuff of which cities are made, but has a **picturesque silhouette.** The congregation was originally French Cana-dian.

METROPOLITAN MUSEUM VICINITY

[M 1.] Metropolitan Museum Historic District, Along the E side of Fifth Ave. from E. 78th St. to E. 86th St. running irregularly through the Fifth-Madison blocks. ★ Buildings within the district are de-no'ted by ☆.

[M 1a.] N.Y.U. Institute of Fine Arts/originally **James B. Duke resi-dence,** 1 E. 78th St., NE cor. Fifth Ave. 1912. Horâce Trumbauer. Interior remodeled, 1958, Robert Venturi, Cope & Lippincott. ★ ☆

Reputedly a push here and a pull there made a Bordeaux Château into this austere and elegant town house, originally built for the **Dukes,** whose resources were those of the **American Tobacco Company.** Now it serves New York University graciously.

[M 1b.] Cultural Services, Embassy of France/formerly **Payne Whit-ney residence,** 972 Fifth Ave., bet. E. 78th and E. 79th Sts. 1906. McKim, Mead & White. ★ ☆

A pale neighbor to the grand Dukes adjacent.

[M 1c.] N.Y.U. Institute of Fine Arts: Conservation Center/originally **Albert Morgenstern residence/**later **Mr. & Mrs. Andrew J. Miller resi-dence,** 14 E. 78th St., bet. Madison and Fifth Aves. 1887. Facade altered for the Millers, 1917, Harry Allan Jacobs. ☆ Altered for N.Y.U., 1983, Michael Forstl.

Behind the simple 4-story-plus-roof 1917 facade are 15 levels of conservation facilities, including a cascade of floors built atop the old roof. The added structure catches north light but is invisible from the street.

[M 2.] The Rabbi Joseph Lookstein Upper School, of the Ramaz School, The Morris B. and Ida Newman Educational Center, 60 E. 78th St., bet. Madison and Park Aves. 1980. Conklin & Rossant. ☆

Five brownstone row houses of Finch College removed and, in their place, an Orthodox Jewish school inserted. Its **pewter gray aluminum facade** is an echo of its predecessors' presence, **a witty visual play of fact and fiction.** But the metallic skin is not a friend to 78th's masonry.

[M 3.] 157, 159, 161, 163–165 East 78th Street (row houses), bet. Lexington and Third Aves. 1861. Henry Armstrong, builder. ★

Vernacular row houses informed by an awareness of the Italianate style, **popular in the city** in the 1850s and 1860s. The tall parlor windows, retained in all 5, are rare in these parts.

East 79th Street, between Fifth and Madison Avenues:

[M 4a.] Ukranian Institute of America/originally **Isaac D. Fletcher residence/**then **Harry F. Sinclair residence/**then **Augustus** and **Ann van Horn Stuyvesant residence,** 2 E. 79th St., SE cor. Fifth Ave. 1899. C. P. H. Gilbert. ☆

A French Gothic palace. The precedents are limited: few in the Middle Ages ever achieved commercial wealth. The classic comparison is **the house of Jacques Coeur** (*ca. 1450*) at Bourges.

[M 3.] 157-165 E. 78th Street: French doors embellish the parlor floors

[M 4b.] Hanae Mori (boutique)/formerly **Richard Feigen Gallery,** 27 E. 79th St., bet. Fifth and Madison Aves. Altered, 1969, Hans Hollein and Baker & Blake.

A chromium cylinder dominates this cubistic stucco entrance.

[M 5a.] New York Society Library/originally **John S. Rogers residence,** 53 E. 79th St., bet. Madison and Park Aves. 1917. Trowbridge & Livingston. ★

The library of the New York Society (rather than a library for members of society). Anyone may join for a yearly membership fee; **225,000** volumes and a quiet reading room.

[M 5b.] Originally John H. Iselin residence, 59 E. 79th St., bet. Madison and Park Aves. 1909. Foster, Gade & Graham. ★ **[M 5c.]** Originally **Thatcher M. Adams residence,** 63 E. 79th St. 1903. Adams & Warren. ★ **[M 5d.]** Originally **George and Sarah Rives residence/** now **Consulate of Greece,** 67-69 E. 79th St. 1908. Carrère & Hastings. Altered and expanded upward, 1962, Pierre Zannettos. ☆

An imposing trio in 3 different styles, each tied to Classical themes: neo-French Renaissance, neo-Georgian, neo-French Baroque, respectively.

[M 5e.] 72-76 East 79th Street (row, town houses)/converted to **apartment tower,** bet. Madison and Park Aves. **Nos. 72-74,** 1884, Anson Squires. ☆ **No. 76,** 1884, James E. Ware. ☆ Conversion, 1988, Conklin & Rossant.

A daring, setback tower addition to a trio of Victorian houses that had been abandoned in the midst of an earlier redevelopment project.

[M 6a.] 895 Park Avenue (apartments), SE cor. E. 79th St. 1929. Sloan & Robertson.

Art Deco hasn't quite been accepted by these talented architects, nor has neo-Classicism been given a warm farewell. A handsome structure, nonetheless.

[M 6b.] Belgravia (apartments), 124 E. 79th St., bet. Park and Lexington Aves. 1985. Gruzen & Partners.

A suave dark red infill to the wall of tall 1920s (and post-World War II) apartments that line wide 79th.

[M 6c.] Hunter College School of Social Work, CUNY, Lois and Samuel Silberman Fund Building, 127-135 E. 79th St., bet. Park and Lexington Aves. 1967. Enlarged, 1988. Both by Wank Adams Slavin Assocs.

The 5¢ Staten Island Ferry ride is **a dim memory.** But the **nickel-a-year rent remains,** here, **thanks to the Silberman Fund,** which owns the building and rents it to the school via a 20-year lease charging one dollar! On occasion of the first 20 years expansion was called for, but only in the usable space for teaching; the yearly rent—until 2007 at least—remains 5¢. The building itself sports an interesting facade of **vertically incised window openings** in a gray terra-cotta (bottom) and white iron-spot brick (top) wall.

[M 7a.] 45 East 80th Street (apartments), NE cor. Madison Ave. 1987. Liebman Liebman & Assocs.

Twenty-seven demure stories, faced with Italian granite and Indiana limestone, growing out of a Post Modern plinth that continues Madison Avenue's 2 stories of shops and services.

[M 2.] Ramaz Lookstein Upper School   **[M 7b.]** Manhattan Church of Christ

[M 7b.] Manhattan Church of Christ, 48 E. 80th St., bet. Madison and Park Aves. 1967. Eggers & Higgins.

Cast concrete and thick stained glass energize this facade.

[M 8.] East 80th Street, Park to Lexington Aves.

Roll call: No. 116: Originally **Lewis Spencer Morris residence** (*1923. Cross & Cross.*) ★ Neo-Federal. **No. 120:** Originally **George Whitney residence** (*1930. Cross & Cross.*) ★ Neo-Georgian. **No. 124:** Originally **Clarence Dillon residence** (*1930. Mott B. Schmidt.*) ★ Neo-Federal. **No. 130:** Originally **Vincent Astor residence**/now **Junior League of the City of New York** (*1928. Mott B. Schmidt.*) ☆

These houses form a grand grouping of wide neo-Georgian Regency town houses, a quartet of the last to be built in this grand scale in New York. **No. 130** rises above its neighbors, a stately travertine facade **in the manner of the Brothers Adam.**

[M 9a.] The Terrace, Stanhope Hotel, 997 Fifth Ave., SE cor. E. 81st St. 1965. (Hotel, 1926, Rosario Candela.) ☆

A pleasurable addition to an old and elegant hotel. The sights equal those offered to café-sitters worldwide: the passing fair, the Metropolitan Museum, tottering dowagers, Jaguars, and the near-jet set.

[M 9b.] 998 Fifth Avenue (apartments), NE cor. E. 81st St. 1910. McKim, Mead & White. ★ ☆

A pacesetter in the design of Fifth Avenue, Peek at the **Japanese garden trellis** over the wall behind (along 81st Street).

[M 9c.] La Résidence (apartments), 1080 Madison Ave., bet. E. 81st and E. 82nd Sts. W side. 1981. Thierry W. Despont, designer; Emil N. Steo, architect.

A serene midblock high-rise addition to Madison Avenue that minimizes its tower by a setback from a carefully detailed base. All things considered, a good neighbor.

[M 10.] 940 and **944 Park Avenue (apartments),** NW cor. E. 81st St. Late 1920s.

Neo-Romanesque and Art Deco side by side.

From Fifth Avenue and 82nd Street to Madison Avenue:

[M 11a.] 1001 Fifth Avenue (apartments), bet. E. 81st and E. 82nd Sts. 1979. Johnson/Burgee, design architects. Philip Birnbaum & Assocs. associated architects. ☆

High-rise limestone pretentiousness with an **openly ersatz** mansard roof whose true nature is apparent to any who care to look. An architectural conceit raised to new heights.

[M 11b.] Originally **Benjamin N. Duke residence,** 1009 Fifth Ave., SE cor. E 82nd St. 1901. Welch, Smith & Provot. ★ ☆

It's hard to believe that this spectacular mansarded palace was a speculative house. Built by Upper East Side developers W. W. and T. M. Hall, it was quickly snapped up by a founder of the American Tobacco Company. Developers were different then.

[M 11c.] East 82nd Street, Fifth to Madison Aves., on axis of the main entrance of the Metropolitan Museum. **Nos. 2-22, 3-19.** ☆

Rich facades as a group frame the Met's main entrance, as if they housed the court of **the palace** of art. *Worth a special stroll.*

[M 12.] Metropolitan Museum of Art, in Central Park facing Fifth Ave. bet. E. 80th and E. 84th Sts. **Rear facade** (now visible only within Lehman Wing), 1880. Calvert Vaux & J. Wrey Mould. **SW wing and facade,** 1888, Theodore Weston. **Central Fifth Avenue facade,** 1895–1902, Richard Morris Hunt and Richard Howland Hunt. **Side wings along Fifth Ave.,** 1906, McKim, Mead & White. **Thomas J. Watson Library,** 1965, Brown, Lawford & Forbes. **Front stairs, pools, Lehman Wing, and Great Hall renovations.** 1969–1975. **Sackler Wing for the Temple of Dendur,** 1979. **American Wing,** 1980. **Michael C. Rockefeller Wing for Primitive Art,** 1981. **Dillon Galleries for Far East Art,** 1981. André Meyer Galleries for European **Paintings,** 1981. **Egyptian Wing,** 1982. **Wallace Galleries for 20th Century Art,** 1986. **Iris and B. Gerald Cantor Roof Garden,** 1987. **Tisch Galleries,** 1988. **European Sculpture and Decorative Art Wing,** 1989. All by Kevin Roche John Dinkeloo & Assocs. **Open to the public.**

The neo-Renaissance design example for this elegant warehouse of art was revealed at the **World's Columbian Exposition of 1893,** at which the opposing Romanesque Revival style lost its position of preeminence.

Vaux's earlier **Ruskinian Gothic kernel** is now largely encased: the Fifth Avenue frontage filled in with a **City Beautiful palace** in the manner of Versailles, the behind encased and devoured by the Lehman Wing, a flashy glass pyramid flanked by walls designed to screen what Roche and Co. considered the vulgar excesses of Vaux. It is a rich and confusing mélange—exciting, grand, controversial, often elegant, sometimes banal. The **main hall** is still **one of the great spaces** of New York, the city's only suggestion of the great visionary neo-Roman spaces of the **18th**-century Italian draftsman and engraver, Piranesi.

Since 1969 the museum has undergone a reconstruction and expansion **unrivaled by any museum** in America (if not the world) designed by architect Kevin Roche. Many are offended by their impact on Central Park.

The works within are without peer. Savor them moment by moment, year by year. (Mandatory contribution—an oxymoron—on entry.)

[M 12.] The Metropolitan Museum's American Wing displays the old Assay office

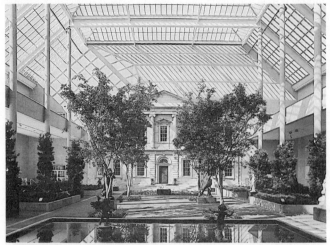

[M 9b., 11a., 11b.] A Fifth Avenue trio   **[M 15a.]** St. Ignatius Loyola RC Church

[M 13.] 25 East 83rd Street (apartments), NW cor. Madison Ave. 1938. Frederick L. Ackerman and Ramsey & Sleeper. Altered, 1986.

A modern monument, not in its external elegance but in its pacesetting technology: the first centrally air-conditioned apartment building in the city (note that there are no grilles penetrating the walls—air is drawn in at the roof and distributed by interior ductwork). In the 1980s the glass block "windows" thought necessary for economical cooling were removed in favor of clear glass, surprisingly giving the building **a new lease on life.**

[M 14a.] Marymount School/originally **Jonathan Thorne residence,** 1028 Fifth Ave., SE cor. E. 84th St. 1902. C. P. H. Gilbert. ☆

Praise to the Church for preserving this handsome mansion by default. The school also occupies **Nos. 1026** and **1027** (*1903. Van Vleck & Goldsmith.*)

[M 14b.] 3 East 84th Street (apartments), bet. Fifth and Madison Aves. 1928. Howells & Hood. ☆

Cubistic modeling and pressed-metal spandrels presage Raymond Hood's later **News** and **RCA Buildings.**

[M 14c.] 1128 Madison Avenue (stores), SW cor E. 84th St. 1986. Rosenblum/Harb.

A brilliant expansion and recladding of a dull 2-story taxpayer, turning it **from a pumpkin into Cinderella's coach.** Through talent, not magic.

[M 14c.] 1128 Madison Ave. building: commerce raised to new aesthetic heights

[M 16a.] John H. Duncan's charming row houses, Madison Ave. at East 84th St.

[M 15a.] Church of St. Ignatius Loyola (Roman Catholic), 980 Park Ave., SW cor. E. 84th St. 1898. Schickel & Ditmars. ★

Vignola (mannerist Italian architect) in the American manner, with a **German** accent. Limestone, superscaled, air-conditioned; grim, proper, and **Park Avenue-ish.** The chapel downstairs is an ethnic balancer, dedicated to **St. Laurence O'Toole,** titular saint of Yorkville's mid 1800s Irish settlers.

[M 15b.] Regis High School (Roman Catholic), 55 E. 84th St., bet. Madison and Park Aves. 1917. Maginnis & Walsh. ★

Eight grand **Ionic** columns are the armature of this facade.

[M 16a.] Row houses: 21 East 84th Street, bet. Fifth and Madison Aves. and 1132 and 1134 Madison Ave., NW cor. E. 84th St. 1892. John H. Duncan.

A brick and terra-cotta terrace (English grouping of jointly de-signed town houses), now sullied by unhappy storefronts on the avenue.

[M 16b.] 30 East 85th Street (apartments), SW cor. Madison Ave. 1986. Schuman, Lichtenstein, Claman & Efron.

A 2-story Post Modern base continues Madison Avenue's retail activities in both flame-finished and polished granite. Above are the apartments in a desert sand–colored brick. Fine detailing.

[M 17a.] New World Foundation/formerly **Lewis Gouverneur Morris residence,** 100 E. 85th St., SE cor. Park Ave. 1914. Ernest Flagg. ★

The radical English architect and urban designer **Richard Norman Shaw** (1831–1912) converted Georgian fantasies into such rich and complex places as this. A sprightly collision of quarter-round windows, widow's walks, and dormers flying in all directions. Among Flagg's best.

[M 17b.] Park Avenue Christian Church (Disciples of Christ)/origi-nally **South Reformed Church,** 1010 Park Ave., SW cor. E. 85th St. 1911. Cram, Goodhue & Ferguson.

Native materials, here Manhattan schist, were assembled with in-spiration from the **Sainte Chapelle in Paris.** Such were the words of Cram, but the inspiration seems to have been effective largely for the *flèche.* (Sainte Chapelle is a glass box with incidental stone supports; this is a stone box with incidental glass.)

[M 17c.] Originally **Reginald DeKoven residence,** 1025 Park Ave., bet. E. 85th and E. 86th Sts. E side. 1912. John Russell Pope. ★

An urban adaptation of Jacobean Revival that was somehow over-looked in the serial redevelopment of Park Avenue. DeKoven (1859–1920) was a composer of popular light opera; his "O Promise Me" was a wedding standby for generations.

[M 18.] YIVO Institute for Jewish Research/formerly **Mrs. Cornelius Vanderbilt residence**/originally **William Starr Miller residence, open to the public.** Fifth Ave., E 86th St. 1914. Carrère & Hastings. ☆

An elegant émigré—from the **Place des Vosges** without the **Place;** a town palace of limestone and brick, encrusted with Ionic pilasters, crowned with a slate mansard roof. Now **an archive of Yiddish culture** (watch for unusual exhibition subjects).

CARNEGIE HILL AND BEYOND

Carnegie Hill is most pronounced as you move uptown along Madison Avenue above 86th Street or downtown on Park at 96th Street, where trains bound for Grand Central dive into the 2½-mile tunnel which burrows beneath the glitter and swank of Park Avenue [see M Manhat-tan/Grand Central/Park Avenue P 1.]. The area covered here runs from 87th to 106th Streets east of Fifth; over to Lexington and environs *below* 96th, over to Park and environs *above* 96th. Remember, the Carnegie Hill Historic District (in two parts) is just a fraction of this area.

[C 1a.] Liederkranz Club/originally **John S. Phipps residence,** 6 E. 87th St., bet. Fifth and Madison Aves. 1904. Grosvenor Atterbury.

The relocated sculpture in the eastern side yard *(1896. G. Moretti, sculptor.)* commemorates the semicentennial of the German music soci-ety (1847–1897) that vacated its earlier quarters at **115 East 58th Street** in 1949 (demolished since).

[C 1b.] Phelps-Stokes Fund/formerly **Buttinger residence,** 10 E. 87th St., bet. Fifth and Madison Aves. 1958. Felix Augenfeld & Jan Hird Pokorny.

Built as a residence around a private library, which occupies a handsome, 2-story glass-walled place.

[C 2.] Park Avenue Synagogue, 50 E. 87th St., SE cor. Madison Ave. 1980. James Rush Jarrett and Schuman Lichtenstein Claman & Efron, associated architects.

The facade is clad in "Mankato stone, cut in a rusticated manner." Heavy-handed.

[C 3.] Solomon R. Guggenheim Museum, Fifth Ave. bet. E. 88th and E. 89th Sts. 1959. Frank Lloyd Wright. Addition along E boundary facing E. 89th St. Taliesin Associated Architects. **Aye Simon Reading Room,** 1978, Richard Meier & Assocs.

The Guggenheim's central space is one of the greatest Modern interiors in the world: a museum **more important as architecture** than for the contents it displays. To appreciate it, take the elevator (half round) to the skylighted top and meander, literally, between the structural baffles, down the helical ramp. The crudely formed, painted exterior concrete has not aged happily. And the side-street addition is a labored affair, a decorative parody of Wright by son-in-law **William Wesley Peters.**

[C 3.] T. M. Prentice, Jr. solves two expansion problems: Guggenheim and Whitney

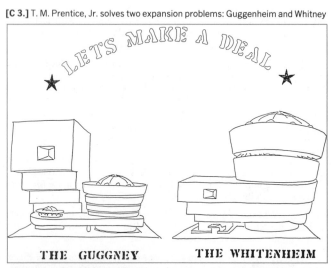

[C 3.] Wright's Guggenheim Museum   [C 4a.] The 60 East 88th Street apts.

An addition to the Guggenheim, to occupy the site of the 89th Street wing, but to be larger in size and less derivative in appearance, was pursued with great energy by the museum's administration. Its controversial design underwent a number of changes devised by its architects, Gwathmey Siegel & Associates, in 1987.

[C 4a.] 60 East 88th Street (apartments), bet. Madison and Park Aves. 1987. Beyer Blinder Belle.

A restrained **midblock handshake** between the traditions of the 1920s and those of the Post Modern. A rusticated limestone base, surrounding a bull's-eye window and supporting a brass 'n' glass canopy, is the lower element of a finely crafted red brick superstructure terminating in a modern mansard. A particularly fine detail is the French-doored balconettes outfitted in flat metal railings. Everything works together here. **A splendid work . . .** Oh, were Manhattan only to have more like it!

[C 4b.] 1082 Park Avenue (apartments), bet. E. 88th and E. 89th Sts. W side. Altered, ca. 1927.

Tuscany in terra-cotta.

[C 5a.] National Academy of Design, 3 and 5 E. 89th St., bet. Fifth and Madison Aves. and 1083 Fifth Ave. **No. 3,** 1914. Ogden Codman, Jr. **No. 5,** 1958, William and Geoffrey Platt. **No. 1083,** remodeled, 1915, Ogden Codman, Jr. **Open to the public.**

Once a center of conservatism in the arts, in recent years it has become a **refreshing repository** for imaginative exhibitions. Founded in 1825, it includes architects, painters, and graphic designers.

[C 5b.] St. David's School/originally the **Cutting residences,** 12, 14, and 16 E. 89th St., bet. Fifth and Madison Aves. 1919. Delano & Aldrich.

John-John Kennedy's attendance at this school brought notoriety to these handsome neo-Georgian town houses.

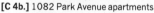
[C 4b.] 1082 Park Avenue apartments   **[C 5c.]** Entry: The Graham House apts.

[C 5c.] Graham House (apartments), 22 E. 89th St., SW cor. Madison Ave. ca. 1892.

If for no other reason the **serendipitous entrance ornament** makes this a wonderful addition to the city.

[C 6.] 45 East 89th Street, along Madison Ave., bet. E. 89th and E. 90th Sts. E side. 1969. Philip Birnbaum and Oppenheimer, Brady & Lehrecke, associated architects.

A notch above its competition, particularly at the lower levels. The handsome red-brown brickwork was designed by **Thomas Lehrecke** around a basic body by **Philip Birnbaum.** The body is a blockbuster, a state of affairs that can't be condoned, regardless of other virtues.

[C 7a.] 50 East 89th Street (apartments), bet. Madison and Park Aves., through to E. 88th St. 1974. Emery Roth & Sons.

A modest Modern **midblock good neighbor,** well conceived and well executed in exposed concrete and dignified dark brick.

[C 7b.] Church of St. Thomas More (Roman Catholic)/originally **Beloved Disciple Protestant Episcopal Church/**later **East 89th Street Reformed Church,** 59-63 E. 89th St., bet. Madison and Park Aves. 1873. **Rectory,** 65 E. 89th St. 1892.

A **country church** of **great quality** and **modest scale** which survives in the percolating real estate caldron of the Upper East Side. Over the years, its worth has been recognized by a number of different religious denominations.

East 90th Street, between Fifth and Madison Aves:

[C 8a.] Church of the Heavenly Rest (Episcopal), SE cor. Fifth Ave. and E. 90th St. 1929. Hardie Philip of Mayers, Murray & Philip, architects. Pulpit Madonna, Malvina Hoffman, sculptor. Exterior sculpture, Ulrich Ellerhausen.

Stripped Gothic, with some of the strong but austere massing that prefigures modern as a style if not a fact.

[C 7b.] RC Church of St. Thomas More   **[C 8a.]** Church of the Heavenly Rest

[C 8b.] Originally **M. Louise McAlpin residence,** 11 E. 90th St. 1903. Barney & Chapman. ★

Inspired, the Landmarks Preservation Commission report tells us, by the classical traditions of the 18th-century French *hôtel particulier.*

[C 8c.] Originally **Emily Trevor residence,** 15 E. 90th St. 1928. Mott B. Schmidt. ★

Neo-Federal with Flemish-bond brick, a tepid 1920s favorite in many of the park blocks.

[C 8d.] Originally **Harriet S. Clark residence,** 17 E. 90th St. 1919. F. Burrall Hoffman, Jr.

A neo-Georgian house with **an unusual arcaded loggia** in the European tradition.

Sinclair Lewis and Dorothy Thompson, husband and wife, lived in the undistinguished apartment block at 21 East 90th Street in the early 1930s. They maintained two sitting rooms so they could entertain guests separately.

[C 9.] 1261 Madison Avenue (apartments), NE cor. E. 90th St. 1901. Buchman & Fox. ★

Built to house only 14 families, this **gracious Beaux Arts** apartment building enhances Carnegie Hill.

[C 10.] Carnegie Hill Historic District. Two separate midblock areas: **[C 10a.]** Bet. Madison and Park Aves. along parts of E. 90th, E. 91st, and E. 92nd Sts. **[C 10b.]** Fifth and Madison Aves. along parts of E. 92nd, E. 93rd, and E 94th Sts. ★

A landmark district created more to preserve the handsome local midblock scale and texture than any pervasive or consistent architectural quality.

East 91st Street, between Fifth and Madison Avenues:

[C 11a.] **Cooper-Hewitt Museum, the Smithsonian Institution's National Museum of Design/**formerly the **Columbia School of Social Work/**originally **Andrew Carnegie residence,** 2 E. 91st St., SE cor. Fifth Ave. to E. 90th St. 1901. Babb, Cook & Willard. ★ Museum alterations, 1977, Hardy Holzman Pfeiffer Assocs. **Open to the public.**

When Carnegie built this château, **squatters were his neighbors.** Louise and Andrew Carnegie lived here from 1901 until the surviving Louise's death in 1946. Its new life is as houser and exhibitor of the great collection **originally assembled for the Cooper Union** by the Cooper and Hewitt families: the decorative arts, from wallpaper to furniture *and* as **a stage for wonderful and imaginative exhibitions** in the decorative arts, architecture, graphics, and you-name-it.

[C 11a.] Cooper-Hewitt Museum viewed through fence of its generous garden

[C 11b.] Orig. the Otto Kahn residence   [C 11c.] Orig. James A. Burden, Jr. res.

[C 11b.] **Duchesne Residence School faculty residence** a.k.a. **Convent of the Sacred Heart/**originally **Otto Kahn residence,** 1 E. 91st St., NE cor. Fifth Ave. 1918. J. Armstrong Stenhouse with C. P. H. Gilbert. ★

A Leviathan house (145 feet of frontage, 6 lots wide): an American version of an English version of an Italian Renaissance palace (cf. Palazzo della Cancelleria in Rome). It is rich but subdued, as expected in Boston or Florence.

[C 11c.] Duchesne Residence School/originally **James A. Burden, Jr., residence,** 7 E. 91st St. 1905. Warren & Wetmore. ★

Built by the industrialized ironmonger from Troy, N.Y., whose commercial legacy was the American Machine and Foundry Company (AMF). A freestanding mansion with a side court.

[C 11d.] Consulate of the U.S.S.R./originally **John H. Hammond residence,** 9 E. 91st St. 1903. Carrère & Hastings. ★ Alterations, 1976, William B. Gleckman.

Hammond's world was recorded in popular history when Benny Goodman became his son-in-law. The Soviet government appreciates style and bought it for their first New York consulate since 1942. **A palace worthy of anybody.**

[C 11e.] Originally **John B. Trevor residence,** 11 E. 91st St. 1921. Trowbridge & Livingston. ★

A pale neighbor of the magnificence to the west.

[C 11f.] The Spence School, 22 E. 91st St. 1929. John Russell Pope. Addition, 1988, Fox & Fowle.

A high-rise, watery neo-Georgian by someone who should have known better, John Russell Pope, whose National Gallery of Art is one of Washington's most elegant oases. The Spence addition means not to compete.

[C 12a.] The Dalton School, the First Program, 61 E. 91st St., bet. Madison and Park Aves. ca. 1925.

A large neo-Georgian town house of good scale.

[C 12b.] Brick Presbyterian Church, 1140-1144 Park Ave., NW cor. E. 91st St. 1938. York & Sawyer; Lewis Ayres, designer. **Chapel of the Reformed Faith,** 1952, Adams & Woodbridge.

The safe bumpety-brick and limestone-lanterned **neo-Georgian** of the 1930s.

Sarabeth's Kitchen (restaurant/food shop), 1295 Madison Ave., in Hotel Wales, bet. E. 92nd and E. 93rd Sts. E side.

Sarabeth Levine, president of this enterprise, offers inspired meals, desserts, breads, jams, and other comestibles in a cozy and very cordial atmosphere.

[C 13a.] 1107 Fifth Avenue (apartments) SE cor. E. 92nd St. 1925. Rouse & Goldstone.

Mrs. Marjorie Merriweather **Post (Toasties)** Close Hutton (later) Davies May commissioned this vertically stacked town palace to allow herself a superb **54-room triplex** vantage point in space. Note the elegant auto entrance on 92nd Street.

[C 13b.] The Jewish Museum/originally **Felix M. Warburg residence,** 1109 Fifth Ave., NE cor. E. 92nd St. 1908. C. P. H. Gilbert. **Albert and Vera List Wing,** 1963, Samuel Glazer. **Open to the public.**

A Gothic château (with a **Miami Beach** annex) that has become a center for **extremely fine exhibitions.**

[C 14.] "Night Presence IV" (sculpture), on the Island in Park Ave., N of E. 92nd St. 1972. Louise Nevelson, sculptor.

This purposely rusty (self-weathering) steel construction is **a forlorn Modern loner** in these neo-Renaissance precincts.

[C 15.] 120 and **122 East 92nd Street (residences),** bet. Park and Lexington Aves. ca. 1853. ★

Wooden houses from rural times. Even in their isolation, they had to conform to the commissioners' (grid) plan of 1811. They have a homely scale.

Note: Part of the Carnegie Hill Historic District ★ lies in the park blocks of East 92nd, 93rd, and 94th Streets [see C 10b.].

East 93rd Street, between Madison and Park Avenues:

[C 16a.] 1321 Madison Avenue (row house), NE cor. E. 93rd St. 1891. James E. Ware. ★

Craggy Queen Anne: mysterious and so rich in detail that the later Madison Avenue storefront insertions can almost be overlooked. Almost.

The Corner Bookstore, 1313 Madison Ave., SE cor. E. 93rd St.

Featured subjects are cooking, gardening, children, art and architecture, and a selection of standbys, old and new, hard and soft. All are displayed in a modern tailored shop that will age graciously.

[C 16b.] Smithers Alcoholism Center, St. Luke's-Roosevelt Hospital Center/formerly **Billy Rose residence**/originally **William G. Loew residence,** 56 E. 93rd St. 1932. Walker & Gillette. ★

The last great mansion, it has the **manners of John Soane,** the avant-garde Regency architect who used classic parts with a fresh attitude toward form and space.

[C 16c.] Lycée Français de New York/formerly **Permanent Mission of Romania to the United Nations**/originally **Virginia Graham Fair Vanderbilt residence,** 60 E. 93rd St. 1930. John Russell Pope. ★ Altered to Lycée, 1976, William B. Gleckman.

Look at the voussoirs: each has the face of a different woman.

[C 16d.] Originally intended as **George F. Baker, Sr. residence,** 67 E. 93rd St. 1931. Delano & Aldrich. ★ **[C 16e.]** Originally **addition to, and courtyard for George F. Baker, Jr. residence,** 69 E. 93rd St. 1929. Delano & Aldrich. ★ **[C 16f.]** Originally **Francis F. Palmer residence**/later **George F. Baker, Jr. residence**/now **The Synod of Bishops of the Russian Orthodox Church Outside of Russia,** 76 E. 93rd St. 1918; northern addition, 1928, both by Delano & Aldrich. ★

A beautifully fashioned urban complex, all by Delano & Aldrich, in the neo-Federal style built (or rebuilt) for the Bakers, father and son. George, Sr. (known as the dean of American banking) died in 1931 and left George, Jr.—already wealthy in his own right—a $60 million bequest, hence allowing **a rare architectural moment** in crowded, costly Manhattan. The Synod has owned **Nos. 69-75** since 1958.

A lesson in town design in itself, and in how to respect and reinforce the form of street and avenue while creating both private garden space and richness and variety of architectural form. The "French" courtyard is worthy of an *hôtel de ville.*

[C 17.] The triple ogee-arched entrance to 1185 Park Avenue's interior court

[C 17.] 1185 Park Avenue (apartments), bet. E. 93rd and E. 94th Sts. E side. 1929. Schwartz & Gross.

A full blockfront with **an interior court** resembling the West Side's Ansonia or its downtown Park Avenue neighbors near Grand Central, now all gone.

[C 18.] 128 East 93rd Street (residence), bet. Park and Lexington Aves. ca. 1865.

A slate mansarded frame house restored to look like a life-size dollhouse. Too much restoration can also put out the flame.

[C 19a.] International Center of Photography/formerly **National Audubon Society**/originally **Willard Straight residence,** 1130 Fifth Ave., NE cor. E. 94th St. 1914. Delano & Aldrich. Remodeled, 1974, Robert Simpson. ★

Elegant, distilled, refined; a sharp, precise, intellectually studied American neo-Georgian house with a **homely residential scale.** The Center is a pleasant, low-keyed use of its original rooms.

[C 19b.] 5-25 East 94th Street (row houses) bet. Fifth and Madison Aves. 1892–1894. Cleverdon & Putzel. In Carnegie Hill Historic District. ☆

A speculator's row of brownstone, whitestone, and rock-face ashlar **Romanesque Revival** houses with a variety of detail for individuality. **Nos. 15, 17, 21,** and **25** are the most vigorous of the lot.

[C 20.] Carnegie Hill Tower (apartments), 40 E. 94th St., SE cor. Madison Ave. 1983. Edward Giannasa.

Well tailored in pale brick. In a curious way its sliced-off corner pays its respects to the gutsier cylindrical tower of the armory, across the street.

[C 21a.] The demolished Park Avenue (east) facade of Squadron A Armory

[C 21a.] West facade of Squadron A Armory, 8th Regiment, N.Y. National Guard, Madison Ave., bet. E. 94th and E. 95th Sts. E side. 1895. John Rochester Thomas. ★

A fantasy of the brickmason's virtuosity: arches, corbels, crenellations; plastic, neomedieval modeling. Now a **play castle,** a backdrop for the open space of **Hunter's** facilities to the east.

[C 21b.] Hunter College Campus Schools/formerly **Hunter High School**/originally **Intermediate School 29, Manhattan,** Park Ave. bet. E. 94th and E. 95th Sts. W side. 1969. Morris Ketchum, Jr. & Assocs.

Castellated brick complementing its old machicolated neighbor, the west facade of which is **preserved as a monument** along Madison Avenue. But why didn't they use the same elegant colored mortar?

[C 22.] Originally **Mr. & Mrs. Ernesto Fabbri residence**/now **The House of the Redeemer,** 7 E. 95th St., bet. Fifth and Madison Aves. 1916. Grosvenor Atterbury.

A **limestone palazzo** with iron gates and a pillared entrance. For the couple's first house, on 62nd Street, see [G 6e.].

East 96th Street, between Fifth and Madison Avenues:

[C 23a.] Lycée Français de New York/formerly **Mrs. Amory S. Carhart residence,** 3 E. 95th St. 1913. Horace Trumbauer. ★

A French school in a **Francophile town palace.** The carriage (garage) doors with a people-door inset are a typical French division between the public world and the private house and garden.

[C 23b.] Manhattan Country School/originally **Ogden Codman, Jr., residence,** 7 E. 96th St. 1915. Ogden Codman, Jr. ★

Painted limestone, a shuttered **cartoon** of the **Renaissance** from a talented amateur night.

[C 23c.] Carnegie Hill School/formerly **The Emerson School**/originally **Mrs. Robert Livingston residence,** 12 E. 95th St. 1916. Ogden Codman, Jr.

Another Codman design for this block [see above and below]. Note the garlanded swags.

[C 23d.] 14 East 96th Street (apartments). 1986.

An out-of-place 17-story sliver that beat out the zoning restrictions imposed later. One of a dozen or so sprinkled throughout the Upper East side, mostly from Lexington Avenue eastward.

[C 23e.] Originally **Lucy Drexel Dahlgren residence**/later **Pierre Cartier residence**/later **St. Francis de Sales Convent,** 15 E. 96th St. 1915. Ogden Codman, Jr. ★

A **masterful** limestone town house, extremely **disciplined** yet **lively** with French Renaissance motifs. Owner Cartier was of the jewelry firm. Codman (who lived at **No. 7**) was something of a Francophile: he compiled an index of all known French châteaux, some 36,000!

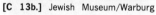

[C 13b.] Jewish Museum/Warburg   **[C 24a.]** Florence Nightingale Home

[C 24a.] Florence Nightingale Nursing Home, 175 E. 96th St., bet. Lexington and Third Aves. 1967. William N. Breger Assocs.

A penthouse provides a giant, hovering "cornice" over an open roof deck [also see **Long-Term Care Facility, E Harlem E 2.**]

Nineteen stories or thirty-one? The higher numbers, according to the developer of the apartment tower at 108 East 96th Street; the lower, according to the city's Building Department, the Board of Standards and Appeals, and a succession of state courts. The excess stories were spotted in 1986 by the president of a local community group, CIVITAS. The city's subsequent stop-work order was followed (because of a loophole) by a furious effort on the part of the developer to complete the building, working from the top of the converted dozen stories *downward.* Confirmation of the stop-work order, litigation, appeals, and the citing of hardship kept the controversy simmering for years.

[C 24b.] Upper East Side Cultural Center (mosque), 201 E. 96th St., NE cor. Third Ave. 1989. Skidmore, Owings & Merrill.

Built askew of Manhattan's grid, the mosque is traditionally oriented toward Islam's Mecca, in Saudi Arabia. Also slated for the site are a minaret and administration wing.

[C 25.] St. Nicholas Russian Orthodox Cathedral, 15 E. 97th St., bet. Fifth and Madison Aves. 1902. John Bergesen. ★

An exotic form among the dour surroundings created by predominantly rich northern European Protestants. **High Victorian, Ruskinian,** polychromatic (red brick, blue and yellow tile), crosses, arches, ornations, and a bunch of **delicious onion domes.**

[C 26.] St. Bernard's School, 4 E. 98th St., bet. Fifth and Madison Aves. 1918. Delano & Aldrich.

For boys, not the dogs of monks. An awkward **neo-Georgian.**

Mt. Sinai Medical Center:

[C 27.] Mt. Sinai Medical Center, E. 98th to E. 102nd Sts., Fifth to Madison Aves. Original buildings, 1904, Arnold W. Brunner. **[C 27a.] Magdalene and Charles Klingenstein Pavilion,** 1952, Kahn & Jacobs. **[C 27b.] Annenberg Building,** 1976, Skidmore, Owings & Merrill. **[C 27c.] North Pavilion, Phase 1,** 1989; **Phase 2,** 1991. Both by I. M. Pei & Partners.

It tried to grow within the grid (absorbing two cross streets), rebuilding itself in the same manner as Roosevelt, Lenox Hill, and so many other hospitals; the body remains and gradually changes its appearance.

The high-rise **Annenberg Building** at center block, surrounded by a plaza space, is a great, rusty, cadaverous blockbuster of a building, an incursive hulk that dominates the skyline of East Harlem (to its east).

Sphere (1967. Arnaldo Pomodoro.) is a sophisticated punctuation to the plaza space.

The **Metzger Pavilion** (by Brunner) faces Annenberg at midblock, a French Baroque Revival delight.

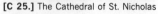
[C 25.] The Cathedral of St. Nicholas **[C 28a.]** Baum-Rothschild Staff Res.

[C 28a.] Baum-Rothschild Staff Pavilion, Mt. Sinai Medical Center (apartments), 1249 Park Ave., SE cor. E. 97th St. 1968. Pomerance & Breines.

A snappy, slender tower with balconies that presides over the portal of the Park Avenue tunnel into Grand Central Terminal.

[C 28b.] Jane B. Aron Residence Hall, Mt. Sinai Medical Center, 50 E. 98th St., SW cor. Park Ave. 1984. Davis, Brody & Assocs.

A composition of rectangular prisms, cylinders, and subtle tapestries of golden-hued brick, interspersed with green-framed windows, inset air-conditioning grilles, and splashes of glass block. **A consummate achievement.**

[C 29a.] New York Academy of Medicine, 2 E. 103rd St., SE cor. Fifth Ave. 1926. York & Sawyer. **Library open to the public.**

Literal eclecticism—a little bit of **Byzantine** detail and mannerism, a pinch of **Lombardian Romanesque**—monolithic and massive (windows and doors are tiny apertures).

What may be the world's largest collection of cookbooks is surprisingly housed here, the gift of **Dr. Margaret Barclay Wilson.** She (if not all physicians) believed that the enlightened, disciplined and/or enriched palate led to well-being of the mind and/or body.

[C 29b.] Statue of Dr. J. Marion Sims, M.D., LL.D., Fifth Ave. along Central Park, opp. E. 103rd St. ★

Tribute to a surgeon, philanthropist, and founder of Women's Hospital.

[C 29c.] Museum of the City of New York, 1220 Fifth Ave., bet. E. 103rd and E. 104th Sts. 1932. Joseph H. Freedlander. ★

The product of a competition between 5 invited architects, this is **a bland neo-Georgian building.** The contents try to make up for any architectural deficiencies: "dioramas" demonstrate the physical form and history of New York. Savor Indians, maps, Dutch and English colonists, antique toys, Rockefeller rooms, period rooms, ship models, portraits, a mishmash.

Seek out the model (on the first floor) of the Castello plan (1660) of New Amsterdam, the best visualization available of that Dutch beaver-trading town.

Alexander Hamilton and **DeWitt Clinton** face Central Park from niches in the facade (*Adolph A. Weinman, sculptor*).

[C 29d.] El Museo del Barrio/originally **Heckscher Foundation for Children (settlement house),** 1230 Fifth Ave., bet. E. 104th and E. 105th Sts. E side. **Open to the public.**

The museum of Puerto Rican art, history, and culture.

[C 30.] Terence Cardinal Cooke Health Care Center/formerly **Flower & Fifth Avenue Hospitals/**originally **The Fifth Avenue Hospital,** 1240-1248 Fifth Ave., bet. E. 105th and E. 106th Sts. 1921. York & Sawyer.

One of York & Sawyer's lesser works; compare with their *later* New York Academy of Medicine, on 103rd. [See above.]

EAST OF EDEN

If the expanse of the Upper East Side flanking Fifth Avenue is a veritable Garden of Eden, then this precinct, lying between that ultrachic neighborhood and York Avenue's health care and research row, can be called **East of Eden.** It begins at Third Avenue and ranges to just short of York, from the Queensboro Bridge to East 79th Street.

[E 1.] Roosevelt Island tramway station, Second Ave. SW cor. E. 60th St. 1976. Prentice & Chan, Ohlhausen.

A **spectacular exercise** in great transit architecture. If the **aerial tramway** in itself were not enough, this glassy box, perched high astride—and slightly askew of—Second Avenue, only adds to the ski-slope drama. Within the beautifully detailed industrial container is the **colorful mechanism** (out of Chaplin's *Modern Times*) that propels the cars across the East River's West Channel to the Roosevelt Island terminal. **A silent, bird's-eye view** of city and river, a moving observation deck. *Take a trip!*

Serendipity 3 (restaurant), 225 E. 60th St., bet. Second and Third Aves.

A boutique upstairs, and mostly trivia below, in this former shop with restaurant that has become a restaurant with shop.

[E 2a.] Evansview (apartments)/originally **Memphis Uptown,** 305 E. 60th St., bet. First and Second Aves. to E. 61st St. 1987. Abraham Rothenberg and Gruzen Samton Steinglass.

The *ultimate* sliver: lanky, proud, colorful, and witty. A fine addition to the area if not ultimately lost amid a sea of lesser towers.

[E 2b.] Day & Meyer, Murray & Young Corporation (storage warehouse), 1166 Second Ave., bet. E. 61st and E. 62nd Sts. E side. ca. 1928.

One of a **fast disappearing urban form:** a largely windowless, highrise storage warehouse, beautifully detailed in brick and terra-cotta.

[C 28b.] The Jane B. Aron residence   [E 2a.] The slender Evansview apts.

[E 3a.] The Savoy (apartments), 200 E. 61st St., SE cor. Third Ave. to E. 60th St. 1986. Philip Birnbaum & Assocs. **[E 3b.] Trump Plaza (apartments),** 167 E. 61st St., NW cor. Third Ave. to 62nd St. 1984. Philip Birnbaum & Assocs.

Two 30-story-plus **"boomerang plan"** projects by the same architect that became the subjects of a lawsuit brought by developer Donald J. Trump against the Savoy's Morton Olshan. It was settled out of court through the intercession of state supreme court justice Edward J. Greenfield, who imposed design changes on The Savoy (the later structure) that would ensure visual differences between these two titans (the buildings, not the developers).

 [E 4.] Treadwell Farm Historic District, generally both sides of the midblocks of E. 61st and E. 62nd Sts. bet. Second and Third Aves. ★

Two blocks of brownstone houses on the lands of Adam Treadwell's farm: **uniform rows of human scale** sought by the affluent among surrounding commercial blocks. See [V Manhattan/Astor Place A 8a.] for another Tredwell memory—the family spelled it both with and without the *a,* this time Seabury Tredwell's **Old Merchant's House.**

 [E 4a.] Trinity Baptist Church, 250 E. 61st St., bet. Second and Third Aves. 1931. Martin G. Hedmark. In Tredwell Farm Historic District. ☆

Sandwiched among the brownstones of the historic district is this early (for New York) Modern church which **echoes Swedish motifs** like the Hansa gables and other elements preserved in Stockholm's outdoor Skansen Museum. The yellow brick facade is **a celebration of brick—** corbeled, arched, stepped, pierced, grilled—it's a mason's triumph. (In fact, it's a false front, almost twice the height of the interior space beyond.) A great event!

[E 5.] The Vertical Club, 330 E. 61st St. bet. First and Second Aves. 1982. Eugene Ho, engineer.

Tier after tier of sports facilities perched above a knockoff entrance from Frank Lloyd Wright's V. C. Morris Shop, San Francisco.

[E 6a.] 400 East 61st Street (mixed use), bet. First and York Aves. 1990. Apartments, Costas Kondylis of Philip Birnbaum & Assocs. Offices and retail, Hellmuth, Obata & Kassabaum. Thomas Balsey Assocs., landscape architects.

A pair of 44-story cylinders rising from a 6-story base. More glitz from Glick?

[E 6b.] The Abigail Adams Smith Museum, Colonial Dames of America/earlier **Abigail Adams Smith residence**/earlier **Mt. Vernon Hotel** (1826–1833), 421 E. 61st St., bet. First and York Aves. 1799. **Open to the public.**

A unassuming but real Federal **ashlar stone** building. Built as a stable by William S. Smith, son-in-law of President John Adams, it served a **never-completed manor house** (across today's 61st Street) that burned to the ground in 1826. The stable was subsequently promoted in status and served as a hotel, until converted to use as a private house in 1833.

[E 7.] The Royale (apartments), 188 E. 64th St., SW cor. Third Ave. 1986. Alfredo De Vido Assocs., design architects. Schuman Lichtenstein Claman & Efron, architects. Voorsanger & Mills Assocs., lobby spaces. Quennell-Rothschild Assocs., landscape architects.

Well intentioned, taking its cues from a classical column: base, shaft, capital. But tall and awkward, like many a teenager.

[E 8a.] Our Lady of Perpetual Help Church/Infant of Prague National Shrine (Roman Catholic) and **Rectory of the Redemptorist Fathers,** 321 and 323 E. 63rd St., bet. First and Second Aves. 1887. **[E. 8b.]** Originally **Convent**/now **apartments,** 329 E. 63rd St. ca. 1870. Converted, expanded, ca. 1977.

Once a coherent group of structures serving an immigrant working-class parish. The thoughtless, insensitive conversion of a fine Gothic Revival convent makes clear the need: without landmark designation and regulation, this can too often occur.

[E 9a.] The Phoenix (apartments), 160 E. 65th St., SW cor. Third Ave. 1968. Emery Roth & Sons.

A very competent Modern concrete grid—too competent, too tailored. There are no surprises.

[E 9b.] 200 East 65th Street (apartments), SE cor. Third Ave. to E. 64th St. 1987. Ulrich Franzen & Assocs.

Residents must love the tiers of 5-sided corner windows, which combine with the 49 stories of even-colored, rangeless brick to make a stark intrusion into the neighborhood. The controversial project had originally been named MILRO Tower after developers Paul **MIL**stein and **R**obert **O**lnick.

[E 10.] The Rio (apartments), 304 E. 65th St., SE cor. Second Ave. 1987. Gruzen Samton Steinglass.

Split personality: the bottom and top are a curious contrast in this, perhaps the penultimate sliver: [see E 2a.].

[E 11.] City and Suburban Homes Company, First Avenue Estate (model tenements), E. 64th to E. 65th Sts. bet. First and York Aves: 1168-1190, 1194-1200 First Ave. 1898. James E. Ware. 403-423 E. 64th St. 1901. James E. Ware. 404-416 E. 65th St. 1900. James E. Ware. 429 E. 64th St. and 430 E. 65th St. 1915. City and Suburban Homes Architectural Department: Philip H. Ohm.

Experimental housing for the working classes by a do-good organization in the era **before governmental intervention.** The apartment groups are 6-story walk-ups similar to the ones at 79th Street [see E 37.]: straightforward design, successful background buildings. Ware, architect of the majority of the structures, won second prize in the City and Suburban Homes Company **Model Tenement Competition of 1896.**

Manhattan House to Tower East:

This unnamed hillcrest runs from 66th to 72nd Streets, falling away toward the north, the south, and Second Avenue. Until 1955 its spine was the clanking steel and wood-grilled elevated trestle along Third Avenue, an economic and social wall limiting migration to its east. When the el was scrapped (reducing the convenience of rapid transit for this neighborhood) the eastern blocks blossomed with high-rise luxury.

 [E 12.] Manhattan House (apartments), 200 E. 66th St., bet. Second and Third Aves. through to E. 65th St. 1950. Skidmore, Owings & Merrill and Mayer & Whittlesey.

This is the closest Manhattan offers, conceptually, to the "blocks" of **Le Corbusier,** his **machines for living** (misinterpreted by many as implying a mechanistic way of life).

The subtle aesthetic decision to choose pale gray glazed brick and white-painted steel windows by itself raised this block above its coarse new neighbors (white glazed brick + aluminum sash = pasty). The balconies become the **principal ornament,** but unfortunately they are small and precarious for those with any trace of vertigo. (Sometime in the 1980s the original windows were replaced—with regrettable aesthetic results.)

The block was occupied from 1896 to 1949 by the Third Avenue Railway System car barns where horsecars and then electric streetcars were housed. It was an elaborate French Second Empire mansarded "palace."

[E 12.] Manhattan House in 1952, with its white steel casement windows intact

[E 12a.] Café Marimba, 1115 Third Ave., NE cor. E. 65th St. (entrance on E. 65th St. in rear of Manhattan House). 1984. Sam Lopata, restaurant designer.

An elegant sign on the street wall announces this elegant eatery tucked under the Manhattan House shops facing Third Avenue.

One life for my country: The Dove Tavern, a landmark for travelers on the Boston Post Road, stood at the northwest corner of what is now Third Avenue and East 66th Street, a block north of its latter-day namesake. It had been established sometime prior to 1763 and flourished for over 30 years. Commemorative plaques and statues elsewhere notwithstanding, Captain Nathan Hale was hanged by the British on September 22, 1776, in the Artillery Park near the tavern. Captured while reconnoitering British forces on Long Island, he was executed immediately—denied even the attendance of clergy. Though his last letters to his mother and friends were destroyed, his last words remain familiar to many.

 [E 12b.] 265 East 66th Street (apartments), NW cor. Second Ave. 1978. Gruzen & Partners.

A tall, suave, glass residential tower with 4 rounded corners—the equivalent, in architectural terms, of **the gray flannel suit.** A welcome subtlety is its developer's decision not to employ an ostentatious name, rare for most recent luxury apartment towers.

[E 13a.] Janovic Plaza, Inc. (decorating supplies), 1150 Third Ave., NW cor. E. 67th St. 1982. Voorsanger & Mills Assocs.

The first redesign of a line of Post Modern, historicist, home-decorating shops, the one that led the design revolution for the chain. For decorators, painting contractors, and amateurs, all.

[E 13b.] Fox Television Center/originally **Central Turn-Verein,** 215 E. 67th St., bet. Second and Third Aves. 1887. Albert Wagner.

Opera yielded to TV (Channel 5) here after World War II. Pompous glitz. See next item for restrained glitz.

[E 13c.] 222-242 East 67th Street (row houses), bet. Second and Third Avenues. 1984. Attia & Perkins.

Before choosing an architect, developer Sheldon Solow conducted a competition attracting entries from such world-class architects as England's James Stirling, Gruzen & Partners, and Richard Meier. Architect Eli Attia was chosen.

In a city superbly enriched by an amazing inventory of row houses of virtually every description, it's hard to understand why these 11 fail to capture any of the abundant spirit and charm of their linear antecedents, save the use of party walls. Right across the street is this row of gems designed for horses, carriages, and grooms:

[E 13d.] 223, 225, 227 East 67th Street (carriage houses), bet. Second and Third Aves. ca. 1900.

Three **fine recalls** of the horse-and-carriage era. Their rich facades shame more recent examples intended for residential purposes.

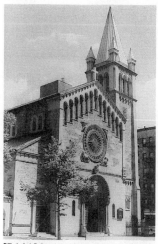

[E 14d.] St. John Nepomucene Church   **[E 13d.]** 223–227 E. 67th St. stables

[E 14a.] St. Catherine's Park (playground), First Ave. bet. E. 67th and E. 68th Sts. W side. Redesigned, 1971, Jay Fleishman. Re-redesigned, 1988, Blumberg & Butter.

A 1970s aesthetic of concrete bunkers converted to a 1980s aesthetic of visibility from the street. **Capricious.** The name refers to the church to the northeast:

[E 14b.] St. Catherine of Siena Church (Roman Catholic)/Shrine of St. Jude Thaddeus, 411 E. 68th St., bet. First and York Aves. 1931. Wilfred E. Anthony.

A departure for the architect: bare red brick neo-Gothic inside and out, revealing the influence of the **English Arts and Crafts movement** and William Lethaby (1857–1931).

[E 14c.] Bethany Memorial Church (Reformed in America), 400 E. 67th St., SE cor. First Ave. 1910. Nelson & Van Wagenen.

A **quaintly fashioned** church structure, much more demure (Protestant) than St. John of Nepomuk next door (Catholic).

[E 14d.] St. John Nepomucene Church (Roman Catholic), 411 E. 66th St., NE cor. First Ave. 1925. John Van Pelt.

A wonderfully **romantic paean to the Romanesque style** for a Slavic (St. John of Nepomuk) congregation. Another version by the same architect, **Guardian Angel,** is in Chelsea. [See M Manhattan/ Chelsea H 8.]

[E 15.] 210 East 68th Street (apartments), SE cor. Third Ave. 1928. George & Edward Blum.

An Art Deco essay with kelly green terra-cotta embellishments. [For another, see M Manhattan/Four Squares E 5c.]

[E 16a.] First Magyar Reformed Church of the City of New York, 346 E. 69th St., bet. First and Second Aves. 1916. Emery Roth.

The elder Roth *before* his Beresford and San Remo. Here, **white stucco** and **bright faience** vernacular transported, as if by magic carpet, from Hungary to this cramped East Side site.

[E 16b.] Stuarts Restaurant, 1288 First Ave., bet. E. 69th and E. 70th Sts. E side. 1985. Alfredo De Vido Assocs., architects. Steven Fineberg, graphic designer. Nicholas Fedder, lighting design.

Green on green on green exterior. Soft, carefully detailed, heavenly interior.

[E 17a.] 180 East 70th Street (apartments), SW cor. Third Ave. 1986. Kohn Pederson Fox Assocs.

One of those new Post Modern structures that's supposed to *look* as though it's been here longer than it has. (This building replaced the old Pinehurst Garage.) Upon reflection, the **superscaled allusions to classicism** are perhaps a bit farfetched, with any subtlety parboiled out. But its new ornament is refreshing both above street level and in the tempietto on high.

[E 17a.] 180 East 70th Street apts.   **[E 18.]** Kingsley apartments, E. 70th

[E 17b.] 220 East 70th Street (apartments), bet. Second and Third Aves. 1988. Ted Reeds Assocs.

A midblock midrise crafted of two tones of red brick and some modest, inoffensive Post Modern ornament. The **setback** at the height of neighboring row houses is an **important acquiescence** to the Upper East Side side street.

[E 17c.] Lenox Hill Station, U.S. Post Office, 221 E. 70th St., bet. Second and Third Aves. 1935.

W.P.A. neo-Georgian, now beginning to come into its own.

[E 18.] The Kingsley (apartments), 400 E. 70th St., SE cor. First Ave. 1984. Stephen B. Jacobs & Assocs.

The tower is an effective use of **rounded balconies** for rhythm; the base is less effective.

East 71st Street, between Second and Third Avenues:

[E 19a.] 203, 207, 209, 211 East 71st Street (town houses), Altered, 1980s. **[E 19b.] 213 East 71st Street (row house),** ca. 1880.

A lesson in how not to design neighboring house facades. The site of **Nos. 203–209** was earlier a residence of the Dominican Sisters and later the Retreat for Ladies and Homeless Girls. **No. 213** retains a largely untouched facade, a foil to its western show-offs.

[E 19c.] 251 East 71st Street (row house), bet. Second and Third Aves. Altered, ca. 1975.

Star Trek? Elliptical bubbles in aluminum frames punctuate a white stucco facade.

[E 20a.] Provident Loan Society of America branch, 180 E. 72nd St., bet. Lexington and Third Aves. ca. 1895.

An exquisitely tiny **temple of finance,** in the shadow of:

[E 20b.] Tower East (apartments), 190 E. 72nd St., SW cor. Third Ave. to E. 71st St. 1962. Emery Roth & Sons.

A sheer, freestanding tower: 4 apartments per floor, all with magnificent views. One of the earliest departures here toward **quality Modern high-rise** design. Built on the site of the Loew's 72nd Street movie house.

[E 21a.] 235 East 72nd Street (apartments), bet. Second and Third Aves. Altered, 1947. Lewis J. Ordwein.

Early Modern redesign, now very dated.

[E 21b.] St. John the Martyr Catholic Church/originally **Knox Presbyterian Church,** 252 E. 72nd St., bet. Second and Third Aves. ca. 1888. Rededicated, 1904.

Congregation Bohemian in origin. Rock-faced and smooth brownstone Romanesque Revival.

[E 22a.] Le Chambord (apartments), 350 E. 72nd St., bet. First and Second Aves. 1987. Costas Kondylis of Philip Birnbaum & Assocs.

Twenty-three stories of condos with a pudgy Post Modern plinth that **replaced a much beloved Trans-Lux** neighborhood movie theater. Movies *are* more fun.

[E 22b.] Marcello (restaurant), 1354 First Ave., bet. E. 72nd and E. 73rd Sts. E side. 1986. Gian Luigi Perrone.

A fancy fake Florentine front (opaque) that leads to an elegant Italian restaurant (velvety).

[E 23a.] Originally **Murry and Leonie Guggenheim Dental Clinic/**now **New York Hospital Dialysis Center,** 422-428 E. 72nd St., bet. First and York Aves. 1930.

Ranks of closely spaced, multistory, neo-Romanesque sandstone columns give a distinctive texture to the facade. A lovely composition.

[E 23b.] Sokol Hall/originally **Čech Gymnasium Association,** 420 E. 71st St., bet. First and York Aves. ca. 1897.

The local community's neo-Classical gymnasium.

[E 23c.] Sotheby's (auction gallery)/earlier **Sotheby, Parke-Bernet York Avenue Gallery/**originally **Eastman Kodak Company,** 1334 York Ave., SE cor. E. 72nd St. to E. 71st St. ca. 1929. Converted to gallery, 1980, Lundquist & Stonehill. Expanded, 1989, Michael Graves.

An effective initial redesign in elegant flamed granite resulting in suave architecture totally appropriate to the new use. Success called forth yet another redesign.

[E 24a.] River Terrace (apartments), 515 E. 72nd St., E of York Ave. 1985. Schuman Lichtenstein Claman & Efron.

A blockbuster. From far away, the one with the **very big clock.** From up close, nothing very special.

[E 24b.] 525 E. 72nd St (apartments), E of York Ave. through to E. 73rd St., bet. York and FDR Drive. 1987. Davis, Brody & Assocs.

An elegant tower design occupying a *back street* site (73rd) but with a *main street* address (72nd).

[E 25.] East 73rd Street, between Lexington and Third Avenues.

A stable block . . . of stables.

Manhattan's gridiron plan, unlike those of other cities, didn't provide back alleys for service. Therefore, in New York's horsedrawn era, certain blocks were assigned the role of **service streets,** addressing the needs of those four-legged beasts of burden. These **smelly, noisy, noisome** places were often **located a distance from the properties** of their well-to-do owners. Typically, the carriages were garaged in the front, the horses stabled in the rear, and grooms' quarters were above. Later, garages came, as new structures or as conversions.

Roll call of **carriage houses** on S side: **No. 166:** Originally **Henry G. Marquand's**/later **Joseph Pulitzer's**/now **Central Gospel Chapel,** 1884, Richard Morris Hunt. ★ **No. 168:** Originally **William Baylis'**/ later **Charles Russell Lowell Putnam's,** 1899, Charles Romeyn. ★ **No. 170:** Originally **George C. Clausen's**/later **Henry T. Sloane's**/later **James Stillman's** 1891, Frank Wennemer. ★ **No. 172–174:** Originally **James B. Layng's,** 1889, Frank Wennemer. ★ **No. 178:** Originally **Charles I. Hudson's,** 1902. John H. Friend. ★ **No. 180:** Originally **Max Nathan's**/later **George D. Widener's garage,** 1891, William Schickel & Co. ★ **No. 182:** Originally **S. Kayton & Company (commercial stable),** 1890, Andrew Spense Mayer. Ground floor altered, 1908, Edward L. Middleton. Expanded upward, 1938, James J. Gavigan. ★

Roll call of **carriage houses** on N side: **Nos. 161 and 163:** Originally **William H. Tailer's,** both 1897; both by Thomas Rae. ★ **Nos. 165, 167:** Originally **Henry H. Benedict's,** both 1904, both George R. Amoroux. ★

[E 25a.] 171 East 73rd Street (row house). 1860. Vestibule and garden wall added, 1924, Electus Litchfield, architect and owner. ★
[E 25b.] 175 East 73rd Street (row house)/later **blacksmith shop** on ground floor. 1860. Ground floor altered into smithy, 1896. Restored, 1926, Francis Livingston Pell, architect and owner. ★

Two separated **"broken teeth"** are all that remain of the block's original group of 6 Italianate row houses. They reveal the **earliest stage of development,** as a modest street for lower middle-class families. The others were demolished in order to build the adjacent carriage houses.

[E 25c.] Originally **J. Henry Alexandre carriage house,** 173 E. 73rd St. 1903. Hobart C. Walker. ★

Alexandre lived at 35 East 67th Street (extant), whose facade he had altered (by another architect).

 [E 25d.] Originally **Automobile Realty Company garage,** 177-179 E. 73rd St. 1906. Charles F. Hoppe. ★

A proud, exquisitely detailed Beaux Arts container for the newly emerging automobile. A **rare surviving example** of the city's early response to the needs of the *horseless* carriage.

 [E 26a.] Buckley School, The Hubball Building, 210 E. 73rd St./209 E. 74th St., bet. Second and Third Aves. 1974. Brown, Lawford & Forbes.

Replacing a Con Ed substation is this through-block essay in New Brutalist concrete, red brick, and freestanding smokestack.

[E 26b.] 220, 230, 225, 235 East 73rd Street (apartments), bet. Second and Third Aves. ca. 1929.

Four substantial apartment blocks, each rising 10 sheer stories on opposite sides of the street. Their detail and subtle ornament make them urban grace notes despite their large scale.

[E 27.] Bohemian National Hall/Národní Budova, 321 E. 73rd St., bet. First and Second Aves. ca. 1895.

A little soap and water would do wonders for this overblown but very dignified structure built to meet the needs of the Czech community that is still in evidence here. *Note the lions' heads.*

[E 28a.] Petaluma (restaurant), 1356 First Ave., SE cor. E. 73rd St. 1985. Edward Linenschmidt.

Popular Post Modern dining spot.

[E 28b.] Ronald McDonald House (children's residential facility), 407 E. 73rd St., bet. First and York Aves. 1989. The Spector Group.

The facade owes a great deal to the design ideas of Michael Graves.

Eats along Third Avenue:

[E 29a.] Anabelles (restaurant), 1294 Third Ave., bet. E. 74th and E. 75th Sts. W side. 1987. Sam Lopata, designer.

Copper and black, but not one of Lopata's inspired efforts.

[E 29b.] Mezzaluna (restaurant), 1295 Third Ave., bet. E. 74th and E. 75th Sts. E side. 1984. Robert Magris.

A very Italian, very informal place, breezily outfitted for those in a rush on their way up.

[E 29c.] Ciaobella (restaurant), 1311 Third Ave., NE cor. E. 75th St. 1986. Federica Marangoni and Fabrizio Plessi, designers.

The awnings welcome; the interior comforts. At Ciaobella it's always a sunny day.

Brighton Grill (restaurant), 1313 Third Ave., bet. E. 75th and E. 76th Sts. E side.

Seafood served in the simplest—and most apt—deep blue and white settings.

Jim McMullen (restaurant), 1341 Third Ave., bet. E. 76th and E. 77th Sts. E side.

A granddaddy (1977) of such yuppie places on Third Avenue. It takes a lot to be able to celebrate a decade (or more) of service to a fickle clientele. Handsome front, Gaelic atmosphere, and straightforward cooking continue to do it here.

East 74th Street, between First and Second Avenues:

[E 30a.] 306-310 East 74th Street (apartments). ca. 1936.

Art Moderne but unusual in its **red brick livery** (ruined by poor repointing); most of the city's is in orange or cream brick.

The East River shore at the turn of the century: playgrounds and garbage scows

[E 30b.] Greek Orthodox Archdiocesan Cathedral of the Holy Trinity/Hellenic Eastern Orthodox Church of New York, 319 E. 74th St. 1931. Kerr Rainsford, John A. Thompson, Gerald A. Holmes.

A little-known but much-admired neo-Romanesque red brick and limestone-trimmed edifice by the firm that later designed the vastly different neo-Gothic **Hunter College Uptown** (now Lehman College) in the Bronx, under the name **Thompson, Holmes & Converse.**

[E 30c.] The Forum (apartments), 343 E. 74th St. to E. 75th. 1986. The Vilkas Group.

At 25 stories, this uses air rights from the two churches that are its bookends. Tall *midblock* structures like this one were later made more difficult by the 59th-96th Street Upper East Side **midblock downzoning,** which went into effect after this project was on its way.

[E 30d.] Jan Hus (Bohemian Brethren) Presbyterian Church, 347 E. 74th St. 1880. **[E 30e.] Church House** a.k.a. **Jan Hus House,** 351 E. 74th St. 1915.

Jan Hus *house* is better known—citywide—for the **dramatic, musical, and light opera** events held in its auditorium, than the parent church next door.

Mama Leah's Blintzeria, Ltd. (restaurant), 1400 First Ave., bet. E. 74th and E. 75th Sts. E side.

Brunch, lunch, and dinner featuring favorites derived from the **east European shtetl** served in a crisp, well-designed, and homey setting. It's presided over by Mama Leah herself, who hails from Hastings-on-Hudson—the unlikely drop, it would seem, for these gustatorial secrets.

[E 31.] Church of the Epiphany (Episcopal), 1393-1399 York Ave., NW cor. E. 74th St. 1939. Wyeth & King. Eugene W. Mason, associated architect.

The distinctive squat spire is a rare romantic interlude along Manhattan's avenuescapes. What a great silhouette!

[E 32.] Consolidated Edison (power plant)/originally **Manhattan Elevated Railway/**later **Interborough Rapid Transit Company/**later **N.Y.C. Board of Transportation,** 535 E. 74th St., NW cor. FDR Drive to E. 75th St. ca. 1900. C. Wellesley Smith.

Classicized to make it a good neighbor despite its size and smoke. Its coal was barged to the site before the FDR Drive landlocked the facility.

[E 33a.] 310 East 75th Street (apartments), bet. First and Second Aves. ca. 1936.

Steel casemented Art Moderne, in golden yellow, orange, and red brick. The corner windows were not only stylish but also an **exciting spatial event** for the tenants.

[E 33b.] The Saratoga (apartments), 330 E. 75th St., bet. First and Second Aves. 1984. Schuman, Lichtenstein, Claman & Efron.

The avenue tower and the sidestreet low-rise wing are **neatly articulated** with a V-notch. Nicely detailed, with a **sidewalk clock** to count the hours.

[E 34a.] The Promenade (apartments), 530 E. 76th St., SW cor. FDR Drive to E. 75th St. 1987. Costas Kondylis of Philip Birnbaum & Assocs.

To develop its enormous riverfront bulk, this glitzy tower utilizes air rights from the low-rise Town School, around which it wraps.

[E 34b.] The Town School, 540 E. 76th St., SW cor. FDR Drive. 1973. Armand Bartos & Assocs. Altered, 1978, R. M. Kliment & Frances Halsband.

Stylish brickwork with incised windows and entry.

[E 35.] 430 East 77th Street (apartments), bet. First and York Aves. Converted, 1971.

A conversion from tenement to luxury apartments with **style.** Brick piers and arches and iron railings give this a rich order unmatched by the marble-framed and plastic-plant-festooned lobbies of its vulgar competitors.

[E 36a.] John Jay Park, Cherokee Place (E of York Ave.) bet. E. 76th and E. 78th Sts., to FDR Drive. E side. **Bath house,** 1908. Stoughton & Stoughton.

A small neighborhood park with swimming pool and playground; intensively used. It carries a lush parasol of trees.

[E 20b.] Tower East apts., E. 72nd St.   **[E 36b.]** Orig. Shively Sanitary apts.

[E 36b.] Originally **Shively Sanitary Tenements (apartments)**/later **East River Homes**/now **Cherokee Apartments,** 507-515, 517-523 E. 77th St., 508-514, 516-522 E. 78th St., W side of Cherokee Place. 1911. Henry Atterbury Smith.

The progressive environmental ideas of Dr. Henry Shively, intended to help cure those with tuberculosis (the second leading cause of death in the early 20th century), were translated into these **model tenements** with the assistance of **Mrs. William Kissam Vanderbilt.**

A **second glance** here is well deserved. These simple buildings are **rich** in architectural thoughts new for their time: the triple-hung windows allow a tenant to step onto a **narrow French balcony** and view the river; and even without taking the step, one has a dramatic sense of space and view. The units are entered through **Guastavino tile-vaulted tunnels** opening into central courtyards from which, at each corner, stairs rise 5 flights. Note the **wrought-iron seats** and iron-and-**glass canopies** sheltering the stair climber from the rain.

[E 37.] City and Suburban Homes Company, York Avenue Estate (model tenements), E. 78th to E. 79th Sts. bet. York Ave. and FDR Drive: 1194-1200 York Ave. 1901. Harde & Short. 503-509 E. 78th St. 1904. Percy Griffin. **Bishop Henry Codman Potter Memorial Buildings,** 510-528 E. 79th St. 1912. City and Suburban Homes Architectural Department: Philip Ohm, chief architect. 519-539 E. 78th St. and 536 E. 79th St. 1913. City and Suburban Homes Architectural Department: Philip Ohm. **[E 37a.]** Originally **Junior League Hotel**/later **East End Hotel for Women**/now **apartments,** 541 E. 78th St. (once 1 East River Drive). ca. 1913. City and Suburban Homes Architectural Department: Philip Ohm.

Experimental **housing for the working classes** (and a hotel for women operated by the **Junior League**): The apartment groups are 6-story walk-ups but without the charm of the neighboring Shively group on Cherokee Place. Ware, architect of the earliest group on this site, won second prize in the **City and Suburban Homes Company Model Tenement Competition of 1896.** R. Thomas Short (of Harde &

Short) was first-prize winner in the **Charity Organization Society Competition of 1900.** [Also see the other full-block complex, E 11.]. The onetime hotel originally had balconies overlooking the East River and a windswept, wood-trellised roof garden.

York Avenue was originally Avenue A, as the incised street names reveal at the corners of Public School 158, Manhattan, at 1458 York Avenue (between East 77th and East 78th Streets). The thoroughfare was renamed in 1928 in honor of the nation's greatest World War I hero, Sergeant Alvin C. York. Single-handedly he killed 25 enemy soldiers, took 132 prisoners, and silenced 35 machine guns—all in one morning's skirmish.

 [E 38a.] 180 East 78th Street (taxpayer), SW cor. Third Ave. to E. 77th St. 1938. E. H. Faile, engineer. Adjacent caretaker's house, 1939, Richard B. Thomas.

A bland exterior hides one of the cleverest urban ideas in Manhattan: row houses **piggybacked over shopping.** When the **Third Avenue el** was still up, the small windows facing the avenue (and the el's noise and grime) provided minimum vision and air required by the City's building code.

East 78th Street, between Second and Third Avenues:
[E 38b.] 208, 210, 212, 214, 216, 218 East 78th Street (row houses). 1865. Warren and Ransom Beman, John Buckley, builders. ★ **[E 38c.] 235 East 78th Street (row house).** ca. 1870. Altered, 1964, Bruce Campbell Graham. **[E 38d.] 237-241 East 78th Street (row houses).** ca. 1870. **[E 38e.] 255-261 East 78th Street (row houses).** ca. 1870.

A block of wonderful Victorian row houses; **Nos. 208-218** are only 13'-4" wide!
No. 235 has been modernized with the addition of brick walls and wrought iron to accommodate the separate needs of an upper and lower duplex renovation. The others reveal a relatively pristine urbanity that was perhaps not adequately appreciated in the 1960s.

[E 37a.] The East End Hotel for Women   [E 40.] Yorkville Branch, The N.Y.P.L.

[E 39.] 450, 450A, 450B East 78th Street (taxpayer), bet. First and York Aves. ca. 1855.

A combination of shops below and residential above in this 2-story **wood frame** structure clad in clapboard. Manhattan miracle.

 [E 40.] Yorkville Branch, New York Public Library, 222 E. 79th St., bet. Second and Third Aves. 1902. James Brown Lord. ★ Interior redesigned, 1987, Gwathmey Siegel & Assocs.

A Palladian, neo-Renaissance London club—but for the masses, not the classes, with an exquisite interior redesign.

HOSPITAL ROW

The York Avenue corridor between the Queensboro Bridge and 71st Street, once the land of the tenement but now—cutting off the East River shoreline—the site for more and more facilities for health care and research. The upland area has become increasingly desirable to those seeking housing (and who can afford the high costs), and so the gargantuan institutions have had to build their own backup residential facilities in order to lure qualified staff and students.

Rockefeller University

[H 1a.] Faculty House, Rockefeller University (apartments), 500 E. 63rd St., SE cor. York Ave. 1975. Horace Ginsbern & Assocs.

A superior apartment building, from an era when not too many high-rise apartments in the Upper East Side were actually *designed.*

[H 1b.] Scholars Building, Rockefeller University (apartments), 510 E. 63rd St., over FDR Drive. 1988. Abramowitz Harris & Kingsland.

Its architecture, closely keyed to **Faculty House,** never admits that it hovers atop the drive on massive trusses, a license that no reputable architect of the 1950s–1970s would have enjoyed.

[H 2.] Rockefeller University/originally **Rockefeller Institute for Medical Research,** 1270 York Ave., bet. E. 64th and E. 68th Sts. Site acquired, 1901. 1903–1910. York & Sawyer.

A campus for research and advanced education **occupies a high bluff** overlooking the East River; the site was once the summer estate of the Schermerhorn family of Lafayette Street. The first building opened in 1903.

Caspary Auditorium (*1957. Harrison & Abramovitz.*) is the gloomy dome adjacent to York Ave. It **once sparkled with blue tile,** but weather problems caused its re-roofing with what might whimsically be thought of as gutta-percha.

The **President's House** (*1958. Harrison & Abramovitz.*) is a limestone and glass country house tucked in a corner at the bluff's edge. *Ask the guard for permission to look around.*

Memorial Sloane-Kettering Cancer Center

[H 3.] Memorial Sloane-Kettering Cancer Center, 1275 York Ave., bet. E. 67th and E. 68th Sts. W side. **Main Building,** 444 W. 68 St. 1938. James Gamble Rogers, Inc. Additions. **[H 3a.] Arnold and Marie Schwartz International Hall of Science for Cancer Research/**earlier **James Ewing Memorial Building/**originally **James Ewing Memorial Hospital, N.Y.C. Department of Hospitals,** First Ave. bet. E. 67th and E. 68th Sts. E side. 1950. Skidmore, Owings & Merrill. **[H 3b.] Rockefeller Research Laboratories,** 430 E. 68th St., bet. York and First Aves. 1988. Davis, Brody & Assocs. and Russo+Sonder. **[H 3c.] Sloane-House (nurses' residence),** 1233 York Ave., bet. E. 66th and E. 67th Sts. W side. 1965. Harrison & Abramovitz.

A full city block (and more) bulging with cancer care and research facilities.

[H 4.] The Premier (apartments), 333 E. 69th St., bet. First and Second Aves. 1963. Mayer, Whittlesey & Glass; William J. Conklin, designer.

A simple, crisp, but forceful facade of exposed concrete and pale brick. The contained balconies are far more **usable** and **weather-resistant** than the toothy ones punctuating innumerable lesser buildings.

[H 5a.] Jacob S. Lasdon House, Cornell Medical College (apartments), 420 E. 70th St., bet. First and York Aves. 1975. Conklin & Rossant.

Concrete and glass, elegant and crisp: a friendly, cool, and handsome neighbor.

[H 5b.] Laurence G. Payson House, New York Hospital (apartments), 435 E. 70th St., NW cor. York Ave. to E. 71st St. 1966. Frederick G. Frost, Jr. & Assocs.

Three staggered slabs straddle two service corridors: a dramatic freestanding form.

New York Hospital-Cornell Medical Center

[H 6.] New York Hospital-Cornell Medical Center, York Ave. bet. E. 68th and E. 71st Sts. to FDR Drive. 1933. Coolidge, Shepley, Bullfinch & Abbott. Altered and expanded. **[H 6a.] William and Mildred Lasdon Biomedical Research Center,** York Ave. bet. E. 68th and E. 69th Sts. 1988. Payette Assocs., architects. Rogers, Burgun, Shahine & Deschler, Inc., associated architects.

The word **massing** could have been invented to describe the original structures of this **great medical complex.** It has steadily expanded upland and one day will **grow, extend, and replace itself** on a platform over the drive (to the river's edge, as Carl Schurz Park covers the drive in the 80s, and Rockefeller University and apartment buildings do to the south.) **Lasdon** is an example, one that makes a successful 1980s statement in the context of the original.

[H 6.] New York Hospital-Cornell Medical Center complex on a 1930s postcard

[H 9a.] Cornell Medical Coll. S Bldg.   [H 4.] The Premier apts. on E. 69 St.

[H 7.] C. V. Starr Pavilion, New York Hospital, spans E. 70th St. bet. York Ave. and FDR Drive. 1986. Perkins & Will.

The 1880s **stained-glass seal** in the lobby, by Louis Comfort Tiffany, says **"Go and do likewise."** It has traveled northward with the hospital: from its installation in the hospital's first building at Broadway near Duane Street; to West 15th Street off Fifth in 1877; to the nurses' quarters at 525 East 70th Street in 1932, until that structure was demolished in the 1970s; and now here, the first major hospital expansion in 50 years.

[H 8a.] Hospital for Special Surgery, 535 E. 70th St., NW cor. FDR Drive to E. 71st St. 1955. Rogers & Butler. Operating room addition and portico, 1981.

A hard-to-find adjunct to Cornell-New York enjoying river views. The new entrance is terrific.

[H 8b.] Helmsley Medical Tower (mixed use), 1320 York Ave., bet. E. 70th and E. 71st St. E side. 1987. Schuman, Lichtenstein, Claman & Efron.

A smooth, **very smooth** reinterpretation of the medical center's already smoothed neo-Gothic originals, but at the 1980s superheated scale: tall. Staff apartments and, at street level, administrative and retail space.

[H 9a.] S Building, Cornell University Medical College/originally **Institute for Muscle Diseases, Muscular Dystrophy Association of America,** 515 E. 71st St., bet. York Ave. and FDR Drive. 1961. Skidmore, Owings & Merrill.

Neat, well designed, and dull.

[H 9b.] The Belair (apartments), 525-535 East 71st St., bet. York Ave. and FDR Drive. 1989. Frank Williams & Assocs.

A 38-story tower where once was a 5-story garage.

YORKVILLE

This northeastern quadrant of the **Upper East Side** is named for the village originally centered on 86th Street and Third Avenue. **86th Street** later became the city's **German-American** Hauptstrasse (Main Street). In the 1930s Fritz Kuhn led parades of the German-American Bund until Pearl Harbor finally put an end to such antics. Other central European groups also found this area to their liking: there is still considerable evidence in church names, settlement houses, and older restaurants of the Hungarian and Czech communities. Architectural interest is scattered: because wealthy latecomers migrated only to the upper riverside near Carl Schurz Park [see the Gracie Square section], the bulk of the area's building became, until recently, housing for the lower middle class. The area is now punctuated by many new towers (some of them those damnable midblock slivers) for the *nouveaux riches,* and gentrification is particularly evident in the shops and restaurants along the avenues.

For the purposes of this guide Yorkville begins above 79th Street and runs to 96th, from Lexington Avenue to the East River, except for the area around East End Avenue, described in the next section, **Gracie Square and Environs.**

[Y 1a.] Hungarian Baptist Church, 225 E. 80th St., bet. Second and Third Aves. ca. 1890.

An exotic brick and terra-cotta takeoff on an Italian palazzo.

[Y 1b.] 249 East 80th Street (residence), bet. Second and Third Aves.

Mansarded houses are hardly rare in many parts of Manhattan, but in this precinct this one is lonely and special.

Püski-Corvin Magyar Könyvesház (Hungarian bookstore), 251 E. 80th St., bet. Second and Third Aves.

The spot to get the Hungarian books you've always wanted.

[Y 1c.] Pig Heaven (Chinese restaurant), 1540 Second Ave., bet. E. 80th and E. 81st Sts. E side. 1984. Sam Lopata, designer.

A visual **running gag** on the theme of porkers, executed on a limited budget. One of Lopata's most playful commissions.

[Y 2.] Lexington House (apartments), 1190-1192 Lexington Ave., NW cor. E. 81st St. 1983. Noah Greenberg.

One of the early wave of sliver buildings that were later outlawed (at least in midblock locations). Others, occupying corner sites like this one, *are* still possible.

[Y 3.] Duplex 81 (apartments), 215 E. 81st St., bet. Second and Third Aves. 1983. William B. Gleckman.

For Milan perhaps, not for Gotham.

[Y 4.] 420 East 81st Street (apartments), bet. First and York Aves. ca. 1986.

Six stories of purply brick. For infill, a little can go a long way.

Le Refuge Restaurant, 166 E. 82nd St., bet. Lexington and Third Aves.

Like a provincial eatery miles from Paris.

[Y 5.] Originally **row houses,** 1220, 1222, 1224 Lexington Ave., bet. E. 82nd and E. 83rd Sts. W side. 1880.

A gray marble **Italianate trio** with the year 1880 carved in the central pediment. Its streetfront shops join it to its neighbors, causing most to overlook the drama overhead. *Crane your neck.*

[Y 6.] American Federation for Hungarian Education & Literature, Ltd., 213-215 E. 82nd St., bet. Second and Third Aves.

A pair of houses set back a short distance from the street and connected with a wrought-iron balcony. *Note the plaque marking the visit of Cardinal Mindszenty of Hungary in 1973.*

[Y 7.] 306 and **306A East 82nd Street (row house and backhouse),** bet. First and Second Aves. ca. 1855.

A pair of very well preserved 2-story structures.

[Y 8.] St. Stephen of Hungary Church and **School (Roman Catholic),** 408 E. 82nd St., bet. First and York Aves. 1928. Emil Szendy.

Yellow ocher brick in the neo-Romanesque style, sporting a tile hip roof.

Nagy Magyar Ünnep New Yorkban!
AZ AMERIKAI MAGYAR KATHOLIKUSOK
FÉLMILLIÓ DOLLÁROS ALKOTÁSA AZ
UJ SZENT ISTVÁN TEMPLOM,
ISKOLA ÉS DISZTEREM
406—412 EAST 82ND STREET, NEW YORK

VASÁRNAP, DECEMBER 2-IKÁN

A templom ünnepélyes fölszentelését

ESTE HÉT ÓRAKOR DISZBANKET
A HOTEL ASTORBAN!

Bankett-jegy ára személyenkint 5 dollár!

[Y 9b.] St. Elizabeth of Hungary Ch.   **[Y 8.]** Consecration of St. Stephen's

Martell's (restaurant), 1469 Third Ave., SE cor. E. 83rd St.

Claims to be the oldest bar (since 1883) in Yorkville. One of the first singles joints in the Upper East Side.

[Y 9a.] Polo Grounds (restaurant), 1472 Third Ave., bet. E. 83rd and E. 84th Sts. W side. 1987. Stephen Lepp Assocs.

"Big drinks, good food, great sports." Despite the allusions that older folks may find between the name and Coogan's Bluff, this carefully designed bar and restaurant caters—with its sea of TV sets—to whatever sporting event may be on the tube.

[Y 9b.] St. Elizabeth of Hungary Roman Catholic Church, 211 E. 83rd St., bet. Second and Third Aves. 1918.

A superior, spired neo-Gothic exterior, but **the treat is within:** ascend the stairs to view a just heavenly groin-vaulted ceiling painted in the **colors of Ravenna's mosaics.**

[Y 9c.] 222 East 83rd Street (row house), bet. Second and Third Aves.

The one with the *big* red rose in front (from when it housed a florist, **Bouquets à la Carte**). A treat for the street.

[Y 9d.] 331 East 83rd Street (row house), bet. First and Second Aves. ca. 1880.

Hardly tetched b' time; a gem in a time warp. Too bad about the clumsy rooftop addition.

[Y 10a.] Formerly **Mayo Ballrooms,** 1493 Third Ave., NE cor. E. 84th St. ca. 1927.

Eclectic romance in the Art Deco style, utilizing polychromed terra-cotta bas-relief ornament for great effect.

[Y 10b.] Sidewalk clock, in front of 1501 Third Ave., bet. E. 84th and E. 85th Sts. E side. ca. 1885. ★

Street furniture protected by the Landmarks Preservation Commission. Hooray!

[Y 10c.] Originally **Labor Temple of the Workmen's Educational and Home Association**/then **Hungarian Workmen's Home**/then **lofts,** 245 E. 84th St., bet. Second and Third Aves. 1907.

Some buildings, like cats, have many lives.

[Y 11.] Zion St. Mark's Church/earlier **Zion Lutheran Church**/originally **Deutsche Evangelische Kirche von Yorkville,** 339 E. 84th St., bet. First and Second Aves. 1888.

A **frothy reminder** of the early days of **German immigration** to this precinct. A blessed survivor.

[Y 12.] 1578-1600 York Avenue (tenements), bet. E. 84th to E. 85th Sts. E side. ca. 1870.

An almost original blockfront of "first-class flats." Looks like a Hollywood backlot setting, but it's genuine.

[Y 13.] Manufacturers Hanover Trust Company, Yorkville Branch (bank), 1511 Third Ave., NE cor. E. 85th St. ca. 1915.

A bank of the old school: neo-Renaissance tailored stonework.

[Y 14.] The America (apartments), 300 E. 85th St., SE cor. Second Ave. 1987. Murphy/Jahn.

As American as apple pie. *This?* Thirty-six stories of boring beige and gray surface decoration? A bore from the normally flashy Chicago architect Helmut Jahn.

[Y 15a.] 406, 408, 410 East 85th Street (row houses), bet. First and York Aves. ca. 1865.

Charmingly small in scale, with mansards and some fine ironwork.

[Y 15b.] 412 East 85th Street (dwelling), bet. First and York Aves. ca. 1855.

A rare clapboard single house, set **deep in the row:** perhaps that's what's kept this frame house with us.

[Y 16a.] RKO 86th Street Twins (movie theaters), 125 E. 86th St., and **180 East 87th Street (apartments)**/originally **Gimbel's East (department store),** SW cor. Lexington Ave. to E. 86th St. Abbott, Merkt & Co. Converted to apartments, 1989, Skidmore, Owings & Merrill.

Once a windowless, sheet metal-clad, anonymous box—no wonder it failed to attract customers! Following the **dissolution of the Gimbel's department store chain** in 1986, a **new use** had to be found: a 1920s style structure was planned to emerge from the rebuilding. The theaters remain.

[Y 16b.] Uptown Racquet Club, 151 E. 86th St., bet. Lexington and Third Aves. 1976. Copelin, Lee & Chen.

A serene, stylish form in ribbed concrete block crowns a group of bustling ground-floor commercial establishments of the 86th Street corridor, who pay it no heed.

[Y 17a.] Bremen House (offices), 220 E. 86th St., bet. Second and Third Aves. ca. 1974.

Carven dark red brick marking the coming of a new, nontraditional 86th Street.

[Y 17b.] The Montgomery (linked tenements), 230-240 E. 86th St., bet. Second and Third Aves. ca. 1883.

Four stories of urbane facadism whose ground floor is a container for German tradition and 80s gentrification: **Kleine Konditorei (cafe-restaurant), Karl Ehmer Wurst Haus (butcher), Flemings Bar & Restaurant.**

[Y 17e., b.] The Manhattan apartments at the corner; The Montgomery midblock

[Y 17c.] 225 East 86th Street (apartments), bet. Second and Third Aves. 1982. Stephen B. Jacobs & Assocs.

Post-Baroque fun with windows.

[Y 17d.] The Far East (apartments), 235 E. 86th St., bet. Second and Third Aves. 1983. Liebman Liebman & Assocs.

A high style, purply brick design statement, but embodying a quality more appropriate to Milan than 86th Street.

[Y 17e.] The Manhattan (apartments), 244 E. 86th St., SW cor. Second Ave. 1878.

A 6-story mild Queen Anne apartment block that was home to the family of Senator Robert F. Wagner, Sr. Developers were the Rhinelander family.

[Y 17f.] Milan's (restaurant) 1647 Second Ave., bet. E. 85th and E. 86th Sts. W side.

A curious neo-medieval facade executed in stucco to look like concentric stone eyebrows. What people won't think of!

 [Y 18.] Grand Union (supermarket), 350 E. 86th St., bet. First and Second Aves. Altered, 1982. Milton Glaser, graphic designer. Jordan Steckel, sculptor.

The **Brobdingnagian green Bartlett pear** (made of colored plasticized fiber glass), sitting on the sidewalk, announced the first of this chain grocers' empire-wide redesign. The interior is an excitement as well.

[Y 19.] Channel Club Condominiums (apartments), 451 E. 86th St./1637-1639 York Ave., near NW cor. E. 86th St. 1987. Wechsler, Grasso & Menziuso.

Forty stories of softly modeled glitz in a neatly designed tower.

[Y 20a.] Group Residence for Young Adults, Jewish Board of Guardians, 217 E. 87th St., bet. Second and Third Aves. 1968. Horace Ginsbern & Assocs.

Bold, plastic, **New Brutalist** (but not brutal). Classy, personal, distinguished: a Modern monument.

[Y 20b.] 247 East 87th Street (apartments), NW cor Second Ave. to E. 88th St. 1966. Paul & Jarmul.

The same economics, the same materials, the same zoning and building laws as its speculative apartment house peers, here in the hands of someone who cared. The bold massing of the balconies reads with great richness on the avenue. This notable facade was the setting for the film version of Neil Simon's *The Prisoner of Second Avenue* (1975).

[Y 21.] St. Joseph's Catholic Church of Yorkville, 408 E. 87th St., bet. First and York Aves. 1895. William Schickel & Co.

A charming country basilica-form church with a flat neo-Romanesque facade in limestone.

Herbert Glaser Bake Shop, 1670 First Ave., bet. E. 87th and E. 88th Sts. E side.

An old-fashioned neighborhood bakery preparing and purveying the real article (behind a grim green modernized front). Mmmm—the aroma!

[Y 20b.] 247 East 87th Street apts.   **[Y 22.]** Row houses, 146-156 E. 89th

[Y 22.] 146-156 East 89th Street (row houses), bet. Lexington and Third Aves. 1887. Hubert, Pirrson & Co. ★

Six spectacularly romantic Queen Anne remainders of a row of ten single-family houses; all except **No. 146** are 12½ feet wide, half a city lot. Originally commissioned by **developer William Rhinelander,** whose family's philanthropy can be seen at the Holy Trinity complex on East 88th [see Y 24a.].

[Y 23.] 230 East 88th Street (apartments), bet. Second and Third Aves. 1968. David Todd & Assocs.

The access to the living units is via open, grilled galleries, allowing "floor through" apartments throughout. Ah, the cross-ventilation!

[Y 24a.] Church of the Holy Trinity (Episcopal), St. Christopher House/ Rhinelander Memorial (parish house) and **Parsonage,** 312-332 E. 88th St., bet. First and Second Aves. 1897. Barney & Chapman. Cloister chapel stained glass, Robert Sowers. All ★.

A remarkable and wonderful enclave for this precinct, for Manhattan, and for the city as a whole. Using the **romantic forms of the French Renaissance (François I)** in golden brick and terra-cotta, the architects here created a touch of the Loire Valley embracing a garden oasis surmounted by **one of New York's great bell towers.** To come upon this verdant treasure by accident is one of the city's greatest experiences.

The entire complex was a gift of Serena Rhinelander as a memorial to her grandfather and father.

[Y 24b.] Rhinelander Children's Center, Children's Aid Society, 350 E. 88th St., bet. First and Second Aves. Vaux & Radford.

Once a school for crippled children, another beneficence (like Holy Trinity) of the Rhinelanders. Unfortunately, the masonry facade of this fine Vaux design has been slushed with mortar.

[Y 25.] Our Lady of Good Counsel Church D.O.M. (Roman Catholic), 236 E. 90th St., bet. Second and Third Aves.

Robust, undisciplined, deeply three-dimensional: a great side-street facade, now revealed by the opening up of the Ruppert site across the way. [Also see the school, below: Y 26b.]

[Y 26a.] 1716–1722 Second Avenue (apartments), NE cor. E. 89th St. ca. 1880.

A pair of apartment buildings whose remaining detail reminds one of Calvert Vaux's model tenements.

[Y 26b.] Our Lady of Good Counsel School (Roman Catholic), 325 E. 91st St., bet. First and Second Aves.

The rosé-colored pressed brick, the limestone trim, and the generous mansard **overcome the regrettable loss** of detail and scale contributed by this monument's original windows.

[Y 27a.] River East Plaza (apartments)/formerly **garage,** 402 E. 90th St., bet. First and York Aves. 1983.

High upon the east, lot-line wall is a palimpsest of a former life: very powerful neo-Baroque forms. A puzzlement.

[Y 24a.] The Church of the Holy Trinity   [Y 27a.] River East Plaza apartments

[Y 27b.] East River Tower (apartments), 1725 York Ave., bet. E. 89th and E. 90th Sts. W side. 1970. Horace Ginsbern & Assocs.

A clever pattern: 33 stories of alternating balconies that zig and zag between projected columns.

[Y 28a.] The 92nd Street Y/a.k.a. **Young Men's and Young Women's Hebrew Association,** 1395 Lexington Ave., SE cor. E. 92nd St. 1930. Necarsulmer & Lehlbach and Gehron, Ross & Alley. Expanded and altered.

A citywide center for cultural affairs, the **Y's Kaufmann Auditorium** holds readings from the resident **Poetry Center** in addition to concerts and lectures of more general interest.

[Y 28b.] Originally **Richard Hibberd residence,** 160 East 92nd Street, bet. Lexington and Third Aves. 1853.

A rare (in congested Manhattan) wood frame residence embellished with a brace of Corinthian-capitaled porch columns. Once the home of Eartha Kitt.

A block south:

[Y 28c.] 160 East 91st Street (apartments), bet. Lexington and Third Aves. ca. 1880.

Eight stories of softly bowed red-brick bays enhanced by strings of wrought-iron fire escapes fashioned in the curves of a violin.

Jacob Ruppert's Brewery, together with Ehret's and Ringler's, occupied the multiblocks between **90th** and **93rd** Streets, **Second** and **Third Avenues** for the glory of the German beer hall (this is **Yorkville**). Thirty-four buildings accrued over three-quarters of a century. Where there were originally almost 100 breweries in New York, now there are only small breweries, established in the 1980s, once the loss became painful: the larger enterprises of beermaking removed to automated stainless steel factories in places like **Wichita, Kansas, Cranston, R. I.,** and **Allentown, Pennsylvania.**

[Y 29.] Ruppert and **Yorkville Towers (apartment complexes),** E. 90th to E. 92nd Sts. bet. Second and Third Aves. 1976. Davis, Brody & Assocs. **Ruppert Park,** E. 89th St. NW cor. Second Ave. 1979. Balsley & Kuhl, landscape architects.

Bulky modeled form. **Notches, slots, cut corners** from the vocabulary initiated by this firm at Waterside [see M Manhattan/Four Squares E 8b.]. The density is immense and overwhelming. Given that millstone, the architects have handled an unfortunate program in a sophisticated manner. Talent can't save us from behemoths.

Adjacent to the original high-rise towers along Third Avenue are the last elements in the Ruppert Urban Renewal Project, housing for the elderly and luxury apartments:

[Y 30a.] Arthur B. Brown and William B. Brown Gardens, New York Foundation for Senior Citizens (housing for the elderly), 225 E. 93rd St., bet. Second and Third Aves. 1985. Davis, Brody & Assocs.

A low budget is outwitted here by thoughtful architectural touches: half-Tootsie Roll window sills, striped brick bands, and, best of all, open-air 2-story solariums facing southeast. Hooray!

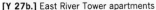

[Y 27b.] East River Tower apartments   **[Y 30b.]** Carnegie Park apartments

[Y 30b.] Carnegie Park (apartments), 200 E. 94th St., SE cor. Third Ave. 1983. Davis, Brody & Assocs.

Here a 31-story tower is set off from its related lower neighbors by rounding off the corners.

Ruppert's (restaurant), 1662 Third Ave., NW cor. 93rd St.

Having purloined its moniker from the brewery once located across the way, this comfy place modestly calls itself "A restaurant/bar in the New York Tradition." Pubby fun.

[Y 31.] 176 East 93rd Street (row house), bet. Lexington and Third Aves. 1973. Gueron & Lepp.

A brick tour de force: apartments for 3 families. **Arched** . . . and **arch.**

The Marx Brothers: While best known for their raucous Hollywood comedies Leonard "Chico" Marx (1891–1961), Adolph Arthur "Harpo" Marx (1893–1964), and Julius Henry "Groucho" Marx (1895–1977) were all Manhattan natives. Their boyhood home ("ancestral" was their term) was a 3-bedroom apartment in the row house at 179 East 93rd Street.

[Y 32a.] Astor Terrace (apartments/row housing), 245 E. 93rd St., NW cor. Second Ave. to E. 94th St. Schuman, Lichtenstein, Claman & Efron.

An avenue tower of dignified purply brick, plus a dozen midblock row houses surrounding a green central space, evoke some of the urban residential values of the past. The blandness of these row house facades, however, is no match for the richness of their century-old predecessors.

 [Y 32b.] The Waterford (apartments), 300 E. 93rd St., SE cor Second Ave. 1987. Beyer Blinder Bell and Vinjay Kale.

Like the **Irish crystal** for which it is named, this is a particularly **elegant piece of craftsmanship.** The 48-story tower stands out (for now) from the surrounding urban fabric of this once not very fashionable area.

[Y 33.] Stanley Isaacs Houses, N.Y.C. Housing Authority, First Ave. bet. E. 93rd and E. 95th Sts. E side. 1966. Frederick G. Frost, Jr. & Assocs.

The poor sometimes have the best views—and breezes—in New York. Open-access corridors modulate the standard brick and aluminum windows of this small (coat-, not vest-pocket) housing project. The **barrel-vaulted community center** was thought an architectural and social step to give place for participation in the community to project residents.

GRACIE SQUARE AND ENVIRONS

The corridor along East End (until 1890 called Avenue B) Avenue's length, running from East 79th to East 92nd Streets.

[S 1a.] 1 East End Avenue (apartments), bet. E. 79th and E. 80th Sts., E side to FDR Drive. 1929. Pleasants Pennington and Albert W. Lewis.

A 14-story apartment building shoehorned into a narrow, trapezoidal site, 29 feet wide at the south end, 51 feet at the north, 204 feet away. Its east facade once fronted on **Marie Curie Avenue,** the name of the marginal street widened to create the Drive.

[S 1b.] N.Y.C. Board of Higher Education Headquarters/originally **Welfare Island Dispensary, N.Y.C. Department of Hospitals,** 535 E. 80th St., NW cor. East End Ave. 1940. Louis E. Jallade.

A Classical/Art Deco/Art Moderne composite that is a cousin—at least once removed—to the old Board of Transportation Building. [See WC Brooklyn D 8b.].

Gracie Square/Gracie Terrace/Carl Schurz Park

Robert Moses, André Kostelanetz, Gloria Vanderbilt, Benno Schmidt, Constantine Sidamon-Eristoff, Osborn Elliott, mayors since Fiorello La Guardia, and other well-connected New Yorkers have lived in these surrounds. Changes in the original low-scale and working-class demeanor were first made in the 1920s when **Vincent Astor** built the apartments at 520 and 530 East 86th Street. The zoning change of 1928 permitted residential developments along East End Ave below 84th Street, the easternmost block of which is called **Gracie Square;** the corresponding block of 83rd is **Gracie Terrace.**

Maria Bowen Chapin erected a new neo-Georgian building for her girls' school (*1928. Delano & Aldrich.*) at East End Avenue and 84th. Brearley soon followed suit (*1929. Benjamin Wistar Morris.*) directly on the riverfront, a site since compromised by the construction of FDR Drive—but resulting in the deck built over Finley Walk to compensate the school for the loss.

[S 2.] John H. Finley Walk, over FDR Drive, bet. E. 81st St. and E. 84th St./Gracie Sq. 1941.

This elevated promenade was named for Finley (1863–1940), editor of *Harper's Weekly,* president of City College, associate editor of the *New York Times,* and inveterate walker, shortly after his death. What makes it special are the **memorable cutout identification signs** that line the pathway, a collaboration between **cartoonist Edwin Marcus** and **architect Harvey Stevenson.** The walk connects with Carl Schurz Park's Esplanade.

[S 3.] 52-54 East End Avenue (apartments), SW cor. E. 82nd St. 1988. Michael Lynn Assocs.

A 40-story corner sliver, a stratospheric spike on a 4,000-square-foot postage stamp-sized lot.

[S 4.] 91 East End Avenue (apartments), bet. E. 83rd St./Gracie Terrace and E. 84th St./Gracie Sq. E side.

A black stucco, stylish exterior with a *very* large house number.

[S 5.] 525 East 85th Street (residence), bet. York and East End Aves. 1958. Paul Mitarachi.

Two-storied and sheathed in glass. Gardens both in front and rear allow the raised living room (via its wood balustered balcony) to overview its own garden to the south.

[S 6a.] 420 East 86th Street (apartments), bet. First and York Aves. ca. 1936.

A 6-story apartment building that looks as out of place in these parts today (a rare example here of Grand Concourse Art Moderne) as it must have when built. Refreshing nevertheless, particularly the polychrome brick spandrels.

[S 6b.] Henderson Place Historic District, ★ 549-553 E. 86th St., NW cor. East End Ave. ☆ 6-16 Henderson Place, E side. ☆ 140-154 East End Ave., W side. ☆ 552-558 E. 87th St. ☆ 1882. All by Lamb & Rich.

A charming cul-de-sac provides the name for 24 (of the original 32) dwellings that survive: tiny, **zesty Queen Anne row houses** that transport unwary romantics to other climes and another era. Regrettably **overwhelmed and vulgarized** by the **monster apartment** to the west.

[S 7.] Carl Schurz Park/originally **East River Park,** E. 84th St./Gracie Sq. to E. 90th St., bet. East End Ave. and the East River. 1876, 1891. Reconstructed, Harvey Stevenson, architect; Cameron Clarke, landscape architect.

A brilliant solution to the intersection of city, river, and highway. Suspended over FDR Drive is **a sinuous expansive esplanade** overlooking **Hell Gate's churning waters.** It is edged with a curved, **user-friendly** wrought-iron fence so effective that its form was appropriated for the Battery Park City Esplanade; Brooklyn Heights Promenade would benefit as well. "Imitation is the sincerest form of flattery," Charles Caleb Colton, 1780–1832.

Carl Schurz (1829–1906): general, minister, senator, secretary of the interior, and editor, was the most prominent German immigrant of the 19th century.

From the edge, view:

Triborough Bridge, opened 1936: an elevated viaduct on Wards and Randalls Islands connected by four overwater bridges—one between the two islands, and three to the three boroughs. The views from automobiles are handsome, particularly approaching Manhattan from Queens; even better from the same route on foot.

Hell Gate Bridge *(1917. Gustav Lindenthal, engineer.)* is the reason Pennsylvania Station is a **station** rather than a terminal. Traffic brought under the Hudson River from the old terminal point in Jersey City can continue underground and under-river to Queens, thence over the Hell Gate and Little Hell Gate (now filled in) to the Bronx, Westchester, and Boston. The **bowstring trusses** (both upright and inverted) are handsome engineering.

Randalls Island became a park and headquarters of the Triborough Bridge and Tunnel Authority when the new Triborough Bridge made it accessible—the stadium is a sometime center of European football-soccer matches and summer concerts.

Wards Island: the Ward brothers farmed here in the 1780s. Now it's occupied by a sewage disposal plant (to the east of the Triborough's roadway), Manhattan State Hospital, and a small but lovely and very rural park connected to Manhattan by an **ungainly footbridge** (improved through a later non-institutional color scheme) with spectacular views. The bridge was predicated on the development of the whole island as a park, but the hospital, originally scheduled to be demolished, was reincarnated in a vigorous program of mental health facilities.

[S 8.] Gracie Mansion, official residence (since 1942) **of the Mayor/** earlier **Museum of the City of New York/**originally **Archibald Gracie residence,** Carl Schurz Park, East End Ave. opp. E. 88th St. ca. 1799. Expanded, 1804–1808. Restored, 1936, Aymar Embury II; 1985, Charles A. Platt Partners. **Susan Wagner Wing,** added, 1966, Mott B. Schmidt. ★ **Mansion open to public on a restricted basis.**

A remote country residence in its day, Gracie's house has been through the mill of reconstruction and restoration. The 1966 addition permits the mayor to use the house while others think *they* are using it. The 1985 restoration makes it (particularly on the interior) a true executive mansion. Its country peers from the same era include the Hamilton Grange *(1802)*, Abigail Adams Smith House *(1799)*, Jumel Mansion *(1765)*, and Van Cortlandt Mansion *(1748)*.

[S 8.] Gracie Mansion, since 1942 the official residence of New York City mayors

[S 9.] Gracie Square Gardens (apartment complex), 515, 525 E. 89th St. and 520, 530 E. 90th Sts., bet. York and East End Aves. ca. 1939.

An **unpretentious quartet** of 6-story red brick apartment buildings with neo-Baroque entry trim, whose principal charm is their scale and lovely central garden for residents.

 [S 10a.] Originally **Municipal Asphalt Plant/**now **Asphalt Green Sports and Arts Center** a.k.a. **George and Annette Murphy Center,** 655 E. 90th St., NW cor. York Ave./FDR Drive, to E. 91st St. 1944. Kahn & Jacobs. ★ Altered, 1982, Hellmuth, Obata & Kassabaum, associated architects. Pasanella+Klein, design architects. **[S 10b.]** Proposed **Asphalt Green Swim and Sports Training Center,** 1990? Foster de Jesus and Robert Wagenseil.

Exposed concrete over a parabolic, arched steel frame that was **once a single giant space** containing the equipment for mixing the city's asphalt. Now **divided into levels** for neighborhood athletic activities. An ambitious (separate) expansion is planned.

[S 10a.] The old Municipal Asphalt Plant recycled as a sports and arts center

[S 11.] **Fireboat House Solar Energy Education and Demonstration Center**/former **Fireboat Station,** East River along FDR Drive at E. 90th St. Altered, 1981, Steven Robinson, architect, and Total Environmental Action, Inc.

A curious mélange of old, new, and solar-oriented forms **recycled** by a community group—with lots of governmental subsidy—out of **a riverside facility** that once serviced City fireboats.

THE HEIGHTS AND THE HARLEMS

MORNINGSIDE HEIGHTS • HAMILTON HEIGHTS
HARLEM • EAST HARLEM

North of Cathedral Parkway, Central Park North, and 110th Street, for the most part, lie the areas of Morningside and Hamilton Heights, Harlem, and East Harlem, the last extending southward to 97th Street east of Park Avenue. **The Heights precincts** are known for their **college complexes**—Columbia, Barnard, Teachers, the **seminaries** below the 125th Street valley, and CCNY above it; the **Harlems** are the city's best-known **black and Hispanic ghettos.** All four areas offer relics of the past, signs of **revitalization as well as of decay,** and a display of **diverse life-styles** which reflect their **varied populations.** There is much to tempt the eye . . . and the mind.

N

0   1000   2000
feet

THE BRONX

Harlem
River

H60
H59

H35
H33 H34
H31 H32
H29 H30
H28

E23

E22
E21
E20
E19
E18
E17

Mount Morris/
Marcus Garvey
Memorial Park
H22
23
H21
H20
H19
H17
18
H16

E16
East Harlem
E15
E14
E13
E12
E11
E9   E10
E8
E7
E4   E5 E6
E3
E2
E1

Upper
East
Side

MORNINGSIDE HEIGHTS

From Cathedral Parkway north to West 125th Street, the western hilly side of Manhattan Island is Morningside Heights. Between **the steep escarpment** of Morningside Park on the east and the **gentle slopes** along the Hudson lie many of Manhattan's **most impressive** visual, architectural, and cultural delights. The site of a 1776 Revolutionary War skirmish, Morningside Heights became the site of the Bloomingdale Insane Asylum in 1818 and of the Leake and Watts Orphan Asylum 20 years later. The opening of Morningside Park in 1887, Riverside Drive three years later, and the simultaneous settlement here of major cultural institutions permitted the development of **several magnificent groups** of buildings, each in a **well-designed** setting. High-density housing along Riverside and Morningside Drives provided **people power** for the institutions and for an active community life.

Tips for touring: In general, Morningside Heights is a walker's area. Landmarks are densely spaced; students and residents populate the streets. The same can't be said for the other three precincts, where a car is the best means of locomotion and guarantee of security. A word to the wise: stay out of Morningside, Colonial, and St. Nicholas Parks. They are not policed and are avoided by local residents, sensitized to the danger of assault that empty paths and heavy greenery portend.

West of Broadway:

[M 1.] The Hendrik Hudson (apartments), 380 Riverside Dr., bet. Cathedral Pkwy. and W. 111th St. 1907. **Broadway addition/**now **College Residence Hotel,** 601 Cathedral Pkwy., NW cor. Broadway. 1908. Both by William L. Rouse.

The Hendrik Hudson was originally a grandiose apartment building in a Tuscan villa style, jacked up in scale to fit its Riverside Drive site: projected balconies, bracketed Spanish tile cornices, and two Palladian-styled towers capped with overhanging hipped roofs. These **embellishments** and both interior and exterior elegance **have been reduced** by time, economics, and the elements. What remains largely undiminished is the **bold, expressive ornament,** particularly on the Broadway addition (and also **on a relative** at the northeast corner of Broadway and West 111th Street).

[M 2.] Bank Street College of Education, 610 W. 112th St., bet. Broadway and Riverside Dr. 1970. Harry Weese & Assocs.

A **tall, distinguished, reserved** composition. A suave sliver of mirrored glass chamfers the corners of the **muted brick prism.** This teachers' training school had its beginnings on Bank Street in Greenwich Village, hence its name.

St. John the Divine to Carl Schurz's statue:

[M 3a.] Cathedral Church of St. John the Divine (Episcopal), Amsterdam Ave. at W. 112th St. E side. 1892–1911. Heins & La Farge. Work continued, 1911–1942. Cram & Ferguson. **[M 3b.] Deaconesses' House.** 1911. La Farge & Morris. **[M 3c.] St. Faith's House.** 1912. Heins & La Farge. **[M 3d.] Synod House.** 1913. Cram & Ferguson. **[M 3e.] Choir School.** 1913. Cook & Welch. **[M 3f.] Bishop's Home and Deanery.** 1914. Cram & Ferguson. **[M 3g.] Open-Air Pulpit.** 1916. Howells & Stokes.

Bishop Henry Codman Potter (1834–1908) was responsible for initiating this enormous **architectural coronet** to crown Morningside Heights. In 1891 he arranged to purchase the site of the Leake and Watts Orphan Asylum (whose 1840s Greek Revival building still remains) and, after **an architectural competition,** commissioned **Heins & La Farge** to design the church. The apse, choir, and crossing bear their **Byzantine-Romanesque influence.** By 1911 the bishop and both architects had died (Potter's tomb is in the church's St. James Chapel), and a new **architectural figure** came upon the scene: **Ralph Adams Cram** of Cram & Ferguson. Cram's style was **the French Gothic,** though over the years other versions of Gothic (and other architects: Thomas Nash, Henry Vaughan, Carrère & Hastings) were employed, all **working** within Cram's grand scheme. By 1942, the year of Cram's death, only his great nave and the west front (minus its towers) were complete. There **the work stopped,** halted by our entry into World War II.

Completion is not imminent, but work resumed in 1979 under the surveillance of **Bishop Paul Moore, Jr.** and **Dean James Parks Morton,** who combine the happy interests of social activism, avant-garde art and music, and a heavy and heady interest in architecture. **James Bambridge,** a British master stonemason, came to New York on the bishop's invitation to train a cadre of youths in stonecutting. The first efforts are raising the south Amsterdam Avenue tower; the north tower will then follow. Finally the great lantern over the crossing will be built in accordance with Cram's original design (see the model in the Cathedral gift shop), replacing the "temporary" dome that has sheltered the worshiping flock for nearly a century. Built of Guastavino vaulting, a process developed by Spanish architect Rafael Guastavino, **it required no interior support** during the course of construction. Craftsmen worked from the completed vault (of three staggered laminations) as they laid the remaining swirls of tile **using a special adhesive mortar.** The resulting underside, handsomely patterned, is **visible from within,** although the plans had originally called for concealing it with mosaics.

Despite its incompleteness and mix of styles it is **an impressive interior,** enormous not only in plan but also in volume, its side aisles being built as high as the nave. Do **visit the baptistry and ambulatory chapels** radiating from the apse.

On the landscaped grounds are a number of **ancillary buildings,** among them the Synod House on Cathedral Parkway, whose Amsterdam Avenue portal is embellished with sculpture **from Alexius to Zinzendorf.**

Were St. John the Divine to be completed it would be the world's largest cathedral, even though it is not as large as St. Peter's in Rome. St. Peter's, large as it is, is not a cathedral. The Pope, as bishop of Rome, maintains his seat (his **"cathedra"**) at the Church of St. John Lateran, outside the Vatican's walls. Size does not a cathedral make.

[M 4a.] Amsterdam House (nursing home), 1060 Amsterdam Ave., NW cor. W. 112th St. 1976. Kennerley, Slomanson & Smith.

An elegantly designed multistory slab for the care of the elderly. The use of naturally finished wood-framed windows is **a masterful touch.**

[M 4b.] 113th Street Gatehouse, New Croton Aqueduct, W. 113th St., SW cor. Amsterdam Ave. ca. 1890. **[M 4c.] 119th Street Gatehouse,** W. 119th St., SE cor. Amsterdam Ave. ca. 1890.

Construction **labor was cheap** in the 1880s when the New Croton Aqueduct was built, and a manufactured item, such as **cast-iron pipe, was expensive.** It was more economical, therefore, to minimize the use of pipe when water pressures were minimal and to use **masonry aqueduct** instead. Between 119th and 113th Streets such a masonry aqueduct, **horseshoe-shaped in cross section,** ran under Convent and Amsterdam Avenues until 1987 when steel pipe replacements were installed. These **extraordinarily finely crafted** stone gatehouses stand above the shafts at both ends of the aqueduct portion where pipes join it from the north and continue to the south.

[M 5a.] St. Luke's Hospital, Morningside Dr., bet. W. 113th and W. 114th Sts. W side. Original building, 1896. Ernest Flagg.

The western pavilions have been replaced, and the handsome baroque drum and dome are **in danger** of being lost; but the high mansard roofs and the profusion of Classical detail give the original buildings their **dignity and charm.**

[M 5b.] Église de Notre Dame (Roman Catholic), Morningside Dr., NW cor. W. 114th St. **Apse,** 1910. Dans & Otto. **Rectory,** 1915, 1928. Cross & Cross. ★

Like the nearby cathedral, **this church is also unfinished.** The interior must be lighted artificially because the oversized drum and dome, designed to bring skylight into the church, were never built. For a sense of what completion would bring, **visit nearby St. Paul's Chapel** at Columbia [see M 8d.] whose drum and dome **are in place.**

A **surprising contrast** to the smooth pale stone interior of the church is the rough dark stone replica of the **grotto at Lourdes** behind the altar.

[M 6.] 44-47, 50, and 54 Morningside Drive (apartments), bet. W. 114th and W. 116th Sts. ca. 1910.

They look comfortable from the outside, and just imagine the views. Many on the Columbia faculty call these home.

[M 7a.] Statue of Carl Schurz, Morningside Dr. at W. 116th St. E side. 1913. Karl Bitter, sculptor. Henry Bacon, architect.

This is an excellent place from which to view Harlem from afar. Rising from the patchwork quilt roofscape below is a tall white building to the north, the Harlem State Office Building. A reformer, avid conservationist, and editor of the *New York Evening Post* and the *Nation,* Schurz (1829–1906) has his own **park** too [see E Manhattan/Gracie Square S 7.], but you can't see that from here.

[M 7b.] President's House, Columbia University, 60 Morningside Dr., at W. 116th St. W side. 1912. William Kendall of McKim, Mead & White.

Built, as is much of Columbia, of Stony Creek granite, Indiana limestone, and overburned brick. Most presidents have elected to live elsewhere.

Eats and drinks: The acclaimed watering place of Morningside Heights is the dark, cavernous, and notorious **West End Cafe,** 2911 Broadway, between 113th and 114th, a bar which has attracted the locals for decades and in the 1940s was where beat writers William Burroughs, Jack Kerouac, and Allen Ginsberg hung out. For pastry and coffee, try **The Hungarian Pastry Shop,** 1030 Amsterdam Avenue near 111th. For heavier dining there's **The Symposium** (Greek), 544 W. 113th, midblock between Broadway and Amsterdam. **The Caffè Pertutti,** 2862 Broadway, is a popular newcomer with a Little Italy ambience; **Tom's Restaurant,** 2880 Broadway, a hardy perennial with a **lunch counter** for **penny counters.** And **The Mill Luncheonette,** 2895 Broadway, offers homemade food and *echt* egg creams in 1950s surroundings.

Columbia University:

[M 8.] Columbia University campus, W. 114th to W. 120th Sts., bet. Broadway and Amsterdam Aves. Original design and buildings, McKim, Mead & White. Construction begun, 1897. Additions and changes by others.

Columbia is one of the nation's **oldest, largest, and wealthiest** institutions. Prior to relocating here on the Heights, Columbia **occupied two other campuses,** the first southwest of the current City Hall and later a site east of Rockefeller Center's buildings. (The university, up until 1987, owned Rockefeller Center real estate, from which it derived **a substantial income.**) Today's main campus occupies land bought from the **Bloomingdale Insane Asylum.**

The earliest buildings, north of 116th Street (now a pedestrian walkway), are situated **on a high terrace,** two flights of stairs above surrounding streets and separated from them by high, forbidding granite basements. The south campus, **a later addition** south of West 116th Street, is terraced below the level of the 116th Street pedestrian way.

Arranged along Classical lines, the campus is **dominated** by the great, domed, limestone Low Library. The Italian Renaissance-style **instructional buildings,** of red brick, limestone trim, and copper-green roofs, are **arranged around the periphery** of the campus and are **augmented** by planting, tasteful paving, statues, plaques, fountains, and a variety of Classical ornament and detail. All of this, however, **fails to animate the campus** into either a dramatic or picturesque composition. The old buildings except for Low Library and St. Paul's Chapel, and the new except for Fairchild, are lifeless.

It must be said that McKim, Mead & White's **original concept** of a densely built-up campus, with a narrow central quadrangle and six intimate and sheltered side courts, **was never followed.** Only the court between Avery and Fayerweather Halls was completed, and this is now changed by the subterranean extension of Avery Library. The alternative to the compact plan, plus the university's explosive growth, resulted in the **spread of Columbia's buildings** to the remainder of Morningside Heights, with even **an ill-fated attempt** to build a gymnasium in Morningside Park.

[M 8a.] Low Memorial Library, N of W. 116th St., bet. Amsterdam Ave. and Broadway. 1897. McKim, Mead & White. ★   Interior ★.

Columbia University's most noteworthy visual symbol, familiar to millions of Americans as the backdrop for the 1968 student riots, is the **monumental, domed, and colonnaded** Low Library, named not for its height but for its donor, **Seth Low** (1850–1916), mayor of Brooklyn, president of Columbia, and mayor of New York. Set atop of three tiers of graciously proportioned steps, this **dignified centerpiece** for the campus so **dominates its open space** that for many years a small sign cautioned the unfamiliar "THIS IS NOT BUTLER LIBRARY." The reference is to the fact that Low is no longer the university library, its interior spaces being more **suited to ceremonial and administrative uses** than to shelf space and reading rooms. Off the rotunda to the east is a small **library of Columbiana** with items of interest to those who wish to trace the university's march northward through Manhattan from its 18th-century beginnings downtown as King's College.

[M 8b.] Alma Mater. 1903. Daniel Chester French, sculptor.

Centered on the formal stair one tier below Low is *Alma Mater,* the once-gilded bronze statue which forms the background of nearly every university graduation ceremony. An **evocative sculpture,** the enthroned figure extends her hand in welcome as she looks up from the mighty tome of knowledge lying open in her lap. Secreted in the folds of her robes on her left side is her **familiar,** an owl. **As a symbol,** *Alma Mater* has understandably **elicited both love** (a protest in 1962 which caused a newly applied gilding to be removed in favor of the more familiar green patina) **and hate** (in 1968 she survived a bomb blast during that period of student unrest).

Charles Follen McKim: Despite the commonly held belief to the contrary, *not* all buildings produced by the architectural firm of McKim, Mead & White were by its most famous partner, Stanford White. Chief architect for the Columbia campus was Charles Follen McKim (1847–1909), commemorated in a bronze plaque set into the pavement in front of *Alma Mater.* The Latin inscription can be translated as "An artist's monuments look down upon us throughout the ages."

[M 8c.] Butler Library/originally **South Hall,** W. 114th St. bet. Amsterdam Ave. and Broadway. 1934. James Gamble Rogers.

This is Columbia's **major library.** Its collections are notable but it is overshadowed architecturally by Low across 116th Street. Named for **Nicholas Murray Butler,** Columbia's president between 1902 and 1945, the period of the university's enormous growth.

[M 8d.] St. Paul's Chapel (Episcopal), N campus, E of Low Library. 1907. Howells & Stokes. ★

In the **initial period of development** of the Morningside Heights campus, general planning and design were **almost entirely a McKim, Mead & White monopoly.** One of two exceptions (the other was Arnold W. Brunner's School of Mines) is this especially fine chapel, **the best of all Columbia's buildings.** It is a gift of Olivia Egleston Phelps Stokes and Caroline Phelps Stokes, sisters of wealthy financier and philanthropist Anson Phelps Stokes (1838–1913). The beautifully executed work was the design of Howells & Stokes, one of whose partners, Isaac Newton Phelps Stokes (author of *The Iconography of Manhattan Island*) was their nephew. The interior is filled with **exquisite Guastavino vaulting; magnificent light** pours down from above. A visit during a performance of antique works by one of Columbia's musical groups will also reveal its sonorous acoustics. **Pro Ecclesia Dei.**

The last surviving building of the Bloomingdale Insane Asylum, on whose site Columbia was built, is East Hall (1878), just south of St. Paul's. As part of the asylum it was called the Macy Villa. It now serves as the home of the Temple Hoyne Buell Center for the Study of American Architecture.

[M 8e.] Law School, 435 W. 116th St., NE cor. Amsterdam Ave. 1963.
[M 8f.] School of International Affairs, 420 W. 118th St., SE cor. Amsterdam Ave. 1971. Both by Harrison & Abramovitz.

The blocklong bridge that links this pair of **whiter than white** high-rise extensions to the campus makes a **gloomy tunnel** of Amsterdam Avenue below. Looking up at Law's south facade from the terrace you almost expect a dictator **to strut out** onto the cantilevered box **to harangue the multitudes.** An enormous sculpture by **Jacques Lipchitz** was a 1977 addition to the west facade.

[M 8g.] Casa Italiana, 1161 Amsterdam Ave., bet. W. 116th and W. 118th Sts. E side. 1927. William M. Kendall of McKim, Mead & White.

An appropriately Renaissance palazzo for Ivy Leaguers seeking Italian culture.

[M 8h.] Avery Hall, N campus, N of St. Paul's Chapel. 1912. McKim, Mead & White. Underground addition and courtyard to E, 1977, Alexander Kouzmanoff & Assocs.

One of 9 similar instructional buildings, Avery Hall houses the School of Architecture and **Avery Library,** the nation's **largest architectural library.**

[M 8i.] Marcellus Hartley Dodge Physical Fitness Center, NW campus. 1974. The Eggers Partnership.

This fancily named gym addition eventually replaced the **abortive project** that was to occupy a site off Morningside Drive in the park, opposition to which sparked the student riots of the late 1960s.

[M 5a.] St Luke's Hospital Chapel   **[M 8j.]** Fairchild Life Sciences Ctr.

[M 8j.] Sherman Fairchild Center for the Life Sciences, NE campus. 1977. Mitchell/Giurgola Assocs.

A radically designed building which **shields the campus** from the banal facade of Seeley W. Mudd Hall. Fairchild is clad with a screen that seems a **vertical extension** of the **red tile pavers** covering Columbia's terraces.

[M 8k.] Computer Science Department Building, NE campus, partially under Fairchild Center for the Life Sciences, sharing terrace with Mudd Engineering and facing Amsterdam Ave. 1983. R. M. Kliment & Frances Halsband.

An **interstitial weaving** of 3 buildings, a plaza, and a street. A subtle architectural and urbanistic coup that makes this campus extension a better precinct.

[M 8l.] Uris Hall addition, N campus, N of Low Library. 1986. Peter L. Gluck & Partners.

Anything that could mask **Uris** would be a plus, and here is a shallow (in depth not character) and handsome **Post Modern** building to do the job.

[M 8m.] East Campus complex (residence hall and offices), SW cor. 118th St. and Morningside Drive. 1982. Gwathmey Siegel & Assocs.

A sleek, gray and red tile residence slab with glass block. This is the swan song of the International Style, or is it perhaps a rooster crowing the Post Modern [PoMo] neo-International 1930s Renaissance? In any categorization, it is both elegant and handsome.

[M 9a.] Morris A. Schapiro Hall (dormitory), 615 W. 115th St., bet. Broadway and Riverside Dr. 1988. Gruzen Samton Steinglass.

An infill building in the city streetscape, outside the formal boundaries of McKim, Mead & White's Renaissance university. It is a good neighbor to those next door, with architectural remembrances of the main campus in the color and texture of its brickwork.

When at its front door, turn around and view the huge **terra-cotta grotesques** atop **No. 612** across the street. Has Columbia missed the boat **again** in its hopefully up-to-date styling of new adjunct units? Or is neo-Baroque another style yet to be revived?

[M 9b.] Originally **The Alpha Club,** 434 Riverside Dr., bet. W. 115th and W. 116th Sts. 1903. Wood, Palmer & Hornbostel.

An elaborate frat house in the Beaux Art mode, so stylish in its time.

[M 9c.] The Colosseum (apartments), 435 Riverside Dr., SE cor. W. 116th St. 1910. Schwartz & Gross.

Like a heavily embroidered tapestry, this unusual curved facade, together with its opposite-handed sibling across West 116th Street, frames the main entrance of the Columbia campus atop the hill—best seen from the Drive.

[M 9d.] Originally **Eton Hall** and **Rugby Hall (apartments),** 29 and 35 Claremont Ave. **[M 9e.] Peter Minuit Hall (apartments),** 25 Claremont Ave. All bet. W. 116th and W. 119th Sts. W side. 1910. Gaetan Ajello.

Eton and Rugby constitute one opulent facade of white-glazed brick embellished with bold, white-glazed terra-cotta ornament. Minuit is a slightly lesser relative to the south. All are by the **unsung architectural hero** of Morningside Heights and the Upper West Side, **Gaetan Ajello.** Between 1910 and 1930 he designed some 50 apartment buildings in these areas for the Paterno and Campagna real estate interests—the "C" emblazoned on the terra-cotta shields here stands for Campagna [see R Bronx R 7e.]. Neatly incised on the cornerstones of these apartments (as on many of his other works) is his architectural calling card: GAETAN AJELLO, ARCHITECT.

Barnard College:

[M 10.] Barnard College campus, W. 116th to W. 120th (Reinhold Niebuhr Place) Sts., bet. Broadway and Claremont Ave. **[M 10a.] Milbank Hall,** comprising **Milbank, Brinckerhoff,** and **Fiske Halls,** 606 W. 120th St., N end of campus. 1896–1898. Lamb & Rich. **[M 10b.] Brooks Hall (dormitory).** 1907. Charles A. Rich. **[M 10c.] Barnard Hall.** 1917. Arnold W. Brunner. **[M 10d.] Hewitt Hall (dormitory).** 1924. Charles A. Rich. **[M 10e.] Lehman Hall/Wollman Library.** 1959. O'Connor & Kilham. **[M 10f.] Reid Hall (dormitory).** 1961. **[M 10g.] Millicent McIntosh Center.** 1969. Vincent G. Kling & Assocs. **[M 10h.] Helen Goodhart Altschul Hall.** 1969. Vincent G. Kling & Assocs. **[M 10i.] New Dormitory.** 1988. James Stewart Polshek & Partners.

In its original **Lamb & Rich** quadrangle, crowned with Arnold Brunner's 1917 **Barnard Hall,** Barnard obviously aped Columbia's architecture across Broadway. Later and lesser architects added Lehman, McIntosh, and Altschul, **modern** in their stance but without reference to the context of street or campus. Quality control has been reestablished with the construction of the new dormitory.

Barnard was established to be the undergraduate women's equivalent of Columbia by Frederick A. P. Barnard (1809–1899), the Columbia president who had championed the cause of **equal rights** for women in higher education. Since Columbia itself has been coeducational since 1983, a "women's college" (with some male students) is somewhat of an anachronism within a world of unisexism.

The Lehman Library's grilled facade is the work of **solar consultants** Victor and Aladar Olgyay, Hungarian emigrés who somehow got their north arrow confused: the grillage faces slightly south of east, where there is negligible sun loading. They were, however, concerned more with architectural ideology than with its reality.

[M 10h.] Barnard's Altschul Hall   **[M 13.]** Public School 36, Manhattan

[M 11.] Main Hall, the first Teachers College building (photo ca. 1893)

Terrace Restaurant Atop Butler Hall, 400 W. 119th St., SW cor. Morningside Dr.

The **highest** public restaurant in upper Manhattan. Continental cuisine and atmosphere; superb views of the city. (To get equally good views without food or drink, visit the upper-floor lounge of the School of International Affairs [see M 8f.].)

Yushima (Japanese restaurant), 420 W. 119th St., bet. Morningside Dr. and Amsterdam Ave.

Down the block from Butler Hall in a converted ground-floor apartment. Very unpretentious atmosphere. Remembered by old-timers as the Aki Tea Room—it didn't serve sushi then.

North of the Columbia Campus:

[M 11.] Teachers College, Columbia University, 525 W. 120th St., bet. Amsterdam Ave. and Broadway. **[M 11a.] Main Hall.** 1892. William A. Potter. **[11b.] Macy Hall**/originally **Macy Manual Arts Building,** N of Main Hall. 1894. William A. Potter. **[M 11c.] Frederick Ferris Thompson Memorial Hall,** W of Main Hall. 1904. Parish & Schroeder. **[M 11d.] Russell Hall,** E of Main Hall. 1923. Allen & Collens. **[M 11e.] Thorndike Hall,** NW of Main Hall. 1973. Hugh Stubbins & Assocs. **[M 11f.] Whittier Hall (dormitories),** Amsterdam Ave. bet. W. 120th and W. 121st Sts. W side. 1901. Bruce Price.

Tightly squeezed into a full city block, this semiautonomous branch of Columbia offers **a rich range of red brick architecture** largely from the turn of the **20th century.** Peeking above the composition from West 121st Street—it is entered through a court from West 120th Street—is **a sleek new high-rise addition,** 81 years removed from the earliest building.

[M 11g.] Originally **Horace Mann School**/now **Horace Mann Hall, Teachers College,** Broadway bet. W. 120th and W. 121st Sts. E side. 1901. Howells & Stokes and Edgar H. Josselyn.

Horace Mann School was founded in 1887 as the laboratory school for Teachers College, but those activities are now conducted in the suburban Riverdale campus. Its charming forms, however, continue to **enliven the Broadway blockfront** it commands, as it now serves TC in other capacities.

[M 12.] Bancroft Hall (apartments), Teachers College, 509 W. 121st St., bet. Amsterdam Ave. and Broadway. 1911. Emery Roth.

Tucked away on a dark side street in the shadow of Teachers College is this **ebullient eclectic warhorse** of a facade: aggressive, bold, charming, mysterious. An altogether wonderful discovery, with verdigris copper-clad bay windows and a timber **Italianate Tuscan** roof.

[M 13.] Public School 36, Manhattan, The Morningside School, 123 Morningside Dr., NE cor. Amsterdam Ave. 1967. Frederick G. Frost, Jr. & Assocs., architects. William Tarr, sculptor.

This school is actually a group of separate buildings situated on top of rock outcroppings on a **site demapped from Morningside Park.** Simple brick stair towers, cast concrete construction, and large rectangular windows mark the earliest arrival of **the New Brutalism** in upper Manhattan. The **self-weathering steel** sculpture is a particularly **harmonious element** in the overall design.

[M 14.] Jewish Theological Seminary, 3080 Broadway, bet. W. 122nd and W. 123rd Sts. E side. 1930. Gehron, Ross, Alley, architects. David Levy, associate architect. **[M 14a.] Seminary expansion** and **Library,** 1985. Gruzen & Partners.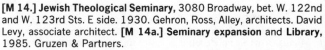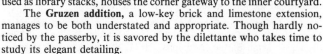

This **clunky,** oversized neo-Georgian building is the **central institution** of the Conservative movement in American Judaism. The tower, used as library stacks, houses the corner gateway to the inner courtyard.

The **Gruzen addition,** a low-key brick and limestone extension, manages to be both understated and appropriate. Though hardly noticed by the passerby, it is savored by the dilettante who takes time to study its elegant detailing.

[M 15.] Union Theological Seminary, W. 120th (Reinhold Niebuhr Place) to W. 122nd Sts., bet. Broadway and Claremont Aves. 1910. Allen & Collens. Altered, 1952, Collens, Willis & Beckonert. ★

A stronghold of **theological modernism** and **social consciousness** is housed in a Collegiate Gothic quadrangle of rock-face granite with limestone trim. Two handsome perpendicular towers, an exquisite chapel, library, refectory, and dormitories **recall medieval Oxbridge.**

Rabbi Mordecai Kaplan (1881–1983), founder of the Jewish Reconstructionist movement, taught at the Jewish Theological Seminary from 1909 to 1963 and established the Society for the Advancement of Judaism in 1922. He defined Judaism as a "civilization," embracing language, custom, and culture beyond the conventional limitations of religious belief.

An early champion of equal rights for women, Rabbi Kaplan is credited with having created the *bat mitzvah,* the rite marking a girl's arrival at the age of Jewish duty and responsibility. In 1922 Rabbi Kaplan's daughter, Judith, became the first bat mitzvah.

[M 16.] Interchurch Center, 475 Riverside Dr., bet. W. 119th and W. 120th Sts. 1958. Voorhees, Walker, Smith, Smith & Haines.

A bulky work that attempts to harmonize with—but only detracts from—lyrical Riverside Church to the north.

[M 15.] Union Theological Seminary

[M 17.] Riverside Church in 1959

[M 17.] Riverside Church (Baptist), 490 Riverside Dr., bet. W. 120th and W. 122nd Sts. 1930. Allen & Collens and Henry C. Pelton. Burnham Hoyt, designer. S wing, 1960. Collens, Willis & Beckonert.

The **ornament of Chartres** adapted to a 21-story high-rise **steel-framed church.** Funded by John D. Rockefeller, Jr., this church enjoys the finest in available materials, stone carving, and stained glass of its era. Its 392 foot-high tower (largely an office building disguised as a place of bells) is surmounted by the 74-bell **Laura Spelman Rockefeller Memorial Carillon,** with its 20-ton tuned bass bell. Both carillon and bell are **the largest in the world.** Commanding an imposing site along Riverside Drive, the church was criticized upon completion for its opulence, as "a late example of bewildered eclecticism." Nevertheless, despite problems of scale which seem to make it smaller than it is (particularly when up close), it is easily **the most prominent architectural work** along the Hudson from midtown to the George Washington Bridge. Within the church is the lovely **Christ Chapel.**

Take an elevator to the carillon and climb the open stairway past the bells to the **lofty windblown observation deck.**

[M 18a.] Manhattan School of Music/originally **Juilliard School of Music/Institute of Musical Art,** 120 Claremont Ave., NE cor. W. 122nd St. 1910. Donn Barber. Additions, 1931, Shreve, Lamb & Harmon. **[M 18b.] Mitzi Newhouse Pavilion.** 1970. MacFadyen & Knowles.

Innocuous limestone with a neat concrete and glass cafeteria.

[M 19.] International House, 500 Riverside Dr., N of Sakura Park, N of W. 122nd St. 1924. Lindsay & Warren, Louis Jallade, partner-in-charge.

The multistory residence for the **numerous foreign** (and other) **students** who attend the nearby centers of higher learning. A structure

made important by its setting—the formal plantings of **Sakura Park**—
rather than by any particular architectural merit of its own.

[M 20.] Grant's Tomb/General Grant National Memorial, Riverside
Dr. at W. 122nd St. 1897. John H. Duncan. Mosaic benches, 1973.
Pedro Silva, Cityarts Workshop. ★ Interior ★.

The contributions of 90,000 subscribers paid for this **pompous
sepulcher,** the design of which was chosen in an architectural competition. It is a free copy of **Mausoleus' tomb** at Halicarnassus (present-day
Turkey) of 350 B.C.—one of the Seven Wonders of the Ancient World:
hence a **mausoleum.** As attention-getting as this pile of granite is from
Riverside Drive, here parted to create its spacious lawned site, it is **a far
better work inside.** There, through the massive bronze doors in a great
solemn white marble setting, President and Mrs. Grant rest side by side
in identical **polished black sarcophagi.**

A sinuous, colorful, amusing mosaicked bench rings the tomb's
plaza but, curiously, doesn't compete with the tomb itself. It is a
"beautification effort" which involved community residents in this monument on their doorstep. Shades of **Gaudí** and his **Parque Güell** in
Barcelona—the mosaics are wonderful.

To the memory of an amiable child: Almost lost at the edge of the
monumental space commanded by Grant's Tomb is a tiny fenced area
across and down a few steps from the west driveway. Here stands a
modest stone urn "Erected to the Memory of an Amiable Child, St.
Clair Pollock," a five-year-old who fell to his death from these rocks on
July 15, 1797. When the property was sold, the child's uncle asked that
the grave remain inviolate; and despite the bureaucratic problems involved, the request has been honored through the years. The views of
the Hudson Valley are particularly beautiful from this tranquil spot.

[M 21a.] 560 Riverside Drive (apartments), N of Tiemann Place.
1964. **[M 21b.] 2 St. Clair Place (offices),** W of W. 125th St. 1969.
Brown, Guenther, Battaglia, Seckler.

An enormous apartment complex for individuals and families connected with Columbia and its sister institutions on the Heights. Gleaming white, beveled, concrete picture-framed windows repeat and repeat
and repeat in the low office wing.

HAMILTON HEIGHTS

This precinct, west of St. Nicholas and Colonial Parks from 125th Street
north to Trinity Cemetery, includes the old **village of Manhattanville,**
the once-famous **Sugar Hill,** and the **City College campuses.** The precinct takes its name from the country estate of Alexander Hamilton. His
home and other 19th-century houses, churches, and institutional buildings survive, but most of the existing buildings here date from the
construction of the Broadway-Seventh Avenue IRT subway, which
opened in 1904.

[T 1.] St. Joseph's Church (Roman Catholic), 401 W. 125th St., NW
cor. Morningside Ave. 1889. Herter Brothers.

An unpretentious church of **modest scale and detail.** The north end
features an interesting intersection of 4 roof gables. Note the blind oculi
around the rear doors.

Manhattanville: Along the west end of the valley that **cleaves** Morningside Heights (on the south) and Hamilton Heights (on the north)
grew the village of Manhattanville. It straddled both sides of today's
West 125th Street, which leads to the former landing of the ferry to
Fort Lee. **A bustling village** more in the **New England mill town tradition** than that of New York City, the settlement supported a **pigment
factory,** D. F. Tiemann & Company (below 125th Street), **a worsted
mill** (on 129th Street west of Broadway), **Yuengling Brewery** (128th
Street east of Amsterdam), as well as a grammar school, post office,
and a sprinkling of churches. **Manhattan College began** in 1853 along
Broadway at 131st Street before relocating to Riverdale. The area still

retains in its structures vestiges of its **19th-century industrial beginnings.**

[T 2a.] IRT Broadway Line viaduct, along Broadway spanning W. 125th St. 1904. William Barclay Parsons, engineer. ★

The sweeping latticed arch and its abutments are **worthy of Eiffel.** Best seen from the west, where the Transit Authority's gross billboard is less evident.

[T 2b.] Prentis Hall (Department of Chemical Engineering), Columbia University/originally **Sheffield Farms Milk Company,** 632 W. 125th St., bet. Broadway and St. Clair Place. 1906. Edgar J. Moeller.

Milky white glazed terra-cotta, now somewhat yellowed and begrimed, is this **ex-dairy's face to the world.** How appropriate (poetically, at least) that it is now a chemical engineering laboratory.

Where 125th Street turns today it once did not. The diagonal street in the valley between Morningside and Hamilton Heights was called Manhattan Street. It ran obliquely to the street grid only because the topography made the valley the natural route for a wide thoroughfare—along it ran the streetcars to the Fort Lee Ferry. In 1920, however, it was decided that Manhattan Street should be renamed West 125th Street, and the old part of the original West 125th Street, west of Morningside Avenue, was renamed LaSalle Street. Now 125th Street has vanished entirely—at least on official maps, supplanted by Martin Luther King, Jr. Boulevard. But the A train will still take you to 125th.

The city fathers also bestowed other new names: Moylan Place for West 126th Street (now eradicated by General Grant Houses), Tiemann Place (after the old color works) for 127th Street, and St. Clair Place for 129th Street. Incidentally, the oblique route of 125th follows a geological fault line similar to California's San Andreas but not nearly so active.

[T 3.] The wondrous skeleton of the rebuilt Riverside Drive viaduct

[T 3.] Riverside Drive viaduct, bet. W. 124th and W. 135th Sts. 1901. F. Stewart Williamson, engineer. Totally rebuilt, 1987.

From Morningside Heights to Hamilton Heights this lacy (from below) steel viaduct steps off 26 bays of **filigreed steel arches** across the 125th Street valley.

[T 3a.] Harlem on the Hudson Esplanade, 125th St. at the Hudson River. 1987. Rod Knox.

A filigree of pipe-frame scaffolding, a bed of grass, and potted trees make this stretch of the river salubrious once more. Concerts of a modest scale lend a note of grace.

[T 3b.] Riverside Drive retaining wall and viewing platforms, W. 135th to W. 153rd Sts. 1873–1910. Frederick Law Olmsted, Jr.

Smooth granite **retains the Drive,** crowned with a neo-Classical balustrade (between 141st and 147th Streets). Once the face of a **seemingly fortified city,** it is masked by the Henry Hudson Parkway, the old Hudson River Railroad freight line, and the new North River Water Pollution Control Plant. The **best view** is from the plant's roof: the new state park by Richard Dattner.

[T 4a.] Templo Biblico/originally **Engine Company No. 37, N.Y.C. Fire Department,** 503 W. 126th St., bet. Amsterdam Ave. and Old Broadway. 1881. Napoleon LeBrun.

Old firehouses are sturdy and readily reusable—this one is a case in point. The structure stands on a block originally devoted to **a sprawling charitable institution** called **Sheltering Arms,** today a city park and swimming pool. West on West 126th Street are other community-oriented buildings.

[T 4b.] Manhattanville Neighborhood Center/originally **The Speyer School,** 514 W. 126th St., bet. Amsterdam Ave. and Old Broadway. 1902. Edgar H. Josselyn.

Built as a **demonstration school** for Teachers College and as a neighborhood settlement, it is now defunct. Note the **Flemish Renaissance** silhouette of its parapet.

[T 4c.] St. Mary's Church-Manhattanville (Episcopal), 521 W. 126th St., bet. Amsterdam Ave. and Old Broadway. 1909. Carrère & Hastings and T. E. Blake. **[4d.] Rectory.** ca. 1850.

Its name cut into stone in Old English characters and its archaic forms preserve the image of Manhattanville as **a remote 19th-century village.** The mid 19th-century white frame rectory, set back from the street to the west of the church, is a delightful surprise.

[T 4e.] Originally Bernheimer & Schwartz Pilsener Brewing Company, W end of block bounded by W. 126th and W. 128th Sts. E side of Amsterdam Ave. ca. 1885.

A phalanx of 19th-century red brick brewery buildings (a descendent of the earlier occupant of this site, Yuengling Brewery), now applied to a variety of contemporary uses. The most charming is the stable (?) at 454-458 West 128th, almost at the end of the dead-end street.

The Met's tin shed: The grimy shed sheathed in corrugated iron occupying some two-thirds of an acre at 495 West 129th Street, east of Amsterdam Avenue, shelters all manner of bulky sets for the Metropolitan Opera House at Lincoln Center. It was built around 1895 as a storage shed for Amsterdam Avenue streetcars. The expanse of sloping roof, unusual for Manhattan, is best seen from the hill behind, along 130th Street.

[T 5a.] Riverside Park (apartments), 3333 Broadway, bet. W. 133rd and W. 135th Sts. W side. 1976. **[T 5b.] Intermediate School 195, Manhattan, The Roberto Clemente School,** 625 W. 133rd St., bet. Broadway and Twelfth Ave. 1976. Both by Richard Dattner & Assocs., Henri A. LeGendre & Assocs., and Max Wechsler Assocs.

The local leviathan: a great slab-sided half octagon that embraces river views and the sun. A N.Y.C. Educational Construction Fund project, this oyster has as its pearl the new local school.

[T 6.] Our Lady of Lourdes Church (Roman Catholic), 467 W. 142nd St., bet. Convent and Amsterdam Aves. 1904. O'Reilly Bros. ★

A bizarre reincarnation made from parts of three important buildings. The gray and white marble and bluestone facade on West 142nd Street includes elements salvaged from the Ruskinian Gothic-influenced **National Academy of Design** (*1865. Peter B. Wight*), which stood at what is today the northwest corner of East 23rd Street and Park Avenue South. The apse of the church and parts of its east wall are built from the architectural elements of the **Madison Avenue end of St. Patrick's Cathedral,** removed to build the Lady Chapel that is there today. And the elaborate pedestals flanking the steps which lead up to the church are relics of department store magnate A. T. Stewart's white marble mansion, (*1869. John Kellum*), which embellished the northwest corner of 34th Street and Fifth Avenue until 1901.

[T 7.] Originally **Academy of the Holy Child (Roman Catholic)/**then **St. Walburgas Academy,** 630 Riverside Dr., NE cor. W. 140th St. ca. 1910.

A dark **forbidding** building with a rock-face stone raiment.

𝔑𝔞𝔱𝔦𝔬𝔫𝔞𝔩 𝔄𝔠𝔞𝔡𝔢𝔪𝔶 𝔬𝔣 𝔇𝔢𝔰𝔦𝔤𝔫,

[T 6.] The National Academy of Design became a facade: Our Lady of Lourdes

[T 8.] North River Water Pollution Control Plant City of New York, W. 137th to W. 145th Sts. W of the Henry Hudson Pkwy. to the Hudson River. 1986 (partial service) to 1991. Theodore Long, architect at Tippetts-Abbett-McCarthy-Stratton; Feld, Kaminetsky & Cohen; Gibbs & Hill; all engineers. **[T 8a.] State Park** on top, 1991. Richard Dattner & Assocs.

Various designers have attempted to assuage the Harlem community in return for positioning this 22-acre monster facility on their doorstep. In effect, this is the processing plant for all sewage on the West Side from Morton Street to the Spuyten Duyvil, the effluents of more than a million people. Park designers, in order, have included Philip Johnson, whose proposed grand decorative fountains were misinterpreted as sewage-aerating devices; Gruzen & Partners; and Bond-Ryder Associates. Richard Dattner's work is to be built—an activity center connected to the Riverside Drive bluff by two umbilical bridges.

City College:

[T 9.] The City College of the City University of New York (CUNY)/ originally **City College,** a.k.a. **CCNY,** W. 138th to W. 141st Sts., St. Nicholas Terr. to Amsterdam Ave. 1903–1907. Including **[T 9a.] Baskerville Hall/**originally **Chemistry Building; [T 9b.] Compton Hall/** originally **Mechanical Arts Building; [T 9c.] Goethals Hall/**originally **Technology Building; [T 9d.] Wingate Hall/**originally **Gymnasium;** and **[T 9e.] Shepard Hall.** All by George B. Post. 1903–1907 ★ Renovation of Shepard Hall, 1989: interior, William Hall & Assocs.; exterior, The Stein Partnership.

This, the second campus of what is still referred to as **CCNY,** is clad with the by-product of the city's transit system. **Manhattan schist,** excavated during construction of the **IRT Broadway subway,** adorns the original quadrangle, trimmed with white glazed terra-cotta. Its **cathedral** is Shepard Hall, a towered, skewed, Gothic bulk encrusted with terra-cotta quoins, finials, voussoirs, and other detail. Shepard's satellites to the west, across Convent Avenue, also in Gothic fancy dress, are party however to a formal **neo-Renaissance** plan and courtyard.

[T 9f.] Steinman Hall (School of Engineering), Convent Ave. bet. St. Nicholas Terr. and W. 141st St. E side. 1962. Lorimer & Rose.

Glass-block Modern, with the inescapable white glazed brick of the 1960s. The "modernism" of that decade could not understand that an appropriate relationship might somehow have been created with the original campus next door. See also Cohen Library below.

[T 9g.] Mahoney Hall (Science and Physical Education), Convent Ave. S of 138th St. E side. 1971. Skidmore, Owings & Merrill.

Exposed concrete grillage on a battered rocky precast concrete base; an unfriendly place to the pedestrian. Its elevated terrace and bridge were once intended to be the first link in a total campus plan that, fortunately, was aborted.

[T 12.] Hamilton Hts. Historic Dist.   **[T 9.]** Finialed City College skyline

[T 9.] The neo-Renaissance City College, embellished with neo-Gothic detail, 1966

[T 9h.] North Academic Center, W. 135th to W. 138th Sts., bet. Convent and Amsterdam Aves. 1983. John Carl Warnecke & Assocs.

This megastructure's skewed geometry was justified by old Shepard Hall's 45 degree tilt to the city's grid. It sits on the site of **Lewisohn Stadium,** a winter sport's field and once a summer mecca for outdoor concertgoers, where symphony orchestras held sway until the overbearing noise of planes in a landing pattern for LaGuardia Airport squelched its acoustic usefulness.

NAC crowns Hamilton Heights, the next hill from Columbia's Morningside Heights. Though perhaps an acropolis for Harlem, the

Center is more likely a stranded aircraft carrier amid these small-scaled tenement and town house blocks.

[T 10.] South Campus/formerly **Manhattanville College of the Sacred Heart**/originally **Academy and Convent of the Sacred Heart,** W. 130th to W. 135th Sts. bet. Convent Ave. and St. Nicholas Terr. ca. 1840–1865 **[T 10a.] Nursery**/onetime **President's House**/originally **Gatehouse, Manhattanville College,** Convent Ave. NE cor. W. 133rd St. 1912.

The Roman Catholic **academy** and **convent** for its teachers, the Ladies of the Sacred Heart, was established here in 1847, also giving name to the **adjacent Convent Avenue.** In 1952 the college and the sisters moved to Westchester, and the City bought the complex for City College. Old Finley Hall has been demolished in favor of a sports complex. The newest buildings include:

[T 10b.] Originally **Morris Raphael Cohen Library,** within the South Campus, Convent Ave. SE cor. W. 135th St. 1957. Lorimer & Rose.

A glass-block Modern encore. In this era of Post Modern reconsideration of all history, including the various phases of "modern" architecture, such works pique the attention of young architects.

[T 10b.] Cohen Library on City College's South Campus: glass-block Modern

[T 10c.] Aaron Davis Hall for the Performing Arts, within the South Campus, Convent Ave., SE cor. W. 135th St. 1979. Abraham W. Geller & Assocs. and Ezra D. Ehrenkranz & Assocs.

An expression of complexity, this intricate building was designed to house three theaters within and to serve one—an open-air amphitheater—without.

Near the City College campuses:

[T 11.] 135th Street Gatehouse, New Croton Aqueduct, W. 135th St. SW cor. Convent Ave. 1890.

A rock-face brownstone (top) and granite (bottom) fort. This is the end of the 12 foot-diameter **masonry aqueduct** from High Bridge [see U Manhattan 6b.]. Here the water is distributed into a **network of pipery** whose next stop is the 119th Street Gatehouse [see Morningside Heights M 4c.].

[T 12.] Hamilton Heights Historic District, generally along Convent Ave. bet. W. 141st and W. 145 Sts., including parts of Hamilton Terr., W. 140th, W. 141st, W. 142nd, W. 143rd, W. 144th, and W. 145th Sts. ★

Until the extension of elevated rapid transit up Columbus and Eighth Avenues in 1879, this was a rural area **dotted with the country houses** of the affluent. Among them was Alexander Hamilton's **Grange** on a site that is today the south side of West 143rd Street between Amsterdam and Convent Avenues.

The advent of the el brought a period of **speculative expansion** in the 1880s. Since Convent Avenue ended at West 145th Street, and

Hamilton Terrace formed **a closed loop** denying access to through traffic, this area became a protected enclave, ideally suited to **high-quality residential development.** That flurry of construction, dating from 1886 to 1906, resulted in the **picturesque row houses** which are the richness of these blocks, houses designed by architects William E. Mowbray, Adolph Hoak, William Ström, Robert Kelly, George Ebert, Henri Fouchaux, John Hauser, and the firm of Neville & Bagge. **Punctuating the horizontality** of these groups of 3- and 4-story houses **are three churches** marking **gateways** to the district: Convent Avenue Baptist, St. James Presbyterian, and St. Luke's. It was St. Luke's purchase of Hamilton's Grange that caused the Grange to be moved in 1889 to its current site, where it served as the congregation's chapel during construction of the adjacent church between 1892 and 1895.

The **romantic appearance** of the district and its varied row houses had **a special appeal** for professors and staff from neighboring City College who, after the campus opened in 1907, began to take up residence here. The area's popularity later waned, but the **brownstone revival movements** of the 1960s and 1970s have resulted in an upswing.

[T 12a.] 280-298 Convent Avenue (row houses), bet. W. 141st and W. 142nd Sts. W side. 1899–1902. Henri Fouchaux. **320-336 Convent Avenue (row houses),** bet. W. 143rd and W. 144th Sts. W side. 1890–1892. **311-339 Convent Avenue (row houses),** bet. W. 142nd and W. 144th Sts. E side. 1887–1890. Adolph Hoak. ☆

Picturesque houses all, with a profusion of ornament and roots in a variety (and intermix) of ancient styles: Flemish, Tudor, and Romanesque. Those at the north end further enhance the streetscape by being set back behind gently raised front yards.

[T 12b.] St. Luke's Church (Episcopal), Convent Ave., NE cor. W. 141st St. 1892. R. H. Robertson. ☆

A brownstone Romanesque Revival structure, massive in scale and volume, making the most of **contrasts in texture** in the working of the stone surfaces. It is unfortunate that the **monumental tower** above the arched corner doorway, which would have completed the composition, **was never finished.** Note the **stately arcade** of half-round arches across the Convent Avenue front.

[T 12c.] Hamilton Grange National Monument, 287 Convent Ave., bet. W. 141st and W. 142nd Sts. E side. 1802. John McComb, Jr. ★ ☆ **Open to the public.**

This, the **country home** of Alexander Hamilton for the last two years of his life, has been stored here since 1889 awaiting a suitable permanent site.

A **frame house** in the Federal style now bearing the cream-colored paint of the Park Service, it stands **squeezed** between St. Luke's and a group of apartment buildings, a **discomfiting posture** for so historic a structure. The interior has not been refitted for public visitation either, beyond the bland installation of some furnishings in the parlor floor rooms—a disappointment.

[T 12d.] Convent Avenue Baptist Church/originally **Washington Heights Baptist Church,** 351 Convent Ave., SE cor. W. 145th St. 1899. Lamb & Rich. ☆

This Gothic Revival church has a **checkerboard** stone facade usually associated with Romanesque Revival buildings. Squat and ungainly.

Aunt Len's Doll and Toy Museum, 6 Hamilton Terr., N of W. 141st St. W side. **Open to the public—call first.**

A former schoolteacher, Mrs. Lennon Holder Hoyte (known to everyone in the community as Aunt Len), has over her many years collected an **astounding range of dolls and toys** which cheerfully clutters every **nook and cranny** of a typical Hamilton Terrace row house.

[T 12e.] St. James Presbyterian Church and Community House/formerly **St. Nicholas Avenue Presbyterian Church,** St. Nicholas Ave., NW cor. W. 141st St. 1904. Ludlow & Valentine. ★ ☆

As the century turned, the competence and richness of Gothic Revival church architecture ebbed. This bland work's urban design value is **to mark entry** to the district to those approaching from the east, the Harlem Valley. The tower, however, is a major local landmark.

Vintage street lamp: The lazily meandering route of the old Bloomingdale Road across northern Manhattan is marked today by the diagonal of Hamilton Place. Where this street meets Amsterdam Avenue, creating the triangle of space known officially as Alexander Hamilton Square, stands an early cast-iron street lamp. It is not of the bishop's crook variety, but a more monumental version with a baronial base and two lamps rather than one. These relics can still be found infrequently throughout Manhattan. Long may they shine.

Vintage street lamp: urban sculpture   **[T 13a.]** Lower Wash. Hts. Nghbd. Ctr.

 [T 13a.] Lower Washington Heights Neighborhood Family Care Center, 1727 Amsterdam Ave., NE cor. W. 145th St. 1975. Abraham W. Geller & Assocs.

A corner plaza is the main contribution of this over-scaled salmon brick structure.

 [T 13b.] Hamilton Grange Branch, The New York Public Library, 503 W. 145th St., bet. Amsterdam Ave. and Broadway. 1906. McKim, Mead & White. ★

All the **ruffles and flourishes** of a Florentine palazzo transferred to a New York street. The same architects' later 115th Street Branch is far superior.

[T 14.] Public School 153, Manhattan, The Adam Clayton Powell, Jr. School, 1750 Amsterdam Ave., bet. W. 146th and W. 147th Sts. W side. 1975. Bureau of Design, N.Y.C. Board of Education.

Simple massing and neat brick details mark this work, **appropriately restrained;** this community is already **busy with street life** and the **ornate relics** of earlier architects.

[T 15.] Row houses, W. 147th St., bet. Broadway and Riverside Dr. S side. ca. 1900–1905.

These houses are not extraordinary, but perched **on this steep hill** they make it a special street: San Francisco in New York.

[T 16.] Originally **Temple B'nai Israel (synagogue),** 610 W. 149th St., bet. Broadway and Riverside Dr. 1920.

Limestone facade, battered walls, and a handsome verdigris-copper high dome. Although later converted to a church, it is now abandoned.

[T 17.] Church of the Crucifixion (Anglican), Convent Ave., NW cor. W. 149th St. 1967. Costas Machlouzarides.

An airfoil roof is the hat on these curved concrete forms. One can only wish the luxuriant ivy well as it encloses this overdesigned **tour de force:** a kind of **hallucinogenic version** of Le Corbusier's Ronchamp.

[T 18.] City Temple, Seventh-Day Adventists' Church/originally **Mt. Neboh Temple (synagogue)**, 564 W. 150th St., bet. Amsterdam Ave. and Broadway. 1917. Berlinger & Moscowitz.

From temple (Jewish) to temple (Christian) in a half-century. A Spanish tile roof tops this **adventure** in clinker brick masonry and intricate dark brown terra-cotta. Sober but proud.

[T 19a.] Dawn Hotel (former residence), 6 St. Nicholas Place. ca. 1888. **[T 19b.] 8 St. Nicholas Place (former residence)**, SE cor. W. 150th St. 1885.

A neglected row house (**No. 6**) adjoined by the Shingle Style **extravaganza** on the corner (**No. 8**). All in all, a curious enclave left over from the early days of urbanization. The most notable of the group is across West 150th Street:

[T 19c.] Originally James Anthony Bailey residence/now **M. Marshall Blake Funeral Home**, 10 St. Nicholas Place, NE cor. W. 150th St. 1888. Samuel B. Reed. ★

Rock-face granite **stylishly Dutch-gabled** and corner-towered. Once it was a major mansion owned by **circus entrepreneur** Bailey, who joined with showman **Phineas T. Barnum** in 1881 to form the Barnum & Bailey circus.

[T 19d.] 14 St. Nicholas Place (residence), bet. W. 150th and W. 151st Sts. E side. ca. 1890.

Another of these exuberant houses.

[T 20.] Originally Joseph Loth & Company "Fair and Square" Ribbon Factory, 1828 Amsterdam Ave., bet. W. 150th and W. 151st Sts. W side. 1886.

In 1893, *King's Handbook of New York* praised this local version of **a New England textile mill**: "Good taste and a degree of public spirit were shown by the firm in so designing the outward aspect of their establishment as to avoid the prosiness of business and keep in harmony with the surroundings." Six hundred workers produced the ribbons **known to seamstresses across the country** in 15 widths, 200 colors, and up to 90 styles. Note the radiating wings visible from the side streets.

[T 21.] Originally 32nd Precinct, N.Y.C. Police Department, 1854 Amsterdam Ave., SW cor. W. 152nd St. 1872. Nathaniel D. Bush.

A wonderful **Victorian relic**—long may it serve! Brick with brownstone graining and a dignified mansard roof trimmed with cast-iron cresting against the sky.

[T 22a.] Upper Manhattan Medical Group: reveals thoughtful window placement

[T 22a.] Upper Manhattan Medical Group, 1865 Amsterdam Ave., NE cor. W. 152nd St. 1953. Nemeny, Geller & Yurchenko.

Red brick within a gray-painted concrete grid: windows **happen where needed** rather than as part of an abstract composition. The central courtyard is an intimate sunswept delight.

[T 22b.] 473 W. 152nd Street (residence) on Old Croton Aqueduct right-of-way bet. St. Nicholas and Amsterdam Aves. ca. 1870.

A scene out of Tennessee Williams. Set way back from the street—actually behind a diagonal swath through the street grid **reserved for the Old Croton Aqueduct**—is a sagging but symmetrical clapboard villa.

Milestone: Remarkably preserved in front of the villa at 473 West 152nd Street is one of Manhattan's ancient milestones, marked 1769. It reads "9 MILES FROM N. YORK." (It was moved here from its original site, 133rd Street, in 1813.) For a display of other milestones, visit the New-York Historical Society.

[T 22c.] Dance Theatre of Harlem/formerly **garage,** 466 W. 152nd St., bet. St. Nicholas and Amsterdam Aves. ca. 1920. Altered, 1971, Hardy Holzman Pfeiffer Assocs.

An early adaptive-reuse effort by a firm of architects who **champion the ordinary** both in what they begin with and what they add. Pipes, ducts, bare lighting fixtures, old walls—all get used and, **miraculously,** become much more in the process.

[T 22d.] 456, 458, and **460 West 152nd Street (row houses),** bet. St. Nicholas and Amsterdam Aves. ca. 1890.

A trio framed by bay-windowed projections: half-cylindrical on the west, half-hexagonal on the east. **Romanesque Revival.**

[T 22e.] Wilson Major Morris Community Center of St. John's Baptist Church, 459 W. 152nd St., bet. St. Nicholas and Amsterdam Aves. 1970. Ifill & Johnson.

Before being shuttered in steel to resist the wear and tear of vandalism, this was a **modest study** in beige brick, precast exposed aggregate, and glass with a particularly neat parapet treatment. Morris was founder of **St. John's Church** across the street at **No. 448.**

[T 23a.] St. Luke A.M.E. Church (African Methodist Episcopal)/originally **Washington Heights Methodist Episcopal Church,** 1872 Amsterdam Ave., SW cor. W. 153rd St.

The **barn-red-painted church,** both of whose symmetrical spires have disappeared, and its adjacent **barn-red-painted rectory** are bright spots in the community. This is **one of four churches** along this block of West 153rd Street across from the stillness of Trinity Cemetery. The other three:

[T 23b.] Church of St. Catherine of Genoa (Roman Catholic) and Rectory, 504-506 W. 153rd St., bet. Amsterdam Ave. and Broadway. 1890. **[T 23c.] Russian Holy Fathers Church (Russian Orthodox),** 526 W. 153rd St. ca. 1925. **[T 23d.] Christ Evangelical Lutheran Church**/originally **Washington Heights German Evangelical Lutheran Church,** 544 W. 153rd St. 1896. Altered, 1921.

Across from Trinity Cemetery, it seems, is a particularly suitable place for building churches. St. Catherine's is of golden-hued brick with a **stepped gable;** its rectory is an interesting asymmetrical study. The Russian Church, **set back** some 10 feet from the adjacent housing, seems reticent to reveal its **lovely blue onion dome** surmounted by a golden, three-armed cross. The Evangelical Church has, regrettably, **seen better days.**

[T 24a.] 411-423 West 154th Street (row houses), bet. St. Nicholas and Amsterdam Aves. **[T 24b.] 883-887 St. Nicholas Avenue,** bet. W. 154th and W. 155th Sts. W side. ca. 1890.

Despite the **all-too-visible results** of Perma Stone veneer hucksters, these mansard-roofed row houses in a high-above-the-side-street setting make them **a robust addition** to the community. The magnificent elms on West 154th Street help too. The south side's row houses are newer, more reminiscent of Central Park West's park blocks.

HARLEM

> ". . . there is so much to see in Harlem."
> —Langston Hughes

To those who haven't been above 110th Street, Harlem means the black ghetto, wherever it may be. But **New York is different** from all other cities, and **its Harlem is different** from all other ghettos. This Harlem consists of a variety of contrasting little Harlems, some distinct, some overlapping. Saturday night Harlem is one place; it is a very different place on Sunday morning. There is also literary Harlem, political Harlem, religious Harlem, West Indian Harlem, black nationalist Harlem, and philanthropic Harlem.

In other cities the ghettos either radiate from the oldest and most dilapidated neighborhoods or are relegated to the wrong side of town, where they sorely lack transportation and social facilities. But Harlem became New York's black ghetto when its housing was relatively new. Here we find **churches and institutions** set on **wide boulevards** or facing **well-designed parks and plazas.** Three major subway lines give Harlem access to other parts of the city. The stores, restaurants, and hotels of 125th Street retained their largely white clientele long after the departure of the area's white population.

The railroad's powerful stone walls separate Harlem and East Harlem

The village of **Nieuw Haarlem** was established by Peter Stuyvesant in 1658 in what is now East Harlem and was connected with New Amsterdam, ten miles to the south, by a road built by the Dutch West India Company's black slaves. Eight years later the British governor, Richard Nicolls, **drew a diagonal** across Manhattan, from the East River at 74th Street to the Hudson River at 129th Street, to separate New York from Harlem, which was henceforth to be known as **Lancaster.** Early in the 19th century **James Roosevelt** cultivated a large estate along the East River before moving to Hyde Park. A country village existed at 125th Street and First Avenue.

The **opening** of the New York and Harlem Railroad in 1837 marks the beginning of Harlem's development **as a suburb for the well-to-do.** Many of the handsome brick and brownstone rows of this era still survive. The **extension of the elevated** to Harlem in 1879 was **followed by the construction** of tenement houses along the routes of the els and apartment houses—**some on a lavish scale**—along the better avenues. These were augmented by schools, clubs, theaters, and commercial buildings.

Completion of the IRT Lenox Avenue Subway in 1904 encouraged **a real estate boom** in Harlem, but many more apartments were built than could be rented, and entire buildings adjacent to Lenox Avenue near 135th Street remained unoccupied. Just at this time **the** blocks west of Herald Square, where a large part of the city's black population was living, were **being redeveloped.** The construction of Pennsylvania Station, Macy's department store, large hotels, offices, and loft buildings was forcing blacks **to seek living space** elsewhere. But in no other parts of the city were they welcome.

The black settlement in the high-prestige neighborhood of Harlem was made possible by **Philip A. Payton, Jr.** (1876–1917), a remarkable black realtor who founded the Afro-American Realty Company in 1904. Alert to both the **opportunity in Harlem** and the **desperate housing situation** in the Tenderloin, he was able to open Harlem's many vacant apartment buildings to blacks by **assuming the management** of individual buildings and **guaranteeing premium rents** to their landlords. The availability of good housing was unprecedented; the **hard-pressed black community flocked** to Payton's buildings, often paying **exorbitant rents** but, for a short while at least, **enjoying good housing.**

Renaming city streets: In the olden days, surnames of dignitaries became the official titles of city thoroughfares. In this fashion Sixth Avenue **above** Central Park became Lenox Avenue after James Lenox, philanthropist, bibliophile, and founder of what became the New York Public Library's Lenox Collection. Later, however, the style changed, to include longer names. That same Sixth Avenue **below** Central Park is officially Avenue of the Americas, though few use that title. To honor Harlem civil rights champion, provocative preacher, and flamboyant congressman Adam Clayton Powell, Jr., Seventh Avenue north of Central Park was officially proclaimed a boulevard and redubbed with **all** of Powell's names, thus creating an unwieldy mouthful for addresses or directions. Similarly, Central Park West—or Eighth Avenue, if you will—is officially Frederick Douglass Boulevard as it progresses northward to the Harlem River; and 125th Street both **East** and **West** is Martin Luther King, Jr. Boulevard. The first governor of Puerto Rico is honored by Luis Muñoz Marin Boulevard, as 116th Street east of Lexington is officially known. In the interests of simplicity, the guide uses the traditional names—as do most New Yorkers—with no offense intended.

Since Payton's day, Harlem's troubles have been due not to the area's physical shortcomings but to the **abuse and exploitation** that our society visits upon its black members. The great influx of blacks during the 1920s, instead of being allowed to spread, **was bottled up** in this one area. The **privations** of the Great Depression, the **inadequacy** of public and private measures to deal with poverty, and the **failures** of urban renewal have further burdened Harlem and its people.

In spite of exploitation, neglect, and the passing of time, **Harlem has survived** as one of New York's places of interest. Fine **patrician rows** of private houses and **excellent** churches, communal buildings, and commercial blocks—which **"progress" has erased** from more fashionable neighborhoods—**survive, neglected, in Harlem.**

Northwest of Central Park: St. Nicholas to Morningside Avenues

[H 1.] Semiramis (apartments), 137 Central Park N., bet. St. Nicholas and Seventh Aves. ca. 1905. Renovated into condominiums, 1987.

Rough-cut stone and maroon brick were combined to produce a facade which lives up to its name: **Semiramis was a mythical Assyrian queen** known for her beauty (and to whom is ascribed the building of Babylon). Unfortunately the cornice is no more.

[H 2.] Towers on the Park (apartment complex), Cathedral Pkwy. and Frederick Douglass Circle, bet. Manhattan and Frederick Douglass (Eighth) Aves. N side. 1987. Bond Ryder & James.

Condominium apartments here anchor the northwest corner of Central Park, as do the Schomburg Towers to the northeast. Crisp but bland. They bow, however, to the circle and consciously make a corner for the park.

[H 3.] Morningside Park, bet. Cathedral Pkwy. and W. 123rd St., Manhattan and Morningside Aves. and Morningside Dr. Preliminary plan, 1873. Revised plan, 1887. Both by Frederick Law Olmsted and Calvert Vaux. Western retaining wall and bays, 1882. J. Wrey Mould.

This narrow strip of park land contains **the high and rocky cliff** that **separates Harlem,** below and to the east, **from Morningside Heights,** above and to the west. It preserves a bit of **primeval Manhattan** as a dramatic foreground to the Cathedral of St. John the Divine, visible at its crest. Proposals of the mid 1960s aimed at solving both the social problems of Harlem and the space problems of the institutions on the Heights by cluttering the park with buildings. Public School 36 [see Morningside Heights M 13.] **ate away** the northwest corner of the park, and a proposed Columbia University gymnasium **was to** have usurped two additional acres of public park. The scar visible in the park is what remains of that abortive plan, canceled by the student riots of 1968.

[H 4.] Junior High School 88, Manhattan, The Lydia F. Wadleigh School, 215 W. 114th St., bet. Seventh and Eighth Aves. 1905. C. B. J. Snyder.

This red brick school is embellished with stained glass, installed when it was built as a prestige high school for girls. Later it became dense Harlem's *only* high school—this time coed.

[H 5.] 115th Street Branch, The New York Public Library, 203 W. 115th St., bet. Seventh and Eighth Aves. 1908. McKim, Mead & White. ★

Rusticated limestone, arched windows, and a carved seal of the City, guarded by a pair of angels, recall the **Pitti Palace** in Florence. One of New York's handsomest branch libraries.

[H 6.] First Corinthian Baptist Church/originally **Regent Theatre,** 1910 Seventh Ave., SW cor. W. 116th St. 1913. Thomas W. Lamb.

Venice's **Doge's Palace** adapted to the needs of the early motion picture. **S. L. Rothafel** (1882–1936), later famous as **"Roxy,"** began his career here as a picture palace impresario successfully steering the theater out of its initial, catastrophic management failings. It is now a flamboyant Hollywood set for religion.

[H 7.] Graham Court (apartments), 1923–1937 Seventh Ave., bet. W. 116th and W. 117th Sts. E side. 1901. Clinton & Russell.

Commissioned by William Waldorf Astor, this, the most luxurious apartment house in Harlem, contains 8 **elevators.** Surrounding a court, it is entered through **a splendid arched passageway,** 2 stories high. These architects later designed the Apthorp, another courtyarded apartment.

[H 7.] Graham Court apartments, anchor of an important Harlem intersection

[H 8.] St. Thomas the Apostle Church (Roman Catholic), 260 W. 118th St., SE cor. St. Nicholas Ave. 1907. Thomas H. Poole & Co.

Beserk eclecticism reminiscent of the filigrees of Milan's Cathedral or of many Flemish or Venetian fantasies. It is unnameable but wonderful.

[H 9.] Originally Schinasi Brothers Cigarette Company/now **Champ Morningside Children's Center,** 311 West 120th St., bet. Eighth and Manhattan Aves. ca. 1905.

Two **mysterious medallions** adorn this otherwise plain facade: one bears a crowned and pyramided seal of **Egyptian Prettiest;** the other displays a bas-relief bust of one Eliel Constan Tiusperpavov. The plaques relate to the original use of the structure, the manufacture of **expensive Turkish cigarettes** popular at the turn of the 20th century. The purveyors were the **Schinasi Brothers,** two of whose freestanding mansions still overlook the Hudson River from Riverside Drive.

[H 10a.] Church of the Master (United Presbyterian), 86 Morningside Ave., bet. W. 121st and W. 122nd Sts. 1972. Victor Christ-Janer and

Roger Glasgow. [H 10b.] Originally **Morningside Avenue Presbyterian Church,** 360 W. 122nd St., SE cor. Morningside Ave. 1904.

The newer building, of vertically arranged gray concrete block resembling **masonry shingling,** overshadows (stylistically) the traditional orange brick church to the north.

[H 11.] Former **Dwyer Warehouse/**originally **O'Reilly Storage Warehouse,** 258-264 St. Nicholas Ave., NE cor. W. 123rd St. 1892. Cornelius O'Reilly.

In 1915, three storage warehouses occupied this block of St. Nicholas Avenue; today only the orange brick shell of this one, and its annex on West 124th Street, remain. Note the flush quoins in contrasting red brick.

[H 12.] **28th Precinct, N.Y.C. Police Department,** 2271 Eighth Ave., bet. W. 122nd and W. 123rd Sts. to St. Nicholas Ave. 1974. Lehrecke & Tonetti.

Set in a triangular space left over after the chaotically arranged streets took their share, this carefully designed 2-story police station is **a superb architectural work** with a subtle and witty respect for materials not unlike **Louis Kahn's** late efforts.

Between Fifth and St. Nicholas Avenues to the 125th Street Corridor

[H 13a.] **Public School 208, Manhattan, The Alain L. Locke School,** 21 W. 111th St., bet. Fifth and Lenox Aves. [H 13b.] **Public School 185, Manhattan, The John Mercer Langston School,** 20 W. 112th St. Both 1968. Katz, Waisman, Weber.

A modest pair of schools in brick and exposed aggregate trim, set back to back on the through-block site. The schools are identified in **elegantly fashioned** bronze and colored porcelain enamel letters.

[H 14.] **Memorial Baptist Church/**originally **Northminster Presbyterian Church,** 141 W. 115th St., bet. Lenox and St. Nicholas Aves. 1905.

Powerful circular and arched **openings framed in limestone** set into a field of dark red and black tapestry brickwork. A **robust** facade.

[H 15.] **Malcolm Shabazz Mosque No. 7/**formerly **Muhammad's Temple of Islam/**originally **Lenox Casino,** 102 W. 116th St., SW cor. Lenox Ave. Converted to temple, 1965, Sabbath Brown.

An innocent translation of the forms of a Middle Eastern mosque into the vernacular materials of 20th-century shopping centers. The aluminum pumpkin-shaped dome is surmounted by a forever-spinning golden crescent. **Vulgar.**

[H 16.] **Refuge Temple of the Church of Our Lord Jesus Christ/** formerly **Harlem Casino,** 2081 Seventh Ave., NE cor. W. 124th St. Interior renovated, 1966, Costas Machlouzarides.

The Refuge Temple was founded in 1919 by the Reverend Robert C. Lawson, who **criticized the lack of emotionalism** in Harlem's more established churches and offered recent migrants the **fire, brimstone, and personal Christianity** with which they were familiar down South. Marble and granite **jazz.**

Frawley Circle to Mount Morris

[H 17.] **Arthur A. Schomburg Plaza (apartment complex),** E. 110th to E. 111th Sts., bet. Fifth and Madison Aves. 1975. Gruzen & Partners and Castro-Blanco, Piscioneri & Feder.

Two **handsome,** 35-story **octagonal prisms** mark the northeast corner of Central Park—Frawley Circle—intended to be an elegant traffic circle but long a backwater of gas stations and urban blight. Sharing the site are an 11-story rectangle along Madison Avenue and a one-story midblock garage podium that provides for varied outdoor activities on its **inviting wood-trellised deck.** A project of the N.Y.S. Urban Development Corporation.

[H 18.] Originally **The Brewster (apartments)/**then **The State Bank,** 1400 Fifth Ave., NW cor. W. 115th St. ca. 1897.

Furnished rooms now occupy this distinguished Renaissance Revival limestone structure. It must have been an experience **worthy of the Medicis** to enter this banking palace.

[H 19.] Originally **Engine Company No. 58, N.Y.C. Fire Department,** 81 W. 115th St., bet. Fifth and Lenox Aves. 1892. Napoleon LeBrun & Sons.

Another former firehouse, one of many designed by **the architects of the Metropolitan Life tower.** They gave an appropriate amount of attention to each.

[H 20.] Originally **The Avon (apartments),** 1770 Madison Ave., NW cor. E. 116th St. ca. 1896.

A sea of closely spaced, freely interpreted Doric columns. The upper floors are gone. Now a local church.

[H 21.] Bethel Church, once a temple   **[H 17.]** Schomburg Plaza apartments

[H 21.] Bethel Way of the Cross Church of Christ/originally **Congregation Shaari Zadek of Harlem,** 25 W. 118th St., bet. Fifth and Lenox Aves. 1900. Michael Bernstein.

Fanciful forms borrowed from Islamic architecture grace the facade of what, in another culture, might have been **a harem.** Here its beginnings were as a synagogue, later converted to church uses when demographic tides shifted. **Painted.**

The Mount Morris Area west to Lenox:

[H 22.] **Marcus Garvey Memorial Park/**formerly **Mt. Morris Park/** originally **Mt. Morris Square,** interrupting Fifth Ave. bet. 120th and 124th Sts., Madison Ave. to Mt. Morris Park W. Land purchased by the city, 1839.

Truly a mount springing out of the flat plain of central Harlem, a logical platform for the fire watchtower which still remains. The park's **unruly rocky terrain** caused it to be largely left alone by park planners until the 1960s, when two major buildings were inserted. In 1973 the **park was renamed** in honor of black leader **Marcus Garvey** (1887–1940).

[H 22a.] **Fire watchtower,** in park SW of Madison Ave. and E. 121st St. 1856. Julius Kroehl, engineer. ★

The **lone survivor** of many fire towers that once surveyed New York for signs of conflagration. The structure employs a post-and-lintel cast-iron frame similar to that used by **John Bogardus** in his warehouses.

[H 22b.] **Mt. Morris Recreation Center and Amphitheater, N.Y.C. Department of Parks & Recreation,** in park, along Mt. Morris Park W. opp. W. 122nd St. 1969. Lundquist & Stonehill.

Despite the ill-advised community-painted murals added later, this intrusion into the park is **a dignified one.**

[H 22c.] Mt. Morris Park Swimming Pool and Bathhouse, N.Y.C. Department of Parks & Recreation, in park, SW of Madison Ave. and W. 124th St. 1969. Ifill & Johnson.

This intrusion, in contrast to [H 22b.], is **crude.**

[H 23.] Mt. Morris Park Historic District, Mt. Morris Park W. to W of Lenox Ave., bet. W. 119th and W. 124th Sts. ★

Stately residences along the west flank of the hilly picturesque park, and others along the side streets, reflect the **varied Victorian styles** of the late 19th century that characterize the fabric of this small district. Interrupting the **warp and woof** are a sprinkling of fine churches and other institutional buildings which date from the area's urbanization as a fashionable and highly desirable community. Fortunately the area has **retained its architectural character** over the decades. Among the architectural firms represented in the district, in addition to those responsible for the buildings listed below, are Thom & Wilson, James E. Ware, and George F. Pelham.

[H 24.] Mt. Morris Presbyterian Church/originally **Harlem Presbyterian Church,** Mt. Morris Park W. at SW cor. W. 122nd St. 1905. T. H. Poole. ☆

By the time this Classically inspired church was built, the effects of the Chicago World's Fair's **White City** were being felt.

[H 25.] Row houses, Lenox Ave. bet. W. 120th and W. 121st Sts. E side. 1888. Demeuron & Smith. ☆

A Victorian row of 9 with distinctive mansard roofs. Of an original ten, one tooth (**No. 204)** is missing.

[H 22a.] Fire Watchtower, Garvey Park   **[H 26.]** Mount Olivet Baptist Church

[H 26.] Mt. Olivet Baptist Church/originally **Temple Israel,** 201 Lenox Ave., NW cor. W. 120th St. 1907. Arnold W. Brunner. ☆

Once one of the city's most prestigious synagogues, this neo-Roman structure dates from the period when **German Jewish** families were **taking up residence** in town houses formerly occupied by families of Dutch, English, and Irish descent. Except for the baptismal pool, the **lavish marble interior** of the synagogue **remains intact.**

 [H 27.] St. Martin's Episcopal Church and Rectory/originally **Holy Trinity Episcopal Church,** 18 W. 122nd St., SE cor. Lenox Ave. 1888. William A. Potter. ★ ☆

In the spirit of Richardsonian Romanesque but not of the quality of the style's originator. The bulky tower houses **one of America's finest carillons:** a group of 40 bells, which places it **second in size** in the city to the 74 at Riverside Church.

[H 28.] Ephesus Seventh-Day Adventist Church/formerly **Second Collegiate Church/**originally **Reformed Low Dutch Church of Harlem,** 267 Lenox Ave., NW cor. W. 123rd St. 1887. J. R. Thomas. ☆

A lofty spire makes this edifice an important Lenox Avenue landmark.

[H 29a.] Bethelite Community Baptist Church/originally **Harlem Club,** 36 W. 123rd St., SE cor. Lenox Ave. 1889. Lamb & Rich. ☆

When this splendid Romanesque Revival brick club opened it served the local elite. Today its handsome forms serve the local community as a church.

[H 27.] Sturdy St. Martin's Church   **[H 29a.]** Originally the Harlem Club

[H 29b.] Greater Bethel A.M.E. Church (African Methodist Episcopal)/originally **Harlem Free Library,** 32 W. 123rd St., bet. Mt. Morris Park W. and Lenox Ave. 1892. Lamb & Rich. ☆

This present-day religious building adjacent to the old Harlem Club was originally built to serve as one of the city's many free libraries. In 1904 it joined the New York Public Library system, and a new branch building for the area was built in 1909 at 9 West 124th Street, with **Carnegie funds.**

[H 30.] Ethiopian Hebrew Congregation/originally **John Dwight residence,** 1 W. 123rd St., NW cor. Mt. Morris Park W. 1890. Frank H. Smith. ☆

A mansion in the neo-Renaissance style, first introduced into these parts by architects McKim, Mead & White. Now occupied by **a congregation of black Jews.**

[H 31.] Originally **The Morris (apartments)/**then **Mt. Morris Bank and Safety Deposit Vaults,** 81-85 E. 125th St., NW cor. Park Ave. 1889. Lamb & Rich.

Begrimed by the incessant passage of commuter trains rattling by on the adjacent Park Avenue viaduct, this once elegant building is now **almost** restored. Look carefully—its Richardsonian Romanesque arches are there!

Northern Fifth and Madison Avenues above 125th Street:

Studio Museum in Harlem, 144 W. 125th St., bet. Lenox and Seventh Aves. **Open to the public.**

Museum and cultural center for local and national black art.

[H 32.] Mt. Moriah Baptist Church/originally **Mt. Morris Baptist Church,** 2050 Fifth Ave., bet. E. 126th and E. 127th Sts. W side. 1888. Henry F. Kilburn.

Gone are the brownstone mansions, the **gently pitched stoops** spilling out onto the **wide sidewalks,** and the **generous trees.** What remains, among other relics of Fifth Avenue above 125th Street, is this **green-gray stone** church, now even more morose in appearance than when new.

[H 33.] Metropolitan Community Methodist Church/originally **St. James Methodist Episcopal Church,** 1975 Madison Ave., NE cor. E. 126th St. 1871. **[H 33a.] Rectory,** 1981 Madison Ave. 1871.

Very proper and somber Victorian brownstone clads this Gothic Revival edifice. In **charming contrast** is the **prim,** mansarded minister's house to the north, whose **cast-iron cresting** still remains.

[H 34.] St. Andrew's Church (Episcopal), 2067 Fifth Ave., NE cor. E. 127th St. 1891. Henry M. Congdon. ★

A dour and rugged rock-face granite church whose tall clock tower is set not at the corner of the intersection but, rather, **in a more dynamic location,** against the south transept along East 127th Street. The corner, therefore, is available for a picturesque, south-facing side entrance.

[H 35.] Intermediate School 201, Manhattan, The Arthur A. Schomburg School, 2005 Madison Ave., bet. W. 127th and W. 128th Sts. 1966. Curtis & Davis.

A rectangular windowless masonry doughnut raised on concrete stilts offers **no glassy temptations** for vandals. Despite the rich brick and concrete textures with which the architects adorned the school's exterior, and though a pleasing composition in the abstract, the public space under the building is dark, oppressive, and uninviting.

[H 31.] Originally The Morris apts.   **[H 35.]** Intermediate School No. 201

Wretched refuse: On the morning of March 21, 1947, police converged on 2078 Fifth Avenue at East 128th Street in Harlem, summoned by a phone tip. There was a dead body, the caller said, in the once fashionable but now decaying brownstone row house in which the strange and reclusive Collyer brothers—Homer and Langley—had been living for 38 years. Though the search was balked by barricades of refuse, Homer's emaciated body, dressed in a tattered gray bathrobe, was soon found. In a massive manhunt for Langley, police plowed through the junk-crammed mansion, while tons of debris were carted off. Buried in the mountains of garbage were five pianos, several guns, thousands of empty bottles and cans, some 1910 pinup pictures, dressmaker's dummies, and a Model T Ford. Finally, Langley's body—smothered by debris rigged to booby-trap burglars—was extracted. It had taken almost three weeks to find it.

[H 36.] 17, 19, 21, 23, and **25 West 129th Street (row houses),** bet. Fifth and Lenox Aves. ca. 1885.

An unusual row because of its **Tudor Gothic details** executed in red brick and red unglazed terra-cotta. **No. 17** is closest to mint condition.

[H 37a.] All Saints' Church (Roman Catholic), E. 129th St. NE cor. Madison Ave. 1894. Renwick, Aspinwall & Russell. **[H 37b.] Rectory,** 47 E. 129th St. 1889. Renwick, Aspinwall & Russell. **[H 37c.] School,** 52 E. 130th St. 1904. W. W. Renwick.

The best of Harlem's ecclesiastical groupings. The Gothic tracery and terra-cotta ribboning of the buff, honey-colored, and brown brick wall surfaces make **a confection** of these related buildings designed by the successor firms of James Renwick, Jr. Its patterned brickwork is reminiscent of Siena.

[H 38.] St. Ambrose Church (Episcopal)/originally **Church of the Puritans (Presbyterian),** 15 W. 130th St., bet. Fifth and Lenox Aves. 1875.

The original name of this rock-face granite Gothic Revival structure came **as the price** of its construction: **a gift was proferred** with the condition that the congregation (then the Second Presbyterian Church of Harlem) **take on the name** of the Church of the Puritans, which had just sold its lease on Union Square. The gift—and name—were accepted.

The 125th Street Corridor: Lenox to Eighth Avenues

[H 39.] 125th Street Medical Building/originally **H. C. F. Koch & Company (dry goods store),** 132-140 W. 125th St., bet. Lenox and Seventh Aves. 1893. William H. Hume & Son. Altered.

This was the first of the old established **dry goods merchants** of lower Sixth Avenue to move northward. It moved **too far;** its success as Harlem's chief department store lasted **only some 30 years.** Its name remains in the building's pediment.

[H 40.] Harlem State Office Building, 163 W. 125th St., NE cor. Seventh Ave. 1973. Ifill Johnson Hanchard.

Built to provide a state resource and symbol within the Harlem community, this monumental work set in a monumental plaza was a tangible outgrowth of 1960s racial unrest. It is a second cousin to Albany's Empire State Plaza **edifice complex**—both architecturally and politically.

[H 39.] Orig. Koch & Company store   [H 40.] Harlem State Office Building

[H 41.] Theresa Towers (office building)/originally **Hotel Theresa,** 2090 Seventh Ave., bet. W. 124th and W. 125th Sts. W side. ca. 1910. George & Edward Blum. Altered, 1971.

Long **a favored meeting spot** in Harlem, the Theresa attracted Cuba's Prime Minister **Fidel Castro** as his New York hotel when he visited the U.N. in 1960. **Khrushchev** came to Harlem to visit *him.* It has since been converted to office use.

[H 42.] M. W. King Solomon Grand Lodge, A.F. & A.M. and **Star of Hope Grand Chapel, D.E.S. (Masonic temple)/**originally **Alhambra Theater,** 2114 Seventh Ave., SW cor. W. 126th St. 1905. J. B. McElfatrick & Co. Altered, 1976. Alterations, 1988, Beyer Blinder Belle and Roger Glasgow.

A Beaux Arts tour de force in Flemish-bond brick and fancifully mixed terra-cotta ornaments by a firm of well-known theater architects. Now in limbo.

[H 43.] Sydenham Hospital Clinic/originally **Commonwealth Building,** 215 W. 125th St., bet. Seventh and Eighth Aves. 1971. Hausman & Rosenberg.

Developed jointly by a local community group (black and Puerto Rican) and a suburban real estate company (white), this crisp, white concrete, precast facade is a happy addition to West 125th Street. The rear facade, on West 126th, is less pretentious but equally handsome.

[H 43.] The Commonwealth Office Building was a welcome newcomer to Harlem

[H 43a.] Apollo Theatre, 253 W. 125th St., bet. Seventh and Eighth Aves. 1914. George Keister. ★ Interior ★.

Although it dates from 1914, the Apollo, at 253 West 125th Street, did not become one of Harlem's high spots until 1934. That year the old **Hurtig & Seaman Theatre,** with a white-only admissions policy, was taken over by Leo Brecher and Frank Schiffman, who renamed it the Apollo and opened its doors to the black community. Since then it has been known as **the** Harlem showplace for black entertainers. For years it was the attraction that drew white audiences to Harlem. **Bessie Smith,** America's "Empress of the Blues," appeared that first year, followed by other blues singers such as **Billie Holiday** and **Dinah Washington.** Huddie **(Leadbelly)** Ledbetter sang from its stage in the 1930s shortly after doing time for intent to murder. **Duke Ellington's** sophisticated style and **Count Basie**'s raw-edged rhythms filled the house later. Following World War II bebop had its fling: the names of **Charlie (Bird) Parker, Dizzy Gillespie, Thelonius Monk,** and, more recently, such entertainers as **Gladys Knight** and **Aretha Franklin** have glittered on its marquee. Beginning in the 1980s it has had another cultural renaissance.

[H 44.] Originally Pabst Concert Hall, 243-251 W. 124th St., bet. Seventh and Eighth Aves. ca. 1900.

Though the entrance to this concert hall was originally on bustling 125th Street, the **fantastic arched roof** is best seen from the rear on 124th. Note how the curve of the roof is expressed by the brick facade.

North of 125th Street: Schomburg Center, Strivers' Row, Sugar Hill

[H 45.] Originally Methodist Third Church of Christ/now **Baptist House of Prayer,** 80 W. 126th St., bet. Fifth and Lenox Aves. 1889.

This converted building and its neighbors make a fine Romanesque Revival combination. The columns at the roof are vigorous.

[H 46.] **Metropolitan Baptist Church/**originally **New York Presbyterian Church,** 151 W. 128th St., NE cor. Seventh Ave. 1884. John R. Thomas. ★ Auditorium, 1890, Richard R. Davis.

A rock-face white stone edifice, **enlivened at the entrance** by polished orange granite columns bearing Romanesque **"Afro" capitals** and, over the side chapel, by a majestic half-cone of a roof.

[H 47.] **Salem United Methodist Church/**originally **Calvary Methodist Episcopal Church,** Seventh Ave. NW cor. W. 129th St. 1887. Enlarged, 1890.

This church once had the largest Protestant church auditorium and membership in the city. The simple brick structure is embellished by a **carefully detailed** bell tower and **splendid arched paneled** doors.

[H 48.] **The Astor Block (row houses),** 8-62 W. 130th St., bet. Fifth and Lenox Aves. S side. 1883. Charles Buck. ★

Three-story brick, single-family row houses with wooden porches and large front and side yards. A **restrained beauty** which has been tarnished by years of economic distress. Opposite is an almost intact terrace of brownstones.

[H 46.] Metropolitan Baptist Church/originally New York Presbyterian Church

[H 49.] **Row houses,** W. 130th St. bet. Lenox and Seventh Aves. N and S sides. ca. 1885–1890.

Two wonderful rows of brownstones flank this street, many displaying their original stoops and cast-iron balustrades, which were once painted to simulate brownstone. Large trees contribute to the **enviable** environmental qualities.

[H 50.] **Lionel Hampton Houses (apartments),** 273 W. 131st St., NE cor. Eighth Ave., 201 W. 130th St., NW cor. Eighth Ave., 410 St. Nicholas Ave., bet. W. 130th and W. 131st Sts. 1974. Bond Ryder Assocs.

One tall and two low apartment buildings, as well as a 2-story retail/office structure, make up this **appealing** masonry composition, which straddles an irregular site on both sides of St. Nicholas Avenue. Note how the L-shaped window openings and the through-wall air-conditioners develop a pattern, which then becomes the **dominant theme** of the facades.

Liberation Bookstore, Lenox Ave. NW cor. W. 131st St.

A bookshop that prides itself, rightfully, on its stock of books related to black history and black studies.

[H 51a.] **Williams Christian Methodist Episcopal Church/**formerly **Lafayette Theatre,** 2225 Seventh Ave., bet. W. 131st St. and W. 132nd St. E side. ca. 1910.

Since 1951 this church has occupied this 3-building complex, **origi-nally designed** as a complete **neighborhood entertainment center,** with a large theater, ballroom, restaurant, tavern, public meeting rooms, and offices. For three decades the Lafayette was the nation's leading black theater. The critically acclaimed production of *Darktown Follies* (1913) is credited with having started the vogue of outsiders' coming to Harlem for entertainment.

[H 51b.] Site of the Tree of Hope, center island of Seventh Ave. at W. 131st St. N side.

The tree which once grew in the middle of the avenue across from the old Lafayette Theater is gone, as is its replacement contributed by dancer **Bill "Bojangles" Robinson** (1878–1949)—see his bronze plaque set into the pavement!

[H 52.] St. Aloysius' Roman Catholic Church, 209 W. 132nd St., bet. Seventh and Eighth Aves. 1904. W. W. Renwick.

Deep purple brickwork and pale green glazed brick trim harmo-nize with terra-cotta that **resembles Belgian lace.** Together they pro-duce an evocative and delicate facade, evocative of the exuberant **Certosa** at Pavia.

 [H 53.] Engine Company No. 59, Ladder Company, No. 30, N.Y.C. Fire Department, 111 W. 133rd St., bet. Lenox and Seventh Aves. 1962. Giorgio Cavaglieri.

Perhaps fashionable in its time, this **bright red glazed brick** plus **Miesian-framed** firehouse negates the more enduring architectural val-ues of its older tenement neighbors, with their richly worked, twisted steel fire-escape railings and intricate cut-stone plinths.

Beale Street: Life in Harlem stimulated the curiosity of outsiders for the forbidden, particularly during the Roaring Twenties. Exploiters ar-ranged specially trumped-up visits (for those who could pay) to see what was ballyhooed as "the primitive essence of Harlem Life." The night spots along West 133rd Street between Lenox and Seventh Avenues, such as Dickie Wells', Mexico's, Pod's and Jerry's, and the Nest, were in the center of such activity. A similarity to Beale Street in Memphis, made famous by black composer and blues compiler W. C. Handy, caused the name to be popularly applied to the street in Harlem. The Great Depression curtailed most of these goings-on.

 [H 54a.] St. Philip's Church (Episcopal), 214 W. 134th St., bet. Sev-enth and Eighth Aves. 1911. Vertner W. Tandy and George W. Foster.

This spare, northern Gothic church in salmon-colored Roman brick, was founded in the notorious **Five Points** section of the Lower East Side in 1809. A century later it was able to sell its properties in the Tenderloin for almost $600,000. With this **windfall** the church **pur-chased its present site,** as well as a row of 10 apartment houses on West 135th Street previously restricted to whites. When the congregation began its move to Harlem, white tenants living in the apartment houses were evicted, and their places were made available to blacks.

The church design was a collaborative effort of **two black ar-chitects;** Vertner W. Tandy was **the first black** to be granted an **architec-tural registration** in New York State.

[H 54b.] Public School 92, Manhattan, The Mary McCleod Bethune School, 222 W. 134th St., bet. Seventh and Eighth Aves. 1965. Perci-val Goodman.

A **gentle blend** of creamy cast-in-place concrete framing, Hudson River red brick, and yellow-ocher of exposed aggregate precast span-drels make for **a thoughtful design** with **no architectural fireworks** employed. It has not worn too well.

 [H 55a.] Schomburg Center for Research in Black Culture, The New York Public Library, 515 Lenox Ave., bet. W. 135th and W. 136th Sts. W side. 1978. Bond Ryder Assocs. **[H 55b.]** Originally housed in the **135th Street Branch,** 103 W. 135th St., bet. Lenox and Seventh Aves. 1905. McKim, Mead & White. ★

The 135th Street library was the **unofficial headquarters** of the **black literary renaissance** of the 1920s. Arthur A. Schomburg (1874–1938), a Puerto Rican black, privately undertook the task of **collecting the raw materials of black American history,** which were then in danger of loss through neglect by the academic community. In 1926 the **Carnegie Corporation** of New York **purchased the collection** and had it deposited here with **Schomburg** himself **as curator.** In 1972 the Schomburg Collection was formally renamed as a research center.

In 1978 the long-awaited Schomburg Center opened with proper facilities for storing, conserving, and disseminating the archive's treasures.

[H 55c.] Countee Cullen Branch, The New York Public Library, 104 W. 136th St., bet. Lenox and Seventh Aves. 1942. Louis Allen Abramson. Restored, 1988.

This Art Moderne library, named for a poet of the Harlem Renaissance, **Countee Cullen,** was built as an extension to the original home of the Schomburg Center [see H 55a. and H 55b.].

Madame C. J. Walker: Born to freed slaves shortly after the Civil War, this enterprising promoter rose from washerwoman to become reputedly the richest black woman in New York, through the development and sale of hair-straightening products. Her home and adjacent hair parlor occupied the site on which the Countee Cullen Branch Library was built. She died in 1919 in Irvington, N.Y., where she had bought a house on the main street—to the consternation of her white neighbors.

[H 56.] Harlem Branch, YMCA, 180 W. 135th St., bet. Lenox and Seventh Aves. 1932. James C. Mackenzie, Jr.

A stately red-brown brick Y not to be confused with its 1919 vintage predecessor across the street. Note the pair of **broken-pediment** entranceways built from the same brick.

[H 57.] Row houses, W. 136th and W. 137th Sts. bet. Seventh and Eighth Aves. ca. 1895–1905.

A row house flock equal to any of the Upper West Side's park blocks—except that **these are in Harlem.** The ones on West 136th Street are a few years older.

[H 58.] Row houses, 26-46 Edgecombe Ave., bet. W. 136th and W. 137th Sts. E side, and 321 W. 136th St., bet. Edgecombe and Eighth Aves. ca. 1885.

Victoriana set along a triangular intersection (Dorrence Brooks Square), the backdrop for which is St. Nicholas Park. Before the park's greenery was cut back to provide mediocre recreation space, the contrast between nature and architecture must have been vivid. **No. 26** at the corner of West 136th Street, though down at the heels, is particularly noteworthy. Bay windows enliven the masonry facades.

[H 59a.] Union Congregational Church/originally **Rush Memorial A.M.E. Zion Church (African Methodist Episcopal),** 60 W. 138th St., bet. Fifth and Lenox Aves. ca. 1910. **[H 59b.] St. Mark's Roman Catholic Church/**originally **Church of St. Mark the Evangelist,** 65 W. 138th St. 1908.

A curious juxtaposition on opposite sides of the street: two small pinkish red-painted brick churches trimmed with Gothic-style light-colored stone, each with a pair of ornately fashioned wood entrance doors.

[H 60.] Abyssinian Baptist Church, 132 W. 138th St., bet. Lenox and Seventh Aves. 1923. Charles W. Bolton.

A random ashlar "Princeton Gothic" church, **a landmark** in Harlem due to the charisma, power, and notoriety of its spellbinding preacher, **Adam Clayton Powell, Jr.** (1908–1972). Powell's **reform accomplishments** while a member of the House of Representatives, **and his flamboyance** were known across the country. The church has established **a memorial room,** open to the public, containing artifacts from his life. Call before you visit.

[H 61.] Casino Renaissance, 2351 Seventh Ave., SE cor. W. 138th St. ca. 1925.

The casino and adjacent theater constitute a commercial community center, combining a great variety of entertainments. In disrepair.

[H 62.] St. Nicholas Historic District (The King Model Houses), generally W. 138th to W. 139th Sts., bet. Seventh and Eighth Aves., including 202-250 W. 138th St. and 2350-2354 Seventh Ave. 1891. James Brown Lord. 203-271 W. 138th St., 202-272 W. 139th St., and 2360-2378 Seventh Ave. 1891. Bruce Price and Clarence S. Luce. 203-267 W. 139th St. and 2380-2390 Seventh Ave. 1891. McKim, Mead & White. ★

By the time David H. King, Jr. built these **distinguished row houses and apartments,** he had already been widely **recognized as the builder** responsible for the old **Times Building** of 1889 on Park Row, Stanford White's **Madison Square Garden,** and the base of the **Statue of Liberty.** Displaying rare vision, King commissioned the services of three different architects at one time to develop this group of **contiguous blocks** for the well-to-do. The results are **an urbane grouping** reflecting the differing tastes of the architects: all with similar scale, varied but harmonious materials, and related styles—Georgian-inspired in the two southern blocks, neo-Italian Renaissance in McKim, Mead & White's northern group. In addition, they share **the amenity of rear alleys** with entrances from the side streets. No wonder they were so prized by their original, white, occupants.

As Harlem became **first a refuge for blacks** and **then a ghetto,** the homes and apartments **retained their prestige** and attracted (by 1919) many ambitious as well as successful blacks in medicine, dentistry, law, and the arts (such as W. C. Handy, Noble Sissle, and Eubie Blake). As a result, **Strivers' Row** became a popular term for the district in the 1920s and 1930s.

[H 54b.] Public School 92, Manhattan   [H 63.] West 139th Street Playground

[H 62a.] Victory Tabernacle Seventh-Day Christian Church/originally **Equitable Life Assurance Company,** 252 W. 138th St., bet. Seventh and Eighth Aves. 1895. Jardine, Kent & Jardine.

Ill-advised signs and billboards fail to conceal this **Moorish temple.** It was built **to sell life insurance** to residents of this newly opened "suburb" of Harlem, particularly **to** those living in the King Model Houses.

[H 63.] West 139th Street Playground, N.Y.C. Department of Parks & Recreation, Lenox Ave. bet. W. 139th and W. 140th Sts. W side. 1971. Coffey, Levine & Blumberg, architects and landscape architects. Henri A. LeGendre, consultant. Mural, 1971. Children's Art Carnival. Repainted, 1976.

One of **the most successful reconstructions** of an existing City playground. The space has been modulated, the levels altered, and play equipment introduced in a confident way which responds to the needs of a typically diverse community. Missing are **cutesy-pie forms** or **bomb shelter boldness:** a model for the future. Thanks go to the *Reader's Digest* people for their funding.

[H 64.] St. Charles Borromeo Church (Roman Catholic), 211 W. 141st St., bet. Seventh and Eighth Aves. 1888. Altered, 1973, L. E. Tuckett & Thompson.

The destruction of the nave by fire provided the opportunity for contemporary reuse by building a **modern miniature sanctuary** within the walls of the original. Limestone and brick neo-Gothic.

[H 65.] Harlem School of the Arts, 645 St. Nicholas Ave., N of W. 141st St. W side. 1977. Ulrich Franzen & Assocs.

A distinguished Harlem institution, once housed next door at St. James' Presbyterian Church Community House. It now occupies its own **intricately programmed building,** nuzzled against the **craggy hillside** of Hamilton Terrace's backyards.

[H 66.] Row houses, Bradhurst Ave., bet. W. 143rd and W. 145th Sts. W side. ca. 1888.

Stoop removal and general lack of maintenance have hurt this **inventive row** of Victorian houses. Nevertheless their wit prevails.

[H 67.] Jackie Robinson Play Center/originally **Colonial Play Center (swimming pool and bathhouse),** in Jackie Robinson (formerly Colonial) Park, Bradhurst Ave. bet. W. 145th and W. 147th Sts. W side. 1936. N.Y.C. Parks Department. Aymar Embury II, consulting architect.

The **most dramatic** of the city's WPA-built pools. Cylindrical volumes squeeze the abutting sidewalk and alternate with an assortment of half-round arches. These spring from varied Romanesque-inspired capitals to create **a powerful statement** in bold, red brick masonry worthy of its Roman aqueduct (hence "Romanesque") forebears. The **confident design** of this outdoor natatorium **overcomes the shortcomings** of its unskilled masons: bricks in some archways bunch up as they reach their crests, giving them almost the shape of a pointed arch. This free diversity of embellishment and unevenness in craftsmanship appropriately echoes the Romanesque style.

Sugar Hill: The model of the sweet life in Harlem was identified, between the 1920s and 1950s, with a stretch of Edgecombe Avenue west of (and overlooking) the escarpment of Colonial Park and the Harlem Valley below. The multiple dwellings which line Edgecombe above West 145th Street as it ascends Coogan's Bluff were the accommodations to which upwardly mobile blacks aspired and in which those who had achieved fame lived: Cab Calloway, Duke Ellington, Walter White, Roy Wilkins, Thurgood Marshall, W. E. B. DuBois, Langston Hughes. Down by the Harlem River, the Flats below the Hill, were the old Polo Grounds, where the New York Giants once played; now a housing project.

Riverbend, Dunbar, and Harlem Houses:

[H 68.] Riverbend Houses (apartments), Fifth Ave. bet. E. 138th and E. 142nd Sts. E side. 1967. Davis, Brody & Assocs.

Social and aesthetic concerns meld into a single, eminently successful apartment development **respectful of street lines** along Fifth Avenue. Dense, compact, and of imaginatively used vernacular materials, it has 625 apartments in the sky for moderate-income families. The tall end towers consist of flats; the 8- and 10-story structures in between contain duplexes reached by outdoor passages which provide tenants with **semiprivate terraces** overlooking the Harlem River. **A monumental breakthrough** in urban, publicly subsidized housing.

[H 68.] A renaissance of publicly assisted housing started at Riverbend Houses

A revolution in brick began at Riverbend Houses as a result of the skyrocketing costs of laying brick following World War II. To achieve economy and to introduce a new scale in exterior masonry units, architects Davis, Brody & Assocs. developed the giant brick (5½″ high × 8″ wide) first used at Riverbend.

[H 69.] 369th Regiment Armory, N.Y. National Guard, 2366 Fifth Ave., bet. W. 142nd and W. 143rd Sts. W side. 1923. Van Wart & Wein. ★

A superb example of the bricklayer's art. In this case the mason's efforts are in **deep purpley-red** and exhibit a Moderne style rather than an attempt to reconstruct a medieval fortress.

[H 70.] Dunbar Apartments, 2588 Seventh Ave., bet. W. 149th and W. 150th Sts. to Eighth Ave. 1928. Andrew J. Thomas. ★

Named for black poet **Paul Laurence Dunbar** (1872–1906), these 6 apartment buildings, grouped around a landscaped inner court, have been **home to such notables as** Countee Cullen, W. E. B. DuBois, A. Philip Randolph, Bill "Bojangles" Robinson—and Matt Henson, who, as part of the Peary expedition, was the first westerner to set foot upon the North Pole in 1909. Financier John D. Rockefeller, Jr. conceived the project **to be a model for solving Harlem's housing problem;** under the pressures of the Great Depression, however, he finally foreclosed his mortgages and sold the property. It has been a rental development ever since.

[H 71.] Harlem River Houses, N.Y.C. Housing Authority, bet. W. 151st and W. 153rd Sts., Macombs Place and Harlem River Dr. 1937. Archibald Manning Brown, chief architect in association with Charles F. Fuller, Horace Ginsbern, Frank J. Forster, Will Rice Amon, Richard W. Buckley, John L. Wilson. Michael Rapuano, landscape architect. Heinz Warnecke, assisted by T. Barbarossa, R. Barthé, F. Steinberger, sculptors. ★

Riots in Harlem in 1935 precipitated the planning and design of this, **the city's first** federally funded, federally owned, and federally built housing project. Writing in 1938 of the 4-story apartment buildings, grouped around open landscaped courts embellished with sculpture, **Lewis Mumford** exuberantly stated that the project offers "the equipment for decent living that every modern neighborhood needs: sunlight, air, safety, play space, meeting space, and living space. The families in the Harlem Houses have higher standards of housing, measured in tangible benefits, than most of those on Park Avenue." Perhaps he was being too exuberant.

EAST HARLEM

East Harlem, once **Italian Harlem,** is today **Spanish Harlem.** Unlike Central Harlem, it was **never a prestigious** residential district: its remaining older housing stock **reveals** its **working-class beginnings.** For over a century it has been the home of laborer immigrants and their families, including large German, Irish, Jewish, and Scandinavian populations. The sizable Italian community, now virtually gone, sank its roots here prior to 1890. Today, East Harlem is **El Barrio, "the neighborhood,"** overwhelmingly Puerto Rican in population, heritage, and culture, whose first settlers came here around the time of **World War I.**

From the ubiquitous family-owned **bodegas,** or grocery stores, found on practically every street, to **El Museo del Barrio,** the sophisticated local museum on Fifth Avenue, East Harlem is **an important link** to the unique traditions of a significant and growing number of Hispanic residents.

[E 1.] Baum-Rothschild Staff Pavilion, Mt. Sinai Medical Center, 1249 Park Ave., SE cor. E. 97th St. 1968. Pomerance & Breines.

A snappy, slender tower with balconies that presides over the portal of the Park Avenue tunnel into Grand Central Terminal.

[E 2.] Long-Term Care Facility, Florence Nightingale Nursing Home, 1760 Third Ave., bet. E. 97th and E. 98th Sts. 1974. William N. Breger Assocs.

Confident sculptural handling here of the oversize-brick massing produced a physical asset to the streetscape.

[E 3.] Electrical substation, N.Y.C. Transit Authority/originally **Manhattan Railway Company,** 1782 Third Ave., SW cor. E. 99th St. ca. 1902.

The two blocks between East 98th and 99th Streets stretching from Third Avenue west to Park are today the site of the apartment towers of Lexington Houses. In 1879 they were occupied by the **newly built 99th Street yard** of the Manhattan Railway Company's **Third Avenue el.** It was **not until** 1902 that **electric-powered** elevated trains were first used—until then the trains pulled by **smoke-belching miniature steam locomotives**—had been creating **the need for substations** such as this. **All that remains** of the elevated railway is this grimy but handsome orange brick structure and a stretch of rough stone retaining wall on East 98th Street.

[E 4.] MaBSTOA Bus Garage/once **Metropolitan Street Railway Company (trolley barn),** E. 99th to E. 100th Sts., Lexington to Park Aves. ca. 1885.

Try to imagine this building in 1907, perhaps the heyday of trolley transportation in Manhattan, when its owner, the Metropolitan Street Railway Company, controlled **47 streetcar lines** and **300 miles of track.** That year its 3,280 cars handled 571 million passengers—not all from this barn, thank goodness—which limited its activities only to the Lexington Avenue and the Lexington-Lenox Avenue lines. Today the brick structure, minus tracks, serves as a **considerably less colorful** diesel bus garage. The **acronym** is for Manhattan and Bronx Surface Transit Operating Authority.

[E 5.] Church of the Resurrection, East Harlem Protestant Parish, 325 E. 101st St., bet. First and Second Aves. 1965. Victor A. Lundy.

A windowless painted brick pillbox, somewhere between a fallout shelter and a Maginot Line fortress. Designed for a setting among grimy tenements, most of which have since been demolished, **its starkness was meant as a bold and powerful contrast.** Today it seems contrived, sitting like a cocked hat among vacant lots. Economy dictated the substitution of a built-up roof for the planned brick pavers. The interior is more inviting.

[E 6a.] Metro North Plaza/Riverview Apartments, bet. E. 100th and E. 102nd Sts., First Ave. and FDR Drive. 1976. **[E 6b.] Public School 50, Manhattan, The Vito Marcantonio School.** 1975. Both by Conklin & Rossant.

Exposed cast-concrete frames with ribbed-block infill make **high-rise and low-rise** housing here arranged in **a chaste, symmetrical pattern.** The school, approached on a ramp at the far east end of the complex, makes a **dramatic statement** within the discipline of the same materials. A combined effort of the state's Urban Development Corporation and the city's Educational Construction Fund.

The painted bridge: All structural steel bridges must be painted regularly to protect their vulnerable surfaces against corrosion. It is rare, however, that the colors chosen vary much from gunmetal gray or bureaucratic green. Fortunately for all of us, the idea that bridges could be painted richer, happier colors struck architects William Conklin and James Rossant just as the Wards Island Pedestrian Bridge—over the East River above Metro North—was up for periodic rehueing. In 1976 the bridge came out blue-violet (towers), cadmium yellow (walkway), and vermillion (trim), making it urban sculpture of the finest sort. A spectacular improvement! Now repainted with more sober blue and green towers, and a blue span.

[E 6a. & 6b.] Metro North Plaza apartments and the contiguous public school

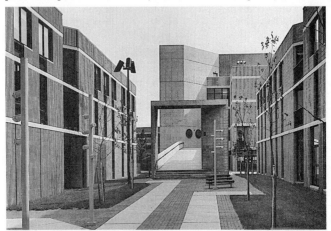

[E 7.] Combined police/fire stations   **[E 8.]** Smotrich & Platt's Exodus Hse.

[E 7.] 23rd Precinct, N.Y.C. Police Department, and **Engine Company No. 53, Ladder Company No. 43, 4th Division, N.Y.C. Fire Department,** 1834 Third Ave., SW cor. E. 102nd St. 1974. Milton F. Kirchman.

A sloping site and a combination of clients—the Police Department, the Fire Department, and the Department of Public Works, the city's coordinating agency—gave rise to this **three-dimensional cubist composition.**

[E 8.] Exodus House, 309 E. 103rd St., bet. First and Second Aves. 1968. Smotrich & Platt.

A **spartan work** in the style of the **New Brutalism.** No fancy materials or details in this nonprofit drug-treatment center, no sanctimonious messages in its simple forms. **Gutsy** but badly deteriorated.

[E 9a.] The Church of the Living Hope, 161 E. 104th St., bet. Lexington and Third Aves. Altered, ca. 1969. **[E 9b.]** Originally **Engine Company No. 53, N.Y.C. Fire Department,** 179 E. 104th St. ca. 1898. **[E 9c.] Hope Community Hall**/originally **29th Precinct, N.Y.C. Police Department,** 177 E. 104th St. 1884.

A **curious trio** of buildings, two of which began as the area's fire and police outposts. The **explosive expansion** of the City's construction program in the 1960s and 1970s replaced them [see E 7.] and **enabled reuse** as a community amenity. The ogee curves in the wrought-iron balconies on the police station are lovely.

[E 10.] Park East High School/originally **Manhattan School of Music,** 230-240 E. 105th St., bet. Second and Third Aves. 1928. Donn Barber. Additions, Francis L. Mayer.

A **refined set of facades** as befits an institution dedicated to fine music, the Manhattan School of Music. That institution moved to Morningside Heights **in a game of musical chairs** with the Juilliard School of Music, which moved to Lincoln Center.

[E 11a.] St. Cecilia's Church (Roman Catholic), 120 E. 106th St., bet. Park and Lexington Aves. 1887. Napoleon LeBrun & Sons.

This ornately embellished facade is one of East Harlem's **special treasures.** The material of the facade is primarily glazed terra-cotta **worked with great skill and imagination.** The facade is enhanced by a huge bas-relief of St. Cecilia as a youthful organist.

[E 11b.] Originally Public School 72   [E 14.] Aguilar Branch, N.Y. Pub. Lib.

[E 11b.] Harlem Council for Community Improvement/formerly **Massive Economic Neighborhood Development (MEND)**/originally **Public School 72, Manhattan**/then **Public School 107,** 1680 Lexington Ave., bet. E. 105th and E. 106th Sts. W side. ca. 1892.

Patterned brickwork and a handsome tower give **solidity and authority** to this venerable onetime schoolhouse, while paint hides its age.

[E 12.] Franklin Plaza Cooperative/originally **Franklin Houses, N.Y.C. Housing Authority,** bet. E. 106th St. and E. 108th St., First and Third Aves. 1959. Holden, Egan, Wilson & Corser. Plaza and play areas altered, 1961, Mayer & Whittlesey.

One of **the most graceful groups** of residential towers of its period and patrimony in Manhattan. First intended as subsidized public housing, this development became a cooperative under the auspices of community groups. The gardens and play areas were later redesigned in an early attempt to enrich the ground plane.

[E 13.] 1199 Plaza (apartment complex), bet. E. 107th and E. 110th Sts., First Ave. and FDR Drive, plus extension to E. 111th St. along the

Drive. 1975. The Hodne/Stageberg Partners, architects. Herb Baldwin, landscape architect.

Four U-shaped red brick configurations each step down from 32-story towers of flats to 10-, 8-, and 6-story wings of duplexes, to house humanely a high density of residents, 450 to the acre. The complex achieves **an effective though not impolite** separation between public entry and shopping space along First Avenue and the varied outdoor spaces overlooking the East River, areas that the cooperator-tenants and their guests may enjoy in comparative privacy and safety. Curiously enough, this **very handsome project**—make sure to see it both from First Avenue and from FDR Drive—was designed by a Minneapolis architectural firm on the basis of its winning entry (not used) in a 1963 architectural competition to develop the site. Twelve years of redesign, red tape, and construction resulted in one of the city's **most impressive and most livable** works of multifamily housing. Incidentally, 1199 is not an address but the name of the project's sponsors, **District 1199** of the National Union of Hospital and Health Care Employees, AFL-CIO.

[E 13.] 1199 Plaza cooperative housing, a distinguished competition winner

 [E 14.] Aguilar Branch, The New York Public Library, 174 E. 110th St., bet. Lexington and Third Aves. 1899. Expanded and new facade added, 1905. Both by Herts & Tallant.

A **triumphal gateway to knowledge,** 3 stories high, replaces an earlier and even better one, half as wide, by the same architects. The present one comprises **two monumentally scaled Classical columns** and a cornice framing a 20th-century cast-iron multistory facade within. Originally founded in 1886 as an independent library to serve immigrant Jews (**Grace Aguilar** was an English novelist of Sephardic descent), it was brought into the New York Public Library system and expanded by a Carnegie gift. It now serves a newer, Hispanic population.

[E 15.] "La Marqueta" (enclosed market), under Park Ave. railroad viaduct bet. E. 111th and E. 115th Sts.

A **hothouse of small merchants.** Under rumbling commuter trains is one of the most **colorful, fast-moving, fragrant, and boisterous** of New York's **commercial pageants.** A mecca for both bargain hunters and those who love to bargain. It is under new renovation.

[E 16a.] James Weldon Johnson Houses, N.Y.C. Housing Authority, bet. E. 112th and E. 115th Sts., Third to Park Aves. 1948. Julian Whittlesey, Harry M. Prince, and Robert J. Reiley.

Within the genre of publicly assisted housing projects of the 1940s and 1950s (of which a cluster can be seen from First all the way to Lenox Avenues) this is **one of the best.** Well-proportioned buildings of varying heights and a large plaza, small courts, and sculpture all contribute to the quality.

[E 16b.] Public School 57, Manhattan, The James Weldon Johnson School, 176 E. 115th St., SW cor. Third Ave. 1964. Ballard, Todd & Snibbe.

An overhanging cornice, generous small-paned windows, and molded bricks make this school a warm, safe, and friendly place. The scale of this building **would enhance and respect** a block of row houses; but in its present setting, amid large housing projects, its attention to scale is largely unnoticed.

[E 17a.] St. Paul's Church (Roman Catholic), 121 E. 117th St., bet. Park and Lexington Aves. **[E 17b.] Rectory,** 113 E. 117th St. Both 1908. Neville & Bagge.

The handsome towers contribute to this especially fine church, a very late Romanesque Revival design.

[E 18.] Assemblea de Iglesia Pentecostal de Jesucristo/originally **First German Baptist Church of Harlem,** 220 E. 118th St., bet. Second and Third Aves. ca. 1895.

An **ebullient** facade with a wide, inviting half-round arch entrance now painted cream and brown.

[E 19.] Iglesia Luterana Sion/originally **St. Johannes Kirche (Lutheran),** 217 E. 119th St., bet. Second and Third Aves. 1873.

An early masonry church for this community, which was then remote from the city's center. The church began as a home for a German-speaking congregation; today it serves those who speak Spanish.

[E 20.] Harlem Courthouse, 170 E. 121st St., SE cor. Sylvan Place bet. Lexington and Third Aves. 1893. Thom & Wilson. ★

This handsome brick and stone courthouse is **a model** 1890s **palace** of justice, now used for far more humble government functions. A rich array of forms (gables, archways, the imposing corner tower) and materials (water-struck red brick, bluestone, granite, terra-cotta, and copper) make this fine work both **a Landmark** and **a landmark.**

[E 21a.] 1-7 Sylvan Court, E. 121st St. N of Sylvan Place bet. Lexington and Third Aves. ca. 1885.

Seven brick town houses grouped around a pedestrian off-street walkway that suffers from a regrettable lack of care.

[E 21b.] Elmendorf Reformed Church, 171 E. 121st St., bet. Sylvan Place and Third Ave. ca. 1910.

A small church with an unusual but undistinguished limestone facade is the **oldest congregation in Harlem** and the successor to the Dutch church founded here in 1660.

[E 22.] Chambers Memorial Baptist Church/originally **Carmel Baptist Church/**then **Harlem Baptist Church,** 219 E. 123rd St., bet. Second and Third Aves. 1891.

The gabled brick front wall of this church is modulated with **a witty array** of windows and doors.

[E 23.] Iglesia Adventista del Septimo Dia/originally **Our Saviour (Norwegian) Lutheran Church,** 237 E. 123rd St., bet. Second and Third Aves. ca. 1912.

A humble facade enriched by an arched entryway and Spanish tile cladding on its gently pitched gable roof.

[E 24.] Taino Towers (apartment complex), bet. E. 122nd and E. 123rd Sts., Second and Third Aves. 1979. Silverman & Cika.

Unlike most government-subsidized housing, this project was neither conceived, designed, nor financed by the local housing authority: it was sponsored by **a persistent coalition** of local residents and community leaders together with the project's architects. As a result it is no predictable masonry fortress; it reminds you more of the **hotel architecture of Miami Beach.** Its crisp, 35-story towers reflect the sky in enormous picture windows of tautly stretched glass set in articulately framed white concrete. The towers **contrast** not only **with the mundane** red brick forms of typical low-rent, high-rise housing for the poor, but even more with the **easygoing squalor** of the adjacent **Barrio.**

The financing scheme, dependent upon leasing 225,000 square feet of commercial space on the first 6 stories to rent-paying community services, **ran into trouble** with the **1975–1976 recession** and the City's fiscal crisis. The large glass areas, designed before the energy crunch of 1974, prove to be yet **another serious headache.** Still only partially occupied.

[E 25.] East Harlem Triangle Community Service Building, 2322 Third Ave., NW cor. E. 126th St. 1974. Herbert Tannenbaum.

Built to serve the community's organizational needs (early-childhood center, social services, meeting rooms, etc.), this structure has **the look of Olivetti's social service buildings** in Italy back in the 1950s.

UPPER MANHATTAN

WASHINGTON HEIGHTS • INWOOD • MARBLE HILL

Upper Manhattan is the finger pointing northward toward the Bronx, a slender finial on the otherwise fat island. The district's southern boundary is marked by **Trinity Cemetery** at 155th Street, that northern ending of the **1811 commissioners plan** beyond which New York "could never grow."

Indian cave dwellers once lived in **Inwood Hill Park.** The father of our country not only gave part of this area its name—**Washington Heights**—but also slept here (and headquartered) in what is now named the **Morris-Jumel Mansion.** This area was once a country preserve of the wealthy, and some of those estates have remained intact in a variety of forms, although the rich live elsewhere. Museums, a park, a medical center, a bus terminal, and a university now occupy such lands; and other sacred and profane institutions ornament this urban district. It is filled mainly with apartment houses, creating one of the city's most densely populated sectors; its parks, institutions, and dramatic river views make it one of the most livable. The **IRT Broadway-Seventh Avenue subway,** which reached Dyckman Street and Fort George Hill in **1906,** was the major impetus for development of the eastern section. The **IND Eighth Avenue subway** arrived in **1932,** encouraging still more apartment house construction.

Within **Upper Manhattan,** and particularly in the sector called **Washington Heights,** there have been a maze of ethnic subcommunities. The long-departed **Irish** have been replaced by **blacks, Hispanics,** and, surprisingly, **yuppies,** who are rediscovering the virtues of this enclave. **Greek** and **Armenian** populations were once large; and in the 1930s, after **Hitler's** accession to power, so many German-Jewish refugees settled here that the area was termed the **Fourth Reich.**

[U 1a.] Trinity Cemetery, Amsterdam Ave. to Riverside Dr., W. 153rd to W. 155th Sts. Boundary walls and gates, 1876. Gatehouse and keeper's lodge, 1883. Vaux & Radford. Grounds, 1881. Vaux & Co., landscape architects. **W section open to the public.**

Here is **bucolic topography:** the cemetery climbs the hill from the river to Amsterdam Avenue, affording some idea of the topography of Manhattan Island before man cut, molded, and veneered it with brick, concrete, and asphalt. This was once part of the farm of **John James Audubon,** (1785–1851), the great artist-naturalist, whose home, **Minniesland,** was near the river at 155th Street and who is buried here. On Christmas Eve carolers visit the grave of **Clement Clarke Moore,** author of "A Visit from Saint Nicholas." This was the rural cemetery of Wall Street's **Trinity Church.**

Sadly missing today is the suspension bridge over Broadway (Vaux, Withers & Co., architects; George K. Radford, engineer), which linked the cemetery's halves. It was demolished in 1911 to build:

[U 1a.] Gatehouse, Trinity Cemetery   **[U 1b.]** The Chapel of the Intercession

[U 1b.] Church of the Intercession (Episcopal) and **Vicarage,** 550 W. 155th St., SE cor. Broadway. 1914. Bertram Goodhue of Cram, Goodhue & Ferguson. ★

Set in **Trinity Cemetery,** this was the largest chapel of Trinity Parish, now promoted to the status of independent church. Here is the dream of the Gothic Revivalist come true: a large "country" **church, tower and cloister, parish house and vicarage**—all mounted on a bucolic bluff overlooking the Hudson. Inside, stone piers support a wood hammer-beam roof, washed in light from glass that is seemingly from 13th-century France. Loose chairs, rather than pews, make it seem even more French. *See the charming cloister off the 155th Street entry.*

The memorial to the church's architect, Bertram Grosvenor Goodhue (Lee Lawrie, sculptor. 1929) gives a Protestant interpretation to the royal tombs of St. Denis: THIS TOMB IS A TOKEN OF THE AFFECTION OF HIS FRIENDS. HIS GREAT ARCHITECTURAL CREATIONS THAT BEAUTIFY THE LAND AND ENRICH CIVILIZATION ARE HIS MONUMENTS. This is perhaps the only New York memorial to an architect **within** one of his own major works.

[U 2.] Audubon Terrace Historic District, Broadway bet. W. 155th and W. 156th Sts. W side. Master plan, 1908. Charles Pratt Huntington. ★

Three small museums, a church, and the National Institute of Arts and Letters share an awkwardly proportioned court, part of the **Renaissance Classical Revival** of the early 20th century. As a cul-de-sac with no ground-floor activity (restaurants, shops, people, or movement), it has become an unused—and sometimes ill-used—backwater. **Boring.**

[U 2a.] Museum of the American Indian, Heye Foundation, Audubon

Terr., 3745 Broadway, NW cor. W. 155th St. 1916. Charles Pratt Huntington. ☆ **Open to the public.**

Originally the private collection of George Heye, this is now a comprehensive museum concerned with the prehistory of the Western Hemisphere and with the contemporary American Indian, continentwide. All is clad in **miniature Ionic** limestone Renaissance Revival. This remote site, although rather grand in its way, has a hazy future: it may give way to a new museum. The vacated palazzo here will then be available for other community uses.

[U 2b.] Boricua College/originally **American Geographical Society,** Audubon Terr., 3755 Broadway, SW cor. W. 156th St. 1911. Charles Pratt Huntington. ☆

In a world of jet travel, communications satellites, and computers, a physically central place for information storage is less than vital. The Society's map collection, the largest in the Western Hemisphere, was therefore lured to Milwaukee, where the University of Wisconsin offered better quarters and more generous financing. The building's subsequent tenant, **Boricua College,** is obviously more a part of this minority community than were the curators of cartography.

[U 2c.] Hispanic Society of America, Audubon Terrace. W Building, 1908, Charles Pratt Huntington. E Building and additions to W Building, 1910–1926, Charles Pratt Huntington, Erik Strindberg, and H. Brooks Price. ☆ **Open to the public.**

A happy irony hovers over this site: the Hispanics in question were mostly those of Iberia and, sometimes, of **equidistant Latin America.** Another Hispanic group now surrounds this symbolic site, making it an appropriate centerpiece to a newly arrived population.

The richly appointed storehouse of Hispanic painting, sculpture, and the decorative arts confronts a pompous **neo-Baroque** sunken court (part of this unfortunate cul-de-sac) filled with lots of dull and academic bronze sculpture. Would you believe **El Cid** plus a deer, a doe, a fawn, and four **heroes?**

[U 2d.] American Numismatic Society, Audubon Terr., S side. 1907. Charles Pratt Huntington. ☆ **Open to the public.**

A museum of money and decorations: paper, coins, medals, and whatever. Here the art of commerce is expressed in the media for trading, and the honor of special events and activities is equally celebrated—a marriage of the printed franc, dollar, and yen, silver and gold coinage, with the Victoria Cross and the Congressional Medal of Honor.

[U 2e.] National Institute of Arts and Letters/American Academy of Arts and Letters, Audubon Terr. **Administration Building,** 633 W. 155th St. 1923. William M. Kendall of McKim, Mead & White. **Auditorium and Gallery,** 632 W. 156th St. 1930. Cass Gilbert. ☆ **Museum open to the public.**

An Anglo-Italian **Renaissance club** that houses both an institute and an academy honoring distinguished persons in literature and the fine arts. The administration building contains a permanent exhibition of the works of the American impressionist Childe Hassam, a library, and a museum of the manuscripts of past and present members.

Above it all the cornice is emblazed: ALL ARTS ARE ONE, ALL BRANCHES ON ONE TREE . . . HOLD HIGH THE FLAMING TORCH FROM AGE TO AGE.

[U 2f.] Church of Our Lady of Esperanza (Roman Catholic), 624 W. 156th St., bet. Broadway and Riverside Dr. 1912. Charles Pratt Huntington. Remodeled, 1925, Lawrence G. White of McKim, Mead & White.

The green and gold interior contains stained-glass windows, a skylight, and a lamp—all given by King Alfonso XIII of Spain at its opening in 1912.

[U 3.] Engine Company No. 84, Hook & Ladder No. 34, N.Y.C. Fire Department, 515 W. 161st St., bet. Amsterdam Ave. and Broadway. 1906. Francis H. Kimball.

Beaux Arts rusticated limestone, with infilled brick à la Henri IV. Look up to an eagle, swags, and festoons.

IRT's Hoosick: Named after the Hoosick Tunnel near North Adams, Mass., which holds the record as the longest two-track tunnel in the U.S. The tunnel, for the IRT Broadway-Seventh Avenue Line, is cut through solid rock under Broadway and St. Nicholas Avenue between W. 157th Street and Fort George.

[U 4.] Jumel Terrace Historic District, around Jumel Terr. bet. W. 160th and W. 162nd Sts., Edgecombe Ave. and St. Nicholas Ave., including 50 row houses. ★

[U 4a.] Morris-Jumel Mansion, 1765 Jumel Terr., bet. W. 160th and W. 162nd Sts. 1765. Remodeled, ca. 1810. ★ ☆ Interior ★. **Open to the public.**

Built by **Roger Morris** as a summer residence for his family, it served during the Revolution as Washington's headquarters. But for most of that war the house was in British hands (as was all of Manhattan and, therefore, all of New York of that day). After the war it served as a farmhouse and tavern until 1810, when Stephen Jumel purchased it and partially renovated the house in the then-modern **Federal** style. The **finest view in Manhattan** is blocked by bulky apartment buildings to the south.

In **Tuscan-columned, Georgian-Federal style,** with a facade of wood boards and quoins simulating stone, and a shingled behind. The hipped roofs to balustraded captain's walks are admirable cornices to this classic square linked to an octagon. **Open to the public.**

[U 4a.] Morris-Jumel Mansion, in the Tuscan-columned Georgian-Federal style

[U 4b.] 10-18 Jumel Terrace (row houses), bet. W. 160th and W. 162nd Sts. W side. 1896. Henri Fouchaux. ☆

Lime- and **brown**stone stalwarts worthy of the Upper West Side park blocks.

[U 4c.] 1-19, 2-20 Sylvan Terrace (row houses), bet. Jumel Terr. and St. Nicholas Ave. 1882. Gilbert Robinson, Jr. ☆

Wooden 2-story houses: savor the wooden canopy at **No. 20** and the doors at **No. 5.** Here are green shutters, brown hoods, and cream clapboards. This is a revived memory of very old New York.

[U 4d.] West 160th Street (row houses), bet. Edgecombe and St. Nicholas Aves. S side. **No. 418,** 1890. Walgrove & Israels. **Nos. 420-430,** 1891. Richard R. Davis. ☆

Brick and brownstone, with **up-and-down** picturesque profiles.

Washington Heights: see map p. 3

[U 4e.] **430-438 West 162nd Street (row houses),** bet. Jumel Terr. and St. Nicholas Ave. 1896. Henry Fouchaux.

Look at the bas-relief in the side of **No. 430,** the corner house.

Columbia-Presbyterian complex:

[U 5a.] **Audubon Research Park**/originally **Audubon Theatre** and **Ballroom**/then **Beverly Hills Theatre**/later **San Juan Theatre,** Broadway at W. 165th St. E side. 1912. Thomas W. Lamb. Alterations, 1990, Perkins & Will and Bond Ryder James.

A former 2,368-seat theater whose terra-cotta glazed polychromy along the Broadway facade is corniced and encrusted, in counterpoint to **Babies' Hospital** opposite, which is detail-less — except for its babies. In 1965, in the second-floor ballroom, Black Muslim leader Malcolm X was assassinated during a rally.

Movie palaces such as this once provided **architectural** romance equal to the movies themselves.

[U 5b.] **Columbia-Presbyterian Medical Center,** W. 165th to W. 168th Sts., Broadway to Riverside Dr. 1928–1947. James Gamble Rogers. 1947–1964, Rogers & Butler. 1964–1974. Rogers Butler & Burgun.

The original complex of this vast teaching hospital, situated on a bluff over the Hudson. The architecture is both bulky and pallid, the streetscape a bore. Inside, however, medical wonders are performed. Perhaps one would forgive the architects and their companion clients, medical administrators, if it were a hospice for the blind.

Later buildings, cited below, promised some respite from this megalopolitan stance; but, unfortunately, fat buildings unrelated to the street and the city proliferate.

[U 2c.] Hispanic Society's forecourt [U 5f.] Bard-Haven residence towers

[U 5c.] **Presbyterian Hospital expansion,** W. 165th to W. 166th Sts., Broadway to Riverside Dr. 1989. Skidmore, Owings & Merrill.

A tall glassy entry, 4 flying bridges, and an exquisitely appropriate Post Modern/neo-Art Deco addition overlooking the Hudson.

[U 5d.] **Julius and Armand Hammer Health Sciences Center,** 701 Fort Washington Ave., bet. W. 168th and W. 169th Sts. W side. 1976. Warner, Burns, Toan & Lunde.

A somber blockbuster in self-weathering steel and rose brick. For its soul mate, look at Mt. Sinai's **Annenberg Center,** an equally bulky centerpiece of that medical complex.

[U 5e.] **N.Y.S. Psychiatric Institute addition,** 722 W. 168th St., extended N along Haven Ave. W side. 1987. Herbert W. Riemer.

In stylish brown brick with sloping sills: the monolithic image and posture of the 1970s.

[U 5f.] Bard-Haven Towers, (medical center staff housing) 100 Haven Ave., bet. W. 169th and W. 171st Sts. W side, overlooking Henry Hudson Pkwy. 1971. Brown, Guenther, Battaglia & Galvin.

Tall cliff-hangers (literally) that cling to the escarpment and enjoy wonderful Hudson views. The corbeled lower stories are a dramatic event to drivers who approach the George Washington Bridge.

Freud's library: In the Freud Memorial Room of the Neurological and Psychiatric Institutes is shelved part of Sigmund Freud's personal library.

[U 6.] Highbridge Park, W. 155th to Dyckman Sts., Edgecombe and Amsterdam Aves. to the Harlem River Dr. 1888. Calvert Vaux and Samuel Parsons, Jr. Altered.

Once the site of an amusement park, marina, and promenade, this park gains its beauty from a steep slope and rugged topography. An excellent vantage point to survey the **Harlem River Valley.**

[U 6a.] Adventure Playground, in Highbridge Park, Edgecombe Ave. bet. W. 163rd and W. 165th Sts. E side. 1973. Richard Dattner & Assocs.

Tunnels, mountains, and slides create an **imaginative world** for child's play.

[U 6b.] Engine Company No. 67, N.Y.C. Fire Department, 518 W. 170th St., bet. Amsterdam and Audubon Aves. 1901. Flagg & Chambers.

An uptown work by those who brought you the great firehouse on Great Jones Street [see V Manhattan/Astor Place A 6.]

[U 6c.] High Bridge/originally **Aqueduct Bridge,** Highbridge Park at W. 174th St. 1839–1848. New central span, 1923. ★

This is the **oldest remaining bridge** connecting Manhattan to the mainland. It was built to carry Croton water to Manhattan. The bridge originally consisted of closely spaced masonry piers and arches, but the central group was replaced by the present cast-iron arch when the **Harlem River Ship Canal** was built. The pedestrian walk has been closed for many years.

[U 6d.] Highbridge Tower, Highbridge Park at W. 173rd St. 1872. Attributed to John B. Jervis. ★

This landmark tower, originally used to equalize pressure in the **Croton Aqueduct,** now simply marks the Manhattan end of **High Bridge.** Adjacent is the site of a large and well-used public outdoor swimming pool.

[U 7.] Henry Hudson Parkway, from Van Cortlandt Park to and across Henry Hudson Bridge. **[U 7a.] Pavilion,** in Fort Washington Park on Riverside Dr. at W. 180 St. W side. 1913. Jaros Kraus.

Driving south into Manhattan on this Hudson-hugging parkway is one of New York's **great gateway experiences.** From **Riverdale** (the affluent West Bronx) one passes over the **Henry Hudson Bridge** (a dramatic object from the distance but a bore at first hand) before descending to the banks of the **Hudson.** Next, the Cloisters, romantically surmounting a hilltop, lonely and wondrous; through a wooded area; then under the majestic **George Washington Bridge.** All of a sudden the skyline of Manhattan materializes, and the **rural-urban transition** is complete.

[U 8a.] Fort Washington Presbyterian Church/originally **West Park Presbyterian Church,** 21 Wadsworth Ave., NW cor. W. 174th St. 1914. Carrère & Hastings.

Brick and limestone English Baroque: its **Tuscan** columns and pilasters, broken pediments, and console-bracketed tower bring us back to **Christopher Wren's** 17th-century reconstruction of London.

[U 8b.] United Church/originally **Loew's 175th Street Theatre,** Broadway NE cor. W. 175th St. 1930. Thomas W. Lamb. Altered.

The **Reverend Ike** once held forth here in splendor reminiscent of archaic Miami Beach. This terra-cotta place was at the apogee of movie palace glamour in those long-gone days when Hollywood ruled the world and free crockery on Wednesday nights was an added fillip.

[U 9.] George Washington Bridge, W. 178th St. and Fort Washington Ave. over the Hudson River to Fort Lee, N.J. 1931. O. H. Ammann, engineer, & Cass Gilbert, architect. Lower level added, 1962.

"The **George Washington Bridge** over the **Hudson** is the most beautiful bridge in the world. Made of cables and steel beams, it gleams in the sky like a reversed arch. It is blessed. It is the only seat of grace in the disordered city. It is painted an aluminum color and, between water and sky, you see nothing but the bent cord supported by two steel towers. When your car moves up the ramp the two towers rise so high that it brings you happiness; their structure is so pure, so resolute, so regular that here, finally, steel architecture seems to laugh. The car reaches an unexpectedly wide apron; the second tower is very far away; innumerable vertical cables, gleaming against the sky, are suspended from the magisterial curve which swings down and then up. The rose-colored towers of New York appear, a vision whose harshness is mitigated by distance."

—**Charles Edouard Jeanneret (Le Corbusier)**
When the Cathedrals Were White, 1947.

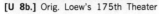

[U 8b.] Orig. Loew's 175th Theater   [U 9.] The George Washington Bridge

[U 9a.] Little Red Lighthouse/originally **Jeffries Hook Lighthouse,** Fort Washington Park below the George Washington Bridge. 1921.

Directly under the east tower of the George Washington Bridge, the lighthouse was built to steer grain barges away from the shoals of Jeffrey's Hook. When navigational lights were mounted on the bridge, it was no longer used and was put up for auction in 1951. A barrage of letters from children who had read *The Little Red Lighthouse and the Great Gray Bridge,* by **Hildegarde Hoyt Swift** and **Lynd Ward,** saved the lighthouse. The City now maintains it.

[U 10a.] George Washington Bridge Bus Station, Fort Washington and Wadsworth Aves., W. 178th to W. 179th Sts. 1963. Port of New York Authority and Pier Luigi Nervi.

A **concrete butterfly** shelters a bus terminal at the end of the bridge, interlocking with the IND Eighth Avenue subway. The shape is excused as a form for natural ventilation for the noxious buses; it also provides the opportunity for a formal tour de force for **Dr. Nervi,** an engineer more comfortable with Italian economics, where his skills provide the cheapest, as well as the most exciting, forms. Here, with the millstone of the Port Authority engineering staff, his forms were labored and the economics absent.

[U 10b.] Bridge Apartments, bet. W. 178th and W. 179th Sts., Wadsworth and Audubon Aves. 1964. Brown & Guenther.

An early experiment in residential air rights over a highway; but fumes, dirt, and noise rise to the unfortunate dweller above. The depressed bridge approaches **should have been** decked over to provide artificial ground for the residents, and the fumes **should have been** mechanically exhausted. The curtain wall buildings are, therefore, ensmogged and, incidentally, fussily detailed.

[U 11a.] Alexander Hamilton Bridge, Highbridge Park bet. W. 178th and W. 179th Sts. over the Harlem River to the Bronx, 1964.

The bridge bringing the Cross-Bronx Expressway to the George Washington Bridge approaches in Manhattan: serviceable but dull.

[U 11b.] Washington Bridge, W. 181st St. and Amsterdam Ave. over the Harlem River to the Bronx. 1884. William R. Hutton, Chief Engineer, N.Y.C. Bridge Commission.

A magnificent arched bridge not to be confused with the **George** Washington Bridge. A great filigree of steel is enjoyed by the **Major Deegan** or **Harlem River** driver; to those crossing on top it's just a flat plane.

The bridge is the product of a competition won by C. C. Scheider (first prize) and W. Hildebrand (second prize)—with the final design based on the work of both prizewinners; the revised bracing system was modified by the N.Y.C. Bridge Commission and its consultants, Edward H. Kendall, architect, and William J. McAlpin and Theodore Cooper, engineers.

Yeshiva University area

[U 12.] Yeshiva University campus, W. 183rd to W. 187th Sts., along Amsterdam Ave.

A mixed bag of architectural tricks, more a collection of separate opportunities, successes, and failures than an integrated whole or sum.

[U 12a.] Main Building, Yeshiva University, 2540 Amsterdam Ave., SW cor. W. 187th St. 1928. Charles B. Meyers Assocs.

This is one of the great romantic structures of its time. Domes, towers, and turrets can be seen from miles away; and the architect's lavish use of orange stone, copper and brass, ceramic tile, and **Middle Eastern eclectic** architectural detail makes a visual treat.

[U 12b.] Mendel Gottesman Library, Yeshiva University, 2520 Amsterdam Ave., bet. W. 185th and W. 186th Sts. W side. 1967. Armand Bartos & Assocs. **Museum (in the library) open to the public.**

A rich composition of brick, terra-cotta and glass **highly articulated** to make the best of sun, shadow, and view. **Super** bay windows.

[U 12c.] Science Center, Belfer Graduate School of Science, Yeshiva University, 2495 Amsterdam Ave., at W. 184th St. E side. 1968. Armand Bartos & Assocs.

Bulky brick piers for a warehouse of science.

[U 13.] Isabella Neimath Home and Geriatric Center, 525 Audubon Ave., bet. W. 190th and W. 191st Sts. E side. 1965. Joseph D. Weiss.

A home for the elderly, providing small apartments designed to meet their special needs. The pitched and folded roof was designed ostensibly in deference to its older neighbor (the original home), which no longer exists: it was later replaced by an addition to this addition. Oh, well . . .

[U 14a.] Fort Washington Collegiate Church, Fort Washington Ave. NE cor. W. 181st St. 1907.

This small **country church** dates from the time when Washington Heights was really country; brick and timber Gothic Revival.

Washington Heights: see map p. 3

The highest point: In Bennett Park, along the west side of Fort Washington Avenue between 183rd and 185th Streets, is a rock outcropping that is the highest natural point in Manhattan, 267.75 feet above sea level. An added bonus is the outline of Revolutionary War Fort Washington, marked by stone pavers.

[U 14b.] Hudson View Gardens (apartments), 116 Pinehurst Ave., bet. W. 183rd and W. 185th Sts. W side. 1925. George F. Pelham.

Collegiate Gothic encrusted with Virginia creeper, of brick with simulated half-timbering. This **romantic and urbane cluster** of multiple dwellings embraces private gardens and enjoys, from many parts, romantic river views.

[U 12a.] The Main Building, Yeshiva University, with Middle Eastern eclectic detail

[U 14c.] Castle Village (apartment complex), 120-200 Cabrini Blvd., bet. W. 181st and W. 186th Sts. W side. 1938. George F. Pelham II.

At **Hudson View,** Pelham *père* embraced his public space; at **Castle Village** Pelham *fils* planted himself in it. Each floor of these cruciform buildings contains 9 apartments, 8 of which have river views. The site was formerly occupied by the Paterno estate; its massive retaining walls still retain the present building site.

[U 14d.] 16 Chittenden Avenue, at W. 186th St. (Alex Rose Place)

The guest house of the former **Paterno** estate perches on a great pier that drops to the parkway's edge below.

[U 15.] Fort Tryon Park, W. 192nd to Dyckman Sts., Broadway to Riverside Dr. 1935. Frederick Law Olmsted, Jr. Planting plan, James W. Dawson. ★

A gift of the Rockefeller family to New York City, this site was formerly the **C. K. G. Billings estate** (the triple-arched driveway from Riverside Drive was its entrance). The park is famous for its flower gardens.

The fort's grand site still remains; a plaque states

THE NORTHERN OUTWORK OF FORT WASHINGTON, ITS GALLANT DEFENSE AGAINST THE HESSIAN TROOPS BY THE MARYLAND AND VIRGINIA REGIMENT, 16 NOVEMBER 1776, WAS SHARED BY MARGARET CORBIN, THE FIRST AMERICAN WOMAN TO TAKE A SOLDIER'S PART IN THE WAR FOR LIBERTY.

[U 15a.] The Cloisters, Metropolitan Museum of Art, Fort Tryon Park. 1934–1938. Charles Collens of Allen, Collens & Willis. Alterations to

receive the Fuentadueña Chapel, 1961, Brown, Lawford & Forbes. ★
Open to the public.

Named for the French and Spanish monastic cloisters imported and reassembled here in concert with a **12th-century chapter house,** the **Fuentadueña Chapel,** and a **Gothic and a Romanesque chapel.** The concept and the reality are both very romantic; the siting at this river-viewing crest is an overwhelming confrontation between the city and a Hudson River School painter's view of—not surprisingly—the Hudson River.

The contents are the majority of the medieval art collection of the Metropolitan Museum of Art; most impressive are the **Unicorn tapestries.** Concerts of medieval and Renaissance music are held here from time to time.

[U 14b.] Hudson View Gardens apts.   **[U 15a.]** Arcaded scene, The Cloisters

De profundis: The two deepest subway stations in the city are near here (why deepest? the land merely gets higher and the tracks get—at least relatively—lower!): the IRT-Broadway Seventh Avenue station at 191st Street and Saint Nicholas Avenue (180 feet below the street, or the street is 180 feet above the subway); and the IND Eighth Avenue station at 190th Street and Fort Washington Avenue (165 feet down). In both cases elevators whisk passengers up and down: level-equalizers.

INWOOD

[U 16.] Dyckman House, Broadway NW cor. W. 204th St. 1783. ★
Open to the public.

The site is monumental, the porch lovely. Rebuilt by **William Dyckman** after the British destroyed the previous building, this is the **only 18th-century farmhouse** remaining in Manhattan. With its gambrel roof and brick and fieldstone lower walls, the house shows a strong Dutch influence. The interior, with random-width chestnut floors and original family furnishings, is well worth a visit.

[U 17a.] Columbia University Stadium, in Baker Field, W. 218th St., NW cor. Broadway. 1986. Richard Dattner & Assocs.

Cool concrete. A simple, graceful understated settee for Ivy League football watchers.

[U 17b.] Charles and Frances Allen Pavilion, Presbyterian Hospital, 5145 Broadway, opp. W. 220th St. W side. 1988. Skidmore, Owings & Merrill.

A 3-story community hospital satellite of the main hospital in Washington Heights, this built on unused lands of Columbia's Baker Field.

For Marble Hill, that part of Manhattan now physically joined to the Bronx, see R Bronx.

THE OTHER ISLANDS

In addition to Manhattan and Staten, which are islands unto themselves, and Long, the western part of which is occupied by the city's two largest boroughs (Queens and Brooklyn), the city is infested with yet **other islands.** Some are so **small or low-lying** that the tides keep them under water most if not all of the time. Others appear in official documents but are in fact **submerged** by the city's offal in numerous landfill projects. Yet others are **joined,** either to each other or to some "mainland," so that they are no longer truly **islands.** Jamaica Bay, within the jurisdiction of both Brooklyn and Queens, has bits of mucky land which fall into all of the above categories. Luckily for municipal officials already overwhelmed by less arcane issues, the **National Park Service** now worries about most of Jamaica Bay's islands, pols, marshes, and hassocks as part of its **Gateway National Recreation Area.**

Among the larger, inhabited (or once inhabited) islands within the city's waterways—in some cases not normally open to the public—are

Liberty Island
Known until 1956 as Bedloes Island, after Isaac Bedlow, an English merchant who owned it in the 17th century.

[O 1.] Statue of Liberty (National Monument), National Park Service, built atop Fort Wood. 1886. Frédéric Auguste Bartholdi, sculptor; Alexandre Gustave Eiffel, engineer; Richard Morris Hunt, architect of the base. Additions to the base, 1972. Refurbished, 1986, Thierry Despont and Swanke Hayden Connell. **Open to the public.**

Bartholdi's colossal sculpture *Liberty Enlightening the World* is indeed colossal: she stands 151 feet high, the tip of the flaming torch in her upraised hand rises some 395 feet above the harbor's waters, her index finger is 8 feet long, her eyes each 2½ feet wide. Journey to Liberty Island via the privately operated, regularly scheduled ship, and ascend the 168-step helical stair through the verdigrised sheets of $3/32$-inch-thick copper to the observation platform in the seven-spiked crown. There—if the crowd behind allows you enough time to gaze—you will see the city's great harbor spread before you.

The New Colossus: The symbolic relationship between Liberty's welcoming form and the millions of immigrants arriving in steerage in New York harbor was not formally established until 1903. It was then that a plaque was affixed to the base bearing the lines of a poem written in 1883 by Emma Lazarus as part of a fund-raising effort for the statue. Its last lines capture the cry of Liberty's silent lips:

> *"Give me your tired, your poor,*
> *Your huddled masses yearning to breathe free,*
> *The wretched refuse of your teeming shore.*
> *Send these, the homeless, tempest-tost to me,*
> *I lift my lamp beside the golden door!"*

To the disappointment of many who climb the stair to the top, the poem is not inscribed on the tablet grasped in Liberty's left hand—that inscription reads JULY IV MDCCLXXVI.

Long before Liberty was planned as a symbol of the centennial relationship between the French and American people, Bartholdi had conceived of a colossus of similar scale for the entrance of the Suez Canal; Liberty's progenitor would have stood guard there as a **sentry** to honor that French ditch. Happily for America, the concept was quickly switched to the more gracious job of greeting the traveler and immigrant to New York harbor (but **who greets their grandchildren** at Kennedy Airport?). Bartholdi's most extravagant work (although small) is his fountain in the Place des Terreaux of Lyons; here the waterworks are in the form of water vapor spewing from the nostrils of horses arising from their fountain pool.

Not only the statue but also the lawns and walkways are open to the public, under the jurisdiction of the National Park Service.

Ellis Island

[O 2.] Originally **U.S. Immigration Station**/now **Ellis Island National Monument, National Park Service.** 1898. Boring & Tilton. Reconstructed and restored, 1991, Beyer Blinder Belle and Notter Finegold & Alexander. **Open to the public.**

Successor to the old Immigrant Landing Station once housed in Castle Clinton, this **extravagant eclectic** reception structure was created to greet (or is it process?) the **hordes of European immigrants** arriving at the turn of the century: 1,285,349 entered in 1907 alone, the peak year.

Fanciful **bulbous turrets** bring to the heavily Eastern European population arriving a remembrance of ornately detailed public buildings left behind. Restoration makes the main hall and its lesser companions **a vast memorial** to the principle that created America and imported all its peoples, except for the hardy but not numerous Native Americans. *Take a trip over.*

Governors Island

Its name derives from an act of the New York legislature in 1698 which set the land aside **"for the benefit and accommodation of His Majesty's governors."** Since then it has also served as a sheep farm, quarantine station, racetrack, and game preserve. It is best known for its use as **a military fortification** until 1966, when the U.S. Coast Guard took command. Public visitation is **strictly limited** to special **open-house weekends** in the warm-weather months, when the forts, green spaces, and a Coast Guard cutter or two are available for inspection. Bring a picnic lunch. The ferryboat leaves from the Battery and is free—no visitors' cars are allowed. Call Coast Guard public information for dates. *It's worth waiting for.*

Apocrypha: After the British evacuation of New York in 1783, Governors Island was owned by Columbia College. The first volunteers to work on the construction of Fort Jay included its students. (Columbia, then King's College, was located in Lower Manhattan at the time.) A few years later (1811), the island's major fort, Castle Williams, a much more potentially potent place, was added to guard the Battery of Manhattan.

While forts were created to guard the waterways, the island's inner land was used as a racetrack. The land was later infilled with the houses, housing, and barracks of the U.S. Army—a curious choice: the land-based military here at sea.

In 1934 Mayor La Guardia proposed that Governors Island become a municipal airport. Fortunately, that idea did not succeed, for although the planes of 1934 could have landed on such a potentially short landing strip (and flying boats could use the harbor), it would be useless for modern jets.

Mayor O'Dwyer had a better idea in 1945: the United Nations, where it could have been in "splendid isolation" from the commercial city.

In the end some elegant and lusty 19th-century architecture has survived these various fantasies. May the Coast Guard long reign on this stationary guardian-place of the harbor.

[O 3a.] Fort Jay a.k.a. **Fort Columbus** (1808–1904), entrance to E of ferry landing on Andes Rd. 1798. Rebuilt, 1806. ★

The officers' dwellings set within the walls of the fort add a note of domesticity **that diminishes the fearsomeness** of this now **dry-moated fortress,** built in a pentagonal, star-shaped plan. The brownstone Federal entranceway is a felicitous effort bearing a **handsome sculptural composition.**

[O 3b.] Castle Williams, Andes Rd. W cor. Hay Rd., W of ferry landing.

1811. Lt. Col. Jonathan Williams, chief engineer, U.S. Army. Converted to military prison, 1912. ★

Appearing from the harbor to be fully circular in shape (hence its onetime nickname, **The Cheesebox**) this 200-foot-diameter red sandstone fortification **is actually chevron-shaped** in plan on its inland side. Together with Castle Clinton at the Battery [see L Manhattan/Financial District F 1c.], it was built to crisscross the intervening waterway with cannonballs during the War of 1812. They were never used.

Williams, its designer, was Benjamin Franklin's nephew and the individual for whom Williamsburg, Brooklyn, was named.

[O 2.] Orig. Ellis Is. Immigration Sta.   [O 3b.] Castle Williams, Governors Is.

[O 3c.] Originally **The South Battery**/now incorporated into **Officers' Club,** Comfort Rd. W cor. Barry Rd., SE of ferry landing. 1812.

Built to command Buttermilk Channel, the harbor's waterway between Governors Island and Brooklyn, this fort is now largely hidden by additions made to accommodate its later use as the island's officers' club.

[O 3d.] Chapel of St. Cornelius the Centurion (Episcopal), Barry Rd. W cor. Evans Rd., SE of ferry landing. 1905. Charles C. Haight.

Built by **Trinity Parish** during the period (1863–1924) when the War Department did not see fit to assign an official Army chaplain to the military reservation. **Inside** the Gothic Revival chapel hang **87 battle flags and regimental colors** from all periods of American history.

[O 3e.] The Blockhouse, Building 9, Barry Rd. SE of ferry landing. 1843. Martin E. Thompson. Altered. ★

Spare Greek Revival now minus its entrance steps.

[O 3f.] The Admiral's House/originally **Commanding General's Quarters, Building 1,** Barry Rd. S of Andes Rd., SE of ferry landing. 1840. ★

This imposing brick manor house, porticoed front and rear with slender white 2-story Doric colonnades, served such illustrious generals as Winfield Scott, John J. Pershing, Omar N. Bradley, and Walter Bedell Smith.

[O 3g.] The Dutch House, Building 3, Barry Rd., S of Andes Rd., SE of ferry landing. 1845.

Built to resemble the typical house of a New Amsterdam settler but used initially as a commissary storehouse. Now officers' quarters.

[O 3h.] The Governor's House, Building 2, W cor. Andes and Barry Rds., SE of ferry landing. ca. 1708. Altered, 1749 and later. ★

The island's oldest structure, **truly Georgian** in style since its official use as residence for the British governors required **textbook adherence** to the style of the motherland. An unpretentious yet dignified Flemish-bonded brick manor house.

[O 3i.] Brooklyn-Battery Tunnel Ventilator Building, Triborough Bridge and Tunnel Authority, off Governors Island, SE of ferry landing. 1950.

This prominent white octagonal prism contributes little to the harbor panorama but subtracts a lot with its bulk and unfriendly scale.

Erosion and landfill: Governors Island, called Nooten Eylandt (or Nuts Island) in the Dutch period (1625–1664), then encompassed 170 acres. But by the early 1900s the harbor's tides had washed away the southwestern portion, reducing the acreage to a mere 70. At that point the south seawall ran roughly between Castle Williams and the South Battery along today's Hay, Clayton, and Comfort Roads. The placement of material dredged from the harbor's channels together with rock excavated from subway construction subsequently extended the island to its present 173 acres.

Roosevelt Island

"Instant City" is what some people call Roosevelt Island but **"New Town in Town"** was the catch phrase preferred by the State's Urban Development Corporation. Back in 1971, UDC won the opportunity to create a high-density residential community in the center of the 2-mile-long, 600-foot-wide sliver of land in the East River then known as Welfare Island, a cordon sanitaire for the city's poor, destitute, and chronically ill. An **ambitious master plan by Philip Johnson and John Burgee** evoked **a community for pedestrians** arranged along a network of streets which flowed north from the island's subway stop on the 63rd Street Crosstown Line. Residents' and visitors' **cars are stored in a megagarage** at the foot of the small lift bridge to Long Island City, and **a bus system** links the garage at the north with the tramway and subway at the south.

Changes in thinking about the number of people, the height of buildings (the 8 to 10 stories in the master plan being increased to 20 along the main street), the need to coordinate construction with the demolition of existing buildings, delays in the completion of the subway link, double-digit inflation, and finally UDC's fiscal collapse all **contributed to departures** from the master plan. The most significant consequence of the changes was the reduction (forced by UDC's collapse) of population from the minimum **"critical mass"** of 18,000 needed to sustain shopping, a hotel, restaurants, and entertainment. As a result only **Southtown,** with 2,138 units, less than half of the number originally contemplated, was built at first. **Northtown,** in the space between today's residential enclave and the subway station, is only partially built.

The silent but **exhilarating aerial voyage** via overhead tramcar (a subway token's fare each way) is an appropriate way to reach Roosevelt Island. (Cars must enter via the bridge from Queens and park in the Motorgate garage.) The **silent ride** is echoed by **the curious silence** on the island, **a stone's throw** from Manhattan's elegant east shore. The quiet is broken only by the **buzz of auto tires** along FDR Drive across the channel to the west and **the hum of "Big Allis,"** Con Edison's turbine generator, on the opposite shore. Infrequently, the eerie stillness is interrupted by the **staccato beat of rotors** overhead from aircraft using the 60th Street Heliport. Beyond these sounds are only the gentle noises of harbor craft and the splash of the East River waters along the seawalls which gird the island.

Walk along the length of the **gently zigzagged** residential spine called, naturally, **Main Street,** as far as Motorgate, which contains the parking garage and the community's only supermarket. On both sides of Main Street are arranged the apartment blocks, each a variation on a **U-shaped plan.** The open sides of the U's face the river, with the highest sections making **a not displeasing canyon** of Main Street and the lower tiers of apartments stepping down toward the island's east and west promenades.

A walk through the community should include a saunter along the two perimeter walks, which offer entrancing views.

The Central Part

[O 4a.] Aerial Tramway Station, N of Queensboro Bridge. 1976. Prentice & Chan, Ohlhausen.

This is the main point of pedestrian arrival at Roosevelt Island until completion of the subway (which will never compete successfully with the **sensuous delights** of this aerial voyage). The form of this tramway station conjures up **images of Switzerland,** its steep skislope roof being very different from its Manhattan mate [see E Manhattan/ East of Eden E1.]

[O 4b.] Old Welfare Island Service Building, N of Aerial Tramway Station. 1942. Moore & Hutchins and Percival Goodman.

Combined in a structure reminiscent of **constructivist architecture** are an enormous central laundry, service vehicle garage, and fire station for the island hospital's needs. Scheduled for demolition.

[O 4c.] Sports Park, S of Queensboro Bridge. 1977. Prentice & Chan, Ohlhausen.

A long, earth-colored, ground-hugging gymnasium building, plus outdoor accouterments. Swimming pool, basketball.

[O 4d.] Blackwell Farmhouse, Blackwell Park, E side of Main St., S of Eastwood. 1796–1804. Restored, 1973, Giorgio Cavaglieri. ★
[O 4e.] Blackwell Park. 1973. Dan Kiley & Partners, landscape architects.

This modest clapboard dwelling is the rebuilt home of the Blackwells, who owned and farmed this island, once named for the family, from the late 1660s to 1828, when it was purchased by the City. With the construction of a penitentiary the following year, the house became the residence for the first of the many island institutions' administrators.

[O 4f.] Eastwood (apartments), 510, 516, 536, 546, 556, 566, 576, and 580 Main St. E side, opp. "Big Allis," generator of Consolidated Edison. 1976. Sert, Jackson & Assocs.

The crisp, undulating accretion of buildings whose **unifying arcades** line the east side of Main Street. The occupants of its 1,000 units are **low-, middle-, and moderate-income** tenants. Their windows face the **candy cane-striped smokestacks** of Con Ed's erratic electric generator, "Big Allis" (for Allis Chalmers, its manufacturer), and the **industrial dreariness** of that part of Long Island City. (The wealthier live on the west side of Main Street.) **Bright red accents** on the brown ribbed-block facades, **a trademark** of the architects, have become **the theme color** for the whole development as well.

Schools: A radical innovation in the city's public education policy divides the Roosevelt Island community's public school system into five separate minischools built in conjunction with each of the apartment towers. Blackwell Primary School (grades K–2) just north of the farmhouse, Island House Middle School (3–4), Westview Upper School (5–6), Rivercross Intermediate School (7–8), and Eastwood Arts School (shared facilities) constitute Public School/Intermediate School 217, Manhattan. Athletics for all are centralized at Sports Park [O 4c.].

[O 4g.] Rivercross (apartments), 505, 513, and 541 Main St. W side, opp. Rockefeller University. 1975. Johansen & Bhavnani, architects. Dan Kiley & Partners, landscape architects.

Brightly painted **nautical ventilating funnels** announce the southernmost of the island's three luxury buildings, this one a cooperative. Like its neighbor to the north [O 4j.], it relies on dun-colored cement asbestos panels as cladding for much of its exterior. The material imparts a sober, urbane look from afar (good) but a thin, expressionless surface up close (bad).

[O 4h.] Originally **Chapel of the Good Shepherd (Episcopal)**/now **Good Shepherd Community Ecumenical Center,** 543 Main St. W side. 1889. Frederick Clarke Withers. Restored, 1975, Giorgio Cavaglieri. ★ **Plaza,** 1975, Johansen & Bhavnani, architects. Lawrence Halprin Assocs., landscape architects.

A stroke of genius to have preserved—and handsomely restored—this **vigorously designed** 19th-century country chapel for 20th- (and 21st-) century use. The old bronze bell (cast in 1888 by Mencely & Co., West Troy, N.Y.) has been placed on the plaza as **a charming sculptural note.**

Eats: Light meals are available along the Eastwood arcade at the Capri Restaurant & Pizzeria. But good weather and the wondrous river views suggest a picnic: fixins available at either the M.&D. Delicatessen (579 Main Street in Island House) or at Sloan's supermarket (in Motorgate).

[O 4i.] East and West Promenades. 1975. Zion & Breen, landscape architects.

Both are beautifully detailed: the west promenade, facing Manhattan, is the more complex, utilizing multilevels; the east promenade is modest, more subtle, and equally enjoyable.

[O 4j.] Island House (apartments), 551, 555, 575 and 595 Main St. W side, opp. Cornell-New York Medical Center. 1975. Johansen & Bhavnani, architects; Lawrence Halprin Assocs., landscape architects.

More housing for the wealthier. Island House is entered, **as an ocean liner,** via gangplanks, brightly painted in orange and yellow. As in Rivercross to the south [O 4g.], there is a prominent skylight-enclosed year-round indoor pool on the river frontage.

[O 4k.] Westview (1) **[O 4f.]** Eastwood   **[O 4n.]** Motorgate garage complex

[O 4k.] Westview (apartments), 595 and 625 Main St. W side, opp. Hospital for Special Surgery. 1976. Sert, Jackson & Assocs.

Dark gray-brown brick plus the **idiosyncratic bright red accents** mark Sert's Manhattan-facing effort for the wealthier, as contrasted with his more extensive project across Main Street for the less well-to-do, built of masonry block.

[O 4l.] Northtown, Main St. W side., opp. Motorgate garage complex. 1989. Gruzen Samton Steinglass.

The infill of this long vacant strip provides the final segments of Roosevelt Island's development. **GSS** and its predecessor firms have produced (as has Davis, Brody & Assocs.) some of the city's most distinguished housing. Compare **Chatham Green, Chatham Towers, and Schomburg Towers,** all architecture for the moderate-incomed and middle class—but with more **class** than most luxury efforts.

[O 4m.] Roosevelt Island Bridge/originally **Welfare Island Bridge,** over East Channel, East River, connecting 36th Ave., Queens, with Motorgate garage and the Roosevelt Island street system. 1955. Repainted, 1971, 1985.

Now silver gray after a period of blue-violet and crimson—a sobering event similar to that of the Wards Island pedestrian bridge [see H Manhattan/East Harlem ff. E 6a.]

[O 4n.] Motorgate (garage complex), N of Roosevelt Island Bridge. 1974. Kallmann & McKinnell.

A parking garage with initial capacity for 1,000 cars and expansion capability for 1,500 more. The dramatic, glass-enclosed entrance structure for pedestrians is a structural tour de force.

[O 4o.] AVAC Complex/Fire Station, N of Motorgate. 1975. Kallmann & McKinnell.

Fire engines are housed in this terminal of the **Disney World-proven** refuse collection system, a giant underground vacuum collector connected to the rubbish chutes of all the new buildings.

The Southern Part

[O 5a.] Goldwater Memorial Hospital, City of New York/originally **Welfare Hospital for Chronic Diseases,** S of Sports Park. 1939. Isador Rosenfield, senior architect, N.Y.C. Department of Hospitals; Butler & Kohn; York & Sawyer. Addition to S, 1971.

Low-rise chevron-shaped balconied wings extend from a central north-south spine, giving patients confronted with long confinements **a maximum** of sunlight and river views.

[O 5b.] Formerly **City Hospital/**originally **Island Hospital/**then **Charity Hospital,** in proposed Landmark Park, S of Goldwater Memorial Hospital. 1859.

A grim reminder of the 19th-century medical ministrations to the needy. Built of stone quarried on the island by **convicts** from the adjacent penetentiary.

[O 5c.] Originally **Strecker Memorial Laboratory,** in proposed Landmark Park, SE of City Hospital overlooking E channel of the East River. 1892. Withers & Dickson. 3rd story added, 1905. ★

A neo-Renaissance work which contrasts in both scale and style with its 19th-century neighbors to the north and south. In its day it was the city's **most sophisticated** medical research facility.

[O 5d.] Smallpox Hospital, in proposed Landmark Park, SW of Strecker Memorial Laboratory. 1856. James Renwick, Jr. S wing, 1904. York & Sawyer. N wing, 1905, Renwick, Aspinwall & Owen. ★

Years of **disuse and exposure** to the elements have made this into a natural **Gothick** ruin. Its official landmark designation further encourages such a role in quoting architectural historian **Paul Zucker** on the qualities of ruins: "an expression of an eerie romantic mood . . . a palpable documentation of a period in the past . . . something which recalls a specific concept of architectural space and proportion." The designation suggests that the structure possesses all of these. It does.

[O 5e.] Delacorte Fountain, S tip of island. 1969. Pomerance & Breines, architects.

An artificial geyser of prechlorinated river water which, despite the 250-foot maximum height of its **white plume,** failed—even when operating—to carry the day against the vast panorama of the city. It has been out of action since 1985.

The Northern Part

[O 6a.] Originally **Octagon Tower, N.Y.C. Lunatic Asylum**/later **Metropolitan Hospital,** in proposed Octagon Park, N of Northtown. 1839. Alexander Jackson Davis. Mansard roof and entry stair added, ca. 1880, Joseph M. Dunn. ★

A romantic tower that was once surmounted by a later convex mansard "dome"—now also minus the two wings which once extended from it (demolished in 1970). UDC's fiscal problems prevented its intended total restoration as a *folie* in as-yet-unbuilt Octagon Park. A ruin in Westchester marble.

[O 6b.] **Bird S. Coler Hospital, City of New York,** N end of island. 1952. Addition to S, 1954.

An undistinguished design left over from the late 1930s. Construction was delayed by World War II and was finally begun in 1949.

[O 6c.] **Lighthouse,** in Lighthouse Park, N tip of island. 1872. James Renwick, Jr., supervising architect, Commission of Charities and Correction. ★ **Lighthouse Park,** 1979, Quennell-Rothschild Assocs.

Built on a tiny island just off the tip of today's Roosevelt Island (and since joined to it) under the direction of the Board of Governors of the City's Commission of Charities and Correction, whose supervising architect at the time was Renwick. The lamps for this "private" lighthouse were later furnished by the U.S. Lighthouse Service. An octagonal form of rock-face Fordham gneiss—its crocketed cornice is sensuous. The park is a modest, green, ground-swelling place, with simple timber retaining walls.

The legend of John McCarthy: An inscription carved on the local gray gneiss ashlar of the Roosevelt Island Lighthouse adds credence (of a sort) to the legend that a 19th-century patient at the nearby lunatic asylum was permitted to build this structure:

THIS IS THE WORK/WAS DONE BY/JOHN MCCARTHY/WHO BUILT THE LIGHT/HOUSE FROM THE BOTTOM TO THE/TOP ALL YE WHO DO PASS BY MAY/PRAY FOR HIS SOUL WHEN HE DIES

Though official records are vague, there may be some truth to the tale.

Wards Island/Randalls Island

Located in the vicinity of the turbulent Hell Gate at the junction of the East and Harlem Rivers, these were once separate islands but today are joined as a result of landfill operations. **Randalls,** the northernmost, houses the Triborough Bridge interchange as well as the administrative headquarters of the Triborough Bridge and Tunnel Authority. Entertainment and sporting events as well as the Festival of San Juan, the patron saint of Puerto Rico, are held in Downing Stadium.

Wards Island, a recreation area joined to Manhattan by a pedestrian bridge [see H Manhattan/East Harlem ff. E 6a.] at East 103rd Street, is the site of a number of City and State facilities. Among them are

[O 7a.] Originally **Firemen's Training Center**/now **Firefighters' Training Center, N.Y.C. Fire Department,** Wards Island, NE part of island opp. Astoria Park, Queens. 1975. Hardy Holzman Pfeiffer Assocs.

This Urban Development Corporation project, built to substitute for the old firemen's training center demolished on Roosevelt Island, is **a confident work** of architecture and **a witty one,** too—shades of those wonderfully exuberant Napoleon LeBrun & Sons' firehouses of the 1890s! To the left of the entrance road sits a great shed-roofed space rising from **a berm of earth** (which seems to throw off water too quickly to support vegetation) entered through corrugated steel **culverts.** To the right lies **a mock city** (built of brown vitrified tile block) meant to be set afire and extinguished as part of the firemen's training. Unfortunately for visitors, the complex is fenced in and guarded by a gatehouse—though sometimes not by a gatekeeper.

[O 7a.] The Firefighters' Training Center, by Hardy Holzman Pfeiffer Associates

[O 7b.] Rehabilitation Building, Manhattan Psychiatric Center, N.Y.S. Department of Mental Hygiene/formerly **Manhattan State Hospital,** Wards Island, S of hospital buildings. 1970. Caudill Rowlett Scott.

A 2-story halfway house in the stern shadow of an earlier generation's high-rise mental hospital.

[O 7c.] Manhattan Children's Treatment Center, N.Y.S. Department of Mental Hygiene, Wards Island, opp. E. 107th St. recreation pier. 1972. Richard G. Stein & Assocs.

Campus style low-rise residence, teaching, and treatment facilities for mentally retarded and emotionally disturbed children. Vitreous block in variegated tones of brown enrich the appearance of this handsome grouping.

The other Other Islands: New York is filled with islands, many of them inaccessible to the public either because of official edict or simple geography. In the first category are such City-owned (and guarded) examples as Rikers Island, in the East River just north of LaGuardia Airport (reached by a bridge from Hazen Street in Queens but under the jurisdiction of the Bronx), the home of many penal institutions; North Brother Island, adjacent to Rikers, site of the now-abandoned Riverside Hospital—"Typhoid Mary" Mallon was its best-known resident; and Hart Island, east of City Island in Long Island Sound, where the city's potter's field is located.

Quite visible but inaccessible because of geography (the currents of the East River) are tiny bits of land such as Belmont Island, south of Roosevelt opposite the United Nations; and Mill Rock, just east of 96th Street. But the richest assortment of islands, the nesting ground of thousands upon thousands of birds that migrate along the Atlantic Flyway, is the myriad group scattered in the semiaquatic wonderland of Jamaica Bay, now part of the National Park Service's Gateway National Recreation Area.

THE BRONX

NEW
JERSEY

N

R 11
N. Riverdale
R 10
R 9
R 16
R 8
Riverdale
R 7
R 14
R 6
R 5
R 12
Fieldston
R
R 4
Spuyten
Duyvil
R 3
Kingsbridge
R 2
R 1
Marble
Hill
Fordham
W 27
Heights
W 30
W 29 W 16
W 26
Kingsbridge
W 15
Heights
W 25
University
Heights
W 24
W 14
W 23
W 22
W 13
W 21
Morris
Heights
W 11 W 12
W 20 W 10
W
W 19
W 8
W 9
Grand
W 7
W 18 W 6
Highbridge
W 4
Start
Concourse
Tour
W 3
W 2
W 1
Melrose

Van
Cortlandt
Park
R 15

Woodlawn
R 13

Woodlawn
Cemetery
W 38

W 28
W 31
Bedford
Park
W 17
End
Concourse
Tour
W 34
W 33
Fordham
University
C 3
C 2
Belmont
C 4
Twin Parks
C 1
C 6
S 18
Crotona
Park
S 17
S 16
Morrisania
S 15
S 14
S 13
Longwood
S 20
S 19
S 12
S 11
S 10
S 8
St. Mary's
S 9
Park
S 2
S 3 S 5
Mott Haven S 6
S 4

W 37

N 17
Woodlawn

W 36
W 35

N 4

C 11
N.Y.
Botanical
Gardens
Bronx
Park
C 10
Bronx
Zoo
C 9
West
Farms
C 7
C 8
Van
Nest
E 6

Cross

Bronx
E 2

C 5
C

Hudson River

Concourse

MANHATTAN

River

Harlem

S 21
E 1
Soundview
S 22
Bronx
River
E 3

S 23 Hunts
Point
Market

Hunts Point
Bruckner

S 7
Port Morris

North
Brother
Island

South
Brother
Island

Triborough
Bridge

Rikers Island

0   1   2
miles

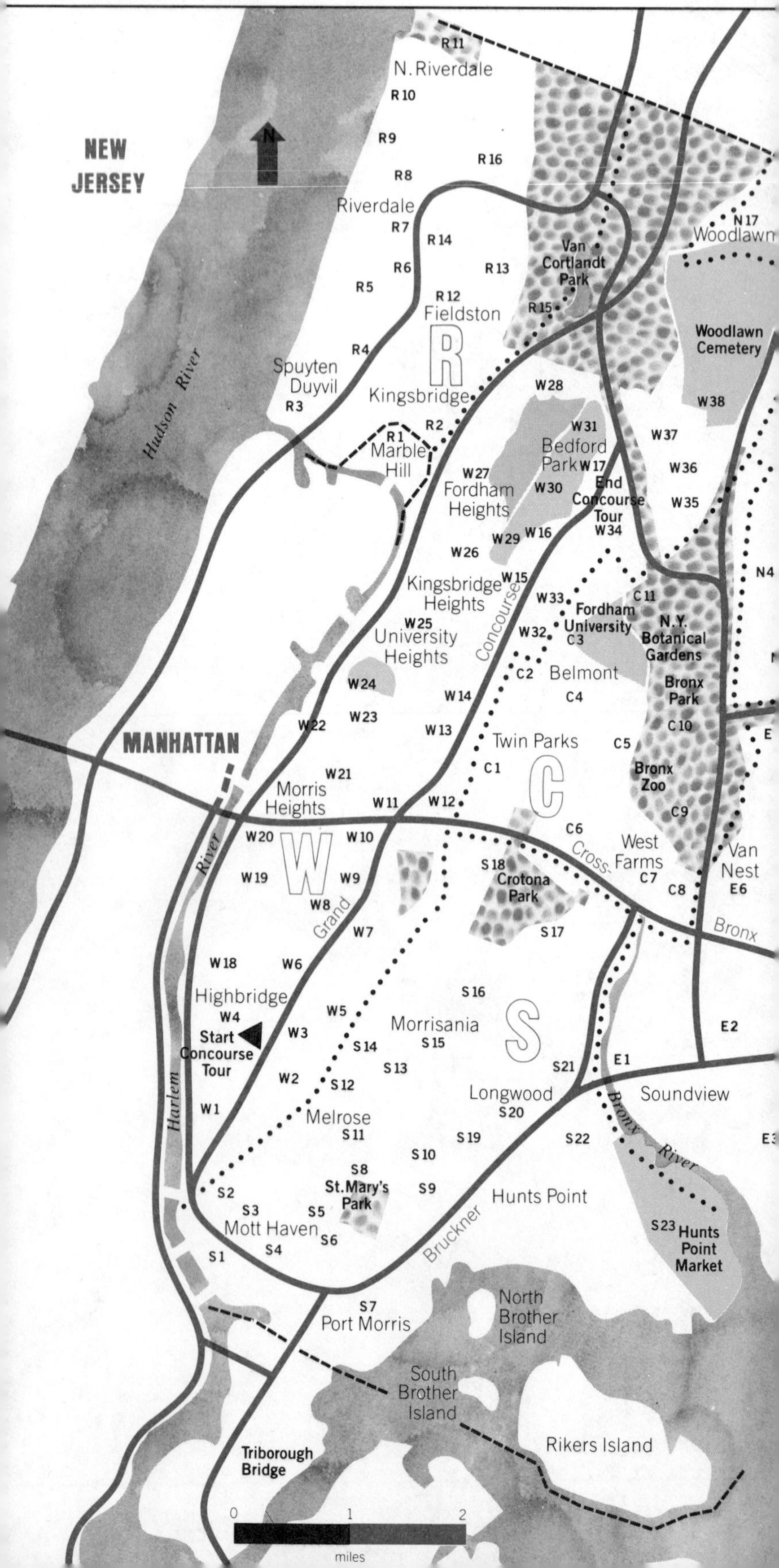

THE BRONX

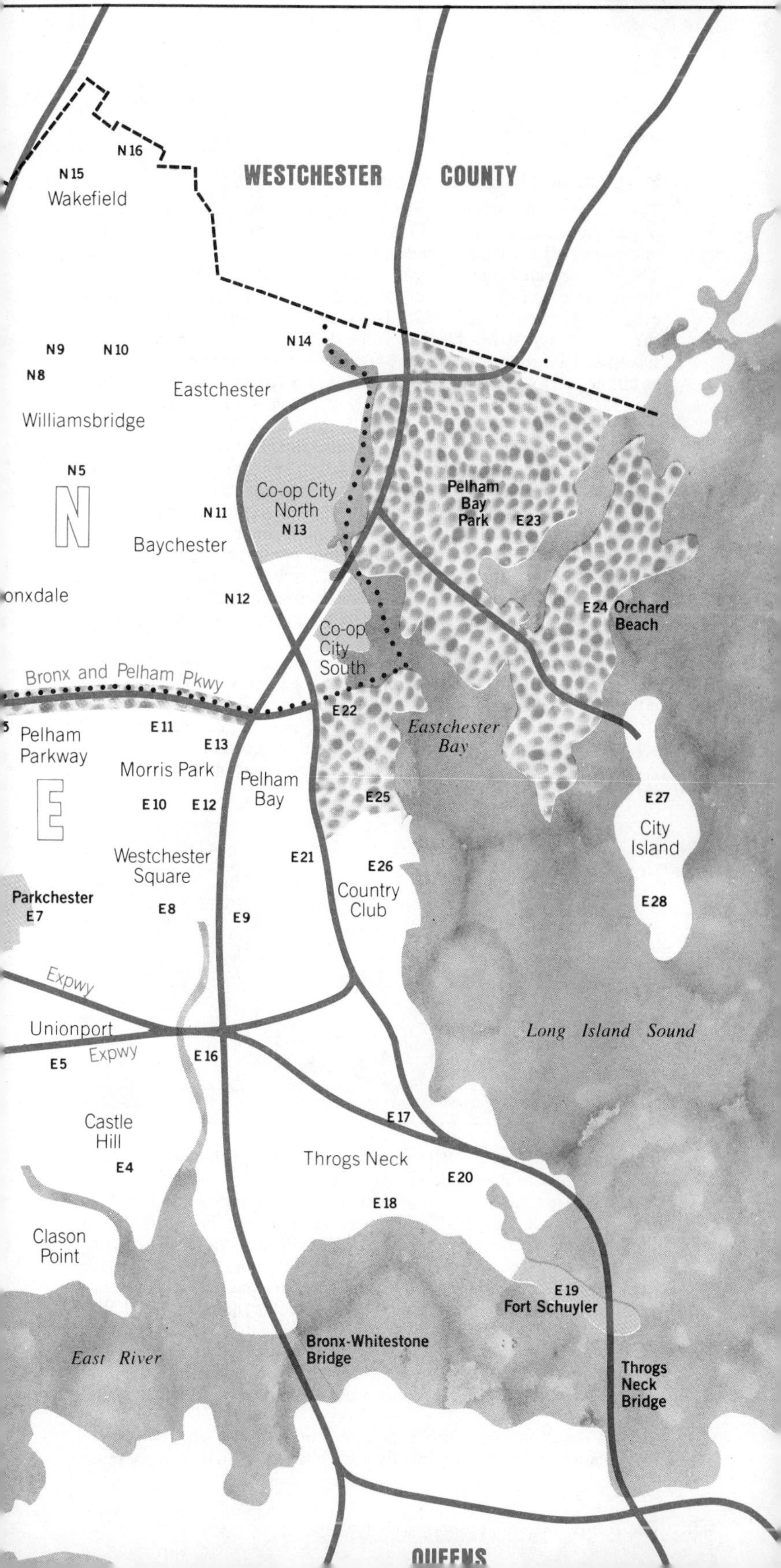

WESTCHESTER COUNTY

N 16

N 15
Wakefield

N 14

N 9   N 10

N 8

Eastchester

Williamsbridge

N 5

N

N 11

Co-op City
North

Pelham
Bay
Park

E 23

Baychester

N 13

onxdale

N 12

E 24 Orchard
Beach

Co-op
City
South

Bronx and Pelham Pkwy

E 22

Eastchester
Bay

5

Pelham
Parkway

E 11

E 13

E

Morris Park

E 25

Pelham
Bay

E 27

City
Island

E 10   E 12

E 21

E 26

E 28

Westchester
Square

Country
Club

Parkchester
E 7

E 8

E 9

Expwy

Long   Island   Sound

Unionport

E 5   Expwy

E 16

E 17

Castle
Hill

E 4

Throgs Neck

E 20

E 18

Clason
Point

E 19
Fort Schuyler

East   River

Bronx-Whitestone
Bridge

Throgs
Neck
Bridge

QUEENS

2

THE BRONX

Borough of The Bronx/Bronx County

The northernmost of New York City's five boroughs, this is the only one
physically joined to the North American mainland; the others are (or
once were) either islands by themselves or parts of another, Long Island.
The only wrinkle is the *borough* of Manhattan, which is no longer quite
the equivalent of the *island* of Manhattan, not since the straightening
out of the Harlem River in 1895. This major **earth-moving effort** severed
the community of Marble Hill from the northern tip of Manhattan
Island and joined it instead, some fifteen years later, to the Bronx, using
as fill the earth dug out of the **excavations for Grand Central Terminal.**

Like the County of Westchester, of which it was a part for some
200 years, Bronx County's topography consists of **hills and valleys** in
the west end and what was originally a **marshy plain** to the east. To this
day are visible the rocky outcroppings and streets of steps which characterize many areas of the West Bronx. The east is, as a result of **nonstop
landfill** and a recent **population explosion** in red brick housing, less
identifiable as a marsh. But a drive or walk through Pelham Bay Park
will reveal some of the borough's **sylvan, preurbanized reeded landscapes** along the peninsulas which extend into Long Island Sound.

In the 19th century the Bronx was covered with farms, market
villages, embryo commuter towns, country estates, and a number of
rambling charitable institutions. It was then a place of **rural delights.**
In 1874 the western portion of the Bronx (designated Western, Riverdale, Central, and Southern Bronx in this guide) was annexed to the
city. Bridgebuilding and the extension of elevated rapid transit lines
from Manhattan, and then a growth of population, industry, and
schools followed **political union.** The eastern Bronx (designated as Eastern and Northern Bronx in this guide) became part of New York City
in 1895.

Except for parts of Riverdale, the westernmost, hilliest, and least
accessible part of the borough, the physical vestiges of the old villages
with such names as West Farms, Morrisania, Kingsbridge, and Middletown were submerged by 20th-century development. The **extension of
the rapid transit lines** along Jerome Avenue, Boston Road, White Plains
Road, Westchester Avenue, and finally along Grand Concourse made
the Bronx the next step in **upward mobility** for hundreds of thousands
of families of average but improving means. But the post-World War
II suburban exodus drained away many of their offspring. And governmental housing policy relocated many of the older generation who
remained, eastward to Co-op City, a huge development of thirty-five-
story apartment towers, bedding down, in aggregate, some 55,000
people.

As the Bronx approaches the 21st century it has become home to
a population that is predominantly nonwhite and to an inordinate num-

ber of poor. Though stable communities continue to flourish with populations drawn from all racial and economic backgrounds, much of the South, Central, and West Bronx carries the appellation **"Fort Apache,"** with areas approaching the appearance of a burned-out wilderness, scenes not unlike those in **war-ravaged** cities.

In contrast to the visible decay of many of its communities, however, is the **green leafy** camouflage of the borough's larger **parks** and the **parkways** which link them. They are the result of a plan by local visionaries devised back in 1883 and executed largely in the two decades that followed. Though the parks and parkways show the scars of economic deprivation and personal as well as municipal poverty—broken benches, broken glass, broken tree limbs—they continue to make up the **most generous park system** in the city. The ability of nature to rejuvenate itself (fully one-fifth of the Bronx's area—5,861 acres—is parkland, although admittedly large amounts are not yet developed) coupled with the foresight of the borough's early planners may offer guidelines for future development.

Prospect Theatre, Bronx, New York City.

Tips on touring: The Bronx, the smallest of New York's outer boroughs, is still quite large. Its southwestern quadrant, south of Fordham Road and west of the Bronx River (except for some notably healthy parts such as Belmont), is a large area beset by economic and social problems. The northwest, Riverdale, is picturesque, convoluted, and very hilly. The Bronx east of the Bronx River is simply vast. All this adds up to a recommendation that **touring be best done by car** with enough stop-offs to stretch your legs and to permit looking with greater care—so much can be missed, even when driving at a crawl. A car can provide a needed sense of protection in a devastated area, but be prepared to **roll up your windows** in hot weather when approaching a fire hydrant being used to provide relief from the heat. Otherwise some playful kids will cup their hands around the spray and inundate you. It's nothing personal on their part, but it's no fun driving with a puddle in your lap. Get a **street map** before embarking. The pocket atlases of the city are large enough to read but small enough to maneuver in the confines of a car.

For those **intrepid pedestrian wanderers** a good option is a mix of Bronx Park (zoo and botanical garden), Fordham University's Gothic-styled campus, and (except on Sundays) the nearby Italian community of Belmont and its wonderful European shopping street, Arthur Avenue. [See **Central Bronx** for the details.] **Mass transit** to a good starting point: Take the subway (D train or Jerome Avenue Line train) to the Fordham Road Station. Then change (another fare—exact change, please) for Bus Bx 12 eastbound to Southern Boulevard and East Fordham Road, where you will find the zoo's Rainey Gate a short walk east on the south side of the street, the garden on the north. (IRT expresses to the East 180th Street Station drop you at the south end of the zoo, very near the Boston Road Gate.)

Remember there is **safety in numbers.** Don't walk in desolate areas. Don't tour at night. Do take a friend along—it's more fun that way.

Meanwhile, there is much to see:

SOUTHERN BRONX

MOTT HAVEN • PORT MORRIS • MELROSE • MORRISANIA
CROTONA PARK • LONGWOOD • HUNTS POINT

South Bronx

Though their names persist into the present, the country villages that once existed in the South Bronx have long disappeared. Soon after the **Civil War** the farms that survived from colonial days began to give way to private homes and tenement rows. In more recent days these have given way to **arterial highways** and **public housing** developments. The rapid growth of other parts of the Bronx in the 20th century eclipsed the South Bronx and shifted the focus of commerce, entertainment, and government to other parts of the borough. Successive waves of immigrants and industries have passed in and out of the South Bronx, but their **footprints** are hard to find. Without money, power, or prestige, the area has been unable to cultivate its ornaments. **Landmarks** venerated in other places are overlooked here. Some have completely disappeared; others are marked for demolition. Many have been burned down, but some survive and wait to be rediscovered.

MOTT HAVEN

[S 1a.] Formerly **Mott Iron Works,** Third Ave. bet. Harlem River and E. 134th St., opp. Bruckner Blvd. to former Mott Haven Canal (filled-in). W side. 1828–1906.

Jordan L. Mott, **inventor of a coal-burning stove,** established a factory west of Third Avenue, between East 134th Street and the Harlem River, in 1828. The venture prospered and grew. Some buildings of the ironworks can still be seen from the western walkway of the Third Avenue Bridge. *Note the company's name in relief in the south wall's brickwork.* It was Mott, who **founded the village of Mott Haven,** whose monogram "MH" persists in the mosaics of the 138th and 149th Street Stations of the Jerome Avenue subway.

[S 1a.] The former Mott Iron Works' presence in 3-dimensional brick letters

The Broncks: The first European settlers of this area were Jonas Bronck, a Dane from Amsterdam, and his family, whose farmhouse is believed to have been located east of the Third Avenue Bridge. Though some say the borough's **official** name, **The Bronx,** owes its initial article to friends of the settlers saying "Let's pay a visit to the Broncks," the less romantic but more accurate explanation lies elsewhere. As it was common to speak of the Army of **the** Potomac or the valley of **the** Hudson, each taking its name from a river, so it was with the lands along the banks of the local river here, **the** Bronx River.

Piano Town:

[S 1b.] Formerly **Krakauer Brothers Piano Company (factory)**, 307-309 E. 132nd St., bet. Lincoln and Alexander Aves. N side. ca. 1890.
[S 1c.] Formerly **Kroeger Piano Company (factory)**, Alexander Ave. NW cor. E. 132nd St. ca. 1890. **[S 1d.]** Formerly **warehouse**, 82-96 Lincoln Ave., bet. E. 132nd St. and Bruckner Blvd. E side. 1888. C. C. Buck. **[S 1e.]** Formerly **Estey Piano Company (factory)**, E. 132nd St. bet. Lincoln and Alexander Aves. N side. 1885. A. B. Ogden & Son.

In the last decades of the 19th century, as an emerging urban middle class was able to amass enough surplus income to seek the finer things, **pianos came into demand.** In the Bronx they were player pianos after the process for a "pianola" was patented in 1897. The local German immigrant population included skilled workers employed in these former piano factories, as others similarly skilled were employed across the East River at the **Steinway** and **Sohmer** factories in **western Queens** [q.v].

[S 1e.] Orig. Estey Piano Co. factory   **[S 4.]** Bertine Block on E. 136 Street

[S 2a.] Branch, **Chase Manhattan Bank**/originally **North Side Board of Trade Building**, 2514 Third Ave., SE cor. E. 137th St. 1912. Albert E. Davis.

After the Bronx became part of Greater New York, but before it became a county of its own, it was the **North Side** of New York County (or Manhattan). This neo-Classical terra-cotta structure served as headquarters of the borough's board of trade.

[S 2b.] **2602 Third Avenue (warehouse)**, NE cor. E. 140th St. ca. 1890.

Arches of all varieties penetrate the substantial brick walls, making this warehouse special.

[S 2c.] **Intermediate School 183, Bronx, The Paul Robeson School**, 339 Morris Ave., NW cor. E. 140th St. 1974. Stein & Stein.

A severe **New Brutalist** cast-in-place concrete structure. The later addition of mesh window grilles only intensifies the building's prisonlike qualities.

[S 3.] **Mott Haven Historic District,** ★ generally along both sides of Alexander Ave. bet. E. 137th and E. 141st Sts., including **[S 3a.] St. Jerome's Roman Catholic Church**, 230 Alexander Ave., SE cor. E. 138th St. 1898. Delhi & Howard ☆ **[S 3b.] St. Jerome's School**, 222 Alexander Ave., NE cor. E. 137th St. ☆ **[S 3c.] 40th Precinct, N.Y.C. Police Department**, 257 Alexander Ave., NW cor. E. 138th St. 1924. Thomas E. O'Brien. ☆ **[S 3d.] Mott Haven Branch, N.Y. Public Library**, 321 E. 140th St., NW cor. Alexander Ave. 1905. Babb, Cook & Willard. ☆ **[S 3e.] Tercera Iglesia Bautista (Third Spanish Baptist Church)**/originally **Alexander Avenue Baptist Church**, 322 Alexander Ave., SE cor. E. 141st St. 1902. Ward & Davis. ☆

This is the old Bronx at its best. Not only are there well-designed row houses and apartments—by such architects as Carl A. Millner, Charles Romeyn, Arthur Arctander, and others—but five fine institutional buildings as well, two of which, the churches, handsomely define the district at its south and north ends. No. 280 Alexander Avenue was the home of **Edward Willis,** a local land developer for whom nearby Willis Avenue is named.

Mott Haven's other "brownstones":

[S 4.] The Bertine Block (row houses), E. 136th St. bet. Willis Ave. and Brown Place: **[S 4a.] 408-412 East 136th Street.** S side. 1878. Rogers & Browne. **[S 4b.] 414-432 East 136th Street.** S side. 1891. George Keister. **[S 4c.] 415-425 East 136th Street.** N side. 1893. John Hauser. **[S 4d.] 434-440 East 136th Street.** S side. 1895. Adolph Balshun, Jr.

The Bertine Block devives its name from the decorative grouping of low-stooped row houses of yellow face brick commissioned by **developer Edward D. Bertine** between 1891 and 1895. The earlier houses precede Bertine's involvement and are in the less picturesque neo-Grec style.

[S 4e.] Plaza Borinquen: view from the courtyard of the low-rise apartments

[S 4e.] Plaza Borinquen, 3 sites: 1) E. 137th St. bet. Willis Ave. and Brown Place. 2) E. 137th St. NW cor. Brown Place. 3) E. 138th St. to E. 139th St., bet. Willis and Brook Aves. 1974. Ciardullo-Ehmann.

Eighty-eight triplex apartments contained in groups of row houses thoughtfully planned to fill three different kinds of **scattered sites** within the existing housing fabric. The red-brown masonry, with similarly toned mortar and bright highlights in the orange and red air conditioner covers, heralds a new look for the South Bronx. **Borinquen** is the name given the island of Puerto Rico by its original settlers, the **Taino people.**

Between Willis and Brook Avenues:

(Brook Avenue is one-way south.)

[S 5a.] 403-445 East 139th Street (row houses). N side. **408-450 East 140th Street (row houses).** S side. 1888. William O'Gorman.

Neo-Grec 2½-story, red brick, **mini-"brownstones"** heavy with cast-iron railings on the stoops.

[S 5b.] 409-427 East 140th Street (row houses). N side. 1897. William Hornum.

Here the houses across 140th Street echo Dutch and Flemish influences in their detail.

[S 5b.] Row houses at 409–427 East 140th St., with Dutch/Flemish echoes

[S 5c.] Originally **Willis Avenue Methodist Episcopal Church,** 330 Willis Ave., NE cor. E. 141st St. 1900. George W. Kramer.

A very interesting composition of tiered windows distinguishes this church. Were the steeple still in place, this would be a real prize.

[S 5d.] 404-450 East 142nd Street (row houses). S side. 1897. William O'Gorman.

Again, neo-Grec returns.

[S 5e.] Originally **Congregational Church of North New York,** 415 E. 143rd St., bet. Willis and Brook Aves. N side. 1903. Dodge & Morrison.

Anchoring the small-scale row houses midblock is this late Romanesque Revival, creamy gray, rock-faced stone church. What a **welcome relief** to the humorless red brick high-rise "projects" so evident nearby!

[S 5f.] 419-437 East 143rd Street (row houses). N side. 1887. H. S. Baker. **[S 5g.] 404-446 East 144th Street (row houses).** S side. 1887. H. S. Baker.

And yet more neo-Grec.

[S 6a.] St. Ann's Church (Episcopal) and Graveyard, 295 St. Ann's Ave., bet. E. 139th and E. 141st Sts. W side. 1841. ★

An old stone-walled church turned slightly askew to the street grid and facing a space that is neither street nor true oasis, St. Ann's is an echo from the Bronx's dim past. **Mysterious hummocks** in front of the edifice mark burial vaults in which early parishioners' remains are entombed. Adjacent is the weathered wood of play equipment installed as a 1960s social response to the neighborhood's deprived children. Memories of those once-hopeful days swirl around you along with the dust at your feet.

[S 6b.] José de Diego-Beekman Houses, 346 St. Ann's Ave., bet. E. 141st and St. Mary's Sts. E side. ca. 1901. Rehabilitation, 1975, Beyer Blinder Belle.

Some early 20th-century tenements are being turned around into late 20th-century housing resources. This is but one of a number of examples in the South Bronx. It is believed by some that the renewal of existing housing stock is a **more realistic** (if not the most glamorous) solution to the pressing human need for urban shelter.

[S 6c.] Centro de Salud Segundo Ruiz Belvis, (neighborhood family-care center), E. 142nd St. NW cor. St. Ann's Ave. 1972. Frost Assocs., architects; William Tarr, sculptor.

An important step forward: not just a needed community health center but a physical symbol of hope in the cityscape.

[S 6d.] Originally **Henry W. Boetteger Silk Finishing Factory**/later **Boetteger & Heintz Silk Manufacturing Company,** 401 Brook Ave., SW cor. 144th St. 1888. Robert Otz and George Butz.

Were the window openings to be unstuccoed, this factory complex would rival the old mill buildings of New England.

[S 6e.] St. Pius V Roman Catholic Church, 416 E. 145th St., bet. Willis and Brook Aves. 1907. Anthony F. A. Schmidt.

Its **strong silhouette** suggests a 19th-century utilities building, but in fact this substantial red brick church is an early 20th-century paean to God.

PORT MORRIS

East of the Bruckner Expressway and the Bronx approaches to the Triborough Bridge and south of East 141st Street lies a peninsula of industry **largely forgotten** by the wheels of progress: Port Morris. It was developed as a **deepwater port** by the Morris family during the mid 19th century, in the hope of rivaling New York. The Hell Gate Plant of the Consolidated Edison Company is located here.

 [S 7a.] Bronx Grit Chamber of Wards Island Water Pollution Control Plant, City of New York, 158 Bruckner Blvd., bet. St. Ann's and Cypress Aves. S side. 1936. McKim, Mead & White. ★

An impressive exercise in the neo-Baroque but a little late in this century for such antics.

[S 7b.] Bronx approach, Hell Gate Bridge, E. 132nd St. bet. Willow and Walnut Aves. S side. 1917. Gustav Lindenthal, engineer. Henry Hornbostel, architect.

Looking through the **seemingly endless row** of concrete arches that support the structure of this railroad viaduct is positively mesmerizing.

[S 7c.] Philip Knitting Mills (factory)/formerly **Bogart Piano Company**/ originally **Mothers Friend Shirt Waist (factory),** Willow Ave. bet. E. 135th and E. 136th Sts. E side. ca. 1888. Entry altered, ca. 1935.

Another former piano factory—the southern Bronx had many— with a later, gently Art Deco entry. [See S 1b., c., d., e.]

[S 7d.] Originally **James P. Lenihan, Inc. (factory),** 841 E. 135th St., bet. Willow and Walnut Aves. N side. 1925.

A utilitarian, corrugated-steel, 4-story shed. Its adjoining masonry office addresses the street with a **handsomely carved** limestone sign panel identifying its owner.

MELROSE

Dominating this community is the traditional business and entertainment center of the borough, **called the Hub,** the intersection of five busy streets: East 149th Street, Third, Willis, Melrose, and Westchester Avenues. Old-timers can recall the area as a **bustling entertainment center,** with fare ranging from silent flicks and burlesque to operatic performances, and with trolley lines converging from every direction. The Bronx stretch of the Third Avenue el, which once clattered overhead, was removed in the 1970s, but the pace on the street remains **furious and chaotic,** an expression of the coming together of the many Hispanic and black communities, of which Melrose and the rest of the South Bronx is today composed. If there is a word to sum up the Hub's purpose it is **"buy!"** Alexander's first store at 2952 Third Avenue and a onetime branch of 14th Street's Hearn's, which still bears the name, are the flagships for hundreds of smaller merchants.

[S 8a.] St. Mary's Park, St. Ann's to Jackson Aves., St. Mary's to E. 149th Sts. Reconstructed, 1936.

This park is named for **St. Mary's Church,** a wooden country church that stood on Alexander Avenue and East 142nd Street until its demolition in 1959. The crest of the hill at the north end of the park is a good place from which to survey this neighborhood. It was once known as **Janes' Hill** and belonged to Adrian Janes, whose family's **famous ironworks** was located nearby.

The Capitol dome: On the south side of Westchester Avenue between Brook and St. Ann's Avenues is the site of what was once the Janes, Kirtland & Company Iron Works. It was here, in one of America's largest foundries of its time, that were cast such lowly devices as iron furnaces and such elegant items of architectural ironwork as Central Park's Bow Bridge. But literally crowning partners Janes' and Kirtland's many achievements was the casting and erection (using horsepower) of the 8,909,200 pounds of iron which became the Capitol Dome in Washington, D.C., completed in 1863.

West of St. Mary's Park:

[S 8b.] Public School 27, Bronx, 519 St. Ann's Ave., bet. E. 147th and E. 148th Sts. W side. 1895. C. B. J. Snyder.

Built 5 stories tall for children with good legs and good lungs. The carved **limestone escutcheon** over the main entrance is an effulgent work of sculpture.

East of St. Mary's Park:

[S 9a.] Former **Ward Bread Company (bakery),** 367 Southern Blvd., bet. E. 142nd St. and St. Mary's St. to Wales Ave. W side. ca. 1900.

Abutting the **old Port Morris Branch** of the New York, New Haven & Hartford Railroad is this 6½-story white, glazed terra-cotta bakery. Note the name in brick down its chimney.

[S 9c.] Saint Roch's: neo-Plateresque   **[S 11b.]** Lincoln Medical & M.H. Center

[S 9b.] Originally **Samuel Gompers Industrial High School,** 455 Southern Blvd., along Tinton Ave. bet. E. 145th and E. 146th Sts. W side, to Wales Ave. 1932. Walter C. Martin.

A handsome statuesque symmetric composition in a form of stripped-down neo-Romanesque.

[S 9c.] St. Roch's Church and Rectory, 425 Wales Ave., bet. E. 147th and E. 149th Sts. W side. 1931. DePace & Juster.

The style employed here is **neo-Plateresque,** the Landmarks Preservation Commission staff believes, inspired by the architecture of 16th-century Spanish Renaissance forms.

North of St. Mary's Park:

[S 10a.] 560-584 Eagle Avenue (2-family housing), bet. E. 149th St. and Westchester Ave. E side. ca. 1986, *(Eagle Ave. one-way south.)*

A **brilliant solution** for reasonably priced housing. Very three-dimensional in concept, with **real backyards** for the apartment dwellers.

[S 10b.] 600, 610, 620 Trinity Avenue (apartments), bet. E. 149th St. and Westchester Aves. ca. 1939.

These unusual-for-this-area, 6-story, cream and brown brick, **Art Moderne** buildings reek of the West Bronx and Grand Concourse. What a surprising housing resource—don't let them burn!

[S 10c.] Hunts Point Multi-Service Center, 630 Jackson Ave., NE cor. E. 151st St. 1974. Bond Ryder Assocs.

One of a number of new institutions which grew out of the Model Cities Program in the South Bronx, this building seems out of place with its rich, yellow tan block and almost opaque-seeming, dark-tinted sheets of glass.

[S 10d.] St. Anselm's RC Church: its rich volumes are best seen from the rear

[S 10d.] St. Anselm's Church (Roman Catholic), 673 Tinton Ave., bet. E. 152nd St. and Westchester Ave. W side. ca. 1907. Anton Kloster.

This church's exterior is bare-bones brick practically everywhere except around the entrance, where some poetically illustrated glazed tile plaques and neo-Romanesque ornament soften the bluntness of the masonry. But as the exterior is **bold and forceful,** the interior is **soft and supple,** its details a combination of Byzantine and Romanesque motifs created by brothers of the Benedictine order who came here from Germany in the 1920s. A **blue-green light** floats down upon the sanctuary from a circular, stained glass clerestory as though lighting a grotto. The walls **shimmer** with the brothers' ceramic tile **tesserae.** It is both a surprising and moving experience.

The Hub:

[S 11a.] Fashion Moda (art gallery), 2803 Third Ave., bet. E. 146th and E. 148th Sts. W side. Open to the public.

A neighborhood showplace for off-Madison Avenue art founded by Stefan Eins and Joe Lewis in 1979.

[S 11b.] Lincoln Medical & Mental Health Center, N.Y.C. Health & Hospitals Corporation, Morris Ave. SW cor. E. 149th St. 1976. Max O. Urbahn Assocs. Brick bas-relief mural, Aleksandra Kasuba.

The brickwork of this up-to-date health care facility is just too much of a good thing. Of an indescribably strident earth color, it aggressively grabs your attention, as does what must be the largest bronze anodized-aluminum identification sign in the world. On the other hand, the swirled brick **bas-relief** on the 149th Street side is a handsome addition to the streetscape.

 [S 11c.] Immaculate Conception Church of the Blessed Virgin Mary (Roman Catholic), 389 E. 150th St., NW cor. Melrose Ave. 1887. Henry Bruns. **[S 11d.] School Hall,** 378 E. 151st St., SW cor. Melrose Ave. 1901. Anthony F. A. Schmitt.

This austere yet handsome brick Romanesque Revival church boasts the highest steeple in the borough. It recalls the days when the **Germans were the most populous ethnic group** in the Bronx and their prominence in the building trades, brewing, and the manufacture of musical instruments was of central importance to the borough's prosperity. The facades of the rectory on the west, the church in the center, and the Redemptorist Fathers home on the east make **a handsome composition** of brick detail and arched windows. A later auditorium on the southwest corner of 151st Street and Melrose Avenue is a reserved Beaux Arts composition.

[S 11e.] 614 Courtlandt Avenue (apartments), NE cor. E. 151st St. 1872. Altered, 1882, Hewlett S. Baker. ★

In a neighborhood where the tides of change are everywhere apparent, here is a miraculously intact 3-story town house complete with intricate detailing on a mansard roof.

[S 11f.] Engine Company 41, N.Y.C. Fire Department, 330 E. 150th St., bet. Courtlandt and Morris Aves. S side. 1903.

Civilization in the midst of chaos.

[S 11g.] Michelangelo Apartments, E. 149th to E. 150th Sts., bet. Morris and Park Aves. 1976. Weiner & Gran and Jarmul & Brizee.

If this project's flat, uninteresting facade on 149th Street was meant as a foil to the more colorful, more three-dimensional one of Lincoln Medical Center across the street, it succeeds. But there must have been a better way. A project of the state Urban Development Corporation.

[S 11h.] Maria Lopez Plaza (apartments), 635 Morris Ave., NW cor. E. 151st St. 1982. John Ciardullo Assocs.

Designed in 1975 and delayed by the City's financial crisis but well worth waiting for: white columns, half-cylindrical balconies, and thoughtful fenestration raise this housing to a level considerably above the norm. And what only the residents see—in the block-square, green interior courtyard—is brilliant housing design united with enlightened urban living.

[S 11d.] Immaculate Conception Ch.   **[S 11h.]** The Maria Lopez Plaza apts.

[S 12a.] 153rd Street Viaduct, connecting Park Ave./Concourse Village E. with Concourse Village W.

When you can't afford to repair it, close it! Four ill-maintained **lacy steel trusses** cross the former New York Central Melrose Yard, but only pedestrians use it—they've cut a hole in the fence.

Humble churches:

[S 12b.] Greater Universal Baptist Church/originally **Church of the Holy Trinity (Italian Presbyterian),** 253 E. 153rd St., bet. Morris Ave.

and Concourse Village E. N side. 1911. **[S 12c.] Greater Victory Baptist Church**/originally **St. Matthew's Lutheran Church,** 374 E. 156th St., bet. Courlandt and Melrose Aves. S side. 1895. **[S 12d.]** Originally **Reformed Church of Melrose,** 742 Elton Ave., NE cor. E. 156th St. 1874. Henry Piering. **[S 12e.]** Originally **Elton Avenue (German) Methodist Episcopal Church,** 790 Elton Ave., SE cor. E. 158th St. 1879. John Rogers or H. S. Baker.

The world around this remarkable array of religious buildings may be in chaos, but their congregations and ministers persevere . . . and the churches survive.

MORRISANIA

[S 13a.] Formerly **Ebling Brewery,** St. Ann's to Eagle Aves., N of E. 156th St. **[S 13b.]** Formerly **Hupfel Brewery,** St. Ann's to Eagle Aves., bet. E. 159th and E. 161st Sts. Both ca. 1875.

The South Bronx being a German neighborhood in the 19th century, there was a continuing demand for **lager beer.** Before the advent of refrigeration, the brewing of lager (from the German *liegen,* to lie still) required a **chilled place to age.** Caves cut into hillsides made it possible to pack the beer kegs with naturally cut ice and then to seal the openings temporarily until the beer had aged. No surprise then that these former breweries backed up to the Eagle Avenue **escarpment** (it is **so steep** that Eagle Avenue negotiates East 161st Street over a high bridge). The caves are used today for less romantic manufacturing purposes. During Prohibition, both caves and breweries were converted into **indoor mushroom farms.**

[S 13c.] Model Cities Site 402 (housing), Eagle to Cauldwell Aves., bet. E. 156th and E. 161st Sts. 1987. Shelly Kroop.

Three-story concrete block housing, the color of bubble gum. An attempt to brighten up the neighborhood no doubt.

[S 13d.] Sts. Peter & Paul Ch. Rectory   **[S 13e.]** Old Bronx Boro Courthouse

[S 13d.] Church of Sts. Peter and Paul (Roman Catholic), 840 Brook Ave., NE cor. E. 159th St. 1932. **Rectory,** 833 St. Ann's Ave., bet. E. 159th St. and E. 161st St./Third Ave. W side, 1900. Michael J. Garvin.

The church is in handsome granite ashlar, looking more as though it was commissioned by the Episcopal diocese than the Roman Catholic—but very beautiful nonetheless. The rectory is a charming reminder of the parish's earlier days.

[S 13e.] Originally **Bronx Borough Courthouse**/then **Criminal Court of the City of New York, Bronx County Branch,** occupying triangle bet. E. 161st St., Brook Ave., and Third Ave. 1906. Michael J. Garvin. ★

Strong vertical forms set against the fine horizontal lines cut into its base make this Beaux Arts structure a monument as well as a building. In spite of many decades of smoke, grime, neglect, and the rattling of the now-gone Third Avenue el, it remains grand, even though its windows are missing, its metalwork is tarnished, and its walls are covered with soot. The leaf-crowned statute of **Justice by G. E. Roine,** which peered into every passing train for so many years from the south facade, may not be there much longer . . . a feeble replacement courthouse has opened nearby [see W Bronx W5.].

[S 13f.] 42nd Precinct, N.Y.C. Police Department/originally **36th Precinct,** 3137 Third Ave. (entry on Washington Ave.), opp. E. 160th St. at George Meade Plaza. 1904. Charles Volz.

This station house has seen its designation change often, the evidence being apparent over the door: the plaque reads 36th; the recut frieze says 46th; the most recent stenciled version, 42nd. This neo-Classical structure appears in exterior shots of *Fort Apache,* a movie about life in the South Bronx. The **real Fort Apache** was actually the **Simpson Street station house** [see S 20c.].

[S 14a.] Melrose Courts (apartments), 3203-3213 Park Ave., NW cor. E. 161st St. 1920. Charles Kreymborg, completed by William E. Erb and Paul R. Henkel.

A shambles but still impressive in both size and adornment. Although 6 stories tall, it has no elevators—but elaborate brick, stucco, and tile embellishment.

[S 14b.] Morrisania Air Rights Housing (apartments), over the 4-track Metro North railroad cut straddling Park Ave., bet. E. 158th and 162nd Sts. 1980. Jarmul & Brizee.

It's hard to believe that this area of abandonment, deterioration, and desolation was so overcrowded in the late 1960s that the N.Y.C. Housing Authority was persuaded to commission (and patiently shepherd through years of delay) these extraordinarily expensive structures poised over the wide railroad cut. Despite the **trendy diagonal form** of the base, these are still tall, unfriendly monsters; perhaps their frightening appearance even aggravated the area's problems.

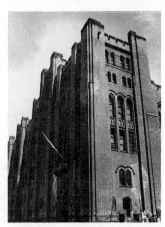

[S 14b.] Morrisania Air Rights Hsg.   [S 15f.] The 105th Artillery Armory

[S 15a.] Charlton Playground, N.Y.C. Department of Parks & Recreation, E. 164th St. bet. Boston Rd. and Cauldwell Ave., midblock. Reconstructed, 1982, Weintraub & di Domenico.

A **welcome anomaly** in these parts of deadening municipal presence: among the surrounding "projects" and blight, a city facility of great imagination and subtlety. A simple but exquisitely sculpted pergola perches atop a sharp rise in the topography. A neighborhood acropolis. Design commissioned by the **N.Y.C. Department of Housing, Preservation & Development.**

[S 15a.] Charlton Playground: a creation of great imagination and subtlety

[S 15b.] **1041-1067 Clay Avenue (row houses),** bet. E. 165th and E. 166th Sts. W side. 1902. **1040-1066 Clay Avenue (row houses),** bet. E. 165th and E. 166th Sts. E side. 1902. All by Warren C. Dickerson. **1038 Clay Avenue (residence),** NE cor. E. 165th St. 1907. Charles C. Clark.

A lovely group of classically inspired row houses on a site that had been the old **Fleetwood Trotting Course** until 1898.

[S 15c.] Former **Sheffield Farms Company (Milk) Bottling Plant,** 1051 Webster Ave., bet. E. 165th and E. 166th Sts. W side. 1914–1921. Frank Rooke.

Though milk is no longer pasteurized or bottled behind this glazed terra-cotta facade, the cows and milk bottles are still visible—in the ornament.

[S 15d.] **1074 Cauldwell Avenue (residence).** 1887. F. T. Camp.
[S 15e.] **1076 Cauldwell Avenue (residence).** 1892. Charles C. Churchill. Both E cor. Boston Rd., S of E. 166th St.

Two gleaming, **well-cared-for,** expansive (for this outlying area) Victorian frame houses preside over a dusty intersection that has seen better days.

[S 15f.] **105th Artillery Armory, N.Y. National Guard,** 1122 Franklin Ave., NE cor. E. 166th St. 1910. Charles C. Haight.

A dark, red brick fortress with slitlike windows looks down on a steep street of stairs. Together with **Hines Park** and the facade of St. Augustine's Church, the armory provides the backdrop for an exciting but forgotten urban space. It is the perfect stage for a **medieval melodrama** or a childhood game of **knights in armor.**

 [S 15g.] **St. Augustine's Church (Roman Catholic),** 1183 Franklin Ave., NW cor. E. 167th St. 1894. Louis C. Giele. [S 15h.] **St. Augustine's School,** 1176 Franklin Ave., bet. E. 167th and E. 168th Sts. E side. 1904.

Renaissance and Baroque elements are combined in the somber but imposing facade of the church. The parish school up the block to the north is distinguished by a sculpture group projecting from the tympanum of its classical pediment.

[S 16.] **Morris High School Historic District,** bet. Boston Rd. and Forest Ave. (incl. Jackson Ave.), bet. E. 166th St. and Home St., plus Trinity Ave. SE cor. E. 166th St. ★ [S 16a.] **Trinity Episcopal Church of Morrisania,** 690 E. 166th St., SE cor. Trinity Ave. 1874. ☆

A district of row houses primarily by architect **Warren C. Dickerson,** as well as others by **John H. Lavelle, Harry T. Howell,** and **Hugo Auden.** Crowning all, however, is:

[S 16b.] **Morris High School,** 1110 Boston Rd., NE cor. E. 166th St. 1904. C. B. J. Snyder. ☆ Interior. ★

A powerful, turreted central tower, gabled green copper roof, buff brick, and terra-cotta trim make this **a superior model of Public School Gothic** and a centerpiece of the neighborhood. When first begun, the school was originally to have been named **Peter Cooper** High School! Why?

[S 16c.] 1266 Boston Road (residence). ca. 1890. **[S 16d.] 1270 Boston Road (residence).** ca. 1890. Both bet. E. 168th and E. 169th Sts. at McKinley Sq. E side. **[S 16e.] McKinley Square.**

Somewhat narrower structures than those 3 blocks away on Cauldwell Avenue, these are in the **Grant Wood/American Gothic mode.** Perhaps it is no accident that they survive: one is surrounded by a high, chain link fence; the other is cheek by jowl with a firehouse.

[S 16f.] Originally **Eichler Mansion**/now **Department of Mental Health, Bronx-Lebanon Hospital Center, Fulton Division,** 1285 Fulton Ave., SW cor. E. 169th St. 1890. De Lemos & Cordes.

A plethora of riches: yet *another* residential relic of the 19th century, this time of red brick and terra-cotta. Eichler was a **beer magnate** and his mansion sat on the hill looking west to his **brewery,** once located at Third Avenue south of East 169th Street.

[S 16g.] Originally **Temple Adath Israel,** 551 E. 169th St., bet. Fulton and Third Aves. N side. 1889? Altered later.

This modest edifice is considered by some to be the first Jewish synagogue built in the Bronx. It has since served the Puerto Rican community as a Baptist church.

[S 15g.] Saint Augustine's Church   **[S 16g.]** Orig. Temple Adath Israel

[S 16h.] Lewis S. Davidson, Sr., Houses, N.Y.C. Housing Authority, 810 Home St., bet. Union and Prospect Aves. S side. 1150, 1152 Union Ave., bet. E. 167th and Home Sts. E side. 1221 Prospect Ave. W side. 1973. Paul Rudolph.

Exposed cast-in-place concrete frames with dark gray, ribbed block infill, these 8-story low-rent apartment buildings are a refreshing change from the monotonous red brick towers previously bestowed upon the city's neighborhoods by the Authority.

[S 16i.] Engine Company 82, Ladder Company 31, N.Y.C. Fire Department, 1213 Intervale Ave., NW cor. E. 169th St.

This Beaux Arts firehouse figures heavily in the 1972 fiction bestseller about fire fighting in the South Bronx, Dennis Smith's *Report from Engine Co. 82.*

[S 16j.] Walls A.M.E. Zion Church (African Methodist Episcopal)/ formerly **Holy Trinity Lutheran Church**/originally **Free Magyar Reform Church,** 891 Home St., NE cor. Intervale Ave. 1909. Thompson & Frohling.

A charmingly conceived yellow brick church which effectively makes use of a triangular spit of land just across from **Engine Company 82.**

CROTONA PARK

[S 17a.] Junior High School 98, Bronx, The Herman Ridder Junior High School, 1619 Boston Rd., SW cor. E. 173rd St. 1932. Walter C. Martin.

Named for the philanthropist who was publisher of the *New York Staats-Zeitung*. On a difficult irregular site the architect has employed a handsome multifaceted tower as a focal point for the limestone-clad building. The design is a **late-blooming** combination of Beaux Arts classicism and Art Deco.

[S 17b.] Charlotte Gardens (residences), along the spine of Charlotte St. and Louis Nine Blvd. (formerly Wilkins Ave.) radiating out toward Crotona Park, Minford Place, and E. 170th St. Edward J. Logue, governmental developer.

This is the center of the notorious **South Bronx,** something of a geographical misnomer. **President Jimmy Carter** made Charlotte Street a rallying point when, on a personal visit in October 1977 amid the burned-out hulks of 5- and 6-story apartments, he called for reconstruction, as **Churchill** did **after London's blitz.** The reconstruction, these 1½-story ticky-tacky suburban dwellings, with nary a tree in sight (except for gnarled back-alley survivors), reveals another kind of destruction: of valuable, close-in, urban land through **underutilization.**

[S 18.] Crotona Park, Fulton, Third, E. Tremont, and Arthur Aves., Crotona Park North, East, and South, and a small jog to Southern Blvd. and E. 175th St. Reconstructed, 1936. **[S 18a.] Crotona Play Center, N.Y.C. Department of Parks & Recreation,** in Crotona Park, Fulton Ave. at E. 175th St. E side. 1936. N.Y.C. Parks Department and Aymar Embury II.

Formerly the estate of the Bathgate family (for whom the nearby avenue was named), Crotona Park is one of six sites for parks selected by a citizens' committee in 1883. Named for **Croton,** an **ancient Greek city** renowned as the home of many **Olympic champions,** the park contains a vast array of sports facilities which are in sad disarray today. The best and, at least to the eye, the most enduring is the play center (actually a bathhouse and swimming pool), one of the **great red brick WPA structures** built in the 1930s.

[S 18b.] Technical Center, Bathgate Industrial Park, Third Ave. SE cor. E. 174th St. 1987. Port Authority of N.Y. & N.J. Architectural Design Team.

The handsomest of the structures in the industrial park which lies between the Cross-Bronx Expressway and Claremont Parkway from Washington to Fulton Avenues.

LONGWOOD

[S 19.] Longwood Historic District and Extension, parts of Macy Place, Hewitt Place, Dawson, Kelly, Beck, and E. 156th Sts., bet. Prospect Ave. and Fox St., from Leggett to Longwood Aves. ★

Largely an **enclave of intact masonry row houses,** complete with stoops, wrought-iron railings, and magnificent brownstone embellishments, designed primarily by architect **Warren C. Dickerson** and completed in the years 1897 to 1901.

[S 19a.] Patrolman Edward P. Lynch Center, Police Athletic League/ formerly **The Martinique Club, The Longwood Club/**originally **Samuel B. White residence,** 974 E. 156th St., SW cor. Beck St. ca. 1850. Altered. ☆

Turned at an angle to today's street grid, this much altered country house has seen a long series of adaptive reuses. When this area's developer, **George B. Johnson,** bought the Samuel B. White estate he used this building as his real estate office to market his row houses.

[S 19b.] United Church/originally **Montefiore Hebrew Congregation,** 764 Hewitt Place, bet. E. 156th St. and Longwood Ave. E side. 1906. Daumer & Co. ☆

This lyrical, pastel-painted, white-trimmed edifice smiles **beamingly** down its one-block axis, Macy Place, toward busy, noisy Prospect Avenue, one of Hunts Point's main drags. Originally a synagogue patterned after the Eastern European model, it nevertheless was crowned with twin onion domes! Today, reflecting ethnic and religious shifts in the community, a crucifix occupies the space between the domes.

[S 19c.] **Engine Company 73, N.Y.C. Fire Department,** 655 Prospect Ave., NW cor. E. 152nd St. 1900. Horgan & Slattery.

A Beaux Arts-Baroque municipal embellishment.

[S 19d.] **711, 713, 715 Prospect Ave. (residences),** bet. E. 155th and E. 156th Sts. W side. ca. 1885.

A wonderful trio in a marvelously eclectic block.

[S 19b.] Old Montefiore Hebrew Cong.   **[S 19c.]** Engine Company 73, N.Y.F.D.

[S 19d.] Sprightly row houses: 711, 713, 715 Prospect Avenue, in Longwood

[S 20a.] **Tiffany Plaza,** Tiffany St. SE cor. Fox St., opp. St. Athanasius Roman Catholic Church. 1981. Weintraub & di Domenico.

A **public plaza** of patterned paving blocks focused on a freestanding white-and-pink stucco-and-glass-block wall, **built in defiance** of the South Bronx's nefarious image by the N.Y.C. Department of Housing, Preservation & Development.

[S 20b.] Hunts Point Branch, N.Y. Public Library, 877 Southern Blvd., NW cor. Tiffany St. 1928. Carrère & Hastings.

The architects of *the* public library in Manhattan here tried their hand on a modest branch with brilliant success: a knockoff of **Brunelleschi's Ospedale degli Innocenti** in Florence. The arcade of brick arches is memorable.

[S 20c.] 41st Precinct, N.Y.C. Police Department/originally 62nd Precinct/a.k.a. The Simpson Street Station, 1086 Simpson St., bet. Westchester Ave. and E. 167th St. E side. 1914. Hazzard, Erskine & Blagdon.

An Italian palazzo—note those massive stone voussoirs radiating out from the entranceway—now standing in not-so-splendid isolation. This is the *real* **Fort Apache.** [See S 13f.]

[S 21.] Longfellow Gardens: provides both visual relief and material relaxation

[S 21.] Longfellow Gardens, Longfellow Ave. bet. E. 165th St. and Lowell Place. E side. 1983. Weintraub & di Domenico.

Another **great open space** brought to you by the folks at NYC HPD: a pergola set within a handsomely fenced space, providing **visual relief** and **material relaxation** from everyday toil.

HUNTS POINT

[S 22a.] Originally **American Bank Note Company (factory),** Lafayette Ave. NE cor. Tiffany St. 1911. Kirby, Petit & Green.

The **peninsular portion** of the Hunts Point community is separated from the rest of the South Bronx not by a waterway but by a deep railroad cut, once the tracks of the **New York, New Haven & Hartford,** and by the massive elevated **Bruckner Expressway.** Guarding a main entry to the "peninsula" is this dark and spare masonry fortress which served to guard its own valuable contents as well. Printed within were **billions** of pesos, cruzeiros, colons, sucres, and gourdes for Mexico, Brazil, Costa Rica, Ecuador, and Haiti (respectively), stock certificates, travelers' checks, and even lottery tickets.

[S 22b.] Corpus Christi Monastery, 1230 Lafayette Ave., at Baretto St. E side. 1890. William Schickel.

The best time to visit this cloistered community of Dominican nuns is on Sunday afternoon, when they sing their office. The church, with its beautiful polished mosaic floor, bare walls, and scores of candles, is then fully lighted.

[S 22c.] Spofford Juvenile Center, N.Y.C. Department of Juvenile Justice/originally Bronx Youth House for Boys, 1221 Spofford Ave., NE cor. Tiffany St. 1958. Kahn & Jacobs.

This institution shares a superblock with the Corpus Christi Monastery. The Spofford Center, sterile in appearance (its white brick walls help), continues to attract headlines not for its architecture but for the notoriety associated with the quality of its social services. Security now includes a second fence, topped with coils of razor wire.

[S 22d.] Engine Company 94, Hook & Ladder Company 48, N.Y.C. Fire Department, 1226 Seneca Ave., SW cor. Faile St. ca. 1925.

An open-air roof gallery and colorful terra-cotta shields embellish this firehouse.

[S 22e.] Bright Temple A.M.E. Church (African Methodist Episcopal)/ formerly **Temple Beth Elohim (synagogue)/**formerly **Peter A. Hoe residence/**originally **"Sunnyslope,"** William W. Gilbert residence. 812 Faile St., NE cor. Lafayette Ave. ca. 1870. ★

Askew to today's street grid, like the Samuel B. White residence [see S 19a.], is this picturesque gray stone Gothic Revival mansion. It once stood on a large estate close to the now demolished **"Brightside,"** the frame country house of **Col. Richard M. Hoe,** the famed **inventor of the rotary printing press.** (Peter was his younger brother.)

The Hunts Point Market:

Built on the site of the Con Ed Hunts Point coke plant.

[S 23a.] New York City Terminal Market, along Halleck St. bet. Lafayette and East Bay Aves. 1965. Skidmore, Owings & Merrill.

Spacious facilities for trailer trucks and railroad cars are provided in this **decentralized wholesale fruit and vegetable market** (the Hunts Point markets were a keystone in the city's planning strategies of the 1960s and 1970s). A model of SOM efficiency, enhanced by black-painted steel, blue-tinted glass, and occasional walls of carmine red brick.

[S 23b.] Hunts Point Cooperative Meat Market, Hunts Point Ave. S of East Bay Ave. 1976. Brand & Moore.

Most dramatic of the facilities which constitute the **second stage** of the Hunts Point Market, these long, low, yellow-ocher masonry blocks **capture the spirit** of the wholesale market very well. Their smaller Stage II neighbors, by other architects, do considerably less well.

Drake Park: In the center of this forgotten plot of land at Hunts Point and Oak Point Avenues stands an iron fence enclosing the graves of many early settlers of the area, including members of the Hunt family itself, for which the point is named. Poet Joseph Rodman Drake (1795–1820) is also buried here, hence the name of the park and nearby Drake Street. Other poets honored by streets in the surrounding, ill-kempt industrial area: Halleck, Whittier, Longfellow, and Bryant.

CENTRAL BRONX

TWIN PARKS WEST/TREMONT • FORDHAM • BELMONT

TWIN PARKS EAST/EAST TREMONT • WEST FARMS

BRONX ZOO • NEW YORK BOTANICAL GARDEN

The Central Bronx includes the Bronx Zoo, the New York Botanical Garden, Fordham University, and the district encompassing the Webster Avenue corridor on the west and the Bronx River area on the east.

Its south boundary is the **gash** of the Cross-Bronx Expressway. Within this area can be found a **great variety** of flora, fauna, land uses, housing types, and building conditions. Institutions of **world prominence** are within sight of **humble** and **exotic** neighborhood establishments. Long-forgotten landmarks lie close to excellent new community structures that may one day become landmarks for future generations.

TWIN PARKS WEST/TREMONT

The **twin parks** referred to in the urban renewal catch phrase are Bronx and Crotona, which very roughly bracket, on the north and south, this geographic area of the Bronx. In 1966–1967, when renovation of existing housing stock was unfashionable and building economics had not made arson and abandonment the way of life in multistory communities such as this, a **scattered site, infill-housing** location study was financed by the **J. M. Kaplan Fund.** The results, translated into architecture by talented and mostly young architects, form more than twenty projects scattered along the east and west flanks of a mile-square area. They are a **model** of governmentally influenced **urban design** and **notable** low- and moderate-income **high-rise apartment architecture** as well. Sponsors included the N.Y.C. Educational Construction Fund (ECF), the N.Y.C. Housing Authority (NYCHA), and—most significant and influential of all—the N.Y.S. Urban Development Corporation (UDC). While Twin Parks projects were on their way up, however, much of the rest of Tremont and East Tremont went down.

[C 1a.] 1880 Valentine Avenue (apartments), bet. Webster Ave. and E. 178th St. E side. (Twin Parks project.) 1973. Giovanni Pasanella.

On an almost unbuildable narrow triangle commanding the undisciplined open space of a complicated street intersection and a **hilly green ether** once called Echo Park is this brilliant solution to a difficult problem. Stepping its way **hither and yon** and **up, up, up** is this dark red, oversized-brick-clad UDC building for elderly tenants. It's perfect.

[C 1b.] 1985 Webster Avenue (apartments), bet. E. 178th and E. 180th Sts. W side. **[C 1c.] 2000 Valentine Avenue Apartments,** bet. E. 178th and E. 180th Sts. E side. **[C 1d.] 2100 Tiebout Avenue Apartments,** NE cor. E. 180th St. (Twin Parks project.) 1973. Giovanni Pasanella.

The most controversial buildings in Twin Parks: 1) Elevators service duplex split-level apartments by stopping every 2½ floors, thus eliminating 60% of the normal corridors and creating many very livable floor-through apartments—but at the same time irritating the buildings' contractors, who were out for profits, not challenges. 2) The buildings are powerful sculptural statements, vaguely reminiscent of Le Corbusier's **Unité d'Habitation** in Marseilles; their dark red brick walls add to their assertiveness. 3) A number of details were overlooked. The most glaring: a meaningful handling of the open space between the Webster and Valentine Avenue buildings.

[C 2a.] Twin Parks West Sites 1 & 2 Apartments, N.Y.C. Housing Authority, 353, 355, 360, 365 Ford St., 355, 365 E. 183rd St., W of Webster Ave. 1974. Giovanni Pasanella.

Though these low-income projects utilize the same **skip-stop elevator** concept as the Pasanella-designed UDC apartment buildings a few blocks to the south, they are less self-assertive. Differing-height wings (rather than a bold rectangular ground plan), the elimination of cantilevered projections at the elevator-served floors, and the introduction of small fire-exit projections, which **add punctuation to the facades,** make this housing a bit more conventional in appearance.

[C 2b.] Patrolman Andrew F. Giannone-Webster Community Center, Police Athletic League, 2255 Webster Ave., NW cor. Ford St. (Twin Parks project.) 1974. Smotrich & Platt.

With a name that is almost longer than the building, this is a refreshingly disarming small-scale community amenity built by UDC.

[C 2c.] 333 East 181st Street (apartments), at Crane Sq., Tiebout Ave., and Folin St. E side. (Twin Parks project.) 1973. Prentice & Chan, Ohlhausen, architects. R. T. Schnadelbach, landscape architect.

Given a complex program of studio-to 5-bedroom apartments by their client (UDC) and a cliffside site that had always served as a **natural line of demarcation** between two neighborhoods, these architects tackled both problems head on. Elimination of an elevator corridor on every third floor and the use of duplex apartments (resulting in **lyrical window patterns** on the two main facades) were the responses to the problems posed by the program. Construction of a **long ramped stairway** along the face of the cliff resolved the problem of access. An exceptionally satisfying statement—as though this building was always meant to occupy this site.

[C 1c.] Twin Pks. apts/Valentine Ave.   **[C 2b.]** Giannone-Webster PAL Center

[C 2d.] Intermediate School 137, Bx.   **[C 2e.]** Twin Parks apts/E. 184th St.

[C 2d.] Intermediate School 137, Bronx, The Angelo Patri School, 2225 Webster Ave., bet. Folin St. and E. 181st St. W side. (Twin Parks project.) 1975. The Architects Collaborative.

Named for educational philosopher Angelo Patri, a hero in the nearby Italian-American community (he was principal of P. S. 45, Bronx), this **exuberant colorful** cast-concrete structure makes one wonder what was ever wrong with public school. If the education within matches the **verve** and **imagination** of the architecture, a victory will have been achieved. Another UDC project.

[C 2e.] 355, 365 East 184th Street (apartments), bet. Marion and Webster Aves. N side. 1973. Prentice & Chan, Ohlhausen, architects. R. T. Schnadelbach, landscape architect.

Tackling another rough site, this architect/landscape architect team began at the beginning, with a strong site plan. The result is a **sunken courtyard** embraced on 3½ sides by a set of continuous brick-walled apartment blocks, this time with a smooth, serene window pattern. Note the neat **diagonal recesses** at the block's **reentrant corners;** they solve an old bugaboo: how to light a room in such a location without having windows wind up at one end or the other. Here those spaces are living rooms, and the windows are in the very center—but on the bias. **Consummate artistry** is evident here. Unfortunately, the power of water to erode is all too evident from the scars in the courtyard's landscaping.

FORDHAM

[C 3e.] Keating Hall, Fordham University: most imposing building on campus

[C 3.] **Fordham University, Rose Hill Campus,** generally E of Webster Ave., N of E. Fordham Rd., S and W of Southern Blvd. [C 3a.] **Administration Building**/central part formerly **Rose Hill Manor House.** 1838. ★ [C 3b.] **University Church**/officially **Our Lady, Mediatrix of All Graces,** 1845, William Rodrigue. Transept, chancel, crossing and lantern added, 1929. ★ [C 3c.] **St. John's Residence Hall,** 1845, William Rodrigue. ★ [C 3d.] **Thebaud Hall**/originally **Science Hall,** 1886, Eugene Kelly. [C 3e.] **Keating Hall,** 1936, Robert J. Reiley. [C 3f.] **Alumni House**/originally **William Rodrigue residence.** 1840. William Rodrigue. ★

A Jesuit institution since 1846, the university began as St. John's College in 1841, founded by the **Right Reverend John Hughes** (later New York's first Catholic archbishop) and guided initially by its first president, **John McCloskey** (later America's first cardinal). Hughes commissioned his brother-in-law, **William Rodrigue,** to design a residence hall and church for the fledgling institution to accompany the already existing Rose Hill Manor House—for which this campus is named. Later Rodrigue associated with **James Renwick, Jr.,** in the design of the new St. Patrick's Cathedral, which upon completion was dedicated by then **Cardinal McCloskey.** (Detect a closeness here?)

Fordham derived its present name in 1905 from that of the old manor, later village, of Fordham—**not the other way around,** as some well-meaning community people would have you believe. The campus's physical presence, along heavily traveled East Fordham Road, is very strong. Mature trees, dense shrubs, brilliantly green lawns, and a group of harmonious gray stone **Collegiate Gothic** buildings (built mostly from designs by **architect Emile G. Perrot** between 1911 and 1930) offer a distinguished contrast to the tacky commercial architecture of the Bronx's waning automobile row adjacent to the campus. The best of Fordham's buildings, save the early **Manor House,** a rough-stone, country-style Greek Revival masterpiece, is the last in the Collegiate

Gothic style, **Keating Hall.** A picturesque work carefully sited, it is diminished in quality only by the steel transmitting antenna of the university's radio station, WFUV.

Two literary tales relate to the campus. It is said that the 98-acres were the setting for James Fenimore Cooper's novel, *The Spy.* And it is also said that the bell in the University Church (appropriately dubbed "Old Edgar") was the inspiration for Poe's poem, *The Bells.* [He lived nearby—see W Bronx W 33a.].

[C 3g.] Fordham Plaza (office building), 1 Fordham Plaza, E. Fordham Rd. SE cor. Third Ave. to Washington Ave. and E. 189th St. 1986. Skidmore, Owings & Merrill.

The ill-defined open space to the west of the building, best recalled as a pedestrian's nightmare, has always been called Fordham Plaza, at least ever **since the Bronx's urbanization.** A highly decorative office tower has been inserted to further mark the amorphousness. The black granite, multicolored brick and glass-block wedding cake, even though all glitzed up, doesn't help.

BELMONT

The Bronx's Little Italy: The fork in the street grid where Crescent Avenue diverges from East 187th Street (just a few blocks southeast of Fordham University) provides a space which, straight **out of the Mediterranean tradition,** has fostered a great marketplace for the cohesive Italian-American community of Belmont. Along East 187th Street, past Belmont Avenue and the area's religious and social rallying point, **Our Lady of Mt. Carmel Roman Catholic Church,** and into busy, colorful Arthur Avenue, you will find a multitude of small retail shops resembling those which were once the mainstay of New York's streets. Long may they prosper here! Freshly baked Italian breads, salami, and olive oil. *Latticini freschi,* fresh fish, and clams on the half shell from a common plate served on a wooden sidewalk stand (with unlimited lemons). Drop into the European-feeling New York City Retail Market, a **Fiorello LaGuardia morality gesture** of 1940 that removed Arthur Avenue's pushcart peddlers but, thankfully, not the street life. It's all worth an extra special good weather visit . . . every day but Sunday, of course.

Dominick's Restaurant, 2335 Arthur Ave., bet. E. 186th St. and Crescent Ave. W side.

A restaurant without a menu. Small, hearty, delicious, reasonably priced. Try it at lunchtime, when the neighborhood regulars drop in.

[C 4.] Belmont Branch/Enrico Fermi Cultural Center, N.Y. Public Library, 610 E. 186th St., SW cor. Hughes Ave. 1981. Joseph Daidone.

A sleek design reflecting in yet another way the **pride** found in this ethnic community, so evident everywhere.

White Castle (eatery), 550 E. Fordham Rd., SE cor. Lorillard Place. 1930. Remodeled, 1961.

This is not a recommendation for food (what can a 35¢ hamburger be made of?) or for atmosphere—it's **all rather utilitarian:** stainless steel and aluminum, cramped, and dingy. Rather, this purveying machine for fast food, open twenty-four hours a day, is a lesson in how unresponsive a 20th-century structure can be to basic human environmental requirements. **Free parking.**

[C 5a.] Keith Plaza (apartments)/Public School 205A, Bronx (grades 1-4), 2475 Southern Blvd., bet. E. Fordham Rd. and E. 187th St. W side. **[C 5b.] Kelly Towers North Apartments,** 2405 Southern Blvd., NW cor. E. 187th St. **[C 5c.] Kelly Towers South Apartments/Public School 205B, Bronx (early childhood center),** 2375 Southern Blvd., SW cor. E. 187th St. (Twin Parks projects.) 1975. Giovanni Pasanella.

Pasanella, the architect of these three apartment blocks, was the most prolific of those associated with the Twin Parks renewal effort [see C 1a., b., c., d., 2a.]. Though the apartment plans used here are the most conventional of any of those projects, the resulting buildings, in subtle shades of tan, are among his most convincing when seen as elements in the cityscape. Keith Plaza, the graceful, 30-story tower at the north end of the trio, acts as a **pylon** to mark an **important gateway** into the community; it is located close to the point where busy East Fordham Road (U.S. 1) crosses Southern Boulevard. Unfortunately, the actual corner site could not be used; it had long been occupied by a unit of a nationwide **orange-roofed ice cream** and **fried clam chain,** a **somewhat older** local landmark.

[C 5a.] Keith Plaza apts/PS 205A, Bx.   **[C 6i.]** Twin Pks. apts/Crotona Avenue

[C 5d.] 2841 Crotona Avenue (former residence), NW cor. E. 189th St. ca. 1900.

Hidden behind Keith Plaza is this **old residence,** a stalwart stone symbol of wealth antedating Twin Parks and now partly concealed by a humdrum hamburger stand.

TWIN PARKS EAST/EAST TREMONT

[C 6a.] 2111 Southern Boulevard (apartments), NW cor. E. 180th St. **[C 6b.] 800, 820 East 180th Street (apartments),** SW cor. Southern Blvd. (Twin Parks projects.) 1973. James Stewart Polshek & Assocs.

Sponsored by UDC, these [and not Keith Plaza, see C 5a.] were intended to be the "urban designer" gateway to Twin Parks from the east. They fail to live up to the intention despite the brash two-dimensional, black on tan striping of the brickwork on both the 31-story tower and its 9-story neighbor to the south. A satisfying note: the inclusion of retail stores at the base of both buildings **attracts street life** to "the project."

[C 6c.] Ella Rivers Memorial Swimming Pool and Bathhouse, N.Y.C. Parks & Recreation Department, E. 180th St. bet. Prospect and Mapes Aves. S side. (Twin Parks project.) 1971. Heery & Heery.

Theoretically, good-looking outdoor swimming pools are a political asset. In addition to providing **warm-weather diversions,** they don't cost the city too much to operate, since 9 out of every 12 months they lie dormant. Judging from the hostile graffiti on this one, some of the locals must have caught on to this callous game.

[C 6d.] Intermediate School 193, Bronx, The Whitney M. Young, Jr., School, 1919 Prospect Ave., bet. E. 176th St. and E. Tremont Ave. W side. 1975. William A. Hall & Assocs.

A brick structure that begins to insert physical stability into a 1970s ravaged neighborhood.

[C 6e.] 730 Oakland Place (apartments). [C 6f.] 750 East 179th Street (apartments). [C 6g.] 740 East 178th Street (apartments), all bet. Prospect and Clinton Aves. All S side. (Twin Parks projects.) 1974. Skidmore, Owings & Merrill.

Crisp, modular, precast-concrete 16-story rectangular prisms with crisp, modular, precast-concrete balconies. **Veddy, veddy spiffy**—but what have these to do with life in the Bronx, or anywhere for that matter? Precast in sections a few miles away, the buildings were erected here as one of UDC's experimental HUD-aided Operation Breakthrough projects.

[C 6h.] 2311 Southern Boulevard, 760 East 183rd Street (apartments), SW cor. **[C 6i.] 2260 Crotona Avenue (apartments)**, bet. E. 183rd and Grote Sts. E side. **[C 6j.] 725, 735 Garden Street (apartments)**, bet. Prospect and Crotona Aves. N side. (Twin Parks projects.) Richard Meier & Assocs. 1974.

These 3 dark red, oversized-brick-clad, UDC-sponsored buildings are the **most successful** in all of Twin Parks in graciously recognizing the adjacent neighborhood without pandering to existing materials, building heights, or details. Through careful volumetric, spatial, and detailing decisions, the simple, stepped-brick masses **add to**, rather than fight with, **the neighborhood's fabric.** They offer the plus of making the existing even more visible and, therefore, more interesting, as well. The design has so many **good things** about it that you tend to miss the out-of-place *Titanic* ship railings and the bland treatment of the ground plane. The chain link fencing added later under the buildings is, on the other hand, hard to miss . . . and regrettable.

WEST FARMS

[C 7a.] Intermediate School 167, Bronx, The Lorraine Hansberry School, 1970 West Farms Rd., SE cor. E. Tremont Ave. 1973. Max O. Urbahn Assocs.

Defining part of the south edge of old West Farms Square [see C 7c.] is this **crisply designed** city school, **a far cry** from most of its predecessors of the 1940s and 1950s. It uses a cast-concrete structural frame and dark, rough-ribbed concrete block infill to achieve its neat and dramatic geometry. Its site was once that of the **Bronx Bleachery**, a well-remembered industry probably because of its **negative impact** upon the purity of the adjacent Bronx River.

[C 7b.] Former **Peabody Home**/now **Circle Missions, Inc.**, 2064 Boston Rd., NE cor. E. 179th St. 1901. E. A. Sargent.

Now sandwiched between the Lambert Houses properties and in the shadow of the IRT elevated lumbering overhead, this fine red brick building in a Tudor Gothic style adds a **syncopated note** to the area's ambience. It was once a home for the aged; it is now occupied by the followers of the late **Father Divine.**

[C 7c.] Lambert Houses (apartments), Shopping Plaza, and Parking Garage, along Boston Rd. bet. Bronx Park S. and E. Tremont Ave. 1973. Davis, Brody & Assocs., architects; A. E. Bye Assocs., landscape architects.

These distinctive sawtooth-plan apartment, shopping, and parking structures south of Bronx Park were commissioned by **Phipps Houses,** a nonprofit foundation concerned with building **better housing** in the city. They utilize a special 8"-thick single-wythe bearing wall of special dark red-clay bricks as a unifying construction material in all the buildings. In the 6-story residential buildings, wood joists bear on the walls to form floors and roofs. The south end of the shopping plaza bounds **old West Farms Square,** once a **trolley car hub** and a secondary commercial center for the entire borough.

[C 7d.] Old West Farms Soldier Cemetery, E. 180th St. NE cor. Bryant Ave. (now a pedestrian walk). 1815. ★

Forty veterans of four wars lie in repose amid trees and shrubs in this **oasis of calm** adjacent to the west edge of Lambert Houses: tombstones of soldiers from the War of 1812, the Civil War, the Spanish-American War, and World War I may be seen through the fence surrounding this ⅔ acre site. After many years of neglect and desecration, the locally organized **Civil War Memorial Committee,** reconstituted about 1950, came to the rescue, restored the site and memorial statue, and achieved its recognition as an official landmark.

[C 7e.] Beck Memorial Presbyterian Church, 980 E. 180th St., bet. Vyse and Bryant Aves. S side. 1903.

A somber stone sentinel overlooking the old cemetery across the street.

Across the Bronx River to the east:

[C 8a.] Originally **The Bronx Coliseum**/now **N.Y.C. Transit MaBSTOA Bus Repair Facility (Manhattan and Bronx Surface Transit Operating Authority),** E. 177th St. bet. Devoe and Bronx Park Aves. S side. 1928.

Built originally as the Auditorium Convention Hall for the **Sesquicentennial Exposition** of 1926 in Philadelphia and subsequently dismantled and reerected here. Prior to World War II the bulky bowstring arched structure was the site of indoor **automobile races** and **boxing matches**—it seated 15,000 people. During the war it was requisitioned as a U.S. Army ordnance repair facility, which is not too different from its use today. To its west was once the **amusement park** and **swimming center** called **Starlight Park** on the east bank of the Bronx River.

[C 8b.] Fire Alarm and Telegraph Bureau, N.Y.C. Fire Department, 1129 E. 180th St., bet. Devoe and Bronx Park Aves. N side. 1923.

A buff-brick Italian Renaissance Revival structure dedicated to housing **the high tech** of the 1920s.

[C 8c.] Originally **New York, Westchester & Boston Railway Company Administration Building**/now **entrance to E. 180th Station of the IRT Dyre Avenue Subway,** 481 Morris Park Ave., NW cor. E. 180th St. 1912. Fellheimer & Long, Allen H. Stem, associated. ★

Twin towers capped with red tile roofs and walls of warm-hued, bush-hammered concrete identify this headquarters building in the **Italian Villa style** for a railroad **that never made it.** The N.Y., W. & B. was to have been a suburban line that would glamorously and swiftly transport commuters to the suburbs developing around White Plains and Port Chester prior to World War I; the **picturesque** architecture was to set the tone. The enterprise, having never made a profit, finally **failed in 1937.** The N.Y.C. Transit Authority's IRT Dyre Avenue Line still uses some of the city route [see E Bronx E 15e.].

BRONX ZOO

[C 9.] The Bronx Zoo/officially **New York Zoological Park,** Bronx Park, S of E. Fordham Rd. Opened in 1899. Original architects, Heins & La Farge. **Open to the public.**

At the Bronx Zoo's opening ceremonies, visitors were officially welcomed not to one of the "small closed zoological gardens of Europe" but to "a free Park, projected upon a scale larger than has ever been attempted before." By today's standards its 252 acres are cramped in comparison to more modern and expansive zoos in other cities. And though the zoo is "free" in the sense of rambling meadows, pastures, and dusty plains, rising costs have severely limited the times when admission is gratis.

Nevertheless, the Bronx Zoo is the **largest** of the city's five zoos—though privately run it occupies city parkland and receives a city subsidy—and is **the most ambitious** in both **concept** and **execution.** The area is divided into basically two parts. At the north end is **Baird Court,** a large space around whose grassy plots and sea lion pool are formally arrayed many of the zoo's original buildings. This part is more like a zoological garden, with indoor and outdoor caged species and a pavilion housing **animal heads and horns,** trophies of some of the naturalist-hunter founders. The remainder of the zoo's acreage is devoted, more or less, to a more naturalistic zoological *park,* culminating in **moated exhibitions,** the African Plains, and the **forest** along the Bronx River displaying the wildlife of Asia. To shorten walking distances between all these places the management introduced an aerial **"Skyfari"** and a monorail people-mover in the Asian area.

[C 9a.] Jungle World/Tropical Asia Rain Forest, 1985. Herbert W. Riemer.

An **exotic structure** that suggests the mysteries of the fauna of Asia and then helps to remove some of them, partly through a motorized outdoor trip, labeled **Bengali Express,** through the Wild Asia grounds.

For those old enough to remember, General Motors pioneered this kind of trip (through a city of tomorrow) at the 1939–1940 World's Fair.

[C 9b.] The African Plains, near the Boston Rd. zoo entrance. 1941. Harrison & Fouilhoux, architects. Harry Sweeney, designer.

Moats rather than bars protect the public from the lions, while other moats protect the other animals of the **savannah** from both lions and visitors. Full-size replicas of indigenous buildings attempt to recreate an African landscape in the Bronx. Notable as an early effort **to make more natural** the visual relationship between animals and visitors.

[C 9c.] Carter Giraffe Building. 1982. Harold Buttrick & Assocs.

Twenty-one feet high and a replacement for the original, which dated from 1908. When it opened, the *New York Times* said it looked "more like a Columbus Avenue bar than a zoo space." See for yourself. And giraffes are among nature's greatest wonders.

[C 9d.] Aquatic Bird House. 1964. Goldstone & Dearborn. **[C 9e.] The World of Darkness.** 1969. Morris Ketchum, Jr., & Assocs. **[C 9f.] The World of Birds.** 1972. Morris Ketchum, Jr., & Assocs.

Three works of modern architecture of the 1960s–1970s can be found in the zoo: the Aquatic Bird House; the World of Darkness, a windowless building that **reverses day and night** for the visitor in order to display cave-dwelling and nocturnal animals; and the World of Birds, the most effective of the three. This display of some 550 birds in 25 **different habitats** is a plastic, flowing composition of rounded, rough-faced concrete-block forms dramatically illuminated within by skylights. Visitors here walk in rooms *with* birds, not on the other side of grilles separated from them . . . it makes a lot of difference.

[C 7c.] Lambert Houses apartments   **[C 9f.]** The World of Birds, Bronx Zoo

[C 10a.] Paul J. Rainey Memorial Gate. 1934. Paul Manship, sculptor; Charles A. Platt, architect of gate lodges and gateposts. ★ **[C 10b.] Rockefeller Fountain.** 1910. ★ Both at E. Fordham Rd. entrance.

Manship's beautifully scaled Art Deco-inspired bronze gates, a gift of **Grace Rainey Rogers**—they are dedicated to her brother—open upon an earlier, handsomely detailed Italian garden. In the center of the driveway's turnaround is an early 18th-century Italian fountain picked up near **Lake Como** by benefactor **William Rockefeller,** John D. Sr.'s brother.

[C 10c.] Baird Court: [C 10d.] Lion House. 1903. **[C 10e.] Primate House.** 1901. **[C 10f.] Administration Building.** 1910. **[C 10g.] Main Bird House.** 1905. **[C 10h.] Elephant House.** 1911. Heins & La Farge. **[C 10i.] Heads and Horns Building.** 1922. Henry D. Whitfield. All surround Baird Court. H. A. Caparn, landscape architect.

The zoo's formal Baird Court was a direct outgrowth of the **City Beautiful** precepts of the **World's Columbian Exposition** of 1893. It was a controversial afterthought to what had been a desire to treat the zoo grounds as **a naturalistic park.** The elephant house, a classical palace with a Byzantine interior, a high dome, and terra-cotta decoration, could serve as **capitol of a banana republic.**

NEW YORK BOTANICAL GARDEN

[C 11.] New York Botanical Garden, Bronx Park, N of E. Fordham Rd. Site, 1895. Calvert Vaux and Samuel Parsons, Jr. **Open to the public.**

The Botanical Garden, incorporated in 1891 and patterned after the **Royal Botanical Gardens** at Kew, England, is one of the world's leading institutions of its kind. Its scientific facilities include a conservatory, museum, library, herbarium (a collection of dried plants), research laboratory, and a variety of groves and gardens. The selection of this site within Bronx Park, as recommended by **Vaux and Parsons,** enables the garden to perform a second valuable function: it contains and preserves the **beautiful gorge** of the Bronx River, a **virgin hemlock forest,** and some of the **historic buildings** which were here before the park was created. It occupies 240 acres of city parkland at the northern extreme of Bronx Park.

[C 10a.] Paul J. Rainey Memorial Gate: Pelham Parkway entrance, Bronx Zoo

[C 11a.] Enid A. Haupt Conservatory at N.Y. Botanical Garden (1976 photo)

[C 11a.] Originally **Conservatory Range**/now **Enid Annenberg Haupt Conservatory,** 1902. William R. Cobb for Lord & Burnham, greenhouse manufacturers. Altered, 1938, 1953. Restored, 1978, Edward Larrabee Barnes & Assocs., architects. Kiley, Tindall, Walker, landscape architects. Vignelli Assocs., graphics. ★

A great group of greenhouses in the tradition of Decimus Burton's Great Palm House at Kew, and Joseph Paxton's Crystal Palace. Many years of deterioration threatened the glass fairyland and its wide-ranging plant species, but at the last minute, restoration (rather than replacement with an elaborate cubical box) won out—a victory for plants and people alike.

[C 11b.] Museum Building. 1902. Robert W. Gibson. Addition, 1973.
[C 11c.] Laboratory Building. 1957. Brown, Lawford & Forbes.

Two contrasting works in purpose, scale, design, and age which share a formal axis near the original main entrance to the garden.

[C 11d.] Old Lorillard Snuff Mill. ca. 1840. Restored, 1954. ★

This building, together with a later gatehouse and stables, is the only improvement that remains from the extensive local landholdings of **the Lorillards,** a family whose name is still associated with the **tobacco industry.** Built of local fieldstone, the mill once used the adjacent waters as power **to grind snuff,** a more popular tobacco product in the 19th century than it is today. Fortunately the mill building, a fine example of **local industrial architecture,** was adapted into a public snack bar (open summer months only), and its new terrace is a lovely place to nibble to the bubbly sounds of the adjacent river.

The Bronx River Gorge: Just north of the snuff mill is an arched stone footbridge, a great spot from which to view the gorge of the Bronx River and the turbulent waters that carved it over the millennia. It is yet another surprising event in a city filled with them. The nearby hemlock forest is the last remaining part of a stand of trees that once covered much of New York City.

WESTERN BRONX

THE GRAND CONCOURSE • HIGHBRIDGE
MORRIS HEIGHTS • UNIVERSITY HEIGHTS
KINGSBRIDGE HEIGHTS • FORDHAM HEIGHTS
BEDFORD PARK • NORWOOD

The West Bronx

The West Bronx was known as a place of wholesome blandness, at least until wholesale population shifts, followed by burnouts and abandonments in the 1970s and 1980s made it look like the South Bronx. The pairs of diminutive cast-stone lions that guard the entrances to so many of the area's apartment houses were an attempt at **elegance** but resulted in a **dreary sameness.** But a closer look at this area will yield some surprises. It is the spot in America, second to none, to see the **largest single array** of **Art Deco- and Art Modern-inspired** ornament—on apartments built between 1927 and 1942. An array of housing, schools, parks, hospitals, industries, and public works of social and architectural interest are all located here. This, too, though you may not believe it at first, is a place of urban diversity.

[W 1a.] Formerly **Cashman Laundry,** Gerard Ave. NE cor. E. 140th St. 1932. R. G. and W. M. Cory.

A stylistic little brother to the same architects'/engineers' Starett-Lehigh Building in Manhattan.

[W 1b.] Bronx Terminal Market, City of New York, Exterior St., Cromwell Ave., and E. 151st St. (entrance at W. 149th St.). North buildings, 1925, Albert W. Lewis and Samuel Axhandler. South buildings, 1935.

Originally, these 37 acres of land, the multistory yellow brick fortress/refrigerated warehouse, and the four-towered "castle" west of the Major Deegan Expressway were developed by Mayor John Hylan (1918–1925) to remove the city's fruit and vegetable markets from

downtown congestion. His $17 million effort failed. Wishing, a decade later, to transform **"Hylan's Folly"** into **a LaGuardia success,** that reform mayor invested another $1.7 million to build the ten low, white brick buildings over the remainder of the site plus a curvilinear-steel-arcaded "farmers' square." Though successful, it failed also to unseat Manhattan's centrally located, if inefficient, wholesale markets.

In the 1960s and 1970s, **Hunts Point** became the city's policy commitment for food wholesaling [see Bronx S 23a, b.], and the future of the old Bronx Terminal Market became clouded. As one wag said at the time, "If you ever defrost it, the whole thing would collapse!" It still stands.

THE GRAND CONCOURSE

The Grand Boulevard and Concourse (as it is officially named, but rarely called), one of the grand thoroughfares of New York, was designed in 1892 by Louis Risse as the **Speedway Concourse** to provide access from Manhattan to the large parks of the "annexed district" of the Bronx. The original design provided **separate paths** for horse-drawn vehicles, cyclists, and pedestrians, and for grade separation through underpasses at all major intersections.

[W 1c.] Public School 31, Bronx, The William Lloyd Garrison School/ once temporarily **Theodore Roosevelt High School,** 425 Grand Concourse, bet. E. 144th and E. 146th Sts. to Walton Ave. W side. 1899. C. B. J. Snyder. ★

Known locally as **The Castle on the Concourse** because of its Collegiate Gothic style. A runthrough for the same architect's later Morris High School [see S Bronx S 16b.].

[W 1d.] Hostos Community College, CUNY, Grand Concourse bet. W. 144th and W. 149th Sts. W side. Master plan, Gwathmey Siegel & Assocs. and Sanchez & Figueroa. **[W 1e.]** Originally **Security Mutual Insurance Company,** 500 Grand Concourse, SE cor. W. 149th Sts. 1965. Horace Ginsbern & Assocs.

The community college, many of whose students are drawn from the **large Hispanic population** of the Bronx, is expanding from its site on the east side of the Concourse (which included the reuse of Security Mutual building, the Bronx's first office building constructed in 25 years). The western campus addition will be reached via an overhead walkway.

[W 1f.] IRT subway junction, beneath E. 149th St. and Grand Concourse. Lower level, 1904. Upper level, 1917.

Here two subway stations have been built one below the other, separated by a mezzanine. (The trains on the upper level are marked "Woodlawn Road," a **nonexistent street.**) The lower station, in the **Parisian** manner, is one large **barrel vault.** Despite uninspired decoration, poor lighting, and minimal maintenance, this station is one of the **exciting** spaces of the subway system. On the southwest corner of the intersection above is a former entrance to the station which bears the name **Mott Avenue,** the thoroughfare which preceded Grand Concourse in these parts.

[W 1g.] General Post Office, The Bronx/originally **Bronx Central Annex, U.S. Post Office Department,** 558 Grand Concourse, NE cor. E. 149th St. 1937. Thomas Harlan Ellett, architect; Louis A. Simon, supervising architect. ★

The chaste gray brick walls and windows set in tall arches fail to achieve the dignity they seek. The best to be said for the building is that it has WPA murals by **Ben Shahn** in the public lobby.

[W 2a.] Cardinal Hayes High School (Roman Catholic), 650 Grand Concourse, SE cor. E. 153rd St. 1941. Eggers & Higgins.

Made reticent by its uninspired buff brick, the school is in the form of a quarter circle, therefore effectively creating an inviting green forecourt. Building embellishments are also reticent but in the Art Deco mode.

[W 2b.] Originally **Morgan Steam Laundry Company,** 700 Grand Concourse, bet. E. 153rd and E. 156th Sts. E side. ca. 1920.

An intriguing octagonal smokestack together with flat-roofed, precociously modern boxy forms distinguish this maroon brick industrial structure. It serves other purposes today.

Franz Sigel Park: Named for a Civil War general, this craggy park, on the west side of Grand Concourse north of East 153rd Street, is the repository of graffitied concrete "park furniture" installed by overzealous governmental bureaucrats in the early 1970s in the mistaken belief that physical amenities—*any* amenities—will cure acute social and economic ills.

A Grand Concourse Driving Tour:

Art Deco/Art Moderne and other styles:

The Roaring Twenties gave some families the needed economic lift that allowed them to move from their relatively shabby Manhattan digs to **spanking new quarters** in outlying places like the Bronx. The IRT Jerome Avenue elevated, running parallel to the Concourse down the hill to the west, had been finished in 1918. By the late 1920s the City was **digging a trench** down the center of the Grand Concourse to install the northern leg of its own Independent subway, which would open on July 1, 1933, in the depths of the Great Depression. Nevertheless, the subway did connect to Manhattan's business districts, to the Garment Center, and to the reemerging Upper West Side. The **convenience was unmistakable,** and developers seized the opportunity to buy potential apartment sites along the Concourse deflated in price by the economic downturn.

During the 1930s, the **golden age of the Concourse, two Paris expositions** were having great effect upon American style. The 1925 Exposition Internationale des Arts Décoratifs et Industriels Modernes had given birth to the **ornamentalism of Art Deco;** and the 1937 Exposition Internationale des Arts et des Techniques Appliqués à la Vie Moderne evoked the **streamlined forms of Art Moderne,** which were paralleled in the New York World's Fair of 1939–1940. The former influenced the use of decorative terra-cotta, mosaics, ironwork doors, and etched glass so rampant in the entry and lobbies of West Bronx apartments. The latter gave rise to the use of **striped brick** patterns, **cantilevered corners,** steel **casement windows** and particularly corner windows, and the use of highly **stylized letter forms.** The amalgam of these styles was concentrated along and near the Bronx's premier boulevard in dozens of 6-story apartments; these and similar works of residential architecture could be characterized as **the Concourse Style.** Sprinkled between the older dour apartment blocks of the 1920s are the now somewhat grimy gems:

START at Grand Concourse and East 153rd Street. The tour continues north along the entire length of the Concourse with a number of divergences along the way. While on the Concourse use service road except to make left turns, permitted only from center section.

[W 3a.] 730 Grand Concourse (apartments), bet. E. 153rd and E. 156th Sts. E side. 1939. Jacob M. Felson. **[W 3b.] 740 Grand Concourse (apartments),** bet. E. 153rd and E. 156th Sts. E side. 1939. Jacob M. Felson.

Both of these suffer from a lack of a second color of brick.

[W 3c.] 750 Grand Concourse (apartments), SE cor. 156th Sts. E side. 1937. Jacob M. Felson.

Timid despite two colors of brick. Chalk it up to shallow modeling of the brick planes.

[W 3d.] Thomas Garden Apartments, 840 Grand Concourse, bet. E. 158th and E. 159th Sts. E side. 1928. Andrew J. Thomas.

A block-square development of 5-story pre-Art Deco walk-up buildings grouped about a westernized **Japanese garden** in a sunken central court. All of the units are reached through the court by walking past concrete lanterns, a water course, and charming bridges. The short flights of steps leading down into the court effectively **separate the building** entrances from the busy Concourse traffic outside. This project, **named for its architect,** is one of two [see H Manhattan's Dunbar Apartments] designed for John D. Rockefeller, Jr., who hoped to solve the problems of the slums by investing in middle-income housing. (This project was originally undertaken by the ILGWU, using the state's new limited-dividend housing law.)

[W 3e.] The Bronx County Building, 851 Grand Concourse, SW cor. E. 161st St., at Lou Gehrig Plaza. 1934. Joseph H. Freedlander and Max Hausle, architects. Sculpture at four entrances: Adolph A. Weinman, sculptor; Edward F. Sanford, George Snowden, Joseph Kisselewski, associates. Frieze, Charles Keck. ★

An enormous, 10-story-high mostly limestone pile whose ponderous form is, luckily, relieved by sleek Moderne sculpture, both in the round and on friezes which beribbon its walls.

Divergences:

[W 4a.] Bronx House of Detention for Men/originally **Bronx County Jail,** 653 River Ave., SW cor. E. 151st St. (W of the Concourse.) 1931. Joseph H. Freedlander. Additions.

A curiously handsome high-rise penal institution, by the architect of the nearby Bronx County Building.

[W 4b.] Yankee Stadium, E. 161st St. SW cor. River Ave. (W of the Concourse.) 1923. Osborn Engineering Co. Rebuilt, 1976, Praeger-Kavanagh-Waterbury.

Built by brewery magnate Colonel Jacob Ruppert for the team he owned and for its most valuable player, Babe Ruth (the short right field helped him to set his home run record). In the early 1970s someone got the idea that the New York Yankees were the key to the neighborhood's, the Bronx's, and New York City's economic salvation; and so the whole stadium—as well as acres of adjacent fallow land—were rebuilt at a cost of some $100 million, a sum the city will probably never stop paying interest upon. There are fewer columns to obstruct vision and many, many more parking spaces, but the adjacent community seems, if anything, to have increased its rate of decay.

[W 5.] Criminal Court/Family Court, City of New York, 215 E. 161st St., bet. Sheridan and Sherman Aves. N side. (E of the Concourse.) 1977. Harrison & Abramovitz.

If architecture is expressive of the social order, then this bulky structure tells us that justice must be **ponderous, rigid, and self-righteous.**

Alex and Henry's Restaurant, 862 Courtlandt Ave., S of E. 161st St. E side. (E of the Concourse.)

Wherever you find a courthouse you also find where the lawyers and judges eat. This is it for the **Bronx's justice system,** a tacky-looking building with presumably presentable food.

Back to the Concourse:

[W 6a.] 888 Grand Concourse (apartments), SE cor. E. 161st St. 1937. Emery Roth.

A constipated effort on an important corner, across from the former **Concourse Plaza Hotel,** by an architect whose earlier, better designs can still be found along Broadway and Central Park West.

[W 6b.] The Lorelei Fountain, Joyce Kilmer Park, Grand Concourse, SW cor. E. 164th St. 1899. Ernst Herter, sculptor.

The fountain honors the author of "Die Lorelei," Heinrich Heine, whose bas-relief portrait is on the south side of the base. The statue was presented to the city by a group of New Yorkers of German ancestry in 1893 after the sculptor's gift had been **rejected by Düsseldorf,** Heine's birthplace. The donors wanted it placed at Manhattan's Grand Army Plaza, where the Sherman statue now stands. But Heine's ethnic background—he was both a German and a Jew—together with the statue's questionable artistic merits, **made that site unavailable.** After six years of debate the statue was placed in its present location. But even here **its troubles continued.** After its unveiling the fountain was vandalized, restored, and then for a time put under constant police protection. Judging from the graffiti which covers it today, protection is once again required.

[W 6c.] 1000 Grand Concourse (apartments), NE cor. E. 164th St. 1935. Sugarman & Berger.

Whatever marginal character it had *with* small-paned casements was lost through the substitution of ungainly aluminum double-hungs.

[W 7a.] Andrew Freedman Home, 1025 Grand Concourse, SW cor. McClellan St. 1924. Wings, 1928. Joseph H. Freedlander and Harry Allan Jacobs.

This subdued, gray and yellow limestone palace is French-inspired, but its setting in a garden gives it the air of a large English country house. It is a home for the aged endowed by Freedman, a leading **subway contractor** and owner of the baseball team which became the **N.Y. Giants.** The panic of 1907 made him fearful of losing the comforts to which he had become accustomed, and he established this home for **aged indigents** who could show that they had once enjoyed affluence. (A retired **czarist general** was a guest here for a time.)

[W 7b.] The Bronx Museum of the Arts/originally **Young Israel Synagogue,** 1040 Grand Concourse, NE cor. E. 165th St. 1961. Simon B. Zelnik. Expansion, 1988, Castro-Blanco, Pischioneri & Feder. **Open to the public.**

Using a vacant post-World War II synagogue building, this community museum has brought **many intriguing displays** of both art and history to the Bronx, utilizing a high level of curatorial skill. It began in the lobby of the Bronx County Building.

[W 7d., e.] 1166 & 1188 Grand Conc.   **[W 8b.]** 1227 Grand Concourse apts.

[W 7c.] 1150 Grand Concourse (apartments), NE cor. McClellan St. 1936. Horace Ginsbern. **[W 7d.] 1166 Grand Concourse (apartments),** bet. McClellan St. and E. 167th St. 1936. Horace Ginsbern. **[W 7e.] 1188 Grand Concourse (apartments),** SE cor. E. 167th St. 1937. Jacob M. Felson.

A full block of now-casementless apartments, No. 1188 being the most impressive with its sawtooth patterns.

More divergence from the Concourse: South on E. 167th Street:

[W 7f.] 1210 Sherman Avenue (apartments), NE cor. E. 167th St. 1937. Charles Kreymborg. **[W 7g.] 1212 Grant Avenue (apartments),** NE cor. E. 167th St. 1936. Horace Ginsbern.

Two very colorful Art Moderne works somewhat sacked by time. Their polychromed brick makes them special.

[W 7h.] Daughters of Jacob Geriatric Center: Main Building/formerly **Home and Hospital of the Daughters of Jacob,** 321 E. 167th St., bet. Findlay and Teller Aves. N side. 1920. Louis Allen Abramson. **[W 7i.] Findlay House/Weinstein-Ratner Pavilion,** 1175 Findlay Ave. W side. 1971. Louis Allen Abramson. **[W 7j.] Geriatric Center,** 1160 Teller Ave. E side. 1973. Blumenkranz & Bernhard.

Another, this time less fashionable-looking, home for the aged: the ungainly, **tall Roman colonnade** and pediment which rests against the entrance to the original building was supposed to give it a dignified appearance. It is *that* building, built as eight **radiating-spoked wings** set at the end of a generous **Italian garden,** that is of interest. The radiating plan was common for hospitals (and penitentiaries) always seeking more efficient centralized control.

More divergence from the Concourse:

This time, west.

[W 8.] Morrisania Neighborhood Family Care Center, 1225-1257 Gerard Ave., bet. E. 167th and E. 168th Sts. W side. (W of the Concourse.) 1973. Armand Bartos & Assocs.

A strongly modeled geometric mass of square brick units, across from the **abandoned Morrisania Hospital.**

[W 8a.] 44th Precinct, N.Y.C. Police Department, Jerome to Gerard Aves., bet. E. 168th and E. 169th Sts. 1989. Gatje Papachristou Smith.

A 5-sided 2-storied combination station house and vehicular service facility built on a steeply sloping site.

Back to the Concourse:

[W 8b.] 1227 Grand Concourse (apartments), bet. E. 167th and E. 168th Sts. W side. ca. 1938.

A narrow little Art Moderne orphan with a **vane of masonry** at its north end, looking like a movie house sign, but of brick.

[W 8c.] Grand Concourse Seventh-Day Adventist Temple/originally **Temple Adath Israel (synagogue),** 1275 Grand Concourse, SW cor. 169th St. 1927.

Predates the Concourse's Deco-Moderne heyday. Dignity here is **achieved by restraint:** smooth blank walls relieved by sparing use of ornamented neo-Classical columns and pilasters. The incised lettering of the original institution remains, as does the cornerstone.

[W 9a.] Originally **Roosevelt Gardens (apartments)/**later **Roosevelt Court,** 1455–1499 Grand Concourse, bet. E. 171st and E. 172nd Sts. to Wythe Place. W side. 1924. Altered, ca. 1986.

Stripped of its original Mission Style details, this once-romantic giant is now a **neat but barren** visual remnant of the Concourse's discovery by an emerging middle class in the 1920s. The 1980s guard station at the entrance, however, reveals a *re*discovery.

[W 9b.] 1500 Grand Concourse (apartments), NE cor. E. 172nd St. 1935. Jacob M. Felson.

The parapet limestone has been carved into folds, like velvet. Note the orange and brown brick, meander-pattern spandrels, and three-over-three windows. Spectacular.

[W 9c.] 1505 Grand Concourse (apartments), NW cor. E. 172nd St.

This, of 8 stories, is a galaxy of cream brick, but subtle . . . too subtle.

Self-Expression: The urge to create is not limited to credentialed professionals: Harold Swain, an attorney by trade, had such a desire to build. And build he did, between 1908 and 1955, on the north side of East 172nd Street just west of the Concourse. Parked cars and weeds obscure what remains of his little house, garage, indoor swimming pool, and other structures, but it's still possible to spy them, built of crazily patterned bricks, stones, tiles, and discarded bottles and scraps of glass.

[W 10a.] Bronx-Lebanon Hospital Center, Concourse Division/originally **Lebanon Hospital,** 1650 Grand Concourse, NE cor. Mt. Eden Ave. at Chet Henderson Sq. 1942. Charles B. Meyers. Expanded, 1991, Cannon/Mason Da Silva Assocs.

Monumental, fussy, very European in appearance.

[W 10b.] 1675 Grand Concourse (apartments), SW cor. E. 174th St. (street is below the Concourse) through to Walton Ave. 1936. Jacob M. Felson.

Poetic, graceful, **inlaid designs** in contrasting brick colors.

[W 9b.] 1500 Grand Concourse apts.   **[W 9b.]** 1500 Grand Conc. (detail)

 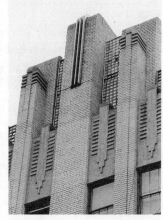

[W 10b.] 1675 Grand Concourse apts.   **[W 14a.]** 2121 Grand Conc. (details)

[W 10c.] 1750 Grand Concourse (apartments), bet. E. 173rd St. and Cross-Bronx Expwy. (both below the Concourse). E side. 1937.

Geometric ornament, with steel casements still in place.

[W 11a.] Lewis Morris Apartments, 1749 Grand Concourse, NW cor. Clifford Place. (outdoor public stairway). 1923. Edward Raldiris.

A 13-story Grecian high rise. Once, *the* place to live on the Concourse.

[W 11b.] Bell Telephone Building, 1775 Grand Concourse, SW cor. E. 175th St. ca. 1923. McKenzie, Voorhees & Gmelin.

A curious Florentine palazzo in cream brick and limestone, expanded upward as telephones increased in number.

[W 11c.] 1791 Grand Concourse (apartments), SW cor. E. 175th St. 1936. Edward W. Franklin.

Ruined by the loss of its delicately detailed, multipaned casement windows.

[W 11d.] Pilgrim United Church of Christ/originally **Christ Congregational Church,** 1808 Grand Concourse, NE cor. E. 175th St. 1910. Hoppin & Koen.

A strong presence on the Concourse: a **neo-Georgian front** and a **Hagia Sophia rear.**

[W 11e.] 1835 Grand Concourse (apartments), NW cor. E. 176th St. 1939. H. Herbert Lillien.

Also makes the best of another oddly shaped site.

[W 11f.] 1855 Grand Concourse (apartments), SW cor. Mt. Hope Place. 1936. Thomas Dunn.

Very subtle, oblique, planar modeling.

A brief divergence, downhill to the east:

[W 12a.] Originally **Elizabeth M. Shuttleworth residence,** 1857 Anthony Ave. SW cor. Mt. Hope Place. 1896. Neville & Bagge. ★

A private residence in the form of a miniature chateau of rock-faced gray stone with finely carved limestone trim. Note particularly the modeling of the faces within the **circular medallions** near the roof. A mimosa tree and other verdant vegetation almost conceal this welcome relic in an otherwise drab area.

[W 12b.] Tremont Towers (apartments), 333 E. 176th St., NW cor. E. Tremont Ave., opp. Echo Park. 1937. Jacob M. Felson.

Making the best of a curved site downhill from the Concourse.

Return to the Concourse:

[W 13a.] Mt. Hope Court (apartments), 1882 Grand Concourse, SE cor. Monroe Ave., at E. Tremont Ave. 1914. Otto Schwarzler.

[W 13a.] Bronx Flatiron: Mt. Hope Ct.   **[W 14a., b.]** 2121, 2155 Grand Conc.

[W 11d.] The Pilgrim United Church of Christ: a strong spiritual presence

The Bronx's own **Flatiron Building,** built on a sharply acute-angled site and, for many years, the **borough's tallest building,** at 10 stories. Predictions that residential elevators would make the Bronx a borough of 10-story structures didn't materialize until the advent of red brick "projects," beginning with Parkchester [see E Bronx E 7.].

[W 13b.] Morris Avenue Historic District ★, 1969-1999 Morris Ave., bet. E. Tremont Ave. and E. 179th St. W side. ☆ 1966-1998 Morris Ave., bet. E. Tremont Ave. and E. 179th St. E side. ☆ 60 and 108 E. 179th St., SW and SE cor. Morris Ave. ☆ 1906–1910. All by John Hauser.

A complete row of bowfront, 3-story row houses with wrought-iron detail, stonework, stoops, and cornices largely intact.

[W 13c.] 1939 Grand Concourse (apartments), SW cor. E. 178th St. ca. 1940.

Art Moderne. One of the zigzag-plan fronts.

[W 14a.] 2121 Grand Concourse (apartments), SW cor. E. 181st St. 1936. Horace Ginsbern.

If a cantilevered corner was the key to being stylish, then this zigzag plan tried to be the most stylish of all. **Art Moderne at its best,** but it needs to keep those original steel casement windows and to be delivered of those dreadful plastic store signs. Note the richly molded, gray cast-stone entry around the corner on East 181st.

[W 14b.] 2155 Grand Concourse (apartments), NW cor. E. 181st St. to Creston Ave. 1939. H. Herbert Lillien.

Yet another zigzag facade. Not as wonderful. (Down East 181st and around the corner on Creston Avenue are yet other examples.)

[W 14c.] 2186 Grand Concourse (apartments), NE cor. Anthony Ave. ca. 1939.

A poor cousin to the group above.

[W 14d.] 2195 Grand Concourse (apartments), SW cor. E. 182 St. 1938.

Neo-Classical sashaying into Art Moderne. Note the original fine ironwork on the entry doors.

[W 14e.] 2255 Grand Concourse (apartments), bet. E. 182nd and E. 183rd Sts. W side. 1936. Horace Ginsbern.

The casement windows here are subtly bowed. Note the three-dimensional, red-and-black granite entry surround. A tailored work.

[W 14f.] 2230 Grand Concourse (apartments), NE cor. E. 182nd St. (Entry on E. 182nd.) ca. 1937

Pinstripe orange and brown brick spandrels.

For the commercial structures around the intersection of the Grand Concourse and East Fordham Road, see **Highbridge/Morris Heights/University Heights,** which follows [W 17b.].

[W 15a.] 2615 Grand Concourse (apartments), bet. E. 192nd and E. 193rd Sts. W side. 1938. Charles Kreymborg.

Plain-Jane Moderne.

[W 15b.] 2665 Grand Concourse (apartments), NW cor. Kingsbridge Rd. E. 1922. Margon & Glaser. **[W 15c.] Brockman Manor (apartments),** 2701 Grand Concourse, bet. Kingsbridge Rd. E. and E. 196th St. W side. ca. 1927. H. I. Feldman. **[W 15d.] McAlpin Court (apartments),** 2825 Grand Concourse, NW cor. E. 197th St. ca. 1927. H. I. Feldman.

These three structures are Renaissance Revival in overall style; and the latter two, at only 6 stories, are crowned with very handsome Chicago School cornices, still intact.

[W 16a.] Town Towers (apartments), 2830 Grand Concourse, NE cor. E. 197th St. 1931. Horace Ginsbern.

Its brick piers and crenellated parapet **shimmer hello** as thousands drive past it. Take a peek at the **spectacular lobby.** Dismiss the remaining original 1930s Apartments Available sign . . . things are different today.

[W 16b.] 2910 Grand Concourse (apartments), bet. E. 198th and E. 199th Sts. E side. ca. 1940.

Beige stone models the entry; corner windows and steel casement remain. Bland.

[W 16a.] The Town Towers apartments

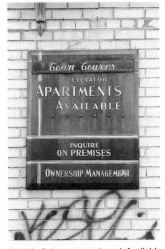

[W 16a.] Apartments (once) Available

[W 16c.] 2939 Grand Concourse (apartments), SW cor. Bedford Park Blvd. 1937. Leo Stillman.

Gutsy. The windows are in Art Deco (rather than an Art Moderne) style: three-over-three double-hung.

[W 17a.] 3155 Grand Concourse (apartments), NW cor. E. 205th St. 1936. Jacob M. Felson.

A curious pergola entry and some etched glass in the lobby. Corner casement windows. Best of all: the **vertical pinstripes** of spandrel brick.

[W 17b.] Dornhage (apartments), 2914 Jerome Ave. **[W 17c.] Edna (apartments),** 2928 Jerome Ave. Both bet. Minerva Place and Bedford Park Blvd. E side. 1936. William I. Hohauser.

Reverse the syllables of **Dornhage** and you have the client's name, **Hagedorn.** Art Deco with terrific polychromed terra-cotta.

END of Grand Concourse Driving Tour.

HIGHBRIDGE/MORRIS HEIGHTS/UNIVERSITY HEIGHTS

These neighborhoods lie west of Grand Concourse and follow the University Avenue ridge and the Harlem River from Macombs Dam Park below West 161st Street northward to the vicinity of Kingsbridge Road. They contain hundreds of the **familiar** Bronx apartment houses, older one-family wooden homes, and a **variety** of institutions, public works, and landmarks, many of **national fame** and importance. Highbridge, the area south of the Cross-Bronx Expressway, was settled in the 1830s by Irish workers who built the Old Croton Aqueduct and High Bridge as well as the railroad which soon appeared on the east bank of the Harlem River.

[W 18a.] Unused IRT Subway Tunnel, bet. Jerome Ave. at Anderson Ave. W side, to Major Deegan Expwy. below W. 161st St. E side. 1918.

The **steep ridge** which forms this part of the West Bronx has barely begun before it is penetrated by this now-abandoned subway tunnel. Barely three blocks long, it was built to connect the Ninth Avenue el at the old site of the Polo Grounds baseball stadium in Manhattan with the IRT Jerome Avenue elevated line—some of the structural steel for the connecting shuttle can still be seen nearby at River Avenue and East 162nd Street. Neither tunnel portal is particularly visible; the west one can be glimpsed fleetingly from the Major Deegan Expressway. Once there were plans to use the tunnel, following its closing in 1955, for a trolley museum.

[W 18b.] Muhammad's Mosque of Islam/originally **American Female Guardian Society and Home for the Friendless,** 936 Woodycrest Ave., NE cor. Jerome Ave. ca. 1901. William B. Tuthill.

Built as an eclectically styled mansion, this institution sits on **a commanding precipice** overlooking the valley of Macombs Dam Park and Yankee Stadium. Never as elegant as its Park Avenue (Manhattan) counterparts, it nevertheless **adds a needed note of grandeur** to this community.

Macombs Dam Park: This park, at Jerome Avenue and West 161st Street, together with the Macombs Dam Bridge into Manhattan, recalls the nearby site of Robert Macomb's 1813 dam across the Harlem River. The dam used the waterway's tidal flow to power a mill until Macomb's neighbors demolished the dam in 1838, in order to open the river to shipping. Considering the *river's* later success as a vital ship canal, the park and bridge should perhaps have been renamed for Macomb's prophetic neighbors.

[W 18b.] Old Female Guardian Soc.   **[W 18d.]** The Park Plaza Apartments

[W 18c.] Macombs Dam Bridge/a.k.a. Central Bridge, over the Harlem River bet. Jerome Ave., The Bronx, and W. 155th St., Manhattan. 1895. Alfred P. Boller, engineer.

With the replacement of the original **University Heights Bridge** [see W 22d.] with a larger look-alike, this stands out as the city's finest example of 19th-century swing bridges. While it looks flimsy now, in 1895 it was one of the heaviest drawbridges ever built.

[W 18d.] Park Plaza Apartments, 1005 Jerome Ave. bet. Anderson Ave. and E. 165th St. W side. 1928. Horace Ginsbern. ★

One of the earliest (and one of the best) Art Deco-inspired apartment buildings in the Bronx. Influenced both by the 1925 Exposition Internationale des Arts Décoratifs et Industriels Modernes in Paris, and motifs from **Mayan architecture** then fashionable. Note the elaborate polychromed terra-cotta ornament.

[W 19a.] West 167th Street housing, bet. Nelson and Woodycrest Aves. S side. ca. 1985.

Well executed 3-story attached housing.

[W 19b.] Noonan Plaza (apartments), 105-145 W. 168th St., NW cor. Nelson Ave. 1931. Horace Ginsbern.

These 7-story apartments, arranged to form a quadrangle, are entered diagonally through **a highly decorative masonry arcade** which leads to a central court, the original splendors of which can only be guessed at today. Art Deco-*cum*-Mayan was the idiosyncratic style of the Ginsbern firm at the time. One of the West Bronx's key Depression monuments.

[W 19c.] Union Reformed Church of Highbridge, 1272 Ogden Ave. bet. W. 168th and W. 169th Sts. E side. 1889. Alfred E. Barlow.

A quaint stone church which contrasts beautifully with the Moderne decor of Noonan Plaza immediately adjacent.

[W 19d.] Public School 11, Bronx/formerly **Grammar School No. 91,** 1257 Ogden Ave., bet. W. 168th and W. 169th Sts. W side. 1889. G. W. Debevoise. ★

A **picturesque gem** of an old multistory school building. Note the carving of its original designation right into the stonework. A lot was lost architecturally when the late Victorian love of decoration disappeared—fortunately remnants such as this remain.

[W 19e.] 1182 Woodycrest Avenue (residence), bet. W. 167th and W. 168th Sts. E side. ca. 1875.

A surviving cream and white Victorian country house.

[W 19f.] 1200 Woodycrest Avenue (apartments), bet. W. 167th and W. 168th Sts. E side. 1936. Franklin, Bates & Heindsmann.

Art Moderne, now totally neglected.

[W 20a.] Carmelite Monastery, 1381 University Ave., opp. W. 170th St. W side. 1940. Maginnis & Walsh.

When the walkway of adjacent High Bridge was open to pedestrians, the house of this **cloistered community** was best seen from there, from the riverside. Hugging the steep slope of the hill, which tumbles down to the Harlem River valley, this latter-day, **medieval-style** building—with its tower, cells, chapel, cloister, and gardens—became visible without revealing the life of contemplation within its walls. Today only its carefully crafted University Avenue facade is readily available to visitors. Serenity amidst devastation.

[W 20b.] Washington Bridge, over the Harlem River, from University and Ogden Aves., The Bronx, to W. 181st and Amsterdam Ave., Manhattan. 1888. C. C. Schneider, original designer. John McAlpine and William R. Hutton, successive chief engineers. ★

Not the *George* Washington but just plain *Washington* Bridge and, in its own intricate way, **a superior bridge.** Two soaring sets of arches: one spanning the water, the other the river valley's flood plain. Schneider won **the design competition,** but cost overruns forced the substitution of steel latticework under the roadway. A happy compromise, particularly from the deck of a leisurely Circle Liner below.

[W 21a.] 1660 Andrews Avenue (NYCHA rehabilitated apartments), bet. W. 175th and W. 176th Sts. E side. ca. 1925. Altered, 1987, Shelly Kroop and James McCullar.

Those City-aided balconies add oomph to a tired stretch of street that needs them.

[W 21b.] South Bronx Job Corps Center/formerly **Salvation Army Training College/**originally **Messiah Home for Children,** 1771 Andrews Ave., SW cor. W. Tremont Ave. 1908. Charles Brigham.

A rare example in New York City of the **neo-Jacobean** style, a valuable, visually enriching addition to this currently down-at-the-heels neighborhood. (Brigham designed the **Christian Science Mother Church,** in Boston.)

Along the banks of the Harlem River:

Once this was decaying riverside frontage. It had been the site of miscellaneous coal docks and the Consolidated Ship Building Corporation and was **cut off** from the adjacent residential community by the tracks of the Penn Central Railroad and the Major Deegan Expressway. Beginning in the late 1960s these valuable land resources were **returned to public** use by the combined efforts of the City of New York, the New York State Park Commission for New York City, and the New York State Urban Development Corporation. As the projects were completed, the state park was renamed for Roberto Clemente, a local **baseball hero** killed in a plane crash; the housing was renamed, naturally, River Park Towers, to reflect their setting.

[W 22a.] Roberto Clemente State Park/originally **Harlem River Bronx State Park,** Matthewson Rd. off W. Tremont Ave. Bridge along Harlem River. 1973. M. Paul Friedberg & Assocs., landscape architects; Dean McClure, architect for recreation building.

The first of a planned series of state parks in the city, this intricately designed **recreation playland** offers swimming, diving, gymnasium events, and a **wonderful stroll** along the seawall of the adjacent Harlem River. It may not have the verdancy of an upstate park, but its **lively forms** animate an otherwise isolated urban setting.

[W 22b.] River Park Towers (apartments), 10, 20, 30, 40 Richman Plaza, off Cedar Ave. Bridge along Harlem River. 1975. Davis, Brody & Assocs., architects; M. Paul Friedberg & Assocs., landscape architects.

A variation of the earlier Waterside project in Manhattan, these two intricate and tall brick apartment towers (actually two pairs of buildings joined) form a **dramatic landmark** from both sides of the river and to the millions of motorists who pass by them every year. To those who live in the towers (and those who visit) they are **equally satisfying** up close—particularly the combination **pedestrian and vehicular plaza** on which the apartment towers, parking garage, and retail stores front and from whose edges the tall shafts rise seemingly **to infinity.** The pedestrian plaza facing the river, however, is too large and too bleak.

[W 19d.] Public School 11, The Bronx   **[W 22b.]** The River Park Towers apts.

[W 22c.] Public School 229, Bronx/Junior High School 229, Bronx, The Roland N. Patterson School, 225 Harlem River Park Bridge, NE cor. Richman Plaza. 1977. Caudill Rowlett Scott.

Utilizing the air rights over the railroad tracks, this is a most unorthodox school in appearance, having only the bare minimum of windows but a very dramatic exterior appearance.

Old Croton Aqueduct: Completed in 1842, the Old Croton Aqueduct was the first dependable source of drinking water for the growing city. It runs a 32-mile downhill course from Croton Reservoir in Westchester County to High Bridge. In this area of the West Bronx it is particularly apparent, since much of its course is **topped by a green walkway** and sitting areas. Its most visible part is its southern edge along University Avenue just above West Tremont Avenue, but the green ribbon is available for public use for some fifteen blocks along a route which parallels University Avenue some 30 yards to the east. *Take a stroll.*

[W 22d.] University Heights Bridge, over the Harlem River bet. W. Fordham Rd., The Bronx, and W. 207th St., Manhattan. 1895. William H. Burr, consulting engineer, with Alfred P. Boller and George W. Birdsall. Relocated, 1908, Othniel F. Nichols, chief engineer. ★

The 1895 **Tinkertoy bridge** that occupied the site once spanned the Harlem River at Broadway between West 220th and 225th Streets. When the IRT Broadway Line elevated came to the Bronx, that bridge was no longer purposeful. So, rather than waste a bridge, **it was floated a mile or so** down the Harlem to this West 207th Street site. But in the affluent 1980s, just years after the city faced bankruptcy, a second reuse to accommodate increased traffic couldn't be justified, and so the lacy, latticework structure was demolished (but only *after* politically desirable landmark designation) so that a wider, stronger, modern bridge using superficially similar forms could be erected in its place.

Back along University Heights:

[W 23a.] Calvary Methodist Church, 1885 University Ave., bet. W. Tremont and W. Burnside Aves. W side. 1924.

This church's rough stone walls contrast with its refined stained glass windows. The **small but strongly composed** building appears as a bastion against the changes which are sweeping the area. Built and physically endowed by a moneyed community in the 1920s, it now serves a congregation which must struggle to maintain the fine qualities of the edifice.

[W 23b.] Gatehouse, New Croton Aqueduct, W. Burnside Ave. SW cor. Phelan Place. ca. 1890. Benjamin S. Church, engineer.

One of a **series** of stone buildings built in the Bronx and Manhattan to service the city's **second** water supply system, the New Croton Aqueduct (1885–1893). The gray stone structure is detailed to **reflect pride** not only in the **reliability** and **pureness** of the drinking water but also in the **skills** of the stonecutters who crafted it.

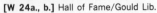

[W 24a., b.] Hall of Fame/Gould Lib.   **[W 29.]** Kingsbridge Armory, N.Y.N.G.

The Old N.Y.U. Uptown Campus

[W 24.] Bronx Community College, CUNY/formerly **New York University, University Heights Campus,** University Ave. bet. W. 180th St. and Hall of Fame Terr., W side, to Sedgwick Ave. and vicinity. Original grounds and Ohio Field, 1894. Vaux & Co., landscape architects.

Begun in the 1890s, this 50-plus-acre campus was the uptown campus of New York University until 1973. In that year the **properties were sold** to the City of New York for use as a campus for Bronx Community College, CUNY, and the N.Y.U. College of Engineering was absorbed into a newly renamed Polytechnic Institute of New York, in downtown Brooklyn.

Today's campus seems overpopulated by buildings placed in a disturbingly **helter-skelter**—as opposed to charmingly picturesque or classically formal—fashion. Its planning has been criticized almost from the beginning for not taking advantage of the views down into the **still-beautiful valley** of the Harlem River.

[W 24a.] The Hall of Fame for Great Americans, entrance on Hall of Fame Terr. 1901, 1914. McKim, Mead & White. ★ **Open to the public.**

Not a hall at all but a roughly semicircular **Classical arcade** between whose columns are arrayed bronze busts of great Americans. They are picked by a college of more than **100 electors** chosen from the fields of higher education, science, jurisprudence, and business and from among others in public life. The colonnade was conceived by N.Y.U. **Chancellor MacCracken** to camouflage, from Sedgwick Avenue below, the unsightly high foundation walls underpinning **Stanford White's** Library, Philosophy Hall, and Language Hall.

[W 24b.] Gould Memorial Library ★ and interior ★, **Cornelius Baker Hall of Philosophy** ★, **Hall of Languages** ★, 1900. All by McKim, Mead & White.

These three buildings—Gould is the domed one in the center—together with the Hall of Fame Arcade, are the *pièce de résistance* of this campus, and their design is attributed to architect Stanford White himself. Looked at in terms of their **exquisitely detailed** stone exteriors, they achieve a grand Classical Revival composition. Unfortunately, the spaces within the halls lack that grandeur.

[W 24c.] Gould Hall of Technology/Begrisch Lecture Hall. 1964. Marcel Breuer & Assocs. **[W 24d.] Julius Silver Residence Center and Cafeteria.** 1964. Marcel Breuer & Assocs. Robert F. Gatje, associate. **[W 24e.] Technology Two.** 1972. Marcel Breuer & Assocs., Hamilton Smith, associate.

Three additions to the campus before the N.Y.U. administration got its signals straight about the future. Both technology halls suffer from a concrete pomposity.

[W 24d.] Orig. Julius Silver Residence Center and Cafeteria, New York Univ.

[W 24f.] South Hall/formerly **Gustav H. Schwab Residence.** 1857. **[W 24g.] Butler Hall**/formerly **William Henry W. T. Mali Residence.** ca. 1859. **[W 24h.] MacCracken Hall**/formerly **Henry Mitchell MacCracken Residence**/originally **Loring Andrews Residence.** ca. 1880. Hall of Fame Terr. bet. Loring Place and Sedgwick Ave. N side.

Three mansions that predate the campus. Schwab was New York representative for the North German Lloyd Steamship Company. Mali was the Belgian consul general in New York. MacCracken was chancellor of N.Y.U. and founder of the Heights campus. Loring Andrews was owner of much of the land that formed the campus.

[W 24i.] Sedgwick Residence Hall, W. 183rd St. bet. Loring Place and Sedgwick Ave. N side. 1969. La Pierre, Litchfield & Partners.

Before leaving its uptown campus, N.Y.U. succeeded in integrating this large new building in a community of small old ones. No longer in use, since Bronx Community College doesn't need dorms.

Beyond the old N.Y.U. Campus:

[W 25a.] St. Nicholas of Tolentine Church (Roman Catholic), University Ave. SW cor. Fordham Rd. 1928. Delaney, O'Connor & Schultz.

Using a design vocabulary derived from Gothic antecedents, this gray stone church heralds the important event of the intersection of two broad thoroughfares.

[W 25b.] Fordham Hill Cooperative Apartments/originally **Fordham Hill Apartments,** Sedgwick Ave. NE cor. Webb Ave. 1950. Leonard Schultze & Assocs.

On the former site of the Webb Academy & Home for Aged Ship Builders are these nine pristine 16-story apartment towers developed for the Equitable Life Assurance Society by an architect of the Waldorf-Astoria. Bland.

László Moholy-Nagy's widow, architectural historian Sibyl, and their two children moved into Fordham Hill Apartments after the death, in 1946, of the former Bauhaus instructor, photographer, and theorist. A refugee from Hitler's Germany, Moholy-Nagy had relocated to Chicago, where he founded the New Bauhaus and then the Institute of Design. In all the family stayed in these accommodations for about a year.

KINGBRIDGE HEIGHTS

[W 25c.] Originally **U.S. Veterans Hospital No. 81/**now **Kingsbridge Veterans Hospital,** 130 W. Kingsbridge Rd., bet. Webb and Sedgwick Aves. S side. **New Hospital,** 1979. Max O. Urbahn Assocs, Inc. **[W 25d.] Nursing Home Care Unit,** 1984. Urbahn Assocs., Inc. **[W 25e.] Old Chapel.**

This commanding green hillside site with spectacular views, across the Harlem Valley, of upper Manhattan has provided for the needs of diverse occupants over the years. During the British occupation of New York it was a site for one of their forts. Later it was a private estate and served as the Catholic Orphan Asylum before becoming a veterans' hospital in the 1920s. The 1979 all aluminum-clad replacement hospital calls even more attention to itself than did its immense neo-Georgian predecessor. The Home Care Unit is a particularly handsome addition, just as the old chapel is a welcome holdover.

[W 26.] The Jewish Home and Hospital for the Aged. [W 26a.] Salzman Pavilion, 100 W. Kingsbridge Rd., bet. Webb and University Aves. S side. 1975. **[W 26b.] Greenwall Pavilion,** 2545 University Ave., at W. 192nd St. W side. 1972. Both buildings by Weiss Whelan Edelbaum Webster.

On what was once the site of the Hebrew Infant Asylum are two imposing additions to an institution for the elderly.

[W 26c.] 2751 University Avenue (apartments), NW cor. W. 195th St. 1936. Edward W. Franklin.

Art Deco in cream, orange, and brown brick, with its entry still intact.

[W 26d.] Rosenor Gables (apartments), 2757 Claflin Ave., bet. W. 195th and W. 197th Sts. W side. ca. 1928.

Deeply modeled neo-Tudor. **Imposing** except for the post-energy-crisis, brown anodized aluminum windows.

[W 26e.] Rectory, Our Lady of Angels Roman Catholic Church, 2860 Webb Ave. bet. W. 197th St. and Reservoir Ave. ca. 1900.

Impressive and asymmetric, its ground floor is of **undressed field-stone.** Catch that carved wood *porte cochère.*

North along Kingsbridge Terrace:

[W 27a.] 2744 Kingsbridge Terrace (residence), N of W. Kingsbridge Rd. E side. 1912.

Close by the vast veterans' hospital is this tiny monument, a stucco castle with numerous gables, balconies, crenellated turrets, a weather vane, a TV antenna, and a tunnel reputedly leading from the "dungeon" to the street.

[W 27b.] Kingsbridge Heights Community Center/originally **50th Precinct, N.Y.C. Police Department,** 3101 Kingsbridge Terr., SW cor. Summit Place. 1902. Horgan & Slattery. ★

Referring to the political connections of this structure's successful architects, Seth Low in 1902 called for the **"disorganizing and unslatterifying"** of municipal architecture as one of his mayoral promises.

[W 27c.] Sholom Aleichem Houses/Yiddish Cooperative Heim Geselshaft (cooperative apartments) 3451 Giles Place, 3470 Cannon Place, 68 W. 238th St., 3605 Sedgwick Ave. Entry via Giles Place (one-way north and east) from Kingsbridge Terr. 1927. Springsteen & Goldhammer.

Four **unembellished** red-brick apartments atop a hill overlooking the Harlem River valley. Built around a **meandering courtyard** by a Jewish community whose common goal was the preservation of Eastern European Yiddish culture (as contrasted with the Hebrew religious culture) through membership in the *Arbeiter Ring* (Workmen's Circle).

[W 28a.] Amalgamated Cooperative Apartments, N of Sedgwick Ave., bet. Saxon and Dickinson Aves. 1927. Springsteen & Goldhammer.
[W 28b.] Amalgamated Cooperative Apartments extensions, S of Van Cortlandt Park S. bet. Giles Place, Orloff Ave., Sedgwick Ave., and Hillman (once Norman) Ave. 1929–1937. Springsteen & Goldhammer.

Among the earliest housing completed in New York City under the 1926 Limited-Dividend Housing Companies Law was the easternmost of this accretion of 5-story (walkup) and 6-story (elevator) romantic brick-and-ashlar, **Gothique-styled** structures, which remain a credit to their sponsors, designers, builders, and management boards. Amalgamated refers to the **Amalgamated Clothing Workers of America,** whose best-known leader was Sidney Hillman (hence the street-name change).

The Old Jerome Park Reservoir, and its surrounding institutions:

Jerome Park Reservoir: First filled in 1905, this concrete-lined water-storage facility holds **773 million** gallons. Goulden Avenue, its eastern boundary, sits atop a combination of the **Old Croton Aqueduct** and a masonry dividing wall which was to separate it from another part of the reservoir planned as a second stage. The second basin, with a capacity almost twice that of the first, was excavated to the east of the present reservoir, extending to Jerome Avenue between West Kingsbridge Road north to Mosholu Parkway. **Abandoned in 1912, the pit was filled in** and now serves as the site for the Kingsbridge Armory, Lehman College, two subway yards, three high schools, a park, and a couple of publicly aided housing developments!

The reservoir and nearby Jerome Avenue take their name from the **Jerome Park Racetrack,** which occupied this site from 1876 until 1890. Leonard W. Jerome, Winston Churchill's grandfather, was a prime mover in the sponsoring American Jockey Club which strived (with success) to elevate horse racing in this country to the status of an aristocratic sport.

[W 29.] Kingsbridge Armory, 29 W. Kingsbridge Rd., bet. Jerome and Reservoir Aves. N side. 1912. Pilcher & Tachau. ★

Called the largest armory in the world, this picturesque 20th-century fortress, the **Carcassonne of The Bronx,** is probably better known for peacetime activities such as indoor bicycle races than for the putting down of civil insurrection.

[W 30.] Herbert H. Lehman College, CUNY/originally **Hunter College Uptown,** Goulden Ave. SE cor. Bedford Park Blvd. Original buildings,

1932. Thompson, Holmes, & Converse. **[W 30a.] Library and Shuster Hall,** 1960. Marcel Breuer & Assocs.; Robert F. Gatje, associate. **[W 30b.] Carman Hall (classrooms and cafeteria),** 1970. DeYoung & Moskowitz. **[W 30c.] New Library, Speech and Theater, and Auditorium Buildings,** along Paul Ave. 1980. David Todd & Assocs. and Jan Hird Pokorny.

The older buildings never had the architectural glue to pull them together as a composition; the newer ones along Paul Avenue, interrupted by the City's financial crisis, are quite impressive.

[W 31a.] High Pumping Station, Jerome Reservoir, of the former **N.Y.C. Department of Water Supply, Gas & Electricity,** 3205 Jerome Ave., bet. Van Cortlandt Ave. E. and W. Mosholu Pkwy. S. W side. 1905. George W. Birdsall. ★

Deceptively simple, this straightforward gabled masonry form in red brick is **detailed with consummate skill.** The result is a superb example of industrial architecture.

[W 31b.] Tracey Towers, 20 and 40 W. Mosholu Pkwy. S., SW cor. Jerome Ave. 1974. Paul Rudolph.

The tallest structures in the Bronx, these two apartment buildings (one 41 stories, the other 38) offer their residents phenomenal views in all directions. Similarly, the gray, ribbed-block towers are themselves visible from afar, resembling sand castles with overactive thyroids.

FORDHAM HEIGHTS

[W 32a.] Intermediate School 115, Bronx, The Elizabeth Browning School/formerly **Bronx High School of Science**/earlier **Evander Childs, Walton, De Witt Clinton High Schools**/originally **Public School 9, Bronx,** E. 184th St., bet. Creston and Morris Aves. S side. 1915.

Physically, a very ordinary N.Y.C. public school, but this is where the Bronx High School of Science began in 1938 (and where its Nobel Prize-winning scientists were trained). **Bronx Science** is now in a custom-built structure opened in 1959 north of Lehman College, CUNY.

[W 32b.] Loew's Paradise Theater/now divided into **Paradise Twins 1 and 2,** 2417 Grand Concourse, bet. E. 184th and E. 188th Sts. W side. 1929. John Eberson.

Stars and clouds were what made the Paradise special, surely not its reserved terra-cotta facade on the Concourse, a facade minus any projecting marquee (because of the Concourse's special zoning limitations). Inside, this theater was an extravaganza of **ornament, ornament, and more ornament,** surmounted by a deep blue ceiling over the auditorium, **twinkling stars,** and projected **moving clouds.** Considered by one connoisseur of such things the "most beautiful and elaborate" of Eberson's designs.

[W 32c.] Creston Avenue Baptist Church, 114 E. 188th St., bet. Creston and Morris Aves. S side. 1905.

Crushed on both sides by retail shops reaching out for customers in this competitive shopping strip, this playful, castlelike church hangs on.

[W 32d.] Alexander's (department store)/originally **Wertheimer's,** Fordham Rd. NW cor. Grand Concourse. 1933. Altered into Alexander's, 1938, Starrett & Van Vleck. Additions, 1953–1960, Ketchum, Giná & Sharp, Morris Ketchum, Jr., & Assocs.

Less important for its design—horizontal bands of glass block across its curved but otherwise unadorned facade—than for being a shopping magnet and local landmark of the Fordham Road retail district. It occupies a dramatic site at the crest of the hill toward which Fordham Road ascends.

[W 32e.] Dollar Dry Dock Bank/originally **Dollar Savings Bank,** 2530 Grand Concourse, bet. Fordham Rd. and E. 192nd St. W side. 1932. Halsey, McCormack & Helmer. Addition, 1951.

This work, with **a great clock,** is by the deans of outer-borough bank designers: their well-known Brooklyn's Williamsburgh Savings

Bank tower [see WC Brooklyn/Boerum Hill/Times Plaza B 15b.], and others.

[W 33a.] Poe Cottage, Poe Park, Grand Concourse SE cor. E. Kingsbridge Rd. 1816. ★ **Open to the public.**

The cottage was moved into the park from its original site across Kingsbridge Road in 1913. Edgar Allan Poe lived here from 1846 until a few months before his death in 1849. He came here in the hope that the clear country air would aid his ailing young wife. (She died during their first winter in the small house.)

[W 33b.] St. James Church (Episcopal), 2500 Jerome Ave., NE cor. E. 190th St. 1863. Dudley & Diaper. ★

A stone Gothic Revival church in the shadow of the IRT Jerome Avenue elevated. The greenery of the churchyard and adjacent St. James Park (1901) seems to block out some of the clatter.

[W 33c.] St. James Park Recreation Center, N.Y.C. Department of Parks & Recreation, 2530 Jerome Ave., bet. E. 190th and E. 192nd St. E side. 1970. Richard G. Stein & Assocs.

The design principles of the International Style, **carefully applied** and with worthy effect.

BEDFORD PARK

[W 34a.] Bedford Park Presbyterian Church, 2933 Bainbridge Ave., NW cor. Bedford Park Blvd. 1900. R. H. Robertson. Addition, 1929.

Another stone church which bestows a distinguished tone upon a heavily trafficked street.

[W 34a.] The ashlar neo-Tudor Bedford Park Presbyterian Church (1968 photo)

[W 34b.] 52nd Precinct Station House/originally **41st Precinct, N.Y.C. Police Department,** 3016 Webster Ave., NE cor. Mosholu Pkwy. 1906. Stoughton & Stoughton. ★

Responding to the ambience of a quasi-rural setting at the turn of the century, the architects of Manhattan's Soldiers' and Sailors' Monument on Riverside Drive created a romantic **Tuscan villa-inspired** solution to this precinct house commission. The tower bears polychromed terra-cotta clock faces and deeply projecting eaves—a high point in such romantic design in the city.

[W 34c.] Bedford Park Congregational Church (United Church of Christ), E. 201st St. NE cor. Bainbridge Ave. ca. 1890.

Tiny, but its ashlar and wood frame construction are special.

[W 35a.] Ursuline Academy (Roman Catholic)/originally **Mount St. Ursula Convent,** 330 Bedford Park Blvd./2885 Marion Ave. ca. 1888. Arthur Arctander.

Don't let the cream-colored paint job on the old building deceive you. This is **the real stuff.**

NORWOOD

[W 35b.] Mosholu Parkway, connecting Bronx and Van Cortlandt Parks.

One of the few completed links in the **network of parkways** that was proposed to connect the major parks of the Bronx. At the eastern entrance to the parkway the **Victory Monument** serves to divide traffic.

[W 34b.] 52nd Precinct Sta., N.Y.P.D.   **[W 35c.]** St. Brendan's Catholic Ch.

[W 35c.] St. Brendan's Church (Roman Catholic), Perry Ave. bet. E. 206th and E. 207th Sts. W side. 1966. Belfatto & Pavarini.

St. Brendan is the patron saint of navigators, so it should come as no surprise that this church was built to resemble the **prow of a ship.** There are two churches in this building, and the slope of the site permits us to enter both at ground level. The flat-ceiling lower church is entered from West 206th Street. The upper church, entered from East 207th Street, is under the **steeply sloped roof.** Near the entrance the ceiling is **low** and the church **dark,** but as we move toward the altar the **space and light** around us grow. The steeple, part of the upswept roof, forms the prow. The stained glass, **boldly colored,** is particularly beautiful. It is best to visit when the church is in use.

[W 36a.] Valentine-Varian House/Museum of Bronx History, 3266 Bainbridge Ave., bet. Van Cortlandt Ave. E. and E. 208th St. E side. 1775. ★ **Open to the public.**

A well-proportioned fieldstone farmhouse moved in the 1960s from its original location across the street on Van Cortlandt Avenue East. Today it is also the home of **The Bronx County Historical Society** and the site of a museum of local history: photos, postcards, old beer bottles, arrowheads and cartridges . . . and topical exhibits.

Williamsbridge Oval: The embankment behind the Valentine-Varian House continues to curve around to form an oval which today encloses an elaborate city playground. Between 1888 and 1923 the embankment formed a dam to contain the waters of the Williamsbridge Reservoir, part of the city's water supply system. After its abandonment tunnels were cut through, and play equipment and benches were introduced. Appropriately named, the surrounding streets are called Reservoir Oval East and West.

[W 36b.] Former **Keeper's House, Williamsbridge Reservoir,** Reservoir Oval E. NE cor. Putnam Place. ca. 1890. Benjamin S. Church, engineer.

One of the many rock-faced stone buildings built for the city's water supply system. This one, however, was meant as a residence and office rather than as a gatehouse or service facility. It has outlived the effective life of the abandoned reservoir across the street.

[W 37.] Montefiore Hospital and Medical Center, E. Gun Hill Rd. bet. Kossuth and Tryon Aves. S side. Original buildings, 1913. Arnold W. Brunner. **[W 37a.] Henry L. Moses Research Institute,** E. Gun Hill Rd.

SE cor. Bainbridge Ave. 1966. Philip Johnson & Assocs. **[W 37b.]** **Annie Lichtenhein Pavilion,** Kossuth Ave. bet. E. Gun Hill Rd. and E. 210th St. E side. 1970. Gruzen & Partners and Westermann/Miller Assocs. **[W 37c.] Loeb Pavilion,** E of Lichtenhein Pavilion. 1966. Kelly & Gruzen and Helge Westermann. **[W 37d.] Montefiore Apartments II,** 3450 Wayne Ave., bet. E. Gun Hill Rd. and E. 210th St. E side. 1972. Schuman, Lichtenstein & Claman.

Like most hospital campuses nurtured over decades and responding to growth in population and changes in treatment techniques, this one is chaotic in appearance. It speaks well for administration and donors that the newer additions are **exemplary in their architecture,** beginning with Philip Johnson's 1966 work. The Montefiore II Apartments is one of the tallest in the borough; its dark red-brown brick volume is **impressive** from **both near and far.**

[W 37e.] North Central Bronx Hospital, N.Y.C. Health & Hospitals Corporation, Kossuth Ave. NE cor. E. 210th St. 1976. Westermann/ Miller Assocs.; Carl Pancaldo; Schuman, Lichtenstein & Claman.

Considering the limitations of the site (space made available from the existing Montefiore complex), this is a **spectacularly successful** hospital design when viewed as public architecture. Crisp, neat, bold forms of brick and precast concrete articulate the street facades and present a **confident** and **inviting** appearance.

[W 37d.] The Montefiore II apartments   **[W 37e.]** North Central Bronx Hospital

[W 38.] Woodlawn Cemetery, entrances at Jerome Ave. N of Bainbridge Ave. E side and at E. 233rd St. SW cor. Webster Ave. **Open to the public.**

A lavish array of tombstones, mausoleums, and memorials in a richly planted setting. Many **wealthy and distinguished people** are buried here. Tombs and mausoleums are replicas and small-scale reproductions of several famous European chapels and monuments. **Jay Gould,** the Woolworths, and Mayors **John Purroy Mitchel** and **Fiorello LaGuardia** are among the many famous people interred at Woodlawn.

RIVERDALE

MARBLE HILL (MANHATTAN) • KINGSBRIDGE
SPUYTEN DUYVIL • RIVERDALE • NORTH RIVERDALE
FIELDSTON • VAN CORTLANDT PARK

In this precinct, extending from Broadway west to the banks of the Hudson River, can be found **lush estates** and **lavish mansions,** low-rent subsidized housing, and block after block of very ordinary, **middle-class apartments.** It differs most from the rest of the Bronx, however, in that some parts—such as the private-street community of **Fieldston** and the slopes of the old community of **Riverdale-on-Hudson**—house some of the borough's most affluent and most influential people. **Kingsbridge,** the flat area along Broadway below West 242nd Street, preserves the name of the earliest settlement (which grew up around the first bridge to Manhattan, built in 1693). **Spuyten Duyvil** is the hilly southwestern tip of this precinct, from which the graceful arch of the Henry Hudson Bridge springs to its opposite abutment in Manhattan. **Marble Hill** is the area between Spuyten Duyvil and Broadway and is actually a part of Manhattan though separated physically by the channel of the Harlem River Ship Canal. Since it is *not* officially part of the Bronx, it will be given short shrift here. Its name describes it well: a steeply sloped mound of Inwood marble (a misnomer for a local limestone) turned upon itself as the result of its old street pattern.

MARBLE HILL (MANHATTAN)

[R 1.] St. Stephen's Methodist Episcopal Church, 146 W. 228th St., SE cor. Marble Hill Ave. 1897.

The church stands as a marker and a sign of welcome to **Manhattan's orphaned Marble Hill community,** cut off from its mother island and physically connected to the Bronx by the technologies of canal digging and earth moving. A **picturesque Shingle Style work** with a commanding presence.

KINGSBRIDGE

[R 2a.] Church of the Mediator (Episcopal), 3045 Kingsbridge Ave., SW cor. W. 231st St. 1913. Henry Vaughan.

A fine, gray ashlar granite Gothic Revival sanctuary neatly sited on a prominent corner by an architect of Washington's National Cathedral.

[R 2b.] Originally **George H. Moller residence**/formerly **Residence, Brothers of the Christian Schools,** 3029 Godwin Terr., bet. W. 230th and W. 231st Sts. W side. ca. 1875.

Set back a bit from the adjacent 1920s brick multiple-dwelling construction, atop a black stone retaining wall, is this mansard-roof, stuccoed house, **moved from its original site** a few hundred feet west and clearly left over from another era. The romantic front porch is shaded by a tall evergreen. Note the public stairway at the north end of the street up to Naples Terrace.

Donaghy Steak House, 5523 Broadway, N of W. 230th St. W side.

For meat-and-potato lovers this is a straightforward restaurant with good food and thoughtful service.

Ehring's Tavern, 228 W. 231st St., W of Broadway at Godwin Terr.

Good food with a German tang and, as a tavern would have it, good drink, too.

Stella D'oro Restaurant, 5806 Broadway, S of W. 238th St. E side.

Italian cuisine served out at a wholesale scale by the makers of all those little packaged breads and pastries.

West on W. 230th Street and south up hill to Kappock Street:

SPUYTEN DUYVIL

Spuyten Duyvil, an early Dutch name for the region where the Harlem and Hudson Rivers meet, is also the name of the **steeply sloped area** of the Bronx which overlooks the confluence of the waters. It has been overbuilt with tall undistinguished apartments.

[R 3a.] Edgehill Church of Spuyten Duyvil (United Church of Christ)/ originally **Riverdale Presbyterian Chapel,** 2550 Independence Ave., at Kappock St. S side. 1888. Francis H. Kimball. ★

Occupying a spit of property between two roads that set off in different directions at different grades is this **exquisitely picturesque** eclectic sanctuary: a base of Richardsonian Romanesque, a top of Gothic Revival, and a smattering of Tudor details.

[R 3b.] 2475 Palisade Avenue (apartments), SW cor. Independence Ave. ca. 1930. **[R 3c.] Villa Charlotte Brontë (apartments),** 2501 Palisade Ave., NW cor. Independence Ave. 1926. Robert Gardner.

A small apartment house, 5 stories plus attic, of brick, rubblestone, and shingle designed around casement windows; and the Villa, two **romantic, intricate, visually intriguing** wings containing sixteen units, some partly above, some below street level. Together these habitations occupy the southwesternmost edge of the Spuyten Duyvil escarpment, one of **the city's finest sites,** overlooking the confluence of the **Harlem and Hudson Rivers.** These responsible works of architecture were intended to enhance both the street and the view. Would that their grotesque post-WW II neighbors had been so skillfully designed.

[R 3c.] Villa Charlotte Brontë apts.   **[R 6a.]** "Greyston," W. E. Dodge res.

[R 3d.] Henry Hudson Memorial Column, Henry Hudson Park, Kappock St. NW cor. Independence Ave. 1912. Babb, Cook & Welch. Column by Walter Cook of Cook, Babb & Willard. Sculpture of Hudson, 1938. Karl Bitter and Karl Gruppe.

The 100-foot Doric column and base were erected on this high bluff by public subscription following the **Hudson-Fulton Celebration of 1909.** The 16-foot bronze of Hudson gazing out at his river from atop the column was **not installed until long after.** It was the work of Karl Gruppe working from a plaster model by his teacher, the noted sculptor Karl Bitter.

[R 4a.] Spuyten Duyvil Branch, N.Y. Public Library, 650 W. 235th St., bet. Independence and Douglas Aves. S side. 1971. Giorgio Cavaglieri.

A dignified building in an area characterized by chaotic and unrelated building development.

[R 4b.] Seton Park playground, N.Y.C. Department of Parks & Recreation, W. 235th St. SW cor. Douglas Ave. 1975. M. Paul Friedberg & Assocs., landscape architects.

The playground occupies part of the heavily overgrown former site of the **Seton Hospital for Consumptives,** a Roman Catholic institution dating from 1893.

RIVERDALE

Riverdale, the northwest strip of this precinct, which slopes romantically down to the Hudson's banks, was once a name reserved for the area immediately around the Riverdale station of the onetime New York Central & Hudson River Railroad. Then it was called **Riverdale-on-Hudson** at West 254th Street. Today, all too many high-rise apartment hulks along Henry Hudson Parkway have **diminished the exclusivity** of both name and community. Fortunately, however, a cadre of tenacious residents, a couple of foreign governments, and some eleemosynary institutions still preserve the mansions, the lovely landscapes, and the tranquil beauty of the older community.

A note of caution: The Riverdale area north of West 240th Street and west of Henry Hudson Parkway is an obstacle course for the unwary. Narrow, winding, hilly streets are commonplace. Without much notice they sometimes narrow first into lanes, then driveways, and then abruptly stop. Street signs are often missing or misleading. Since many of the smaller thoroughfares are not officially mapped and others are private (Fieldston's boundaries, east of the parkway, are comparatively easy to determine from the large private-street signs), maps don't help much. The condition of the streets in the area is frequently abominable, partly a result of the high cost of maintenance and partly because residents wish to discourage idle visiting. Not only do potholes abound but in some areas asphalt bumps have been added to discourage reckless driving, since walking and cycling are popular.

All of this has probably contributed to preserving this extra special part of New York. Contributing too are the barking dogs that remain even when the homeowners have taken their cars on an errand. Whether walking, bicycling, or driving, be careful . . . and beware.

[R 5a.] Delafield housing estate/originally **"Fieldston Hill,"** Edward C. Delafield residence and estate/later **Delafield Botanical Estates, Columbia University,** 680 W. 246th St., SW cor. Hadley Ave. ca. 1865. Residence altered, 1916, Dwight James Baum. Converted into housing estate, 1986, James Stewart Polshek & Partners.

The large fieldstone home of Riverdale's old family, the Delafields, and their **lush overgrown estate,** sold by Columbia University and then converted into 33 condominium units.

[R 5b.] Edward A. Ames residence, 709 W. 246th St., W of Independence Ave. N side. 1971. Hobart Betts & Assocs.

Down a private drive sits this gem of a house, sheathed in natural cedar and glass.

[R 5c.] Eric J. Schmertz residence, 4550 Palisade Ave., S of W. 247th St. E side. 1971. Vincent A. Claps.

Turned diagonally to the quiet road, this 2-story stained-wood-sheathed house is subtly modeled and detailed. One of Riverdale's best contemporary houses.

[R 6a.] Originally **"Greyston,"** William E. Dodge residence/later **Greyston Conference Center, Teachers College,** 690 W. 247th St., SW cor. Independence Ave. 1864. James Renwick, Jr. ★ **[R 6b.]** **Gatehouse.** ca. 1864.

As Riverdale became a country retreat in the 1860s, this was one of the earliest houses commissioned. The Dodge family was instrumental not only in the establishment of Teachers College in 1887 but also in the transfer to TC in 1961 of this large, many-gabled, many-chimneyed mansion. The **gatehouse,** an asymmetric composition with jerkin head roofs, is in the style of A. J. Downing and Calvert Vaux's books on cottage design.

Riverdale's mansions and views: To call attention to every house worth mentioning in this architectural treasure chest of a community would require a tome in itself. Some of its narrow lanes (and the homes that border them) are particularly rewarding. Sycamore Avenue above West 252nd Street has buildings so picturesque that you won't believe you're in the city. Try Independence Avenue between West 248th and 254th Streets. The best view of Riverdale and the Hudson beyond is from a point just north of West 252nd Street. And visit Wave Hill, whose entrance is at West 249th Street, for a view that Mark Twain and Arturo Toscanini enjoyed.

 [R 6c.] "Alderbrook," formerly **Percy Pyne residence,** then **Elie Nadelman residence,** 4715 Independence Ave., S of W. 248th St. W side. ca. 1880.

An Andrew Jackson Downing-inspired Gothic Revival brick house full of gables and crockets, long the home and studio of sculptor **Elie Nadelman (1882–1946).** Adjacent is a group of houses snugly occupying a private community now called Alderbrook, after the estate whose lands it shares.

[R 7a.] Riverdale Country School, River Campus, W. 248th St./Spaulding's Lane, bet. Independence and Palisade Aves. N side. **[R 7b.] Perkins Study Center,** 1967, R. Marshall Christensen. **[R 7c.]** Originally **"Parkside" George H. Foster residence,** ca. 1871. **[R 7d.]** Originally **"Oaklawn," Henry F. Spaulding residence,** ca. 1863. Thomas S. Wall.

The Study Center's roof is special: two concave surfaces which **approach** one another **but never quite kiss,** leaving a skylight at the ridge. The older structures, particularly the northernmost, **Oaklawn,** are survivors from 19th-century estates, now used for school purposes.

[R 7e.] Formerly **Count Anthony Campagna residence,** 640 W. 249th St., at Independence Ave. 1929. Dwight James Baum.

Placed exquisitely at the end of a short cobblestoned drive, this stucco-walled and tile-roofed mansion is an **aristocratic building,** somehow more traditionally European in feeling than American. It was commissioned, however, by a Manhattan builder who struck it rich in the Roaring Twenties.

[R 7f.] Coachman's residence, Henry F. Spaulding estate, 4970 Independence Ave., NE cor. W. 249th St. 1879. Charles W. Clinton. ★

A Stick Style picturesque cottage, moved from the west side of Independence Avenue in 1909. **Glorious.**

[R 8.] Wave Hill Center for Environmental Studies, 675 W. 252nd St., SW cor. Sycamore Ave. Entrance on Independence Ave. at W. 249th St. W side. **Open to the public. [R 8a.] "Wave Hill," (northern building):** center section, 1844; north wing, late 19th century; armor hall, 1928, Dwight James Baum; south wings, after 1933; general renovation, 1975, Stephen Lepp. ★ **[R 8b.] "Glyndor II," (southern building)/** now **CUNY Institute of Marine and Atmospheric Sciences at City College,** early 20th century.

Early conservationist and J. P. Morgan partner George Walbridge Perkins bought this estate and two others which form the adjacent River Campus of the Riverdale Country School [see R 7a.], in the early 20th century. The neo-Georgian **Glyndor mansion,** which he built soon after, bears his initials on the metal downspouts at the roof. The older **Wave Hill building** he rented out to distinguished individuals, continuing its early role as a residence for the famous, such as publisher William H. Appleton, Theodore Roosevelt, and Mark Twain; he also rented to guests such as William Makepeace Thackeray, John Tyndall, T. H. Huxley, and Herbert Spencer. Before Perkins' descendants presented both buildings to the city in 1960, Wave Hill was also the home of **Arturo Toscanini** and the official residence of the United Kingdom's ambassador to the United Nations. Perhaps Wave Hill's most **intriguing tenant** was **Bashford Dean,** builder of the armor hall. He was curator of arms and armor at the Metropolitan Museum of Art and also curator of reptiles and fishes at the American Museum of Natural History. Between 1906 and 1910 he held both posts **simultaneously.**

John F. Kennedy 1917–1963: While a youngster attending the nearby Riverdale Country School on Fieldston Road, John F. Kennedy lived in **Charles Evans Hughes'** former boxy stucco house on West 252nd Street at the southeast corner of Independence Avenue (officially 5040 Independence). That was from 1926 through 1928.

[R 8c.] H. L. Abrons residence, 5225 Independence Ave., NW cor. W. 252nd St. 1980. Harold Sussman, Horace Ginsbern & Assocs.

The complex form of this frame house may provide superb interiors, but the job of architecture is to integrate both inside with outside, and also the outside with its site and neighbors. Well . . . ?

[R 8d.] Nicholas deB. Katzenbach residence/originally **Robert Colgate residence, "Stonehurst,"** 5225 Sycamore Ave., bet. W. 252nd and W. 254th Sts. W side. 1861. ★

Hidden by newer homes on Sycamore Avenue and by dense trees is another of the **great stone mansions** of Riverdale (such as Greyston or Wave Hill) and the Bronx (Van Cortlandt, Bartow). Katzenbach was **U.S. Attorney General** and Undersecretary of State; Colgate, an **early entrepreneur** in lead and paint.

[R 8e.] Sycamore Avenue barns, bet. W. 252nd and W. 254th Sts. E side. ca. 1853. **[R 8f.] William S. Duke barn,** 5286 Sycamore Ave., SE cor. W. 254th St. ca. 1856. Altered into carriage house, 1888, Frederick C. Withers.

These barns, in various stages of reuse, once served the country homes atop the hill to the east along today's Independence Avenue.

[R 9a.] Salanter Akiba Riverdale Academy, 655 W. 254th St., bet. Independence and Palisade Aves. N side. 1974. Caudill Rowlett Scott Assocs.

Given a hill which slopes, slopes, slopes, and a need for a structure to join the educational activities of what were once **three Hebrew day schools,** what better solution than a stepped building? This one is primarily a series of classroom floors and skylighted roof tiers stepping down the slope (providing all with **cross-the-river views**), and unified by a roof structure paralleling the earth's slope. Shades of Harvard's Gund Hall—but here a result of the topography, not whim. Regrettably, its unrelenting form and weather-resistant materials have prevented it from better blending into its surroundings.

[R 9a.] Salanter Akiba Riverdale Academy: its classrooms follow the terrain

[R 9b.] Housing cluster, Palisade Ave. NW cor. W. 254th St. 1980s.

Woodstock in Riverdale. Cutesy, but that's not enough.

NORTH RIVERDALE

[R 9c.] Ladd Road, off Palisade Ave. bet. W. 254th St. and Sigma Place. E side. **[R 9d.] James Strain residence,** 731 Ladd Rd. E side. 1970. Keith Kroeger Assocs.

A group of houses all built since 1957, clustered along a cul-de-sac around a private swimming pool. The site is the former estate of **Dr. William Sargent Ladd** (hence the name of the road), whose original stone gateposts guard the entrance. The Strain house embodies a geometrical clarity which gives the enclave a center of focus.

[R 9e.] Gethsemane-on-Hudson Monastery and **Cardinal Spellman Retreat House, Passionist Fathers and Brothers,** 5801 Palisade Ave., opp. Sigma Place. W side. **[R 9f.] Riverdale Center of Religious Research/**formerly **Old Residence.** ca. 1895 **[R 9g.] New Residence and Chapel.** 1967. Brother Cajetan J. B. Baumann, O.F.M.

Neither the old residence, a 3-story shingled Victorian country house, nor the new, an undistinguished orange brick dorm, is of special interest. It is the new chapel, almost hidden from the road, that is a dramatic expressionistic architectural/sculptural work.

[R 10.] The Hebrew Home for the Aged at Riverdale, 5901 Palisade Ave., S of W. 261st St. W side. **Additions: [R 10a.] Goldfine Pavilion (south building).** 1968. Kelly & Gruzen. **[R 10b.] Palisade Nursing Home (north building).** 1975. Gruzen & Partners. **[R 10c.] East Pavilion.** 1987. Gruzen Partnership.

This institution awakened precociously to the benefits and satisfactions of **high-quality architecture for the elderly.** The early work combines exposed concrete and stacked red brick and seems to express in its windows a response to the temptations of the spectacular 270° river views. The newer, 7-story all-brick north building seems carved from **a monumental cube** almost as sculptor Gutzon Borglum attacked the Black Hills of South Dakota. Even the utility building off the road shows the architect's care and talent.

[R 9d.] The James Strain residence: a very elegantly detailed crystaline prism

[R 11a.] College of Mount St. Vincent: tiered porches survey the Hudson

[R 11.] College of Mount Saint Vincent on Hudson/originally **Convent and Academy of Mount Saint Vincent,** Riverdale Ave. and W. 263rd St. W side. **[R 11a.] Original College Building,** central section, 1857–1859. Henry Engelbert. Additions: 1865, 1885, 1908, E. Wenz.

1952. ★ [R 11b.] **Library**/formerly **"Fonthill," Edwin Forrest residence,** 1846. ★ [R 11c.] **Louise LeGras Hall**/originally **St. Vincent's Free School,** W. 261st St. opp. Netherland Ave. N side. 1875. [R 11d.] **Marillac Hall**/originally in part **E. D. Randolph residence,** ca. 1855. [R 11e.] Originally **"Fonthill" cottage and stable,** 1846. ★

The **Sisters of Charity,** who operate the college, purchased this site from actor **Edwin Forrest** (his feud with William Charles Macready in 1849 touched off the **Astor Place Riot**) when their original quarters in Manhattan were to be destroyed by the construction of Central Park. Forrest's house, Fonthill, is as eccentric a building for New York as the **"folly"** it was patterned after was for England: William Beckford's **Fonthill Abbey.** Though this is the best-known building on the campus, the old red brick college itself, four stories high and oh *so* long, is an unfamiliar and more spectacular sight. Its 180-foot tower rises some 400 feet above the level of the Hudson. LeGras Hall was, between 1875 and 1910, the sparsely settled Riverdale's only elementary school. It is a charming building, accessible directly from adjacent West 261st Street.

[R 11b.] "Fonthill," Edwin Forrest res.

Verdant scene in Fieldston community

FIELDSTON

A community of **private streets** and romantic, **English-inspired** homes of the 1920s grouped along the streets north of Manhattan College Parkway; Fieldston Road, with its green central mall, is the quiet main thoroughfare. Among the many charms of the area is **the oak tree preserved** in the center of the intersection of Delafield and Iselin Avenues. If you are bicycling or driving, beware of the street paving. Potholes can be the rule.

[R 12.] **The Fieldston Schools,** Manhattan College Pkwy. SW cor. Fieldston Rd. [R 12a.] **Original buildings.** 1926. Clarence S. Stein and Robert D. Kohn. [R 12b.] **Tate Library.** 1971. Murphy & Mackey.

A group of private schools, operated by the New York Ethical Culture Society, huddling together on their hilly rise. The early buildings are unassuming in their mixture of traditional materials. The newer Tate Library attempts to bridge the design gulf between then and now.

[R 12c.] **Riverdale-Yonkers Ethical Culture Society,** 4550 Fieldston Rd., NE cor. Manhattan College Pkwy. 1965. William N. Breger Assocs.

A simple painted concrete-block structure, almost engulfed by the lush landscape.

[R 12d.] **3875 Waldo Avenue (apartments),** SW cor. Manhattan College Pkwy. to Dash Place. 1928. Horace Ginsbern.

The romance of Fieldston penetrated beyond its own **sentineled** streets. This neo-Tudor apartment is very much part of the 1920s Riverdale scene.

[R 12e.] **S. L. Victor residence,** 200 W. 245th St., SW cor. Waldo Ave. 1968. Ferdinand Gottlieb.

A formal, dignified contemporary design in now-gray redwood siding. Slate-paved stairs **ceremoniously** lead to a pair of lovely paneled doors which are the formal entry. The street side of the house is discreet with slender windows; the rear, private, opens to the **lush backyard.** A wonderful house.

[R 12e.] S. L. Victor residence: strict geometry in a rambling green setting

[R 13d.] Orig. C. E. Chambers res.　**[R 14a.]** Con. Synagogue, Riverdale

[R 13.] Horace Mann High School, 231 W. 246th St., NE cor. Tibbett Ave., **[R 13a.] Pforzheimer Hall.** 1956. Victor Christ-Janer. **[R 13b.] Prettyman Gymnasium.** 1968. Charles E. Hughes III. **[R 13c.] Gratwick Science Wing Addition** and **Pforzheimer Hall renovation.** 1975. Frost Assocs.

Once located next to **Teachers College** in Manhattan, Horace Mann High School (and Horace Mann-Barnard Elementary School south of West 246th Street) now occupies this more verdant campus. Pforzheimer, Prettyman, and particularly Gratwick are **interesting** newer buildings.

[R 13d.] Originally **C. E. Chambers residence,** 4670 Waldo Ave., bet. College Rd. and Livingston Ave. E side. ca. 1923. Julius Gregory.

A picturesque suburban house, reminiscent of the best in English country house design, by a master architect of such. Gregory did quite a number of similar fine homes in Fieldston.

[R 14a.] Conservative Synagogue of Riverdale, Congregation Adath Israel, Henry Hudson Pkwy. NE cor. W. 250th St. 1962. Percival Goodman.

Strong forms in concrete and dark red brick give this synagogue considerable character.

[R 14b.] Henry Ittleson Center for Child Research, Jewish Board of Guardians, 5050 Iselin Ave., N of W. 250th St. E side. 1967. Abraham W. Geller; M. A. Rubenstein, design associate.

A neatly arranged and dramatically designed community of tan block pavilions capped by standing-seam metal roofs. The group, for the treatment of disturbed children, is set well back from the street.

 [R 14c.] Christ Church (Episcopal), Henry Hudson Pkwy. SE cor. W. 252nd St. 1866. Richard M. Upjohn. ★

A small, picturesque church, of brick and local stone, with a simple pierced-wall belfry. Minimal alterations and careful maintenance have preserved this delightful edifice.

A detour west across the Parkway:

[R 14d.] Riverdale Presbyterian Church and **Manse: The Duff House,** 4765 Henry Hudson Pkwy. W., at W. 249th St. W side. 1863. James Renwick, Jr. Both ★

A pair of Renwick designs fortunately framed from distractions on either side by heavy greenery. The Duff House is curious in that its original design called for both a **mansard roof** and Gothic Revival **gables and dormers.**

East across the Parkway and downhill to Broadway:

VAN CORTLANDT PARK

[R 15a.] Van Cortlandt Swimming Pool, Van Cortlandt Park, Broadway at W. 242nd St. E side. 1970. Heery & Heery.

The largest of a series of system-designed, system-built pools. It was completed in a successful crash program intended to break the city's normal, **slow-as-molasses** schedule for government-financed construction.

[R 15b.] Van Cortlandt Mansion Museum, Van Cortlandt Park, Broadway bet. W. 242nd and W. 246th Sts. E side. 1748. ★ **Open to the public.**

A carefully preserved fieldstone country house for a wealthy landed family. A simple exterior hides a **richly decorated interior.** It stands south of the area that was once its farm, today an enormous meadow used for a variety of **sporting events,** particularly cricket (enjoyed by the city's large West Indian population) and **model airplane trials.**

[R 16b.] The Riverdale Branch, The N.Y. Public Library: a light-gathering gable

Vault Hill, overlooking the Van Cortlandt Mansion, contains the Van Cortlandt family vault. When the British occupied New York in 1776, Augustus Van Cortlandt, the city clerk, hid the municipal records in the vault. In 1781, General Washington had campfires lit here to deceive the British, while he marched to Yorktown for the battle against Cornwallis.

On high ground, this time north of the Parkway:

[R 16a.] Diplomatic Residence, United Nations Mission, Union of Soviet Socialist Republics, 355 W. 255th St., NE cor. Mosholu Ave./ One Scharansky Square. 1975. Skidmore, Owings & Merrill.

Nineteen stories of apartments built **from the top down** on two cast-in-place concrete masts which form the building's cores, a process called **"lift-slab construction."** Each floor was fabricated on the ground and **jacked up** to its position in the structure along the masts. The Russians pursued the **patented construction system** after an early conventional design was shelved, to save a million dollars.

The new address emerged in 1982 when the Bronx borough president renamed the block in honor of the then imprisoned Russian-Jewish dissident, **Anatoly Shcharansky.** The square and the dissident's name differ in spelling . . . it's The Bronx, after all.

[R 16b.] Riverdale Branch, N.Y. Public Library, 5540 Mosholu Ave., opp. W. 256th St. E side. 1967. Robert L. Bien.

A simple and appropriate composition whose great gable **gathers the light** necessary to read by.

EASTERN BRONX

SOUNDVIEW • CLASON POINT • CASTLE HILL • UNIONPORT

VAN NEST • PARKCHESTER • WESTCHESTER SQUARE

MORRIS PARK • PELHAM PARKWAY • THROGS NECK

PELHAM BAY • COUNTRY CLUB AREA • CITY ISLAND

Until war clouds foreshadowed the start of World War II, this was a **sleepy area** of the Bronx. In its center was a large green space shaded by majestic trees, called the **New York Catholic Protectory,** an institute for destitute children. The neighborhoods around it were largely residential, with one-, two-, and four-family houses, stray apartment buildings, and all kinds of minor commercial, industrial, and institutional establishments. And **many empty lots.** To the north, along Pelham Parkway, and to the west, down to the Bronx River, were groups of six-story apartment buildings. To the south and east were marshland and peninsulas **jutting out** into the East River and the Long Island Sound: Clason Point, a **resort** and **amusement center** with a ferry to College Point, Queens; Ferry Point; and Throgs Neck. To the east were the remnants of the old **Village of Westchester,** called Westchester Square, hardly recognizable with the coming of the IRT elevated in 1920. And beyond lay Pelham Bay Park, **the borough's largest,** stretching north to the Westchester County line, and City Island, an oasis in the Sound.

Then the New York Catholic Protectory grounds were purchased by the Metropolitan Life Insurance Company, and in February 1940 the first of the 40,000 tenants who were to populate **red brick,** high-rise **Parkchester** moved in. **The die was cast.** Empty lots, cattail-filled swamp, even parts of Pelham Bay Park were to be decimated by the **crush** of a new population.

Today, the area south of Bruckner Boulevard is a phalanx of **other red-brick housing** projects. Hospital facilities occupy the marshy lands which fed Westchester Creek, now diminished by the construction of a **behemoth high school** only yards from Westchester Square. Two of the peninsulas are springboards for suspension bridges to Long Island. A pleasant stretch of Pelham Bay Park along the banks of Eastchester Bay may one day become an **urban ski slope,** elevated by countless truck-loads of smelly garbage deposited there, politely called landfill. "Progress" has come to the Eastern Bronx. Its effects are profound.

SOUNDVIEW

The community lying between the Bronx River and the parkway bearing the river's name. Cartoonist/playwright **Jules Feiffer** was raised here on Stratford Avenue when the area was predominantly Jewish, beginning with the arrival of the **IRT Pelham Bay elevated** in 1920. The area today is Hispanic. Don't confuse it with adjacent Clason Point, the peninsula that really does have a view of Long Island Sound. (The Sound seems to have been renamed East River by some non-tradition-bound cartographers.)

[E 1.] Public School 152, Bronx, 1007 Evergreen Ave., NW cor. Bruckner Expwy. 1975. Kahn & Jacobs.

A handsomely composed earth-colored brick school structure that adds a note of **gentle majesty** to a physically humdrum neighborhood. It presents a particularly good appearance to users of the expressway.

Just east of Soundview:

[E 2.] 1341 Noble Avenue (folk art), bet. E. 172nd and E. 174th Sts.

Semidetached brick houses are commonplace here and so, it would seem, the occupants of this particular one decided to give it some added character, adorning the exterior with the **shiny detritus** of our planned-to-be-obsolescent society: hubcaps, chrome-plated bumpers, etc. *Don't miss a peek down the driveway.*

CLASON POINT

A protuberance into either Long Island Sound or the East River, depending on your geographical alliances. It has, over the years, been labeled after its successive occupants: **Snakipins** (the native American settlement), **Cornell Point** (after Thomas Cornell, 1642), and finally **Clason Point** (after Isaac Clason). Between 1883 and 1927 it was the home of **Clason Military Academy,** operated by a Roman Catholic order. Before the trolley came, in 1910, public access was via boat, launch, or steamer from Long Island, Mott Haven, and Manhattan. The waters were not polluted then. The attractions were dance halls and hotels, picnic grounds and a bathing pier, restaurants, a saltwater pool, and places with names like **Dietrich's, Gilligan's Pavilion and Killian's Grove, Higg's Camp Grounds, and Kane's Casino.** (Kane's Casino held out until it caught fire in 1942.) Between 1923 and 1938 the City operated a popular ferry service to College Point, in Queens. Tragedy came in 1924 when a freak wind squall blew down the Clason Point Amusement Park's ferris wheel (on the site of Shorehaven Beach Club, now endangered) killing 24. Prohibition, pollution, and competition (from filtered pools like easily accessible Starlight Park in nearby West Farms) finally doomed the resort area.

[E 3a.] Holy Cross Roman Catholic Church, 600 Soundview Ave., NE cor. Taylor Ave. 1968. Brother Cajetan J. B. Baumann, O.F.M.

Powerful geometric brick masonry forms that cry out "modern." But they cry too loud.

[E 3b.] Bethlehem Evangelical Lutheran Church, 327 Bolton Ave., bet. O'Brien and Soundview Aves. W side. ca. 1915.

White aluminum clapboard-sided church with neo-Federal trim. An antique touch to the community.

Harding Park, named for President Harding, was well described by the *Times* in 1981: "a folksy ramshackle village with an aura of another era. Its narrow macadam roads wander here and there, without benefit of sidewalks or street lamps, diverging off into muddy lanes and alleys. There are junked cars in driveways and wash drying on lines. Winterized bungalows of every size and shape . . . stand under tall trees." A haphazard, sewerless, but proud community that emerged from Clason Point's resort years, it abuts the waterfront south of O'Brien Avenue between White Plains Road and Leland Avenue.

CASTLE HILL

Another peninsula projecting into the Sound/River, separated from Clason Point by an inlet called Pugsley Creek.

[E 4a.] Formerly **Lacombe Iron Works Corporation,** 2058 Lacombe Ave., SW cor. Screvin Ave. ca. 1920.

A small but handsome masonry structure with proud corner towers. It apparently had a more ambitious purpose in its first life . . . who knows what it might have been?

[E 4b.] Castle Hill Jewish Community Center, 486 Howe Ave., SE cor. Lacombe Ave. ca. 1970.

Embattled in appearance behind a high chain link fence, the synagogue's large, green marble tablets proclaim **the Ten Commandments** in gilded Hebrew lettering to an apparently hostile community.

[E 4c.] Castle Hill Pool, Castle Hill Ave. SW cor. Norton Ave. ca. 1925.

Architecturally undistinguished but one of the city's few remaining *pre-*World War II private swimming pools, where every summer anyone who could afford it bought a season ticket good for a locker and unlimited admissions. Adolescence for many Bronxites began here.
  Midget auto races were held nearby, at Zerega and Lafayette Avenues, in the 1920s and 1930s, and the **roar of the speeding cars** accelerating after the turns was heard for miles across the flat, featureless landscape.

UNIONPORT

[E 5a.] Boulevard Manor (apartments), 2001 and 2045 Story Ave., bet. Pugsley and Olmstead Aves. N side. 1974. Gruzen & Partners.

Among the enormous number of multistory housing developments dropped helter-skelter in the area south of Bruckner Expressway in the 1960s and 1970s, these two buildings alone deserve commendation for their architecture. No unique technology has been employed here, nor any exotic building materials—only a desire to delight the eye of residents and passersby.

[E 5b.] White Plains Gardens (apartments), 1221, 1223, 1225, 1227 White Plains Rd., bet. Gleason and Westchester Aves. W side. ca. 1929.

A privately sponsored **for-profit** miniproject: four 6-story elevator apartment houses wrapped around a green center court that is entered through a neo-Gothic gateway. The plan provided for the introduction of treed "play yards" in the empty side spaces obligated by the Multiple Dwelling Law. (The sunnier one, to the south of the buildings, was, of course, the most played in.) [See also **Starling Gardens** E 7b.]. **Enlightened middle-class housing.**

VAN NEST

[E 6a.] Church of St. Dominic (Roman Catholic), 1739 Unionport Rd., bet. Van Nest and Morris Park Aves. W side. 1926.

An **asymmetrically** placed bell tower and a prominent spoked rose window in this neo-Romanesque edifice brighten the narrow path of ancient Unionport Road. DOMINE · DILEXI · DECOREM · DOMUS · TUAE (Lord, I have loved the beauty of Thy house).

[E 6b.] 1808-1814 Amethyst Street (row houses), bet. Morris Park and Rhinelander Aves. E side. ca. 1895.

Common in Mott Haven, rare in Van Nest: masonry row houses, in this case 2½ stories and of orange salt-and-pepper brick with brownstone trim.

PARKCHESTER

[E 7.] Parkchester (apartment development), E. Tremont Ave., Purdy St., McGraw Ave., Hugh J. Grant Circle, White Plains Rd. 1938–1942. Board of Design: Richmond H. Shreve, chairman; Andrew J. Eken, George Gove, Gilmore D. Clarke, Robert W. Dowling, Irwin Clavan, and Henry C. Meyer, Jr.

"A city within a city" was what it was called in its early days. Across the street was subway access to Manhattan. It contained a large movie theater, over 100 stores including Macy's first branch, a bowling alley and bar/restaurant, parking garages for 3,000 cars, and 40,000 residents at **a density of 250,000 people per square mile!** As planning goes, however, this was an exceptionally thoughtful enterprise. Curving streets, lots of well-kept lawn, shrubbery, and trees, carefully planned pedestrian routes and recreation areas, and playful colored terra-cotta sculpture and face block—all calculated to inspire and delight whenever visual boredom set in. **Metropolitan Life Insurance Company,** its sponsor, maintained it for almost 30 years until about the time N.Y.C.'s Human Rights Commission accused it of maintaining a white-only policy. In 1968 Parkchester was sold to real estate giant **Helmsley-Spear, Inc.,** who proceeded to co-op it, quadrant by quadrant.

[E 7.] Parkchester apt. complex: Metropolitan Oval fountain (1960 photo)

[E 7a.] Parkchester Branch, N.Y. Public Library, 1985 Westchester Ave., bet. Hugh J. Grant Circle and Pugsley Ave. N side. 1985. Richard Dattner & Assocs., architects. Marcia Dalby, sculptor.

Of red patterned brick, defining a sturdily fenced semicircular forecourt which bids welcome, via a **freestanding brick archway,** to those walking by under the noisy Pelham Bay elevated. Apparently, the first to have entered the fenced enclosure were oversized plasticized beasties (thanks to the city's 1% for art program).

[E 7b.] Starling Gardens (apartments), 2141, 2143, 2145, 2147 Starling Ave., bet. Odell and Purdy Sts. N side. ca. 1929.

A clone of **White Plains Gardens** [see E 5b.] except here occupying a full blockfront. Enlightened housing for middle-class families.

[E 7c.] Westchester-Bronx YMCA, 2244 Westchester Ave., bet. Castle Hill and Havemeyer Aves. S side. 1971. William A. Hall & Assocs.

This neat juxtaposition of basic geometric volumes is a more utilitarian replacement for the red brick Victorian country house, **once the rectory** of St. Peter's Church down the street [see below], whose rooms were the previous answer to this Y's needs.

Dominick's Restaurant, 2356 Westchester Ave., NE cor. Parker St.

For over a century a good place to eat. Italian food. Down a few steps from the street.

WESTCHESTER SQUARE

The now cut-up green was the center of the old **Village of Westchester,** founded in 1653 and known as **Oostorp** under the Dutch. Between 1683 and 1759, while under British rule, the village was the seat of the **County of Westchester,** of which the Bronx was then part. It is now the focus of neighborhood shopping and a stop on several bus lines.

[E 8a.] St. Peter's Church in the Village of Westchester (Episcopal), 2500 Westchester Ave., opp. St. Peter's Ave. E side. 1855. Leopold Eidlitz. Clerestory addition and restoration, 1879. Cyrus L. W. Eidlitz. ★ **[E 8b.] Originally St. Peter's Chapel/**now **Foster Hall.** 1868. Leopold Eidlitz. ★ **[E 8c.] St. Peter's Graveyard.** ★

A tribute to the vitality of this picturesque Gothic Revival composition is that it has withstood the **vibration** and the **visual pollution** of passing trains on the adjacent IRT Pelham Bay elevated structure and has survived to be dubbed an official city landmark.

[E 8d.] Huntington Free Library and Reading Room/originally **The Van Schaick Free Reading Room,** 9 Westchester Sq., bet. Westchester and Tratman Aves. W side. 1882. Frederick Clarke Withers. Addition to rear, 1891. William Anderson.

When advised of the cost of its upkeep, local taxpayers refused to accept this gift of a fellow resident, **Peter Van Schaick.** It was not opened until 1891, together with an extension to the rear, through the efforts (and added funding) of railroad magnate **Collis P. Huntington,** who maintained a summer residence in nearby Throgs Neck [see E 18a.]. The original library is a **modest but joyful** red brick creation. Unfortunately the humorless orange brick addition to the south overwhelms Withers' work.

[E 7b.] Starling Gardens apartments   **[E 8d.]** The Huntington Free Library

[E 8e.] The Owen Dolen Golden Age Center addition adds life to an old area

[E 8e.] Owen Dolen Golden Age Center, N.Y.C. Department of Parks & Recreation, Benson St., NW cor. Westchester Ave., Westchester Sq. ca. 1920. Altered, 1983, John Ciardullo Assocs.

Dramatic use of concrete and **brightly painted industrial forms** gives life to a preexisting senior citizens' center totally hemmed in by asphalt and traffic in this East Bronx hub.

[E 8f.] Consolidated Edison Customer Service Facility, 55 Westchester Sq., SE cor. Ponton Ave. 1982. Richard Dattner & Assocs.

An étude in masonry and glass. The skillful use of color, texture, and transparency give it just the correct degree of prominence in this **working-class neighborhood.**

[E 8g.] 44-53 Westchester Square (linked row houses), bet. Ponton and Roberts Aves. E side. ca. 1912.

One must look carefully but the time spent reflecting on this structure's unified glazed surfaces will be well spent: glazed brick and glazed terra-cotta wherever there are no windows or doors. A **fascinating work** of facade architecture.

[E 8h.] Ferris Family Cemetery, Commerce Ave. E of Westchester Sq., bet. Westchester Ave. and Butler Place. S side. 18th century.

As Woodlawn Cemetery is large, Ferris is small . . . but **very** well kept, considering that its once bucolic surroundings are now a grimy industrial area.

[E 9a.] Herbert H. Lehman High School, E. Tremont Ave. at Hutchinson River Pkwy. S side. 1972. The Eggers Partnership, architects. Roger Bolomey, sculptor.

Built in response to the 1960s population explosion of the East Bronx, this school itself explodes over its site. Its gymnasium **straddles the adjacent highway;** its athletic facilities sit on filled-in Westchester Creek. An angular **rust-brown steel** sculpture boldly marks the entrance to the smooth, precast-concrete-sheathed building.

[E 9b.] 1st Presby. Ch./Throgs Neck   **[E 11d.]** Rose F. Kennedy Res. Center

[E 9b.] First Presbyterian Church in Throgs Neck, 3051 E. Tremont Ave., bet. Ericson Place and Dudley Ave. N side. ca. 1880.

Perched comfortably on a hill above a series of stone retaining walls, this red brick, white-trimmed church (and its graveyard to the rear) seem **oblivious to the changes** evident along the avenue below. Its steeple is particularly noteworthy.

MORRIS PARK

Morris Park/Pelham Pkwy/Eastchester Road hospital complex:

[E 10.] Albert Einstein College of Medicine, Yeshiva University, 1300 Morris Park Ave., SW cor. Eastchester Rd. **[E 10a.] Forchheimer Medical Science Building.** 1955. Kelly & Gruzen. **[E 10b.] Robbins Auditorium, Friedman Lounge, Gottesman Library.** 1958. Kelly & Gruzen. **[E 10c.] Ullman Research Center for Health Sciences.** 1963. Kiesler & Bartos. **[E 10d.]** Originally **Bassine**/now **Belfer Educational Center for Health Sciences.** 1971. Armand Bartos & Assocs. **[E 10e.] Chanin Cancer Research Center.** 1976. Schuman, Lichtenstein, Claman & Efron.

Like Topsy (and many other college and hospital campuses), **this place just grew.** Most of the buildings are competent enough, but as a group they are a failure. Belfer, one of the newest, is by far the most distinguished . . . perhaps there is hope.

[E 10f.] Originally **Physur Building (professional offices),** 1180 Morris Park Ave., NE cor. Hering Ave. 1973. Oppenheimer, Brady & Vogelstein.

An appropriately reserved and dignified building of dark brownish-gray brick with deeply recessed slope-sill window openings that add interest to the composition and dignity to the neighborhood.

Across Morris Park Avenue to the north:

[E 11a.] Max and Evlynne Low Residence Complex, 1925, 1935, 1945 Eastchester Rd., NW cor. Morris Park Ave. 1972. Pomerance & Breines. **[E 11b.] Anne and Isidore Falk Recreation Center,** Morris Park Ave., NW cor. Eastchester Rd. 1986. Steven Robinson & Assocs., architects. Schuman, Lichtenstein, Claman & Efron, associated architects.

An interesting composition of three high-rise apartment towers and a gymnasium **for the staff** of Albert Einstein College and its medical facilities.

[E 11c.] Bronx Municipal Hospital Center, N.Y.C. Health & Hospitals Corporation, Morris Park Ave. to Pelham Pkwy. S., W of Eastchester Rd. Original buildings: **Abraham Jacobi Hospital** and **Nathan B. Van Etten Hospital.** 1955. Pomerance & Breines. **[E 11d.] Rose Fitzgerald Kennedy Center for Research in Mental Retardation and Human Development, Albert Einstein College of Medicine,** 1410 Pelham Pkwy. S. S side. 1970. Pomerance & Breines.

The same architectural firm, over a period of some 15 years, designed buildings for this hospital complex. Note the difference in approach in their later design.

[E 11e.] 49th Precinct, N.Y.C. Police Department, 2121 Eastchester Rd., opp. Rhinelander Ave. W side. 1985. Smotrich & Platt, architects. Ivan Chermayeff, sculptor, Chermayeff & Geismar Assocs.

A geometric fantasy of a station house fronted by its own stand of—**not** trees—blue-painted steel **bulrushes.** Guess how many?

[E 11f.] Calvary Hospital, 1740 Eastchester Rd., bet. Waters Place and Amtrak right-of-way. E side. 1978. Rogers, Butler & Burgun.

A **very abstract** composition of dark square windows set flush into a deep red, square-gridded geometric form. **Too abstract** for the healing arts of a hospital.

The world's first air meets: On a 307-acre site, south of today's Pelham Parkway, between Bronxdale Avenue and Williamsbridge Road down to the former New Haven railroad right-of-way, some of the earliest public trials of powered aircraft were held in 1908 and 1909. Aviation pioneers Glenn H. Curtiss (and his partner Alexander Graham Bell) and Samuel P. Langley (of the Smithsonian) were drawn to the meets, as were as many as 20,000 spectators. The site had been, between 1889 and 1902, the Morris Park Racecourse, replacement for the earlier Jerome Park Racetrack, whose grounds in the West Bronx had been acquired to build the reservoir bearing the same name. Horse racing moved to Belmont Park in 1903; airplane meets moved too; and in 1910 a spectacular fire wiped out many of the remaining stables/hangars. Nary a trace of the course remains today save a blocked-up tunnel portal under Bronxdale Avenue, where crowded railroad coaches once deposited visitors to this onetime recreation mecca in the Bronx.

Bronx State Hospital campus:

[E 12a.] Bronx State Hospital Rehabilitation Center, N.Y.S. Department of Mental Hygiene, 1500 Waters Place, bet. Eastchester Rd. and Hutchinson River Pkwy. N side. 1971. Gruzen & Partners.

Intricate in plan, with many reentrant corners and projecting stair towers; yet the forms fall together with an effortlessness that is rare. **A very unassuming** but **very fine** work.

[E 12b.] Bronx Children's Psychiatric Hospital, N.Y.S. Department of Mental Hygiene, 1000 Waters Place, bet. Eastchester Rd. and Hutchinson River Pkwy. N side. 1969. The Office of Max O. Urbahn.

An attempt to lessen the oppressive institutional quality of the earliest Bronx State Hospital buildings (by the same firm) through the introduction of a domestically scaled collection of interlinked shed-roofed units.

[E 12a.] Rehabilitation Center, Bronx State Hospital, gently hugging its site

[E 13.] Bronx Developmental Center: elegant summation of modern technology

[E 13.] Bronx Developmental Center, N.Y.S. Department of Mental Hygiene, Waters Place bet. Eastchester Rd. and Hutchinson River Pkwy. N side. 1976. Richard Meier & Assocs.

The advances of 20th-century technology are summed up in the forms and materials of this center for the mentally retarded. Dramatically located on a **spacious and serene** site along the edge of the Hutchinson River Parkway, its long, prismatic forms evoke the majesty of a **rectilinear dirigible.** Clad in a tightly stretched skin of natural anodized aluminum panels, it looks as if it were fabricated by an **aircraft manufacturer,** not by **earthbound** building contractors. Windows, resembling enormous elongated portholes, add to the machine-age look, as does the **proud expression** of the intricate and colorful central mechanical system which controls the building's inner environment. It is a **consummate work** of architecture and is sure to be ranked among the great buildings of its time.

PELHAM PARKWAY NEIGHBORHOOD

[E 14a.] Former **Bronxdale Swimming Pool (abandoned),** Bronxdale Ave. NE cor. Antin Place. ca. 1928.

Crowds of kids, mommas, and poppas no longer wait to plunge into the cool, chlorinated waters of this answer to the city's **steamy summers.** But the polychromed Art Deco terra-cotta ornament is still there, resisting the elements.

[E 14b.] 2009 Cruger Avenue (apartments), ca. 1930. **2039, 2055 Cruger Avenue (apartments),** ca. 1937. All bet. Bronxdale and Brady Aves. W side. **[E 14c.] 2095, 2105 Cruger Avenue (apartments),** bet. Brady Ave. and Maran Place. W side. ca. 1938.

It's the **West Bronx** which is Art Deco/Art Moderne heaven, but No. 2009 here (opposite the old Bronxdale Pool) is a strong Deco work whose **vermilion glazed terra-cotta** singles it out; its owners thoughtlessly removed its period metalwork after 1978. The casement windows of its Moderne neighbors up the block have been refenestrated, but the round-cornered fire escapes remain. Thank goodness!

[E 14d.] Bronx and Pelham Parkway, connecting Bronx Park and Pelham Bay Park.

Rarely referred to by any name other than just Pelham Parkway, this **wide** and **luxuriant greenway** has not suffered from the widenings and removal of ancient trees that other thoroughfares in the city have undergone. Prior to World War II the center lanes were closed off on Sunday mornings for bicycle racing.

[E 14e.] 2166 and **2180 Bronx Park East (apartments),** bet. Lydig Ave. and Pelham Pkwy. S. E side. ca. 1937.

Six-story Art Moderne housing overlooking the lawns and trees of Bronx Park. Keep those casements!

[E 14e.] 2166 Bronx Park East apts.   **[E 15.]** Morningside Hse. for the Aged

Kosher pizza, bagels and lox, brisket and flanken: Unassuming Lydig Avenue (a block south of the Pelham Parkway Station of the IRT 241st Street-White Plains Road Lines), for about five blocks east of White Plains Road, is a busy, happy, prosperous shopping street of a vital Jewish community. How long it will stay this way is anybody's guess, but if you're nearby it's worth a visit . . . and a nosh.

[E 14f.] Hooper's Choice (restaurant), 2221 Boston Rd., NW cor. Pelham Pkwy. N. 1987.

A bold Post Modern design occupying a strategic corner.

[E 14g.] Alhambra Gardens (apartments), 750-760 Pelham Pkwy., bet. Holland and Wallace Aves. S side. 1927. Springsteen & Goldhammer.

Unrepentantly **romantic.** The name **Alhambra** tells it all: Spanish tile, Spanish ironwork, Spanish detail all around a lush green courtyard. It's hard to reconcile oneself to the idea that these are just **well-planned** 6-story elevator apartments. **Hooray!**

[E 15.] Morningside House (residence for the aged), 1000 Pelham Pkwy. S. **[E 15a.] Reception Building,** bet. Lurting and Hone Aves. S side. **[E 15b.] Administration and Medical Services Building,** bet. Lurting and Haight Aves. S side, through to Esplanade. All 1974. Johnson-Burgee.

A rare architectural **tribute to the dignity** of our society's aged citizenry. An urbane pair of buildings with a carefully controlled, resortlike exterior.

[E 15c.] Bronx House (settlement house), The Harris and Sarah Lichtman Building, 990 Pelham Pkwy. S., bet. Bogart/Paulding and Hone Aves. S side. 1970. **[E 15d.] S. H. and Helen R. Scheuer Swim Center,** 1973. All by Westerman/Miller Assocs.

Whatever architect said "God is in the details" should look at those employed on this building. They are much too fussy and self-conscious.

[E 15e.] Morris Park Station, IRT Dyre Avenue Line/originally on the former **New York, Westchester & Boston Railway,** The Esplanade at Paulding Ave. 1912. Fellheimer & Long, architects. Allen H. Stem, associated architect.

The Spanish Colonial Revival focus of the visual axis created by **The Esplanade,** the diagonal thoroughfare that marks the 3,940-foot-long, cut-and-cover subway in which the defunct N.Y., W.& B. commuter line bypassed treelined Pelham Parkway. [For the railway's original administration building, see Bronx C 8c.]

THROGS NECK

Spelled with one or two g's and sometimes with an apostrophe, the name once referred to the outermost peninsula of land beyond East Tremont Avenue's end. Its name is derived from **John Throckmorton,** who settled here in 1643 while New York was still under Dutch rule. Until the early part of the 20th century this area was covered with estates. Today its inhabitants are modest, home-owning families.

[E 16a.] St. Joseph's School for the Deaf (Roman Catholic)/originally **St. Joseph's Institute for the Improved Instruction of Deaf Mutes,** 1000 Hutchinson River Pkwy., SE cor. Bruckner Blvd. **[E 16b.] St. Helena's (**now **Commercial) High School (Roman Catholic)/**originally also **St. Joseph's School for the Deaf,** 55 Hutchinson River Pkwy., SW cor. Bruckner Blvd. Both ca. 1898. Schickel & Ditmars.

When the Hutchinson River Parkway was built in 1939 as the approach to the Bronx-Whitestone Bridge, the **right-of-way** cut St. Joseph's campus in two. Later, when the children of Parkchester [see E7.] grew in numbers to be of high-school age, the parish of St. Helena's established **a new secondary school,** using the west half of St. Joseph's holdings. From a distance at least, these seem the **epitome of 19th-century gloom,** now coming back into style.

[E 17a.] Engine Company 72, Ladder Company 55 (deactivated), N.Y.C. Fire Department, 3929 E. Tremont Ave., NE cor. E. 177th St. 1972. Arthur Witthoeft.

Firemen still slide down **brass poles** from their second-floor bunk-rooms. In this firehouse the poles are set into tall elegant cylinders at the outside of the building.

 [E 17b.] Fort Schuyler House (retirement home), 3077 East 177th St., bet. Logan Ave. and Throgs Neck Expwy. N side. 1971. Weiss & Whelan.

Mixed tones of orange brick, exposed concrete balconies, raked stair tower roofs, and a particularly interesting east facade of this 8-story apartment make it a happy landmark at the confluence of the Cross-Bronx and Throgs Neck Expressways.

[E 18a.] Preston High School (Roman Catholic)/formerly "Homestead," Collis P. Huntington (summer) residence/**originally Frederick C. Havemeyer residence,** 2780 Schurz Ave., SE cor. Brinsmade Ave. ca. 1870.

It is so rare that a summer house with a recorded history **survives this long** that one is prepared to forgive its lack of architectural distinction. (Huntington and family—whose wealth came from the railroads—contributed to a number of fine buildings in the city [see E8d. and U Manhattan U3]. Original owner Havemeyer was a sugar king.) The newer additions for high school use are unfortunate. The house became a school in 1924.

[E 18b.] White Beach Condominiums and Marina, 2716 Marina Dr./Schurz Ave., bet. Balcom and Huntington Aves. S side. 1985. Mario Procida.

White stucco domestic resort architecture **enlivened** with **yellow awnings** and terraced with **blue ships' railings.** Quite appropriate in its waterfront setting between the Bronx-Whitestone and Throgs Neck bridges. Order amidst the ordinary.

Marina Del Rey (caterers), 1 Marina Dr./Schurz Ave., SE cor. E. Tremont Ave.

Planted in the 1980s at the end of one of the Bronx's **longest,** most **undulating** thoroughfares, Tremont Avenue, is this Nouveau Riche stucco-plus-brown anodized aluminum announcement (to some) that they have arrived.

[E 18c.] Silver Beach Gardens Corporation, Pennyfield and Schurz Aves. to Long Island Sound. (Entrance: Chaffee Ave. at Pennyfield Ave.) **[E 18d.]** Originally **Abijah Hammond residence**/now **Offices, Silver Beach Gardens Corporation,** ca. 1800. **[E 18e.] The Park at Edgewater,** Throgs Neck Expwy. Extension, at Theodore Karony Sq. (Entrance: W of Miles Ave. along the Expressway's north service road, a two-way street.)

Two of the three **waterside communities** in the Bronx where only the building is owned by the occupant, and ground rent is paid to the owner of the land (the third is **Harding Park** on Clason Point). These buildings were originally summer cottages, but they are now winterized. Silver Beach Gardens' Indian Trail affords excellent views of the Sound.

The Hammond house, featuring Federal detail, was built by a wealthy trader who emigrated here after serving in the Revolution in Massachusetts. Later, sugar king **Frederick C. Havemeyer's** family [see E 18a.] occupied the house until 1914.

Both of these communities consider their streets private (even though Edgewater is regularly traversed by a city bus line).

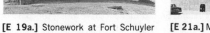

[E 19a.] Stonework at Fort Schuyler   [E 21a.] Middletown Plaza apartments

[E 19.] Fort Schuyler/now **SUNY Maritime College,** E end of Pennyfield Ave. **[E 19a.] Fort Schuyler.** 1834–1838. Capt. I. L. Smith. ★ Conversion to **Maritime College,** 1934–1938. Conversion of fort's dining hall to the **Adm. Stephen Bleecker Luce Library,** William A. Hall, 1967. **[E 19b.] Vander Clute Hall (dormitory, dining).** 1963. **[E 19c.] Riesenberg Hall (health and physical education).** 1964. **[E 19d.] Marvin-Tode Hall (science and ocean engineering).** 1967. All by Ballard Todd & Assocs.

A drive along the perimeter road (it changes names a number of times) of this narrow neck of land will reveal views of Long Island Sound that make looking at the college's architecture difficult. Old Fort Schuyler itself is well worth a stop to visit its interior court **(called St. Mary's Pentagon)** and for views from its ramparts. Another 19th-century fortress (and landmark), Fort Totten, across the Sound, is more easily seen from here than from its home borough of Queens. It's hard to believe that the old fort lay abandoned between 1878 and 1934, when WPA funds enabled restoration for reuse.

Protecting our sea approaches: America's seacoast fortifications were developed in three stages. The **First System** was started in 1794 when it was feared that we might be drawn into the European wars that followed the French Revolution. The **Second System,** begun in 1807, was motivated by the potential danger from Great Britain that ended with the War of 1812. The **Third System,** unlike the first two (which had been responses to external threats), was initiated in a peaceful era in 1817 and continued until the time of the Civil War. Both Fort Schuyler and Fort Totten (1862–1864) were built as part of this Third System, to be able to rake with cannon fire any enemy approaching the port of New York via the Long Island Sound.

[E 20a.] St. Frances de Chantal Church (Roman Catholic), 190 Hollywood Ave., SE cor. Harding Ave. 1971. Paul W. Reilly.

It's hard to miss this church. Perhaps that's one of its faults. No faulting its stained glass, however—**colorful chunks** in the **European style** precast into concrete window panels.

[E 20a.] St. Frances de Chantal RC Church: a curvilinear brick composition

[E 20b.] Monastery of St. Clare (Roman Catholic), 142 Hollywood Ave., bet. Schurz Ave. and Monsignor Halpin Place. N side. 1933. Robert J. Riley.

A peaceful composition built of masonry by those who were especially skilled in the craft of bricklaying. EGO · VOS · SEMPER · CVSTODIAM (I will always watch over you).

[E 20c.] 714 Clarence Avenue (residence), bet. Randall and Philip Aves. NE side. ca. 1920.

The views over Long Island Sound make a drive along this part of Clarence Avenue unlike any other in the city. **No. 714** is covered by mosaics applied in a vernacular style. So is the garage—even the birdhouse. Regrettably, the large red brick clubhouse of the American Turners of New York at nearby **No. 748** is a bulky intrusion in this simple wood-framed community.

PELHAM BAY

Named for the adjacent park, this community lies west of it, contained by the Hutchinson River Parkway, Bruckner Boulevard/Expressway, and on the south by St. Raymond's (Roman Catholic) Cemetery.

[E 21a.] Middletown Plaza (apartments), N.Y.C. Housing Authority, 3033 Middletown Rd., bet. Hobart and Jarvis Aves. NW side. 1973. Paul Rudolph.

A tall, dramatic cast-concrete frame, gray ribbed block infill, gray window sash, united by architect Rudolph's **limitless imagination,** make this housing for the elderly his best work in the borough and one of the Bronx's most notable architectural works.

[E 21b.] Pelham Bay Branch, N.Y. Public Library, 3060 Middletown Rd., SE cor. Jarvis Ave. 1976. Alexander A. Gartner.

A modest modern library with an inviting plaza. It shares the block with the American Indian museum's annex. [See below.]

[E 21c.] Museum of the American Indian, Heye Foundation Annex, Bruckner Blvd. SW cor. Middletown Rd.

This is a warehouse and research center for the museum whose public galleries were, at least in 1987, on Audubon Terrace in Manhattan. Totem poles, Indian houses, and wigwam replicas are displayed on the lawns, but **you can't go inside.**

[E 21d.] St. Theresa of the Infant Jesus (Roman Catholic) Church, 2855 St. Theresa Ave., NW cor. Pilgrim Ave. 1970. Anthony J. DePace.

Orange brick **pylons** make the church look a bit like an exhibition pavilion. Heavily ornamented with robust stained glass and mosaic tile tesserae. The **old church bell** is displayed across the street, and the inscription locates the original church at Pilgrim and *Morris Park* Avenues. (A look at a street map will reveal that St. Theresa Avenue is the eastern extension of Morris Park Avenue; its name was changed in 1968.)

[E 21e.] Addition, Greek Orthodox Church of Zoodohos Peghe, 3573 Bruckner Blvd., SW cor. Arnow Place. ca. 1975.

A radically modern addition to the original 1930s church building. The waterfront of **the Country Club community,** across Bruckner Boulevard from this church, is the home of many prosperous Greek-Americans.

Pelham Bay Park:

The largest of the six parks purchased as a result of the new Bronx parks program of 1883. At that time this one was **outside the New York City limits.** It contains two golf courses, an archery range, bridle paths, the Police Department firing range (private), and ample facilities for hiking, cycling, horseback riding, and motoring. Shell racing is held in the North Lagoon. Between 1910 and 1913 a **monorail** traversed the park from the New Haven Railroad line to City Island.

[E 22.] Pelham Bay Park World War Memorial, Shore Rd. E of Bruckner Expwy. SE side. ca. 1925. John J. Sheridan, architect. Belle Kinney, sculptor.

One of the handsomest and best-maintained monuments (unlike nearby Rice Stadium) in the entire city.

[E 23.] Bartow-Pell Mansion Museum, Pelham Bay Park, Shore Rd. near Pelham-Split Rock Golf Course, S side. 1675. Alterations, 1836–1845 attributed to Minard Lafever. Restoration, 1914. Delano & Aldrich. ★ **Open to the public—limited hours.**

Lords of the Manor of Pelham once owned this house, which was later enlarged, renovated, and remodeled in the Federal style. The mansion became the home of the **International Garden Club** in 1914. The Pell family plot, a magnificent formal garden, a view of Long Island Sound from the grounds, and rare and tasteful furnishings within combine to make a visit worthwhile.

[E 24.] Orchard Beach, N.Y.C. Department of Parks & Recreation, E shore of Pelham Bay Park on Long Island Sound. 1936. N.Y.C. Parks Department, Aymar Embury II, architectural consultant.

A large, sandy, crescent-shaped beach reopened in 1936 after extensive remodeling by the WPA and the Department of Parks. The bathhouses are enhanced by a strong set of concrete colonnades, chastely decorated with blue terra-cotta tiles. The beach cafeteria is under the spacious entry terrace. This is a good public place, **monumental without being overpowering,** and efficient without being crowded with needless details.

[E 25.] Rice Memorial Stadium, Pelham Bay Park, NW of Middletown Rd. and Stadium Ave. 1922. Herts & Robertson.

This concrete stadium is unusual because of the small **Greek temple** atop the bleachers which frames Louis St. Lannes' heroic statue *The American Boy.* The stadium was given to the city by the widow of **Isaac L. Rice** as part of a complex of other athletic facilities including a 330-foot-long swimming pool, bathhouse, bleachers, and a decorative 100-foot-high white marble Doric column. **All but the stadium are gone today.** The Rices' mansion still stands along Riverside Drive at West 89th Street.

[E 25.] Rice Stadium, Pelham Bay Park

[E 28d.] Grace Episcopal Ch., City Is.

Watt, Ampère, Ohm: In gratitude for Julia Rice's gift of athletic facilities in her husband's honor, the city fathers named nearby streets after units of electrical measurement, since Rice's name had long been associated with developments in electric storage batteries for automobiles and submarines. Rice was also the inventor of the Rice gambit, a chess opening.

COUNTRY CLUB AREA

Country Club Road leads to the **Westchester Country Club** (named for the Bronx when it was still part of Westchester County) at the water's edge. This area has long been known for its large homes on generous sites, now the residences of affluent Italian- and Greek-Americans.

[E 26.] Providence Home for Aged Women/Generoso Pope Memorial, Sisters of St. John the Baptist (Roman Catholic), Stadium Ave. opp. Waterbury Ave. E side. ca. 1920. Additions 1936, 1957, 1967, 1979.

A comfortable place to spend one's golden years, overlooking the Sound, named for the publisher of the longtime Italian-language newspaper, *Il Progresso Italiano,* and a mover in the sand and gravel business.

CITY ISLAND

A tight little island which is part of New York City by law but has scarcely any other connections. Its first industry was the **Solar Salt Works,** which made salt by **evaporating seawater.** That was in 1830. Then came oystering and eventually **yacht building.** (Though this activity has declined, City Island's shipwrights have built a number of our entries in the America's Cup race including the 1967 and 1970 winner, *Intrepid.*) **Filmmaking** came to the island around 1900, together with D. W. Griffith, Douglas Fairbanks, and the Keystone Kops, who filmed a scene on Fordham Street. Fish and seafood fanciers are today's most important asset to the island's economy: City Island Avenue is filled with **restaurants of every description.** As the Hispanic population of the borough burgeons, more and more of City Island's signs seek to cultivate a Spanish-speaking clientele.

On the streets that run perpendicular to the fishbone spine of City Island Avenue are **more than a handful of old quality homes,** now engulfed in latter-day lightweights. There is space to mention only a few:

[E 27a.] 21 Tier Street (residence), W of City Island Ave. N side. ca. 1894.

Shingle Style and of quality. Compare it with its self-consciously modernized neighbor at **No. 33.**

[E 27b.] Originally **Public School 17, Bronx**/now **City Island Museum,** 190 Fordham St., E of City Island Ave. S side. 1898. C. B. J. Snyder. **Open to the public—limited hours.**

A masonry school, by the dean of New York City's early school architects, that dates from the very year of the city's consolidation. This one, properly, is **a modest work** befitting a remote outpost of the municipality.

[E 27c.] 284 City Island Avenue (apartments), bet. Fordham and Hawkins Sts. E side. ca. 1898.

A 19th-century high rise, at least in the context of City Island's environment. Five stories tall (including its attic) but only 20 feet wide. Its gambrel roof and Palladian window **add just the right zest!**

[E 27d.] Boatyard Condominium overlooks Long Island Sound at City Island

[E 27d.] The Boatyard Condominium, 210 Carroll St., E of City Island Ave. Both sides. 1986. William Milo Barnum & Assocs.

A **genuinely appropriate colony** of wood-frame, modestly proportioned structures offering 70 units fronting on the waters of the Sound.

Schofield Street: West of City Island Avenue.

[E 28a.] 65 Schofield St. (residence). N side. ca. 1865. **62 Schofield St. (residence).** S side. ca. 1865.

Two Italianate examples of somewhat differing quality.

[E 28b.] 84-86 Schofield St. (residence). S side. ca. 1875.

Only one-story in height but with a grand mansard top hat. Note the monumental porch and the **abundantly scaled** French doors (instead of windows) onto it. Poorly maintained, but let's hope it will be rescued. Be sure to look at **No. 90.**

[E 28c.] 95 Pell Place (residence), W of City Island Ave. N side. 1930.

A bungalow purchased right out of the **Sears Roebuck catalog.** The Oriental influence is unmistakable and a refreshing note of variety in this conservative community.

[E 28d.] Grace Church (Episcopal), 104 City Island Ave., SE cor. Pilot St. 1867. **[E 28e.] Rectory,** ca. 1862.

A pair of gems that befits an off-the-beaten-track seafaring community. The church is a **paragon** of Gothic Revival wood craftsmanship. The rectory is a modest wood frame structure which derives from the Italian Villa Style.

[E 28f.] 141 Pilot Street (residence), NE cor. City Island Ave. ca. 1862.

More of the same, this house has lathe-turned porch posts and eyebrow windows.

[E 28g.] 175 Belden Street (residence), E of City Island Ave. N side. ca. 1880. ★ (Down a single lane, dead-end street: *walk.*)

A very well preserved picturesque cottage, **rare in the city,** located almost at the southernmost tip of the island.

NORTHERN BRONX

BRONXDALE • WILLIAMSBRIDGE • BAYCHESTER
EASTCHESTER • WAKEFIELD • WOODLAWN

The Northern Bronx has been the site of some settlement since the 17th century, and for some two months in the 18th century **the nation's executive mansion** was here; but most of this area's modest homes and scattered groups of apartment houses (as well as gargantuan Co-op City) date from the 20th.

BRONXDALE

[N 1a.] New York Institute for the Education of the Blind, 999 Pelham Pkwy. N., bet. Bronxwood Ave. and Williamsbridge Rd. 1924. McKim, Mead & White.

An inoffensive campus of neo-Georgian buildings for the elementary and college-preparatory education of the blind and visually handicapped.

[N 1b.] Frampton Hall, New York Institute for the Education of the Blind, Astor Ave. NW cor. Paulding Ave. 1971. Eggers & Higgins.

If blindness is not enough of a challenge then mental retardation plus blindness is. This neatly designed facility is for the treatment of just this combination of afflictions.

[N 2.] 2440 Boston Road, N.Y.C. Housing Authority (apartments), bet. Waring and Mace Aves. E side. 1972. Davis Brody & Assocs.

Twenty stories of housing predominantly for the elderly in one tower, count them, two. With a bit of visual **sleight of hand,** an otherwise bulky prism is made to look like **two slender shafts** offset slightly from one another. And to top off this architectural **legerdemain,** the tower is broader at the top (to accommodate larger apartments) than at the bottom. The adjacent one-story community center is a carefully contrasted foil for the tower.

[N 3.] Lourdes of America, on grounds of **St. Lucy's Roman Catholic Church,** Bronxwood Ave. NW cor. Mace Ave. 1939. **Open to the public.**

An amazing sight. Out-of-doors in a stone grotto rising high above the adjacent sidewalks are **hundreds** of **twinkling candles** in tiny red-glass containers, placed there by the devout who have come to share in the many cures claimed for this replica of **the famous French shrine.** (If St. Lucy's sounds strange to your ears, think of the parish as Santa Lucia's.)

[N 2.] 2440 Boston Road apartments   **[N 6a.]** Private Chapel of F. Lisanti

[N 4.] Worker's Cooperative Colony/"The Coops" (apartment development), Bronx Park E. bet. Allerton and Arnow Aves. to Barker Ave.
[N 4a.] First House, S of Britton St. 1927. Springsteen & Goldhammer.
[N 4b.] Second House, N of Britton St. 1929. Herman J. Jessor of Springsteen & Goldhammer.

Walk-ups built under the sponsorship of the United Workers Cooperative Association, consisting largely of unionized **Eastern European Jewish garment workers,** a group with strong left-wing political attachments. That may explain the use of **hammer-and-sickle motifs** above the entry doors of First House (otherwise designed in a neo-Tudor style quite commonly found in the Bronx in the 1920s). The later Second House dispensed with both the political symbolism *and* the picturesque stylizing. The "Coops" (pronounced COOPS, not CO-ops) are believed to be the first cooperative housing built in the city since the successful efforts of the Finnish community in Brooklyn's Sunset Park [See WC Brooklyn S3.]. Since the "Coops'" advanced financing techniques were not matched by effective management, the Colony became insolvent in 1943 and has been privately owned since. Following World War II, Jessor was architect of many large garment-union-sponsored housing developments as well as the immense Co-op City development.

WILLIAMSBRIDGE

Hillside Homes:

[N 5.] Hillside Homes (apartment development), almost five city blocks, W of Boston Rd. bet. Wilson Ave. and Eastchester Rd. through to Hicks St. bet. Wilson and Fenton Aves. 1935. Clarence S. Stein.

Is it high land costs or planning prejudices that seem to make it **impossible to duplicate** this highly successful moderate-rental housing development? Most of the buildings here are only 4 stories high, and they occupy one-third of the land. A large central playground and community center are provided for school-age children, while sandboxes and tot lots are placed away from street traffic inside 7 large **sunken interior courts** reached through tunnel passageways. The design builds upon Stein's earlier **Sunnyside Gardens.** [See W Queens W 34a.]

Despite new red fascia panels at the parapets, the original skillful brickwork and casement windows make the architecture here quite substantial. Were only this true on the Boston Post Road shopping strip . . . chaotic to say the least.

Nineteenth-century Williamsbridge: The discontinuous street pattern found in the dozen blocks northeast of the East Gun Hill Road–White Plains Road intersection marks a charmingly serendipitous 19th-century wood-frame residential community that is worth a brief visit. The houses reflect the 1980s adulteration of architectural integrity and detail resulting from the gullibility of naive owners swallowing the fast talk of aluminum window and siding dealers. A great loss.

[N 6a.] Private Chapel (Roman Catholic), E. 215th St. bet. Holland and Barnes Ave. S side. 1905. Frank Lisanti.

In contrast to the public devotions at Lourdes of America [see N 3.], this is a place for private meditations: a humble chapel transposed from the slopes of southern Italy. Below the bell and the ornate wrought ironwork cross is carved:

F. LISANTI
IN DEVOZIONE
DELL' IMMACOLATA
PER SE E FAMIGLIA
ERESSE
1905

(F. Lisanti erected [this] for himself and his family in devotion to the Immaculate. 1905.)

[N 6b.] Regent School, Kindergarten and Primary Grades, 719 E. 216th St., bet. White Plains Rd. and Barnes Ave. N side. ca. 1915.

Four economically spaced Doric columns carry **a substantial pediment** ornamenting a sprightly (if somewhat officious-appearing) structure in this modest, lower-middle-class community.

[N 7a.] Emmanuel Baptist Church, 3711 White Plains Rd., bet. E. 216th and E. 217th Sts. W side. ca. 1895.

A contented masonry edifice resting its bones atop an earthen berm that **predates** the adjacent IRT elevated structure.

[N 7b.] Miracle Provider Church/originally **St. Luke's Episcopal Church,** 661 E. 219th St., bet. Carpenter Ave. and White Plains Rd. opp. Willett Ave. N side. ca. 1885.

A **country church** of shingles, stucco, and half timber, engulfed by an early, urbanizing Bronx.

[N 8a.] Peter Gillings Apartments, 737 E. 219th St., bet. White Plains Rd. and Barnes Ave. N side. ca. 1905.

The **rock-faced stone facade** of this early (for this neighborhood) 3-story multiple dwelling proudly proclaims its developer's name.

[N 8b.] St. Peter's Evangelical Lutheran Church, 741 E. 219th St., bet. White Plains Rd. and Barnes Ave. N side. ca. 1898.

A "constructivist" Shingle Style church with intact brown-stained shingles and white trim. Ever see **wood-shingled buttresses** before? Quite wonderful.

[N 8c.] St. Valentine's (Roman Catholic) Church and **Parish Hall,** 809 E. 220th St., bet. Barnes and Bronxwood Aves. N side. ca. 1890.

Skip the newer masonry church on East 221st Street, and gaze upon the old wood frame hall behind—was it the **original meeting place** of the congregation?—before it falls to the march of progress. (The church was originally built for a Polish congregation.)

[N 9a.] 3925 Barnes Avenue (tenement), NW cor. E. 223rd St. ca. 1885.

A 3-story wood frame building redolent of the late 19th century, even to its street-level commercial occupants: **a corner grocer** and **a barber shop.** This antique, together with the houses two blocks north, contains the seeds of the Bronx's own Old Sturbridge Village.

[N 9b.] 777 East 225th Street (residence) and **3981 Barnes Avenue (residence),** NW cor. E. 225th St. ca. 1875.

A pair of diminutive, wood-shingled, gabled houses, each with a tiny front porch. The former house is contained within **a gritty white picket fence,** and an ungainly 20th-century garage separates the houses at the most important corner of their joint site. It is still a miracle that they have survived with their exterior integrity largely intact.

[N 9c.] First Presbyterian Church of Williamsbridge and **Rectory,** 730 E. 225th St., bet. White Plains Rd. and Barnes Ave. S side. 1903. John Davidson.

The church is asymmetrically disposed with a square belfry to one side, bearing an **unexpected ogival roof** balanced atop four slender colonnettes. All of this is executed in wood shingles using an eclectic array of stylistic influences. **A provincial masterpiece.** The rectory is more conservative, in a neo-Colonial mode.

[N 9b.] 777 East 225th Street res.   **[N 9c.]** 1st Presby. Ch., Wmsbridge.

[N 10.] 47th Precinct, N.Y.C. Police Department, 4111 Laconia Ave., bet. E. 229th and E. 230th Sts. W side. 1974. Davis, Brody & Assocs.

It's not unreasonable to conceive of a police station as an updated medieval castle. But when dreams become brick-and-mortar reality, problems can surface. They do here in this overly contrived design.

BAYCHESTER

[N 11a.] Haffen Park Pool, N.Y.C. Department of Parks & Recreation, Burke Ave. SW cor. Ely Ave. 1970. Heery & Heery. **[N 11b.] Haffen Park,** redevelopment, 1973, Coffey, Levine & Blumberg.

A precast concrete, systems-built pool, constructed as part of a crash program to influence an election campaign (as many public works are intended to do). **Neat detailing** and **early supergraphics** commend the design, but the lush greenery in Haffen Park, preserved in the park's development, is the most welcome sight.

[N 12a.] Junior High School 144, Bronx, The Michelangelo School, 2545 Gunther Ave., SW cor. Allerton Ave. 1968. The Office of Max O. Urbahn.

Entirely of cast-in-place concrete, more fashionable as an advanced building material then than now, this well-intentioned design has not aged well. Most regrettable are the later additions of metal mesh screens over the windows to deter stone-throwing vandals.

[N 12b.] Waldbaum's Shopping Center, 1750 Gun Hill Rd., E of Gunther Ave. S side. 1985. R.A.L. Design Assocs.

If a supermarket-plus-parking makes a "strip," let all strips look as good as this one.

[N 13a.] Co-op City. Northern section: E of New England Thruway/Baychester Ave. bet. Co-op City Blvd. and Bartow Ave. **Southern section:** E of Hutchinson River Pkwy. E., bet. Bartow and Boller Aves. 1968–1970. Herman J. Jessor, architect. Zion & Breen, landscape architects.

Out in the middle of nowhere, on marshy land that was once the site of an ill-fated amusement park named **Freedomland,** a group of government officials, union representatives, and housing developers **dreamed the impossible dream.** Today the dream may better be described as **a coma.** From out of the **pumped-sand fill** rises a mountain range of 35-story residential towers, **35 of them,** plus 236 clustered two-family houses and eight multistory parking garages. In addition, there are three shopping centers, a heating plant, a firehouse, and an educational park consisting of two public schools, two intermediate schools, and a high school. In this total **non-environment,** largely designed by bureaucrats with **not a scintilla of wit,** live some 55,000 souls, many of whom vacated sound accommodations in the West Bronx (in many cases Art Deco apartment blocks) to move here.

Let's be thankful for the **landscaping.** It's the **best thing** at Co-op City.

[N 13b.] Bay Plaza (shopping center), Hutchinson River Pkwy. W., NW cor. New England Thruway (Baychester Ave.). 1988. Gruzen Samton Steinglass.

Finally, a shopping center to serve Co-op City's denizens, and their many neighbors.

EASTCHESTER

When that part of the Bronx lying east of the Bronx River was **lopped off** Westchester County in 1895, the dividing line ran right through the village of Eastchester. As a result, the old village green lies **a stone's throw** outside city limits. This community of the northeasternmost Bronx is still referred to, however, by its **colonial name.** It is largely a wasteland, unfortunately: automobile repair shops, fast-food operations, marginal industry and the like. But at its edges and even within are some bright spots.

[N 14a.] Originally **Vincent-Halsey House,** 3701 Provost Ave., bet. Light and E. 233rd Sts. W side. mid 18th century.

Regrettably this historic house (not open to the public) has been overwhelmed by its ugly industrial neighbors. Today a nondescript old building, it was once a colonial farmhouse set among Eastchester's furrowed fields. **John Adams** moved the **presidential mansion** here in 1797 to **escape a yellow fever epidemic** raging in Philadelphia, then the national capital. Adams governed the nation from this place for two months, but **tragedy did not escape him** here. One of his sons drowned while swimming in nearby Eastchester Creek.

[N 14b.] Church of the Nativity of Our Blessed Lady (Roman Catholic), 1510 E. 233rd St., SW cor. Secor Ave. 1975. Don Shepherd, designer.

A minor work which calls attention to itself because of its location and the **pre-rusted structural steel crucifix** that dominates the corner of the site.

[N 14c.] Public School 15, Bronx (Annex to P.S. 68, Bronx)/formerly **Public School 148, Bronx**/originally **Village of Eastchester public school,** 4010 Dyre Ave., bet. Dark and Lustre Sts. E side. 1877. ★

An architectural "pot of gold" at the end of the (once upon a time?) **rainbow-graffitied** Dyre Avenue IRT Line: a gingerbread brick-and-wood-trimmed schoolhouse which wound up on the New York City side of the boundary when Eastchester was split in two. Its cheerful forms can't help but bring a smile to your face.

WAKEFIELD

[N 15.] St. Anthony's Roman Catholic Church, 4501 Richardson Ave., NW cor. E. 239th St. 1975. Belfatto & Pavarini.

Strongly articulated brick forms topped by **a tall slender pylon** carrying a carefully detailed cross.

[N 16a.] St. Paul's Slovak Evangelical Lutheran Church, 729 Cranford Ave., bet. White Plains Rd. and Barnes Ave. N side. 1928. Altered, 1962.

A small but out-of-the-ordinary ashlar stone church distinguished by a **trio of bronze** bells embraced by the very top of its facade.

[N 16b.] 4577 Carpenter Avenue (residence), SW cor. W. 240th St. ca. 1880.

A house in the **Eastlake Style** with imbricated shingles on the Carpenter Avenue frontage and clapboard siding elsewhere. Look carefully—the mature fir trees tend to conceal.

WOODLAWN

Snug against the **Yonkers city line,** this is the only clearly demarked community in the Northern Bronx—thanks to its neighbors, Van Cortlandt Park on the west, Woodlawn Cemetery on the south, and the Bronx River Parkway and the old **New York & Harlem Railroad** right-of-way (now Metro North) on the east. The opening of that railroad commuter route encouraged settlement here in the 19th century.

[N 14c.] Public School 15, The Bronx   **[N 16a.]** St. Paul's Slovak Church

[N 15.] St. Anthony's Catholic Church: A modern note in a traditional locale

[N 17.] 125 East 238th Street (residence), bet. Oneida and Kepler Aves. N side. ca. 1925.

A cramped site and a cheap, one-color (white) paint job conceal the merits of this catalog-item bungalow that you could once purchase from **Sears Roebuck.** In 1977 the stucco was cream-colored, and the wood was a deep brown. What a difference a shade makes!

BROOOKLLYN

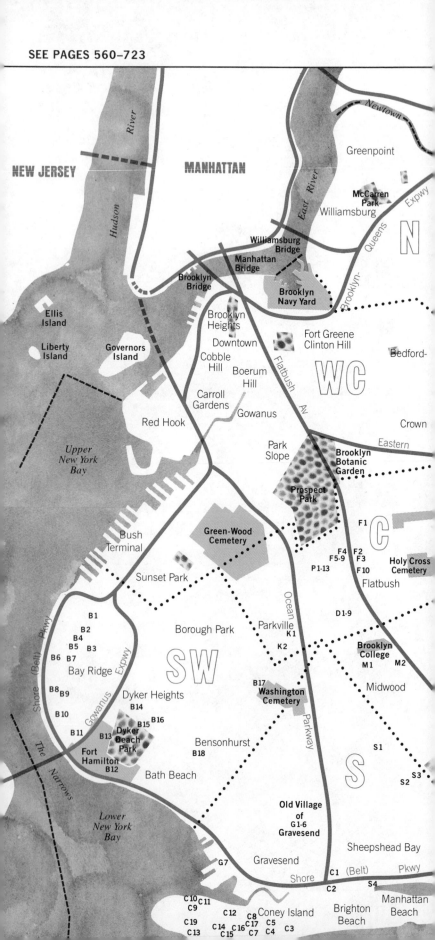

NEW JERSEY

MANHATTAN

Newtown

Greenpoint

East River

McCarren Park–
Williamsburg

Hudson River

Queens Expwy

N

Williamsburg
Bridge

Manhattan
Bridge

Brooklyn
Bridge

Brooklyn
Navy Yard

Brooklyn-
Queens Expwy

Ellis
Island

Liberty
Island

Governors
Island

Brooklyn
Heights

Downtown

Cobble
Hill

Boerum
Hill

Carroll
Gardens

Gowanus

Red Hook

Fort Greene
Clinton Hill

Bedford-

Flatbush Av

WC

Crown

Upper
New York
Bay

Park
Slope

Brooklyn
Botanic
Garden

Prospect
Park

Eastern

Bush
Terminal

Green-Wood
Cemetery

Sunset Park

F1

C

F4 F2
F5-9 F3
F10

P 1-13

Holy Cross
Cemetery

Flatbush

Shore (Belt) Pkwy

B1

B2
B4
B5   B3
B6 B7

Bay Ridge

B8 B9

B10

B11

Gowanus Expwy

Borough Park

Parkville

Ocean

D 1-9

K1

K2

Brooklyn
College

M1   M2

Midwood

SW

Dyker Heights

B14

B15 B16

B13

Dyker
Beach
Park

B17
Washington
Cemetery

Bensonhurst

B18

Parkway

S1

S

S3

The Narrows

Fort
Hamilton

B12

Bath Beach

Lower
New York
Bay

G7

Old Village
of
G 1-6
Gravesend

Gravesend

Shore

Sheepshead Bay

C1 (Belt) Pkwy

C2

S4

S2

Manhattan
Beach

C 10 C 11
C 9

C 12

C 19

C 13

C 14
C 15

C 8
C 16 C 17
C 7

C 5
C 4   C 3

Coney Island

Brighton
Beach

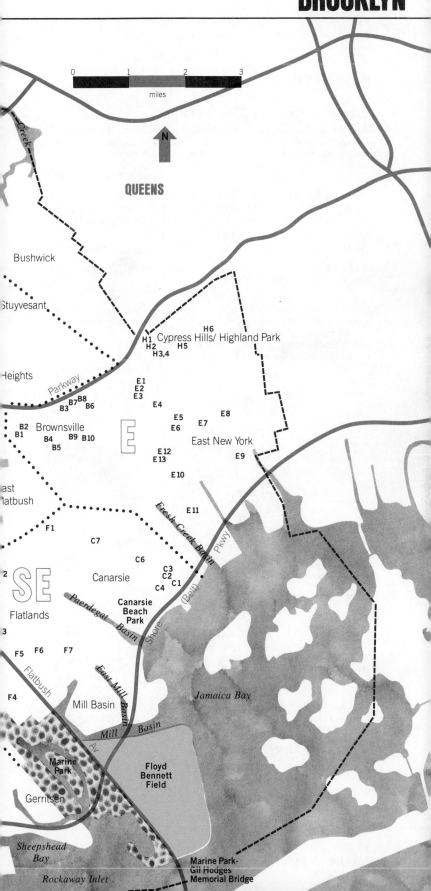

0   1   2   3
miles

N

QUEENS

Bushwick

Stuyvesant

H1 Cypress Hills/ Highland Park
H2   H5   H6
H3,4

Heights

Parkway

E1
E2
E3
E4
B3 B7 B8
B6
E5   E8
E6   E7
B2 Brownsville
B1
B4   B9 B10
B5
East New York
E9

E
E12
E13

E10

ast
Flatbush

E11

F1

Fresh Creek Basin

C7

Pkwy

C6

SE
C3
C2
C4 C1
Canarsie

(Belt)

Flatlands

Paerdegat Basin

Canarsie
Beach
Park

Shore

F5 F6   F7

East Mill Basin

Jamaica Bay

F4

Mill   Basin

Mill Basin

Av

Marine
Park

Floyd
Bennett
Field

Gerritsen

Sheepshead
Bay

Marine Park-
Gil Hodges
Memorial Bridge

Rockaway Inlet

3

BROOKLYN

Borough of Brooklyn/Kings County

"Brooklyn's situation for grandeur, beauty, and salubrity is unsurpassed probably on the whole surface of the globe: and its destiny is to be among the most famed and choice of the half dozen cities of the world . . ."

—**Walt Whitman,** 1861.

"New York is Babylon; Brooklyn is the truly holy City. New York is the city of office work, and hustle: Brooklyn is the region of home and happiness . . . There is no hope for New Yorkers, for they glory in their skyscraping sins; but in Brooklyn there is the wisdom of the lowly."

—**Christopher Morley,** 1917.

"It'd take a guy a lifetime to know Brooklyn t'roo an' t'roo. An' even den, yuh wouldn't know it all."

—**Thomas Wolfe,** 1935.

"Terribly funny, yes, but Brooklyn is also a sad brutal provincial lonesome human silent sprawling raucous lost passionate subtle bitter immature innocent perverse tender mysterious place, a place where Crane and Whitman found poems, a mythical dominion against whose shores the Coney Island sea laps a wintry lament."

—**Truman Capote,** 1946.

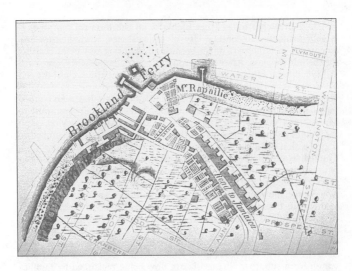

Legions of row houses march across the varied precincts of old and middle-aged Brooklyn (1820–1920), punctuated by apartment blocks sometimes new and viable, sometimes old and burned out, and marred with the scars of **peacetime wars.** In further reaches, two-, three-, and single family houses flood the plains washed out from the glacier's last bluffs (terminal moraine), atop which **old** Brooklyn sits. Litter, stickball in the summer, roller skate hockey in the winter, steeples silhouetted against a sometimes smoggy sky—all edge against the imperious towers of the skyline that lies across the bay. These are the traditional caricatures of Brooklyn, valid in essence but only part of a **rich civic fabric** that is both **urban** and **suburban,** and that bears an extant architectural history older and richer than its more urbane fellow borough (sometime **competing** separate city), Manhattan.

The physical objects themselves have not undergone serious transformation; with certain notable exceptions they seem only to age and become begrimed. In large measure it is our way of seeing them that changes. Brooklyn today, even to many of its residents, is very often the **image** absorbed from a car on a limited-access highway: the **industry** of the north end, the **spin** along the Narrows with the Verrazano Bridge punctuating the **contrast** between people and nature. Motorists also remember the intricate spider web of Coney Island's **Wonder Wheel,** the endless stretches of **swampland** at Jamaica Bay, or the sinuous curves of the parkway along verdant Interboro Parkway (1935). The placement of our highways and the speed of our cars tend to obscure the essence of most of Brooklyn as a **pedestrian-streeted** residential community of variegated neighborhoods, and to mark its peripheral monuments as **separate objects** divorced from the borough's basic context.

Old Brooklyn today (that **highland** on the **terminal moraine**) is largely a nineteenth-century city of brownstones, town houses, and tenements, in large part intact because of enduring service as housing for the middle class. After the borough's consolidation with New York in 1898, much of the population emigrated to Manhattan. Until the end of World War II, the **brownstone, whitestone,** and **brick** row houses became—by default—the refuge of middle-class families, who banded together neighborhood by neighborhood. After their daily commute to Manhattan (**New York** or **The City** to Brooklyn natives), they retreated each night to their homes across the river. As architects succumbed to their passion for all things new and modern, Brooklyn was forgotten. The **rediscovery** in the late 1960s of vast stretches of brownstone Brooklyn, led by a young and sophisticated upper-income middle class, marked a change in the way the borough was perceived.

Viable and venerable residential communities, seeming backwaters in the mainstream of physical change, such as **Brooklyn Heights, Park Slope,** the **Hills (Clinton, Cobble,** and **Boerum), Carroll Gardens, Prospect Heights**—their renaissance will undoubtedly spur the exploration of much of Brooklyn's other precincts—**Williamsburg** and **Greenpoint, Sunset Park** and **Dyker Heights.** Places abandoned by families in their search for a suburban Shangri-la are now being reclaimed by families who savor the architecture and life of a streetfronted, park-studded, subway-served Brooklyn.

WEST CENTRAL BROOKLYN

CIVIC CENTER/DOWNTOWN BROOKLYN
BROOKLYN HEIGHTS • FULTON FERRY DISTRICT
COBBLE HILL • CARROLL GARDENS • GOWANUS • RED HOOK
SUNSET PARK AND ENVIRONS • BOERUM HILL/TIMES PLAZA
FORT GREENE • CLINTON HILL • NAVY YARD • PARK SLOPE
PROSPECT PARK/GRAND ARMY PLAZA • INSTITUTE PARK
BEDFORD-STUYVESANT • CROWN HEIGHTS

Town of Brooklyn/Breukelen

Established as a town before **1658**, incorporated as a city in **1834**. Annexed the City of Williamsburgh and the Town of Bushwick in **1855**, Town of New Lots in **1886**, Towns of Flatbush, Gravesend, and New Utrecht in **1894**, and Town of Flatlands in **1896**. Consolidated into greater New York City in **1898**.

The original **Town,** later **City,** of **Brooklyn** encompassed all the brownstone neighborhoods again fashionable today, mostly atop the high ground left by the last glacier, the terminal moraine. The residential precincts of Brooklyn Heights, Fort Greene, Clinton Hill, Park Slope, Bedford-Stuyvesant, Crown Heights, Cobble Hill, and Boerum Hill are all within the boundaries of the original town—as are the **Brooklyn Civic Center** and the shopping mall along the newly renovated **Fulton Street.** In addition, the teeming waterfront facilities from the Manhattan Bridge south to the deactivated Brooklyn Army Terminal lie within the area, as do the backup residential communities of **Red Hook, Gowanus,** and **Sunset Park.** And within the old town's boundaries are half of both Prospect Park and Green-Wood Cemetery as well.

Although the extent of the old town can still be accurately charted, it is of **little significance** in any overall sense today when compared to the **individual communities** that it comprises.

The independent **City of Brooklyn** moved quickly to give form to its identity by building a city hall, which still stands as its seat of borough affairs. As the **19th century** progressed, Brooklyn's population and wealth grew, and so did its civic center. With city hall as the focus, there soon emerged a variety of richly embellished governmental and commercial buildings, hotels, and shopping emporia. But to a visitor to Downtown Brooklyn during this era of expansion, the most apparent features were not its richly ornamented buildings but the **spindly iron trestles** that inundated many of its major streets, throwing **zebra-striped** shadows. For this part of Brooklyn was to be not only the city's hub of government and shopping but of **transportation** as well, and the elevateds crisscrossing overhead made their way down Fulton Street and Myrtle Avenue to their connections to Manhattan. It was not until after World War II that the elevated filigrees were demolished and today's **Cadman Plaza Park** built.

Civic Center/Downtown Brooklyn Walking Tour: From Borough Hall to the Flatbush Avenue-Fulton Street intersection, about a half-mile walk. (Subway to the Borough Hall Station of the IRT Lexington and Seventh Avenue Lines, or the BMT Court Street Station, Court Street exit.)

The first buildings are gathered around Cadman Plaza. Walk north from Joralemon Street to Tillary Street and beyond.

[D 1a.] Brooklyn Borough Hall/formerly **Brooklyn City Hall,** 209 Joralemon St., at Cadman Plaza W. and Court St. N side. 1846–1851. Gamaliel King. Cupola, 1898. Vincent C. Griffith and Stoughton & Stoughton. Statue of Justice installed and building restored, 1987, Conklin & Rossant. ★

A **Greek Revival Palace,** later crowned with a Victorian cupola, it presents a bold face to Cadman Plaza, particularly monumental due to the broad, steep mass of steps rising to its entrance colonnade. First intended to be a lesser copy of New York's City Hall (**1802–1811**) across the river, the project went through four designs. In the elapsed time aesthetic moods changed, and the Franco-Georgian design of **1802** became the **Greek Revival** world of the **1830**s and **1840**s. According to Brooklyn's city directory, King was a grocer until 1830, then a carpenter—not unusual in an era when **Thomas Jefferson** designed the University of Virginia, and the Capitol of the United States was built according to the competition-winning design of a physician, **William Thornton.**

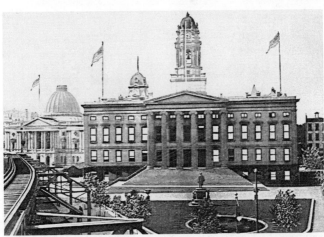

[D 1a.] Brooklyn Borough Hall (ca. 1905 postcard). County Courthouse at left

[D 1b.] Brooklyn Municipal Building, 210 Joralemon St., SE cor. Court St., opposite Borough Hall. 1926. McKenzie, Voorhees & Gmelin.

The **background building** where much of the municipal bureaucracy functions, as contrasted with the foreground building, Borough Hall, the ceremonial center. A grand set of Tuscan columns presents an entrance to the subway.

[D 1c.] Borough Hall Station, IRT Lexington Avenue Line, below Jora-
lemon St., E of Court St. 1908. Samuel B. Parsons, chief engineer.
Heins & La Farge, architects. Redesigned and restored, 1987, Mayers
& Schiff. ★

A series of richly modeled and colored faience plaques carries the
abbreviation BH, and subtly colored mosaic tesserae and pink marble
further humanize the **straightforward engineers' works** in this Contract
2 station, opened four years after completion of the original IRT Contract 1 work at Manhattan's City Hall Station. **Ornate bronze dedication plaques** located on the mezzanine's north wall (no fare required)
explain the sequence further.

[D 1d.] Temple Bar Building, 44 Court St., NW cor. Joralemon St.
1901. George L. Morse.

Three verdigris cupolas crown this office building, Brooklyn's
highest when it was built, heralding the arrival of the 20th century.
Tacky at street level.

[D 2a.] Cadman Plaza (officially S. Parkes Cadman Plaza), bounded
by Cadman Plaza W., Court, Joralemon and Adams Sts., and the Brooklyn Bridge approaches. 1950–1960. Designed by various city and borough agencies. Christopher Columbus monument: statue, 1867, Emma
Stebbins, sculptor; base and installation at this site, 1971, A. Ottavino.
Senator Robert F. Kennedy sculpture, 1972, Anneta Duveen, sculptor.

Scarcely a plaza, this is an **amorphous park** created by demolition
of several blocks east of Brooklyn Heights. A principal goal was to
create a graceful setting for new Civic Center buildings that would
complement Borough Hall. Almost equally important **fringe benefits**
were the **elimination of the elevated tracks** that crossed the Brooklyn
Bridge and crowded Fulton Street and the easing of automobile traffic
through street-widening. Stebbins' statue of Columbus originally stood
in Central Park. It was carved two years after she completed the **Angel
of the Waters** and supporting cherubs for the Bethesda Fountain.

[D 2b.] N.Y.S. Supreme Court, 360 Adams St., S part of Cadman Plaza
opposite Montague St. 1957. Shreve, Lamb & Harmon.

Unlike the nation's Supreme Court, New York's **Supreme** Court
is the lowest court, where legal action first commences. Shreve, Lamb
& Harmon are best known for the Empire State Building (1931). A
handsome set of **architectural nostalgia** is the pair of lamps from the
now-demolished Hall of Records (**1905.** R. L. Daus).

[D 2c.] Statue of Henry Ward Beecher   [D 3a.] Brooklyn General Post Office

[D 2c.] Statue of Henry Ward Beecher, near Johnson St., S part of
Cadman Plaza. 1891. John Quincy Adams Ward, sculptor; Richard
Morris Hunt, architect of the base.

Mr. Beecher, the preacher and brother of Harriet Beecher Stowe,
was relocated from his perch confronting Borough Hall to decorate the

expanse of the new Cadman Plaza. The fence and lawn surrounding the sculpture are **unfortunate,** for Ward's strong concept should allow people to **join the figures** already touching the base at Beecher's feet.

[D 3a.] Brooklyn General Post Office, 271 Cadman Plaza E., NE cor. Johnson St. 1885–1891. Mifflin E. Bell (original design); William A. Freret, successor. North half, 1933. James Wetmore. ★

The original building to the south is in an exuberant Romanesque Revival. Deep reveals and strong modeling provide a rich play of light. The taller addition is a **humorless tail** attempting to wag its lusty dog. Recent interior alterations are worthy only of a developer's **cut-rate boondocks motel.**

[D 3b.] Federal Building and Courthouse, 275 Washington St., NE cor. Tillary St., on Cadman Plaza. 1961. Carson, Lundin & Shaw.

The **embassy** to Brooklyn from Washington.

[D 3c.] Brooklyn War Memorial, N part of Cadman Plaza, opposite Orange St. 1951. Eggers & Higgins, architects. Charles Keck, sculptor.

Though its innards contain a small museum and other community facilities, its primary role is **as a wall,** completing the plaza's formal composition of terrace, paths, shrubs, trees, and lawn.

Return to Tillary Street and follow it east.

[D 4a.] New York City Technical College, CUNY, Tillary Street, bet. Jay and Adams Sts., S side. Expanded, 1987, Edward Durrell Stone Assocs.

A vast new greenhouse links the two earlier buildings that separately front on Adams and Jay. The resulting plaza is a welcome new urban space.

Turn left on Jay Street.

[D 4b.] St. James Cathedral (Roman Catholic), Jay St. bet. Cathedral Place and Chapel St. E side. 1903. George H. Streeton.

Neo-Georgian, with a handsome, verdigris copper-clad steeple. The first church on this site (**1822**) became the cathedral of Brooklyn in **1853;** but in **1896,** with the succession of Brooklyn's second bishop, it was officially renamed the procathedral. **Pro,** in this instance, means in place of, for that bishop was planning an elaborate new cathedral of his own, the giant Immaculate Conception Cathedral, which never materialized. The **pro**cathedral did not become the cathedral once again until **1972.** (Cathedral means literally that church which contains the **cathedra,** or chair of the bishop. Size does not a cathedral make but, rather, ecclesiastical function. Therefore there can be only one cathedral in any diocese or see).

Return to Tillary Street and turn left. Walk two blocks, turning right into Bridge Street.

[D 5.] Originally **First Free Congregational Church**/later **Bridge Street African Wesleyan Church**/now **Polytechnic Institute of New York Student Center,** 311 Bridge St., bet. Johnson St. and Myrtle Ave. E side. 1844. ★

A **Greek Revival temple** in brick with a Doric-columned porch and entablature. Chaste, apart from the later Victorian stained glass, which is exuberant even from the outside. Once a major stop on the **underground railroad,** it provided sanctuary for runaway slaves and those blacks fleeing the 1863 draft riots. As the Bridge Street **AWE** Church it was the first black congregation in Brooklyn (**1854–1938).**

At Willoughby Street turn right.

[D 6a.] New York Telephone Company, Long Island Headquarters, 101 Willoughby St., NE cor. Bridge St. 1931. Voorhees, Gmelin & Walker.

Brick with a **graded palette,** a delicate aesthetic. Note the equally elegant **Art Deco** grillages over the ground-floor windows.

[D 6b.] Originally **New York & New Jersey Telephone Company Building,** 81 Willoughby St., NE cor. Lawrence St. 1898. R. L. Daus.

A grand **Beaux Arts-Renaissance Revival** palace, Brooklyn's first telephone headquarters. Look closely at the carved entrance surrounds: the intertwined **TC** (for telephone company) over the door; the free use of bells, earpieces, and ancient wall telephones that were worked into the classical **Beaux Arts** ornament. And hovering over it all is a grand copper-clad cornice.

Turn right at Jay Street.

[D 7.] Originally **City of Brooklyn Fire Headquarters,** 365-367 Jay St., bet. Willoughby St. and Myrtle Ave. E side. 1892. Frank Freeman. ★

This is a building to write home about. A powerful **Romanesque Revival,** brick, granite, and tile structure, it is the New York branch (with **Louis Sullivan**'s Condict Building) of the Chicago School. Freeman learned much from afar by viewing **H. H. Richardson**'s work, as did Sullivan.

[D 7.] The former Jay Street Firehouse   **[D 9b.]** Once Brooklyn Public Library

[D 8a.] Originally **Edison Electric Illuminating Company, Central Station for Brooklyn,** 358-362 Pearl St., N of Fulton St. W side. 1891.

Another Romanesque Revival remnant.

[D 8b.] Originally **N.Y.C. Board of Transportation Building**/now **N.Y.C. Transit Authority Headquarters,** 370 Jay St., NW cor. Willoughby St. 1950. William E. Hauggard & Andrew J. Thomas.

Home of the subway systems' managers . . . and bureaucracy. The two gracious though dingy lobbies to the subway, at north and south ends, are **fringe benefits** gained from a building contiguous to its subway lines. Windows here read as skin, rather than holes punctured in masonry, by the device of detailing the glass flush with its limestone surrounds. Nightly money trains bring the take from all boroughs directly to a spur in the building's bowels.

[D 8c.] Originally **Brooklyn Law School**/now **Brooklyn Friends School,** Pearl St. N of Fulton St., E side. ca. 1930. Thompson, Holmes & Converse.

A curious Art Moderne building with a crowning of Romanesque Revival arches.

Follow Jay Street across Fulton—at this point its name becomes Smith—to Livingston Street.

[D 9a.] N.Y.C. Board of Education Headquarters/originally **Benevolent Protective Order of Elks,** 110 Livingston St., SW cor. Boerum Place. 1926. McKim, Mead & White.

MM&W were deflated after **Stanford White'**s death, shot by a jealous husband in **1906.** The partnership's other powerful talent, **Charles Follen McKim,** died in **1909** (Mead was the business partner). The staff thereafter produced occasional wonders, as with Manhattan's Municipal Building of 1914. But for the most part the production, as here, was **pallid** and **boring.**

[D 9b.] Long Island College Hospital Therapeutic Nursery/originally **Brooklyn Public Library,** 67 Schermerhorn St., bet. Boerum Place and Court St. N side. ca. 1890. **[D 8f.]** Originally **German Evangelical Lutheran Church,** 63 Schermerhorn St., bet. Boerum Place and Court St. N side. 1888. J. C. Cady.

A bold pair of buildings designed at the height of Brooklyn's **Romanesque Revival.** The arched entry of No. 67 is a worthy but distant neighbor to that at Frank Freeman's **Jay Street Firehouse.**

[D 9c.] N.Y.C. Transit Authority Museum, Schermerhorn St. NW cor. Boerum Place. Downstairs, in the former IND Court Street subway station. **Open to the public.**

A wonderful **underground museum** on an inactive spur of the subway system. Here are trains, turnstiles, and tesserae of varying vintages. **Admission by a token.**

[D 10.] Originally **St. Vincent's Home for Boys,** Boerum Place SW cor. State St. Chapel, 1927, McGill & Hamlin.

More interesting for who did it than what it is. **Talbot Hamlin** was professor of architectural history at Columbia, most noted for his great book, *Greek Revival Architecture in America* (1944).

[D 11.] Brooklyn Men's House of Detention, 275 Atlantic Ave., bet. Smith St. and Boerum Place. N side. ca. 1950. LaPierre, Litchfield & Partners.

Cheerfully described as the **Brooklyn Hilton,** this facility holds mostly those awaiting trial who cannot post bail, as well as those considered too dangerous to roam before trial.

[D 12a.] Brooklyn Friends Meetinghouse, 110 Schermerhorn St., SE cor. Boerum Place. 1854. Enoch Straton, builder. ★

Once a freestanding structure in simple **Quaker** brick, it is overpowered by the Central Court Building adjacent to its contiguous former school.

[D 12b.] Central Court Building, 120 Schermerhorn St., SW cor. Smith St. 1932. Collins & Collins.

Similar in bulk to 110 Livingston Street [see D 9a.], this Renaissance Revival **hulk** adds to the cityscape through its deep entrance porch, articulated by 3 great neo-Renaissance arches.

[D 13.] Proposed **Livingston Plaza,** a block surrounded by Smith, Livingston, Schermerhorn Sts., and Boerum Place. 1989. Murphy/Jahn.

Low-rise jazz to come from the people who gave us 425 Lexington Avenue.

[D 14.] Fulton Street Mall, along Fulton St. and DeKalb Ave. bet. Flatbush Ave. Ext. and Adams St. 1985. Seelye, Stevenson, Value & Knecht, engineers. Pomeroy, Lebduska Assocs., architects.

The magnetism of the Fulton Street shopping area already fills the sidewalks with people. The mall has bestowed a blessing upon the commotion by widening the sidewalks, limiting vehicles to buses, and adding covered **bus stops, kiosks, benches,** and **lighting.**

Gage & Tollner's Restaurant, 372 Fulton St., bet. Smith St. and Red Hook Lane. Building ca. 1875 ★ Interior, 1892. ★

Except for an ungainly vertical sign, building and restaurant are much as they were the day they opened: a Victorian interior of plush velvet, cut glass, mirrors, gaslight, mahogany, and bentwood chairs. It would do justice to a **Mississippi River steamboat.** A broad menu of fish, shellfish, and crustaceans is cooked to order. Elegant architecturally; more than satisfactory gastronomically.

[D 15a.] Abraham & Straus (department store), 420 Fulton St., bet. Gallatin Place and Hoyt St. Main building S side. 1929 and 1935. Starrett & Van Vleck. Secondary building NE cor. Gallatin Place and Livingston St. 1885. **[D 15b.]** Originally **Liebmann Brothers Building,** 446 Fulton St., SW cor. Hoyt St. 1880s. Parfitt Brothers.

Eight interconnected buildings jointly form the **great department store of Brooklyn,** in a similar blockfilling manner to its Manhattan counterpart, **Bloomingdale's.** The main building is a subdued **Art Deco,** but the small Romanesque Revival gem at Gallatin Place is distinguished in **Roman brick,** brownstone, and granite. Some of the wondrous earlier **cast-iron and brownstone facades** commissioned by Abraham Abraham peek over later street- and storefront modernizations aside the main block.

[D 15c.] Hoyt Street Station, IRT Seventh Avenue Line, below Fulton St. at Hoyt St. 1908. Samuel B. Parsons, chief engineer. Altered. W end redesigned, 1986, Mayers & Schiff.

The western parts of this station's platform walls, below the A&S facade, now carry a **tailored look**—horizontal maroon pencil stripes but at a properly enlarged **civic architecture scale**—giving it a classy look it never enjoyed during its first three-quarters of a century of service.

[D 16.] Formerly **Offerman Building**/originally **Wechsler Brothers Block,** 503 Fulton St., bet. Bridge and Duffield Sts. N side. 1891. Lauritzen & Voss.

Grossly altered. The Duffield Street facade preserves some of the Romanesque Revival detail, even at ground level, that once embellished the whole body of the building. Look up at a **great incised sign.** The sleazy covering of, and alteration to, the Fulton Street facade have destroyed distinguished architecture that might well have been reinforced, rather than mutilated. But still, **look up.**

[D 17.] Dime Savings Bank of New York: glories of Rome on the Fulton Mall

[D 17.] The Dime Savings Bank of New York, 9 DeKalb Ave., NE cor. Fleet St., off Fulton St. 1907. Mowbray & Uffinger. Expanded, 1932, Halsey, McCormack & Helmer.

A domical, columned **Roman Revival** palace. The interior is remarkable; plan to visit it during banking hours. Gilded, monumental Liberty-head dimes are the predominant motif. Money must have been well managed by those who could afford such grandeur.

Follow DeKalb Avenue past the Dime to the far side of Flatbush Avenue Extension.

On the site of the Albee Square Mall (1980. Gruen Associates) stood the **RKO Albee** movie theater, one of downtown Brooklyn's last great picture **palaces,** demolished in 1977. It was a neo-Renaissance fantasy of columns and star-twinkling ceilings, a vast place of 2,000 seats. Edward F. Albee, a vaudeville impresario, was the foster father of playwright **Edward Albee.** The theater's swan song included a screening of *Who's Afraid of Virginia Woolf?* based on the younger Albee's great play.

[D 18.] Long Island University, Brooklyn Center, 385 Flatbush Ave. Ext., bet. DeKalb Ave. and Willoughby St. E. side. **[D 18a.] Campus entry arch, Long Island University,** Flatbush Ave. Ext. N of DeKalb Ave. E side. 1985. Park, Quennell-Rothschild Assocs., landscape architects. Arch design, Nicholas Quennell.

A latter day brightly colored **triumphal arch** fashioned from structural steel sections and a steel grid. It stands in a tiny park that **replaced a ragtag gas station** that for years debased the L.I.U. campus entrance. **A cheery welcome** to both campus and to Brooklyn for the heavy traffic entering via the nearby Manhattan Bridge, but hardly competition the **real thing** at Grand Army Plaza, two miles further up Flatbush Avenue [see A 2.].

[D 18c.] The Humanities Building of L.I.U., once the Maltz warehouse

[D 18b.] Arnold and Marie Schwartz Athletic Center and **Tristram W. Metcalf Hall, Long Island University**/originally **Brooklyn Paramount Theater and offices.** 1928. Altered, 1950, 1962.

Brooklyn's **leading movie palace** was converted in two stages to university use: the office block in **1950,** the **4,400**-seat auditorium in **1962.** The intervening years witnessed the **swan song of popcorn** in these marble halls. Adjacent to the north are two distinguished new campus buildings:

[D 18c.] Humanities Building, Long Island University/originally **Maltz Building,** 1967. Davis, Brody & Assocs. and Horowitz & Chun.

The structure of an existing warehouse was here reclad and extended in brick. New guts and a new envelope on an existing skeleton, with fine materials, elegant detailing, and handsome spaces, make this **an extraordinary work.** Developer **B. M. Maltz** created the original loft building in **1925.** (The highly visible—but misleading—sign of the Pharmacy College pertains to the donors' gift elsewhere on the campus.)

[D 18d.] Library-Learning Center, Long Island University, 1975. Davis, Brody & Assocs. and Horowitz & Chun.

Linked to the earlier Humanities Building by a bright red-painted, **Vierendeel-trussed,** glass-caged bridge, this crisp complex begins to knit together the disparate older buildings of the reworked **Brooklyn Center** campus.

Leave the L.I.U. campus and turn left on Flatbush Avenue Extension.

[D 19.] New York Telephone Company Office Building, 395 Flatbush Ave. Ext., bet. DeKalb Ave. and Fulton St. E side. 1976. Skidmore, Owings & Merrill. **[D 20.] Consolidated Edison Company, Brooklyn Division,** 30 Flatbush Ave., bet. Nevins and Livingston Sts. 1974. Skidmore, Owings & Merrill.

These two buildings are at the heart of Brooklyn's former entertainment center; where Con Ed stands was the **Brooklyn Fox,** a movie and vaudeville showplace **(1928–1971).** N.Y. Tel's building erased the scars of a major rebuilding of the BMT subway interchange below. Though by the same firm, the **two buildings are of very differing expressions.** Architecturally, at least, Con Ed has emerged the **victor** in this battle of the utilities.

END of Civic Center/Downtown Brooklyn Walking Tour: The subway station here at Nevins and Flatbush offers both the IRT Lexington and Seventh Avenue service. The DeKalb Avenue Station, a block back along Flatbush Avenue Extension, provides connections to both BMT and IND subways.

[D 13.] Prop. Livingston Plaza Bldg.   **[D 20.]** Con Edison, Brooklyn Division

[D 21.] Metrotech, roughly bet. Flatbush Ave., Tillary, Jay, and Willoughby Sts., excepting a NW quadrant including N.Y.C. Board of Education Channel 25 and Westinghouse High School; and a SW quadrant of commercial buildings largely facing Willoughby St. 1989–   Master plan, Haines Lundberg Waehler.

Here are 10 proposed blocks and $770 million of sadly gargantuan neighbors for this firm's ancestral talent, Ralph Walker, whose Voorhees, Gmelin & Walker 1931 telephone building **[D 6a.]** is a local elegance. This is an unfortunate reprise of the "urban renewal" of the 1960s, such as that which obliterated and "renewed" a vast portion of Manhattan's Upper West Side. The architecture proposed seems a cut-rate rip-off of Cesar Pelli's **World Financial Center** in Manhattan.

A handsome aside to the north:

[D 22.] Originally **Thompson Meter Company Building,** Bridge St. bet. York and Tillman Sts. 1910. Louis Jallade. Henry J. Hardenbergh, designer.

Glazed terra-cotta crowns and girds this lush concrete industrial building.

BROOKLYN HEIGHTS

Colonized by well-to-do merchants and bankers from the city across the river, Brooklyn Heights is the **suburban product** of a combined **land** and **transit** speculation; in this case the transit was the new steam-powered ferry. In **1814 Robert Fulton's** invention, with financial backing from

Hezekiah Pierrepont, first connected the newly renamed **Fulton** Streets of New York and Brooklyn by fast boats, giving occasion to Pierrepont and others (**Middagh, Hicks, Remsen, Livingston**) for profitable division and sale of their heights **"farmland."** With the new ferry it was quicker and easier to go by water from **Fulton to Fulton** than to travel by omnibus on Manhattan Island. This status continued until the **New York and Harlem Railroad** provided a route to the northern "frontier": in **1832** horsecars linked the distant town of Harlem, and in **1837** steam trains crossed the Harlem River to Westchester. A **surveyor's grid** marked the Heights into **25 × 100**-foot lots as the system for parcel sales. Although other subdivisions were made by speculators, those dimensions remain the **basic module of the Heights.**

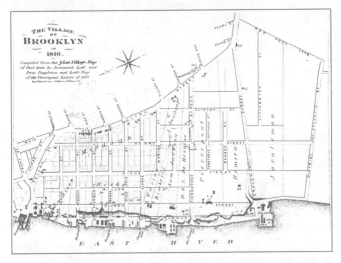

That the oldest building was built in **1820** (24 Middagh Street) is not surprising. Lots did not come on the market until **1819,** and even as late as **1807** there had been but **7 houses on the Heights,** with perhaps 20 more at or near the ferry landing at the river's edge below. By **1890** the infill was **substantially complete,** and the architectural history of the Heights primarily spans those **seventy** years. Occasional buildings were built much later in random locations, but the principal **pre-1890** urban fabric was still intact in 1965, when the district was designated a **historic district** under the city's newly enacted **Landmarks Preservation Law.** Vacant lots on Willow Place afforded architects Joseph and Mary Merz a chance to add buildings in serious modern architectural terms, but within the scale of the surrounding environment. These, plus a few others, have extended (with the approval of the **Landmarks Preservation Commission**) a previously **truncated architectural history** to the present: the others include Ulrich Franzen's building for the **Jehovah's Witnesses** on Columbia Heights [H 46.], Alfredo De Vido's brownbrick at 222 Columbia Heights [H 26a.], and a motley assortment of old and new residential buildings on Poplar Street by Wids de la Cour, David Hirsch, and Charles Platt [H 58.].

[H 1.] Brooklyn Heights Historic District, generally bounded on the W and N by the Brooklyn-Queens Expwy. and Cadman Plaza W., on the S by Atlantic Ave., on the E by Henry St. to Clark St., and an irregular line to Court St. and Atlantic Ave. ★

The **first** district to be designated (1965) under the **Landmarks Preservation Law**—a logical choice, as the Heights was the city's foremost, discrete and substantially intact enclave of architecture.

All the listings below **lie within** the historic district where noted with the district symbol. ☆

South Heights Walking Tour: A circuit that begins at Court and Remsen Streets (across from Borough Hall) and ends nearby at Livingston and Clinton Streets (subway to Borough Hall Station of the IRT Lexington and Seventh Avenue Lines or Court Street Station of the BMT).

[H 1a.] Originally **The Franklin Building,** 186 Remsen St., bet. Court and Clinton Sts. S. side. ca. 1890. Parfitt Bros.

One of four **Romanesque Revival-Queen Anne** red-brick extravaganzas in the vicinity by these fraternal architects. [Also see H 19a., H 19b., H 21a.]. Rock-face brownstone supports brick pilasters, large and small. Sturdy granite piers articulately support the entrance archway.

[H 1b.] Originally (1857–1895) **Brooklyn Gas Light Company Headquarters/**later (1895–1914) **Brooklyn Union Gas Company Headquarters/**now (since 1962) **McGarry Library, St. Francis College,** 180 Remsen St., bet. Court and Clinton Sts. S side. 1857.

A miraculously saved Tuscan-columned **classical temple** which has seen a variety of uses in its more than 130 years. The gas company moved next door in 1914 to:

[H 1c.] Originally (1914–1962) **Brooklyn Union Gas Company Headquarters/**now **St. Francis College,** 176 Remsen St., bet. Court and Clinton Sts. S side. 1914. Frank Freeman.

One of 3 downtown Brooklyn buildings with **classical colonnades** on the upper stories. Compare it with 110 Livingston Street and the Central Court Building [Civic Center/Downtown Brooklyn D 9a. and D 12b.]. The husky Tuscan columns at the entry are fluted and sport entasis, that delicate swelling of the column's profile that gave (and gives) so much visual strength to Greek temples.

At this point you enter the Brooklyn Heights Historic District.

[H 2a.] The Brooklyn Club, 131 Remsen St., bet. Clinton and Henry Sts. N side. ca. 1858. ☆

The paired **Corinthian** columns are a strong portal to this bland brownstone.

[H 1b.] Brooklyn Union Gas Company   **[H 2b.]** Portico, Brooklyn Bar Assn.

[H 2b.] Brooklyn Bar Association/formerly **Charles Condon residence,** 123 Remsen St., bet. Clinton and Henry Sts. N side. ca. 1875. ☆

Here are relatively **jazzy chromatics** of white limestone and dark red brick. It is an exuberant note on Remsen Street. Atop is a curved and slated mansard roof. The stonework is incised with Eastlake detail.

[H 2c.] Our Lady of Lebanon Roman Catholic Church (Maronite Rite)/originally **Church of the Pilgrims (Congregational),** 113 Remsen St., NE cor. Henry St. 1846. Richard Upjohn. ☆

Certainly, Upjohn was **avant-garde:** this has been called the earliest example of Romanesque Revival in this country, a bold massing of ashlar stonework, a solid, carven image. The spire was removed due to deterioration and the high cost of its replacement. The doors at both the

BROOKLYN HEIGHTS

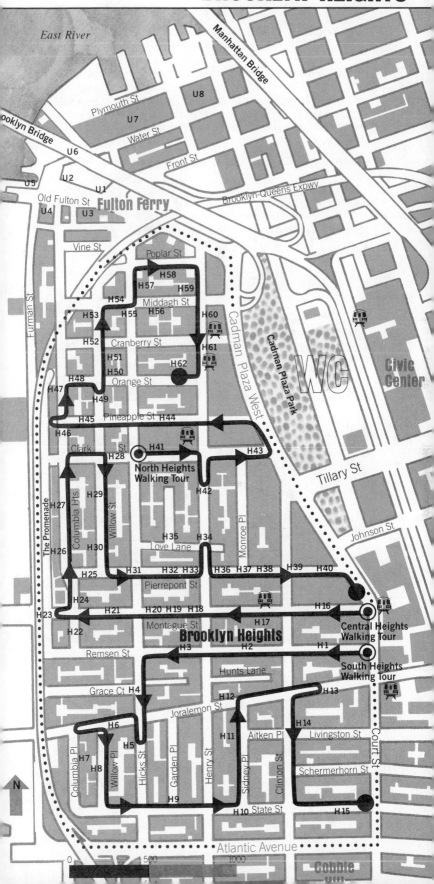

East River

Manhattan Bridge

Brooklyn Bridge

Plymouth St

U8

U7

Water St

Front St

U6

Brooklyn-Queens Expwy

U5

U2

U1

Old Fulton St

Fulton Ferry

U4

U3

Vine St

Poplar St

H58

H57

H59

H54

Middagh St

H53

H55

H56

H60

H52

Cranberry St

H61

H51

H62

H50

Orange St

H48

H49

H47

Pineapple St

H45

H44

H46

Clark St

H41

H28

North Heights Walking Tour

H43

H42

Columbia Hts

H29

H27

Willow St

H26

H30

H35

H34

Love Lane

Monroe Pl

The Promenade

H25

H31

H32 H33

H36 H37 H38

H39

H40

Pierrepont St

H24

H21

H20 H19 H18

H16

H23

H22

Montague St

H17

Brooklyn Heights

H2

H1

Central Heights Walking Tour

Remsen St

H3

South Heights Walking Tour

Hunts Lane

Grace Ct

H4

H12

H13

Joralemon St

H14

H6

H11

Aitken Pl

Livingston St

H5

Columbia Pl

H7

Willow Pl

Hicks St

Garden Pl

Henry St

Sidney Pl

Clinton St

Schermerhorn St

Court St

H8

H9

H10 State St

H15

N

0   500   1000

Atlantic Avenue

Cadman Plaza West

Cadman Plaza Park

WC

Civic Center

Tillary St

Johnson St

cobble

west and south portals were salvaged from the ill-fated liner *Normandie,* which burned and sank at its Hudson River berth in **1942.** Note the images of Norman churches and Norman-built ocean liners.

The **Church of the Pilgrims** moved in with Plymouth Church [H 62a.] in **1934,** and its **Tiffany windows** were moved to an annex, Hillis Hall, of the combined congregation.

[H 3a.] 70 Remsen Street (apartments), bet. Henry and Hicks Sts. S side. 1929. H. I. Feldman. ☆

Sturdy neo-Romanesque decorated arches over marble columns and spreading neo-Byzantine capitals give considerable style to a simple apartment block. Feldman similarly decorated the old Pierrepont Hotel [H 32a.].

[H 3b.] Exotic 87 Remsen Street house

[H 2c.] Original Church of the Pilgrims

[H 4c.] 14 Grace Ct. Alley carriage hse.

[H 4a.] Grace Church's entry courtyd.

[H 3b.] 87 Remsen Street, bet. Henry and Hicks Sts. N side. ca. 1890. ☆

An exotic brick mansion with a mélange of brownstone and terracotta detailing. Note the copper roof against the sky.

Turn left on Hicks Street.

[H 4a.] Grace Church, 254 Hicks St., SW cor. Grace Court. 1847. Richard Upjohn. **Parish House** to the west. 1931. ☆

After a **radical venture** completing the **Church of the Pilgrims** [H 2c.], **Upjohn** went **"straight,"** back to the more academic brownstone neo-Gothic. A bit of urban charm is the entrance court, off Hicks Street at the south side, leading to the parish house. A backwater for pedestrians, it is crowned by the **umbrella of a glorious elm** some 80 feet tall. Benches are available.

[H 4b.] Grace Court. W of Hicks St. ☆

Its charm originally derived from the **juxtaposition** of Grace Church and the double-deep backyards of Remsen Street's houses. In the 1960s the construction of a **banal** 6-story red-brick apartment building on some of those yards changed all that. The eastern half of this one-block **cul-de-sac** is still lovely.

[H 4c.] Grace Court Alley. E of Hicks St. ☆

A real mews (for Remsen Street and Joralemon Street mansions). A walk to its end and then a turnabout will reveal many delights not visible from Hicks Street. **No. 14**'s arched bearing wall of tooled brownstone is lusty. Many of these carriage houses still retain their iron **hay cranes,** some used today only for holding potted plants. Note the crisp **contrasting brownstone quoins** on Nos. **2** and **4.**

[H 4d.] 263 Hicks Street, bet. Joralemon St. and Grace Court Alley. E side. ca. 1860. Alterations ca. 1885. ☆

A Renaissance Revival brownstone up-styled in the 1880s with a new stoop, replete with Norman zigzag ornamentation, a rock-face brownstone frieze, and a dormered tile roof.

[H 5a.] 262-272 Hicks Street, SW cor. Joralemon St. ca. 1885. ☆

A **Shingle Style** terrace, designed as a group composition. The corbeled brickwork, shingles, and picturesque profiles are romantic: they confer an identity on the various occupants. Each is different from its neighbor but part of an **overall architectural composition.**

[H 5b.] Engine Company 224, N.Y.C. Fire Department, 274 Hicks St., bet. Joralemon and State Sts. W side. 1903. Adams & Warren. ☆

A **house** for fire engines **in scale** with its house neighbors. A Renaissance Revival building, with copper-clad dormers.

[H 5c.] 276-284 Hicks Street, bet. Joralemon and State Sts. W side. ☆

Five brick arches—two half-round, three half-ellipses—once swallowed carriages. Note the sculptured **woman's head** on the dormer of No. 276. More carriages resided across the street at Nos. **291** and **293.**

[H 5d.] 277-283 Hicks Street (apartments)/formerly **St. Charles Orthopedic Clinic,** bet. Joralemon and State Sts. Altered, 1921, 1985. ☆

A nonindustrial use of the spiral stair as a fire exit, a handsome and elegant form that **enriches the street.**

[H 6a.] 58 Joralemon Street, bet. Hicks St. and Willow Place. S side. ca. 1847. Converted to present use, 1908. ☆

The world's only **Greek Revival subway ventilator.** It permits release of air pressure built up by IRT Lexington Avenue Line express trains rushing through the East River tunnel, deep beneath Joralemon Street. And it affords stranded passengers an emergency exit to the surface.

[H 6b.] 29-75 Joralemon Street, bet. Hicks and Furman Sts. N side. 1844–1848. ☆

Twenty-five Greek Revival houses (several have been altered) step down Joralemon's hill. The row has a **pleasant rhythm,** with each pair stepping down roughly 30 inches from its neighbors. The missing tooth at **No. 33** is now being replaced by architects **Joseph** and **Mary Merz.**

[H 6c.] 25 Joralemon Street/formerly **High Pressure Fire Service, Main Pumping Station,** bet. Hicks and Furman Sts. N side. ☆

Before superpumper fire trucks were available, this served to increase the pressure in fire mains to reach high-rise fires. Now it has joined the myriad building types converted to co-ops and condominiums.

[H 7a.] Riverside (apartments), 4-30 Columbia Place, SW cor. Joralemon St. 1890. William Field & Son. ☆

On the river's side they stood, until **truncated** by the Brooklyn-Queens Expressway. The original contained a central garden, partially remaining between the extant units and the expressway's wall.

[H 7a.] The radical Riverside Apts.   **[H 5b.]** Engine Co. 224, N.Y.F.D.

Alfred T. White, a prominent and paternalistic Brooklyn businessman, whose motto was **"philanthropy plus 5 percent,"** commissioned these, as well as the Tower and Home buildings [see Cobble Hill C 4a., 4b., 4c.]. They are the **original** limited-profit housing, predating the City and State's first "limited-dividend" projects (Stuyvesant Town) by 57 years. White also was a major participant in the creation of **Forest Hills Gardens** [see Central Queens C 53.].

[H 7b.] 7-13 Columbia Place, bet. Joralemon and State Sts. E side. ☆

Four charming small and modest houses, whose porches give a friendly scale to the block.

Now back a few steps to Willow Place and turn right.

[H 8a.] 2-8 Willow Place, bet. Joralemon and State Sts. W side. ca. 1847. ☆

Gothic Revival detail decorates simple brick row houses. In the battle of the Revival styles, the basic plan and spatial arrangement of row houses were almost constant: their cornices, lintels, doorways, and portals are **the variables** that identify the Federal (1820s), Greek Revival (1830s), and Gothic Revival (1840s) styles. Many Federal houses were updated to the fashionable Greek Revival and, subsequently, from **Greek** to **Gothic.** The later Renaissance Revival houses had, however, both an extended plan and inflated volume.

[H 8b.] 26 Willow Place, bet. Joralemon and State Sts. W side. ca. 1880. ☆

A retired chapel that is now host to the **Roosa School of Music,** the **Heights Players,** and a nursery school. Ruskinian Gothic in the era of St. Ann's [H 13b.]

[H 8c.] 43-49 Willow Place, ca. 1846. ☆

This recently restored Greek Revival wood colonnade joins four town houses, from an era when **colonnades denoted class.**

[H 8d.] 40, 44, and 48 Willow Place, NW cor. State St. 1966. Joseph & Mary Merz. ☆

These 4 town houses (one is a double residence) gave new life to **Willow Place** while **respecting the scale and nature** of their older neighbors. Garages occupy ground-floor space; and cement block, in a special

8-inch-square size and used with sensitivity and imagination, assumes a dignity that most thoughtless users miss by a mile. Note the compact integration of garage, rear garden terrace, and handsome wood fence on the **State Street** side of **No. 48.**

Turn left on State Street.

[H 9.] Garden Place, bet. Joralemon and State Sts. ☆

A handsome urban space, one block long, contained on four sides. Note the terra-cotta, brick, and limestone Queen Anne at **No. 26,** the Hansel and Gretel carriage house **(No. 21),** the intruders from Queens **(Nos. 17, 19, 19a.),** and the lush lintels at **No. 34. Nos. 40** through **56** form a handsome terrace. Locals describe this as the **Scarsdale of Brooklyn Heights,** where the affluent nest in this **cul-de-sac.**

[H 8c.] 43–49 Willow Place. Brooklyn's last terrace of colonnaded houses

[H 8d.] Merz, Clyne, and Garment row houses, 48, 44, and 40 Willow Pl.

[H 10a.] 103-107 State Street, NW cor. Sidney Place. ca. 1848. ☆

A trio, but only **No. 107** still has the elegant cast-iron balcony that allows **French doors** to open to the parlor floor.

[H 10b.] 118 State Street, bet. Henry St. and Sidney Place. S side. Converted, 1980s, Eli Attia. ☆

A converted warehouse that displays a vast skylight in profile.

Turn left onto Sidney Place.

[H 10c.] Sidney Place, bet. State and Joralemon Sts. ☆

A more varied, more interesting version of Garden Place. Its architecture includes everything that Garden Place offers, while adding a church, **St. Charles Borromeo,** and such specialties as a 7-story Greek Revival house! The **front gardens** on the east side between **Aitken Place** and **State Street** are unusual [also see H 30b.].

[H 11a.] St. Charles Borromeo Church (Roman Catholic), 21 Sidney Place, NE cor. Aitken Place. 1869. P. C. Keely. ☆

A simplified brick Gothic Revival in maroon-painted brick. The plain interior is decorated with wood **Carpenter Gothic** arches and trim.

[H 11b.] 18 Sidney Place (apartments), opposite Aitken Place. W side. ca. 1838. ☆

At first glance it seems one has found the **world's first 7-story Greek Revival town house** (to match the world's only Greek Revival subway ventilator, around the corner). Three stories were added in the late nineteenth century to create a girl's residence.

Turn right on Joralemon Street.

[H 12a.] 135 Joralemon Street, bet. Henry and Clinton Sts. N side. ca. 1833. ☆

An opposite-hand plan from **24 Middagh Street** [see H 54.]. Their similarities are concealed by a post-Civil War cast-iron porch, and the house is dwarfed by two bulky later buildings.

[H 12a.] Rare wood Federal house   **[H 13b.]** Saint Ann's Episcopal Church

[H 12b.] 129 Joralemon Street, bet. Henry and Clinton Sts. N side. ca. 1891. C. P. H. Gilbert. ☆

A grandly scaled outpost of the **Chicago School** in Roman brick is sadly squeezed between a banal apartment building and a doctor's office more appropriate to Archie Bunker Land than to the Heights' urbane streets.

Turn right on Clinton Street.

[H 13a.] Packer Collegiate Institute, 170 Joralemon St., bet. Court and Clinton Sts. S side. 1854. Minard Lafever. Addition, 1957 (Katherine Sloane Pratt House), 1957. ☆

This is a parody of a British Victorian businessman's Gothick **castle.** The understated addition tries to remain a background neighbor. Collegiate only in the sense that it prepares students for college, not a college itself.

[H 13b.] Originally St. Ann's Church (Episcopal)/now **Auditorium of Packer Collegiate Institute,** Clinton St. NE cor. Livingston St. 1869. Renwick & Sands. ☆

Brownstone and terra-cotta of different colors and textures make an exuberant and unrestrained extravaganza. **Renwick** had produced more academically correct Gothic Revival churches at Manhattan's

Grace and **St. Patrick's**—perhaps by the time of St. Ann's his confidence had mushroomed. The copybooks of the **Pugins** used at **Grace** were discarded in favor of current architectural events, particularly the "new" museum at Oxford, by **Deane & Woodward,** designed and built with the eager assistance of theorist **John Ruskin**—hence **"Ruskinian Gothic."**

St. Ann's is a monumental but comforting presence on these tight, row-housed streets, its diminutive chapel adjacent forming an articulate transition to the Packer gym to the north.

[H 14.] 140-142 Clinton Street, bet. Joralemon St. and Aitken Place.ʼ W side. ca. 1855. ☆

Lintels and a cornice lush with volutes and garlands, both in **cast iron.** The detail and profiles survived well in comparison with those **carved** in erodible brownstone. It looks as if its many eyebrows were surveying St. Ann's Church across the street.

[H 15.] 168-170 State Street, bet. Clinton and Court Sts. S side. ca. 1890. ☆

Robust twin tenements with handsome bay windows from a time when architecture for the lower-income population was still **architecture.**

Home of the Excelsiors: A plaque on the carefully groomed row house at 133 Clinton Street, southeast corner of Livingston Street, identifies this building as the onetime clubhouse of the **Jolly Young Bachelors.** By 1854 that social club had evolved into the **Excelsiors,** an amateur baseball club with the distinction of having as their pitcher **James Creighton,** credited with having pitched the first **curve** ball! With the removal from Brooklyn first of the **Dodgers,** and then of their ball park, **Ebbets Field,** this brownstone remains one of the last vestiges of organized baseball in the borough.

END of South Heights Walking Tour: To reach the Borough Hall/ Court Street subway stations, return to Joralemon Street and walk one block east. If you are filled with energy, two other Brooklyn Heights walks follow. For a change of pace, respite, and refreshments, walk south to Atlantic Avenue [See **Cobble Hill**].

Central Heights Walking Tour: Starts and ends at Court and Montague Streets. (Subways to Borough Hall Station of the IRT Seventh Avenue and Lexington Avenue Lines, or east escalator of Court Street Station of the BMT local.)

Montague Street: Throughout the 19th century and until the end of World War II, this was the road to the Wall Street Ferry, dipping down the bluff to its wateredge terminal. Pier 4 now occupies that site. There were companion ferries to the north, the Fulton Ferry, and to the south at Atlantic Avenue, South Ferry. The latter is remembered in name only on its Manhattan end by the terminus of the IRT Seventh Avenue local.

A **stone bridge** by Minard Lafever **(1855)** and a later passerelle called the **"Penny Bridge,"** both located between Pierrepont Place and Montague Terrace, once carried the brow of the Heights over Montague Street's steep incline, with its appropriate **cable car** line.

Walk west on Montague Street.

[H 16a.] Crossland Savings Bank/originally **Brooklyn Savings Bank,** 205 Montague St., NW cor. Cadman Plaza W. 1962. Carson, Lundin & Shaw.

Urban renewal swallowed the Brooklyn Savings Bank's great **Frank Freeman** edifice that stood at the northeast corner of Pierrepont and Clinton Streets, his one exercise in **Roman pomp.** Freeman's eclectic palette produced the neo-**Renaissance** Crescent Athletic Club [see H 39.] and the great **avant-garde** Hotel Margaret (see Necrology).

Here the bank built a neat work that holds the three **street lines** it confronts, an important effort where Cadman Plaza Park tends to create an amorphous scene.

[H 16b.] Originally **National Title Guaranty Building,** 185 Montague St., bet. Cadman Plaza W. and Clinton St. N side. 1930. Corbett, Harrison & MacMurray. Entrance altered.

A bold early **Art Deco** building from the team that immediately after shared the design responsibility for Rockefeller Center. The bold **3-D** massing remains fresh to this day.

 [H 16c.] Citibank/originally **People's Trust Company,** 183 Montague St., bet. Cadman Plaza W. and Clinton St. N side. 1903. Mowbray & Uffinger. Pierrepont St. rear addition, 1929, Shreve, Lamb & Harmon.

This is a D. W. Griffith version of a **Roman temple.** The bank, unfortunately, is neither staffed nor patronized by **bacchanalian revel-** •**ers,** so that the total effect is a little wistful, like an abandoned movie set. Built of marble, not just wire lath and plaster, it provides a sense of security to its depositors . . . and who is now around to drive the moneylenders from the temple?

The sculpture in the pediment is unconscious **Pop Art,** particularly when overlaid with antipigeon spikes.

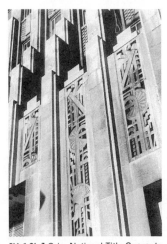 

[H 16b.] Orig. National Title Guaranty   [H 16d.] Manufacturers Hanover Trust

 [H 16d.] Manufacturers Hanover Trust Company/formerly **Brooklyn Trust Company,** 177 Montague St., NE cor. Clinton St. 1915. York & Sawyer.

The bottom and top of this rich Italian palace is copied from Verona's **Palazzo della Gran Guardia** (1610). In between the model was stretched vertically to supply more floors for commerce. Corinthian engaged columns rest on **rusticated** tooled limestone.

At this point you enter the Brooklyn Heights Historic District.

 [H 17a.] Originally **Franklin Trust Company (office building),** 164 Montague St., SW cor. Clinton St. 1891. George L. Morse. ☆

A granite, rock-face base, sunk within a moat, bears limestone arches and, in turn, brick and terra-cotta piers, columns, and arches. All are capped with a dormered red tile roof. A **gem.**

 [H 17b.] St. Ann's & the Holy Trinity (church)/originally **Holy Trinity Protestant Episcopal Church,** 157 Montague St., NW cor. Clinton St. 1847. Minard Lafever. Stained glass, William Jay Bolton. ☆

Brownstone, unfortunately, weathers poorly. Here the **New York Landmarks Conservancy** has lead the counterattack by citing this great neo-Gothic church as a **cause célèbre.** Concerts and theater of the **avant-garde** have aided its slow restoration, but with a citywide constituency that gives heart to serious landmark preservation and restoration.

The interior is cast and painted terra-cotta rather than carved stone, as it might appear at first glance. Reredos by **Frank Freeman.** The whole is, unfortunately, minus its original brownstone spire.

A bust of its controversial former pastor, John Howard Melish, by sculptor **William Zorach,** is bracketed from the north side of the entrance vestibule.

Montague, the shopping street: Only 4 blocks long, Montague is a chameleon in that short stretch: it serves residents of the Heights at its west and denizens of the Civic Center to the east. With astronomically rising rents, the local stalwarts have slowly been squeezed out in favor of **"chains"** or have been ensnared in real estate owners' fantasies about the potential profits of this chic center of Brooklyn. Empty stores stand cheek by jowl with the latest trendy boutique. Sadly, the successful repopulation of Brooklyn Heights by a conservative, family-oriented young and middle-aged middle class has brought with it flocks of conspicuously affluent yuppies, both resident and influxing by day. They have created a market along the street much like that of the Upper West Side's Columbus Avenue, itself a mercantile wasteland 15 years ago and now a Gold Coast for conspicuous spending (in boutiques, not barbershops). Montague trails that landlord's nirvana, happily, but aspires to the same fantasyland.

[H 17b.] St. Ann's/Holy Trinity Ch.

[H 21b.] Dutch gables crown casino

[H 18.] Montague Mews, NW cor. Montague and Henry Sts. Remodeled, 1987, Wronsky/Lehman. ☆

A simple commercial 2-story taxpayer has been Brooks Brothered: careful detail, somber colors, and neat lettering have transformed schlock disorder into the architectural equivalent of the gray flannel suit.

[H 19a.] The Berkeley/The Grosvenor, 111 and 115 Montague St., bet. Henry and Hicks Sts. N side. 1885. Parfitt Bros. ☆

Twin Queen Anne brownstone, terra-cotta, and brick apartment houses. Ground-floor shopfronts demean the wondrous architecture above; **look up!** There is a 2-story Parisian-style mansard roof up there.

[H 19b.] The Montague, 105 Montague St., bet. Henry and Hicks Sts. N side. 1902. Parfitt Bros. ☆

Another Queen Anne extravaganza. Here a brooding face peers down from its terra-cotta pediment, leaning over a **console bracket.**

[H 20.] Hotel Bossert, 98 Montague St., SE cor. Hicks St. 1909. Matching addition to S, 1912. Both by Helme & Huberty. ☆

Now a **Jehovah's Witnesses** hostel, this "modern" hotel was in the 1920s a fashionable center of New York social life. The **Marine Roof,** decorated in a yachting spirit by designer **Joseph Urban,** offered dining, dancing, and an unequaled view of the Manhattan skyline. The home of its founder, millwork manufacturer, **Louis Bossert,** still stands [see N Brooklyn/Bushwick-Ridgewood B 11.].

[H 21a.] The Arlington, 62 Montague St., bet. Hicks St. and Montague Terr. S side. ca. 1900. Attributed to Parfitt Bros. ☆

And yet another apartment house. These three complexes [see H 19a., 19b.] were the **modest housing** of the **middle class** at a time when grand brownstones on adjacent Pierrepont and Remsen Streets housed single families and their servants. Shopkeepers, foremen, and others lived here next to the upper-income families of the **Heights.** Note the corner tower for the resident **Rapunzel.**

[H 21b.] The Heights Casino, 75 Montague St., bet. Hicks St. and Pierrepont Place. N side. 1905. Boring & Tilton. ☆

Its founders described this **indoor** squash and tennis club as a **"country club in the city."** A handsome stepped gable dominates; the rich brickwork was later copied in the adjacent 200 Hicks Street. This apartment house stands on the former site of the Casino's **outdoor** tennis courts; the members required that architectural unity be retained as a condition for selling the land.

Boring also designed the major buildings of the Ellis Island immigration station.

[H 22.] 1-13 Montague Terrace, bet. Remsen and Montague Sts. ca. 1886. ☆

A complete **terrace** in the English sense: a **set** of row houses. It is another urbane remnant greater than the sum of its parts. Thomas Wolfe wrote *Of Time and the River* here in 1933–1935. The cornice holds the whole block together.

Take a detour to see the Manhattan skyline.

[H 23.] The Esplanade, W of Montague Terr., Pierrepont Place, and Columbia Heights, bet. Remsen and Orange Sts. 1950–1951. Andrews, Clark & Buckley, engineers. Clarke & Rapuano, landscape architects. ☆

The **Promenade,** as it is known locally, is a fringe benefit from the construction of this section of the Brooklyn-Queens Expressway, at first proposed by Robert Moses to bisect the Heights along Henry Street. A **cantilevered esplanade**—one of the few brilliant solutions for the relationship of auto, pedestrian, and city—was projected from the crest of the Heights to overlook the harbor on a fourth level, over two levels of highway and a service road (Furman Street) for the piers below. It is simple and successful: mostly hexagonal asphalt paving block, painted steel railings, hardy shrubbery, and honey locust trees. The lesson was most recently and happily repeated at the Battery Park City Esplanade.

Return to the street and turn left on Pierrepont Place.

[H 24.] Originally **Alexander M. White and Abiel Abbot Low residences,** 2 and 3 Pierrepont Place, bet. Pierrepont and Montague Sts. W side. 1857. Frederick A. Peterson. ☆

The most **elegant** brownstones remaining in New York, two of an original three, all by the architect of **Cooper Union.** No. 1, the **Henry E. Pierrepont** residence, was demolished in 1946 in favor of a playground at the time of the esplanade-expressway construction.

Alfred Tredway White, Brooklyn philanthropist (Tower and Home and Riverside Apartments and the Botanical Garden's Japanese Garden), was born and brought up at **No. 2.**

Seth Low, father of **Abiel,** was a New Englander who made a killing in the **China trade.** Seth Low, son of **Abiel,** was mayor of Brooklyn, president of Columbia College, and then mayor of a consolidated New York lived at **No. 3.**

A peek at Pierrepont Street and then back onto Columbia Heights.

[H 25a.] Originally **Mrs. Hattie I. James residence,** 6 Pierrepont St., bet. Pierrepont Place and Willow St. S side. ca. 1890. Parfitt Bros. ☆

Romanesque Revival with a strong, rock-face brownstone stair, elaborate foliate carved reliefs, and a bay window, **overlooking** the bay.

[H 25b.] 8-14 Pierrepont Street, bet. Pierrepont Place and Hicks St. S side. ca. 1901. ☆

Another **terrace** where the whole is greater than the sum of its parts. The bow windows form a gracious breast for these English town houses.

[H 26a.] 222 Columbia Heights, NW cor. Pierrepont St. 1982. Alfredo De Vido Assocs. ☆

Brown, glazed modern brick, with torii (rounded moldings) to assuage its Renaissance Revival flank. The bay window and garage door spoil this **hearty attempt** at landmark infill.

[H 26a.] Alfredo De Vido's brown infill apartments at 222 Columbia Heights

[H 26b.] 210–220 Columbia Heights: the best remaining brownstone group

[H 26b.] 210-220 Columbia Heights, bet. Pierrepont and Clark Sts. W side. 1852–1860. ☆

Two pairs and two singles. Altered, but the best remaining examples of group mansions in brownstone; some have been painted light colors. Note **No. 210's** rich Corinthian capitals and also the varied mansard roofs and dormers, which create a picturesque silhouette.

[H 27a.] 145 Columbia Heights, bet. Pierrepont and Clark Sts. E side. ca. 1845. ☆

Exquisite Corinthian columns on a simple brick volume.

[H 27b.] 160 Columbia Heights (apartments), SW cor. Clark St. 1937. A. Rollin Caughey. ☆

An orange brick Art Deco/Art Moderne work with corner casement windows overlooking grand views of Manhattan.

Turn right up Clark Street.

[H 28.] Originally **Leverich Towers Hotel**/now **Jehovah's Witnesses Residence Hall,** 25 Clark St., NE cor. Willow St. 1928. Starrett & Van Vleck. ☆

Comfortably affluent materials borrowed from Romanesque architectural history: brick over random ashlar stonework over granite, with lots of molded terra-cotta decoration. The 4 **arched and colonnaded towers** were once **spotlighted** nightly after sunset.

Turn right again onto Willow Street.

[H 29a.] Dansk Sømandskirke, 102 Willow St., bet. Clark and Pierrepont Sts. W side. ☆

A brownstone **happily converted** into the Danish Seamen's Church.

Willow Street offers a variety of buildings, all of which together form an urban allée of happy variations. Buildings of note other than those described below include **No. 104,** a shingled remnant, gray and white, with a Federal fanlight; **No. 106,** with interesting Eastlake incised lintels; **Nos. 118, 120, 122,** with neo-Gothic window hoods and cast-iron railings; **No. 124,** with a stepped neo-Amsterdam gable and weather vane; and **No. 149,** a vigorous tenement, bay-windowed and reclaimed.

[H 29b.] Originally **S. E. Buchanan residence,** 109 Willow St., bet. Clark and Pierrepont Sts. E side. 1905. Kirby, Petit & Green. ☆

This neo-Federal house is gross, with fat columns, ill-proportioned window panes and muntins, crudely cast concrete lintels, and thick joints in the brickwork. People who embrace what they believe to be **archaeology** often **miss the point** of the styles they wish to emulate [as at H 30b.].

[H 29a.] 102 and 104 Willow Street   **[H 29c.]** The Shingle Style in Brooklyn

[H 29c.] 108, 110, and 112 Willow Street, bet. Clark and Pierrepont Sts. W side. ca. 1880. ☆

The **Shingle Style** in Brooklyn. Picturesque massing and profiles produce odd internal spaces and balconies for our contemporary fun. Terra-cotta reliefs, elaborate doorways, bay windows, towers, and dormers. The English architect **Richard Norman Shaw** (1831–1912) was group leader for these fantasies; in his bailiwick he produced what was strangely termed **Queen Anne.** This is New York's finest example.

Queen Anne: A style of English architecture introduced to this country in the British pavilion at the 1876 **Philadelphia Centennial Exposition,** it remained popular for some twenty years. Its name is deceiving. Queen Anne of England died in 1714, a century and a half before the style was so dubbed, but it was during her 12-year reign that some of the **Gothic** and **Renaissance** elements found in this romantic style were earlier revived.

[H 30a.] 151 Willow Street, bet. Clark and Pierrepont Sts. E side. ca. 1870. ☆

Allegedly a link in the **underground railroad,** it is aligned with an earlier town plan, set back and skewed.

[H 30b.] 155-159 Willow Street, bet. Clark and Pierrepont Sts. E side. ca. 1829. ☆

Three elegant Federal houses equal to **No. 24 Middagh** [H 54.] but in brick. The glass pavers set into **No. 157**'s sidewalk bear an apocryphal tale that they skylit a tunnel leading to **No. 151,** which served the **underground railroad** leading slaves to northern freedom. The three houses are **askew** from Willow Street as they were built to the earlier geometry of Love Lane, which once extended this far west.

Take a left onto Pierrepont Street.

[H 31a.] 35 Pierrepont Street (apartments), bet. Willow and Hicks Sts. N side. 1929. Mortimer E. Freehof. ☆

The roofscape and silhouette of this apartment block have all stops pulled out. A pleasantly synthetic—or is it **precocious**—Post Modern, bag of tricks?

[H 31b.] 36 Pierrepont Street (apartments), bet. Willow and Hicks Sts. S side. 1846. ☆

A freestanding neo-Gothic house and garden. Its newly recreated Pierrepont Street stoop has recently reincarnated ogees and trefoils.

[H 32a.] Originally Hotel Pierrepont, 55 Pierrepont St., bet. Hicks and Henry Sts. N side. 1928. H. I. Feldman. ☆

From the days when even speculative hotels bore lion finials and griffin gargoyles. Now a neatly maintained home for the elderly. See 70 Remsen Street for more Feldman neo-Romanesque.

[H 32b.] The Woodhull, 62 Pierrepont St., bet. Hicks and Henry Sts. S side. 1911. George Fred Pelham. ☆

The dowdy ground floor belies the extravagant Belle Époque Parisian architecture above. Had it been built in London, it would be Edwardian.

[H 30b.] 157 Willow Street entrance   **[H 33.]** Orig. Herman Behr residence

[H 33.] 84 Pierrepont Street/originally **Herman Behr residence/** later **Palm Hotel/**later **Franciscan House of Studies/**now a **residential condominium.** SW cor. Henry St. 1890. Frank Freeman. ☆

After Behr, this mansion had a **profane** and then **sacred** existence prior to being converted in 1977 into apartments. In the Palm Hotel's declining years it was said to have housed the local **Xaviera Hollander** and her lovelies. It then served as a residence for Franciscan brothers. Despite the structure's social vagaries, **Freeman's** design remains a distinguished monument on the Heights streetscape.

[H 34a.] 161 Henry Street (apartments), NE cor. Pierrepont St. 1906. Schneider & Herter. ☆

A **peer** of 62 Pierrepont. In the last **40** years, the external appearance and the view from **without** have been of little or no concern. Interior decoration and a view from within are the requirements. For most architects the **citizen** of the street is **eyeless.** This vigorous building's strong character shows that architecture was once part of the resident's basic needs. Here it bestows identity to the occupants in the process, as does Manhattan's **Dakota.**

A short one-block detour to the left to Love Lane.

[H 34b.] 137, 141, 143 Henry Street, bet. Pierrepont and Clark Sts. E side. 1870s. ☆ No. 143 restored, 1987, Susan Podufaly.

Three of a former **quartet.** Their restored painted clapboard splendor modulates the street, with bay windows and porches reinforcing the rhythm of the stoops.

[H 35.] Love Lane and **College Place,** both in the block bet. Henry and Hicks Sts. N of Pierrepont St. ☆

The names of these two **byways** are more charming than the reality, but the mystery is worth a detour. Note that Love Lane is skewed from the grid's rectilinear geometry.

[H 36a.] 104 Pierrepont Street/originally **Thomas Clark residence,** bet. Henry and Clinton Sts. S side. 1856. ☆

A brownstone row-mansion. Note the ornate console brackets and the verdigris bronze railing atop the majestic stoop.

[H 36b.] 108 Pierrepont Street/originally **P. C. Cornell house,** at Monroe Place. S side. 1840. ☆

The harried remains of a great **Greek Revival** double house; the only original part is the **anthemion-ornamented** pediment over the front door. Once two stories and basement, it was raised to three and a post-Civil War cornice was added.

[H 36c.] 114 Pierrepont Street/originally **George Cornell residence,** later **Alfred C. Barnes residence,** at Monroe Place. S side. 1840. Totally altered, 1887. Further remodeled, 1912. ☆

Once the **siamese** twin of **No. 108,** this was "**modernized**" in 1887 for publisher Barnes, a transmogrification of staggering impact. A simple brick building became a **Wagnerian** stage set: Romanesque Revival with some random eclectic tricks thrown in. Aside from its melodramatic architectural history, its social history includes use as a residence, as the **Brooklyn Women's Club** (after 1912), as a **Christian Science Church,** and, most recently, the fate of most if not all venerable buildings: condominiums.

Monroe Place: A 700-foot-long, 80-foot-wide space, a quiet backwater on axis with the Cornell house described above. The **proportions** of the street and its containment at both ends are far more important than the buildings that line it; for this, like **Sidney, Garden,** and **Willow** Places, is the product of the **staggered grid** that fortuitously made this area so much richer than most of grid-planned Manhattan or Brooklyn. Do take a look at two houses at the north end: **No. 3** (1849), with its later cast-iron planter and goldfish pond; and **No. 12** (1847), where shutters have been returned to the facade.

[H 36d.] Appellate Division, N.Y.S. Supreme Court, Monroe Place, NW cor. Pierrepont St. 1938. Slee & Bryson. ☆

A prim and proper freestanding **Classical Revival** monument of the 1930s, with a pair of powerful **Doric** columns confronting Monroe Place. This is the sort of building that fell into disrepute under **modernists'** manifestos but is now pleasantly admired, if not embraced.

[H 37.] First Unitarian Church/properly **Church of the Saviour,** Pierrepont St. NE cor. Monroe Place. 1844. Minard Lafever. ☆

Lafever, a carpenter by training, was a talented and prolific architect who practiced in many styles (including an **Egyptian Revival** church in Sag Harbor). He wrote a well-known and well-used copybook for builders, *The Beauties of Modern Architecture.* The cast-iron fence is guarded by 6 **crenellated** castelets.

[H 38.] Brooklyn Historical Society/originally **Long Island Historical Society,** 128 Pierrepont St., SW cor. Clinton St. 1881. George B. Post, architect. Olin Levi Warner, facade sculptures. ★ ☆ Interior ★. **Open to the public.**

Post used a bright but narrow range of **Italian reds** at a time when earth colors were popular, from the polychromy of **Ruskin** [see H 13b.] to the near-monochromy of **Richardsonian Romanesque,** such as the Jay Street Firehouse [D 7.].

Note the tower over the entrance stair, hall, and elevator, bearing a **slate-sheathed** pyramid. The monochromatic palette here tempers an exuberant range of detail: pilasters, arches, medallions, cornices, and sculpture. At the entrance a **Viking** and an **Indian** flank the doors over Corinthian pilasters.

This is one of the city's great architectural treasures, both outside and in. There are usually small exhibits and always a great local history collection.

[H 34a.] 161 Henry St. apartments   **[H 36d.]** Appellate Div., Supreme Ct.

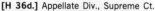

[H 37.] Unitarian Ch. of the Saviour   **[H 38.]** The Brooklyn Historical Society

[H 39.] St. Ann's School/originally **Crescent Athletic Club,** 129 Pierrepont St., NW cor. Clinton St. 1906. Frank Freeman. ☆

Once one of Brooklyn's most prestigious men's clubs, it boasted a swimming pool, squash courts, gym, and three grand 2-story spaces surrounded by mezzanines. After the club folded in 1940, it served as an office building until 1966, when St. Ann's Episcopal Church School bought and remodeled it.

[H 40.] One Pierrepont Place (office tower) a.k.a. **Morgan Stanley Building,** Pierrepont St. bet. Clinton St. and Cadman Plaza W. N side. 1988. Haines Lundberg Waehler.

Brobdingnag comes to Lilliput. This **behemoth** not only looms over the Heights but has become an obese silhouette to much of Brooklyn. The mansarded crest gives a flashy hat to this dumpy matron.

END of Central Heights Walking Tour: If you are hungry, Montague Street's eateries are only a block away, as is the BMT local Court Street subway station at Montague and Clinton Streets. The IRT is a block further east, at Court.

[H 40.] Morgan Stanley office building

[H 41a.] Orig. St. George Hotel in 1967

[H 42a.] The First Presbyterian Church

[H 44.] 70 Pineapple Street condos

North Heights Walking Tour: Of the three walks through Brooklyn Heights this offers the greatest contrasts: old and very new, affluent and modest, tiny and large, domestic and institutional.

START on the southwest corner of Clark and Hicks Streets, less than a block west of the IRT Seventh Avenue Station turnstiles within the old St. George Hotel arcade. Walk east along Clark Street across from the old hotel, take a brief detour south into Henry Street, and then return to Clark and continue east.

[H 41a.] Originally St. George Hotel, bet. Hicks and Henry Sts., Clark and Pineapple Sts. 1885. Augustus Hatfield. Additions, 1890–1923, Montrose W. Morris & others. **Tower Building,** 1930. Emery Roth. ☆

The contrasts of the **North Heights** are properly introduced by those of the old **St. George,** a set of architectural **accretions** that occupies a full city block, and that once was the city's **largest** hotel (with

2,632 rooms). Now divided into separate properties, the oldest buildings, opposite **52 Clark Street,** are abandoned; the **Tower Building** (111 Hicks Street) has become a towering condominium. Other segments are in various stages of development (the 70 Pineapple Street building is also a co-op). The **St. George,** the **Bossert,** the **Standish Arms,** and the **Towers** served Brooklyn and lower Manhattan as topnotch hostelries up to World War II; the last three are now **Jehovah's Witnesses** residences, and the St. George **Hotel** holds on only as the corner **Weller** building at 100 Hicks Street, over the subway entrance at Clark and Henry.

[H 41b.] Clark Lane (apartments), 52 Clark St., bet. Hicks and Henry Sts. S side. ca. 1927. Slee & Bryson. ☆

Eclectic architects found a **style** for every occasion. These, later the designers of the **Appellate Courthouse** [see H 36d.], chose a Romanesque arcade and Gothic gargoyles for this apartment hotel.

[H 43.] Cadman Towers & town hses.   **[H 46.]** Jehovah's Witnesses annex

[H 42a.] First Presbyterian Church, 124 Henry St., S of Clark St. W side. 1846. W. B. Olmsted. Memorial doorway, 1921, James Gamble Rogers. ☆   **[H 42b.] German Evangelical Lutheran Zion Church/** originally **Second Reformed Dutch Church.** 1840. ☆

These two churches occupy sites almost opposite each other. The **Presbyterian** is solid, stolid, and self-satisfied. The **Lutheran** is spare, prim, and denuded of its northern spire. Sometimes a single **thistle** can be more rewarding than a **bouquet of roses.**

The route around Cadman Towers and through Pineapple Walk takes you briefly outside the Brooklyn Heights Historic District.

[H 43.] Cadman Towers, 101 Clark St., bet. Henry St. and Cadman Plaza W. N side; 10 Clinton St., at Cadman Plaza W. W side; plus row housing along Clark St., Monroe Place, and Cadman Plaza W. 1973. Glass & Glass and Conklin & Rossant.

Urban renewal, usually a disastrous incision into the city's fabric, was tempered here by an especial concern with urban design: low-rise town house elements form facades that here bridge the scale from the **towers** proper to the contiguous 19th-century **Heights** streetscape. Tower and town houses alike are clad in handsome and well-detailed concrete and ribbed concrete-block.

Turn left at Cadman Plaza West and left again into the pedestrian mall called Pineapple Walk. Continue west along Pineapple Street itself (back into the Historic District), through the dark backside of the St. George Hotel's original block, its rear mysteriously more intriguing than its bland Clark Street facade.

[H 44.] 70 Pineapple Street (condominiums), bet. Hicks and Henry Sts. S side. ☆

A renovated **segment of the old St. George Hotel,** cleaned of its dour gray paint down to the roseate brick. A gracious improvement of this somber street.

[H 45.] 13 Pineapple Street (residence), bet. Willow St. and Columbia Heights. N side. ca. 1830. ☆

An unusually wide, gray-shingled, freestanding, white-trimmed single house **redolent** of these North Heights days before the masons took over.

[H 46.] Jehovah's Witnesses Dormitory and Library Facility, 119 Columbia Heights, SE cor. Pineapple St. 1970. Ulrich Franzen & Assocs. ☆

An early and sensitive design under the new **Landmarks Law.** The three row-house facades south of this new building are integrated internally with the new structure. The stoops, with entries now closed off, are therefore no longer functional but still add to the **visual enrichment** of the block. Prior to the designation of the **Heights** as a historic district, row houses like these were wantonly destroyed by the same organization to build **Nos. 124** and **107** further along the street.

If you haven't savored the lower Manhattan skyline from these bluffs, cross Columbia Heights and walk to the right along the Promenade. The tour picks up one block north at:

[H 47.] Jehovah's Witnesses Residence, 107 Columbia Heights, SE cor. Orange St. 1960. Frederick G. Frost, Jr., & Assoc. ☆

One of a number of pre-Landmarks Law high-rise dormitories that proliferated in the Heights for these proselytizers of their faith. Relatively new buildings such as this, and older ones remodeled for the sect's needs, are concentrated along Columbia Heights and nearby streets. Local residents continue to fear that too much of the Heights is being gobbled up for the **Witnesses'** seemingly endless expansion.

[H 48.] The Margaret (apartments) 97 Columbia Heights, NE cor. Orange St. 1988. The Ehrenkrantz Group & Eckstut. ☆

This new apartment house (purchased by Jehovah's Witnesses) fills the site of the great **Hotel Margaret** by Frank Freeman (**1889**). Under extensive renovation as condominium apartments, that magnificent structure [see Necrology] burned disastrously in **1980.** The replacement has been the subject of a major legal and landmarks battle. City zoning laws, in tandem with the Historic District designation, limit the height of new construction to **50** feet. Here the owner pleaded that because his distinguished landmark building had been vastly taller, and its economics based upon that, he should be allowed to replace its bulk. A **compromise** allows something in between. Too orange/too green.

[H 48.] Freeman's Margaret (demol.) **[H 48.]** The Margaret apartments

[H 49.] 70 Willow Street/originally **Adrian van Sinderen residence,** bet. Orange and Pineapple Sts. W side. ca. 1839. ☆

A wide **Greek Revival** house, originally freestanding, now **cheek by jowl** with **Jehovah's Witnesses** to the north. Former owners filled the southern gap with a set-back-from-street stair tower. Stage designer **Oliver Smith** rescued this from the Red Cross, to whom it had been bequeathed, restoring its **multipaned** windows and making other corrections.

[H 50.] **54 Willow Street (apartments),** bet. Orange and Cranberry Sts. W side. 1987. Alfredo De Vido Assocs. ☆

A simplistic infill of a vacant lot, here appearing neither old nor new—nor particularly noticeable. The columns are nice to have but naive.

[H 51a.] **57 Willow Street/**originally **Robert White residence,** NE cor. Orange St. ca. 1824. ☆

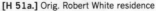

The **Orange** Street wall is a lusty composition of real and blind windows, chimneys, and pitched roofs. But much of it is clothed in dense ivy in the summer, perhaps adding a subtle **suggestive dress** to the **naked form.**

[H 50.] The 48 Willow St. apartments   **[H 51a.]** Orig. Robert White residence

[H 52.] 19 Cranberry Street in a vista looking southward along Willow Street

[H 51b.] **47-47A Willow Street (residences),** bet. Orange and Cranberry Sts. E side. ca. 1860. ☆

The **apocrypha** here state that there were two daughters and one site, riven to create a half for each. The internal guts are complicated by the need for tucking a stair into each 12-foot-wide unit.

[H 52.] **13, 15,** and **19 Cranberry Street (residences),** NW cor. Willow St. ca. 1829–1834. ☆

Greek Revival houses modernized, most extravagantly at **No. 19.** Here a mansard roof made this a fashionable grande dame when the spare classicism of the early nineteenth century gave way to elaboration. The **Empire** gown acquired a **sturdy bodice and a bustle.**

[H 53.] **20-26 Willow Street (residences),** SW cor. Middagh St. 1846. ☆

No-nonsense Greek Revival, this painted brick and brownstone **terrace** is straightforward, austere, yet elegant. The 2-story porches at the rear look out upon the harbor, their views framed by projecting masonry walls. **Henry Ward Beecher** lived at **No. 22.**

[H 53.] The two-story porches of 20–26 Willow Street overlook the harbor

[H 54.] 24 Middagh Street/formerly **Eugene Boisselet residence,** SE cor. Willow St. 1824. ☆

The **queen** of Brooklyn Heights houses (**Nos. 2** and **3** Pierrepont Place are the twin kings): a wood-painted, **gambrel-roofed** Federal house with a garden cottage connected by a garden wall. Note especially the exquisite **Federal doorway** with its **Ionic** colonnettes and the quarter-round attic windows. Proportion, rhythm, materials, and color are **in concert** throughout.

Having turned the corner into Middagh Street, continue east.

[H 55.] Middagh Street, bet. Willow and Hicks Sts. ca. 1817. ☆

One of the earliest streets on the Heights, it contains most of the remaining wood houses. Aside from the glorious **No. 24,** they are now a motley lot: **No. 28,** 1829, mutilated beyond recognition; **No. 30,** 1824, Federal entrance and pitched roof still recognizable in spite of the tawdry asphalt shingles; **No. 25,** 1824, mutilated; **No. 27,** 1829, early Italianate here in wood shingles with painted trim; **No. 29,** similar to 27; **Nos. 31** and **33,** 1847, mutilated.

[H 56.] 56 Middagh Street (residence), bet. Hicks and Henry Sts. S side. 1829. Porch added, ca. 1845. ☆

Bold Doric columns provide both **guts** and **style,** with a rather **blatant** blue body behind.

[H 57a.] Originally **Joseph Bennett residence,** 38 Hicks St. ca. 1830. Restored, 1976. **[H 57b.]** Originally **Michael Vanderhoef residence,** 40 Hicks St. ca. 1831. Restored, 1976. **[H 57c.] 38A Hicks Street (residence),** behind No. 38. All bet. Middagh and Poplar Sts. W side. ☆

An urbane trio now happily restored. The alley leading to **No. 38A** is effectively their common ground, a dense city's private street of identity, as are **Patchin** and **Milligan** Places in Greenwich Village.

The block between Poplar, Hicks, and Henry Streets and the Expressway (referred to by technocrats as Block **207**) contains an interesting new and reconditioned residential enclave comprising a **tenement,** an **orphan asylum,** a former **flophouse,** and modern infillings—all under one developer's sponsorship:

[H 58a.] 55 Poplar Street, bet. Hicks and Henry Sts. N side. 1987. Wids de la Cour and David Hirsch. ☆ **[H 58b.]** Originally **Brooklyn Children's Aid Society Orphanage**/now **apartments,** 57 Poplar St., bet. Hicks and Henry Sts. N side. 1883. Restored, 1987, Wids de la Cour and David Hirsch. ☆

Built as a home for **indigent newsboys,** this ornate Victorian pile was abandoned during the urban renewal craze of the **1960s**—it was then being used as a machine works—before adaptive reuse tardily came to it in the late **1980s**. The heavy hands that razed the blocks between Henry Street and Cadman Plaza, Poplar and Clark Streets, spared this odd gem and the candy factory [H 59.] to the south.

[H 58c.] 61-75 Poplar Street, bet. Hicks and Henry Sts. N side. 1987. Charles A. Platt Partners. ☆

A modern row recapturing some—but only some—of the appropriate scale and detail of the Heights. The remodeled units at the corner of Henry Street had been the former branch of the **Bowery-in-Brooklyn,** a minimal overnight bunkhouse for the homeless (restored, 1987, Wids de la Cour and David Hirsch).

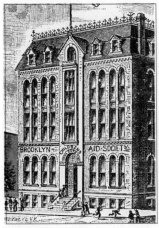

[H 58b.] Bklyn. Children's Aid Society   **[H 59.]** Henry Street Studios building

[H 59.] Henry Street Studios/originally **Mason Au & Magenheimer Candy Company,** 20 Henry St., NW cor. Middagh St. 1885. Theobald Engelhardt. Reconstructed, 1975. Pomeroy, Lebduska Assocs., architects. Martyn and Don Weston, associate architects. ☆

A light industrial building of **mill** construction. Its bold brick bearing walls, timber columns, and heavy plank flooring provide loft space for real and would-be artists. The north facade is designer **Lee Pomeroy**'s modern face where a blank wall formerly stood. **Mouthwatering** memories for older sweet teeth are conjured by the repainted lettering on the south facade: **Peaks** and **Mason Mints.**

[H 60a.] Cadman Plaza North (apartments), 140 Cadman Plaza W., N of Middagh St. W side. 1967. **[H 60b.] Whitman Close (town houses),** 33-43, 47-53, 55-69 Cadman Plaza W., S of Middagh St. W side. **[H 60c.] Whitman Close (apartments),** 75 Henry St., at Orange St. E side. **[H 60d.] Pineapple Walk,** Pineapple Walk bet. Henry St. and Cadman Plaza W. N. side only. 1968. All by Morris Lapidus & Assocs.

These early, ungainly urban renewal projects attempted to heal the **urban wound** left by the **excision** of Cadman Plaza from the cityscape. The removal of elevated lines was a civilized advance, but it was accompanied by the demolition of blocks of sturdy Heights-scaled buildings. **Token row houses** (Whitman Close) and a grilled garage (Cadman Plaza North) matching the height, if not the scale, of the other side of the street, were the prosthetics. They fail, however, to define the intervening streets as **urban spaces** (rather than simply surfaces on which autos navigate), one of the principal qualities of the **Heights.** They are as inappropriate as a **Greek Revival** house from **Willow Street** would be on an acre in Scarsdale.

[H 61.] The Cranlyn (apartments), 80 Cranberry St., SW cor. Henry St. 1931. H. I. Feldman. ☆

Art Deco on the Heights. Here the style presents glazed terracotta bas-reliefs, a bronze-plaque fantasy over the entrance, and jazzy brickwork [see also H 27b.]. Feldman contributed two other multiple dwellings of interest to the Heights, both with Romanesque detail: 55 Pierrepont [see H 32a.] and 70 Remsen [H 3a.].

[H 62a.] Plymouth Church of the Pilgrims/originally **Plymouth Church,** Orange St. bet. Henry and Hicks Sts. N side. 1849. Joseph C. Wells. **[H 62b.] Parish House and connecting arcade,** 75 Hicks St., NE cor. Orange St. 1914. Woodruff Leeming. ☆

Henry Ward Beecher preached here from **1847** to **1887**. Excepting the porch, his church was an **austere brick box of a barn** on the exterior, articulated by relieving arches. (The **Tuscan** porch was added long after Beecher left.) The parish house, of an **eclectic** Classical Revival, happily encloses—together with its connecting arcade—a handsome garden court. Here Beecher, as seen through the eyes and hands of sculptor **Gutzon Borglum,** holds forth—or perhaps holds **court.** Unfortunately, in this era of vandalism, the churchyard, which could be a pleasant place of repose, is locked.

In **1934** the Congregational **Church of the Pilgrims** abandoned its own church building, which is now today **Our Lady of Lebanon** [see H 2c.], and merged with Plymouth Church, causing the combined renaming. The **Pilgrims'** Tiffany windows were relocated at that time to Hillis Hall, behind **Plymouth.**

[H 62a.] Originally Henry Ward Beecher's Plymouth Church of the Pilgrims

[H 62b.] 1914 Plymouth Parish Hse.   **[H 62b.]** Henry Ward Beecher statue

END of North Heights Walking Tour: The nearest subways are the IRT Seventh Avenue Line in the St. George Hotel or, via the Whitman Close town houses at Cranberry Street, the IND Eighth Avenue Line. If your legs are still nimble you may wish to visit the **Fulton Ferry District,** the waterfront, and the dramatic view of the **Brooklyn Bridge** as it leaps across the waters of the East River.

This flat riverfront beneath the **Heights** might well be termed **Brooklyn Bottoms.** The shore of these tidal waters, it was the natural place for a ferry landing, bringing hardy New Yorkers to the rural wilds of Long Island and exporting the produce of lush, flat Long Island farms to the **city.** Rowers and **sailors** plied across this narrow link at first, a tenuous connection because of shifting tides and winds. And in **1776** it became the unhappy port of embarkation for Washington's troops fleeing Long Island under cover of darkness and fog after their defeat in the **Revolution's** first major battle. The first steam-powered ferry came in 1814 and, with it, an ever-increasing flow of ferry traffic that was honored by a **grand Victorian** ferry house in **1865.** After **1883,** with the opening of the new **New York and Brooklyn Bridge,** which still looms over this edgewater, the area was doomed as a commercial center, losing its river commuters slowly until the ferry service was discontinued in **1924.** The spectacular revival of the **Heights** and neighboring brownstone communities has sparked the authorization of a new ferry service, a comforting alternate to the subway commute under the river.

During much of the 19th century, **Fulton Street's** downward curving route to the river (now renamed Cadman Plaza West or, in places, **Old Fulton Street**) was a bustling place, easily accessible by streetcar and elevated, lined with all manner of commercial structures, and graced by places to eat, drink, and rest one's **weary bones.** Some of these **buildings**—if not activities—remain today. Remember as you walk along Front Street that it received its name as the **last thoroughfare** above water. Landfill in the early 19th century pushed the **bulkhead** and **beach** further west. In retrospect, it seems strange that **New York** (that is, Manhattan today) was mapped to Brooklyn's high-water line, thereby assigning the water—and the islands floating within it—to Manhattan. Boaters, swimmers, divers, gulls, and garbage floating on the East River are in Manhattan.

[U 1.] Fulton Ferry Historic District, generally bounded by Water and Main Sts., the East River, Furman and Doughty Sts., and from Front St. to Water St. on a line in back of the buildings along Cadman Plaza W. (Old Fulton St.). ★ **[U 1a.] Ferrybank Restaurant**/originally **Long Island Safe Deposit Company,** 1 Front St., N cor. Old Fulton St. 1869. William Mundell. ☆

A cast-iron Renaissance **palazzo.** This monumental bank overshadowed its older neighbors in the prosperous post-Civil War era. The Brooklyn Bridge's diversion of commuting traffic after 1883 forced the bank to close its doors in **1891.** Now an elegant restaurant, opened by a waiter alumnus of Gage & Tollner's.

[U 2.] Harbor View Restaurant/originally **Franklin House (hotel),** 1 Old Fulton St., E cor. Water St. 1835. Altered, 1850s. ☆

This simple relic of the ferry's balmy days and its neighbors recall the time before the **Brooklyn Bridge,** when the traffic of people and produce passed up **Old Fulton Street.**

[U 3.] Eagle Warehouse (residential cooperative)/originally **Eagle Warehouse and Storage Company of Brooklyn,** 28 Old Fulton St., SE cor. Elizabeth St. 1893. Frank Freeman. Condominium alteration, 1980, Bernard Rothzeid. ☆

A stolid medieval revival warehouse, now recycled as condominiums. The **machicolations** (a word every cocktail party one-upman should know) are equaled only in a few remaining scattered Brooklyn armories. The bronze lettering, a lost art, articulates the grand **Romanesque Revival** arched entry, and the clock's glass face is the window of a spectacular studio loft. Note also the lusty ironwork at the entrance and over the streetside windows. Freeman, **Brooklyn's greatest architect,** designed two buildings tragically lost to fire [see Necrology]: the **Bushwick Democratic Club** and the **Margaret Hotel.**

[U 4.] 8 Old Fulton Street (apartments)/originally **Brooklyn City Railroad Company Building,** SE cor. Furman St. 1861. Remodeled, 1975, David Morton. ★ ☆

When the ferryboat was **queen,** horsecars would line a row of gleaming tracks inlaid in the cobbled pavement, waiting to transport commuters into the heart of Brooklyn. What more appropriate place for the headquarters of that transit combine than here, overlooking the **ebb and flow** of both **tide and passengers?**

[U 5a.] Fulton Ferry Museum, National Maritime Historical Society/ originally **Marine Company 7, N.Y.C. Fire Department (fireboat),** foot of Old Fulton St. 1926. ☆

This simple neglected structure bears a tower for the traditional drying of fire hoses, a churchlike symbol on the site of the former ferry terminal. The latter expired in 1924.

[U 1a.] The Ferrybank Rest. in 1967   **[U 3.]** Eagle Warehouse condos

[U 5b.] Fulton Ferry Pier, N.Y.C. Department of Ports & International Trade & Commerce, foot of Old Fulton Street, at the East River. 1976. ☆

A **sliver of river** is again available to the people, in anticipation of a renewed Fulton to Fulton ferryboat. The **iron railings,** strangely enough, were salvaged from Park Avenue's "parks," removed to improve motorists' sight lines in 1970.

[U 5c.] Bargemusic, foot of Old Fulton Street, moored to the **Fulton Ferry Pier.**

Here a lump of floating nonarchitecture houses wonderful music on occasion. Call.

[U 5d.] River Café, 1 Water St., foot of Old Fulton Street, secretly sitting on piles.

A place to be **in,** not look **at.** Here the picture postcard of lower Manhattan is displayed live. Sit at the bar and savor the **finial** towers of the 1930s, the fat boxes of the 1950s, and the constant river traffic . . . for a price. Reservations are recommended at any pseudo-popular moment. River-hopping celebrities can clutter the stage.

[U 6.] Brooklyn Bridge, East River bet. Adams St., Brooklyn, and Park Row, Manhattan. 1883. John A. and Washington Roebling. Reconstructed, 1955. David Steinman, consulting engineer [see **Bridges** for statistics]. ★ ☆

Perhaps New York's supreme **icon,** this may also be its most wondrous man-made object. The **spider web** of supporting and embracing cables **richly enmeshes** anyone strolling across its boardwalk, a highly recommended walk into the skyline of Manhattan. Start at the entrance stair on Washington Street where Cadman Plaza intersects the bridge. The current colors are reputed to be copies of the original subtle coffee and white, rather than the Public Works Gray that blunted lines and form in the 1930s through 1960s. New ramps for pedestrians and bicyclists opened in 1986, allowing, save for street crossings at each end, movement from island to island without stairs or steps.

 [U 7a.] Empire Fulton Ferry State Park. [U 7b.] Proposed **N.Y.S. Maritime Museum/**originally **Tobacco Inspection Warehouse,** 25-39 Water St., bet. New Dock and Dock Sts. N side. ca. 1860. **[U 7c.] Empire Stores,** 53-83 Water St., bet. Dock and Main Sts. N side. Western 4-story group, 1870. Eastern 5-story group, 1885. Thomas Stone. ☆

A clutch of post-Civil War warehouses that serviced the freighters bearing goods to the Orient and Australia. Forgotten by New Yorkers, they were **rediscovered** by photographer Berenice Abbott in the **Federal Art Project** of the **WPA**. Forgotten again, they were bought by Con Edison for a potential generating plant and were then considered by the City as a relocation site for the Brooklyn meat market. Happily, all that folly is past, and the buildings and open space are to be a symbiotic **Maritime Museum** and park, with loft housing on the buildings' upper floors. The views of the skyline through the Brooklyn Bridge are **Hollywoodian.**

[U 8.] The Walentas Building/originally Gair No. 7, a corrugated-cardboard factory

[U 8.] The Walentas Building lobby

[U 7c.] Empire Stores on Water Street

[U 8.] Walentas Building/originally **Gair Building No. 7,** 1 Main St. ca. 1888. William Higginson. Altered, 1986, John T. Fifield & Assocs.

One of a gaggle of early, reinforced-concrete loft buildings erected by Robert Gair, an early entrepreneur in the corrugated box industry. His dozen structures filled this lowland between the Brooklyn and Manhattan Bridges. They are some of the earliest concrete engineering in America. The Walentas Building bears a square tower with a crowning hipped roof, and a 4-sided clock. Note the new lobby.

COBBLE HILL

South of Atlantic Avenue, just below fashionable Brooklyn Heights, lies the community of **Cobble Hill** with vast rows of distinguished housing, many institutions, and numerous fine churches, although some of the latter have given place to **condominiums** within their neo-Gothic guts. It was overlooked by the urbane young middle class until the 1950s, when an enterprising real estate broker rediscovered the name **Cobles hill** on the **1766 Ratzer** map of New York and Brooklyn and updated

COBBLE HILL/

East River

Brooklyn Heights

Cobble Hill

Carroll Gardens

Red Hook

WC

D3

D2

D1

D9

D13

D10

D12

D11

C1

C16

C17

C15

C2

C14

C3

C4

C11

C12

C13

C5

C10

C9

C8

C6

C7

O8

O7

G9

G1a

G2

G8

G3

G4

G7

G5

G1

G10

G6

G11

O9

CARROLL GARDENS/BOERUM HILL

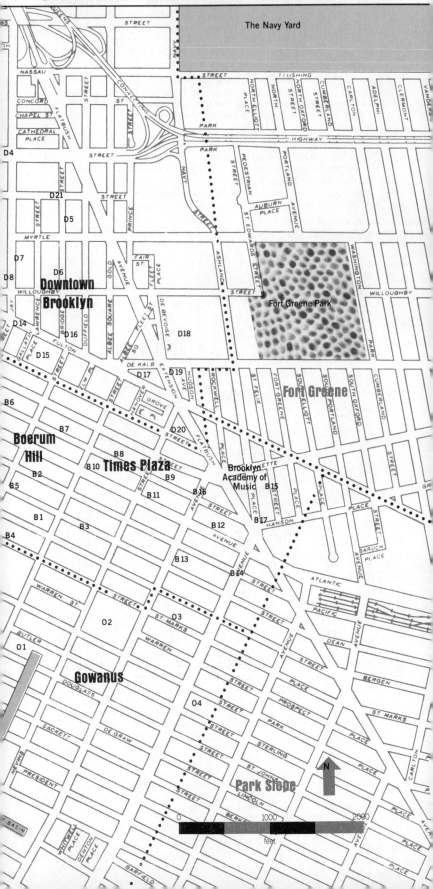

The Navy Yard

Fort Greene Park

Downtown
Brooklyn

Fort Greene

Boerum
Hill

Times Plaza

Brooklyn
Academy of
Music

Gowanus

Park Slope

N

0   1000   2000
feet

its spelling. As the Heights filled with a new brownstone apartment-dwelling population, and rents soared, Cobble Hill became an attractive alternate, with equivalent housing just a bit further from the bridge and skyline. **Coblehill,** or **Ponkiesbergh,** referred to the steep conical hill (since removed) near the intersection of Court Street and Atlantic Avenue. Its peak, during the Revolution, was the site of an important **Continental army** fortification during the **Battle of Brooklyn.**

 [C 1a.] E. M. Fuller Pavilion, Long Island College Hospital, 70 Atlantic Ave., SE cor. Hicks St. 1974. Ferrenz & Taylor. **[C 1b.] Polak Pavilion, Long Island College Hospital,** Hicks St. bet. Atlantic Ave. and Amity St. 1984. Ferrenz & Taylor. Addition, 1988, Ferrenz, Taylor, Clark & Assocs.

These bulky **monoliths** are the heart of Long Island College's rebirth as a major medical institution. Their deeply articulated brick forms are an appropriate understatement for the position at the joint between the Brooklyn Heights and Cobble Hill **Landmarks Districts.** The hospital is a testament to the 19th-century German immigrants who lived here and established this institution to serve the community.

[C 1a.] E. M. Fuller Pavilion, Long Island College Hospital (1967 photo)

Atlantic Avenue: A Near Eastern **bazaar** of exotic foods and gifts, cresting on the block between Court and Clinton Streets: halvah, dried fruit, nuts, pastries, dates, olives, copper and brass work, goatskin drums, inlaid chests. And Near Eastern restaurants too, serving hommus, baba ghannouj, kibbe, stuffed squash, cabbage, and grape leaves, and wonderful yogurt delicacies. Since the 1970s Atlantic Avenue has become a milelong bazaar for antique hunters, stretching from **Hicks Street** to **Times Plaza** at the LIRR Station. For example, in the blocks between **Smith Street** and **3rd Avenue** there are myriad dealers in 19th-century oak furniture. And each September the community stages the **Atlantic Antic,** a Sunday street fair that draws a million people to its shops, booths, rides, music, and general festivities.

Under Atlantic Avenue, from the Long Island Railroad Station at Times Plaza to the East River, is a **tunnel (1844)** that originally linked the **Station** with the Ferry Terminal to Manhattan's **South Ferry.** The tunnel, a grim void, caused the elimination of the mall and trees that originally made this stretch an early sort of Park Avenue for Brooklyn. **Tunnel now reopened to the public—limited hours.**

[C 1c.] Prospect Heights Pavilion, Long Island College Hospital, 349 Henry St., NE cor. Amity St. 1963. Beeston & Patterson.

The earliest stroke in the renewal of **L.I.C.H.** Its exposed concrete frame was once considered stylish. How architectural fashions change . . .

[C 2.] Cobble Hill Historic District, Atlantic Ave. to DeGraw St., Hicks to Court Sts., excepting the NW corner lands of Long Island College Hospital. ★

Within the district are **all** of the following:

[C 2a.] Dudley Memorial, Long Island College Hospital, 110 Amity St., SE cor. Henry St. 1902. William C. Hough. ☆

Richly adorned and in dark red brick, this latter-day miniature **Henry IV "hotel particulier"** recalls the architecture of the Place des Vosges and the Hôpital St. Louis in Paris. It is a fitting neighbor to its adjoining **bourgeois** row houses.

[C 3a.] St. Peter's, Our Lady of Pilar Church (Roman Catholic), Hicks St. NE cor. Warren St. 1860. P. C. Keely. **[3b.]** Originally **St. Peter's Academy.** 1866. **[3c.]** Originally **St. Peter's Hospital**/now **Cobble Hill Nursing Home,** 274 Henry St., bet. Congress and Warren Sts. W side. 1888. William Schickel & Co. ☆

Once a full block to minister to the community's **spiritual** (church), **educational** (academy), **social** (home for working girls at Hicks and Congress Streets), and **health** (hospital) needs. The red painted brickwork held it all together. Things have changed. The church retains its sturdy, buttressed forms in brick, brownstone, and terra-cotta, crowned with a **squat tower.**

[C 4a.] Tower Buildings (left), **[C 4c.]** Home Buildings (right). On Hicks St.

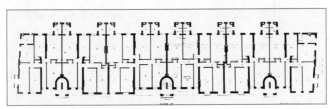

[C 4a.] Plans of the Tower Buildings show floor-through apartment units

[C 4a.] Tower Buildings (apartments), 417-435 Hicks St., 136-142 Warren St., 129-135 Baltic St., E side of Hicks St. 1879. ☆ **[C 4b.] Workingmen's Cottages,** 1-25 and 2-26 Warren Place, bet. Hicks and Henry Sts., 146-154 Warren St. S side. 139-147 Baltic St. N side. 1879. ☆ **[C 4c.] Home Buildings (apartments),** 439-445 Hicks St. and 134-140 Baltic St., SE cor. Hicks St. 1877. All by William Field & Son. Restored, 1986, Maitland, Strauss & Behr. ☆

Completion of the **"sun-lighted tenements"** in newly socially conscious late Victorian London inspired these 226 low-rent apartments and 34 cottages financed by businessman **Alfred Tredway White.** White's dictum, **"philanthropy plus 5%,"** made him the first builder of **limited-profit** (and hence low-rent) housing in America. Innovations such as outside spiral stairs and open balconies that serve as access corridors achieved **floor-through** apartments with good **ventilation.**

Common bathing facilities were originally provided in the basement. The tiny **11½-foot-wide** cottages line a wondrous private pedestrian **mews,** Warren Place. There are no rear gardens, but twin alleys provide rear access.

The Tower Buildings embrace a **garden courtyard.**

[C 5.] 412-420 Henry Street (row houses), bet. Kane and Baltic Sts. W side. 1888. George B. Chappell. ☆

Upon completion, these houses were sold to **F. A. O. Schwarz,** the toy king. **Nos. 412, 414, and 416** retain their original doorways, low stoops, and some of the original ironwork.

Winnie's Mom didn't live here: At 426 Henry Street, just south of Kane, a plaque claims that **Winston Churchill**'s mother, **Jennie Jerome,** was born in that house in 1850. Actually, she was born in 1854 in a house on Amity Street near Court. The confusion results from the fact that Jennie's folks had lived with her uncle, Addison G. Jerome, at 292 (now renumbered 426) Henry Street prior to her birth.

[C 6a.] Originally **Strong Place Baptist Church**/now **St. Francis Cabrini Chapel (Roman Catholic),** DeGraw St. NW cor. Strong Place, 1852. Minard Lafever. **[C 6b.]** Originally **Strong Place Baptist Church Chapel**/ now **Strong Place Day-Care Center,** 56 Strong Place. 1849. Minard Lafever. ☆

A stolid, brownstone Gothic Revival church, charmingly pock-marked as the stucco veneer flakes off. **Lafever** was one of Brooklyn's greatest architects.

[C 7.] South Brooklyn Seventh-Day Adventist Church/originally **Trinity German Lutheran Church,** 249 DeGraw St., bet. Clinton St. and Tompkins Place. N side. 1905. Theobald Engelhardt. ☆

A simple brick church in the **second** Gothic Revival. The **first** flowered in the 1840s, the second at the turn of the century.

[C 8a.] Originally **Dr. Joseph E. Clark residence,** 340 Clinton St., bet. DeGraw and Kane Sts. W side. ca. 1860. ☆

The widest single house in Cobble Hill, **asymmetric** and crowned with a slate mansard roof. Note the **sinuous** ironwork.

[C 8b.] 334 Clinton Street (residence), bet. DeGraw and Kane Sts. W side. ca. 1850. Remodeled, 1888, James W. Naughton. ☆

A **kooky** mansard-roofed **Queen Anne** miniature, created by Naughton's remodeling of the original simple body. Note particularly the corner tower and the lovely wrought-iron strapwork. As architect for the Brooklyn school system, Naughton later built the great **Boys' High School** [see Bedford-Stuyvesant Y 24.].

[C 9a.] Christ Church and Holy Family (Episcopal), 320 Clinton St., SW cor. Kane St. 1842. Richard Upjohn. Altar, altar railings, reredos, pulpit, lectern, chairs, 1917, Louis Comfort Tiffany. ☆

English Gothic cut ashlar brownstone by the elder of the father-and-son architects, the **Upjohns.** They lived on Clinton Street at **No. 296.** [see C 10a. and 10b.]. Four strong finials form an appropriate skyline apex in these low-rise blocks. A **1939** fire destroyed most but not all of the Tiffany windows. The red **Episcopal** doors give lively contrast.

[C 9b.] 301-311 Clinton Street (residences), 206-224 Kane Street, and 10-12 Tompkins Place, 1849–1854. ☆

Nine **classy pairs** of narrow **Italianate** houses developed by New York lawyer **Gerard W. Morris.** The street is pleasantly modulated by the rhythm of the projecting bays.

[C 9c.] Kane Street Synagogue, Congregation Baith Israel Anshei Emes/formerly **Trinity German Lutheran Church**/originally **Middle Dutch Reformed Church,** 236 Kane St., SE cor. Tompkins Place. ca. 1856. ☆

Originally a brick and brownstone Romanesque Revival, its present stuccoed exterior is bland but waterproof. The congregation is descended from a splinter group of Brooklyn's oldest synagogue, once located at State Street and Boerum Place.

[C 10a.] Originally **Richard Upjohn residence,** 296 Clinton St., NW cor. Baltic St. 1843. Richard Upjohn & Son. **[C 10b.] Addition to Upjohn residence,** 203 Baltic St., W of Clinton St. 1893. Richard M. Upjohn. ☆

The younger Upjohn's Romanesque Revival addition retains some of the elegant detail obliterated in the older corner house on its conversion to a multiple dwelling. This is more interesting for the **architects** who lived here than the **architecture.**

[C 8b.] 334 Clinton St., Queen Anne

[C 9a.] Christ Church and Holy Family

[C 11a.] Verandah Place, S of Congress St., bet. Clinton and Henry Sts. ca. 1850. ☆

A pleasant mews, long neglected but now reclaimed as charming residences. **Thomas Wolfe** (1900–1938) lived here once. The bland playground is a pleasant amenity for parents and children but is out of scale with the carriage houses it confronts. Why can't street lighting in such tight and quaint surrounds be bracketed from the buildings proper; as it is in so many older European cities?

Around the corner at 268 Clinton Street is the **Verandah Restaurant,** with a Victorian interior filled with plants.

Church of the Holy Turtle was the affectionate nickname of the Second Unitarian Church, which stood for more than a century on the site of today's Cobble Hill Sitting Park. As built from designs of **J. Wrey Mould** in **1858,** there was no denying that the little edifice resembled a tortoise with a high carapace. (Mould's earlier, Manhattan work, the Unitarian Church of the Saviour, boasted a striped facade and was named the **Church of the Holy Zebra.** It too is gone.) With the Reverend Samuel Longfellow, the poet's brother, as its first minister, Second Unitarian quickly became known for the cultural interests and abolitionist views of both pastor and his transported New England flock. By the 1950s, however, the church had been abandoned, and the site was purchased for a new supermarket. Community intervention prevented this—and resulted in the creation of the park.

[C 11b.] 166, 168, and **170 Congress Street (row houses),** bet. Clinton and Henry Sts. S side. **[11c.] 159, 161,** and **163 Congress Street (row houses),** bet. Clinton and Henry Sts. N side. ca. 1857. ☆

Two triads of Anglo-Italianate row houses, each designed to read as a single unit. The southern group has segmental arched upper-floor windows; the northern group, square-headed ones.

[C 12a.] St. Paul's, St. Peter's, Our Lady of Pilar Church, Court St. SW cor. Congress St. 1838. Gamaliel King. Steeple, early 1860s. Brownstone veneer, 1888. Additions of new sanctuary and sacristy. 1906.
[C 12b.] Rectory, 234 Congress St., bet. Court and Clinton Sts. S side. 1936. Henry J. McGill. ☆

Its tall verdigris copper-sheathed steeple is a giant finial along Court Street for blocks in both directions. It takes careful study to understand the **Greek Revival** form behind the later steeple. King was the **carpenter** who designed Brooklyn's City Hall, now Borough Hall.

[C 12c.] 223 Congress Street (residence), bet. Court and Clinton Sts. N side. 1851. Mansard roof, ca. 1880. ☆

A large Gothic Revival house originally built as a rectory for St. Paul's opposite and the **Free School for Boys.** The mansard roof has been desecrated with—of all things—white aluminum clapboard.

[C 13a.] 194-200 Court Street (apartments), bet. Congress and Warren Sts. W side. 1898. William B. Tubby. ☆

FOSTER in the pediment names this turn-of-the-century block of tenement apartments. The storefronts are miraculously preserved in almost their original condition. Two shades of brick articulate the facade.

[C 13b.] St. Paul's Parish School (Roman Catholic), 205 Warren St., bet. Court and Clinton Sts. 1887. ☆

An eclectic Victorian brick building with Corinthian-capped pilasters. Education seemed more serious in such monumental and dignified surroundings.

[C 14.] Former R. L. Cutter residence: an oriel window and Flemish flourishes

[C 14.] Formerly **Ralph L. Cutter residence/**originally **Abraham J. S. DeGraw residence,** 219 Clinton St., SE cor. Amity St. 1845. Altered, 1891, D'Oench & Simon. ☆

In the early and sparsely built development of Cobble Hill, there were freestanding houses that could view the harbor from their parlor windows. As the blocks infilled, the view was barred, inspiring here a

tower for viewing the harbor over the rooftops beyond. Still freestanding, with a grand garden, it sports a **rock-face brownstone stoop** with both cast and wrought ironwork.

[C 14a.] 146 Amity Street (apartments), SW cor. Clinton St. 1986. Saltini/Ferrara. ☆

A modest modern infill building, trying to look as if it has always been there. Bay windows and ironwork add to the simple brown form.

[C 14b.] 232-236 Clinton Street, NW cor. Amity St. ca. 1885. ☆

The ornate brownstone hooded windows and frieze give rich detail to these late eclectic houses.

Jennie Jerome, born January 9, 1854: Cut stone veneer conceals the original body of No. 197 (once No. 8) Amity Street, where a baby girl was born to Mr. and Mrs. Leonard Jerome. Jennie grew up to marry Lord Randolph Churchill and to give birth, in turn, to a son, Winston. The veneer was obviously added in the hope of **"modernizing" and "improving"** this "old-fashioned" building, an aesthetic akin to placing iron deer, polished spheres, and assorted gnomes on one's front lawn in suburbia.

Cousins (restaurant/bar), 160 Court St., NW cor. Amity St. ☆

This local watering hole provides jazz.

[C 15.] 214 Clinton Street and **147 Pacific Street (apartments),** NW cor. Clinton St. 1892, H. W. Billard. ☆

Queen Anne, in rock-face brownstone and rough brick. See the face in the pediment at **No. 214.** The sheet-metal bay windows are ornamented with **iron studs** and **sinuous** Ionic colonnettes.

[C 15a.] 174 Pacific Street (apartments)/formerly Public School 78, Brooklyn, bet. Clinton and Court Sts. S side. 1889. ☆

A strong **prim** brick school building, looming over its row house neighbors.

[C 16a.] 191 Clinton Street (apartments)/originally South Brooklyn Savings Bank, SE cor. Atlantic Ave. 1871. E. L. Roberts. Restored, 1986. ☆

A noble **Eastlake** commercial building in **Tuckahoe marble.** The bank's move to the east end of the Atlantic Avenue block in **1922** initiated years of decay. Happily, it has now been restored to a position as **prominent citizen.** Note the incised carvings in the lintels.

[C 16b.] 164-168 Atlantic Avenue (lofts), bet. Clinton and Court Sts. S side. 1860–1864. ☆

Merchant princes of the 19th century were more concerned with the quality of their architecture than are those of the 20th. Note the stone quoins and bracketed roof cornices . . . and the horrible storefront at street level.

[C 17a.] 180 Atlantic Avenue (lofts), bet. Clinton and Court Sts. S side. 1873. ☆

A rich and unusual—for these parts—**cast-iron** facade with **wrought-iron** railings modulating the window openings. The sidewall is **sullied** by a garish sign painted on aluminum clapboarding.

[C 17b.] Main Office, Independence Savings Bank/formerly South Brooklyn Savings Institution, 130 Court St., SW cor. Atlantic Ave. 1922. McKenzie, Voorhees & Gmelin. Addition, 1936, Charles A. Holmes. ☆

A **Florentine Renaissance** anchor marking the northeast corner of the Cobble Hill Historic District. A **hundred eagles** bear its cornice on their shoulders. The bank changed its name to unload its "Brooklyn only" image. **South** Brooklyn was Cobble Hill, Carroll Gardens, and Red Hook—the true **south** in Brooklyn's early days, before annexation of the vast southern, eastern, and northern precincts.

END of Cobble Hill Historic District.

CARROLL GARDENS

Historically considered part of **Red Hook** or **South Brooklyn,** the area was renamed **Carroll Gardens** in the blooming gentrification of the 1960s. It has always been physically distinguished from its surrounding neighbors by its unique cityscape, created by land surveyor **Richard Butts.** His **1846** map provided for a series of unusually deep blocks fronting today's **1st Place** through **4th Place** between Henry and Smith Streets. His plan, providing for **deep frontyards** as well as standard backyards, was then extended eastward to Carroll, President, and Second Streets between Smith and Hoyt (Union Street is wider also, but without the gardens). Between row house facades and the narrow sidewalks are **wonderful and lush front gardens,** syncopated with front stoops, that gave the area its name. The sight is as urbane as any in the city. It's unfortunate that **Butts'** creativity has never been publicly honored.

[G 1.] Carroll Gardens Historic District, generally resembling a keystone on its side, including President and Carroll Sts., bet. Smith and Hoyt Sts., and Hoyt St. bet. President and 1st Sts. ★

Only 2 of the 11 fine spaces of Carroll Gardens were designated as the **Landmark District,** an unhappy oversight. Much of the district therefore lies outside the official boundaries.

[G 1a.] 360 Court Street (apartments)/formerly **South Congregational Church,** NW cor. President St. 1857. ★ **[G 1b.] South Congregational Church,** formerly **Ladies' Parlor,** to the W on President St. 1889. Charles Merry. ★ **[G 1c.] Rectory,** 255 President St., bet. Court and Clinton Sts. N side. ★

One of several Brooklyn churches converted into condominium apartments by hook, crook, and the **shrinking** of the borough's Protestantism (G2. below is a neighbor). The dour facade presents a series of stepped planes in brick, a counterpart in masonry to a theater proscenium's contoured velvet curtain. Its silhouette of verdigris-colored finials contrasts with the deep red masonry body.

The present church, in the former **ladies' parlor,** is a sturdy Romanesque Revival with rich terra-cotta ornament; the parish house, a Romanesque Revival delight.

[G 2.] St. Paul's Episcopal Church of Brooklyn, 423 Clinton St., NE cor. Carroll St. 1867–1884. Richard Upjohn & Son.

A severe gray stone building with terra-cotta trim and a steeple that was never completed. Judging from the corner tower, it would have been enormous had it been finished. **Grim Protestants** were here first.

[G 3.] F. G. Guido Funeral Home/originally **John Rankin residence,** 440 Clinton St., SW cor. Carroll St. 1840. ★

A **grand** brick Greek Revival survivor. Somber gray granite supports rosy brick and articulates **sills, lintels,** and **capitals.** Once a lone mansion amid farmland, it overlooked the **Upper Bay** in the same posture and **prospect** as the Litchfield Mansion in Prospect Park.

[G 4.] 450 Clinton Street (apartments)/formerly **Den Norske Sjømannskirke/**originally **Westminster Presbyterian Church,** NW cor. 1st Place. ca. 1865.

Another church, in **stolid** and **eclectic** brownstone, converted to apartments. The air conditioning units punctuating the clerestory spaces form a **bizarre** frieze. Whither the Norwegian seamen?

[G 5.] 98 First Place, SW cor. Court St. ca. 1860.

An **Italianate** corner villa.

[G 6.] 37-39 Third Place (residences), bet. Henry and Clinton Sts. N side. ca. 1875.

A **Charles Addams** mansarded outpost in these precincts. Note the cast-iron grillage in profile against the sky.

[G 3.] Grk. Rev. Guido Funeral Home   **[G 7.]** A 'lighthouse' for the Church

[G 7.] Originally **Catholic Seamen's Institute/**now **Institutional Services, Roman Catholic Diocese of Brooklyn,** 653 Hicks St., NE cor. Rapelye St. 1943. Henry V. Murphy.

From the era of heavy maritime activity in this precinct. The faux **Art Moderne** lighthouse was intended as a **moral beacon:** "A challenge of the church to the barrooms of the river front."

[G 8.] Sacred Hearts of Jesus and Mary and St. Stephen's Church (Roman Catholic)/originally **St. Stephen's Church,** Summit St. NE cor. Hicks St. ca. 1860. P. C. Keely.

A heavy and hearty **Gothick** complex turned out by the prolific Keely, who is believed to have designed 700 churches across the country. Unfortunately, he was no match for Upjohn.

[G 9.] Columbia Terrace, 43-57 Carroll St., N side. 250-260 Columbia St., W side. 43-87 President St., S side. 46-90 President St., N side. 1987. Wids de la Cour and Hirsch & Danois.

Some rather bleak and understated rows infilling the blocks of this neighborhood orphaned by the slashing separation of the **Brooklyn-Queens Expressway**'s cut. Why not cover this wound and allow the healthy neighborhood of Cobble Hill to be sutured to its western reaches?

Carroll Gardens: see map pp. 600–601   **609**

[G 9.] Columbia Terrace: row housing orphaned by Brooklyn-Queens Expwy. gash

[G 10a.] Formerly **South Brooklyn Christian Assembly Parsonage,** 295 Carroll St., bet. Smith and Hoyt Sts. N side. 1878.

Victorian Gothic.

[G 10b.] 297-299 Carroll Street, bet. Smith and Hoyt Sts. N side. 1986.

Twin infill row houses that replace the old church of the **South Brooklyn Christian Assembly,** consumed by fire. A brave and simple modern attempt, complete with stoops.

[G 11.] Formerly **Calvary Baptist Church of Red Hook/**originally **South Congregational Chapel,** 118 4th Place, bet. Court and Smith Sts. 1890.

This robust rotund chapel is **Friar Tuck** to its more restrained heroic Robin Hood, the former South Congregational Church [see G 1a.].

Optical illusions? You can tell for sure only from a land book such as E. Belcher Hyde's of 1912, for example, but it is certain that the street facades of the Carroll Gardens row houses framing Carroll and President Streets are **not** parallel. As a matter of **fact,** the difference is considerable. At the Smith Street end they are **100** feet apart; at Hoyt Street the space increases to **129** feet. The surveyor's **prestidigitation** is concealed, however, by the length of these blocks and their lush greenery.

GOWANUS

A shabby, mostly dull part of Brooklyn, but nevertheless one occasionally finds buildings of interest and pockets of urban charm. Among its most interesting features are the **bridges** and **viaducts** that cross the waterway bearing its name. Before **1911** the fetid **Gowanus Canal** was known derisively as **Lavender Lake.** At that time the **Butler Street**

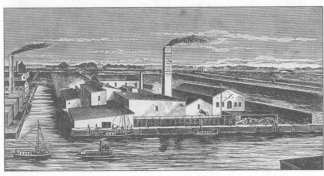

pumping station at its northern terminus began delivering the **stale waters** into New York Harbor's **Buttermilk Channel,** inviting freshwater to enter by **hydraulic action.** A new facility will greatly increase the flow and thus reduce stagnation.

[O 1.] Butler Street Pumping Station, City of New York, Butler St. bet. Nevins and Bond Sts. S side. New facilities, 1987.

A bold and elegant wall screens the hardware from the street while giving it proper **urban** completion.

[O 2.] Wyckoff Gardens, N.Y.C. Housing Authority, Nevins St. to Third Ave., Wyckoff to Baltic Sts. 1966. Greenberg & Ames.

Here the **Housing Authority** omits red brick from its palette and constructs modeled slabs with a variety of setbacks. It is a modest but welcome change in public housing, more successfully followed by those **low-rise, high-density** programs of the early 1970s which produced **streetfronted** 6- and 8-story buildings in Brownsville, East New York, and Bedford-Stuyvesant.

[O 3.] St. Mark's Avenue, bet. Third and Fourth Aves., both sides. ca. 1865.

If this street weren't so poor, it would be famous. Here are brownstones for the lower middle class, 3-story and basement **"English"** tenement buildings marching up **Park Slope** like a provincial brigade.

[O 4a.] Butler/Baltic Street row houses, bet. Fourth and Fifth Aves. Both sides of Butler St., and S side of Baltic St. 1986.

Cut-rate **Post Modern** here provides simulated rusticated stone facades to these two blocks. The corniced gables are reminiscent of **nuns'** hats.

[O 4b.] Originally **N.Y.C. Public Bath No. 7,** 227-231 Fourth Ave., NE cor. President St. ★

A glazed terra-cotta relic awaiting reuse.

[O 4c.] Carroll Street Bridge, over the Gowanus Canal. 1889. George Ingram, engineer-in-charge; Robert Van Buren, chief engineer; both of the Brooklyn Department of City Works. ★

A retractile bridge, one that slides askew to a berth on the west side of the canal to allow waterborne traffic to pass. The oldest of four such bridges extant in the country. A gritty relic from the era when Brooklyn's public works were designed by its own municipal government.

[O 5.] Vechte-Cortelyou House, in James J. Byrne Memorial Playground, 3rd St. SW cor., Fifth Ave. Originally built, 1699. Replica, 1935.

Known as the **old stone house** in Gowanus, the building now occupying the site was **recreated** by the City's Parks Department in 1935, using old sketches and what were believed to be **old stones.** The original house had long before fallen into **total ruin.** In its recreated state it served as a playground office and comfort station until it was vandalized—and once again restored.

The most severe fighting in the Revolutionary War's **Battle of Long Island** (1776) took place here. **General Stirling's** Continental troops fought a delaying action against **Cornwallis'** superior number of redcoats, thus permitting **Washington's** successful retreat.

[O 6.] IND Subway high-level crossing, Smith and 9th St. Station, over Gowanus Canal. 1933.

The land in these parts proved so uneconomical for tunnel construction that the **IND** subway emerges here, rising over 100 feet to meet the **Canal's** navigational clearance requirements. This leaves the **Smith and 9th** Street subway station **high and dry,** and embraced in a latticework of steel. **A spectacular** construction, it lacked an **Eiffel** to make it equally significant visually.

[O 7.] St. Agnes Church (Roman Catholic), 417 Sackett St., NE cor. Hoyt St. 1905. Thomas F. Houghton.

The community's dominant structure save for the **IND** crossing, **St. Agnes** is the local quasi-cathedral in these low row-housed precincts. Here is dressed Manhattan schist ashlar, with limestone detailing, pushing multi-finials to the sky.

[O 5.] The Vechte-Cortelyou House: known formerly as the Old Stone House

[O 6.] The IND subway high-level crossing over Gowanus Canal (1967 photo)

Where the Dodgers played: The James J. Byrne Memorial Playground (along the west side of Fifth Avenue south of 3rd Street) is named for the owner of the forebears of the Brooklyn Dodgers. At the time (1854) the team was playing there, the site was the first Washington Park baseball field. Byrne then moved them to Eastern Park, near today's Broadway Junction. Failing to attract crowds to what was then a remote location, Charles Ebbet persuaded the team to return to these precincts, to a new Washington Park, this time on the west side of 4th Avenue between 1st and 3rd Streets. From there the Dodgers moved to the more commodious stadium on Bedford Avenue named for their new owner, Ebbets Field (1913–1957), which Brooklynites will never forget.

[O 8.] Engine Company 204, N.Y.C. Fire Department, 299 DeGraw St., bet. Court and Smith Sts. N side. ca. 1880.

A holdover from the times when fires were fought by **fire laddies** stoking horsedrawn steam pumpers. This one began as **Engine Company 4, Brooklyn Fire Department,** as cast into the old terra-cotta shields. Brick-and-brownstone Gothic Revival, with an **Italianate** hat.

[O 9a.] St. Mary's Star of the Sea Church (Roman Catholic), 471 Court St., bet. Nelson and Luquer Sts. E side. ca. 1870. P. C. Keely. **[O 9b.] Girls' School,** 477 Court St., NE cor. Nelson St. **[O 9c.] Rectory,** 467 Court St., SE cor. Luquer St.

Painted brick humility—a parish church trio for a 19th-century, immigrant working-class parish. Compare it with other nearby Catholic churches by architect **Keely.** The raw, red brick body behind the painted facade has a more pleasant texture.

Don't miss taking a peek at Dennett Place, just behind St. Mary's.

Dennett Place delivers an atmospheric flavor that's redulent of Maxwell Anderson

Dennett Place: An atmospheric street that seems more like a stage set for **Maxwell Anderson's** *Winterset* than a brick-and-mortar reality. Lying between Court and Smith Streets, it connects Luquer with Nelson Street. It is what we more commonly term a **mews.**

RED HOOK

Like an **Edward Hopper** painting, Red Hook constantly presents excerpts from his stark visions. Here are scattered residential blocks, mixed industry, and neighborhoods generally squalid. The most impressive things here are docks, warehouses, and ships. The immense Red Hook Houses of the 1930s are simply that: **immense.** Only 6 stories, they fail to supply the happy scale of Williamsburg Houses [see Northern Brooklyn W24.]. Fortunately, attempts at urban quality are still in the works: **Ciardullo Associates'** row housing on Visitation Place was an early attempt at infilling this poorly toothed precinct. A bit of what Red Hook looked like **100 years** ago can be savored on Coffey Street between Conover and Ferris Streets and on Pioneer Street between Van Brunt and Richards.

[R 1a.] 71-79 Visitation Place (row houses), bet. Van Brunt and Richards Sts. S side. **[R 1b.] 2-12 Verona Street (row houses).** N side. **[R 1c.] 9-19 Dwight Street (row houses).** E side. 1972. John Ciardullo Assocs.

Federally subsidized low-rent housing sponsored by the New York Urban Coalition, this is a promising example of what can be done without overbearing municipal authority. Sixty-four streetfronted units in 3-story brick and block houses. This success led to further work in Eastern Brooklyn [E 8.].

[R 2.] Originally **Brooklyn Clay Retort & Firebrick Works,** 76-86 Van Brunt St., 99-113 Van Dyke St., 106-116 Beard St. ca. 1860.

Two sturdy granite ashlar warehouses and a **manufactory** with its original masonry chimney are all that remain. They are powerful relics from an era of grand industrial architecture. This great enterprise brought clay from South Amboy, N.J., to the nearby **Erie Basin,** where it was converted to firebrick.

Nos. 76-86 was the firebrick storehouse, **Nos. 99-113** the firebrick factory, and **Nos. 106-116** the boiler house, carpentry shop, and engine room.

 [R 3a.] Originally **Beard & Robinson Stores,** 260 Beard St., along Erie Basin, SE cor. Van Brunt St. 1869. **[R 3b.] Van Brunt's Stores,** 480 Van Brunt St., along Erie Basin, S of Beard St. ca. 1869.

Half-round arch openings and down-to-earth brickwork commend these and other nearby post-Civil War **wharfside warehouses,** the epitome of the **functional tradition.** Compare them with the better-known **Empire Stores** [Fulton Ferry U 7c.]. A cut-stone marker modestly marks the streetside southernmost point of Beard & Robinson. **Look up.** With the declining need or desire for this type of warehousing, these would make magnificent waterfront residential lofts.

[R 2.] Orig. Brooklyn Clay Retort & Firebrick Works: an ashlar stone hulk

Erie Basin: The scythe-shaped breakwater creating this placid harbor was the brainchild of railroad contractor William Beard, who completed it in 1864. He charged ships seeking to haul American cargoes 50¢ per cubic yard for the **privilege** of dumping the rock carried as ballast from overseas ports—thus, a free breakwater. The **longest dead-end street** in New York is Columbia Street, at the Erie Basin. Unfortunately, new works by the Port Authority have closed it off much of the time to auto traffic. If the gate is open, drive the length of the scythe and **see the sea.**

[R 4.] Originally **Port of New York Grain Elevator Terminal, N.Y.S. Barge Canal System,** Henry St. Basin. 1922.

Concrete silos dramatically aligned to receive grain shipments from the Midwest, through the Great Lakes and Erie Canal. The decline of grain traffic to New York harbor led to their deactivation in 1955. The best view is from Columbia Street.

 [R 5.] Red Hook Recreation Center, N.Y.C. Department of Parks & Recreation, Bay St. bet. Clinton and Henry Sts. N side, through to Lorraine St. 1936. N.Y.C. Parks Department, Aymar Embury II, consulting architect. Altered.

A **WPA** pool-bathhouse complex, now with added basketball and boxing. Savor the arches and massive piers.

SUNSET PARK AND ENVIRONS

A neighborhood named for its park, a sloping **green baize oasis** facing the setting sun. Here are sweeping views of the harbor. Once almost exclusively **Scandinavian,** the community shelters a broad ethnic mix, with a large proportion of **Hispanic** population. On the flats between the elevated **Gowanus Expressway** (over Third Avenue, and a continuation of the Brooklyn-Queens Expressway) and the waterfront lie the **Bush Terminal** at the north and the old **Brooklyn Army Terminal** at the south. Beginning a few blocks north of Sunset Park's park is the enormous and very beautiful Victorian burying ground, **Green-Wood Cemetery.**

[S 1.] Green-Wood Cemetery, Fifth Ave. to Macdonald Ave. and Fort Hamilton Pkwy., 20th to 37th Sts. 1840. **[S 1a.] Main Entrance Gate and Gatehouse,** 5th Ave. opp. 25th St. E side. 1861. Richard Upjohn & Son. ★ **[S 1b.] Fort Hamilton Parkway Gate and Gatehouse,** 37th St. W of Ft. Hamilton Pkwy. 1875. Richard M. Upjohn. **Open only to relatives and friends of those interred.**

Opened in 1840, these lands were Brooklyn's first park by default, long before Prospect Park was created. Here, on the highest points in Brooklyn, 478 acres of rolling landscape offered opportunities for Sunday strolling among the hills, ponds, plantings, and superb views of the harbor. Most of the more than half-million buried here (including **Henry Ward Beecher, Nathaniel Currier and James Ives, Peter Cooper, Samuel F. B. Morse, "Boss" Tweed, and Lola Montez**) are memorialized by extraordinary mausoleums and monuments. A veritable history of New York **Victoriana** is indexed by the gravestones, pyramids, obelisks, cairns, temples, and lesser markers. At the **main entrance,** appropriately, is an especially wondrous gatehouse, the **Gothic Revival** counterpart to a pair of Roman triumphal arches. Both a building and a gate, it was called the culmination of the Gothic Revival movement in New York by historian Alan Burnham. Inquire at the office to the right for permission to view the grounds.

[S 1.] Green-Wood Cemetery: the Fort Hamilton Parkway Gate and Gatehouse

[S 2.] McGovern Florist/formerly **Weir & Company Greenhouse,** Fifth Ave. SW cor. 25th St. G. Curtis Gillespie. ca. 1900. ★

Sadly, this once-charming miniature **crystal palace** is in decline. Signs and poor maintenance have marred its stature as a garden showplace serving Green-Wood opposite. One apocryphal story says that it was moved to Brooklyn from the St. Louis World's Fair of 1904.

[S 3.] Alku Toinen (Finnish cooperative apartments), 826 43rd St., bet. Eighth and Ninth Aves. S side. 1916.

Reputedly the **first** cooperative dwelling in New York City. Modest architecturally, it wears a palette of tan Scandinavian brick.

[S 4.] Sunset Play Center, N.Y.C. Department of Parks & Recreation, in Sunset Park at 7th Ave., bet. 41st and 44th Sts. W side. 1936. N.Y.C. Parks Department. Aymar Embury II, consulting architect.

One of several similar sports and aquatic centers built during the depression by the **WPA** (Red Hook and McCarren are others).

[S 5.] St. Michael's Roman Catholic Church, 4200 Fourth Ave., SW cor. 42nd St. 1905. Raymond F. Almirall.

A small replica of Paris' **Sacré Coeur** atop a spire dominates the local skyline.

[S 6.] Formerly **68th Precinct Station House and Stable, N.Y.C. Police Department,** 4302 Fourth Ave., SW cor. 43rd St. 1886. Emile M. Gruwé. ★

Although nearly a ruin, its Romanesque Revival (Venetian and Norman division) is so powerful that the remnants retain vigor even in their time of despair.

[S 7.] Bush Terminal, 28th to 50th Sts., Upper Bay to 2nd Ave. (irregular) buildings 1-4 1911. 5-13 and 19-26 various years to 1926. William Higginson.

Irving T. Bush opened these flats to industrial buildings in 1890. Block after block of 8-story, white-painted buildings are the reality of this mammoth industrial and warehousing enterprise, each unit of which allows a colossal 3 acres on any one floor. In the neighborhood are older brick industrial structures around 1st Avenue and the 40s:

[S 5.] Saint Michael's R.C. Church   **[S 6.]** Old 68th Pct. House & Stable

[S 8.] A wonderous neo-Gothic tower   **[S 9.]** The present 68th Precinct Hse

[S 8.] Originally **National Metal Company**/now **loft space,** 4201-4207 First Ave., SE cor. 42nd St. ca. 1890.

A crenellated Gothic Revival tower is the local campanile. A wonderful mark in the landscape—and an enigma.

[S 9.] 68th Precinct, N.Y.C. Police Department, 333 65th St., bet. Third and Fourth Aves. N side. 1970. Milton F. Kirchman.

An aggressive, arbitrary, tricky, cubistic set of volumes and voids. In the loose civic commissions of the mid and late 1960s architectural histrionics were in favor, rather than any truly urbane attempts to blend into the scale and style of the neighborhood. Here there is at least some excuse, due to the visual chaos created by highway, railroad, and air-rights construction.

[S 10.] Originally **New York Port of Embarkation and Army Supply Base,** a.k.a. **Brooklyn Army Terminal**/officially **Military Ocean Terminal,** Second Ave. bet. 58th and 65th Sts. W side. 1918. Cass Gilbert.

These utilitarian warehouses in exposed concrete are vast and appropriately devoid of extraneous ornament. The innards contain long **skylit** central galleries. Gilbert, who was not known for decorative restraint, embellished with ornament and sculpture his better-known buildings—the Woolworth Building in Manhattan and Washington's Supreme Court, among many other confections. But when military functionalism was the order of the day, he could be as austere as Gropius.

[S 11.] Originally **N.Y.S. Arsenal**/now **Keeper's Self-Storage Warehouse,** Second Ave. bet. 63rd and 64th Sts. E side. 1925.

A grim, precast-concrete former ordnance and quartermaster facility, with limestone quoins and a battered base. Unhappily, its new owners have stripped the facade of the ivy that had once muted these bleak walls.

BOERUM HILL/TIMES PLAZA

Boerum Hill is another new sobriquet for a community that has revived from a neglected past, following in the gentrified footsteps of **Cobble Hill** and **Carroll Gardens.** Although the area claimed by the neighborhood association is larger, the most interesting blocks are on State, Pacific, Dean, and Bergen Streets, east of Court Street and west of 4th Avenue. The Historic District is but a small segment of it all. In the mid 19th century this was a **fashionable district,** as the fine row housing itself indicates. Visitors to the area included **Washington Irving, James Fenimore Cooper, and William Cullen Bryant.** Sidney Lanier lived briefly at 195 Dean Street. Today's residents are a **racial and ethnic mix** that adds special flavor to the community. **Times Plaza** is the eastern terminus of this area. The scale is smaller than that of the Heights or Cobble Hill. Three-story row houses and a greater share of sky give the treed blocks a **softer and homier** aspect, rather than the urbane character of, say, Pierrepont Street.

Charles **Hoyt** and his partner, Russell **Nevins,** acquired the area around their self-named streets in 1834. The oldest houses, from the mid **1840**s, are in the Greek Revival style, with simple pediments and pilasters.

[B 1.] **Boerum Hill Historic District,** irregular, generally lying bet. the Wyckoff St./Hoyt St. intersection on the SW, and the Pacific St./Nevins St. intersection on the NE, including sections of Pacific, Dean, and Bergen Sts. ★

The area chosen for designation includes some of the finest rows of housing as well as some of the precinct's architectural **eccentricities,** which enliven the streetscape. The row houses, single houses, and apartments listed below are among the many contained within the district's boundaries. Nevertheless, whole streets become a joint architectural ensemble and can be savored for their overall urban design, as well as in their separate parts. Buildings within the district are marked with a ☆.

[B 2a.] First Baptist Church, Pacific St. bet. Smith and Hoyt Sts. N side. 1860s.

A small **Hansel and Gretel** confection. The tower, turrets, and manse jointly make a picturesque skyline.

[B 2b.] 360 Pacific Street (single house), bet. Hoyt and Bond Sts. S side. ca. 1861. ☆

A lone painted clapboard house, presenting a **Corinthian-**columned porch to the street and crowned with a cornice bearing dentils.

[B 2c.] 372 and **372½ Pacific Street (row houses)/**bet. Hoyt and Bond Sts. S side. ☆

A pair of small mansarded houses with double entrance doors.

[B 2d.] 374 Pacific Street (row house), bet. Hoyt and Bond Sts. S side. ca. 1850. ☆

A unique example of the Gothic Revival, unfortunately **stripped** of much of its detail. The district is otherwise largely homogeneous, with the earlier Greek Revival houses and later Renaissance Revival. Here is **Lucky Pierre,** always in the middle. The **ornate bronze balcony** fronting the parlor floor was moved from a house in Fort Greene.

[B 3a.] 245 Dean Street (row houses), bet. Bond and Nevins Sts. N side. 1853. John Dougherty and Michael Murray, builders. ☆

This house, one of 30 in a continuous row, remained in the ownership of one family for **many generations.** That typical aspect of history in this neighborhood explains the well-maintained facades. Note the intricately built-up entrance doors.

[B 3b.] 240 and **244 Dean Street (row houses),** bet. Bond and Nevins Sts. S side. 1858. Wilson & Thomas, builders. ☆

Two surviving and carefully restored examples of what were originally **four** Victorian clapboard cottages.

[B 3b.] 157 Hoyt Street Italianate   **[B 4d.]** Boerum Hill Café & Restaurant

[B 4.] Hoyt Street (group of single houses), bet. Bergen and Wyckoff Sts. S side. **[B 4a.] 157 Hoyt Street.** ca. 1860. **[B 4b.] 159, 161, 163 Hoyt Street.** 1871. **[B 4c.] 163½** and **165 Hoyt Street.** ca. 1854. ☆

The north-south streets in this area tend to be through-traffic arteries, and therefore houses on **them** have been altered at their ground floors into **retail space.** This grouping is an exception. **No. 157** bears an Italianate gabled roof; **Nos. 159-163** are mansarded, with vestiges of cast iron against the sky. **Nos. 163½ and 165** are innocuous, but their former deep-set front garden offers ailanthus trees in what might be kindly termed a tiny plaza.

[B 4d.] 148 Hoyt Street (apartments), SW cor. Bergen St. 1851. Thomas Maynard, builder. Renovated, 1880s. ☆

Two stories of painted brick over a former tavern, now the home of the chic **Boerum Hill Café.** The florid sheet-metal work dates from the 1880s alterations.

END of Boerum Hill Historic District. All the Boerum Hill buildings which follow are outside the district.

[B 5.] Hospital of the Holy Family, 155 Dean St., bet. Hoyt and Bond Sts. N side. 1888.

The street facade looks more to be a stew than a design, since Queen Anne was more a stew than a style. Note the **1888** interwoven in the unglazed terra-cotta ornament. The **Romanesque** arched windows step up the facade with the stair they light.

[B 6.] "The State Street Houses," 291-299 State St., bet. Smith and Hoyt Sts. N side. 290-324 State St., bet. Smith and Hoyt Sts. S side. ca. 1860. ★

A group of lovingly preserved Renaissance Revival brownstones with most of the original detail. **Nos. 293-297** have their original cast-iron balustrades. **Nos. 295-299** retain the original portals supported by console brackets. Outside the Historic District, these 22 houses are individually landmarked.

Other worthy buildings nearby, out of the district and **not landmarked:**

[B 7a.] St. Nicholas Antiochian Orthodox Cathedral, 355 State St., bet. Hoyt and Bond Sts. N side.

Cut ashlar schist with limestone detailing describe this **English country church.** The 6 dormer windows with curved eaves at each side of the nave roof provide an **elfic** Victorian quality.

[B 7b.] 371 and **375 State Street,** bet. Hoyt and Bond Sts. N side. 1890.

The **Albemarle** and the **Devonshire** are a pair of aging but spruce dowagers: brick and terra-cotta monoliths over rock-face brownstone. Savor the regal bas-reliefs in the separate pediments.

[B 8.] Engine Company 226, N.Y.C. Fire Department, 409 State St., bet. Bond and Nevins Sts. N side. ca. 1880.

A simple neighborhood civic building embellished with corbeled brick and a perfect **cast-iron crest** against the sky. It has been painted a garish red.

[B 9a.] 443-451 State Street (tenements), bet. Nevins St. and Third Ave. N side. ca. 1895.

Six sprightly tenements, with alternating round and polygonal cornices. Note the carved brownstone and limestone work at the entries and the cast- and wrought-iron balustrades.

[B 9b.] 492-496 State Street (row houses), bet. Nevins St. and Third Ave. S side. ca. 1900.

Stoopless **"English"** row houses. One enters the main floor directly, rather than by walking up a stoop to the parlor floor, as in most of Brooklyn's brick and brownstone houses.

[B 10.] Byelorussian Autocephalic Orthodox Church, 401 Atlantic Ave., NE cor. Bond St.

A simple **Gothick** brick church, articulated with buttresses and bands.

[B 11.] House of the Lord Pentecostal Church, 415 Atlantic Ave., NE cor. Nevins St.

A picturesque late Romanesque Revival church with banded brick arches and a **dour** painted ocher brick body.

[B 12a.] Atlantic Gardens, 525-535 Atlantic Ave., bet. Third and Fourth Aves. late 19th century.

Developer Ted Hilles gathered this cluster of simple brick buildings into a cooperative entered through a **central portal** into the gardens behind. The Victorian storefronts are **happy remnants** in wood, whose bayed fronts give modulation to the street.

[B 12b.] 554-552 Atlantic Avenue, bet. Third and Fourth Aves. S side.

An **Arabian Nights** building, fortunately now reclaimed by Arabs. Its spiral central column is a glazed candy cane, or **Hollywood Bernini,** with accompanying grand arches to each side.

[B 13a.] Originally **Brooklyn Printing Plant, New York Times,** 59-75 Third Ave., bet. Dean and Pacific Sts. E side. 1929. Albert Kahn.

This monumental neo-Classical limestone work **hardly hints** at the avant-garde industrial facilities that this architect would shortly create at the **Dodge Half-Ton Truck Plant** in Detroit (1938). The large windows along Third Avenue permitted the public to view the **printing, collating, and folding** of newspapers along a half-block-long printing press. The papers were then distributed from the through-block alley to the east.

 [B 13b.] Bethlehem Lutheran Church/ originally **Swedish Evangelical Bethelem Lutheran Church,** SW cor. Third Ave. and Pacific Sts. 1894.

A **very North** European brick church with 2 **marvelous** verdigris copper-framed rose windows. It has a crisp hardness, like Saarinen **père.**

[B 12b.] Like a glazed candy cane   **[B 13b.]** The Bethlehem Lutheran Ch.

[B 14b.] Pacific Branch, Bklyn. Library   **[B 15b.]** Williamsburgh Savings Bank

[B 14a.] Church of the Redeemer (Episcopal), Fourth Ave. NW cor. Pacific St. 1870. P. C. Keely.

Presiding over the chaotic intersection, this rock-face ashlar church offers polychromatic **Ruskinian** voussoirs and a sturdy tower set back from Fourth Avenue on Pacific.

 [B 14b.] Pacific Branch, Brooklyn Public Library, 25 Fourth Ave., SE cor. Pacific St. 1904. Raymond F. Almirall.

If the Church of the Redeemer, across Fourth Avenue, is an architectural symphony, this branch library is a Sousa march—self-satisfied, robust, and stridently **Beaux Arts.** Note the cornice with torchères and swags, and the gargantuan consoles over the first floor.

Times Plaza: The 5-way intersection of 3 major routes—Atlantic, Flatbush, and Fourth Avenues—together with 2 secondary ones, Ashland Place and Hanson Place, forms Times Plaza, named for the **Brooklyn Daily Times,** once published nearby. It is now dominated by Brooklyn's tallest building, the **Williamsburgh Savings Bank tower.** It is at this chaotic starfish that the Long Island Railroad has its decrepit **Atlantic Avenue Terminal.** It is destined to be supplanted by major new office facilities.

[B 15a.] Originally **IRT Atlantic Avenue subway kiosk,** in the triangle formed by Flatbush, Atlantic, and Fourth Aves. 1908. Heins & LaFarge. Added enveloping structure, 1977, Stephen Lepp.

A sorry fate overtook this anchor on the IRT subway lines. Constructed in 1908 to celebrate and advertise the new underground connection with Manhattan, it was abandoned as a working entrance and then buried within a filigree intended to revitalize it visually and commercially. Heins & LaFarge's distinguished work for the subway system faintly survives on these lines, mostly in the restored mosaic works.

[B 15b.] **Williamsburgh Savings Bank Tower,** 1 Hanson Place, NE cor. Ashland Place. 1929. Halsey, McCormack & Helmer. ★ ☆ (BAM Historic District.)

Inadvertently, this was New York's most **phallic** symbol (Manhattan's **Cityspire** is taking up the torch), its slender tower dominating the landscape of all Brooklyn. A crisp and clean tower, it is detailed in **Romanesque-Byzantine** arches, columns, and capitals. The **26th** floor includes outdoor viewing space, accessible after a change of elevators. In these upper regions, **all** of Brooklyn's **orthodontists** seem to have roosted. All in all, it is **512** feet of skyline.

Records set, records broken: While the Williamsburgh Savings Bank Tower is still the tallest office building in Brooklyn, it is **not** the tallest structure. That honor goes to the Board of Education's lacy radio and television transmission tower for **WNYE-FM** and **WNYE-TV** atop nearby Brooklyn Technical High School, 29 Fort Greene Place (**597** feet). Similarly, the Williamsburgh's illuminated clock was the largest 4-sided clock in the nation (**27** feet in diameter) until the **40-foot-**diameter clocks on the Allen Bradley Building in Milwaukee were finished in 1962. An up-close look at the grotesquely large hands and illuminated numbers from the tower's observation deck is a worthwhile and surrealistic experience [see B 15b. above].

[B 15c.] Hanson Place Methodist Church: stores occupy some of its frontage

[B 15c.] **Hanson Place Central Methodist Church,** 88 Hanson Place, NW cor. St. Felix St. 1930. ☆ (BAM Historic District.)

Gothic restyled in **modern dress,** an exercise in massing brick and tan terra-cotta that might be termed a cubistic **Art Moderne.** The street level contains stores, a surprising but **intelligent** adjunct to ecclesiastical economics. This building replaced its predecessor, on the site from **1847** to **1927.**

 [B 16a.] Baptist Temple, 360 Schermerhorn St., SW cor. Third Ave. 1894. Rebuilt, 1917.

This **Romanesque Revival** fortress bears gables and a machicolated tower. The lighted cross emblazons the **fundamentalist preaching** within. The intersection before it, officially **Temple Square,** understandably acquired the nickname **Brimstone Square.**

[B 16b.] N.Y.C. Board of Education Certificating Unit/formerly **Public School 15, Brooklyn/**originally **Brooklyn Boys' Boarding School,** 475 State St., NE cor. Third Ave. ca. 1840.

A dour red-painted institutional remnant that is the far-flung **outpost** of the bureaucracy centered at 110 Livingston Street.

[B 17.] Brooklyn Academy of Music Historic District, bet. Lafayette Ave., Ashland, Hanson, and Fort Greene Places, plus parts of the N side of Fort Greene Place and both sides of S. Elliott Place. ★

The row houses of St. Felix Street are a **surprising** and **charming** foil to the bulky neo-Renaissance Academy.

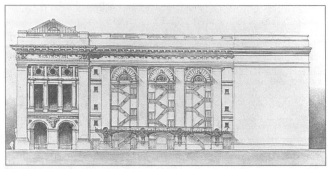

[B 17a.] The Brooklyn Academy of Music's original grand corniced facade

 [B 17a.] Brooklyn Academy of Music (BAM), 30 Lafayette Ave., bet. Ashland Place and St. Felix St. 1908. Herts & Tallant. ☆

This modest building was originally crowned with a great Renaissance Revival **cornice,** its external architectural essential. Its loss puts the building in the role of **queen of England** without a hat. A multichambered performing arts center two generations before Lincoln Center, it still houses a **Symphony Hall, Opera House, Chamber Music Hall,** and other spaces that are rich, handsome, and of excellent acoustic quality. Culturally, it is where the great avant-garde experiments occur in New York, a veritable **Vesuvius** of talent in dance, theater, and music.

FORT GREENE/CLINTON HILL/THE NAVY YARD

"To the rear of the **boisterous** city hall quarter was Brooklyn's other fine residential district, the Hill. Located in the center of the city and surrounded by **diverse elements,** its position was not unlike that of the **Heights;** but its elegant residences were fewer in number and their owners slightly further removed from the traditions of **genteel respectability.** It abounded in churches and middle class houses, the majority of whose owners worked in New York, but took pride in **living** in Brooklyn." **Harold C. Syrett,** *The City of Brooklyn, 1865–1898.*

Fort Greene and Clinton Hill rank with **Cobble Hill** and **Boerum Hill** as rediscovered sectors of urban delight. Clustering around **Fort Greene Park** and **Pratt Institute** are blocks of distinguished brownstones, many **mansions,** and a surprisingly rich inventory of **churches and other institutions.** The communities' edges at **Fulton Street, Flatbush Avenue,** and along the old Navy Yard are roughened by cheap commercial areas and by neighborhoods of urban renewal still in flux. But the body is, for the most part, **solid and handsome.**

FORT GREENE/CLINTON HILL

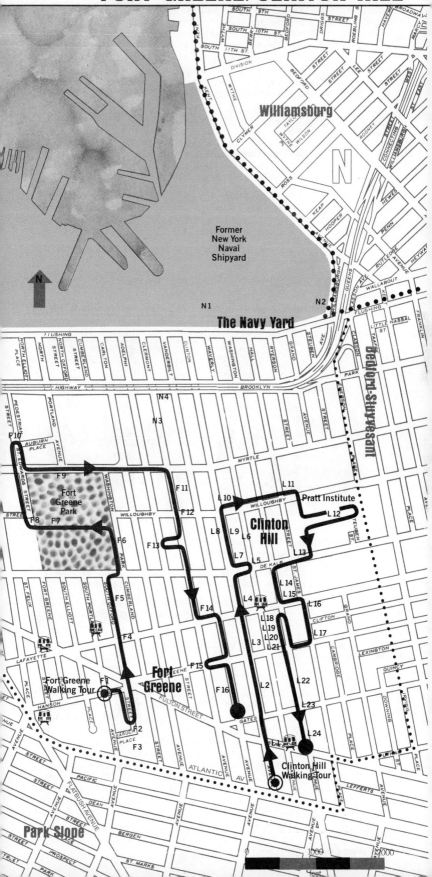

Williamsburg

N

Former
New York
Naval
Shipyard

N1   N2

The Navy Yard

Bedford-Stuyvesant

N4

N3

F10

Fort
Greene
Park

F9

F8 F7

F11

F12

F13

F6

F5

F4

F1

Fort Greene
Walking Tour

Fort
Greene

F14

F15

F16

F2

F3

L10   L11   Pratt Institute
L12

Clinton
Hill

L8 L9 L6

L7   L13

DE KALB

L14
L15

L16

L4

L18
L19
L20
L21

L3

L17

L2

L22

L23

L24

Clinton Hill
Walking Tour

Park Slope

0   1000   2000

feet

FORT GREENE

Fort Greene Walking Tour: Start at Hanson Place and South Portland Street, about four blocks east from either the Atlantic Avenue Station of the IRT, BMT, and Long Island Railroad or the Pacific Street Station of the BMT (all at Times Plaza), or the Lafayette Avenue Station of the IND. The walk ends on Vanderbilt Avenue at Gates. Continue to Fulton Street and turn left to Clinton Avenue to reach the IND subway, one stop farther away from Manhattan. Buildings surrounding Times Plaza are covered in the **Boerum Hill/Times Plaza** section.

[F 1a.] Hanson Place Seventh-Day Adventist Church/originally **Hanson Place Baptist Church,** 88 Hanson Place, SE cor. S. Portland Ave. 1860. ★

A glorious **Corinthian-columned** portico fronts on Hanson Place, with pilasters along the South Portland flanks. Cream columns, trim, and pediments over a dark red body. Victorian milk glass.

[F 2a.] Oxford Nursing Home/originally **Lodge No. 22, Benevolent Protective Order of Elks,** 144 S. Oxford St., bet. Hanson Place and Atlantic Ave. W side. 1912. H. Van Buren Magonigle and A. W. Ross. Altered, 1955, Wechsler & Schimenti.

The glorious **bracketed cornice** is a wide-sweeping catholic hat on this body abused in alteration.

[F 2b.] 143 and **145 South Oxford Street (row houses),** bet. Hanson Place and Atlantic Ave. E side.

A handsome pair of Corinthian-columned porches, **alive and loved.**

[F 1a.] Elegant Corinthian pilasters   [F 2c.] Italianate lawn, Fort Greene

[F 2c.] 158 South Oxford Street (single house), bet. Hanson Place and Atlantic Avenue. W side. ca. 1860.

A freestanding shingled Italianate house with a Carpenter Gothic porch set on a unique podium for these blocks: **a raised lawn.**

[F 2d.] Originally **New York & Brooklyn Casket Company,** 187 S. Oxford St., bet. Hanson Place and Atlantic Ave. E side. 1927. Vincent B. Fox.

A lonely limestone **neo-Georgian** remnant now squeezed between tennis courts and devastation.

Atlantic Avenue Urban Renewal Area

Plotted on a map, this 20-year-old urban renewal area looks faintly like a comet pointing northwest to **Downtown Brooklyn** and the **Civic Center.** Its body is the still decaying **Atlantic Avenue Terminal** of the Long Island Railroad's Brooklyn section. Its tail is contained within Hanson Place and Fulton Street to the north, and Atlantic Avenue to the south. It has eliminated the old **Fort Greene Meat Market** and has constructed new housing projects [F3a., 3b., and 3c.], but it has still to reconstruct the **Terminal** and its related commercial facilities. Once upon a time Baruch College was to have been here, in concert with a grand new terminal; but now commercial space will occupy that proposed volume over the station and yards.

[F 3a.] 170 South Portland Avenue and **161 South Elliott Place (apartments),** bet. Hanson Place and Atlantic Ave. **[F 3b.] 455 and 475 Carlton Avenue (apartments),** bet. Fulton St. and Atlantic Ave. E side. **770 Fulton Street (apartments),** bet. Carlton Ave. and Adelphi St. S side. All buildings, 1976. Bond Ryder Associates.

Residential blocks sheltering a variety of apartments, expressed by the **staccato** placement of the **windows.** The spaces between the buildings are urbanely designed and arranged for playgrounds and plazas.

[F 3c.] Atlantic Terminal Houses, N.Y.C. Housing Authority, 487-495 Carlton Ave., NE cor. Atlantic Ave. 1976. James Stewart Polshek & Assocs.

These larger blocks seemingly use contrasting brick stripes to **camouflage** their ungainly appearance.

[F 4.] 98 South Oxford Street (row house), bet. Greene and Lafayette Aves. W side. ca. 1855.

A **Corinthian** columned porch is a welcome variant on the street.

Here we enter the **Fort Greene Historic District.**

[F 4a.] Fort Greene Historic District, bounded by Willoughby and Vanderbilt Aves., S. Elliott Place, and an irregular line N of Fulton St., plus Fort Greene Park. ★

[F 4b.] Lafayette Avenue Presbyterian Church, 85 S. Oxford St., SE cor. Lafayette Ave. 1862. Grimshaw & Morrill. ☆

This Romanesque Revival, cut-ashlar brownstone church, with a sturdy tower (a polygon over a square) bearing four finials, corners South Oxford and Lafayette. It is noted more, however, for its numerous Tiffany windows. The major one in the Underwood Chapel, installed in 1920, was the **last work** of the Tiffany firm. Dr. Theodore L. Cuyler, a **renowned preacher,** was its minister—hence **Cuyler Park,** the triangle at Fulton Street.

[F 4c.] 99 Lafayette Avenue (apartments), bet. S. Portland Ave. and S. Oxford Place. 1937. Jacob Mark, engineer. A. Markewich, designer.

High-style Art Deco for its time in these brownstone blocks. Red-brown brick arranged with **articulations** and ornament.

[F 4d.] The Roanoke/originally **The San Carlos Hotel,** 69 S. Oxford St., bet. Lafayette and DeKalb Aves. E side. ca. 1893. Montrose W. Morris. ☆

A proud multiple dwelling in brick and limestone, recently gutted by fire. The Landmark Preservation Commission has blessed its reconstruction—a veritable phoenix.

[F 5a.] South Oxford Street and **South Portland Avenue,** bet. Lafayette and DeKalb Aves. ☆

Two handsome, tree-shaded blocks of brownstones. South Oxford's offer a range from the early 1850s to the end of the 19th century. South Portland's are mostly Renaissance Revival from the later 1860s. This district sports not only these **fashionable London street names** but also **Adelphi, Carlton, Cumberland,** and **Waverly.**

At the end of these blocks rises Fort Greene Park, a later stop on the tour. Turn right on DeKalb Avenue, and left at the end of the park onto:

[F 6.] Washington Park (residences), that portion of Cumberland St. facing Fort Greene Park. DeKalb to Myrtle Aves. ☆

These 2 blocks of brownstones were once the equal in **social stature** of any in Brooklyn.

[F 6a.] 192 Washington Park (residence), bet. DeKalb and Willoughby Aves. E side. ca. 1880. Marshall J. Morrill. ☆

Queen Anne, with a mansard roof that bears projecting bay windows, ending with a columned dormer at the crest.

[F 6b.] 179-186 Washington Park (residence), bet. DeKalb and Willoughby Aves. E side. 1866. Joseph H. Townsend, builder. ☆

A mansarded ensemble with **paired dormer windows** in each slated roof. Note the stained-glass fanlight at **No. 182** and the several wood-framed cut-glass doors. Publisher **Alfred C. Barnes** lived at 182.

[F 6c.] 173-176 Washington Park (residences), bet. Willoughby and DeKalb Aves. E side. ca. 1867. Thomas B. Jackson, builder. ☆

Lesser lights than [F 6b.] above, they housed among others William C. Kingsley at **No. 176** and his partner, Albert Keeney, next door at **No. 175. Kingsley and Keeney** were among Brooklyn's most affluent contractors, builders of streets and sewers, a reservoir further out on Long Island, and much of Prospect Park. In **1867,** when Kingsley bought his house, he was known to be the driving political force behind the **Brooklyn Bridge;** he later became its largest individual stockholder.

Enter Fort Greene Park and climb the hill to the base of the giant Doric column.

[F 7.] Fort Greene Park/originally **Washington Park,** DeKalb Ave. to Myrtle Ave., Washington Park St. to Edwards St. 1867. Frederick Law Olmsted & Calvert Vaux. Additions, 1908, McKim, Mead & White. Altered, 1972, Berman, Roberts & Scofidio. ☆

The **prospect** of the harbor and Manhattan skyline from its **summit** suggests that **this** might better have been the park named **Prospect.**

[F 7a.] Prison Ship Martyrs Monument, center of Fort Greene Park. 1908. McKim, Mead & White, architects. A. A. Weinman, sculptor. ☆

A tall **Doric column,** crowned with a bronze brazier, remembers the 11,500 American patriots who died in the 11 British prison ships anchored in Wallabout Bay **(1776–1783).** The old Navy Yard infilled this former East River body of water. Weinman's brazier, 148 feet above the park summit, once held an eternal flame. The tower's stair is not open to the public. Nearby, what was built as the world's **most elegant comfort station,** a square, **distyle in antis** Doric temple, is now the park's visitors' center. **Visit.**

Entries **F 8., F 9., F 10., & F 11.** are an aside **outside** the Historic District.

[F 8.] The Brooklyn Hospital, DeKalb Ave. to Willoughby St., from Fort Greene Park to Ashland Place. 1920. J. M. Hewlett. Altered and expanded, 1967, Rogers, Butler & Burgun. 1985. Rogers, Burgun, Shahine & Deschler. **[F 8b.] Staff Residence (apartments),** NE cor. of site, Willoughby St., SW cor. St. Edwards St. 1976. Walker O. Cain & Assocs.

The residential tower plays with some **cubist carving** at its crest, but the new wing springing out to DeKalb Avenue is sleek and elegant in brown brick and glass.

[F 9a.] Walt Whitman Houses and **[F 9b.] Raymond V. Ingersoll Houses/**originally **Fort Greene Houses, N.Y.C. Housing Authority,** Myrtle to Park Aves., Carlton Ave. to Prince St. 1944. Rosaria Candela, André Fouilhoux, Wallace K. Harrison, Albert Mayer, Ethan Allen Dennison, William I. Hohauser, Ely Jacques Kahn, Charles Butler, Henry Churchill, and Clarence Stein.

Thirty-five hundred apartments **(14,000 persons)** on 38 acres, completed during World War II as high-priority housing for Brooklyn's wartime industrial labor force. Within its bounds are the **Church of St. Michael and St. Edward, Cumberland Hospital,** and **P.S. 67.** Its architects are a roster of New York's greatest talents in the 1930s and 1940s. Nevertheless, it is a bland place—perhaps another case of **too many cooks.**

[F 10.] Church of St. Michael and St. Edward (Roman Catholic)/ originally **Church of St. Edward,** within the bounds of Ingersoll Houses, 108 St. Edward's St., bet. Myrtle and Park Aves. W side. 1902. John J. Deery. Altar, 1972, Carol Dykman O'Connor. Cross, 1972, Robert Zacharian.

Twin conical-capped towers in the manner of a 16th-century **Loire Valley château.** The interior is **Pop Art** plaster, with huge sheets of pictorial stained glass (done by a Norman Rockwell of the medium).

The altar and cross incorporate parts of the old **Myrtle Avenue el,** which once rumbled down the street next door.

For those who remember the dappled gloom of Myrtle Avenue as it suffocated under the el, a walk east on the wide, sunlit thoroughfare will be refreshing. Turn right at Clermont Avenue.

[F 11.] Formerly **3rd Battery, New York National Guard**/now **Encumbrance Warehouse, N.Y.C. Department of Sanitation,** 181 Clermont Ave., bet. Myrtle and Willoughby Aves. E side. ca. 1890.

The **un**encumbered space of this stark, bland onetime National Guard armory is now used to store and auction the encumbrances (household belongings) of unfortunate New Yorkers dispossessed from their homes.

[F 7a.] Originally this "temple" was the world's most elegant comfort station

[F 7a.] The Prison Ship Martyrs Mon.   **[F 12.]** Église Baptiste Française

Now reenter the Historic District.

[F 12.] Église Baptiste d'Expression Française/formerly **Jewish Center of Fort Greene/**originally **Simpson Methodist Church,** 209 Clermont Ave., SE cor. Willoughby Ave. 1870. ☆

The capsule history of a neighborhood's demographic change is here illustrated: first **WASP,** then **Jewish,** now **Haitian.** Here the northern Italian **raiment** of **Lombardian Romanesque** was adapted to the needs of a 19th-century Brooklyn Church. Note the **Star of David** still ensconced above the portals.

Turn for a detour through the midblock playground to Adelphi Street.

[F 13.] Church of St. Michael and St. Mark, (Anglican) Adelphi St. bet. Willoughby and DeKalb Aves. W side. 1888. ☆

A picturesque asymmetrical ensemble in rough brownstone, entowered.

Return to Clermont Avenue.

 [F 14a.] Again **The Brooklyn Masonic Temple**/briefly **Medgar Evers Community College**/originally **The Brooklyn Masonic Temple,** 317 Claremont Ave., NE cor. Lafayette Ave. 1909. Lord & Hewlett and Pell & Corbett. ☆

They took the word **"temple"** literally in 1909. Some of the vigorous polychromy that archaeologists believe was painted onto 5th century B.C. Greek temples is **recalled here** in fired terra-cotta.

[F 14a.] The Brooklyn Masonic Temple   **[F 14b.]** Our Lady Queen of All Saints

 [F 14b.] Our Lady Queen of All Saints School, Church and **Rectory (Roman Catholic),** 300 Vanderbilt Ave., NW cor. Lafayette Ave. 1913. Gustave Steinback. ☆

George Mundelein, later cardinal at Chicago, commissioned this complex while he was pastor of this local parish. A glassy church (**stained**) and a glassy school (**clear**) suggest on the one hand that stained-glass glory, the **Sainte Chapelle** in Paris, and, on the other, the sunlit aspects of modern school buildings. Inside, the church's aisles are, perhaps, the world's narrowest. Outside, 24 saints stand guard over the facade. To enter the church one, in fact, tunnels through the school.

  [F 14c.] Originally **Joseph Steele residence**/now **Skinner residence,** 200 Lafayette St., SE cor. Vanderbilt Ave. 1812. Altered. ★

An extraordinary relic from the days when these precincts were farm country. Greek Revival, with elegant narrow clapboards, a bracketed cornice with eyebrow windows, and a **widow's walk** with a view of the harbor in those open, early days. It wears its age well, with dignity. The original **Federal cottage** is the eastern wing, the tail of the later Greek Revival dog.

[F 15a.] Formerly **Residence, Roman Catholic Bishop of Brooklyn**/now **The Chancery,** 367 Clermont Ave., NE cor. Greene Ave. 1887. P. C. Keely. ☆

Dour. Hollywood would cast it as an orphan asylum in a **Charlotte Brontë** novel. The neatly dressed granite blocks and mansard roof may be austere, but they were **meant** to be subdued in contrast to the proposed but **never built** neighboring cathedral [see below].

[F 15b.] 80 Greene Avenue (apartments), SE cor. Clermont Ave. 1986. Warren Gran & Assocs. ☆

A well-scaled modern infill building, with great balconies that happily corner this intersection. The beehive-crowned **Church of the Messiah** stood here until it burned (see **Necrology**).

[F 16.] 378-434 Vanderbilt Avenue (row houses), bet. Greene and Gates Aves. W side. ca. 1880. ☆

An almost perfectly preserved row of **29 Renaissance Revival** brownstones steps down a gentle hill. At either end their march is stopped in a dignified way: **Nos. 378** and **434** return to the building line, embracing a long narrow space modulated with front stoops and front gardens. Note that the balustrades are **cast iron** painted to look like brownstone. Industrialization rears its head.

Memories of an unbuilt monument: The entire block bounded by Vanderbilt, Clermont, Lafayette, and Greene Avenues was acquired in 1860 as the site for what was to be one of the world's largest churches, the **Cathedral of the Immaculate Conception.** Patrick Charles Keely, one of the 19th century's most prolific architects, was chosen to execute the commission. Foundations were laid and walls rose to heights of ten to twelve feet. The **Chapel of St. John,** the largest of the cathedral's proposed six, was completed in 1878 and the **Bishop of Brooklyn's** residence, nine years later. Then funds dried up and all work stopped. The incomplete walls remained for decades, a challenging playground for imaginative neighborhood children. After Keely's death in 1896, John Francis Bentley, architect of Westminster Cathedral in London, was asked to draw new plans; but he too died, and his plans remained incomplete. The walls stood until 1931, when they and the chapel were demolished to build Bishop Loughlin Memorial High School, a tribute to the prelate who had the original dream in 1860. The only relic is the bishop's residence, now used by the brothers who teach at the high school.

END of Fort Greene Walking Tour: The nearest subway is the IND, a block south and a block east, at Fulton Street and Clinton Avenue. If you're hungry or want a glimpse of adjacent Clinton Hill, walk north on Clinton Avenue.

Relax, refresh, refect, revive: Conveniently located in the center of gravity between the imprecisely defined communities of Fort Greene and Clinton Hill are a few places to eat and browse. Antique shops and boutiques are always opening and closing, too. On the DeKalb Avenue block between Clermont and Vanderbilt Avenues are **Two Steps Down,** a restaurant, at **No. 240;** and **Cino's Italian Restaurant** at **No. 243.** Nearby are two other Italian **trattorie,** the **Venice** at 454 Myrtle Avenue and **Joe's Place,** occupying a nondescript carriage house at 264 Waverly Avenue, north of DeKalb. All are pleasant and reasonably priced.

Farther afield:

[F 17.] Royal Castle Apartments, 20-30 Gates Ave., SW cor. Clinton Ave. 1912. Wortmann & Braun. ★

A 6-story exhuberant Beaux Arts structure, intended to rise to the high style of older Clinton Avenue residences. The ornament smacks of a familiarity with the *Sezession* movement, the Austrian variant of Art Nouveau.

CLINTON HILL

Clinton Hill Walking Tour: Starts at Clinton Avenue and Fulton Street, at the Clinton-Washington Station of the IND train, and ends near the same station. In between you will pass what remains of the homes on the **Hill** that were built by the merchant and industrial **kings** of Brooklyn: the **Bedfords, Pfizers, Underwoods,** and—most prominent of all— the **Pratts.** These monumental buildings present great individuality and vigorous architectural forms, with many monumental porches that make this wide avenue more plastic than typical brownstone blocks.

Walk south along Clinton Avenue. It and Washington Avenue are the wide avenues on which the most fashionable families settled.

[L 1.] Clinton Hill Historic District, generally bet. Willoughby at the N, Vanderbilt Ave. on the W, then a line N of Fulton St., and an eastern line on Downing St. N to Gates Ave., then Grand St. N to Lafayette Ave., then W to Hall St., then N to the Willoughby Ave. start. ★

[L 1a.] Church of St. Luke & St. Matthew (Episcopal)/originally **St. Luke's Episcopal Church,** 520 Clinton Ave., bet. Fulton St. and Atlantic Ave. W side. 1889. John Welch. ★

In the 1880s and 1890s the Episcopalians begat what seemed to be **Baptist temples:** eclecticism gone **beserk** manifested in battered greenish stone walls, Romanesque arches, and Ruskinian Gothic **polychromy** in three shades of brownstone. It all adds up to a **great facade.**

Now turn around and go north on Clinton, past Fulton Street.

[L 1b.] 487 Clinton Avenue (apartments), bet. Gates Ave. and Fulton St. E side. 1892. Langston & Dahlander. ☆

A **Loire Valley château,** towered, machicolated, and mated with a Richardsonian Romanesque entry.

[L 1a.] A 19th-century agglomeration   **[L 1b.]** 487 Clinton Avenue château

[L 2a.] Originally **Morgan Bogart residence,** 463 Clinton Ave., bet. Gates and Greene Aves. E side. 1902. Mercein Thomas. ☆

Unique Renaissance Revival limestone in these parts. Note the Ionic-columned bay window, quoins, and rustications. An **exile** from Manhattan's Upper East Side.

[L 2b.] 457 Clinton Avenue (residence), bet. Gates and Greene Aves. E side. ca. 1870. ☆

A porch with 4 fluted Doric columns and a mansard roof ornament this crisp gray and white building.

[L 2c.] Originally **David Burdette residence,** 447 Clinton Ave., bet. Gates and Greene Aves. E side. ca. 1850. ☆

Now the **Galilee Baptist Church,** this Italianate brick hulk has sandstone quoins and wears two tired **Tuscan** columns at its front porch.

[L 2d.] Originally **William H. Burger residence,** 443 Clinton Ave., bet. Gates and Greene Aves. E side. 1902. Hobart A. Walker. ☆

An eclectic mélange, with fluted and banded **Tuscan** columns and a picturesque pair of gables against the mansard roof.

[L 2e.] Originally built by **Frederick A. Platt,** 415 Clinton Ave., bet. Gates and Greene Aves. E side. ca. 1865. ☆

A **General Grant** box, mansarded with gray slate; the porch is borne by sturdy Composite columns.

[L 2f.] Originally **Charles A. Schieren residence,** 405 Clinton Ave., bet. Gates and Greene Aves. E side. 1889. William Tubby. ☆

A Romanesque Revival/Queen Anne massive mansion.

[L 2g.] Originally **Cornelius N. Hoagland residence,** 410 Clinton Ave., bet. Gates and Greene Aves. W side. 1882, Parfitt Bros. ☆

An Eclectic Queen Anne mansion with picturesque dual chimneys. Note the dentils and swags.

[L 2h.] Originally **C. Walter Nichols** and **Henry L. Batterman residences,** 406 and 404 Clinton Ave., bet. Gates and Greene Aves. E side. 1901. Albert Ulrich. ☆

A Renaissance Revival pair, with a shared **Tuscan**-columned porch.

[L 3a.] Originally **John W. Shepard residence,** 356 Clinton Ave., bet. Greene and Lafayette Aves. E side. 1905. Theodore C. Visscher. ☆

A stuccoed mansion, but the **green tile** roof is something else.

[L 4a.] Originally **James H. Lounsberry residence,** 321 Clinton Ave., bet. Lafayette and DeKalb Aves. E side. ca. 1875. Ebenezer L. Roberts. ☆

A **super**-brownstone, in the same monumental class as Nos. 2 and 3 Pierrepont Place in the **Heights.**

[L 4b.] Originally **John Arbuckle residence,** 315 Clinton Ave., bet. Lafayette and DeKalb Aves. E side. 1888. Montrose W. Morris. ☆

Robust red brick, brownstone, and terra-cotta. Don't miss the intricately molded terra-cotta soffit below the bay window. **Arbuckle** was a coffee merchant who made his fortune from **Yuban** coffee.

[L 4c.] Originally **William Harkness residence,** 300 Clinton Ave., bet. Lafayette and DeKalb Aves. W side. 1889. Mercein Thomas. ☆

Here are strong bay windows surmounted by a tiny Queen Anne balcony that gives stature to a child in the attic.

Take a short detour to the right along DeKalb Avenue and then resume your northern walk on Clinton.

[L 5a.] **282-290 DeKalb Avenue (residences),** SW cor. Waverly Ave. 1890. Montrose W. Morris. ☆

Quintuplets unified by a pediment over the central trio and symmetrical cylindrical turrets at each end. A terrific **tour de force,** rare for both its design and its state of preservation.

[L 5b.] **285-289 DeKalb Avenue,** NW cor. Waverly Ave. 1889. Montrose W. Morris. ☆

This time a **trio,** with pyramidal and conical roofs connected by an intervening mansard. Brownstone, gray stone, terra-cotta, and brick both flat and curved.

[L 5b.] Pyramids, cones, and a mansard here propose an exuberant facade

[L 6.] **Waverly Avenue,** bet. Gates and Myrtle Aves. ☆

This narrow **service street** is sandwiched between the mansions of Clinton and Washington Avenues. Its many stables and carriage houses, remnant of service facilities for those wealthy neighbors, have been recycled as apartments, restaurants, and other independent units.

Back to Clinton Avenue.

[L 7a.] Originally **William W. Crane residence,** 284 Clinton Ave., bet. DeKalb and Willoughby Sts. W side. ca. 1854. ☆

A Newport **Stick and Shingle** Style house with wonderful serpentine jigsaw and carved work in its gables. The cut shingles give it a rich texture, and the varied picturesque gables provide a profile against the sky. **Snazzy.**

[L 7b.] Originally **Behrend H. Huttman residence,** 278 Clinton Ave., bet. DeKalb and Willoughby Sts. ca. 1884. ☆

Bizarre columns mark a sturdy porch, with alternating smooth and rough drum segments. A **neo-Baroque** oddity.

[L 7c] 274 Clinton Avenue, bet. DeKalb and Willoughby Ave. W side. 1879, Charles A. Mushlett, Stoop altered, 1900, Albert Korber. ☆

The stoop is miraculous: tubular rails seem to ride on **verdigris** discs. Unique.

[L 8.] St. Joseph's College/formerly **Charles Pratt residence,** 232 Clinton Ave., bet. DeKalb and Willoughby Aves. W side. 1875. Ebenezer L. Roberts. ☆

The original manor house and gardens of **Pratt père:** Italianate, freestanding brownstone mansion. His sons across the street ventured into more daring architectural experiments.

Charles Pratt, refiner of kerosene at Greenpoint, joined his oil empire with that of John D. Rockefeller's Standard Oil Company in 1874. At the marriage of each of Pratt's first 4 sons, the couple was presented with a house opposite their father's place for a wedding present. Of these, 3 remain: those of **Charles M., Frederic,** and **George. Harold,** succumbing to the changing fashion stimulated by the consolidation of Brooklyn and New York, built his nuptial palace on Park Avenue at 68th Street. Fifth son, **John,** also chose to live (more modestly than Harold) in Manhattan.

[L 2f.] The neo-Flemish Renaissance   [L 9a.] Orig. Frederick B. Pratt res.

[L 9a.] Caroline Ladd Pratt House (foreign students' residence of Pratt Institute)/originally **Frederic B. Pratt residence,** 229 Clinton Ave., bet. DeKalb and Willoughby Aves. E side. 1898. Babb, Cook & Willard. ☆

Attached on one side and freestanding on the other, it forms a neat and handsome urban transition. The pergolaed entry supported by truncated **caryatids** and **atlantides** does the trick. The house proper is gray and white **Georgian Revival.** To the garden's rear, view another sturdy pergola borne by a dozen **Tuscan** fluted columns and, at the entry, a most venerable wisteria.

[L 9b.] Residence, Bishop of Brooklyn (Roman Catholic)/originally **Charles Millard Pratt residence,** 241 Clinton Ave., bet. DeKalb and Willoughby Aves. E side. 1893. William B. Tubby. ☆

Richardsonian Romanesque, this presents a great arch to the street, one that offers a penetration to the garden and garage behind; the garage, a **porte cochere,** is part of the whole building's volume, not an add-on. The detailing in smooth, rounded forms makes this place both powerful and sensuous. Note particularly the spherical bronze lamp at the entrance and the semicircular **conservatory** high on the south wall.

[L 9c.] St. Joseph's College/originally **George DuPont Pratt residence,** 245 Clinton Ave. (N wing only), bet. DeKalb and Willoughby Sts. E side. 1901. Babb, Cook & Willard. ☆

Red brick and limestone, quoined and corniced, this is Georgian revival that reeks of Englishness—it might well be the British embassy. The additions by the college to the south are properly unprepossessing.

[L 9b.] Orig. Charles Millard Pratt res./now Residence, Bishop of Brooklyn

Turn right on Willoughby Avenue.

[L 10.] Clinton Hill Apartments, Section 1, Clinton to Waverly Aves., Willoughby to Myrtle Aves. 1943. Harrison & Abramovitz. Irwin Clavan.

World War II housing for the families of naval personnel (the old Navy Yard, now an industrial park, is a short walk away). Blue and white **nautical motifs** are included as ornament at the entrances, despite wartime restrictions on just about everything else. (Section 2 was completed by the same architects further south between Lafayette and Greene Avenues.)

[L 11.] Willoughby Walk Apartments, Hall St. to Classon Ave., Willoughby to Myrtle Aves. 1957. S. J. Kessler.

Undistinguished slabs dominating the landscape, these marked the coming of urban renewal to this area. Federal subsidies absorbed 90 percent of the cost of land and demolition, making it feasible to create apartments for middle-income families.

[L 12.] Pratt Institute Campus, Willoughby Ave. to DeKalb Ave., Classon Ave. to Hall St. 1887– . Various architects.

Originally 5 blocks and the streets that served them. **Urban renewal** gave the Institute opportunity to make a single, **campus-style** superblock. As the separate buildings were built to conform to the former street pattern, and the intervening buildings were removed, the result became surreal: a kind of abstract chessboard, where the pieces sit on a blank board without a grid.

A **professional school** of art and design, architecture, engineering, and computer information and library sciences. **Charles Pratt** ran it as his **personal** philanthropic fiefdom until his death in 1891. A similar case study to that of **Cooper Union,** with its patron, **Peter Cooper.**

[L 12a.] Memorial Hall, Pratt Institute, S of Willoughby Ave. on Ryerson Walk. E side. 1927. John Mead Howells. ★

Howells **reversed history.** Instead of grafting Byzantine capitals onto Roman columns to produce a Romanesque vocabulary, he grafted this whole building, a neo-Byzantine eclectically detailed hall, onto the adjacent Romanesque Revival Main Building.

[L 12b.] Main Building, Pratt Institute, S of Memorial Hall on Ryerson Walk. E side. 1887. Lamb & Rich. ★

A gung-ho Romanesque Revival, where sturdy, squat columns bear a porch embellished with an organically ornamented frieze. At each side, wrought-iron cradles bear spherical iron lanterns.

Looking backward: To enter the Pratt Institute engine room, located on the ground floor of the East Building (originally Machine Shop Building, 1887, William Windrim), is to pass through a time warp. Inside spin a gleaming trio of late 19th-century Ames Iron Works steam engines (actually installed in 1900), whose electrical generators still supply one-third of the campus buildings with 120 volt D.C. service. These and other antique artifacts form a veritable museum of industrial archaeology. On display is a name plate of the DeLavergne Refrigerating Machine Company, chandeliers from the Singer Tower's boardroom, and a "No Loafing" sign from the Ruppert Brewery complex, among other industrial memorabilia.

To your right across the campus green is the library.

[L 12c.] Library/originally **Pratt Institute Free Library,** Hall St. bet. Willoughby and DeKalb Aves. E side. 1896. William B. Tubby. Altered, 1936, John Mead Howells. Altered again, 1982, Giorgio Cavaglieri & Warren Gran. ★

Tubby's stubby: strongly articulated brick piers give a bold face to Hall Street and adjacent flanks. A free Romanesque Revival but with a classical plan. Originally Brooklyn's first **free** public library, it was restricted to Pratt **students** in 1940.

Walk east along the campus's long axis. At the far end is Pratt's newest building.

 [L 12d.] Pratt Activity/Resource Center, E of Steuben St. 1975. Activity center (upper part), Daniel F. Tully Assocs. Resource center (lower part), Ezra D. Ehrenkrantz & Assocs.

Here are sensational and sinuously housed tennis courts. Architectural fashions come late to Brooklyn, and this one was **outdated** some time ago. These enormous hyperbolic-paraboloidal tents were, apocryphally, the response to the student unrest of the late 1960s and are now a big, bulky east-ending of this amorphous campus.

[L 12e.] Children's Portico, NW cor. of the Activity/Resource Center. 1912.

Here a much later appendage of the library [L 12c.] was dismantled and relocated to the other side of Pratt Campus. It is said to be a copy of part of the **King's School,** Canterbury Cathedral: a Norman Revival Chevron-ornamented remnant.

[L 12f.] Pratt Row, 220-234 Willoughby Ave., S side. 171-185 Steuben St. E. side. 172-186 Emerson Place. W side. ca. 1910. Hobart C. Walker. ★

These were preserved despite the mandates of the same federal **urban renewal** legislation that produced **Willoughby Walk**—mandates to declare a certain percentage of existing units substandard. The 27 that remain are faculty housing. Note the alternating **Dutch** and triangular gables.

[L 12g.] Thrift Hall, Pratt Institute, Ryerson Walk, NE cor. DeKalb Ave. 1916. Shampan & Shampan.

The Thrift, as its classical lettering proclaims atop a neo-Georgian limestone and brick body, was built to be a bank but now houses offices behind those Corinthian pilasters. Charles Pratt, Sr., initiated the idea of student savings in 1889, shortly before his death (his original building was demolished to make way for Memorial Hall). The Thrift closed as a bank in the early 1940s.

[L 13.] St. James Towers/originally **University Terrace (apartments),** DeKalb to Lafayette Aves., St. James Place to Classon Ave. 1963. Kelly & Gruzen.

The balconies are **recessed** within the body of these high-rise slabs rather than projecting. Their containment on three sides not only solves a design problem but also reduces the possibilities for **vertigo.**

[L 14a.] Originally **Graham Home for Old Ladies,** 320 Washington Ave., bet. DeKalb and Lafayette Aves. W side. 1851. J. G. Glover. ☆

A simple neo-Georgian brick building of an almost industrial scale, now painted slate gray. The inset and incised stone plaque speaks of **earlier days** and **earlier uses.** Now it claims to be the **Bull Shippers Plaza Motor Inn.**

The original patron organization was deftly titled **The Brooklyn Society for the Relief of Respectable, Aged, Indigent Females,** to whom paint manufacturer, John B. Graham, donated this building.

[L 12b.] The Main Building, Pratt Inst.   **[L 14a.]** Graham Home for Old Ladies

[L 15a., b.] Apostolic Faith Church (left) & Emmanuel Baptist Church (right)

[L 14b.] Underwood Park, Lafayette Ave. bet. Washington and Waverly Aves. N side. ☆

Mostly the site of the former **John T. Underwood** (of typewriter fame) mansion plus adjacent row houses, demolished at the direction of his widow, who saw Clinton Hill decline precipitously and did not want the grand house she shared with her husband to decline and deteriorate in concert. Fortunately for the rest of the neighborhood, decline was checked and then reversed in the 1960s. Happy for the neighborhood; sad that we lost this one.

[L 15a.] Apostolic Faith Church/originally **Orthodox Friends Meeting House,** 273 Lafayette Ave., NE cor. Washington Ave. 1868. Attributed to Stephen C. Earle. ☆

A simple Lombardian Romanesque brick box, **polychromed** with vigor, in red and white paint, by its current tenants.

[L 15b.] Emmanuel Baptist Church, 279 Lafayette Ave., NW cor. St. James Place. 1887. Francis H. Kimball. ★ ☆

Yellow Ohio sandstone was carved here into an approximation of a **13th-century** French Gothic facade. The interior, in startling contrast, is a **Scottish Presbyterian** preaching space, with radial seating fanning from the pulpit and baptismal font.

[L 16.] Higgins Hall, Pratt Institute/originally **Adelphi Academy,** St. James Place bet. Lafayette Ave. and Clifton Place. N wing, 1869. Mundell & Teckritz. S wing, 1887. Charles C. Haight. ☆

The brickmasons have been loose again, with piers, buttresses, round arches, segmental arches, reveals, and corbel tables. The nature of the material is **exploited** and **exaggerated.** Henry Ward Beecher laid the cornerstone of the north building, and Charles Pratt donated $160,000 for the latter. The north building is somewhat bedraggled these days, as schools of architecture (Pratt's is within) seem to be the **cobbler's children;** the south building is in a sturdy and well-kept Richardsonian Romanesque.

[L 17c.] William Tubby's wonderful mansard streetscape for Cambridge Place

[L 16.] Higgins Hall of Pratt Institute   [L 18b.] Queen Anne 361 Washington

[L 17a.] St. James Place, the southerly extension of Hall St. **[L 17b.] Clifton Place,** running E from St. James Place. ☆ **[L 17c.] Cambridge Place,** starting S at Greene Ave., bet. St. James Place and Grand Ave. ☆

Three **Places** that are really **places.** Each is a showpiece of urban row-house architecture built for the Brooklyn middle class between the

1870s and 1890s. When bored by the monotony of a uniform row, architects turned to **picturesque** variety, giving identity of detail and silhouette to each owner, as in **Nos. 202–210** St. James Place.

Nos. 179-183 St. James Place are a Flemish Revival trio built in 1892 by William B. Tubby. **Nos. 127-135 Cambridge Place,** bet. Gates and Putnam Aves., are a quintet from 1894, also by Tubby.

If you wish a peek at Cambridge Place, turn left at Greene Avenue for a short block and then return. If not, turn right on Greene and right again at Washington Avenue, for a half-block excursion.

[L 18a.] 357-359 Washington Avenue, bet. Greene and Lafayette Aves. E side. ca. 1860. Attributed to Ebenezer L. Roberts. ☆

Twin wood-clapboarded painted Victorian neighbors.

[L 18b.] Originally **Henry Offerman residence,** 361 Washington Ave., bet. Greene and Lafayette Aves. E side. 1888. ☆

Queen Anne brick body, with brownstone quoins and trim, a high mansard roof, and terra-cotta friezes. It boldly thrusts its bayed form out into the streetscape.

[L 19.] The Mohawk (apartments)/formerly **The Mohawk Hotel**/originally **The Mohawk (apartments),** 379 Washington Ave., bet. Greene and Lafayette Sts. E side. 1904. Neville & Bagge. ☆

A **Beaux Arts** latecomer to the **Hill,** festooned with limestone quoins and monumental carved pediments. By the turn of the century, the idea of apartment living—they were termed **French flats**—had begun to catch on. Recently restored, it is again a distinguished residence for the middle class, after many years of seedy life as a hotel.

[L 20.] Clinton Hill Branch, Brooklyn Public Library, 380 Washington Ave., bet. Lafayette and Greene Aves. W side. 1974. Bonsignore, Brignati, Goldstein & Mazzotta.

Here a library **program** is in obvious conflict with the scale and character of the neighborhood. A much better solution would have been to purchase one of the grand mansions available inexpensively in the 1970s. Here the one-story stripped-down modern structure is an alien eyesore.

[L 21a.] Originally **William H. Mairr** and **Raymond Hoagland residences,** 396 and 398 Washington Ave., bet. Greene and Lafayette Aves. W side. 1887. Adam E. Fischer. ☆

Bearded giants in the gables. Vermilion terra-cotta **Queen Anne.**

[L 21b.] 400-404 Washington Avenue (row houses), NW cor. Greene Ave. 1885. Mercein Thomas. ☆

A trio of **Romanesque Revival** beauties, with a variegated silhouette, a corner oriel window, and entrance archways with strong character.

[L 22.] 417 Washington Avenue (residence), bet. Greene and Gates Aves. E side. ca. 1860. ☆

Once upon a time there were expert carpenters (and shinglers and lathers and millworkers), and this gem is the result of such talent. Luckily for us, its owner treasures it and its upkeep. Note this frame dwelling's vigorous scale but miniature size. The lathework in the porch friezes is elegant.

[L 23.] Brown Memorial Baptist Church/originally **Washington Avenue Baptist Church,** 484 Washington Ave., SW cor. Gates Ave. 1860. Ebenezer L. Roberts. ☆

A pinch of Lombardian Romanesque decorates a highly articulated square-turreted **English Gothic** body. The brownstone water tables (white-painted) against red brick are perhaps too harsh.

[L 24.] Originally **College of the Immaculate Conception,** Washington Ave. NE cor. Atlantic Ave. 1916. Gustave Steinback.

A **neo**-neo-Gothic school building of great charm and elegance in brick and limestone.

END of Clinton Hill Walking Tour: The IND stops on Fulton Street at the Clinton-Washington Station. Make connections with the IRT or BMT at Manhattan's Broadway-Nassau/Fulton Street Station.

THE NAVY YARD

[N 1.] Formerly **Brooklyn Navy Yard**/officially **The New York Naval Shipyard**/now **Brooklyn Navy Yard Development Corporation,** Flushing Ave. to the East River, Hudson and Navy Sts. to Kent Ave.

Brooklyn's oldest industry, a shipyard founded here in the body of Wallabout Bay, was purchased by the Navy in **1801** and was abandoned in **1966.** During World War II, 71,000 naval and civilian personnel toiled in this city within the city. In the late 1960s some of its abandoned buildings were converted into an industrial park operated by a quasi-governmental, acronymed organization called Commerce, Labor, and Industry of the County of Kings: **CLICK**

[N 1a.] Formerly **Commandant's House, Quarters A, New York Naval Shipyard,** S of Evans and Little Sts. (E of Hudson Ave.) 1806. Attributed to Charles Bulfinch, associated with John McComb, Jr. ★

Only a glimpse of the rear is possible, for the **old Navy gates** intervene. For most people—at least below the rank of admiral—a photograph had to suffice.

[N 1a.] Formerly Commandant's House, Quarters A, New York Naval Shipyard

[N 1b.] Dry Dock No. 1 of the former New York Naval Shipyard, Dock St. at the foot of 3rd St. 1851. William J. McAlpine, engineer. Thornton MacNess Niven, architect and master of masonry. ★

Considered one of the great feats of **19th-century American engineering,** this granite-walled dry dock has serviced such ships as the **Niagara,** the vessel that laid the **first transatlantic cable,** and the **Monitor,** the Civil War's **cheesebox on a raft.** The **Niagara** was conceived and financed by a consortium headed by the painter-inventor **Samuel F. B. Morse** and the entrepreneur-philanthropist **Peter Cooper.**

[N 2a.] Originally **U.S. Marine Hospital**/later **U.S. Naval Hospital,** Flushing Ave. bet. Ryerson St. and Williamsburg Place. N side. 1838. Martin E. Thompson. ★

This austere Greek Revival hospice was built of **Sing Sing** marble, quarried by those hapless prisoners. Later "classical modernists" used similar spartan lines for simplistic public buildings of the 1930s and 1940s, culminating in the pompous buildings of **Albert Speer's** visions for Hitler's Berlin or Mussolini's "Third Rome." Thompson was a talented Greek Revivalist who muted his palette for such a functional program as this.

[N 2b.] Surgeon's House, Quarters R1, 3rd Naval District, on grounds of U.S. Naval Hospital, opp. Ryerson St. 1863. True W. Rollins and Charles Hastings, builders. ★

A spacious 2-story brick house crowned with a **French Empire** concave-profiled mansard roof. Such was the privileged residence of the Naval Hospital's chief surgeon.

[N 3.] Public School 46, Brooklyn, The Edward Blum School, 100 Clermont Ave., bet. Park and Myrtle Aves. 1958. Katz, Waisman, Blumenkranz, Stein, Weber.

An austere, white glazed-brick body, with a blue-banded base. The canopies, with their turned-up noses, are stylish and thus now out of style. The sculpted horses by Constantino Nivola that once cavorted in the play yard have been exiled in favor of a no-nonsense dual-use playground. Edward Blum was the son-in-law of **Abraham Abraham,** inheriting in turn the presidency of **Abraham & Straus,** Brooklyn's key department store.

[N 3.] The now-dated, onetime avant-garde Edward Blum School/P.S. 46 K

[N 4.] Formerly **U. S. Naval Receiving Station**/now **N.Y.C. Department of Correction facility,** 136 Flushing Ave., bet. Clermont and Vanderbilt Aves. to Park Ave. 1941.

A transient facility for naval personnel arriving, leaving, and/or tarrying at the old Naval Yard. It has that Art Moderne stylishness that went with the end of the depression and the beginning of World War II. The sailors have been replaced by the prison overflow of New York's drug dealers and other felons.

PARK SLOPE

A somber-hued wonderland of **finials, pinnacles, pediments, towers, turrets, bay windows, stoops,** and **porticoes:** a **smorgasbord** of late **Victoriana** and the successor to the **Heights** and the **Hill** as the bedroom of the middle class and wealthy. These three districts are together the prominent topographical precincts of old brownstone Brooklyn: the **Heights** sits atop a bluff over the harbor, the **Hill** is a major crest to the northeast, and the **Slope** slopes from **Prospect Park** down to the **Gowanus Canal** and the flatlands beyond.

Despite its proximity to the park, the area was slow to develop. As late as **1884** it was still characterized as **"fields and pasture."** Edwin C. Litchfield's **Italianate villa,** completed in **1857,** alone commanded the **prospect** of the harbor from its hill in present-day Prospect Park. By **1871** the first stage of the park had been constructed, yet the **Slope** lay quiet and tranquil, bypassed by thousands of persons making their way on the Flatbush Avenue horsecars to this newly created recreation area. By the mid **1880s,** however, the potential of the **Slope** became apparent, and mansions began to appear on the newly laid out street grid.

The lavish homes clustered around **Plaza Street** and **Prospect Park West** eventually were christened the **Gold Coast.** Massive apartment buildings invaded the area after World War I, feeding upon the large, unutilized plots of land occupied by the first growth. These austere **Park Avenue-like** structures, concentrated at **Grand Army Plaza,** are in contrast to the **richly imaginative** brick dwellings of **Carroll Street** and **Montgomery Place,** the mansions, churches, and clubs that still remain, and the remarkably varied row houses occupying the side streets as they descend toward the Manhattan skyline to the west.

[P 1.] Park Slope Historic District, generally along the S flank of Flatbush Ave. and Plaza St., and the W flank of Prospect Park W.; W to Sixth Ave. N of Union St., W to Seventh Ave. N of 4th St., and W to Eighth Ave. N of 15th St. ★

The first draft of the Historic District originally included only the **park blocks.** The **Slope,** emerging as the latest brownstone rediscovery of the upper middle class, was soon recognized as a precinct containing a rich fabric of row housing both within and beyond those initial arbitrary boundaries. The district finally designated reaches northwesterly from the park blocks to encompass part of the richness of **6th Avenue** between Berkeley and Sterling Places.

Park Slope Walking Tour A: From the newsstand where Flatbush Avenue joins Grand Army Plaza (at the surface of the IRT Grand Army Plaza Station) south into Park Slope and return.

Cross Plaza Street and admire:

[P 1a.] The Montauk Club, 25 Eighth Avenue, NE cor. Lincoln Place. 1891. Francis H. Kimball. ☆

A **Venetian Gothic palazzo,** whose canal is the narrow lawn separating it from its cast-iron fence. Remember the **Ca' d'Oro?** But here in brownstone, brick, terra-cotta, and verdigris copper. It bears the name of a local tribe, which explains the 8th Avenue friezes at the 3rd and 4th stories, honoring these former local natives.

[P 1a.] The Montauk Club, a Venetian palazzo moored at Grand Army Plaza

Continue on Plaza Street and turn right into Berkeley Place.

[P 2.] Originally **George P. Tangeman residence,** 276 Berkeley Place, bet. Plaza St. and Eighth Ave. S side. 1891. Lamb & Rich. ☆

Brick, granite, and terra-cotta **Romanesque Revival,** paid for by Cleveland Baking Powder. Cupid caryatids hold up the shingled pediment, with bulky Ionic columns supporting a frieze of scallop shells.

[P 3.] 64-66 Eighth Avenue (row houses), bet. Berkeley Place and Union St. W side. 1889. Parfitt Brothers. ☆

Two bold whitestone and granite residences by popular architects of that period. They bear carved foliate bas-reliefs worthy of **Louis Sullivan.**

Take a peek to the right down Union Street.

[P 4a.] 889-905 Union Street, bet. Seventh and Eighth Aves. N side. 1889. Albert E. White. ☆

Crown Heights

Park Slope

Walking Tour B

Walking Tour A

WC

Grand Army Plaza

Brooklyn Botanic Garden

Institute Park Walking Tour

The Zoo

Prospect Park Walking Tour

Prospect Park

Prospect Lake

Parade Grounds

N

1000   2000 feet

More **Queen Anne,** a picturesque **octet** with eclectic mediaval and classical parts. Note the brownstone friezes and bay windows.

[P 4b.] 905-913 Union Street, bet 7th and 8th Aves. N side. 1895. Thomas McMahon. ☆

A **Queen Anne** quintet in brick, brownstone, and shingles.

[P 5a.] 869 President Street (apartments)/originally **Stuart Woodford residence,** bet. Seventh and Eighth Aves. N side. 1885. Henry Ogden Avery. ☆

Two bracketed oriel windows punctuate the painted brick facade, articulated by **Viollet-le-Duc-**inspired struts. Woodford was **onetime** ambassador to Spain.

[P 5b.] 876-878 President Street (row houses), bet. Seventh and Eighth Aves. S side. 1889. Albert E. White. ☆

Roman brick and brownstone in a bay-windowed Queen Anne. Note the remarkably **lusty** rock-face brownstone stoops.

[P 5c.] 944-946 President Street (row houses), bet. Prospect Park W. and Eighth Ave. S side. 1886–1890. Attributed to Charles T. Mott. ☆

An extravagant duet in brick and brownstone, with rich wrought iron, stained glass and terra-cotta. There is a picturesque profile against the sky.

[P 6.] Montessori School, 105 Eighth Avenue, bet. President and Carroll Sts. E side. 1916. Helme & Huberty. ☆

A limestone **Regency Revival** mansion with a bowed, Corinthian-columned entry.

[P 7.] 18 and **19 Prospect Park West (residences),** SW cor. Carroll St. 1898. Montrose W. Morris. ☆

An eclectic set in limestone Renaissance Revival. Note the 2nd- and 3rd-floor Ionic pilasters and the hemispherical glass and bronze entrance canopy at **No. 18.**

[P 8.] Carroll Street, bet. Prospect Park W. and Eighth Ave. 1887-1911. Various architects. ☆

The **north** side of this street is as **calm, orderly, and disciplined** as the **south** side is **picturesque.** This block of Carroll Street is visual evidence of significant changing styles, viz.,

North Side

863	1890	Napoleon LeBrun & Sons
861-855	1892	Stanley M. Holden. A quartet of yellow Roman brick and brownstone **Romanesque Revival:** stained glass, carved faces, and other decorations.

South Side

878-876	1911	Chappell & Bosworth. **Park Avenue Georgian.**
872-864	1887	William B. Tubby. Queen Anne/Shingle Style.
862	1889	F. B. Langston. Dour polychromed brick and sandstone.
860	1889	Romantic in the spirit of Philadelphia's Wilson Eyre.
858-856	1889	Brownstone underpinning orange Roman brick.
848	1905	William B. Greenman. A narrow bay-windowed neo-classical exile from the Upper East Side.
846-838	1887	C. P. H. Gilbert. Three 40-foot-wide brownstone and brick beauties and the beast.

[P 9.] Originally **Thomas Adams, Jr., residence,** 119 Eighth Ave., NE cor. Carroll St. 1888. C. P. H. Gilbert. ☆

This, and the adjacent matching house at 115 Eighth Avenue, are rock-face brownstone and Roman brick. The Carroll Street arch is worthy of **Louis Sullivan,** incised with naturalistic bas-reliefs in his organic ornamental fashion, and supported by clusters of **Romanesque-**capped columns. These are major **Romanesque Revival** buildings.

[P 10.] 123 Eighth Avenue (residence), SE cor. Carroll St. 1894. Montrose W. Morris. ☆

Gray brick and terra-cotta in a free version of the **Italian Renaissance,** complete with pilasters, columns, and an entrance tympanum; here are **ornate** foliage and a **gloating satyr.**

[P 11.] Old First Reformed Church, 126 Seventh Ave., NW cor. Carroll St. 1893. George L. Morse.

A bulky, gloomy granite and limestone **neo-Gothic** monolith.

[P 12.] 195 Garfield Place (apartments), bet. Sixth and Seventh Aves., N side. Remodeled, 1986, Saltini/Ferrara.

A **quintet** of renewed Eastlake brick tenements: moated, the renovation is a respectful understatement.

[P 7.] 18 Prospect Park West res.   **[P 5a.]** Orig. Stuart Woodford res.

[P 13.] 12, 14, and 16 Fiske Place   **[P 9.]** Former Thomas Adams, Jr., res.

[P 13.] 12-16 Fiske Place (row houses), bet. Carroll St. and Garfield Place. W side. 1896. ☆

A trio where **bay** windows are presented as an academic design exercise—a **square,** a **semicircle,** and a **triangle**—creating a picturesque ensemble. Back to back through the block, the same grouping occurs similarly at **11-17 Polhemus Place.**

Turn left onto Garfield Place, and left again onto Eighth Avenue. Note, as you pass, that James A. Farrell, elected president of the United States Steel Corporation in 1911, lived at **249 Garfield Place** during his presidential tenure.

What shall we call it? Naming apartment buildings to give them panache may have begun with Manhattan's **Dakota.** At the northwest corner of Garfield Place and 8th Avenue are four more modest works: the **Serine,** the **Lillian,** and the **Belvedere.** But the Gallic influence determined number four: the **Ontrinue** (or was that **Entre Nous?**).

[P 14.] Congregation Beth Elohim (synagogue), NE cor. Eighth Ave. and Garfield Place. 1910. Simon Eisendrath & B. Horwitz. ☆

A domed Beaux Arts limestone extravaganza, its corner chamfered.

[P 15.] Montgomery Place, bet. 8th Avenue and Prospect Park W. 1888–1904. ☆

One of the **truly great** blocks in the world of urbane row housing, built as a real estate development by **Harvey Murdock.** Seeking the **picturesque,** he commissioned noted architect **C. P. H. Gilbert** to create the **scene.** An **Art Moderne** amber brick apartment house closes the vista at 8th Avenue—an accidental and successful containment of the street's space.

North Side: 11, 17, 19, 1898. C. P. H. Gilbert. **21, 25,** 1892. C. P. H. Gilbert. **27, 29, 31,** 1904. Unattributed. **35,** 1889. Hornium Bros. **37-43,** 1891. George B. Chappell. **45,** 1899. Babb, Cook & Willard. **47,** 1890. R. L. Daus.

South Side: 14-18, 1888. C. P. H. Gilbert. **20-28,** 1898. Unattributed. **30-34,** 1896. Robert Dixon. **36-46,** 1889. C. P. H. Gilbert. **48-50,** 1890. C. P. H. Gilbert. **52,** 1890. T. Williams. **54-60,** 1890. C. P. H. Gilbert.

Gilbert's works are in a powerful **Romanesque Revival,** with rock-face brownstone, brick, and terra-cotta strongly arched and linteled. Dixon contributed a fussy neoclassicism. The ensemble, however, is a symphony of materials and textures.

[P 15.] 60 Montgomery Place house   **[P 15.]** 40–42 Montgomery Place

Turn right on Prospect Park West, and proceed south.

[P 16.] Woodward Park School/formerly **Brooklyn Ethical Culture School/**originally **Henry Hulbert residence,** 50 Prospect Park W., bet. 1st and 2nd Sts. W side. 1883. Montrose W. Morris. ☆

A cadaverous rock-face and foliate-carved Romanesque Revival. The polygonal and round corner towers compete for attention.

[P 17.] Brooklyn Ethical Culture Society Meeting House/originally **William H. Childs residence,** 53 Prospect Park W., NW cor. 2nd St. 1901. William B. Tubby. ☆

A **Jacobean** loner in these turgid stone precincts, erected by the **inventor** of Bon Ami. Here a **cleansing-**powder fortune built this monument, as opposed to the **baking** powder at [P 2.].

[P 18.] Originally **Litchfield Villa**/or **Ridgewood**/or **Grace Hill Mansion**/now **Brooklyn Headquarters, N.Y.C. Department of Parks,** Prospect Park W. bet. 4th and 5th Sts. E side. 1857. Alexander Jackson Davis. ★ Annex, 1913 Helme & Huberty. ★

This is the villa of **Edwin C. Litchfield,** a lawyer whose fortune was made in midwestern railroad development. In the **1850s** he acquired a square mile of virtually vacant land extending from 1st through 9th Streets, and from the **Gowanus Canal** to the projected line of **10th Avenue,** just east of his completed mansion, a territory that includes a **major portion** of today's **Park Slope.**

The mansion is the best surviving example of Davis's **Italianate style** (he also created **Greek Revival Temples** and **Gothick castles**). More than 90 years of service as a public office have **eroded** much of its original richness: the original exterior stucco, simulating cut stone, has been stripped off, exposing **common brick** behind. Note the **corncob capitals** on the glorious porch colonnades, an Americanization of things Roman—**Corinthian** or **Corn-inthian?** The bay window facing west contains a lush frieze of **swags** and **goddesses.**

Go in, look around, ye fellow citizen and part owner. Renovations, first to the exterior, later to the interior, are scheduled for the 1990s.

[P 18.] Alexander Jackson Davis' highly romantic, Italianate Litchfield Villa

[P 19.] 108-117 Prospect Park West (apartments), bet. 6th and 7th Sts. W side. 1896. ☆

A Roman brick terrace, pristine and proud Renaissance Revival.

[P 20.] 580-592 Seventh Street, bet. Prospect Park W. and Eighth Ave. S side. ☆

Dutch **neo-Renaissance** gables give special syncopation to this handsome block.

END of Park Slope Walking Tour A: *Walk north on Prospect Park West to the Grand Army Plaza subway station.*

Park Slope Walking Tour B: From the newsstand where Flatbush Avenue joins Grand Army Plaza (at the surface of the IRT Grand Army Plaza Station) to the Bergen Street Station of the same lines. Proceed south on St. John's Place. The silhouetted spires that you see on this lovely street are those of:

[P 21.] Memorial Presbyterian Church, 42-48 7th Ave., SW cor. St. John's Place. 1883. Pugin & Walter. **Chapel,** 1888. Marshall & Walter. ☆

An ashlar brownstone sculpted monolith. **Tiffany** glass windows embellish both church and chapel.

[P 22.] Grace United Methodist Church and **Parsonage,** 29-35 7th Ave., NE cor. St. John's Place. 1882. Parsonage, 1887. Parfitt Brothers. ☆

Particularly intriguing is the **Moorish-Romanesque** facade along St. John's Place. The parsonage is a deft transition between the church and the Ward residence *cum* town houses to the north.

[P 23.] Formerly **Lillian Ward residence**, 21 7th Ave., SE cor. Sterling Place. 1887. Laurence B. Valk. ☆

A fanciful corner **oriel** worthy of the 16th-century French Renaissance guards this corner, all crowned with a slated and finialed roof. This special place (**mansion** to the locals) and its neighbors at **Nos. 23-27** were built by Valk for investor **Charles Pied,** a rare and rich group to be so well preserved.

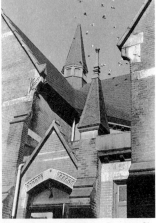

[P 23.] Originally Lillian Ward res.   **[P 30.]** Sixth Avenue Baptist Ch.

Plane crash: In the morning mist of **December 16, 1960,** two airliners collided over **Staten Island.** The pilot of one attempted an emergency landing in Prospect Park but made it only to the intersection of 7th Avenue and Sterling Place. The plane sliced the cornice off a small apartment building west of 7th Avenue (the light-colored brick marks the spot) and came to a rest with its nose on the doorstep of the old **Ward Mansion.** A church on Sterling Place was destroyed by the resulting fire, but miraculously the **mansion** was untouched.

Retrace your steps on 7th Avenue south to St. John's Place. On your right, between Sixth and Seventh Avenues are St. John's Episcopal Church at No. 139, and two robust Victorian town houses across the way at Nos. 176 and 178.

[P 24.] **St. John's Episcopal Church,** 139 St. John's Place, bet. Sixth and Seventh Aves. N side. Chapel, 1870. Edward Tuckerman Potter. Church, 1885. John R. Thomas. ☆

Victorian Gothic in varied hues and tones of brownstone; another **English country gardened church** for Brooklyn. Cut rock-face, random ashlar with, at the arched openings, alternating cream- and brownstone Ruskinian voussoirs.

[P 25.] Originally **William M. Thallon** and **Edward Bunker residences,** 176 and 178 St. John's Place, bet. Sixth and Seventh Aves. S side. 1888. R. L. Daus. ☆

Brownstone and brick eclectic mélange, with some flavor from the **Loire Valley,** some from the **Black Forest.** Note the **caduceus** in **No. 178**'s gable: not surprisingly, both **Thallon** and **Bunker** were physicians.

[P 26.] **Brooklyn Conservatory of Music**/formerly **Park Slope Masonic Club**/originally **M. Brasher residence,** 58 Seventh Avenue, NW cor. Lincoln Place. 1881. S. F. Evelette. ☆

An austere brick and brownstone remnant.

[P 27.] **214 Lincoln Place (residence),** bet. Seventh and Eighth Aves. S side. 1883. Charles Werner. ☆

Brick and brownstone Queen Anne for Charles Fletcher, a gas company president.

[P 28.] Lincoln Plaza (apartments)/formerly **F. L. Babbott residence,** 153 Lincoln Place, bet. Sixth and Seventh Aves. N side. 1887. Lamb & Rich. Enlarged, 1896. ☆

A squat tower corners this **Romanesque Revival** mansion.

[P 29.] Originally **John Condon residence,** 139 Lincoln Place, bet. Sixth and Seventh Aves. N side. 1881. ☆

Another **Romanesque Revival,** with a **lion's head** corbel. Condon was a cemetery florist with his greenhouse opposite the 5th Avenue gate of Green-Wood Cemetery.

[P 30.] Sixth Avenue Baptist Church, Sixth Ave. NE cor. Lincoln Place. 1880. Lawrence E. Valk. ☆

A small-scale brick church, **de-steepled** in the 1938 hurricane.

[P 31.] Helen Owen Carey Child Development Center, 71 Lincoln Place, bet. Fifth and Sixth Aves. N side. 1974. Beyer Blinder Belle.

A strongly modeled brown brick facility, **happily in scale** with the neighboring townscape.

[P 31.] Helen Owen Carey Child Cen.   **[P 33.]** Saint Augustine's RC Church

[P 32.] 99-109 Berkeley Place, bet. Sixth and Seventh Avenues. N side.

Three pairs of brick and rock-face brownstone tenements with terra-cotta friezes and grand arched entryways. Here **tenement** is not a **pejorative** word. ☆

[P 33.] St. Augustine's Roman Catholic Church, 116 Sixth Ave., bet. Sterling and Park Places. W side. 1897. Parfitt Brothers.

Sixth Avenue is one of Park Slope's grandest streets, block after block containing rows of amazingly preserved brownstones. **St. Augustine's** is a rich and monumental foil to such a streetscape. The crusty tower, with its mottled rock-face brownstone, anchors a nave with finials and flèche, presenting an elegant angel **Gabriel. Victoria's best awaits you within.**

[P 34.] 182 Sixth Avenue, SW cor. St. Mark's Place.

Here is a gorgeous bayed parlor floor, housing the best of 19th-century neighborhood commercial space.

[P 35.] Cathedral Club of Brooklyn/originally **The Carleton Club,** 85 Sixth Ave., SE cor. St. Mark's Ave.

Built as an exclusive clubhouse, it was progressively the **Monroe Club,** the **Royal Arcanum Club,** and in 1907, through the efforts of a young priest, the **Cathedral Club,** a Roman Catholic fraternal organization. The priest went on to become **Cardinal Mundelein** of Chicago. The

St. Mark's facade is continued in spirit by the adjacent **Montauk (Nos. 80-82)** and **Lenox (Nos. 76-78)** apartment buildings, bay-windowed in brick and brownstone, a handsome tiled pyramid centered atop.

[P 36.] Tiger Sign Company, 245 Flatbush Ave., bet. Sixth Ave. and Bergen St.

A crisp triangular building housing a sign shop with residence above: beige brick with a brownstone frieze. Here the signs are the Pop Art successor to those formerly on Pintchik's across the avenue. WE ALSO DO PERSPECTIVES.

[P 36.] Pop Art: The Tiger Sign Co.   [P 40.] 14th Reg't. Armory, N.Y.N.G.

 [P 37.] 78th Precinct, N.Y.C. Police Department, NE cor. Bergen St. and Sixth Ave. 1925.

Another Anglo-Italianate neo-Renaissance limestone palazzo. The cornice is super—consoled and dentiled.

END of Park Slope Walking Tour B: The Bergen Street Station of the IRT is close-by.

Miscellany: Further afield are the following entries mostly outside the Historic District, except where noted ☆ .

[P 38a.] Public School 39, Brooklyn, The Henry Bristow School, 417 Sixth Ave., NE cor. 8th St. 1877. Samuel B. Leonard, Superintendent of Buildings for the City of Brooklyn Board of Education. ★

A mansarded Victorian school house in rose-painted, articulated brick. The Second Empire influence reached even these then open fields of Brooklyn.

[P 38b.] Originally **William B. Cronyn residence/**later **Charles M. Higgins Ink Factory,** 271 Ninth St., bet. Fourth and Fifth Aves. N side to 10th St. ca. 1855. Altered, 1895, P. C. Keely. ★

This freestanding **French Second Empire** house is crowned with a cupola, slate mansard roof, and cast-iron crests against the sky. **India ink,** that intense black fluid so misnamed—it should be Chinese ink—was made here for draftsmen, designers, artists, and calligraphers.

[P 39.] Public School 107, Brooklyn, The John W. Kimball School, 1301 Eighth Ave., SE cor. 13th St. 1894. J. M. Naughton. ☆

A simple Romanesque Revival schoolhouse of orange-brown brick. This stern and stately building served a newly mushrooming population.

 [P 40.] 14th Regiment Armory, N.Y. National Guard, 1402 Eighth Ave., bet. 14th and 15th Sts. W side. 1895. William A. Mundell.

Picturesque massing, including battered walls, machicolations, and other **heroic** brick detailing, make this a special event among the rows of brownstones. This is a place where boiling oil might be poured on mythical attackers. The statue of the doughboy remembers World War I (*1923, Anton Scaaf*).

[P 41.] Ansonia Court/originally **Ansonia Clock Company Factory,** 420 12th St., bet. Seventh and Eighth Aves. 1881. Remodeled, 1982, Hurley & Farinella, architects. Zion & Breen, landscape architects.

Here 1,500 workers toiled in the **world's largest clock factory.** The brick functionalist tradition in 19th-century industrial building forms a handsome low-key envelope for apartments surrounding a central land-scaped garden court.

[P 42a.] Ladder Company 122, N.Y.C. Fire Department, 532 11th St., bet. Seventh and Eighth Aves. S side. 1883. **[P 42b.] Engine Company 220, N.Y.C. Fire Department,** 530 11th St. 1907.

The older **Italianate** firehouse once was adequate for the neighborhood's needs. As the row houses filled every vacant parcel up to Prospect Park's edge, the **Classical adjunct** to the west was added.

PROSPECT PARK/GRAND ARMY PLAZA

[A 1.] Grand Army Plaza, within Plaza St. at the intersection of Flatbush Ave., Prospect Park W., Eastern Pkwy., and Vanderbilt Ave. 1870. Frederick Law Olmsted & Calvert Vaux. Scenic landmark. ★

[Fig. A] Original land allocation for Prospect Park, before Olmsted & Vaux

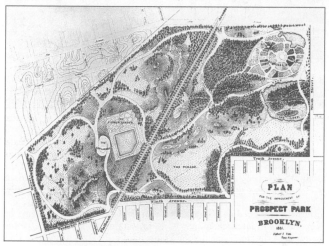

[Fig. B] Olmsted & Vaux' revised "taking" of land for their Prospect Park design

Olmsted & Vaux designed this monumental oval plaza in the spirit of Paris' **Étoile** (now the **Place Charles de Gaulle**), that circular 12-spoked traffic *rond point* that bears in its central island the **Arc de Triomphe.** A masterstroke of city planning, this **nexus** joins their great **Eastern Parkway,** and their **Prospect Park,** with the avenues that preceded it on other geometries. **This** triumphal arch did not arrive for 22 years: the **Soldiers' and Sailors' Memorial Arch [A 2.]** ★ by John H. Duncan, architect of Grant's Tomb, was completed in **1892,** commemorating Union forces that perished in the Civil War. The arch provides, as in its Parisian inspiration, an excellent armature for sculpture, the most spectacular of which is **Frederick MacMonnies'** huge **quadriga** on top **(1898).** Inside the arch itself is more subtle work, bas-reliefs of **Lincoln (Thomas Eakins)** and **Grant (William O'Donovan),** both installed in **1895.** On the south pedestals are two bristling groups representing **The Army and the Navy** by MacMonnies **(1901).** A museum within the arch is open to the public.

[A 2.] The Soldiers' and Sailors' Memorial Arch, a grand Civil War memorial

The oval island to the north of the arch is of a more homely scale, with a double ring of formally trimmed London plane trees surrounding a generous complex of stairs and terraces, and a fountain. Around the **John F. Kennedy Memorial [A 3.]** at the north end **(1965,** Morris Ketchum, architect; Neil Estern, sculptor), the scale shrinks noticeably. This little memorial, the city's only official monument to **Kennedy,** was originally designed as a monolithic marble cube topped by a flame on top, but it was later abandoned as an unsuitable aping of the perpetual flame at Arlington Cemetery's Tomb of the Unknown Soldier. This present form is a compromise, with Kennedy's bust bracketed from the side. Budget makers demeaned it all by causing the cube to be merely a box built of thin butted marble slabs. The **Bailey Fountain** (1932, Egerton Swartwout, architect; Eugene Savage, sculptor) **[A 4.],** a lush interweaving of athletic **Tritons** and **Neptunes** in verdigris bronze, is a delight when in action (unfortunately **rarely** in this water-conscious city).

While the arch was being embellished, a **necklace** of Classical ornaments, designed by Stanford White, was strung across the park entrances facing it (completed in 1894) **[A 5.].** Rising out of entangling fasces, four 50-foot Doric columns are topped with exuberant eagles (by **MacMonnies),** railings, bronze urns, and lamp standards; and two **12-sided** templelike gazebos. Of the whole ensemble, the **gazebos,** with their polished granite **Tuscan** columns, **Guastavino** vaulting, and bronze finials, show **White's** talents most richly.

 [A 6.] Main Library, Brooklyn Public Library (Ingersoll Memorial), Grand Army Plaza at the intersection of Flatbush Ave. and Eastern Pkwy. 1941. Githens & Keally, architects; Paul Jennewein, sculptor of bas-reliefs; Thomas H. Jones, sculptor of the screen over the entry.

Streamlined Beaux Arts, or an example of how the **Ecole des Beaux Arts** developed the **Art Moderne** of the **Paris Exposition of 1937.** In effect it is a formal participant in the geometry of avenues radiating from the **Soldiers' and Sailors' Arch;** but its Moderne/Beaux Arts idiom allowed it to be stylishly modern in its costume as well as classical in its conformance to the grand plan. Inside is lots of grand space.

PROSPECT PARK

Once past **Stanford White's** grand entrance, one sees **Olmsted & Vaux's** park much as they conceived it. They considered it a better work than their first collaboration, **Central Park,** for several reasons, none of which reflects on that earlier work. Principally, as this commission did not result from a competition, with its inevitably fixed site and program, they could change the program first given—and they did. Delay of construction due to the **Civil War** aided their efforts. Almost half of the land set aside for a park by the City of Brooklyn in the **1850s** lay to the northeast of Flatbush Avenue, the main artery to **Flatbush,** which was still a town in its own right: it centered around the reservoir on **Prospect Hill** (since filled in and used as a playground). **Olmsted & Vaux** rejected a scheme [figure **A.**] in which Flatbush Avenue completely bisected the proposed park, recommending instead that the allotted land be expanded to the south and west [figure **B.**]. In severing the land to the northeast, they lost the hill that gave the park its name, but they also got rid of its reservoir (a major part of Central Park to this day) and provided, by default, a tract on which related institutions (the **Library,** the **Brooklyn Museum,** and the **Brooklyn Botanic Garden**) could be located without consuming park space (as the Metropolitan Museum of Art does in Manhattan). Another encumbrance considerably reduced here is the roads. With a more compact shape—and without transverse cuts—**Prospect Park** yielded much less area to wheeled traffic.

[A 7.] Prospect Park, Grand Army Plaza, Prospect Park W., Prospect Park SW., Parkside Ave., Ocean Ave., and Flatbush Ave. 1866–1874. Frederick Law Olmsted & Calvert Vaux. Various alterations. Scenic landmark. ★

Prospect Park Walking Tour: Grand Army Plaza (IRT subway to Grand Army Plaza Station) to southeast entrance at Parkside and Ocean Avenues (Parkside Avenue Station).

Enter between the east (left) pair of Doric columns. Note the statue of **James Stranahan** (1891, Frederick MacMonnies, sculptor), whose personal 24-year crusade is largely responsible for both **Prospect Park** and Olmsted & Vaux's other great contributions to Brooklyn, **Ocean,** and **Eastern** Parkways. Note also the pine grove along the walk; it is replicated on the opposite corner, where the symmetrical entrance composition merges with the park's picturesque layout. Like all walks entering this park, this one quickly loses visual connection with the point of entrance, through its twisting route and the modeling of the terrain's topography.

Turn right at the first fork to **Endale Arch [A 8.],** the first structure completed **(1867);** a dramatic tunnel transition takes you into broad daylight and a ½-mile vista down the **Long Meadow.** The arch is a bucolic vault of **Ruskinian Gothic** in brick and sandstone, once festooned with **crockets, bosses,** and **finials,** and lined with a wooden interior (only traces of all this remain).

Once through the arch, note the corresponding but architecturally unique **Meadow Port Arch [A 9.]** to the right, at the west entrance to the meadow: it is a barrel vault rather than a Gothic one. Follow the path to the left along the edge of the meadow. The recreation on the meadow itself is deftly separated but still visible from the tree-dotted hillsides along the encircling walks. The undulations of the meadow, sculpted by **Olmsted,** offer a sense of place, and topographical variation allows participants to perceive the mass of people present—**impossible** on flat ground. This same trick is the basis of St. Peter's Square in the Vatican, a series of ups and downs within a vast dish that displays to each participant the scale of the whole crowd.

About 500 feet ahead a set of steps rises to the left. Go a bit beyond for a better view of the meadow, then back, up the steps, and across the road. On the other side go left, then right at the next fork down a curving walk to the **Rose Garden [A 10.]** (1895, designer unknown). This space is lovely even without any apparent rosebushes these days. Turning right across the center of the circle, take the steps leading down to the **Vale of Cashmere [A 11.]:** meandering free-form pools with **once-upon-a-time** classical balustrades, now **fallen.** Deep in a hollow facing due south, the **Vale** once supported a lush stand of bamboo (green year-round) and multitudes of birds, some uncommon in New York.

Follow the brick path along the east side of the **Vale** (left as you enter) straight out along the little meadow, from which there are glimpses of the **Long Meadow** across the road. Continue over a modest crest and down the wooded slope to **Battle Pass.** The park road at this point follows roughly the alignment of the original road from **Flatbush** to **Brooklyn,** and it was at this pass that Revolutionary volunteers put up brief resistance against British troops advancing toward **New York** in **1776.**

[A 8.] Endale Arch, a dramatic tunnel   **[A 12.]** Heffalumps once resided here

The Zoo [A 12.]: An optional and recommended detour at this point is to the **Prospect Park Zoo,** just to the south. The zoo offers formal but intimate confrontations with animals, and those in need of services will find rest rooms and fast food. Its neat semicircle of formally planned, understated brick buildings (**1935,** Aymar Embury) was decorated with bas-reliefs and murals by **WPA** artists, including Hunt Diederich, F. G. R. Roth, and Emele Siebern, representing scenes from **Rudyard Kipling's** *Jungle Books.*

Of particular architectural interest is the central pavilion, an octagonal blue-tiled dome of **Guastavino** vaulting with 24 oculi windows. Once there were **pachyderms** under this **pantheon**—rhinoceroses, hippos, and heffalumps—but the heffalumps were removed to the **Bronx Zoo** when all of the City's zoos were placed under that society's aegis. To the west along the park drive is a charming sculpture of a lioness and her cubs (**1899,** Victor Peter).

At **Battle Pass,** cross the road and climb the stairs ahead to a plateau that was once the site of the **Dairy [A 13.]** (1869, Calvert Vaux). Turn left at the top of the stairs, and follow the brow of the plateau across the bridle path, past the red brick service building, then right to cross the high **boulder bridge** (very romantic **rocky rock**), passing over a return loop of the bridle path. From the bridge, bear right, then left up the steps, and then left again at a T-intersection along a walk that skirts the knoll on which the **John Howard Payne** monument [A 13a.] stands (1873, **Henry Baerer,** sculptor). Climb to the crest for a sweeping view of the Long Meadow. The red brick picnic house is directly across the meadow; the more elegant Palladian **Tennis House [A 14.]** (1910, **Helmle & Huberty**) is to its left. Return to the walk below, and take your first left on the walk along the slope's edge. At the next T-intersection go right and then down the steps. Stop where the walk takes a sharp right for a view of the fantastic **boulder bridge** crossed earlier.

Continue your descent into a deep rocky glen, through which a brook gurgles happily. Turn left at the bottom, crossing a smaller boulder bridge, and follow the path along the brook. Turn right at the end of this walk, and pass through the triple **[A 15.] Nethermead Arches** (1870, **Calvert Vaux**), where walk, brook, and bridle path separately pass under the **Central Drive.** The arches are crowned with a **trefoil** sandstone balustrade; the bridge is supported by barrel vaults of brick, granite, and more sandstone. Continue along the brook, past some

specimen trees and into the **Music Grove.** Here a "music pagoda," a
faintly Japanese bandstand, is the site for summer concerts. Cross
Music Grove and bear right on the walk that crosses **Lullwater Bridge.**
From the bridge there is a fine view of the white terra-cotta-faced, newly
restored **Boathouse [A 16.]** (1905, **Helmle & Huberty**) ★ . From the
other side of the bridge there is a long view down the **Lullwater,** meandering toward the **Lake.** Note that the sides of the Lullwater are hard-
edged stone. At the end turn of the bridge turn left for a closer look at
the **Boathouse;** note particularly its elegant black iron lamp standards.
The Boathouse is a pleasant terra-cotta remembrance of **Palladian** architecture. From the Boathouse take the path south past the **Camperdown Elm,** a weeping, drooping Japanese **Brobningnagian bonsai** of a
tree: aged, gnarled, arthritic, and eternal. Then turn left through the
Cleft Ridge Span [A 17.] (1872, **Calvert Vaux**), with its two-toned
incised-tile inner surface enriching this barrel vault.

Through this span is the formal **Garden Terrace [A 18.]** with the
Oriental Pavilion (1874, **Calvert Vaux**), now happily restored after a
disastrous fire. The view down this Beaux Arts-inspired garden to the
Lake has suffered more than the Pavilion, for the semicircular cove at
the foot of the **Terrace** is now filled by the **Kate Wollman** Skating Rink,
a banal place, one of three that originally scarred this and Central Park.
Recreational intrusions, particularly those which inflict buildings foreign to the spirit of the landscape, no matter how noble their intentions
should be banned from the wondrous landscape art of such as **Olmsted
and Vaux.** In this garden, on axis, is *Lincoln* (1869, **H. K. Brown,**
sculptor). Follow Lincoln's gaze to the high wire fence and exposed
refrigeration equipment at what was, until **1961,** the edge of the lake.
Lincoln seems to gesture with his right hand: "Take it away." To the
left is the **Skating Shelter [A 19.]** (1960, Hopf & Adler).

Turn left around this unhappy intrusion, and then pass a **World
War I Memorial** (1920, **A. D. Pickering**). Continuing around the edge
of the lake, you will find a **landing shelter.** This is a 1971 reconstruction
of the **original** (1870, **Calvert Vaux**), the sole survivor of many rustic,
log-braced shelters that once bordered the lake, creating a kind of
mini-Adirondacks image. From here follow the path along the lake's
edge; then bear left across the drive, and continue straight out of the
park through the **Classical porticoes,** crowned with redwood trellises
(1904, **McKim, Mead & White**), to the intersection of **Ocean** and **Parkside** Avenues.

[A 16.] Palladian Lullwater Boathse   **[A 20.]** Stanford White's Croquet Shltr

For further views of the lake and a look at some of the park's finest
Classical structures: Don't leave the park at this point, but instead
follow the walk along the park's south side, between Parkside Avenue
and the **drive,** to the **Croquet Shelter [A 20.]** (**1906,** McKim, Mead &
White, restored, 1967). ★ This Corinthian-columned pavilion of
limestone, with terra-cotta capitals, frieze, and entablature, is supported
within by **Guastavino** vaults. But there are no croquet mallets here;
those **Anglophile** players have departed for Central Park.

INSTITUTE PARK

The green triangle contained by Eastern Parkway and Flatbush and Washington Avenues, formerly known as **Institute Park** after the Brooklyn Institute of Arts and Sciences (which Olmsted & Vaux rejected in their plan for Prospect Park), was **reserved for related institutional uses.** It now accommodates the **Brooklyn Botanic Garden,** the **Brooklyn Museum,** and the main branch of the **Brooklyn Public Library.** The garden and museum are contiguous and offer more than the expected horticultural specimens and works of art. The garden has some interesting examples of landscape architecture, and the museum houses extensive decorative craft collections, **25** period rooms, a *whole* **Dutch Colonial** house, one of the world's *great* **Egyptian collections,** and, in a garden behind, a collection of **exterior architectural building parts** (columns, friezes, sculptures, plaques) from demolished New York buildings.

Botanic Garden to Brooklyn Museum Walking Tour: From the BMT Prospect Park Station on Flatbush Avenue near Empire Boulevard (can also be reached from Grand Army Plaza Station by B41 bus) to the IRT Eastern Parkway Station. Cross the street to the Lefferts Homestead, go back along Empire Boulevard to the Fire Department Bureau of Communications, and *then* enter the Botanic Gardens.

[I 1.] Flatbush Turnpike Tollgate, Empire Blvd. entrance road to Prospect Park. N side. ca. 1855.

A wooden guardhouse moved from its old position at **Flatbush Turnpike** (*now Flatbush Avenue*) is all that remains of the days when roads were privately built and tolls were charged for their use.

 [I 2.] Lefferts Homestead, Flatbush Ave. N of Empire Blvd. W side. In Prospect Park. 1783. ★

Six slender **Tuscan** colonnettes support a **"Dutch"** eave, the edge of a gambrel roof. Painted shingle body, stained shingle roof. The English built many such copies of the basic Dutch house. Its predecessor, in 1776, was burned in the **Battle of Long Island** to prevent its use by the British.

[I 2.] Lefferts Homestead. "Dutch" house built 119 years after New Amsterdam

[I 3.] Brooklyn Central Office, Bureau of Fire Communications, N.Y.C. Fire Department, 35 Empire Blvd., bet. Flatbush and Washington Aves. N side. 1913. Frank J. Helmle. ★

Brunelleschi in Brooklyn: its arcades are those of his foundling hospital in Florence.

[I 4.] Brooklyn Botanic Garden, 1000 Washington Ave., bet. Empire Blvd. and S side of Brooklyn Museum, W to Flatbush Ave.

Enter the garden through the Palladian south gate at Flatbush Avenue and Empire Boulevard. Its 50 acres are intensively planted with *almost every* variety of tree and bush that will survive in this climate.

The most popular attraction, and one that generates traffic jams at the end of April, is the grove of **Japanese cherry trees,** the finest in America. For a simple tour of the garden follow the east side, consistently staying to your right. For seasonal attractions (the cherry blossoms, roses, lilacs, azaleas) not on this route, ask the guard (on a motor scooter) for directions. On the east edge of the garden, a few hundred feet from the south entrance, is a reproduction of the garden from the **Ryoanji Temple, Kyoto [I 5.].** Constructed with painstaking authenticity in **1963,** this replica lacks all of the atmosphere that history and a natural setting give to the original, but it offers an opportunity unique in this area to contemplate a **Zen-inspired,** virtually plantless landscape composition: rock islands in a sea of raked pebbles. Now closed to the public, in a state of restoration.

[I 6.] B.B.G.'s new greenhouses: hexagonal "icebergs" over sunken displays

[I 8.] Japanese Garden: eclectic design resembling a Momoyama stroll garden

Just north of the **Ryoanji** are the greenhouses, facing a plaza with pools of specimen water lilies. The new units **[I 6.]** (1987, Davis, Brody & Assocs.) are harsh hexagonal **"icebergs"** over sunken climatic gardens—somewhat agressive forms that don't share the serenity of the adjacent garden. This conservatory has a tropical jungle section, and a desert section, but its prize exhibit is the collection of bonsai (Japanese miniature trees) **unequaled** in the Americas. North of the conservatory is another formal terrace planted with magnolias (a *dazzling* display in **early to mid-April**) in front of the garden's **School-Laboratory-Administration Building [I 7.]** (1918. McKim, Mead & White), originally painted white but now aquatic green. Farther north is the **Japanese Garden [I 8.]** (1915. Takeo Shiota, designer), gift of philanthropist **Alfred Tredway White.** It resembles a stroll garden of the **Momoyama** period but it is not copied from any one particular example. Around its small pond are examples of almost every traditional plant and device; this overcrowding fails to achieve the serenity of really good Japanese prototypes. **North of the Japanese Garden** is the gate to the parking field which leads to the Brooklyn Museum. Walk out to Washington Avenue and enter the museum via its front entrance on Eastern Parkway, now barren of its monumental staircase removed in the 1930s.

[I 9.] Brooklyn Museum, 200 Eastern Pkwy., SW cor. Washington Ave. 1897–1924. McKim, Mead & White. Addition, 1978, Prentice & Chan, Ohlhausen. Second Addition, 1987, Joseph Tonetti. ★ Master plan competition winner, 1987, Arata Isosaki. James Stewart Polshek & Partners, associate architects.

[I 9.] McKim, Mead & White's presentation rendering of the Brooklyn Museum

One quarter of the grand plan envisioned for **Brooklyn** in the year before consolidation with New York. After the borough was incorporated in the larger metropolis, support for its museum waned. But what it lacks in sheer size, it makes up for in quality: inside is one of the world's greatest **Egyptian** collections.

Note the two sculptured female figures representing **Manhattan and Brooklyn** (1916. Daniel Chester French, sculptor). Although they look as if created for this location, they were placed here in 1963 when their seats at the **Brooklyn** end of the Manhattan Bridge were destroyed in a roadway improvement program.

The austere architecture of the lobby dates from its remodeling in the **1930s** under **WPA** sponsorship. The lobby was moved downstairs from the "parlor floor" to the basement, and the monumental exterior stairway was removed. **Stark functionalism** replaced **Classical monumentality:** a sorry loss. The information desk will offer directions to the collections as well as information on concerts, lectures, and movies in the museum. Among the outstanding exhibits in architecture and interior design are the **Jan Martense Schenck House** (originally built in 1675 in the Flatlands section of Brooklyn), dismantled in 1952 and reconstructed inside the museum, and a suite of rooms from the **John D. Rockefeller Mansion,** built in 1866 at 4 West 54th Street, Manhattan, and redecorated in 1885 in the Moorish style by **Arabella Worsham.**

In the rear, adjacent to the new addition and parking lot, is the **Frieda Schiff Warburg Sculpture Garden** (1966. Ian White, designer). Here are pieces of McKim, Mead & White's **Pennsylvania Station** (a column base and a capital; a figure that supported one side of a huge clock), Coney Island's **Steeplechase** Amusement Park (a roaring lion's head and a lamp standard) and capitals from the first-floor columns of Louis Sullivan's **Bayard** (Condict) building, still standing on Manhattan's Bleecker Street.

Curios and antiquities: Just inside the south (parking area) entrance of the museum is the **Gallery Shop,** once the nation's largest museum shop, with an extensive stock of handcrafted toys, jewelry, textiles, and ceramics from all over the world.

END of Botanic Garden-Brooklyn Museum Walking Tour: The IRT Eastern Parkway subway stop is directly in front of the museum.

[I 9a.] Eastern Parkway, designated a scenic landmark between Grand Army Plaza and Ralph Ave. 1870–1874. Olmsted & Vaux. ★

The first parkway in the nation, intended to bring open space into all areas of the city as part of a comprehensive park system, as yet unbuilt (and unplanned).

BEDFORD-STUYVESANT

Bedford-Stuyvesant is the amalgam of two middle-class communities of the old **City of Brooklyn: Bedford,** the western portion, and **Stuyvesant Heights,** to the east. Today's Bedford-Stuyvesant is one of the city's two major **black enclaves;** the other is its peer **Harlem.** Bed-Stuy differs from its Manhattan counterpart in its much larger percentage of home owners, although **Harlem** is following its lead in gentrifying its own blocks. The southern and western portions comprise masonry row housing of **distinguished architectural quality** and vigorous churches whose spires contribute to the area's frequently **lacy skyline.** The northeastern reaches have considerable numbers of wooden tenements, containing some of the nation's worst **slums.** But on the whole, **Bed-Stuy** has a reputation that doesn't fit with reality: a stable community with hundreds of blocks of well-kept town houses.

Where **Bedford-Stuyvesant** has distinguished architecture, it is **very** good. Its facades of brownstones and brickfronts create a magnificent townscape as good—and sometimes better—than many fashionable areas of **Brooklyn** and **Manhattan.** Parts of **Chauncey, Decatur, MacDonough,** and **Macon** Streets, and the southern end of **Stuyvesant Avenue,** are superb. **Hancock Street,** between **Nostrand** and **Tompkins** Avenues, was considered a showplace in its time (why not **now** too?). **Alice** and **Agate** Courts, short cul-de-sacs isolated from the macrocosm of the street system, are particularly special places in the **seemingly** endless, anonymous grid.

Bed-Stuy comprises roughly **2,000** acres and houses **400,000** people, making it among the **30** largest American cities. It should be toured by car because the sites are dispersed.

[Y 1.] Friendship Baptist Church, 92 Herkimer St., bet. Bedford and Nostrand Aves. S side. 1910.

A **Hollywood Moorish** facade crowned with sheet-metal onion domes and a sturdy cornice over yellow patterned brickwork.

[Y 2.] Brevoort Place, S of Fulton St., bet. Franklin and Bedford Aves. 1860s.

A handsome block of brownstones in **excellent** condition, with their original detail mostly undamaged by the crass moderization of the city's **richer** areas.

[Y 3.] Bethel Seventh-Day Adventist Church/originally **Church of Our Father,** 457 Grand Ave., NE cor. Lefferts Place. ca. 1885.

The **obtuse** angle of this intersection suggested a stepped form to this architect. The brickwork is **piered, arched, corbeled,** and **articulated,** presenting **pinnacles, finials** and **oculi.** A wonderful and vigorous brick monolith.

[Y 4.] Independent United Order of Mechanics of the Western Hemisphere/originally **Lincoln Club,** 67 Putnam Ave., bet. Irving Place and Classon Ave. N side. 1889. R. L. Daus. ★

CROWN HEIGHTS

Williamsburg

The Navy Yard

Y15

Y16

Y12 Y13 Y14

Y11

Y10

Y9

Y17 Y18

Y20
Tompkins
Y19 Park

Y57

Bedford-Stuyvesant

Y58

Y8 Y6 Y7

Y4

Y5

Y21

Y22 Y23

Y24

Y3

Y26

Y25
Y31 Y32 Y33
Y28 Y29 Y30

Y34 Y36
Y2 Y35 Y37
Y1

Y40
Y39

Y41
Y43

Y38

W2
W3 W4
W5 W6
W7
W8

W24

W23

W13 W12

W9 W10

W25

W16 W17 W19
W14 W15
W18
Brower
Park

W11

W21

W20

W22

Park
Slope

Brooklyn
Botanic
Garden

Crown
Heights

W27

W34

W35

W26

W32

W41

W40

W42
W39

W36
W37

W38

W33

Prospect

Park

Prospect Park

The Lake

QUEENS

Bushwick

Y56

Y55

Y54

Y53

Y52

Y45

Y46 Y47

Y50

Y48

Y49

Y51

W30

W29

W31

W28

WC

B7
B8
B9
B10
B11 B12
B13
B14
Y54

2000

feet

Elegant **Republicans** left this florid structure, marking the memory of these streets with a remembrance of better times. The bracketed tower is in the **Wagnerian** idiom popularized by the fantastic 1850s **Bavarian** royal castle of Ludwig II, **Neuschwanstein.**

[Y 5.] Miller Memorial Church of the Nazarene/formerly **Aurora-Grata Scottish Rite Cathedral/**originally **East Reformed Church,** 1160 Bedford Ave., NW cor. Madison St. Rebuilt, 1888.

Bedford Avenue in these blocks is nondescript commercial, and this gray and buff fantasy is a welcome relief. Its history dates back to **1877,** when the **Aurora-Grata Lodge of Perfection,** a Masonic local, bought the old **East Reformed Church** on this site and rebuilt it for **Masonic** purposes. The belfry is still capped by the flat silhouette of a **mystic, mythic** bird, the Scottish Rite emblem in bronze. The **Masons** are gone, and the church is **once again** a church.

[Y 3.] Bethel 7th-Day Adventist Church   **[Y 4.]** Orig. Lincoln (Republican) Club

[Y 5.] The former Aurora-Grata Lodge   **[Y 11.]** Taafe Pl. warehouses in 1966

 [Y 6.] Evening Star Baptist Church/originally **Latter-Day Saints Chapel,** 265 Gates Ave., NW cor. Franklin Ave. 1917. Eric Holmgren.

Superficially reminiscent of Frank Lloyd Wright's **Unity Temple** in Oak Park (1904), this church is a unique cubist experiment for New York. Perhaps it could be termed "**homespun** Schindler" after Richard **Schindler,** the Austrian-born disciple of Wright who followed this idiom in southern California.

[Y 7.] 118 Quincy Street (apartments), SE cor. Franklin Ave. ca. 1890.

A modest example of the lavish apartment buildings built in this community in the **last decade** of the **19th** century. Battered stone walls support arched and rock-linteled brick. Note the fortuitously intact frieze and cornice.

[Y 8.] 418-422 Classon Avenue, bet. Gates Ave. and Quincy St. W side. ca. 1885.

An **exuberant** Romanesque Revival trio arranged as a single composition: brick, brownstone and terra-cotta.

[Y 9.] 361 Classon Avenue and **386-396 Lafayette Avenue,** SE cor. of Classon and Lafayette Aves. ca. 1888.

A **picturesque** and **romantic** Victorian "terrace," partially gutted by fire. Compare this rich massing and detail with the high-rise public housing across the street: charm and personality confronted by **tombstones.**

[Y 10.] 88th Precinct, N.Y.C. Police Department, 300 Classon Ave., SW cor. DeKalb Ave. ca. 1890. South extension, 1924.

Mini-**Romanesque Revival,** it packs an arcuated castle into a tight site and at a small scale.

[Y 11.] Warehouses, 220-232 Taaffe Place, bet. Willoughby and De-Kalb Aves. W side. ca. 1885.

No-nonsense **Romanesque Revival** with virile, vigorous brickwork and arches that **bound and abound; H. H. Richardson** would have been pleased. Some clod, however, has infilled some of these glorious voids with concrete block and sheet metal.

[Y 12.] St. Mary's Episcopal Church, 230 Classon Ave., NW cor. Willoughby Ave. 1858. Renwick & Auchmuty. ★

A very comfortable **English Gothic** country chapel in dressed-brownstone ashlar, with a **verdigris copper** steeple, by a couple of Scots. A flying Gothic arch leads to a pleasant close.

[Y 13.] Convent of the Sisters of Mercy (Roman Catholic), 273 Willoughby Ave., bet. Classon Ave. and Taaffe Place. N side. 1862. P. C. Keely.

A **gloomy** mansarded red brick pile.

Rope walks: Not for crossing jungle swamps or the River Kwai but long narrow buildings created for spinning rope. In **1803** one was erected in the 2 blocks north of the **Convent of the Sisters of Mercy.** It was so long (1,200 feet) that a tunnel was built for it to pass beneath intersecting **Park Avenue.**

[Y 14.] St. Patrick's Roman Catholic Church, Kent Ave. NW cor. Willoughby Ave. **Rectory,** 285 Willoughby Ave. **Academy,** 918 Kent Ave. bet. Kent Ave. and Taaffe Place, N side. 1856. P. C. Keely.

Painted **Gothic Revival.** Its rectory is an arch-windowed, mansarded, brick-and-brownstone **Charles Addams.**

[Y 15.] The Wallabout Warehouse, a robust pile that started as a brewery

[Y 15.] Wallabout Warehouse/formerly **Franklin Brewery/**originally **Malcolm Brewery,** 394-412 Flushing Ave., bet. Franklin and Skillman Aves. S side. E section, 1869. W, section, 1890. Both by Otto Wolf.

A **truncated pyramid** crowns this pile of many-arched brickwork. Its distinctive silhouette provides a **landmark** to thousands of motorists passing it daily on the nearby **Brooklyn-Queens Expressway.**

[Y 16.] Engine Company 209, Ladder Company 102, 34th Battalion, N.Y.C. Fire Department, 850 Bedford Ave., bet. Myrtle and Park Aves. W side. 1965. Pedersen & Tilney.

"Modernists" first enjoyed widespread commissions for New York's public buildings in the **1960s** and **1970s.** Their valiant attempts (including this one) now seem to **pall** in light of a new understanding of architectural history and **historical context.** The **1869** station that this replaced, down the block between **Myrtle** and **Willoughby** Avenues, has unfortunately been demolished.

[Y 17.] CABS (Community Action for Bedford-Stuyvesant) Nursing Home & Related Health Facility, 270 Nostrand Ave., bet. Kosciusko and DeKalb Aves. W side. 1976. William N. Breger & Assocs., architects. Leeds Assocs., interiors.

A **stylish,** elegant stacking of cubist brickwork crowned with a space-frame skylight. **Superb.** The atrium within is a delightful greenhouse filled with a **"bamboo jungle,"** long antedating **IBM's** atrium-jungle at 56th Street and Madison Avenue in Manhattan.

[Y 17.] CABS Nursing Home & Related Health Facility: a bamboo atrium

[Y 18.] Bedford-Stuyvesant Community Pool/a.k.a. People's Pool, N.Y.C. Department of Parks & Recreation, Marcy Ave. bet. Kosciusko and DeKalb Aves. W side. 1969. Morris Lapidus & Assocs.

A reinforced-concrete swimming stadium, startlingly free of **graffiti.** It has worn well and provides recreational relief for residents of this crowded neighborhood.

[Y 19.] Tompkins Park Recreational and Cultural Center, N.Y.C. Department of Parks & Recreation, Tompkins Park, surrounded by Lafayette, Tompkins, Greene, and Marcy Aves. 1971. Hoberman & Wasserman.

Stylish pitched roofs over concrete forms in another of the parks inspired by London's **Bloomsbury.** Olmsted & Vaux designed the original Tompkins Park, but their traces are invisible today.

[Y 20a.] Magnolia grandiflora, in front of 679 Lafayette Ave., bet. Marcy and Tompkins Aves. N side., opp. Tompkins Park. 1885. ★
[Y 20b.] 677, 678, 679 Lafayette Avenue/The Magnolia Tree Earth Center (row houses). 1883. ★

One of two landmark trees in New York (the other is the **Weeping Beech** in Flushing). Here an expatriate **southerner** has survived many of its brownstone neighbors of the same vintage. A third wonder, the

Camperdown Elm, still graces Prospect Park. The brownstones were designated landmarks to insure their continued protection of the tree from north winds.

[Y 21.] John Wesley United Methodist Church/originally **Nostrand Avenue Methodist Episcopal Church,** Quincy St. SW cor. Nostrand Ave. 1880.

A church of timbered gables—some parallel and some skewed to the two streets. All of them surmount a brick body with milky **Tiffany-style** stained glass.

Governors: Between Marcy and Stuyvesant Avenues, streets were named for New York governors: **William L. Marcy, Daniel D. Tompkins, Enos T. Throop, Joseph C. Yates, Morgan Lewis,** and the Dutch director general, **Peter Stuyvesant.** Yates Avenue became Sumner when confusion arose between it and Gates. (The City is currently flirting with many street name changes—is nothing sacred?—so beware.)

[Y 22.] Onetime **IBM Systems Products Division/**formerly **Empire State Warehouse/**originally **Long Island Storage Warehouse and Jenkins Trust Company,** 390 Gates Ave., SW cor. Nostrand Ave. 1906. Helmle, Huberty & Hudswell.

Grand, paired **Beaux Arts** entry portals join the corner at this intersection. A rusticated base supports the patterned brickwork of this sturdy office-building monolith. Lost is a neo-**Baroque** tower that once crowned these low brownstone blocks.

[Y 23.] St. George's Episcopal Church, 800 Marcy Ave., SW cor. Gates Ave. 1887. Richard Upjohn. ★

A fat and friendly **Ruskinian Gothic** country church in the city, in brick, brownstone and slate. The **octagonal** tower is a **delightful lilliputian.**

[Y 24.] Originally **Boys' High School,** 832 Marcy Ave., bet. Putnam Ave. and Madison St. W side. 1891. James W. Naughton. ★

A **major** Brooklyn landmark, in splendid **Romanesque Revival:** arched, quoined, towered, and lushly decorated in terra-cotta in the manner of **Louis Sullivan.**

[Y 24.] Old Boys' High School: one of Brooklyn's major Romanesque Revivals

[Y 25.] Brownstone Blocks, Jefferson Ave. bet. Nostrand and Throop Aves. 1870s.

Merely 3 blocks out of dozens in the area with staid Renaissance Revival brownstones. **F. W. Woolworth** moved here in **1890** (to **No. 209**). Changing fashion and vastly increasing wealth led him across the East River to 990 Fifth Avenue, where his later (1901) residence was designed by C. P. H. Gilbert. Compare the similar migration of **Harold I. Pratt** from **Clinton Hill** to **68th Street** and Park Avenue.

[Y 26.] Most Worshipful Enoch Grand Lodge/originally **Reformed Episcopal Church of the Reconciliation,** Jefferson Ave. SE cor. Nostrand Ave. 1890. Heins & Lafarge.

A churchly place, its octagonal corner tower rising above milky stained glass, brick, and terra-cotta. Now a **Masonic temple.**

[Y 27.] Renaissance Apartments, 488 Nostrand Ave., SW cor. Hancock St. 1888. Montrose W. Morris. ★

Cylindrical, conically capped towers are borrowed from **Loire Valley** châteaus. Its abandoned brick and terra-cotta body is in the grandest **neo-Renaissance** manner.

[Y 28.] 232 Hancock Street, SE cor. Marcy Ave. 1886. Montrose W. Morris.

A mansarded "palace"—oriels, gables, pediments—a **Queen Anne** wonder.

[Y 29.] 236-244 Hancock Street (residence), bet. Marcy and Tompkins Aves. S side. 1886. Montrose W. Morris.

Pompeian-red terra-cotta and brick form a rich tapestry in the manner of **George B. Post's** Brooklyn Historical Society.

[Y 30.] 246-252 Hancock Street (residence), bet. Marcy and Tompkins Aves. S side. 1880s. Montrose W. Morris.

Terra-cotta, stained glass, elliptical arches, and **Byzantine** columns, mansarded and pedimented against the sky.

[Y 31.] Originally **John C. Kelley residence,** 247 Hancock St., bet. Marcy and Tompkins Aves. N side. 1880s. Montrose W. Morris.

A formal freestanding neo-Renaissance town house (the **Renaissance** would have termed it a palazzo) on a triple-width site (**81** feet) built for an **Irish** immigrant who made good. Legend claims that the brownstone was selected piece by piece to guarantee quality. The **irony** is that it is now crumbling and **painted.**

[Y 31.] Neo-Renaissance Kelley res.   **[Y 34.]** 74 Halsey Street's iron railings

[Y 32.] 255-259 Hancock Street (residence), bet. Marcy and Tompkins Aves. N side. 1880s. Montrose W. Morris.

Round stone and elliptical brick arches give vigorous shade and shadow to this trio.

[Y 33.] 273 Hancock Street (residence), bet. Marcy and Tompkins Aves. N side. 1890. J. C. Reynolds & Son.

A lion-faced keystone guards this entry.

[Y 34.] 74 Halsey Street, bet. Nostrand Ave. and Arlington Place. S side. 1880s.

A **wild** Queen Anne place, with exuberant wrought-iron railings and canopy. Imagine **bounding up** those front steps.

[Y 35.] Alhambra Apartments, 29 Macon St., 86 Halsey St., bet. Macon and Halsey Sts. W side of Nostrand Ave., 1880s. Montrose W. Morris. ★

Morris did better here than for Kelley [see Y 31.], with a richer collection of terra-cotta and brick—arcaded, mansarded, chimneyed, and dormered. Now abandoned, it was first desecrated by the shop-fronted additions along Nostrand Avenue. Morris and **Frank Freeman** were Brooklyn's greatest architects.

[Y 36.] N.Y.C. Board of Education Brooklyn Adult Training Center/ formerly **Girls' High School**/originally **Central Grammar School,** 475 Nostrand Ave., bet. Halsey and Macon Sts. E side. 1885. James W. Naughton. Additions, 1891, 1911. ★

A **High** Victorian painted Gothic Revival hulk.

[Y 37.] 64 and 68 Macon Street (residences), bet. Nostrand and Marcy Aves. S side. 1880s.

The intervening "garden" space sets off these two classy houses, allowing **No. 64's** oriel window to view this urbane street and any resident **Rapunzel** to let down her hair. **No. 68** is Romanesque Revival in brick and terra-cotta. Look for the overseeing face in the dormered roof. The second-story corner porch is an elegant incision and a counter-pointing place of overview to **No. 64's** oriel.

[Y 38.] Bedford-Stuyvesant Restoration Plaza, 1360 Fulton St., SE cor. New York Ave. 1976. Arthur Cotton Moore.

Brown brick, brown glass, banners, and a floating **Victorian** facade recalling this block's history give a simple face to the street but also embrace an **urbane** compound-plaza that is **Brooklyn's** answer to San Francisco's **Ghirardelli Square.** Stylish new and renewed buildings mix on this block, including the **Billie Holliday Theater** next door.

[Y 38.] Bed-Stuy's Restoration Plaza **[Y 45.]** 13th Reg. Armory, N.Y.N.G.

[Y 39.] First African Methodist Episcopal Zion Church/originally **Tompkins Avenue Congregational Church,** 480 Tompkins Ave., SW cor. MacDonough St. 1889. George B. Chappell.

The **immense** campanile that dominates the neighborhood is reminiscent of **St. Mark's** in Venice. Brick is everywhere. Once the nation's largest Congregational congregation, it was often referred to as **Dr. Meredith's** church, after its well-known preacher.

[Y 40.] Stuyvesant Heights Christian Church, Tompkins Ave. NW cor. MacDonough St. 1880s.

Painted **Gothic Revival.** A modest form yet with grandly scaled windows.

[Y 41.] Our Lady of Victory Roman Catholic Church, NE cor. Throop Ave. and MacDonough St.

Dressed **Manhattan schist** and limestone in a late, many-pinnacled Gothic Revival. ca. 1890.

[Y 42.] Stuyvesant Heights Historic District, an L-shaped area between Chauncey and Macon Sts., from Stuyvesant to Tompkins Aves. 1870–1920. ★

The wondrous row housing, particularly along Decatur, Bainbridge, and Chauncey Streets, is a cross section of Bedford-Stuyvesant vernacular architectural history. The locally designed buildings encompass attitudes from freestanding suburbia to the best of Victorian row housing and provide a sampling of modest apartment units.

[Y 43.] Fulton Storage Building/originally **New York and New Jersey Telephone Company (branch office),** 613 Throop Ave., NE cor. Decatur St. ca. 1895.

Roman brick and **Renaissance** arches; the spandrels between are richly decorated in sculpted terra-cotta.

[Y 44.] 81 Decatur Street/originally **Clermont Apartments,** bet. Throop and Sumner Aves. N side. 1900.

A **shrunken palace:** here Roman brick, limestone, and pressed metal produce an **Azay-le-Rideau** for families of modest means.

[Y 45.] 13th Regiment Armory, New York National Guard, 357 Sumner Ave., bet. Jefferson and Putnam Aves. E side. 1894. Rudolph L. Daus. Extended, 1906, Parfitt Brothers.

A great granite arch gives support to twin battlemented towers: here are **crenellations, machicolations,** and a **battered base.** It is a powerful presence in this small-scale neighborhood.

 [Y 46.] Mt. Lebanon Baptist Church, 230 Decatur St., SE cor. Lewis Ave. 1894. Parfitt Brothers.

A **superb** Richardsonian Romanesque building in Roman brick and brownstone. The terra-cotta shingled tower is a remembrance of a **Loire Valley** castle's turret.

[Y 47.] Bainbridge Street's town houses: a picturesque Victorian silhouette

[Y 47.] 113-137 Bainbridge Street (row houses), bet. Lewis and Stuyvesant Aves. N side. ca. 1900.

The **studied variegations** of these **13** houses—pyramids, arches, and cones—alternately punctuate the sky. Such a picturesque romance contrasts sharply with the normally sober regularity of **mid** 19th-century Renaissance Revival brownstones.

[Y 48.] Fulton Park, Chauncey to Fulton Sts. at Stuyvesant Ave.

The rumble of the subway **train** doesn't affect the serenity of this sliver of green space along Fulton Street. The neighborhood to the north is named after the park and, because of its well-maintained houses and stable population, is considered an important asset in the work of renewing **Bedford-Stuyvesant.** North of the park along **Chauncey Street** is a fine row of small-scale town houses with intact stoops. In the park's center is a statue of **Robert Fulton** holding his first steam ferryboat to Brooklyn, the *Nassau.* Originally placed in a niche at the Brooklyn ferry terminal, below the Brooklyn Bridge, the statue disappeared. It was later discovered and placed here in 1930 by the **Society of Old Brooklyn.**

City center: The geographical center of New York City lies within Bedford-Stuyvesant—to be exact, within the block bounded by **Lafayette, Reid (Malcolm X Boulevard), Greene** and **Stuyvesant** Avenues, the present site of a less than distinguished public school.

[Y 49a.] 1660-1670 Fulton Street, opp. Fulton Park, bet. Troy and Schenectady Aves. 1976. Henri LeGendre.

Medium-rise housing with a broken and **cadaverous** form that works happily with this predominantly low-rise neighborhood. The elegant tan brick composition is a **star** in the history of Brooklyn's modern architecture.

[Y 49a.] 1660 Fulton St., some handsome, cadaverous medium-rise housing

[Y 49b.] Lawrence H. Woodward Funeral Home, 1 Troy Ave., SE cor. Fulton St. 1976. Henri LeGendre.

A handsome, cubistic, tan brick satellite of **No. 1660.**

[Y 50.] Remsen Court (apartments), 120 Chauncey St., bet. Reid (Malcolm X Boulevard) and Stuyvesant Aves., Chauncey and Fulton Sts. 1976. Tuckett & Thompson.

Broken brick forms enclose private courtyards; the corner windows are stylish. Like **1660** Fulton Street, across the park, it is a New York State Urban Development Corporation project **(UDC)** from that heady period in the 1970s when high-quality architecture was being delivered to the outer boroughs.

McDonald's Dining Room, 327 Stuyvesant Ave., NE cor. Macon St.

A good eating and drinking place in a community that has few elegant bars and restaurants.

[Y 51.] Gabled garden apartments, bet. Fulton St. and Atlantic Ave., E of Utica Ave. 1986.

A **Post Modern** complex in tan and pink concrete block that is an almost **festive addition to this handsome neighborhood.**

[Y 52.] 587-611 Decatur Street, bet. Howard and Saratoga Aves. N side. 1891. J. Mason Kirby.

Pyramids and arches **punctuate** this picturesque group of low-scaled row houses built of **assorted stone.**

[Y 53.] Saratoga Park, bet. Halsey and Macon Sts., Saratoga and Howard Aves.

A lovely **Bloomsbury**-scaled park surrounded by appropriate row houses—none distinguished, all pleasant.

 [Y 54a.] Originally **RKO Bushwick Theater,** SE cor. Howard Ave. and Broadway. 1920s.

Egyptian goddesses crown lavish and fantastic white-glazed terra-cotta oculi that are simultaneously embraced by **giant cupids.** The circular pediments abound with masks, swags, and festoons.

[Y 51.] "Dutch"-gabled garden apts.   **[Y 54a.]** Former RKO Bushwick Thtr.

 [Y 54b.] Engine Co. 233, Ladder Co. 176, N.Y.C. Fire Department, Rockaway Ave. NE cor. Chauncey St. 1987. Eisenman/Robertson.

A fresh piece of contrapuntal geometry in gray and white block, tile and metal panels. It could be a bit of the Paris Exposition of 1925: fortunately it respects the street and plays with diagonals in its superstructure.

[Y 54c.] Public School No. 73, Brooklyn, 241 MacDougal St., NE cor. Rockaway Ave. 1888. Addition, 1895. Both by James W. Naughton.
★

Robust Romanesque Revival in brick, terra-cotta, and limestone. A gem of a facade.

[Y 55.] Originally **Public School 26, Brooklyn**/now **Junior Academy,** 856 Quincy St., bet. Patchen and Ralph Aves. S side. 1891. James W. Naughton.

Romanesque Revival brick and terra-cotta with a series of gables that give a **serrated silhouette.** Sturdy brick colonnettes at the second floor support rock-face lintels; their third-floor companions bear arches.

[Y 56.] Originally **St. John's College** and **Church,** Lewis Ave. bet. Hart St. and Willoughby Ave. E side. 1870. P. C. Keely.

The church behind the college building is in rough-cut brownstone ashlar, a vigorous **Renaissance Revival** bulk.

[Y 57.] Originally **Public School 19, Brooklyn,** Kosciusko St. bet. Throop and Sumner Aves. N side. 1889.

A vast abandoned Romanesque Revival brick and terra-cotta wonder. Study the bas-relief tympanas. Who can rescue such a loner in the wilderness?

 [Y 58.] Ebenezer Gospel Tabernacle, 470 Throop Ave., bet. Gates Ave. and Quincy St. W side. 1891.

A lusty and miniature **Romanesque Revival** gem.

CROWN HEIGHTS

The name **Crown Heights** is applied to the area east of **Washington Avenue** between **Atlantic Avenue** on the north, **Empire Boulevard** on the south and **East New York Avenue** on the east. Included is the handsome portion surrounding **Grant Square** at Bedford Avenue and Bergen Street that was originally the center of **Bedford;** that community's southern boundary is now considered **Atlantic Avenue.**

Crown Heights, the 19th-century **Crow Hill,** actually includes a succession of hills south of **Eastern Parkway.** The old designation derisively recalls the black colony of Weeksville along the former **Hunterfly Road,** with extant buildings now both preserved and restored. Another old thoroughfare is **Clove Road,** once a 2-mile, north-south link from the village of **Bedford** to **Flatbush,** dating from **1662.** Only a block of Clove Road remains, above **Empire Boulevard** east of **Nostrand Avenue.**

The community has been in transition for a generation with, in sectors, an original Jewish population first declining, then reinforced, by a reinfusion of the **Orthodox.** Many **West Indian** immigrants reside in the area, with **Haitian** French and **British** English often heard in the streets.

Frank H. Taylor wrote early in the 20th century: "In the heart of the St. Mark's section are located many beautiful mansions, products of the master hand of the architect, the artist, and the modern mechanic. These beautiful homes are seldom offered for sale. They are cherished as homes and will probably pass from one generation to another, fine demonstrations of the great confidence our wealthy men have in the stability of Brooklyn."

[W 1.] Crown Heights North area, from Rogers Ave. at Grant Sq., along a line between Pacific and Dean Sts. to Albany Ave.; then along a line down to St. John's Place, and back to Grant Sq.

This was an enclave of Brooklyn wealth equal to its **peers** in **Brooklyn Heights, Clinton Hill,** and **Bedford.** The vagaries of social change exiled many Brooklynites to Manhattan after the consolidation of **1898,** but a vast reservoir of luscious architecture was left behind.

[W 2.] 23rd Reg. Armory in 1892   [W 2.] 23rd Reg. Armory, N.Y.N.G.

[W 2.] 23rd Regiment Armory, New York National Guard, 1322 Bedford Ave., bet. Atlantic Ave. and Pacific St. W side. 1892. Fowler & Hough. ★

With its eight great round towers, one soaring over its peers, and arched entry complete with portcullis, this crenellated brick-and-brownstone "fortress" for the **National Guard,** lacks only a moat to be out of **King Arthur's** realm.

[W 3.] Formerly **Medical Society of the County of Kings,** 1313 Bedford Ave., bet. Atlantic Ave. and Pacific St. E side. 1903. D. Everett Waid and R. M. Cranford.

A neo-**Regency** play written in a **Georgian** vocabulary. To a future archaeologist, its tiered **Tuscan** and **Ionic** columns could seem to be a **1980s Post Modern** arrangement of the 18th century.

[W 4.] St. Bartholomew's Episcopal Church, 1227 Pacific St., bet. Bedford and Nostrand Aves. N side. 1893. George B. Chappell. ★

A charming and romantic place: **squat and friendly,** with stone and brick, and trimmed in terra-cotta. The tower is crowned with **"fish scales"** in a sinuous profile. All in a **bosky bower.**

[W 5.] Imperial Apartments, 1198 Pacific St., SE cor. Bedford Ave. 1892. Montrose W. Morris. ★

Erected on an **imperial** scale, with great paired Corinthian terra-cotta columns and arches along both **Pacific Street** and **Bedford Avenue.** Advertised in their time as "elegant and well conducted" and "in the fashionable part of Bedford," the immense apartments have since been subdivided.

[W 5.] The terra-cotta Imperial Apts.   **[W 7.]** The Ulysses S. Grant statue

[W 8.] Formerly the Union League Club of Brooklyn: a Republican stronghold

[W 6.] 1164-1182 Dean Street, bet. Bedford and Nostrand Aves. S side. 1890. George P. Chappell.

Ten Queen Anne houses in a mélange of brick, limestone, terra-cotta, wooden shingles, and Spanish tile, with alternating stepped, peaked, and domed gables.

[W 7.] Ulysses S. Grant Statue, Grant Sq. at Dean St. and Bedford Ave. 1896. William Ordway Partridge, sculptor.

A youthful **Grant** bestrides his charger in this amorphous square.

[W 8.] Bhraggs Grant Square Senior Citizens' Center/formerly **Union League Club of Brooklyn,** Bedford Ave. SE cor. Dean St. 1890. P. J. Lauritzen.

Brooklyn's most resplendent club, built to serve the social needs of Republican party stalwarts of **Bedford,** of which this area was considered a central part. Brownstone **Richardsonian Romanesque** arches support an eclectic body above; note **Lincoln** and **Grant** in the arches' spandrels, and the monumental **American eagle** supporting the great bay window.

[W 9.] 673 St. Mark's Avenue, bet. Rogers and Nostrand Aves. N side. 1888. E. G. W. Dietrick.

Black Forest Queen Anne: an eccentric adventure that continues the experimental vitality of St. Mark's Place, where a whole history of 19th-century experimentation will greet you.

[W 10.] 675 and **677 St. Mark's Avenue,** bet. Rogers and Nostrand Aves. N side. ca. 1890.

Romanesque Revival from the **Chicago School.**

[W 11.] Ancient Divine Theological Baptist Church, 814 Park Place, bet. Rogers and Nostrand Aves. S side. ca. 1890.

A neo-Flemish brick church with a stepped gable.

[W 12.] Union United Methodist Church/originally **New York Avenue Methodist Church,** 121 New York Ave., bet. Bergen and Dean Sts. E side. 1892. J. C. Cady & Co.

A smooth and rounded **Romanesque Revival** red brick monolith.

[W 13.] Hebron French-Speaking Seventh-Day Adventist Church/ originally **First Church of Christ Scientist,** New York Ave. SW cor. Dean St., 1909. Henry Ives Cobb.

An octagonal eclectic building, torn between the **Romanesque** and the **Classical Revival** of the 1893 Chicago World's Fair. Savor the rare, flat terra-cotta shingles (as opposed to Spanish or Roman terra-cotta tiles more commonly used).

[W 14.] William Breger's Marcus Garvey Nursing Home, a modern elegance

[W 14.] Marcus Garvey Nursing Home, 810 St. Mark's Ave., bet. New York and Brooklyn Aves. S side. 1977. William N. Breger & Assocs.

A simple form of terra-cotta colored brick, sculpted, modeled, and beautifully detailed, that replaces three major mansions, including that of **Abraham Abraham,** cofounder of Abraham & Straus (**A&S**).

[W 15.] 828-836 St. Marks Avenue, bet. New York and Brooklyn Aves. S side. ca. 1914.

Five small neo-**Georgian** houses. Note how **No. 828's** eaves have been received by an incision in the nursing home next door!

Abraham Abraham was first a partner in **Wechsler and Abraham,** the forerunner of today's **Abraham & Straus,** Brooklyn's very own department store. Among his many philanthropic accomplishments was the founding of **Brooklyn Jewish Hospital,** built in **1894** as Memorial Hospital for Women and Children. His son-in-law **Edward Blum** and grand-son-in-law **Robert A. M. Blum** carried on both the business and philanthropic tradition. In the **1960s** the latter Blum was board chairman of both **Abraham & Straus** and the **Brooklyn Institute of Arts and Sciences.**

[W 16.] St. Louis Senior Citizens' Center/originally **Dean Sage Residence,** 839 St. Marks Ave., NE cor. Brooklyn Ave. 1869. Russell Sturgis. ☆

Stolid **rock-face** brownstone **Romanesque Revival.** Sturgis was more noted as a critic and writer, and was author of the magnificent **1902** *Dictionary of Architecture.*

[W 17.] 855 and **857 St. Mark's Avenue,** bet. Brooklyn and Kingston Aves. N side. 1892. Montrose W. Morris. ☆

An eclectic **Romanesque Revival** brick and limestone twin-mansion, with an elegant corner tower capped by a belled cupola.

 [W 18.] Brooklyn Children's Museum, Brower Park, entrance at SE cor. of Brooklyn Ave. and St. Mark's Ave. 1976. Hardy Holzman Pfeiffer Assocs.

Earth- and **metal**works worthy of a missile-launching station and festooned with the architecture of movement. **Highway signs** and an entrance through a **transit kiosk** lead into the bowels tunneled within the bermed earth mounds. The structure is analogous to an iceberg: the pinnacle visible from outside gives few signals of the wonders within. Have a child bring you here.

[W 18.] The Brooklyn Children's Museum, a delightful and exciting iceberg

Lost mansions: The 1976 **Brooklyn Children's Museum** replaces the original, organized in **1899,** which occupied two Victorian mansions on this site: the **L. C. Smith** (typewriter) **residence,** an Italianate villa of the **1890s;** and the **Adams residence** of **1867,** the low mansarded home of historian **James Truslow Adams.**

[W 19.] St. Mark's Avenue, bet. Kingston and Albany Aves. Both sides. 1966. I. M. Pei & Partners, architects. M. Paul Friedberg & Assocs., landscape architects.

A **plaza playground** here interrupts St. Mark's Avenue in a heady attempt to bring stability to a once-decaying neighborhood. In retrospect it seems more a device to create parking than a true piece of urbanity.

[W 20.] Originally **Brooklyn Methodist Church Home,** 920 Park Place, bet. Brooklyn and New York Aves. S side. 1889. Mercein Thomas.

It has the **look** of an asylum in its literal sense: a place of refuge for the indigent. Victorian brick with appropriate Victorian planting: traces of formerly abundant **hydrangeas.**

[W 21.] 979 Park Place (residence), bet. Brooklyn and New York Aves. N side. 1888. George P. Chappell.

Could well be a prototypical model for Vincent Scully's great 1955 book *The Shingle Style.* With its projections, recessions, bay windows, and porches, this is an essay in American **"neo-mediaevalism,"** although the Middle Ages never enjoyed such middle-class grandeur.

[W 22.] St. Gregory's Roman Catholic Church, 224 Brooklyn Ave., NW cor. St John's Place. 1915. Frank J. Helmle.

In brick, limestone, and terra-cotta, this is **Roman** revival, remembering **early Christian** churches and the very idea of a basilica. Its inspiration might well have been **San Paolo Fuori le Mura** in Rome.

Further afield:

[W 23a.] Public School 111, Brooklyn/originally **Public School 9, City of Brooklyn,** 249 Sterling Place, NE cor. Vanderbilt Ave. 1868. Samuel B. Leonard. ★ **[W 23b.]** Originally **Public School 9 Annex, City of Brooklyn,** 251 Sterling Place, E of Vanderbilt Ave., 1887. James W. Naughton. ★

A brownstone, terra-cotta, and brick **Renaissance Revival** school with an infusion of some **Romanesque Revival** detail . . . such was the course of eclecticism in the **1890s.** Grand Corinthian pilasters march around the third and fourth floors. Deteriorating rapidly. **HELP!**

[W 24.] Originally **Knox Hat Factory,** 369-413 St. Marks Ave., NE cor. Grand Ave. ca. 1890.

An increasingly hatless male population spelled the doom of once of Brooklyn's once flourishing industries. The grand Manhattan headquarters of **Knox** still stand next to the Public Library at 40th Street and Fifth Avenue.

[W 25.] Nursing Home, Jewish Hospital Medical Center of Brooklyn, Classon Ave. bet. Prospect and Park Places. 1977. Puchall & Assocs. and Herbert Cohen.

The former site of the **Romanesque Revival** Brooklyn Home for Aged Men, it continues to serve the elderly community as one of several nursing homes in the **Crown Heights/Bedford-Stuyvesant** communities.

This is a handsome and elegantly detailed construction of brown brick.

[W 26.] 49-57 Crown Street, NW cor. Franklin Ave. 1976.

This slender tower is a dominant silhouette looming over the Botanic Garden.

[W 27.] 42nd Supply and Transport Battalion, New York National Guard/originally **Troop C Armory,** 1579 Bedford Ave., bet. President and Union Sts. E side. 1908. Pilcher, Thomas & Tachau.

The last stand of the cavalry and a **mighty fortress** to this day. The great arched roof, silhouetted on the outside, is a tribute to the principles of mid-**Victorian** train sheds, still prolific in European capitals. The front fort is in somewhat fussy brick and limestone.

[W 28.] Public School 390, Brooklyn, The Maggie Walker School, Sterling Place, NW cor. Troy Ave. 1977. Giorgio Cavaglieri.

A **highly articulated** modern classroom building, its stair towers elegantly detailed with corner window slots, unfortunately now crudely screened for security. The exposed concrete frame and concrete-block infill are not **weathering** too gracefully.

[W 29.] Weeksville houses, along old Hunterfly Road, bet. St. Mary's Place and Bergen St., bet. Buffalo and Rochester Aves. ★

Four simple wood houses occupied by James Weeks and friends (free **black men**) between 1830 and 1870. The architecture, in painted clapboard, is that of the 19th-century common man. It is the oldest **black** residential landmark in New York.

[W 30.] Berea Baptist Church, Bergen St. bet. Utica and Rochester Aves. N side. 1894.

The small original church to the east, though overpowered by its westerly addition, remains a charming, **castellated** neo-**Romanesque** place.

[W 29.] Weeksville, on Hunterfly Rd.   **[W 31.]** Ocean Hill Intermediate Sch.

[W 31.] Intermediate School 55, Brooklyn, The Ocean Hill Intermediate School, Bergen and Dean Sts., Hopkinson and Rockaway Aves. 1968. Curtis & Davis.

A **grim, "fortified"** place of brown brick with narrow slit windows. Its edge against the sky simulates crenellations.

[W 32.] Crown Gardens (apartments), Nostrand Ave. bet. President and Carroll Sts. E side. 1971. Richard Kaplan. Stevens, Bertin, O'Connell & Harvey, associate architects.

A modest slab shares a courtyard with 3 quadrants of stacked town houses. Here brown brick and exposed concrete presents to the neighborhood one of its most **urbane** blocks. There is a **rhythmic** display of balconies and stair towers in **counterpoint.**

Another closely packed precinct with many blocks of **urbane** interest:

[W 33.] Crown Heights South area, generally including President and Union Sts., bet. New York and Troy Aves., and Carroll St. from New York Ave. to Albany Ave. Mostly 1910–1930.

Eleven blocks of rich row, semidetached, and freestanding **houses,** inhabited by **black** and **Hasidic Jewish** families, who developed a harmonious relationship after initial friction.

[W 34.] 1361-1381 Union Street (residences), bet. New York and Brooklyn Aves. N side. 1912. Axel Hedman.

An eccentric neo-Renaissance row of bowed and bayed limestone fronts. They are crowned with **curious** geometric parapets above their modillioned cornices: triangular, semicircular, rectilinear.

[W 35.] 1485-1529 Union Street (residences), bet. Kingston and Albany Aves. N side. 1909. F. L. Hine.

Alternating bow and bay windows modulate the streetfront. Note the **friezes** between the first and second floors and under the cornice.

[W 36.] 1476-1506 Union Street (residences), bet. Kingston and Albany Aves. S side. 1909. Harry Albertson.

A more **exuberant** set than those across the street, these are alternately crowned with **conical** and **pyramidal** hats, to match their bowed and bayed windows below.

[W 37.] 1483-1491 President Street (residences), bet. Kingston and Albany Aves. N side. 1913. J. L. Brush.

The **whole facade** here becomes a bow in these English-basement houses.

[W 38.] 1401-1425 Carroll Street (residences), bet. Kingston and Albany Aves. N side. 1913. J. L. Brush.

Similar to **Nos. 1483-1491** but with small stoops.

[W 39.] 1311A-1337 Carroll Street (residences), bet. Brooklyn and Kingston Aves. N side. 1913. Slee & Bryson.

A **Federal Revival** brick row with crisp white trim, strangely crowned with eclectic slate mansard roofs. The bay windows pleasantly **modulate** the street.

[W 32.] Crown Gardens Apartments with stacked town houses around a court

[W 40.] 1294 President Street (residence), bet. New York and Brooklyn Aves. S side. 1911. William Debus.

This double house is on the imposing scale of an English **Renaissance** palace.

[W 41.] 1319 President Street (residence), bet. New York and Brooklyn Aves. N side. 1930. H. T. Jeffrey.

Mock Tudor, complete with small, leaded panes, an asymmetrical composition playing the **gabled bay** against a pair of decorated brick chimneys.

[W 42.] 1362 President Street (residence), bet. Brooklyn and Kingston Aves. S side. 1921. Cohn Brothers.

A florid and showy intruder into these mostly modest and serene surroundings. The vocabulary comes from a smorgasbord of French Renaissance ingredients.

NORTHERN BROOKLYN

BUSHWICK-RIDGEWOOD • WILLIAMSBURG • GREENPOINT

Town of Bushwick/Boswijck-"Wooded District"

Established as a town in 1660; Town of Williamsburg separated from
in 1840; annexed to the City of Brooklyn in 1855.

This area, including the three communities of **Bushwick-
Ridgewood, Williamsburg,** and **Greenpoint,** was often referred to as
the **Eastern District** after the merger of **1855,** to distinguish it from the
original area of the **City of Brooklyn,** the **"Western."** In general the
term has fallen into disuse except in connection with the names of a local
high school and a freight terminal (with some logic, as the **Eastern**
District is now the **northern** tip of Brooklyn and **South** Brooklyn is, in
fact, at Greater Brooklyn's **northwest** corner).

Much of this part of Brooklyn is devoted to working-class residential areas clustered between industrial concentrations strung along the
East River and **Newtown Creek.** It is in this precinct that many fortunes
were made in sugar, oil, rope, lumber, shipbuilding, brewing, and glue.

BUSHWICK-RIDGEWOOD

Malt and hops, barley and barrels, beer and ale. **Obermeyer and Liebmann, Ernest Ochs, Claus Lipsius, Danenberg and Coles.** The history
of Bushwick has been the history of brewing. **Beer** came to **Bushwick**
in the middle of the **19th** century when a large **German** population
emigrated here after unsuccessful uprisings in **the Fatherland** in **1848**
and **1849.**

In its early years the community was noted largely for farming, the
produce being sold locally as well as ferried to Manhattan's markets. By
the 1840s **Peter Cooper** had moved his glue factory here, since land
values in **Manhattan's Murray Hill** had risen so sharply that an odorif-
erous glue factory was no longer of economic sense there. **Cooper,**
always a shrewd businessman, chose this undeveloped area of Brooklyn
near main roads connecting the ferries to **New York** with the farms on
Long Island. His site is that of **Cooper Park Houses,** a low-rent housing
project. It is named after the adjacent park given to the City of Brooklyn
in **1895** by the Cooper family.

[B 1.] Originally **Arion Hall**/now **Arion Mansions (catering hall),** 13
Arion Place, bet. Bushwick Ave. and Broadway. E side. 1887.

Once, rich embellishment encrusted this hall, redolent of those
days when the Arion Männerchor, the Eastern District's leading Ger-

man singing society, met and sang here. Now a somewhat seedy catering establishment.

Bushwick Avenue once contained 20 blocks of impeccable and stolid mansions, **freestanding** (in contrast to Brooklyn Heights) town palaces advertising the wealth and taste of local industrial **magnates.** Originally a **gloomy** set of Victorian buildings, they nevertheless revealed the spirit of their times: **wealth** was a burden, and the owners' moral duty to **uplift** the masses was somberly fulfilled through dour stonework. Bushwick is now lined with Black Muslim and Rastafarian enclaves that have absorbed most of the extant palaces: several of the more glorious places have burned, most tragically the Old Bushwick Democratic Club, at the northwest corner of Bushwick Avenue and Hart Street, perhaps the greatest single piece of architecture Bushwick ever knew (see Necrology).

[B 2.] Formerly **Vicelius & Ulmer's Continental Lagerbier Brewery/** later **William Ulmer Brewery,** Beaver St. bet. Locust and Belvidere Sts. SW side. 1872.

A **sad and ghostly** remnant of this brick brewery complex. Of particular note is the brewery office on Belvidere Street, a **mansarded,** cast-iron **crested** "house" that sets a point of style for the industry around it. Ulmer's mansion was on Bushwick Avenue a few blocks east [B 4.]

[B 3.] St. Mark's Lutheran Church and School/originally **St. Mark's Evangelical Lutheran German Church,** 626 Bushwick Ave., SW cor. Jefferson St. 1892.

The verdigris-clad copper-sheathed spire dominates Bushwick Avenue for most of its length. Up close there is brick and terra-cotta trim.

[B 4.] Davis Medical Building/originally **William Ulmer residence,** 670 Bushwick Ave., SW cor. Willoughby Ave. ca. 1885.

A stolid, solid Romanesque Revival brick fortress, as befits a stolid, solid brewer. **Dr. Frederick A. Cook,** a later owner, was a well-known but ill-heralded **Arctic** explorer. He claimed to have discovered the North Pole but lost in court to the navy: **Admiral Robert E. Peary.**

[B 5.] Originally **Mrs. Catherine Lipsius residence,** 680 Bushwick Ave., SE cor. Willoughby Ave. ca. 1886. Theobaold Engelhardt.

A brewer's **widow** commissioned this strangely proportioned Italianate Revival house. Note the **windows** in the frieze.

[B 6.] South Bushwick Reformed Church, 855 Bushwick Ave. NW cor. Himrod St. 1853. ★

A New England **outpost** in these dour and turgid streets; late **Greek Revival** with imposing Ionic columns. Neglect of the parish house, to the rear on Himrod Street, has apparently made possible the

Newtown Creek

East
River

G10
G7 G6
G8
G9
G11 13 18 19 G20
G12 14 15 16 17
G21
G22
G5

Greenpoint

G4 G3

G24 G25

G23

G1
McCarren
Park

G2

W27

W23

W32
W33

W31

Williamsburg

W16 W21
W15 W18 W22
W17 W19 W20
W14

W24

W12

W13
W30

W25
W26

W10
W11 W9
W28

W8
W7
W6
W3

W5

W4

W2
W1

Navy
Yard

W29

Bedford-Stuyvesant

WC

Pratt
Institute

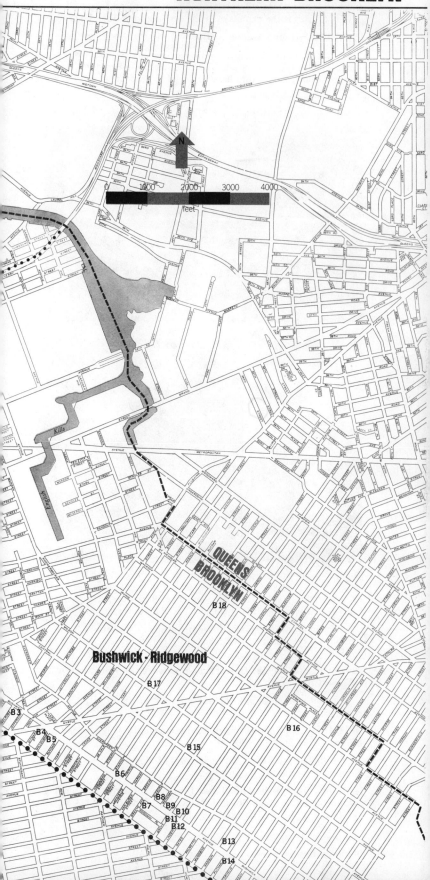

Bushwick - Ridgewood

good care of the parent church next door, with its delicate clapboard and purple and white milk glass.

The street is the namesake of the first minister, **John Himrod.**

[B 7.] 1090 Greene Avenue (residence), NE cor. Goodwin Place.

Mustard-yellow clapboard with red trim and an exuberant bay window on the Goodwin facade. There are lunettes in the frieze, Tuscan columns below. It is said to have belonged to the founder of the **"Bohack's"** grocery chain.

[B 4.] Originally William Ulmer res.   **[B 6.]** South Bushwick Reformed Ch.

[B 5.] Mrs. Catherine Lipsius commissioned this strangely windowed frieze

[B 8.] Originally **John F. Hylan residence,** 959 Bushwick Ave., bet. Bleeker and Menahan Sts. N side. 1885. John E. Dwyer.

One in a row of **unpretentious** brownstones **(Nos. 945-965),** noted particularly because it was the home of the **mayor** of New York **(1918–1925).**

 [B 9.] Originally **Gustav Doerschuck residence,** 999 Bushwick Ave., NW cor. Grove St. ca. 1890.

Another **Romanesque Revival** brewer's mansion, in brick and rock-face granite.

[B 10.] Originally **Charles Lindemann residence,** 1001 Bushwick Ave., NE cor. Grove St. ca. 1890.

A Shingle Style loner, turreted, porched, dormered, and decrepit. Note the bas-reliefs in the stone piers.

[B 11.] Bushwick United Head Start Program/formerly **Arion Singing Society/**originally **Louis Bossert residence,** 1002 Bushwick Ave., SE cor. Grove St. 1887. Theobold Englehardt.

A dour red-brick box crowned with a mansarded slate roof presents Gothic bracketed dormers to the street. **Bossert** was a successful millwork manufacturer who later built **Brooklyn Heights'** Bossert Hotel.

Grove Street owes its name to **Boulevard Grove,** a park at the intersection of that street with **Bushwick Avenue.** Picnics were held there as early as **1863.**

[B 12.] 1020 Bushwick Avenue (residences), SW cor. Linden St., and **37-53 Linden Street,** bet. Bushwick Ave. and Broadway. W side ca. 1885.

Richly decorated Queen Anne brick and terra-cotta town houses. The corner house is special, enriched with a cast-iron crenellated mansard roof. These dark-red monoliths bear superb friezes: **brow** and **waist.** The wrought ironwork on the Linden Street stoops is magnificent.

[B 13.] Bushwick Avenue Central Methodist Episcopal Church, 1130 Bushwick Ave., NE cor. Madison St. 1886–1912.

The octagonal **Renaissance Revival** tower is a local landmark, in polytonal red sandstone and gray brick.

[B 9.] Former Gustav Doerschuck res.

[B 12.] 1020 Bushwick Avenue house

[B 14.] The Bethesda Baptist Church: note the altered campanile (1967 photo)

[B 14.] Bethesda Baptist Church/formerly **Bushwick Avenue Congregational Church,** 1160 Bushwick Ave., SW cor. Cornelia St. 1896. Parfitt Brothers.

A powerful **campanile** corners this handsome brick church. An unfortunate plastic skin girds the original open porch under its conical hat. Note the Renaissance Revival brownstone and brick **parish house** next door.

 [B 15.] St. Barbara's Roman Catholic Church, Central Ave. NE cor. Bleeker St. 1910. Helme & Huberty.

Gleaming white and cream **Spanish Baroque.** The towers are wedding-cake icing: edible. Built to serve a parish at first German, then **Italian** and now largely **Hispanic.** Named not only for the saint but for Barbara Eppig, whose father, brewer **Leonard Eppig,** was a major contributor to its construction.

[B 15.] The Spanish Baroque Revival Saint Barbara's Roman Catholic Church

[B 16.] New Life Child Development Center, 295 Woodbine St., bet. Knickerbocker and Irving Aves. E side. 1973. Paul Heyer.

Carefully arranged brown brick clads this lone understated modern building, a **small token** of renewal in this sad neighborhood.

 [B 17.] 83rd Precinct, N.Y.C. Police Department/originally **20th Precinct, Brooklyn Police Department,** 179 Wilson Ave., NE cor. DeKalb Ave. 1895. William B. Tubby. ★

A powerful Romanesque Revival monument, crenellated, machicolated, and with a columned porch bearing incised **Sullivanesque** ornament. At its dedication the commissioner of the **Brooklyn Department of Police and Excise** declared it to be "commodious, architecturally ornate, and thoroughly equipped . . . the handsomest and most convenient police office in the world." The exaggeration is forgivable, for it is an architecturally distinguished station house. "Kojak" was filmed against this exterior background.

[B 18.] Wyckoff Heights Hospital/originally **German Hospital,** St. Nicholas Ave. bet. Stanhope and Stockholm Sts. S side. 1894.

Smooth. North European rounded brickwork with powerful masonry piers.

WILLIAMSBURG

Right! Without the final "h," even though the Williamsburgh Savings Bank spells its name the old way (the "h" fell when it consolidated with the **City of Brooklyn** in **1855**).

Though it shares its current spelling with the well-known restoration in **Virginia,** the resemblance ends there. This **Williamsburg,** formerly part of the **Town of Bushwick,** later a village and city in its own right, was named after **Col. Jonathan Williams,** its surveyor and grandnephew of **Benjamin Franklin. Richard M. Woodhull** started the community when he purchased thirteen acres of land at the foot of today's **South 2nd Street,** in 1802. He commissioned **Williams** to survey it, established a ferry to **New York** (Manhattan), and quickly went bankrupt **(1811).**

Thomas Morrell and **James Hazard** picked up where **Woodhull** had left off. They also established a ferry, this time to the **Grand Street**

Market at **Corlear's Hook,** providing an outlet for the farmers of **Bushwick** to sell their produce in New York. The impetus to the area's growth, however, was the establishment of a distillery in **1819.** The distillery is gone (as is the **Schaefer** brewery that followed it on the same site). Booze and beer helped build **Williamsburg** but now are only drunk here, not distilled or brewed.

The most telling impact on the community came from the opening of the **Williamsburg Bridge** in **1903.** Overnight the community changed from a fashionable resort with hotels catering to such sportsmen as **Commodore Vanderbilt, Jim Fisk,** and **William C. Whitney** to an immigrant district absorbing the overflow from **New York's Lower East Side.** (*The New York Tribune* of the period characterized the bridge as **"The Jews' Highway."**) Its elegant families moved away, and its mansions and handsome brownstones from the post-Civil War era fell into disuse and then were converted to multiple dwellings.

Bedford Avenue: The sequence is **north,** with the direction of traffic; the house numbers **decrease** as we proceed.

[W 1.] 667-677 Bedford Avenue, bet. Heyward and Rutledge Sts. E side.

An entire blockfront of tenements magnificently encrusted with stone: **rock-face** and **smooth,** brown, tan, and gray. Architecture for the people follows here in the steps of the grander and more monumental mansions further **north.** Granite colonnettes with **Byzantine** capitals.

[W 2.] Formerly **Public School 71, Brooklyn**/now **United Talmudic Academy,** 125 Heyward St., bet. Lee and Bedford Aves. N side. 1888. James W. Naughton. ★

From the French **Second Empire,** with a mansarded central block over brick and brownstone.

[W 3a.] Williamsburg Christian Church, Lee Ave. SE cor. Keap St., adjoining the Brooklyn-Queens Expressway. ca. 1885.

A **super**arched brick outpost maintains Christianity in this now mostly **Orthodox** land.

Hasidic community: Along **Bedford Avenue** are arrayed a group of brownstones, mansions, and apartment houses such as described above. Occupying these precincts is one of New York's most concentrated **Hasidic** (Jewish) communities. This unique settlement of the Satmarer Hasidim, recalling late medieval **Jewish** life in dress and customs, is a result of the persecution of the Eastern European Jewish community during **World War II.** In **1946, Rebbe Joel Teitelbaum** and several of his flock reached these shores and chose **Williamsburg**—even then a heavily **Orthodox** area—as their home. At the end of the war, the remaining survivors from **Poland** and **Hungary** migrated to the new settlement and reestablished their lives there. As the community grew, parts of it split off and moved to other parts of Brooklyn and to the suburbs. Beards and uncut earlocks identify the men; shaved but wigged heads identify the women. Long frock coats and skullcaps are in evidence everywhere among its male population, young and old; and in the winter, the fur-trimmed hat, the *shtreiml,* is certain to make its appearance. Evidence of its residents' heritage is everywhere apparent, from the proliferation of **Hebrew** signs on the mansions to the identification of small business establishments catering to the group.

[W 3b.] Rutledge Street, bet. Lee and Marcy Aves. N side.

One of Williamsburg's loveliest streets. This block is redolent of the best of **Brooklyn Heights.**

[W 4a.] 17th Corps Artillery Armory/formerly 47th Regiment Armory/ originally **Union Grounds,** Marcy to Harrison Aves., Heyward to Lynch Sts. 1883.

The **Harrison Avenue** end is a squat fort: double clerestoried, with crenellated and machicolated corner towers.

The **Union Grounds** were the site of early baseball games in the **1860s,** between the Cincinnati **Red Stockings,** the Philadelphia **Athletics,** the New York **Mutuals,** and the Brooklyn **Eckfords.** ·

[W 4b.] Primary School 380, Brooklyn, The John Wayne Elementary School, Marcy Ave. bet. Lynch and Middleton Sts. 1977. Richard Dattner & Assocs.

A somber **Pompeiian-red** brick construction, formed from clustered polygons and happily appropriate for this dour and solid neighborhood. The painted skirt covers graffiti, but the upper body is the natural brick.

[W 5.] Bedford Gardens (apartments), generally bet the Brooklyn-Queens Expwy., Wythe Ave., and Ross St. Most addresses are along Ross St. 1975.

One project in a nationwide federal effort to stimulate industrial rather than on-site production of buildings. These are in precast concrete—and crude. They look cheap but aren't.

[W 6.] Monsey New Square Bus Trails/formerly **Yeshiva Jesode Hatorah of Adas Yerem,** 571 Bedford Ave., bet. Keap and Rodney Sts. E side. ca. 1890.

Rock-face brownstone and an obviously affluent client made this a showplace. The elliptical bay window is elegant; note the **cherubs** in the copper frieze, roof finials, and all the rest.

[W 7.] Bais Yaakov of Adas Yereim/formerly **Hanover Club/**originally **Hawley Mansion,** 563 Bedford Ave., SE cor. Rodney St. ca. 1875. Remodeled, 1891. Lauritzen & Voss.

Yellow painted brick with brownstone quoins—cast iron against the sky. The *other* **William Cullen Bryant** (1849–1905), publisher of the Brooklyn *Times,* was president of the **Hanover Club.**

The Tree That Grows in Brooklyn: Williamsburg, a swampy, low-lying area, became the ideal spot for the culture of the ailanthus tree (a tree of fernlike leaves similar to those of the mimosa and locust). First imported from China about 1840, the tree was intended for use as the grazing ground of the cynthia moth's caterpillar, a great, green, purpleheaded, horned **monster** (¾ inch in diameter, 3 inches long) that spins a cocoon prized for its silk threads. The **mills of Paterson, N.J.,** were to be its beneficiaries. Its grazing role proved uneconomical (the grazing still goes on, however, without cocoon collection), but the tree was believed to have another virtue for the locals: supposedly providing power to dispel the "disease-producing vapors" presumed to come from swampy lands. See **Betty Smith's** 1943 novel of **Williamsburg** life, *A Tree Grows in Brooklyn.*

[W 8.] 559 Bedford Avenue (residence), NE cor. Rodney St. ca. 1890.

An imposing terra-cotta **castle,** now minus the conical, Spanish tile crown over its round corner tower. The bay on Bedford Avenue gives glassy contrast to the basic body, and an **owl** is perched on Rodney's pediment.

[W 9.] Yeshiva Yesoda Hatora of K'Hal Adas Yereim/formerly **Congress Club**/originally **Frederick Mollenhauer residence,** 505 Bedford Ave., NE cor. Taylor St. 1896. Lauritzen & Voss.

A neo-Renaissance brick mansion with a limestone porch, built by a son of **John Mollenhauer,** founder of the Mollenhauer Sugar Refinery **(1867),** which evolved into the **National Sugar Refining Company** and is more popularly known as **Jack Frost.** The original refineries were at **Kent Avenue** and **Rush Street,** then at **South 11th Street.**

[W 9.] Orig. Frederick Mollenhauer res.   [W 18.] American Savings Bk. branch

[W 10.] Congregation Tifereth Israel, 491 Bedford Ave., SE cor. Clymer St. 1976. Castro-Blano, Piscioneri & Feder.

An isolated well-detailed modern synagogue, unhappily out of scale and context with this once grand neighborhood.

[W 11.] Formerly **the Rebbe's House,** 500 Bedford Ave., NW cor. Clymer St.

Once the home of Grand Rabbi Josel Teitelbaum **(the Rebbe),** who led the bulk of the **Hasidim** from Europe to Williamsburg.

[W 12.] Epiphany Roman Catholic Church/originally **New England Congregational Church,** 96 S. 9th St. bet. Bedford and Berry Aves. S side.

A Lombardian Romanesque brick church with arched corbeltables, a sturdy tower, and flaking paint.

[W 13.] Light of the World Church/originally **New England Congregational Church,** 179 S. 9th St., bet. Driggs and Roebling Aves. N side. 1853. Thomas Little. ★

A giant **super-brownstone** in wood, sheet metal, and stone, this Italianate church bears extraordinary console brackets.

[W 14.] 396 Berry Street, NW cor. S. 8th St. ca. 1885.

This **smooth** terra-cotta and brick warehouse is a **monolith** of narrow joints and virtuoso brickwork.

[W 15.] 103 Broadway (factory), bet. Bedford Ave. and Berry St. N side. ca. 1875.

Elegant cast iron with **glassy** elliptical bays now contains studio lofts. Note the console brackets that form the visual keystones, and its **great** Corinthian columns.

[W 16.] Fruitcrest Corporation/formerly **Bedford Avenue Theater,** 109 S. 6th St., bet. Bedford Ave. and Berry St. N side. 1891. W. W. Cole, builder.

Opened by actress **Fanny Rice** in a farce, *A Jolly Surprise.* Its history as a theater was brief.

[W 17.] H. Fink & Sons Building/formerly **Nassau Trust Company,** 134-136 Broadway, SW cor. Bedford Ave. 1888. Frank J. Helmle.

Neo-Renaissance limestone and granite.

[W 18.] American Savings Bank/originally **Kings County Savings Bank,** 135 Broadway, NE cor. Bedford Ave. 1868. King & Wilcox. William H. Wilcox. ★

Bands of smooth and vermiculated **Dorchester** stone and slender Ionic and Corinthian columns alternate to enliven the exterior of the banking floor of this splendid **Second Empire** masterpiece. **Victorian** at its best, even the interior is carefully preserved, the gaslit chandeliers all present (but wired for electricity). Look at the plaited Indian hut in the entry pediment.

[W 19.] Williamsburgh Savings Bank, 175 Broadway, NW cor. Driggs Ave. 1875. George B. Post. Additions, 1906, 1925. Helme, Huberty & Hudswell. ★

The **eclectic** Victorian crossbreeding of **Renaissance** and **Roman** parts produced one of Brooklyn's great landmarks, particularly to those who pass by train or car over the Williamsburg Bridge. It is a sharp, hard, gray place reminiscent of the work of **Brooklyn's** own great architect, **Frank Freeman,** at the old, long since demolished, **Brooklyn Trust Company** (below the dome). One great and two good, but more modest, Williamsburg restaurants:

Peter Luger's Steak House, 178 Broadway, bet. Driggs and Bedford Aves.

Alfred Hitchcock called its steak the "best in the universe." In this **spartan** outpost of polished oak and white aprons, far from the habitat of its elegant clientele, steak reigns supreme—all else being decoration or fodder for those who can't contend with greatness. It all began as **Charles Luger's Cafe, Billiards, and Bowling Alley** in **1876.** Expensive. **No** credit cards. **No** vegetarians.

Cresci's Restaurant, 593 Lorimer St., bet. Skillman and Congelyea Sts. W side.

Hearty **Italian** food in the center of a neatly maintained Italian community within **polyglot** eastern Williamsburg. It's good to see businessmen (at lunch) and families (at dinner) enjoying the flavorful food and bustling atmosphere.

Bamonte's Restaurant, 32 Withers St., bet. Union Ave and Lorimer St. S side.

The front of this Italian restaurant is a **dark bar** with color TV. But the back is like a theater, and the brightly lighted, glass-fronted, sparkling white kitchen is **onstage** in every way. Lower-keyed than **Crisci's,** more relaxed. Good, sauce-y food.

[W 20.] 195 Broadway/originally **Sparrow Shoe Factory Warehouse,** bet. Driggs Ave. and New St. N side. 1882. William B. Ditmars.

Cast-iron, with exuberant console brackets and fluted, floral-decorated pilasters.

[W 21.] Holy Trinity Church of Ukrainian Autocephalic Orthodox Church in Exile/formerly **Williamsburg Trust Company,** 117-185 S. 5th St., NW cor. New St. 1906. Helmle & Huberty.

Built as a bank, this **opulent** terra-cotta monument is now a **cathedral,** the reverse of the common progression from religious to sectarian use; compare the various churches of Brooklyn Heights and Cobble Hill that are now **condominiums.** The architecture is the natural result of the **World's Columbia Exhibition** (1893), the inspiration for the **American Renaissance.**

[W 22.] Washington Plaza, S. 4th St. to Broadway, New to Havemeyer Sts.

Formerly the **ganglion** for half of Brooklyn's trolley empire, the Plaza is now a depot for nondescript buses belching forth diesel fumes between runs. Some of the old sheds and a signal tower remain, but the web of overhead copper wires is now only a memory. Furthermore, the space is cut into pieces by the elevated subway and the **Brooklyn-Queens Expressway,** which slice through it with abandon. The forecourt for the **Ukrainian Cathedral,** in the plaza's northwest corner, is formally executed and the only part of the whole deserving of the title

"plaza." It contains, among disintegrating **Renaissance Revival** ornaments, a fine verdigris equestrian statue, *George Washington at Valley Forge* (Henry M. Shrady, **1906**).

[W 23.] Formerly **Manufacturers Trust Company/**originally **North Side Bank,** 33-35 Grand St., bet. Kent and Wythe Aves. N side. 1889. Theobald Engelhardt.

Lusty, gutsy, **rock face Romanesque,** arched, cast-iron corniced, wrought iron. A **super,** lonely building.

The Fourteen Buildings: The turn Grand Street takes at Union Avenue marks the beginning of the site of the **Fourteen Buildings.** The street was laid out between **Union** and **Bushwick** Avenues so that it would pass through the property of a group of men who then built for themselves a series of **Greek Revival** frame dwellings in 1836. Each had a dome and a colonnaded porch of fluted wood columns. The houses were arranged one per block on both sides of **Grand Street,** with two extras slipped in. By **1837** each of the men had suffered the consequences of that year's financial panic, and the houses changed hands. In **1850** all fourteen still remained, but by **1896** only one was left. Today there is no sign on this **busy shopping street** of that **bygone elegance** apart from the bend itself.

[W 24.] Williamsburg Houses, N.Y.C. Housing Authority, Maujer to Scholes St., Leonard St. to Bushwick Ave. 1937. Board of Design: Richmond H. Shreve, chief architect; with James F. Bly, Matthew W. DelGaudio, Arthur C. Holden, William Lescaze, Samuel Gardstein, Paul Trapani, G. Harmon Gurney, Harry Leslie Walker, and John W. Ingle, Jr, associate architects.

The **best** public housing project **ever built** in New York but also the first and most expensive (in adjusted dollars). Its 4-story buildings embrace semiprivate spaces for both passive and active recreation. Reinforced concrete and brick infill is **punctuated** by pedestrian ways that connect sequential courtyards through stepped and columned portals. The apartments themselves are reached without benefit of corridors by an entry system that opens directly off the stair landings (as in **Princeton Collegiate Gothic,** here in serene modern dress). The new aluminum doublehung windows are a **clunky alteration,** replacing elegant slender-mullioned, but unhappily deteriorated, steel casements.

[W 25a.] 174 and 178 Meserole Street, bet. Graham and Humboldt Aves. S side. ca. 1880s.

Exuberant, painted wood tenements—No. 174 in **Queen Anne,** No. 178 in **Renaissance Revival**—two of the city's best. **"Tenement"** is pejorative today; in fact it describes a walk-up apartment house that covers most of its building site. Here the light in the back rooms is minimal, but the visible architecture is **magnificent.**

[W 25b.] 182 Graham Avenue (residence), SE cor. Meserole Ave. ca. 1885.

Above a sullied ground floor rises a **Belle Époque** confection with a curved Second Empire mansard roof and ornate and wondrous details. It's a parody of the elegantly dressed businessperson with scruffy unshined shoes.

[W 25c.] New York Telephone Company Communications Center, 55 Meserole St., NE cor. Manhattan Ave. 1975. John Carl Warnecke & Assocs.

Gargantuan hooded windows contribute to a powerful and inhuman place for telephone equipment. This stylish and expensive iron-spotted brick form gives **Ma Bell** additional leverage in its never-ending rate battle.

[W 26.] Holy Trinity Roman Catholic Church, Montrose Ave. bet. Manhattan and Graham Aves. S side. 1882.

A huge twin-towered reprise of Manhattan's **St. Patrick's** Cathedral—or perhaps of the **Abbaye aux Hommes** in Caen.

[W 27a.] 492-494 Humboldt Street, bet. Richardson and Herbert Sts. E side., and 201 Richardson Street, bet. Humboldt and N. Henry Sts. N side. ca. 1850.

These were severed parts of a formerly great Brooklyn **colonnade row;** only one still exists, on Willow Place, in Brooklyn Heights. Here the decline is not one of abandonment but of cultural desecration: **No. 492** has been "improved" downhill, by cladding its natural columns with fluted sheet metal, false shutters, and turgid stone wainscoting. Good intentions have succeeded here only in **destroying** a bit of architectural heritage.

[W 21.] Form. Williamsburg Trust Co.   [W 27a.] A sadly mutilated colonnade

---

Colonnade Rows: Only records remain of the least-known of Brooklyn's four colonnade rows, on the east end of Kent Avenue between **South 8th** and **South 9th** Streets, in Williamsburg. The last section of this ensemble was destroyed in the **1920s.** Among the families who shared the extraordinary views across the river were the **Walls** and the **Berrys. Dr. Abraham Berry** became the first mayor of the city of **Williamsburgh** in **1852. William Wall** became the second—and last—mayor in **1854.**

[W 27b.] **St. Paul's Center,** 484 Humboldt Street, SE cor. Richardson St. ca. 1885.

Iron-spotted bricks and Romanesque Revival.

[W 28.] **Bnos Yakov of Pupa/**originally **Temple Beth Elohim,** 274 Keap St., bet. Marcy and Division Aves. S side. 1876.

This **Hebrew** congregation was the first in Brooklyn, dating from 1851. **Ruskinian Gothic** polychromy in brick and painted brownstone, terra-cotta, stained glass, and tile. Note the lush ironwork gates.

[W 29.] **Woodhull Medical and Mental Health Center,** SW cor. Broadway and Flushing Aves. 1977. Kallman & McKinnell/Russo & Sonder, associated architects.

Almost a **space odyssey** alit at this juncture of Williamsburgh, Bedford-Stuyvesant, and Williamsburg, this **machine for health** was the most technologically and architecturally up-to-date, and the most expensive, hospital of its time. The self-weathering steel has acquired a deep purple-brown patina on this bold, cubistic place. Great human-high trusses span **69** feet, within which workers can adjust the complex piping and tubing that serve the rooms and laboratories above and below these interleaved service levels. **Kallman and McKinnell's** first and major monument was the competition-winning **Boston City Hall.** With this machine for medicine they have created a **superbuilding,** a somewhat scary ode to health, dedicated more to the efficiency of **health economics** than to the serenity of its clients. Widely reviewed in architectural literature, it has won many prizes.

[W 30a.] **Iglesia Pentecostal Misionera/**originally **Deutsche Evangelische St. Petri Kirche,** 262 Union Ave., NE cor. Scholes St. 1881.

That **dour** German brickwork now softened in spirit by a Hispanic congregation.

[W 30b.] Formerly **Public School 69, Brooklyn/**originally **Colored School No. 3,** 270 Union Ave., bet. Scholes and Stagg Sts. E side.

An **Italian Romanesque** miniature for a school flock of Williamsburg's more rural days.

[W 30c.] Iglesia Metodista Unida de Sur Trés/originally **South Third Street Methodist Church,** 411 S. 3rd St., bet. Union Ave. and Hewes St. N side. 1855.

Simple **Lombardian Romanesque,** painted red.

[W 29.] Woodhull Medical and Mental Health Center, a machine for medicine

[W 30b.] An Italian Romanesque miniature for the former Colored School No. 3

[W 31.] American Sugar Refining Company/formerly **Havemeyer and Elder's Sugar Refining Company,** 292-350 Kent Avenue, bet. S. 5th and S. 2nd Sts. W side. ca. 1890.

Between 2nd and 3rd, and again between 4th and 5th, are bulky, bold **Romanesque Revival** behemoths.

[W 32.] Iglesia Bautista Calvario/formerly **St. Matthew's First Evangelical Lutheran Church,** 197-199 N. 5th St., bet. Roebling St. and Driggs Ave. N side. 1864.

Battered buttresses flank this painted brick and glass-blocked church. The shell survives.

[W 33a.] Church of the Annunciation (Roman Catholic), 255 N. 5th St., NE cor. Havemeyer St. 1870. F. J. Berlenbach, Jr.

A crisply detailed and lovingly maintained **Lombardian Romanesque** basilica. Its related convent was across the street.

[W 33b.] 56-64 Havemeyer Street/originally **Convent of the Order of St. Dominic.** 1889. P. J. Berlenbach.

A hearty Romanesque Revival institution, now revived as a condominium.

[W 30c.] Now Iglesia Metodista Unida   **[W 33a.]** Church of the Annunciation

[W 31.] Orig. Havemeyer & Elder's Sugar Refinery, viewed from the East River

Subway kiosks: the late-lamented cast-iron **IRT** subway kiosks were cast in the **Hecla Iron Works** on **Berry Street** in the northern part of **Williamsburg.** The recent reconstruction of one at **Astor Place** near **Cooper Union,** in Manhattan, is a wondrous revival of these great glass and metal canopies.

GREENPOINT

Greenpoint (pronounced **Greenpernt** in those gangster movies of the 1930s) is a quiet, ordered, and orderly community of discrete ethnic populations, with a central charming historic district all but unknown to outsiders, even those in neighboring sectors of Brooklyn.

Its modern history began with the surveying of its lands in **1832** by **Dr. Eliphalet Nott,** president of Union College, in Schenectady (America's first architecturally planned campus), and **Neziah Bliss.** Within two years the whole area was platted for streets and lots. Much of it was purchased for development by **Ambrose C. Kingsland,** mayor of New York (1851–1853), and **Samuel J. Tilden,** who went on to fame in politics and who is happily remembered for the establishment of a free **public library** in New York (parallel with that of **Astor** and **Lenox**).

The area soon became a great shipbuilding center. It was here, at the **Continental Iron Works** at **West** and **Calyer** Streets, that **Thomas F. Rowland** built the ironclad warship *Monitor* from plans created by **John Ericsson.** The "Yankee cheesebox on a raft' was launched on **January 30, 1862,** and battled the Confederate *Merrimack* at Hampton Roads, Va., two months later. Later that year the *Monitor* foundered off **Cape Hatteras** and was lost.

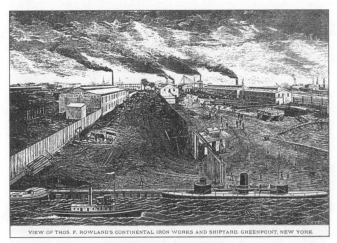

VIEW OF THOS. F. ROWLAND'S CONTINENTAL IRON WORKS AND SHIPYARD, GREENPOINT, NEW YORK.

By **1860** the so-called five black arts (printing, pottery, gas, glass, and iron) were firmly established in **Green Point,** as it was first known. In **1867,** Charles Pratt established his kerosene refinery (Astral Oil Works)—the first successful American **oil well** had flowed in **1859** at **Titusville, Pa. Pratt's** product later gave rise to the slogan, "The holy lamps of **Tibet** are primed with **Astral Oil.**" Astral Oil provided the wealth which later made possible **Pratt Institute,** myriad Pratt family mansions, as well as **Greenpoint's** Astral Apartments.

[G 1.] McCarren Park Play Center, N.Y.C. Department of Parks & Recreation, McCarren Park, Lorimer St. bet. Bayard St. and Driggs Ave. E side. ca. 1936. N.Y.C. Department of Parks. Aymar Embury II, consultant.

Gutted by fire in 1987, this ceremonially arched pavilion, with its imposing clerestory, announced the grand dip behind. It is one of 4 **WPA**-built swimming pools erected in Brooklyn during the Depression; the others are **Red Hook, Sunset Park,** and **Betsy Head.**

[G 2.] Russian Orthodox Cathedral of the Transfiguration, 228 N. 12th St., SE cor. Driggs Ave. 1921. Louis Allmendinger. ★

The **Winter Palace** at St. Petersburg is remembered in the yellow and beige tones of this magnificent cathedral, crowned with 5 verdigris-copper onion-domed cupolas. The real treat, however, is within: the space is small (only **250** seats), and the central cupola is supported on 4 great columns painted to simulate richly veined marble. The triple-altared eastern end is separated from the body of the church by the **iconostasis,** a hand-carved wooden screen on which icons were painted by the monks in the **Orthodox Monastery of the Caves** in **Kiev.** A visit

[G 1.] Entrance pavilion, McCarren Park Play Center & Swimming Pool in 1967

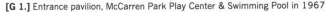

should include the celebration of **Divine Liturgy:** architecture, incense, ritual, and sound, combined in many tongues, create a deeply moving **saturation of the senses.**

[G 3.] Public School 34, Brooklyn, The Oliver H. Perry School, Norman Ave. bet. Eckford St. and McGuinness Blvd. N side. Central block, 1867. Samuel B. Leonard. Wings, James W. Naughton. ★

An austere mixture of Renaissance and Romanesque revivals.

[G 4.] Greenpoint Branch, Brooklyn Public Library, Leonard St., NE cor. Norman Ave. 1972. Hausman & Rosenberg.

A white **mansard** concrete hat floats over a brick base. One misfortune of modern architecture has been its obsession with placing institutional buildings all on one level, violating the scale of multistoried row-housed blocks such as these. Here the excision of the cityscape that is created is no happier than that caused by a **7-11** shop; there is, however, stylish detailing.

Brackets, asphalt, and pictorial masonry: The wood entrance canopy brackets at 117 Norman Avenue next door are a pair of the most monumental in Brooklyn. Such parts are unsung heroes of Victoriana-Brooklyniana, which enriched endless rows of simple houses, in the same fashion that stoops modulated seas of brownstones. Unfortunately, the relentless process of modernization rips these handsome ornaments off houses at the same time that it veneers wood-clapboarded sides with picture-book asphalt pretending to look like stone or brick—or anything other than it really is. One must go to the poorest neighborhoods to find real but decrepitly authentic materials.

[G 5.] Greenpoint Historic District, roughly from Java to Calyer Sts., Franklin to Manhattan Aves. ★

[G 5a.] Greenpoint Savings Bank, 807 Manhattan Ave., SW cor. Calyer St. 1908. Helmle & Huberty. ☆

Roman pomp under a pantheon dome, shingled delightfully in a **fish-scaled** pattern in slate. The Pantheon in Rome was similarly shingled but in bronze, stolen for valuable metal in medieval times. This grand Doric-columned bank is of limestone over a granite base.

[G 6.] St. Elias Greek Rite Catholic Church/formerly **Reformed Dutch Church of Greenpoint,** 149 Kent St., bet. Manhattan Ave. and Franklin St. N side. **Church,** 1870. William B. Ditmars. **Sunday school,** 1880. W. Wheeler Smith. ☆

Bulky brick, brownstone, and whitestone, with the neo-Gothic polychromy (note the alternating red and gray voussoirs) promoted by writer-architectural historian **John Ruskin** and hence termed Ruskinian Gothic. Note the cast-iron fence with its Gothic crests, and the octagonal Sunday school.

[G 7.] Church of the Ascension (Episcopal), 129 Kent St., bet. Manhattan Ave. and Franklin St. N side. 1866. Henry Dudley. ☆

Granite ashlar with brownstone trim, a double-pitched silhouette, and **red** Episcopal doors. Its low and friendly scale is reminiscent of an English country church. Note the 3 oval oculi.

[G 8.] 130 Kent Street (row house), bet. Manhattan Ave. and Franklin St. S side. 1859. Neziah Bliss, builder. ☆

A star on this handsome street of town houses. Here the boldest porch enlivens the streetscape of this block.

[G 9.] Originally **Mechanics and Traders Bank,** 144 Franklin St., NE cor. Greenpoint Ave. ca. 1895. ☆

Gloomy but wonderful Pompeian red Renaissance Revival in terracotta, brick, and rock-face brownstone, with grand pilasters crowned by fantastic composite capitals. Savor the terra-cotta frieze among other riches adorning this lovely building.

[G 10.] The Astral Apartments, 184 Franklin St., bet. Java and India Sts. E side. 1886. Lamb & Rich. ★ ☆

Commissioned by **Charles Pratt** as housing for his kerosene refinery workers, by the same architects who created his **Pratt Institute Main Building**. This many-entried block was patterned after the **Peabody Apartments** in London. **Alfred Tredway White** had initiated such housing experiments in Brooklyn at **Riverside** in Brooklyn Heights and the **Tower & Home Apartments** in Cobble Hill. Here we see patterned brickwork, rock-face brownstone arches and lintels, and structural steel storefronts with the **rivets** themselves as decoration. It has recently been painted and rewindowed. Hurray.

[G 6.] Sturdy Ruskinian-Gothic church   **[G 11.]** 93–103 Milton Street houses

[G 10.] The Astral Apartments by the kerosene-magnate patron Charles Pratt

Milton Street: This rich block between **Franklin Street** and **Manhattan Avenue** is crowned on axis by **St. Anthony's Church**. It sums up the finest urban values of **Greenpoint**, here reaching the **urbane**.

[G 11.] 93-103 Milton Street. N side. 1874. James R. Sparrow, builder. ☆

Six brickfronted houses (Nos. 105-109 were originally three more in a set of nine) that retain their delicate archivolts over their entrance doors, curved **Renaissance Revival** window lintels, each facade now painted individually for identity.

[G 12.] 118-120 Milton Street. S side. 1868. Thomas C. Smith. ☆

This Second Empire pair has been sullied on one side by a defaced mansard roof, on the other by a bastardized cornice. Where was the Landmarks Preservation Commission when we needed it?

[G 13.] 119-121, 123-125 Milton Street. N side. 1876. Thomas C. Smith. ☆

The left pair survive as a single composition; the right pair have been desecrated. No. 125 bears the ubiquitous metal canopy vended to the Brooklyn innocent, as ugly as a clutch of iron deer on the same family's suburban front lawn.

[G 14.] 122-124 Milton Street. S side. 1889. Theobold Engelhardt. ☆

Brick and brownstone Queen Anne. The bracketed canopies over the entrances are both vigorous and intact.

[G 15.] 128-134 Milton Street. S side. 1909. Philemon Tillion. ☆

Three cool, corniced, and bay-windowed tenements, well-kept and well loved, in brick and limestone.

[G 16.] Greenpoint Reformed Church/originally **Thomas C. Smith residence,** 138 Milton St. S side. 1867. Thomas C. Smith. ☆

Italianate Greek Revival (those warring peoples could combine in style on occasion). Before **1891** this congregation resided at what is now **St. Elias Church,** two blocks north on Kent Street.

[G 17.] 140-144 Milton Street. S side. 1909. Philemon Tillion. ☆

The streetscape here is enriched by neo-Classical porches.

[G 18.] 141-149 Milton Street. N side. 1894. Thomas C. Smith. ☆

Arched and recessed loggias at the third floor enliven the plastic quality of this street.

[G 19.] St. John's Lutheran Church, 155 Milton St. N side. 1897. Theobold Engelhardt. ☆

In somber painted brick, this **German Gothic Revival** is a stolid place incised with its original name, **Evangelische-Lutherische St. Johannes Kirche.** Token flying buttresses and lancet windows enliven the facade.

 [G 20.] St. Anthony of Padua Church (Roman Catholic), 862 Manhattan Ave., at the end of Milton St. E side. 1874. Patrick C. Keely. ☆

Attired in red brick and white limestone, the **quasi-cathedral** on this religious block offers a little **fancy dress** to this dour neighborhood. Its **240**-foot spire, at a bend in Manhattan Avenue, is a visual pivot not only for **Milton Street** and **Manhattan Avenue** but for all of **Greenpoint.**

Little Europe Restaurant, 888 Manhattan Ave., bet. Greenpoint Ave. and Milton St. E side.

With a former theater called **Chopin** up the street and a wedding caterer grandly titled the **Polonaise Terrace,** it should come as no surprise that this modest restaurant serves **Middle** and **Eastern** European food. Try the fruit-filled dumplings.

 [G 21.] Union Baptist Church/originally **First Baptist Church of Greenpoint,** 151 Noble St., bet. Manhattan Ave. and Franklin St. N side. 1863. ☆

An early **Romanesque Revival** dissenter from the **English Gothic Revivalism** of the Protestant Episcopal church—a lusty architectural route for some lusty Protestant congregations.

[G 22a.] Greenpoint Home for the Aged, 137 Oak St. N side, at the head of Guernsey St. 1887. Theobold Engelhardt. ☆

An eclectic brick pile with Italianate massing and Romanesque Revival arches.

[G 22b.] Sidewalk clock, in front of 752 Manhattan Ave. E side. ★

One of the city's few remaining freestanding cast iron clocks, now protected by landmarks designation.

[G 23.] St. Stanislaus Kostka Vincentian Fathers Church (Roman Catholic), 607 Humboldt St., SW cor. Driggs Ave. ca. 1890.

Two complex, assymetrical, octagonal spires of this, the largest **Polish Catholic** congregation in Brooklyn, **dominate** the local skyline. Humboldt Street and Driggs Avenue are here renamed **Lech Walesa Place** and **Pope John Paul II** Plaza with the fervency that only a monolithic local ethnic population can supply. The spires' heavy encrustation of stone ornament is in rich contrast to the painted aluminum clapboard and asbestos shingles that line the local streets like exterior wallpaper, **Archie Bunker style.**

[G 24.] 650 and **694 Humboldt Street,** bet. Driggs and Nassau Aves. E side.

Two unsullied remnants of wood housing: **No. 650** built for a single family, **No. 694** a tenement in multicolored paint. Together they demonstrate the texture and color of the community prior to the street's recladding in artificial aluminum, genuine asbestos, and real what-have-you.

[G 25.] Monsignor McGolrick Park, Driggs to Nassau Aves., Russell to Monitor Sts. **[G 25a.] Shelter Pavilion,** 1910. Helmle & Huberty. ★

A park on the scale of London's **Bloomsbury,** with surrounding row houses too low to supply the same architectural containment. Within is a monument (Antonio de Filippo, sculptor), to the *Monitor* and its designer, **John Ericsson,** and the Shelter Pavilion, in 18th-century French neo-Classical style.

CENTRAL BROOKLYN

CENTRAL FLATBUSH • PROSPECT PARK SOUTH
DITMAS PARK • EAST FLATBUSH/RUGBY
WINDSOR TERRACE • PARKVILLE

Town of Flatbush/Vlackebos—"Level Forest"

Established as a town in **1652;** Town of New Lots separated from Flatlands in **1852.** Annexed to the City of Brooklyn in **1894.**

Until the **1880s Flatbush** was a quiet place with a rural character. The introduction of the **Brooklyn, Flatbush & Coney Island Railroad,** now the Brighton Line, encouraged the real estate speculation and development that transformed the farmland into a **fashionable suburb** by the turn of the century. The names of these subdivisions are still used in some cases, only dimly remembered in others: **Prospect Park South,** the most affluent of those extant, **Vanderveer Park, Ditmas Park, Fiske** and **Manhattan Terraces,** and a host of others like **Matthews Park, Slocum Park,** and **Yale Park.**

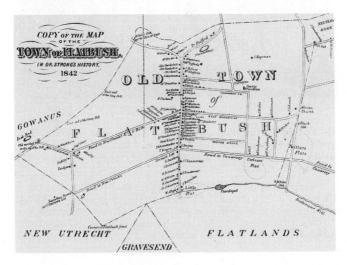

Earlier there had been a series of abortive attempts to impose grids of houses on the countryside, such as **Parkville,** the off-axis grid surrounding **Parkville Avenue** (1852); and **Windsor Terrace,** between **Vanderbilt Street** and **Greenwood Avenue** in the corridor separating **Green-Wood Cemetery** from **Prospect Park** (1862). These projects were never as successful as those in the quiet, lightly trafficked cul-de-sacs created by the railroad's cut on its way to **Brighton Beach.**

Older names, such as **Midwood,** a corruption of the Dutch **Midwout,** are still used in areas that once constituted only a portion of that Dutch enclave.

[L 1.] Prospect-Lefferts Gardens Historic District, roughly bounded by Flatbush Ave., Fenimore St., Rogers Ave. (with a tail that loops almost to Nostrand Ave.), and Empire Blvd. beyond Bedford Ave. ★

This is a neighborhood of simple, early 20th-century houses in a variety of styles: **Romanesque Revival,** neo-**Renaissance,** neo-**Georgian,** neo-**Federal,** and neo-**Tudor.** Here is a classic case where the whole **is** greater than the sum of its parts, where the ensemble—rather than individual buildings—is the landmark.

CENTRAL FLATBUSH

[F 1.] 111 Clarkson Avenue (residence), bet. Bedford and Rogers Aves. N side. ca. 1885.

A fairyland place that might be termed **beserk eclecticism.** The onion domes are redolent of **John Nash's** Royal Pavilion at **Brighton** (England, not **Beach**). Unfortunately, a tacky shop has been installed where part of the front porch once stood.

[F 1.] 111 Clarkson Avenue, a "berserk eclectic" gem, sadly mutilated (1967)

 [F 2a.] Erasmus Hall Museum/originally **Erasmus Hall Academy,** in the courtyard of **Erasmus Hall High School,** 911 Flatbush Ave., bet. Church and Snyder Aves. E side. 1786. ★ **[F 2b.] Erasmus Hall High School.** 1903. C. B. J. Snyder.

Established as a private academy by the **Flatbush Reformed Dutch Church** across the street. The site was previously occupied by the first public school in **Midwout** (Midwood), erected in **1658** by the New Netherlands Colony. The Academy building is **Georgian-Federal** with a hipped-gambrel roof and a **Palladian** window over a delicate **Tuscan-**columned porch.

[F 2a.] Original freestanding Erasmus Hall Academy: view engraved in 1883

Warning: Rule 9, Erasmus Hall Academy, 1797: "No student shall be permitted any species of gaming nor to drink any spiritous liquors nor to go into any tavern in Flat Bush without obtaining consent of a teacher."

[F 3.] Originally **Flatbush Town Hall,** 35 Snyder Ave., bet. Flatbush and Bedford Aves. N side. 1876. John Y. Cuyler. ★

Flatbush did not become part of **Brooklyn** until **1894.** This lusty **Ruskinian Gothic** building is happily being preserved as a community center.

[F 4.] Flatbush Reformed Dutch Church, 890 Flatbush Ave., SW cor. Church Ave. 1793–1798. Thomas Fardon. ★ **[F 5.] Parsonage,** Kenmore Terrace NE cor. E. 21st St. Moved in 1918 from 900 Flatlands Ave. 1853. ★

A rough, horizontally coursed stone ashlar (**Manhattan schist**) church with **Romanesque arched** windows and doors. Crowning it all is a **Georgian** white-painted octagonal tower, with **Tuscan** colonnettes surmounted by urns. The first of three churches built according to the mandate of **Governor Peter Stuyvesant** (the others were the **Flatland Dutch Reformed Church** and the **First Reformed Church**), this is the third building to occupy the site.

Walk through the churchyard from **Church** Avenue, and you will pass delicately incised brownstone gravestones with elegant calligraphy. (Strangely, the limestone markers have eroded, washing off their graphics, while the brownstone survives.) Continue past the meetinghouse of the 1930s onto Kenmore Terrace. On the right is the **Parsonage,** a beautifully detailed late **Greek Revival** painted-shingled house presenting a gracious **Corinthian**-columned veranda, with a handsome cornice of dentils and **Italianate** modillions.

[F 5.] The eclectic Greek Revival parsonage of the Flatbush Reformed Church

[F 6.] Albemarle-Kenmore Terraces Historic District, includes all row houses on the two streets listed below. ★ **[F 7.] Kenmore Terrace,** E of E. 21st St., bet. Church Ave. and Albemarle Rd. South houses, 1918–1920. Slee & Bryson. ☆

The **Flatbush Reformed Church Parsonage** forms one flank, and these pleasant English **Arts** and **Crafts Revival** row cottages, the other.

[F 8.] Albemarle Terrace, E of E. 21st St., bet. Church Ave. and Albemarle Rd. 1916. Slee & Bryson. ☆

Charming **Georgian Revival** row houses in a cul-de-sac that says dead end but that is far from dead. The simple brick architecture is enlivened by alternating bay windows, Palladian windows, entry porches, and dormers in the slate mansard roofs.

[F 9.] Knickerbocker Field Club, 114 E. 18th St., at W. end of Tennis Court. 1886. Parfitt Brothers. ★

Now concealed between apartment buildings on East 18th Street and the subway cut, this is a sprawling **Shingle Style** building. From the parking lot at Albemarle Road and East 17th Street, one can view its **gambrel roofs** and Tuscan-columned porches.

[F 10.] Loew's Kings Theater, Flatbush Ave. bet. Tilden Ave. and Beverly Rd. E side. 1929. C. W. Rapp & George L. Rapp.

With its ornate eclectic terra-cotta facade, this is one of the last **movie palaces** of that vibrant era when going to the movies was as much an adventure as watching the movie on the screen.

PROSPECT PARK SOUTH

The streets between **Church Avenue** and **Beverly Road,** and between **Coney Island Avenue** and the open cut for the **Brighton Line** subway, contain as unique a community as any in the city. The entrances to most of the streets are guarded by pairs of sturdy brick piers bearing cast-concrete plaques with the letters **PPS** in bas-relief. The area is **Prospect Park South,** characterized at the time of its initial development as *rus in urbe,* or "the country in the city," a description not inappropriate even today. Here is an environment that ranks with **Forest Hills Gardens** and **Kew Gardens** in Queens as an architecturally distinguished precinct of grand freestanding turn-of-the-century single-family houses.

PPS is a monument to the vision of the realtor **Dean Alvord.** What he conceived was a garden park within the confines of the grid, abandoning the row house urbanization that had infilled most of old Brooklyn, from the **Heights** to the **Bedford-Stuyvesant,** from **Greenpoint** to **Park Slope.** To these ends he installed all the utilities and paved all the streets before selling one plot of land. Trees were planted not along the curb but at the building line, giving the streets a greater sense of breadth. Alternating every **20** feet were **Norway maples,** for permanence, and **Carolina poplars,** for immediate shade. The short-lived poplars, **Alvord** and his architect, **John Petit,** reasoned, would die out as the maples reached maturity.

[P 1.] Prospect Park South Historic District, generally bet. Church Ave. and Beverly Road, and from a line E of Coney Island Ave. to the Brighton Line's subway cut. ★

[P 2.] Originally Russell Benedict residence, 104 Buckingham Rd., bet. Church Ave. and Albemarle Rd. W side. 1902. Carroll H. Pratt. ☆

A stately portico with **Composite** columns greets the street on this painted shingle residence. A stylish place that has seen better times . . . and owners with better taste.

[P 3.] Originally William H. McEntee residence, 115 Buckingham Rd., bet. Church Ave. and Albemarle Rd. E side. 1900. John J. Petit. ☆

A **volumetric exercise** in the **Shingle Style:** a gambrel-roofed volume, incised for a porch and anchored by a corner "bell"-capped tower. It would be happier with natural, weathered shingles than with its **garish** paint job.

[P 4.] Originally **George U. Tompers residence,** 125 Buckingham Rd., bet. Church Ave. and Albemarle Rd. E side. 1911. Brun & Hauser. ☆

Corinthian columns and finely scaled clapboard. An Americanized **Roman** temple as seen through **Renaissance** eyes.

[P 5.] Originally **Frederick S. Kolle residence,** 131 Buckingham Rd., bet. Church Ave. and Albemarle Rd. E side. 1902. Petit & Green. ☆

This wears **Japanese** fancy dress of a sophisticated sort on a stucco body. Sticks and struts, corbels and brackets, give a timber-structuralist look to what is a rather plain box **underneath.** Alvord's advertisement in *Country Life* described the interior as "a faithful reflection of the dainty Japanese art from which America is learning so much."

[P 3.] The 115 Buckingham Road res.   **[P 5.]** The 131 Buckingham Road res.

[P 6.] Originally **William A. Norwood residence,** 143 Buckingham Rd., NE cor. Albemarle Rd. 1906. Walter S. Cassin. ☆

A re-revival of the **Italian Villa** style best exemplified in Brooklyn at the **Litchfield Mansion** (1857) in Prospect Park.

Backyards: Today's 4-track **Brighton Line,** which abuts the rear yards of the houses on the east side of **Buckingham Road,** was at the time of the original development only a 2-track operation. In **1907** the **Brooklyn Rapid Transit Company,** successors to the original railroad and precursors of the later **BMT,** widened the cut, thus narrowing the backyards of these houses to the nominal amount visible today.

[P 7.] Originally **Louis McDonald residence,** 1519 Albemarle Rd., NE cor. Buckingham Rd. 1902. John J. Petit. ☆

To complement the adjacent **Roman** temple, **Italian** villa, and **Japanese** house, here is an **all-American** example influenced by the **Chicago School.** Note the angels in the bay windows' panels and the corbeled **caryatids.**

[P 8.] Originally **Maurice Minton residence/**now **McAllister residence,** 1510 Albemarle Rd., SE cor. Marlborough Rd. 1900. John J. Petit. ☆

A **stately mansion** with a grand conservatory and stable. The latter's huge-scale composite columns support the roof in the manner of many **Roman** buildings, such as the **Temple of Vesta,** where old columns got a **new hat** too small for them.

[P 9.] Originally **J. C. Woodhull residence,** 1440 Albemarle Rd., SW cor. Marlborough Rd. 1905. Robert Bryson and Carroll Pratt. ☆

Another **Queen Anne/Colonial Revival** hybrid, sullied by the inappropriate asphalt shingles that replaced its original painted clapboarding.

[P 10.] Originally **Francis M. Crafts residence,** 1423 Albemarle Rd., NW cor. Marlborough Rd. 1899. John J. Petit. ☆

A veritable **Queen Anne** gem: shingled, gabled, with a bump here and a shimmy there. It reeks of romance.

[P 11.] Originally **John S. Eakins residence,** 1306 Albemarle Rd., bet. Argyle and Rugby Rds. S side. 1905. John J. Petit. ☆

Colonial Revival is expressed here in the **Tuscan**-colonnaded porch rather than in its exotic profile of multifaceted roofs. The house has been reclad with aluminum siding, a ghastly mistake.

[P 12.] Originally **G. Gale residence,** 1305 Albemarle Road, NE cor. Argyle Rd. 1905. H. B. Moore. ☆

A well-preserved **Classical Revival** house, with eccentric second-story balconies behind the main colonnade . . . similar in a way to **Harry Truman's** efforts at that **other** White House.

[P 12.] The 1305 Albemarle Road res.   **[D. 11]** The George W. Van Ness res.

[P 13.] Originally **Herman Goetze residence,** 156 Stratford Rd., bet. Hinckley and Turner Places. 1905. George Hitchings. ☆

Four-columned **Roman** temple with a **Palladian-windowed** bedroom in the pediment. There are elegant **Corinthian** columns and pilasters, narrow clapboard, and stone quoins simulated in wood.

DITMAS PARK

[D 1.] **Ditmas Park Historic District,** generally surrounded by Ocean, Dorchester, and Newkirk Aves., and the Brighton Line Subway cut. ★

Another significant turn-of-the-century development in the spirit of **Prospect Park South** but at a more modest level. Builder **Lewis Pounds** and architect **Arlington Isham,** in particular, created a district of Bungalow Style, Colonial Revival, and neo-Tudor houses.

[D 2.] **East 16th Street,** Newkirk to Ditmas Aves., and a stretch N of Ditmas Ave. Nos. 511, 515, 519, 523, 549, E side., and Nos. 490, 494, 500, 510, 514, 518, 522, 550, W side. 1908–1909. Arlington Isham. ☆

Bungalows, in the **Shingle Style,** with steeply pitched roofs over front porches supported by columns frequently fat, sometimes polygonal, occasionally round. These are the brethren of myriad **bungalows** born in California and dotting the Midwest, which supposedly are in the **Bengal** style: sun-shielded and deeply sheltered from the heat. Here they are a pleasant mannerism rather than a necessity.

[D 3.] Originally **Harry Grattan residence,** 543 E. 17th St., bet. Ditmas and Newkirk Aves. E side. 1906. Arlington D. Isham. ☆

A special example of the **Queen Anne/Colonial Revival** houses in Ditmas Park.

[D 4.] Originally **Thomas A. Radcliffe residence,** 484 E. 17th St., bet. Dorchester Rd. and Ditmas Ave. W side. 1902. Arlington Isham. ☆

A polygonal corner tower bears a finialed **hat;** and then there are multiple gables with picturesque profiles against the sky.

[D 5.] Originally **Paul Ames residence,** 456 E. 19th St., bet. Dorchester Rd. and Ditmas Ave. W side. 1910. Arne Delhi. ☆

A **Spanish Mission** style structure with a bracketed tile roof, intersected by a third-story pediment. An exotic composition in the **exotic** and **eclectic** spirit of a Norwegian architect practicing in Brooklyn.

[D 6.] Originally **Arthur Ebinger residence,** 445 E. 19th St., bet. Dorchester Rd. and Ditmas Ave. E side. 1931. Foster & Gallimore. ☆

Slate-roofed, tapestry-brick cottage, with a multifaceted chimney at the street—the fantasy of **England** brought to Brooklyn suburbia. **Ebinger** and his brothers still provide, in name, baked goods purchased daily in our local supermarkets.

[D 7.] Originally **George U. Tompers residence,** 1890 Ditmas Ave., SW cor. E. 19th St. 1904. Arlington Isham. ☆

A sprawling, stately **Shingle Style/Colonial Revival** mansion with steeply shingled roofs and a corner tower. The vast porch has an Italianate cornice with **Tuscan** columns. Seven years later **Tompers** purchased the **Roman** temple at 125 Buckingham Road [see P 4.].

[D 8.] **242 Rugby Road (residence),** bet. Beverly and Cortelyou Rds. W side. ca. 1890. ☆

An exceptional **Shingle Style** house with a polygonal onion-domed tower. The porch is incised into the building's volume. Most neighbors present a typical columned projecting **Colonial Revival** porch in these precincts.

[D 9.] Flatbush-Tompkins (originally **Flatbush) Congregational Church Parish House,** 451 E. 18th St., SE cor. Dorchester Rd. 1899. Whitfield & King.

A bold polygonal dark Shingle Style parish house that, if it were a complete form, would have **16** sides.

[D 10.] Originally **George Ramsey residence,** 900 Ocean Ave., bet. Dorchester and Ditmas Aves. W side. 1910. Charles G. Ramsey.

A classy **Queen Anne/Colonial Revival** house complete with **Ionic-**columned porte cochere.

[D 11.] Originally **George Van Ness residence,** 1000 Ocean Ave., bet. Ditmas and Newkirk Aves. W side. 1899. George Palliser.

The **Corinthian** columns that graced this great pediment have vanished, and square columns now replace them. Look at **No. 1010** next door to see what history has lost.

[D 12.] Originally **Thomas H. Brush residence/**now **Community Temple Beth Ohr,** 1010 Ocean Ave., NW cor. Newkirk Ave. 1899. George Palliser.

A grand **Georgian** mansion in red brick and white limestone, presenting **Composite Ionic** columns and pilasters to the street. The **Palladian** window in the pediment is another bedroom, a trick that the **Parthenon** missed.

[D 13.] **2693 Bedford Avenue (residence),** bet. Foster Ave. and Farragut Rd. E side. ca. 1892.

The juxtaposition of deeply shadowed circular recesses and rectangular windows in this **Shingle Style** house produces a feeling of a powerful volumetric interplay.

EAST FLATBUSH/RUGBY

[E 1.] **SUNY Downstate Medical Center.**

This complex occupies an area roughly bounded by Clarkson, New York and Albany Aves., and Winthrop St., stepping down to Lenox Rd., bet. New York and Brooklyn Aves.

The various buildings listed next are within the rubric of this **Center.**

[E 2.] Hospital and Intensive Care Unit, 445 Lenox Rd. N side. 1966. Max O. Urbahn.

Concrete graph paper from a time when that meant Style. Certainly, the rigid progeny of **Mies van der Rohe** were honored in their austere discipline. We now seem to honor the reverse: **license** in architecture is bringing willful chaos, and this now inspires only **boredom** and **yawns.**

[D 13.] The 2693 Bedford Avenue res.   [E 2.] Hospital and Intensive Care Unit

[E 3.] Dormitories, New York Ave. bet. Lenox Rd. and Linden Blvd. E side. 1966. Max O. Urbahn.

Nurses' and interns' dwellings with **Miami Beach** styling, behind what appear to be **stacked picture frames.** All this seems to be part of an alien colony in these East Flatbush blocks.

[E 4.] Kings County Hospital, Clarkson Ave. bet. Brooklyn and Albany Aves. N side. 1931. Leroy P. Ward, architect. S. S. Goldwater, M.D., consultant.

The **Bellevue** of Brooklyn. A high rise with bay windows, a brick body, and Spanish tile roofs, all crowned with marvelous towers and finials. This is rich architecture, reminding us that hospitals don't have to **look** like machines.

[E 5.] Student Center, 394 Lenox Rd., bet. New York Ave. and E. 34th St. 1969. Victor Christ-Janer & Assocs.

A **virtuoso** statement that is simultaneously out of context and of superb quality, the result of a common disease caught by talented architects. Perhaps such bravura should be the **norm,** with the surroundings subordinate to **it.** The pleasant garden courtyard is shared with the dormitories above.

WINDSOR TERRACE

[W 1.] Engine Company 240, N.Y.C. Fire Department, 1309 Prospect Ave., bet. Greenwood Ave. and Ocean Pkwy. E side. 1896.

Brick, rock-face limestone, and slate: castellated **Romanesque Revival** with a corner oriel (its hat has gone) and an arched corbel table. **Louis Sullivan** could have been here.

PARKVILLE

[K 1.] Ocean Parkway, designated a scenic landmark from Church to Seabreeze Aves. 1874–1876. From an idea by Olmsted & Vaux. ★

Six miles of tree-planted malls linking Prospect Park to Coney Island. An addition to the system of parkways proposed by Olmsted & Vaux when planning Eastern Parkway [see WC Brooklyn I 9a.].

[K 1a.] Parkville Congregational Church, 18th Ave. NW cor. E. 5th St. 1895.

The stepped and shingled brackets of the gable, with its hipped roofed belfry, bring exotic detail to this lovely remnant. Note the Victorian milk glass.

[K 2.] Philip Hirth Academy, Beth Jacob School, 4419 18th Ave., bet. McDonald Ave. and Dahill Rd. S side. 1971. William N. Breger Assocs.

Stylish and smartly scaled red-brick cubism.

SOUTHWESTERN BROOKLYN

BAY RIDGE/FORT HAMILTON/DYKER HEIGHTS • BOROUGH PARK
BENSONHURST/BATH BEACH

Town of New Utrecht/Nieuw Utrecht

Established as a town in 1662; annexed to the City of Brooklyn in 1894.

The old **Town of New Utrecht** includes the present-day communities of **Bay Ridge, Fort Hamilton, Dyker Heights, Borough Park, Bath Beach,** and much of **Bensonhurst.** At various times in its past, other, barely remembered communities were identified within its boundaries—**Blythebourne, Mapleton, Lefferts Park,** and **Van Pelt Manor**—and the area was largely rural until the beginning of the 20th century.

BAY RIDGE/FORT HAMILTON/DYKER HEIGHTS

Some of Brooklyn's most desirable residential sites lay along the high ground overlooking the **Narrows** and **Gravesend Bay.** Inevitably this best of topography became the site of magnificent mansions along **Shore Road** and the sometimes higher ground behind and along **Eleventh Avenue** in **Dyker Heights.** The ornate villa of **E. W. Bliss,** of **Greenpoint** fame; **Neils Poulson's** cast-iron fantasy, by the founder of Williamsburg's **Hecla Iron Works; Fontbonne Hall,** the home of **Tom L. Johnson,** the "three-cent mayor of Cleveland"; and many others lined the bluff overlooking the harbor. In the **Chandler White** residence the group headed by **Cyrus Field** and **Peter Cooper** first gathered to discuss the laying of the **Atlantic cable.** The **Bliss** mansion was once the home of **Henry Cruse Murphy,** who, in 1865, met there with **William C. Kingsley** and **Alexander McCue** to formulate the original agreement for the construction of the **Brooklyn Bridge.** Except for **Fontbonne Hall,** now a private school, all the mansions have been supplanted by endless ranks of elevator apartment buildings, forming a palisade of red brick along the edge of **Shore Road.**

[B 1.] Bay Ridge Masonic Temple/ originally **New Utrecht N. Y. Exempt Firemen's Association,** 257-259 Bay Ridge Ave., bet. Ridge Blvd. and 3rd Aves. N side. ca. 1890. Addition to west and conversion to Masonic Temple later.

A *fine exercise* in above-ground archaeology. Look carefully at the entrance cornice and the keystones over the windows. They bear the old volunteer fire company's seals and names (including the now disappeared community of **Blythebourne**) on the east portion of the building, and the **Masonic** symbols (in the stained glass, too) only in the west. The structure was once symmetrical around its ornate entrance. Subtle changes in the brick coloring reveal the line of the addition.

The Pier at the foot of Bay Ridge Avenue gives a promontory for viewers of the whole bay: tankers tug at anchors surrounding, and the distant views of the **Verrazano Bridge, Staten Island,** and the **lower Manhattan skyline,** make this a Brooklyn version of Battery Park.

[B 1a.] 146 67th Street (residence), bet. Sedgwick Place and Ridge Blvd. S side. ca. 1885.

A neo-Gothic Shingle Style villa, towered and with ogee arches—here sullied by asbestos shingles . . . but it is a tree-hooded extravaganza, a loner among the philistines.

[B 1b.] Madeline Court, 68th St. bet. Ridge Blvd. and Third Ave. ca. 1940s.

An urban space in this **in-town suburbia,** brick and slate-roofed, where the **whole** is again serving as master of its parts.

[B 1c.] Salem Evangelical Lutheran Church, 355 Ovington St., bet. Third and Fourth Aves. N side. ca. 1940.

Stepped gables on a north German-Swedish-Dutch vernacular make handsome profiles against the sky.

[B 1d.] Bay Ridge United Methodist Church, 7002 Fourth Ave., SW cor. Ovingston St. ca. 1895.

A green ashlar body with **brown**stone trim makes this a lovely cared-for local confection, with its chocolate joints **oozing.**

[K 1a.] Parkville Congregational Ch.   **[B 2.]** Flagg Court apartments in 1967

[B 2.] Flagg Court (apartments), 7200 Ridge Blvd., bet. 72nd and 73rd Sts. W side. 1933–1936. Ernest Flagg.

Flagg Court, named for its renowned architect (Singer Buildings, Scribner Building), is a 422-unit housing development contained in 6 contiguous buildings. Among the project's avant-garde features were reversible fans below the windows (long since gone), window shades on the outside of windows (the intelligent heat shield, also gone), concrete slabs serving as finished ceilings (commonplace in current architecture), and an auditorium of vaulted concrete. Note the pendant **Carpenter Gothic** cornice on the 8th floor.

[B 3.] Nightfalls Restaurant, 7612 Third Ave., bet. 76th and 77th Sts. W side. 1983. Voorsanger & Mills.

This insertion into a typical Bay Ridge blockfront fills its interior with an **Art Deco** revival. Outside, things are placid, except for the fixed glass panes that infill the former window spaces, giving a commercial crassness to the streetscape.

[B 4.] 112 Bay Ridge Parkway (residence), bet. Ridge Blvd. and Colonial Rd. S side. ca. 1900.

A formal stucco near-mansion with a handsome **Palladian** window and a cleverly suppressed garage.

[B 5a.] 131 76th Street (residence), bet. Ridge Blvd. and Colonial Rd. N side. 1865.

A gray neo-Georgian stuccoed mansion, with a white composite-columned porch.

[B 5b.] 122 76th Street (residence), bet. Ridge Blvd. and Colonial Rd. S side. ca. 1900.

A Gothic Revival mansion perched (with **No. 131** above) on a bluff rising **61** steps from **Colonial Road;** pedestrians—for once—are king here. A hexagonal tower overlooks the Upper Bay. Dr. Elliot, founder of the **Blue Cross,** and his family, dwelled here.

[B 6.] 8220 Narrows Avenue (residence), NW cor. 83rd St. 1916. J. Sarsfield Kennedy.

A mansion disguised as a witch's hideaway. **Black Forest Art Nouveau.** Bumpety stone and **pseudothatchery** make this **Arts and Crafts** revival one of Brooklyn's greatest **private fantasies.**

[B 5b.] Residence at 122 76th Street   **[B 6.]** Black Forest pseudothatch

[B 7.] 175 81st Street (residence), bet. Ridge Blvd. and Colonial Road. N side. ca. 1880.

Shingle Style, conical capped, stepped gables. Note the round-cut shingles on the brick body.

[B 7a.] Shore Court, bet. Colonial Rd. and Narrows Ave. S side. 1930s.

Mock Tudor paired houses embracing a cul-de-sac paved in Belgian block. Wonderful conifers line this urban space.

[B 8.] Shore Hill Apartments (senior citizens' residence), 9000 Shore Rd., bet. 90th and 91st Sts. E side. 1976. Gruzen & Partners.

A **looming** presence in this low-scaled neighborhood. Its tan brick, anodized-windowed facade might better befit a Middle American motel.

[B 9.] Visitation Academy, Visitation Nuns (Roman Catholic), 91st to 93rd Sts., Colonial Rd. to Ridge Blvd. **Convent** and **Chapel,** 1913.

A fortification for **virgins,** with a 20-foot stone and concrete wall to protect first- through eighth-graders from sight. The attached chapel is brick **Italian neo-Renaissance.** Unwalled, it serves as the religious doorkeeper to the Academy.

[B 10.] Originally **James F. Farrell residence,** 119 95th St., bet. Marine Ave. and Shore Rd. N side. ca. 1849.

A splendid **Greek Revival** wood house inundated but not drowned in an adjacent sea of red brick apartment blocks. Painted cream and white, with a Tuscan-columned porch and green shutters (they work!), it is a distinguished architectural remnant **miraculously** preserved among bland multiple dwellings.

[B 11.] St. John's Episcopal Church, 9818 Fort Hamilton Pkwy., NW cor. 99th St. 1890. **Rectory,** 1910.

A **homely** cottage-scaled country church in the looming shadow of the Verrazano Bridge and its ramps. Stone and shingles clad a timbered body enriched with red, white, and gold polychromy. Called the **Church of the Generals,** it attracted numerous military leaders from adjacent Fort Hamilton.

[B 12a.] Fort Hamilton Veterans' Hospital, 800 Poly Place, bet. Seventh and Fourteenth Aves. S side. 1950. Skidmore, Owings & Merrill.

A **sleek** slab with soothing views for veterans.

[B 12b.] Fort Hamilton Officers' Club/originally **casemate fort,** in Fort Hamilton Reservation, Shore Pkwy. E of Verrazano Bridge approaches. 1825–1831. ★ Altered. **Not open to the public.**

A granite military fort now used as an officers' club.

[B 12c.] Harbor Defense Museum, in Fort Hamilton Reservation, 101st St. and Fort Hamilton Pkwy. **Open to the public.**

A small but fascinating military museum charting the defenses of New York Harbor and housed in part of the original fort.

 [B 13.] Poly Prep Country Day School/originally **Brooklyn Polytechnic Preparatory School,** 92nd Street bet. 7th and Dahlgreen Aves. 1924.

A **neo-Georgian** boys' school with spreading athletic fields on what is, for the city, a vast campus. It is now **coeducational.**

[B 10.] James F. Farrell residence, an extraordinary Greek Revival remnant

[B 14a.] 8302 Eleventh Avenue (residence), SW cor. 83rd St. **[B 14b.] 8310 Eleventh Avenue (residence),** bet. 83rd and 84th Sts. W side. **[B 14c.] 1101 84th Street (residence),** NE cor. 11th Ave. All in Dyker Heights.

The **mad dwarfs** who built the **manse** at 8220 Narrows Avenue [see B 6.] moved a mile to build these country cousins. Note, particularly, the **amber** conservatory.

[B 15.] 1265 86th Street (residence), bet. 12th and 13th Aves. N side. ca. 1885.

A handsome **Shingle Style** house, facing Dyker Beach golf course.

 [B 16.] National Shrine of St. Bernadette (Roman Catholic), 8201 13th Ave., bet. 82nd and 83rd Sts. E side. 1937. Henry V. Murphy.

A polygonal exterior, with a verdigris copper roof, houses parabolic concrete arches within. The nave is awash with colored light and features a **kitsch** rock-piled shrine to St. Bernadette at its east end.

BOROUGH PARK

Largely built up during the **1920s** with numerous one- and two-family houses as well as apartment buildings, this section had still been rural, apart from scattered villages, at the turn of the century. Perhaps the most interesting settlement was **Blythebourne,** which lay southwest of the intersection of **New Utrecht Avenue** and **55th Street** along the old **Brooklyn, Bath Beach & West End Railroad,** today's West End subway line. It was founded in the late **1880s** by **Electus B. Litchfield,** the son of **Edwin C. Litchfield** of **Prospect Park** fame. A number of houses were quickly built, as well as a series of **Queen Anne** cottages and two churches. But before the community could take hold, a politician purchased the area north of **Blythebourne** and east of **New Utrecht Avenue** and named it **Borough Park.** A real estate agent at the time warned the **Litchfield** family to sell its holdings, explaining that the pogroms of **Eastern Europe** would soon cause a mass migration to the outskirts of **Brooklyn,** forcing land values down. **Mrs. William B. Litchfield,** who controlled the property at the time, decided not to sell. The prediction was partially fulfilled: the **Borough Park** section did become a heavily **Jewish** community, but the land values, instead of falling, rose tremendously. As a result, **Blythebourne** was swallowed by **Borough Park** and is remembered today only in the name of the local post office, **Blythebourne Station.** The area also embraces a second-generation **Hasidic** community, transposed from **Williamsburg.**

[B 17.] Franklin Delano Roosevelt High School, 5801 19th Ave., bet. 55th and 59th Sts. E side. 1965. Raymond & Rado.

A **graph-paper** facade in concrete brings a note of modernity to this bland and monotonous area.

BENSONHURST/BATH BEACH

This lower-middle-class residential area preserves the family name of **Charles Benson,** whose farm was subdivided into the gridiron we see today. At **New Utrecht** and **18th Avenues** the original village of **New Utrecht** was settled in **1661,** on a site now marked by the **New Utrecht Reformed Church.**

[B 16.] Nat. Shrine, St. Bernadette   [B 18a.] New Utrecht Reformed Ch.

[B 18a.] New Utrecht Reformed Church, 18th Ave. bet. 83rd and 84th Sts. E side. 1828. ★

A **Georgian Gothic** granite ashlar church, its brick-framed Gothic windows filled with **Tiffany**-like **Victorian** milk glass. An eneagled (gilt) liberty pole stands in front of the church; its predecessors date back to **1783** and have been replaced 6 times since.

Liberty Poles: To harass **British** garrisons, or to signify their defeat, Revolutionary patriots erected flagpoles, called **liberty poles,** on which to raise the flag of independence. Lightning and dry rot have taken their toll of the originals, but in some communities a tradition has developed to replace them.

[B 18b.] New Utrecht Reformed Church Parsonage, 83rd St. bet. 18th and 19th Aves. S side. ca. 1885.

A **Shingle Style** home for the pastor, with a generous **Tuscan**-columned porch.

[B 18c.] New Utrecht Reformed Church Parish House, 1827 84th St., bet. 18th and 19th Aves. N side. 1892.

Robust **Romanesque Revival** in a class with **Frank Freeman's** Jay Street Fire House.

SOUTHERN BROOKLYN

GRAVESEND • SHEEPSHEAD BAY
MANHATTAN AND BRIGHTON BEACHES • CONEY ISLAND

Town of Gravesend/'s-Gravesande
Established as a town in **1645**; annexed to the **City** of Brooklyn in **1894**.

Of the six original towns that now constitute Brooklyn, **Gravesend** is unique in a number of ways. **First** of all, it was settled by **English** rather than **Dutch** colonists. **Second,** its list of patentees was headed by a **woman,** a precocious admission of the equality of the sexes. **Third,** Gravesend Village was organized using a set of sophisticated town-planning principles more recognized at **New Haven, Philadelphia,** and **Savannah.** Remnants of the plan survive in the neighborhood street layout, a tiny parallel to the Dutch plan of New Amsterdam extant as the armature of lower Manhattan.

In **1643** Lady Deborah Moody and her Anabaptist flock founded **Gravesend** after a bitter sojourn in **New England,** where they had encountered the same religious intolerance from which they had fled in **"old"** England. The free enjoyment of most religious beliefs, which characterized the **New Netherlands** colony, made **Gravesend** an obvious haven for them, an English social island in this Dutch-named place.

GRAVESEND

In the **19th** century the territory of **Gravesend** became a great resort. No less than three racetracks were built within its bounds at various times, one northeast of **Ocean** and **Jerome** Avenues in **Sheepshead Bay,** another southeast of **Ocean Parkway** and **Kings Highway,** just north of the original village square. Before the development of **Coney Island** as a public beach and amusement area, Gravesend had fashionable hotels and piers, immense pinnacled wooden structures benefiting from the imagination and wit of **Victorian** elaboration. Regrettably, there is almost nothing left of its raucous spirit and lively architecture. **Coney** was revived after World War I following the completion of subway connections to **Manhattan** and the **Bronx;** but it has lost its popularity as a recreation area, surpassed by more attractive suburban resorts accessible by automobile on **Robert Moses**-built highways. The streets, the beach, and the sea remain, but there is little of the physical and social vitality that once made this the **Biarritz** of the middle class. Travel in pairs and only in daylight; watch your wallet.

[G 1.] The Old Village of Gravesend, Village Rd. N. to Village Rd. S., Van Siclen St. to Village Rd. E., centered on the intersection of Gravesend Neck Rd. and McDonald (formerly Gravesend) Ave.

The bounds of **Lady Moody's** town plan, now remembered only in its streets and the **turf** on the cemetery.

 [G 2.] Hicks-Platt residence/a.k.a. **Lady Moody House,** 17 Gravesend Neck Rd., bet. McDonald Ave. and Van Siclen St. N side. 17th cent.

In the **1890s, William E. Platt,** a real estate developer, publicized this as **Lady Moody's** own home, thereby becoming one of the earliest American hucksters of history. The fake stone veneer is **ludicrous;** *bring back the clapboard!* The fluted white **Tuscan** columns provide a visual strength that even **Perma Stone** can't kill!

[G 3.] Ryder-Van Cleef residence, 38 Village Rd. N., bet. McDonald Ave. and Van Siclen St., S side. ca. 1750.

The partial remnant of a narrow **Dutch** gambrel-roofed house, with later additions.

[G 4.] Originally **Elias Hubbard Ryder residence,** 2138 McDonald Ave., bet. Ave S. S and T. W side. ca. 1750.

Located in a **vegetable jungle** next to the McDonald Avenue **el.** This is scraping the barrel for vestigial architecture. The 2-story wing was a **1925** addition.

[G 5.] Trinity Tabernacle of Gravesend/formerly **Gravesend Reform Church,** 145 Gravesend Neck Rd., NW cor. E. 1st St. 1894. J. G. Glover.

This **neo-Gothic** place, built for the Reform church, replaced their original building **(1655)** at **Neck Road** and **McDonald Ave.** The architecture deviated considerably from the plain white wooden churches of **Dutch Reform congregations.**

[G 5.] Trinity Tabernacle of Gravesend   **[S 1.]** The 1766 Wyckoff-Bennett res.

[G 6.] Old Gravesend Cemetery, Gravesend Neck Rd. bet. McDonald Ave. and Van Siclen St. S side. 1643. ★

This shares history with the **First Shearith Israel Graveyard** as burial grounds for early religious exceptions to the mainstream Dutch Reform church. Protestant **Anabaptists** were interred here; whereas Sephardic Jews immigrating from Brazil were buried at **Shearith Israel,** starting in **1683. Lady Moody's** own grave is somewhere within, but its location is lost, although many old stone markers remain. The cemetery is open **4 days a year.**

[G 7.] Brooklyn School for Special Children, 376 Bay 44th St., SW cor. Shore Pkwy. service road. 1975. Edgar Tafel & Assocs.

A low institutional structure in this **wasteland** outside the Parkway, seemingly at the edge of the world. Articulated brickwork in 3 colors and sizes surrounded by an elegant metal fence with **red-squared** finials.

America's only Social Security office that doesn't bear the name of the neighborhood in which it's located is that on Avenue X: if traditions had been followed, it would be the **Gravesend** office.

SHEEPSHEAD BAY

[S 1.] Wyckoff-Bennett residence, 1669 E. 22nd St., SE cor. Kings Highway. 1766. ★

A **rural idyll:** the **most impressive** of all the early Brooklyn houses in the **Dutch style,** and still in private ownership. This one is dated by a number cut into one of the wooden beams. Used as quarters by **Hessian** troops during the Revolutionary War, it contains this inscription scratched into a **4- by 7-**inch pane:

TOEPFER CAPT OF REGT DE DITFURTH
MBACH LIEUTENANT V HESSEN HANAU ARTILERIE

Savor the 6-columned porch, picket fence, ample grounds, and towering trees. This is a bit of Brooklyn from the time before **suburbia** was invented.

[S 1a.] 1996 East 5th Street (residence), bet. Aves. S and T. W side. 1986. Robert A. M. Stern.

An exquisitely detailed Post-Modern detached house in a small enclave of others that date from the 1920s. A real surprise.

[S 2.] Elias Hubbard Ryder residence, 1926 E. 28th St., bet. Aves. S and T. W side. ca. 1834. Altered, 1929. ★

Here is a **squeezed form** between two sets of row house neighbors—**Dutch Colonialism** usurped by neighboring middle-class funk. The **funkiness** is compounded by the **specious** shutters and use of outdoor **gaslight** standards that reek of Brooklyn Union Gas Company's "ye olde" publicity.

Gerritsen: A community of approximately **1,600** lilliputian bungalows on **lilliputian** plots, with narrow streets barely wide enough for cars to pass. It has a volunteer fire company and **lots** of community spirit. Centered on **Gerritsen Avenue** adjacent to developing **Marine Park.**

[S 3.] Good Shepherd Roman Catholic Church, Rectory, Convent, and **School,** Ave. S bet. Brown and Batchelder Sts. S side. **School,** 1932, McGill & Hamlin. **Church,** 1940. **Rectory,** 1950. Both by Henry J. McGill. **Convent,** 1956, John B. O'Malley.

McGill brought a modified **Mission Style** church complex to this Marine Park section of Sheepshead Bay.

 [S 4.] Junior High School 43, Brooklyn/The James J. Reynolds School, 1401 Emmons Ave., bet. E. 14th and E. 15th Sts. N side. 1965. Pedersen & Tilney.

The long, low facades along the side streets, often the weakness in recent public school design, are the most successful aspects of this serious modern building. The cast-in-place concrete has weathered remarkably well.

[S 4.] A modern outpost: Junior High School 43, The James J. Reynolds School

---

Fishing and fish: A flotilla of fishing boats moored along Emmons Avenue from Ocean Avenue east to East 27th Street offers you the chance to catch **blues, stripers,** and **miscellany**—but you will have to rise **early** or go to bed **late.** Generations of compleat anglers have returned bearing far more fish than their extended families could eat. And at Ocean Avenue for several generations stood a restaurant where the vast fruit of the sea was consumed: **Lundy's,** a big, brash, noisy place in a strangely appropriate **Spanish Mission** style building that once served as many as **5,000** meals a day. It is now only a shell. May it have an **early reincarnation.**

MANHATTAN AND BRIGHTON BEACHES

The eastern peninsula of what once was Coney **Island** is isolated, affluent, sometimes green, often dull. Its middle reaches harbor vast hordes of Russian Jewish immigrants; its tip houses the old **World War II**

Naval Training Station, now infilled with the campus of **Kingsborough Community College.** Along the ocean sits the **Brighton Beach Bath and Racquet Club,** a privately owned enclave of summer fun in stylish contrast to the public sands of Coney Island proper to the west. Here developers propose six colossal towers that would complete the Brobdingnagian landscape of this onetime resort and entertainment island.

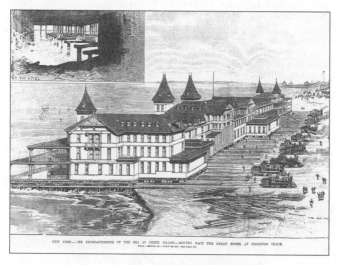

NEW YORK.—THE ENCROACHMENTS OF THE SEA AT CONEY ISLAND—MOVING BACK THE GREAT HOTEL AT BRIGHTON BEACH.

[M 1.] Kingsborough Community College, CUNY, main gate at the end of Oriental Blvd. bet. Sheepshead Bay and the Atlantic Ocean. Master Plan, 1968. Katz, Waisman, Weber, Strauss. Various buildings by KWWS, James Stewart Polshek & Assocs., Lundquist & Stonehill; Warner, Burns, Toan & Lunde; Gruzen Samton Steinglass.

A sprawling **complex** complex, with some stylish modern forms, particularly in profile when seen from the Belt Parkway.

CONEY ISLAND

[C 1.] Coney Island Hospital, 2601 Ocean Pkwy., NE cor. Shore Pkwy. 1957. Katz, Waisman, Blumenkranz, Stein & Weber.

A **land**mark to motorists arriving at the Ocean Avenue gateway to **Coney Island,** even though it's on the other side of the road. Now a period piece of modern architecture, it displays the articulation of its functional parts, with sunshades the major decoration permitted. It grew in the period when **elimination of ornamentation** was an almost holy mission, here well done by fervent acolytes of Walter Gropius.

[C 2.] William E. Grady Vocational High School, 25 Brighton 4th Rd., bet. Brighton 4th and Brighton 6th Sts. N side. 1956. Katz, Waisman, Blumenkranz, Stein & Weber.

Concrete is honored in the parasol vaults over the gymnasium and auditorium, but the effort is dated by its fervent **modernism.** Like its neighbor (by the same architects) across the parkway, it tells of that brief moment in the 1950s and 1960s that still rejected any **token** of architectural historicism.

[C 3.] New York Aquarium, The Boardwalk at NE cor. W. 8th St. **Exhibit Building,** 1955. Harrison & Abramovitz. **Osborn Laboratories of Marine Sciences,** 1965. Goldstone & Dearborn.

To be visited for the contents rather than the envelope, although both are the pressured product of the conflicting needs of **museum** and **amusement** park. The substantial things to see are the **whales, penguins, octopi,** and **electric eels,** but there are other natural and unconscious entertainments. Children, **please touch**—the horseshoe crabs can be **fondled.**

[C 4.] Coney Island Amusement Area, bet. W. 8th St. and W. 16th St., Surf Ave. and The Boardwalk.

Most rides are becoming vacant land, fodder for new housing. The immense **spider web** of the Wonder Wheel, at West 12th Street and the Boardwalk, still offers wondrous Eiffel-like engineering, startling views, and frightening routines to the Ferris-children it attracts; but **Luna Park** and **Steeplechase Park** are long gone. The rusting **parachute jump,** moved here from the **1939–1940 World's Fair,** is a romance for those who wishfully hope for restoration. Roller coasters, carrousels, and **Dodg'em** cars remain; the Cyclone is the most impressive remnant. The **Bowery,** a circus midway between the **Boardwalk** and **Surf Avenue,** provides some taste of the old **charm** and **vulgarity** of Coney's history. Don't overlook the great **Greek Revival** autoscooter rink between 12th and Stillwell. All this is vanishing as the middle class motors down the interstates to other pleasure grounds, bland places like "Great Adventure" and "theme parks" that invent a history that never was. **Rides** remain, as do games of **skill, corn on the cob,** slices of **watermelon,** and—thank God—**cotton candy.** The rides and buildings reveal all sorts of architectural **styles** and **fantasies,** many vernacular in origin, the work of creative local carpenters. It would be pointless to single out any special event, as "progress" is the battle cry. Look around, for there is **plenty** to see and enjoy.

[C 3.] The Osborn Laboratories of Marine Sciences at the New York Aquarium

[C 5.] Nathan's Famous (the original), Surf Ave. SW cor. Stillwell Ave.

After **Luna** and **Steeplechase** were erased, **Nathan's Famous** remains as Coney Island's most venerable institution. **Once upon a time** it cost a nickel on the subway to reach **Coney,** and a **nickel** bought a hot dog at **Nathan's (1987:** $1.45). Open all year for stand-up treats, such as delicatessen sandwiches, clams on the half shell, and **"shrimp boats"** (shrimp cocktails in miniature plastic dinghies). We hope it lasts.

[C 6.] Steeplechase Pier, The Boardwalk at W. 17th St.

A **retired** monument, it is still a **favored fishing dock.** A walk along its 1,000 feet offers cool breezes and wonderful vantage points for summer fireworks or the setting sun. Try your hand at catching **fluke, blues, flounder,** or **stripers.** The **park** that went with the pier provided fantastic competition for the younger set on wooden horses that pursued tracks around a vast block, the **steeples** of the **chase** in question. The **horses** in question were stolen.

[C 7.] Abe Stark Center, N.Y.C. Department of Parks & Recreation, W. 19th St. at The Boardwalk. 1969. Daniel Chait.

A **would-be** Nervi created these once-stylish structural forms to house a skating rink, where precocious figure-skating stars and promising hockey teams vie for space in the midnight hours. Dull architecturally.

[C 8.] Our Lady of Solace Church (Roman Catholic), 2866 W. 17th St., NW cor. Mermaid Ave. 1925. Robert J. Reiley.

A plain brick neo-**Romanesque** church with a refreshingly austere exposed brick interior: arches, limestone columns, timbered roof.

Gargiulo's Restaurant, 2911 W. 15th St., bet. Mermaid and Surf Aves. Restaurant founded 1907; here since 1928.

A **princely palace** in **plebian** surroundings—vast, **vulgar,** wonderful. Elsewhere it would be yet another unimportant restaurant; here it is an **oasis. Expensive.**

Once upon a time architects and politicians got together under the leadership of **Edward J. Logue** and the New York State Urban Development Corporation. Here power delivered to Logue by Governor Rockefeller, with the advice and consent of Mayor Lindsay, changed the rules of public housing and urban design. Coney Island was picked as one of three crucibles of experimentation (Twin Parks in the Bronx and Roosevelt Island were the others). The several projects listed below were all **risk-taking** experiments in **urban design** not attempted by the **New York City Housing Authority** since their late 1930s glories at **Williamsburg Houses** and **Harlem River Houses.**

[C 9.] Sea Rise I (apartments), Neptune and Canal Aves., bet. W. 33rd and W. 37th Sts. 1976. Hoberman & Wasserman.

The **best** of the Coney Island **UDC.** In its successful fulfillment of a **first-rate** architectural school design, it seemed too good to be true. But here is the miracle of architectural glory. Coney Island is honored by this and its **siblings.**

[C 9.] The superb Sea Rise I housing   **[C 12.]** Low-income tower & town hses.

[C 10.] 2730 West 33rd Street (apartments), bet. Bayview and Neptune Aves. 1975. Skidmore, Owings & Merrill.

Stacked **cubist** balconies on a white concrete tower: mechanical, orderly, and dull.

[C 11.] Town houses, Bayview Ave. SW cor. W. 33rd St. 1975. Davis, Brody & Assocs.

Brown brick, concrete-corniced, unassuming, understated row houses, whose broken form surrounds a garden court. **Lovely.**

[C 12.] Apartment tower and town houses, Neptune Ave. bet. W. 24th and W. 25th Sts., S side. 1975. Tower, Skidmore, Owings & Merrill. Town houses, Davis, Brody & Assocs.

A reprise of **[C 10. and C 11.]** above.

[C 13.] Housing for the Elderly, Surf Ave. bet. W. 36th and W. 37th Sts. N side. 1975. Hoberman & Wasserman.

The stepped terraces are remarkably empty; residents willfully cluster around the trafficked streets below, where the action is—not in their architect-assigned space. As **Jane Jacobs** articulated so strongly, **streets** are for people.

[C 14.] Sea Park East (apartments), bet. W. 28th and W. 29th Sts. Midblock bet. Mermaid and Surf Aves. 1975. Tower, Skidmore, Owings & Merrill. Town houses, Davis, Brody & Assocs.

Another reprise.

[C 15.] Sea Park East (apartments), Surf Ave. bet. W. 27th and W. 29th Sts. N side. 1975. Hoberman & Wasserman.

Lesser versions of **Sea Rise I** [see C 9. above].

[C 16.] Ocean Towers (apartments), Surf Ave. bet. W. 24th and W. 25th Sts. N side. 1975. Prentice & Chan, Ohlhausen.

A variety of floor plans offers the facade a **mosaic** of windows, rather than the **stacked regularity** of many apartment towers.

[C 17.] 2920 and 2940 West 21st Street (apartments), NW cor. Surf Ave. 1974. James Doman & Emil Steo.

A bland 7-story block.

[C 18.] Former **Fire Service Pumping Station City of New York,** 2301 Neptune Ave., bet. W. 23rd and W. 24th Sts. N side. 1937. Irwin S. Chanin.

This streamlined but decaying remnant recalls the **Art Moderne** stimulated by the **Paris Exposition** of **1937.** The entrance of this symmetrical modern palace was once guarded by two pairs of prancing steeds, now removed to the Brooklyn Museum sculpture garden. **Too bad.** Coney needed to keep this piece of architectural history.

[C 19.] 2837 West 37th Street, bet. Neptune and Mermaid Aves. E side. ca. 1924.

Mykonos in Brooklyn, once a siamese twin, now severed. Its textured stucco and whitewashed flanks bring Mediterranean memories to this remote spit of Brooklyn.

SOUTHEASTERN BROOKLYN

MIDWOOD • FLATLANDS • CANARSIE

Town of Flatlands/Nieuw Amersfoort

Established as a town in 1666; annexed to the City of Brooklyn in 1896.

The name **Flat**lands aptly describes this area. It is a billiard table, much of it still marshy; a considerable part bordering Jamaica Bay was recaptured as landfill, a **no-no** in present-day environmental circles. The old town included much of what is now **Midwood** to the north, but a good deal of the inland area is still termed **Flatlands,** part of which is a substantial industrial park. At its southern edges are the shorefront areas of old **Floyd Bennett Field, Bergen Beach, Mill Basin,** and **Canarsie,** tidal and aquatic edges now filled with middle-class homeowners yearning to have a powerboat at their lawn and bulkhead's edge. Boaters with sails dwell elsewhere.

MIDWOOD

[M 1.] Van Nuyse-Magaw residence, 1041 E. 22nd St., bet. Aves. I and J. E side. 1800. ★

Originally built at **East 22nd Street and Avenue M,** this farmhouse was moved here around **1916** and was turned perpendicular to the street, to fit its new and narrow lot. The distinctive **Dutch gambrel** roof is therefore the end, or street, facade. Columns at the entrance are from a **1952** "restoration"—or perhaps "improvement." They should be swept away.

[M 1a.] Congregation Kol Israel (synagogue), 3211 Bedford Ave., NE cor. Ave. K. Entrance on Ave. K. 1988. Robert A. M. Stern, architect. Dominick Salvati & Son, consulting architects.

A Post-Modern synagogue attempting to look harmonious in its semi-suburban residential setting.

[M 2.] Johannes Van Nuyse residence, sometimes called the **Coe House,** 1128 E. 34th St., bet. Flatbush Ave. and Ave. J. W side. 1744, 1793, 1806. ★

A well-dressed neighbor in a **tacky** neighborhood, like a Harris tweed jacket among polyster leisure suits. Neat and squeaky clean, it is a mecca for devotees of architectural **Williamsburg** (Virginia style, that is).

FLATLANDS

[F 1.] Originally **Pieter Claesen Wyckoff residence,** 5902 Clarendon Rd., at intersection of Ralph and Ditmas Aves. SW cor. ca. 1641. ★ Restored, 1982. Oppenheimer, Brady & Vogelstein, architects.

A lonely **ancestor** in a neat fenced park, marooned in these industrial precincts. A vast lawn and minimal trees surround this modest place, which remembers the **New Netherlands** with its handsome eaves and shingled body. It is, perhaps, more in the idiom of **Disney** recreations than a part of neighborhood history. **Open to the public.**

[F 2.] Vitagraph Company, Inc./Warner Brothers Pictures, Inc., 791 E. 43rd St., bet. Farragut and Glenwood Rds. E side. ca. 1925.

Movie film was once the most inflammable material that could be stored: here a ventilation system to reduce **built-up heat** within (long before air conditioning was available) allowed natural convection to temper the potential danger. The result is a **roofscape** of startling and dramatic forms.

[F 3.] Flatlands Dutch Reformed Ch. **[F 4.]** The Dutch Colonial Lott res.

[F 3.] Flatlands Dutch Reformed Church, 3931 Kings Highway, bet. Flatbush Ave. and E. 40th St. 1848. Henry Eldert, builder. ★

One of three Brooklyn churches established by order of Governor Peter Stuyvesant—the others are the **Flatbush Reformed Dutch** and the **First Reformed.** Handsomely sited in a tree-filled park, this simple **Georgian-Federal** building stands where two earlier churches stood. The first, built in **1663,** was octagonal in plan. Note the names in the adjacent cemetery: **Lott, Voorhees, Sprong, Kouwenhoven, Wyckoff.**

[F 4.] Hendrick I. Lott residence, 1940 E. 36th St., bet. Fillmore Ave. and Avenue S. W side. 1676. Altered, 1800.

Here some elbowroom allows this **Dutch Colonial** house to be a happy resident of its garden. Modest owners have provided care, but it needs an extra infusion. The small wing is the original structure of **1676;** the main body was built by **Lott** himself in **1800.** The projecting **Dutch** eaves, more usually cantilevered, are supported by columns square on one side and round on the other.

 [F 5.] Originally **Stoothof-Baxter-Kouwenhoven House,** 1640 E. 48th St., bet. Aves. M and N. W side. Before 1796. ★

The form of this lonely enfenced Dutch outpost remains, but its skin has been **modernized . . .** to its discredit.

[F 6.] Douwe Stoothof residence/a.k.a. **John Williamson residence,** 1587 E. 53rd St., bet. Aves. M and N. E side.

Another poorly altered **Dutch Colonial,** veneered with asphalt-impressed false brick. Nevertheless the **shape** is there under that dowdy fabric.

[F 7.] The serene Mill Basin Branch of the Brooklyn Public Library (1974)

 [F 7.] Mill Basin Branch, Brooklyn Public Library, 2385 Ralph Ave., NE cor. Ave. N. 1974. Arthur A. Unger & Assocs.

A serene outpost of graceful modernism in brick that is carved and curved without overkill—in contrast to the **Jamaica Bay Branch** below.

CANARSIE

[C 1.] Bay View Houses, N.Y.C. Housing Authority (apartments), Shore Parkway, NE cor. Rockaway Parkway, 1955. Katz, Waisman, Blumenkranz, Stein & Weber.

A superior example of the Authority's work in those years from **1936** to **1966** when bland brick towers sprouted in enclaves all around town. Here the **mere 8** stories are a blessing, and careful detailing raises the product to a level above the ordinary.

[C 2.] Jamaica Bay Branch, Brooklyn Public Library, 9727 Seaview Ave., NW cor. E. 98th St. 1972. Leibowitz, Bodouva & Assocs.

A **histrionic** little building for such a simple purpose. Ribbed concrete block, slots, notches, cantilevers, and splayed sills created a plasticity now made **ironic** by the blacking out of the windows that all this fuss created.

 [C 3.] Seaview Jewish Center (synagogue), 1440 E. 99th St., bet. Seaview Ave. and Ave. N. W side. 1972. William N. Breger Assocs.

Carved stucco **vanilla ice cream.** Stylish and a world apart from the surrounding **banality.** Make certain to see it from the south.

[C 4.] Waxman Building, Hebrew Educational Society of Brooklyn,
9502 Seaview Ave., SE cor. E. 95th St. 1968. Horace Ginsbern &
Assocs.

A modest building housing a society that moved, along with its
community, from **Brownsville** to **Canarsie.**

[C 5.] Canarsie Pier, Gateway National Recreation Area, S of Shore
Pkwy. at the foot of Rockaway Pkwy.

Jutting into Jamaica Bay, this is a place to fish, rent boats, or just
bask. One day, let's hope, pollution control will make it possible to
gather clams and oysters once again. A restaurant, **On The Pier,** offers
sustenance.

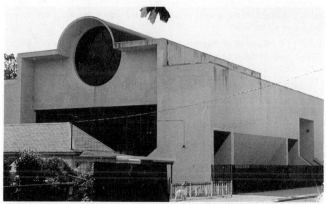

[C 3.] Seaview Jewish Center, stylish in white stucco, like carved ice cream

[C 6.] Bankers Federal Savings, Canarsie Branch, 1764 Rockaway
Pkwy., SW cor. Ave. L. 1961. LaPierre, Litchfield & Partners.

A classic example of self-destruction by the owners of a once
sophisticated modern building. The brutal air-conditioning penthouse
was added without thought, and the ensemble painted in tan enamel
that demeans the product.

[C 7.] Playground, Public School 114, Brooklyn, Remsen Ave. NE cor.
Glenwood Rd. 1972. Norman Jaffe, architect. Robert Malkin, landscape
architect.

One of the experimental playgrounds jointly operated by the Department of Parks and the Board of Education. Here a **brutal concrete
bunker** dominates this austere place: **hard as nails.**

EASTERN BROOKLYN

HIGHLAND PARK • CYPRESS HILLS • BROWNSVILLE
EAST NEW YORK

Town of New Lots

Separated from the Town of Flatbush in 1852; annexed to the City of
Brooklyn in 1886.

Three major neighborhoods exist within this sector. **Highland
Park,** also known as **Cypress Hills,** lies north of Atlantic Avenue.

Brownsville occupies the roughly triangular area between **Remsen Avenue, East New York Avenue,** and the tracks of the **Long Island Railroad. East New York** is the remainder south to **Jamaica Bay** and east to the **Queens** boundary, or **city line,** as its residents often call it—a relic of the days when **Brooklyn** was a separate city.

HIGHLAND PARK/CYPRESS HILLS

[H 1.] 279 and **361 Highland Boulevard (residences),** bet. Miller Ave. and Barbey St. N side. ca. 1900.

Two gracious mansions surviving from a precinct that originally had a myriad; many were displaced by apartment houses seeking these **spectacular views. No. 279,** in gray Roman brick and white limestone, presents a great composite **Ionic**-columned porte cochere. **No. 361** is now a Lithuanian cultural center, with a **banal** modern auditorium attached to its side.

[H 2.] 101 Sunnyside Avenue (apartment house), bet. Hendrix St. and Miller Ave. N side. ca. 1930.

Nestled into the sharp precipice between **Highland** and **Sunnyside Avenues,** this presents a **Classical Renaissance** plan to the Sunnyside Avenue approach: a formal, symmetrical subplaza from which to **rise** to the view.

A row of town houses, on **Sunnyside Avenue,** between **Barbey** and **Miller** Streets, presents a series of porches with paired Tuscan columns and supporting bracketed shedding roofs. The group is a **powerful** statement of this modest area.

[H 3.] 130 Arlington Avenue, 69 Schenck Avenue (residences), SE cor. 1908–1912. Altered, 1977, Rosemary Songer.

Two grand **Classical Revival** houses of Roman brick with great Ionic-columned porches. Wealth was **once** here.

[H 3.] Grand columns: onetime wealth   [B 1.] Rutland Plaza apt. complex

[H 3a.] Originally **James Royal residence,** 18 Ashford St., cor. Ridgewood Ave. 1904. John Petit.

A Queen Anne/Shingle Style gem, pedimented and towered, swathed in green shingles.

[H 3b.] 68 Ashford Street (residence), bet. Ridgewood and Arlington Aves. W side. ca. 1885.

Clapboard and shingles, with a square-in-a-circle oriel balcony of great charm.

[H 4.] St. Joseph's Anglican Church/originally **Trinity Episcopal Church,** 131 Arlington Ave., NE cor. Schenck Ave. 1886. Richard M. Upjohn.

A bulky, vigorous, comforting, buttressed, brick and sandstone church with a friendly, **squatting** scale. It shows a **Romanesque** body, with **Gothic** finials.

[H 5.] Public School 108, Brooklyn, 200 Linwood St., NW cor. Arlington Ave. 1895. James W. Naughton. ★

Roman brick with brownstone that is both rough and smooth. Handsome **Romanesque Revival** arches.

[H 6.] Public School 65, Brooklyn, 158 Richmond St., bet. Ridgewood and Arlington Aves. W side. 1870. Expanded, 1889, James W. Naughton. ★

A somber painted red-brick outpost of education on the early frontier of urbanization.

[H 6a.] Andrews Methodist Church/originally **Wesleyan Methodist Episcopal Church,** Richmond St. bet. Etna St. and Ridgewood Ave. E side. 1892. Attributed to George Crammer.

Romanesque Revival/Shingle Style. A glorious rose window intersects upper shingles and lower rosy brick. A lovely, lonely "country" church.

BROWNSVILLE

Brownsville shares the bottom of the city's economic ladder with the South Bronx. It is largely Hispanic and black, with old and dilapidated housing predominating, much banal public housing, and an isolated intrusion of relatively elegant architecture by the **New York State Urban Development Corporation (UDC).** The neighborhood was first subdivided in 1865 by **Charles S. Brown,** to whom the community owes its name. In **1887** a group of real estate entrepreneurs purchased portions and began to encourage **Jewish** immigrants in the congested **Lower East Side** to move here. The arrival of the **Fulton Street el** in **1889** stimulated the influx, and the settlement became a great concentration of poor **Eastern European Jews.** The community was not free of the problems normally associated with deprived neighborhoods; some of **Murder, Incorporated's** most notorious leaders grew up in these streets. The completion of the **New Lots** branch of the **IRT** subway in **1922** further improved rapid transit connections to Manhattan, and the area grew mildly prosperous. **Pitkin Avenue** is still a major shopping street for the surrounding population, although in the **1920s** through **1940s** it attracted shoppers from a much larger region—such is the fate of our assorted downtowns. The neighborhood's movie house, at **Pitkin** and **East New York** Avenues,—in a brief renaissance the **Hudson Temple Cathedral** and now a furniture store—was once one of the city's great fantasy movie palaces. Following **World War II** the Jewish population moved to more middle-class precincts (most lately Staten Island), and the area declined. Major renewal has been effective only in islands of activity, most notably at **Rutland Plaza, Marcus Garvey Village,** and the various recent row-housed blocks of the **Nehemiah Plan.** In between, vast scars still record the wounds sustained in **peacetime** wars.

[B 1.] Rutland Plaza, East New York Ave. and Rutland Rd., E. 92nd to E. 94th Sts. 1976. Donald Stull & Assocs.

One of the best of the **UDC** incisions into the cityscape (others are at **Roosevelt Island, Coney Island,** and the **Twin Parks** section of the Bronx). Bold form and color rise over the neighboring landscape with style, but the later signs and graphics are **awful.**

[B 2.] Public School 398, Brooklyn, The Walter Weaver School, East New York Ave. bet. E. 93rd and E. 94th Sts. S side. 1976. Perkins & Will.

In an era of **open classrooms,** when schools were conceived as shopping centers of education, this barrel-vaulted **basilica** could offer partitioning (or nonpartitioning) in the most flexible manner. Terracotta brick, with bronze-anodized aluminum.

[B 3.] Originally **Loew's Pitkin Theater**/later **Hudson Temple Cathedral**/now **3 Guys Furniture,** 1501 Pitkin Ave., NW cor. Saratoga Ave. 1930. Thomas W. Lamb.

A land**mark** on this brassy shopping street. Its carefully ornate brick and terra-cotta exterior screened one of those fantasy, fairy-tale auditoriums conjured up by **Lamb** and his peers in the great **picture-palace** era of the late 1920s, complete with twinkling stars and moving clouds across its **ceiling-sky.**

[B 4.] Banco de Ponce/originally **The East New York Savings Bank,** Kings Highway and Rockaway Pkwy., E. side. 1962. Lester Tichy & Assocs.

Tichy brought a bit of Hollywood to Brownsville, **tinseltown** in the slums. Some remember his equally violent ravaging of old Pennsylvania Station's main waiting room with a luminous canopy analogous to a Steven Spielberg visitation from the film *E. T.*

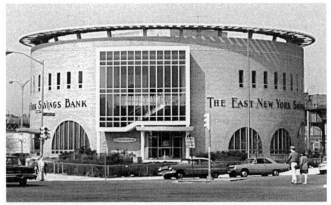

[B 4.] Banco de Ponce, once E. New York Sav. Bk.: Hollywood in Brownsville

 [B 5.] Engine Company 238, Squad Company 4, N.Y.C. Fire Department, 885 Howard Ave., SE cor. Livonia Ave. 1974. Giovanni Pasanella.

Red-brown square brick clads this simple, strong modern fire station, skylit at its rear. A **class act.**

[B 6.] Formerly **Belmont Avenue pushcart market,** Belmont Ave. bet. Rockaway and Christopher Aves.

Once one of the city's most vigorous **street** markets, filled with the itinerant pushcarts of Jewish merchants, **Belmont** still spills from storefronts onto its sidewalks, now thronged with Hispanic and black residents. The **push**carts are gone but not the merchandise, piled high on planks spread over sawhorses and milk crates.

[B 7.] Brownsville Multi-Service Center, Strauss St. bet. Pitkin and East New York Aves. W side. ca. 1972.

A simple but refreshing modern building in ribbed brown concrete block.

 [B 8.] 73rd Precinct, N.Y.C. Police Department, 1546 East New York Ave, SE cor. Strauss St. 1982. Swanke Hayden Connell.

A striking, serrated facade adorns this **understated** precinct station, an island of architectural success in this vast sea of banality.

[B 9.] Betsy Head Memorial Playground Bathhouse, N.Y.C. Department of Parks & Recreation, Strauss St. to Hopkinson Ave., Dumont to Livonia Aves. 1940. John Matthews Hatton.

Liberal use of glass block and a parasol roof delicately balanced on parabolic ribs distinguish the **WPA** bathhouse that serves an immense swimming pool.

 [B 10.] Marcus Garvey Village (row housing), Dumont Ave. to a point S of Riverdale Ave., from W of Bristol St. to Chester St. and including a portion of Rockaway Ave. 1976. Prototypical design, Theodore Liebman of the N.Y.S. Urban Development Corporation and Kenneth Frampton of the Institute for Architecture and Urban Studies. Construction documents by David Todd & Assocs.

The **UDC's** pretentious experiment in low-rise high-density housing: row houses with stoops, embracing paved and planted play and sitting areas. **Austere** and reminiscent of the fanatically regimented Amsterdam housing of the 1920s, it is more a scholastic architectural thesis than a prototype for urban redevelopment.

[B 3.] Loew's Pitkin Theater in 1967   **[B 10.]** Rowhouse Marcus Garvey Vill.

The shtetl: What Brownsville lacked in physical amenities it once made up for in the richness of its social life. Here the immigrant Jewish population recalled the life of the **shtetl**, their former communities in **Eastern Europe. Pitkin Avenue** was the street for the grand promenade, its Yiddish-speaking community addicted to thrashing out the social and political problems of the hour while *shpatzeering* down the avenue. At one time **Hoffman's** cafeteria was the area's modest but glittery version of a **Delmonico's** of another era and social class. **Amboy Street,** the turf of a youth gang immortalized in Irving Shulman's *The Amboy Dukes* (1947), became in **1916** the home of the first birth-control clinic in **America,** established by **Margaret Sanger.** The Jewish population, more affluent than their grandparents, has left what they had perceived to be the **asphalt jungle** and emigrated en masse to suburbia. On Pitkin Avenue, **Yiddish** has been replaced by **Spanish.**

EAST NEW YORK

[E 1.] Grace Baptist Church/originally **Deutsche Evangelische Lutherische St. Johannes Kirche,** 223 New Jersey Ave., bet. Liberty and Glenmore Aves. ca. 1885.

Gothic Revival in banded brown bricks, crowned with a slated high-hatted steeple.

[E 2.] Holy Trinity Russian Orthodox Church, Pennsylvania Ave. SE cor. Glenmore Ave. 1935.

One great and one minor onion dome sheathed in **verdigris** copper crown a salmon brick base. The porch on Glenmore Avenue, with its fat columns and steeply pitched pediment, is an **eclectic fantasy.**

[E 3.] East New York Neighborhood Family Care Center, 2094 Pitkin Ave., bet. Pennsylvania and New Jersey Aves. S side. 1976.

A decent modern building in orange-brown brick, its deeply incised windows a popular stylistic **mannerism** of the 1970s. As is usual in these unsophisticated sectors of the city, the signs **disgrace** the architecture.

[E 4.] Bradford Street, bet. Sutter and Blake Aves.

This street preserves a sense of the early urbanization of **East New York.** Gaily painted, the block retains a **charm** that most of Eastern Brooklyn has lost to the **ravages** of blockbusting, poverty, and neglect.

[E 5.] Originally **Christian Duryea residence,** 562 Jerome St., bet. Dumont and Livonia Aves. ca. 1787.

Yet another farmhouse later surrounded by the city's grid. Here the **hallmark** eaves have been stripped, leaving the form without evidence of its Dutch design origins. Only the **bones** within are a remembrance of its true history.

[E 6.] New Lots Reformed Dutch Church, 630 New Lots Ave., SE cor. Schenck Ave. 1823. ★

Built by the latter-day **Dutch** farmers of this area when weekly trips to the **Flatbush** church became too arduous. A painted wood-shingled body, with Gothic Revival openings. The adjacent parish house is an unfortunate lump.

[E 6.] New Lots Reformed Dutch Ch.   **[E 6.]** New Lots Reformed Dutch Ch.

[E 7.] Essex Terrace apt. complex   **[E 8.]** City Line 1 Turnkey Public Hsg.

[E 7.] Essex Terrace (apartments), bounded by Linden Blvd., Hegeman Ave., Linwood and Essex Sts. 1970. Norval White.

Crisp and well cared-for, this union-sponsored low-rise high-density project surrounds its own central **private plaza.** The corner gates allow residents to admit or restrict the neighborhood at their discretion. Discretion now means **permanently locked.**

[E 8.] City Line 1 Turnkey Public Housing, N.Y.C. Housing Authority, 460-470 Fountain Ave., and 1085-1087 Hegeman Ave., NW cor. Fountain Ave., and 1052-1064 Hegeman Ave., and 768-774 Logan St. SW cor. Hegeman Ave. 1975. Ciardullo-Ehmann.

Quasi-town houses that attempt to emulate the **fussy** scale of their row house neighbors. The attempt is noble but the product is crude. Note particularly the rainwater leaders that wander aimlessly across the facades.

[E 9.] Brooklyn Developmental Center, N.Y.S. Department of Mental Hygiene, 888 Fountain Ave., S of Flatlands Ave. W side. 1974. Katz, Weisman, Weber, Strauss.

At the **edge** of the world, past junkyards, debris, and squatters, sits this handsome, sprawling group of ribbed concrete-block buildings for the care, residence, and education of retarded children.

[E 10.] Public School 306, Brooklyn, 970 Vermont Ave., NW cor. Cozine Ave. 1966. Pedersen & Tilney.

An intelligent, no-nonsense, cast-in-place concrete school in an area whose flat monotony is being broken by towers sprouting everywhere. Note the stylish **1960s** stair towers.

[E 11.] Starrett City, bet. Flatlands Ave. and Shore Pkwy., Seaview and Louisiana Aves. 1976. Herman Jessor.

A **surreal** experience. Great building blocks, housing 5,881 apartments, are placed in the manner of a **supermodel** in this boondock landscape. Jessor's other giant antiurban fantasies include **Co-op City** in the Bronx. The **architecture** of the building blocks is bland. Self-contained, the **City** has its own schools, churches, and synagogues and generates its own heat, light, and power.

[E 9.] Brooklyn Developmental Ctr.   **[E 9.]** Interior, Bklyn Developm'l. Ctr.

[E 12.] Schwartz Comprehensive Health Care Center, Brookdale Hospital Medical Center, Rockaway Pkwy. NE cor. Linden Blvd. 1974. William Breger & Assocs. and Unger/Napier Assocs.

Simultaneously bold and fussy, its pale brown bulk is festooned with vanes that swoop out from its facade.

[E 13.] Baird Special Care Pavilion, Brookdale Hospital Medical Center, 1235 Linden Blvd., NW cor. Rockaway Pkwy. 1968. Horowitz & Chun.

Somber brown brick makes a strong, well-scaled, and serene statement in this pallid part of town. Both private physicians' offices and clinics are contained within.

QUEENS

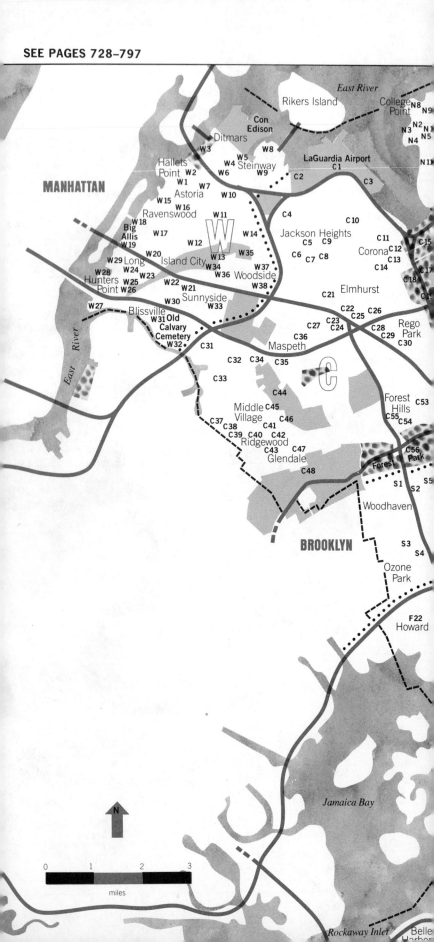

East River

Rikers Island

College **N8** **N9**
Point

N2 **N1**
N3 **N5**
N4

N1

Con
Edison

Ditmars
W3

W5 **W8**
Steinway

Hallets **W4**
Point **W6** **W9**

LaGuardia Airport
C1

C3

MANHATTAN

W1 **W7**

Astoria **W10** **C2**

W15

Ravenswood **W16** **C4** **C10**

Big **W18** **W11** Jackson Heights **C11**

Allis **W17** **W14** **C5** **C9** Corona **C12**

W19 **W12** **C6** **C7** **C8** **C13** **C15**

W20 **W35** **C14**

W29 Long **W13** **C18** **C1**

W28 **W24** Island City **W34** **W37**

Hunters **W23** **W36** Woodside **W38**

Point **W25** **W22** **W21** Elmhurst

W26 **W30** Sunnyside **C21**

W27 **W33** **C22** **C26**

Blissville **C27** **C23** **C25** **C28** Rego

East **W31** Old **C24** **C29** Park

River Calvary **C36** **C30**

W32 Cemetery Maspeth

C31 **C32** **C34** **C35**

C33 **C44**

Middle **C45**

Village **C46**

C37 **C41**

C38 **C42** Forest **C53**

C39 **C40** Hills

C43 Ridgewood **C47** **C55** **C54**

Glendale **C56**

C48 Forest Park

S1 **S2** **S5**

Woodhaven

BROOKLYN **S3**

S4

Ozone
Park

F22
Howard

Jamaica Bay

N

0   1   2   3

miles

Rockaway Inlet
Belle

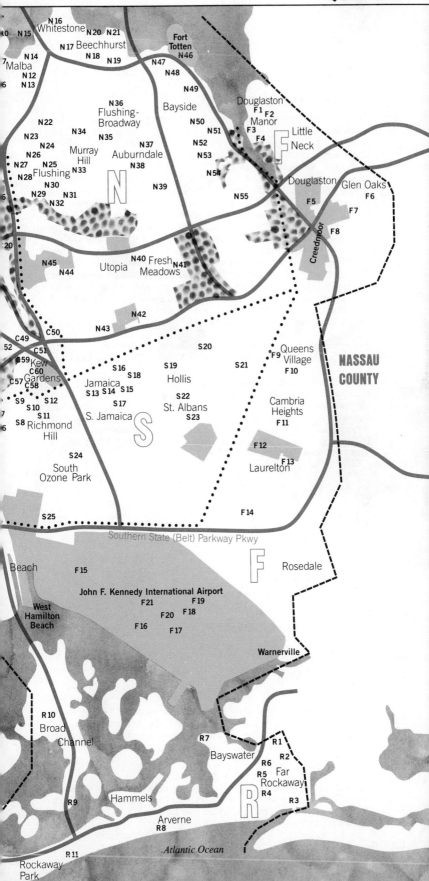

QUEENS

N16
Whitestone N20 N21
N0 N15
N17 Beechhurst
7 Malba N18 N19
N14
N12
N6 N13

Fort
Totten
N46
N47
N48
N49

Douglaston
F1 F2
Manor
F3
F4

Little
Neck

N22
N23
N24
N26
N27 N25 N33
N28 Flushing
N30
N29 N31
N32

N36
Flushing-
Broadway
N34
N35

Bayside

N37
Auburndale
N38

N39

N50
N51
N52
N53

N54

N55

F

Douglaston Glen Oaks
F5 F6
F7

Creedmoor

F8

N
Utopia

N40 Fresh
N41
Meadows

N45
N44

N42

N43

C49 C50
C51
52
C59
C60
Kew
Gardens C58
C57
S9 S12
S10
S7 S11
S8 Richmond
Hill

S20

S16
S18
Jamaica
S13 S14 S15
S17

S19
Hollis

S22
St. Albans
S23

S

S24
South
Ozone Park

S25

S21

F9 Queens
Village
F10

NASSAU
COUNTY

Cambria
Heights

F11

F12

F13
Laurelton

F14

Southern State (Belt) Parkway Pkwy

F

Beach F15

West
Hamilton
Beach

John F. Kennedy International Airport
F21 F19
F20 F18
F16 F17

Rosedale

Warnerville

R10
Broad
Channel

R7

R1
R2
R6
R5 Far
R4 Rockaway
R3

Bayswater

R

R9

Hammels

R8
Arverne

Rockaway
Park

R11

Atlantic Ocean

4

QUEENS

Borough of Queens/Queens County

Queens is the home of *two* of the three metropolitan airports—**La-Guardia** and **Kennedy International.** Its residents are unable to forget that fact, the drone of jets and props ever reminding them as planes swoop out of the sky and into these all-weather aerodromes. Awareness of modern technology is balanced by contact with nature—postage-stamp-sized front lawns or the vastness of the **Jamaica Bay Wildlife Refuge** (now a part of the **Gateway National Recreation Area**), not to mention the borough's other parks: **16,397** acres in all. **Queens** is the largest borough: **114.7** square miles (**126.6** including inland waters), constituting almost a *third* of the city's entire area, almost *twice* the area of Staten Island alone. In population, it ranks second only to **Brooklyn.**

As a borough it is predominantly a bedroom community. The last great open spaces of **New York** were here until the late 1940s, allowing developers to meet the need for detached dwellings: suburbia within the city limits. However, a good deal of industry also thrives within its boundaries: in **Long Island City** and **Maspeth** and along the **Long Island Rail Road** are manufacturers of a wide variety of products.

Before **Queens** became a borough, it was a far larger county, encompassing its present-day area as well as that of **Nassau** (a new county created as a by-product of consolidation into **Greater New York** in **1898**). The borough is named for Catherine of Braganza, **Queen** of Charles II.

The vastness of **Queens** and its relatively late development have encouraged the retention of the old town, village, and subdivision names for its various communities. From a strong sense of pride and identification with the outlying suburbs, residents never refer to themselves as "Queensites" but rather as living in **Jamaica,** or **Flushing,** or **Forest Hills,** or **St. Albans.** If pressed further, the response to "Where do you live?" becomes **"Long Island."**

WESTERN QUEENS

HALLETS POINT • DITMARS • ASTORIA • STEINWAY
RAVENSWOOD • LONG ISLAND CITY • HUNTERS POINT
BLISSVILLE • SUNNYSIDE • WOODSIDE

Long Island City

Separated from the town of Newtown in 1870.

Between 1870 and 1898, when it was consolidated into Greater New York, Long Island City was, in fact, itself a city. It encompassed not only the area we still identify with its name but also the adjacent communities to the north, northeast, and east.

GREATER ASTORIA

The peninsula projecting into Hell Gate's once turbulent waters is named for the family of **William Hallet,** who received it as a grant from Governor Peter Stuyvesant in 1652. From his family's early settlement and that of **Stephen Alling Halsey,** the Father of Astoria, the village of Astoria developed. As a Manhattan suburb its growth followed the introduction of steam-powered ferries in 1815. By 1839 the area had been incorporated, with friends of **John Jacob Astor** winning a bitter factional fight in naming Astoria for him.

The year 1842 saw the completion of the turnpike to Greenpoint. Soon a shipping trade was established in lumber, particularly in exotic foreign woods. Just north of the cove on the mount called **Hallets Point,** lumber and shipping magnates built mansions, a few of which remain but deprived of their former splendor and spacious view-laden grounds. Nearby, at the foot of Astoria Boulevard, the area's most significant **ferry service** to Manhattan, linking easily accessible East 92nd Street, plied the waters between 1867 and the advent of the Triborough Bridge.

The availability of fine lumber and cheap land persuaded piano manufacturer **William Steinway** in the early 1870s to extend his activities from Manhattan to a company town of some 400 acres, purchasing **a superb stone house** for his family at the foot of Steinway Street. The mansion, workers' housing, and both old and new factories all remain.

HALLETS POINT

[W 1a.] Good Church of Deliverance, Pentecostal, and **First Reformed Church of Astoria**/originally **Reformed Dutch Church of Hallets Cove,** 27-26 12th St., bet. 27th Ave. and Astoria Blvd. W side. 1889. Steeple, 1900.

A terra-cotta, brick, and verdigris copper **squat Goth.** Bold, monolithic, and homely.

[W 1b.] Originally **Dr. Wayt residence,** 9-29 27th Ave., NW cor. 12th St. ca. 1845.

Crumbling Italianate mansion.

[W 1c.] Originally **Remsen residence,** 9-26 27th Ave., SW cor. 12th St. ca. 1835.

Greek Revival house, handsomely maintained with rural grounds, rubble garden walls, iron fence, slate sidewalk.

To reach the following entries by car begin at Astoria Park South: Take 14th St. (one-way) south; take 26th Ave. (one-way) east; take 14th Place (one-way) north. Or walk, for smashing views of the Triborough Bridge, Ward's/Randall's Island, Manhattan.

[W 1d.] Astoria Branch, Queens Borough Public Library, 14-01 Astoria Blvd., NE cor. 14th St. 1904. Tuthill & Higgins.

One of many branch libraries embodied in the **gift from Andrew Carnegie,** this has an unusual and welcome appearance. Its public entrance is set at a diagonal to the intersection, thus creating a small plaza, all the better to view its unusual architecture, derived from **North European Renaissance** antecedents.

[W 2a.] Originally **Robert Benner residence,** 25-37 14th St., bet. Astoria Park S. and 26th Ave. E side. 1852.

Two-story Doric, **a grand Southern mansion,** built by James L. Stratton and occupied by Manhattan lawyer Robert Benner, who was known as a fancier of flori- and arboriculture. Hence the magnificent copper beech tree that helps (along with the deep setback from the street) to conceal this house.

[W 2b.] 25-45, 25-47 14th Place (two-family residences), bet. 26th Ave. and Astoria Park S. E side. ca. 1910.

A pair of well-designed (and maintained) houses whose common 2-story porches tie them together as a single, strong architectural composition. *Down the hill, at the corner is:*

[W 2c.] 14-22 Astoria Park South (four-family house), SW cor. 14th Place. 1965. Guy G. Rothenstein, designer.

A successful solution to urban housing using large expanses of glass and precast, preinsulated concrete wall panels. The rear roof terrace has a **Corbusier-inspired** colored glass and stucco wall, à la Ronchamp. Lush border landscaping helps make this Modern structure less obtrusive in an older area. For a number of years the designer worked for Corbu.

[W 2d.] Our Lady of Mt. Carmel Cemetery/originally **site of Our Lady of Mt. Carmel Church (Roman Catholic),** 21st St. NW cor. 26th Ave. 1844–1926.

Site of the original church between 1844 and 1870. [See W 7a.] Since the cemetery's fencing and cleanup in 1983, it has become **an asset to the community.**

DITMARS

Con Edison/Astoria: Put into operation in 1906, and covering hundreds of acres north of 20th Avenue and west of 37th Street, the enormous Con Ed power plant is an unsung landmark of the Ditmars area of Astoria. Built by one of Con Ed's predecessors, the Consolidated Gas Company of New York, it was the world's largest cooking-gas generating plant when completed. It serves both Manhattan and the Bronx via underwater tunnels. Today, both natural gas and electricity are distributed from the site, which has since been considerably expanded using landfill to absorb Berrian Island.

[W 2a.] Orig. Robert Benner residence: the trick is to find this 2-story mansion

[W 2b.] 25-45, 25-47 14th Place res.   **[W 4b.]** Immaculate Conception Ch.

[W 3.] Astoria Park, Shore Blvd. to 19th St., Ditmars Blvd. to Astoria Park S. **[W 3a.] Astoria Play Center and Swimming Pool, N.Y.C. Department of Parks & Recreation,** in Astoria Park. 1936. J. M. Hatton.

A tilted piece of green giving picnic views of the Triborough and Hell Gate Bridges and the Manhattan skyline. Within is an expansive WPA-era pool complex and bathhouse.

[W 3b.] Triborough Bridge, O. H. Ammann, engineer. Aymar Embury II, architect. 1936.

A whole highway system, trestled and bridged, of which this, the **Hell Gate** span, is the greatest part.

[W 3c.] Hell Gate Bridge/officially the **East River Arch Bridge of the New York Connecting Railroad.** 1917. Gustav Lindenthal, engineer. Henry Hornbostel, architect.

The through connection for the **Penn Central** (now **Amtrak**) on its way from **Washington** through **New York** to **Boston** (it tunnels under both the **Hudson** and **East Rivers,** rising in **Queens** to pass over and through these great over- and underslung bowstring trusses).

River Crest Sanitarium: Today the multiblock site is occupied by St. John's Prep (formerly Mater Christi Roman Catholic High School), but it was once a well-known therapeutic facility (founded in 1896 on the old Wolcott estate by a local congressman, Dr. Jonathan Joseph Kindred) "for Mental and Nervous Diseases with Separate Buildings for Alcoholic and Drug Habituation." The grounds extend south from 21st Avenue between Crescent and 27th Streets.

[W 4a.] Arleigh Realty Company row housing and apartments, 21-11 to 21-77, 21-12 to 21-72 28th St., both sides. 21-12 to 21-72 29th St., W side, bet. 21st Ave. and Ditmars Blvd. ca. 1925.

Speculative midblock rows straddling a gentle rise in topography, designed to offer a picturesque composition despite the redundancy of the ingredients. Here, **architecture enriches a locale** and gives it identity, an accomplishment largely missing in postwar speculative rows.

[W 4b.] Church of the Immaculate Conception (Roman Catholic), 29-01 Ditmars Blvd., NE cor. 29th St. 1950. Henry V. Murphy.

Latter-day Italian neo-Romanesque. The unusual corbeled brick bell tower is a dramatic sight, up and down Ditmars Boulevard.

[W 4c.] Metropolitan Life Insurance Company apartments, 33rd to 36th Sts., 21st Ave. to Ditmars Blvd. (One square block.) 1924. Andrew J. Thomas and D. Everett Waid.

The **first Metropolitan venture** into direct development of housing (later to result in Parkchester in the Bronx and Stuyvesant Town/Peter Cooper Village in Manhattan). Two **muted rows** of 5-story, red brick apartments, defining a blocklong verdant garden. In 1974, the project's semicentennial year, residents joined to honor an individual they had found important to their lives by erecting a (slightly misspelled) plaque on the Ditmars Boulevard fence. Commonplace in Vienna, such a **display of affection** is rare in New York:

ALFRED GESCHWIND
July 3, 1908–August 9, 1974
WITHOUT WHO'S LOVE IT WOULD NOT HAVE GROWN

[W 5.] Lawrence Family Graveyard, 20th Rd. SE cor. 35th St. 1703. ★

A memorable location in history. Don't bother to look.

[W 6a.] St. Irene Chrysovalantou (Greek Orthodox) Church, 36-25 23rd Ave., bet. 36th and 37th Sts. N side. Altered from two former row houses, 1980.

The entire north side of this block is a charming vernacular residential composition crowned by the midblock church. The real delight is within: a folk art religious extravaganza, something like walking into a box by **artist Joseph Cornell.** *Plan to visit when open.*

[W 6b.] Bohemian Park and **Hall,** 29-19 24th Ave., NE cor. 29th St. 1910.

A **mittel-Europa beer garden** with picnic tables, lights strung on wires. A place to lift a stein, listen to music, or dance, all behind a less-than-picturesque stuccoed wall. Alas, the last of Queens's many turn-of-the-century picnic grounds. Operated by the **Bohemian Citizens' Benevolent Society of Astoria.**

ASTORIA

[W 7a.] Our Lady of Mt. Carmel Roman Catholic Church, 23-35 Newtown Ave., NW cor. Crescent St. Narthex, 1915. Nave, 1966.

The Newtown Avenue facade is a dignified, wonderful, French Gothic evocation in limestone, an architectural treat for all. **Mt. Carmel Institute,** the parish hall, across the avenue to the southwest, is an intriguing Italian Renaissance foil. The site of an earlier church remains as a small cemetery [see W 2d.].

[W 7b.] HANAC/formerly **74th Precinct, N.Y.C. Police Department,** 23-16 30th Ave., bet. 23rd and Crescent Sts. ca. 1890.

A Romanesque Revival symphony. An important architectural-cultural anchor in a neighborhood showing many conflicting tides of development. (**HANAC** stands for **Hellenic American Neighborhood Action Committee,** a social-services agency for the area's large Greek community.)

[W 7c.] Episcopal Church of the Redeemer and **Chapel,** 30-30 Crescent St., NW cor. 30th Rd. 1868. Consecrated, 1879.

A dark, brooding stone church. Instead of a spire, the bell tower supports an internally illuminated cross.

[W 7d.] Good Shepherd United Methodist Church/originally **First Methodist Episcopal Church of Astoria,** 30-40 Crescent St., SW cor. 30th Rd. 1908.

Another church, across the intersection, to keep Redeemer company.

STEINWAY

William Steinway: The individual from whom the community derives its name was a brilliant 19th-century entrepreneur. Besides being a manufacturer of pianos, Steinway was a transit magnate (today's Steinway Transit Corporation), builder of an underwater tunnel (today's Flushing Line East River crossing), and developer, together with beer baron George Ehret, of a working-class resort, North Beach (site of today's LaGuardia Airport).

[W 8.] Formerly William Steinway residence: the piano maker's summer home

[W 8.] Formerly **William Steinway residence/**a.k.a. **Steinway Mansion/** originally **Benjamin T. Pike, Jr., residence,** 18-33 41st St., bet. Berrian Blvd. and 19th Ave. E side. 1856. ★

On a minimountain in a deciduous jungle inhabited by barking dogs, old cars, and trucks. **William Steinway's** (originally optician Benjamin Pike, Jr.'s) dark gray granite house was a showplace in its time. (The piano factory [1872] is still at the northwest corner of **19th** Avenue and **38th** Street.)

The mountain: The area between 42nd and Hazen Streets, north of 19th Avenue, dominates today's view east from the Steinway Mansion. The 60-foot mountain of tailings from some long forgotten municipal project is now under the jurisdiction of the Port Authority. Given the enormity of the environmental desecration, the authority's neat little signs are ironic: NO DUMPING.

[W 9a.] Originally **Steinway workers' housing,** 41-17 to 41-25, 40-12 to 41-20 20th (Winthrop) Ave., bet. Steinway, 41st (Albert) St. and 42nd (Theodore) Sts. Both sides. 20-11 to 20-29, 20-12 to 20-34 41st St., bet. 20th Ave. and 20th Rd. Both sides. 1877–1879.

Trim, painted Victorian brick row houses, originally rented by the Steinways to their workers. **Loved.** Note the carved stone nameplates on the corner houses bearing the **streets' original names,** those of Steinway family members.

[W 9b.] Steinway Reformed Church/originally **Union Protestant Church,** 41-01 Ditmars Blvd., NE cor. 41st St. 1891.

In 1891 neighbor William Steinway contributed the pipe organ to this **rural Gothic Revival gem** (and no doubt thereby to its change of name and denomination). The regrettable cladding in asbestos shingles has not totally negated its beauty.

[W 9c.] Stern's department store warehouse/originally **Steinway & Sons piano factory,** 45-02 Ditmars Blvd., bet. 45th and 46th Sts. S side. 1902.

A 6-story H-plan mill (along with developments on both adjoining blocks) built by the Steinways to allow for the **1909 departure** from their Park Avenue factory.

[W 9d.] St. Francis of Assisi Roman Catholic Church, 45-04 21st Ave., SE cor. 45th St. 1930.

A Shingle Style church of the Great Depression. Genuine wood detail, inside and out. Great!

[W 9e.] Orig. Abraham Lent residence: a well-preserved "Dutch" homestead

[W 9e.] Originally **Abraham Lent residence,** 78-03 19th Rd., at 78th St. N side. ca. 1729. ★

Weathered shingled dormers and clapboard siding—**a well-preserved "Dutch" farmhouse**—nesting amid lush foliage which also embraces the family cemetery of the Lent and Riker families.

South of Grand Central Parkway:

[W 10.] 114th Precinct, N.Y.C. Police Department, 34-16 Astoria Blvd. S., SW cor. 35th St. 1973. Holden, Yang, Raemsch & Corser.

Neatly articulated, New Brutalist, cast-in-place concrete and brick, but not brutalist enough.

[W 11a.] Sidewalk clock, in front of 30-78 Steinway St., bet. 30th and 31st Aves. W side. ★

One of a group of sidewalk clocks officially designated by the Landmarks Preservation Commission. An inspired decision.

[W 11b.] American Savings Bank, Steinway Branch, 31-02 Steinway St., SW cor. 31st Ave. 1974. Edward Larrabee Barnes Assocs.

Dark brown brick and **sheer glass;** *elegance,* urbanity, and chic in an older, stolid, somber, middle-class community.

Scheutzen Park: The popular 7-acre picnic park/beer garden, established in 1870 at the southeast corner of Steinway Street and Broadway, contained dancing pavilions, shooting galleries, picnic tables, and groves of trees. It was the site of thousands of social events staged by members of the city's German community until it succumbed to development beginning in 1924.

[W 11c.] Church of the Most Precious Blood (Roman Catholic), 32-30 37th St., bet. Broadway and 34th Ave. 1932. McGill & Hamlin. Stations of the cross, D. Dunbar Beck. St. Theresa and St. Anthony statues, Hazel Clerc. Stained glass, Richard N. Spiers & Son.

Henry J. McGill's masterpiece. Only the 37th facade is clad in stone, reflecting both **medieval** and **Modernistic** influences in its boxy forms and octagonal tower capped in a decorative aluminum screen. Inside, however, is a celebration of superior ecclesiastical decorative arts of the twenties and thirties. [Also see Central Queens C 9e.] In 1934, partner **Talbot Hamlin** retired to become **Avery Librarian** at Columbia University.

[W 12a.] Kaufman Astoria Studios/orig. Famous Players Lasky Corp. in 1966

[W 12.] Kaufman Astoria Studios/formerly **U.S. Army Signal Corps Pictorial Center**/formerly **Eastern Service Studios**/originally **Famous Players Lasky Corporation (Paramount Pictures),** irregular site along 35th Ave. bet. 34th and 38th Sts. Both sides. **[W 12a.]** Former **Building No. 1,** 35-11 35th Ave., bet. 35th and 36th Sts. N side. 1921. Fleischman Construction Co., designer. ★ **[W 12b.] Museum of the Moving Image,** 36-11 35th Ave., bet. 36th and 37th Sts. N side. Altered into museum, 1988, Gwathmey Siegel & Assocs.

One of several **old movie studios** that can still be found in New York, this **sprawling example** is the largest in the city—*and* in the East. In the silent era, Gloria Swanson, Rudolph Valentino, W. C. Fields, and other stars, performed there. After talkies arrived, *Beau Geste, The Emperor Jones,* and the W.P.A. film *One Third of a Nation* were filmed here. Following the studios' rebirth in the 1970s, *The Wiz* and other widely heralded productions were filmed here.

[W 13.] Weeks Office Products, Inc. (warehouse), 42-42 Northern Blvd., SE cor. 42nd Place. 1983. Michael Harris Spector & Assocs.

A stucco (in the style of cast concrete) box. An asset to the industrial landscape as a result of its **very sculptural detailing.**

[W 14.] Boulevard Gardens (apartments), 54th St./Hobart St. to 57th St., 30th Ave. to 31st Ave. 1929. Theobald Engelhardt. Adolph M. Dick, consultant.

Early, limited-dividend, privately built housing. Now aluminum-windowed, with its red brickwork cement-washed for waterproofing (surely not for aesthetic) purposes. Its original neo-Georgian detailing was intended to give it character, something the stripped nonarchitecture of later public boxes would lack.

RAVENSWOOD, LONG ISLAND CITY, HUNTERS POINT, BLISSVILLE

These four areas form the industrial concentration of **New York City,** in appearance, if not in fact. Laced by **IRT** and **BMT** elevateds, the passenger yards of the *old* **Penn Central** (now **Amtrak**) and the Long Island Rail Road (now part of the **Metropolitan Transit Authority**) are in an open cut; the **IND** is underground. It is a great transportation nexus. From the els, from a car, or on foot, the factory agglomeration makes itself felt: above, alongside, and even below you as you cross endless trestles over deep scars in the flat landscape.

Ravenswood, along the East River above the Queensboro Bridge, is a low-density area with a mixture of waterside industry, like Con Ed's **Big Allis,** and high-rise public housing. What is currently called **Long Island City** is the site of the bridge approaches, recycled factories, and railroad yards falling into disuse. **Hunters Point** at the south, approaching Newtown Creek, was formerly the center of government and is now the focus of major development projects by Citicorp, the Port Authority, and others.

RAVENSWOOD

[W 15a.] Adirondack Building/originally **Sohmer Piano Company (factory),** 31-01 Vernon Blvd., SE cor. 31st Ave. 1886. Top story and mansard added, 1910.

One of Steinway's competitors also established himself in this area in a multileveled factory. The top floors were added as business flourished. Now a loft building.

[W 15b.] Socrates Sculpture Park, 31-42 Vernon Blvd., bet. 31st Dr. and Broadway. W side on the bank of the East River. 1986. **Open to the public.**

A fallow riverside site converted into an enormous outdoor sculpture garden through the combined efforts of the **Athena Foundation,** and the City's Departments of Parks & Recreation, and Cultural Affairs. (The danger is that the City **has its eyes on the site** for 20-story residential towers!) On display can be found, at various times, the work of Mark Di Suvero (the foundation's founder), Sonfist, Stankiewicz, Tucker, and others.

[W 15c.] Isamu Noguchi Garden Museum, 32-61 Vernon Blvd., NE cor. 33rd Rd. (Entrance on 33rd Rd. bet. 9th and 10th Sts.) 1985. Isamu Noguchi, sculptor; Shogi Sazao, architect. **Open to the public.**

South of Noguchi's combination lamp factory, workshop, and studio is this museum of his work.

[W 15d.] Kraus Company (administrative offices), 33-01 Vernon Blvd., bet. 33rd Rd. and 34th Ave. E side. ca. 1985.

Dark gray salt-and-pepper glazed brick and trendy circular wall-cutouts here only equal conspicuous consumption.

[W 15e.] Structural Display Inc./originally **Barkin-Levin factory (Lassie Coats),** 12-12 33rd Ave., SW cor. 13th St. 1958. Ulrich Franzen.

Built for an expatriate clothing manufacturer from the overcrowded garment district of Manhattan. Exquisitely crisp architecture that has been ill maintained.

[W 16a.] 31-41 12th Street (residence), SE cor. 31st Dr. (one-way east). ca. 1860.

Freestanding 2½-story Italianate **rural house** inundated with brown-green composition, asphalt-shingle siding that nevertheless allows the window detail, the wood trim, and the house's basic form to carry the day.

[W 16b.] 12-17 31st Drive (residence), bet. 12th (one-way north) and 14th Sts. N side. ca. 1885.

A portico of two **finely crafted** columns; the rest of the house is a testament to the **effective sales pitch** of the aluminum siding and storm-door salesman.

[W 15e.] Originally the Barkin-Levin factory (Lassie Coats), in a 1958 photo

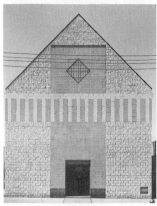

[W 16c.] Community Church of Astoria   Lonely brownstone at 11-41 30th Rd.

[W 16c.] Community Church of Astoria, 14-42 Broadway, bet. 14th Place and 21st St. S side. 1952. Total reconstruction, 1986, Alfredo De Vido Assocs.

A suave, subtle reconstruction and extension of a church serving a congregation with limited means. It's **amazing** what concrete block can be made to do. The site around it is scheduled to become a public high school.

Lone curiosities

Lonely brownstones: At various, totally unexpected points in the largely wood-frame or brick-front **Ravenswood** and **Astoria** communities, appear late 19th-century, richly worked, 2-story sandstone-facade row houses that contrast smooth with rock-face brownstone. They are simply beautiful and always come as a surprise: **34-55 9th St.,** bet. 34th and 35th Aves. E side., **11-41 30th Rd.,** bet. Vernon Blvd. and 12th St. N side., **12-29 to 12-35 30th Drive** (one-way east), bet. 12th and 14th Sts. N side. And there are others! In **Hunter's Point,** see [W 24b, 24c.]

[W 17a.] Summit, 13-15 37th Ave., bet. 13th and 14th Sts. N side. 1985. William Gleckman.

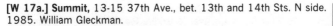

Testing the limits of **minimalist architecture:** bold, stylish, generous in scale, an exercise in gray on gray. But, what exactly is it? (Answer: a waterproofing and restoration company.)

[W 17b.] Scalamandré Silks (factory), 37-46 24th St., NW cor. 38th Ave. ca. 1910.

A contrast: Scalamandré's sumptuous silks/Scalamandré's gritty factory.

Big Allis and southward:

To Roosevelt Island: At the foot of **36th** Avenue as it crosses **Vernon Boulevard** is the bridge to **Roosevelt Island** (formerly **Welfare Island**): Beginning in 1976 it had a brief life in blue and purple, a welcoming spectrum in contrast to its earlier grim **Department of Public Works** *eye-ease* green. Alas, no longer.

[W 18.] Ravenswood Plant, Consolidated Edison Company of New York, Inc., 36th to below 40th Aves., Vernon Blvd. to East River. 1961.

Natural landmarks from all directions are these candy-striped smokestacks, two @ 450 feet, one @ 500 feet. This is the home of **Big Allis,** the enormous (and, for a time, quite cranky) electrical generator manufactured by **Allis-**Chalmers.

[W 19a.] Queensboro Bridge, from Queens Plaza to E. 59th-E. 60th Sts. in Manhattan. 1909. Gustav Lindenthal, engineer. Palmer & Hornbostel, architects. ★

This ornate (note the **Hornbostel** finials) cantilevered bridge formed the backdrop for views from swank **New York** apartments in countless **Hollywood** films of the 1940s. Surprisingly, its completion in **1909** did not lead to the migration across the river that the **Williamsburg** and **Manhattan Bridges** had caused. The last trolley car to see service in New York shuttled across the **Queensboro,** stopping at the (now demolished) elevator tower on **Welfare** (now **Roosevelt**) Island. The trolley and vehicular elevators were discontinued in **1955,** when a bridge was completed between the island and **Queens.** Passenger elevator operation continued until **1975.**

[W 19b.] Old NY Archl. Terra-Cotta Co.   **[W 23b.]** Orig. L.I. City Courthouse

[W 19b.] Originally **New York Architectural Terra-Cotta Company (office),** 42-16 Vernon Blvd., bet. Queens Plaza S. and 43rd Ave. W side. 1892. Francis H. Kimball. ★

Tudor Revival amber brick jewel with Sullivanesque terra-cotta trim. It stands proudly among the artifacts of industrial blight. Look at the chimney pots. (Fear not. It's currently in mothballs.)

[W 19c.] Queensbridge Houses, N.Y.C. Housing Authority, Vernon Blvd. to 21st St., 40th Ave. to Bridge Plaza N. 1939. William F. R. Ballard, chief architect. Henry Churchill, Frederick G. Frost, Burnett C. Turner, associate architects.

One of the *best* of City housing projects, in a handsome light brown brick, now minus its red window frames. Once it was the largest public housing project in the country: **3,149** units in **26** six-story buildings, occupying six superblocks. In the very center is an octagonal plaza with shops, a community center, and a small-town feeling.

[W 19d.] Silvercup Studios (video production studios)/originally **Gordon Baking Company (commercial bakery),** Queens Plaza S. to 43rd Ave., bet. 21st and 22nd Sts. ca. 1939.

The old Silvercup bakery was always reduced to a subsidiary role as pedestal for the **magnificent giant neon sign** advertising its product. Visible in Manhattan across the river, the refurbished sign now proclaims the bakery building's new role in media.

LONG ISLAND CITY

[W 20a.] Originally **Brewster Building,** 27-01 Queens Plaza N., bet. 27th and 28th Sts. 1910. Stephenson & Wheeler.

Bulky brick, surmounted by a "constructivist" clock tower, the clock long since departed. This is where **Brewster** produced his horse-drawn carriages and later assembled **Rolls-Royces,** shipped knocked down from **England,** as well as Brewster fighter planes during World War II.

[W 20b.] Formerly **Chase Manhattan Bank Building/**originally **Bank of the Manhattan Company,** 29-27 41st Ave., at Queens Plaza. 1927. Morrell Smith.

The crenellated clock tower commands this giant tangle of elevated train viaducts.

[W 20c.] Municipal Parking Garage, Bridge Plaza S., 28th St., 42nd Rd., and Jackson Ave. 1976. Rouse, Dubin & Ventura.

They worked hard to raise a common garage to an uncommon status. Stylish smooth and ribbed concrete: too stylish.

[W 20d.] St. Patrick's Roman Catholic Church, 39-50 29th St. (one-way north), NW cor. 40th Ave. 1898.

Renaissance Revival, save for the neatly louvered boxes atop the unfinished twin bell towers.

[W 21a.] LaGuardia Community College, CUNY, Main Building/originally **White Motor Company Factory,** 31-10 Thomson Ave., bet. 31st St. and 31st Place. S side to 47th Ave. ca. 1920. Converted, 1977, Stephen Lepp & Assocs. **[W 21b.] East Building/**originally **Equitable Bag Company,** 31st Place to Van Dam St. S side, to 47th Ave. 1949. Addition, 1957. Conversion expected, 1990, Warner, Burns, Toan & Lunde.

The main building is a delicious, caramel-colored marvel with a sculpted vermilion entry gate and similarly painted window frames. Yum, yum, yum.

[W 22.] International Design Center 29-10 Thomson Ave. **[W 22a.] Center No. 1/**originally **Adams Chewing Gum factory,** 30-30 Thomson Ave., bet. 30th Place and 31st St. S side. 1919. Ballinger & Perot. **[W 22b.] Center No. 2/**originally **American Eveready Building (factory),** 29-10 Thomson Ave., bet. 30th St. and 30th Place. S side. 1914. **[W 22c.] Center No. 3/**originally **Loose-Wiles Sunshine Biscuit Company,** Skillman Ave. bet. 29th and 30th Sts. S side. 1914. William Higginson. Conversion, Center Nos. 1 and 2, 1986; No. 3, 1988. Master plan, I. M. Pei & Partners. Gwathmey Siegel & Assocs., architects. Stephen Lepp Assocs., assoc. architects. Graphics, Vignelli Assocs.

From a Thomson Avenue vantage point, these behemoths, part of the pre-World War I Degnon Terminal and Realty Company development of this Dutch Kills area, continue to look like typical, large Long Island City factories (No. 2 was the famed Sunshine bakery with the famed thousand windows). From 47th Avenue, the project's south side, another world emerges, this one Post Modern. Too bad the replacement window framing is so flat—it emasculates the factories' gutsy World War I-era architecture, some of it paying late tribute to that of Otto Wagner. The new interiors are **breathtaking!**

HUNTERS POINT

[W 23a.] Citicorp office building/former site of **St. John's Hospital (Roman Catholic),** 44th Dr. to 45th Ave., W of Jackson Ave. **Citicorp parking garage,** S of courthouse. 1989. All by Skidmore, Owings & Merrill.

The tower rises 48 stories, some 663 feet, making it the city's **tallest structure outside of Manhattan.** During construction, signs (cynically?) identified the owners as PERENIALLY GREEN, INC. of 153 East 53rd Street, the address of the Citicorp Tower.

[W 23b.] N.Y.S. Supreme Court, Long Island City Branch/originally **Long Island City Courthouse,** 25-10 Court Sq., at Jackson and Thomson Aves. 1876. George Hathorne. Rebuilt, 1908, Peter M. Coco. ★

Beaux Arts Baroque: limestone, brick, and three kinds of granite (smooth gray, rock-face pink, and rock-face slate gray). The present building was built upon the walls of its **burned ancestor.** It was in this courthouse that the **famed 1927 murder trial** of Ruth Snyder and her lover, Henry Judd Gray, took place and where **Willie ("the Actor") Sutton** was asked why he robbed banks. His reply: "Because that's where the money is."

[W 24a.] Hunters Point Historic District, 21-09 to 21-51, 21-12 to 21-48 45th Ave., bet. 21st and 23rd Sts. Both sides. 44-70 23rd St., bet. 45th Ave. and 44th Dr. W side. Early 1870s. Spencer B. Root, John P. Rust, builders, and others. ★

A street of **virgin row houses,** complete with original stoops and cornices. They are faced in Westchester stone, a material more resistant than brownstone to weathering.

[W 24b.] 21-49 45th Rd. (row house), [W 24c.] 21-33, 21-35, 21-37 45th Rd. (row houses), bet. 21st and 23rd Sts. (*45th Rd. one-way east.*) N side. ca. 1890.

The first, a grand symphony in Romanesque Revival; the others, a melodic classical trio, 2-story **brownstones of a rare sort** that can sometimes be found between here and Astoria.

[W 25.] P. S. 1 (artists' studios)/formerly **Public School 1, Queens/**originally **Ward 1 School,** 21st St. bet. 46th Rd. and 46th Ave. 1892. Altered, 1976, Shael Shapiro.

Now converted to lofts in a continuing process of adaptive reuse for the city's artist community, this stolid **Romanesque Revival** building was built when "Battle Ax" **Gleason** was mayor of **Long Island City.** It once supported a clock tower. Contrast the school's zest with the effete WPA-era post office across the way.

Warning!: In the country it's not unusual to find notices warning of underground telephone cable, and natural gas or oil pipelines. But it is disconcerting to find evidence of them under the concrete and asphalt of the inner city. To wit: warning disks on lampposts throughout the Hunters Point area suggest that you not cut a hole in the pavement without first calling a special telephone number. Tread lightly!

[W 26a.] Engine Company 258, Ladder Company 115, N.Y.C. Fire Department, 10-40 47th Ave. (one-way west), bet. Vernon Blvd. and 11th St. S side. 1903. Bradford L. Gilbert.

A **robust multistory firehouse** with stepped super-Dutch gable. Gilbert was a nationally recognized railroad architect.

[W 26b.] St. Mary's Roman Catholic Church, 49-01 Vernon Blvd., SE cor. 49th Ave. 1887. P. C. Keely.

A painted brick church, its steeple an (unofficial) local landmark. As the area gentrified, **the color of the church changed** from working-class red (like the brick at 48-20 across the boulevard) and became closer to the muted color of a Yuppie's suit.

[W 26c.] 108th Precinct, N.Y.C. Police Department/originally **75th Precinct,** 5-47 50th Ave. (one-way east), bet. 5th St. and Vernon Blvd. N side. 1903. R. Thomas Short.

Like the nearby firehouse, this offers an exquisite municipal presence, particularly the **extravagant torchères** that frame the entrance. Short is better known as partner in Harde & Short.

[W 26a.] Engine Co. 258, Ladder Co. 115, N.Y.F.D.: a grand stepped gable

[W 27a.] Port Distributing Corp. bldg.

[W 30b.] St. Raphael's RC Church

The Steinway Tunnels: The twin tubes of the Flushing Line under the East River were originally begun in 1892 by piano king William Steinway as a trolley car connection to Manhattan. A serious explosion, the Panic of 1893, and Steinway's death in 1896 interrupted the project until August Belmont, the IRT financier, revived it in 1902. The tunnel, with reversing loops at each end, became the first connection between Manhattan and Queens in 1907, though it was not put into regular use until converted to subway operation in 1915.

[W 27a.] Port Distributing Corporation, 55-01 2nd St., SE cor. 55th Ave. 1986. David Bilow.

Extremely sophisticated architectural modeling, particularly for this confused industrial enclave. **Hurrah!** (This is where the city's bottled beers emerge: Amstel Light, Budweiser, Michelob, Heineken . . .)

[W 27b.] Formerly **New York Daily News printing plant,** 55-02 2nd St., SW cor. 55th Ave. at Newtown Creek. 1972. Harrison & Abramovitz.

A dated gray ghost on what for a while was called **News Point.** It occupies the former site, until World War II, of the **National Sugar Refining Company,** manufacturers of **Jack Frost sugar.** Slated for demolition as part of an area wide redevelopment by the Port Authority.

[W 27c.] Norval Concrete Corporation storage silos, 2nd St. opp. 54th Ave. W side. 1964–1969.

Eight slip-formed concrete silos whose major function seems to be a giant signboard (on the Manhattan-facing surfaces) for the first name of one of our coauthors.

[W 28a.] Prudenti's Vicino Mare (restaurant)/originally **Hunters Point Branch, Queens County Savings Bank,** 51-02 2nd St., NW cor. Borden Ave. ca. 1895.

A coat of **battleship gray paint** camouflages a robust Romanesque Revival branch bank.

[W 28b.] Queens Ventilating Building, Queens Midtown Tunnel, center of Borden Ave., bet. 2nd and 5th Sts. 1939.

A larger-than-life structure whose utilitarian purpose is obscured by its architecture.

[W 28c.] Originally **Pennsylvania Railroad generating plant/**later N.Y. & Queens Electric Light & Power Company, 2nd St. bet. 50th and 51st Aves. E side. 1909. McKim, Mead & White.

This brick **Renaissance Revival** plant bears 4 great stacks, rampant on the **Queens** skyline. Note the Renaissance window guards in its granite base. Occupants include assorted manufacturing establishments and indoor tennis courts.

[W 28d.] Pepsi-Cola sign, Pepsi-Cola Bottling Company, 45-00 5th St. (one-way south), bet. 46th Ave. and 46th Rd. W side. Riverfront buildings, 1910–1920. Sign, 1936, Artkraft Sign Co.

The upland side of this great sign hardly compares with the **colossal neon-lighted front** along the East River opposite the UN and Beekman Place. But without the building's staunch support how would Manhattan residents be able to see the sign and feel the thirst?

[W 29.] Con Ed Skills Testing & Devel./Overhead Line Constr. Training Center

[W 29.] Consolidated Edison Skills Testing and Development/Overhead Line Construction Training Center, 43-82 Vernon Blvd., bet. 43rd Rd. and 44th Ave. W side. ca. 1975.

A forest of telephone poles, transformers, and wire. Why here, overlooking Manhattan's skyline? Why not? Installation techniques have to be learned somewhere. (A lesson in **land banking.**)

44th Drive: This unusually wide thoroughfare leading to nowhere is the footprint for the louvered IND subway tunnel below, whose tube to East 53rd Street in Manhattan begins under your feet. Both flanks of the Drive are host to a miscellany of municipal activities, including a subway ventilator dating from 1931. The Water's Edge restaurant, at the end, is a licensee of the adjacent N.Y.C. Department of Ports, International Trade & Commerce, which just happened to have jurisdiction over the water rights.

BLISSVILLE

[W 30a.] N.Y.C. Fire Department Repair and Transportation Unit, 48-58 35th St. (one-way north), NW cor. Hunters Point Ave., to 34th St. ca. 1935.

A tall radio-transmission tower and the series of exposed roof ribs identify this **barrel-vaulted** municipal garage where the city's fire trucks go for repairs—or to die. Once part of the city's fire college.

[W 30b.] St. Raphael's Roman Catholic Church, 35-20 Greenpoint Ave., SW cor. Hunters Point Ave. 1885.

A **lonely church** perched at the top of a hill astride the Long Island Expressway and across from Calvary Cemetery, its steeple visible from great distances.

[W 31a.] City View Motor Inn/originally **Public School 80, Queens,** 33-17 Greenpoint Ave., bet. Gale and Bradley Aves., off Borden Ave. 1905. Altered, 1986.

This former elementary school, now cleaned and reworked (with characterless bronze-colored aluminum windows), shares the **barren Blissville hill** with St. Raphael's and Calvary's gatehouse.

[W 31b.] Gatehouse, Old Calvary Cemetery (Roman Catholic), Greenpoint Ave. entrance opp. Gale Ave., off Borden Ave. S side. 1892.

A romantic, vernacular, **spectacular Queen Anne gem.** Others of its genre have almost all been confiscated by time. (By 1916, this first part of the accretive 4-section cemetery, had received 1,170,455 interments!)

[W 32.] Chapel, Old Calvary Cemetery (Roman Catholic), Laurel Hill Boulevard (formerly Penny Bridge). Entrance at Review Ave. N of Laurel Hill Blvd. ca. 1895.

A squat set of limestone beehives with Spanish tile roofs, surrounded by huddled small Roman temple-mausoleums.

On axis with the chapel (cemetery section 3b) is the **Halloran Mausoleum.** An example of Victorian neo-Grecian: Philadelphia's **Frank Furness** and Berlin's **Karl Schinkel** could have been in partnership for this.

The **Johnston Mausoleum,** a small domed neo-Baroque "chapel," crowns a hill 1,000 feet away.

Cemetery within a cemetery: When the Roman Catholic Diocese of New York purchased the first lands for Calvary, in 1846, from the Alsop family, the deal depended upon the diocese permitting the existing Alsop Burying Ground to remain—which it still does—241 feet from the old Penny Bridge Entrance. It contains 34 monuments dating from 1743 to 1889.

SUNNYSIDE

A residential area triggered by the arrival of the **IRT Flushing Line** along **Queens Boulevard** and **Roosevelt Avenue** in **1917.** Though surrounded by industry and cemeteries, its proximity and excellent access to **Manhattan** have assured its stability. Its most noted feature is **Sunnyside Gardens.**

[W 33.] Celtic Park Apartments, 48th Ave. bet. 42nd and 44th Sts., partly to 50th Ave. 1931. 4 units bet. 42nd and 43rd Sts., Ernest Flagg. 8 units bet. 43rd and 44th Sts., Springsteen & Goldhammer.

Six-story **City and Suburban Homes Company** limited-dividend developments entered through beautifully ornamented archways that lead to verdant central courtyards. Built on the site of Celtic Park, the former home of the **Irish-American Athletic Club.** (The name of the adjacent one-block diagonal Celtic Avenue—originally Bowery Bay Road—recalls the earlier use.)

[W 34a.] Sunnyside Gardens, bet. 43rd and 48th Sts., Skillman and Barnett Aves. to 39th Ave., plus parts of 49th and 50th Sts. along Skillman Ave. 1924–1928. Clarence S. Stein and Henry Wright. Frederick Ackerman.

Seventy-seven acres of barren, mosquito-infested land were transformed into a great and successful experiment in urban housing design by the **City Housing Corporation,** headed by Alexander M. Bing, a New York real estate mogul. Forced into using the preordained street grid, architects Stein and Wright arranged row housing to face both the street and the interior garden spaces. *Walk under umbrellas of London plane trees along the paths that penetrate each block,* an urban delight, where the architecture is unimportant—even insipid—but the urban arrangements a source of great community delight.

[W 34b.] Formerly **Naarden-UOP Fragrances (factory)/**originally **Knickerbocker Laundry Company,** 43-23 37th Ave., bet. 43rd and 48th Sts. N side. 1932. Irving M. Fenichel.

Art Moderne concrete, seemingly molded of **streamlined ice cream.** Difficult to find if you're walking or driving but a familiar monument to the hundreds of thousands of daily commuters who speed by on the adjacent LIRR into Manhattan. (Contrast this ebullient work with the dour municipal facility to the east, marked **N.Y.C. Water Supply Distribution, First Ward Station,** built in Mayor Jimmy Walker's time, in 1931.)

[W 34c.] Phipps Gardens (apartments), 51-01 39th Ave., bet. 50th and 52nd Sts. N side. 1931. 52-02 to 53-20 Barnett Ave., bet. 50th and 52nd Sts. S side. 1935. Isador Rosenfeld, office of Clarence S. Stein.

A 4-, 5-, and 6-story architectural incunabulum surrounding a 2-square-block lush, green, private, center-courted world. The architecture here is clearly secondary to **a sense of place.** (Also, there's a second grouping *behind* the first.)

WOODSIDE

Just across the former Long Island City boundary.

[W 34d.] J. Sklar Manufacturing Company/formerly **Lathan Lithography Company,** 38-04 Woodside Ave., bet. Barnett and 39th Aves. W side. 1923. McDonnell and Pearl.

A **Tudor** campus set on manicured lawns disguises this manufactory of surgical instruments. For once a factory becomes a visual amenity in the community.

[W 35.] Originally **New York & Queens County Railroad Company (trolley barn)/**now **gateway to shopping center,** Northern Blvd. SE cor. Woodside Ave. ca. 1895. Altered, 1988.

With the electrification of the **Steinway Railway Company's streetcar system,** a trolley barn was built on this site, which was taken over in 1896 by a Philadelphia syndicate that renamed the operation NY&QCR. The structure endured a number of reuses until the spring of 1987, when much of it was **demolished in favor of a shopping center.** Neighborhood preservation stalwarts prevailed in a last-ditch effort to keep the wrecking ball from completing its task.

[W 36a.] Mathews & Company flats, 52nd St. E side, 53rd St. both sides, 54th St. W side, bet. Skillman and Roosevelt Aves. 52-01 to 53-31 Skillman Ave., bet. 52nd and 54th Sts. N side. 1924. **[W 36b.] Mathews Apartment Building,** 51-45 52nd St., NE cor. Roosevelt Ave. 1924.

Three-story row house apartments, and a single, corner apartment house, all of **yellow Kreischerville (Staten Island) brick,** by developers who helped make early 20th-century Ridgewood a special place. [See ff. C Queens C 37.]

[W 35.] Orig. N.Y. & Queens County Railroad Co. trolley barn (1966 photo)

[W 37.] St. Paul's Episcopal Church of Woodside, 39th Ave. SW cor. 61st St. ca. 1873.

An exquisitely rare, rural, board-and-batten Gothic Revival wooden church. Let there be a miracle: save this church as a living memorial to its motto, CITY CHURCH/COUNTRY FRIENDLINESS.

[W 38a.] Queens Landmark Condominiums/originally **Bulova Watch factory,** 62-10 Woodside Ave., bet. 62nd and 63rd Sts. S side. 1926. Altered, 1985, Ralph Wuest.

Arde Bulova's high-rise watch factory with its prominent clock tower, for decades a **special event in the ho-hum Queenscape** to riders on the LIRR and the Flushing Line, was externally defaced in 1985, its tower removed—and all for the sake of condos. Then the developers had the *chutzpah* to name it Landmark, to help with the sales.

[W 38b.] Bulova School of Watchmaking, 40-24 62nd St. E side. **[W 38c.] Arde Bulova Dormitory,** 40-25 61st St., bet. Woodside and 43rd Aves. W side. 1958.

The Bulova Woodside empire remains only in this small midblock educational compound, appearing like **neo-Georgian dollhouses.**

Ⓒ

CENTRAL QUEENS

NORTH BEACH • JACKSON HEIGHTS • CORONA
FLUSHING MEADOWS-CORONA PARK • ELMHURST
REGO PARK • MASPETH • RIDGEWOOD • MIDDLE VILLAGE
GLENDALE • FOREST HILLS • KEW GARDENS

Town of Newtown/Middleburg

Settled in 1642; chartered by the Doughty Patent of 1640.

The old **Town of Newtown** encompasses present-day communities that form central Queens. Its western reaches comprise endless blocks of old frame buildings, whereas the eastern and central parts have become dense apartment districts. **Jackson Heights** developed between the two world wars, and the trunk along **Queens Boulevard** in both

Rego Park and Forest Hills branched out after World War II. Forest Hills was named (1901) by developer Cord Meyer and immortalized by Forest Hills Gardens, the magnificant town-planning/real estate scheme of the Russell Sage Foundation, to whom Meyer had sold vast land. Rego Park is named for the developing/building Rego (Real Good) Construction Company that pioneered building in that area.

The center of "New Towne," the outgrowth of Middleburg by 1665 and an English Puritan settlement under Dutch auspices, occupied the winding stretch of Broadway north of Queens Boulevard. Vestiges of the community remained well into the 20th century, but only a single church building still stands.

After consolidation with New York in 1898 the name Newtown quickly fell into disuse, and the immediate community became known as Elmhurst. Newtown pippins, grown in the apple orchards of this area were prized by the English, to whom they were exported for the manufacture of cider!

NORTH BEACH

North Beach is a community no more. But prior to World War I it was Queens County's Coney Island on the Sound, as Rockaway was the borough's resort on the ocean. North Beach was an outgrowth of the working-class resort named Bowery Bay Beach, which opened in 1887 through a joint investment of piano maker William Steinway, beer king George Ehret, and patent-medicine manufacturer Henry Cassebeer. Bad associations with the name Bowery resulted in a renaming (1891): North Beach. Located on Queens' north shore, between 81st Street and Flushing Bay, it flourished until Prohibition. The picnic grounds and dance halls, the ferris wheels and carrousels, and the promenades and the steamboat pier emptied of their summer crowds with the banning of alcohol. In 1930 the site became Glenn H. Curtiss Airfield. The City rented it in 1935 to develop what was first dubbed North Beach Airport and, in 1939, renamed LaGuardia Field.

[C 1c.] Helical ramps into the Central Parking Garage, LaGuardia Airport

[C 1.] LaGuardia Airport/originally North Beach Airport, N of Grand Central Pkwy. bet. 81st St. and 27th Ave. (Entries at 94th St. and 23rd Ave.) [C 1a.] Remaining original buildings. 1939. Delano & Aldrich. [C 1b.] New Central Terminal and Control Tower. 1965. Harrison & Abramovitz. [C 1c.] Central Garage. 1976. Staff of the Port of New York Authority. [C 2.] Marine Terminal, entry at 82nd St. and Ditmars Blvd. 1939. Delano & Aldrich. ★ Interior. ★ [C 3a.] Eastern Airlines Shuttle Terminal. 1980. Port Authority of N.Y. & N.J. Architectural Design Team. [C 3b.] Delta Airlines Terminal. 1983. Leibowitz Bodouva & Assocs.

Built for the New York World's Fair of 1939–1940 as New York's second (chronologically) municipal airport (after Floyd Bennett Field in Brooklyn). The 1965 main terminal, in a great glass arc, bears a parasol roof as a symbol of flight—no function intended for it—while the control towers wears a stylish hyperbolic shape. Within the terminal's curved embrace now rests a new garage, a weathered steel grillage accessible by helical concrete ramps (the steel weathers by rusting to a final hard purple-brown patina).

Flanking the main terminal are the old hangars of **1939** vintage (the original main building, too small for post-**World War II** traffic, was demolished) and the **Marine Terminal,** lurking on the northwestern edge of the field. Originally built to serve flying boats of the 1930s (remember the **Yankee Clipper?**), today the **Marine Terminal,** a *fantastic* **Art Deco** extravaganza, is a short-distance shuttle facility (now without benefit of water).

[C 4.] Lexington School for the Deaf, 30th Ave. bet. 73rd and 75th Sts. N side. 1967. Pomerance & Breines.

A modern campus for deaf children.

JACKSON HEIGHTS

Beginning in 1913 on what is today 82nd Street, between Roosevelt Avenue and Northern Boulevard, a venture calling itself the **Queensboro Corporation** initiated the development of the residential community of Jackson Heights, named for **John C. Jackson,** who laid out Northern Boulevard. Elevated transit service along Roosevelt Avenue would not arrive until 1917; and the lands, called **"the cornfields of Queens,"** were still being tilled as market gardens, with some of them serving the special needs of the **Chinatown community.**

At first, the Corporation's units were rental, but after 1919 they were also marketed as cooperatives. In 1923, the choice expanded to include small **"garden apartments"** in the form of convertible single houses. Advanced design and marketing ideas were used over the many decades of construction and operation: the country's first low-rise elevators, the introduction of **dinettes** and **sun parlors** into apartment plans, and the use of the new medium of radio in the 1920s to advertise the co-ops. Because of careful management, good maintenance, and—anti-Semites may insist—the restrictive rental practices of the earliest years, this housing remains to this day very appealing and desirable. The theater on Northern Boulevard **predates talkies** and was designed by one of Broadway's most prolific theater architects.

[C 6a.] Towers Apts. in Jackson Hts.　　**[C 6b.]** Chateau Apts. in Jackson Hts.

[C 5.] Jackson Heights, lying within an irregular, diamond-shaped area between Northern Blvd. and Roosevelt Ave., from 73rd to 88th Sts. **[C 5a.] Laurel Court (apartments)** (the earliest), 33-05, 33-11, 33-15 82nd Street, SE cor. Northern Blvd. 1914. George Henry Wells. **[C 5b.]** Originally **Boulevard Theater,** 82-28 Northern Blvd., bet. 82nd and 83rd Sts. S side. 1925. Herbert J. Krapp. **[C 6a.] Towers Apartments,** 34th Ave. bet. 80th and 81st Sts. N side. 1923. Andrew J. Thomas. **[C 6b.] Chateau Apartments,** 34th Ave. bet. 80th and 81st Sts. S side. 1923. Andrew J. Thomas. **[C 6c.] Dunolly Gardens (apartments),**

78-11 35th Avenue, 78th to 79th Sts., bet. 35th and 37th Aves. 1939. Andrew J. Thomas. **[C 6d.] Graystone (apartments)**, 35-15 to 35-51, 35-16 to 35-52 80th St., bet. 35th and 37th Aves. Both sides. 1917, 1916. George Henry Wells. **[C 7a.] Fillmore Hall (apartments)**, 83-10 35th Ave., bet. 83rd and 84th Sts. S side. 1936. Joshua Tabachnik. **[C 7b.] Spanish Gardens (apartments)**, midblock only, bet. 37th and Roosevelt Aves., 83rd to 84th Sts., 1923. Andrew J. Thomas. **[C 7c.] Linden Court (apartments)**, midblock only, bet. 37th and Roosevelt Aves., 84th to 85th Sts., 1919. Andrew J. Thomas. **[C 8.] English Convertible Country Homes (from single houses into apartments)**, E of 82nd St. 1920s. Various architects, including Robert Tappan. **[C 9a.] Griswold Hall (apartments)**, 86-10 34th Ave., bet. 86th and 87th Sts. S side. 1936. Joshua Tabachnik.

A vast residential community whose livability remains high to this day, even though many avenue frontages originally intended as **end-block parks** were developed as lesser works of architecture . . . *and* of habitability.

[C 9b.] 34-19 to 34-47 90th Street, 34-20 to 34-48 91st Street (apartments), bet. 34th and 35th Aves. 1931. Henry Atterbury Smith.

Two sets of three 6-story apartments, similar to the same architect's **Shively Sanitary Apartments** on Manhattan's East 77th Street, turned diagonal to the street grid. Only the central structure of each group had an elevator; upper-floor tenants had to use roof bridges to reach adjacent buildings.

[C 9c.] 87th to 90th Streets, 30th to 31st Avenues (row housing), Both sides. ca. 1939.

Latter-day "brownstones," in the sense that these too are embellished row houses, but in a simplified French **neo-Norman** style.

[C 9d.] 115th Precinct, N.Y.C. Police Department, 92-15 Northern Blvd., bet. 92nd and 93rd Sts. N side. 1985. Gruen Assocs.

Dark brown brick and terra-cotta make an unconvincing municipal fortress. What are they afraid of? The entrance doors recall those into a castle, but the brick arch that levitates around them gives it all away: lots of bravado but short on guts.

[C 9e.] Blessed Sacrament Church complex (Roman Catholic), 35th Ave. bet. 93rd and 94th Sts. N side. Auditorium, 1933, McGill & Hamlin. Convent, 1937, Henry J. McGill. Church, 1949, Henry J. McGill. Additions.

The 1930s works are the best here, influenced by Lutyens, Dudok, and Sir Giles Gilbert Scott. The church was built a decade after being designed and lacks the great thirties' decorative art flourishes.

CORONA

A Tribute to Satchmo: An exhuberant mural to Louis Armstrong [see C 11a.] embellishes the otherwise ho-hum design of Intermediate School 227, which bears the trumpeter's name. (32-02 Junction Boulevard, SW corner 32nd Avenue.) Designer and team director, Lucinda Luvaas, of City Arts Workshop. 1981.

[C 10.] First Baptist Church of East Elmhurst, 100-05 31st Ave., NE cor. 100th St. 1961.

An **inadvertent**, proto-space-age **Hawksmoor-influenced** facade. The pure cylindrical columns, avoiding any taper or entasis, are nevertheless awkwardly sandwiched between a traditional base and capital.

[C 11a.] Formerly Louis Armstrong residence, 34-56 107th St. (one-way north), bet. 34th and 37th Aves. W side. 1910, later additions.

Satchmo's home. As sensitive as this jazz great was to music, so, it appears, was he unconcerned with the niceties of architecture (or the neighborhood context). Armstrong lived here with his wife from 1943 until his death in 1971; his wife till hers, in 1983.

[C 11b.] Shaw A.M.E. Zion Church (African Methodist Episcopal)/ originally **Northside Hebrew Congregation**, 100-05 34th Ave., bet. 100th and 101st Sts. N side. ca. 1910.

A generous pediment and 4 Ionic columns make a modest monument in the context of humility.

[C 11c.] Florence E. Smith Community Center, Corona Congregational Church, 102-19 34th Ave., bet. 102nd and 103rd Sts. N side. 1981. Medhat Abdel Salam.

Strong, simple, necessary. The strongly **planar portico** makes a dignified entry.

A trip down 104th Street:

One-way southbound.

[C 12a.] Our Lady of Sorrows Roman Catholic Church, 104-01 37th Ave., NE cor. 104th St. 1899. **Convent,** ca. 1895.

Originally built of red brick set in red mortar, this handsomely crafted church was recently painted a cream color in the hope of sprucing it up. Regrettable. **Get out the paint remover!** The robust convent, adjacent, is a welcome foil.

[C 10.] 1st Baptist Ch., E. Elmhurst   **[C 13c.]** Orig. Edward E. Sanford res.

[C 12b.] Emanuel Lutheran (Evangelical) Church, 37-53 104th St., SE cor. 37th Dr. **Rectory,** 37-57 104th St., bet. 37th Dr. and 38th Ave. W side. ca. 1910.

Church: very plain brick. Rectory: very lovely wood frame, set back deeply from the street.

[C 13a.] 104-08 Roosevelt Avenue (former residence)/now commercial offices, SE cor. 104th St. ca. 1885.

A strange but wonderful adaptive reuse: a proud freestanding house, complete with original iron fence, seemingly all **dunked in whitewash.** Now rented out to sundry commercial tenants whose gaudy signs bedeck the intact architecture. Preserve it just this way!

[C 13b.] Iglesia Metodista/originally **Corona Methodist Church,** 42-15 104th St., NE cor. 43rd Ave. ca. 1905.

Today of whitewashed rock-face block composed in an archaic style.

Along 47th Avenue:

One-way westbound.

[C 13c.] Originally **Edward E. Sanford residence,** 103-45 47th Ave., bet. 102nd and 104th Sts. N side. ca. 1871. ★

A rare, largly intact survivor of the 19th-century **village of Newtown,** a freestanding rural house whose "fancifully carved elements . . . transform a humble, domestic structure into an architectural delight," according to the Landmarks Preservation Commission designation.

Nicholas Coppola, Sr. At the headquarters of The Corona Community Ambulance Corps, at 104-38 47th Ave., between 104th and 108th Sts., one finds a humble front yard, an often used outdoor fireplace facing the street (and the community), and a large bronze marker dedicated in 1967 to the corps' founder, Mr. Coppola: A MONUMENTAL PILLAR OF COMPASSION AND BENEVOLENCE FOR HIS FELLOW MEN.

[C 13d.] Union Evangelical Church of Corona, National St. NW cor. 42nd Ave. 1873.

The ill-advised aluminum siding that now clads the church conceals much, but not the basic form, the stained glass, and—miracle of miracles—the **cast-iron cresting** atop the belfry.

[C 14a.] Hook & Ladder Company 138/Engine Company 289, N.Y.C. Fire Department, 97-28 43rd Ave., bet. 97th Place and 99th St. S side.

A fine firehouse of brick and limestone echoing French architectural influences.

[C 14b.] 97-37 43rd Avenue (residence), NW cor. 99th St. ca. 1885.

A **lovely rural holdout** standing free in what has, over a century, become a densely built-up place. Too bad about the new "stylish" veneers that its owners have added.

[C 14c.] Former **Tiffany & Company (factory),** 97th Place bet. 43rd and 44th Aves., N of LIRR. W side. ca. 1885.

While Tiffany Studios sold its handcrafted merchandise from a Madison Avenue address, much of the work was done in this **dowdy industrial building** alongside the Port Washington Branch of the LIRR. Sharp eyes will still discern the faded old painted TIFFANY signs on the 44th Avenue and 97th Place facades (placed there to be read by commuters from Long Island's north shore).

FLUSHING MEADOWS-CORONA PARK

"This is a valley of ashes . . ." In *The Great Gatsby,* F. Scott Fitzgerald wrote of the Corona Dumps, the landfilled marshes that once straddled the Flushing River, navigational facility to the Village of Flushing. The Dumps, worked by the old Brooklyn Ash Company, achieved park status when selected as the site for the 1939–1940 New York World's Fair, with a repeat performance in 1964–1965. Remnants of both remain in Flushing Meadows-Corona Park. A sense of the area that Fitzgerald captured can still be glimpsed, metaphorically at least, in the junkyards east of Shea Stadium's parking lot.

[C 15.] Shea Stadium, bet. Northern Blvd. and Roosevelt Ave., Grand Central Pkwy. to 126th St. 1964. Praeger-Kavanaugh-Waterbury.

The simplicity and sheer bulk of this home for the **Mets** dominate the flat landscape for miles. The original **arbitrary exterior appliqué** of pastel panels (the "wire basket in a windstorm" look) gave way the year after the team's 1986 World Series victory to the equally inspired "douse everything with Mets blue" look. Piercing!

[C 16.] U.S.T.A. National Tennis Center/originally **Singer Bowl, 1964–1965 World's Fair,** Roosevelt Ave. opp. Willets Point Blvd. S side. 1964. Tennis center, 1978, David Kenneth Specter & Assocs. Village Market, 1983, David Kenneth Specter & Assocs., architects. Schnadelbach Partnership, landscape architects.

A slick, snappy, substitute for the **West Side Tennis Club's** beloved but undersized stadium at Forest Hills (extant), resulting from TV's promotion of tennis into a really **big-time spectator sport.** Except for its silhouette, it is difficult to see from Roosevelt Avenue. Better, wait for the **U.S. Open** on the tube.

[C 17.] The Unisphere, 1964–1965 World's Fair. 1964. Peter Muller-Munk, Inc., designer. Bradford Clarke, landscape architect.

A 380-ton, stainless-steel spherical grid representing the earth (together with orbiting satellites), 12 stories tall, perched on a 70-ton, 20-foot-high weathered-steel base. Weighty.

[C 18.] New York Hall of Science, Flushing Meadows-Corona Park at 111th St. opp. 48th Ave. 1964. Harrison & Abramovitz. **Open to the public.**

An undulating tapestry of stained glass set in precast concrete panels, flashy but ill-suited for museum use. It adjoins its own space park, an array of secondhand American spacecraft. Efforts to expand the facility by adding a large, useful wing have not succeeded.

A panorama of New York City: An impressive model of the whole of the city—835,000 buildings—plus streets, rivers, bridges, piers, and airports—is on view at the **Queens Museum** in the old 1939–1940 World Fair's **New York City Building.** Well worth a special visit. An elevated platform offers an airliner's view of the enormous diorama, updated regularly since built for the 1964–1965 World's Fair. The rest of the museum is also a treat. **Open to the public.**

[C 19.] New York State Pavilion, 1964–1965 World's Fair, Flushing Meadows-Corona Park. 1964. Philip Johnson and Richard Foster, architects. Lev Zetlin, structural engineer.

One of the few pavilions of **1964** that attempted to use fresh technology as a generator of form. In this case **tubular perimeter columns** (as well as those supporting the observation deck) were **slip-formed** of concrete in a continuous casting operation which proceeded vertically. The roof, originally sheathed in translucent colored plastic, is a double diaphragm of radial cables separated by vertical pencil rods to dampen flutter. Together with the **Spanish Pavilion** (now reerected in **St. Louis!**) it was an architectural star of the fair: a happy park building working with park space.

[C 19.] NYS Pavilion, '64 World's Fair   **[C 21a.]** Newtown High School bldg.

[C 20.] N.Y. S. Marine Amphitheater/originally **Billy Rose's Aquacade, 1939–1940 World's Fair.** 1939. Sloan & Robertson.

"See Johnny Weissmuller, Eleanor Holm. 4 shows daily. 10,000 seats. Admission 40¢ to 99¢."

ELMHURST

[C 21a.] Newtown High School, 48-01 90th St., bet. 48th and 50th Aves. to 91st St. E side. 1897. C. B. J. Snyder.

A character-filled edifice that sums up in its silhouette and charming ornamental touches the **florid style** found in northern European civic structures of the Baroque period.

[C 21b.] Reformed Dutch Church of Newtown, and **Fellowship Hall,** 85-15 Broadway, SE cor. Corona Ave. **Church,** 1831. **Hall,** 1858. ★

Georgian-Greek Revival in white clapboard, wearing **Tuscan** columns. The stained glass is **Victorian.**

[C 21c.] St. James Parish Hall/originally **St. James Episcopal Church,** Broadway SW cor. 51st Ave. 1734.

Carpenter Gothic additions updated this, the original **St. James,** built on land granted by the town. The steeple on the west end of this somber Colonial relic was removed at the turn of the century. A new **St. James** at the northeast corner of **Broadway** and **Corona Avenue** was built in **1849:** now burned. Its replacement is no match for its predecessor's quality.

[C 22a.] James Rudel Center, LaGuardia Medical Group, H.I.P. of Greater New York/originally **Queens Boulevard Medical Building,** 86-15 Queens Blvd., bet. Broadway and 55th Ave. N side. 1957. Abraham Geller & Assocs.

This medical building sits atop the **IND subway tunnel,** thus requiring heating and air-conditioning equipment normally placed in a basement to be on the roof. The splendid resulting form, **a sophisticated cubist construction,** bears good materials and detailing. It *suffers* from poor maintenance and ugly signs. A cemetery, to its east, was a welcome forelawn until some enterprising exploiter bought the space, moved the bodies, and built a **gross** 6-story apartment house.

[C 22a.] James Rudel Center in 1957 w/ cemetery and municipal courthouse

[C 21b.] Ref. Dutch Church, Newtown   **[C 23b.]** Newtown First Presb. Manse

[C 22b.] Macy's Queens, 88-01 Queens Blvd., bet. 55th and 56th Aves. N side. 1965. Skidmore, Owings & Merrill.

Take a difficult site, consider that a department store requires exterior walls only as enclosure, calculate the parking problem, add the **SOM** touch, and you get **Macy's Queens,** a circular department store girded by a concentric parking garage. What could be more logical?

Luckily, a recalcitrant property owner refused to part with the southwest parcel, forcing a notch to be cut into the squat cylinder of precast concrete panels; a welcome punctuation. The owner died in the early 1980s, and the intruding house was demolished in favor of a modern mediocrity.

[C 22c.] Citibank, Elmhurst Branch/originally **First National City Bank,** 87-11 Queens Blvd. (next to Macy's). 1966. Skidmore, Owings & Merrill.

A considerably **smaller cylinder** than Macy's, by the same architects, but this time in bronzed aluminum and glass. Apparently, circles were briefly in fashion.

[C 22d.] Jamaica Savings Bank, 89-01 Queens Blvd., NE cor. 56th Ave. 1968. William Cann.

A **showy form** (hyperbolic paraboloid) more concerned with advertising than useful space. Too tiny for such a spirited form.

[C 23a.] First Presbyterian Church of Elmhurst/originally **First Presbyterian Church of Newtown,** Queens Blvd. SE cor. 54th Ave. 1893. **[C 23b.] Manse,** 54-03 Seabury St., NE cor 54th Ave. **[C 23c.] Sunday School,** 54-05 Seabury St., bet. 54th and 55th Aves. ca. 1925.

The church, on a prominent Queens Boulevard corner, is a **sober rock-faced granite composition** with an 85-foot tower and brownstone trim. The manse behind it, however, is a **domestic delight** of Shingle Style architecture, currently displaying stylish olive-green garb.

[C 24.] St. John's Queens Hospital, Division of Catholic Medical Center of Brooklyn & Queens, 90-02 Queens Blvd., bet 57th Ave. and Woodhaven Blvd. S side. 1950–1963. Queens Blvd. wing, 1981. Ferrenz & Taylor.

A Modern dignified presence on frenetic, heavily trafficked Queens Boulevard.

[C 25.] Queens Center (shopping mall), Queens Blvd. NE cor. 59th Ave. 1973. Gruen Assocs.

A sparkling 3-story space within is clad in glazed brick and metal panels: a *modernistic* reprise to the 1930s. The concrete garage behind is no-nonsense. Branches of **Steinbach's** (once Ohrbach's), **A & S** (Brooklyn's Bloomingdale's), and **Herman's** ("discount" sporting goods) dominate.

[C 26.] Lefrak City (apartment complex), Junction Blvd. to 99th St., 57th Ave. to Long Island Expwy. **[C 26.]** 1962–1967. Jack Brown.

Hardly a city, it is *red brick forever.* The rental sign, pitched to the **sluggish suburban traffic** on the expressway, once read, IF YOU LIVED IN LEFRAK CITY YOU'D BE HOME BY NOW.

All by itself:

[C 27.] Mathews Company row housing, in the triangle formed by the embankments of the LIRR Main Line, the former New York Connecting Railway, N of Grand Ave., along Calamus and Ankener Aves., Elk Rd., and 82nd St. ca. 1930. Louis Allmendinger.

A very unusual group of " 'tween the wars" low-rise housing, built of the same yellow and brown Kreischerville brick that vast stretches of Ridgewood and Astoria used in the period before World War I. But here, the forms are knockoffs of what was then the *dernier cri* in European housing architecture: casement windows, three-dimensional brick patterns, ocean liner railings, boxy undecorated forms. **Absolutely unique!**

REGO PARK

[C 28a.] AT&T, Rego Park Communications Center, Queens Blvd. bet. 62nd Ave. and 62nd Dr. N side. 1976. Kahn & Jacobs.

A bold, monumental brick mass set on a battered granite base. **Telephone equipment in fancy dress.**

[C 28b.] Alexander's Rego Park, Queens Blvd. NW cor. 63rd Rd. 1959. Addition, 1967. Both by Francis X. Giná & Assocs.

The first of the branch department stores to invade this part of **Queens.** Vermilion glazed brick.

[C 29.] Walden Terrace (apartment complex), 98th to 99th Sts., bet. 63rd Dr. and 64th Rd. 1948. Leo Stillman.

Almost 2 full blocks of 8-story apartment structures whose exposed concrete frames gave them a **precocious Continental look** when they were erected right after World War II. The long, narrow, midblock courtyards are a green treat.

[C 28a.] AT&T Communications Cent.   **[C 34d.]** Church of the Transfiguration

[C 30.] Max and Dorothy Cohn High School, 66-35 108th St., bet. 66th Rd. and 67th Ave. E side. 1971. William N. Breger Assocs.

Stylish brown brick forms, with artfully composed openings. A private religious school.

MASPETH

[C 31a.] Maspeth Branch, The Bank of New York/originally **Branch, Long Island Trust Company,** 54-12 48th St., bet. 54th Rd. and 54th Ave. W side. ca. 1985.

A sophisticated modern banking temple in an area of industrial slurb.

[C 31b.] United Parcel Service Distribution Center, 56th Rd. bet. 44th and 48th Sts. N side. 1967. Francisco & Jacobus.

Superscaled distribution by conveyor belts dictated the fingered form of this pink-mansarded complex.

[C 32a.] St. Saviour's Church (Episcopal), Rust St. bet. 57th Rd. and 57th Dr., to 58th St. 1848. Richard Upjohn. Fire damaged, 1970. **[C 32b.] Parish Hall,** and **Rectory.**

In this primarily industrialized section of Maspeth, paralleling Newtown Creek, is this full block of **sycamore protoforest** surrounding an **ecclesiastical compound.** The structures themselves are a paradise of gray asphalt siding. The original church was severely damaged in a fire just before Christmas in 1970.

[C 33.] 59-37 55th Street (residence), bet. Flushing and Grand Aves. E side, N of LIRR. *(55th St. one-way south.)*

The wood-clapboard frame house, together with the railroad-crossing gate, makes an unusual vignette from the past.

[C 34a.] St. Stanislaus Kostka Roman Catholic Church, 57-01 61st St., SE cor. Maspeth Ave. 1913.

A neo-Romanesque structure turned diagonally to the intersection. Note the inset decorative bricks, **gilded and polychromed,** that subtly embellish the exterior walls.

 [C 34b.] Holy Cross Roman Catholic Church, 61-21 56th Rd., bet. 61st and 64th Sts. N side. 1913.

The voluptuous curvilinear verdigris copper steeple makes this church special. Serves the **local Polish community.**

[C 34c.] Polish-American National Hall, 61-60 56th Rd., bet. 61st and 64th Sts. S side. 1934.

The plaque reads POLSKI DOM NARODOWY, which sounds more exotic than its translation, Polish National Home.

[C 34d.] Church of the Transfiguration (Roman Catholic), Rear, 64-10 Clinton Ave., bet. 64th St. and Remsen Place. S side. Front, 64-21 Perry Ave. E of 64th St. N side. 1962.

The Clinton Avenue facade has hints of 1930s Art Moderne ecclesiastical design; the Perry Avenue front is a kind of **A-frame Modern.** The **prickly detail** of the skylight along the continuous roof peak unite the two. The inscription MANO NAMAI MALDOS NAMAI (My house is a house of prayer) reveals this to be **a Lithuanian congregation.**

[C 34e.] Replica, Lithuanian roadside shrine, in front of 64-25 Perry St. 1981. N side. Arthur Nelson, designer and builder.

An exquisitely fashioned work of the master carpenter's traditional art/craft, contributed by the **Knights of Lithuania, Council 110.**

 [C 35.] Maspeth United Methodist Church/also **United Methodist Korean Church of Central Queens,** 66-39 58th Ave., bet. 66th St. and Brown Place. N side. 1907.

A Gothic Revival country church, now unfortunately clad in wide white bogus clapboard.

[C 36a.] Maspeth Town Hall, Inc./originally **Public School 73, Queens/** formerly **112th Precinct, N.Y.C. Police Department,** 53-35 72nd St., bet. 53rd Rd. and Grand Ave. E side. *(72nd St. one-way south.)* 1897.

The people saved this one. A municipal building from the time before Queens was even part of the city: of wood frame, covered in wood clapboard siding, with large windows so that schoolchildren would have plenty of light. It has given the community lots of service and, like grown children taking care of their aging parents, its neighbors have taken to caring for this building in *its* later years. (It's the town hall spiritually, not officially.)

[C 36b.] Elmhurst gas tanks, Brooklyn Union Gas Company, bet. Grand and 57th Aves. S of 79th and 80th Sts. E side.

Judging from their frequent mention by **helicopter traffic spotters,** the Elmhurst tanks' most important function is to direct traffic into LaGuardia Airport. Take them away and planes will get lost.

Surprisingly, the grounds around these giant telescoping gas containers are immaculately landscaped and very well maintained.

RIDGEWOOD

Ridgewood developed at and after the turn of the century into a dense, low-rise residential community as the growing German-immigrant population of adjacent Bushwick, in Brooklyn, relocated. Electric streetcars came in 1894 and the Myrtle Avenue Line, in 1906 (the elevated part extended in 1915). Many local families had members who worked across the county border in the numerous breweries bearing German names.

 [C 37.] The Adrian Onderdonck House, 1820 Flushing Ave., bet. Cypress and Onderdonck Aves. S side. 1731.

Once a burned and mutilated hulk and the only remnant of the group of **"Dutch" Colonial** farmhouses in this area that had withstood the onslaught of heavy industry onto their farmlands in the early part of this century. Restoration was accomplished by the **Greater Ridgewood Historical Society.**

The Yellow Brick Houses and Mathews Model Flats:

Between 1895 and 1920 some 5,000 working-class structures were built during **Ridgewood's housing boom.** The earlier ones were of wood frame. But beginning around 1905 the expansion of **fire limits** forced brick construction on the developers, and a veritable city of 2- and 3-story yellow-brick row houses, tenements, and flats emerged.

One of the area's best-known builders was **Gustave X. Mathews** who, with his architect Louis Allmendinger, developed the **Mathews Model Flats,** considered so advanced in their planning that the City's **Tenement House Department** exhibited them at the **1915 Panama-Pacific Exposition,** in San Francisco.

The idiosyncratic yellow brick employed by three of the area's most prolific architects, Louis Berger & Company, Louis Allmendinger, and Charles Infanger, was speckled (or *iron-spot*) brick made in the kilns of the **Kreischer Brick Manufacturing Company** in what was then Kreischerville (now renamed Charleston), Staten Island. [See Staten Island S 19c., 20.]

Thousands of row houses built of yellow brick line the streets of Ridgewood

Block after golden block of **these happy abodes remain,** some of the best, urbanistically speaking, being the setback Mathews Company rows along Bleecker and Menahan Streets, north of Cypress Avenue, across from Public School 81, Queens. Some 60 percent of the total number are recognized in what was, in 1983, the **largest designation** made to the **National Register of Historic Places.** A few special examples:

[C 38.] Stockholm Street, between Onderdonk and Woodward Avenues. 1862 to 1868, 1870 to 1894 Stockholm Street (row houses), W side. 1867 to 1893 Stockholm Street (row houses), E side. 376, 380 Woodward Avenue (apartments), SW cor. and SE cor. Stockholm St. ca. 1905. Louis Berger & Co.

Ridgewood's own yellow brick road. Here, Kreischerville brick not only clads the matching rows of narrow houses, **peeking from behind their white-columned piazzas,** but also makes up the street bed, which rises gently to meet the green ether of **Linden Hill Cemetery.**

[C 39a.] Roman Catholic Church of St. Aloysius, and **Rectory,** 382 Onderdonk Ave., SE cor. Stockholm St. 1907, 1917. Francis J. Berlenbach. **[C 39b.] St. Aloysius Convent,** 1817 Stanhope St. ca. 1893.

Six 5-globed cast-iron lampposts guard this neo-Renaissance church, with its **165-foot twin towers,** and the adjacent stuccoed rectory. But the true gem is the convent around the corner, *despite* its cladding in green hexagonal composition shingles. When this parish began, the area was called **Old Germania Heights.**

[C 40a.] 1912-1936 Grove Street (row apartments), bet. Woodward and Fairview Aves. E side. **[C 40b.] 11A, 15, 17 St. John's Road (row apartments)** bet. Grove and Menahan Sts. N side. 1908–1910. Louis Berger.

While many of Ridgewood's houses set off the yellow masonry with gray limestone trim, not all keystones bear carved human faces, as these groups do.

Sammet's Restaurant, 651 Onderdonk Ave. NE cor. Linden St.

Middle European cooking in a longtime neighborhood establishment.

[C 41a.] 63-41 Forest Avenue (residence), bet. Grove and Menehan Sts. N side.

Freestanding frame house with asphalt shingles.

[C 41b.] Formerly **J & C Platz, Inc. (store),** 65-25 Forest Ave., NW cor. Gates Ave.

Look carefully behind the roll-down security shutters: A hardware and paint store whose wooden fixtures take one back at least 75 years: oiled floors, pressed-metal ceilings, a gold leaf sign lovingly applied to the glass transom. **Call a Hollywood set decorator, quick!**

[C 41c.] 59-11 Gates Avenue (residence), bet. Forest Ave. and 60th Place. ca. 1880.

A wood-frame holdout with carefully carved modillions.

[C 39b.] St. Aloysius Church Convent   **[C 41d.]** 66-45 Forest Avenue house

[C 41d.] 66-45 Forest Avenue (row house), bet. Gates and Palmetto Sts. N side. ca. 1885. ★

Miraculous that this clapboard frame house has survived **largely intact** (meaning: it has not been entirely reclad with composition, asphalt, asbestos, aluminum, vinyl, Perma Stone, stucco, or "face" brick!) from the earliest days of Ridgewood's urbanization, before the **stringent fire laws** of the nearby **City of Brooklyn** dictated the use of masonry for densely spaced housing like this.

A group of bronze bells graces the lawn to the east of Trinity Reformed Church, at 60th Place and Palmetto St., a 1926 addition to this neighborhood. The bells themselves, however, are older, a present from congregant J.B. of the German Evangelical St. Peters Church, Brooklyn, Eastern District. They were cast in 1880 by the Buckeye Bell Foundry: RUFE DAS VOLK ZUM LOBE DES HERRN (I call the people to praise the Lord).

[C 42.] 66–75 Forest Avenue (originally **residence**)/now **knitting mill,** NW cor. Putnam Ave. 1906. Louis Berger & Co.

A generous—perhaps even pompous—porched mansion occupying a prominent corner site, today relegated to adaptive reuse as **a knitting mill,** a common "cottage industry" in modern-day Ridgewood.

Movie Set: To find a location to film Neil Simon's *Brighton Beach Memoirs* (1986), Hollywood came to the NW corner of Seneca Avenue and Palmetto Street, where the Metropolitan Avenue el structure and adjacent early 1900s buildings permitted the reincarnation of Brooklyn's BMT Brighton Beach elevated of an earlier day. With the right light it is possible to read the set decorator's addition to the outside of the station mezzanine: RIDE THE OPEN AIR ELEVATED.

[C 42.] 66-75 Forest Ave. factory

[C 51a.] F. MacMonnies' *Civic Virtue*

[C 43a.] St. Matthias Roman Catholic Church, 58-25 Catalpa Ave., bet. Onderdonk and Woodward Aves. N side. 1926. **[43b, c.] Parish Hall, Rectory,** 1909. Francis J. Berlenbach.

A yellow-brick ecclesiastical ensemble. In its earlier years, the church published postcards that located it **across the nearby Brooklyn border,** no doubt the fulfillment of a wish by either the parish or the printer (or both).

Yugoslav bakery, 68-64 Forest Ave., bet. Catalpa and 69th Aves. W side.

Yet another ethnic group enriching this multiethnic neighborhood, as well as the whole city. **Come early on Saturday or Sunday;** the bread and pastry move quickly.

MIDDLE VILLAGE

[C 44.] Gatehouse, Mt. Olivet Cemetery, Eliot Ave. NE cor. Mt. Olivet Crescent. ca. 1910.

The cemetery guarded by this picturesque gatehouse has not only originally interred remains but also the contents of other, discontinued burial places. For example, the remains from the vaults of the **Bedford Street Methodist Episcopal Church,** in Manhattan, were transferred here in November 1913; the remains from the **Hallet Family Cemetery** in April and May 1905.

[C 45.] Fresh Pond Crematory/originally **United States Columbaria Company,** 61-40 Mt. Olivet Crescent, NW cor. 62nd Ave. 1901. Otto L. Spannhake. South addition, 1929. Chapel, 1937.

A pompous pale brick and limestone crematory sited across from the **undulating landscape** of **Mt. Olivet Cemetery.** The neo-Gothic chapel to the north is actually a delightful (but recessive) composition, set back from the crescent as it is.

[C 46.] Rentar Plaza, Metropolitan Ave. at 65th Lane. S side. 1974. Robert E. Levien Partners.

An **aircraft carrier gone astray** that parks 1,200 cars on its flight deck. Glazed brown brick, rounded stair forms. One floor is equal in area to half the Empire State Building; three floors, to an entire tower of the World Trade Center.

Niederstein's Restaurant, 69-16 Metropolitan Ave., at 69th St. S side. 1854. Badly remodeled, 1974.

A roadside tavern on the road from **Greenpoint** to **Jamaica,** now architecturally destroyed by a plastic mansard roof, fake leaded windows; the *philistines* were here without knowing they were philistines. We mention it only because it had a generous history and is the only place in these parts with pretentions to the service of food.

The **Niederstein family** took over in **1888** to serve the **German** population making pilgrimages to the **Lutheran Cemetery** nearby.

GLENDALE

[C 47.] 70-12 Cypress Hills Street (residence), opp. 62nd St. W side. ca. 1860.

Compromised by time, this Italianate frame house is nevertheless important because its strong **distinctive porched form** is today a **rare event** for this neighborhood.

[C 46.] The Rentar Plaza shopping center: an aircraft carrier gone astray

[C 48.] Fourth Cemetery of the Spanish-Portuguese Synagogue, Congregation Shearith Israel, Cypress Hills St. N of Cypress Ave./Interboro Pkwy. W side. **Chapel and Gate,** 1885, Vaux & Radford. Restoration, Harmon Goldstone, 1962.

High atop a gentle rise, amid cemeteries representing many faiths, is this **small burial ground,** the latest of this Central Park West congregation whose three earlier ones are landmarks. The gate and chapel here are magnificent—though largely overlooked—works of **Calvert Vaux.**

FOREST HILLS

North of Queens Boulevard:

[C 49a.] Forest Hills South, bet. Queens Blvd. and Grand Central Pkwy. Service Rd., 76th Dr. and 78th Ave. 1941. Philip Birnbaum.

Neo-Georgian architecture surrounding and serving the real purpose and joy of this complex: a grand mall that presents a lush park to the pedestrian in the spring, in the space **113th Street** would have passed, here claimed for people. The southern view is axial with:

[C 49b.] Forest Hills Tower (offices), 118-35 Queens Blvd., NW cor. 78th Crescent. 1981. Ulrich Franzen & Assocs.

A tall, prominent and exquisitely detailed 15-story office complex, by far **the best large-scale architecture in these parts.** Yet, too tall, too prominent, too exquisitely detailed *here.*

[C 50.] The "Pretzel" Highway Intersection, Grand Central Pkwy., Union Tpke., Van Wyck Expwy., Interboro Pkwy. 1939–1964.

A highway engineer's fantasy come true. The best view is from the upper-floor windows of the Queens Borough Hall, or from a helicopter passing from Manhattan to Kennedy Airport.

[C 51a.] **Civic Virtue (statue)**, NE cor. Queens Blvd. and Union Tpke. 1922. Frederick MacMonnies, sculptor.

Once directly in front of **City Hall** in **Manhattan**, this **Nordic** male chauvinist was banished to these boondocks by popular pressure (note that the writhing women are not being stepped upon, however). **MacMonnies**, Brooklyn's great sculptor (see *The Horse Tamers* at **Prospect Park**), was in his dotage when this was carved: a sorry reprise to a brilliant career.

[C 51b.] **Queens Borough Hall**, Queens Blvd. bet. Union Tpke. and 82nd Ave. N side. 1941. William Gehron & Andrew J. Thomas.

A pompous neo-**Classical** building in red brick and limestone. Thomas was capable of much better.

South of Queens Boulevard:

THE Forest Hills, and its neighbors.

[C 52.] **Arbor Close** and **Forest Close**, from the back of Queens Blvd. storefronts to Austin St., 75th Ave. to 76th Ave. side 1925–26. Robert Tappan.

Picturesquely profiled row houses, clad in brick, slate, and half-timbering. The garden within offers privacy hedged at its edges. A charming, urbane place.

My Kitchen Bistro, Inc., 72-24 Austin St., bet. 72nd Ave. and 72nd Rd. S side.

A nice place for a bite.

[C 52.] Arbor Close and Forest Close   [C 53.] Forest Hills Gardens in 1967

[C 53.] **Forest Hills Gardens**, 71st (Continental) Ave. to Union Tpke., Long Island Railroad right-of-way to an uneven line south of Greenway South. 1913–present. Grosvenor Atterbury, architect. Frederick Law Olmsted, Jr., landscape architect.

"Apart from its convenient location, within a quarter of an hour of the center of Manhattan Island, the Forest Hills Gardens enterprise differentiates itself . . . from other suburban development schemes most notably in that its size permits a *unique layout* of winding streets, open spaces and building lots and thus permits the development of an ideally attractive neighborhood, while its financial backing is such that the realization of the well studied plans is assured in advance beyond peradventure." **Alfred Tredway White** in a promotional booklet of 1911.

White, who had pioneered in housing for the working class [see WC Brooklyn C 4a, 4b, 4c.] would not have been disappointed. This project, sponsored by the **Russell Sage Foundation,** has become one of Queens's **most exclusive residential enclaves.** It is also a splendid combination of good planning and of romantic, picturesque architecture.

[C 54.] North Forest Park Branch, Queensborough Public Library, 98-27 Metropolitan Ave., bet. 69th Rd. and 70th Ave. N side. 1975. Kaminsky & Shiffer.

Late New Brutalist in style, softened through use of a ranged, terra-cotta-colored, square brick. **Adds character** to a humdrum shopping street.

[C 53.] Forest Hills Gardens: postcard of picturesque Church in the Gardens

[C 55.] Remsen Family Cemetery, adjoining 69-43 Trotting Course Lane, NE cor. Alderton St. (N of Metropolitan Ave. *Both the Lane and Street are one-way northish.*) Mid 18th to mid 19th centuries. ★

Typical of the small private cemeteries of Long Island, of which few remain. In this one, a handful of very old tombstones cohabits with a group of more recent memorials. Cherry trees line the triangle of land. Of course, the adjacent family homesteads are long gone.

All by itself:

[C 56.] Forest Park Jewish Center, 90-45 Myrtle Ave., E of Woodhaven Blvd. N side. 1962. Expanded, 1970, Donald J. Steingisser.

Dignified gray salt-and-pepper glazed brick clads the sophisticated **acute-angle forms** that make up the street facade of this edifice. Perhaps **too "midtown" an appearance** for this Queens neighborhood.

KEW GARDENS

A community abounding in English allusions, not the least of which is its name, designed to echo—and to derive prestige from—its **London suburb namesake.** Kew Gardens was developed by a Manhattan lawyer, **Albon Platt Man** (and later by his son, **Alrick Hubbell Man**) for those who, in that placid era before World War I, were already wearying of city life and desirous of finding a garden spot only a short railroad trip from Manhattan. The Mans built some 300 houses and sold them, in the prices of those years, for between $8,000 and $20,000. Kew Gardens straddles the LIRR cut south of Forest Hills and is contained by major areas of greenery, **Forest Park** on the northwest and **Maple Grove Cemetery** on the east. The heavily trafficked Union Turnpike and Queens Boulevard mark its northern boundaries and 85th Avenue and 127th Street its southerly ones.

Murder in the night: Adjacent to the LIRR station on quiet Austin Street, near the location of the beloved Austin Book Store (now gone), is the site of the heavily publicized murder, in 1964, of Catherine (Kitty) Genovese, who was killed as 38 neighbors ignored her screams for help.

[C 57a.] Mayfair Road, bet. Park Lane South and 116th St.

The most notable residences are **Nos. 115-19** (Italian stucco with Spanish tile roof), **115-18,** and **115-27.**

[C 57b.] Grosvenor Lane, bet. Park Lane S. and 116th St.

Particularly note **No. 115-01,** at the Park Lane South corner, and **No. 115-24.**

Abingdon Rd:

[C 57c.] Kew Gardens Jewish Center Anshe Sholom, 82-52 Abingdon Rd., NW cor. 83rd Ave. 1970. Laurence Werfel.

The zeal to translate religious needs into architecture here promotes an **impassioned** but **awkward** design solution: a copper-clad enclosure for the **ark of the covenant** slashes into a corner of the dark brick sanctuary.

[C 57d.] Abingdon Road, bet. 83rd Ave. and Lefferts Blvd.

A street of wonderful freestanding homes of the early 20th century: **Nos. 83-26, 83-36, 83-42, 83-48,** and **83-66** on the Boulevard's corner: what a splashy portico!

[C 58a.] Congregation Shaare Tova (synagogue), 82-33 Lefferts Blvd., SW cor. Abingdon Rd. 1983. Richard Foster.

A very sophisticated design for the sanctuary of the **Mashhadi community,** Iranian Jews. An exercise in cubical solids and circular voids, both at top of its walls and in its skylights. Yet all out of place on Abingdon Road.

[C 58b.] 84-36, 84-40 Abingdon Road (residences), bet. Lefferts Blvd. and Brevoort St. S side. ca. 1910.

Two of the finest **Colonial Revival** single houses in these parts. Love those great porches!

[C 59a.] 82-16, 82-18, 82-20, 82-22 Beverly Road (residential grouping), bet. Onslow and Audley Places. W side. ca. 1925.

A group of charming slate-roofed homes arranged around an intimate circular commons.

[C 59b.] 80-55 Park Lane (residence), bet. 80th Rd. (Quentin St.) and Onslow Place. E side. ca. 1925.

Veddy symmetric, veddy proper!

[C 59c.] Stucco houses with Spanish tile roofs, Grenfell St., Kew Gardens

[C 59c.] Grenfell Street, bet. Quentin St. (80th Rd.) and Onslow Place. E side. ca. 1920.

Especially note **Nos. 80-57, 80-63, 80-67, 80-83.**

[C 59d.] 119-33 to 119-43 80th Road (residences), bet. Austin St. and Queens Blvd. ca. 1920.

Four homes with **red tile roofs** form a welcome enclave on a tree-shaded street whose other houses, each individually designed, are relatively bland.

[C 60a.] Kew Hall Cooperative Apartments, 83-09 Talbot St., bet. 83rd Dr. and Lefferts Blvd. ca. 1929.

An almost-block-square structure, surrounding an inner green space **so large it admits car traffic** (if you belong). The replacement in the 1980s of its original wood windows has cost it much of its original character.

[C 60b.] 84-62 Austin Street (apartments), nr. 84th Ave. W side. 1981. Peter Casini.

Unusually radical facades along the LIRR Main Line in a structure built on a leftover sliver of land.

NORTHEASTERN QUEENS

COLLEGE POINT • MALBA • WHITESTONE • BEECHHURST
FLUSHING • MURRAY HILL • BROADWAY-FLUSHING
AUBURNDALE • UTOPIA • FRESH MEADOWS • BAYSIDE

Town of Flushing/Vlissingen
Settled in 1642; chartered in 1645.

The town **Flushing** is commonly associated with the growth of religious freedom in the **New World.** Founded by **English** settlers, it received its patent from **Dutch Governor Kieft,** who stipulated in its text that the freedom of conscience of its townspeople was to be guaranteed. **Kieft's** successor, **Peter Stuyvesant,** attempted to suppress the **Quaker** sect, a number of whose adherents had settled in **Flushing. Quaker** and **non-Quaker** residents banded together against **Stuyvesant** and were successful in having the patent's stipulation recognized and observed. Among these settlers was the **Bowne** family, whose house, dating from the **17th** century, can still be seen. The old **Quaker Meeting House** of the same period also remains as a testament to this struggle for religious liberty.

COLLEGE POINT

This community is named for an ill-fated Episcopal divinity school founded in **1836** by the **Rev. William A. Muhlenberg** but never opened. Before religion found it, it was called Strattonsport, after **Eliphalet Stratton,** who had purchased the land in 1790 from the **Lawrence** family, noted early settlers. See their graveyard in **Astoria/Steinway** [see Queens W 5.] At first, **College Point** was virtually an island separated from the **Village of Flushing** by creeks and flooded marshland and connected by a route known as **College Point Causeway** (now Boulevard). Landfill and recent developments have begun to change this, but the area's isolation is still visible in the flats near the remains of Flushing Airport, once a private aircraft facility, now slated for development as an industrial park.

In the Civil War era the district became a lusty industrial community, only a few vestiges of which remain. It attracted large **German** and **Swiss** populations whose beer gardens and picnic groves were the focus of Sunday outings by German-born **Manhattanites.** Following the war the **Poppenhusen** family (Conrad was majority stockholder in the **Long Island Rail Road**) purchased large amounts of property and established an institute still bearing its name.

[N 1a.] Poppenhusen Branch, Queensborough Public Library, 121-23 14th Ave., NW cor. College Point Blvd. 1904. Heins & LaFarge.

One of many public library branches in the city funded by a gift from Andrew Carnegie. This structure is similar in style to the contemporaneous Bronx Zoo designs of its architects.

[N 1b.] Playground/Parking Area/originally site of **Public School 27, Queens,** College Point Blvd. SW cor. 14th Ave. 1988. Richard Dattner & Assocs.

Until the 1980s the site of a public school.

[N 1c.] Beech Court (residential grouping), particularly **10 Beech Court (residence),** N of 14th Ave. bet. College Point Blvd. and 121st St.

Granite entry pylons still mark this kempt and venerable oasis (behind the library) that was once the Herman Funke estate. Now the site of a handsome array of homes surrounding a grassy, treed central green, including **a rare Art Moderne intruder** of stucco, glass block, and steel casement, at **No. 10.**

[N 1d.] Originally **Boker residence/**then **College Point Clubhouse/**now **apartments,** 12-29 120th St., NE cor. Boker Court (at N end of 120th St., N of 14th Ave.)

A relic of the era when this part of College Point was a group of adjacent estates, such as **Herman Funke's,** next door. [See N1c.]

[N 2.] First Reformed Church of College Point and **Sunday School,** 14th Ave. NW cor. 119th St. 1872.

A rare NYC example of the **Eastlake style in full bloom.** One of Queens's—and New York City's—finest!

[N 2.] 1st Reformed Ch., College Pt.   **[N 5.]** Flessel's College Pt. Restrnt.

[N 3.] EDO Corporation, Governmental Systems Division, 14th Ave. bet. 110th and 112 Sts. N side. West unit, 1983. East unit, 1985. Steven B. Rabinoff & Assocs.

No accident that this is at one of College Point's many waterfront edges: EDO (the acronym of its founder, **Earl Dodge Osborn**) was formed in 1922 as **Edo Aircraft Corporation,** producers first of seaplanes and later of metal pontoons. To accommodate its diversification, EDO commissioned this sleek metallic and blue newcomer in the **"American Corporate" style.** Well designed, but truly meant for a place other than College Point.

Chilton Paint Company, at the foot of 15th Avenue, at 110th Street, with its bold painted sign facing LaGuardia Airport across the bay, was once the site of the **W. Patrick Torpedo Works,** where, prior to World War I, emissaries from foreign powers came to inspect the exotic armament produced here.

[N 4.] Poppenhusen Institute, 114-04 14th Rd., SE cor. 114th St. 1868. Mundell & Teckritz. ★

A somber **Second Empire** place painted cream and chocolate brown. It sheltered one of the nation's **earliest free kindergartens** and provided adult education courses so that local workers could better themselves. **A philanthropy of Conrad Poppenhusen.**

[N 5.] H. Flessel Restaurant/originally **Witzel's Hotel,** 14-24 119th St., NW cor. 14th Rd. ca. 1890. Later additions.

Time warp. The exterior of this accretive, village hotel-restaurant complex seems totally **untouched by time,** save for a neon sign (clearly of the 1930s) that hangs out over the corner. Founder Witzel's other enterprise was his nearby **Point View Island.** [See N 10.] Interior sports a pooltable, family dining, and great fun.

[N 6a.] St. Fidelis [of Sigmaringen, Martyr] Roman Catholic Church, 14-10 124th St., NW cor. 15th Ave. 1894.

Founded in 1856 for the 26 Catholic families then residing hereabouts. A sweet memorial (carved in German and later in English) for its founder, the **Reverend Joseph Huber,** stands next to the **handsome octagonal baptistry.** Inside, bold 1981-vintage wood sculptures hang over the altar.

[N 6b.] Pair of magnolia grandiflora trees, 124-11 15th Ave., bet. 125th and 126th Sts. N side.

Like the single specimen designated a city landmark in Brooklyn in 1970 [see WC Brooklyn Y 20.], this *pair* of **"laurel magnolias,"** native to warmer southern climes, survives in a less than accommodating climate. It is even **farther north** than its Brooklyn cousin.

[N 7a.] Originally H.A. Schleicher residence/later **Grand View Hotel** 11-41 123rd St., opp. 13th Ave. E side. 1860.

An early showplace of College Point that predates the street grid, hence its island setting. This stretch of 13th Avenue was once called **Schleicher Court,** perhaps giving rise to the neighborhood rumor that the mansion was the village *court*house. Actually, Schleicher was into **selling arms to the Confederate army.**

[N 7b.] Poppenhusen Memorial, College Point Blvd., College Place, 11th Ave. 1884.

Set in an immaculate green triangle, this modest, bronze portrait bust atop a **granite stele** marks the area of Conrad Poppenhusen's home, a mansard-roofed structure that once commanded **panoramic views** from the top of this promontory.

[N 8.] Hermon A. McNeil Park/formerly **College Point Shorefront Park/**originally **Chisholm Estate,** Poppenhusen Ave. bet. 115th St./Powell's Cove Blvd. and College Place. N side.

This was to have been the site of the ill-fated **St. Paul's College,** after which College Point is named. The founder's sister built the **1848 Chisholm mansion,** which became—in pre-air-conditioning 1937—**Mayor LaGuardia's summer city hall.** Robert Moses soon demolished it in favor of a park.

[N 9a.] 5-27 College Point Boulevard (residence), NE cor. 6th Ave.
[N 9b.] 122-07 6th Avenue (residence), bet. College Point Blvd. and 123rd St. N side. ca. 1986.

A pair of pert 2½-story brick houses with **strong silhouettes** and **thoughtful fenestration** and detailing. A rare example, in these parts, of high-quality speculative residential design.

[N 10.] Originally Tallman's Island Sewage Treatment Works, N.Y.C. Department of Public Works/now **Tallman's Island Water Pollution Control Plant, N.Y.C. Department of Environmental Protection,** Powells Cove Blvd. (extension of Lax Ave.) opp. 128th St. N side. 1939. Expanded, 1976.

A stunningly clean green oasis (despite its utilitarian purposes) studded with **Art Moderne concrete and glass-block** detail on the former site of a 19th-century amusement park, Joseph Witzel's **Point View**

Island. (The view *today* is of the Whitestone Bridge.) Another Witzel property, his nearby hotel, is extant. [See N 5.]

[N 11.] Originally **India Rubber Company**/then **Hard Rubber Comb Company**/then **I. B. Kleinert Rubber Company**/now **miscellaneous industries,** intersection of 127th St. and 20th Ave. 1889, 1921.

Industrial archaeology. Poppenhusen founded this complex of rubber-products manufactories in 1877. They later became the home of **Kleinert** dress shields and earmuffs. At their tops the buildings still bear faded signs that reveal bits of their history. *Look up!*

College Point Industrial Park:

Along the west flank of the Whitestone Expressway *(one-way south)* between 14th and 20th Avenues.

[N 11.] Old Poppenhusen rubber wks.   **[N 15b.]** Art Moderne house in Malba

[N 12.] Holy Trinity Roman Catholic Church, Whitestone Expwy. S of 14th Ave. W side. (a.k.a. 14-51 143rd St. E side.) 1986.

Lined up alongside slick structures of the industrial park is this fireproof echo of a provincial, southern European church.

[N 13a.] Octagon (office building), 17-50 Whitestone Expwy., S of 14th Ave. W side. 1984.

An 8-sided **black-on-black prism** that is more an icon for the building's name than a building.

[N 13b.] Greater New York Automobile Dealers, 18-20 Whitestone Expwy., S of 14th Ave. W side. 1986. Laurence Werfel & Assocs.

Another **minimalist geometric abstraction,** this time in stretched aluminum arranged in a quarter-round, pie-shape plan.

MALBA, WHITESTONE, BEECHHURST

The original community saw its major growth in the streets radiating from **14th** Avenue and **150th** Street. Though settled in **1645,** it took the establishment of **a tinware factory** to convert it from a rural settlement into a thriving manufacturing center. A bit of industry survives, but the area is best known for its housing resources, such as the adjacent, formerly private, community of **Malba,** west of the **Bronx-Whitestone Bridge; Beechhurst;** and the **Levitt House** development, now known as **Le Havre,** in the shadow of the **Throgs Neck Bridge:** upper-middle-income enclaves of special qualities and character.

MALBA

A small enclave, founded in 1908, of **wide, sweeping, high-crowned** residential streets that were **private** until recently. Few of the picturesque community-installed street signs remain, but the air of separateness still pervades the quiet scene.

[N 14.] 42 North Drive (residence), at 141st St. S side. ca. 1925.

Among Malba's many older houses is this Italian-influenced gem, distinguished by its **unusually dignified design** (note the inset wall tiles), **continuing care,** and **commanding site,** on a green berm where North and Center Drives meet.

[N 15a.] Malba Pier, at the end of Malba Dr. next to the Whitestone Bridge.

A **private fringe benefit** for this upper-middle-class community. The view of the bridge is melodramatic.

[N 15b.] Kempf/Ball residence, 143-08 Malba Dr., at the East River. ca. 1937.

Rounded, stuccoed concrete block in the **Art Moderne** style of the **Paris Exposition** of **1937.**

WHITESTONE

What little industry remains occupies newer, undistinguished buildings. Churches of every description today identify the community. Its older houses have largely been compromised, with only a few exceptions.

[N 16.] Formerly **Dr. George W. Fish residence,** 150-10 Powells Cove Blvd. Entrance via private drive bet. 2-15 and 2-55 149th St., N of Powells Cove Blvd. E side. ca. 1870.

A mansarded, emporched General Grant house, magnificently sited to overlook this inland sea and preserved, no doubt, because of its difficulty of access. **For an effort-filled peek,** take curving 150th Street north to its cul-de-sac end; the house is beyond the parking area fence.

[N 16.] Old Dr. G. W. Fish residence: mansarded, emporched, and well hidden

[N 17a.] Martin A. Gleason Funeral Home/formerly **residence,** 10-25 150th St., NE cor. 11th Ave. ca. 1890.

The **crucial corner** of this generous house, now seeing reuse, is a **wedding cake** of Ionic-columned tiered porches.

[N 17b.] Holy Cross Greek Orthodox Church/originally **Epworth Methodist Episcopal Church,** 150-05 12th Ave., NE cor. 150th St. ca. 1885.

Fishtail shingled: white wood on its walls, colored slate on its roof. A **saintly structure** that suffers the later architectural histrionics of the International Style (1967) in the Immanuel Lutheran Church's colossal black cross, diagonally across the intersection.

[N 18a.] Whitestone Hebrew Center (original sanctuary, now school) 12-41 Clintonville St., SE cor. 12th Rd. 1948. John J. McNamara. Addition, 1966. **[N 18b.] Whitestone Hebrew Centre (sanctuary),** 12-25 Clintonville St., NE cor. 12th Rd. 1960.

The earliest part, now the school, is late Art Moderne. The cantilevered corners, steel sash windows, rounded wall intersections, and bold 1930s incised lettering suggest the architecture of the Grand Concourse in the Bronx, which congregants may have then viewed as a **symbol of middle-class arrival.** By the time the *new* sanctuary had been commissioned, other concerns were evident: CENTER had become CENTRE.

[N 18c.] Grace Episcopal Church and Sunday School, 140-15 Clintonville St., bet. 14th Ave. and 14th Rd. E side. 1859. Gervase Wheeler. Additions, 1904, 1939, 1957.

The belfry is key here, an intriguing work of sculpture executed in fine red brickwork, with a single bronze bell and a simple rope to toll it. Damn those **electronic** carillons!

[N 18d.] Whitestone Branch, Queensborough Public Library, 151-10 14th Rd., SE cor. Clintonville St. 1970. Albert Barash.

Competent Institutional Modern.

[N 18e.] St. Nicholas Russian Orthodox Church of Whitestone, 14-65 Clintonville St., bet. 14th Rd. and Cross Island Expwy. (North service road). E side. 1969. Sergei Padukow.

Intersecting, gleaming, metallic roofing and **white stuccoed parabolic forms,** glaringly out of place in this small-scale community.

[N 19.] 156-15 Cross Island Expressway (residence), North service road (one-way west), bet. 156th and 157th Sts. N side. ca. 1860.

Finely proportioned, in the Italianate mode. Let's hope no one ever paints those **blue-green-stained shingles** that clad the upper story!

[N 20a.] Foster Medical Corporation/originally **THC Systems,** 152-15 10th Ave., bet. 152nd and 154th Sts. N side. 1978. Wax Assocs.

A columned Modern temple for corporate administration, built on what was once a remote freight yard of the LIRR and its predecessor, the **Northside R.R.,** at the former **Whitestone Landing.**

BEECHHURST

A theatrical enclave: The 1920s saw the secluded location of Beechhurst on Long Island Sound become a favored location for Broadway theater people. Only minutes away from Manhattan via the LIRR branch whose terminal was Whitestone Landing, the area attracted actress-singer Helen Kane, Thurston the Magician, entertainer Harry Richman, and producers Joseph Schenck and Arthur Hammerstein.

[N 20b.] Single houses, on drive at 154-59 Riverside Dr., bet. 154th Place and 158th St. N side. 1987.

A group of trendy, Modern, shed-roofed frame structures.

[N 21a.] Le Havre Houses (apartments)/originally **Levitt House Development,** 162nd to Totten St., Powells Cove Blvd. to 12th Ave. 1958. George G. Miller.

Thirty 8-story beige and henna apartment buildings built by **William (Levittown) Levitt's brother, Alfred,** an amateur architect, working with Miller, a pro. Actually, a very inviting housing estate, much in the style of postwar British models.

[N 21b.] Cryder House (apartment tower), 166-25 Powells Cove Blvd., opp. 166th St. N side. 1963. Hausman & Rosenberg.

A *lone* apartment slab standing out dramatically—too dramatically?—from lesser construction in its vicinity. Its inhabitants **enjoy great views.**

[N 21c.] "Wildflower," originally **Arthur Hammerstein residence/** later **Ripples Restaurant,** 168-11 Powells Cove Blvd., E of 166th St. at Cryder's Point. 1924. Dwight James Baum. Additions. ★

An asymmetrically massed, deeply shadowed, intricately detailed, **neo-Tudor masterpiece** designed for Arthur, Oscar Hammerstein I's second son. (Oscar II, the *My Fair Lady* Hammerstein, was Arthur's nephew.) Wildflower's owner was a **successful Broadway producer** who worked with Gershwin, Kern, Romberg, Friml, Youmans, and Victor Herbert. "A.H. Thys Hovse was bvilt in the Yere of owre Lorde MCMXXIV," read the tiles at the entrance.

FLUSHING

Until the end of World War II, **Flushing** was a charming **Victorian** community laced with some 6-story **Tudor** apartments constructed in the late 1920s and early 1930s. Many of its streets were lined with rambling white clapboard and shingle (**Classical Revival** and **Shingle Style**) houses dating from the last quarter of the **19th** century. On its outskirts were vast reaches of undeveloped rolling land.

The construction of the **Bronx-Whitestone Bridge** together with its connecting highways for the **1939–1940 New York World's Fair** set the stage for a change that was nipped in the bud by Pearl Harbor. After the end of the war the rush to build was on.

Two blocks of modest mansions:

Bayside Avenue, east of Parsons Boulevard, and 146th Street to 29th Avenue.

[N 22a.] 145-15 Bayside Avenue (residence). N side. ca. 1920.

Behind a dense evergreen hedge.

[N 22b.] 145-38 Bayside Avenue (residence). S side. ca. 1880.

A mansarded gem (and barn) blessed with loving care.

[N 22c.] 29-34 to 29-45 146th Street (residences), bet. Bayside and 29th Aves. Both sides. ca. 1925.

A full, verdant, short block of 1920s Tudor, entered twixt a pair of low stone gateposts of a 19th-century estate.

A pleasant excursion:

For a taste of pre-World War II Flushing, drive a loop from Union to 150th Streets on 32nd and 33rd Avenues.

[N 23.] St. John Vianney Church (Roman Catholic), 34-21 Union St., SE cor. 34th Ave. 1974. Bentel & Bentel.

A simple, powerful, dark-brick box form modified by a curved garden wall and greatly enhanced by its landscaping.

Then, a taste of Flushing's oldest:

[N 24a.] Bowne House, 37-01 Bowne St., bet. 37th and 38th Aves. E side 1661, with later additions. ★ **Open to the public.**

Built by **John Bowne,** a **Quaker,** this house was the first indoor meeting place of the forbidden **Society of Friends;** earlier they had met clandestinely in the nearby woods. **Bowne** was a central figure in the dispute with **Governor Peter Stuyvesant** over religious freedom. The carefully maintained interiors contain a wide variety of colonial furnishings.

[N 24b.] The Weeping Beech Tree, 37th Ave. W of Parsons Blvd. N side. 1847. ★

An immense canopy of weeping branches hangs about its broad trunk, almost creating a natural shelter. On a cul-de-sac that makes a peaceful place for it and the adjacent **Kingsland Homestead.**

[N 24c.] Originally **Kingsland Homestead/**once **William K. Murray residence/**now home of **Queens Historical Society,** 143-35 37th Ave., W of Parsons Blvd. N side. ca. 1785. ★ Moved from 40-25 155th St. to current site in 1968. **Open to the public.**

A gambrel-roof, English-Dutch shingled house, once the home of the family for which Manhattan's **Murray Hill** was named.

[N 25a.] Bowne Street Community Church/originally **Reformed Church of Flushing,** 143-11 Roosevelt Ave., NE cor. Bowne St. 1891.

Northern European brick Romanesque Revival, with a tower from Prague.

[N 25b.] 144-85 Roosevelt Avenue (residence), bet. Parsons Blvd. and 147th St. N side. 1885.

A perfectly preserved but (in inner Flushing, at least) rapidly disappearing breed: a Shingle Style single house.

Next, move west along Northern Boulevard from Union Street:

The New Orient: Beginning in the 1970s Flushing became the center of an enormous and diverse oriental community comprising Chinese, Japanese, Koreans, and those from the Indian subcontinent. A visit to Union Street south of Northern Boulevard will reveal a vast array of signs in Eastern tongues.

[N 26a.] Flushing Armory, 137-58 Northern Blvd., bet. Main and Union Sts. S side. 1905.

A minifort: brick over brownstone, with a battered and crenellated and machicolated tower.

[N 26a.] Flushing Armory on postcard   **[N 25a.]** Old Reformed Ch., Flushing

[N 26b.] Flushing's old Town Hall, 1864–1898, now finding new adaptive uses

[N 26b.] Originally **Flushing Town Hall/**later **Municipal Courthouse/** later **dinner theater, restaurant,** 137-35 Northern Blvd., NE cor. Linden Place. 1864. William Post. ★

A well-preserved **Romanesque Revival** brick pile of the **Civil War** era. It served as **Flushing's Town Hall** until 1898, when **Flushing** became part of **New York City.** A theater and restaurant have made this splendid building once more part of community life. Now other uses are sought.

[N 26c.] Friends' Meeting House, 137-16 Northern Blvd., bet. Main and Union Sts. S side. 1694–1717. ★

Austere and brooding, this medieval relic looks out timidly upon the never-ending stream of cars on **Northern Boulevard.** On its rear facade, facing the quiet graveyard, are two doors, originally separate entrances for men and women. The wood-shingled, hip-roofed structure has been used continuously since the **17th** century for religious activities by the **Society of Friends,** except for a hiatus as a **British hospital,** prison, and stable during the **Revolution.**

[N 26d.] Formerly **RKO Keith's Flushing Theater,** Northern Blvd. opp. Main St. N side. 1928. Thomas Lamb. **Partial interior.** ★ Altered, 1988, Robert Meadows.

The future of the theater is **clouded**—only its entry and lobby are protected landmarks.

Prince's nursery: North of **Northern Boulevard,** from the site of the former **RKO Keith's** Theater, was a tree nursery, the first in the country, established by **William Prince** in **1737.** The 8 acres had, by **1750,** become the **Linnaean Botanic Garden.** All traces of the site are erased, but not its produce. To this day **Flushing** displays **140** genera, consisting of **2,000** species of trees that are, in large part, the progeny of **Mr. Prince.**

[N 27a.] Main Street Tower (office building), 36-25 Main St., SE cor. Northern Blvd. 1987. Leo Sakler.

Sleek, slick, smooth, dated before its time.

[N 27b.] Ebenezer Baptist Church, 36-12 Prince St., bet. 36th Ave. and 36th Rd. W side. 1973. Pedro Lopez.

At the eastern outskirts of downtown Flushing is this ambitious, **dramatically fashioned** house of worship: striated concrete block and lots of amber stained glass—actually plastic—for an upwardly mobile black congregation.

[N 28a.] St. George's Episcopal Church, Main St. bet. 38th and 39th Aves. W side. 1854. Wills & Dudley.

Miraculously, this stately **Gothic Revival** church has withstood the commercial, cacophonous onslaught on Main Street. **Francis Lewis,** a signer of the **Declaration of Independence,** was a church warden in the original building, completed in **1761.** Manhattan schist ashlar and brownstone; it would be more convincing without the later wood-shingled steeple.

[N 28b.] Korean Commercial Bank of New York, 136-88 39th Ave. (one-way west), bet. Union and Main Sts. 1985. Bo Yoon & Assocs.

Post Modern wearing a livery of Georgian red brick and limestone.

[N 29a.] The Free Synagogue of Flushing, 41-60 Kissena Blvd., NW cor. Sanford Ave. 1927. Maurice Courland.

A stately neo-Baroque presence turned diagonally to a difficult intersection of streets.

[N 29b.] The Windsor School, 136-23 Sanford Ave., bet. Main St. and Kissena Blvd. N side. ca. 1845.

Greek Revival mansion (the capitals have gone back to Corinth) with a mansarded, balustraded roof.

[N 29c.] U.S. Post Office, Flushing, Main St. SE cor. Sanford Ave. 1932. Dwight James Baum and William W. Knowles, architects. James A. Wetmore, supervising architect, U.S. Treasury Dept.

A tasteful neo-Georgian building from an era when taste was all one had to hold on to; a safe and comforting neighborhood monument.

[N 30.] The Waldheim Neighborhood (East Flushing Residential Blocks), bounded by Franklin Ave., Parsons Blvd., a line bet. Cherry and 45th Aves., and Bowne St. 1875–1900.

Porches, chimneys, mansards, and gambrels; Shingle Style, Queen Anne, and eclectic miscellany. **A wonderful small district** that our apocrypha say was preserved by a "preservation" action in the late 1920s after completion of the **apartment house** at **42-66 Phlox Place**—an anticipation of the Landmarks Preservation Commission forty years later.

Wander off Bowne St. and down Ash: **143-10 Ash Ave.,** in "Moorish" glossy (!) stucco; **143-13 Ash Ave.,** Shingle Style, well hedged; **143-19 Ash Ave.,** a Palladian Buddhist temple; **143-32 Ash Ave.,** a bungalow with bumpety stone and a squat Palladian window; **143-40 Ash Ave.,** early concrete block (1908); **143-63 Ash Ave.,** awkward Classical Revival; **143-64 Ash Ave.** and **143-61 Beech Ave.,** two that might as well be in Oak Park, Ill.; and **143-37 Beech Ave.,** New England Georgian in stained wood shingle. Where a junior Newport "cottage" stood, at Ash Ave., SW cor. Parsons, is one of:

A group of oriental temples:

[N 30a.] Nichiren Shoshu Temple, Daihozan Myosetsu-Ji, 42-32 Parsons Blvd., SW cor. Ash Ave. 1984. Ashihara Assocs.

Serenity without dullness: a testament to the expressive possibilities of **thoughtful architecture,** even when rendered in ribbed concrete block. This temple is constructed to serve the needs of a 13th-century form of Japanese Buddhism. NAM-MYOHO-RENGE-KYO.

[N 29c.] United States Post Office, Flushing: a safe and comforting monument

[N 30b.] Won Buddhist Temple, Song Eun Building, 43-02 Burling St., SW cor. Cherry Ave. 1986. Bo Yoon & Assocs.

A Korean Buddhist temple, black-and-white in concept as well as coloration.

[N 31.] Hindu Temple Society of North America, 45-57 Bowne St., bet. 45th and Holly Aves. E side. 1977. Baryn Basu Assocs. architects. Sculpture by Department of Endowments, Andhra Pradesh, India.

The exquisitely ornate Indian sculpture that totally overwhelms the temple's exterior is *so* out of place in this modest middle-class community that it somehow fits!

[N 32.] Martin Lande House (apartments)/originally **Kissena II Apartments,** 137-47 45th Ave., off Kissena Blvd., bet. 45th and Geranium Aves. N side. 1970. Gruzen & Partners.

Articulated, well-proportioned, and, happily, not an architectural statement in excess of its duties. The brick, glass, and sash, framed in a cast-concrete grid, are beautifully detailed.

MURRAY HILL

[N 33.] 149-19 Elm Avenue (residence), bet. 149th and Murray Sts. N side. 1895.

A midblock wonder, sporting a half-round second-story porch. Dig those extremely **finely spaced, square wood balusters** betwixt Ionic columns.

[N 34.] North Shore Oldsmobile, 149-04 Northern Blvd., SE cor. 149th St. 1963. Rigoni & Reich.

An elegant modern pavilion for the sale of cars: 4 cruciform piers bear a hovering, bulky roof. But surrounded on all sides by the **leering front ends** of cars, what can really look good?

BROADWAY-FLUSHING

[N 35.] St. Andrew Avalino Roman Catholic Church, 157-01 Northern Blvd., NE cor. 157th St. 1940. Henry V. Murphy.

A combination of neo-Romanesque and Art Deco, using materials so **lovingly designed** (inside and out) and **finely crafted** that the building itself could convert infidels to the faith. Attend a mass!

[N 32.] The Martin Lande House apts.   **[N 33.]** House at 149-19 Elm Avenue

[N 36.] 29-12 to 29-60, 29-01 to 29-61 167th Street (row houses), bet. 29th and 32nd Aves. Both sides. ca. 1925.

A romantic composition of row houses, with rear central driveways and garages for the emerging motor car.

AUBURNDALE

[N 37.] 189-10 to 189-30, 189-11 to 189-29 37th Avenue (residences), bet. Utopia Blvd. and 190th St. N and S sides. ca. 1925.

A remarkably effective use of neo-Tudor design to create a feeling of warmth and friendliness on an otherwise ubiquitous street.

Joseph Cornell (1903–1973), shy, reticent creator of exquisite and often mysterious works of art in the form of boxes, lived in an Archie Bunker kind of 1920s detached wood frame house at 37-08 Utopia Parkway, between 37th and 39th Avenues.

[N 38.] Temple Beth Sholom, 42-50 172nd St., NW cor. Northern Blvd. to Auburndale Lane. 1954. Unger & Unger. South addition, 1964. Stanley H. Klein.

In contrast to the original, the addition's fabriclike curves of green slate and brick are a welcome relief from the excesses of the Northern Boulevard strip.

[N 39.] St. Nicholas Greek Orthodox Church Chapel and **William Spyropoulos School,** 196-10 Northern Blvd., SE cor. 196th St. 1974. Raymond & Rado.

A **spartan octagonal auditorium** is crowned with a **spherical dome:** bold concrete and brick. The chapel is a lilliputian version of the main church: the form, a sort of romantic "brutalism."

UTOPIA

Utopia Land Company: In June 1905 the *New York Times* noted a plan to develop a 50-acre tract, to be called Utopia, for relocated residents of Manhattan's Lower East Side. The new community, a local Queens newspaper later said, would "carry out Communistic ideas." Utopia lay between today's 164th Street and Fresh Meadow Lane, from the Long Island Expressway to Jewel Avenue. But back then the north-south streets were intended to bear Lower East Side names like Houston, Stanton, Rivington, Delancey, Clinton, and Broome etc. The scheme failed, and the land was sold in 1911.

FRESH MEADOWS

[N 40.] Fresh Meadows Housing Development, 186th to 197th Sts., Long Island Expwy. to 73rd Ave. (irregularly). 1949. Voorhees, Walker, Foley & Smith; 20-story addition, 1962. Voorhees, Walker, Smith, Smith & Haines.

This **166-acre** development on the site of the old **Fresh Meadows Country Club** was a post-World War II project of the **New York Life Insurance Company.** Its (then) avant-garde site plan, including a mix of row housing, low- and high-rise apartments, regional shopping center, theater, schools, and other amenities, scores as excellent planning but *dull* architecture.

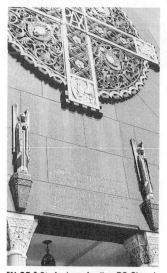

[N 35.] St. Andrew Avalino RC Church   **[N 44a.]** Queens Coll. Science Bldg.

[N 41.] Long Island (Vanderbilt) Motor Parkway: [N 41a.] 73rd Avenue overpass, Cunningham Park W of Francis Lewis Blvd. **[N 41b.] Hollis Court Boulevard overpass,** N of Union Tpke and Richland Ave. **[N 41c.] Springfield Boulevard overpass,** N of Kingsbury Ave. All 1909.

These funky reinforced-concrete overpasses date from the construction of America's first "super highway." The road was built by race car enthusiast William K. Vanderbilt especially for automobiles, stretching **a total of 45 "dustless" miles** from a toll lodge at Hillside Avenue to Lake Ronkonkoma, in Suffolk County. Cars were narrower then: the road was only 16 feet wide, making it ideal for its current reuse (in Queens, at least) as a grade-separated bikeway.

[N 42.] St. John's University, Queens Campus (Roman Catholic), Union Tpke. SW cor. Utopia Pkwy., to Grand Central Pkwy. Relocated from Brooklyn, beginning 1955. **[N 42a.] Frumkes Hall,** 1971. Carson, Lundin & Thorsen. **[N 42b.] Sun Yat-sen Hall, Center of Asian Studies.** 1973. Herman C. Knebel.

In the vast 105 acres of this campus, mighty little architecture of note exists. S.Y.S. Hall, however, a *faux* Chinese temple and polychromed gate, adds a **brilliant splash of color** to an otherwise drab setting.

 [N 43a.] Originally **Queens General Hospital,** now **Queens Hospital Center, N.Y.C. Health & Hospitals Corporation,** 82-68 164th St., bet. Goethals Ave. and Grand Central Pkwy. 1937. Sullivan W. Jones, John E. Kleist, Jacob Lust. Additions.

Art Deco orange brick, built long before the post-World War II building boom in Queens.

 [N 43b.] Originally **Triborough Hospital for Tuberculosis** (now part of Queens Hospital Center), Parsons Blvd. NE cor. 82nd Dr. 1940. Eggers & Higgins.

A light, bright, softly modeled high-rise hospital turned to the sun and bedecked with south-facing tiers of balconies and solariums, designed when TB was still a scourge and sunlight was believed to be its salvation.

 [N 44.] Queens College, CUNY, 65-30 Kissena Blvd., bet. Long Island Expwy. and Melbourne Ave., to Main St. **[N 44a.] New Science Building,** 1987. Davis Brody & Assocs. **[N 44b.] Benjamin Rosenthal Library,** 1987. Gruzen Samton Steinglass.

When it opened in 1937, Queens College occupied 9 Spanish Mission Style tile-roofed buildings built in 1908 for use as the **New York Parental School,** a special school for incorrigibles and truants. The current 52 acres contain a **hodgepodge of architecture** ranging from a few of the original structures to the sophisticated new Science and Rosenthal Library buildings, linked by a bridge. Paul Klapper, for whom a college building and an adjacent elementary school are named, was the college's first president.

[N 44c.] Queensboro Hill Branch, Queensborough Public Library, 60-05 Main St., NE cor. Long Island Expwy. 1980. Stephen Lepp Assocs.

Carven brick architecture. Simple and sure.

[N 45.] Public School 219, Queens, The Paul Klapper School, 144-39 Gravett Rd., E of Main St. N side. 1966. Caudill, Rowlett & Scott.

A domed set of open classrooms, from the era when open classrooms were guaranteed to deliver a great elementary education—and a headache for the teacher by the end of the school day.

BAYSIDE

Bayside is located northeast of **Flushing** and has an attractive suburban character maintained by an abundance of detached houses and low-rise apartments. Originally settled by **William Lawrence** in **1664,** it remained largely rural until linked to **Manhattan** by the **LIRR's East River tunnels** in **1910.**

Fort Totten:

Entry from 212th Street, North of Bell Boulevard. **Open to the public.**

This military reservation dates from 1857, but it wasn't until 1898 that it was designated Fort Totten by **President McKinley** in honor of **General Joseph G. Totten,** Director of the War Department's Bureau of Seacoast Defense.

 [N 46a.] Originally **Officers Club, The Fort at Willets Point, Fort Totten,** Murray and Totten Aves. opp. Weaver Ave., Fort Totten. S side. ca. 1870. Enlarged, 1887. ★

Castellated Gothic Revival in the spirit of Alexander Jackson Davis and Andrew Jackson Downing. Wood here simulates masonry grandeur in what began as "the castle," a casino for officers.

[N 46b.] Fort Totten Battery, Fort Totten. 1864. William Petit Trowbridge, engineer. ★ **Open to the public** (obtain permission at main gate).

A monumental, tooled granite-block fortification. Arched ways along its **embrasured walls** are arranged in a V-shape plan, with a bastion at its prow worthy of ancient Rome. It was built to protect, with **Fort Schuyler** across the strait, **the east entry** to New York Harbor.

[N 46c.] Ernie Pyle U.S. Army Reserve Center, Fort Totten. First right turn after main gate. 1984. Burkavage & Evans.

A mark of the *new* U.S. Army: BIG. A very very long, low, **unrelentingly red** masonry structure that relates not at all to the size, scale, materials, or details of the typical buildings that characterize the *older* U.S. Army at charming Fort Totten.

Leaving Fort Totten:

[N 47a.] Bay Bridge at Bayside (condominium housing)/formerly the site of **General Telephone & Electronics Laboratories,** Cross Island Pkwy., South Service Rd., bet. Clearview Expwy. and 208th Place. S side. Entry at Estates Lane. 1984. Liebman Liebman Assocs.

A heavy-handed development, turned inward, that *seems* to go on forever, designed by those who must fancy themselves latter-day Mansarts.

[N 47b.] Bay Terrace Jewish Center (synagogue), 209th St. SW cor. Bell Blvd. to 209th Place. 1962. Arthur Silver.

A narrow sliver of land between two closely spaced streets, put to good use for a religious complex.

[N 48a.] Birchwood Park/The Towers at Waters Edge (housing development) 215th St., bet. 17th and 23rd Aves. to Waters Edge Drive. Entry at 215th St. opp. 18th Ave. 1967–1969.

Three freestanding apartment towers plus lots of attached duplex row houses, all decorated in the same cream-and-brown color scheme of Santa Fe Railroad outbuildings when left too long unrepainted.

[N 46a.] Officers Club, Fort Totten   **[N 55.]** Queensboro Comm. College

[N 48b.] Scheuer House (retirement home), 208-11 26th Ave., NW cor. Corp. Kennedy St., at Clearview Expwy. 1981. The Gruzen Partnership.

A well-designed residential facility operated by **Self-Help Community Services, Inc.**

[N 49.] St. Mary's Hospital for Children (Episcopal), 29-15 216th St. (dead end), S of 29th Ave. 1951. George B. Post & Sons. Addition, 1984. Breger & Terjesen.

It would seem that Post, the 19th-century founder of the architectural firm, was a figure of enormously greater talent than his offspring.

[N 50a.] Crocheron Park, entry drive via 35th Ave. off Corbett Rd., at 216th St.

One of Queens's best kept secrets: **Mickle Pond** at the southeast corner of this park, literally **only a few feet** from the fast-moving traffic of Cross Island Parkway. Overlooking it are:

[N 50b.] 217-63, 217-67, 217-71, 217-75, 217-79 Corbett Road (residences), bet. 217th and 221st Sts. N side. 1986.

Pretentious (get a load of those two-car garages!) but mildly credible despite the aluminum siding and fussy arches.

[N 50c.] Former **James J. Corbett residence,** 221-04 Corbett Rd., SE cor. 221st St. ca. 1900.

The plaque on the boulder reveals that **world's heavyweight champion,** "Gentleman Jim" Corbett lived here between 1902 and his death in 1933. He held the title from 1892 to 1897. He evidently also had taste in architecture.

[N 50d.] 35-26 221st Street (residence), SW cor. Corbett Rd. ca. 1900.

Corbett's contemporaries had taste, too.

[N 50e.] Riverview Montessori School addition, 221-21 Corbett Rd., NE cor. 221st St. 1987. Richard Frank.

Cast-in-place concrete, glass block, chain-link-fenced roof play area. Very visible, on its **promontory site,** to parkway traffic below.

Via 38th Avenue, east from 222nd Street:

[N 51a.] "The White House," 38-03 223rd St., opp. 38th Ave. E side. ca. 1985.

A bright white trapezoidal extravaganza that **screams** for attention in this once serene neighborhood.

[N 51b.] Formerly **Columbian Fathers Residence/now Les Clochettes (private school),** 35-55 223rd St. (dead end), NE cor. 37th Ave. ca. 1900. Altered, 1987, John Bruscella, Steven Gaetano, Joseph Cacioppo.

Just a large old house with a cylindrical bumpety, stone tower to give it that extra fillip. Now stripped of some detail for energy-efficient use.

[N 51c.] 35-49 223rd St. (residence), dead end N of 37th Ave. 1987.

A bit of Amagansett grafted onto Bayside. The neighborhood has others.

Nearby:

[N 52.] All Saints Episcopal Church, 39-30 215th St., NW cor. 40th Ave. 1962.

A dignified graystone neo-Gothic edifice with **an especially interesting belfry** form that gives this heavily treelined neighborhood even more class.

South of the LIRR tracks:

[N 53a.] 215-37 43rd Avenue (apartment complex), NW cor. 216th St. 1931. Benjamin Braunstein.

Half-timbered, stucco and brick, slate-roofed: a **meandering medieval close** offers access, light, intimacy *and* privacy, and great charm. *Meander through;* there are entries to the close on both streets.

[N 53b.] Lawrence Family Graveyard, 216th St. bet. 42nd Ave. and LIRR. W side. 1830. ★ **Not open to the public.**

A tiny private cemetery of the ubiquitous Queens family [see W Queens W 5.].

[N 54a.] Merrill Lynch Realty (offices), 218-10 Northern Blvd., bet. 218th and 219th Sts. (Springfield Blvd.). N side. 1986.

A textured, mirrored box, which holds its own very well amid the **cacophony of the strip.** At least it does in daylight.

[N 54b.] Oakland Lake, Alley Park, Springfield Blvd. to Cloverdale Blvd., S of 46th Ave. Reconstructed, N.Y.C. Department of Parks & Recreation Design Staff, 1986. **Open to the public.**

An oasis in the Olmstedian mode; note the **naturalistic joining** of land and water, rarely done well in a City park. It was re-created through design.

[N 55.] Queensborough Community College, CUNY/formerly the site of **Oakland Golf Course and Club,** 56th Ave. NW cor. Cloverdale Blvd. to Garland and Kenilworth Drs. 1967 Master Plan: **[N 55a.] Library, Science, Humanities, Gymnasium, Campus Center,** 1967–1970. Frederick Wiedersum & Assocs. and Holden, Egan, Wilson & Corser. 1970–1975 Master Plan: **[N 55b.] Administration Building,** 1977. Percival Goodman. **[N 55c.] Medical Arts Building,** 1977. Armand Bartos & Assocs.

Built from scratch in just 10 years on a large portion of the **old Oakland Golf Course.** The first round of structures is precast concrete and brick, straightforward and simple. The later 2 structures are examples of **stylish form-making** for its own sake. At the crest of the grand outdoor stair is the former clubhouse, now the **Oakland Building,** a welcome survivor.

SOUTHERN QUEENS

WOODHAVEN • OZONE PARK • RICHMOND HILL • JAMAICA
HOLLIS • ST. ALBANS • SOUTH OZONE PARK

Town of Jamaica/Rustdrop

Settled in 1656; chartered in 1660.

The communities lying within the boundaries of the old **Town of Jamaica** contain, as a group, the widest contrasts of any section of **Queens.** Some, like **Ozone Park, Richmond Hill,** and **Woodhaven,** are quiet residential communities. **Jamaica** itself, on the other hand, is a bustling marketplace with department stores, specialty shops, and theaters. Affluence is everywhere visible in **Jamaica Estates** along **Grand Central Parkway;** poverty and squalor mark the black slums of **South Jamaica;** in the **St. Albans** area, though, is a lovely, treelined, middle-income black community. Parts of **Jamaica** date from the **17th** and **18th** centuries; **Richmond Hill, Queens Village,** from the **19th.**

WOODHAVEN, OZONE PARK

[S 1a.] Fire Alarm Telegraph Station, N.Y.C. Fire Department, 83-98 Woodhaven Blvd., NW cor. Park Lane S. ca. 1915.

A *retardataire* container for 1920s high tech.

[S 1b.] Christ Church Congregational, 85-27 91st St. *(one-way north),* SE cor 85th Rd. 1914. Addition, 1928.

The imaginative carpentry at the belfry cornice (and the rooster weather vane) distinguish this **grayed stucco edifice.** But that neon-outlined crucifix, that's *another* matter.

[S 2.] St. Matthew's Episcopal-Anglican Church, 1901. R. F. Schirmer and J. A. Schmidt. **Parish Hall,** and **Rectory,** 85-36 96th St. *(one-way southbound),* bet. 85th Rd. and 86th Ave. E side.

The **peaceful green compound** formed by these three structures is a **gift to 96th Street.** The particularly lovely neo-Gothic church is built of an extremely good-looking ashlar, whose joints have been deeply raked, giving the structure **great character** in an otherwise softly configured neighborhood.

Midblock cemetery: Immediately behind St. Matthew's is the private Wyckoff-Snediker Cemetery, accessible to the families' descendants via a lane that begins at 97-01 Jamaica Avenue.

[S 3a.] Former **Lalance & Grosjean kitchenware factory/**now largely the site of **Pathmark Shopping Center,** Atlantic Ave. bet. 89th and 92nd Sts. to 95th Ave. 1876. Shopping center, 1986, Niego Assocs.
[S 3b.] Originally **Lalance & Grosjean clock tower and factory,** Atlantic Ave. SW cor. 92nd St. 1876.

Until most of the antique, red-painted brick structures were wasted in the mid 1980s to form yet *another* shopping center, this intricate array of 19th-century mill buildings was a remarkable relic of the era when the Village of Woodhaven claimed a **nationally known tinware and agateware manufacture.** Its products graced many an American kitchen for generations, and the Lalance & Grosjean factory employed hundreds.

In the end, saving the **squat clock tower** atop one of the old factories became a sop to those preservation interests which sought to save more of the historic building complex from destruction.

Pop's Restaurant and Ice Cream Parlor, 85-22 Jamaica Ave., bet. 85th and 86th Sts. S side.

An old-fashioned shop in a 1907 structure.

Schmidt's Confectionery, 94-15 Jamaica Ave., bet. 94th and 96th Sts. N side.

Original store fixtures and a history of chocolate-making dating to 1925 make this a special place.

[S 3c.] Originally **The Wyckoff Building (office building),** 93-02 95th Ave., SE cor. 93rd St. 1889.

A distinguished 19th-century commercial corner that was originally **a real estate exchange** and the office of the **Woodhaven Bank.** In this part of low-rise Queens, its four stories (plus corner egg-shaped dome) must have made it the **local skyscraper** when first opened.

[S 3d.] Originally **Lalance & Grosjean workers' housing,** 85-02 to 85-20 95th Ave. and 85-01 to 85-21 97th Ave., bet. 85th and 86th Sts. Both sides. 1884.

Modest wood-frame row houses built as a paternalistic gesture to its employees by *the* local company.

Mae West's early career: The brassy movie queen was born in nearby Brooklyn but is said to have begun her career performing in Louis Neir's Hotel, a combination tavern-hotel. The 2-story structure still exists (in remarkably original shape) at 87-48 78th Street, at the northwest corner of 88th Avenue. (The streets here are all one-way, somehow always the *wrong way:* 78th runs *northbound* below Jamaica Avenue, where Neir's is now a bar.)

A brief excursion into Ozone Park:
[S 4.] **Mullins Furniture sign,** 92-16 101st Ave., bet. 92nd and 93rd Sts. S side. Sign on W wall, ca. 1910.

Palimpsest. A furniture company's outdoor, wall-size ad, weatherbeaten but still robust in graphic design.

RICHMOND HILL

West of Jamaica and south of Forest Park's hills lies the community of Richmond Hill. Its plan was evolved and its streets laid out by Manhattan lawyer **Albon P. Man** (also responsible for adjacent Kew Gardens) and his English landscape architect, **Edward Richmond,** in the years

1867 through 1872. Like **Kew Gardens,** Richmond Hill also owes its name to a London suburb.

Richmond Hill Driving Tour:

A meandering drive through part of Richmond Hill's finest streets ending at The Triangle.

Using a good street map or pocket atlas, begin with the former factories at the south flank of Forest Park at Park Lane South and 101st Street. Then scoot around and follow 86th Avenue (two-way) eastward as a rough spine for the trip. Take detours up and down the streets (mostly one-way) as you choose:

[S 5a.] Formerly **William Demuth & Company–S. M. Frank & Company/** now **apartments,** 84-10 101st St., SW cor. Park Lane. ca. 1895. Converted, 1987.

Backing up on the old **LIRR Rockaway Beach Division** siding, a factory where briar was turned and polished to manufacture **Frank Medico smoking pipes.** Built at a time when every man could afford a pipe and conversations centered on which shape burned coolest to the taste. The often unkempt **green center mall** dividing 101st Street is nevertheless a civilizing 19th-century touch.

[S 5b.] Public School 66, Queens, The Brooklyn Hills School, 85-11 102nd St., bet. 85th Rd. and 85th Dr. E side. 1901. Additions. *(102nd St. is two-way.)*

Many coats of paint have muffled the terra-cotta ornament, but the Art Nouveau molded terra-cotta sign still reads **loud and clear.** The **bell tower** has lost both its bell *and* its pyramidal cap sometime along its journey. At the turn of the century this part of Richmond Hill took its name from the (former) great City of Brooklyn to the west, hence the school's name: **Brooklyn Hills.**

[S 5c.] 85-58, 85-54 104th Street (residences), bet. 85th and 86th Aves. W side. ca. 1900. *(104th St. is one-way north here.)*

A pair of large gambrel-roof single houses, still bearing their original combination of large wood-shingle-and-stucco siding and **diagonal wood muntins** dividing the second-floor window sash.

[S 6.] Trinity Methodist Church, 107-14 86th Ave., bet. 107th and 108th Sts. S side. ca. 1910.

The church's **florid neo-medieval** column capitals are provincial, yet very charming.

[S 7a.] Richmond Hill War Memorial, edge of Forest Park, Park Lane S., NE cor. Memorial Drive, at Myrtle Ave. and 109th St. J. P. Pollia, sculptor. ca. 1925.

The poignant bronze sculpture of an **innocent young lad** caught up in a war not of his making sits atop a granite stele with an inscription that makes use of an uncommon gender for such memorials:

ERECTED BY THE PEOPLE OF RICHMOND HILL
IN MEMORY OF HER MEN
WHO SERVED AND DIED IN THE WORLD WAR
1917–1918

Note also the small-scale but exquisitely crafted bronze flagpole base, adjacent.

[S 7b.] 85-12 110th Street (residence), bet. 85th and 86th Aves. W side. ca. 1900. *(110th St. is one-way south.)*

Symmetric gambrel-roofed, with asymmetric detail. Unusual.

[S 7c.] 84-16 110th Street (residence), bet. Myrtle and 85th Aves. W side. ca. 1900.

Complex pyramidal geometry and an **intermix** of rectangular and half-round openings make this frame house special.

[S 7d.] 85-28 111th Street (residence), bet. Myrtle and 86th Aves. W side. ca. 1900. *(111th St. is two-way.)*

A fine home retaining most of its original Shingle Style livery.

[S 8.] Church of the Holy Child Jesus (Roman Catholic), 85-80 112th St. *(one-way south),* NW cor. 86th Ave. 1931. Henry V. Murphy.

Neo-Romanesque *cum* Art Moderne, of orange brick and exquisitely carved limestone. Reminiscent, inside and out, of **later Bertram Goodhue** work. The bell tower is a gem.

[S 9a.] 84-37 113th Street (residence), NE cor. 85th Ave. *(113th St. is one-way north.)* ca. 1875.

Note the **shy Japanese touches** at the edge of the roof beams, from a time when some architects were flirting with oriental motifs.

[S 7a.] Richmond Hill War Memorial   **[S 7b.]** 85-12 110th St. residence

[S 9a.] 84-37 113th Street residence   **[S 8.]** Holy Child Jesus RC Church

114th Street (two-way) between 85th and 86th Avenues.

(114th St. is one-way south, below Myrtle only.)

[S 9b.] 85-04 114th Street (residence), SW cor. 85th Ave. ca. 1900.

Fun architectural compositions like this house caused Victorian houses first to *lose* their stylishness . . . and more recently to *regain* it. Thank God!

[S 9c.] 85-10, 85-14, 85-20 114th Street (residences), W side. ca. 1900.

A smashing group!

[S 9d.] 85-03 114th Street (residence), SE cor. 85th Ave. ca. 1900.

The original porch has been partly enclosed, but above it much of the **architectural interest** survives.

[S 10.] Union Congregational Church/United Church of Christ, 86-10 115th St. *(one-way north),* SW cor. 86th Ave.

Built of **black stone,** pointed in a projecting V-joint profile.

116th Street, south of Jamaica Avenue:

(One-way south.)

[S 11a.] Landmark Tavern Building/originally **Richmond Hill Branch, Bank of Jamaica,** 116-02 Jamaica Ave., SE cor. 116th St. ca. 1900.

Gentrification has given new life to this distinctive, turn-of-the-century corner commercial building. In the mid 1980s the prescription for real estate success in this locale was **"Call it a landmark."** In this case, it *is* one (though still unofficial).

[S 11b.] 87-72, 87-78 116th Street (residences), bet. 89th and Jamaica Aves. W side. ca. 1885.

Imagine when all the single homes on this block looked as **pristine** as these two.

The Triangle:

Actually, many triangles are formed where **Lefferts Boulevard** crosses the **intersection of Myrtle and Jamaica Avenues,** a special event in the otherwise ho-hum local street grid. The complex streetscape is further enriched by the route of the **old LIRR Montauk Division viaduct,** which—using its *own* geometry—passes *over* the streets but *under* the old BMT Jamaica Line's elevated structure. A block west sees the northbound **birth of Hillside Avenue,** which swings around a quarter turn, dips beneath the LIRR viaduct, and merrily spins its way east to **the Nassau County line.**

The immediate area is filled with curiosities:

[S 12a.] Richmond Hill Republican Club, 86-15 Lefferts Blvd., bet. Hillside and Jamaica Aves. E side. 1920.

A temple to the party of **President Abraham Lincoln** (archery range in basement). Richmond Hill was even more heavily Republican **before the Great Depression.**

[S 12b.] Richmond Hill Branch, Queens Borough Public Library, 118-14 Hillside Ave., SW cor. Lefferts Blvd. 1905. Tuthill & Higgins.

One of many yellow-brick Carnegie gifts, this on a green triangle of its own, early on called **Library Square.**

[S 12c.] Triangle Hofbrau (restaurant)/formerly **Triangle Hotel,** Myrtle Ave. bet. 117th St. and Jamaica Ave. 1864.

A rambling restaurant and bar whose walls are **bedecked** with **old photos** and **arcane memorabilia.** A plaque from the **Native New Yorkers Historical Association** claims this is Long Island's **oldest tavern** in continuous operation. In the 1890s, during the bicycle craze, it was called **Wheelmen's Rest.** A friendly place to eat a hearty meal.

Frappes and sundaes: Frank Jahn's is a neo-real 1890s ice cream parlor at 117-03 Hillside Avenue (near 117th Street and Jamaica Avenue). Complete with marble countertops, leaded-glass Coca-Cola chandeliers, and wild—just *wild*—ice cream concoctions.

END of Richmond Hill Driving Tour.

JAMAICA

[S 13.] King Mansion, King Park, Jamaica Ave. bet. 150th and 153rd Sts. N side. North section, 1730; west section, 1755; east section, 1806. ★ **Interior** ★

A large bland white house, more interesting for its *social* history than its architecture, set on a greensward which also contains a wonderful Victorian pergola once used for band concerts.

[S 14a.] Federal Social Security Administration, Jamaica Ave. SW cor. Twombly Place (Parsons Blvd.) to Archer Ave. 1987. The Gruzen Partnership and The Ehrenkrantz Group.

This big, bulky, brick, bureaucratic block proves there *was* BIG GOVERNMENT, even during the conservative Reagan administration, whose legions built it. **Mammon,** here government's version, overwhelms a pair of spiritual neighbors:

[S 14b.] First Reformed Church of Jamaica, 153-10 Jamaica Ave., SE cor. 153rd St. S side. 1859. ★

Almost entirely of red brick used in a variety of Romanesque Revival arched forms as doorways, windows, corbel tables, and relieving arches—**all three-dimensional.**

[S 14c.] Grace Episcopal Church and **Graveyard,** 155-03 Jamaica Ave., bet. 153rd St. and Parsons Blvd. 1862. Dudley Field. Additions, 1901–1902. Cady, Berg & See. ★ **Graveyard,** ca. 1734.

A brownstone monolith from grass to finial. English country **Gothic.**

Along 160th Street:

Between Jamaica and 90th Avenues *(one-way north)*. E side.

[S 11b.] 87-72 116th St. residence   **[S 14c.]** Grace Episc. Church, Jamaica

[S 13.] King Mansion, more interesting for social history than its architecture

[S 14d.] Formerly **Roxanne Swimsuits,** 90-33 160th St., bet. Jamaica and 90th Aves. ca. 1936.

A sophisticated **mastaba** of Art Deco origins which has seen better days.

[S 14e.] Iglesias de Dios Mission Board, 90-25 160th St. ca. 1925.

Friendly Tudor.

[S 14f.] Bethany French Baptist Church/originally **First Independent Hebrew Congregation,** 90-21 160th St. ca. 1910.

Until the mid 1980s a wood-frame provincial synagogue. Now **bedecked** with all sorts of fast-talk salesmanship: aluminum siding, Perma Stone, razor wire.

Beyond:

[S 14g.] Title Guarantee Company/formerly **Suffolk Title & Guarantee Building,** 90-04 161st St. 1929. Dennison & Hirons.

The decoration here is more important than the building: Art Moderne at the **third-floor spandrels** and the **sky:** blue, beige, orange and black.

[S 15a.] Originally **Jamaica Savings Bank,** 161-02 Jamaica Ave., bet. 161st and 162nd Sts. S side. 1898. Hough & Dewell.

Second Empire **Beaux Arts** cheek by jowl with the Renaissance Revival club below.

[S 15b.] **Jamaica Arts Center**/formerly **Jamaica Register Building,** 161-04 Jamaica Ave., bet. 161st and 162nd Sts. S side. 1899. A. S. Macgregor. ★

A Renaissance Revival **English club,** now happily preserved as an arts center.

[S 15c.] **Sidewalk clock,** in front of 161-11 Jamaica Ave., bet. 161st and 162nd Sts. N side. ★

One of the city's officially designated **street furniture** landmarks.

The Revolution: The Battle of Long Island, in the closing days of August 1776, had its skirmishes in Jamaica as well as Brooklyn. **Boulder Crest,** at the terminal moraine's summit overlooking the outwash plain on which the Jamaica business district was built, held the rifle pits of the retreating Continental soldiers. A commemorative glacial boulder and plaque can be found on the lawn at the southwest corner of 150th Street and 85th Drive.

[S 16.] **Jamaica Learning Center**/formerly **Hillcrest High School Annex**/formerly **Jamaica Vocational High School**/originally **Jamaica Training School,** 162-10 Hillside Ave., bet. 162nd and 163rd Sts. S side.

A green oasis.

[S 17a.] Originally **J. Kurtz & Sons (furniture store),** 162-24 Jamaica Ave., SW cor. Guy R. Brewer Blvd. 1931. Allmendinger & Schlendorf. ★

Six **spectacular** stories of **Art Deco commercial architecture,** only minimally compromised since the Kurtzes left, in 1978.

South of the LIRR embankment:

[S 17b.] York College, CUNY: A generous plaza for the red brick buildings

[S 17b.] **York College, CUNY,** 94-20 Guy R. Brewer Blvd., S of LIRR to Liberty Ave. W side. 1983. The Gruzen Partnership.

The **cascade of steps** at the boulevard entry enriches the neat, low, carefully controlled architecture of this campus. The Union Hall Street arched pedestrian underpass (1913) through the LIRR embankment from Archer Avenue is **an intriguing way** to reuse the former path of a now discontinued street.

[S 17c.] Originally **St. Monica's Roman Catholic Church (vacant),** 94-20 160th St., S of LIRR. 1857. Anders Peterson, master mason. ★

Deserted by its congregation and its former neighbors. A forlorn reminder that buildings, like people, are mortal.

[S 17d.] Prospect Cemetery, 159th St. SW cor. Beaver Rd. 1662. ★

The first public burial ground of **Jamaica.** In the early years of this community the wealthy were mostly buried in church—laymen under their pews, clergymen in the chapel or beneath the pulpit. Less affluent parishioners were interred in the churchyard. The rest were buried in **Prospect Cemetery.**

[S 18.] Tabernacle of Prayer/originally **Loew's Valencia Theater,** 165-11 Jamaica Ave., bet. 165th St. and Merrick Blvd. N side. 1929. Drew Eberson.

One of the city's **great motion picture palaces,** now seeing service as a church. With the Jamaica Avenue elevated gone, the decorative terra-cotta facade is more readily visible.

America's first supermarket: It all began in June 1930 when King Kullen opened a large self-service grocery store, complete with "unlimited parking," at 171-06 Jamaica Avenue. It later became the machine shops of Thomas Edison Vocational High School. The unlimited parking area is now the site of a taxpayer.

[S 19.] Bethesda Missionary Baptist Church/originally **Jamaica First German Presbyterian Church,** 179-09 Jamaica Ave., NW cor. 179th St., opp. 179th Place. 1900.

A substantial white gem of a wood church.

HOLLIS

[S 20a.] 191-01 Hollis Avenue (residence), a.k.a. **99-21 Hollis Avenue,** bet. 191st St. and 100th Ave., opp. Farmers Blvd. N side. ca. 1875.

Occupying a large piece of property and commanding an ancient intersection: Hollis Avenue was once **Old Country Road** leading east into Long Island; **Farmers Boulevard** was the route to the farms of southeastern Queens, the large freestanding elaborately ornamented Italianate house is **a remarkable throwback** to the area's 19th-century roots.

[S 19.] Bethesda Missionary Church   **[S 20c.]** Gatepost marking Hollis Pk.

[S 20b.] First United Methodist Church of Hollis, 91-31 191st St., bet. Jamaica and Woodhull Aves. E side. ca. 1885.

A handsome combination of shingles and slate.

[S 20c.] Hollis Park development: entrance gateposts, various locations, including 193rd St. at Jamaica Ave. N side.

The cast stone inserts on these particular brick guardians read FULTON STREET (once Jamaica Avenue's name), HOLLIS PARK BOULE-

VARD. Many 1920s land speculators in the area east of Jamaica used such **brick entrance posts** to lend prestige to the communities they were developing, in the style of 19th-century suburban developments, in Brooklyn or nearby New Jersey.

[S 20d.] Hollis Unitarian Church, 195-39 Hillside Ave., opp. 195th Place. N side. 1961. Blake & Neski.

A *spartan* pale brick box.

[S 21.] 211-02 Hollis Ave. (residence), opp. 211th St. S side. ca. 1875.

Cartoonist **Charles Addams** couldn't have captured the spirit any better. Undergoing renovation; will its integrity survive?

ST. ALBANS

[S 22.] Formerly **Sol Cafe Division, Chock Full O'Nuts Coffee Corporation,** 109-09 180th St., NE cor. Brinkerhoff Ave. ca. 1955.

An 11-story curiosity astride the old LIRR Far Rockaway Division embankment: **a lone skyscraper** seeking a reason for having been built.

[S 23.] Murdock Avenue, bet. Linden Blvd. and LIRR. Addisleigh Park.

On either side of Murdock Avenue and on many streets nearby in greater **St. Albans** lies **a superb suburban neighborhood,** with well-kept homes and vast, immaculately manicured lawns. Here an affluent black community **does itself proud** and firmly lays to rest the rednecks' biased prophesies.

SOUTH OZONE PARK

[S 24.] St. Teresa of Avila Roman Catholic Church, 109-71 130th St., bet. 109th and 111th Aves. W side. 1937.

Of low silhouette in the 1930s intermix of yellow brick and Art Deco/Classical styles. As the neighborhood changed from Italian at the parish's founding to black now, it is not unusual to hear **spirituals** being sung during collections.

[S 25.] Aqueduct Racetrack, Rockaway Blvd. to North Conduit Ave., IND Rockaway Line right-of-way to 114th St. 1894. Reconstruction, 1959. Arthur Froehlich & Assocs.

The **Big A,** as it is commonly known, is the last racetrack entirely within the city limits. As land values increase, these enormous operations sell to developers (cf. **Jamaica Racetrack,** now **Rochdale Village**). The name relates to the **Ridgewood Aqueduct, Brooklyn** and **Queens's** first large-scale water system, which still follows **Conduit Avenue,** the service road of Southern Parkway, in from its reservoirs on **Long Island.**

FAR QUEENS

DOUGLASTON MANOR • DOUGLASTON • LITTLE NECK
GLEN OAKS • CREEDMOOR • QUEENS VILLAGE
CAMBRIA HEIGHTS • LAURELTON • SPRINGFIELD GARDENS
JFK AIRPORT • HOWARD BEACH

Out beyond Cross Island Parkway and Springfield Boulevard, lying along the **Nassau County border** or abutting the northern shores of Jamaica Bay, is the area we call **Far Queens.** The northern parts, such as Douglaston Manor along the east side of Little Neck Bay, are among Queens's **most exclusive neighborhoods.** The areas to the southeast comprise an immense—largely unknown to residents of Manhattan—group of **middle-class black suburban communities.** To the south of this Queens "frontier" is the **megaworld** of Kennedy Airport and, to its west, the large community of Howard Beach and a few smaller ones.

DOUGLASTON MANOR, DOUGLASTON, LITTLE NECK, GLEN OAKS

Douglaston Manor, Douglaston, and **Little Neck** lie east of the **Cross Island** (Belt) **Parkway,** New York's circumferential highway, and, as a result, many assume they are part of adjacent **Nassau County.** The part above **Northern Boulevard** certainly lends credence to this belief, since the area resembles the prosperous commuter towns on the adjacent **North Shore.** Originally the peninsula was **all Little Neck,** but in **1876** the western part was renamed **Douglaston** after **William B. Douglas,** who had donated the LIRR station there. It is a rocky, treed knoll with sometimes narrow, winding streets **chockablock** with Victorian, stucco, shingled, myriad individual houses of romance, many with splendid views of water, sunsets, and sailboats.

DOUGLASTON MANOR

[F 1.] Douglaston Club/formerly **George Douglas residence/**originally **Wynant Van Zandt residence,** 32-03 Douglaston Pkwy. (West Drive), SE cor. Beverly Rd. Before 1835, with numerous additions.

A large, homely country house with a **Tuscan-columned** porch; now a tennis club.

[F 2.] Allen-Beville residence, 29 Center Dr., SW cor. Forest Rd. 1848–1850. ★

A Greek Revival snuggling up to the new Italianate style of the time. White shingles, Tuscan porch, octagonal widow's walk overlooking Little Neck Bay.

[F 3.] Cornelius Van Wyck residence, 37-04 Douglaston Pkwy. (126 Drive), SW cor. Alston Place. 1735. Numerous Additions. ★

The original "Dutch" house is barely visible, engulfed as it is by later accretions.

[F 4.] 233-34, 233-38, 233-40 Bay Street (residences), bet. 234th St. and Douglaston Pkwy. S side.

A challenge: find these three Shingle Style-Victorian gems tucked away along this bosky lane. The last embraces an early **gambrel-roof** neighbor to its east wall.

DOUGLASTON

[F 5a.] North Hills Branch, Queensborough Public Library, 57-04 Marathon Pkwy., opp. 57th Ave. W side. 1987. Abraham W. Geller & Assocs.

Round and domed and bright blue and red, with a yellow canopy: a *very* colorful addition to the **beige burbs.**

[F 5b.] Douglaston Manor Restaurant/originally **North Hills Golf Course Clubhouse,** 63-20 Commonwealth Blvd., opp. Marathon Pkwy. W side. ca. 1925. Additions.

A romantic Spanish-tile-plus-beige-stucco **confection** occupying the **high ground** atop a city golf course. When the leaves aren't too thick the setting allows patrons to dine while watching **endless streams of traffic** maneuver sinuous Grand Central Parkway as far as the eye can see, almost all the way to Manhattan's skyscrapers in the hazy distance.

GLEN OAKS

[F 6a.] North Shore Towers: Coleridge, Beaumont, Amherst (apartment towers), 269-10, 270-10, 271-10 Grand Central Pkwy., at the Nassau County line. (Entry via Grand Central Parkway's south service road, from Little Neck Pkwy.) 1975.

Ever wonder what those tall, strongly silhouetted residential towers are, just as you **cross the line** from Nassau County into Queens? It's too soon to be Manhattan. Hmmmm . . . Well, *these* are they: three of them, each 33 stories tall, a total of 1,848 units.

Long Island Jewish Hospital-Hillside Medical Center:

Like most hospitals this one just started to grow and **things got out of hand.** But amid the physical confusion some **fine architectural works** stand out:

[F 6b.] Ronald McDonald House (residential facility), 76th Ave. opp. 267th St. N side. 1986. Lee Harris Pomeroy Assocs.

A 2-story structure, semicircular in plan, it **welcomes visitors** by employing an exterior color scheme that Michael Graves would also understand. A muted, dignified, convincing design.

[F 6b.] Ronald McDonald House, LIJH   **[F 13.]** Laurelton Estates row houses

[F 6c.] Helen and Irving Schneider Children's Hospital, 269-01 76th Ave., opp. 269th St. N side. 1983. The Architects Collaborative. **[F 6d.] Radich Therapy Pavilion,** 1987. The Architects Collaborative.

Suave in color and form without, bright and cheery in color and form within: **a perfect hospital equation.** Perhaps one day the entire campus will boast such qualities.

[F 6e.] Norma and Jack Parker Pavilion, Jewish Institute for Geriatric Care, 271-11 76th Ave., opp. 271st St. N side. 1972. Katz Waisman & Blumenkranz.

A bold, high-rise, cast-in-place concrete slab punctuated with well-detailed balconies. The composition pays homage, in a way, to **Le Corbusier's Salvation Army building** on the outskirts of Paris. Very impressive.

CREEDMOOR

Creedmoor: In 1873 the extensive lands of today's state hospital became a National Rifle Association firing range where state militia, rod-and-gun clubs, and NRA members trained and competed. Too many wild shots and too much unruly behavior caused Governor Charles Evans Hughes to shut the range down in 1907. It was Conrad Poppenhusen [see N Queens, College Point] who had sold NRA the property, a farm formerly owned by B. Hendrickson Creed, hence the name. Nearby Springfield and Winchester Boulevards and Musket, Pistol, Sabre, and Range Streets are all reminders of Creedmoor's earlier use.

[F 7a.] Queens County Farm Museum/originally **Samuel Cornell farmhouse,** a.k.a. **Adriance Farmhouse,** a.k.a. **Creedmoor farmhouse,** 73-50 Little Neck Pkwy., bet. 73rd Rd. and 74th Ave. W side. ca. 1750. Additions, ca. 1840, 1875, 1885, 1900. ★ **Open to the public.**

An early farmhouse preserved by the happy accident of its location: protected by the lands of the enveloping state institution (though now officially occupying City park property).

[F 7b.] Federal Aviation Administration, air traffic control facility, 63rd Ave. bet. 251st and 252nd Sts. N side. ca. 1948.

These 5 **blue lacy metal towers** are part of the complex beacon system that guides air traffic through the array of airports that serve the metropolitan area. It's not often that such high tech is so **approachable,** particularly amid a community of well-kept suburban homes.

 [F 8.] Rehabilitation Center, Creedmoor Psychiatric Center, State of New York, Commonwealth Blvd. bet. Grand Central Pkway. and 76th Rd. W side. 1969. William Lescaze & Assocs.

Low in scale, inauspicious, muted in color, in contrast with the hospital's nearby **gargantuan** 18-story Medical/Surgical Building.

QUEENS VILLAGE

[F 9.] Public School 34, Queens, The John Harvest School, 104-12 Springfield Blvd., SW cor. Hollis Ave. ca. 1905. Addition, 1930.

Ornate limestone scrolls and other ornament **elevate** the old elementary school's dark brick exterior to **architectural heights.**
For a time beginning in 1844, the site of today's 2-acre school playground was the **potter's field** for poorhouse inmates of Jamaica, Flushing, Newtown, Hempstead, North Hempstead, and Oyster Bay, *all* of which were then part of Queens County. Nassau was lopped off in 1898 as part of the deal to create a Greater New York.

[F 10a.] Little Sisters of the Poor Convent (Roman Catholic), 110-39 Springfield Blvd., bet. 110th and 112th Ave. E side. Entry opp. 110th Rd. ca. 1900. Later additions. **[F 10b.] Queen of Peace Residence,** 110-30 221st St. Entrance from 221st St. N of 112th Ave. ca. 1975.

The order of the Little Sisters has quietly retrenched its urban outposts, once sprinkled on what has become prime land, in favor of this **more remote location** in Far Queens. Here it also operates a pompous-appearing facility for the elderly at the eastern end of its property, behind a convent's high masonry walls.

CAMBRIA HEIGHTS

 [F 11.] Martin's Garden Center/originally **residence,** 119-03 Springfield Blvd., SE cor. 119th Ave. at Francis Lewis Boulevard. ca. 1860.

An Italianate Villa Style wood frame mansion, complete with cupola, all seemingly **dipped in whitewash** and given a new existence as a garden center. Poetic?

LAURELTON

[F 12.] Springfield Cemetery Chapel, 122-01 Springfield Blvd., opp. 122nd Ave. E side. 1849.

Venerable Springfield Cemetery is contained on three sides by newer Montefiore, but the old board-and-batten chapel remains.

[F 13.] Laurelton Estates (row houses), 224th St. E side; 225th St. both sides; 226th St. both sides, bet 130th and 133rd Aves. Also, 229th St. bet. 130th and 131st Aves. Both sides. ca. 1925.

A **spectacular display** of what architectural **imagination,** builders' **skills,** and a reasonable **budget** can do to craft the repetitive facades of row housing into a satisfying, memorable, picturesque composition. Is even *this* 20th-century skill forever lost to us?

SPRINGFIELD GARDENS

 [F 14a.] Originally **Peter Nostrand residence,** 186-19 140th Ave., bet. Southgate Plaza and Springfield Blvd. N side. ca. 1865.

Yet another Italianate Villa Style frame house surviving in eastern Queens.

[F 14b.] Holiday Inn, Kennedy Airport, 144-02 135th Ave., opp. 144th St. S side. 1987. Alesker, Reiff & Dundon.

A **crisp 12-story prism** that visually far surpasses its corny neighbors in the hotel business.

JFK AIRPORT

[F 15–21.] John F. Kennedy International Airport/formerly **Idlewild Airport/**originally **Anderson Field,** Southern Pkwy., Rockaway Blvd., and Jamaica Bay. Entry via Van Wyck Expwy. 1942 to present.

With land claimed by fill in the swampy waters of **Jamaica Bay,** Kennedy's **4,900** acres are roughly equivalent in area to Manhattan Island south of **34th Street.** It is so large that it's possible to run up several dollars' tariff on your taxi meter between the terminal and the airport's edge; **Manhattan** lies **15** miles further west. The fare will be well spent, however, for the trip will take you past every architectural cliché of the past four decades, some very handsome works, and some less distinguished hangovers from earlier periods as well.

Kennedy is best known for its **Terminal City,** housing the various passenger terminals, a control center, a central heating and cooling plant, three chapels, and a multitude of parking places. In addition the airport has many cargo complexes and service and storage facilities for the airline companies, as well as a hotel, a federal office building, and other service structures.

[F 15a.] Viscount Hotel/originally **International Hotel,** Van Wyck Expwy. at Southern Pkwy. 1958. Additions, 1961, William B. Tabler.

The *gateway* building, by default, to this aircraft empire.

[F 15b.] Federal Office Building. 1949. Reinhard, Hofmeister & Walquist.

Neo-frumpy, by some of the guys who helped build New York's greatest commercial wonder, **Rockefeller Center.**

[F 15c.] J.F.K. Branch, Citibank/originally **First National City Bank,** along main access road. 1959. Skidmore, Owings & Merrill.

The stilts holding this **exquisite glass box** above its roadside site express just the right amount of diffidence about becoming associated with the rest of **Terminal City.**

[F 16a.] Eastern Airlines. 1959. Chester L. Churchill.

Skip it.

[F 16b.] Northwest Airlines et al. 1962. White & Mariani.

A forest of mushroom columns at its portals masks this simple box behind.

[F 16c.] Pan American's original terminal, a simple concrete parasol, in 1961

[F 16c.] Pan American Airways et al. 1961 with additions. Tippetts-Abbett-McCarthy-Stratton; Ives, Turano & Gardner, associate architects. Zodiac figures: Milton Hebald, sculptor.

A **tour de force** produced a parasoled pavilion unfortunately marred from the beginning by gross details (i.e., the meandering drainpipes around the great piers). Now, expanded manyfold into a complex as large and confusing as the **Palace of Knossos** (the Minotaur's labyrinth), the parasol is but an entrance canopy to this depressing maze.

[F 17.] International Arrivals Building, 1957. Skidmore, Owings & Merrill.

The principal place of **Customs,** and hence a string of international airlines flank a grand, vaulted central pavilion. Once a place of sumptuous lounges and bars where one could stroll past the glass arrivals hall to see and greet incoming passengers passing through Customs, it is now comparatively drab and dull. A screen bars the arrivee's view, and the international airline bars are degraded or gone. The affluent travelers of the 1950s have been overwhelmed by the populist travelers of the 1970s who seek a **McDonald's** world: noisy, dirty, inelegant, crowded—fast food amid cacophony.

[F 17.] The International Arrivals Building and control tower in a 1964 photo

[F 18a.] Trans World Airlines Terminal A: voluptuary, soaring, and sinuous

[F 18a.] TWA Terminal A/originally **Trans World Airlines Terminal.** 1962. Eero Saarinen & Assocs. Additions. **Freestanding canopy addition,** 1978, Witthoeft & Rudolph.

Romantic voluptuary: soaring, sinuous, sensuous, surreal, and for a long time, controversial. Well worth a visit to see for yourself what all the debate was about. Unfortunately, trips through the **"umbilical cord"** to the original plane loading pod-lounge are forbidden to all but ticketed passengers, because of security precautions against hijackings.

[F 18b.] TWA Terminal B/originally **National Airlines Sundrome.** 1972. I. M. Pei & Partners.

A classy, classic building, **the best architecture at Kennedy:** rich travertine walls and floors under a great columned and corniced roof.

This **serene temple** to transport was, in its *original* corporate incarnation, the **"portal to Florida"** for many taking the bargain flights. With National Airline's demise, TWA took over the facility.

[F 19.] British Airways Terminal. 1970. Gollins Melvin Ward & Partners.

Heavy-handed battered concrete over heavy-handed battered glass. An awkward tour de force.

[F 20a.] Chapels. 1966. **Our Lady of the Skies (Roman Catholic),** George J. Sole. **Protestant,** Edgar Tafel & Assocs. **Jewish,** Bloch & Hesse.

All three are labored and self-conscious "modern": the **Protestant** is the best of the lot. Underutilized and endangered.

[F 18b.] TWA Passenger Terminal B/originally the National Airlines Sundrome

[F 20b.] Kennedy Airport Central Heating and Refrigeration Plant (in 1966)

[F 20b.] Central Heating and Refrigeration Plant. 1957. Skidmore, Owings & Merrill, architects. Seelye, Stevenson, Value & Knecht, mechanical and electrical engineers.

On axis with the **International Arrivals Building,** across the fountain-studded megamall, this glass display case for condensers, compressors, pumps, and pipes is a multicolored fantasy: splendid and wonderful.

[F 21a.] American Airlines. 1960. Kahn & Jacobs. Stained glass, Robert Sowers.

The world's largest stained-glass wall is screened from the public passenger by private offices, small rooms that enjoy its colored light privately. A strange and frustrating experience for the uninitiated observer.

 [F 21b.] United Airlines Passenger Terminal, 1961. Skidmore, Owings & Merrill.

A fastidiously detailed, subtly curving building that is, at Kennedy, second only to the **TWA Terminal B** for classic serenity.

[F 21a.] The American Airlines Term.   **[F 21b.]** The United Airlines Terminal

[F 21c.] Gulf Station. 1959. Edward D. Stone & Assocs.

A pretentious and unintended joke in the form of a miniature of Stone's **American Embassy, New Delhi.**

Warnerville: Squeezed between the eastern end of Kennedy Airport and the Nassau County town of Inwood is a waterbound settlement, many of whose houses are built on pilings, like those of Bangkok. Traffic along Rockaway Turnpike is rarely calm enough to allow a leisurely notice of the entrances to this curious community split between Queens and Nassau: at East Dock Street, 1st, or 3rd Streets. Picturesque, certainly, but hardly gentrified . . . yet.

HOWARD BEACH

Spreading out east and west behind the false fronts of **Cross Bay Boulevard's** glitzy/tawdry **fast-food and amusement strip** intended to catch the eye of Rockaway Beach-bound motorists, Howard Beach lies south of Southern (Belt) Parkway and west of Kennedy Airport. It is the belated outgrowth of an early 20th-century Jamaica Bay shorefront resort of **William J. Howard's** (the LIRR first came to nearby onetime **Ramblerville** and **Hamilton Beach** in 1880). The area is a flat, featureless, largely post-World War II development that, save for the strip that divides it in two, boasts few notable **punctuations** of its humdrum texture.

 [F 22a.] Rockwood Park Jewish Center, 156-45 84th St., bet. 157th Ave. and Shore Pkwy. E side. ca. 1972. Hausman & Rosenberg.

Dignified—if trendy—forms nevertheless create a badly needed visual punctuation in the graph-paper texture of tract development.

 [F 22b.] St. Helen's Church (Roman Catholic), 157th Ave. SW cor. 83rd St. 1979.

The yellow brick of the parish's earlier, conservatively designed buildings is here employed in a **lively, asymmetrical, self-conscious** bit of ecclesiastical **expressionism.**

West Hamilton Beach: waterfront homes along lanes ending at Hawtree Creek

West Hamilton Beach lies at the eastern flank of Howard Beach. Sandwiched between the banks of Hawtree Creek and Basin, a placid inland waterway, and the speeding trains of the Transit Authority (once LIRR) Rockaway Division right-of-way, lies this little-known, isolated water-oriented community. Boats are everywhere. Car access is via Lenihan's Bridge (the neighborhood name) into one north-south street (103rd according to maps, 104th if you believe street signs); pedestrians can use the modern 163rd Avenue bridge. For local Tom Sawyers summers here are great—they can jump into the water whenever they feel like it. Sitting on damp, marshy soil or on pilings are hundreds of tiny homes along a string of threadbare lanes that dead end at water's edge. Most are barely one car-width wide, demarked by wooden telephone poles that sit in the gutter, rather than on sidewalks much too narrow to accommodate them. About the only way to determine the area's name is from reading it on the trucks of its volunteer fire company (before Kennedy Airport lopped off the eastern part, it was called Hamilton Beach).

THE ROCKAWAYS/JAMAICA BAY

FAR ROCKAWAY · BAYSWATER · ARVERNE · BROAD CHANNEL
ROCKAWAY PARK · RIIS PARK · ROCKAWAY POINT

Portion of Town of Hempstead/Hemstede
Settled and chartered in 1664.

This narrow spit of land, a breakwater for **Jamaica Bay** (Floridians would term it a key), was so inaccessible prior to the coming of the railroads in **1868–1878** that it was an exclusive resort second only to **Saratoga Springs.** The accessibility afforded by rail connections by **1900** drove society leaders to more remote parts of Long Island's south shore in and around the **Hamptons. Neponsit** and **Belle Harbor** retain traces of this former splendor. (The IND subway, here not sub- but on grade or elevated, replaced the LIRR as the operator of the trestled connection to Long Island and the continent.)

After the departure of high society the area became a resort for the middle class. But in much of the peninsula, this too has changed: the **Hammels** and **Arverne,** both east of the terminus of the **Cross Bay Bridge,** became squalid slums. **Arverne** never achieved the aims intended by urban renewal, its renewing momentum crushed by the cost spiral and the lack of interest by **Presidents Nixon** and **Ford** in public and publicly assisted housing. Some public and publicly assisted housing for low- and middle-income families dots the area. Unfortunately, all but **Roy Reuther Houses** are grim in appearance and amazingly unresponsive to their beachfront sites. The potential development of a great recreational area at **Breezy Point,** thanks to the successful fight waged by a number of civic-minded citizens, holds out the greatest promise for the area. **Breezy Point** is a unit of the **Gateway National Recreation Area.**

FAR ROCKAWAY

[R 1.] Sage Memorial Church, The First Presbyterian Church of Far Rockaway, 13-24 Beach 12th St. Best seen from Central Ave. bet. Sage Place and Beach 12th St. N side. 1909. Cram, Goodhue, & Ferguson.

Across the immaculate Central Avenue lawn is this exquisite memory of Far Rockaway in the first decade of this century. (Sage is philanthropist **Russell Sage,** of **Forest Hills Gardens fame.**) On the lawn is a 1919 tablet to Teddy Roosevelt by the **Village Beautiful Association.** Ah, those were the days.

[R 1.] Sage Memorial Presb. Church   [R 3.] Roy Reuther Houses aptmts.

[R 2.] Congregation Knesseth Israel, 728 Empire Ave., NW cor. Sage St. 1964. Kelly & Gruzen.

An octagonal sanctuary; the **local monument** is now somewhat dated stylistically.

[R 3.] Roy Reuther Houses (apartments), 711 Seagirt Ave., bet. Beach 8th and Beach 6th Sts. S side. 1971. Gruzen & Partners.

Middle-income housing sponsored by the **United Auto Workers:** a great, stepped series of monolithic slabs faces the ocean across Atlantic Beach, **Nassau County's** first key. **Outstanding** in more ways than one.

[R 4.] Richard Cornell Graveyard, center of block and bounded by Mott, Caffrey, and New Haven Aves., Gateway Blvd. (old Greenport Rd.). 18th and 19th centuries. ★

To see this overgrown 67 × 75-foot tombstoneless midblock site where rest the remains of an ancestor of **Ezra (University) Cornell,** rent a helicopter. On second thought, don't bother.

[R 5a.] 101st Precinct, N.Y.C. Police Department/originally **79th Precinct,** 16-12 Mott Ave., NE cor. Scott A. Gadell Place. 1923.

One of many precinct houses of this era of city expansion modeled after **Renaissance palazzi.**

[R 5b.] Beth El Temple (church)/originally **St. John's Episcopal Church,** Mott Ave. NW cor. Beach 18th St. ca. 1885.

Picturesque 19th-century wood chapel, up to its ears in 20th-century dissonance.

[R 5c.] Intermediate School 53, Queens, The Brian Piccolo School, 1045 Nameoke St., bet. Cornaga Ave., Mott Ave., Beach 18th St., and Foam Place. 1972. Victor Lundy.

A many-bay-windowed volume surrounding a central courtyard to which there is a grand, monumentally staired entry—the intended main entrance—now barred because of security problems. The skylight setbacks on Foam Place make **great scaffolding** for graffiti makers. *See it from both Nameoke and from Beach 18th/Foam (one-way north).*

[R 5b.] Orig. St. John's Episc. Church   **[R 6b.]** 1518 Central Avenue bldg.

[R 6a.] Formerly **National Bank of Far Rockaway,** 1624 Central Ave., bet. Mott Ave. and Bayport Place N side. ca. 1900. H. Gardner Sibell.

Renaissance Revival in white glazed terra-cotta with great **Corinthian** pilasters. The **lattice of steel** for its once prominent sign remains an element on the local skyline.

[R 6b.] 1518 Central Avenue (commercial structure)/originally **Masonic Hall,** bet. Mott Ave. and Bayport Place. N side. ca. 1890.

The ground floor is now broken up for **crass commerce,** but the handsome symmetrical facade reveals a more distinguished history.

BAYSWATER

A peninsula on a peninsula, located on Far Rockaway's *north shore,* in Jamaica Bay, between Norton and Mott Basins. *Take Mott Avenue west, out of the business district.*

[R 7a.] Formerly **Maimonides Institute/**originally **private residence,** 3401 Mott Ave. (at west end). 1907. Altered. Damaged by severe fire, mid 1980s.

An extraordinarily lavish brick and terra-cotta country mansion, bearing **monograms of LaH,** at the very tip of the Bayswater peninsula, later crudely reused as a private school and, regrettably, badly damaged in a fire. The **picturesque ruins** remain visible through the gateway at Mott Avenue's terminus.

[R 7b.] "Sunset Lodge" (residence), 1479 Point Breeze Ave., N of Mott Ave. W side. ca. 1910. **[R 7c.] 1478 Point Breeze Avenue (residence),** N of Mott Ave. E side. ca. 1910.

Two of Bayswater's fine single homes. **Sunset Lodge,** whose name is on gateposts, seems abandoned. Great loss.

ARVERNE

[R 8a.] Ocean Village, Rockaway Beach Blvd. to the Boardwalk, bet. Beach 56th Place and Beach 59th St. 1976. Carl Koch & Assocs.

Prefabricated, precast-concrete and brick slabs and towers surrounding a central courtyard at the edge of the sea: multifamily urban renewal in a sea of unrenewed weeds.

[R 8b.] Originally **Congregation Derech Emunah (synagogue),** 199 Beach 67th St., SE cor. Rockaway Blvd. 1903. William A. Lambert.

Neo-Georgian in the Shingle Style.

BROAD CHANNEL

The community of Broad Channel occupies the southern end of Jamaica Bay's largest island, sharing it with **Big Egg Marsh** and, at the north, with **Black Bank Marsh** and **Rulers Bar Hassock.** Together these three constitute the Jamaica Bay Wildlife Refuge, one of Robert Moses' genuine achievements and now part of the National Park Service's **Gateway National Recreation Area.** This is the bay's only island accessible by vehicles other than boats—it even has a subway station on the IND Line to the Rockaways. Broad Channel supports a devoted and proud, **water-oriented community** along narrow lanes that fan out from Cross Bay Boulevard like fish bones from a spine.

 [R 9.] St. Vergilius School (Roman Catholic) Recreation Building, 19-02 Cross Bay Blvd., NE cor. E. 20th Rd. ca. 1937.

An Art Moderne facade set far back from the busy boulevard link to the Rockaways across Jamaica Bay. Motorists are so busy paying the tolls at the booths only a few yards away that this **wonderfully whimsical building** is entirely overlooked.

 [R 10.] Visitors' Center, Jamaica Bay Wildlife Refuge, Gateway National Recreation Area, U.S. Department of the Interior, National Park Service/originally N.Y.C. Department of Parks. Cross Bay Blvd. one mile N of Broad Channel settlement's border. W side. 1971. Fred L. Sommer & Assocs. with Elliot Willensky. **Open to the public.**

Serene, concrete and fluted concrete block, appropriately noncompetitive with its surrounding vegetation. The individual whose **vision and incredibly hard work** transformed the dunes and marshes into an invaluable public accommodation, once Robert Moses gave it the go-ahead, was **Herbert Johnson,** a sainted parkie.

The wildlife refuge, most importantly a bird sanctuary boasting both freshwater and saltwater ponds—and innumerable wild denizens changing with the seasons—is well worth a visit. However, you must phone before coming!

ROCKAWAY PARK

[R 11.] Rockaway Playland, Rockaway Beach Blvd. to Shore Front Blvd. bet. 97th and 98th Sts. 1901.

The vestiges of the older, somewhat larger Rockaway Beach amusement park, Queens's (much smaller) ocean version of Coney Island. For roller coaster riders and such, this was Queens's **ocean option;** North Beach amusement park, now replaced by LaGuardia Airport was the **North Shore choice,** located on the Sound. Playland remains a popular summer attraction to its devotees, a summertime shorefront carnival.

RIIS PARK

 [R 12.] Jacob Riis Park, Gateway National Recreation Area, U.S. Department of the Interior, National Park Service/originally N.Y.C. Department of Parks, Beach 149th to Beach 169th Sts., Atlantic Ocean to Rockaway Inlet. 1937. Frank Wallis, designer. Aymar Embury II, consulting architect.

A *mile* of sandy beach graced by simple, handsome, WPA-era buildings. In addition to swimming, there are **other recreational possibilities,** such as handball, paddle tennis, and shuffleboard, as well as a boardwalk for strolling. In the winter this is a haven for **Polar Bear Club** enthusiasts, and the **13,000-car** parking lot becomes an aerodrome for radio-controlled model aircraft flights. Now a Gateway unit, refreshments are available year round, as are lockers during the swimming season (nominal charge).

[R 13a.] Breezy Point, Gateway National Recreation Area, U.S. Department of the Interior, National Park Service/originally N.Y.C. Department of Parks. **[R 13b.] Breezy Point Cooperative, Inc.,** 202-30 Rockaway Point Blvd.

Appropriately named, these windswept dunes are the site of a private, largely one-story, cooperative shorefront community—the guard at the gatehouse **ensures continued privacy**—with onetime ferry access to Sheepshead Bay, Brooklyn. For many years, its most conspicuous landmarks were the **abandoned concrete frames** for an ill-fated **high-rise** apartment development. In 1963, owing to pressure from a group of public-spirited citizens, City authorities **courageously acquired title** to the site, adjacent to the cooperatives, for future recreational use and **saved Breezy Point** from becoming another high-rise jungle. With the establishment of Gateway, the area—added to Riis Park and Fort Tilden to its east—forms 3½ miles of uninterrupted Atlantic shorefront under the managerial aegis of the National Park Service's **Smokey the Bear.**

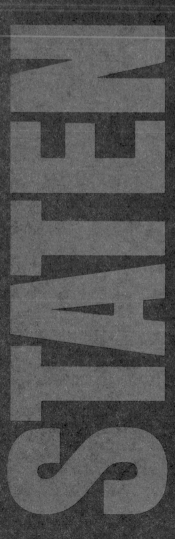

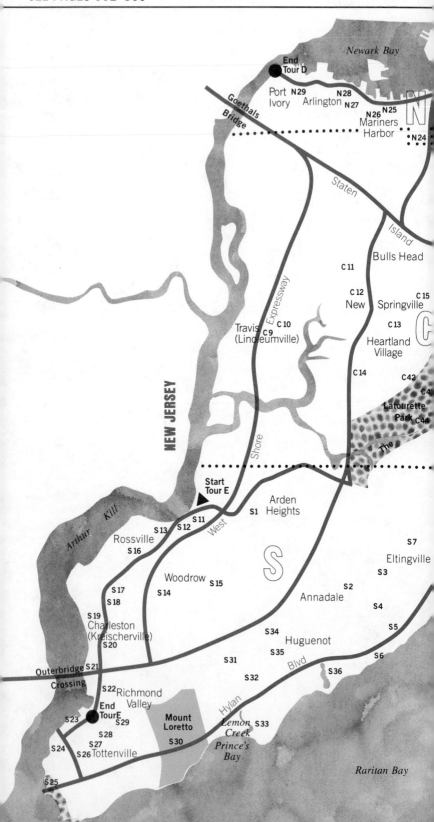

Newark Bay

End Tour D

Port Ivory   N29   N28
Arlington   N27
N26   N25
Mariners Harbor
N24

N

Goethals Bridge

Staten Island

Bulls Head

C 11

C 12   New   Springville   C 15

C 13

Travis (Linoleumville)   C 9   C 10

Heartland Village

C 14

C 42

C 4

Latourette Park   C 44

The

NEW JERSEY

Expressway

Shore

Start Tour E

Arden Heights   S 1

Arthur   Kill

Rossville

S 13   S 12   S 11
West

S 16

S 7

Eltingville

S 3

S

Woodrow   S 15

S 17
S 18

S 14

S 2

Annadale

S 4

S 5

S 19
Charleston (Kreischerville)
S 20

S 34   Huguenot

S 35

Blvd

S 6

Outerbridge   S 21
Crossing

S 31

S 32

S 36

S 22   Richmond Valley

Hylan

End Tour E   S 29

Mount Loretto

Lemon Creek   S 33

Prince's Bay

S 23

S 28

S 30

S 27
S 24   S 26   Tottenville

S 25

Raritan Bay

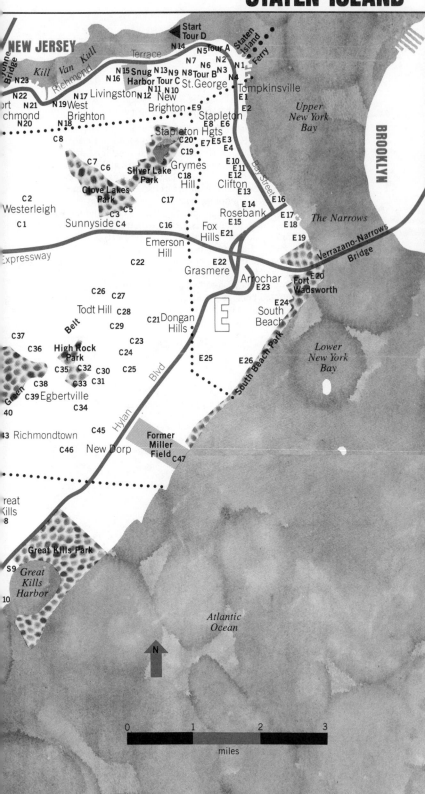

STATEN ISLAND

NEW JERSEY

Bayonne Bridge

Kill Van Kull

Richmond Terrace

Start Tour D

Staten Island Ferry

N14
N5 Tour A
N7 N6 N2
N8 Tour B N3
N9 N1
N4
Tompkinsville

N15 Snug N13
N16 Harbor Tour C
N11 N10
N12 New
Brighton

St. George

E1
E2

Upper New York Bay

BROOKLYN

N23
N22 N21
N20 N18 N19 West Brighton
N17 Livingston

Port Richmond

C8

C7 C6
C2 Clove Lakes Park
Westerleigh
C1
Sunnyside C4
C3 C5
Silver Lake Park

Stapleton Hgts
C20
C19
C18 Grymes
C17 Hill

E9
E8 E6
E7 E5 E3
E4

Stapleton

E10
E11
E12
E13 Clifton

Bay Street

E16

The Narrows

C16
Emerson Hill

Fox Hills
Rosebank
E14
E15 E21

E17
E18
E19

Verrazano-Narrows Bridge

Expressway

C22

Grasmere
E22

Arrochar
E23

Fort
E20
Wadsworth

C26 C27
Todt Hill C28
Belt C29
C21 Dongan Hills

E24
South Beach

C37
C36 High Rock
C35 C32 Park
C38 C33 C30
C39 Egbertville C31
C34
C23
C24
C25

Green Belt

Blvd

E25

E26

South Beach Park

Lower New York Bay

40
43 Richmondtown
C45
C46 New Dorp

Hylan

Former Miller Field
C47

reat
Kills
8

Great Kills Park

S9 Great Kills Harbor

10

Atlantic Ocean

N

0   1   2   3
miles

5

STATEN ISLAND

Borough of Staten Island/Richmond County

For most tourists, Staten Island is nothing more than the terminus of a **spectacular ferry ride.** Few venture ashore to explore. From such thoroughfares as Bay Street or Hylan Boulevard the views are very discouraging: drab brick houses, huge gasoline stations, and gaudy pizza parlors predominate. Persevere. Behind the listless dingy facades are **hills as steep as San Francisco's,** with breathtaking **views of the New York harbor;** mammoth, crumbling mansions surrounded by **mimosa and rhododendron,** rutted dirt roads, four-foot black snakes and fat, **wild pheasant.** There are Dutch farmhouses, **Greek temples,** Victorian mansions beyond Charles Addams' wildest **fantasies,** and ridges where archaeologists still find Indian artifacts.

The roughly triangular island is 13.9 miles long and 7.5 miles wide. It is 2½ times the size of Manhattan and ranks **third in area** among the city's boroughs. **Population** is close to Manhattan's in 1845, approaching 400,000, a mere ten persons per acre. The density continues to rise as a result of the completion of the Verrazano Bridge, and the demand for housing in the city.

11961— Board Walk at Midland Beach, STATEN ISLAND, N.Y.

Hills and dales: One always is aware of being on an island. A slight, salty **dampness** in the air, a **brackish** smell, a buoy **braying forlornly** in the distance, a feeling of isolation, proclaim the fact.

Down the backbone of the island, from St. George to Richmondtown, runs a range of hills formed by an outcropping of **serpentine rock.** These hills—Fort, Ward, Grymes, Emerson, Todt, and Lighthouse— are dotted with elegant mansions of the 19th and 20th centuries, many of them taken over by **private schools** and **charitable institutions.** Others remain palatial residences protected from the hoi polloi by high fences and private roads. (Private associations pay for streetlamps, telephone poles, and upkeep.) **Todt Hill,** often proclaimed the **highest point** on the Atlantic coast, is a dinky 409.2 feet compared with Cadillac Mountain at 1,532 on Maine's Mt. Desert Island. The views, however, are justly famous.

Links to the Mainland: In the north, the steel arch of the **Bayonne Bridge,** opened in 1931, connects Port Richmond and Bayonne. In the northwest, the **Goethals Bridge,** a cantilever structure built in 1928, joins Howland Hook and Elizabeth. In the southwest is the **Outerbridge Crossing**—named not for its remoteness from Manhattan but for Eugenius H. Outerbridge, first chairman of the Port of N.Y. Authority. It also opened in 1928 and spans the Arthur Kill between Charleston and Perth Amboy. The **Verrazano-Narrows Bridge,** completed in 1964, provides a crossing to Brooklyn and is responsible for the land (and people) boom which has swelled Staten Island's population ever since.

Once upon a time: The island is rich in historical associations. Indians and Dutch colonialists seem absurdly distant and irrelevant in Manhattan. The crush of **towering skyscrapers** inhibits the play of the imagination on which a sense of history thrives. On Staten Island, however, miles of forest form the enormous Greenbelt, and farmhouses in the Dutch mode can still be found. Here it is still possible to envision the life of our forebears.

History books notwithstanding, Staten Island was first "discovered" by the Algonquin Indians. It was first *seen* by a European, **Giovanni da Verrazano,** in 1524, and was named **Staaten Eylandt** 85 years later by Henry Hudson while on a voyage for the **Dutch East India Company.** Following a number of unsuccessful attempts, the first permanent settlement, by 19 French and Dutch colonists, was established in 1661 near the present **South Beach.** The island was renamed **Richmond** (after King Charles II's illegitimate son, the duke of Richmond) following the English capture of New Amsterdam in 1664.

Until the Revolution, inhabitants went quietly about their business, farming, fishing, oystering, shipbuilding. The revolution brought 30,000 hungry, lusty **redcoats** and **Hessian mercenaries** who occupied the island from 1776 to 1783. Initially Loyalist in sentiment, islanders greeted **Admiral Howe** with boisterous celebrations. But the 3,000 islanders were hard put to provide food, fuel, and hay for the occupying army and rapidly lost some of their fondness for the British. The island was the scene of several **skirmishes** between patriots, encamped on the Jersey shore, and the king's troops.

At the beginning of the 19th century a sixteen-year-old's $100 investment in a passenger-and-produce ferry across New York harbor marked the first successful business venture of a native-born islander, **Cornelius Vanderbilt.** [See E18a, C32.] As a result of such improved access across New York Bay the island began, in the 1830s, to develop into a **summer retreat** for wealthy, if not particularly prominent, families from New York and the South, who moved into the New Brighton area. A small literary colony sprang up around the eminent eye specialist **Dr. Samuel MacKenzie Elliott.** [See N 16b.] James Russell Lowell, Henry Wadsworth Longfellow, and Francis Parkman came to Elliott for treatment and stayed on the island to recuperate. Here Italy's patriot, **Giuseppe Garibaldi,** lived in exile, and **Frederick Law Olmsted** opened an experimental wheat farm. But Staten Island's connection with famous people has always been rather tenuous; more typical were **gentleman farmers, shipbuilders,** and **oyster captains.**

The **Civil War** may have benefited oyster captains, but other islanders suffered the dislocation of a new army. The island became the **assembly point for Union regiments** in the process of organization. Fields and orchards were turned into **camps** and **training fields,** exacerbating an already touchy situation. Confederate sympathies were strong on the island; many Southerners had sent their wives and children up from Virginia and Maryland to the comparative safety of Staten Island's hotels. Lootings, burnings, and riots of the **antidraft citizenry** plagued the island, and **abolitionists** had a hard time protecting their homes from the **angry mobs.**

After the war the island continued to develop, albeit slowly. The industrial revolution brought **brick and linoleum factories,** breweries, dye and chemical plants, **wagon and carriage makers.** Farming continued to be a leading occupation. Growth was so sluggish, however, that in 1871 the Legislature appointed a committee to study the problem. This report, **penned by Olmsted** and amazingly fresh even today, was the first of endless analyses of Staten Island's **lack of growth** or (as is more popular today) **excessive growth.** It pointed to the **prevalence of malaria** (mosquitos prospered in the island's marshes) and **poor ferry service.** Indeed, the preceding decades had seen one ferry's hull crushed by ice, another blown up as the result of a boiler explosion. Prospective passengers were understandably alarmed.

The rural nature of the island, however, did attract the sporting set from across the bay. Here the **first lawn tennis court in America** was built in 1880, and the **first American canoe club** founded. Lacrosse, cricket, rowing, fox hunting, fishing, bathing, and cycling engaged **weekend enthusiasts.** But by the beginning of the 20th century, the island's popularity had begun to wane. Fantastic schemes worthy of **Barnum and Bailey** were developed in a last-ditch attempt to lure the tourist trade. One promoter imported **Buffalo Bill's Wild West Show,** complete with **sharpshooting Annie Oakley,** "Fall of Rome" spectacles, and herds of girls and elephants.

Advice for touring: A good street map or street atlas is an absolute necessity. A newspaper stand inside either the Manhattan or St. George ferry terminals *may* accommodate you, but its safer to plan in advance. (Even with such assistance, don't be surprised to discover unexpected dead ends, nonexistent streets, thoroughfares that zig when they're supposed to zag, and of course the one-way bugaboos—Staten Island has more than its fair share.) A car is not a necessity but offers distinct advantages—remember, though: not all ferry boats are equipped to take cars. Call before leaving.

Walking tours: There are two. **Tour A** is a short loop from the St. George ferry terminal that takes you through the immediate Civic Center area. **Tour B** begins near the ferry and takes in the heights overlooking St. George. It offers the option of either walking or driving.

Carless tours: If you have exact change (in coins for now), Bus S 113 will take you leisurely to Richmondtown Restoration, where a great deal of concentrated touring is possible. Bus S 113 will also take you from there to Tottenville to see the Conference House. Return by Staten Island Rapid Transit (S.I.R.T.) in smooth-running, sleek stainless steel subway cars, where, as on a commuter system, the conductor collects the fare (same amount as for the subways in the other boroughs) and issues a ticket.

Driving tours: The island cannot be done in a day. Despite any misimpressions created by the reduced-scale insets of the island in some city maps, Staten Island is the city's third largest borough. Distances are deceptively great, roads poorly marked, and buildings hard to find. Nevertheless, the way to discover Staten Island is to be independent and take some chances. The street map will help enormously. But for those who enjoy a guided tour, here are four driving tours:

Tour B: A short ramble (which can also be walked, as in **Tour A,** above) around St. George/Fort Hill/Brighton Heights, the communities overlooking the ferry's point of arrival.

Tour C: A midlength jaunt to and through New Brighton, a residential community atop a series of hillocks, featuring the 19th-century suburb named Hamilton Park.

Tour D: A generous excursion extending the length of the North Shore, along the waters of Kill Van Kull via Richmond Terrace to Port Ivory, with a number of optional side trips to the near interior.

Tour E: A South Shore drive along Arthur Kill Road beginning in Rossville—more than halfway down the island's length—which encompasses some of the island's least developed areas and surveys the impact of both old and new industries on island life. It terminates in Tottenville, opposite Perth Amboy, N.J.

Today and tomorrow: During the last half-century the dangers threatening the island's natural advantages of space, air, grass, and trees have increased. Park areas are being **menaced by expressways.** On humid, stagnant days, lawns shrivel up and die from chemical fallout, and citizens hastily retreat to the safety of air-conditioned homes. Meadows have been **scraped clean of trees,** natural streams buried, **hills leveled** in preparation for jerry-built housing developments. Wild salt marshes are now city garbage dumps. The outlook is grim—particularly to anyone who remembers what rural Staten Island was once like. But to those who know how rare **a blade of grass** is in Manhattan or Queens, the island, by contrast, is positively pastoral. The recession of the 1970s slowed highway development. The National Park Service, through its Gateway National Recreation Area, now controls much of the island's ocean and bay shoreline. The state wetlands act offers protection against indiscriminate destruction of marshlands. South Richmond, the least developed part of the island, has been the subject of many studies to control its growth. And first steps to protect the Greenbelt have been taken by enacting zoning legislation for a special natural area district. Whether the island's remaining opportunities will be used with care or recklessly squandered is the big question for Staten Islanders (and other New Yorkers) in the decades to come.

Restaurants: The island is not known for its restaurants, but the steadily increasing population has expanded choices in recent years. They are listed geographically in the text.

Staten Island Ferry Ride

> *We were very tired, we were very merry—*
> *We had gone back and forth all night on the ferry.*
> —Edna St. Vincent Millay

Drawbridges and rusty chains **clank,** engines **shudder** and grunt, the throaty whistle **blasts,** and **the ferry churns out** into the oily waters of New York harbor. Petulant gulls hover aloft; commuters, inured to the spectacular, settle behind newspapers, while tourists crowd to the rail. Children and even some adults become very merry.

Ferries leave frequently during daylight hours, less so on weekends. Upon boarding, move to the far end of the upper deck. From this position, **Brooklyn** lies to the left, and **Governors Island** is immediately ahead; **Ellis Island,** the old immigration station, and the **Statue of Liberty,** bound to produce **a lump in the throat** for even the most callous, appear in succession on the right.

The **first glimpse** of Staten Island is attractive. Steep, wooded hills rise behind the civic center of St. George; **Greek Revival porticos** appear along the waterfront, and **Gothic spires** and **Italianate towers** of schools and churches top hills on the right. On a misty or, more likely, smoggy day, the aspect is momentarily reminiscent of **a small Italian town.** Romance is quickly dispelled by the brutally efficient red brick ferry terminal at St. George, with its eye-ease green tile interior—more suggestive of a gymnasium shower room than of a **gateway.**

NORTHERN STATEN ISLAND

ST. GEORGE • FORT HILL • BRIGHTON HEIGHTS
NEW BRIGHTON • LIVINGSTON • WEST BRIGHTON
PORT RICHMOND • MARINERS HARBOR • ARLINGTON
PORT IVORY

The North Shore

Don't be like most people, who return to Manhattan without having taken even a stroll through nearby St. George. If on foot, do take a short walk (Tour A) or a slightly more strenuous one up to Fort Hill (Tour B) before taking the ferry back.

ST. GEORGE/FORT HILL/BRIGHTON HEIGHTS

Walking Tour A: Through St. George's Civic Center: After negotiating the length of the rambling, many-fingered bus terminal (upland of the Ferry Terminal), you arrive at the harbor side of an incomplete row of structures that were to have formed Staten Island's civic center. The first buildings of consequence are arrayed along Richmond Terrace on the right (west); the lesser ones behind the brick wall at Bay Street on the left (east) are for the return stroll back to the ferry.

Richmond Terrace:

Between Borough Place and Hamilton Avenue.

A grand (but incomplete) scheme of civic structures initiated by Staten Island's first borough president, George Cromwell.

[N 1a.] Staten Island Borough Hall, Richmond Terr. NW cor. Borough Place. 1906. Carrère & Hastings. ★

With its picturesque form, this elegant brick structure, in the style of **a French town hall** welcomes those arriving to the island by ferry.

[N 1a.] Staten Island Borough Hall, as depicted on a pre-World War I postcard

 [N 1b.] Richmond County Court House, 30 Richmond Terr., SW cor. Schuyler Place. Designed, 1913. Completed, 1919. Carrère & Hastings. ★

A design **totally different** from neighboring Borough Hall. Purists object, but the effect is pleasing.

Montezuma's La Fosse aux Loups (restaurant), 11 Schuyler St., off Stuyvesant Place.

A stone's throw from the ferry. Begun as **Montezuma's Revenge** in the early 1970s, it has graduated to being one of the island's handsomest and most dependable restaurants. *Save it for the end of your visit.*

 [N 2a.] 120th Precinct, N.Y.C. Police Department/originally **66th Precinct/Borough Police Headquarters,** 78 Richmond Terr., NW cor. Wall St. 1922. James Whitford, Sr.

The form of an Italian Renaissance palazzo adapted to the island's security needs, but **pale in comparison** with Whitford's smaller effort in Tottenville. [See Staten Island S 24b.]

[N 2b.] Richmond County Family Courthouse, 100 Richmond Terr., bet. Wall St. and Hamilton Ave. W side. Sibley & Fetherston. 1933.

Finely detailed Ionic columns and a delicately ornamented facade (all in softly glazed terra-cotta) **look pleasantly remote** from the heavy problems that are pondered within.

A walk up Hamilton Avenue and a left turn onto Stuyvesant Place will take you to the local museum, a resting place before you return to the ferry.

 [N 3a.] N.Y.C. Department of Health Building, 51 Stuyvesant Place, bet. Wall St. and Hamilton Ave. E side. ca. 1935. Henry C. Pelton.

Modest Municipal mid-Depression Art Deco. Doesn't hold a candle to the **Ambassador Apartments,** on nearby Daniel Low Terrace (Tour B.)

[N 3b.] Staten Island Museum, Staten Island Institute of Arts and Sciences, 75 Stuyvesant Place, NE cor. Wall St. 1918, 1927. Robert W. Gardner. Open to the public.

A sleepy museum, bulging from its small Georgian Revival building and waiting for the day when it will move to **larger accommodations** at Snug Harbor Cultural Center.

If you're filled with energy and want an extended walk in this area, turn to Driving/Walking Tour B. If it's time to return to the ferry, follow Stuyvesant Place east past the upland side of the Courthouse and Borough Hall. Then walk downhill to the far end of the Ferry Terminal entry area, Bay Street. Along the way:

[N 4a.] St. George Branch, N.Y. Public Library, 10 Hyatt St., SE cor. Central Ave. 1906. Carrère & Hastings. Altered, 1987, David Paul Helpern. Stained glass, David Wilson.

One of a group of **four Carnegie gifts** that began to bring a semblance of culture to the rural island early in the century.

Behind the Bay Street wall:

Best seen from the sidewalk leading back into the Ferry Terminal.

[N 4b.] Formerly **Chief Physician's Residence, U.S. Coast Guard Base, St. George,** 1 Bay St., S of Ferry Terminal. 1815.

The gambrel roof of this handsome, Federal-style building can be seen from Bay Street, picturesquely peeking over the base's curving high brick wall, **studded with star anchors.** The fussy dormers and scalloped roof are later additions. The structure predates the use of the site by the **Lighthouse Service** (1868) and the **Coast Guard** (1939), when the area was first the **Quarantine** (1799) and later in part turned over to customs use.

[N 4c.] Formerly **Administration Building, U.S. Coast Guard Base, St. George**/originally **Office Building, U.S. Lighthouse Service, Third District Depot,** 1 Bay St., S of Ferry Terminal. 1871. A. B. Mullett, Supervising Architect of the Treasury. Additions, 1901. ★

Three mansard-roofed stories of granite and red brick, in the center of the compound, designed in the French Second Empire style by its American master, **Alfred Bult Mullett.** He was architect of that other (much larger) gem, Washington's old **State, War, and Navy Department Building** (now the Executive Office Building).

END of Tour A. *Ferries to Manhattan run frequently during the daytime hours.*

Walking or Driving Tour B: A short trip through St. George/Fort Hill/Brighton Heights: This brief—but steep—tour of the nearby hills above the ferry landing is undulating, both laterally and vertically. It is best taken by foot or by slowly moving car (put your blinkers on), and is arranged to follow the one-way street pattern.

From the Ferry Terminal exit (at Bay Street and Richmond Terrace), walk or drive up hill on short Borough Place, and take a mandatory soft left onto the steep upgrade of Hyatt Street. [For the branch library, see N 4a., above.]

(If you've come by car and wish to leave it conveniently parked, use the Municipal Parking Field at the top of Hyatt Street—the entrances are off Central Avenue and St. Mark's Place—above Borough Hall.)

START *across from parking field at St. Mark's and Fort Pls.*

St. Mark's Place:

Between Fort Place and Westervelt Avenue, north side.

[N 5a.] Brighton Heights Reformed Church, 320 St. Mark's Place, SW cor. Fort Place. 1866. John Correja. ★

A delicate, 19th-century white wood-framed church, almost entirely overwhelmed everywhere one looks by **intrusive 20th-century competitors.**

Proceed northerly (then westerly) along St. Mark's Place.

[N 5b.] Curtis High School, St. Mark's Place, NW cor. Hamilton Ave. 1904, 1922. C. B. J. Snyder. Additions, 1925, 1937. Continued alterations. ★

Collegiate Gothic as applied to secondary-school education. Its lofty site and strong architectural forms add appropriately to its physical prominence as Staten Island's **first municipal structure to be** completed after Richmond County was absorbed into Greater New York in 1898.

Hotel Castleton was opened in 1889, in the days when Brighton Heights was a well-known resort. It was a 400-room wood-frame behemoth by architect C. P. H. Gilbert, just across St. Mark's Place from today's Curtis High School, where two large apartment towers now stand. The hotel was destroyed in 1907 in a spectacular fire, a depiction of which can be found among Borough Hall's lobby murals.

St. Mark's Place turns softly to the west at Nicholas Street.

[N 5c.] Originally **Henry H. Cammann residence,** 125 St. Mark's Place. 1892. Edward Alfred Sargent. **[N 5d.]** Originally **Vernon H. Brown residence,** 119 St. Mark's Place. 1890. Edward Alfred Sargent. **[N 5e.]** Originally **Frederick L. Rodewald residence,** 103 St. Mark's Place. 1894? Edward Alfred Sargent. All bet. Nicholas St. and Westervelt Ave. N side.

Three **exemplary reminders** (particularly the well-maintained **No. 119,** painted a handsome olive green) of what this remarkable row of **Queen Anne Revival** wood-shingled houses once looked like. Unique in all New York. **No. 125** was purchased by silent film star Mabel Normand in 1916 for use by her father, a stage carpenter.

[N 5c.] Orig. Henry H. Cammann res.   **[N 5e.]** Orig. Frdk. L. Rodewald res.

[N 5f.] 75 St. Mark's Place (residence), bet. Nicholas St. and Westervelt Ave. N side. ca. 1880.

Shingle Style with delicate Doric columns. The rear boasts **three tiers of porches** peering out at Manhattan across the harbor.

[N 5g.] St. Peter's Roman Catholic Church, 49 St. Mark's Place, N side. 1903. Tower, 1919. Both by Harding & Gooch. **Rectory,** 1912, George H. Streeton.

For its first decade and a half, this was just a symmetric cream-colored brick church perched atop **the Brighton Heights escarpment,** whose design recalled transitional Romanesque-Gothic forebears. Then in 1919 the symmetry was broken with the completion of St. Peter's extremely tall, **slender bell tower,** an impressive local landmark ever since. It came to be known as the **Cardinal's Tower** after its dedication by New York's **John Cardinal Farley.** (The complicated forms of the church complex as they hug the cliff are best seen from Richmond Terrace, below, on Driving Tour D.)

[N 5h.] 17, 19 St. Mark's Place (double house), ca. 1875.

Sumptuously mansarded.

[N 5i.] 1, 5 St. Mark's Place (double house), NE cor. Westervelt Ave. ca. 1860.

A craggy and mysterious structure designed to properly turn the corner onto Westervelt.

Along Westervelt Avenue:

Turn left slowly and, as you do, look carefully across the avenue and down the hill on Westervelt:

[N 6a.] 42 Westervelt Avenue (residence), W side. ca. 1860.

An expansive clapboard house painted the Staten Island (or muted) version of a San Francisco **"painted lady"** color scheme.

[N 6b.] 36-38, 30-32 Westervelt Avenue (double houses), W side. ca. 1855–1860.

Two wonderful but very different structures: the near one, in wood frame simply clad in clapboard, is **in marvelous contrast** to the far one, in intricately laid Italianate dark red brick.

Take the first left at the fork onto Hamilton Avenue (at the Glorious Church of God in Christ), and stop at the tiny cul-de-sac at the left, Phelps Place.

Phelps Place:

A time warp. Three frame 19th-century houses on one flank and, on the other, a large, raw-brick low-rise apartment complex—St. George Garden Apartments, recovering from the wounds of its use as welfare housing. (It's ironic that the apartments occupy the site of the **opulent Anson Phelps Stokes mansion.**) In the distance, ever in view, is St. Peter's **slender tower** and cross.

[N 6c.] 7, 8, and 9, 10 Phelps Place (double houses), W side. 1891. Douglas Smyth. **[N 6d.] 11 Phelps Place (residence),** N end. ca. 1880.

Tudor shingle double house twins are the first off the street; Shingle Style further within the enclave. Note the porte cochere on No. 11.

Continue on Hamilton Avenue and take a right turn onto Daniel Low Terrace:

[N 6d.] Ambassador Apartments, 30 Daniel Low Terrace, bet. Crescent Ave. and Fort Hill Circle. W side. 1932. Lucian Pisciatta.

Art Deco at its best, at least on Staten Island. Six stories of subdued, cream-colored brickwork with **black accents,** enlivened by colored, molded terra-cotta ornament that culminates over the main entryway. The metalwork on the entrance doors, done in a **peacock pattern,** is exquisite.

Turn right at Fort Hill Circle and follow it around past a charming collection of freestanding houses. Then take a right turn onto the second intersection with Daniel Low Terrace and follow it downhill.

[N 6e.] 117 Daniel Low Terrace (residence), NE cor Fort Place. ca. 1885.

An essay in reds: brick with terra-cotta ornaments and narrow-chested window proportions.

END of Tour B. *Time now to return to the ferry or to your parked car, or to consider staying longer. Fort Place will take you downhill to both the parking field and the ferry. (The other tours require a car.)*

Driving Tour C: A trip through New Brighton: This condensed tour begins along steeply sloping Jersey Street, for many decades a poor black community whose slum dwellings have been replaced with low-rise public housing. It quickly enters the heights of New Brighton, where vestiges of the 1836 development plan for hillside terraces, as well as evidence of the 1851 Hamilton Park planned community, will be found.

START *at Richmond Terrace and Jersey Street. Drive slowly and put your blinkers on for safety.*

NEW BRIGHTON

A development begun in 1836 by Thomas E. Davis, a Manhattan speculator.

[N 7a.] Richmond Garden, N.Y.C. Department of Housing, Preservation & Development, Jersey St., bet. Richmond Terr. and Crescent Ave. W side. 1986. Weintraub & di Domenico.

An intricate cast-iron-trimmed fence, gazebos, and other traditional elements of **parkmaking** greatly **distinguish this simple green space.** It was designed to complement the adjacent, thankfully small-in-scale but otherwise not especially noteworthy, yellow-and-brown brick **Richmond Gardens Apartments.**

[N 7b.] St. Stanislaus Kostka Roman Catholic Church, 109 York Ave., bet. Carlyle and Buchanan Sts. E side. 1925. Paul R. Henkel.

The interesting forms that constitute the rear of this church are visible atop the heights overlooking Richmond Garden.

Take a right turn (west) onto Pauw Street, zigzag across York Avenue, and follow the very steep hill up to a right turn (north) on Harvard Avenue.

Hamilton Park:

A number of suburban country dwellings of 12 to 14 rooms (nevertheless dubbed "cottages" at the time) are to be found here from the 19th-century planned community, Hamilton Park. In 1853, the same year as West Orange, N.J.'s Llewellyn Park, developer **Charles Kennedy Hamilton** began a suburban development planned along the romantic precepts of landscape gardener **Andrew Jackson Downing.** The area even then was only a half hour by steam ferry from Manhattan's tip, pretty much the same as today. (Whether steam- or diesel-powered, ferry speed seems determined by the drag of its hull in the water rather than by the medium of propulsion.) The Hamilton lands lay **on the heights** between today's East Buchanan, Franklin, Prospect, and York.

[N 8a.] 119 Harvard Avenue (residence), bet. Prospect Ave. and Park Place, opp. Nassau St. ca. 1859.

Charming brick Gothic Revival cottage for Hamilton Park.

[N 8b.] 32 Park Place (residence), SE cor. Harvard Ave. ca. 1864. Additions. Carl Pfeiffer.

Fronting on Harvard but bearing a Park Place address is this **lovingly composed brick house** with a later ogee-curved mansard roof and segmental arched dormers, one of the 12 second-stage Hamilton Park cottages designed by Pfeiffer.

[N 8c.] Originally **Pritchard residence,** 66 Harvard Ave., NW cor. Park Place. 1845. ★

Hidden behind privet hedge, birch trees, and wisteria is this expansive, grand, yellow stucco house with gray trim. Note that its front entrance was placed to command the downhill view to the west—today its large backyard. This is believed to be Hamilton Park's first spec house.

[N 8d.] 29 Harvard Avenue (residence), bet. Park Place and E. Buchanan St. E side. ca. 1864. Carl Pfeiffer.

Another of the "cottages" commissioned by developer Hamilton.

Proceed ahead and take a left turn downhill (west) on narrow East Buchanan Street. Then take another left turn (south) on Franklin Avenue.

[N 9a.] The Hamilton Park Cottage, 105 Franklin Ave., bet. E. Buchanan St. and Cassidy Place. E side. ca. 1859. ★

This triple-arched, porticoed residence is *officially* identified, by virtue of its designation as a City landmark, as one of the 19th-century "cottages" built under Charles K. Hamilton's development plan.

Quick, take that right turn onto curving (south) Pendleton Place.

[N 9b.] Originally **William S. Pendleton residence (2)/**later **T. M. Rianhard residence,** 1 Pendleton Place, SW cor. Franklin Ave. 1861. Charles Duggin.

The **"second" Pendleton house**—see below. **A magnificent work** of freestanding residential architecture whose asphalt-composition "brick" siding does not detract enough from its distinctive **Stick Style silhouette** and robust forms to diminish its visual role in the community.

[N 8c.] 66 Harvard Ave.: the first speculatively built Hamilton Park "cottage"

[N 9b.] The "second" Pendleton res.

[N 10a.] 158 Prospect Ave. residence

[N 9c.] Originally **William S. Pendleton residence (1),** 22 Pendleton Place, bet. Franklin and Prospect Aves. N side at the curve. 1855. Charles Duggin. ★

This is known as **the "first" Pendleton house.** After his business ventures prospered (he was president of the local ferryboat company and dabbled in real estate), Pendleton forsook this wood-shingled **Gothic Revival villa** with crisscrossed muntin windows for the even greater confection across the street known as the "second."

Take a right turn (west) onto Prospect Avenue for an amazing array of fine residences.

[N 10a.] 158 Prospect Avenue (residence), bet. Franklin and Lafayette Aves. S side. ca. 1885.

A very romantic shingled house whose west gable steps out progressively as your eyes rise to the roof's peak.

[N 10b.] 172 Prospect Avenue (residence), bet. Franklin and Lafayette Aves. S side. ca. 1870.

A stately, tall mansard gives this frame dwelling some of the quality of a French Second Empire stone house.

[N 10c.] 180 Prospect Avenue (residence), SW cor. Lafayette St. ca. 1885.

Warm, inviting, Tudor Revival in half-timber over brick.

[N 10d.] 202 Prospect Avenue (residence), SW cor. Lafayette St. ca. 1885.

Brown shingled with an added sloped dormer facing north, no doubt to illuminate **an artist's studio** in the attic.

[N 10e.] 212 Prospect Avenue (residence), bet. Lafayette Ave. and Ellicott Place. S side. ca. 1895.

Three **sunbursts** over the three multipaned windows/doors.

[N 10f.] 232 Prospect Avenue (residence), SE cor. Ellicott Place. ca. 1870.

Shingle Style but the shingles have been painted white somewhere along the way.

Ellicott Place:

Between Lafayette and Clinton Avenues. S side. Two brick gateposts and a green center island mark this one-block enclave, ever lovely in its entirety.

[N 11a.] 15 Ellicott Place (residence), S of Prospect Ave. E side. ca. 1870.

Shingle Style, painted yellow, and terrific!

[N 11b.] 254 Prospect Avenue (residence), SW cor. Ellicott Place. ca. 1885.

A wood frame dwelling in the Queen Anne Revival Style. Complex *and* contradictory.

[N 11c.] 229 Prospect Avenue (residence), bet. Lafayette Ave. and Clinton Court. N side. ca. 1885.

A pale green stunner.

Time for a seventh-inning stretch: get out of the car and stretch your legs by walking back to Lafayette Avenue and turning right (south).

[N 11d.] 270 Lafayette Avenue (residence), bet. Prospect Ave. and Arnold St. W side. ca. 1885.

Brown stained shingles with **delectable diagonal tucks and darts.** But someone fooled with the attic window in the gable!

[N 11e.] 280 Lafayette Avenue (residence), NW cor. Arnold St. ca. 1870.

A prim mansarded house, **the kind they paint** on Mother's Day greeting cards.

[N 11f.] 176 Arnold Street (residence), SW cor. Lafayette Ave. ca. 1900.

This dwelling is built of concrete—that's right, cast-in-place concrete. Take a good look. Clearly an early use of the substance in residential construction.

Back to the car. Proceed west on Prospect Avenue to the Goodhue Home, and follow it around to the right (north) to Clinton Avenue.

[N 12a.] "Woodbrook," Jonathan Goodhue residence/now **Goodhue Children's Center Recreation Building,** 304 Prospect Ave., at Clinton

Ave. S side. ca. 1845. B. Haynard and James Patterson, builders.
[N 12b.] William H. Wheelock Residence Facility, Goodhue Center,
290 Prospect Ave., at Clinton Ave. S side. 1971. Davis, Brody & Assocs.

The driveway at the west end of Prospect Avenue leads to an unusual pair of buildings used by the Children's Aid Society for their work. **Woodbrook,** though it shows its age, still conveys some of the elegance it must have possessed when it was a villa commanding the vast acreage of the Goodhue estate, still largely intact. The **Wheelock Building,** named for a trustee of the center, is an experiment in group living for eight teenagers. Woodbrook's tarnished elegance contrasts with the carefully contrived utilitarian statement of its modern neighbor.

[N 12b.] The William H. Wheelock Residence Facility, at the Goodhue Center

[N 12c.] St. Peter's Boys High School Residence, once a grand private house

[N 12c.] Residence, St. Peter's Boys High School/earlier **Nicholas Muller residence,** 200 Clinton Ave., at Prospect Ave. W side. ca. 1857.

Neat and crisp in dark red with white trim, this house is the most distinguished building on the small St. Peter's campus.

Proceed north on Clinton Avenue, and take a right turn (east) on Fillmore Street.

[N 13a.] Originally **New Brighton Village Hall,** 66 Lafayette Ave., SW cor. Fillmore St. 1871. James Whitford, Sr. ★

The boarded-up windows and years of neglect fail to conceal the prim dignity of this mansard-roofed brick delight. Seeking a viable contemporary use.

[N 13b.] Christ Church (Episcopal), 76 Franklin Ave., SW cor. Fillmore St. 1904. **Parish Hall,** 1906.

A gray ashlar complex featuring as its off-center centerpiece a dignified neo-Gothic church which, together with the Parish Hall, forms a chaste green corner campus.

With one's arrival at Christ Church, Tour C ENDS. *A left turn (north) onto Franklin Avenue and a right turn (east) onto Richmond Terrace will take you back to the Ferry Terminal and Bay Street.*

Driving Tour D: A trip of contrasts between industrial desolation and residential and institutional elegance. Proceeding westerly along Richmond Terrace, the tour follows Kill Van Kull (the waterway that separates Staten Island from Bayonne, N.J.) from the ferry terminal all the way to Port Ivory at the extreme end of the island's North Shore. From there it's easy to get onto the Staten Island Expressway toward Brooklyn or the Goethals Bridge to Elizabeth, N. J., or to retrace the route to the ferry. There are a few diversionary side trips along the way through Livingston, West New Brighton, Port Richmond, and Mariners Harbor.

START *on Richmond Terrace just west of the civic center at Hamilton Avenue.*

At first the tour skirts the bottom of the Brighton Heights escarpment, with the abandoned **Staten Island Rapid Transit North Shore route** (run by the Baltimore & Ohio Railroad) between you and the waterway and some mansarded (and other) homes on the upland side of the Terrace. (The church hugging the cliff is St. Peter's [see N 5g.].)

[N 14a.] 194, 202, 204, 208, 216 Richmond Terrace (residences), bet. Stuyvesant Place and Nicholas St. S side. ca. 1875.

A group of currently (or formerly) mansarded frame houses in various states of repair, sitting with their backs to the high ground and their fronts overlooking the Kill and New Jersey beyond. When built, **theirs was a bucolic view.**

[N 13a.] Old New Brighton Village Hall   **[N 15.]** Old Chapel at Snug Harbor

[N 14b.] Pavilion on the Terrace (restaurant)/formerly **Columbia Hall, Knights of Columbus/**originally **Henry P. Robertson residence,** 404 Richmond Terr., bet. St. Peter's Place and Westervelt Ave. S side. ca. 1835. John Haviland?

This is the last vestige of **Temple Row,** the name given to ten early 19th-century Greek Revival mansions built by **wealthy New Yorkers** and **Southern planters** along Richmond Terrace when the view across the **Kill Van Kull** was more pastoral. Its handsome Doric columns and stately pediment are compromised by years of neglect and recent patch-ups. **No. 404** and four others (all gone) were developed by English-born developer, **Thomas E. Davis.**

[N 14c.] 536 Richmond Terrace (residence), bet. York Ave. and Franklin Sts. S side. ca. 1875.

Another mansard, this one **almost hidden** atop a black ashlar re-taining wall behind dense, luxuriant hedges. What goes on there?

[N 14d.] Originally **Capt. John Neville residence,** 806 Richmond Terr., bet. Clinton Ave. and Tysen St. S side. ca. 1770. ★

Identified by its slender-columned 2-story veranda, it is said that the house reflects the Caribbean journeys of its retired sea captain owner, John Neville. Its proximity to the old **Sailors' Snug Harbor,** just down the Terrace, gave it a period of success as a local tavern, the Old Stone Jug.

[N 15.] Snug Harbor Cultural Center: Old Bldg. C and neighbors (1869 print)

[N 15.] Snug Harbor Cultural Center/originally **Sailors' Snug Harbor,** 914 Richmond Terr., bet. Tysen St., Snug Harbor Rd., and Kissel Ave. S side to Henderson Ave. **Building A,** 1879. ★ **Building B,** 1840, Samuel Thomson & Son. ★ **Building C (central building facing Richmond Terr.),** 1833, Minard Lafever. ★ Interior ★ **Building D,** 1844, Samuel Thomson & Son. ★ **Building E,** 1880. ★ **Center (or north) Gatehouse,** 1873. ★ **West Gatehouse,** 1880. **Chapel,** 1856. ★ Interior, ★ **Iron Fence,** 1842, Frederick Diaper. ★ **Building M, Maintenance,** renovated into the **Staten Island Children's Museum,** 1987, David Prendergast, Jeffrey Hannigan, James Sawyer. Keith Goddard/Works, graphic design. **Music hall,** 1892; restoration-competition winner, 1987, Rafael Viñoly. **Open to the public.**

Five Greek temples serenely surveying an immaculately groomed lawn made Sailors' Snug Harbor an obvious **landmark choice** back in the 1960s. A court action by the Harbor's trustees against designation, their **initial victory,** and their **ultimate defeat** on appeal by City attorneys presaged New York City's purchase of the buildings—and then the remainder of the picturesque site. Whether the city's and the community's vision can, through **adaptive reuse,** be made into a tangible cultural center for Staten Island is still a great local question.

The Harbor was founded by Robert Richard Randall, who con-verted his Revolutionary War privateer-father's bequest into a fund for the support of **"aged, decrepit and worn-out sailors."** For many years, the proceeds from Randall's property in Manhattan's Greenwich Vil-lage supported the Harbor. Following the court of appeals support of landmark designation, the Harbor's trustees moved the institution to a new site on the North Carolina coast. This paved the way, in 1976, for the reuse of the **rich complex** of Greek Revival, Victorian, and early 20th-century edifices, and 60 acres of romantic grounds to the south, for **a new public benefit.**

Among the new facilities that have opened to the public are the **Newhouse Gallery** and the **Children's Museum,** in reworked Building M. The latter opened with a participatory exhibition **Building Buildings** by architect **Lee Skolnick,** an informative and imaginative educational display about architecture that should be kept on view forever.

Losses at Snug Harbor: A number of the Harbor's fine buildings succumbed to the high cost of maintenance long before its landmark status was declared, such demolitions perhaps explaining the public support for designation. Its most opulent structure was architect R. W. Gibson's 1892 **Randall Memorial Church,** with a dome that echoed London's St. Paul's but at a considerably smaller scale. (Five of its stained-glass windows are preserved at Calvary Presbyterian Church [1894], Castleton and Bement Avenues.) The other was the **Hospital,** a neo-Classical structure cruciform in plan (like 18th-century English prisons), with four long wings extending out from a domed central pavilion. It bit the dust in 1951.

R. H. Tugs (restaurant), 1115 Richmond Terr., nr. Bard Ave. N side.

On the bank of the Kill Van Kull with real closeup views of the tugs and other shipping that sail its waters. Yuppie food and drink in a passable atmosphere.

Side Trip 1. through Livingston and West Brighton: *Take a left onto Bard Avenue. In one block, just your side of the park, take a right (west) turn onto Delafield Place. To skip the Side Trip continue west on Richmond Terrace about one mile to Taylor Street just ahead of* [N 19b.].

LIVINGSTON

[N 16a.] Walker Park Recreation Building, N.Y.C. Department of Parks & Recreation, 50 Bard Ave., SW cor. Delafield Place. 1934.

Full-timbered with brick infill, ashlar walls, a red slate roof, and charming casement windows, all built during the nadir of the Great Depression. Spectacularly **ultraromantic** and kept in a truly immaculate state—but surely not by the city's ostensibly poverty-stricken Parks Department.

Walker Park: Mary Ewing Outerbridge brought lawn tennis to Staten Island from Bermuda in 1874 (vying with Nahant, Massachusetts, for the record of hosting the first sets played in this country). In 1880 the first national tennis tournament was played here, in what is now Walker Park. Ms. Outerbridge was the sister of Eugenius H. Outerbridge, for whom the Crossing is named, and the park is named for Mr. Outerbridge's good friend, Randolph St. George Walker, Jr., a casualty of World War I. Today tennis and cricket are played on the grounds.

[N 16b.] Dr. Samuel MacKenzie Elliott residence, 69 Delafield Place, bet. Bard and Davis Aves. N side. 1850. ★

An early eye surgeon of wide repute, Dr. Elliott, as a result of his distinguished patients, became **the focal point** of a small but far-flung **literary colony:** James Russell Lowell, Henry Wadsworth Longfellow, and Francis Parkman, among others. The house itself, one of some fifteen he built in this area, is a straightforward ashlar granite box whose only exterior charm is a frilly, serpentine vergeboard along its gabled roof. (Another Elliott-built house in granite exists at 557 Bard Avenue, south of Forrest Avenue/City Boulevard, E side.) It is unclear where Elliott himself lived.

To the south, across Walker Park:

[N 16c.] Originally **Stewart Brown residence,** 14–17 Livingston Court, bet. Bard and Davis Aves. S side. ca. 1860.

Bold of scale and **rich** of detail—note the many dormers. This fine old house squeezes **Livingston Court,** indicating it was built before the court.

It's easier to see the next venerable structure by walking—rather than driving—a block back to narrow, twisting Richmond Terrace:

[N 16d.] Earlier **Kreutzer-De Groot-Pelton residence,** 1262 Richmond Terr., near Pelton Place. S side. 1722–1836. ★

Typical of the area's colonial residences. First, islanders built a one-room structure, usually of local fieldstone; rooms were later added when needed. The stone cottage on the right dates from 1722; the central shingled section was added in 1770; the 2-story brick section on the left was built in 1836. The man who was to become England's **King William IV** in 1830 was entertained here during the Revolution.

Back to the car: A few left turns will take you three-quarters around Walker Park, squeezing past the Stewart Brown house on Livingston Court. Then a right turn onto Bard Avenue takes you farther south to the next brief stop.

[N 16e.] Originally **George W. Curtis residence,** 234 Bard Ave., NW cor. Henderson Ave. 1850.

Curtis was a **dedicated abolitionist** and **supporter of Lincoln.** In this house he hid Horace Greeley from mobs of angry Staten Islanders, who generally supported the Southern cause. **Curtis High School** is named for this historic figure.

For an interesting detour, continue south on Bard Avenue to Castleton, where a group of structures are within close walking distance of one another. Otherwise make a right turn, west, onto Henderson Avenue to [N 17a.].

Optional Detour:

Area around Bard and Castleton Avenues and the St. Austin Places.

[N 16f.] **Convent, St. Vincent's Medical Center of Richmond**/originally **T. F. McCurdy residence**/later **Henry M. Taber residence**/later **William T. Garner residence**/later **St. Austin's School,** 710 Castleton Ave., opp. Hoyt Ave. N side. ca. 1850. Rear addition, 1898, Samuel R. Brick, Jr. **Gatehouse,** Bard Ave., S of Moody Place. E side. ca. 1850.

A huge Victorian mansion proclaims by size, if not by beauty, the prodigious wealth garnered by 19th-century businessmen (McCurdy was a **wholesaler,** Taber a **"cotton king,"** Garner a **cotton mill owner**). Ulysses S. Grant considered retiring here; but his wife, visiting the house on a warm damp day, was **plagued by mosquitoes** that thrived (and still do!) in Staten Island's marshes and swamps.

St. Austin's Place:

Between North St. Austin's Place and South St. Austin's Place.

[N 16g, 16h.] **Henderson Estate Company residences,** 33 St. Austin's Place. E side. 34 St. Austin's Place. W side. Both, 1893. McKim, Mead & White.

On opposite sides of this short street a pair of dark-brown shingled **neo-Colonial freestanding homes,** designed by the McK, M & W staff as low-budget (for them) houses.

[N 16i.] **St. Mary's Episcopal Church,** 347 Davis Ave., NE cor. Castleton Ave. 1853. Wills & Dudley. **Parish House,** 1914. **Rectory,** 1924. Both by Ralph Adams Cram.

An outgrowth of a then fashionable movement called **ecclesiology,** the design of this small church is patterned after **early 14th-century English precursors.** (Frank Wills was the official architect of the New York Ecclesiological Society.) Cram's later additions were **skillfully related** to the church building's unusual architecture.

Back to the car:

Pick up tour at Henderson Avenue and Broadway:

WEST BRIGHTON

[N 17a.] **Lawrence C. Thompson Park,** Henderson Ave. NW cor. Broadway. **[N 17b.]** **West Brighton Pool, N.Y.C. Department of Parks & Recreation,** Henderson Ave. bet. Broadway and Chappell St. 1970. Heery & Heery. **[N 17c.]** **Recreation Building,** Broadway opp. Wayne St. 1976. Arthur S. Unger & Assocs.

The pool complex is one of some dozen **crash-program** precast-concrete examples found throughout the city, commissioned—**and furiously constructed**—on the eve of a tough **mayoral election campaign.** Its distinctive composition and glossy graphics (and the rakish roof of its later recreation-building neighbor to the northeast) make more **successful designs** than most City-commissioned works, which are often ponderously conceived by less-skilled minds.

West Brighton: The official name of this community is West *New* Brighton, lying as it does to the west of New Brighton. But the "New" has been dropped by all save fuddy-duddy mapmakers and the government officials who advise them. One of the few official recognitions of the vernacular is in the foot-high lettering of the entrance sign of the West Brighton Pool.

Make your way to Castleton Avenue by taking the first permissible left (south) and then a right (west):

Along Castleton Avenue:

[N 18a.] Engine Company 79, N.Y.C. Fire Department/formerly Company 104/originally **Medora Hook & Ladder Company No. 3 (volunteer),** 1189 Castleton Ave., bet. Barker and Taylor Sts., opp. Roe St. N side. ca. 1885. Plaque, 1905, Alexander Stevens, Superintendent of Buildings.

The city took over this ornate 19th-century firehouse with the **advent of paid firemen** in 1905 (hence the plaque), but the building had graced the community for decades as the home of unpaid fire laddies. It continues to grace the community today.

[N 18b.] Keypac Collaborative, Brooklyn Union Gas Company, 1207 Castleton Ave., bet. Barker and Taylor Sts. N side. 1889.

An old brick commercial structure, now seeing a renewed life, **trimmed in terra-cotta** and sporting an ornamental cornice. It beats bronze anodized aluminum any day!

[N 18c.] Our Lady of Mt. Carmel-St. Benedicta Church and Rectory **(Roman Catholic),** 1265 Castleton Ave., NE cor. Bodine St. 1969. Genovese & Maddalene.

Topped by an intricately textured brick screen, this severe geometric edifice is **very prominent** on this commercial strip of Castleton Avenue. Its boldness, however, has a tendency to clash with (rather than dominate) the used car emporia and 2-story frame houses that are its neighbors. The sheet metal sculpture of **the saint that looks down upon parishioners** entering the church and the dramatic skylit altar and rich modern stained glass of the interior are very effective.

Leaving Castleton Avenue: *Immediately after this church on the corner, take a right (north) on Bodine Street, another right (east) on De Groot Place, and a left (north) on Taylor:* Both De Groot and Taylor display a number of fine houses: No. 6 De Groot, Nos. 157, 151–153 Taylor (both to the south), Nos. 128, 119, 90–92, and 83 Taylor. *Stop at one-block-long Trinity Place, where, midblock will be found:*

[N 19a.] Originally **Captain John T. Barker residence,** 9-11 Trinity Place, bet. Taylor and Barker Sts. N side. 1851.

An exceptional Italianate villa restored with taste and restraint to emphasize its wonderful details: the bracketed roof eaves, the center cupola, the porch supported by paired columns. Barker was a **silk dyer** by trade, associated with **Barrett, Tileston & Company,** later **the New York Dyeing and Print Works,** whose establishment near the foot of Broadway gave that area the name **"Factoryville."**

Take a left, again picking up DRIVING TOUR D along Richmond Terrace, to start another side trip at the very next block, Dongan Street.

Side Trip 2 takes in the community of Port Richmond: *Take a left (south) one block beyond Taylor Street, onto Dongan Street. Otherwise, continue on DRIVING TOUR D west about one-half mile on Richmond Terrace—watch those sharp changes in direction—and pick up at [N 22.].*

[N 19b.] 13 Dongan Street (residence), bet. Richmond Terr. and De Groot Place. E side. ca. 1875.

A "painted lady" **in the San Francisco tradition,** this time perhaps *too* made-up in sky blue with blush pink trim.

Follow Dongan Street south to its end, turn right (west) onto Cary Avenue which becomes Post Avenue a block later.

PORT RICHMOND

[N 20a.] Temple Emanu-El (synagogue), 984 Post Ave., bet. Decker and Heberton Aves. S side. 1907. Harry W. Pelcher.

A small-town version of a Classical Revival facade: **heavy Roman columns and pediment,** a tall octagonal domed cupola, even the carefully spelled-out name in relief over the entrance—complete with hyphen. Yet there is **strength of purpose** in both the innocent pretentiousness of the street facade embellished with very **simple stained glass,** and the more straightforward cladding of the remainder of the edifice's wood frame, with **shingles** once stained a **deep forest green.** A wonderful relic of this community's earlier days.

After the synagogue, take an immediate right (north) onto Heberton Avenue:

Along Heberton Avenue:

This is the prime residential thoroughfare of the community, paralleling Port Richmond Avenue, the business street two blocks west. Among its fine older homes, reflecting the onetime affluence of this important commercial community, are **Nos. 272, 253, 252, 233, 198, and 121.**

[N 20b.] Faith United Methodist Church/originally **Grace Methodist Episcopal Church,** 221 Heberton Ave., NE cor. Castleton Ave. 1897. Addition, 1983. George L. Smalle.

An offshoot in 1867 of **West Brighton's Trinity Methodist Church,** this congregation's later Gothic Revival edifice, in dark brick with terra-cotta trim, sits uncomfortably beside its modest 1980s addition.

[N 20c.] Old Public School 20, Richmond, Heberton Ave. NW cor. New St. 1891. **[N 20d.] Addition,** Heberton Ave. SW cor. Vreeland St. 1898.

The original wing marks one of the island's last remaining school buildings of its genre, in which a mandatory **belfry** and **clock** made an important **contribution** to both the school's architecture and community life. School population must have been expanding at a furious rate for the addition, across from **Veterans Park's** south side, to have been built only seven years after the original wing.

Across Veterans Park:

[N 21a.] Park Baptist Church/originally **North Baptist Church of Port Richmond,** 130 Park Ave., NW cor. Vreeland St. 1843. Addition/name change, 1871. **[N 21b.] St. Philip's Baptist Church,** 77 Bennett Ave., bet. Heberton and Park Aves. N side. 1891. Altered, 1926, George Conable.

Park Baptist's congregation, overlooking the park's west edge, established **a mission church** in **1881** for members of the local black community. It became St. Philip's, fronting on the north side of the park.

[N 21c.] Port Richmond Branch, N.Y. Public Library, 75 Bennett St., NW cor. Heberton Ave. 1905. Carrère & Hastings.

One of Andrew Carnegie's many gifts, this library, fronting on the park, was inserted into an already quite urbane island setting in the first decade of the 20th century.

All by itself:

This requires a detour west from Heberton Avenue to Park Avenue and south to:

[N 21d.] Catholic Youth Organization, 120 Anderson Ave., bet. Heberton and Port Richmond Aves., opp. Park Ave. S side. 1926. James Whitford, Sr.

A wonderfully pompous glazed terra-cotta Roman Revival temple facade, at the south end of Park Avenue, regrettably long in need of maintenance and protection.

From Heberton Avenue (to which you return if you've taken the detour) driving north, turn left (west) onto Church Street to see THE church and its chapel; right turn (north) onto Port Richmond Avenue; left turn (west) to rejoin Richmond Terrace and its perimeter TOUR D:

[N 22a.] Staten Island Reformed Church, 54 Port Richmond Ave., bet. old railroad viaduct and Richmond Terr., opp. Church St. W side. 1844.
[N 22b.] Sunday School, 1898, Oscar S. Teale.

Site of the **first religious congregation** on Staten Island, organized in 1663. The present church **replaced three earlier ones** on the site. Read the various plaques outside the church and walk through the **old graveyard.** And visit the Sunday School interior; it's quite incredible. (The school's architect was deeply into magic and later designed Harry Houdini's tomb in Machpelah Cemetery, Queens.)

[N 23a.] 2167 Richmond Terrace (residence), bet. Ferry and North Sts. N side. ca. 1855. **[N 23b.] Faber Pool, N.Y.C. Department of Parks & Recreation,** 2175 Richmond Terr., opp. Faber St. N side. 1932. Sibley & Fetherston. **Open to the public.**

A diminutive, forgotten Italianate villa stands cheek by jowl with a Mission Style public pool that is set across a deep lawn from the road and is named for the **pencil-manufacturing Eberhard Faber family,** who once lived nearby.

[N 23c.] Bayonne Bridge, Willow Brook Expwy. and Hooker Place to Bayonne, N.J. over Kill Van Kull. 1931. O. H. Ammann, engineer. Cass Gilbert, Inc., consulting architects.

A graceful **soaring silvery arch** that rises from the water's edges and sweeps the mind away from the industrial slurbs at either anchorage. For over 40 years the Bayonne **held the record** for the longest arch span, at 1,675 feet longer than even the Sydney Harbor Bridge in Australia. But that record is now (decisively) broken by the **New River Gorge Bridge** along U.S. Route 19 in **West Virginia:** 3,030 feet. (Its roadway is also the highest east of the Rocky Mountains: 876 feet above the New River's waters!)

All by itself:

Detour south along Morningstar Road and return to Richmond Terrace.

[N 24.] Church of St. Adalbert (Roman Catholic), 30 St. Adalbert Place, NE cor. Morningstar Rd. 1968. W. O. Biernacki-Poray.

One of a number of **radically modern** Roman Catholic churches on Staten Island, this structure is **dramatically sited** to be seen by traffic on the Willowbrook Expressway, which it abuts. A more reserved facade greets those entering the church from the local street; and the interior, with its upswept ceiling and modern stained glass, is the best feature of all.

MARINERS HARBOR

"Captains' Row," Richmond Terrace between Van Pelt and De Hart Aves. (and to the east). S side:

In the 1840s and 1850s, before the waters became fouled, wealthy **oyster captains** lived in a row of 2-story homes with columned **2-story porches.** The houses overlooked what was then called Shore Road, along which as many as 40 to 50 oystering sloops could be found, moored in the Kill.

[N 25a.] 2848 Richmond Terrace (residence), ca. 1840.

A Greek Revival porched 2-story Captains' Row house in a state of disrepair, missing one of its four original porch columns, among other things, but a rarity nonetheless.

[N 25b.] 2868 Richmond Terrace (residence), ca. 1875.

A mansarded former mansion, built decades after its neighbors to the east (above), whose walls are now sheathed with an overlay of quatrefoil-patterned composition shingles.

[N 25c.] Originally **Stephen D. Barnes residence,** 2876 Richmond Terr. ca. 1853. ★

A Captains' Row home, **an eclectic combination** of Italianate and Gothic Revivals, unusual for the bull's-eye windows in the attic below the deep cornice. Note the *trompe l'oeil* ground-floor window detail and that of the main entrance door. It camouflages the barricades installed to ward off the vandals.

Take a left (south) onto Union Avenue for a short but worthwhile detour through upland Mariners Harbor:

[N 26a.] Staten Island Seventh-Day Adventist Church/originally **Mariners Harbor Baptist Church,** 72 Union Ave., NW cor. Forest Court. 1858.

Proud, symmetric, stately through the years. **A sonata of fine brickwork** unusual for this era of Staten Island development. This church was founded by members of Port Richmond's North (now Park) Baptist Church.

Take a right turn (west) onto Continental Place and the next right (north) onto Harbor Road.

[N 26b.] 258 Harbor Road (residence), opp. Continental Place. W side. ca. 1845 plus addition.

Columned, battened, ribbed, picket-fenced, but white—always white—and preventing Continental Place from continuing through.

[N 26a.] Orig. Mariners Harbor Bapt.   **[N 26c.]** Summerfield Methodist Ch.

[N 26c.] Originally **Summerfield Methodist Church/**now **Summerfield United Methodist Church,** 104 Harbor Rd. and **[N 26d.] Parsonage,** 100 Harbor Rd., both bet. Leyden Ave. and Richmond Terr. W side. 1869.

A handsome pair of shingled frame structures tinted a pale green with white trim. As refreshing a sight as a crisp salad on a summer's day.

[N 26e.] 74 Harbor Road (residence), bet. Leyden Ave. and Richmond Terr. ca. 1845. W side.

Proof that even red, asphalt-composition, *faux* brick siding cannot entirely defile the character of a Greek Revival "captain's house," with its 4-columned double-height porch. (This is not a testimonial to the siding!)

Continue north and take the next left onto Richmond Terrace (again). The next large intersection (with South Avenue) offers a brief optional diversion for a group of residences in the first (long) block. But return to the Terrace quickly.

South Avenue:

Between Richmond Terrace and Arlington Place.

[N 27a.] 109, 113, 117 South Avenue (residences). All E side.
[N 27b.] 116 South Avenue (residence). W side. ca. 1885.

These four 19th-century freestanding suburban houses, particularly **No. 109,** are outstanding examples in the area.

Continuing on Richmond Terrace:

<u>ARLINGTON</u>

[N 28a.] 3246 Richmond Terrace (residence), bet. South and Arlington Aves. S side. ca. 1845.

An unusual type of **asphalt siding** gives this captain's house the appearance of being built of 1930s concrete block. (What catalog did *it* come from?) The four subtly tapered, **lathe-turned** porch columns are distinctive.

[N 28b.] Arlington Terrace (apartments), 35, 55, 65, 85 Holland Ave., bet. Richmond Terr. and Benjamin Place. E side. 1987. Diffendale & Kubec.

Four towers (with attached low-rise maisonettes) visible from Richmond Terrace (and elsewhere in this low-rise area), wear precast concrete panels. Their facades are punctuated by cantilevered balconies ranked neatly up the dozen stories. These crisp prisms seem a welcome expression of confidence in the face of surrounding chaos.

[N 28c.] Heron Place (apartments), Arlington Place bet. Arlington and Holland Aves. 1988. Stephen B. Jacobs & Assocs.

One hundred ninety units of 2- and 3-story **simplex** and **duplex** living, an extension of the earlier Arlington Terrace [above], by a different architect.

<u>PORT IVORY</u>

[N 29.] Proctor & Gamble Company, Western Ave. S of Richmond Terr. 1907 and additions.

It's **99 and 44/100ths percent pure** industrial archaeology (for some future era), where a 135-acre now-diversified soap company makes many products besides Ivory soap. The soap itself dates from 1878 and an earlier **P & G** stint as candlemakers; the name, from Psalm 45: "All thy garments smell of myrrh, and aloes, and cassia, out of the ivory palaces, whereby they have made thee glad."

On this elevated note **Tour D ENDS.** Western Avenue leads to Forest Avenue (via Gulf Avenue) and the well-marked entrances to both the Goethals Bridge to New Jersey and the Staten Island Expressway to the Verrazano Bridge to Brooklyn. Or you can retrace Richmond Terrace (or an alternate route along Forest Avenue—follow the signs) back to the ferry.

EASTERN STATEN ISLAND

<u>TOMPKINSVILLE</u> • <u>STAPLETON</u> • <u>STAPLETON HEIGHTS</u>
<u>CLIFTON</u> • <u>ROSEBANK</u> • <u>FOX HILLS</u> • <u>GRASMERE</u>
<u>ARROCHAR</u> • <u>SOUTH BEACH</u>

This area is, to most islanders' thinking, **another part of the North Shore;** no one in Staten Island refers to any area as "eastern." But for the purposes of isolating the communities **along the right shoulder** of the island, we've grouped them under this **artificial** rubric.

TOMPKINSVILLE

Established as a village around 1815 through the efforts of **Governor Daniel D. Tompkins;** hence its name. Some of its streets, Hannah and Minthorne (and Sarah and Griffin, since renamed), recall his children's names. A plaque in the park calls it **The Watering Place** where navigators before 1628 replenished their ships' supply of water.

Along or near Bay Street:

[E 1a.] Bay Street Landing (apartments)/originally **American Dock Company, Piers 1-5,** below Bay St. bet. U.S. Coast Guard Base and Victory Blvd. E side. Converted into apartments, 1982. **[E 1b.] Harbour Pointe (apartments),** 80 Bay Street Landing. Converted into apartments, 1987, David Kenneth Specter & Assocs.

Alfred J. **Pouch (of Terminal fame)** established the **American Dock Company** in 1872, but the reinforced-concrete coffee and cocoa warehouses converted to residential use date from the early 20th century. The waterside redevelopment also features restaurants.

Landing Cafe, Pier 4, Bay Street Landing.

A chance to eat and drink on one of the redeveloped piers that jut out into the Upper Bay.

[E 1c.] The Baltimore Flats, 17-23 Victory Blvd., E of Bay St. N side. 1885.

To some, a local eyesore; to others a potential for restoration.

A trip dockside via Hannah Street:

[E 2a.] Joseph H. Lyons Pool, Murray Hulbert Ave. SW cor. Victory Blvd. 1936. **N.Y.C. Department of Parks & Recreation,** Aymar Embury II, consultant.

Squat cylinders of economical red-brick masonry, **helical concrete stairways,** and Art Deco detailing identify this as one of eight city swimming pools built in the **heyday** of municipal construction, the Great Depression of the 1930s. Named for the commander of local V.F.W. and American Legion units.

Great Depression bathhouses: Public works—and works for the public—were a great civic concern during the Great Depression. This concern, plus the availability of subsidized skilled labor, resulted in the building of a group of great public swimming pools and even greater public bathhouses. The superior architectural design of the bathhouses (actually locker and shower facilities for pool users) makes them monuments to their period even decades later. Bronx: Crotona Park; Brooklyn: Betsy Head Park, McCarren Park, Red Hook Park, and Sunset Park; Manhattan: Colonial (now renamed) Park and Highbridge Park; Staten Island: Joseph H. Lyons Pool.

[E 2b.] George Cromwell Center, N.Y.C. Department of Parks & Recreation, Pier 6, Murray Hulbert Ave. at Victory Blvd. E side. 1936.

A port pier converted to recreational use in the 1930s, it sports a fine Art Deco front. Named for the island's **first borough president.**

[E 2c.] Richmond Water Tunnel Chlorination Station, N.Y.C. Department of Environmental Protection, Murray Hulbert Ave. at Victory Blvd. W side. 1974. N.Y.C. Board of Water Supply. **[E 2d.] Tompkinsville Water Pollution Control Facility, N.Y.C. Department of Environmental Protection,** Murray Hulbert Ave. at Pier 7. W side. 1976. Warren W. Gran & Assocs.

What a contrast in these two municipal works built only a few years apart. The sophisticated if too self-conscious shed-roofed control facility cast in Brutalist gray concrete is for society's **waste products.** The prim, handsomely crafted neo-Georgian chlorination station of carefully laid brick, pink granite, and monumental aluminum trim

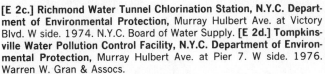

is for another vital need: **pure water.** The architectural message seems clear . . . or does it?

STAPLETON

Governor Tompkins' son, Minthorne, and **William J. Staples** purchased land south of Tompkinsville from Cornelius (later "Commodore") Vanderbilt, a native of Staten Island, and established the village of Stapleton (named after Staples) in 1833. Stapleton became the home of **two large breweries** in the 19th century: **Bechtel's,** at the foot of the cliff along Van Duzer Street (opposite Broad, where evidence still exists), and the **Rubsam & Hohrmann Atlantic Brewery** (1870–1953), later Piel's, which finally closed in 1963 and occupied the long blockfront along Canal Street's north side.

[E 3a.] Paramount Theater, Bay Street   [E 7b.] 387 St. Paul's Ave. residence

[E 3a.] Paramount Theater, 560 Bay St., bet. Prospect St. and Union Place. ca. 1935. C. W. Rapp & George L. Rapp. **[E 3b.] Park Villa,** 70 Beach St., bet. Union Place and Van Duzer St. ca. 1920.

The former, a small but wondrously decorative Art Deco **false-front backdrop** to an altered marquee in orange brick and polychromed terra-cotta. The latter, kind of around the corner, a discotheque rebirth of an eclectically styled 20th-century theater. Stapleton had a few.

Inland and uphill from Bay Street:

[E 4.] Tappen Park/originally **Washington Park,** Bay to Wright Sts., Water to Canal Sts. Park reconstructed, gazebo added, 1982, Quennell Rothschild Assocs. **[E 4a.]** Originally **Edgewater Village Hall,** in Tappen Park, Wright St., bet. Water and Canal Sts. 1889. Paul Kühne. ★

Though it bears the name of **Edgewater,** a 19th-century village (which also included parts of Tompkinsville, Clifton, and Rosebank) all but forgotten today, this fine Victorian edifice is an anchor for another community not at all forgotten, **Stapleton.** The intricately detailed masonry structure sits within **Tappen Park,** shaded by stately old trees which temper the loudness of the many small businesses attempting on every side to destroy the peacefulness of its setting. A picturesque **Victorian** landmark, improved by the addition of a gazebo and information kiosk.

Discover Stapleton: To provide both residents and visitors with insight into the history and environment of Stapleton, a team from High Rock Park's environmental center [see C35.] developed and installed more than a hundred *permanent* illustrated markers along the community's streets during the 1976 national bicentennial. They told of the area's growth and change, recollected people and events, and called attention to the buildings, spaces, and views. Some remain.

[E 4b.] Stapleton Branch, N.Y. Public Library, 132 Canal St., SW cor. Wright St. 1907. Carrère & Hastings.

One of a group of four Carnegie gifts that began to bring a semblance of culture to the **rural island** early in this century. By this time, with the coming of the breweries, the library branch here was quite welcome.

Along Van Duzer Street.

One-way northbound.

[E 5a.] Originally **Richard G. and Susannah Tompkins Smith residence,** 390 Van Duzer St., bet. Wright and Beach Sts. ca. 1835. ★
[E 5b.] Originally **Robert Hazard residence,** 364 Van Duzer St., bet. Beach and Prospect Sts. W side. ca. 1835. ★

Two houses in adjacent blockfronts with "Dutch kick" roofs and 2-story columned porches. **No. 364** is diminutive in scale, No. 390 is positively pompous, with an elegant **tetrastyle** Corinthian portico. (Mrs. Smith was the daughter of Governor, later Vice-President Daniel Tompkins.)

STAPLETON HEIGHTS

Along St. Paul's Avenue.

One-way southbound.

[E 6a.] Formerly **Public School 15, Richmond**/now **N.Y.C. Board of Education Office of Maintenance & Operations, Staten Island.** St. Paul's Ave. SE cor. Grant Ave. ca. 1888. Edward A. Sargent.

A Queen Anne survivor.

[E 6b.] St. Paul's Memorial Church (Episcopal), 225 St. Paul's Ave. *(one-way south),* 1870. Edward T. Potter. ★ **[E 6c.] 231 and 139 St. Paul's Avenue (residences).** ca. 1870. All bet. Clinton St. and Taxter Place. E side.

A lovingly crafted English country church whose traprock walls have **weathered beautifully** over the years. Nearby neighbors are two Shingle Style Victorian houses.

[E 7a.] Originally **Badenhausen residence,** 368 St. Paul's Ave., bet. Cebra and Occident Aves. W side. ca. 1895.

A brewery magnate's house; it looks it.

[E 7b.] 387 St. Paul's Avenue (residence), bet. Cebra and Occident Aves. E side. ca. 1885.

A true architectural extravaganza, **bedecked** with all sorts of **Victorian gingerbread.**

[E 7c.] 400 St. Pauls's Avenue (residence), SW cor. Occident Ave. ca. 1895.

A stucco Tudor Revival hunk that hugs (for dear life) the **steep bank** of Ward's Hill.

[E 7d.] 21 Court Street (residence), bet. Boyd and Van Duzer Sts. S side. 1888.

Commanding a **grand panoramic view** is this red brick house, which proclaims the year of its construction in red terra-cotta, adding **rich ornament** to the facades.

[E 8a.] Originally **Gatehouse**/altered into **James Pietsch residence,** 101 Cebra Ave., bet. Ward Ave. and Rosewood Place. N side. 1927. James Pietsch, builder.

Pietsch redid the existing stone gatehouse to an estate on this site. The result would intrigue Hansel and Gretel, as it does us. He moved from Brooklyn to Staten Island to live in the house.

[E 8b.] 226 Ward Avenue (residence), bet. Cebra Ave. and Austin Place. W side. ca. 1870.

A charming clapboard country house **perched atop a luxuriant hillside garden** overlooking Ward Avenue and the harbor beyond. Too bad about the insensitive concrete-block row houses (1987) that are its latter-day neighbors on both Ward and Cebra Avenues.

(Southward on Ward Avenue, Occident Avenue, Sunrise Terrace, and a right on Louis Street leads you to Howard Avenue and Grymes Hill, areas covered in C Staten Island, Central Staten Island.)

[E 8c.] Originally **Caleb T. Ward residence**/later Sally and Lewis Nixon residence/**called Ward-Nixon Mansion**/now **apartments,** 141 Nixon Ave. (loop), off Ward Ave. (Entrance driveway bet. Nos. 135 and 143.) ca. 1835. George B. Davis, builder. ★

Surmounting the **crest of Ward's Hill** and surrounded on all sides by less grand 20th-century houses, this immensely scaled Greek Revival mansion once sat amid **a 250-acre estate,** eventually sold off by its owners. It still reflects the enormous wealth of its builder and an era when this and nearby areas of Staten Island were fashionable locations for the wealthy. Easier to see **from a distance** than from Nixon Avenue. Its panoramic views are legendary.

[E 8a.] 101 Cebra Ave., a gatehouse totally transformed by its owner-builder

[E 9.] Orig. S. R. Smith Infirmary, as remembered on a postcard, ca. 1905

[E 9.] Originally **S. R. Smith Infirmary**/later **Frost Building, Outpatient Clinic, Staten Island Hospital**/now **Castleton Castle Condominiums,** Castleton Ave. opp. Cebra Ave. N side. (Officially 101 Stanley Ave.) 1889. Alfred E. Barlow. Additions, 1890, 1891, Bradford L. Gilbert.

Four **orotund** towers each surmounted by a shingled dunce cap of a roof, machicolated dormers with stepped brick gables, thick masonry walls freely pierced by varying sizes of windows, and a commanding, hilltop site contribute to making this one of the city's most delightful Victorian fantasies. The failure of the City's Landmarks Preservation Commission to designate it relegated the building to insensitive conversion into yuppie housing marketed under a cutesy name and cost the building the loss of crucial detail.

Back to Stapleton: Harrison Street and surrounds.

Between Quinn and Brownell Streets.

[E 10a.] Harrison Street, bet. Quinn and Brownell Sts. Both sides. ca. 1875–1895. Charles Schmeiser and others.

An amazing enclave. Tightly packed individual homes of great variety and high quality, many in superb states of preservation. The handsome masonry house at **No. 53,** midblock on the N side, was the home of the brewmaster at the nearby Rubsam & Hohrmann brewery.

[E 10b.] First Presbyterian Church, Brownell St. SW cor. Tompkins St. 1894.

The outgrowth of an earlier First Presbyterian Church of Edgewater, the early name of the village. The dark masonry, large rose window, and **distinctive stepped gables,** reminiscent of earlier Dutch Colonial architecture, make this a special event in this backwater of Stapleton.

[E 10c.] 10 Tompkins Street (residence), bet. Brownell and Quinn Sts. S side. ca. 1880.

A curious structure built of granite block.

Back door to America: An important strategy conference brought Winston Churchill to the island's shores during World War II. The prime minister secretly debarked from a British cruiser anchored off Stapleton and took the B&O Railroad directly to Washington to confer with President Roosevelt. Thus you might say the island is the back door to America.

Back to Bay Street: South of Tappen Park.

[E 10d.] Originally **Dr. James R. and Matilde Boardman residence/** later **Capt. Elvin E. Mitchell residence,** 710 Bay St., bet. Broad St. and Vanderbilt Ave. W side. 1848. ★

A large Italianate villa built atop the steep Bay Street slope by the **resident physician** of the nearby Seaman's Retreat Hospital. It was purchased in 1894 by Capt. Mitchell with the proceeds of an award for saving *all* 176 persons aboard a Cunard liner sinking in Long Island Sound a few years earlier.

CLIFTON

[E 11.] Bayley Seton Hospital (Roman Catholic)/formerly **U.S. Public Health Service Hospital/**formerly **U.S. Marine Hospital/**originally **Seaman's Retreat,** Bay St. NW cor. Vanderbilt Ave. Earliest buildings, 1834–1854. **[E 11a.]** Originally **Seaman's Retreat Main Building,** 131 Bay St. 1834–1854. Abraham P. Maybie, builder. ★ **[E 11b.]** Originally **Seaman's Retreat Physician-in-Chief's Residence,** 131 Bay St. 1842. Staten Island Granite Co., builder. ★ **[E 11c.] Later buildings,** 1933–1936, Kenneth M. Murchison, William H. Gompert, Tachau & Vaught, associate architects; J. H. de Sibou, consultant; James A. Wetmore, Louis A. Simon, supervising architects, U.S. Treasury Dept.

Hard to spot through the trees from the exit driveway on Bay Street (but worth the effort) is the old hospital's **imposing stone facade** with 2-story **pierced galleries** and **pedimented pavilions.** Originally operated successively by the state and federal governments—unlike the privately run **Sailors' Snug Harbor** on the island's North Shore [see N15.]—this early marine hospital building spawned the large complex of 1930s buildings which now dominates the site. The well-known **National Institutes of Health,** located in Bethesda, Maryland, had their modest beginnings here in a small laboratory of this old structure. In 1981, after the Feds left, locals established the Bayley Seton, after Dr. Richard Bayley of the old quarantine station, and his daughter who later became St. Elizabeth Ann Seton.

[E 12a.] 110 to 144 Vanderbilt Avenue (residences), bet. Talbot Place and Tompkins Ave. S side. 1900. Carrère & Hastings.

A full blockfront of eight matching, closely spaced, neo-Tudor suburban houses **of extremely high quality.** The firm was responsible for other fine work on the island [and later won the competition to design the **New York Public Library's main building.**] It's a wonder that so many—particularly Nos. 110, 120, 130—are in such a fine state of preservation. The developer was George Washington Vanderbilt, whose enormous estate Biltmore, in Asheville, N.C., was the work of Richard Morris Hunt and Frederick Law Olmsted.

[E 12b.] Originally **Mariners' Family Asylum of the Port of New York/** now **Staten Island Reception Center, New York Foundling Hospital (Roman Catholic),** 119 Tompkins Ave., bet. Vanderbilt Ave. and Hill St. E side. 1855. J. Graham Glauber.

Contiguous with the rear of Bayley Seton Hospital is this building constructed **to care for** the widows, wives, sisters, and daughters of the seamen of the port, who were being treated next door, in those earlier days, at the old Seaman's Retreat.

[E 13a.] 251 Tompkins Avenue (residence), bet. Norwood and Townsend Aves. E side. ca. 1860.

Sprockets at the porch columns and other decorative touches make this a delightful survivor.

[E 13b.] 93 Townsend Avenue (residence), bet. Tompkins Ave. and Bay St. N side.

Carpenter Gothic—but without the Gothic. Too bad about the composition asphalt siding!

[E 13c.] 72 Greenfield Avenue (residence). S side. **[E 13d.] 73 Greenfield Avenue (residence).** N side. Both bet. Bay St. and Tompkins Ave. viaduct. 19th century.

The first of brick with a Romanesque Revival portico, the second, Gothique with a great wraparound porch.

[E 13e.] Originally **Louis De Jonge & Company (factory),** 330 Tompkins Ave., SW cor. Greenfield Ave. (accessible only from Greenfield Ave.) 1918.

Decorative papers were once milled in this reinforced-concrete giant (giant at least for Staten Island).

ROSEBANK

For a very long time a community of Italian Americans.

[E 14a.] Garibaldi-Meucci Memorial Museum, 420 Tompkins Ave., SW cor. Chestnut Ave. 1840. ★ **Open to the public.**

An unlikely refuge for fiery Italian patriot Giuseppe Garibaldi, who lived here with his friend **Antonio Meucci** beginning in 1850. Restlessly awaiting an opportunity to return to Italy, Garibaldi made candles in a nearby factory, killing time by fishing and "shooting thrushes." **The museum** has letters and photographs describing Garibaldi's life and documenting Meucci's claim to **invention of the telephone** prior to Alexander Graham Bell. For a time Meucci operated the house as a tavern and beer garden for **Frederick Bachman,** owner of the **Clifton Brewing Company.**

Fig trees: Italians on the island love ripe figs. Consequently, many backyards are decorated with weird trees bundled up like mummies in winter, laden with clusters of ripe figs in summer. The presence of this tree is a foolproof clue to its owner's nationality. The Garibaldi memorial is no exception: an Italian caretaker lives on the second floor.

[E 14b.] Nicholas DeMatti Playground, N.Y.C. Department of Parks & Recreation, Tompkins Ave. S of Garibaldi-Meucci Museum, bet. Chestnut Ave. and Shaughnessy Lane. W side. ca. 1920.

The *right way* to do a playground. What this recreation area exhibits in *quality* prevails over Robert Moses' claims of *quantity*— his many additions to the city's playground inventory. Quality *does* count.

[E 14c.] Originally **Bachman Flats,** 103-125 Chestnut Ave., bet. Tompkins Ave. and Anderson St. N side. ca. 1865.

Seemingly workers' housing, a group of 10 row houses bracketed by larger ones at each end. Across Chestnut Avenue is the 5-acre factory that was once the **G. Siegle Corporation,** early manufacturers of fine pigments for industry; it later became the **Ansbacher-Siegle Corporation,** a chemicals manufacturer whose painted sign palimpsest was decipherable long after A-S departed.

[E 14d.] **Church of St. Joseph (Roman Catholic),** Tompkins Ave. bet. St. Mary's Ave. and Shaughnessy Lane. S side. 1957. Neil J. Convery.

A *very* orange neo-Romanesque church complemented by a sculptural freestanding bell tower with four bells.

[E 15.] **Our Lady of Mount Carmel Society Shrine** and **Hall,** 36 Amity St., W of White Plains Ave. Established, 1899. (Access via White Plains Ave. from St. Mary's Ave. Parking on Virginia Ave. bet. Fox Hill Terr. and Fletcher St.)

In a guide devoted to architecture it's a particular pleasure to report on this robust outdoor year-round folk art display, fervently honoring **Our Lady of Mount Carmel.** The celebrations culminate here (and at other Mt. Carmel feasts all over the city) every summer, about the second week of July. Beat the crowds, visit another time. It's inspiring.

[E 16.] **St. Mary's Roman Catholic Church,** 1101 Bay St., opp. St. Mary's Ave. E side. 1857.

Tiers of round-arched **triplet openings** enliven the central bell tower that identifies this church set on a berm astride Bay Street (once New York Avenue).

Toward the Narrows along Hylan Boulevard:

[E 17a.] Originally **Henry and Anne McFarlane residence/**later **New York Yacht Club/**later **Frederick Bredt residence,** 30 Hylan Blvd., bet. Bay and Edgewater Sts., inland of Austen House. ca. 1845. Additions. ★

Set back from the Boulevard but enjoying **a fantastic Narrows view.** It was the New York Yacht Club's **second home** from 1868 to 1871 during which time its members viewed at the finish line, the Narrows, the first race in challenge for the **America's Cup** (originally secured by the club in 1851). The house features bay windows framed with Egyptoid forms.

[E 17b.] **The Alice Austen House, "Clear Comfort,"** 2 Hylan Blvd., bet. Bay and Edgewater Sts., overlooking Upper New York Bay. S side. ca. 1691–1710. North extension, porch, dormers added, 1846, James Renwick, Jr.? Restored, 1985, Beyer Blinder Belle. ★ **Open to the public.**

The original portion having been built by a **Dutch merchant** (to take advantage of the still breathtaking view?), this house was purchased and altered by John Austen, a wealthy and cultivated New Yorker, in 1844. His granddaughter, **Alice Austen** (1866–1952), came here in 1868 at the age of two. She is remembered today for her **pioneering work** in what was in her early years a new art and a new science, **photography.** More than 7,000 of her glass-plate negatives are preserved at the Staten Island Historical Society. They depict, with consummate artistry, the world she knew between 1880 and 1930.

The neat restoration somehow removes too many of the qualities that time had wrought. But the restored lawn is breathtaking.

[E 17c.] **Ocean View Condominiums (apartments),** 31 Hylan Blvd., bet. Bay and Edgewater Sts. S side. 1987. Nicholas J. Salvadeo.

Where else but across from Alice Austen's chaste, picturesque, diminutive "Clear Comfort" would a *14-story* apartment building be appropriate? The Zoning Resolution needs a very careful look!

[E 18a.] St. John's Episcopal Church, 1331 Bay St., SE cor. New Lane. 1871. Arthur D. Gilman. **[E 18b.] Parish House,** 1865. ★ **[E 18c.] Rectory,** 1862.

Churches such as this are more likely to be found in the English countryside than on Staten Island. A fine example of Victorian Gothic style built of rose-colored granite with handsome stained-glass windows. Unfortunately, the original steeple has been altered. The first child baptized in the original frame building of this parish was **Cornelius Vanderbilt,** born in nearby Stapleton in 1794.

[E 10a.] 53 Harrison St. residence   **[E 18a.]** St. John's Episcopal Church

[E 17b.] "Clear Comfort," as photographed by Alice Austen in the 19th century

[E 18d.] Originally **"Woodland Cottage" (rental residence)**/later Rectory, **St. John's Episcopal Church,** 33-37 Belair Rd., bet. Bay and Clayton Sts. N side. ca. 1834. Alexander Jackson Davis? Western addition, ca. 1900, James Thompson, builder. ★

The original house is a Gothic Revival gem, with **ultraromantic detailing** and **proportions.** If it wasn't an A. J. Davis creation, it ought to have been—builder Thompson wasn't quite as talented. Between 1858 and 1869 it was nearby St. John's rectory.

[E 19.] Von Briesen Park, Bay St. opp. Wadsworth Ave. E side.

Once the estate of Arthur Von Briesen, the first president of Citizens' Union, this park displays a group of fine trees planted while still an estate and also enjoys **unparalleled views** of New York harbor, the Verrazano Bridge, and the courtyard of Battery Weed next door. The small parking area at Bay Street is rarely full. Stop and **take a walk** to the edge of the cliff for the great view.

Across the northern boundary of the park you will glimpse one of Staten Island's many ponds, this one in the adjacent shorefront residential community of **Shore Acres.**

[E 20a.] Battery Weed, Fort Wadsworth, in a view from the Verrazano Bridge

[E 20.] Fort Wadsworth Military Reservation, S end of Bay St. **[E 20a.] Battery Weed,** 1847–1861. ★ **[E 20b.] Fort Tompkins,** 1861. ★ **Military Museum open to the public.**

The gate and guards look ominous, but actually visitors are welcome. Drive straight ahead; turn left beyond the bridge; follow signs to the **Military Museum** and the closeup view down into the landmarked Battery Weed, built at the water's edge before the Civil War. The three tiers of arched galleries make the interior of the **polygonal fortress** far less formidable in appearance than its severe exterior walls.

Romantic legend depicts Algonquin Indians standing here spellbound by the sight of Hudson's ship, the *Half Moon,* entering the Narrows in 1609. Since those sylvan times, Dutch, British, and Americans in times of war have stood watch here, scanning the horizon for enemy ships.

The fort was known well into the 1970s as the oldest continuously staffed military post in the United States. There are plans to add parts of the site to the holdings of the **Gateway National Recreation Area** if ever the military decides to relinquish them. The Military Museum is a fascinating storehouse of armed forces trivia displayed in the galleries of another old fortress, **Fort Tompkins,** built at the top of the escarpment guarding the Narrows.

FOX HILLS

Named for banker **Lewis Henry Meyer's** estate, **Fox Hill,** this became an emergency army encampment during both world wars in the area between Targee Street and the S.I.R.T. north of Steuben Street; the area was **clumsily urbanized** in the late 1970s and 1980s. Today's still undeveloped parts are where bored Staten Island youth **race their mopeds . . .** and do other, nefarious things?

Teutonic streets: Brooklyn has rows of avenues named for governors of the state and others for the state's major cities. In Fox Hills all of the local (which excludes arterial Targee) streets cut off by the Staten Island Expressway's embankment are named for rivers (or places) in Germany: Rhine, Oder, Britten (misspelled Britton), Hanover, Neckar, Weser, and Elbe; plus Mosel, the only street the highway crosses.

GRASMERE

[E 21.] Ipes Pond, Fox Hills. Visible from N end of Elbe Ave. (dead end).
[E 22a.] Brady's Pond, Grasmere. Visible from Lakeview Terr., reachable from E side of Clove Rd. south of S.I.R.T. underpass via (unmarked) Hillcrest Terr. (one-way streets.) **[E 22b.] Cameron Lake,** Grasmere. Visible from Windemere Road, N off Clove Rd. S of Fingerboard Rd.

Three **small refreshing expanses** of water. The latter two are jealously **guarded from public view** by their waterside residents; the former, across the Staten Island Expressway in Fox Hills, is a kind of no-man's-land guarded by moped fanatics.

ARROCHAR

[N 23a.] St. Joseph's Hill Academy for Girls (Roman Catholic)/original residence named **"Clar Manor"/**later **William M. McFarland estate, "Arrochar,"** 850 Hylan Blvd., NE cor. Major Ave. ca. 1850.

The **Scottish name** of McFarland's estate is now the name of the Arrochar community radiating out from the academy. The old Italianate villa itself has been **compromised over the years,** and the academy's newer architecture is uninspired.

[E 23b.] St. John's Villa Academy Convent, Sisters of St. John the Baptist (Roman Catholic)/originally **"Hawkhurst,"** William H. Townsend residence, 57 Cleveland Place, E of Landis Ave./Chicago Ave. intersection. S side. ca. 1846. Additions.

A brick Gothic Revival fantasy which some attribute to architect James Renwick, Jr., who married a woman from nearby Clifton. *This* structure should have become the standard of quality (if not necessarily the inspiration for the appearance) of the academy's later architecture. It didn't.

[E 23c.] Geller House, Jewish Board of Family and Children's Services, 77 Chicago Ave., bet. Columbia and Landis Aves. N side. ca. 1915.

A **gregarious, substantial, avuncular** house, quite appropriate to its current task.

[N 23d.] 212 Major Avenue (residence), bet. Sand Lane and Wallace Ave. S side. ca. 1920. **[N 23e.] 75 Landis Avenue (residence),** bet. Major and Chicago Aves., opp. Pickersgill Ave. E side. ca. 1920.

Two fine freestanding residences of wood-trimmed stucco bearing similarly conceived details. The rear of the former is equally interesting and visible from MacFarland Ave. to the south.

SOUTH BEACH

[E 24a.] 88-98 Father Capodanno Boulevard (apartments), NE cor. Drury Lane. 1985.

Four stories of **jaunty, nautical, driftwood-gray-trimmed seaside condominiums,** overlooking South Beach, the boardwalk, and the Lower Bay approaches to New York harbor. (Once called Seaside Boulevard, the street is named for a priest killed in the Vietnam War, a winner of the Congressional Medal of Honor.)

[E 24b.] Verrazano-Narrows Bridge monument, Lily Pond Ave. NE cor. Major Ave. 1964.

One of the city's best-kept secrets as far as public sculpture is concerned. This is a **bas-relief** relating the Italian explorer to the bridge named in his honor. It contains stones supposedly removed from the Verrazano castle.

Basilio's (restaurant), 45 Ocean Ave., at Galesville Court, South Beach.

A fixture for **hearty Italian food** (during the warm weather months only) since 1918, with decor that hasn't changed much in the interim. Drivers should use the **back entrance** on Lily Pond Ave. between McLean Ave. and Father Capodanno Blvd. Parking.

H. H. Richardson house: On Staten Island? It's hard to believe—and looking at it today (minus its original shingles) makes it even harder, but the house at 45 McClean Avenue at the northeast corner of Lily Pond Avenue (south of the Verrazano Bridge toll plaza) is an early (1868–1869) design of Henry Hobson Richardson. Later to become the architect of such masterpieces as Boston's Trinity Church and considered one of this country's architectural geniuses, Richardson lived in Staten Island early in his career, between 1867 and 1874.

[E 25a.] Staten Island Hospital, Main Building, 475 Seaview Ave., E cor. Mason Ave. 1978. **[E 25b.] Imaging Center,** on Mason Ave. opp. Alter Ave. SE side. 1987. Both by Bobrow & Fieldman.

The original hospital structure is 4 stories of crisp, creamy, precast concrete applied in long horizontal panels that complement the long, dark, horizontal strip windows. An air of **natty efficiency** permeates the architecture and (let's hope) carries over into the hospital's medical care. In later works **glass-block** cylindrical self-consciousness begins to appear.

The complex is located at the intersection of two 8-lane streets that make this flat place **look more like Florida** than Staten Island. Where are the palm trees?

[E 25c.] Professional Building, 500 Seaview Ave., E of Mason Ave. S side. 1987. Diffendale & Kubec.

Looks like a streamliner: All aboard!

[E 26a.] South Beach Psychiatric Center, N.Y.S. Department of Mental Hygiene, 777 Seaview Ave., NW cor. Father Capodanno Blvd. 1974. John Carl Warnecke & Assocs.

It's very big and was stylish in its time. Now it just seems to go on forever.

[E 26b.] South Beach (officially **Franklin D. Roosevelt Beach and Boardwalk) Gateway National Recreation Area/**originally **South Beach** and **Midland Beach,** along the Atlantic Ocean bet. Fort Wadsworth and former Miller Field. Current appearance, 1938.

In the 1890s these adjacent beaches became private seaside resorts complete with beachfront homes, tent colonies, restaurants, amusement areas, and such, but with **Prohibition** they lost their crowds and their capacity to sustain themselves. (The depressed right-of-way—minus rails—of Staten Island Rapid Transit's South Beach Branch **still threads** through Rosebank and Arrochar to the old **South Beach Station** at Sand Lane.) Just before World War II the **WPA** built the new facilities for the City's Parks Department, and they are once again the federal government's. The S.I.R.T. station was replaced by a **handsome concrete bus shelter** at the end of Sand Lane.

CENTRAL STATEN ISLAND
WESTERLEIGH • SUNNYSIDE • TRAVIS
NEW SPRINGVILLE • BULLS HEAD • HEARTLAND VILLAGE
GRYMES HILL • EMERSON HILL • DONGAN HILLS
CONCORD • TODT HILL • EGBERTVILLE • RICHMONDTOWN
NEW DORP • OAKWOOD

This area of the guide stays clear of the shorefront communities of the North Shore, covered in **Northern** [N] and **Eastern** [E] Staten Island,

and deals with the **central belt of communities** that stretches from the waters of Arthur Kill on the west to Lower New York Bay below South Beach on the east. It embraces the island's **chain of inland hills** like **Grymes** and **Todt** and **Emerson,** and the **Dongan Hills,** and the entire **Staten Island Greenbelt.** That verdant carpet stretches southwesterly from the never completed interchange of the Staten Island Expressway and the unbuilt northern leg of Richmond Parkway to **Richmondtown Restoration.** Once the Village of Richmond, the island's county seat, Richmondtown has many charming old government structures that became the nucleus of **Staten Island's own "Colonial Williamsburg."**

WESTERLEIGH

Earlier begun as **Prohibition Park.**

Outside the area that was Prohibition Park:

[C 1a.] Society of St. Paul Seminary (Roman Catholic), 2187 Victory Blvd., NW cor. Ingram Ave. 1969. Silverman & Cika.

Perhaps Staten Island's most unusual institutional building: a combination of architecture and monumentally scaled sculpture. Its large size and prominent location make it visible from great distances. Though it conveys an **intriguing appearance** from afar, it is **less satisfying** up close—but still well worth a visit. The society is devoted to religious publishing and operates a bookstore and media center open to the public.

Prohibition Park, a community occupying a wooded tract of some 25 acres bounded by today's Watchogue Road and Demorest, Maine, and Wardwell Avenues, was set up in 1887 for teetotalers; lots were sold to prohibitionists throughout the country. Some streets were named for dry states—Maine, Ohio, Virginia; others for Prohibition party presidential candidates—Bidwell, Wooley, Fiske. Another resident was Dr. Isaac Kauffman Funk, who with his associate Adam Willis Wagnalls was preparing *A Standard Dictionary of the English Language* (1890). The area today is known as Westerleigh, but the original street names remain to admonish the unwary of the evils of alcoholic beverages.

[C 1b.] Originally **Garrett Houseman residence,** 308 St. John Ave., NW cor. Watchogue Rd. ca. 1730–1760. ★

Long before this area became the local focus for the **national prohibition movement,** this house was built in a position that is today catercorner to the street grid. Housman was a **Loyalist** during the Revolution. The tiny one-room stone house on the right was undoubtedly built first, with the clapboard addition following 30 years afterward. (St. John Avenue was named after the Prohibitionist governor of Kansas.)

The Boulevard:

This was Prohibition Park's premier thoroughfare. Its 4,000-seat University Temple, a meeting hall **similar to the Methodist facility** in Ocean Grove, N. J., straddled the Fiske Avenue end with an arched entry spanning two bell towers; it burned in 1903. The **Park Hotel,** a large frame building, occupied the site of today's P.S. 30, between Fiske and Wardwell Avenues, on the south side. A number of the Prohibition leaders' fine 19th-century homes also remain:

[C 2a.] Originally **Frank Burt residence,** 42 The Boulevard, SW cor. Deems Ave. ca. 1893. John H. Coxhead.

Sitting atop a one-story ashlar plinth, this is the **most substantial home remaining** on The Boulevard, with its Palladian window, decorative shingles, and sunburst-pattern ornament.

[C 2b.] Originally **Isaac K. Funk residence,** 6, 8 The Boulevard, SE cor. Deems Ave. ca. 1893. Carr, Carlin & Coxhead.

A baronial clapboard double house whose **twin projected bays** on the second floor sandwich an expansive solarium.

[C 2c.] Originally the **Reverend William H. Boole residence,** 682 Jewitt Ave., SW cor. Maine Ave. ca. 1890.

Boole was a well-known evangelist and a cofounder of Prohibition Park. His wife, **Ella Boole,** later became a leader of the **Women's Christian Temperance Union,** the W.C.T.U.

[C 2d.] Westerleigh Park, N.Y.C. Department of Parks & Recreation, Neal Dow to Willard Aves., bet. Maine and Springfield Aves. 1887.

Today's 2.9 acres are all that remain of Prohibition Park's original green space, where **band concerts** and **outdoor lectures** were given. The bandstand in the center is an echo of the early days.

SUNNYSIDE

Victory Boulevard, west of Clove Road:

[C 3a.] Physicians & Surgeons Specialty Building, 1460 Victory Blvd. 1975. **[C 3b.] Annex,** 1478 Victory Blvd. ca. 1983. Both bet. Egan Ave./Little Clove Rd. and Albert St. S side. Both by Charles Azzue, builder.

Swaybacked, skylighted, and stuccoed, these structures do catch your attention but fail to hold it for very long. Designed by their builder. [Also see C 29a, b.].

[C 3c.] Staten Island Obstetrics & Gynecology Associates Building, 1384 Victory Blvd., SW cor. Marx St. 1975.

A well-handled wood frame professional building that calls attention to itself through its **skillful use of contrasts:** vertical and diagonal siding, sweeping circular and tall slit windows, and a distinctive roof line.

[C 3d.] Richmond Kidney & Medical Center, 1366 Victory Blvd., SW cor. Marx St. to Cypress Ave. 1984. Joseph B. Raia.

A Modern essay in colored terra-cotta, which nicely complements it neighbor to the west [see above].

[C 4.] Swedish Home for Aged People/originally L. B. La Bau residence, 20 Bristol Ave., bet. Cypress Ave. and Little Clove Rd. E side. ca. 1870.

The mansarded home, originally, of Commodore Cornelius Vanderbilt's daughter Alicia, who married La **Bau.** Nearby La**bau** Avenue (tin-earedly) recalls the in-law family.

[C 5a.] Staten Island War Memorial Outdoor Skating Rink and Locker Pavilion, N.Y.C. Department of Parks & Recreation, Victory Blvd. at Labau Ave. N side. 1972. Brodsky, Hopf & Adler.

A polygonal wood-shingled roof **peeks up from the hollow** in Clove Lakes Park in which the pavilion was sited. Though the designer exercised care in the choice of ruddy brick and dark wood shingles, the shiny aluminum railings which **form a maze** for crowd control are out of keeping with the setting. So is the exposed cooling tower for chilling the ice . . . an afterthought?

[C 5b.] New Clove Road Pumping Station, N.Y.C. Department of Environmental Protection, Victory Blvd. bet. Ontario and Labau Aves. S side. 1976. Yaroscak & Sheppard.

It is rare that a utilitarian municipal water facility rises to the level of worthy architecture. This poured-in-place reinforced-concrete structure does. It uses **20th-century technology** as effectively as its older neighbor to the east used red brick and cast stone. But it does so with greater panache. Tsk, tsk to the ugly transformer and cage thoughtlessly plunked right in front!

Clove Road:

[C 6a.] Originally **John King Vanderbilt residence,** 1197 Clove Rd., N of Victory Blvd. E side. ca. 1836. Architect unknown. Expanded and restored. ★

A charming Greek Revival frame house built by one of "Commodore" Vanderbilt's cousins. Purchased in 1955 and later restored by Dorothy Vanderbilt Smith:

[C 6b.] Formerly **Dorothy Valentine Smith residence/**originally **John Frederick Smith residence,** 1213 Clove Rd., N of Victory Blvd. E side. 1895. Architect unknown. Expanded and altered. ★

A Queen Anne late Victorian country house, the lifelong residence of one of Staten Island's most devoted chroniclers, Dorothy Valentine Smith.

[C 6c.] Originally **Gardiner-Tyler residence,** 27 Tyler St., bet. Clove Rd.-Broadway intersection and Burgher Ave. N side. ca. 1835. ★

Opposite St. Peter's Cemetery. The elegant portico of this fine home faces west toward a great view. Note the crisply fluted columns with their florid capitals and the chunky scroll brackets that connect the portico to the house proper. **President John Tyler's widow,** a woman of Southern sympathies, resided here during the Civil War. During the conflict, it is said, she was relieved, by **outraged Unionists,** of a Confederate flag which she had displayed.

[C 7.] **Staten Island Zoo,** Clarence T. Barrett Park, 614 Broadway at Colonial Court. W side. Rear entrance from Clove Rd. S of Martling Ave. 1936. N.Y.C. Parks Department. **Open to the public.**

A small zoo, specializing in snakes, and an accompanying children's zoo; the only zoo in America exhibiting **all 32 species** of rattlesnakes. Snake lovers are reassured by the notice: "None of these snakes is fixed—all have full possession of fangs."

[C 8a.] **Scott-Edwards residence,** 752 Delafield Ave., bet. Clove Rd. and Raymond Place. S side. ca. 1730. Altered, ca. 1840. ★

A century after its original construction as a colonial farmhouse with a so-called **Dutch kick roof,** a formal Greek Revival colonnaded porch was added. The original unwhitewashed fieldstone walls are still visible on the side. It's too bad about the addition of dormer and vents to the graceful roof line.

[C 8b.] **397 Clove Road (residence),** bet. Disosway Place and Cornell Ave. E side. ca. 1885.

A great Shingle Style residence occupying a generous site set back from **narrow old Clove Road,** rediscovered (and repainted a golden yellow with white trim) in the 1980s.

TRAVIS

Near the extreme western end of Victory Boulevard is this sleepy community, originally named Long Neck and known since 1930 as Travis. For a quarter of a century it had been renamed **Linoleumville** after a local industry, the **American Linoleum Company,** whose buildings were located on Arthur Kill at the foot of the boulevard (then Richmond Turnpike) between 1873 and the late 1920s. Melvin and Wild Avenues recall **Melvin Wild** who, as the factory superintendent in 1874, invented the process for making inlaid linoleum. The largest landmark in Travis is the **Con Edison power plant**—it occupies the site of the linoleum factory and more.

[C 9.] Originally **District School School No. 3, Long Neck/**now **wing of Public School 26, Richmond,** Wild Ave. S of Victory Blvd. W side, across school yard. 1880. Second floor added, 1896. Francis H. Skeritt, builder.

A holdover whose tiny eroded **marble plaque** set into the upper part of the red brick wall—on the side away from New Jersey's chemical-laden winds—barely reveals the names of the school district's trustees and the builder. (The old outhouse sits in the SW corner of the school yard.)

[C 10a.] **Oceanic Hook & Ladder Company (volunteer),** 4010 Victory Blvd., SE cor. Burke Ave. 1881. **[C 10b.]** **Engine Company 154, N.Y.C. Fire Department,** 3730 Victory Blvd., bet. Baron Blvd. and Travis Ave. S side. 1971. George J. Masumian.

It's always good to discover a remaining **volunteer fire brigade.** While Oceanic's digs are hardly something to write home about, they still have **greater spirit** than the City's labored official version a few blocks east.

NEW SPRINGVILLE/BULLS HEAD

[C 11a.] Our Lady of Pity (Roman Catholic) Church, 1616 Richmond Ave., bet. Victory Blvd. and Merrill Ave. W side. 1987. Tudda, Scherer & Zborowski.

An expanding population gives rise to new parishes. The architecture here is a bit too much.

[C 11b.] Hillside Swim Club Locker Pavilion, 151 Signs Rd., bet. Park Dr. and Victory Blvd. N side. 1984. Joseph B. Raia.

Two genders, therefore two wings. Logical, neatly conceptualized, symmetrically organized, and to top it off, **very well designed and detailed.** A terrific accompaniment to a day in the pool.

[C 11c.] Rustic Woods (row house development), Signs Rd. NE cor. Victory Blvd. 1982. DiFiore & Giacobbe.

One of the few condominum developments on Staten Island that has anything positive going for it. It's only a question of whether time will improve it (through the maturation of landscape) or ruin it (through the vernacular "improvements" its owners will impose).

[C 12.] Son-Rise Charismatic Interfaith Church/originally **Asbury Methodist Episcopal Church,** 2100 Richmond Ave., bet. Rivington Ave. and Amsterdam Place. W side. 1849, 1878. ★

The side walls of this humble church date from 1849; the arch-windowed front and tower were constructed in 1878. In the graveyard lies **Ichabod Crane,** whose name was used by his friend Washington Irving in the story of the **headless horseman.** The church itself was originally named for the circuit-riding Reverend Francis Asbury, the **first American Methodist bishop,** who made his first "circuit" on Staten Island in 1771.

HEARTLAND VILLAGE

Named by real estate developers, this was the area of Staten Island's (and New York City's) **last stand of truck farms.** This heart-shaped enclave lies within the green (on a map at least) embrace of what one day is promised as Fresh Kills Park (the world's largest landfill) on the west, LaTourette Park on the east, and the route of ill-fated Willowbrook Parkway and the grounds of the former Willowbrook State School on the north.

A drive through Heartland Village is a must, if only to see in a condensed version the great post-Verrazano Bridge rape of Staten Island. To see the remarkable variety of tasteless housing of every description take Travis Avenue, in either direction, between Richmond Avenue and Forest Hill Road. Along the way, it will be easy to find some stabilizing institutions:

[C 13a.] Public School 69, Richmond, The Daniel D. Tompkins School, 144 Keating Place, bet. Rockland and Travis Aves. to Merry Mount St. W side. 1976. Belfatto & Pavarini. **[C 13b.] Intermediate School 72, Richmond, The Rocco Laurie School,** 33 Ferndale Ave., bet. Travis and Saxon Aves. to Merry Mount St. E side. 1975. Belfatto & Pavarini. **[C 13c.] Korean Christian Church of Staten Island,** 1250 Rockland Ave., bet. Grissom and Ferndale Ave. S side. 1985. Edward Luders.

On three adjacent blocks is a critical mass of educational, religious, social, and cultural life in this community without a traditional center. But, fear not. Staten Island Mall is only a hitch away.

[C 14.] Staten Island Mall (shopping center), 2665 Richmond Ave., bet. Richmond Hill Rd. and Platinum Ave. to Marsh Ave. 1973. Welton Becket & Assocs.

Compared to the chaotic roadside development everywhere else on the island, Staten Island's first regional shopping facility is a welcome exercise in responsible and disciplined design. Bravo! *A walk inside is enlightening too.* Like every mall, it offers a range of eateries, choices of (if not choice) pit stops, and plenty of parking.

Willowbrook:

[C 15.] Originally **Halloran General Hospital, U.S. Army/**later **Willowbrook State School,** Willowbrook Rd., SW cor. Forest Hill Rd. to Willowbrook Park. 1941. William E. Haugaard, N.Y. State Architect. **[C 15a.]** Originally **N.Y.S. Research Institute for Mental Retardation,** 1050 Forest Hill Rd., on Willowbrook grounds, S of Willowbrook Rd. W side. 1967. Fordyce & Hamby. All eventually to become **College of Staten Island, CUNY, Central Campus,** Master plan for college, 1988, Edward Durrell Stone Assocs.

Built by the State to care for retarded children, these **late Art Deco** facilities were **taken over by the army** in 1941 (and renamed for Col. Paul Stacey Halloran, U.S. Army Medical Corps) to care for the wounded. After 1951, the buildings were **reconverted to serve their intended purpose,** until court action forced their closing as places of inhumane treatment for the developmentally impaired. The later crisp but dull research institute was swept by the same revisionist tide. A 1980s proposal called for yet another **conversion,** this time to a central campus for the now divided activities of the College of Staten Island, the local unit of City University.

[C 15b.] **Homes for people with developmental disabilities,** Forest Hill Rd. S of the former Research Institute. W side. 1988. Stanley Pinska Assocs.

New York State's response to court decisions about its care (or lack thereof) of retarded individuals at the **infamous Willowbrook State School.** Sometimes deinstitutionalization only begets other (architectural) institutionalization.

GRYMES HILL

The hill that lies north of the Clove, the "cleft," the route of the Staten Island Expressway. The main thoroughfare is Howard Avenue, which sinuously winds its way along the shoreward crest northward from Clove Road to Hero Park, at the edge of **Stapleton Heights.**

[C 16.] **Sunrise Tower (apartments),** 755-775 Narrows Rd. N., bet. Richmond and Clove Rds. N side. 1987. Lauria Assocs.

Between today's Emerson and Grymes Hills the declivity, the cleft, the clove had existed for **millennia** prior to the **arrival of Europeans** in America. **Clove Road** was built by early settlers; then, following the completion of the Verrazano Bridge, the concrete ribbons of the **expressway** were laid with federal subsidy. Slowly, other ribbons—this time of **ticky-tacky** housing—began to appear on the slopes, using the lands of institutions that couldn't resist the profits to be made by selling to developers. Inevitably there appear the precast retaining walls to hold back the earth around the parking lots. And above them looms the Clove's **first high rise,** 12 stories of red brick, **stepped back to echo the slope** of Grymes Hill and topped by a health club, with tax-abated condo units offering great views . . . of endless streams of expressway traffic moving below.

(Later in the year Sunrise Tower was completed, the City enacted a **Special Hillsides Preservation District** protecting some of the nearby slopes. Too little too late?)

On or alongside Howard Avenue:
Northerly from Clove Road.

[C 17.] **Wagner College,** Howard Ave. bet. Campus Rd. and Stratford Rds. Both sides.

Founded in Rochester, N.Y., in 1883, Wagner Memorial Lutheran College came to Staten Island in 1918 after purchase of **the Cunard property** 370 feet above sea level on the brow of Grymes Hill. The Cunards were a branch of the English steamship family. The college today is coeducational and nonsectarian.

If you plan to go exploring, it's best done on foot . . . put your car in a parking area.

[C 17a.] Originally **"Oneata," Gen. William Ward Greene residence/** formerly **Music Building, Wagner College,** West campus, Howard Ave. W side, beyond athletic fields. ca. 1865.

The gorgeous view to the east is no doubt responsible for naming this house "Oneata," **Seminole** for "kissed by the dawn." A charming mansard-roofed house, it may soon be kissed by the wrecker's ball to make way for college expansion.

[C 17b.] Mergerle Science and Communications Center. 1968. Perkins & Will. **[C 17c.] August Horrmann Library.** 1961. Perkins & Will. **[C 17d.] Towers Dormitory.** 1964. Sherwood, Mills & Smith. **[C 17e.] Harbor View Dormitory.** 1968. Sherwood, Mills & Smith. **[C 17f.] Student Union.** 1970. Perkins & Will.

These recent additions to the Wagner campus were designed over a 10-year period by **various architects** working within two different architectural firms. The **diversity of approach** is apparent, but visual unity is nevertheless achieved by the acceptance of an imposed discipline of unglazed red face brick as the predominant building material.

[C 17e.] The red brick prisms of Harbor View Dormitory at Wagner College

[C 17g.] Administration Building, Wagner College, East Campus, 631 Howard Ave. E side. 1930. Smith, Conable & Powley.

Handsome brick neo-Tudor. It **reeks of higher education,** as more modern works fail to do.

[C 17h.] Originally **"Bellevue," Sir Edward Cunard residence/**now **Cunard Hall, Wagner College,** East Campus, Howard Ave. E side. ca. 1851.

This old mansion, whose name referred to the glorious view now diminished by new construction, is today used for college offices.

[C 17i.] Originally **Augustinian Academy (Roman Catholic),** 144 Campus Rd., bet. Howard Ave. and Inwood Rd. S side. 1927. Wilson Eyre & McIlvaine.

A rambling neo-Romanesque 2-story school perched at the brow of Grymes Hill overlooking the expressway on the site of Capt. Jacob Hand Vanderbilt's home. **("Captain Jake"** was the **Commodore's brother.)** The academy's palette of colors, burnt umber and red brick with red Spanish tile gabled roofs, makes a very special presence. Two wings extend inland toward visitors, welcoming those entering the driveway. *Its fine site makes it vulnerable to demolition for condos.*

Serpentine Road, the original name of Howard Avenue, is a self-guiding tour of one of Staten Island's poshest areas. Both sides of the thoroughfare are lined with mansions left over from earlier days, the intervening spaces being increasingly filled with less distinguished, more recent works of domestic architecture. The residences on the harbor side have spectacular views. The other, inland side is the site of two educational institutions.

[C 18.] The Staten Island Campus of St. John's University (Roman Catholic)/formerly **Notre Dame College,** 300 Howard Ave., bet. Arlo Rd. and Greta Place. W side.

Beginning in 1934, Notre Dame College utilized **the Gans residence,** a neo-Georgian holdover. Since taking over the campus, **St. John's** has added very white, stone-trimmed structures including an all too visible, probably very economical (but silly-looking in this posh area) inflated dome over its gymnasium.

[C 19a.] Notre Dame Academy (Roman Catholic), 78-134 Howard Ave., bet. Eddy and Louis Sts. W side. Second half, 19th century.

The academy is a girl's private school conducted by sisters of **Montreal's Congregation de Notre Dame.** It uses the grounds of the former Scott, Heyn, and Dreyfus estates.

[C 19b.] "The Enclave at Grymes Hill" (residences), along Howard Circle, at Howard Ave. opp. Eddy St. E side. 1988. Calvanico Assocs., supervising architects.

A plan for 11 million-dollar-plus houses built on the site of the **Davis Mansion,** demolished in 1965, and 40-room **Horrmann Castle,** the brewer's fantasy lost in 1967. The site overlooks the **Serpentine Art and Nature Commons,** an outdoor preserve of steep slopes that tumbles down to Van Duzer Street, in Stapleton Heights.

Hero Park, along the south side of Louis Street between Howard Avenue and Victory Boulevard, was a gift to the City in 1920 by Dr. Louis A. Dreyfus and his wife, Berta Schreiber Dreyfus. The doctor is credited with having invented a water-based permanent house paint as well as an artificial chicle for a chewing gum base. The parklands were an adjunct to his estate along Howard Avenue to the south, now part of Notre Dame Academy. "Hero" refers to the veterans of World War I, as the renaming of Richmond Turnpike to Victory Boulevard recalls the armistice that ended that conflict.

[C 20.] Our Lady of Good Counsel Church and Rectory (Roman Catholic), Victory Blvd. SE cor. Austin Place. 1968. Genovese & Maddalene.

Articulated dark-red brick piers contrast with cast-in-place reinforced concrete to create a **powerful sculptural statement** that effectively controls a difficult hillside site along one of the island's busiest thoroughfares. The 3-story rectory on the Austin Street side is linked to the sanctuary by use of a **handsome brick and concrete bell tower.**

EMERSON HILL

Emerson Hill, marks the south side of the Clove, across from Grymes Hill, and is named for **Judge William Emerson,** brother of poet Ralph Waldo Emerson, who regularly visited him here. The easiest way to see (and probably get lost on) the hill is via Emerson Drive, a turnout (which appears to be an uphill narrow extension of the road that many wrongly take) from Clove Road as it crosses the expressway. The narrow roads and curious homes were largely developed in the 1920s by **Cornelius G. Kolff,** a local civic leader later remembered for a ferryboat named in his honor. **Nos. 3, 93, and 205** Douglas Road are among the more interesting newer houses to be found here. (Don't be surprised if practically every lane you turn onto is called Douglas Road . . . it just *is* that way.) Emerson Hill's quaintness results from the constricted yet rustic development patterns and a never ending feeling of closeness with nature, but don't miss the spectacular long-distance views between the houses and the dense foliage. A memorable spot.

Before good roads were cut through to the summit of Todt Hill, and its **forested slopes** were opened to high-style residential development, the group of hills south of the Clove (the cleft through which the Staten Island Expressway passes between Grymes Hill and Emerson Hill) carried the omnibus name Dongan Hills. Since the opening of the Verrazano Bridge in 1964, practically every Staten Island hillock has been **separately named** to meet the **marketing needs** of the local real estate industry. The area closer to the expressway is called Concord.

Along Richmond Road:

Between Staten Island Expressway and Four Corners Road/Flagg Place.

[C 21a.] St. Simon's Episcopal Church, 1055 Richmond Rd., opp. Columbus Ave., Concord. W side. 1961. James Whitford, Jr.

A simple gabled brick church enhanced by its three-bell freestanding bell tower. Called "the church on the curve" since its forebear "the church in the clove" was destroyed for the expressway.

[C 21b.] The Billiou-Stillwell-Perine House, 1476 Richmond Rd., bet. Delaware and Cromwell Aves. SE side. 1662–1830. ★ **Open to the public.**

Like the **house that Jack built,** this one has additions sprawling in every direction. Looking at the building from the front and reading from left to right, you see rooms dating from 1790, 1680, 1662, and 1830. The original one-room **fieldstone farmhouse** with steep pitched roof, built in 1662, is best seen from the back. Walk around the house; take a look inside and in particular at the magnificent open-hearth fireplace.

Lum Chin, 1771 Hylan Blvd., near Liberty Ave., Dongan Hills.

If it's Chinese food you crave, try their wide range of dishes in as sophisticated an atmosphere as anyone would wish.

Nunzio's Restaurant, 2155 Hylan Blvd., near Midland Ave., Grant City.

This place has a reputation among locals for making the best pizza on the island, if not the city!

TODT HILL

Staten Island's *most* chic residential area. Its **summit at 409.2 feet** above sea level is the **highest point along the Atlantic coastline** south of Cadillac Mountain on Mt. Desert Island, Maine.

Off Ocean Terrace:

[C 22a.] 57 Butterworth Avenue (residence), N of Ocean Terr. at end. E side. ca. 1925.

A gingerbread house.

[C 22b.] 57 Carlton Place (residence), E of Ocean Terr. off Emerson Ave., at end. Emerson Hill. ca. 1925.

If this place looks vaguely familiar it's because the wedding scene at the beginning of *Godfather* was filmed here.

The Country Club Area:

This area of Todt Hill, roughly bounded by Flagg Place and Todt Hill Road, is a very prestigious residential area. It once contained **a group of large estates.** Now it is the site for many of the island's most elaborate residences, both traditional and modern; for the **Staten Island Academy,** a private school; a number of seminaries, and for the **Richmond County Country Club.**

Off and along Flagg Place:

[C 23a.] Richmond County Country Club/originally **"Effingham," Junius Brutus Alexander residence**/later **Meyers residence,** 135 Flagg Place. NW side. (Entrance on The Plaza, SE side.) ca. 1860. Many additions.

A much-altered large old Renaissance Revival house where the **island's society** has played since 1897. Alexander was a wealthy Southern cotton grower who regularly voyaged north during the South's long hot summers.

[C 23b.] 16 East Entry Road (residence), bet. Flagg Place, and The Plaza. SW side. ca. 1975.

A modest Modern essay in intersecting shed roofs.

[C 24a.] "Copper Flagg Estates": former outbuilding expanded into residence

[C 24.] Originally **"Stone Court," Ernest Flagg residence, gatehouse, gate, and site**/in part now **St. Charles Seminary, Pious Society of St. Charles, Scalabrini Fathers (Roman Catholic),** in part now **"Copper Flagg Estates"** [see below], 209 Flagg Place, bet. W. Entry Rd. and Iron Mine Dr. NW side. ★ **Additional landmark site and outstructures** including former **South Gatehouse,** 79½ Flagg Court, NW side. Former **Water tower,** 96 Flagg Court. SE side. Former **Stable,** 79 Flagg Court. NW side. Former **Palmhouse,** 61 Flagg Court, NE side. All part of landmark site ★. Accessible from Coventry Rd. **[C 24a.]** "Copper Flagg Estates" (residences on and adjacent to landmark site): *Within the landmark site:* **Altered South Gatehouse, Stable, Palmhouse,** 1987, Robert A. M. Stern. **New residences: 15, 16, 27, 39, 51, 71 Flagg Court.** Both sides. All 1987, 1988. Robert A. M. Stern. *Outside landmark site:* **New residences: 60, 61, 81 Copperflagg Lane. 255 Flagg Place.** All 1987. Robert A. M. Stern. **15, 25 Copperleaf Terrace, 24, 36, 48, 60, 76, 88, 100 Copperflagg Lane.** All 1987, 1988. Calvanico Assocs., Charles M. Aquavella, Di Fiore & Giacobbe, Joseph Morace, architects; Robert A. M. Stern, architectural design review.

Ernest Flagg (1857–1947) was once one of **Staten Island's largest landowners** as well as a prolific and honored architect. Among his designs were the **U.S. Naval Academy** in Annapolis and many of New York's finest buildings, such as the **Singer Tower** and buildings for the Scribner publishing family. For decades **Stone Court** was his rural palatial residence, a grand house of unusual design which reflects Flagg's interest in, and permutations upon, the local **French Huguenot** colonial tradition. (Disregard the insensitive later additions to the house itself.)

In the early 1980s the City's Landmarks Preservation Commission added the rear of the site to its earlier designation, making a total of 9½ acres, to embrace a number of the estate's outbuildings such as the fieldstone water tower, the stable, and the palm house, and a generous lawn and pool. A developer, working with **architect Robert A. M. Stern,** altered and expanded the existing small structures (the swimming pool, for example, was filled in and became a formal garden), and added new residences—where **Edwin Lutyens'** design influences can be discerned—to encircle the lawn. The ten altered and new units *on* the landmark site were regulated by the commission; the thirteen planned for neighboring lands—were not. There *are* discernably clear differences. The best is **No. 255 Flagg Place:** a miniature variation on the themes of Flagg's "Stone Court."

Ernest Flagg's Todt Hill cottages:

Flagg designed, built, and sold a number of picturesque cottages adjacent to Stone Court on lands originally owned by his Flagg Estate Company.

[C 24b.] Main cottage, 45 West Entry Rd., W of Flagg Place. N side.
[C 24c.] "Bowcot, 95 West Entry Rd., W of Flagg Place. N side. 1918.
★ **[C 24d.] "Wallcot,"** 285 Flagg Place. NW side. 1921. ★ **[C 24e.] "Hinkling Hollow,"** 309 Flagg Place. NW side. 1927. **[C 24f.] Paul Revere Smith residence,** 143 Four Corners Rd., 1924, and **[C 24g.] Paul Revere Smith honeymoon cottage,** 143½ Four Corners Rd. (behind No. 143), both bet. Richmond and Benedict Rds. N side. 1924.

Each house is different in plan and elevation, but all of them share in the use of local stone, serpentine, as one of their principal exterior materials. That, combined with **distinctive pitched roofs,** liberal use of **traditional and inventive dormers,** and **hooded brick chimneys,** gives them all a very special Flagg flavor. **(Shades of the Cotswolds!)**

[C 25.] Originally **The McCall's Demonstration House,** 1929 Richmond Rd., opp. and N of Hunter Ave. NW side. 1925. Ernest Flagg. ★

In 1924–1925, *McCall's* magazine publicized (and sold plans at $15 each) **eight house designs,** ranging from four to seven rooms, responding to the needs of America's middle-class homemakers **"by America's foremost architects."** Flagg was one of the eight, but in his case he actually *built* his, on Richmond Road (a main drag even then), below his estate. Evidently an active self-promoter, he installed a sign that once read:

> THIS HOUSE COST LESS THAN THE ORDINARY
> FRAME HOUSE OF EQUAL SIZE

Along and off Todt Hill Road:

[C 26a.] St. Francis Novitiate, Franciscan Fathers (Roman Catholic seminary), 500 Todt Hill Rd., opp. Whitwell Place. W side. 1928.

A somber red-brick institutional structure that began in 1928 as a prep school for those planning a career in the church. Set amid **a flowing green lawn,** its 86-foot tower surmounts one of Todt Hill's highest elevations.

[C 26b.] 3 Whitwell Place (residence), bet. Todt Hill Rd. and Woodhaven Ave. N side. ca. 1980.

A large Modern house with good massing.

[C 27.] 31 Hunt Lane (residence), bet. Woodhaven Ave. and Buttonwood Rd. N side. 1987.

That it's hilly hereabouts is certainly a fact, but it certainly isn't mountainous. Yet this **extremely lavish,** eclectically designed house, set into a terraced site behind a long sweeping stuccoed retaining wall, is *faintly* reminiscent both of the **Himalayan palace** of Tibet's Dalai Lama and some of the **early work of Frank Lloyd Wright.**

[C 28a.] 275 Benedict Road (residence), bet. Four Corners Rd. and St. George Dr. E side. ca. 1983.

A combination of the Parthenon and the work of Charles F. A. Voysey!

[C 28b.] 60 St. James Place (residence), SW cor. Benedict Rd. ca. 1980.

Heard of half-timber? This thinly veneered neo-Tudor rambling residence might be characterized as "sixteenth-timber."

[C 28c.] 8 Romer Road (residence), E of St. George Dr. E end. 1985. Steven J. Calvanico.

Presents a pretentious neo-neo-Georgian facade to visitors, while reserving the harbor view for only those who are invited to enter.

[C 28d.] Originally **Edward R. Stettinius, Sr., residence**/now **Dongan Hall, Staten Island Academy,** 715 Todt Hill Rd., bet. Circle and Four Corners Rd. 1910.

A grand, neo-Georgian mansion built by the **industrialist-financier father** of U.S. Steel president Edward R. Stettinius, Jr., who would become secretary of state in the Roosevelt and Truman administrations. Converted to classroom use by **the island's premier private school,** it still outshines the later, built-for-purpose, modern architecture that came to clutter the campus.

[C 29a.] Originally **Charles Azzue residence,** 785 Todt Hill Rd., bet. Four Corners Rd. and Cromwell Circle. E side. 1975. Charles Azzue, builder.

The **original white stucco** walls and sharply pitched roof lines initially set this house apart from its subdued Todt Hill neighbors. Other strident designs have since been built nearby, while this one has been **tamed** by a Hershey's **chocolate-brown paint job.** The house was designed by its builder, who is known locally for many dramatic "modern" works.

[C 29b.] Originally **Dr. Rothman residence,** 775 Todt Hill Road, bet. Four Corners Rd. and Cromwell Circle. E side. ca. 1978. Charles Azzue, builder.

House (embellished in sgraffito) and garage, each occupying a separate trapezoidal white stuccoed prism, linked by a wood-clad tube. Apparently, to some people this out-of-the-ordinary design signifies "home."

[C 30a.] Richmond County Country Club Pro Shop, golf course, 1122 Todt Hill Rd., opp. Flagg Place. NW side. 1985. Warner, Burns, Toan & Lunde.

A trim octagonal design.

[C 30b.] New Dorp Moravian Church, 1256 Todt Hill Rd., N of Richmond Rd. W side. 1844. **Parsonage,** ca. 1870. **Parish House,** 1913.

This "new" church is older than many of New York's "old" ones. The pretentious, gray stucco parish house in Classical Revival style was the gift of William H. Vanderbilt, son of Cornelius.

[C 31.] Moravian Cemetery, Entrance, Richmond Rd. opp. Otis Ave. N side.

A large fascinating cemetery in which some of the island's **most distinguished families** are interred, including, in a separate, private area, the extended Vanderbilt family. [See the Vanderbilt Mausoleum, below.] While the **Vanderbilt area is not open to the public,** the remainder of the cemetery's older parts offers beautiful landscapes, walks, and drives.

[C 31a.] Old New Dorp Moravian Church/now **Church School** and **Cemetery Office,** within Moravian Cemetery. 1763.

A good example of Dutch Colonial style. Has **sweeping roof** extending over eaves to form porch. Building originally served as church and parsonage; now it caters to the very young as well as the very old as both church school and cemetery office.

[C 32.] Vanderbilt Mausoleum, rear of Moravian Cemetery. 1866. Richard Morris Hunt, architect. Frederick Law Olmsted, landscape architect. **Not open to the public.**

Seemingly carved out of the "living rock," with an ornate granite entrance and observation terrace added by **Hunt** and **Olmsted.** Buried within the **72 crypts** are **"Commodore"** Cornelius Vanderbilt (who paid in advance for the tomb and was later reinterred there) and members of his family. In the remaining 14 acres of the Vanderbilt plot (there had once been 22) are others of the extended family, including the Sloans.

[C 33.] Originally **New Dorp Light Station**/now **private residence,** N end of Altamont Ave. Best viewed from Beacon Ave. and Boyle St. ca. 1854. ★

A former Coast Guard navigation beacon, it acted as an aid to ships entering New York harbor. Its white clapboard tower is hardly reminiscent of the traditional lighthouse form. Now decommissioned, it sees adaptive reuse as a house.

[C 32.] Vanderbilt Mausoleum, on a private site next to Moravian Cemetery

[C 34.] Gustave Mayer residence/originally **David Ryers residence,** 2475 Richmond Rd., bet. New Dorp Lane and Olin St. NW side. (Entry at 24 St. Stephen's Place, opp. Walnut St.) SE side. 1856.

A stately villa atop the rise overlooking the New Dorp flats.

EGBERTVILLE

Along and off Rockland Avenue:

Rockland Avenue, between Richmond Road and Brielle Avenue, hugs **Egbertville Ravine,** the proposed route of **Robert Moses'** Willowbrook Expressway. The route was chosen, naturally, because it required few relocations of residents and because the costs of acquiring the site would be low. (The area between Manor Road and Brielle Avenue is part of Latourette Park and is known among devoted local naturalists as **Buck's Hollow.**) The fact that the ravine and forest south of Rockland Avenue in this stretch are **a remarkable natural area** within the larger Staten Island Greenbelt was not—at least in Moses' time—much of a concern. As the island's population continues to rise and its traffic jams increase, the question of environmental values will again pose difficult decisions.

[C 35.] High Rock Park Conservation Center, 200 Nevada Ave., at summit of hill. **Open to the public.**

A primarily natural rather than built environment, this hardwood forest preserve is a rarity among New York City's protected green spaces. With about 100 acres it is only a small part of the 1,000-acre Staten Island Greenbelt. There are marked, self-guiding trails, a loose strife swamp, a pond, and a visitors' center where more information is available about this nationally recognized environmental-education center.

[C 36–37.] N.Y.C. Farm Colony/Seaview Hospital Historic District. ★ **[C 36.] Seaview Hospital, N.Y.C. Health and Hospitals Corporation,** 480 Brielle Ave., bet. Manor Rd. and Rockland Ave. E and SE sides. 1914. Raymond F. Almirall. ☆ **Open-air radial pavilions, auditorium, Group Building** additions, 1917, Edward F. Stevens and Renwick, Aspinwall & Tucker. ☆ **Roman Catholic Chapel,** 1927. ☆ **Episcopal Chapel,** 1932. ☆ **[C 37.]** Originally **The N.Y.C. Farm Colony,** Brielle Ave. bet. Walcott and Rockland Aves. W side. 1906. Raymond F. Almirall. 1916, Frank Quimby. 1932, William Flanagan. ☆

The earliest buildings of Seaview, originally described as the world's largest tuberculosis hospital, are Almirall's in the **Spanish Mission Style** with much inset decorative tile and Spanish tile roofs. The Farm Colony ("poorhouse" in less euphemistic language) across Brielle Road consists of many smaller structures in a range of styles in which gambrel roofs and **Colonial Revival** porticoes predominate. The extensive Farm Colony site is slated for private residential redevelopment under the auspices of the City.

Lighthouse Hill:

West of Rockland Road (which follows the Egbertville Ravine), north of Richmond Road, and south and east of Latourette Park.

 [C 38.] Eger Home (Lutheran), 120 Meisner Ave., bet. London Rd. and Rockland Ave. S side. 1971. Quanbeck & Heeden.

The prismatic gray multistory masonry nursing home is too large, too noticeable, and too artificial an intrusion into the natural rhythms of the Staten Island Greenbelt. Founded in Brooklyn by Carl Michael Eger, this institution for aged Norwegians has owned this site since 1924.

[C 39.] Nathaniel J. Wyeth, Jr., residence, 190 Meisner Ave., bet. Lowell Court and Scheffelin Ave. S side. ca. 1850.

A lovely, seemingly deserted, 2-story cube of brick masonry topped by a many-sided, many-windowed monitor in the center of its roof. The house is heavily engulfed on the road side by **lush landscaping,** a siting that offers the privacy that newer homes have sacrificed to wide, showy lawns. On the far side (private) it enjoys a fantastic panorama of the approaches to New York harbor.

[C 40a.] Jacques Marchais Center of Tibetan Art, 338 Lighthouse Ave., W of Windsor Ave. 1947. S side. Jacques Marchais, designer. **Open to the public.**

The largest privately owned **collection of Tibetan art** outside of Tibet. A rare treat if you enjoy Tibetan sculpture, scrolls, and painting.

[C 40b.] "Staten Island Lighthouse"/Ambrose Channel Range Light, Edinboro Rd. bet. Windsor and Rugby Aves. S side. 1912. William E. Platt? ★

This lighthouse, strangely distant from rocks and pounding waves, stands calmly amid lawns and homes. The tapered octagonal structure of yellow brick with fanciful Gothic brackets supporting its upper-level wraparound walkway is a pleasant change from pure white cylindrical lighthouses familiar to yachtsmen. The beacon, on high ground and visible for miles at sea, provides range lights to guide ships along Ambrose Channel. *Most dramatic looking up from Lighthouse Avenue.*

 [C 40c.] "Crimson Beech"/originally **William and Catherine Cass residence,** 48 Manor Court, W of Lighthouse Ave. S side. 1959. Frank Lloyd Wright.

A very long, very low building (its gently pitched, bright maroon, hipped roof goes on and on) that clings precariously to the cliff edge, taking full advantage of the **spectacular ocean views.** One of a number of **prefabricated** homes that were the product of Wright's late career—certainly not of the quality of the great architect's prairie houses. But it *is* the **only Wright-designed residence** within the city limits.

[C 40d.] 426 Edinboro Road (residence), bet. Windsor and Rugby Aves. S side. 1987. Steven J. Calvanico.

A speculative Modern house, built to enjoy the spectacular views from these parts.

In LaTourette Park, accessible from Edinboro Road, Lighthouse Hill, and Richmond Hill Road.

 [C 41.] Originally **David LaTourette Residence/**now **LaTourette Park Clubhouse,** LaTourette Park E of Richmond Hill Rd. 1836. Altered, 1936. ★

Either in silhouette on the brow of the hill or studied more carefully up close, this (minus its 1936 WPA porch addition) is a fine masonry Greek Revival mansion. As the clubhouse for a **City-owned golf course,** however, its interior is a great letdown: mostly barren, dim rooms used for snack bar purposes.

[C 42.] The Sylvanus Decker Farmhouse, Staten Island Historical Society, 435 Richmond Hill Rd., bet. Forest Hill Rd. and Bridgetown St. N side. ca. 1810. Porch addition, 1840. ★

A cozy clapboard Dutch-inspired white-painted farmhouse with barn-red outbuildings. A 1955 gift to the historical society, it will be restored, in conjunction with nearby Richmondtown, as a farmhouse of the 1830s.

RICHMONDTOWN

If you're arriving by car, the best approach is from the heights of LaTourette Park down the hairpin turns of Richmond Hill Road, from which Richmondtown Restoration appears to be a miniature village arranged under a celestial Christmas tree.

Once the county seat of Richmond County. Now the site of an ambitious project involving the **restoration** and **reconstruction** of approximately 31 buildings, and hopes for a trolley museum and operating streetcars, all under the direction of the Staten Island Historical Society.

At its founding in 1685 Richmondtown was humbly known as **"Cocclestown,"** presumably after oyster and clam shells found in streams nearby. Here, in 1695, the Dutch erected the Voorlezer House, their **first meetinghouse,** used for both church services and teaching school. Subsequently a **town hall** and jail were built; by 1730 the town was thriving. It had a new courthouse, one tavern, about a dozen homes, and the Church of St. Andrew. This tiny town was now the largest and most important on the island. As such, the name Cocclestown was considered inappropriate and was changed to the more staid Richmondtown. By the time of the **American Revolution,** when the British occupied it, Richmondtown had a blacksmith shop, a general store, a poorhouse, a tanner's shop, a Dutch Reformed Church, a gristmill, and several more private homes.

[C 43.] Richmondtown Restoration, Staten Island Historical Society, Office and public parking, 411 Clarke Ave., SE of Arthur Kill Rd. N side. Begun 1939. Restored, Wyeth & King, and other architects; various landscape architects. **Open to the public.**

The efforts of interested members of the society, combined with the blessings of Robert Moses, resulted in this **"living historical museum"** built around the physical nucleus of the county seat's remaining government buildings and other nearby survivors. To these have been added **other endangered structures** that were moved from various points on the island to this City-owned site.

[C 43a.] Staten Island Historical Society Museum/formerly **Second County Clerk's and Surrogate's Office,** 302 Center St., NW cor. Court Place. 1848. ★

This charmingly scaled red brick building, which once served a governmental purpose, is today a museum. On display are odd **bits of Americana** of varying interest—china, lithographs, furniture, toys, and a marvelous collection of tools and an exhibit, "Made on Staten Island." Note the photos around the gallery (second floor) of Staten Island buildings, most of which have met wrecking ball fate. To get your bearings, study the model of the Richmondtown Restoration project and get a map showing the buildings open to the public the day you visit.

[C 43b.] Third County Court House, Center St. opp. S end of Court Place. ca. 1837. S side. ★

Frumpy but grand. Succeeds in making clear that it is the architectural dowager of this community. It houses the Visitors' center.

[C 43c.] Stephens House and General Store, Court Place NE. cor. Center St. 1837. ★

Fascinating reconstruction of a 19th-century store—everything from ginger beer to quinine pills. The musty smell of soap and candles delights a modern-day shopper used to antiseptic, cellophane-wrapped goods in supermarkets. The storefront is perfectly plain: no neon signs, no billboards.

[C 43d.] Lake-Tysen House, Richmond Rd. bet. Court and St. Patrick's Place. N side. ca. 1740. ★

One of the best examples of the Dutch Colonial style remaining in the metropolitan area and luckily saved at the last minute from destruction when it was moved in 1962 from original site in New Dorp.

[C 43e.] Voorlezer's House, Arthur Kill Rd. bet. Center St. and Clarke Ave. W side. 1695. ★

An archetypical "little red schoolhouse." In Dutch communities unable to obtain a minister, a lay reader *(voorlezer)* was chosen by the congregation to teach school and conduct church services. It is the **oldest-known elementary school building** in the United States.

Other Richmondtown individual city landmarks: ★

[C 43f.] Basketmaker's Shop, ca. 1810, ★ . **Bennett House,** ca. 1837, ★ . **Boehm-Frost House,** ca. 1770, ★ . **Christopher House** (disassembled and awaiting reerection), ca. 1756, ★ . **Cooper's Shop,** ca. 1790–1800, ★ . **Grocery Store,** ca. 1860, ★ . **Parsonage,** ca. 1855, ★ . **Treasure House,** ca. 1700, ★ . **Van Pelt-Rezeau Cemetery,** one of the city's few remaining private burial grounds, ★ . **Cubberly-Britton Cottage,** ca. 1670. Additions, ca. 1700, ca. 1750. ★

In or near Richmondtown, but not part of the Restoration:

East of Richmondtown Restoration:

[C 43g.] St. Patrick's Roman Catholic Church, 53 St. Patrick's Place, bet. Center St. and Clarke Ave. E side. 1862. ★

A brick church whose window openings carry Romanesque Revival half-round arches, but whose narrow proportions are more in keeping with a Gothic Revival verticality.

[C 43h.] The Moore-McMillen House/formerly **Rectory of St. Andrew's Episcopal Church,** 3531 Richmond Rd., opposite Kensico St. W side. 1818. ★

A very good example of Federal style, with extremely handsome doorway and neatly articulated cornice. Behind the house is a good view of the Staten Island Lighthouse [See C 40b.].

West of Richmondtown Restoration:

[C 40b.] The Staten Island Lighthouse   **[C 44.]** St. Andrew's Episcopal Church

[C 44.] St. Andrew's Episcopal Church, 4 Arthur Kill Rd., SE cor. Old Mill Rd. 1872. William H. Mersereau. ★

A picturesque English country church set in a picturesque Staten Island setting complete with graveyard. Borders the marshlands of Latourette Park.

NEW DORP

Arrayed on either side of **New Dorp Lane,** between both Richmond and Amboy Roads, and Hylan Boulevard, lies the community of New Dorp. It expanded easterly after the opening of the Verrazano Bridge, all the way to the ocean (an area earlier called **New Dorp Beach**). Miller Field, at New Dorp Beach, was once the home of the Vanderbilts and, later, of the U.S. Army Air Corps.

[C 45a.] 245 Rose Avenue (residence), SW cor. 10th St. ca. 1885.

A **robust Victorian house** that controls a suburban residential corner without crushing it to death. The house sports an **octagonal corner cupola** with an ogival roof, imbricated shingles, and a Stick Style railing on a balcony tucked beneath the jerkinhead roof.

[C 45b.] Plaza Professional Complex, Ross Ave. opp. 7th St. N. side. 1987.

Warmly reminiscent of Frank Lloyd Wright, but out of place here.

[C 46.] Monsignor Farrell High School (Roman Catholic), a dramatic building

[C 46.] Monsignor Farrell High School (Roman Catholic), 2900 Amboy Rd., S cor. Tysen's Lane. 1962. Charles Luckman Assocs.

Very **modern** (for its day) and very **sophisticated** (for Staten Island in the 1960s): California Modern.

All by itself on the Ocean:

[C 47.] World War II bunker, on the beach at former Miller Field/now Gateway National Recreation Area, NE of the foot of New Dorp Lane. ca. 1942.

All along the beaches of the east coast during World War II the military built observation posts to **spot potential invaders** by sea. Simple in conception and form, they were tall vertical cylinders of reinforced concrete gashed near the top by a narrow horizontal slot facing oceanward. **When hostilities ended,** the priorities for their removal were less than those that had determined their rapid construction. And so, thankfully, this remains to remind us.

Mauro's Italian Restaurant, 121 Roma Ave., off New Dorp Lane, near old New Dorp Beach.

Italian food prepared the way it used to be, in a community redolent of the old beachfront atmosphere.

OAKWOOD

[C 48.] St. Charles Borromeo Church (Roman Catholic), Penn Ave. SW cor. Hylan Blvd. 1973. Clark & Warren.

A Modern mansard sits atop a brick plinth, the intersection creating a **clerestory window.**

Miller Field, now part of Gateway, was the elaborate New Dorp estate of William Henry Vanderbilt, the Commodore's son and the deliverer of Cleopatra's Needle in Central Park. An extensive plot of land lying between Hylan Boulevard and the ocean, from New Dorp Lane to Elmtree Avenue, it became a U.S. Army airfield (and remained an Army installation long after the reorganization of the military to create a separate Air Force). It was named after James Ely Miller, the first aviator of the American Expeditionary Forces, the A.E.F., to be killed in World War I combat.

SOUTHERN STATEN ISLAND

ARDEN HEIGHTS • ELTINGVILLE • GREAT KILLS • ROSSVILLE
WOODROW • CHARLESTON • RICHMOND VALLEY
TOTTENVILLE • PRINCES BAY • ANNADALE • HUGUENOT

The South Shore

The South Shore is that part of Staten Island **farthest from the Verrazano Bridge** and the St. George ferry, the points of interface with the rest of the city. Therefore it has naturally been the **last part of the island to be developed.** In the 1980s, however, the empty (meaning occupied only by forest, marsh, clay pits, or sand dunes) lands **fast began to disappear,** as the rising demand to live within the five boroughs reached its zenith.

ARDEN HEIGHTS

[S 1.] Village Greens (residential development), along Arden Ave. bet Arthur Kill Rd. and Bunnell St. W side. Completed bet. 1972–1974. Norman Jaffe.

Begun in 1970 as a 2,000-family, 160-acre **"planned unit development"** (PUD), this project is a result of special N.Y.C. zoning legislation intended to foster cluster housing, thereby optimizing available open space for neighborhood needs. **Less than a third of the units were completed.** These appear to be very busy visually, thus intensifying the **cheek-by-jowl** feeling. Such simple expedients for adding variety as color change were avoided; all the clusters are of white aluminum siding. Though not successful visually, the project is far more satisfying than the land-wasting, detached tract housing prevalent elsewhere on the island.

ELTINGVILLE

[S 2.] Holy Child Church (Roman Catholic) and **Parish Center,** 4747 Amboy Rd., NW cor. Arden Ave. 1970. Mignone, Coco & Smith.

The white roof and clerestory of this unusually shaped Modern church make it highly visible at a major Staten Island intersection. Close up, however, it loses a lot of its appeal.

[S 3.] St. Alban's Episcopal Church and **Rectory,** 76 St. Alban's Place (one-way east, formerly Old Amboy Rd.), bet. Winchester and Pacific Aves. S side. 1860. ★

A gem. Board-and-batten Carpenter Gothic style with a steeply pitched roof. The entrance is not opposite the apse area but from one side—an interesting variation.

[S 4.] Public School 55, Richmond, and **playground,** 54 Osborne St., SE cor. Woods of Arden Rd. to Koch Blvd. School, 1965. Playground, 1967. Both by Richard G. Stein & Assocs.

The school is a tame New Brutalist essay but more convincing than most public schools of the 1960s. Its geometry is softened by abstract sculpture by **Constantino Nivola.**

The playground, with sculpture also by Nivola, was heralded at the time of its construction as **a design breakthrough.** Upon completion it proved to be a booby trap, its steep changes of grade and high walls challenging neighborhood children into dangerous acrobatic feats. The "zoo bars," installed afterward as a safety measure, create **an unintentional but pleasing** moiré effect for anyone in motion.

[S 8.] Gatehouse, Ocean View Cem.   **[S 12d.]** 2545 Arthur Kill Road house

[S 3.] St. Alban's Episcopal Church: the skill of its early carpenters is evident

[S 5.] Originally **Poillon residence**/later **Frederick Law Olmsted residence,** 4515 Hylan Blvd., bet. Woods of Arden Rd. and Hales Ave. N side. ca. 1720. Significantly altered. ★

Hard to find—it's set back from road. Extensively remodeled in the 19th century. Before he became a park designer, **Frederick Law Olmsted** lived here, running a fruit farm, planting trees, and experimenting with landscaping. Later, when Olmsted began work on Prospect Park, **he moved up to Clifton,** commuting daily to Brooklyn on the nearby ferry.

[S 6.] 80 Bayview Terrace (residence), E of Peare Place. S side. ca. 1986.

One of a group of **idiosyncratic** modern seaside homes of the 1980s, this symmetric 2-story example evidently was designed to reveal the qualities of brown-stained siding laid up in **a variety of directions:** vertically, horizontally, diagonally. By the looks of it, it must be like living in a giant chiffonier.

Carmen's (restaurant), 750 Barclay Ave., south of Hylan Blvd. near Arden Ave., Annadale.

Spanish and Mexican food in a popular, hacienda setting overlooking Raritan Bay. A bit on the expensive side. Parking.

GREAT KILLS

[S 7.] Originally **Great Kills Masonic Lodge, No. 912,** 4095 Amboy Rd., NW cor Lindenwood Rd. 1928.

A porticoed, pedimented, relic of (not so terribly) old Staten Island. It just goes to show how a reference to the Classical world sets an inevitably archaic tone.

[S 8.] Gatehouse, Ocean View Memorial Park (cemetery)/formerly **Valhalla Burial Park,** Amboy Rd. opp. Hopkins Ave. ca. 1925.

A wonderfully romantic, asymmetric neo-Gothic composition in rough and dressed stone, with fine ironwork. A proper entrance to a place of repose.

[S 9.] The Poillon-Seguine-Britton House/originally **Jacques Poillon residence/**later **Joseph G. Seguine residence/**later **Richard H. Britton residence/**now **Harbor View Health and Beauty Spa,** 360 Great Kills Rd., NE cor. Mansion Ave. ca. 1695. Additions, 1730, 1845. Veranda, 1930, Robert C. Hornfager. ★

Generations of Poillons and Seguines inhabited this house before the Brittons and their successors in the 20th century. The thick stone walls mark the earliest part of this house, very well maintained over centuries.

Windjammer Restaurant, 141 Mansion Ave., NW cor. McKee Ave.

Two stories of dining overlooking the Richmond County Yacht Club and the masts of Great Kills Harbor's legion of small boats.

[S 10.] Port Regálle (residential development), Tennyson Dr., bet. Nelson and Wiman Aves. to Great Kills Harbor. 1988. John Ciardullo Associates. 1987.

A "planned unit development" of **clustered homes** that gather around a new street, Harbour Court, at the mouth of Great Kills Harbour.

South Shore Driving Tour E: Along Arthur Kill Road: A drive from Rossville west, south, and west again along the ancient winding route that very roughly parallels the barrens, brackish waters, and industrial intrusions lining the shore of its namesake, the Arthur Kill. Only at **Rossville** does the road come precipitously close to the murky waters of the Kill itself.

START *at Exit 4, Arthur Kill Road, of the West Shore Expressway, in the westbound/southbound direction (closest to the Kill).*

ROSSVILLE

Rossville, now **a veritable eastern ghost town,** was the site of the old Blazing Star Ferry to New Jersey, in service from 1757 to 1836. Stagecoaches going between New York City and Philadelphia **took the ferry,** propelled by sail or oars, here and in Tottenville.

[S 11a.] 2286 Arthur Kill Road (residence), E of Rossville Ave. S side. ca. 1860.

A mansarded loner.

[S 11b.] Sleight Family Graveyard/Rossville Burial Ground/Blazing Star Burial Ground, Arthur Kill Rd. opp. and E of Rossville Ave. N side. ca. 1750. ★

Rossville was once known as Blazing Star and its connection to

New Jersey, as the Blazing Star Ferry. The graveyard, **one of the island's earliest extant,** sits atop a concrete wall (an addition) that elevates it above the road and the dampness of the salt marshes beyond.

Graveyards—industrial and others: Along Arthur Kill Road between Rossville Avenue and Zebra Place lie three waterside graveyards: two burial grounds containing the remains of the area's early European settlers, and another kind, for manmade marine castaways. The cemeteries are **St. Luke's,** and **Sleight Family/Blazing Star** [see below]. The other, at No. 2453, is **Witte Marine Equipment Company.** It is here, on dozens of mucky underwater acres, that rusting ships and leaky barges spend their last days prior to being liberated of their arcane spare parts for reuse on their still-operable cousins. Such tenants as retired two-stack Staten Island ferryboats, in their now barely remembered crimson-and-black paint jobs, can best be seen from the rise of St. Luke's Cemetery. [See S 13b.].

[S 11c.] 2365 Arthur Kill Road (residence), W of Rossville Ave. N side. ca. 1820.

Venerable. Its condition tells us it has seen a long life.

[S 12a.] 2504 Arthur Kill Road (residence), bet. St. Luke's Ave. and Hervey St. SE side. ca. 1840.

A lesser Greek Revival **"captain's house"** than its neighbor, No. 2512: compare, for example, the girth of their respective Doric-inspired columns.

[S 12b.] Originally **Peter L. Cortelyou residence,** 2512 Arthur Kill Road, NE cor. Hervey St. ca. 1855. Additions.

A **resplendent Greek Revival house** of grand scale, located on a rise on the inboard side of the road. Its 2-story stately wood columns, six rounded freestanding and two square engaged, are Doric in inspiration. In the 1980s its owners built a deep wood deck with **"Grecian" lattice fencing** that gelded the lower parts of the portico from public view.

[S 12c.] 2522 Arthur Kill Road (residence), SE cor. Hervey St. ca. 1840. Additions.

A long, gabled 2-story white-painted shingled house with an attached one-story porch. But look carefully. Note that the second-story windows facing the road are grouped as three and, separately, two. There is a history of accretions to this house.

[S 12d.] 2545 Arthur Kill Road (residence), E of Zebra Place. N side. ca. 1800.

Its location, set back on a deep lawn, and its barn red color—very different from its light-colored neighbors—seem to immunize it from 20th-century intruders.

[S 13a.] Formerly **Mark Winant residence/**later **Dr. Robert H. Golder residence,** 2571 Arthur Kill Rd., bet. Hervey St. and St. Luke's Ave. N side. ca. 1750. Additions, ca. 1820, ca. 1860.

The western 1½-story gabled part is the oldest; additions (such as the porch) were added along the way.

[S 13b.] St. Luke's Cemetery/originally **Woglum Family Burying Ground,** Arthur Kill Rd. opp. Zebra Place. N side. Established as St. Luke's, ca. 1847.

Another old cemetery, once the graveyard of the local Episcopal church established here in 1847, now in the shadow of the enormous 200 feet in diameter steel cylinders built to contain **liquefied natural gas** (LNG). Among the family names: **Guyon, Winant, Disoway.** The grounds are administered by All Saints Episcopal Church in Westerleigh.

A side trip into the South Shore's forested heartland:

WOODROW

Sandy Ground:

The intersection of Bloomingdale and Woodrow Roads was known on maps as **Bogardus Corners**—after the Bogardus family's grocery, established in 1860—or, in modern times, as Woodrow. Part of the integrated community of Woodrow (on some maps, Wood Row) was **Sandy Ground,** a settlement of **free black oystermen** who migrated in the 19th century from the shores of Chesapeake Bay, drawn by the flourishing oyster industry of nearby Princes Bay. They **intermarried** with local black families, and the settlement continues to this day despite the disappearance, long ago, of oystering in these waters.

[S 14.] Rossville A.M.E. (African Methodist Episcopal) Zion Church Cemetery, Crabtree Ave. 450 feet W of Bloomingdale Rd. S side. ca. 1854– . ★

Established as the graveyard for the **1854 church on Crabtree Avenue,** now gone, its surviving gravestones help illuminate the history of Sandy Ground, a story richly told in **Joseph Mitchell's** "Mr. Hunter's Grave," collected in his 1960 book *The Bottom of the Harbor.*

 [S 15.] Originally **Woodrow Methodist Episcopal Church**/now **Woodrow United Methodist Church,** 1109 Woodrow Rd., bet. Rossville and Vernon Aves. N side. 1842. Later addition. ★

This **starkly simple** Greek Revival temple is almost—but not quite—spoiled by the awkward arcaded bell tower added atop its roof in the late 19th century, when simplicity must have gone out of favor.

Return to Arthur Kill Road.

[S 16.] Arthur Kill Correctional Center, N.Y.S. Department of Correctional Services, 2911 Arthur Kill Rd., bet. Chemical Lane and Clay Pit Rd. N side. 1970. Ira Kessler & Assocs.

Judging from the interminable festooning of coiled razor wire atop every fence, this is **no easy place of escape:** Staten Island's **Devils Island.**

[S 17a.] Public School 4, Richmond, The Kreischer School, 4210 Arthur Kill Rd., N of Storer Ave. E side. 1896.

Cream-colored brick with orange brick quoining, trim, and "pediment," constructed of the products of the onetime brick factory for whose **founder** the school is named. It overlooks a tiny old cemetery and, since 1934, the fuel tanks of **Port Socony,** now renamed **Port Mobil.**

[S 17b.] Charleston Cemetery, Arthur Kill Rd. N of Storer Ave. W side.

Another of the tiny community cemeteries that line Arthur Kill Road atop low retaining walls. The name **Storer** is evident on a number of the **extant markers,** as it is on the nearby street sign.

[S 18a.] Originally **John Batchellor residence**/later **Nicholas Killmeyer Hotel & Tavern**/later **Union Hotel**/later **Century Inn,** 4256 Arthur Kill Rd., NE cor. Sharrotts Rd. ca. 1840. Addition, ca. 1853.

A country hotel right out of **a Grade B Western** (in the best sense). It reeks of the frontier.

For nature lovers, a short sidetrip to a preserve: Take a left (east) onto Sharrotts Road for a third of a mile and then a left (north) onto Carlin Street to the end, a few hundred feet:

[S 18b.] Clay Pit Ponds State Park Preserve, N.Y.S. Office of Parks, Recreation, & Historic Preservation, 83 Nielsen Ave., opp. Carlin St. **Open to the public.**

Named for the pits once created by the nearby brick works [see below]. Now some **250 acres of ponds** (like Abraham Pond), **bogs, sandy barrens, mature woodlands, and spring-fed streams.** There are trails and various scheduled interpretive programs. (No picnicking facilities.) Beware of Staten Island's scourge; the mosquitoes; they carry **hunting licenses.**

Return to Arthur Kill Road.

CHARLESTON

Charleston, formerly known as Kreischerville after Balthazar Kreischer, who started a brick factory in 1854, is an area rich in clay.

Old clay pits can still be visited; several brickmaking firms operated here during the 19th century.

[S 19a.] Originally **Nicholas Killmeyer store and residence,** 4321 Arthur Kill Rd., NW cor. Winant Place. ca. 1865.

Mom and Pop seemed to live over the store even in the mansard-roofed era.

[S 19b.] Free Hungarian Reformed Church in America/originally **St. Peter's German Evangelical Lutheran Church,** 25 Winant Place, W of Arthur Kill Rd. N side. 1883.

Kreischer originally built the church **for his Lutheran brethren.** Its early character peeks through despite some unfortunate modernization.

[S 19c.] Originally **workers' housing, B. Kreischer & Sons, firebrick manufacturers,** Kreischer St. S of Androvette St. E side. ca. 1865.

Some remaining examples of Kreischer's version of 19th-century industrial paternalism.

[S 20.] Originally **Charles C. Kreischer residence,** 4500 Arthur Kill Rd., opp. Kreischer St. (bet. Englewood Ave. and Veterans Rd. W.). SE side. ca. 1885. ★

In an otherwise flat, sea-level setting juts up a mound of earth topped with this **Stick Style house.** Its lacy details and delicate turret with open-air balcony might be made of sugar, covered with white icing. To the northwest is the former terra-cotta and brickmaking area once called Kreischerville, after the owner's father. Originally, an identical twin house—but designed opposite hand—occupied the adjacent site to the south, that of his brother, Edward B. Kreischer.

[S 20.] The Kreischer residence: hilltop home of Staten Island brickmakers

[S 21.] Outerbridge Crossing, connecting Richmond Pkwy., Charleston, with Perth Amboy, N.J., over Arthur Kill. 1928. Alexander Waddell, engineer; York & Sawyer, architects.

With the decision to name this ungainly cantilever truss bridge after owner Port of New York Authority's first chairman, **Eugenius Outerbridge,** it became clear this would *never* be called Outerbridge Bridge.

M. J.'s Supper Club, 4846 Arthur Kill Rd., bet. S. Bridge St. and Richmond Valley Rd.

Enjoys unimpaired views of gasoline tanks and the Outerbridge Crossing.

RICHMOND VALLEY

[S 22a.] Originally **Abraham Cole residence,** 4927 Arthur Kill Road, NW cor. Richmond Valley Rd. ca. 1840, additions. **[S 22b.] 4934 Arthur Kill Road** (originally residence/now Richmond Valley Kennels), N of Richmond Valley Rd. E side. ca. 1880. **[S 22c.] 291 Richmond Valley Road (residence),** E of Arthur Kill Rd. N side. ca. 1870.

A trio of houses that dignifies a corner of remote Staten Island with **stylistic idiosyncrasies** decades apart, yet ever in harmony with one another.

END of Tour E. *Try a bit of R & R in the island's southernmost community, Tottenville.*

TOTTENVILLE

The community occupying Staten Island's southernmost tip, across the mouth of Arthur Kill from Perth Amboy, N.J., to which ferry service was available from the last stop of the S.I.R.T. until October 1963.

[S 23a.] 5403 Arthur Kill Road (residence), NW cor. Tyrell St. ca. 1855.

An embellished 2-story cube. Remarkable what a simple bracketed cornice can do to what appears essentially to be an almost flat-roofed house: it resembles **Frank Lloyd Wright** or **Buster Keaton** wearing a **porkpie hat.** The syncopated but generous porch adds yet another special note.

[S 23b.] 5414 Arthur Kill Road (residence), bet. Tyrell and Main Sts. S side. ca. 1870.

A mansarded house, once scoffed at, that came to be painted a pretty combination of cream with tan trim.

Along Main Street:

One-way south.

[S 24a.] 104 Main Street (residence), opp. Arthur Kill Rd. W side. ca. 1835.

The miles of **twisting, turning, ever-surprising** Arthur Kill Road end at this sprightly **Carpenter Gothic** cottage. It makes the trip worthwhile! (Actually Arthur Kill Road jogs a bit north here, but it *seems* to end.)

[S 24b.] 123rd Precinct, N.Y.C. Police Department/originally **70th Precinct,** 116 Main St., bet. Arthur Kill Rd. and Craig Ave. S side. 1924. James Whitford, Sr.

A well-done example of **Italian Renaissance Revival,** as befits a precinct house of the **municipal constabulary.** But how does its urbanity and sophistication feel amid the homey, small-scale residences of "downtown" Tottenville? Out of place. (It was probably built on this Main Street site at downtown's edge in optimistic expectation that it would one day become engulfed in similarly scaled business buildings. It hasn't.)

[S 24c.] 127 Main Street (residence), bet. Arthur Kill Rd. and Craig Ave. E side.

Once, every little 19th-century settlement in America boasted a vernacular Victorian frame house like this, **where the local burgher lived** amid curving porches and gabled wings and dormers. Let us cherish the few, like this, that remain, even though time and economics have taken a toll.

[S 24d.] Tottenville Masonic Temple, 236 Main St., bet. Craig Ave. and Amboy Rd. W side. ca. 1900.

Oh, how the **polychromed ornament** made nearby by skilled local craftsmen of the **Atlantic Terra Cotta Company** has come to festoon this wonderful Main Street work. The site of the factory is today marked by the Atlantic Station of the S.I.R.T.

Conference House area:

The southern tip of Hylan Boulevard.

[S 25a.] The Conference House/originally **Captain Christopher Billopp residence,** Conference House Park, foot of Hylan Blvd. N side. ca. 1680. ★ **Open to the public.**

This manor house was built by **British naval captain Christopher Billopp,** the gentleman mistakenly credited for Staten Island's inclusion in New York State. (Myth had it that he sailed around the island in less than the stipulated 24 hours, thereby winning the island from New Jersey.) The house was the site of a **Revolutionary War conference** (hence the name) during which the British representatives offered "clemency and full pardon to all repentent rebels" should they lay down their arms. **Benjamin Franklin, John Adams, and Edward Rutledge,** representing the unrepentant rebels, politely demurred . . . and the war continued. Had the conference been a success we might have remained a British colony. Behind Conference House, along the west side of Satterlee Street (one-way north), north of Hylan Boulevard.

[S 25a.] Billopp/Conference House: an important Revolutionary War landmark

[S 25b.] Originally **Captain Henry H. Biddle residence,** 70 Satterlee St., opp. Pittsfield St. W side. ca. 1840.

A **clapboard captain's house** (like the ones on Captains' Row, in Mariners Harbor) but with a *pair* of matching tetrastyle 2-story porticoes, one facing Perth Amboy across the narrow Arthur Kill, the other facing inland. The **four masonry corner chimneys** indicate that this was never a very chilly house. The 1980s building boom regretably intruded upon this house's century-and-a-half of solitude.

[S 25c.] 96 Satterlee Street (residence), S of Pittsfield St. W side.

What looks like a very old structure, coaxed through more than a century of life and domestic service.

Easterly, on and off Amboy Road:

[S 26a.] St. Paul's Methodist Episcopal Church, 7558 Amboy Rd., bet. Main and Swinnerton Sts. S side. 1883.

The stolid Romanesque Revival gabled brick sanctuary contrasts with and is enhanced by **spare but frothy** window framing and roof trim.

[S 26b.] 24 Brighton Street (residence and former stable), bet. Amboy Rd. and Pittsfield Ave. opp. Summit St. S side. ca. 1880.

A rare surviving example of a carefully designed and executed country house together with its matching outbuilding—with enough land to convey an accurate sense of 19th-century life.

[S 27a.] Tottenville Branch, N.Y. Public Library, 7430 Amboy Rd., bet. Brighton St. and Yetman Ave. S side. 1904. Carrère & Hastings.

One of a group of four Carnegie gifts on Staten Island that began to bring **a semblance of culture** to the rural island early in this century.

[S 27b.] Originally **Church of Our Lady Help of Christians,** 7398 Amboy Rd., SE cor. Yetman St. ca. 1892.

In this low-rise community at the island's southern tip even this short—but bold—corner **octagonal bell tower** provides an important piece of **visual punctuation** to the streetscape.

[S 27c.] Originally **District School No. 5/now wing of Public School 1, Richmond,** Yetman St. SW cor. Academy St. 1878.

A fine work of 2-story masonry architecture, the secular cousin of St. Paul's Methodist Church. [See S 26a.]

[S 28.] Formerly **Dr. Henry Litvak residence and office,** 7379 Amboy Rd., NW cor Lee Ave. ca. 1895. Altered to present form, 1941, Eugene G. Megnin.

A New York City version of a white stucco and glass-block, Corbusier-inspired *maison,* particularly startling to discover among (and out of context with) Tottenville's vernacular structures.

[S 28.] Formerly Dr. Henry Litvak residence and office: a *faux*-Corbusier *maison*

Yesterday's Restaurant & Lounge, 7324 Amboy Rd., bet. Sleight and Sprague Sts., S side.

A common means of recognizing America's 1980s nostalgia trip (which made its mark nationwide in practically every community that had a stock of 19th-century buildings) is through the opening of a theme restaurant. This is Tottenville's entry.

[S 29.] Bethel Methodist Episcopal Church, 7033 Amboy Rd., NE cor. Bethel Ave. 1886.

The larger-than-life masonry facade of this church is embellished with unglazed terra-cotta trim which no doubt came from the well-known clay works of Atlantic Terra Cotta. *Note the extensive cemetery behind the church.*

Along Hylan Boulevard:

Mount Loretto:

[S 30a.] Church of St. Joachim and St. Anne (Roman Catholic), Mt. Loretto Home for Children, Hylan Blvd. bet. Sharrott and Richard Aves. N side. 1891. Benjamin E. Lowe. New nave, 1976.

A disastrous fire in 1973 destroyed the church except for its main facade. In an **imaginative architectural solution,** the towered Gothic Revival front was saved, and a simple **new A-frame nave** was built against it. Economy, simplicity, harmony. The original church was commissioned by **Father John G. Drumgoole,** founder of the 650-acre home (originally for homeless newsboys).

[S 30b.] St. Elizabeth's Home for Girls (Roman Catholic), Mt. Loretto Home for Children, Hylan Blvd. bet. Sharrott and Richard Aves. S side. 1897. Schickel & Ditmars.

A 5-story central pavilion with 4-story wings on either side, all capped with dormered mansards. Topping everything, **a delicate becolumned cupola** surmounted by a cross. **Very somber** except for its site, a gentle rise overlooking Raritan Bay and the *whole* Atlantic Ocean.

[S 30c.] Originally **Princes Bay Lighthouse and Keeper's House**/now **Residence for the Mission of the Immaculate Virgin, Mt. Loretto Home for Children,** Hylan Blvd. bet. Sharrott and Richmond Aves. S side. ca. 1845.

From Hylan Boulevard just west of Sharrott Avenue there is a good view of the **rusticated brownstone** lighthouse which sits on a rise at the water's edge. Its **beacon** is now replaced by **a statue of the Virgin Mary.** It makes an enviable residence and dining hall for priests who care for nearly 1,000 children from broken homes.

PRINCES BAY

Spelled variously as Princes Bay, Prince's Bay, Prince Bay, Princess Bay.

Once a prosperous fishing and oystering village. Oysters from here were so famous that fashionable restaurants in New York and London carried **"Prince's Bays"** on their menus. An area of run-down shacks with tar paper flapping, paint peeling, and curious developers seeking opportunities for profit.

[S 31a.] Originally **John H. Ellsworth residence,** 90 Bayview Ave., 400 feet S of S.I.R.T. E side. ca. 1879.

A ill-kempt but extremely fine, clapboard, oysterman's house overlooking the Lemon Creek salt meadow.

[S 31b.] Originally **Abraham J. Wood residence,** 5910 Amboy Rd., bet. Kane Court and Seguine Ave. S side. ca. 1840. ★

Unpretentious Greek Revival domestic architecture that has survived, set back from the road on a low knoll, for more than a century. One of many houses built in the area for Princes Bay oystermen.

[S 32.] **Richmond Memorial Hospital and Health Center,** 375 Seguine Ave., NE cor. Keating St. **Addition,** 1987, Ferrenz, Taylor, Clark & Assocs.

Known for their effective use of **red brick** in major hospital work elsewhere in the city, the architects of the addition here **turn to another palette,** perhaps in order to distance it from the uninspired earlier structures. The result may be too slick for the residential context.

[S 33a.] Originally **Joseph H. Seguine residence,** 440 Seguine Ave., bet. Wilbur St. and Hank Place. Set back on W side. ca. 1840. Altered. ★

Grand, but clumsy Greek Revival: the 2-story pillars are fat and chunky; the fanlight in the middle of the pediment, awkward; clapboards conceal original stone walls. Still, the structure's **Southern-style grandeur** is appealing. Joseph Seguine was a descendant of the Seguine family whose earlier homestead is across the road [see below].

A mawkish overblown **New England saltbox** (ca. 1985), designed to look old from the start, stands between Seguine Avenue and the landmark that it will no doubt compromise.

[S 33b.] **The Manee-Seguine Homestead**/originally **Abraham Manee residence**/later **Henry Seguine residence**/later **Homestead Hotel**/ later **Purdy's Hotel,** 509 Seguine Ave., NE cor. Purdy Place. ca. 1690. Additions, ca. 1820. ★

The early home of two families of **French Huguenot descent** who derived their income from harvesting the local oyster beds and farming the surrounding acres. The original house is the eastern part, built in two stages of **rubblestone walls.** The additions to the west and north are of wood frame. It was Henry Seguine's oldest son, Joseph, who built the larger house across Seguine Avenue. In 1874 the Manee-Seguine structure was purchased by **Stephen Purdy** for use as a hotel.

ANNADALE/HUGUENOT

[S 34a.] **Huguenot Reformed Church,** 5475 Amboy Rd., NW cor. Huguenot Ave. 1924. Ernest Flagg.

A refreshingly different church design for its time (and place) by **one of America's most original architects.** Built of native serpentinite, a stone quarried on the architect's estate in the Todt Hill section of the island [see C 24.], the church was dedicated as the national monument of the **Huguenot-Walloon Tercentenary** celebration in 1924.

 [S 34b.] Our Lady Star of the Sea (Roman Catholic) Church, 5411 Amboy Rd., bet. Huguenot Ave. and S. Railroad St. 1983. Belfatto & Pavarini.

Crisply mushy Modern.

[S 35.] Tottenville High School, S of Amboy Rd. at Luten Ave. NW cor. Deisius St. 1972. Daniel Schwartzman & Assocs.

Located in the **community of Huguenot** but **renamed** for the high school it replaced, in **nearby Tottenville.** One of the first problems confronting the school was the removal of the letters H U G U E N O T cast into the cast-in-place concrete facade. A reserved, monochromatic design, whose unconvincing arcades are unnecessary in this low-density part of the island, dark, and far from inviting.

Arbutus Lake:

[S 36a.] St. Joseph's-by-the-Sea High School (Roman Catholic), 5150 Hylan Blvd. S side. 1962.

Overlooking serene Arbutus Lake and a short-lived beach resort, **Arbutus Beach,** is this awkwardly designed parochial school. At one time the summer home of steel magnate **Charles M. Schwab** stood here; it was converted to a children's hospital and later added to by a new structure also known as St. Joseph's-by-the-Sea, run by the same order that runs the school. Eventually the complex was demolished to build the school.

[S 36b.] 85 Chester Avenue (residence), [S 36c.] 59 Chester Avenue (residence), Both bet. Swain and Arbutus Aves. N side. ca. 1925.

Two nearby creamy stuccoed homes of a very domestic, slightly baronial, unlabeled style. **No. 85** boats a Spanish tile roof. Both wonderful.

[S 36d.] Nicolisi Drive (residences), at foot of Arbutus Ave. 1980s.

A 38-site development of lavish, pompous, custom-built, **"mansions"** sandwiched between Arbutus Lake and the ocean.

Annadale-Huguenot: The community of Annadale owes its name to the train station which honored Anna S. Seguine, of the nearby (Princes Bay) Seguine family; Joseph was the railroad's president. "Huguenot" honors the early European settlers who had come here fleeing persecution. The two areas will perhaps be forever linked because of a City urban renewal proposal bearing their hyphenated names. It outlined a disciplined plan for growth for the large tract that was 70% undeveloped, sewerless, and largely City-owned. It tried to preclude the development of yet more thoughtless, uneconomical, and destructive tract housing. After the 1965–1975 freeze on new home construction (during which the Annadale-Huguenot Urban Renewal Plan was scuttled anyway), the City's Health Department ruled on minimum lot sizes for septic tanks, and new construction began. While the seemingly endless, loathsome tracts of Heartland Village [q.v.] were ultimately avoided, Annadale-Huguenot is still hardly a Broad Acre City.

NECROLOGY

NECROLOGY

Mementos of the past are essential in understanding and savoring the changing metropolis. While it's folly to believe that New York should always stay the same, the nature, scale, and motives of change profoundly affect the quality of the city. This necrology merely hints at the **continuing, vast, and rapid transformation.**

MANHATTAN

LOWER MANHATTAN

Seamen's Church Institute, 15 State St., SE cor. Pearl St. 1969. Eggers & Higgins.

The picturesque, plastic, and romantic red brick structure that had replaced its 1907 predecessor at Coenties Slip [see below] **lasted less than 20 years.** The institute, which began as a Gothic Revival chapel on a barge in 1834 to serve the spiritual and social needs of mariners, still exists at rented quarters in a lower Broadway office building.

U.S. Office Building/originally **Aldrich Court,** 45 Broadway, bet. Morris St. and Exchange Alley. W side. 1886. Youngs & Cable.

A Romanesque Revival structure whose 9 stories towered over its neighbors when built and were towered over, **in turn,** by the time of its removal in the 1970s.

U.S. Army Building, 39 Whitehall St., bet. Water and Pearl Sts. E side. 1886. Stephen D. Hatch.

The mirrored recladding—not a demolition—marks the second reconstruction here. Hatch's Victorian, fortlike hollowed brick doughnut **rose from the foundations** of Leopold Eidlitz's 1861 New York Produce Exchange. The Army facility was best remembered by the countless thousands who came here **with fear and trembling** to undergo preinduction physicals.

71 Pearl Street (commercial building), bet. Broad St. and Coenties Alley. N side. Foundations, 1641. Walls, 1700. Facade, 1826. ★

The facade of this official landmark, whose foundations were claimed to be those of the **Dutch Stadt Huys,** New York's first city hall, was carefully dismantled to be reerected at South Street Seaport. **Be patient**—there is some question as to whether all its parts can still be located.

Originally **Franklin National Bank (offices)/**later **European-American Bank,** 132 Pearl St., at Hanover Sq. E side. 1962. Eggers & Higgins.

The culturally bankrupt client—eventually to go bankrupt financially—had called for "Georgian," resulting in an awkward, inflated building. Not an unwelcome addition to the Necrology.

60 Wall Street (offices), bet. William and Nassau Sts. N side through to Pine St. 1905. Clinton & Russell.

The 27-story structure that for a time (via an overhead connecting bridge) gave a Wall Street address (60 Wall Tower) to the old Cities Service Building on Pine Street [see L Manhattan/Broadway-Nassau N 1a.]. After demolition the **enormous site** was, for almost a decade, most notable as a sprawling asphalt-paved *pedestrian* space, *not* a parking field.

Seamen's Church Institute, 25 South St., SW cor. Coenties Slip. 1907. Additions, 1919, 1929. Warren & Wetmore.

The only part of this structure not destroyed to build the 55 Water Street office tower was the verdigris "lighthouse" memorializing the sinking of the *Titanic* [see L Manhattan/South Street Seaport S 1a.].

55, 57, 61 Front Street, bet. Cuylers Alley and Old Slip. S side. **54, 56, 62, 64 Front Street,** bet. Coenties and Old Slips. N side. **96-110 Front Street,** bet. Gouverneur Lane and Wall St. N side. **142 Front Street,** NE cor. Depeyster St. All 1830s.

Such warehouses, **almost entirely gone** from the scene, formed the core of commercial Lower Manhattan in the early 19th century. Even the most utilitarian structures were done in Greek Revival.

Engine Company No. 4, Ladder Company No. 15, N.Y.C. Fire Department, Water Street at Old Slip, through to Front St. E side. ca. 1955.

Porcelain enameled as though it were a gas station, this **severe but naively Modern** 1950s fire station grew more charming as it aged and became more dated. It was demolished for the piazza of Palatina, the recycled First Precinct building; the engines are now tucked into the rear of 1 Financial Plaza.

 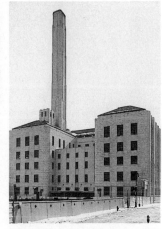

United States Army Building in 1978   United States Assay Building in 1977

U.S. Assay Building, Old Slip bet. South and Front Sts. E side. 1930. James A. Wetmore, Acting Supervising Architect, U.S. Treasury.

A massively sculptural granite monolith **low rise** with a **high-rise** smokestack. The Feds auctioned the site off for $27 million, an astronomical sum for the early 1980s.

Manhattan Landing on the East River between Whitehall Street and South Street Seaport: One of the city's more ambitious plans was aborted during the mid 1970s fiscal crisis: to build out over the water to the pierhead line a phalanx of office structures—including a new New York Stock Exchange and tens of thousands of apartments. Its "reincarnation" is still being awaited (by some).

The Singer Building and **Tower (offices),** 149 Broadway, NW cor. Liberty St. 1908. Ernest Flagg.

The **tallest building ever demolished** (47 stories, 612 feet). One of the city's **great** monuments—demolished for 1 Liberty Plaza. The ornate Beaux Arts lobby alone was worth the price of 10,000 sewing machines. Torn down in broad daylight—**after** the Landmarks Preservation Commission came into existence—this has to be **city's greatest loss since Penn Station.**

Originally **German-American Insurance Company (offices),** 1 Liberty St., at Maiden Lane. N side. 1907. Hill & Stout.

A critical element in one of Lower Manhattan's most cavernous streetscapes, this magnificantly corniced, wonderfully proportioned, appropriately triangulared structure was wasted by the City for a street widening—just to accommodate more cars!

Originally **Morgan Laing Stores (warehouses),** 258-262 Washington St. and 97 Murray St. NW cor. 1848. James Bogardus. Stolen, 1974, 1977. ★

Landmark for a day. Designated a Landmark in 1970, one of the country's earliest prefabricated cast-iron buildings had its facades carefully dismantled, to be reerected as part of the Washington Market

Urban Renewal Project. While waiting, **someone absconded** with the parts—*twice!* (They were not trivial items but weighed more than 6 tons.)

Suerken's Restaurant, 27 Park Place, NE cor. Church St.

While the cast-iron columned facade remains behind a layer of 1980s glitz, the old-fashioned German eatery itself, of **darkened wood, stained glass,** and **tiled floor,** is no more. Gone also are the hearty sauerbraten and dumplings, the bauernwurst, sauerkraut, and hot mustards, and those steins of beer . . . lots of beer.

The Singer Tower on a 1912 postcard   Orig. Ger. Amer. Insurance Co. in 1971

Ross Scientific Apparatus, 81 Reade St., bet. Broadway and Church St. S side.

The gaggle of microscopes, barometers, glass eyes, litmus paper, and beakers of all shapes and sizes was a great feast for even the most scientifically inept. Out of business.

Pedestrian walkway, Brooklyn Bridge, City Hall Park, Manhattan, to Cadman Plaza, Brooklyn. 1883. Washington Roebling.

The raised walkway, interrupted at the pairs of anchorages and towers by stairs, provided one of the most **carefully modulated, peacefully exhilarating,** and **spiritually invigorating** walks in the city. It has been replaced by a predictable, continuous ramp that often becomes a high-speed bikeway, courtesy of the New York City Department of Transportation.

Fordham University, City Hall Division/formerly **Vincent [Astor] Building,** 302 Broadway, SE cor. Duane St. 1899. George B. Post.

Sixteen terra-cotta-trimmed stories demolished to make way for an ill-fated project: a gargantuan municipal office building to accommodate the ever expanding bureaucracy.

H. Bowker & Company (lofts), 101-103 Duane St., bet. Broadway and Church Sts. N side. 1870. Thomas Little. **317 Broadway (lofts),** SW cor. Thomas St. 1865. **10-12 Thomas Street (lofts),** bet. Broadway and Church Sts. S side. 1870. Thomas Little. **64-66 Thomas Street (lofts),** bet. Church St. and W. Broadway. S side. 1867. **43-45 Worth Street (lofts),** bet., Church St. and W. Broadway. N side. 1860. S. A. Warner. **54 Worth Street (lofts),** bet. Broadway and Church Sts. S side. ca. 1860. William Field & Son. **58-60 Worth Street (lofts),** bet. Broadway and Church Sts. S side. 1869. Griffith Thomas. Rebuilt, 1879, J. Morgan Slade. **66-68 Worth Street (lofts),** bet. Broadway and Church Sts. S side. ca. 1870.

Cast-iron "gray ghosts" that are now **truly** ghosts, the ones on Worth and Thomas lost to AT&T's Long Lines tower.

Olliffe's Pharmacy, 6 Bowery, bet. Pell and Doyers Sts. W side. 1803.

In spite of remodelings over the years, this was considered the oldest drugstore in America.

Originally **Olive Branch Baptist Church**/later **Congregation Beth Haknesseth Anshe Sineer (synagogue),** 290 Madison St., SW cor. Montgomery St. 1856.

The **pink synagogue,** isolated amid low- and middle-income housing, was destroyed by fire.

Garden Cafeteria, 165 E. Broadway, SE cor. Rutgers St.

This magnificent dairy café was probably the last visible center for Yiddish intellectuals—artists, writers, journalists—even after the *Jewish Daily Forward* moved from its old building a few doors over. The *Forward*'s editor, **Abraham Cahan,** must have lunched here; it was rumored that **Leon Trotsky** was a frequent diner in his New York days; **I. B. Singer** definitely was. Never to resound again is the GONG! of the ticket machine as you pulled your ticket for the perpetually annoyed counterman to punch in the price of matzo ball soup and kasha varnishkes. Another dairy restaurant, **Galishoff's** on Rivington Street, is also gone.

Mills House No. 2 (hotel), 16 Rivington St., NW cor. Chrystie St. 1897. Ernest Flagg.

A lesser-known Flagg work built as a hostel for low-income guests. It is survived by a larger cousin, now The Atrium in the Village [see V Manhattan/Greenwich Village V 14b.].

St. Alphonsus Church (Roman Catholic)/originally **Church of St. Alphonsus Liguori,** 312 W. Broadway, bet. Canal and Grand Sts. W side. 1872. Rectory, 308 W. Broadway. ca. 1878. Church Hall, 320 W. Broadway. ca. 1885.

The lively combination of fronts was dominated by the asymmetric Lombardian Romanesque facade of the church. Conveniently, as the community's Roman Catholic **population began to sag,** so did the buildings' foundations, resulting apparently from **settlement** into a longforgotten **underground stream.** Closed in 1980 because of danger of collapse, the church and its companions were soon demolished.

THE VILLAGES

Harout's Restaurant, 14 Waverly Place, bet. Christopher and W. 10th Sts. S side. 1961. Haroutiun Dederian.

It very early recognized the values of leaving well enough alone, namely the original architecture. Landmark preservation before the Commission.

Eighth Street Bookshop: When Greenwich Village was the intellectual center of New York, West 8th Street was its main commercial strip. One of the street's great institutions was a *real* bookshop, founded by two brothers, Eli and Ted Wilentz. It opened at No. 30, at the corner of MacDougal Street, until success caused it to move to a much larger multistory space across the street at **No. 17** (*1965. Elliot Willensky*). The genial shop not only attracted casual customers but was a haven for writers and poets as well.

Women's House of Detention, 10 Greenwich Ave., bet. Christopher and W. 10th Sts. E side. 1931. Sloan & Robertson.

Not the architecture, Art Deco, but its ungainly bulk and earpiercing conversations (screamed from barred windows to friends in the street below) led to this jail's demise.

Sutter's French Café, 18 Greenwich Ave., NE cor. W. 10th St.

Croissants, brioches, and all manner of other caloric temptations, a touch of Paris, disappeared when inflation got the better of the proprietors (and their landlord).

Plaque, Greta Garbo Home for Wayward Boys and Girls, 146 W. 11th St., bet. Sixth and Greenwich Aves.

The strange brass plaque on the door of this Victorian row house briefly announced the reclusive star's (perhaps imaginary) philanthropic bent and always evoked a double take from passersby. A hoax?

Elizabeth Bayley Seton Building, St. Vincent's Hospital, 157 W. 11th St., NE cor. Seventh Ave. 1899. Schickel & Ditmars.

Its dark red brick set off by bold rows of light-colored limestone trim, the hospital's main building was the most distinguished element in the complex. Demolished for the **state of the art** George Link, Jr. Pavilion.

Uprooted: When the huge Loew's Sheridan Theater was demolished in the 1970s by St. Vincent's to make way for expansion, the West Village Committee took advantage of a hiatus in the building schedule to create a charming English garden, along with a recycling center for refuse, in the Village Green, bounded by Seventh and Greenwich Avenues and West 12th Street. The hospital eventually undid the greenery for its Materials Handling Center.

Church of St. John's-in-the-Village (Episcopal)/originally **Hammond Street Presbyterian Church,** 220 W. 11th St., SW cor. Waverly Place. 1846.

The original Greek Revival church was destroyed by fire in 1971 and then replaced [see V Manhattan/Greenwich Village D 16a.].

St. Vincent's Hospital (1910 postcard)   B'way Central Hotel (1908 postcard)

Morton Street Pier/originally **Pier 42, North River,** Hudson River at West St.

As a result of West Village pressure, the City renovated the shed-less pier as **community open space.** The two Board of Education **Maritime High School ships** were initially moored alongside. Now closed to the public, with a tall chain-link fence that proclaims PEOPLE NOT WELCOME.

Miller Elevated Highway/better known as **The West Side Highway,** Rector St. to W. 72nd St., over West St., Eleventh and Twelfth Aves. Canal to W. 22nd Sts., 1931. W. 59th to W. 82nd Sts., 1932. W. 22nd to W. 38th Sts., 1933. W. 38th to W. 46th Sts., 1934. W. 46th to W. 59th Sts., 1937. Sloan & Robertson, architects for these sections. Canal St. bridge, 1939. Rector to Canal Sts., 1948.

Potholes, rust, and many other indications of the impact of rock salt, heavy traffic, and **deferred maintenance** were visible along the elevated West Side Highway before December 15, 1973, when the combined weight of an asphalt-laden dump truck and a car finally caused a major collapse—near the Gansevoort Market—thus sealing its doom. For a time, the abandoned roadway attracted bicyclists and artists eager to exploit its **huge concrete canvas.** The elegant steel arch that suspended the highway across Canal Street spent its last days gaily decorated with 140 gallons of pink, purple, and blue paint, a composition called **"Hudson Summer Sunset"** by its creator, **A. Eric Arctander.**

Whither Westway?: After almost ten years of planning and almost another ten of legal debate, the $2 billion Westway proposal, a gigantic real estate development posing as a highway/park project, was defeated. Replacement: a new 6-lane highway *cum* park along the Hudson estimated at only $810 million.

153 Crosby Street (warehouse), bet. E. Houston and Bleecker Sts. E side. ca. 1840.

Once a splendid Greek Revival commercial building.

Originally **Southern Hotel/**later **Grand Central Hotel/**later **Broadway Central Hotel,** 673 Broadway, bet. Bleecker and W. 3rd Sts. W side. 1871. Henry Engelbert.

When this great Beaux Arts lady went, she did so in dramatic fashion—not so much a peaceful demise as a mighty—and deadly—collapse into the center of Broadway's pavement.

Old Church of the Nativity (Roman Catholic), 46 Second Ave., bet. E. 2nd and E. 3rd Sts. E side. 1832. Town & Davis (A. J. Davis, J. H. Dakin, and James Gallier).

By a most distinguished firm, this Greek Revival, Doric columned, white painted wood church grew very old and very decayed. It was finally replaced by a lesser Modern edifice.

Lebost Windmill, atop N.Y.U. School of Education/originally Hebrew Technical School, 34 Stuyvesant St., SE cor. E. 9th St.

This ungainly, out-of-place **windmill-like contrivance** for generating electricity was born of the late 1970s energy crisis; deceased in the early 1980s when the crisis declined. Its supports remain.

Old St. George's Ukrainian Catholic Church, 26 E. 7th St., bet. Second Ave. and Hall Place. 1840.

This Greek Revival temple in stucco with a **mini-onion dome** was demolished in 1976 to provide off-street parking for the congregation's new building next door.

MIDTOWN

CHELSEA

Cavanaugh's Restaurant, 256 W. 23rd St., bet. Seventh and Eighth Aves. 1876.

For many decades the steaks and other Irish and American fare here satisfied the greedy cravings of the likes of **Diamond Jim Brady** and the more modest appetites of generations of ordinary New Yorkers.

Belly dancing: Eighth Avenue between West 28th and West 29th Streets was the heart of a Middle Eastern enclave of modest restaurants and night clubs housed in a rich variety of Victorian buildings. The exotic establishments, their names recalling once faraway places—Ali Baba, Grecian Cave, Egyptian Gardens, Port Said, Istanbul—have all gone. And so have the often well endowed belly dancers.

The Chelsea piers, Hudson River along Twelfth Ave., bet W. 12th and W. 22nd Sts. W side. 1902–1907. Warren & Wetmore.

A group of the North River's last surviving pier structures, long inactive. The head houses' **cast-in-place concrete ornament** (echoing the details of limestone) was appropriately austere, a far cry from the lush carving of the real thing at W & W's Grand Central Station.

441 West 28th Street (model tenement), bet. Ninth and Tenth Aves. 1916.

Originally built as demonstration housing by the Hudson Guild.

403-405 West 28th Street (row houses), bet. Ninth and Tenth Aves.

Two houses which possessed rare, vine-covered verandas.

Lüchow's (restaurant), 110 E. 14th St., opp. Irving Place. 1914.

The **richly ornate** series of mock Victorian spaces was filled with **heavy German fare,** plenty of draft beer, and music: sentimental string instrumentalists as well as **brassy oompah bands.** The interiors remained magnificent if somewhat seedy; the food deteriorated with each change in ownership. While up for both exterior and interior landmark designation since 1978, the Landmarks Preservation Commission never took action. The owner vowed to keep the front.

S. Klein's-on-the-Square (department store), 2-18 Union Sq., bet. E. 14th and E. 15th Sts. E side. Converted, 1921.

The old, frantic, cut-rate department store with the flashy name was actually a cluster of mid 19th-century buildings including the Union Square Hotel, harking back to a time when the square was bordered with such establishments as Tiffany & Company, F. A. O. Schwarz, and Brentano Brothers. After a last-minute, halfhearted effort to save the buildings, they were demolished for the Zeckendorf Towers.

Irving Place Theatre/originally **Amberg's Theatre,** 11 Irving Place, SW cor. E. 15th St. 1888.

After a life as a legitimate theater, burlesque house, home of foreign films, German playhouse, and storage warehouse for S. Klein's, the Moorish style structure was finally demolished in 1985 for Zeckendorf Towers. It was earlier the site of Irving Hall, a Democratic club and chief rival of Tammany Hall.

Wilburt's (home furnishings), 194 Third Ave., bet. E. 17th and E. 18th Sts. W. side. 1964. Space Design Group.

Housewares, glass, china, and ceramics were sold in this preview of Conran's near Gramercy Park. The shop was as handsome as its contents: elegant **and** unpretentious.

Originally **DeMilt Dispensary/**later **American Musical and Dramatic Academy,** 245 E. 23rd St., NW cor. Second Ave. 1851.

A great display of carefully crafted masonry displaced by a lesser work.

Originally **Leonard Jerome residence/**later **Union League, University,** and **Manhattan Clubs,** 32 East 26th St., SE cor. Madison Ave. 1859. Thomas R. Jackson. ★

Famous as the mansion of **Winston Churchill's grandfather,** this Second Empire structure later served as transitory homes for several of New York's **elite clubs.** The building achieved questionable notoriety as one of New York's few officially designated landmarks **to be demolished.**

Belmore Cafeteria, 407 Park Ave. S., bet. E. 28th and E. 29th Sts. E side.

An East Side landmark: the long line of yellow cabs parked outside signaled a taxi drivers' haven. Once filled with Formica, cigar smoke, and cabbies' tales of woe, this local institution succumbed to a condo apartment tower after half a century.

Trinacria Importing Company (gourmet shop), 415 Third Ave., NE cor. E. 29th St.

Greek, Armenian, and Near Eastern foods made this a favorite local takeout. The aroma alone incited the appetite.

Union Square Hotel/later S. Klein's   The 71st Regiment Armory, N.Y.N.G.

Originally **Madison Square Presbyterian Church Mission House,** 432 Third Ave., NW cor. E. 30th St. ca. 1900. Howells & Stokes.

The 4-story golden-hued brick building with severe half-rounded arched openings served the **Reverend Charles Henry Parkhurst's church,** which fronted on Madison Square. The mission house was vacant for many years until torn down for apartments.

HERALD SQUARE AND WEST

Pennsylvania Station, Seventh Ave. bet. W. 31st and W. 33rd Sts. W side to Eighth Ave. 1910. McKim, Mead & White.

An imperial neo-Roman monument built for ordinary people, its **much protested demolition** in 1963 spurred the permanent establishment of New York City's Landmarks Preservation Commission. **Mourning the station's demise,** an editorial in the October 30, 1963, *New York Times* observed: "we will probably be judged not by the monuments we build but by those we have destroyed."

MURRAY HILL

71st Regiment Armory, New York National Guard, Park Ave. bet. E. 33rd and E. 34th Sts. E side. 1905. Clinton & Russell.

The first edition of the *AIA Guide* called it a "burly brick mass topped by a medieval Italian tower." It is now replaced by a combined high school and office tower [see M Manhattan/Murray Hill M 2a.].

J. P. Morgan carriage house, 211 Madison Ave., bet. E. 35th and E. 36th Sts. E side.

This rare remnant from Madison Avenue's early elite era housed the **Anthroposophical Society in America.** The site how supports a sliver.

144 East 39th Street (carriage house), bet. Lexington and Third Aves. **143, 148,** and **152 East 40th Street (carriage houses),** bet. Lexington and Third Aves. Late 19th century.

These 4 carriage houses once afforded passersby a variety of building styles and modest scale among newer monoliths.

Architects Building (offices), 101 Park Ave., NE cor. E. 40th St. 1912. Ewing & Chappell and La Farge & Morris.

In this building, built **by** architects **for** architects, scores of the profession's offices filled the floors above the **Architects' Samples Corporation** exhibition space, which snaked through the lobby level and mezzanine.

Ernest Flagg residence/later **Chess and Athletic Club,** 109 E. 40th St., bet. Park and Lexington Aves. 1905. Ernest Flagg.

Flagg (1857–1947), who resided here until his death, included in his palatial city house an intriguing tiled entrance for his auto, which would be **lowered by elevator** to a garage below street level. The entrance opened onto an opulent multilevel interior space.

113 and **115 East 40th Street (residences)/**formerly **The Architectural League of New York,** bet. Park and Lexington Aves.

For decades these interconnected buildings, one a carriage house, sheltered the **New York Chapter of the AIA,** the Architectural League, and other art and architectural organizations.

Originally **Tiffany & Company stables,** 140 E. 41st St., bet. Lexington and Third Aves. 1904. McKim, Mead & White.

The stables are gone, but Tiffany's old store on Fifth Avenue and 37th Street lives on in another guise. [See M Manhattan/Herald Square Q 23.]

CLINTON

Brittany du Soir (restaurant), 800 Ninth Ave., NE cor. W. 53rd St.

First, Café Brittany went out of business, and then Brittany du Soir, about the last of the city's moderately priced French restaurants. Far from brilliant cuisine but pleasant, cozy, and very pre-yuppie.

Rossiter Stores, Terminal Warehouse Company/later **Gardner Warehouse Company,** Twelfth Avenue NE cor. W. 59th St. 1889. Walter Katté, chief engineer.

A phalanx of solid, masonry warehouses, their walls punctured with tiers of arched openings, each guarded by steel shutters that opened like a butterfly's wings.

TIMES SQUARE AREA

Franklin Savings Bank, 658 Eighth Ave., SE cor. W. 42nd St. 1899. York & Sawyer.

This was one of the architects' earliest banks, in a massive Classical style.

Helen Hayes Theatre/originally **Folies Bergère Theatre/**later **Fulton Theatre,** 210 W. 46th St., bet. Broadway and Eighth Ave. 1911. Herts & Tallant.

One of the finest of Broadway's theaters to disappear, it opened originally as a **theater-restaurant.** The previous *AIA Guide* called its lavish blue and cream terra-cotta facade **"worked by a crochet hook."**

BRYANT PARK AREA

Kress Building (variety store), 444 Fifth Ave., NW cor. W. 39th St. 1935. Edward Sibbert.

The Art Deco structure contained the S. H. KRESS & CO. 5.10.25. CENT STORE as the chunky, incised letters indicated, the epitome of the

20th-century urban general store; over the entrance were neo-Mayan symbols of purchasable goods. Replaced by the tower of the Republic National Bank of New York [see M Manhattan/Bryant Park B 6a.].

Wendell L. Willkie Building of Freedom House/originally **The New York Club,** 20 W. 40th St., bet. Fifth and Sixth Aves. 1907. Henry J. Hardenbergh.

It was home to a gentlemen's club that from the late 1840s had slowly made its way uptown. Its upper floors later housed the New York chapters of the city's architects' and planners' organizations, just beneath the colossal brick gable. **Defaced in advance of consideration** by the Landmarks Preservation Commission and eventually demolished.

The Kinetic Sculpture on Grace Plaza, its official name, was located at the southeast corner of Sixth Avenue and West 43rd Street. Designed by Hugh Greenlee of Greenlee-Hess Industrial Design in Cleveland, it was presented to the people of the City of New York on the occasion of owner W. R. Grace's 125th anniversary. A glass enclosure some 6 feet wide, 27 feet long, and 12 feet high, it contained 700 gallons of gooey, cloudy, white silicone (Dow Corning 200 Fluid), which in all seasons of the year oozed—slowly . . . very . . . slowly—down the inside walls of the enclosure, inspiring some to dub the contrivance **Sperm Bank.** Then, one day in the mid 1980s, it stopped oozing and was quietly removed.

GRAND CENTRAL/PARK AVENUE

Airlines Terminal Building (ticket office/bus terminal), 80 E. 42nd St., SW cor. Park Ave. 1940. John B. Peterkin.

The low but powerful limestone **Art Deco** airline ticket and airport transit center was from the beginning dwarfed by its neighbors, the Lincoln and Pershing Square Buildings. Replaced by the **Philip Morris Building,** the massive eagles now grace a facility of the cigarette manufacturer in Richmond, Va., designed by Hardy Holzman Pfeiffer Associates.

Airlines Terminal Building on East 42nd Street as seen on a 1940s postcard

Hotel Biltmore, Madison to Vanderbilt Aves., E. 43rd to E. 44th Sts. 1914. Warren & Wetmore.

The clock in its ornate lobby was a **favorite meeting place** for college students in the old days. In the early 1980s, as soon as the preservation community got wind of the Biltmore's impending recladding in shiny brown granite veneer by **Environetics** (an architectural firm), the developers quickly stripped the building down to its steel frame. Last-minute attempts to designate at least the lobby a landmark failed.

Acquavella Building, 119 E. 57th St., bet. Park and Lexington Aves.

An enchanting Tudor jewel replaced by an even more enchanting baguette [see M Manhattan/Grand Central/Park Avenue P 22a.].

137 East 57th Street (offices), NW cor. Lexington Ave. 1930. Thompson & Churchill, architects; Charles Mayer, consulting engineer.

As a previous *AIA Guide* edition put it, "A pioneering piece of structural virtuosity: the columns are recessed 9 feet from the skin. Steel tensile straps hang the perimeter floors and walls from roof girders." All this apparently to avoid a stream bed beneath the building's corner. But its inclusion in the Museum of Modern Art's modern architecture exhibition of 1932 was not sufficient to justify landmarking.

UNITED NATIONS/TURTLE BAY

Harcourt Brace Jovanovich Bookstore, in former Harcourt Brace Jovanovich Building, 757 Third Ave., NE cor. E. 47th St. 1964. Cloethiel Woodard Smith & Assocs.

One of America's best-known woman architects designed this handsome bookshop, entered through a cylindrical vestibule with half-round swinging doors.

FIFTH AVENUE

La Potagerie (restaurant), 554 Fifth Ave., bet. W. 46 and W. 47th Sts. W side. 1971. George Nelson & Co.

After the demise of the Brass Rail and Schrafft's, it was difficult to find a **dignified but reasonably priced** Fifth Avenue eatery. Here a variety of soups and desserts were offered in a pleasant, inviting, and carefully designed cafeteria setting. **One of the first** of its type to be **concerned with design,** from the food display down to the napkins.

The sleek, curved glass facade of La Potagerie, a soup restaurant, in 1971

Schrafft's (restaurant)/originally **Knoedler Gallery,** 558 Fifth Ave., bet. E. 45th and E. 46th Sts. W side. 1911. Carrère & Hastings.

Its facade was cosmetized via radical plastic surgery into the Philippine Center (*1974. Augusto Comacho*).

Latter-day double-decker buses: Although only four of them existed, patience was rewarded by taking a grand tour down Fifth Avenue, up Madison, along Riverside Drive, and to the Cloisters on the upper deck of a 1976 vintage, dark red, double-decker bus (made in Britain, of course), all for the price of a transit token each way.

Olivetti-Underwood Showroom, 584 Fifth Ave., bet. W. 47th and W. 48th Sts. W side. 1954. Belgiojoso, Peressutti & Rogers, architects. Wall relief, Constantino Nivola, sculptor.

Olivetti's elegant office equipment roosted on green marble pedestals growing out of the green marble floor.

Brentano's (bookstore), 586 Fifth Ave., bet. W. 47th and W. 48th Sts. W side. Altered, 1965, Warner, Burns, Toan & Lunde.

Until the discount bookstore came on the scene, Brentano's with its multilevel, multipurpose spaces was among midtown's favorites.

Spanish National Tourist Office, 587 Fifth Ave., bet. E. 47th and E. 48th Sts. E side. 1964. Javier Carvajal.

This austere white stucco and oak cave was often obscured by tourist come-ons.

Schrafft's (restaurant) in 1967 photo   The Olivetti Showroom in 1954 photo

Creative Playthings (toy shop), 1 E. 53rd St., bet. Fifth and Madison Aves. Altered, 1970, Godard/Hodgetts/Mangurian/Walker.

This important outlet for educational toys with its comfortable, smooth interior spaces became the Museum of Broadcasting.

West 53rd Street between Fifth and Sixth Avenues: With its juxtaposition of 19th-century Victorian town houses and the "shocking" 1939 International Style Museum of Modern Art (and the later Donnell Library), this vibrant block of evolving midtown, crammed full of art and culture, has been totally diffused. Three daring museums melded the elegance of the older buildings with strong statements of modern design: **The Museum of Contemporary Craft** in the row house at **No. 44** was altered in 1961 by David Campbell and altered again in 1979; its earlier space at **No. 29,** designed in 1956 by Campbell, was a sensitive multilevel carving within another old row house; both are gone. **The Museum of American Folk Art** row house space at **No. 49** was demolished. **The Museum of Modern Art**'s annex was at **No. 23,** the former George Blumenthal residence of 1904 by Hunt & Hunt. It was converted into offices, and then the ground floor was transformed in 1973 and 1975 by Abraham Rothenberg Assocs. and Thomas Lowrie for one of the museum's shops, always leaving the grand Beaux Arts facade intact, until the end. MOMA's own original canopy and penthouse terrace restaurant by Philip L. Goodwin and Edward Durell Stone, and the 1951 west addition by Philip Johnson & Assocs., were removed to accommodate the vast expansion of 1985 which had claimed the Blumenthal annex.

Santiago Shoe Salon/ later **T. Jones,** 697 Fifth Ave., bet. E. 54th and E. 55th Sts. E side. 1965. Morris Ketchum, Jr. & Assocs.

Giant glass shoe boxes, just off the sidewalk, were used to display its wares.

Sona the Golden One (boutique), 7 E. 55th St., bet Fifth and Madison Aves. 1965. Richard Meier, architect. Elaine Lustig Cohen Assocs., designers.

An oriental bazaar of the 1960s.

ROCKEFELLER CENTER AREA

Singer Showroom, 9 W. 49th St., in Maison Française. 1965. Victor Lundy.

The rather bland display of fabrics, notions, and sewing machines was always out of place in this dramatic setting.

Japan Airlines Ticket Office, British Empire Building at Channel Gardens. 1956. Raymond & Rado; Junzo Yoshimura, associate architect.

A tiny semiprecious jewel.

Pot au Feu (soup restaurant), 123 W. 49th St., bet. Fifth and Sixth Aves., in the Exxon Building. 1973. Charles Morris Mount and Judith Kovis Stockman.

A companion to the now disappeared La Potagerie, Pot au Feu served up simple, modestly priced food in a colorful, relaxed space.

Mus. of Contemp. Craft at 29 W. 53rd   Mus. of Modern Art annex in 1978

Sona the Golden One, in a 1965 photo   The New York Coliseum in early 1960s

La Fonda del Sol (restaurant), 123 W. 50th St., bet. Sixth and Seventh Aves., in the Time & Life Building. 1960. Alexander Girard.

An exuberant design in which the forms, spaces, and materials were impeccably controlled. A very special place.

The Ground Floor (restaurant), 51 W. 52nd St., NE cor. Sixth Ave., in the CBS Building. 1965. Eero Saarinen & Assocs.

The elegant, dark, sleek interior, replaced by a series of redesigns, was planned by the Saarinen firm down to the table settings.

CENTRAL PARK SOUTH

Al and Dick's Steak House, 151 W. 54th St., bet. Sixth and Seventh Aves. 1948. Nemeny & Geller.

Its plain wood front led to a straightforward interior of stone, brick, wood, and brass. Design of this refinement was rare in popular restaurants.

The Mill at Burlington House, 1345 Avenue of the Americas, NW cor. W. 54th St. 1970. Chermayeff & Geismar, designers.

An endless carpet led visitors past a **colorful 8½-minute multimedia presentation** on the nature of textiles—Burlington Industries' of course—and an exhilarating time line of American life. The space was subsequently rented to a fur shop.

125 West 55th Street (carriage house), bet. Sixth and Seventh Aves. ca. 1885.

A very rare orphan, this particularly robust and obviously tenacious stable served a wealthy residence nearby. This last vestige of another era seems to have survived quite happily until removed for CitySpire.

Broiling Wall (churrasqueria) at the exuberant La Fonda del Sol restaurant

Broadway Tabernacle (Congregational)/later **Broadway United Church of Christ,** 1750 Broadway, NE cor. W. 56th St. 1905. Barney & Chapman.

Pale buff brick and pale gray terra-cotta and very big, it was extolled by architecture critic Montgomery Schuyler (1843–1914) as the best of Modern Gothic.

New York Coliseum, 10 Columbus Circle, bet. W. 58th and W. 60th Sts. W side. 1956. Leon and Lionel Levy.

One of **Robert Moses' early manipulations** of the federal Title I urban renewal program produced this dreary white brick, **white elephant.** Long before it was outclassed by the Javits Convention Center, it had been relegated to the has-been stage: obsolete the minute it opened.

PLAZA SUITE

Lederer de Paris (leather goods), 711 Fifth Ave., bet. E. 55th and E. 56th Sts. E side. 1939. Morris Ketchum, Jr., architect. Victor Gruenbaum (Victor Gruen), associate. **Ciro of Bond Street (jewelry),** 713 Fifth Ave., bet. 55th and 56th Sts. E side. 1939. Morris Ketchum, Jr.

These were 1930s showroom showpieces, perfect examples of the Fifth Avenue speciality shop.

IBM Showroom, 590 Madison Ave., SW cor E. 57th St. Altered, 1959, Eliot Noyes.

The architecture of display *par excellence* and the pure pleasure of viewing exhibits (some by Charles Eames) from the street; the showroom enabled anyone to participate in an experience without actually having to enter. Replaced by the hovering cantilever of the IBM tower.

D/R Design Research (home furnishings)/formerly **Galerie Norval,** 53 E. 57th St., bet. Fifth and Madison Aves. Altered, 1965, Benjamin Thompson.

The New York branch of the store that Boston architects **Ben** and **Jane Thompson** opened on **Brattle Street in Cambridge.** New York's 4-story primer of good contemporary design was filled with furniture, kitchen gadgets, clothes, and toys—all of good contemporary design.

Georg Jensen (silver/china/jewelry), 601 Madison Ave., bet. E. 57th and E. 58th Sts. E side. Altered, 1974, James Stewart Polshek & Assocs.

Georg Jensen was **never quite the same** once the gift shop left its space at the southeast corner of Fifth Avenue and East 53rd Street and relocated to an entire building on Madison Avenue close to a major competitor, **Bonniers.** Giant mirrored letters formed an elegant graphic facade to the emporium, but its large, handsome, solid silvery entrance door occasionally resulted in bruised noses.

Bonniers (gift shop)/later **Georg Jensen Specials,** 605 Madison Ave., bet. E. 57th and E. 58th Sts. E side. 1949. Warner-Leeds Assocs.

Originally commissioned as a bookstore for the **Swedish publishing house,** the store broadened, selling exquisitely tasteful household and gift items. Its elegantly understated yet unmannered interior and its **gangplank stair** were considered a scripture for modern design.

L'Étoile (restaurant), 3 E. 59th St., bet. Fifth and Madison Aves. 1966. Alexander Girard, designer. Lee Schoen, associated architect.

L'Étoile's design was "French" modern: austere, polished, and with the most elegant graphics.

Originally **Arion Society,** 491 Park Ave., SE cor. E. 59th St. 1887. De Lemos & Cordes.

This Berea sandstone, buff brick, and terra-cotta Italian Renaissance palazzo was topped by **heroic sculptural groups** of Arion and other, mythological figures. The society was responsible for bringing the conductor **Leopold Damrosch** to America in 1871. Many years later the building housed one of the city's first post-World War II art theaters, the Park Avenue.

EAST 57TH STREET

RKO 58th Street Theatre, 964 Third Ave., bet. E. 57th and E. 58th Sts. W side. ca. 1925.

One of central Manhattan's last movie palaces. While its marquee had been streamlined, its interior was **pure Valentino.**

Originally **The Henry Keep Flower Memorial and Halsey Day Nursery, St. Thomas' Parish**/later **Alvin Ailey Dance School,** 229 E. 59th St., bet. Second and Third Aves. 1896. Wolfgang Partridge.

This Gothic Revival holdout was built by New York Governor Roswell P. Flower (1891–1895) in memory of his son. Its replacement: a nondescript 3-story taxpayer.

UPPER WEST SIDE

Proposed **Litho City (mixed use),** W. 59th St. to W. 72nd St., West End Ave. to the Hudson River. 1963. Kelly & Gruzen.

This **aborted riverfront project** would have placed 15,000 people—along with shopping, parks, piers, an international student center, and a new headquarters for the *New York Times*— over existing freight yards and piers. The site has been spared for other megaproposals, among them **Donald Trump's,** which includes plans for the world's tallest building.

Columbia Fireproof Storage Warehouse, 149 Columbus Ave., bet. W. 66th and W. 67th Sts. E side. 1893. G. A. Schellenger.

Its ornate brickwork and soaring verticality were emblematic of a time when the financial bottom line **was not critical** and architects

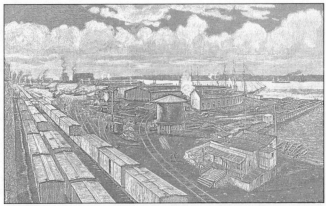

West Side yards, site of proposed Litho City and Trump's Television City

managed to **find urbane solutions** to even the most mundane problems, such as the blank walls of a warehouse.

College of Pharmaceutical Science, Columbia University/originally **College of Pharmacy of the City of New York,** 115 W. 68th St., bet. Columbus Ave. and Broadway. 1894. Little & O'Connor.

A fuddy-duddy building which seemed nevertheless to scoff at its lesser neighbors.

Lincoln Square Center for the Arts/originally **26th Precinct, N.Y.C. Police Department/**later **20th Precinct,** 150 W. 68th St., bet. Broadway and Amsterdam Ave. ca. 1889. Nathaniel D. Bush.

The *AIA Guide* second edition admired its "dignified composition: segmental and semicircular arched openings linteled in neatly carved stone and set into a russet brick field." And, it continued, "Lucky for us that it has found another use." It did—temporarily. Since then it has been replaced by a permanent **hole in the ground,** the entrance to a below-street parking garage for Tower 67.

Originally **St. Nicholas Skating Rink/**later **St. Nicholas Arena/**finally **American Broadcasting Companies Broadcasting Operations and Engineering,** 57 W. 66th St., bet. Central Park W. and Columbus Ave. 1896. Ernest Flagg and Walter B. Chambers.

In spite of the many layers of stucco and different hues of paint—all battleship gray—the gay ornament of the post-Columbian Exposition era came through . . . to the end. Now the site of Capital Cities/ABC Inc. headquarters.

The Lederer de Paris boutique in 1954   Columbia Coll. of Pharmacy in 1978

Christ Church (Episcopal)/later Bible Deliverance Evangelical Church, 211 W. 71st St., bet. Broadway and West End Ave. 1890. Charles C. Haight. Addition, 1925.

Because its entrance was originally on Broadway—until its valuable frontage was sold off in 1925—the nave of the orange brick and terra-cotta Romanesque Revival church ran **parallel to West 71st Street.** An apartment building now fills the site.

Gentrification II: The opening of the restaurant with the curious name P.S. 77, at the southeast corner of Amsterdam Avenue and West 77th Street, was one of the first marks of gentrification on the Upper West Side—before the furious onslaught that began in the late 1970s—and just made it into the previous edition of the *AIA Guide.* P.S. 77 is out of business as is Dino DeLaurentiis's DDL and many other establishments. Already replaced by a newer gentrification, they didn't stay around long enough to make *any* edition.

All Angels' Episcopal Church, 428 West End Ave., SE cor. W. 81st St. 1890. Samuel B. Snook of J. B. Snook & Sons. Altered, 1896, Karl Bitter Studio, sculptors.

The delicacy of this church was made even more fragile by the brilliant placement of its axis **diagonal to the street grid.** Its slow annihilation was all the **more painful** with the triumphant survival of the **giant TV tube** across the street.

Formerly **Mt. Neboh Synagogue/**originally **Unity Synagogue/**later **Adventists' Crossroads Church,** 130 W. 79th St., bet. Columbus and Amsterdam Aves. 1928. Walter S. Schneider.

The fastest landmark in the West—the West Side, that is. The artificial stone and granite Byzantine-style structure must win the record for having been an officially designated **landmark for the shortest time.** The Seventh-Day Adventists bought the building in 1978 and sold it to developers three years later for $2.4 million—$2 million more than they had paid for it. The building was designated in February 1982, de-designated for reasons of economic hardship in February 1983, and demolished soon after. It's now the site of an apartment building.

Street names: Even the city's street names are no longer sacred. What was wrong with West 84th Street (now officially Edgar Allan Poe Street)? Or West 90th Street (now Henry J. Browne Boulevard)? And quick, where is 1 Lincoln Plaza . . . or 1 Astor Plaza . . . or, or, or . . .?

New Yorker Theater/originally **Adelphi Theatre/**later **Yorktown Theatre,** 2409 Broadway, bet. W. 88th and W. 89th Sts. W side. 1915. Rouse & Goldstone. **New Yorker (bookstore),** 250 W. 89th St. SW cor. Broadway.

One of the fine movie theaters that ran films from out of our past, the New Yorker Theater and its colleagues were doomed by upper Broadway's new residential developments and the VCR. The bookshop, around the corner and up the stairs, was **a great place to kill time** (browse?) and even buy a book or two before the show started.

Thalia Theatre, 258 W. 95th St., bet. Broadway and West End Ave. 1931. Ben Schlanger and R. Irrera.

Who doesn't miss the Thalia? You swore you'd never go there again but then couldn't pass up the magnificent flicks—if your seat didn't flip over backward and the old film didn't catch fire at the moment of **Bogart's** and **Bergman's parting.** And those weird sloping floors: **up,** yet! The perfect ambiance for *Strangers on a Train* or *Marat/Sade.* What, the Thalia's coming back? Oh, no . . .

Grace United Methodist Church/originally **Grace Methodist Episcopal Church,** 131 W. 104th St., bet. Columbus and Amsterdam Aves. 1905. Berg & See.

This midblock church, with its orange Roman brick facade, provided a pleasing relief from the drab surroundings.

Bookshops in memoriam: The intelligentsia of the West Side kept a host of idiosyncratic bookshops in business until retail rents skyrocketed during the 1980s real estate boom. Along with the hardware stores, delicatessens, shoe repair shops, and mom-and-pops were Radius on West 72nd Street near West End Avenue, New Yorker at West 89th Street and Broadway, Womanbooks at West 92nd Street and Amsterdam Avenue, and Dolphin on Broadway between West 105th and West 106th Streets. While new bookstores have come to the area, some of that special dust has settled.

CENTRAL PARK

Central Park Zoo, Central Park, SE end, opp. East 64th St. 1934. N.Y.C. Dept. of Parks. Aymar Embury II, consulting architect. Gilmore Clarke, consulting landscape architect.

The group of red brick, WPA-style animal houses was demolished only in part for the zoo's reconstruction [see C Manhattan/Central Park S 25.]. The simple cafeteria, overlooking the sea lion pool, offered mothers and children an enjoyable respite.

UPPER EAST SIDE

Mrs. Marcellus Hartley Dodge residence, 800 Fifth Ave., NE cor. E. 61st St. 1923. R. S. Shapter.

Although undistinguished and unused—its perpetually shuttered windows provoked many juicy rumors—it was one of the avenue's few remaining freestanding mansions.

Daly's Dandelion/formerly **Daly's Bar,** 1029 Third Ave., SE cor. E. 61st St.

An early example of the chicification of a venerable bar. Obviously not chic enough, this one went for a new apartment tower.

7 East 67th Street (town house), bet. Fifth and Madison Aves. 1900. Clinton & Russell. **9 East 67th Street (town house),** bet. Fifth and Madison Aves. 1913. Hiss & Weeks.

A pair of fine residences that were sacrificed on the altar of "progress."

Paraphernalia (boutique), 795 Madison Ave., bet. E. 67th and E. 68th Sts. E side. 1966. Ulrich Franzen.

A neat adaptation of a womenswear shop to an existing architectural situation, this was about the earliest of the young jet-set shops.

Valentino (boutique), 801 Madison Ave., bet. East 67th and E. 68th Sts. E side. Altered, 1970, Aldo Jacober, design architect; George K. Wasser, consulting architect.

One of the pioneer swanky Madison Avenue designer boutiques. This one had a striking 5-story cylindrical show window.

Formerly **Gerrish H. Milliken residence,** 723 Park Ave., NE cor. E. 70th St. ca. 1870.

The **spiral fire stair** at the rear (off 70th Street) of this perfectly ordinary brownstone was an **architectural wonder.** The new Asia Society building occupies the site.

Originally **Elihu Root residence,** 733 Park Ave., SE cor. E. 71st St. 1905. Carrère & Hastings.

This was a neo-Georgian manor built for the distinguished statesman.

54 E. 72nd Street (row house), bet. Madison and Park Aves. 1889. Altered to apartments, 1949, Morris Lapidus.

In this simple, non-showy Modern building, glass was used for light not sight.

Presbyterian Home (residence for the elderly), 49 E. 73rd St., bet. Madison and Park Aves. 1869. Joseph Esterbrook.

An invigorating mansard-roofed institution.

Originally **John Sherman Hoyt residence**/later **James Stillman residence,** 900 Park Ave., NW cor. E. 79th St. 1917. I. N. Phelps Stokes.

In its final years this rich neo-Tudor mansion was the consulate of the United Arab Republic.

Cherokee Club, 334 E. 79th St., bet. First and Second Aves. ca. 1885.

This Romanesque Revival building was once a **Democratic Party clubhouse.** After losing a tardy battle for landmark designation, the ornately carved facade was first defaced, then mutilated, and finally destroyed. A tacky 8-story apartment building is on the site.

Convent of the Little Sisters of the Assumption/originally **Convent of the Sisters of Bon Secours,** 1195 Lexington Ave., NE cor. E. 81st St. 1889. William Schickel.

The picturesque 4-story red brick building was one of the city's last Victorian Gothic structures of its type. A last-ditch effort to designate it an official landmark failed. One less fine reminder of days past.

434 East 84th St. (residence), bet. First and York Aves.

One of the last frame houses of Manhattan with a very homey, un-New York veranda along its front. In the mid 1980s, as it was receiving some notice in the press as a prime example of unchanging New York, a nondescript, 6-story apartment house was already rising in its place.

 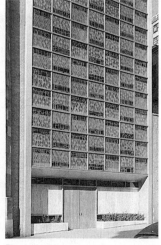

The Presbyterian Home (1967 photo)   The Milton Steinberg House in 1955

New York Turn Verein, 150 E. 85th St., SE cor. Lexington Ave. ca. 1900.

The German Renaissance Revival German sports club was built of sturdy granite, brick, and limestone. The long-gone ground-floor restaurant, **Jaeger House**/earlier **Hans Jaeger,** easily matched in both decor and food **Lüchows,** its rival 70 blocks to the south. Replaced by a plump, otiose apartment tower.

RKO 86th Street Theatre, 137 E. 86th St., NW cor. Lexington Ave. 1920s.

Another of the classy 1920s movie palaces gone, this one for the later defunct Gimbels East.

Milton Steinberg House, Park Avenue Synagogue, 50 E. 87th St., bet. Madison and Park Aves. 1955. Kelly & Gruzen. Stained glass, Adolf Gottlieb.

The *AIA Guide*'s second edition stated: "A sleek stained-glass facade forms a rich nighttime tapestry in front of this activities-and-office building." The glass has been reinstalled within the synagogue.

Jacob Ruppert Brewery, Second to Third Aves., E. 90th to E. 93rd Sts. 1870s and later.

A grand old brewery complex removed for urban renewal [see E Manhattan/Yorkville Y 29.].

Squadron A (Eighth Regiment) Armory, N.Y. National Guard (east section), Park Ave., bet. E. 94th and E. 95th Sts. 1895. John R. Thomas.

The east part was removed in favor of a modern echo, I. S. 29, Manhattan, now Hunter High School; the west part survives as a "ruin" [see E Manhattan/Carnegie Hill C 21a. and C 21b.].

THE HEIGHTS AND THE HARLEMS

Tien Tsin Restaurant, 569 W. 125th St., E of Broadway. **The Shanghai Café,** 3217 Broadway, N of W. 125th St.

It may be hard to believe, but once upon a time there were no **Szechuan or Hunan restaurants** in all of New York City and a lot of chop suey and chow mein. In those years—decades—one ventured to West 125th Street to these stalwarts of rare non-Cantonese cuisine. Uniqueness that bred patronage.

Finley Student Center and **Goldmark Hall**/originally **Main Building** and **Chapel, Convent of the Sacred Heart**/ later **Manhattanville College of the Sacred Heart,** Convent Ave. and W. 133rd St. 1847–1890. Henry Engelbert.

The convent and academy, founded at Houston and Mulberry Streets, occupied these Romanesque Revival stone buildings in **a park-like setting** until moving to Westchester County in the early 1950s. City College took over the complex and eventually demolished these earliest buildings.

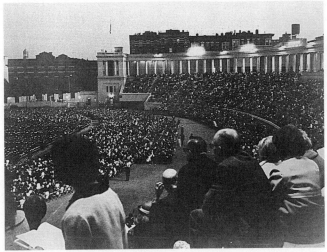

Lewisohn Stadium crowded with music fans at a summer concert (1957 photo)

Lewisohn Stadium, City College of New York, Amsterdam Ave. bet. W. 136th and W. 138th Sts. E side to Convent Ave. 1915. Arnold W. Brunner.

Most warmly remembered for its **concerts, not its architecture,** the colonnaded stadium offered serious music during summers unrelieved by home air conditioners to thousands of New Yorkers at very low prices: **30¢, 60¢, $1.20.** Demolished in favor of academic expansion [see H Manhattan/Hamilton Heights T 9c.].

Elevator entrance and **electrical substation**/originally for **Manhattan Railway Company,** Ninth Avenue elevated, 311-313 Cathedral Parkway, bet. Eighth and Manhattan Aves. N side. 1903. George H. Pegram, engineer.

The villa-style Roman brick structure dated from the addition of a new station to the Ninth Avenue elevated, which turned north here onto Eighth Avenue from Cathedral Parkway after jogging one block over from Columbus (Ninth) Avenue. The site is part of a housing development [see H Manhattan/Harlem H 2.].

Sculpture, site of the **Tree of Hope,** center island of Seventh Ave. at W. 131st St. N side. 1972. Algernon Miller.

The tree which once grew in the middle of the avenue opposite the old Lafayette Theater is long gone. To mark the spot where out-of-work black entertainers **traded gossip and tips** on jobs, **Bill "Bojangles" Robinson** donated another tree, which disappeared. The metal tree sculpture, intended as a permanent reminder, is gone as well.

Engine Company No. 35, N.Y.C. Fire Department, 223 E. 119th St., bet. Second and Third Aves. 1890. Napoleon LeBrun & Sons.

LeBrun's office did most of the city's firehouses at the start of the Gay Nineties. The results weren't bad, and many remain—but not this.

THE OTHER ISLANDS

Torch, Statue of Liberty, Liberty Island. 1886. Frédéric Auguste Bartholdi, sculptor. Numerous alterations. Major alteration, 1916, Gutzon Borglum, sculptor.

Bartholdi apparently was never pleased with the functioning of the statue's **original copper flame torch,** upon which the 1986 replacement was modeled. Almost immediately, it was fussed over, windows were cut through, and lights were added. **Borglum,** the sculptor of the Presidents on **Mt. Rushmore,** later refashioned the torch, cutting the original copper into a lattice. Pesky leaks over the years and dim illumination doomed it to removal and replacement.

Ellis Island (proposals). 1959–1961, Taliesin Associated Architects. 1966, Philip Johnson & Assocs.

Among the sundry ideas for tampering with the island whose name is synonymous with the immigrant experience, several have come from **noted architects.** Based on some sketches made by **Frank Lloyd Wright** shortly before his death, the Taliesin group proposed a semicircular megacomplex of hotel and apartment towers called Key Project, which looked like an early attempt at a NASA space station in New York harbor. Several years later, as part of the new Ellis Island National Park, **Philip Johnson** put forward a monumental, Boullée-inspired, doughnut-shaped pavilion within which the names of all those who passed through the immigration station would have been inscribed.

THE BRONX

SOUTHERN BRONX

Mott Haven Reformed Church, 350 E. 146th St., bet. Third and College Aves. 1852.

Replaced by a modern edifice.

Richard M. Hoe & Company (printing machinery and saw works)/ originally **DeLavergne Company (refrigeration manufacturers),** 910 E. 138th St., from Locust Ave. to W of Walnut Ave. S side. Port Morris. 1846.

These were a collection of robust brick industrial sheds and a more ornate office structure with **Dutch-style stepped roofs.** The Hoe Company—Colonel Hoe had invented the **rotary printing press** back in 1846 —took over the DeLavergne buildings when its own 19th-century complex on Manhattan's Lower East Side was demolished for the Amalgamated Housing. Lost without warning. The colonel's brother's house still stands nearby in Hunts Point [see S Bronx S 22e.].

Schlitz Inn, 737 E. 137th St., NW cor. Willow Ave. Port Morris.

The last restaurant of the many that served the once flourishing German community of the South Bronx.

Old Bronx Borough Hall, in Crotona Park, E. Tremont Ave., SE cor. Third Ave. 1895, 1897. George B. Post.

Situated on a high bluff, the old local seat of government was irreparably damaged by fire while efforts were underway to find an adaptive reuse.

Ellis Island National Park: model of Philip Johnson's proposal, 1966 photo

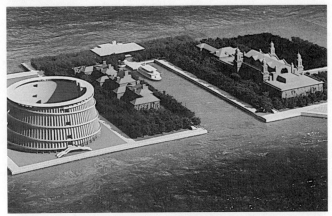

The old Bronx Borough Hall in Crotona Park, with striped awnings, ca. 1910

CENTRAL BRONX

Formerly **Biograph Company Studios,** 807 E. 175th St. and 790 E. 176 St., bet. Marmion and Prospect Aves. East Tremont. 1912.

Founded in 1895 to compete with Thomas A. Edison, the Biograph motion picture company was one of the studios centered in New York before the movie moguls **folded their tents** and **stole away** to Hollywood. In this building, built in what was once the wilds of the Bronx, D. W. Griffith reportedly shot some of his early films.

WESTERN BRONX

Formerly **Bedford Park Casino,** 390 Bedford Park Blvd., bet. Decatur and Webster Aves. S side. ca. 1880.

Although the ground floor was clearly 20th-century, the upper portions of the wood facade revealed the original onetime center for neighborhood recreation. Before its demolition, the building was used by a **violin bow manufacturer.**

RIVERDALE

Administration Building, Salanter Akiba Riverdale Academy/originally **Henry W. Boettger residence,** 655 W. 254th St., bet. Independence and Palisade Aves. 1905.

This multistory orange brick neo-Tudor mansion was the last of conductor **Arturo Toscanini's** several homes in Riverdale.

Barrymore's Inn/formerly **Riverdale Inn,** 6471 Broadway at Mosholu Ave. W side.

The closing of this restaurant marked the real end of an era. The colorful mayor **Jimmy Walker** was said to have tête-à-têted with dancer **Betty Compton** here back in the 1920s, when this spot was truly out of the way.

EASTERN BRONX

Formerly **Rectory, St. Peter's Church (Episcopal)/**later **Westchester-Bronx YMCA,** 2244 Westchester Ave., bet. Castle Hill and Havemeyer Aves. S side. Parkchester. 1850.

A neglected red brick Victorian country residence, one of the last of its type in New York, was replaced by a spanking new Y [see E Bronx E 7c.].

NORTHERN BRONX

Formerly **Engine Company No. 69, N.Y.C. Fire Department,** 243 E. 233rd St., bet. E. 234th St. and Katonah Ave. Woodlawn. ca. 1895.

This lusty wood frame firehouse stood almost in Westchester County. In this outpost of New York, no wonder the structure looked more like a barn than a municipal facility. Replaced by a dull fireproof version.

24th Ward School/later **Evander Childs High School Annex/**later **Resthaven Nursing Home,** 225 E. 234th St., bet. Kepler and Katonah Aves. N side. Woodlawn. 1893. C. B. J. Snyder.

A fake white Colonial portico had obscured a great Romanesque Revival facade. Fire eventually resulted in its demolition.

BROOKLYN

WEST CENTRAL BROOKLYN

Gilbert School, 341 Bridge St., bet. Myrtle Ave. and Willoughby St. E side. Downtown Brooklyn. ca. 1845.

A Greek Revival building drastically altered over the years.

Martin's Department Store: the neo-Romanesque building at 503 Fulton Street in Downtown Brooklyn, designed originally as offices by Lauritzen & Voss in 1891, has been converted back to offices once again but with the unfortunate loss of the area's next to last great retail establishment. Martin's styles were conservative, sturdy, and reliable but always offered at least a few surprises. The closing of the **last** of the old emporia may just be a matter of time.

RKO Albee Theatre, 1 DeKalb Ave., at Albee Sq. Downtown Brooklyn. ca. 1924.

Manhattan isn't the only borough losing its movie memories. This **fine amusement palace** was removed on behalf of the shopping area's revitalization.

Hotel Margaret, 97 Columbia Hts., NE cor. Orange St. Brooklyn Heights. 1889. Frank Freeman. ☆ (Included within the Brooklyn Heights Historic District.)

In the dead of a raw winter night a fire began in the nearly completed apartment conversion of this **once grand old hotel.** Curiously, in a community where fire trucks get to the scene in seconds, here the fire had raged silently within its thick walls for hours. By the time the equipment arrived the flames were out of control, and the structure **burned fiercely** for more than a day. It took tremendous quantities of water to **quell the fire,** causing spectacular icicles to festoon the burned-out facades and turning the nearby streets into **bumpy skating rinks.** The building's exuberant nautical look, with ornate sheet metal panels trimmed in exposed rivet heads, was very appropriate to its harbor-view siting. **A great urban injury.**

Hotel Margaret, in its glory, ca. 1907   Hotel Margaret, after the fire, 1980

Boro Book Shop: The loss of this used bookstore (at No. 152) presaged the loss of the neighborhood quality of Montague Street, the major shopping street of Brooklyn Heights. It was the quintessential book-shop: a rich hoard of books, its crannies ever so slightly mysterious, the steady puffing of the owner's cigar, an old cat or two to trip over, obviously low rent, and an unwritten sign that said GENTRIFICATION KEEP OUT. It didn't.

Hoagland Laboratory, Long Island College Hospital, 335 Henry St., SE cor. Pacific St. Cobble Hill. 1888. John Mumford.

Devastated by fire and later demolished, this eclectic Romanesque Revival building was the first privately founded laboratory in the country devoted to bacteriological, histological, and pathological research. Its early Art Nouveau copper signs were glorious.

Church of the South Brooklyn Christian Assembly/originally **Carroll Park Methodist Episcopal Church/**later **Norwegian Methodist Episcopal Church,** 297-299 Carroll St., bet. Smith and Hoyt Sts. 1873. ☆ (Included within the Carroll Gardens Historic District.)

A memento of **the large Scandinavian population** that settled in South Brooklyn from the late 19th century until the mid 20th, when the Victorian Gothic structure was sold to the last occupant. The church, consumed by fire, was replaced by two town houses.

Church of St. Simon the Cyrenian, 175 S. Oxford St., bet. Hanson Place and Atlantic Ave. E side. Fort Greene. ca. 1895.

A fine residence that spent its last years as a church. The previous *AIA Guide* called it "Black Forest Queen Anne": ornamented stucco, ornamented terra-cotta, ornamented brick.

Church of the Messiah and Incarnation (Episcopal), 80 Greene Ave., SE cor. Clermont Ave. Fort Greene. 1865. James H. Giles. Redesigned, 1892, R. H. Robertson.

Until the church was engulfed by flames and then torn down, it was hard to miss its 130-foot-tall brick and terra-cotta beehive-capped spire, modeled after the 12th-century Byzantine Romanesque cathedral in **Périgueux** in southwest France.

460 Washington Avenue (residence), bet. Greene and Gates Aves. W side. Clinton Hill. ca. 1890.

A Queen Anne porch enclosed this brick and terra-cotta mansion. Boarded up for some years, it was finally demolished.

Second Battalion Armory, N.Y. Naval Militia, 5100 First Ave., bet. 51st St. and 52nd Sts. W side. Sunset Park. 1904. Lord & Hewlett.

A spectacular **parabolic arched naval armory,** visible from both land and harbor. No attempt was made here to conceal its structural form but, rather, to embellish it with a romantic facade of crenellated towers and battlements. **Abandoned for years,** it was demolished mercilessly in favor of a bland 1-story post office.

The Second Battalion Armory, N.Y. Naval Militia, a bold harborside silhouette

71st Precinct, N.Y.C. Police Department, 421 Empire Blvd., NE cor. New York Ave. Crown Heights.

A Florentine palace despite its un-Florentine brick, it was replaced by a modern police station.

374-376 Franklin Avenue (double house), SW cor. Quincy St. Bedford-Stuyvesant. ca. 1865.

This looked as though it came right out of A. J. Downing's Victorian country house design manuals.

212 Gates Avenue (country house), bet. Franklin and Classon Aves. S side. Bedford-Stuyvesant.

Victim of a fire and subsequent "renovations," this Carpenter Gothic house is barely recognizable today.

Originally **Temple Israel (synagogue)/**then **Brooklyn Traffic Court/** then **Bergen Tile (store),** 1005 Bedford Ave., NE cor. Lafayette Ave. Bedford-Stuyvesant. 1893. Parfitt Bros.

When this Byzantine Romanesque house of worship was dedicated by its affluent German-Jewish congregation, it rated front-page coverage in the *Brooklyn Daily Eagle.*

Originally **Abraham Abraham residence,** 800 St. Marks Ave., bet. New York and Brooklyn Aves. S side. Crown Heights. ca. 1890.

Built as a proper mansion for one of Brooklyn's most prominent philanthropists, the founder of A&S. It was demolished for a nursing home [See WC Brooklyn/Crown Heights W 14. and below].

Originally **Ludwig Nissen residence,** 814 St. Marks Ave., bet. New York and Brooklyn Aves. S side. Crown Heights. ca. 1905. Arne Dehli.

Also torn down for the nursing home. The *AIA Guide*'s first edition called it "a miniature of the Potsdam Palace."

820 St. Marks Avenue (residence), bet. New York and Brooklyn Aves. S side. Crown Heights. ca. 1890.

Another mansion removed for the nursing home.

Old Brooklyn Children's Museum, in Brower Park, Brooklyn Ave., bet. St. Marks Ave. and Park Place. Crown Heights. North Building: L. C. Smith residence, ca. 1890. South Building: William Newton Adams residence, 1867.

The museum's new facility replaces its original buildings, two Victorian mansions that were familiar landmarks in Brower Park [see WC Brooklyn/Crown Heights W 18.].

Loehmann's (women's apparel), 1476 Bedford Ave., NW cor. Sterling Place. Crown Heights.

Until it went out of business at this location, this chaotic store, wrapped in **gilded Oriental detail,** was filled with unbelievable bargains. A wonder to little boys who watched the scene in awe—Loehmann's had no fitting rooms for mother! Some **Chinese dragons still lurk** on Sterling Place.

212 Gates Avenue: a country house in Bedford-Stuyvesant's center (1967 photo)

Originally Temple Israel, then a city traffic court, last a tile store, in 1967

St. Mary's Hospital, Division of Catholic Medical Center of Brooklyn and Queens, 1298 St. Mark's Ave., bet. Rochester and Buffalo Aves. S side. Crown Heights. 1882.

This picturesque brick edifice with mansard rooflets had been an outgrowth of St. Mary's Female Hospital, which also helped establish the Hospital of the Holy Family on Dean Street in Cobble Hill.

696 Bushwick Ave. (residence), SW cor. Suydam St. Bushwick.

This wonderfully elaborate Italianate frame mansion simply collapsed one day. Its replacement is a vacant lot.

Bushwick Democratic Club/most recently **Bethesda Pentacostal Church,** 719 Bushwick Ave., NW cor. Hart St. Bushwick. 1892. Frank Freeman. ★

After being ravaged by seemingly endless fires, there was too little left to preserve of this building, one of the city's greatest, **designed by Brooklyn's greatest architect.** Its ornament matched that of **Louis Sullivan,** and its structural forms, such as the negative bay windows behind arches, presaged architecture to come for several generations.

Late, great Bushwick Democratic Club   Williamsburg Gas Light Co., ca. 1905.

Joseph Schlitz Brewing Company/originally **Leonard Eppig's Germania Brewery**/then **Interboro Cereal Beverage Company** (during Prohibition)/then **George Ehret's Brewery,** 24-44 George St., SE cor. Central Ave. Bushwick. ca. 1877.

A richly worked brick behemoth gone to rest, together with the other once world-renowned Brooklyn brewing industries.

20 Bleecker Street (apartments), bet. Bushwick and Evergreen Aves. E side. Bushwick. ca. 1890.

A triumphant, magnificent Victorian wood and bay-windowed tenement, painted a **luscious cream and brown** to show off its finely honed details. A survivor amid the surrounding devastation, the building is not in fact demolished but merely **reclad in aluminum,** its facade and refined details totally concealed.

Originally **Joseph F. Knapp residence**/later **a dancing academy**/later **Yeshiva Umesivta Torah V'Yirah D'Satmar,** 554 Bedford Ave., NW cor. Ross St. Williamsburg. 1894.

Built for the president of the Metropolitan Life Insurance Company, it was replaced for a "more modern" Williamsburg.

Originally **First Reformed Dutch Church of Williamsburg**/later **Congregation Tifereth Israel (synagogue),** 491 Bedford Ave., SE cor. Clymer St. Williamsburg. 1869.

The Gothic Revival structure was destroyed by fire and replaced by a matter-of-fact synagogue.

Originally **Dr. Charles A. Olcott residence**/later **Entre Nous Club,** 489 Bedford Ave., NE cor. Clymer St. Williamsburg.

A relic of this area's more glorious upper-middle-class period.

Originally **Williamsburg Gas Light Company**/later **Brooklyn Union Gas Company,** 324 Bedford Ave., NW cor. S 2nd St. Williamsburg. ca. 1866.

A fine work of architecture, needlessly demolished—cast-iron facade and all. It stood on the site of the old Williamsburgh City Hall.

97 Broadway (offices), bet. Bedford Ave. and Berry St. N side. Williamsburg. 1870.

The cast-iron Second Empire, mansard-roofed edifice once housed the **Kings County Fire Insurance Company.** A 3-story Victorian Baroque porch was reminiscent of the porch on Alfred Mullett's State, War, and Navy Building in Washington—but in iron rather than stone.

CENTRAL BROOKLYN

Boccie: For some years the railroad tracks along 37th Street lay dormant; the railroad's sandy roadbed beneath the abandoned BMT Culver shuttle at 14th Avenue formed an ideal court—the tracks were standard gauge (4'-8½" apart)—for a group of diehard Italian émigrés to play their game of Latin bowls. When the elevated structure was eventually dismantled, so was the game of boccie.

SOUTHWESTERN BROOKLYN

Pollio's Restaurant, 6925 Third Ave., near Bay Ridge Ave. Bay Ridge.

A real Italian mamma's restaurant, this hole-in-the-wall was authentic down to the chilled Chianti. You ate what she had just made. Too few left.

The Ridge (residence), 129 Bay Ridge Pkwy., bet. Ridge Blvd. and Colonial Rd. N side. Bay Ridge. 1900.

A Shingle Style mansion in the sky, perched high on a lawn retained by a giant rubble wall; its **red cedar shingles** were set off with **crisp white trim.** Demolished in favor of apartments.

8205 11th Avenue (residence), SE cor. 82nd St. Dyker Heights. ca. 1870.

This clapboarded and towered Italianate country home sat high on the hill overlooking the bay. It was entered by a generous Tuscan-columned porch.

8756 21st Avenue (residence), just N of Bath Ave. W side. Bath Beach. ca. 1888.

The Shingle Style residence, with its white shingles and blue trim, formed a solid volume with sections cut away for porches and crowned with a bell-like tower. An adjacent gas station doomed it.

Cropsey residence, 1740 84th St., SE cor. Bay 16th St. Bensonhurst. ca. 1860.

A Victorian frame house replaced by a mundane facility for the elderly.

SOUTHERN BROOKLYN

2835 West 37th Street (residence), bet. Neptune and Mermaid Aves. E side. Coney Island. Altered.

The Aegean must have been on the minds of the masons responsible for the **vernacular conversion** of two adjacent two-family houses, complete with whitewashed, textured stucco surfaces. The right half of the pair remains.

Shatzkin's Famous Knishes, 1500 Surf Ave., SE cor. W. 15th St. Coney Island.

The knish was raised to a high art: here one could devour these **pastry-covered delicacies**—filled with apple, blueberry, cherry, cheese, kasha (groats), or, of course, potato.

F. W. I. L. Lundy Brothers Restaurant: While the Spanish mission-style stucco building remains at Emmons and Ocean Avenues in Sheepshead Bay, it has sat empty for years while awaiting settlement of an endless complexity of family squabbles. Lundy's was crowded, noisy, and too large; the waiters were rude and the wait interminable; and the pale green interior walls were slightly sickening. But the food . . . magnificent!

SOUTHEASTERN BROOKLYN

Pepsi-Cola Bottling Plant, 9701 Avenue D, NW cor. Rockaway Ave. Canarsie. 1956. Skidmore, Owings & Merrill.

Not quite lost—its corpus is still there. A **classic curtain-walled structure** sitting amid a **low-lying marsh** and a **railroad siding,** the building has been badly defaced, its windows perfect targets for neighborhood youths. Pepsi added protective grilles, all but canceling any potential for a positive future.

EASTERN BROOKLYN

Mobile home park, Sutter to Pitkin Aves., Herzl St. to W side of Strauss St. Brownsville. 1970. M. Paul Friedberg & Assocs., site planners.

The cheerless dwellings, built by the state's Urban Development Corporation in what the second edition of the *AIA Guide* called "early-Fort Bragg style," were reportedly popular among their residents. Yet the project lasted only a few years. The site is now part of the Nehemiah Plan housing.

Belmont Avenue Baths, 15 Belmont Ave., bet. Thatford Ave. and Osborn St. N side. Brownsville. ca. 1915.

The handsome facade which once sported a fine lettered sign, RUSSIAN AND TURKISH BATHS, is totally unrecognizable.

Parish House, New Lots Reformed Dutch Church, 620 New Lots Ave., SE cor. Schenck Ave. East New York. 1823.

The shingled parish house, a fitting complement to the church, was superseded by a new building.

QUEENS

WESTERN QUEENS

26-35 and **26-41 4th Street (residences),** bet. 26th and 27th Aves. E side. Astoria. ca. 1835.

Two of the last of Astoria's palatial Greek Revival mansions built by shipping and lumber entrepreneurs during the mid 19th century.

26-41 4th Street, one of the last of Hallets Point's great lumber barons' mansions

CENTRAL QUEENS

United States Pavilion, 1964–1965 World's Fair, Flushing Meadows-Corona Park. 1964. Charles Luckman Assocs.

An embarrassing—but perhaps accurate—symbol for America, the huge square doughnut with multicolored plastic walls was built atop four immense piers surrounding a pyramidal entrance structure. Razed in 1977. Hooray!

St. James Episcopal Church, 87-07 Broadway, NE cor. Corona Ave. Elmhurst. 1849.

This mid 19th-century church, destroyed by fire, was an outgrowth of the earlier one, which remains as the Parish Hall [see C Queens C 21c.].

NORTHEASTERN QUEENS

23-27 College Point Boulevard (residence), bet. 23rd and 25th Aves. E side. ca. 1870.

This well-kept Victorian country house, on a large lot with blue mansard roof and cornice, was typical of late 19th-century College Point. Demolished for a brick monster.

The immense United States Pavilion, from the 1964–1965 New York World's Fair

Parish House, the First Congregational Church of Flushing (1967 photograph)

First Congregational Church of Flushing and **Parish House,** Bowne St. bet. 38th and Roosevelt Aves. W side.

Until destroyed by fire, these dignified 19th-century wood-frame structures enhanced the community, set as they were on a green carpet of grass.

143-43 and **143-46 Sanford Avenue (residences),** bet. Bowne St. and Parsons Blvd. S side. Flushing. ca. 1860.

Two **charming survivors** from the mid 19th century. Until the 1960s central Flushing's **gracious treelined streets** were filled with amply proportioned, single-family Victorian frame homes. The number has been reduced to scarcely more than a handful.

St. Thomas Hall (school)/later **St. Joseph's Academy (Roman Catholic),** Kissena Blvd. NE cor. Sanford Ave. Flushing. 1839.

A dour Victorian institutional structure; today the site of a busy shopping complex.

Bell homestead, 38-08 Bell Blvd., bet. 38th and 39th Aves. W side. Bayside. ca. 1845.

Imprudently replaced by Prudential.

THE ROCKAWAYS

Hebrew Institute of Long Island, Seagirt Blvd. bet. Beach 17th and Beach 19th Sts. N side. ca. 1900.

The school occupied four Classical Revival white stucco and Spanish tile mansions, built when the Rockaways had been a classier area. In a decayed state for many years, they were replaced by an apartment complex.

STATEN ISLAND

NORTHERN STATEN ISLAND

Public School 18, Staten Island, Broadway NE cor. Market St. West Brighton. 1890. Edward A. Sargent. Addition, 1898.

The previous edition of the *AIA Guide* advised the visitor to take "a leisurely walk around" the building to "savor its collection of richly configured hip-roofed red brick pavilions, which tilt with one another along Market Street all the way back to Campbell Avenue." The demise of the old multistory school, with its **intricate clock tower,** is a visible **loss to the community.**

P.S. 18, Staten Island, 1910 postcard   Nathaniel Marsh residence, in 1967

Brooks residence, 414-418 Richmond Terr., SE cor. Westervelt Ave. New Brighton. 1835.

A common saga: a mansion allowed to deteriorate and then demolished. In this case, it was a porticoed Greek Revival temple.

EASTERN STATEN ISLAND

Planter's Hotel, 360 Bay St., NW cor. Grant St. Tompkinsville.

A fashionable hotel patronized by wealthy Southerners during the 19th century.

Free port to home port: In 1921 Mayor John Hylan (for whom Staten Island's Hylan Boulevard was named) ordered the building of a series of deepwater piers between Tompkinsville and Stapleton in an attempt to boost the island's maritime economy. The scheme failed and was dubbed **Hylan's Folly.** In 1937 the area was designated Free Trade Zone No. 1, where international cargo could be stored for transshipment without the payment of import duty. This scheme also failed; the truck and airplane had overtaken the ship. After years of neglect and vandalism, the facility was shut down. Taking its place in the 1990s: the home port for the battleship USS *Iowa* and its fearsome complement of nuclear missiles.

Demyan's Hofbrau (restaurant), 742 Van Duzer St., W of Broad St. W side. Stapleton Heights.

Located in part of what had been a brewery on the hill **overlooking Stapleton** and the harbor, the restaurant was filled with **local memorabilia.** Destroyed by fire in 1980.

Nathaniel Marsh residence, 30 Belair Rd., bet. Bay St. and Clayton St. S side. Rosebank. ca. 1860.

This pink brick, wisteria-covered mansion sat atop a shady hill enjoying superb harbor views. Removed to build a residence for the elderly.

CENTRAL STATEN ISLAND

Horrmann Castle (residence), 189 Howard Ave., opp. Greta Place. E side. Grymes Hill. ca. 1915.

A fantasy castle, it was Bavarian, French Renaissance, Flemish, Spanish, and English Queen Anne all heaped together and topped by a crow's nest with an onion-shaped cupola.

The Captain Cole residence, its portico overlooking a sweeping lawn, in 1978

Forest Discount Getty/formerly **Herb & Lloyd Service Station,** 1881 Forest Ave., at Sanders St. N side. ca. 1920.

Aluminum siding has obscured the original integrity of this gas station, a **relic of the early days** of the automobile. Its walls were last painted in subtle earth tones, the roof clad in Spanish tile. Who will know if it's still there until its *re*unveiling—or demolition?

SOUTHERN STATEN ISLAND

Holmes-Cole residence, 3425 Hylan Blvd., SW cor. Justin Ave. Great Kills. ca. 1730.

An early 18th-century house, overlooking Great Kills Harbor, bulldozed for a ticky-tacky subdivision.

J. Winant residence/formerly **Blazing Star Tavern,** 2930 Arthur Kill Rd., bet. St. Luke's and Engert Aves. S side. Rossville. ca. 1750.

One of the oldest buildings in New York City, it had been a cozy **stopping place** for **stagecoach travelers** to and from points south and weary from bouncing over the rutted roads.

Captain Cole residence, 1065 Woodrow Rd., bet. Rossville and Vernon Aves. Woodrow. ca. 1836.

The old Colonial house was a nice complement to the nearby Woodrow United Methodist Church.

Old **Church of St. Joachim** and **St. Anne (Roman Catholic), Mt. Loretto Home for Children,** Hylan Blvd. bet. Sharrott and Richard Aves. N side. ca. 1882.

The towers and main facade of this imposing edifice, destroyed by fire, were saved; the badly damaged nave was demolished and replaced by a modern substitute [see S Staten Island S 30a.].

THE CITY

THAR SHE GROWS

The Population of New York City

	Within Present Limits of N.Y.C.	Manhattan
1790	49,401	33,131
1800	79,216	60,515
1810	119,734	96,373
1820	152,056	123,706
1830	242,278	202,589
1840	391,114	312,710
1850	696,115	515,547
1860	1,174,779	813,669
1870	1,478,103	942,292
1880	1,911,698	1,164,673
1890	2,507,414	1,441,216
1900	3,437,202	1,850,093
1910	4,766,883	2,331,542
1920	5,620,048	2,284,103
1930	6,930,446	1,867,312
1940	7,454,995	1,889,924
1950	7,891,957	1,960,101
1960	7,781,984	1,698,281
1970	7,894,862	1,539,233
1980	7,071,639	1,428,285
1984 estimate	7,164,742	1,456,102

Land Area

	Square Miles	Acres
Manhattan	22.6	14,478
The Bronx	43.1	27,606
Brooklyn	78.5	50,244
Queens	114.7	73,406
Staten Island	60.9	38,947
New York City	319.8	204,681

The Bronx	Brooklyn	Queens	Staten Is.
1,781	4,495	6,159	3,835
1,755	5,740	6,642	4,564
2,267	8,303	7,444	5,347
2,782	11,187	8,246	6,135
3,023	20,535	9,049	7,082
5,346	47,613	14,480	10,965
8,032	138,882	18,593	15,061
23,593	279,122	32,903	25,492
37,393	419,921	45,468	33,029
51,980	599,495	56,559	38,991
88,908	838,547	87,050	51,693
200,507	1,166,582	152,999	67,021
430,980	1,634,351	284,041	85,969
732,016	2,018,356	469,042	116,531
1,265,258	2,560,401	1,079,029	158,346
1,394,711	2,698,285	1,297,634	174,441
1,451,277	2,738,175	1,550,849	191,555
1,424,815	2,627,319	1,809,578	221,991
1,471,701	2,602,012	1,986,473	295,443
1,168,972	2,230,936	1,891,325	352,121
1,172,952	2,253,858	1,911,235	370,595

The City of New York in 1980 had a population that exceeded the combined total of the 10 smallest states:

Alaska	401,851
Delaware	594,338
Idaho	943,935
Montana	786,690
Nevada	800,493
New Hampshire	920,610
North Dakota	652,717
South Dakota	690,768
Vermont	511,456
Wyoming	469,557
	6,772,415

Were the City of New York the 51st state it would rank as the tenth largest in population.

BRIDGES

Type	Bridge	Over	Between/In
S	George Washington	Hudson River	Manhattan-N.J.
S	Throgs Neck	East River	Bronx-Queens
S	Bronx-Whitestone	East River	Bronx-Queens
F	Rikers Island	Bowery Bay	Queens-Rikers Is.
S	Triborough	East River	Queens-Wards Is.
L		Harlem River	Man.-Randalls Is.
F		Bronx Kills	Bx.-Randalls Is.
A	Hell Gate	East River	Queens-Wards Is.
L	Wards Is. (Ped.)	East River	Man.-Wards Is.
L	Roosevelt Island**	East R./E. Channel	Qns.-Roosevelt Is.
C	Queensboro	East River	Man.-Queens
S	Williamsburg	East River	Man.-Brooklyn
S	Manhattan	East River	Man.-Brooklyn
S	Brooklyn	East River	Man.-Brooklyn
S	Verrazano-Narrows	The Narrows	Bklyn.-Staten Is.
A	Henry Hudson	Harlem River	Man.-Bronx
L	Broadway	Harlem River	Manhattan
W	University Heights	Harlem River	Man.-Bronx
A	Washington	Harlem River	Man.-Bronx
A	Alexander Hamilton	Harlem River	Man.-Bronx
A	High Bridge	Harlem River	Man.-Bronx
W	McCombs Dam	Harlem River	Man.-Bronx
W	145th Street	Harlem River	Man.-Bronx
W	Madison Avenue	Harlem River	Man.-Bronx
W	Third Avenue	Harlem River	Man.-Bronx
W	Willis Avenue	Harlem River	Man.-Bronx
T	East 174th Street	Bronx River	Bronx
B	Westchester Avenue	Bronx River	Bronx
B	Bruckner Boulevard	Bronx River	Bronx
B	Unionport	Westchester Creek	Bronx
B	Eastchester	Eastchester Creek	Bronx
B	Hutchinson Riv. Pk. Ext.	Eastchester Creek	Bronx
B	Pelham	Eastchester Bay	Bronx
S	City Island	Pelham Bay Narrows	Bronx
B	Whitestone Expwy.	Flushing River	Queens
B	Flushing (Northern Blvd.)	Flushing River	Queens
F*	Roosevelt Avenue	Flushing River	Queens
F	Little Neck	Alley Creek	Queens
B	Hunters Point Ave.	Dutch Kills	Queens
F	Midtown Highway	Dutch Kills	Queens
R	Borden Avenue	Dutch Kills	Queens
F	Hawtree Basin (Ped.)	Hawtree Basin	Queens
B	North Channel	North Channel	Queens
B	Cross Bay-Veterans' Mem.	Jamaica Bay	Queens
F	Hook Creek	Hook Creek	Queens-Nassau
B	Pulaski	Newtown Creek	Queens-Bklyn.
B	Greenpoint Ave.	Newtown Creek	Queens-Bklyn.
T	Kosciusko	Newtown Creek	Queens-Bklyn.
S	Grand Street	Newtown Creek	Queens-Bklyn.
B	Metropolitan Ave.	English Kills	Brooklyn
B	Union Street	Gowanus Canal	Brooklyn
R	Carroll Street	Gowanus Canal	Brooklyn
B	Third Street	Gowanus Canal	Brooklyn
F	Third Avenue	Gowanus Canal	Brooklyn
B	Ninth Street	Gowanus Canal	Brooklyn
B	Hamilton Avenue	Gowanus Canal	Brooklyn
B	Mill Basin	Mill Basin	Brooklyn
B	Cropsey Avenue	Coney Island Creek	Brooklyn
S	Stillwell Avenue	Coney Island Creek	Brooklyn
F	Ocean Avenue (Ped.)	Sheepshead Bay	Brooklyn
L	Marine Pkwy.-Gil Hodges	Rockaway Inlet	Bklyn.-Queens
A	Bayonne	Kill Van Kull	Staten Is.-N.J.
L	B & O Railroad	Arthur Kill	Staten Is.-N.J.
T	Goethals	Arthur Kill	Staten Is.-N.J.
T	Outerbridge Crossing	Arthur Kill	Staten Is.-N.J.
R	Lemon Creek	Lemon Creek	Staten Island
B	Fresh Kills	Richmond Creek	Staten Island

Note: The city has a total of 2,098 bridges, not counting the Transit Authority's 70 miles of elevated track or MTA's Park Avenue viaduct.

TUNNELS

Tunnel	Under	Between
Lincoln N. tube	Hudson River	Manhattan-N.J.
C. tube		
S. tube		
Holland N. tube	Hudson River	Manhattan-N.J.
S. tube		
Brooklyn-Battery	Upper N.Y. Bay	Manhattan-Bklyn.
Queens-Midtown	East River	Manhattan-Queens

Completed	Max. Span (feet)	Max. Clear. Above M.H.W. (feet)	Engineer/Architect	Operating Agency
1931	3,500	212	O.H. Ammann/Cass Gilbert, Inc.	PA
1961	1,800	142	O.H. Ammann	TBTA
1939	2,300	150	O.H. Ammann/Aymar Embury II	TBTA
1966		52		DOT
1936	1,380	143	O.H. Ammann/Aymar Embury II	TBTA
1936				TBTA
1936	383	55		TBTA
1917	1,087	135	G. Lindenthal/H. Hornbostel	NYCRR
1951	312.2	55/135	Madigan/Hyland	DOT
1955	418	40/103		DOT
1909	1,182	135	G. Lindenthal/Palmer & Hornbostel	DOT
1903	1,600	135	Leffert L. Buck	DOT
1909	1,470	135	G. Lindenthal/Carrère & Hastings	DOT
1883	1,595.5	133	J.A. & W.A. Roebling	DOT
1964	4,260	228	O.H. Ammann	TBTA
1936	800	142.5	E.H. Praeger, C.F. Loyd	TBTA
1962	304	24.3/135		DOT
1908	264.5			DOT
1888	508.8	133.5	William R. Hutton	DOT
1963	1,526	103		DOT
1848	322	102		DPR
1895	408.5	29.2		DOT
1905	300	25.2		DOT
1910	300	25		DOT
1899	300	25.8		DOT
1901	304	25.1		DOT
1928	190	30.5		DOT
1938	83	17.2		DOT
1953	118	26.6		DOT
1953	75	17.5		DOT
1922	127	12.5		DOT
1941	160	35		DOT
1908	80	17.5		DOT
1901	164.8	12.3		DOT
1939	174	35		DOT
1939	107	25		DOT
1925	212	25.6		DOT
1931	44.5	7.3		DOT
1910	71.5	88		DOT
1940	126.5	90		DOT
1908	82	4		DOT
1963	72	18		DOT
1925	123	26.3		DOT
1939	131	17.5		TBTA
1931	34.2	4.1		DOT
1954	176.6	55/135		DOT
1929	180	27.4		DOT
1939	300	125		DOT
1903	227	9		DOT
1933	111	10.7		DOT
1905	56	8.3		DOT
1889	45.2	4.7		DOT
1905	56	7.3		DOT
1889	40.3	13		DOT
1905	56	7.3		DOT
1942	66.3	19		DOT
1940	165	35		DOT
1931	155	11.3		DOT
1929	250	5.7		DOT
1917	46.2	7.8		DOT
1937	400	55/150		TBTA
1931	1,675	150	O. H. Ammann/Cass Gilbert, Inc.	PA
1959	558			C&O
1928	672	135	Alexander Waddell/York & Sawyer	PA
1928	750	135	Alexander Waddell/York & Sawyer	PA
1958	34	4		DOT
1931	81	11.7		DOT

Abbreviations

A	Arch	L	Lift
B	Bascule	R	Retractile
C	Cantilever	S	Suspension
F	Fixed	T	Truss
	W	Swing	
	M.H.W.	Mean High Water	
	Ped.	Pedestrian	

C&O Chessie System
DOT N.Y.C. Department of Transportation
DPR N.Y.C. Department of Parks & Recreation
PA Port Authority of New York & New Jersey
NYCRR New York Connecting Railroad (Amtrak)
TBTA Triborough Bridge & Tunnel Authority

*Originally a bascule bridge
**Originally Welfare Island Bridge

Completed	Length of Tube (Feet)	Engineer	Operating Agency
1945	7,482 N.		PA
1937	8,216 C.	O.H. Ammann, Ralph Smilie, C.S. Gleim	
1957	8,006 S.	John M. Kyle	
1927	8,558 N. 8,371 S.	C.F. Holland, Ole Singstad	PA
1950	9,117	Ole Singstad	TBTA
1940	6,414 N. 6,272 S.	Ole Singstad	TBTA

GEOGRAPHY OF THE CITY

Latitude at City Hall: 40°42′26″ North

Longitude at City Hall: 74°0′23″ West

Elevation above sea level at City Hall: 37 feet

New York is a water city: It is situated at the confluence of a major river and the ocean, waterways that have played a major role in establishing the fundamental form of the city. Through the years they have also influenced its growth.

New York is a port city: Not only is there an abundance of shoreline but also natural deep channels and a harbor well protected from the vicissitudes of an open sea.

New York is an island city: Appropriately, all of New York's boroughs except one, The Bronx, are located on islands: Manhattan, Long Island (shared with suburban Nassau and Suffolk counties), and Staten Island. In addition, the city is encrusted with other bits of land that poke up from its waters: Governors, Roosevelt, and Rikers islands, to name just a few, and the extensive and convoluted collection in Jamaica Bay, some of which forms a wildlife preserve.

Geology: Throughout the city the signposts of its geological development are everywhere apparent. The location of its Midtown (though *not* its Downtown group, whose foundations reach deep but often fail to find bedrock) skyscrapers reflects the place where bedrock comes closest to the surface. Less abstract indications of the city's geology can be found in the New Jersey Palisades along the Hudson River opposite Riverside Drive, in Manhattan's Fort Tryon or Morningside Parks, or in the hilly areas of the West Bronx and central Brooklyn and Queens.

New York's relative youth as a city is in strong contrast to its geological age. Fordham Gneiss, which makes up the ridge of the West Bronx and along whose spine the Grand Concourse winds its way, dates from the 2-billion-year-old Proterozoic (or Late Precambrian) Period. Inwood Marble is next oldest, its white substance clearly visible in the stone cliffs of the community appropriately named Marble Hill. (Examples are best viewed from a round-Manhattan boat tour, just as you leave the Harlem River for the Hudson). Newest is Manhattan Schist (or mica schist), a mass of metamorphic rock covering the deeper limestone stratum, which is the firm bedrock providing the superb foundations for the city's Midtown skyscrapers.

The general physical form of the city and its immediate region, the form we recognize today, dates from the much later, 225 million-year-old Triassic Period. The Palisades and the brown sandstone so ubiquitous in the city's brownstone row houses are now thought to be a product of the more recent (180 million-year-old) Jurassic Period.

The coming of the Ice Age 20,000 to 25,000 years ago provided the finishing touches to the pattern of the city. (The current gorge at the Hudson is glacial in origin.) The glacier pushed ahead of it a mound of gravel, rock, and other debris. This mound is still visible as the terminal moraine which runs from the southern tip of Staten Island (and forms its backbone) to the Narrows, where it is interrupted, only to rise again to form Long Island's spine as well.

South of these hills, particularly in Brooklyn and Queens, is the sandy outwash deposited by the melted glacier, to this day giving rise to such descriptive place names as Flatlands. This melting of the glacier converted the once deeper gorge of the Hudson River into an estuary and filled the shallow depressions with water to form the East and Harlem Rivers (actually tidal straits), Long Island Sound, and the shallow bays of Jamaica and Gravesend.

The geological accidents of history have provided the city with some 578 miles of waterfront, innumerable beaches and overlooks, and, perhaps most important of all, a substratum to support its soaring skyscrapers.

New York Underground: Within the geological strata and below the city's 6,000 miles of streets and its many miles of waterways are a variety of underground channels which most New Yorkers take for granted. A trip on the subway or through a vehicular or railroad tunnel offers only a small indication of the vastness and complexity of New York's underground networks. The subways account for 134 miles of below-the-surface routes, in tunnel and open cut; and other publicly accessible tunnels (under Park Avenue, for example) for perhaps an additional 10 miles. The magnitudes of other underground systems, however, are of an entirely different order: 62,000 miles of electrical wires and services; 7,800 miles of gas mains; 20 million miles of wire (in cables) for telephones; over 50 miles of steam mains that heat fully one-seventh of Manhattan's buildings; not to mention water mains, sewers, coaxial and fiber-optic cable systems, cable and the abandoned pneumatic tubes that once sped mail between post office branches at 30 MPH *below* the streets (rather than 8 MPH *on* them).

The space invested in the subsurface facilities necessary to make the metropolis function, carved through its primeval rock and muck, would support a small city. And within New York there are such underground "cities" even now in Rockefeller Center, at Grand Central Terminal with its below-grade passages to adjacent buildings, and in the World Trade Center.

Though this underground empire functions amazingly well, it remains an enigma, even for those who regularly patrol and repair its nethermost mazes; the diagram on the following two pages gives some indication of their phenomenal complexity.

CORRECTIONS AND ADDITIONS

If you think we've noted something incorrectly or left something out, please let us know! Write clearly, or better yet, print. Send the information on a Xerox copy of this form or on a separate sheet of paper to:

Elliot Willensky
c/o Harcourt Brace Jovanovich
111 Fifth Avenue
New York, N.Y. 10003

PLEASE FORWARD TO AUTHOR

Page: _____ Entry no. [_____]

Name of structure: _____

Correction/Addition: _____

_____

_____

_____

_____

_____

_____

_____

_____

Your name: _____

Your address: _____

City: _____ State: _____ Zip:_____

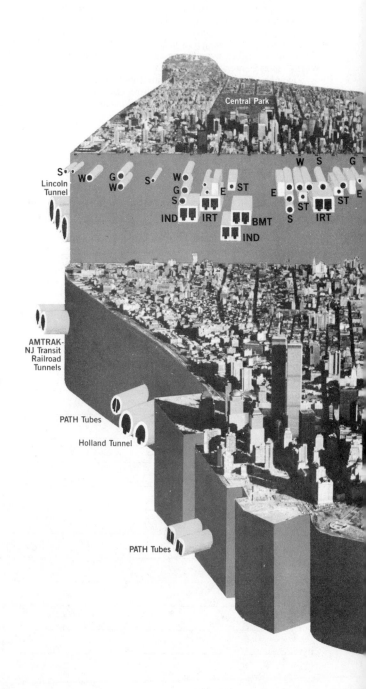

Central Park

S
Lincoln
Tunnel

W
W

G

S

W
G
S

W

E ST

E
S

W S G

E

ST

ST

IND

IRT

BMT

IRT

E

IND

AMTRAK-
NJ Transit
Railroad
Tunnels

PATH Tubes

Holland Tunnel

PATH Tubes

NEW YORK UNDERGROUND

New Jersey

New York

Palisade Diabase

Riverside Drive

Hudson River

River Silt

Triassic Sandstone & Shale

Inwood Marble

Manhattan Mica Schist

Fordham Gneiss

HUDSON RIVER CUTAWAY AT RIVERSIDE DRIVE

th Street

— 10
— 20
— 30
— 40
— 50 Feet

eens Midtown Tunnel

S	Sewer	E	Electric
W	Water	ST	Steam
G	Gas		

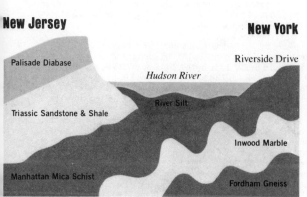

AMTRAK-L.I.R.R. Tunnels

IND Sixth Avenue
Subway

IND Eighth Avenue Subway

City Water Tunnel No. 1
750 ± Feet

IRT Seventh Avenue Subway

BMT Nassau Street Subway
BMT Broadway Subway
IRT Lexington Avenue Subway

oklyn-Battery Tunnel

PHOTO CREDITS

Introduction: *xxii–xxiii* by Jeff Perkell. **Manhattan:** P. 7 collection EW; 8L by NW; 8R by Margaret Latimer; 9 by NW; 11 by NW; 13 courtesy Library of Congress; 14 by EW; 15 by EW; 16 by EW; 17TL by NW; 17TR by EW; 17BL courtesy Kevin Roche John Dinkeloo & Assocs.; 17BR by EW; 18 by NW; 19L by EW; 19R by NW; 21TL/B by NW; 21TR © 1983 Daniel Cornish, courtesy Fox & Fowle; 23TL by NW; 23TR by EW; 23B courtesy Port Authority of NY & NJ; 25L courtesy Fox & Fowle; 25R by NW; 26 by NW; 27L by NW; 27R by EW; 28L by NW; 28R courtesy Fox & Fowle; 29 courtesy Rouse Company, Inc.; 32TL courtesy Beyer Blinder Belle; 32TR courtesy Rouse Company, Inc.; 32B © Steve Rosenthal, courtesy Benjamin Thompson & Assocs.; 33 by NW; 34 © Steve Rosenthal, courtesy of Benjamin Thompson & Assocs.; 36 by Alexandre Georges, courtesy Skidmore, Owings & Merrill; 37L by NW; 37R courtesy Federal Reserve Bank of NY; 38L by Nathaniel Lieberman, courtesy John Burgee Architects with Philip Johnson; 38R by NW; 39L by NW; 39R by EW; 40L by EW; 40R by NW; 41 by EW; 44L courtesy James Stewart Polshek & Partners; 44R courtesy Rothzeid Kaiserman Thomson & Bee; 45TL/TR © Wolfgang Hoyt, ESTO, courtesy Davis, Brody & Assocs.; 45B courtesy Gruzen Samton Steinglass; 47 courtesy Battery Park City Authority; 49L courtesy Port Authority of NY & NJ; 49R courtesy Skidmore, Owings & Merrill; 52 by NW; 53L by NW; 53R courtesy Skidmore, Owings & Merrill; 54TL/BL/BR by EW; 54TR by NW; 56T/BR by EW; 56BL by NW; 57TL by NW; 57TR/B by EW; 59 by EW; 60TL/TR by NW; 60BL/BR by EW; 63 *Harper's Weekly*, collection EW; 64L by EW; 64R courtesy Gruzen Samton Steinglass; 65 by NW; 66L courtesy Gruzen Samton Steinglass; 66R by EW; 67 by NW; 68L by EW; 68R by NW; 69 by NW; 70 by NW; 71 by EW; 73T courtesy Library of Congress; 73BL/BR courtesy Kelly & Gruzen; 74 by NW; 77 by NW; 79 by EW; 80L by EW; 80R courtesy Pasanella+Klein 81T courtesy John T. Fifield Assocs.; 81B courtesy National Archives: Public Housing Administration; 83 by EW; 84 by EW; 85 by EW; 87 by EW; 88 by Nathaniel Lieberman, courtesy Prentice & Chan, Ohlhausen; 89 by EW; 90 by EW; 91 by EW; 95TL by John Ebstel, courtesy Architectural Forum; 95TR courtesy Architectural Forum; 95B by Peter Blake, courtesy Architectural Forum; 97 by EW; 99 by EW; 104 by Ann Douglass; 109TL by NW; 109TR by Margaret Latimer; 109B © Paul Warchol, courtesy James Stewart Polshek & Partners; 111 by Margaret Latimer; 113TL by EW; 113TR by Nathaniel Lieberman, courtesy Philip Johnson & Richard Foster 113BL © Steve Rosenthal, courtesy Benjamin Thompson & Assocs.; 113BR by Gil Amiaga, courtesy Warner, Burns, Toan & Lunde; 114 by EW; 115L by Ann Douglass; 115R by EW; 118T by Ann Douglass; 118BL by Margaret Latimer; 118BR by NW; 120 courtesy Margot Gayle; 121L by Ann Douglass; 121R by Margaret Latimer; 123T/BR by Margaret Latimer; 123BL by EW; 124 courtesy Whittlesey & Conklin; 125L Margaret Latimer; 125R by Alexandre Georges, courtesy Edgar Tafel; 127TL by Margaret Latimer; 127TR by Ann Douglass; 127B *Valentine's Manual*, 1866, collection EW; 128L by Ann Douglass; 128R by Margaret Latimer; 130 by Ann Douglass; 131TL by NW; 131TR by Margaret Latimer; 131B by Ann Douglass; 133 by Margaret Latimer; 135L by Ann Douglass; 135R by Margaret Latimer; 136L by Margaret Latimer; 136R by EW; 137TL/TR/BL by Margaret Latimer; 137BR by Ann Douglass; 138L by Margaret Latimer; 138R by Ann Douglass; 139 courtesy Richard Meier & Assocs.; 142L courtesy Edgar Tafel; 142R by Paul Warchol, courtesy Smith & Thompson; 144 by Margaret Latimer; 145 by Margaret Latimer; 147L by Ann Douglass; 147R courtesy Film Forum; 150 by NW; 152TL/BL/BR by NW; 152TR by EW; 153TL/TR by NW; 153B by EW; 154 by NW; 156 collection EW; 157L © Paul Warchol, courtesy Prentice & Chan, Ohlhausen; 157R by NW; 158 by NW; 159 collection EW; 161L by EW; 161R by NW; 165L courtesy John T. Fifield Assocs.; 165R by EW; 166L © 1987 Wolfgang Hoyt, ESTO, courtesy Voorsanger & Mills Assocs.; 166R by NW; 167 by NW; 173L by John Dixon; 173R collection EW; 174 by Suzan Kunz; 175TL/B by Suzan Kunz; 175TR by John Dixon; 179T by John Dixon; 179BL/BR by Suzan Kunz; 180L by Suzan Kunz; 180R courtesy Stephen B. Jacobs & Assocs.; 181L by Suzan Kunz; 181R courtesy National Maritime Union; 183 by Suzan Kunz; 186L by Suzan Kunz; 186R by EW; 189L by NW; 189R by EW; 191L by Suzan Kunz; 191R by NW; 193 by Suzan Kunz; 196 by NW; 198L by NW; 198R by Suzan Kunz; 200 by Suzan Kunz; 201L by NW; 201R by Suzan Kunz; 203 by Suzan Kunz; 204 by Robert Gray, courtesy Davis, Brody & Assocs.; 205 courtesy I. M. Pei & Partners; 209 by EW; 210L collection EW; 210R by John Dixon; 211 © Nathaniel Lieberman, courtesy I. M. Pei & Partners; 213L courtesy Davis, Brody & Assocs.; 213R courtesy Empire State Building Company; 214L collection EW; 214R by John Dixon; 217 by Suzan Kunz; 219 by Suzan Kunz; 220 by Suzan Kunz; 223 by Suzan Kunz; 225L by Margaret Latimer; 225R by EW; 228 by

Douglas Haskell; 229L by Suzan Kunz; 229R by Ann Douglass; 230L by Suzan Kunz; 230R by Ann Douglass; 231 courtesy Mayers & Schiff; 236L courtesy Edward Larrabee Barnes Assocs.; 236R by Suzan Kunz; 237 by Margaret Latimer; 240T by Bob Serating, courtesy New York Public Library; 240BL by John Dixon; 240BR by Adam Bartos, courtesy Davis, Brody & Assocs.; 241 © Ezra Stoller Assocs., courtesy Skidmore, Owings & Merrill; 242 by Suzan Kunz; 245T by EW; 245BL by J. Alex Langley; 245BR courtesy Union Carbide; 247 by NW; 249L © Ezra Stoller Assocs., courtesy Philip Johnson & Assocs.; 249R by Ezra Stoller © ESTO, courtesy Skidmore, Owings & Merrill; 250L by Suzan Kunz; 250R courtesy Kohn Pederson Fox Assocs.; 251TL/BR by Suzan Kunz; 251TR © 1982 Peter Aaron, ESTO, courtesy Voorsanger Mills Assocs.; 251BL by NW; 253L by John Dixon; 253R by EW; 254 by Ezra Stoller © ESTO, courtesy Ford Foundation; 255 courtesy the United Nations; 256L Kevin Roche John Dinkeloo & Assocs.; 256R by Suzan Kunz; 258 by Suzan Kunz; 259L by Suzan Kunz; 259R by Greg Murphy, courtesy John Burgee Architects; 260L by Suzan Kunz; 260R courtesy Philip Johnson & Assocs.; 261L by Ralph Streiner, courtesy William Lescaze; 261R by Suzan Kunz; 262L courtesy Fox & Fowle; 262R by Suzan Kunz; 264 by John Dixon; 265L by Ann Douglass; 265R by Ben Schnall, courtesy Lester Tichy; 267L courtesy Voorsanger & Mills Assocs.; 267R by John Dixon; 268L courtesy Edward D. Stone & Assocs.; 268R © Scott Frances, courtesy The Museum of Modern Art; 269L © 1986 by Dan Cornish, ESTO, courtesy Fox & Fowle; 269R by Ann Douglass; 270L courtesy University Club; 270R by Gottscho-Schleisner, courtesy Harrison & Abramovitz; 271L by John Dixon; 271R by Beta Csen; 272 collection EW; 274 courtesy Rockefeller Center, Inc.; 276L by John Dixon; 276R by Suzan Kunz; 277L by Suzan Kunz; 277R by NW; 278 by Suzan Kunz; 280 courtesy Library of Congress (Detroit 017416); 281L by NW; 281R courtesy Der Scutt; 283TL © 1984 Cervin Robinson, courtesy Edward Larrabee Barnes Assocs.; 283TR © 1984 Richard Payne, courtesy John Burgee Architects; 283BL by Norman McGrath, courtesy Kahn & Jacobs; 283BR © 1986 Peter Mauss, ESTO, courtesy Der Scutt; 285 courtesy Emery Roth & Sons; 290L by Ezra Stoller, ESTO, courtesy Skidmore, Owings & Merrill; 290R by Gil Amiaga; 291 by Ezra Stoller, courtesy Philip Johnson; 292 by David Hirsch; 294L by EW; 294R by Suzan Kunz; 295 by Suzan Kunz; 296 courtesy Hausman & Rosenberg; 297 by Suzan Kunz; 298L by Suzan Kunz; 298R by EW; 300 by EW; 301 by EW; 303TL by EW; 303TR/B by Suzan Kunz; 304L by EW; 304R collection EW; 306L by EW; 306R by Suzan Kunz; 307L by EW; 307R collection EW; 309 by EW; 310 by Suzan Kunz; 311 by EW; 312L by Suzan Kunz; 312R by EW; 313 by Suzan Kunz; 314 by Suzan Kunz; 315 by Suzan Kunz; 316 by EW; 318 by Suzan Kunz; 319L by Ann Douglass; 319R by Suzan Kunz; 321L by EW; 321R by Suzan Kunz; 323L by EW; 323R by Wurts Brothers, courtesy Emery Roth & Sons; 325L by EW; 325R by Suzan Kunz; 326T courtesy The American Museum of Natural History; 36BL/BR by EW; 328L by EW; 328R by Suzan Kunz; 328TL/TR/BL by Suzan Kunz; 329BR by EW; 332 by Suzan Kunz; 334L courtesy Ifill Johnson Hanchard; 334R by Suzan Kunz; 335T by David Lubarsky, courtesy Rosenblum/Harb; 335BL/BR by EW; 337 by John Albok; 339 collection EW; 340L courtesy Kreisler-Borg Construction Co.; 340R courtesy Abraham Rothenberg Assocs.; 343 collection EW; 344 collection EW; 346L courtesy David Paul Helpern; 346R © Todd Henkels, courtesy Stephen B. Jacobs & Assocs.; 347L courtesy Beyer Blinder Belle; 347R by EW; 348 by EW; 351TL/TR/BL by EW; 351BR courtesy Edward Durell Stone; 352 by EW; 355T by EW; 355BL/BR by NW; 356L by NW; 356R by EW; 357 by NW; 358 by EW; 360 courtesy Cong. Zichron Ephraim/Park East Synagogue; 361 by NW; 362 by NW; 363L by NW; 363R courtesy Ulrich Franzen & Assocs.; 364 by NW; 365 by EW; 368 by NW; 370L by EW; 370R by NW; 371 by NW; 374T courtesy T. M. Prentice, Jr.; 374BL © Ezra Stoller, ESTO, courtesy Marcel Breuer & Assocs.; 374BR by Edmund Stoeklein, courtesy Robert A. M. Stern; 376 by NW; 377L by Wolfgang Hoyt, ESTO, courtesy Conklin Rossant; 377R courtesy the Eggers Partnership; 379T courtesy Kevin Roche John Dinkeloo & Assocs.; 379BL courtesy John Burgee Architects; 379BR by NW; 380T courtesy Rosenblum/Harb Architects; 380B by EW; 382T courtesy T. M. Prentice, Jr.; 382BL by NW; 382BR courtesy Beyer Blinder Belle; 383 by EW; 384L by EW; 384R by NW; 385 by NW; 387 by EW; 388 collection EW; 389L by NW; 389R courtesy William N. Breger Assocs.; 390L by EW; 390R courtesy Pomerance & Breines; 392L © 1984 Wolfgang Hoyt, ESTO, courtesy Davis, Brody & Assocs.; 392R courtesy Gruzen Samton Steinglass; 394 by Salvatore Cavalastro, courtesy Whittlesey & Conklin; 395 by EW; 396L courtesy Kohn Pederson Fox Assocs.; 396R © Todd Henkels, courtesy Stephen B. Jacobs & Assocs.; 399 courtesy The National Archives: Public Housing Administration; 401 by NW; 402L collection EW; 402R by NW; 404T collection EW; 404BL © Ezra Stoller Assocs., courtesy Skidmore, Owings & Merrill; 404BR courtesy Whittlesey & Conklin; 406L by EW; 406R collection EW; 408 by EW; 409L by Louis Reens, courtesy Samuel Paul & Seymour Jarmul; 409R by EW; 410L by NW; 410R by EW; 411L by EW; 411R © Wolfgang Hoyt, ESTO, courtesy Davis, Brody & Assocs.; 414 by David Pickman, courtesy Pasanella+Klein 422L courtesy St. Luke's Hospital; 422R courtesy Mitchell/Giurgola Assocs.; 424TL by EW; 424TR by Alexandre Georges, courtesy Frost Assocs.; 424B courtesy Teachers College; 426L courtesy Union Theological Seminary; 426R courtesy Riverside Church; 428 by Suzan Kunz; 430 collection EW; 431TL by EW; 431TR/B courtesy CCNY; 432 courtesy CCNY; 434L by EW; 434R by Bill Rothschild, courtesy Facilities Development Corp.; 435 by EW; 437 courtesy Abraham W. Geller & Assocs.; 439 by Roger Feinstein; 441L by EW; 441R by David Hirsch, courtesy Gruzen & Partners; 442L by Roger Feinstein; 442R by Bro. David McAdams; courtesy Mt. Olivet Baptist Church; 443 by EW; 444L by EW; 444R by Louis Reens, courtesy Curtis & Davis; 445 by EW; 446 Hausman & Rosenberg; 447 by Roger Feinstein; 450L by Norman McGrath, courtesy Percival Goodman; 450R by George Roos, courtesy Coffey, Levine & Blumberg; 451 by David Hirsch, courtesy Davis, Brody & Assocs.; 454T by Norman McGrath, courtesy Conkin & Rossant; 454BL by EW; 454BR by Norman McGrath, courtesy Smotrich & Platt; 455L by Roger Feinstein; 455R Serating; 456 by Norman McGrath, courtesy Hodne/Stageberg Partners, Inc.; 459 by Richard Dattner; 461 by Louis H. Frohman, courtesy Washington Headquarters Assoc.; 462L by Richard Dattner; 462R courtesy Presbyterian Medical Center; 464L by Richard Dattner; 464R courtesy the Port of New York Authority; 466 courtesy Yeshiva University; 467 collection EW; 467R by Max Jaffe, collection EW; 470L by Margaret Latimer; 470R courtesy U.S. Coast Guard; 471 by Norman McGrath, courtesy Johansen & Bhavnani; 473L by Steve Rosenthal, courtesy Sert, Jackson & Assocs.; 473R by Steve Rosenthal, courtesy Kallmann & McKinnell; 476 by Norman McGrath, courtesy Hardy Holzman Pfeiffer Assocs. **Bronx:** P. 480 collection EW; 481 collection EW; 482 by EW; 483L by EW; 483R by Roger Feinstein; 484 courtesy John Ciardulla Assocs.; 485 by EW; 487L by EW; 487R by Rothschild, courtesy Facilities Development Corp.; 488 by Roger Feinstein; 489L by EW; 489R © Nathaniel Lieberman, courtesy John Ciardullo Assocs.; 490 by EW; 491 by EW; 492 courtesy Weintraub & di Domenico; 493 by EW; 495 by EW; 496 courtesy Weintraub & di Domenico; 499 by EW; 500 courtesy Fordham University; 502 by EW; 505L by Robert Gray, courtesy Davis, Brody & Assocs.; 505R courtesy NY Zoological Society; 506T courtesy NY Zoological Society; 506B courtesy NY Botanical Garden; 511 by EW; 513 by EW; 514 by EW; 516 by EW; 517 by EW; 519L by EW; 519R by Robert Gray, courtesy Davis, Brody & Assocs.; 520L by William R. Simmons, courtesy NYU; 520R by EW; 521 by Ben Schnall, courtesy Marcel Breuer & Assocs.; 525 courtesy Bedford Park Presbyterian Church; 527L by Gil Amiaga, courtesy Schuman Lichtenstein Claman & Efron; 527R by Rothschild, courtesy Facilities Development Corp.; 529 by EW; 532 courtesy Caudill Rowlett Scott; 533T by EW; 533B courtesy College of Mount St. Vincent; 534L by Roger Feinstein; 534R by EW; 535T courtesy Ferdinand Gottlieb; 535BL by EW; 535BR by Alexandre Georges, courtesy Percival Goodman; 536 by Robert L. Bien, courtesy Robert L. Bien; 540 courtesy Metropolitan Life Insurance Co.; 541TL by EW; 541TR collection EW; 541B by Nathaniel Lieberman, courtesy John Ciardullo Assocs.; 542L by EW; 542R by Jack Horner-Pennyroyal, courtesy Pomerance & Breines; 544T courtesy Gruzen & Partners; 544B by Ezra Stoller © ESTO, courtesy Reynolds Metals Co.; 545 by EW; 547L by John R. Kennedy, courtesy Maritime College, SUNY; 547R by EW; 548 courtesy Paul W. Reilly; 550 by EW; 551 by Rothschild, courtesy William Milo Barnum & Assocs.; 553L by Norman McGrath, courtesy Davis, Brody & Assocs.; 553R by EW; 555 by EW; 557 by EW. **Brooklyn:** P. 562 courtesy Brooklyn Historical Society; 563 courtesy Brooklyn Historical Society; 565 collection EW; 566 by NW; 568 by NW; 570 by NW; 571 by David Hirsch; 572L courtesy Cohen Brothers Realty & Construction Corp.; 572R by EW; 573 courtesy Brooklyn Historical Society; 574L courtesy Brooklyn Historical Society; 574R by NW; 576TL by EW; 576TR/BL/BR by NW; 578 by NW; 579T by NW; 579B by Gil Amiaga, courtesy Joseph and Mary Merz; 580 by NW; 582 by NW; 583L courtesy Brooklyn Historical Society; 583R by NW; 585T courtesy Alfredo DeVido; 585B by NW; 586 by NW; 587 by NW; 589TL/TR by NW; 589BL/BR courtesy Brooklyn Historical Society; 590 TL/BL/BR by NW; 590TR by EW; 591L courtesy of Glass & Glass/Conklin & Rossant; 591R courtesy Ulrich Franzen Assocs.; 592L by NW; 592R courtesy Ehrenkrantz/Eckstut Assocs.; 593TL courtesy Alfred DeVido Assocs.; 593TR/B by NW; 594 by NW; 595L courtesy Brooklyn Historical Society; 595R by David Hirsch; 596T courtesy Brooklyn Historical Society; 596BL/BR by NW; 598L by EW; 598R by NW; 599T/BL courtesy John T. Fifield Assocs.; 599BR by NW; 602 courtesy Long Island College Hospital; 603 courtesy Brooklyn Historical Society; 605 by NW; 606 by EW; 608 by Margaret Latimer; 609 by NW; 610T by Suzan Kunz; 610B courtesy Brooklyn Historical Society; 612T courtesy Brooklyn Historical Society; 612B by EW; 613 by EW; 614 by EW; 615 courtesy Brooklyn Historical Society; 616TL/BL by EW; 616TR/BR by NW; 618 by NW; 620 TL/TR/BR by NW; 620BL by EW; 621 by NW; 622 courtesy Brooklyn Historical Society; 624 by NW; 627 by NW; 628 by NW; 630 by NW; 631 by NW; 632 by NW; 633 by NW; 635 by NW; 636 by NW; 638 courtesy the US Navy; 639 by NW; 640 by EW; 643 by EW; 644 by EW; 645 courtesy Brooklyn Historical Society; 646L by NW; 646R by EW; 647L by NW; 647R by EW; 648 by NW; 649 courtesy Brooklyn Historical Society; 650 by EW; 652 by NW; 653 by NW; 654 by EW; 655T by NW; 655B courtesy Brooklyn Botanic Garden; 656 courtesy The Brooklyn Museum; 657 courtesy Brooklyn Historical Society; 660TL/TR/BR by NW; 660BL by EW; 661 courtesy Brooklyn Historical Society; 662 courtesy CABS; 663 courtesy Brooklyn Historical Society; 664 by EW; 665L by NW; 665R courtesy Brooklyn Historical Society; 666 by EW; 667 by NW; 668 by NW; 669 by EW; 670 by EW; 671 by NW; 672 by Norman McGrath, courtesy Hardy Holzman Pfeiffer; 674 by NW; 675

by NW; 676 courtesy Brooklyn Historical Society; 677 courtesy Brooklyn Historical Society; 680TL/B by EW; 680TR collection EW; 681 by EW; 682 by EW; 684
by EW; 685 by EW; 688L by EW; 688R by EW; 689T courtesy NY State Health
and Mental Hygiene Improvement Fund/H. Bernstein; 689B by EW; 690TL/TR by
EW; 690B courtesy Brooklyn Historical Society; 691T courtesy Brooklyn Historical Society; 691B by EW; 693TL/B courtesy Brooklyn Historical Society; 693TR
by EW; 695 courtesy Brooklyn Historical Society; 696 by EW; 697T courtesy
Brooklyn Historical Society; 697B by EW; 699 by EW; 700 by EW; 702L by EW;
702R courtesy Max O. Urbahn & Assocs.; 704 by EW; 705 by EW; 706 by EW;
707 by EW; 709 by EW; 710 by Ben Schnall, courtesy Pedersen & Tilney; 711
courtesy Brooklyn Historical Society; 712 by Bill Rothschild, courtesy Goldstone
& Dearborn; 713L courtesy NY State Urban Development Corp.; 713R by NW;
715L by EW; 715R by NW; 716 by NW; 717 by NW; 718L by EW; 718R by NW;
720 by EW; 721L by EW; 721R by NW; 722TL/TR by EW; 722BL/BR by NW;
723L by Rothschild, courtesy Facilities Improvement Corp.; 723R by Galbraith,
courtesy Facilities Improvement Corp. **Queens:** P. 730 by EW; 732 by EW; 733
by EW; 734 by EW; 736T © Ezra Stoller, courtesy Ulrich Franzen & Assocs.;
736BL by Paul Warchol, courtesy Alfredo De Vido Assocs.; 736BR by EW; 737
by EW; 740 by EW; 741 by EW; 744 by EW; 745 by NW; 746 by EW; 748 by
EW; 750 by EW; 751T courtesy Abraham W. Geller Assocs.; 751BL by NW;
751BR by EW; 753L by NW; 753R by EW; 755 by EW: 756 by EW; 757L by EW;
757R by NW; 758 by Skyviews Survey, Inc. (109621, Aug. 1974); 759L by NW;
759R by EW; 760 collection EW; 761 by EW; 763 by EW; 765 by NW; 766 by
EW; 769TL by EW; 769TR by NW; 769B by EW; 771 by NW; 772L by NW; 772R
by EW; 773L by EW; 773R by Dan Cornish © ESTO, courtesy Davis, Brody &
Assocs.; 775L by EW; 775R by NW; 780 by EW; 782 by EW; 783 © Nathaniel
Lieberman, NYC, courtesy Gruzen Samton Steinglass; 784 by EW; 787L by Norman McGrath, courtesy Lee Harris Pomeroy Assocs.; 787R by EW; 789 by Ezra
Stoller © ESTO, courtesy Pan Am; 790T courtesy The Port of New York Authority;
790B by Ezra Stoller © ESTO, courtesy TWA; 791T by NW; 791B by Gottscho-
Schleisner, Inc., courtesy Skidmore, Owings & Merrill; 792 by EW; 793 by EW;
794L by EW; 794R by NW; 795 by EW. **Staten Island:** P. 802 collection EW; 806
collection EW; 808 by EW; 811T by Mina Hamilton; 811BL/BR by EW; 813T by
Norman McGrath, courtesy Davis, Brody & Assocs.; 813B by EW; 814 collection
EW; 821 by EW; 824 by EW; 826 by EW; 830TL by EW; 830TR by Mina Hamilton;
830B by Alice Austen, courtesy Staten Island Historical Society; 831 courtesy
Municipal Art Society of NY; 839 by Manuel V. Rubio, courtesy Wagner College;
842 by EW; 845 by EW; 848L by EW; 848R by Mina Hamilton; 849 courtesy
Charles Luckman Assocs.; 851TL/TR by EW; 851B by Mina Hamilton; 855 by
Mina Hamilton; 857 by Mina Hamilton; 858 by EW. **Necrology:** P. 863L by EW;
863R by NW; 864L collection EW; 864R by Margaret Latimer; 866 collection EW;
868 *Valentine's Manual,* 1869, collection EW; 869 collection EW; 871 collection
EW; 872 by Norman McGrath, courtesy George Nelson & Co.; 873L by Ann
Douglass; 873R courtesy Olivetti Corp.; 874TL by Renita Hanfling, courtesy
Museum of Contemporary Crafts; 874TR by EW; 874BL by Ezra Stoller © MARIS
(ESTO), courtesy Richard Meier; 874BR collection EW; 875 by Dan Wynn, cour-
tesy Restaurant Assocs.; 877T *Scribner's Magazine,* October 1889, collection
EW; 877BL © Ezra Stoller, courtesy Victor Gruen Assocs.; 877BR by EW; 880L
by NW; 880R courtesy Kelly & Gruzen; 881 courtesy CCNY; 883T © Louis
Checkman, courtesy Philip Johnson; 883B collection EW; 885L collection EW;
885R by EW; 886 by EW; 887 by EW; 888L by EW; 888R courtesy Brooklyn
Union Gas Co.; 890 by EW; 891T courtesy Charles Luckman Assocs.; 891B by
EW; 892L collection EW; 892R by Mina Hamilton; 893 by EW.

GLOSSARY

A

air rights Rights to fill additional airspace with building volume under zoning laws. Nineteenth-century landmarks, for example, usually are of much less volume than current zoning permits; air rights are therefore the rights to the additional unbuilt volume transferred, say, to the new office building next door.

antefix Anthemion-ornamented finials that embellish the edge of a Greek temple above the entablature, covering the open ends of its roof tiles and forming a serrated silhouette.

anthemion A stylized honeysuckle ornament in Greek, Greek Revival, and neo-Grec architecture.

archaeology The study of artifacts and, in particular, buildings of a poorly documented ancient, lost, or even recent but ignored period.

architrave The "chief beam" of a Classical entablature, spanning directly above and between columns, and, in turn, supporting frieze and cornice.

archivolt The decorated band around an arch.

arcuated Composed of arches.

Art Deco A modern style first presented at the Paris Exposition Internationale des Arts Décoratifs of 1925 and rehonored in the late 1970s: a style of geometric ornament rather than form.

articulate To set off and/or emphasize by means of a joint, as a brick is articulated by deeply incised mortar, or a building's wing is articulated by the link that connects it with its parent.

Art Moderne A modern style: streamlined stucco and chromium, as if buildings traveled at the speed of automobiles. Inspired by the Paris International Exposition of 1937.

Art Nouveau When Samuel Bing opened his shop, "Art Nouveau," in Paris (1898), little did he know that the sinuous style that we have inherited would be so named: vegetative ornament that not only became the surface decoration of the then "modern" architecture but also contributed to form, particularly in Hector Guimard's Métro entrances.

ashlar Stone cut for a wall; either regular and in courses, or "random." It implies a rough and variegated stone (as in Manhattan schist or Fordham gneiss), as opposed to the smooth and monolithic sawn granite, limestone, or polished marble.

atrium A center courtyard within a house.

avant-garde The cultural front-runners —artists and architects ahead of the pack.

B

balustrade The assemblage of railing, balusters, and newels that leads you and your hand up and down the staircase.

Baroque The exuberant late Renaissance style supported by the Jesuits in their attempt to lure the flock back to Rome in the face of Luther's Reformation: extravagant architectural stagecraft for the Counter-Reformation.

battered A battered wall is one, the exterior face of which slopes away from its base, thick at its bottom, thinner at the top.

battlements The toothy parapet atop a castle or would-be castle: crenellations.

Beaux Arts Literally "fine arts," from the Parisian architectural school (École des Beaux-Arts) that served as fountainhead for formal American architectural education. The progeny of the school produced grand (sometimes pompous) public architecture: the Paris Opéra, the Chicago World's Fair of 1893, the New York Public Library, Grand Central Station, and so forth.

berm A linear mound of earth; sometimes a landscape device to shield something ugly from a passerby's view, as around a parking lot.

board and batten Flat boards with square trim covering their joints that gave "verticality" to the Gothic Revival wood cottage. Modern architects have used boards and battens on occasion more to be different than meaningful.

bollard A short, fat, round concrete masonry, metal pier, set freestanding into the street, that constrains wheeled traffic but allows pedestrians to pass.

boss A round, decorative, sometimes sculpted ornament, as at a Gothic or neo-Gothic intersection of vaulting ribs—here in stone.

brick Brick is made mostly of kiln-baked clay, but concrete brick also exists as well as the sun-dried adobe of America's southwest, Mexico, and other preindustrial countries. Once brick was mostly in standard sizes, hence **standard** brick. Other popular sizes now include:

> **standard** The brick of early America, of New York's Georgian, Federal, and Greek Revival architecture, from the James Watson house to the Colony Club. It also sheathed most of New York's high-rise housing, from Park Avenue to the vast towers of the Housing Authority: 2¼″ high × 8″ wide.
>
> **Roman** The only size the ancient Romans used and popular in late 19th-century American architecture, particularly with the Chicago School: 2″ high × 12″ wide.
>
> **jumbo** Builders of the 1940s and 1950s found that masons could lay a larger, heavier brick at the same rate as standard brick (and the unions agreed), reducing the cost of a wall. The sizes were modestly different from "standard" visually, resulting in a distorted building scale. Only later, when very much bigger brick was produced, did economics and aesthetics conjoin once more (see double and imperial brick): 2¾″ high × 8″ wide.
>
> **double** A first attempt at producing a brick aesthetic combined with the new masonry economy, particularly in the early work of Davis, Brody & Associates at Riverbend Houses. Here brick simulates the scale of tile: 5½″ high × 8″ wide.
>
> **imperial** The later upscaling of the "double" to a square face: 8″ high × 8″ wide.

Broadacre City A utopian vision of Frank Lloyd Wright where all dwell in single-family freestanding houses on generous lots; an antiurban idea served by automobiles and television, where public transportation and face-to-face meetings are thought unnecessary.

broken pediments Pediments broken apart explosively as in Baroque and neo-Baroque architecture.

brownstone Brown sandstone from the Connecticut River Valley or the banks of the Hackensack River. Soft, porous, and perishable.

Brutalism The bold concrete architecture inspired by Le Corbusier's work and his followers. Also, **New Brutalism.**

butted glass Glass sheets, as in a shopfront, where there is no mullion and the glass, necessarily thicker, meets its neighbor with a joint filled with silicone (plastic). Great transparency results.

C

campanile The freestanding bell tower of an Italian church.

cantilever A stationary lever, the arm of which supports a load, as in a fishing pole.

Carpenter Gothic The jigsaw and lathe allowed carpenters to capture quickly and inexpensively an idea of Gothic in Gothic Revival American wood houses: ogees and finials decorated windows, porches, and cornices.

caryatid At the Erectheum on Athens' Acropolis, erect ladies serve as the columns of its porch (now replaced with concrete copies due to deterioration from pollution). Any such female figures used as architectural supports are caryatids.

casement A hinged window that opens out like a door.

cast iron Liquid iron poured into a shapely mold and thence cast. Fragile in comparison to wrought iron or steel, cast iron is good for compression but shatters if you bend it.

castle Now largely a romantic idea. Strictly speaking, a fortified royal residence.

catacomb A chambered cellar serving as a cemetery in, particularly, ancient Rome.

catenary The natural curve of a hanging string (or a cable, or a suspension bridge), supported at both ends. A discrete mathematical shape.

chamfer To dull, or cut off the edge of, say, a rectangular column.

château A French country castle, with or without fortifications.

Chicago School The early modern style of Louis Sullivan, John Wellborn Root, William Le Baron Jenney, and company: birthschool of the skyscraper.

clapboard Linear shingles that clad (clap) each other in courses. Used in Federal, Greek Revival, and other Victorian stylistic ventures.

classic Of a superior and/or eternal design.

Classical Of and/or relating to the Classical period of architecture and civilization, i.e., Greek and Roman.

Classical Revival A literal revival of Greek and Roman architecture, rather than the Renaissance arrangement of Classical detail in a new fashion.

clinker bricks Bricks overburned in the kiln and then used decoratively in counterpoint to the rest of the normal brick wall which they share.

close The lawn and landscape around an English cathedral or church, usually with other religious buildings defining its limits. Where a French or Italian cathedral would relate to street and plaza, the English one is served by its close.

Colonial The architecture of, particularly, America, when it was a colony. (Strictly speaking before July 4, 1776.)

In Manhattan only one extant building can claim the Colonial title, St. Paul's Chapel of 1766. Other Colonial buildings, now encompassed by an expanded New York, were rural outposts when built.

colonnade A row of columns usually supporting a beam, architrave, or series of arches.

colonnettes Little columns for decorative purposes.

column The vertical sticklike support of a building or structure as opposed to the fatter "pier" or the archaic "pillar." Columns may range from matter-of-fact supports, such as a modern steel column, to those participating in ornate orders of Classical architecture: Doric, Ionic, and Corinthian.

Composite Mixed orders, where Doric and Ionic might share the same column.

concrete Particularly Portland cement concrete: a chemical coalescense of materials (sand, water, and an aggregate such as crushed stone) into an artificial stone. Reinforced with steel bars, it becomes the structure of buildings, roads, or bridges; plain, it fireproofs steel buildings by encasing the structure protectively.

concrete block If your society lacks clay, it may be rich in limestone, and from limestone we create Portland cement. Such cement + aggregate (sand and stones) becomes concrete and thence concrete block for those who need an alternate to brick (made from clay).

console bracket The enscrolled bracket that supports many a Renaissance and neo-Renaissance cornice. Also, **cornice bracket.** See **modillion.**

corbeled Bracketed out; in masonry, bricks are corbeled when each succeeding layer (course) projects slightly over the one below.

corbel table A series of corbeled bricks or stones supports a string of small decorative arches, frequently following the gabled end of an Italian Lombardian Romanesque church or its revival.

Corinthian The late Greek (Hellenistic) and early Roman order of architecture that produced acanthus-leaved capitals (as opposed to Ionic "ram's horns" and Doric austerity).

cornice The crown of a building, its edge against the sky; particularly part of a Classical order's entablature.

course A layer of masonry or wood; brick, block, board, or stone.

crenellated Crowned with a cornice of solid teeth (merlons) that protect the warrior, interrupted by voids that allow him to shoot.

cresting The cast-iron filigreed crest atop a Victorian mansard roof.

crocket The teat on a Gothic finial.

cul-de-sac A dead-end street, alley, or road.

D

dentil The toothy blocks under the cornice of a Greek or Roman entablature, reminiscent of the wood joinery in earlier temples from which Greek architecture in marble was derived.

distyle With two columns, as in a temple.

distyle in antis Two columns flanked by two blank walls.

Doric The austere and elegant set of parts (called an "order") developed in the 6th and 5th centuries B.C. in Greek architecture (particularly Athenian, and of Athenian colonies).

dormer An upright window projecting from a sloping roof. It makes usable a sloping attic space as well as those myriad mansard roofs of Paris, the steep pitch of which provides normal rooms on the inside and a roofclad wall facing the street.

Dutch Colonial The simple house style of New Amsterdam and environs, including those deep-eaved gambrel-roofed rural farmhouses (see Brooklyn's various Wyckoff houses) and the stepped gables of town houses at the tip of Manhattan; the latter have totally vanished; one needs to view Curaçao to see their equivalents built in the same 17th-century period.

E

Eastlake Charles Eastlake (1836–1906), architect, writer, and furniture designer, influenced late 19th-century New York with incised geometric decoration.

eclectic In architecture the borrowing of assorted styles and stylistic details for a single building.

Egyptian Of or relating to Egypt from approximately 3000 B.C. to its conquest by Alexander the Great, 332 B.C.

embrasure The splayed slot through which one might shoot at an approaching enemy. In medieval fortifications the opening without was small and that within, broad.

entablature The set of roof parts in a Classical building that the columns support: i.e., architrave (or first beam over the columns), frieze, and cornice, or top-ending. The frieze is an opportunity for cartoon graphics, as in the animal frieze at the Parthenon (the Zoophorus) or that at Brooklyn's zoo (also animals).

entasis The slight swelling of a Classical column that reinforces the visual impression of strength. The best (i.e., the Parthenon) are so subtle that one is aware of it only after conscious intellectual effort.

esplanade A linear walking part along the water's edge, like that at Brooklyn Heights or Battery Park City.

exedra A large semicircular alcove (annex) to a central space (particularly in Classical architecture).

F

face brick Brick with (at least) one side with a weather and visual finish. Common brick, on the other hand, is used as a backup and for internal invisible structural walls.

faience A fine pottery glaze adapted to architectural decor.

Federal The first "American" style of architecture, based on English Georgian.

festoon A pendant wreath; it also describes any exuberant decoration.

fillet The flat ribbon separating the flutes of an Ionic column.

finial The ultimate end of a Gothic pinnacle decorated with crockets, a finger in silhouette against the sky.

Flamboyant Used to describe the flame-like tracery of late French Gothic; later, to describe anything that is ostentatiously ornate.

French flats At first New York termed apartment houses French flats, for in

Edith Wharton's words in *The Age of Innocence*, "that was how women with lovers lived in the wicked old societies, in apartments with all the rooms on one floor."

frieze The bas-relief (or painting) in a band that decorates the top of a room or participates in a Classical entablature.

G

gable The triangular ending of a two-way pitched roof.

gambrel roof The double-pitched roofs employed by Dutch and later Victorian architects.

garland A collection of flowers, as in a wreath, or festoon.

General Grant The good general was a passive participant in this mid-Victorian eclectic mélange—usually ornate wood houses with mansard roofs that otherwise might be termed "Charles Addams."

Georgian Of the Georges, those imported German kings of England who were in charge when the best of English urban design was around. Simple but elegant brick and limestone.

Gothic Revival The romantic revival of largely Gothic detail in the 1840s. Some felt (like John Ruskin) that the medieval period was filled with **good** people, and a revival of that architecture might make citizens of the 1840s equally good. Bad psychology, but it left some smashing architecture.

Gothick An English-style neo-Gothic building.

granite The hard, fine-textured igneous (solidified from a liquid state) stone of mixed quartz, mica, and other ingredients. Sedimentary stones (limestone, brownstone) erode, wear out; granite is forever.

Greek Revival The Greeks were revived for both archaeological and political honors (the 1820s revolution liberating them from Turkey). In the 1820s, 1830s, and 1840s American houses were decorated with Greek parts, and occasionally whole buildings took on Greek temple form: cf. New York's Federal Hall National Memorial.

H

hammer beam The bracketed wood structure of a Gothic or neo-Gothic hall: a kind of wood supercorbeling.

headers The short ends of bricks in a wall used as ties to connect (bond) two thicknesses (wythes) of brick.

hip roof A roof without a gable and with eaves all around.

hood molds Moldings crowning and enveloping the head (top) of a window, particularly in neo-Gothic architecture.

I

imbricated Bearing overlapping shingles or plates arranged as in the scales of a fish. Victorian roofs, both mansard and single-gabled, frequently were imbricated in several colors.

impost block A block that bears the load, as in those corbeled limestone blocks bearing the ribs or timbers of a Gothic or neo-Gothic vault.

incunabulum A precocious affair; strictly speaking, a book printed from

movable type before 1501, but implying equivalent childlike precocity in
any activity, including architecture.

intaglio An incised pattern or decoration, or a printing block so incised that
will create printed relief.

Ionic The elegant voluted order of
Greek architecture. Its capitals are
sometimes compared to ram's horns.

Italianate Of an Italian character, particularly in mid 19th-century villas
copied from Italian prototypes.

J

jerkinhead roof A gabled roof with a
chamfered, or sliced off, plane at its
ends.

jerry-built Shoddily, cheaply, or unsub-
stantially built.

L

light A windowpane or, technically, the
compartment in which it fits.

limestone Sedimentary stone, mostly
from ancient seabeds; the silted and
pressed product of sand and seashells.
Soft, workable, and subject to erosion
in time.

M

machicolation The stepped-out cornice
of a Gothic structure that allows the
protected to pour boiling oil on an
enemy attempting to scale the walls.

maisonette A British term for duplex
apartments within an apartment
house, like a "little house."

mansard The steep, story or more-high
roofs developed by the French 17th-
century architect François Mansart,
co-opted by Victorian architects of the
19th century (particularly in Paris,
where they squeezed in an extra illegal
floor).

marble Pressed and heated (metamor-
phized) limestone, pressed for extra
eons to a harder, finer texture. It can be
polished to bring out its striations; in
its purest form it is without veins, as in
the Pentelic marble of the Parthenon
or Carrara marble from Italy.

mastaba The battered (sloping-walled)
tomb buildings of early Egyptian no-
bles subordinate to the pyramids which
they surrounded (cf. Gizeh).

merlon The tooth of a crenellated wall;
a solid between two voids (the warrior
behind a merlon shoots between the
merlons).

modillion The horizontal enscrolled
bracket that supports many a Renaissance and neo-Renaissance cornice.
See also **console bracket.**

mullion The vertical member supporting a glass wall, as in a storefront, or
between repetitive windows.

muntin A small bar that divides a window's sash into panes: the little sticks
that make up the framing of six-over-
six double-hung sash and so forth.

N

nave The central space of a Christian
church; the space for people, as opposed to the space for clergy (chancel)
or monastic brethren (transepts).

neo-Grec The late 19th-century style
that brought back Greece for a second
time (Greek Revival in the 1820s,

1830s, and 1840s was the first). Here it
was a more decorative and less columnar affair.

neo-Renaissance A revival of Renaissance buildings and parts, in New
York mostly those of England and
Italy but with an occasional French example. (The New York County Lawyers' Association, the Metropolitan
Club, and the Towers Nursing Home,
respectively.)

New Brutalism A second coming, in
the 1960s, of Brutalism (q.v.).

nosing The projecting edge of a step.

O

oculus An eyelike round window.

ogee The double-curved arch of both
Moorish and French Flamboyant
Gothic architecture. S-shaped.

ogival Having a pointed arch or vault,
as in the nave of a Gothic church.

order The base, columns, and entablature in Classical architecture: Doric,
Ionic, Corinthian, Tuscan, or Composite orders.

oriel A small bay window that captures
a view for its resident.

P

palazzo The super town house of Italian nobility (i.e., palace); later a description of any big, urbane building in
an Italian town.

palimpsest A surface that has been
reused for writing, symbols, or carving,
only partly obliterating a previous message underneath.

Palladian Of and/or relating to the
16th-century Italian architect Andrea
Palladio (Jefferson went bananas over
him); particularly used in reference to
the paired columns flanking an arch, as
at the Basilica of Vicenza.

parapet The wall around a building's
roof (literally a "breast guard").

parge To weatherproof a surface by
coating it, as with stucco, but with a
lighter cement wash—usually where
unseen, below grade, or on the rear
(unseen?) of a building.

pediment The triangular gable end of a
Classical temple and part of that architecture's order; later used separately as
a decorative part of Renaissance architecture.

pergola A trellised walkway, usually
festooned with vines; with grapevines it
would be termed an arbor.

Perma Stone® Fake masonry simulating stonework or brick, composed of
colored stucco with struck joints in a
contrasting color to imply "mortar."

piazza The Italian word for plaza—
and sometimes an American word for
porch (particularly in the Midwest).

pilaster The flat remembrance of a column that articulates a wall, and frequently repeats the rhythm and parts
of an adjacent colonnade. Usually decorative and nonstructural.

pillowed rustication Baroque architects
gave stone the imagery of wormwood,
marshmallows, and other fantasies.
Here, in neo-Baroque, pillows take
over.

pinnacle The tower atop a Gothic but-
tress.

plaza The English (and now American)
version of the Italian piazza: an outdoor space contained by different
buildings. New York has some annexed to private construction (cf. Seagram's Plaza), few publicly created

ones: The Plaza at 59th Street and
Fifth Avenue; the Police Plaza next to
the Brooklyn Bridge; and the World
Trade and World Financial Center
Plazas—the last three all since 1960.

plinth   The base that holds it all up, as
at a column or a wall.

point block   A British term for an apartment tower.

polychromy   Of many colors, particularly in architecture.

Pompeian red   The deep red of Pompeian frescoes.

Post Modern   A catchall term for (1)
the renewed interest of contemporary
architects in the history of architecture, including, in their own work, allusions to a historical vocabulary; and
(2) a permissive approach that allows
many to claim that "anything goes,"
now that they are released from the
constraints of "modern" and "functionalism," with their concomitant
morality and lack of ornament.

Po Mo   Short for Post Modern.

porte cochere   The covered portal to a
house or public building, meant originally for the horse and carriage but
now just as useful for a stretch limo.

Q

Queen Anne Style   Originally the pre-
Georgian style of Queen Anne's reign
(1702–1714), in 19th-century American architecture the style is that of a
mixture of medieval and Classical
parts: Tudor, Federal, and Greek Revival grown fat, bulbous, rich, and encrusted. Eclectic extravaganzas of delight.

quoins   Cornerstones of a building that
articulate that corner; frequently in a
different material, as in the limestone
quoins of a brick Georgian building
(say "coins").

R

range   Particularly in brick, where the
natural baking process in a kiln produces (from the bricks stacked within)
a range of color, some darker, some
lighter, depending on the individual
brick's placement in the kiln's stacks.

rectory   The dwelling of a priest
(whether Catholic or Episcopalian).

reentrant corner   An interior corner.

Renaissance   The rebirth or revival of
the Classical Greek and Roman
worlds, their humanism, individual
creativity, and, in architecture, the adaptation of the Classical vocabulary to
new building types, such as churches
and palazzi.

reredos   A background screen behind an
altar and, occasionally, a major art object itself, like the reredos by Frank
Freeman in Brooklyn Heights' Holy
Trinity Church.

retardataire   Laggard, behind the times,
a Johnny-come-lately to the art or architecture of the moment—but mostly
a pejorative for the avant-garde putting
down the architecture of what went before and then hung on.

reveals   The sides of a window or door
opening, that "reveal" the thickness of
the encompassing walls.

rock-faced   Rock made more rocky by
artful sculpture; neat stones faced with
hewn-rock forms.

Roman   The imperial organizers of the
Classical world who brought engineering to architecture, creating great public works—vaulted, domed baths and
temples, arched aqueducts—all deco-

rated and ordered with the parts developed by 5th-century B.C. Greece.

Romanesque   The round-arched and
round-vaulted sturdy early medieval
architecture of Europe that was succeeded by the more elegant and sinuous Gothic. Its revived forms were
highly popular in the late 19th century
(e.g., Jay Street Firehouse, Brooklyn).

row house   Houses that share common
walls and form a row, or what the English term terraces. Town house is the
elegant social promotion of the same
physical place.

Ruskinian   Relating to the ideas of the
19th-century English writer, art critic,
social theorist, and historian John Ruskin. *See* **Gothic Revival.**

rusticated   Stones that have deeply incised joints to exaggerate their weight
and scale. A Renaissance device.

S

sash   The subframe carrying the pane(s)
of glass in a window, as in one of two
double-hung window sash, or one of
two halves of a casement window.

schist   Laminations of rock, the product
of hot geology, as a napoleon or bak-
lava has layers of pastry. Manhattan
island's skyscraper core is founded on
Manhattan schist.

Second Empire   The period of Napoleon
III in France (1852–1870) that brought
to reality Baron Haussmann's Paris
with its concomitant mansard roofs
and neo-Renaissance detail. In America this style was aped in the 1870s and
1880s.

serpentine   Anything that is serpentlike
in its undulating form. Stone called serpentine has such striations.

sgraffito   The polite antecedent of
graffiti, here enhancing architecture
with an elegance of writing rather than
defacing it, as on the subway cars of
New York.

Shingle Style   The romantic and picturesque style of the 1880s and 1890s that
brought the freestanding architecture
of America to a special apogee: the
plastic forms resulting were clad in
wood shingles. But the style's name extended to woodless buildings, based on
the same picturesque forms.

soffit   The underside of an architectural
part, as the soffit of a balcony, commonly misused to describe the infill
vertical panels to the ceiling above
kitchen cabinets.

spandrel   The space between the window head of one floor and the window
sill of the floor above; opaque masonry
or paneling that conceals the floor construction behind. In Renaissance architecture it was the triangular space between two adjacent arches.

star anchors   Tension rods from front
outer wall to back outer wall stabilized
early 19th-century buildings, and the
hand that held the outside face of a
building inward was often a cast-iron
star, a decorative end to an engineering
need.

stele   The memorial finial or slab set in
the ground that remembers persons,
places, or events. A tombsone is a stele,
as are the Druidic remains of Stone-
henge.

stepped gable   The masonry end (usually) that covers a pitched roof's triangular profile, rising above it in rectilinear steps; a Dutch device that
presented itself to the street (English
gables ran parallel).

strapwork   A 16th-century northern

European decoration similar to leather or fretwork.

surround That framing material which surrounds an opening, window, door, or whatever.

swag A draping of cloth, frequently remembered in stone; also termed a festoon.

T

taxpayer A low (1- or 2-story) modest building where many stories might be permitted by zoning but where the owner, because of limited finances (particularly during the 1930s depression), wished only to have sufficient income to pay the expenses and taxes until better times arrived.

tempietto A little temple in Italian.

tenement A 19th-century, low-rise walk-up apartment house that covers most of its site; now a pejorative term.

terrace A group of row houses (English).

terra-cotta Literally "cooked earth" in Italian, terra-cotta is baked clay. A hard, red-brown material used for pottery, paving, shingles, statuary, and, in late 19th-century New York, for fireproofing steel (by encasing it in terra-cotta blockwork).

tesserae The tiny mosaic tiles (originally of marble) that created Roman floors. Nowadays they may be of glass.

tetrastyle Having four columns, usually in the Greek temple manner.

thermal granite Sawn slabs of granite the surface of which has been treated under intense flames, producing a roughened texture, as at the CBS Building by Eero Saarinen.

torchère A simulated torch powered by gas or electricity.

torus A convex, half-round molding, in Classical architecture at the base of an Ionic column; also used in the Renaissance and neo-Renaissance.

town house Originally the secondary residence of the English country gentleman. Now not necessarily a house in town but one in an urban arrangement: i.e., row house. *Town house* is a classier term—to increase sales. Some of New York's 19th- and early 20th-century town houses are equivalent to the Italian palazzo.

Tuscan The Roman version of Doric, with a simplified capital and, usually, no flutes.

tympanum Within an arched entry the semicircular space above the doors below, sculpted in high relief in Gothic and Romanesque architecture.

U

U.L.U.R.P. Uniform Land Use Review Process, wherein variations in the zoning laws, or large-scale development, are reviewed by the local Community Planning Board, before a final review by the City Planning Commission and Board of Estimate. A lengthy process.

V

veranda The airy porch imported from India, partially screened for outdoor living, not just rocking.

verdigris The green patina (oxide) on weathered copper, brass, or bronze. It is the handsome equivalent on copper of iron's rust, both resulting from oxidation.

vergeboard A board trimming the underedge of a gabled roof, sometimes called a bargeboard.

vernacular The ordinary architecture of a culture without benefit of architect, as in the stuccoed houses of the Mediterranean's rim (Greece, Capri, North Africa) or the verandaed farmhouses of 19th-century America.

viaduct An elevated roadway that is the trafficked equivalent of an aqueduct, supported on many columns or piers; as opposed to a bridge that spans the space in question.

Victorian A loosely defined catchall word. The architecture of the Industrial Revolution was largely coincidental with the reign of Victoria (1837–1901), which spanned from carpenter Greek Revival to the steel-framed skyscraper.

villa A country house for a well-to-do city dweller's escape (Italian).

volutes The scroll-like cresting of, for example, an Ionic capital.

voussoir The wedge-shaped stones or radial bricks of an arch, cut to fit its shape, whether circle, ellipse, or ogee.

W

water table The level of water underground (that may affect a building's foundations); or the deflecting molding that skims water away from a building like a skirt near the ground on the building's perimeter.

wrought iron More easily wrought and less brittle than cast iron, it now serves for railings and decoration. It once served as structural beams and railroad rails, before the more refined steel was invented.

wythe A single plane of brick (usually 4 inches); part of a wall composed of two or more wythes bonded by metal ties or brick "headers." A cavity wall is composed of two wythes with an air space between.

Z

ziggurat The stepped or spiral pyramidal holy places of ancient Babylon.

zoning The legal constraint of building to protect one's neighbors and oneself from noxious uses, to preserve or ensure one's quota of light and air, and to control density of land use.

INDEX

Every building described in the Guide is listed as a primary entry in the INDEX, either by name or by street address. Numbered streets designated as "East" or "West" are listed under those designations, in numerical sequence; all other numbered streets are indexed alphabetically. Streets, avenues, plazas, etc., with the same name but in different locations are further identified by borough, street, or area.

The names of those involved in creating the works listed in the Guide appear in LARGE AND SMALL CAPITAL LETTERS. Unless otherwise indicated, they are architects.

A question mark (?) following a building's name indicates questionable attribution.

A page reference in **boldface type** indicates that an illustration of the building, area, or other work will be found on that page.

The following are the abbreviations used in this Index:

Acad.	Academy	Hosp.	Hospital	Pct.	Precinct
add.	addition(s)	HQ	Headquarters	Pkwy.	Parkway
Admin.	Administration	H.S.	High School	Pl.	Place
Apts.	Apartments	Hts.	Heights	P.O.	Post Office
Assocs.	Associates	Inst.	Institute	Prep.	Preparatory
Assn.	Association	Intl.	International	Presby.	Presbyterian
Ave.	Avenue	Is.	Island	Prot.	Protestant
Bldg.	Building	I.S.	Intermediate	P.S.	Public or
Blvd.	Boulevard		School		Primary
Bklyn.	Brooklyn	JFK	John F.		School
BPL	Brooklyn Public		Kennedy	Pt.	Point
	Library	J.H.S.	Junior High	QPL	Queensborough
Br.	Bridge		School		Public
Bway.	Broadway	Jr.	Junior		Library
Bx.	Bronx	Lab.	Laboratory(ies)	RC	Roman Catholic
Comm.	Community	LI	Long Island	Rd.	Road
Co.	Company	LIC	Long Island	Ref.	Reform(ed)
Corp.	Corporation		City	Rehab.	Rehabilitation
Ct.	Court	Luth.	Lutheran	res.	residence(s)
Ctr.	Center	mag.	magazine	Rest.	Restaurant
Dept.	Department	Manh.	Manhattan	Rgt.	Regiment
Div.	Division	Meth.	Methodist	Rm.	Room
Dorms.	Dormitories	Mt.	Mount	RR	Railroad
E.	East	N.	North	Russ.	Russian
Educ.	Education	NY	New York	S.	South
Eng.	Engine	NYC	New York City	SI	Staten Island
Episc.	Episcopal	NYPL	New York	Soc.	Society
Ft.	Fort		Public Library	Span.	Spanish
Gov. Is.	Governors	NYS	New York State	Sq.	Square
	Island	NYU	New York	St.	Street
GPO	General Post		University	Univ.	University
	Office	orig.	originally	Whse.	Warehouse
Grad.	Graduate	Orth.	Orthodox	W.	West

A

AALTO, ALVAR, 63
  Inst. of Intl. Educ., 257
ABBOTT, MERKT & CO.
  Gimbel's East, 407
  Port Authority Commerce Bldg., 181–82
ABEL, BAINNSON & ASSOCS.
  also ABEL & BAINNSON
  Gateway Plaza, 46
  Olympic Place, 266
Abe Stark Ctr., 712
Abigail Adams Smith Museum, 393
Abingdon Rd., 761
Abraham, Abraham, 672
  res., 886
Abraham & Straus dept. stores, 207, 212, 570, 672, 752
ABRAMOVITZ, MAX
  Philharmonic Hall, 292
  see also HARRISON, AMBRAMOVITZ & HARRIS et seq.
ABRAMOVITZ HARRIS & KINGSLAND
  Brookdale Ctr., Hebrew Union College, 113
  Scholars Bldg., Rockefeller Univ., 403
  see also HARRISON, ABRAMOVITZ & HARRIS et seq.
ABRAMOVITZ KINGSLAND SCHIFF
  Lincoln Ctr. North, 292
  Swiss Bank Tower, 265
ABRAMSON, LOUIS ALLEN
  B'nai Jeshurun Community Ctr., 302
  Countee Cullen Branch, NYPL, 449
  Daughters of Jacob Home and Hosp., 511–12
Abron Arts for Living Ctr., **88**
Abrons, H. L., res., 531
Abyssinian Baptist Church, 449
Academy of Music, 184, 194–95, 226
ACKERMAN, FREDERICK L.
  E. 83rd St., No. 25: 379
  First Houses (apts.), 162

  Sunnyside Gardens (housing), 743
  see also VAN WART & ACKERMAN
Acker, Merrall & Condit Co., 223
Acquavella Bldg., 871–72
Actors Studio, 222
Adam Clayton Powell, Jr., Blvd., 438
Adam Clayton Powell, Jr., School, P.S. 153, Manh., 434
Adams, F. P., 242
ADAMS, HERBERT, sculptor, 114, 238
Adams, James Truslow, res., 672
Adams, John, 145, 556, 857
Adams, Thatcher M., res., 376
Adams, Thomas, Jr., res., 642, **643**
Adams, William N., res., 887
ADAMS & PRENTICE
  Gnome Bakery, 286
ADAMS & WARREN
  Adams res., 376
  Beard res., 361, 364
  Eng. Co. 224: 577, **578**
ADAMS & WOODBRIDGE
  Brick Presby. Church chapel, 386
  Madison Ave. Presby. Church, 372
  Trinity Church wing, 20
Adams Chewing Gum factory, 738–39
Adams Dry Goods Store, 178
ADAMSON & ASSOCS.
  Wintergarden, 46
  World Financial Ctr., 46–47
Adath Jeshuron of Jassy synagogue, **89**
addo-x (showroom), 246
Adelphi Acad., **636**
Adelphi Theatre, 878
Adirondack Bldg, 735
ADLER, DANKMAR
  Carnegie Hall, **278**
Admiral's House, Gov. Is., 470
Adriance Farmhouse, 787
Adventists' Crossroads Church, 878
Adventure Playgrounds
  Central Park, 339, **340**
  Highbridge Park, 463

Baudouine Bldg., 192
BAUM, DWIGHT JAMES
  Campagna res., 531
  Delafield Botanical Estates, 530
  Hammerstein res., 767–68
  U.S.P.O., Flushing, 770, **771**
  Wave Hill Ctr., 531
  West Side YMCA, 292, 293
Bauman & Kessel Films, 176
BAUMANN, BROTHER CAJETAN J. B.
  Cardinal Spellman Retreat House, 532–33
  Gethsemane-on-Hudson Monastery, 532–33
  Holy Cross Church, 538
  Riverdale Ctr. of Research, 532–33
  St. Mary's Church, Byzantine Rite, 196
Baumann's Carpet Store, 184
Baum-Rothschild Staff Pavilion, Mt. Sinai
  Medical Ctr., **390**, 453
BAYARD, HENRY, carpenter, 127–28
Bayard Bldg., **150**, 151, 656
Bay Bridge at Bayside (housing), 775
Baychester, 555–56
Bayer, Laura K., res., 366
BAYLEY, JOHN BARRINGTON
  Frick Collection add., 365–66
Bayley Seton Hosp., 827
Baylies, Edmund L., res., 347
Baylis, William, carriage house, 398
Bayonne Br., 802, 820, 898–99
Bay Plaza (shopping ctr.), 556
Bay Ridge Ave., 703
Bay Ridge/Fort Hamilton/Dyker Heights,
  703–706
Bay Ridge Masonic Temple, 703
Bay Ridge Pkwy., No. 1112: 704
Bay Ridge United Meth. Church, 704
Bayside, 774–77
Bayside Ave., 768
Bay St., Queens, 786
Bay St., SI, 823
Bay Street Landing, SI, 823
Bayswater, 795
Bay Terrace Jewish Ctr., 775
Bayview Houses, Bklyn., 716
Bayview Terrace, SI, 851–52
Beach House (rest.), 53
Beacon Theater, 309
beat generation, 104
Beard, Ruth Hill, res., 361, **364**
Beard, William, 614
Beard & Robinson Stores, 614
Beaudésir (patisserie), 307
Beaux Arts Apt. Hotel, 256
Beaux Arts Inst. of Design, 256
Beaux Arts Studios (orig.), 239
Beaver St., **13**
Be Bop Café, 108
Bechtel's brewery, 824
BECK, D. DUNBAR, artist, 734
Beck, Martin, res., 358
BECKET, WELTON, ASSOCS.
  Bank of Tokyo, **21**
  Barclay Bank Bldg., 27
  SI Mall, 837–38
Beck Memorial Presby. Church, 503–504
Bedford, 669, 671
Bedford Ave., 683
  No. 559: 684
  Nos. 667–677: 683
  No. 2693: 701, **702**
Bedford Ave. Theater, 685
Bedford family, 629
Bedford Gardens (apts.), 684
Bedford Park, 525
Bedford Park Casino, 883
Bedford Park Congregational Church, 525
Bedford Park Presby. Church, **525**
Bedford St.
  No. 3: 144
  No. 75½: 132
  No. 100: 133
Bedford St. Meth. Episc. Church, 757
Bedford-Stuyvesant, 564, 611, 657–68
Bedford-Stuyvesant Comm. Pool, 662
Bedford-Stuyvesant Restoration Plaza, **665**
Bedloes Island, see **Liberty Island**
Bedlow, Isaac, 468
BEEBE, PHILO, builder
  W. 24th St., Nos. 437–459: 176
Beechhurst, 765, 767–68
Beekman, R. Livingston, res. (orig.), 354–**355**
Beekman Downtown Hosp., 41–42
Beekman Pl., 257, 258

Beekman St., 34–35
Beekman St. Hosp., 30–31
Beekman Tower, 257
BEESTON & PATTERSON
  LI College Hosp. Prospect Hts. Pavilion,
  603
Behan, Brendan, 172
Behr, Herman, res. (orig.), **587**
BEHRENS, CHARLES
  Wooster St., No. 105: 100
Beker Chapel, St. Peter's Church, 249
Belair (apts.), 405
Belasco Theater, W. 42nd St., 233
Belasco Theater, W. 44th St., 232
Belden St., No. 175: 552
BELFATTO & PAVARINI
  Church of the Epiphany, 202–**203**
  I.S. 72, SI, 837
  Our Lady Star of the Sea Church, 860
  P.S. 69, SI, 837
  St. Anthony's Church, 556, **557**
  St. Brendan's Church, **526**
Belfer (orig. Bassine) Educ. Ctr., Einstein
  College, 542–43
Belfer Grad. School of Science, Yeshiva
  Univ., 465
BELGIOJOSO, PERESSUTTI & ROGERS
  Olivetti-Underwood Showroom, 872, **873**
Belgravia, 377
BELKIN, ARNOLD, painter, 222
Bell, Alexander Graham, 543
BELL, MIFFLIN E.
  Bklyn. GPO, **566**, 567
Belleclaire, Hotel, 311, **312**
"Bellevue," 839
Bellevue Hosp. Ctr., 204–205
Bell homestead, 892
Bells, The (Poe), 501
Bell Telephone Bldg., 513
Bell Telephone Laboratories, **139**, 210
BELLUSCHI, PIETRO
  Juilliard School of Music, 292
  Pan Am Bldg., 244, **245**
Belmont, 501–502
Belmont, August, 740
Belmont Ave., Bklyn., 720, 890
Belmont Branch, NYPL, Bx., 501
Belmont Is., 476
Belmont Park, 543
Belmore Cafeteria (former), 869
Belnord Apts., 317
Beloved Disciple Prot. Episc. Church (orig.),
  384
Belvedere (apts.), 644
Belvedere Castle, 338, **339**
BEMAN, WARREN AND RANSOM, builders,
  402
Bemelmans, Ludwig, 375
Benchley, Robert, 242
BENCKER, RALPH B.
  Horn & Hardart's Automat, 279
Benedict, Henry, carriage house, 398
Benedict, Russell, res., 698
Benedict Rd., No. 275: 843
Benepe, Barry
  Greenmarket, 141
Benetton (shop), 265
Benner, Robert, res. (orig.), 729, **730**
Bennett, James Gordon, 41, 207
Bennett, Joseph, res. (orig.), 594
Bennett Bldg. (orig.), **40**, 41
Bennett Park, 466
Benson, Charles, 707
Bensonhurst/Bath Beach, 703, 707
BENTEL & BENTEL
  St. John Vianney Church, 768
BENVENGA, CLEMENT J.
  Water Club (rest.), 204
BERDAN, PAMELA, landscape designer, 129
Berea Baptist Church, 674
Beresford (apts.), **326**, 327
BERG, CHARLES I.
  E. 70th St., No. 15: 366
  Kaskel & Kaskel Bldg., 213
  see also CADY, BERG & SEE
BERG & CLARK
  St. John's Evangelical Luth. Church, 136,
  137
BERG & SEE
  Grace Meth. Episc. Church, 878
Bergen Beach, 714
Bergen St., 617
Bergen Tile (store), 886, **887**
BERGER, LOUIS, & CO.
  also LOUIS BERGER
  Forest Ave., Nos. 166–175: 756, **757**
  Ridgewood yellow brick houses, **755**

Blazing Star Burial Ground, 852–53
Blazing Star Ferry, 852, 853
Blazing Star Tavern (former), 894
Bleecker Court (apts.), 150
Bleecker St., Bklyn., No. 29: 888
Bleecker St., Manh., 129–130
Bleecker St. Playhouse, 116–17
BLESCH & EIDLITZ
    St. George's Church, 196
    see also EIDLITZ, LEOPOLD
Blessed Sacrament Church, Manh., **306**
Blessed Sacrament Church complex, Queens,
    747
Bliss, E. W., villa, 703
Bliss, (Mrs.) George T., res., 360, **361**
BLISS, NEZIAH, 690
    Kent St., No. 130: 692
Bliss, (Mrs.) William H., 352
Blissville, 735, 742
BLOCH & HESSE
    Jewish Chapel, JFK Airport, 791
    Stephen Wise Free Synagogue, 323
BLOCH HESSE & SHALAT
    Palladium (disco), 194–95
"Block Beautiful," 197
Block 207, Bklyn., 594
"Bloody Angle," 77
Bloomingdale, (Mrs.) Lyman G., 348–49
Bloomingdale (Bloemendael), 287, 320
Bloomingdale Insane Asylum, 418, 420
Bloomingdale Rd., 287, 305–306
Bloomingdale's (dept. store), 284–85
Bloomingdale School, P.S. 145, Manh., 334
Bloomingdale Sq., 320
Blue Mill (rest.), 132
Blue Willow Café, 151
Blum, Albert, res., 371
Blum, Edward, 672
BLUM, GEORGE & EDWARD
    Blum, Albert, res., 371
    E. 22nd St., No. 235: **203**
    E. 68th St., No. 210: 396
    Hotel Theresa, 445
    West End Ave., No. 838: **304**
Blum, Robert A. M., 672
BLUMBERG & BUTTER
    St. Catherine's Park, 395
    see also COFFEY, LEVINE & BLUMBERG
BLUMENKRANZ, JOSEPH
    Bellevue Hosp., 205
BLUMENKRANZ & BERNHARD
    Daughters of Jacob Ctr., 511–12
    Gouverneur Hosp., 84
    see also KATZ, WAISMAN &
        BLUMENKRANZ et seq.; VIOLA,
        BERNHARD & PHILIPS
BLY, JAMES F.
    Williamsburg Houses, 687
Blythebourne, 703, 706–707
Blythebourne P.O., 707
BMT (subway)
    Brighton Line, 699, 757
    Culver shuttle, 889
    Flatbush interchange, 572
    49th St. Station, Manh., 234
    Jamaica Line, 781
    Queens el, 735
B'nai B'rith, 87
B'nai Israel Kalwarie synagogue, 83
B'nai Jeshurun synagogue, 302
Bnos Yakov of Pupa synagogue, 688
BOAK & PARIS
    Midtown Theater, 320
Boardman, Dr. James R., 827
Boatyard Condominium, **551**
Bo-Bo's Rest., **77**
BOBROW & FIELDMAN
    Imaging Ctr., 833
    SI Hosp., 833
Bobst Library, NYU, 112, **113**
Bodenheim, Maxwell, 105
BODKER, ALBERT JOSEPH
    E. 62nd St., No. 40: **347**, 348
    Turin (apts.), 329
BOEHM, GEORGE A.
    Forward Bldg., 83–**84**
BOEHME, G. A. & H.
    Chalif's School of Dancing, 277
Boehm-Frost House, 848
Boerum Hill Cafe, **618**
Boerum Hill Historic District, 617
Boerum Hill/Times Plaza, 564, 617–622
Boetteger, Henry W., res., 884
Boetteger Silk Factory, 486
BOGARDUS, JAMES, iron founder, 51
    Canal St., Nos. 254–260 (?): 68

Laing Stores, 863–64
    Leonard St., No. 85: **69**
    Nassau St., No. 63 (?): 38
"Bogardus" Bldg., 31, **32**, 51
Bogardus Corners, 854
Bogart, Morgan, res., 630
Bogart Piano Co., 486
BOGERT, JACOB C., builder
    Bank St., No. 68: 141
Bohemian Citizens' Benevolent Soc. of
    Astoria, 731
Bohemian National Hall, 398–99
Bohemian Park and Hall, 731
Boisselet, Eugene, res., 594
Boker res., 763
BOLLER, ALFRED P., engineer
    Macombs Dam Br., 517
    Univ. Hts. Br., 520
BOLLES, ROBERT S. (Bob Steel),
    welder-sculptor, 102
BOLOMEY, ROGER, sculptor, 542
BOLTON, CHARLES W.
    Abyssinian Baptist Church, 449
BOLTON, WILLIAM JAY, glass designer
    Holy Apostles Church windows, 177
    St. Ann's and the Holy Trinity Church,
        582, **583**
BOND RYDER ASSOCS.
    Atlantic Ave. apts., 625
    Hunts Pt. Multi-Service Ctr., 488
    Lionel Hampton Houses, 447
    North River State Park, 430
    Schomburg Ctr., 448, 49
BOND RYDER JAMES
    Audubon Research Park, 462
    Battery Pointe (apts.), 44
    Soundings (apts.), 44
    Towers on the Park (apts.), 438
Bond St., Nos. 1–5: 151, **152**
Bond St. Savings Bank Bldg., 160
Bonniers (shop), 876
BONSIGNORE BRIGNATI & MAZOTTA
    Chemical Bank, Canal St., 76
BONSIGNORE, BRIGNATI, GOLDSTEIN &
    MAZOTTA
    Clinton Hill Branch, BPL, 637
Bookseller's Row, 158
Books, Inc., 373
Boole, Rev. William H., res., 834–35
Booth, Edwin, statue, 197
Booth Theatre, 230, 232
Borden Ave. Br., 898–99
BORGLUM, GUTZON, sculptor
    Beecher statue, 596
    NY Evening Post Bldg., 59
    Statue of Liberty torch, 881
Boricua College, 460
BORING, WILLIAM A.
    E. 73rd St., No. 14, 372
BORING & TILTON
    Heights Casino, **583**, 584
    St. Agatha's School, 302
    U.S. Immigration Station, 469, **470**
Borinquen, Plaza, **484**
Boro Book Shop, 885
Borough Hall Station, IRT Lexington Ave.
    Line, Bklyn., 566
Borough Park, 703, 706–707
Bossert, Hotel, 583, 591
Bossert, Louis, res., 583, 680–81
Boston Road, 480
    Nos. 1266 and 1270: 493
    No. 2440: 552, **553**
Boswijck ("Wooded District"), 676
BOSWORTH, WILLIAM WELLES
    AT&T Bldg., 40
    Cartier, Inc., 266–**267**
    E. 65th St., No. 12: 354
    E. 69th St., No. 12: 364
    Sigel statue base, 305
BOTTOMLEY, WILLIAM LAWRENCE
    E. 73rd St., No. 14: 372
    Turtle Bay Gardens, 262
    Warburg res., 366
BOTTOMLEY, WAGNER & WHITE
    River House, 258
Bouché, Louis, 118
Boulder Crest, 783
Boulevard (apts.), 317
Boulevard (Bloomingdale Rd.), 287, 306
Boulevard (rest.), 317
Boulevard, SI, 834
Boulevard Gardens (apts.), Queens, 735
Boulevard Grove (park), Bklyn., 681
Boulevard Manor (apts.), Bx., 539
Boulevard Theater, 746–47

Bronxdale, 557–58
Bronxdale Swimming Pool, 544
Bronx Developmental Ctr., **544**
Bronx Grit Chamber, 486
Bronx H.S. of Science (former), 524
Bronx House, 546
Bronx House of Detention for Men, 510
Bronx Kills
  Triborough Br., 898–99
Bronx-Lebanon Hosp. Ctr.
  Fulton Div., 493
  Concourse Div., 512
Bronx Municipal Hosp. Ctr., 543
Bronx Museum of the Arts, 511
Bronx Park, 506
Bronx Park East, Nos. 2166 and 2180: **545**
Bronx River, 482, 503, 507, 537
  bridges, 898–99
Bronx State Hosp. Rehab. Ctr., 543–44
Bronx Terminal Market, 507–508
Bronx-Whitestone Br., 768, 898–99
Bronx Youth House for Boys, 496–97
Bronx Zoo, 504–506
Brookdale Ctr., Hebrew Union College, 113
Brookdale Hosp. Medical Ctr., 723
BROOKLYN, 559–723, 884–890
  bridges, 898–99
  land area, 896
  population (1790–1984), 896–97
  town and city of, 564, 676, 682, 695, 708,
    714, 717
  tunnels, 898–99
Brooklyn, City of, Fire HQ, **568,** 569
Brooklyn Acad. of Music, 622
Brooklyn Acad. of Music Historic District,
  622
Brooklyn Army Terminal, 614–15, 617
Brooklyn Ash Co., 749
Brooklyn Bar Assn., **574**
Brooklyn baseball teams, 581, 612
Brooklyn, Bath Beach & West End RR, 706
Brooklyn-Battery Tunnel, 7, 898–99
  Ventilation Bldgs., 8–9, 471
Brooklyn Borough Hall, **565**
Brooklyn Botanic Garden, 654–56
Brooklyn Boys Boarding School, 622
Brooklyn Br., 58, 62–**63,** 64, 91, 566, 597,
  598, 626, 703, 864, 898–99
Brooklyn Children's Aid Soc. Orphanage,
  594–**595**
Brooklyn Children's Museum, **672,** 887
Brooklyn City RR Co. Bldg., 597–98
Brooklyn Civic Center/Downtown Brooklyn,
  564, 565–72
  Walking Tour, 565–72
Brooklyn Clay Retort and Firebrick Works,
  613–**614**
Brooklyn Club, 574
Brooklyn Conservatory of Music, 646
Brooklyn Daily Eagle, 886
Brooklyn Daily Times, 621
BROOKLYN DEPT. OF CITY WORKS
  Carroll St. Br., 611
Brooklyn Developmental Ctr., **723**
Brooklyn Dodgers, 612
Brooklyn Eckfords, 683
Brooklyn Ethical Culture Meeting House and
  School, 644
Brooklyn, Flatbush & Coney Is. RR, 695
Brooklyn Fox Theater, 571
Brooklyn Friends Meetinghouse, 569
Brooklyn Friends School, 568
Brooklyn Gas Light Co. HQ, **574**
Brooklyn Heights, 564, 572–96
  Central Hts. Walking Tour, 581–90
  North Hts. Walking Tour, 590–96
  South Hts. Walking Tour, 573–81
Brooklyn Hts. Esplanade, 24, 63, 584
Brooklyn Hts. Historic District, 573, 602
Brooklyn Hts. Promenade, 24, 63, 584
Brooklyn Hills School, P.S. 66, Queens, 779
Brooklyn Historical Soc., 12, 19, **589**
Brooklyn Home for Aged Men, 673
Brooklyn Hosp. and Staff Res., 626
Brooklyn Inst. of Arts and Sciences, 654,
  672
Brooklyn Jewish Hosp., 672
Brooklyn Law School, 568
Brooklyn Masonic Temple, **628**
Brooklyn Men's House of Detention, 569
Brooklyn Meth. Church Home, 673
Brooklyn Municipal Bldg., 565
Brooklyn Museum, 654, **656**
Brooklyn Navy Yard, *see* **Navy Yard**
Brooklyn Paramount Theater, 571
Brooklyn Polytechnic Prep. School, 706

Brooklyn Public Library, **568,** 569
Brooklyn Public Library, Main Branch, 650,
  654
Brooklyn-Queens Expressway, 584, 609, 686
Brooklyn Rapid Transit Co., 699
Brooklyn Savings Bank, 581
Brooklyn School for Special Children, 709
Brooklyn Soc. for the Relief of Respectable,
  Aged, Indigent Females, 635
Brooklyn Technical H.S., 621
Brooklyn Traffic Court, 886, **887**
Brooklyn Trust Co., **582**
Brooklyn Union Gas Co., **574,** 754, 818, **888**
Brooklyn War Memorial, 567
Brooklyn Women's Club, 588
Brooks Atkinson Theater, 232
Brooks Brothers Stores, 151, **152,** 188
Brooks res., 892
Broome St., 92, 102
  No. 375: **79**
  Nos. 437–441: 94–95
  No. 519: 102
  cast-iron bldgs., 101
Brotherhood in Action Bldg., 226
Brotherhood Synagogue, 198
Brothers of the Christian Schools res., 528
BROWN, ARCHIBALD MANNING
  Harlem River Houses, 452
Brown, Charles S., 719
BROWN, HENRY KIRKE, sculptor, 185, 653
BROWN, JACK
  Gateway Plaza, 56
  Lefrak City, 752
Brown, James, res., 146
Brown, Stephen H., res., 367–68
Brown, Stewart, res., 816
BROWN & GUENTHER
  Bridge Apts., 465
  see also BROWN, GUENTHER *et seq.*
BROWNE, FREDERICK C.
  Croisic Bldg., 192
  Hotel Hargrave, 308
Brown Gardens, 411
BROWN, GUENTHER, BATTAGLIA & GALVIN
  Bard-Haven Towers, **462,** 463
BROWN, GUENTHER, BATTAGLIA, SECKLER
  Riverside Dr., No. 560; and St. Clair Pl.,
    No. 2: 427
  Trinity House/Trinity School, 333
Browning, Edward West, 239, 308
BROWN, LAWFORD & FORBES
  Buckley School, **371,** 372, 398
  Cloisters, **467**
  Metropolitan Museum Watson Library,
    378–79
  NY Botanical Garden Lab., 507
Brown Memorial Baptist Church, 637
Brownstone Blocks, 663
Brownsville, 611, 718, 719–21
Brownsville Multi-Service Ctr., 720
Bruce-Brown, William, carriage house, 365
Bruckner Blvd. Br., 898–99
Bruckner Expressway, 496
BRUMIDI, CONSTANTINO, painter, 201
BRUN & HAUSER
  Tompers res., 699
BRUNNER, ARNOLD W.
  Barnard Hall, 423–24
  Lewisohn Stadium, 881
  Montefiore Hosp., 526–27
  Mt. Sinai Medical Ctr., 390
  Temple Israel, **442**
  23rd St. Public Baths, 204
BRUNNER & TRYON
  Beth-El Chapel, 352
  David Sarnoff Bldg., 84
  Mt. Sinai Dispensary, 359
  Shearith Israel Syn., **323**
Bruno Dessange boutique, 353
BRUNS, HENRY
  Immaculate Conception Church, 488–**489**
BRUSCELLA, JOHN
  Les Clochettes (school), 776
BRUSH, J. L.
  Carroll St., Nos. 1401–1425: 675
  President St., Nos. 1483–1491, 675
Bryant, William Cullen (d. 1878), 237, 336,
  617
  statue, 238
Bryant, William Cullen (d. 1905), 684
Bryant Park, 237–38
Bryant Park Area, 237–43, 870–71
  Walking Tour, 237–43
Bryant Park Bldg., 238
Bryant Park Studios, 239
Bryant Theater, 233

Chemical Bank Canal St. branch, 76
Chemical Corn Exchange Bank, 16
CHEN, PAUL K. Y.
  Playboy Club, 281
CHERMAYEFF, IVAN, designer
  also CHERMAYEFF & GEISMAR;
    CHERMAYEFF, GEISMAR & ASSOCS., 266,
    269, 543, 875
Cherokee Apts., **401**
Cherokee Club, 880
Chess and Athletic Club, 870
Chester Ave., Nos. 85 and 59: 860
Chez Ma Tante (rest.), 143
Chicago Tribune Tower competition, 254, 257
Chicago World's Fair (1893), see World's
  Columbian Exposition
CHILD ASSOCS., landscape architects
  also SUSAN CHILD
  South Cove Park, 43
Children's Aid Soc.
  Goodhue Children's Ctr., 813
  Newsboys' and Bootblacks' Lodging House,
    163–64
  Rhinelander Children's Ctr., 410
  6th St. Industrial School, 164
  Sullivan St. Industrial School, 116
CHILDREN'S ART CARNIVAL
  W. 139th St. Playground, **450**–51
Children's Day Treatment Ctr., **306**
Children's Mansion, 305
Children's Museum of Manh., 236–37
Children's Portico, Pratt Inst., 634
CHILDS, DAVID
  Columbus Ctr., 275
  see also SKIDMORE, OWINGS & MERRILL
Childs, William H., res., 644
Child's Rest. Bldg., 265
Chilton Paint Co., 763
Chinatown/Little Italy, 72–81
Chinatown Mission/Church of Our Saviour
  (Episc.), 75
"Chinese Dragon Restaurant" neon sign, 76
Chinese Merchants' Assn., 76
Chisholm Estate, 764
CHISLING, ELLIOT L.
  St. Vincent Ferrer School, 354
Chittenden Ave., No. 16: 466
Chock Full O'Nuts Coffee Corp., 785
"Choragic Monument of Lysicrates," 59, 64,
  303
Christ and St. Stephen's Church (Episc.), 295
Christ Church (Episc.), Bx., 536
Christ Church (Episc.), Manh., 878
  Rectory, 306
Christ Church (Episc.) and Parish Hall, SI,
  814
Christ Church (Meth.), Manh., 345
Christ Church and Holy Family (Episc.),
  Bklyn., 604, **605**
Christ Church Congregational, Bklyn., 777
Christ Congregational Church, Bx., 513–**514**
CHRISTENSEN, R. MARSHALL
  Perkins Study Ctr., Riverdale Country
    School, 531
Christ Evangelical Luth. Church, Manh., 436
CHRISTIE, DAVID, builder
  Charles St., No. 131: **137**, 138
CHRIST-JANER, VICTOR, & ASSOCS.
  also VICTOR CHRIST-JANER
  Church of St. Matthew and St. Timothy,
    327, **328**
  Church of the Master, 439–40
  Downstate Student Ctr., 702
  Pforzheimer Hall, Horace Mann H.S., 535
  10th Church of Christ, Scientist, **109**
Christodora House, 163, **165**
Christopher House, 848
Christopher Park, 129
Christopher St., 136
  No. 10: 127
  Nos. 18 and 20: 126, **127**
  Nos. 59–61: 143
  No. 95: 136–37
  PATH station, 135, 136
CHRISTY, HOWARD CHANDLER, painter,
  322
Chrysler Bldg., **253**, 285
Chumley's (rest.), 132
CHURCH, BENJAMIN S., engineer
  New Croton Aqueduct Gatehouse, 520
  Williamsbr. Reservoir Keeper's House, 526
CHURCHILL, CHARLES C.
  Cauldwell Ave., No. 1076: 492
CHURCHILL, CHESTER L.
  Eastern Airlines, JFK,.789
CHURCHILL, HENRY S.
  Ft. Greene Houses, 626

  Lowell (apts.), 349
  Queensbridge Houses, 738
  see also THOMPSON & CHURCHILL
Churchill, Hotel, 310
Churchill, Winston, 827
Church Missions' House, 199
Church St., 68, 71, 72
Ciaobella (rest.), 399
CIARDULLO, JOHN, ASSOCS.
  Hamilton Fish Play Center, 92
  Maria Lopez Plaza (housing), **489**
  Owen Dolen Golden Age Ctr., **541**
  Port Regalle (res. development), 852
  Red Hook row houses, 613
CIARDULLO-EHMANN
  City Line 1 Turnkey Public Housing, **722**
  Plaza Borinquen (housing), **484**
Cinema I and Cinema II, 285
Cino's Italian Rest., 629
Circle Missions, Inc., 503
Ciro of Bond St. (shop), 875
Citarella (seafood), 314
CIT Bldg., 283
Citibank branches, 16–17, 78, 192, 582, 752,
  789
Citicorp Ctr., 249
Citicorp bldg. and garage, LIC, 739
Cities Service Bldg., 36
Citizen's Savings Bank, 75
CITY AND SUBURBAN HOMES
    ARCHITECTURAL DEPT.
  First Ave. Estate, 393
  Junior League Hotel, 401–**402**
  York Ave. Estate, 401
City and Suburban Homes Co., 393, 401–**402**,
  742–43
CITYARTS WORKSHOP, muralists, 110, **111**,
  222, 427, 747
City Bank Farmers' Trust Co., **16**
City Ctr. of Music and Drama, 275, 279
City College, CUNY, 430–32, 881
City Hall, 61–**62**
  subway station, IRT Line, 62
City Hall Park, 61, 62
City Hosp., 474
City Housing Corp., 743
City Island, 537, 550–52
City Island Br., 898–99
City Island Museum, 551
City Line 1 Turnkey Public Housing, **722**
City of Brooklyn, 1865–1898 (Syrett), 622
CitySpire (mixed use bldg.), 279, 621
City Temple, Seventh-Day Adventists'
    Church, 435
City Univ. Grad. Ctr., CUNY, 238
City View Motor Inn, 742
CITY WALLS, INC., muralists, 99
Civic Center, 58–72
  Walking Tour, 58–72
Civic Ctr. Synagogue, **68**
Civic Club (orig.), 206
Civic Fame (Weinman), 64
Civic Virtue (Macmonnies), **757**, 759
Civil Courthouse, City of NY, 66–67
CIVILETTI, PASQUALE, sculptor, 307
CLAPS, VINCENT A.
  Schmertz res., 530
Claremont House, 371
Claremont Riding Academy, **318**
Clarence Ave., Nos. 714 and 748: 548
CLARK, CHARLES C.
  Clay Ave., No. 1038: 492
Clark, Edward Severin, 287, 324
CLARK, GEORGE W.
  Manh. Savings Bank branch, 76
Clark, Harriet S., res., 384
CLARK, JAMES L., sculptor
  Roosevelt Memorial, **326**
Clark, Dr. Joseph E., res., 604
Clark, (Mrs.), J. William, res., 361
Clark, Stephen, 317
Clark, Stephen C.
  garage, 368
  residence, 366–67
Clark, William, res. (orig.), 75
CLARK & WARREN
  St. Charles Borromeo Church, 849
CLARKE, BRADFORD, landscape architect
  Unisphere, 1964–65 World's Fair, 749
CLARKE, CAMERON, landscape architect
  Carl Schurz Park, 413
CLARKE, GILMORE D., landscape architect
  Central Park Zoo, 879
  Parkchester, 539–**540**
  Peter Cooper Village, 202
  Stuyvesant Town, 202
  see also CLARKE & RAPUANO

Clarke, Thomas, Capt., 169
Clarke, Thomas B., res., 216
CLARKE & RAPUANO, landscape architects
    Bklyn. Hts. Esplanade, 584
    see also CLARKE, GILMORE D.; RAPUANO,
        MICHAEL
Clark Lane (apts.), 591
Clarkson Ave., No. 111: **696**
"Clar Manor," 832
Clason Military Acad., 538
Clason Pt., 537, 538
Clason Pt. Amusement Park, 538
Classon Ave., Nos. 361 and 418–422: 661
Claudio's (rest.), 129
Clausen, George C., carriage house, 398
CLAVAN, IRWIN
    Clinton Hill Apts., 633
    Parkchester, 539–**540**
    Peter Cooper Village, 202
    Stuyvesant Town, 202
CLAWSON, HARRY M.
    E. 57th St., No. 322: 286
Clay Ave., Nos. 1038, 1040–1066, and
    1041–1066: 492
Clay Pit Ponds State Park, 854
"Clear Comfort," 829, **830**
Clement Clarke Moore Park, 175
CLEMENTE, FRANCISCO, artist, 194–95
Clemente, Roberto, 429, 519
Cleopatra Rest., 318
Cleopatra's Needle, see Obelisk, Central Park
CLERC, HAZEL, sculptor, 734
Clergy House, Grace Church Houses, 157
Clermont Apts., 666
CLEVERDON & PUTZEL
    Central Park W.–W. 76th St. Historic
        District, 325
    E. 12th St., Nos. 36, 37, 42, and 43: 126
    E. 94th St., Nos. 5–25: 388
C.L.I.C.K., 638
Cliff Dwellers Apts., 304
Clifton, 827–28
Clifton Pl., 636–37
Clinton, 221–26, 870
    Walking Tour, 221–26
CLINTON, CHARLES W.
    7th Rgt. Armory, 356, **357**
    Spaulding estate coachmen's res., 531
    see also CLINTON & RUSSELL
Clinton, DeWitt, Park, 221
Clinton, DeWitt, statue, 391
Clinton, Gov. George, 59
Clinton, Hotel, 193
CLINTON & RUSSELL
    Apthorp Apts., **311**
    Astor Apts., 309
    Bway., No. 391: 70
    Cities Service Bldg., 36, 862
    E. 62nd St., No. 4: **346**
    E. 67th St., No. 7: 879
    Graham Court (apts.), **439**
    Langham (apts.), 324
    Level Club, 309
    Mecca Club, 279
    71st Rgt. Armory, 215, **869**
    West End-Collegiate Historic District, 299
    Whitehall Bldg., 8
    Whyte's Rest., 40
    see also CLINTON, CHARLES W.; RUSSELL,
        W. H.; RENWICK, ASPINWALL &
        RUSSELL
Clinton Ave., Bklyn.
    No. 274: 632
    Nos. 415 and 457: 630
    No. 487: **630**
Clinton Court (res. group), 222
Clinton Hill, 564, 622–23, 629–38
    Walking Tour, 629–38
Clinton Hill Apts., 633
Clinton Hill Branch, NYPL, 637
Clinton Hill Historic District, 629
Clinton St., Bklyn.
    Nos. 133 and 140–142: 581
    Nos. 191, 214, and 232–236: 607
    Nos. 296, 301–311: 604
    No. 334: 604, **605**
    No. 450: 609
Clinton Tower (apts.), 224
Clock Tower Gallery, 69
Clocks, sidewalk, see sidewalk clocks
Cloisters, 463, 466–**467**
CLOSE, CHUCK, painter, 80
Clove, The, SI, 838
Clove Rd., Bklyn., 669
Clove Rd., SI, 835–36, 838
CMA DESIGN GROUP, LTD., 129

COBB, HENRY IVES
    First Church of Christ, Scientist, 671
    Liberty Tower, 38
COBB, WILLIAM R.
    Conservatory Range, NY Bot. Garden, **506**
Cobble Hill, 564, 599–607
Cobble Hill Historic District, 602, 603, 607
Cobble Hill Nursing Home, 603
Cobble Hill Sitting Park, 605
"Cocclestown," 847
COCO, PETER M.
    LIC Courthouse, **737,** 739
CODMAN, OGDEN, JR.
    Dahlgren res., 389
    De Wolfe res., 369
    Livingston res., 389
    Metropolitan Club, 345
    National Acad. of Design, 383
    residence, 389
Coenties Slip, 25
coffee houses, 116
COFFEY, LEVINE & BLUMBERG
    Clement Moore Park, 175
    Haffen Park, 555
    W. 139th St. Playground, **450**–51
    see also BLUMBERG & BUTTER
Coffey St., 613
Coffin, William Sloane, 116
Cohan, George M., 226, 229, 231
Cohan & Harris Theater, 232
COHEN, ELAINE LUSTIG, ASSOCS., designers
    873, **874**
COHEN, HERBERT
    Jewish Hosp. Nursing Home, 673
Cohen Library, City College, **432**
COHN BROTHERS
    President St., No. 1362: 675
Coho (rest.), 31
Cole, Abraham, res., 856
Cole, Capt., res., **893,** 894
COLE, JAMES
    W. 95th St., No. 143: 331
Cole, Nat King, 346
COLE, W. W.
    Bedford Ave. Theater, 685
Coles Sports and Recreation Ctr., NYU, 117
Colgate, Robert, res., 532
Colglazier, Duane, res., **142**
Collectors' Club, 216
College of Insurance, 50
College Pl., 588
College Point, 762–65
College Pt. Blvd., 762
    No. 5–27: 764
    No. 23–27: 891
    playground and parking area, 763
College Pt. Causeway, 762
College Pt. Clubhouse, 763
College Pt. Industrial Park, 765
College Pt. Shorefront Park, 764
College Res. Hotel, 418
Collegiate School annex, 300
COLLENS, CHARLES
    Cloisters, 466–**467**
    see also ALLEN & COLLENS; ALLEN,
        COLLENS & WILLIS
COLLENS, WILLIS & BECKONERT
    Riverside Church, **426**
    Union Theological Seminary, 425, **426**
    see also ALLEN & COLLENS; ALLEN,
        COLLENS & WILLIS
COLLINS & COLLINS
    Central Ct. Bldg., Bklyn., 569
Collyer Brothers, 444
Colonial Park, 418
Colonial Play Ctr., 451
Colonnade Row, Manh., 147, **154**–55
Colonnade Rows, Bklyn., 688
Colony Clubs, 194, 348
Colored School No. 3 (orig.), 688–**689**
Colosseum (apts.), 423
COLT, STOCKTON B.
    Emmet Bldg., 194
    see also BARNEY & COLT; TROWBRIDGE,
        COLT & LIVINGSTON
Colum, Padraic, 120
Columbia (apts.), **319**
Columbia Cinema, 320
Columbia College, 60, 469
Columbia Fireproof Whse., 876–77
Columbia Grammar and Prep. School, **329**
Columbia Hts.
    Nos. 145 and 160: 585
    Nos. 210–220: **585**
    Nos. 222: 573, **585**
Columbia Fathers Res., 776

Columbia Pl., Nos. 7–13: 578
Columbia-Presby. Medical Ctr., 462–63, 467
Columbia-Presby. Medical Associates, East
    Side, 346
Columbia School of Social Work, **385**
Columbia St., 614
Columbia Terrace, 609, **610**
Columbia Univ., 420–23
    College of Pharmaceutical Science, **877**
    Prentis Hall, 428
    Teachers College, **424,** 425
Columbia Univ. Club, 241
Columbia Univ. Stadium, 467
Columbus, Christopher, statues, 275, 339, 566
Columbus Ave., 295, 311, 330
    No. 600: 334
Columbus Ctr. (planned), 275
Columbus Circle, 275–76
Columbus House (apts.), 331
Columbus Manor (apts.), 332
Columbus Park Towers (apts.), 332
Columns (apts.), 239
COMACHO, AUGUSTO
    Philippine Ctr., 872, **873**
Commandant's House, NY Naval Shipyard,
    638
Comme des Garçons (boutique), 100
Commerce St., Nos. 39 and 41: 132, 133
Commissioners Plan (1811), 145, 190, 458
Commodities Exchange HQ, 9
Commodore Hotel, 252–53
Common, The, 61
Commonwealth Bldg., **446**
Commonwealth Fund, 373
Community Church of Astoria, **736**
Community Synagogue, Max D. Raiskin Ctr.,
    163
Community Temple Beth Ohr, 701
Complete Traveller (bookshop), 216
Compton, Betty, 884
COMSTOCK, FREDERICK R.
    Second Church of Christ, Scientist, 322
CONABLE, GEORGE
    St. Philip's Baptist Church., 819
Concourse Plaza Hotel, 510
Condict, Silas Alden, 151
Condict Bldg., **150,** 151, 656
Condit, Carl, 151
Condon, Charles, res., **574**
Condon, John, res., 647
CONDON, RICHARD S.
    Front (rest.), 129
Conduit Ave., 785
Con Edison, see Consolidated Edison Co.
    W. 110th St. substation, 336
Coney Island, 563, 710, 711–14
Coney Is. Creek bridges, 898–99
Coney Is. Hosp., 711
Conference House, 856–**857**
Confucius Plaza (apts.), 75
CONGDON, HENRY M.
    St. Andrew's Church, 444
Congregationalist Church of N. NY, 485
Congregations (Jewish houses of worship), *see*
    under synagogue names
Congress Club, **685**
Congress St., 605, 606
CONKLIN, WILLIAM J.
    Butterfield House, **124**
    New School for Social Research, **124**
    Premier, 403, **404**
CONKLIN & ROSSANT
    also CONKLIN ROSSANT
    Bway., No. 938: 188
    Bklyn. Borough Hall, 565
    Cadman Towers, **591**
    E. 79th St., Nos. 72–76: 376
    Hudson View W., 45
    Lasdon House, 403
    Metro North Plaza/Riverview Apts. and
        P.S. 50, Manh., 453–**454**
    P.S. 135, Manh., 258
    Ramaz Lookstein Upper School, 375–76,
        377
    see also MAYER, WHITTLESEY & GLASS;
        ROSSANT, JAMES S.
Conkling, Roscoe, statue, 190
CONRAN DESIGN GROUP, 155
    Broadway, The, **314**
Conran's (home furnishings), 155, 314
Conservative Synagogue of Riverdale, **535**
Conservatory Range, NY Botanical Garden,
    506
Consolidated Edison Co.
    Astoria plant, 730
    Bklyn. Div., **572**

E. 74th St. plant, 400
Front St. substation, 35
Hunts Pt. coke plant site, 497
Ravenswood plant, 471, 472, 737
Training Center, **741**
Travis plant, 836
W. 59th St., powerhouse, 224, **225**
W. 110th St., substation, 335
Westchester Sq. Customer Service, 542
Consolidated Edison Co. Bldg. and Tower,
    194
Consolidated Ship Bldg. Corp., 518
Continental Ctr., 27–28
Continental Illinois Ctr., 269, 270
Continental Iron Works, 690
Convent Ave., 432, 433
Convent Ave. Baptist Church, 433
CONVERY, NEIL J.
    Church of St. Joseph, 829
Coogan Bldg., 178
Coogan's Bluff, 178, 451
Cook, Dr. Frederick A., 677
Cook, Walter, 529
Cook, William A., res., 368
COOK & WELCH
    Cathedral of St. John the Divine Choir
        School, 418–19
    see also BABB, COOK & WELCH; BABB,
        COOK & WILLARD; COOK, BABB &
        WILLARD
COOK, BABB & WILLARD
    Hudson Memorial Column, 529
    see also BABB, COOK & WELCH; BABB,
        COOK & WILLARD; COOK & WELCH
COOLIDGE, SHEPLEY, BULFINCH & ABBOTT
    NY Hosp./Cornell Medical Ctr., **404**
Co-op City, 88, 89, 480, 555–56
COOPER, ALEXANDER, & PARTNERS
    also ALEXANDER COOPER; ALEXANDER
        COOPER & ASSOCS.
    South Park, 43
    Stuyvesant H.S. (proposed), 48
    Trump City, 297
    World Financial Ctr., 43
    see also COOPER, ECKSTUT ASSOCS.
Cooper, Gloria Vanderbilt, res., 359
Cooper, James Fenimore, 501, 617
Cooper, Karen, 146
Cooper, Peter, 156, 615, 638, 676, 703
COOPER, THEODORE, engineer, 465
COOPER, ECKSTUT ASSOCS.
    Battery Park City, 42–43
    Esplanade, 43
    see also COOPER, ALEXANDER, &
        PARTNERS ECKSTUT, STANTON;
        EHRENKRANTZ GROUP & ECKSTUT
Cooper-Hewitt Museum, **385**
Cooper Park Houses, 697
Cooper Sq., No. 69: 164
Cooper Sq. Assembly of God, 165
Cooper Union for the Advancement of
    Science and Art, 150, 155–**156**
Copacabana (night club), 345
COPELAND NOVAK ISRAEL & SIMMON
    Herald Ctr. (shopping mall), 212–13
COPELIN, LEE & CHEN
    Uptown Racquet Club, 407–408
Copley (apts.), 294, **295**
"Copper Flagg Estates," **842**
Copperflagg Lane, Nos. 60, 61, 76, 81, 88:
    842
CORBETT, HARVEY WILEY, 202
    Criminal Courts Bldg. and Men's House of
        Detention, 66
    E. 8th St., Nos. 4–26: 111
    Metropolitan Life N. Bldg., 190
    see also HELMLE & CORBETT; HELMLE,
        CORBETT & HARRISON
Corbett, James J., res. (former), 776
Corbett, Raymond R., Bldg., 202
CORBETT, HARRISON & MACMURRAY
    National Title Guaranty Bldg., 581–**582**
    Rockefeller Ctr., 272–274
    see also HARRISON, WALLACE K.;
        HELMLE, CORBETT & HARRISON
Corbett Rd., 776
Corbin Bldg., 40
CORCHIA-DE HARAK ASSOCS., designers,
    26–**27,** 28
    see also DE HARAK, RUDOLPH
Corinthian (apts.), 220
Corlear's Hook, 683
Corlear's Hook Houses, 89
Cornell, George, res., 588
Cornell, J. B. & J. M., 172–**173**
Cornell, Joseph, 772

Cuyler Park, 625
Cyclone roller coaster, Coney Is., 712
Cypress Hills, 718–19
Cypress Hills St., No. 170–12: 758

D

DaCunha, George W.
  Gramercy Park Hotel, 198
  Greene St., No. 31: 96
Dag Hammarskjold Plaza, 255–56, 257, **259**
Dag Hammarskjold Tower (apts.), 257
D'Agostino Res. Hall, NYU Law School, 114, 115
Dahlgren, Lucy Drexel, res., 389
Daidone, Joseph
  Belmont Branch, NYPL, 501
Daily, Clifford Reed, 133
Daily News printing plant, 741
Daily Worker, 185
Dairy, Central Park, 339
Dairy, Prospect Park, 652
Dakin, J. H.
  Old Church of the Nativity, 867
Dakota (apts.), 72, 280, 287, 317, 324
Dakota Stables, 311
Dalby, Marcia, sculptor, 540
Dalton on Greenwich (apts.), 51
Dalton School, 386
Daly's Dandelion (bar), 879
Damrosch Park, 291
Dance Theatre of Harlem, 436
Danenberg & Coles, 676
Daniel D. Tompkins School, P.S. 69, SI, 837
Daniel Low Terrace, No. 117: 809
Dans & Otto
  Église de Notre Dame, 419–20
Dansk Sømandskirke, 586
Dante Park, 293
Danzig, Philip, mosaic designer, 222
Dattner, Richard, & Assocs.
  also Richard Dattner
  Central Park playgrounds, 337, 339, **340**
  College Pt. playground, 763
  Columbia Univ. Stadium, 467
  Highbridge Park playground, 463
  I.S. 295, Manh., 429
  Manhattan 1 and 2 (theaters), 285
  North River State Park, 429, 430
  Parkchester Branch, NYPL, 540
  P.S. 380, Bklyn., 684
  P.S. 234, Manh., 51
  Riverside Park apts., 429
  Stanton Playground, 205
Daughters of Jacob Ctr., 511–12
Daumer & Co.
  Montefiore Hebrew Congregation, **495**
D'Auria, James D.
  Woods 37th (rest.), 208
Daus, Rudolph L.
  Bklyn. Hall of Records, 566
  Lincoln Club, 657, **660**
  Montgomery Pl., No. 7: 644
  NY & NJ Telephone Co. Bldg., 567–68
  NY County National Bank, 182
  Thallon and Bunker res(s). 646
  13th Rgt. Armory, **665**, 666
Davidson, John
  First Presby. Church of Williamsbridge and Rectory, 554–**555**
Davidson, Lewis S., Sr., Houses, 493
Davies, Lord Llewellyn
  Museum Tower, 268
Davies, Marion, res., 305
Davis, Albert E.
  North Side Board of Trade Bldg., 483
Davis, Alexander Jackson
  Gramercy Park W., Nos. 3 and 4: **198**
  Litchfield Villa, **645**
  Octagon Tower, 475
  Old Church of the Nativity, 867
  "Woodland Church" (?), 830
  see also Town & Davis
Davis, George B., builder, 826
Davis, Michael and John, res. (orig.), 354
Davis, Richard R.
  NY Presby. Church Auditorium, 447
  W. 160th St., Nos. 420, 430: 461
Davis, Shelby Cullom, Museum, 291
Davis, Thomas E., 810, 815
Davis, Brody & Assocs.
  Albany St., Nos. 320–340: **45**
  Boston Rd., No. 2440: 552, **553**
  Bklyn. Botanic Garden greenhouses, **655**
  Brown Gardens (apts.), 411
  Bryant Park NYPL stacks, 237

Carnegie Park apts., **411**
Cathedral Pkwy. Houses, 333–34
Central Park Place (apts.), 276
Coney Is. town houses, 713
Copley (apts.), 294, **295**
Delmonico Plaza (offices), 283
E. 72nd St., No. 525: 398
East Midtown Plaza (apts.), 203, **204**
Fifth Ave., No. 110: 187
47th Pct., 555
Hudson Tower apts., **45**
Lambert Houses, 503, **505**
Lincoln Ctr. North (mixed use), 292
LIU Bklyn. Ctr., 571
Mt. Sinai Medical Ctr. Aron Res. Hall, 390–391, **392**
NY Public Library, 239–240
Queens College New Science Bldg., **773**, 774
Riverbend Houses, 451–**452**
River Park Towers, **519**
Rockefeller Research Labs., 403
Ruppert Towers, 411
Sea Park East (apts.), 714
Waterside (apts.), **204**
Westyard Distribution Ctr., 212, **213**
Wheelock Res., Goodhue Ctr., 812–13
William St., No. 100: 37
Yorkville Towers (apts.), 411
Zeckendorf Towers (mixed use), 185, **186**
Davis Hall for Performing Arts, City College, 432
Davis Mansion, 840
Davis Medical Bldg., 677, **680**
Davison, Henry P., res. (orig.), 363
Dawn Hotel, 435
Dawson, James W., landscape designer
  Ft. Tryon Park, 466
Day, William H.
  Chapel of the Transfiguration, 295
Day & Meyer, Murray & Young, 392
Daytop Village, 239
Dead End Kids, 286
Dean, Bashford, 531
Dean, E. C.
  Turtle Bay Gardens, 262
Dean & DeLuca (gourmet shop), 99
Dean St.
  No. 195: 617
  Nos. 240 and 244: **618**
  No. 254: 618
  Nos. 1164–1182: 670
Deane & Woodward, 581
Dean Witter, 50
DeBevoise, G. W.
  Grammar School 91, Bx., 518, **519**
Debus, William
  President St., No. 1294: 675
Decatur St., 657
  No. 81: 666
  Nos. 587–611: 667–68
Decker, Sylvanus, farmhouse, 847
Decoration and Design Bldg., 286
Deery, John J.
  Church of St. Edward, 626–27
De Forest, Lockwood, res., **118**, 119
DeGraw, Abraham J.S., res., 606–607
DeGraw, John
  Grove St., Nos. 14–16: 134
De Groot Pl., 818
De Harak, Rudolph, designer
  Rivertower, 258–59
De Jonge, Louis, & Co., 828
De Kalb Ave., Nos. 282–290, 285–289: **631**
DeKoven, Reginald, res., 381
Delacorte Fountain, 474–75
Delacorte Memorial Theater, 337, 338
De La Cour, Wids
  Children's Aid Soc. Orphanage, 595–**595**
  Columbia Terrace, 609, **610**
  Poplar St., 573, 594–95
Delafield, Edward D., res. and estate, 530
Delafield housing estate, 530
DeLamar, Joseph, res., **217**, 218
Delamarre, Jacques
  Century Apts., 321
  Chanin Bldg. lobby, 282, **283**
  Majestic Apts., 324
Delaney, O'Connor & Schultz
  St. Nicholas of Tolentine Church, 522
Delano family, 154–55
Delano & Aldrich
  Baker and Palmer res(s)., 387
  Bartow-Pell restoration, 540
  Chapin School, 413

DELANO & ALDRICH (*cont.*)
Colony Club, 348
Cutting res(s)., 383
E. 69th St., No. 11: 364
Greenwich House, 129
Kips Bay Boys Club, 260
Knickerbocker Club, 346
LaGuardia Airport bldgs. and Marine
Terminal, 745–46
Pratt res., 361–**362**
St. Bernard's School, 390
Sloane res., 363
Straight res., 388
Sutton Sq., No. 12: 286
Third Church of Christ, Scientist, 349
Union Club, 365
DeLavergne Refrigerating Machine Co., 634,
882
DELEHANTY, BRADLEY
Lenox School, 368
Delehanty Inst., 159
DE LEMOS & CORDES
Adams Dry Goods Store, 178
Arion Soc., 876
Eichler Mansion, 498
Fulton Bldg., 41
Keuffel & Esser Bldg., 41
Macy's (dept. store), 207–208
NY County National Bank, 182
Siegel-Cooper Store, **180**
DEL GAUDIO, MATTHEW
Civil Courthouse, City of NY, 66–67
Williamburg Houses, 687
DELHI, ARNE
Ames res., 701
Nissen res., 886
DELHI & HOWARD
St. Jerome's Church, 483–84
Délices La Côte Basque (now Succès La Côte
Basque), 372
Delmonico Plaza, 283
Delmonico's Rest., **15**
Delta Airlines Terminal, LaGuardia Airport,
745–46
DeLury, John J., Sr., Plaza, 42
DeMatti, Nicholas, Playground, 828
DEMEURON & SMITH
Lenox Ave. row houses, 442
DeMilt Dispensary, **868**
Demuth, William, & Co.–S.M. Frank & Co.,
779
Demyan's Hofbrau, 892
Dennett Pl., **613**
Dennis, Patrick, 141
DENNISON, ETHAN ALLEN
Ft. Greene Houses, 626
DENNISON & HIRONS
Beaux Arts Inst., 256
Suffolk Title & Guarantee Bldg., 783
DEPACE, ANTHONY J.
St. Theresa of the Infant Jesus Church, 549
DEPACE & JUSTER
St. Roch's Church and Rectory, **487**
DERDERIAN, HAROUTIUN
Caliban's (rest.), 200
Harout's Rest., 865
Marvin Gardens (rest.), 315
Derech Emunah synagogue, 796
DE ROSA, EUGENE
B. S. Moss's Colony Theater, 232
Gallo Theater, 233
DE ROSA & PEREIRA
Bryant Theater, 233
Times Sq. Theater, 233
DESHON, FATHER GEORGE
St. Paul the Apostle Church, 225
DESIGN COALITION: STEPHEN TILLY/ALAN
BUCHSBAUM
Film Forum 1 & 2: 146, **147**
DESKEY, DONALD, designer, 272–**274**
DESPONT, THIERRY W., 378, 468
Deutsch-Amerikanische Schuetzen
Gesellschaft, 165
Deutsche Evangelische Kirche von Yorkville,
407
Deutsche Evangelische Lutherische St.
Johannes Kirche, 721
Deutsche Evangelische St. Petri Kirche, 688
Deutscher Verein, 355
DE VIDO, ALFREDO, ASSOCS.
also ALFREDO DE VIDO
Columbia Hts., No. 222: 573, **585**
Community Church of Astoria, **736**
Royale (apts.), 393
Stuarts Rest., 396
Tra Cho boutique, 353

Willow St., No. 54: **593**
Word of Mouth catering, 371
DeVinne Press Bldg. (orig.), **154**
Devonshire, 619
DeWitt Clinton H.S., Bx., 524
DeWitt Clinton H.S., Manh., **225**
DeWitt Ref. Church, 92
DE WOLFE, ELSIE (Lady Mendl)
Colony Club, 194
E. 71st St. res., 369
"Washington Irving" House, 195
DE YOUNG & MOSKOWITZ
Carman Hall, Lehman College, 524
Fashion Inst. of Technology bldgs., 177
Spear & Co. (orig.), 213–14
Dezer, Michael, Classic Motors, 177
Dianne B. (boutique), 103
DIAPER, FREDERICK
Sailors' Snug Harbor Chapel, **814**, 815–16
see also DUDLEY & DIAPER
DICK, ADOLPH M.
Boulevard Gardens, 735
DICKERSON, WARREN C.
Clay Ave., Nos. 1038, 1040–1066,
1041–1067: 492
Longwood Historic District, 494
Morris H.S. Historic District, 492
DIEDERICH, HUNT, artist, 652
Diego-Beekman Houses, 485
Dietrich's, 538
DIETRICK, E. G. W.
St. Mark's Ave., No. 673: 671
DIFFENDALE & KUBEC
Arlington Terrace apts., 822
Prof. Bldg., Seaview Ave., 833
DiFIORE & GIACOBBE
Copper Flagg Estates, 842
Rustic Woods, 837
Dillon, Clarence, res. (orig.), 377
DILTHY, WILLIAM J.
Charles Broadway Rouss Annex, 98
Dime Savings Bank of NY, Bklyn., **570**
DINKELOO, JOHN, *see* ROCHE, DINKELOO &
ASSOCS. (KEVIN ROCHE JOHN
DINKELOO & ASSOCS.)
Di Roberti's Pasticceria, 167
Disk and Slab (Yang), 27
District School No. 3, SI (orig.), 836
District School No. 5, SI (orig.), 858
District 65 Bldg., 155
Ditmars, 730–31
Ditmars, William, res., 304
DITMARS, WILLIAM B.
Ref. Dutch Church of Greenpoint, 692, **693**
Sparrow Shoe Factory, 686
see also SCHICKEL & DITMARS
Ditmas Park, 700–701
Ditmas Park Historic District, 700
Divine, Father, 503
Divine Paternity Church, **325**
DIXON, ROBERT
Montgomery Pl., No. 30–34: 644
Dobson's (rest.), 295
Dodge, Marcellus Hartley, Fitness Ctr.,
Columbia Univ., 422
Dodge, (Mrs.) Marcellus Hartley, res., 345,
879
Dodge, Robert, res., 75
Dodge, William E.
"Greyston" res., **529**, 530
statue, 238
DODGE & MORRISON
Congregational Church of N. NY, 485
Milbank res., 358
Dodge family, res.
D'OENCH & SIMON
Cutter res., **606–607**
Le Boutillier Bros., 184
D'OENCH & YOST
Germania Life Insurance Co., 186
Doerschuck, Gustav., res., 680, **681**
"Dog of the Ilk," 137
Dollar Savings Bank (now Dollar Dry Dock
Bank), 524–25
Dolphin (bookstore), 879
DOMAN, JAMES
W. 21st St., Nos. 292 and 294: 714
Dominican Acad., 361
Dominick's Rest., Arthur Ave., Bx., 501
Dominick's Rest., Westchester Ave., Bx., 540
Donaghy Steak House, 528
Dongan Hall, SI Acad., 843–44
Dongan Hills/Concord, 841
Dongan St., No. 13: 819
DON-LINN CONSULTANT DESIGN CORP.
W. Bway., Nos. 430, 432, 434: 103

Donnell Library, NYPL, 270, 873
DORAN, JOHN
    St. Joseph's RC Church, **128**
Dornhage (apts.), 516
Dos Passos, John, 110
Dorilton (apts.), 306
Dorrence Brooks Sq., 449
double-decker buses, 872
DOUGHERTY, JOHN, builder
    Dean St., No. 245: 618
Douglas, Adelaide E., res., 218
Douglas, George, res., 786
Douglas Rd., Nos. 3, 93, and 205: 840
DOUGLASS, ALEXANDER, builder
    Bethune St., Nos. 19–29: 141
Douglaston, 786
Douglaston Club, 786
Douglaston Manor, 785, 786
Douglaston Manor Rest., 786
Dove Tavern, 394
Dow Jones & Co. Bldg., 46
Dowling, Robert W.,
    Parkchester, 539–**540**
Downing, Andrew Jackson, 336, 810
Downing Stadium, 475
Downstate Medical Ctr., 701–**702**
Down Town Assn., 36
Downtown Athletic Club, **9**
Downtown Manh. Heliport, 26
DOYLE, ALEXANDER, sculptor, 212
Drake, Joseph Rodman, 497
Drake Park, 497
D/R Design Research, 876
Dreiser, Theodore, 120, 309
Drexel, Burnham, Lambert, Inc., 49
Dreyfus, (Mr. and Mrs.) Louis A., 840
DREYFUSS, HENRY, designer, 246
Driggs Ave., 694
DRISCHLER, FRANK
    E. 69th St., No. 149: **365**
Drumgoole, Father John G., 858
Dry Dock #1, NY Naval Shipyard, 638
Duane Hotel, 218
Duane Park, 56–58
Duane St., **57**, 58, 72
Duarte, Juan Pablo, statue, 147
Dubinsky Student Ctr., Fashion Inst. of
    Technology, 177
DUBOIS, NATALIE
    Union Carbide Bldg., 246
Dubois, W. E. B., 451, 452
DUBOY, PAUL E.
    Ansonia Hotel, 308–**309**
    Soldiers' & Sailors' Monument, **303**
    see also GRAVES & DUBOY
DUBUFFET, JEAN, painter-sculptor, **37**
Duchesne Res. School, **385,** 386
DUCKWORTH, ISAAC F.
    Broome St., No. 467: 101
DUCKWORTH, JAMES F.
    Greene St., 96, **97**
    Leonard St., No. 73: **69**
DUDLEY, HENRY
    Church of the Ascension, 692
    see also WILLS & DUDLEY
DUDLEY & DIAPER
    St. James Church, 525
    see also DIAPER, FREDERICK
Dudley Memorial, LI College Hosp., 603
Dudok, Willem, 213
DU FAIS, JOHN
    6th Pct. (orig.), 76
    9th Pct. (orig.), **138**
Duff House, 536
Duffy, Father Francis P., 227, 231
Duffy Sq., 231
DUGGIN, CHARLES
    Pendleton res(s)., **811**
DUGGIN & CROSSMAN
    21 Club, 267
Duke, Benjamin N., res., 378, **379**
Duke, James B., res., 375
Duke, William S., barn, 532
Dukler Mugain Abraham synagogue, 91
Dunbar, Paul Laurence, 452
Dunbar Apts., 452
Duncan, Isadora, 322
DUNCAN, JOHN H.
    City Hall, 61
    E. 63rd St., No. 15: 348–49
    E. 70th St., No. 11: 366
    E. 84th St., No. 21: **380**–81
    11th Judicial District Court, 236–37
    Grant's Tomb, 427
    Knox Bldg., 239
    Lehman res., 270

Madison Ave., Nos. 1132 and 1134: **380**–81
Milbank res., 358
Soldiers' and Sailors' Memorial Arch, **650**
Wertheim res., 357
W. 76th St., Nos. 8–10: 325
Dunham, Mary D., res. (orig.), 361
DUNN, JOSEPH M.
    Octagon Tower, 475
DUNN, THOMAS
    Grand Concourse, No. 1855: 514
    Holy Trinity Church Rectory, 315
Dunolly Gardens (apts.), 746–47
Duplex (apts.), 406
Duryea, Christian, res., 721–22
Dutch House, Gov. Is., 470
Dutch Kills
    bridges, 898–99
DUVALL, SAM, owner-designer
    Ritz Café, 216
DUVEEN, ANITA, sculptor, 566
Dwight, John, res., 443
Dwight St., Nos. 9–19, 613
DWYER, JOHN E.
    Hylan res., 680
Dwyer Whse., 440
Dyckman House, 467
Dyker Heights, 703–706

E

Eagle Ave.
    Nos. 560–584: 487
    escarpment, 490
Eagle Fire Eng. Co. No. 13: 132
Eagle Whse. and Storage Co. (now apts.),
    597, **598**
Eakins, John S., res., 700
EAKINS, THOMAS, painter-sculptor, **650**
Ear Inn, 146
Earl Carroll's Theater, 235
Earlton studios, 308
East 1st St., 160
East 2nd St., No. 63: **161**
East 3rd St., Nos. 30–38 and 67: 162
East 4th St.
    No. 34: **153**–54
    No. 36: **153**–54
East 5th St., Bklyn., No. 1996: 710
East 6th St., 160, 163
East 7th St., 160
East 8th St., Nos. 4–26: 111
East 10th St.
    No. 7: **118,** 119
    No. 9: 119
    No. 110: 166
    Nos. 114–128: 166, **167**
East 11th St., 159
East 12th St.
    Nos. 35, 36, 37, 39, 42, and 43: 126
    No. 49: 157–58
    No. 201: 168
    No. 234: 168
East 16th St., Bklyn., 700
East 16th St., Manh., No. 9: 187
East 18th St., Nos. 326, 328, and 330: 202
East 22nd St.
    Nos. 134 and 150: 199
    Nos. 220 and 235: **203**
East 28th St., 201
East 29th St., No. 203: 201
East 31st St., No. 22: 194
East 35th St., Nos. 157 and 159: 219–20
East 37th St.
    Nos. 19 and 21: 218
    No. 130: 219
East 38th St., Nos. 125, 149, and 152: 219
East 39th St.
    No. 4: 239
    No. 144: 870
East 40th St.
    Nos. 113, 115, 143, and 152: 870
    No. 148: **219,** 870
East 49th St.
    No. 219: **261**
    No. 212: **260,** 261
    Nos. 303–309: 262
East 50th St., No. 245: 260
East 51st Street subway station, IRT, 247–48,
    249
East 52nd St., No. 301: 260
East 53rd St., Nos. 312 and 314: **258**
East 54th St. Recreation Ctr. and Pool, 259
East 55th St., Nos. 116, 120, 122, and 124:
    250
East 57th St., 284–86, 876
    No. 111: 251

HARRISON & ABRAMOVITZ (*cont.*)
  NY Aquarium, 711
  Philharmonic Hall, 292
  Rockefeller Univ. bldgs., 403
  Socony Mobil Bldg., 253
  Time & Life Bldg., 273
  see also ABRAMOVITZ, MAX;
    ABRAMOVITZ, HARRIS & KINGSLAND;
    HARRISON, ABRAMOVITZ & HARRIS
HARRISON & FOUILHOUX
  African Plains, Bx. Zoo, 505
  Hunter College, 363
  Rockefeller Apts., 220, 270
  see also FOUILHOUX, ANDRÉ; HOOD,
    GODLEY & FOUILHOUX
Harrison St., No. 53: 827, **830**
Harrison St. houses, 52
Harris Theater, 232
Harry's (rest./bar), 15
Harsenville, 307
Hartford (apts.), 310
Hartford, Huntington, 276
Hart Is., 476
HARTMAN, BERTRAM, mosaic designer, 349
Harvard Ave., Nos. 29 and 119: 810
Harvard Club, 241–42
Harvey, Charles, 50
HASENSTEIN, H.
  Barrow St., No. 15: 129
Hassam, Childe, painter, 460
Hastings (tile showroom), 198
HASTINGS, CHARLES
  Surgeon's House, 638–39
HASTINGS, THOMAS
  Carrère Memorial, 304
  Grand Army Plaza, Manh., 279–80, **281**
  see also CARRÈRE & HASTINGS
Hatch, Barbara Rutherford, res., 349–50
HATCH, STEPHEN D.
  A. A. Thompson & Co., 31
  Bond St., Nos. 1–5: 151, **152**
  Duane St., No. 165: **57**
  Duane St., No. 168: 58
  Fleming Smith Whse., 53, 54
  Manh. Savings Inst. Bldg., 151
  NY Life Insurance Bldg., 69, **70**
  NY Plaza, No. 3: **14**, 25
  U.S. Army Bldg., 862
HATFIELD, AUGUSTUS
  St. George Hotel, **590**–91
HATFIELD, ISAAC, carpenter/builder
  Gilsey House, **193**
  Hudson St., Nos. 510–518: 134
HATFIELD, O. P.
  Bway., No. 547: 94
HATFIELD, R. G., engineer
  Grand Central Depot, 243
HATTON, JOHN MATTHEWS
  Astoria Play Ctr. and Pool, 730
  Betsy Head Bathhouse, 720
HAUGAARD, WILLIAM E.
  Halloran General Hosp., U.S. Army, 838
  NYC Board of Transportation Bldg., 568
Haughwout Store, 94, **95**
Haupt Conservatory, NY Botanical Garden,
  506
HAUSER, JOHN
  E. 136th St., Nos. 415–425: **483**, 484
  Morris Ave. Historic District, 515
HAUSLE, MAX
  Bx. County Bldg., 510, 511
HAUSMAN & ROSENBERG
  Commonwealth Bldg., **446**
  Cryder House, 767
  Greenpoint Branch, BPL, 692
  Lincoln Sq. Synagogue, 295, **296**
  National Bank of North America, 264
  Rockwood Park Jewish Ctr., 792
Havemeyer, Frederick C., res., 546, 547
Havemeyer, Henry O., stable, **356**–57
Havemeyer & Elder's sugar refinery, 689, **690**
Havemeyer St., Nos. 56–64: 690
HAVILAND, JOHN
  Robertson res. (?), 814
Havoc, June, 222
"Hawkhurst" (orig.), 832
Hawley, Irad, res. (orig.), 125–26
Hawley Mansion (orig.), 684
Hawtree Basin Br., 898–99
HAYDEL & SHEPARD
  Fabbri res., 347
Hayden House (apts.), 329
Hayden Planetarium, 326
Hayes, Rutherford B., 197
HAYNARD, B., builder
  "Woodbrook," 812–13

Hazard, James, 682
Hazard, Robert, res., 825
HAZLETT, WILLIAM C.
  Ivy Court (apts.), 320
HAZZARD, ERSKINE & BLAGDON, 406
Healy's, Tom (rest.), 197
Hearn, George A., 125, 486
Hearns (dept. store), 486
Hearst, William Randolph, 237
Hearst Mag. Bldg., **237**
Hearth and Home Corp., 116
Heartland Village, 837–38
HEATH, JOHN
  All Saints' Church (?), 85
Heavenly Rest, Church of the, **384**
HEBALD, MILTON, sculptor, 789
HEBERT, MAURICE,
  Schwab, Charles M., res., 299
Heberton Ave., 810
Hebrew Educ. Soc. of Bklyn., 717
Hebrew Home for the Aged at Riverdale, 533
Hebrew Immigrant Aid Soc., 150, 154
Hebrew Infant Asylum, 522
Hebrew Inst. of LI, 892
Hebrew Technical School, 867
Hebrew Union College, 113, 151, 323
Hebron French-Speaking Seventh-Day
  Adventist Church, 671
Heckscher Bldg., 282
Heckscher Foundation, 391
Heckscher Playground, 337
Hecla Iron Works, 703
  subway kiosks, 155, **157**, 690
HEDMAN, AXEL
  Union St., Nos. 1361–1381: 674
HEDMARK, MARTIN G.
  Trinity Baptist Church, 392
Heenan, Frances "Peaches," 308
HEERY & HEERY
  Haffen Park Pool, 555
  Rivers Memorial Swimming Pool and
    Bathhouse, 502
  Van Cortlandt Pool, 536
  W. Brighton Pool, 817–18
THE HEIGHTS AND THE HARLEMS,
  415–58, 881–82
Heights Casino, **583**, 584
Heine, Heinrich, 510
HEINS & LA FARGE
  Astor Place subway station, 155
  Bliss res., 360, **361**
  Bowling Green subway station, 8
  Bx. Zoo, 504–506
  Cathedral of St. John the Divine, 418–19
  City Hall subway station, 62
  Columbus Circle subway station, 275–76
  E. 70th St., No. 17: 366
  Grace Church Clergy House, 157
  IRT subway, 621
  Poppenhausen Branch, QPL, 762–63
  Ref. Episc. Church of the Reconciliation,
    664
  72nd St. subway entrance, 307
  33rd St. subway station, 216
  Wall St. subway station, 21
  see also LA FARGE & MORRIS
HEJDUK, JOHN
  Cooper Union, 155–**156**
Helen Hayes Theater (former), 232, 870
Hellenic Eastern Orth. Church, 400
Hell Gate, 413, 475
Hell Gate Br., 414, 486, 731, 898–99
HELLMUTH, OBATA & KASSABAUM
  Asphalt Green Ctr., 414, **415**
  E. 61st St., No. 400: 393
Hell's Angels, 162
"Hell's Hundred Acres," 92
Hell's Kitchen, 207, 221, 226
HELMLE, FRANK J.
  Bklyn. Bureau of Fire Communications,
    654
  Nassau Trust Co., 685–86
  St. Gregory's RC Church, 673
HELMLE & CORBETT
  Bush Tower, 238
  see also CORBETT, HARVEY WILEY
HELMLE & HUBERTY
  Greenpoint Savings Bank, 692
  Hotel Bossert, 583
  Lullwater, **653**
  McGoldrick Park Pavilion, 695
  Montessori School, Bklyn., 642
  Prospect Park Boathouse, **653**
  Prospect Park Tennis House, 652
  St. Barbara's RC Church, **682**
  Williamsburg Trust Co., 686, **688**

HOWELL, HARRY T.
  Morris H.S. Historic District, 492
HOWELLS, JOHN MEAD
  Panhellenic Hotel, 257
  Pratt Inst. Library, 634
HOWELLS & HOOD
  Daily News Bldg., 254
  E. 84th St., No. 3: 380
  see also HOOD, RAYMOND
HOWELLS & STOKES
  E. 69th St., No. 33: 364–65
  Horace Mann School, 425
  Madison Sq. Presby. Church Mission
    House, 869
  St. John the Divine pulpit, 418
  St. Paul's Chapel, Columbia Univ., 421–22
  Univ. Settlement House, 89
  see also STOKES, ISAAC NEWTON PHELPS
Hows Bayou (rest.), 53
HOYT, BURNHAM, **426**
Hoyt, Charles, 617
Hoyt, John Sherman, res., 880
Hoyt St., **617**, 718
  IRT subway station, 570
Hub, The, Bx., 486, 488–89
Hubball Bldg., 398
Huber, Joseph, 349
HUBERT, PHILIP G., 172, 194
Hubert Home Club, 194
HUBERT, PIRSSON & CO., 172
  Chelsea Hotel, 172–**173**
  Croisic apt. hotel, 192
  E. 89th St., Nos. 146–156: **409**
Hudson, Charles I., carriage house, 398
Hudson, Henry, 803
Hudson & Manh. RR, 135
Hudson-Fulton Celebration (1609–1909), 23,
    529
Hudson Park, 131–32
Hudson River
  George Washington Br., 463, 464, 898–99
  Holland Tunnel, 53–54, 102, 898–99
  Lincoln Tunnel, 207, 211, 898–99
Hudson River Ctr., 211–12
Hudson River Night Line, 140
Hudson River RR, 169, 297
Hudson St., 55–56
  No. 55: 57
  No. 108: 55, **56**
  No. 135: 53, **54**
  Nos. 284 and 288: 146, **147**
  Nos. 473–477, 487–491, and 510–518: 134
Hudson Temple Cathedral, 719–20, **721**
Hudson Theater, 232
Hudson Towers (apts.), **45**
Hudson View East (apts.), 44
Hudson View Gardens (apts.), 466
Hudson View West (apts.), 45
Hughes, Charles Evans, 531, 787
HUGHES, CHARLES EVANS III
  Prettyman Gym, Horace Mann H.S., 535
  Titanic Memorial Lighthouse, 30
Hughes, Rev. John, 500
Hughes, Langston, 451
Huguenot, *see* Annadale/Huguenot
Huguenot Ref. Church, 859–60
Huguenot-Walloon Tercentenary, 860
Hulbert, Henry J., res., 644
Humboldt St., 694
  Nos. 492–494: 687–**688**
  Nos. 650 and 694: 695
HUME, WILLIAM H.
  Altman Dry Goods Store, 180
  H. C. F. Koch & Co., **445**
  Simpson Crawford store, 180
Hungarian Baptist Church, 405
Hungarian Pastry Shop, 420
Hungarian Workmen's Home, 407
HUNT, RICHARD HOWLAND
  Metropolitan Museum, 378–79
  Shepard res., **355**
  see also HUNT & HUNT
HUNT, RICHARD MORRIS
  Arsenal, 350
  Assn. for Relief of Respectable Indigent
    Females, 334
  Astor res., **344**, 352
  Beecher statue, **566**–67
  Carnegie Hall, **278**
  Jackson Sq. Library, 122
  Marquand res., 398
  Metropolitan Museum, 378–79
  Peck Slip, Nos. 21–23: 35
  Roosevelt Bldg., **95**, 96
  Statue of Liberty base, 468
  Trinity Church doors, 20

Vanderbilt Mausoleum, 844, **845**
Washington Sq. N., No. 2: 110
Hunt, Richard Morris, Memorial, 365
Hunt, Wilson, res., 52
HUNT & HUNT
  Blumenthal res., 873
  1st Pct., 26, **27**
  69th Rgt. Armory, **201**
  Vanderbilt res., 266–**267**
  see also HUNT, RICHARD HOWLAND
Hunter College, **363**–64
Hunter College Campus Schools, 388
Hunter College H.S., **363**
Hunter College Uptown, 523–24
Hunter College School of Social Work, 377
Hunter H.S., 388
Hunterfly Rd., 669
Hunters Point, 735, 739–42
Hunter's Point Ave. Br., 898–99
Hunters Point Historic District, 739
HUNTING, W. C., & J. C. JACOBSEN
  American Fine Arts Soc., **277**
HUNTINGTON, ANNA VAUGHN HYATT,
    sculptor, **303**–304
HUNTINGTON, CHARLES PRATT
  Church of Our Lady of Esperanza, 460
Huntington, Collis P., 541
  "Homestead," 546
Huntington Free Library, **541**
Hunt Lane, No. 31: 843
Hunts Point, 496–97, 508
Hunts Pt. Branch, NYPL, 496
Hunts Pt. Cooperative Meat Market, 497
Hunts Pt. Multi-Service Ctr., 488
Hupfel Brewery, Bx., 490
Hupfel Brewing Corp., Manh., 220
HURLEY & FARINELLA
  Ansonia Court (apts.), 649
  Beekman St., No. 12: 41
  Le Gendarme (apts.), **138**
Hurok, Sol, 309
HURRY, WILLIAM
  John St. United Meth. Church, 38
Hurst, Fannie, 322
Hurtig & Seaman Theatre, 446
Hutchinson River Pkwy., 546
Hutchinson River Pkwy. Ext. Br., 898–99
Huttman, Behrend H., res., 632
Hutton, E. F., Bldg., 205, 256, 267
HUTTON, WILLIAM R., engineer
  Washington Br., 465, 518, 898–99
Huxley, Thomas H., 531
Huxtable, Ada Louise, 14, 30, 289
HUXTABLE, L. GARTH, designer, 248
Huyler, Peter, 132
Hyde, William, 133
Hylan, John F., 507, 680, 893
Hylan Blvd., 829

I

IBM Bldg., 282, **283**, 875
IBM Gallery, 282
IBM Showroom (former), 875
IBM Systems Product Div. (former), 663
Ichabod's (rest./bar), 318
Iconography of Manhattan Island (Stokes), 89
Ideogram (Rosati), 48
Idlewild Airport, *see* Kennedy, John F., Intl.
    Airport
IFILL & JOHNSON
  Morris Community Ctr., 436
  Mt. Morris Swimming Pool, 442
IFILL JOHNSON HANCHARD
  Harlem State Office Bldg., **445**
  St. Martin's Tower, 333, **334**
Iglesia Adventista del Septimo Dia, 457
Iglesia Bautista Calvario, 689
Iglesia Católica Guadalupe, 183
Iglesia de Dios, 164
Iglesia de Dios Mission Board, 782
Iglesia Luterana Sion, 457
Iglesia Metodista, 748
Iglesia Metodista Unida de Sur Trés, 689,
    690
Iglesia Pentecostal Misionera, 688
Ike, Reverend, 464
Il Bufalo (rest.), 129
Il Fornaio (rest.), 78
ILGWU Cooperative Village (apts.), 89
ILLAVA, KARL, sculptor, **357**
"I Love You Kathy" (apts.), 200
IMAS, RODOLFO
  Levana Rest., 295
Immaculate Conception, Cathedral of the
    (unbuilt), Bklyn., 629

Kingsborough Community College, CUNY, 711
Kingsbridge, 528
Kingsbridge Armory, **520, 524**
Kingsbridge Heights, 522–24
Kingsbridge Heights Community Ctr., 523
Kingsbridge Terrace, No. 2744: 523
Kingsbridge Veterans Hosp., 522
King's College, *see* Columbia College
Kings County, 562–64
Kings County Fire Insurance Soc., 889
Kings County Hosp., 702
Kings County Savings Bank, 686
King's Handbooks and *King's Views of New York City*, 328
Kingsland, Ambrose C., 690
Kingsland Homestead, 768
Kingsley (apts.), **396**
Kingsley, William C., 626, 703
King Solomon Grand Lodge, A.F. & A.M., 445–46
King St.,
  Nos. 1–49 and 16–54: 145
KINNEY, BELLE, sculptor, 549
kiosks
  Atlantic Ave. subway station, 621
  Bryant Park, 237
  IRT subway, 690
  Lexington and 51st St. subway station, 249
  NY Public Library, 240
Kips Bay, 203–206
Kips Bay Boys Club, 260
Kips Bay Branch, NYPL, 201
Kips Bay Brewing Co., 220
Kips Bay Plaza, 92, **205**–206
KIRBY, J. MASON
  Decatur St., No. 587–611: 667–68
KIRBY, PETIT & GREEN
  American Bank Note Co., 20, 496
  Buchanan res., 586
  see also PETIT, JOHN; PETIT & GREEN
KIRCHMAN, MILTON F.
  23rd Pct., **454**
  68th Pct., 616–17
KIRCHOFF & ROSE
  Palace Theater, 233–34
KISSELEWSKI, JOSEPH, sculptor, 510
Kissena II Apts., 771, **772**
Kissinger, Henry, 247
Kitchen performance space, 101, 182
Kitt, Eartha, 411
Klapper, Paul, 774
KLEIN, MILTON
  French & Co., **352**, 353
KLEIN, STANLEY H.
  Temple Beth Sholom, 772
Kleinert, I. B., Rubber Co., **765**
Kleine Konditorei (rest.), 408
Klein's, S., On the Square (dept. store), 158, 185, 868, **869**
KLEIST, JOHN E.
  Queens General Hosp., 774
Klerk, Michel de, 88
KLIMENT, R. M., & FRANCES HALSBAND
  Columbia Univ. Computer Science Bldg., 422–23
  NY Mercantile Exchange, 55, **56**
  Town School, 400
KLING, VINCENT G., & ASSOCS.
  Altschul Hall, Barnard College, 423, **424**
Klingenstein Pavilion, Mt. Sinai Medical Ctr., 390
KLOSTER, ANTON
  St. Anselm's Church, **488**
Knapp, Joseph F., res., 888
KNEBEL, HERMAN C.
  Sun Yat-sen Hall, St. John's Univ., 773–74
Knesseth Israel synagogue, 794
Knickerbocker Club, Manh., 345, 346
Knickerbocker Field Club, Bklyn., 698
Knickerbocker Hotel, 228–29
Knickerbocker Laundry Co., 743
Knickerbocker Village (apts.), 75
Knight, Gladys, 446
Knights of Columbus Columbia Hall, 814–15
Knoedler Gallery, E. 70th St., 366
Knoedler Gallery, Fifth Ave., 872, **873**
Knoll Intl. Design Ctr., 100
KNOLL PLANNING UNIT, designers, 275
KNOWLES, HARRY P.
  Mecca Temple, 279
KNOWLES, WILLIAM W.
  U.S. P.O. Flushing, 770, **771**
KNOX, ROD
  Harlem on the Hudson Esplanade, 428
Knox Hat Bldg., 239, 673
Knox Hat Factory, 673

Knox Presby. Church, 397
KOCH, CARL, & ASSOCS.
  Ocean Village (apts.), 795
Koch, H. C. F., & Co., **445**
KOEHLER, V. HUGO
  Lyric Theater, 233
KOENIG, FRITZ, sculptor, 48
KOGELNIK, KIKI, designer, 111
KOHN, ESTELLE RUMBOLD, sculptor, 321
KOHN, ROBERT D.
  Ethical Culture School, **321**
  Fieldston Schools, 534
  Macy's, 207–208
  NY Evening Post Bldg., **59**
  NY Soc. for Ethical Culture, 321
  Riverside-West 105th St. Historic District, 305
  Spero Bldg., 188
  Temple Emanu-El, 352
  see also BUTLER & KOHN
KOHN PEDERSEN FOX ASSOCS.
  American Broadcasting Co. studios, 293–**294**, 296
  Capital Cities/ABC Inc. HQ, 294
  E. 57th St., No. 135: **251**, 252
  E. 70th St., No. 180: **396**
  Heron Tower (offices), **250**
  Hoboken-Manhattan ferry, 47
  Home Box Office bldg., 238
  Home Insurance Group plaza, 37
  "Ninth Ave. Tower" and plaza, 212
  Rizzoli/Coty office bldg., 271–72
  Shearson Lehman Plaza (offices), 52–**53**
  WABC Channel 7 & Bldg., 294
KOKKINS & LYONS
  St. Gerasimos Greek Orth. Church, 335
Kolff, Cornelius G., 840
Kol Israel synagogue, 715
Kol Israel Anshe Poland Congregation (orig.), 82
Kolle, Frederic S., res., **699**
KONDYLIS, COSTAS
  also PHILIP BIRNBAUM & ASSOCS.
  Battery Place Apts., 43
  Bromley (apts.), **315**
  Horizon (apts.), 220
  Le Chambord (apts.), 397
  Manh. Plaza (apts.), 206
  Promenade (apts.), 400
KONTI, ISIDORE, sculptor, 276
KORBER, ALBERT
  Clinton Ave., No. 274: 632
Korean Christian Church of SI, 837
Korean Commercial Bank of NY, 770
KORN, LOUIS
  Fifth Ave., No. 91: 187
  Progress Club, Walden School, 328
  Wooster St., Nos. 141–145: 100
Korvette's (discount store), 212, 264
Kosciusko Br., 898–99
Kosciuszko Foundation, **352**, 353
KOUZMANOFF, ALEXANDER, & ASSOCS.
  Avery Hall, Columbia Univ., 422
Krakauer Bros. Piano Co., 483
KRAMER, GEORGE W.
  Willis Ave., Meth. Episc. Church, 485
Kramer, Raymond C., res., 372
KRAMER & KRAMER
  Argosy Print and Book Store, 284
KRAPP, HERBERT J.
  Boulevard Theater, 746–47
  Bway. theaters, 232, 233
KRAUS, JAROS
  Henry Hudson Pkwy., 463
Kraus Co., 735
Kreischer, Balthazar, 854
Kreischer, B., & Sons, workers' housing, 855
Kreischer, Edward, 855
Kreischer, Charles C., res., **855**
Kreischer School, P.S. 4, SI., 854
Kreischerville, 854
Kress Bldg. (former), 870–71
KRETSCHMANN, SERGIO, muralist, 140
Kreutzer-DeGroot-Pelton res., 817
KREYMBORG, CHARLES
  Grand Concourse, No. 2615: 515
  Melrose Courts (apt.), 491
  Sherman Ave., No. 1210: 511
KROEGER, KEITH, ASSOCS.
  Strain res., 532, **533**
Kroeger Piano Co., 483
KROEHL, JULIUS, engineer
  Mt. Morris fire watchtower, 441, **442**
KROOP, SHELLY
  Andrews Ave., No. 1160: 518
  Model Cities site 402: 490
Kuan Sing Dumpling House, 77

Kuhn, Fritz, 405
KÜHNE, PAUL
  Edgewater Village Hall, 824
KUHN, LOEB & CO., 359
Kurtz, J., & Sons, 783
KURZER & KOHL
  Goebel & Co., 133
KUSSKE, CHRISTOPHER, landscape architect
  DeLury Plaza, 42
Kuwait Mission to the UN, 256
KYLE, JOHN M., engineer
  Lincoln Tunnel, 898–99

L

LAANES, CARL, designer, **175**
La Bau, L. B., res. (orig.), 835
Labor Lyceum, 162
Labor Temple of the Workmen's Home Assn.,
  407
Lacombe Iron Works Corp., 539
La Cupole, (rest.), 216
Ladd, Dr. William Sargent, 534
Ladder Companies, NYC Fire Dept.
  No. 1 Manh., 71–72
  No. 4 Manh., 234
  No. 15 Manh., 359
  No. 15 Manh. (former), 863
  No. 18 Manh., **87**
  No. 30 Manh., 448
  No. 31 Bx., 493
  No. 43 Manh., **454**
  No. 55 Bx., 546
  No. 102 Bklyn., 662
  No. 115 Queens, 739, **740**
  No. 122 Bklyn., 649
  No. 176 Bklyn, 668
Ladd Rd., 532
Ladies Mile, 96, 157, 187–89
Ladies' Parlor, 608
Ladies Pavilion, Central Park, 338
Lady Chapel, Church of the Transfiguration,
  192
Lady Chapel, St. Patrick's Cathedral, 266
"Lady Moody House," 708
LA FARGE, JOHN, painter, 126
  Church of the Ascension, 119
  Church of the Incarnation, 217
  Judson Memorial Baptist Church, 114
  St. Paul the Apostle Church, 225
LA FARGE & MORRIS
  Architects Bldg., 219, 870
  St. John the Divine Deaconesses' House,
    418–19
  see also HEINS & LA FARGE; MORRIS,
    BENJAMIN WISTAR
Lafayette (Bartholdi), 185
Lafayette Ave., Bklyn., Nos. 677, 678, and
  679: 662–63
Lafayette Ave., SI, Nos. 270 and 280: 812
Lafayette Ave. Presby. Church, Bklyn., 625
Lafayette St., Manh., 147–50, 154–55
  No. 2: 65
  Nos. 376–380: **152**
  Nos. 400, 401, and 409: 154
  Nos. 440 and 442: 155
Lafayette Theater, 447–48
LAFEVER, MINARD
  Bartow-Pell Mansion (?), 549
  Church of the Holy Apostles, 177
  Church of the Saviour, C. 588, **589**
  Holy Trinity Prot. Episc. Church, 582, **583**
  Packer Collegiate Inst., 580
  Penny Br., 581
  Sailors' Snug Harbor, 815–16
  Strong Pl. Baptist Church and Chapel, 604
La Goulue (rest.), 366
LaGrange Terrace, 147, **154**–55
LaGuardia, Fiorello, 211, 279, 469, 501, 527,
  764
LaGuardia, Fiorello H., H.S., 296–97
LaGuardia Airport, 728, **745**–46
LaGuardia Community College, CUNY, 738
Laing, Morgan, Stores (orig.), 863
Lake-Tysen House, 848
Lalance & Grosjean (factory), 778
LALIQUE, RENÉ, glassmaker, 271–72, **273**
La Maison Japonaise (rest.), 219
LAMANTIA, JAMES
  Belvedere Castle, 338, **339**
  Central Park Dairy, 339
  World Trade Center concourse, **49**
"La Marqueta" (enclosed market), 456
LAMB, THOMAS W.
  Audubon Theater and Ballroom, 462
  Bway. theaters, 232, 233
  Loew's 175th St. Theater, 463–**464**

Loew's Pitkin Theater, 719–20, **721**
Pythian Temple, 295, **297**
Regent Theatre, 439
RKO 81st St. Theatre, 314
LAMB & RICH
  Amsterdam Ave., Nos. 301–309: 309
  Astral Apts., 692–**693**
  Babbott res., 647
  Barnard College bldgs., 423–24
  Berkeley Prep. School, 241
  Harlem Club, **443**
  Harlem Free Library, 443
  Henderson Pl., 413
  La Rochelle (apts.), 310
  Mechanics & Traders Bank, 94
  Morris (apts.), **443**
  Pratt Inst., Main Bldg., 634, **635**
  Tangeman res., 640
  Washington Hts., Baptist Church, 433
  West End Ave., Nos. 341–357: 299
  West End-Collegiate Historic District, 299
  W. 74th St., Nos. 161–169: 309
  W. 76th St., No. 301: 299
  W. 77th St., Nos. 302–306, 299
LAMB & WHEELER
  Cutting res., 358
  E. 68th St., Nos. 8 and 10: 359–60
  Milbank res., 358
Lambert, John, 147
Lambert, Phyllis, 248
Lambert, Sarah R., res., 52
LAMBERT, WILLIAM A.
  Derech Emunah synagogue, 796
Lambert Houses, Shopping Plaza, and
  Parking Garage, 503, **505**
Lambert's Pasta & Cheese, 370
Lambs Club, 229
Lambs Theater, 229
Lamont, Thomas W., res., **364,** 367
Lancaster (apts.), 119
Lancaster (Harlem), 437
land area, NYC, 896
Landing Cafe, 823
Landis Ave., No. 75: 832
Landmarks Preservation Commission, NYC,
  10, 13, 30, 110, 247, 336, 346, 573, 625,
  842, 871
Landmarks Preservation Law, 573, 592
Landmark Tavern, Manh., 223
Landmark Tavern Bldg., Queens, 781
Land's End 1 (apts.), 85
LANG, JEREMY P.
  Banca Commerciale Italiana, 15
Langdon Bldg., 70
Langham (apts.), 324
Langley, Samuel P., 543
LANGMANN, OTTO F., sculptor, 338
LANGSTON, FREDERICK B.
  Carroll St., No. 862: 642
LANGSTON & DAHLANDER
  Clinton Ave., No. 487: **630**
Lanier, James F. D., res., 217
Lanier, Sidney, 617
LANSBURGH, G. ALBERT
  Martin Beck Theater, 233
LAPIDUS, ALAN, ASSOCS.
  Crowne Plaza Hotel, 234
  W. 61st St., No. 43: 289–90
LAPIDUS, MORRIS, & ASSOCS.
  also MORRIS LAPIDUS
  Americana Hotel, 235
  Bedford-Stuyvesant Community Pool, 662
  Cadman Plaza North (apts. and town
    houses), 595
  E. 72nd St., No. 54: 879
LA PIERRE, LITCHFIELD & PARTNERS
  Bankers Federal Savings Bank, 717
  Sedgwick Hall, NYU, 522
La Réserve (rest.), 265
La Résidence (apts.), 378
La Rochelle (apts.), 310
LARSEN-JUSTER
  Minetta Lane Theatre, 115
La Salle St., 428
Lasdon, Jacob S., House, Cornell Medical
  College, 403
Lasdon, William and Mildred, Biomedical
  Research Ctr., 404
Lasker Pool-Rink, Central Park, 337, 340
Last Wound-Up (toy store), 311
Latham Lithography Co., 743
LaTourette, David, res., 846–47
LaTourette Clubhouse, 846–47
LaTourette Park, 837
Latter-Day Saints, Church of Jesus Christ of,
  Lincoln Sq., 293
Latter-Day Saints Chapel, Bklyn. (orig.), 660

956   Index

MacCracken Hall, NYU/Bx. Community
College, 521
MacDONALD, WILSON, sculptor, 339
MacDonough St., 657
MacDougal Alley, **109**
MacDougal St., 115
No. 24: **144**, 145
Nos. 43–51: 145
Nos. 127–131 and 130–132: **115**
**MacDougal-Sullivan Gardens Historic
District,** 116
MacFADYEN & KNOWLES
Newhouse Pavilion, Manh. School of
Music, 426
see also KALLMAN, McKINNELL &
KNOWLES
MacGREGOR, A. S.
Jamaica Register Bldg., 783
MACHLOUZARIDES, COSTAS
Calhoun School Learning Ctr., 301
Church of the Crucifixion, 434
Refuge Temple, 440
MACKENZIE, JAMES C., JR.
Harlem Branch, YMCA, 449
Mackle, Oakley & Jennison (grocers), 33
Macklowe, Harry, developer, 278
Macmillan Co. Bldg., 125
MacMONNIES, FREDERICK, sculptor, 118
Civic Virtue, **757**, 759
Grand Army Plaza eagles, 650
Nathan Hale, 61
NY Public Library fountain, 239–**240**
St. Paul the Apostle Church, 225
Soldiers' and Sailors' Memorial Arch, **650**
Stranahan statue, 651
Washington Arch winged figures, 110, **111**
MacNEIL, HERMAN A., sculptor, 110
Macomb, Robert, 517
Macombs Dam Br., 517, 898–99
Macombs Dam Park, 517
Macon St., 657
Nos. 64 and 68: 665
Macready, William, 155
Macy, Josiah, & Son, 33
Macy, R. H., 184
Macy's
Dry Goods Store, 183–84
Manh., 207
Queens, 751–52
Madeline Ct., 704
MADIGAN/HYLAND, engineers
Wards Is. Br., 898–99
Madison Ave.
No. 121: 194
Nos. 527 and 535: 270
No. 625: 282, **283**
No. 650: 283
No. 667: 346
Nos. 964 and 980: 373
No. 1128: **380**
Nos. 1132 and 1134: **380**–81
No. 1261: 384
No. 1321: 387
Madison Ave. Baptist Church Parish House,
194
Madison Ave. Br., 898–99
Madison Ave. Presby. Church, 372
Madison Sq., 172, 184, 190–91
see also **Four Squares**
Madison Sq. Boys & Girls Club, 206
Madison Sq. Garden, first and second, 192,
234
Madison Sq. Garden Ctr., third, 209
Madison Sq. Park, 190
Madison Sq. Presby. Church Mission House,
869
Madison Sq. Station, U.S.P.O., 199–200
Maestro Café, 293
Maggie Walker School, P.S. 390 Bklyn., 673
Magickal Childe (shop), 180
MAGINNIS & WALSH
Carmelite Monastery, 518
Regis H.S., 380
Magnolia grandiflora (tree), Bklyn., 662–63
Magnolia grandiflora (trees), Queens, 764
Magnolia Tree Earth Ctr., Bklyn., 662–63
MAGONIGLE, H. VAN BUREN
Elks Lodge No. 22: 624
Firemen's Memorial, 304
Maine Memorial, 275
MAGRIS, ROBERT
Mezzaluna (rest.), 399
Mahoney Hall, City College, 431
Maiden Lane
No. 33: **38**
No. 90: 37

Maimonides Inst., 795
Maine Memorial, 275
Main St., Roosevelt Is., 472
Main St., SI, Nos. 104 and 127: 856
Main St. Tower, Queens, 770
Mairr, William H., res., 637
Maison Française, La, 272, 274
MAITLAND, STRAUSS & BEHR
Tower and Home Bldgs. and Workingmen's
Cottages, **603**–604
Majestic Apts., 324
Majestic Theater, 233
Major Ave., No. 212: 832
Major Deegan Expressway, 518
Malba, 765–66
Malcolm Brewery, 661
Malcolm Shabazz Mosque No. 7: 440
Malcolm X, 462
MALHOTRA, AVINASH K.
Archives (mixed use), **135**
Bleecker Court (apts.), 150
West Coast (apts.), 140
W. 53rd St., No. 410: 224
Mali, William W. T., res., 521
MALKIN, ROBERT, landscape architect
P.S. 114, Bklyn., playground, 717
Mall, The, Central Park, 338–39
Mallon, Mary ("Typhoid Mary"), 476
Maltz, B. M., developer, 571
Maltz Bldg., LIU, 571
Mama Leah's Blintzeria, Ltd. (rest.), 400
Man, Albon Platt, 760, 778
Man, Alrick Hubbell, 760
MANCA, ALBINO, sculptor, **8**
Mandarin Inn, Mott St., 76–77
Mandarin Inn, Pell St., 76–77
MANDEL, HERBERT L.
Harbor View Terrace (apts.), 224
Manee, Abraham, res., 859
Manee-Seguine Homestead, 859
Manganaro's Grosseria, 211
MANGIN, JOSEPH
City Hall, 61, **62**
Old St. Patrick's Cathedral, 79
Manhasset (apts.), 320
MANHATTAN, 2–476, 480, 862–82
bridges, 898–99
land area, 896
population (1790–1984), 896–97
tunnels, 898–99
Manhattan, E. 86th St. (apts.), **408**
Manhattan, W. 52nd St. (apts. and offices),
235
Manhattan and Brighton Beaches, Bklyn.,
710–11
Manhattan Ave., Bklyn., No. 752, sidewalk
clock, 694
Manhattan Ave., Manh., 334
Manh. Brewing Co., 102
Manh. Br., 75, 656, 898–99
Manh. Br. Arch and Colonnade, 75
Manh. Ctr., 210
Manh. Children's Treatment Ctr., 476
Manh. Church of Christ, **377**
Manh. Church of the Nazarene, 229
Manh. Club, 868–69
Manh. College, 427
Manh. Community College, CUNY, 51
Manh. Community Rehab. Ctr., 221
Manh. Country School, 389
Manh. Elevated Railway, 400
Manh. House (apts.), **394**
Manh. Life Insurance Bldg., 278–79
Manh. Music Hall, 232
Manh. 1 and 2 (movie theaters), 285
Manh. Opera House, 210
Manh. Place and plaza (apts.), 206
Manh. Plaza (apts.), 222
Manh. Psychiatric Ctr. Rehab. Bldg., 476
Manh. Railway Co.
Cathedral Pkwy. substation, 881–82
Division St. substation, 82–83
99th St. yard, 453
Manh. Refrigeration Co., 140
Manh. Savings Bank, 75, 76
Manh. Savings Inst. Bldg., 151
Manhattan Schist, 900
Manh. School of Music, 426, 455
Manh. State Hosp., 476
Manh. St., 428
Manhattantown scandal (1957), 330
Manh. Trade School for Girls, 199
Manh. Traffic Unit B, 212
Manhattan Transfer (Dos Passos), 110
Manhattan Valley, 334–36
Manh. Valley Town Houses, **335**

MEADOWS, ROBERT E.
  Ctr. for Bldg. Conservation, 35
  RKO Keith's Flushing Theater, 770
Meat market, wholesale, 140
Mecca Temple (Masonic), 279
Mechanics and Traders Bank, Bklyn., 692
Mechanics and Traders Bank, Manh., 94–95
Mechanics and Tradesmen, General Soc. of,
  bldg., 241
Mechanics of the Western Hemisphere,
  Independent United Order of, 657, **660**
Medgar Evers Comm. College, CUNY, **628**
Mediator, Church of the (Baptist), 202
Mediator, Church of the (Episc.), 528
Medical Soc. of the County of Kings, 669
MEGNIN, EUGENE G.
  Litvak res. and office, **858**
MEIER, RICHARD, & ASSOCS.
  also RICHARD MEIER
  Bx. Developmental Ctr., **544**
  Simon Reading Rm., Guggenheim Museum,
  382
  Sona the Golden One, 873, **874**
  Twin Parks projects, **502**, 503
  Westbeth (apts.), **139**
Melish, John Howard, 582
MELLEN, NICHOLAS CLARK
  Berwind res., 350
Mellon, Paul, res. and garage, 367, **368**
Melrose, 486–90
Melrose Courts (apts.), 491
MELTZER, MARVIN H.
  Enclave, 260
  W. 81st St., No. 100: 312, **313**
Melville, Herman, 9, 105, 140
MELVIN, WALTER B.
  Prince St., No. 130: 100
MELZER, ROMAN
  Golden Theater, 233
Memorial Baptist Church, 440
Memorial Hall, Pratt Inst., 633, 634
Memorial Hosp. for Women and Children,
  672
Memorial Presby. Church and Chapel, 645
Memorial Sloane-Kettering Cancer Ctr.,
  403–404
Memphis Downtown (apts.), 138
Memphis Uptown (apts.), 391–**392**
MEND (Massive Economic Neighborhood
  Development), **455**
Mendl, Lady, see DE WOLFE, ELSIE
Mengoni, Giuseppe, 282
Men's House of Detention, 66
Mercantile Library Bldg., 155
Mercedes-Benz showroom, 250
Mercer St., 96, 98–99
Mercer St. Res. Hall, NYU, **113**–14
Merchants Bank, 188
Merchants' Exchange, 16–**17**
Meredith, Dr., 665
Mergene Science and Communications Ctr.,
  Wagner College, 839
Meridies (rest.), 129
Merkin Concert Hall, 294, **295**
Merrill, Charles E., Hall, NYU, 22, **23**
Merrill Lynch Plaza, 39
Merrill Lynch Realty, 776
Merrill Lynch World HQ, 46, 47
MERRITT, MORTIMER C.
  O'Neill Dry Goods Store, **179**
  Wooster St., Nos. 28–30: 100
MERRY, CHARLES
  Ladies' Parlor, 608
MERSEREAU, WILLIAM
  Fraunces Tavern, 14
  St. Andrew's Episc. Church, **848**
MERTIN, ADOLPH
  Volunteer Hosp., 30
MERZ, JOSEPH AND MARY
  Joralemon St., No. 29–75: 577
  Willow Pl., 573
  Willow Pl., Nos. 40, 44, and 48: 578–**579**
Meserole St., Nos. 174 and 178: 687
Messiah, Church of the, 628
Messiah and Incarnation, Church of the, 885
Messiah Home for Children, 518
Metcalf, Tristram W., Hall, LIU, 571
Methodist Book Concern, 188
Methodist Third Church of Christ, 446
Metro Communications Ctr., 76
Metro North Plaza/Riverview Apts., 453–**454**
Metropolis Project, **225**
Metropolitan Ave. Br., 898–99
Metropolitan Baptist Church, **447**
Metropolitan Club, 345
Metropolitan Community Meth. Church, 444

Metropolitan Correction Ctr., 64, **66**
Metropolitan Hosp., 475
Metropolitan Life Insurance Co. Ditmars
  apts., 731
  Main Bldg., Tower, and North Bldg.,
  Madison Ave., 190, **191**
  Parkchester, 537, 540
  Stuyvesant Town, 202
Metropolitan Lumber & Mill Works, 102
Metropolitan Museum of Art, 378–**379**
  Assay Office facade, 19
  Cloisters, 463, 466–**467**
  Fifth Ave. entrance, 95
Metropolitan Museum Historic District, 375
Metropolitan Museum Vicinity, 375–81
Metropolitan Opera House (former), 226
Metropolitan Opera House, Lincoln Ctr., 291
  warehouse, 429
Metropolitan Railway Co., 102, 453
Metropolitan Savings Bank, 165
Metropolitan Tower, 278
Metrotech (proposed), 572
Metro Theater, 320
Metzger Pavilion, Mt. Sinai Medical Ctr., 390
METTAM, CHARLES
  Bway., No. 537: 94
  Greene St., No. 100: 98
Meucci, Antonio, 828
Meyer, André and Bella, Physics Hall, NYU,
  112, 113
Meyer, Cord, 745
MEYER, HENRY C., JR.
  Parkchester, 539–**540**
Meyer, Lewis Henry, estate, 831
MEYERS, CHARLES B., ASSOCS.
  also CHARLES B. MEYERS
  Bellevue Psychiatric Hosp., 204
  Gouverneur Hosp., 84
  Lebanon Hosp., 512
  NYC Criminal Courts Bldg. and Men's
  House of Detention, 66
  NYC Dept. of Health Bldg., **66**
  Ohab Zedek synagogue, 331
  Rodeph Sholom synagogue, 327
  Yeshiva Univ., 465
Meyers' Hotel, 35
Mezzaluna (rest.), 399
Middagh St., 594
  No. 24: 573, 580, 594
  No. 56: 594
Middleburg, 744–45
Middle Collegiate Church, 163
Middle Dutch Ref. Church, 604–605
MIDDLETON, EDWARD L.
  Kayton & Co. (stable), 398
Middletown Plaza (apts.), **547**, 548
Middle Village, 757–58
Midland Beach, 833
Midtown Hwy. Br., 898–99
MIDTOWN MANHATTAN, 169–286,
  867–76
Midtown North Police Pct. House, 236
Midtown South Police Pct. House, 210
Midtown Theatre (orig.), 320
Midwood, 696, 714–15
MIES VAN DER ROHE, LUDWIG, 87, 260
  Seagram Bldg., 248, **249**
MIGNONE COCO & SMITH
  Holy Child Church, 850
Milan (apts.), 178, **179**
Milan House (apts.), 359
Milan Labs., 79
Milan's (rest.), 408
Milbank, Jeremiah, res., 358
milestones, 436
Military Ocean Terminal, see Bklyn. Army
  Terminal
Mill, The, at Burlington House, 875
Millay, Edna St. Vincent, 105, 132
Mill Basin, **714**
Mill Basin Branch, BPL, 716
Mill Basin Br., 898–99
MILLER, ALGERNON, sculptor, 882
Miller, (Mr. and Mrs.) Andrew J., res., 375
Miller, Arthur, 172
Miller, Ebenezer, res., 52
MILLER, E. C.
  Central Park Br. No. 28: 340
MILLER, GEORGE G.
  Levitt House Development, 767
Miller, Glenn, 209
Miller, I., Bldg., 231
Miller, I., Shoe Salon, 282
Miller, James Ely, 850
Miller, William Starr, res., 381
Miller Elevated Highway, 866

Oakland Pl., No. 730, 501–502
"Oaklawn," 531
Oakley, Annie, 804
Oakwood, 849–50
Obelisk, Central Park, 338
Obelisk for Peace (Marantz), 215
Obermeyer & Liebmann Brewery, 676
O'BRIEN, THOMAS E.
    40th Pct., 483–84
Ocean Ave., No. 1010: 701
Ocean Ave. Br., 898–99
Ocean Hill I.S. 55, Bklyn., **674**
Oceanic Hook & Ladder Co. (volunteer),
    836–37
Ocean Pkwy., 702
Ocean Reef Grille (rest.), 31
Ocean Towers (apts.), 714
Ocean View Condominiums, 820
Ocean View Memorial Park Gatehouse, **851,**
    852
Ocean Village (apts.), 795
Ochs, Adolph, 226
Ochs, Ernst, 676
O'CONNOR, ANDREW, sculptor, 6
O'CONNOR, CAROL DYKMAN
    Church of St. Edward altar, 626–27
O'Connor, Johnson, Research Foundation,
    347
O'CONNOR, LAWRENCE J.
    Holy Cross School, 227
    St. Agnes Church., 253
O'CONNOR & KILHAM
    General Theological Seminary, 174
    Lehman Hall/Wollman Library, Barnard
        College, 423–24
    see also MORRIS & O'CONNOR
Octagon bldg., Queens, 765
Octagon Park (proposed) and Tower,
    Roosevelt Is., 475
Odd Fellows Hall, 78
Odeon Rest., 58
O'DONNELL, JAMES
    Dodge res., 75
O'DONOVAN, WILLIAM, sculptor, **650**
O'Dwyer, Mayor William, 649
Offerman, Henry, res., **636,** 637
Offerman Bldg., 570
Officers Club, Ft. Totten, 774, **775**
Officers Club, Gov. Is., 470
OGDEN, A. B., & SON
    piano factories, 483
O'GORMAN, WILLIAM
    E. 140th St., Nos. 403–445 and 408–450:
        484
Ohab Zedek synagogue, W. 95th St., 331
Ohab Zedek synagogue, Norfolk St. (orig.), **90**
OHM, PHILIP H.
    First Ave. Estate (apts.), 393
    Junior League Hotel, 401–**402**
    York Ave. Estate (apts.), 401
Ohrbach's Rego Park (dept. store), 752
O'Keeffe, Michael, 204
Olcott, Dr. Charles A., res., 888
Old Calvary Cemetery Gatehouse and Chapel,
    742
Old Country Rd., 784
Old First Ref. Church, 643
Old Fulton St., Bklyn., 597
    No. 8: 597–98
Old Germania Hts., 755
Old New Dorp Moravian Church, 844
Old Print Shop, 201
Old St. Patrick's Cathedral, Rectory, Chapel,
    Convent, and Girls' School, 79–80
Old Stone Jug (tavern), 815
Old Welfare Is. Service Bldg., 472
Old West Farms Soldier Cemetery, 503
OLGYAY, VICTOR AND ALADAR
    Lehman Library, 424
Oliffe's Pharmacy, 865
Olive Branch Baptist Church, 865
Oliver H. Perry School, P.S. 34, Bklyn., 692
Oliver St. Church, **74**
Olivetti Bldg., 283–84
Olivetti-Underwood Showroom, 872, **873**
Olivotti Bldg., 370
OLMSTED, FREDERICK LAW
    Central Park, 336
    Eastern Pkwy., 656
    Forest Hills Gardens, **759, 760**
    Ft. Greene Park, 626
    Morningside Park, 438
    Ocean Pkwy., 702
    Prospect Park, 651–53, 654
    Riverside Park, 298, 300
    Tompkins Park, 663
    SI residence, 851

SI wheat farm, 803
    Vanderbilt Mausoleum, 844, **845**
OLMSTED, FREDERICK LAW, JR.
    Ft. Tryon Park, 466
    Riverside Dr. retaining walls and viewing
        platforms, 428–29
OLMSTED, W. B.
    First Presby. Church, **590,** 591
Olnick, Robert, developer, 393
Olshan, Morton, 392
Olympia & York, 43
Olympic Airways ticket office, 266–**267**
Olympic Tower, 266
O'MALLEY, JOHN B.
    Good Shepherd Convent, 710
Omo Norma Kamali (boutique), 272
Onderdonck, Adrian, House, 754
O'Neal's Baloon (rest.), 292
"Oneata," 839
1 Fifth Ave. Bar/Rest., 111
104th St., Queens, 748
    Nos. 85–58 and 85–54: 779
110th St., Queens
    No. 84–16: 779
    No. 85–12: 779, **780**
111th St., Queens, No. 85–28: 779
113th St., Queens, No. 84–37: **780**
114th St., Queens, Nos. 85–04, 85–10, 85–14,
        85–20, and 85–03: 780
115th St. Branch, NYPL, Manh., 439
116th St., Queens, Nos. 87–72 and 87–78:
        781, **782**
125th St. Medical Bldg., Manh., **445**
135th St. Branch, NYPL, Manh. 448–49
145th St. Br., 898–99
146th St., Queens, Nos. 29–34 to 29–45: 768
153rd St. Viaduct, Bx., 489
160th St., Queens, 782
163rd Ave. Br., Queens, 793
167th St., Queens, Nos. 189–10 to 189–30 and
        189–11 to 189–29: 777
O'NEIL, JOHN J.
    W. Bway., Nos. 145–147: 58
O'Neill, Eugene, 105
O'Neill, Hugh, Dry Goods Store, **179**
1-2-3 Hotel, **229**
On the Pier (rest.), 717
Ontrinue (apts.), 644
Oostorp, 540
Oppenheimer & Co. Tower, 46
OPPENHEIMER, BRADY & LEHRECKE
    Amsterdam Houses add., 297
    Bankers Trust Co. Bldg., 246
    Bankers Trust Co. Bway. branch, 293
    E. 89th St., No. 45: 383
    Playboy Club, 281
    see also LEHRECKE, THOMAS
OPPENHEIMER, BRADY & VOGELSTEIN
    Harrison St. Houses, **52**
    Independence Plaza North (apts.), 51–**52**
    Physur Bldg., 543
    Wyckoff house, 715
Orchard Beach, 549
Orchard St., **90**
ORDWEIN, LEWIS J.
    E. 72nd St., No. 235: 397
O'REILLY, CORNELIUS
    warehouse, 440
O'REILLY BROS.
    Our Lady of Lourdes Church, 429, **430**
Oriental Pavilion, Prospect Park, 653
Ormonde (apts.), 294
O'ROURKE, JEREMIAH
    Church of St. Paul the Apostle, 225
Orthodox Friends Meeting House, **635**–36
Orwell House, 327–28
OSADKA, APOLLINARE
    St. George's Ukrainian Church, 165
Osborn, Earl Dodge, 763
Osborne Apts., 277
OSBORN ENGINEERING CO.
    Yankee Stadium, 510
Osborn Labs. of Marine Sciences, 711, **712**
OSTROW, ROBERT
    W. 19th St., No. 365: 174
    W. 22nd St., No. 260: 173
OTHER ISLANDS, 468–76, 882
Otis, Elisha Graves, 94
O'Toole, St. Laurence, 380
OTTAVINO, A., stone carver, 566
Ottendorfer Branch, NYPL, 166
OTZ, ROBERT
    Boetteger Silk Finishing Factory, 486
Our Father, Church of (orig.), 657, **660**
Our Lady Help of Christians, Church of
        (orig.), 857–58
Our Lady, Mediatrix of All Graces, 500, 501